LEARNING
CANADIAN
CRIMINAL
PROCEDURE

Twelfth Edition

THOMSON REUTERS®

LEARNING CANADIAN CRIMINAL PROCEDURE

Twelfth Edition

by

DON STUART
B.A., LL.B., Dip.Crim., D.Phil.

*Faculty of Law,
Queen's University*

TIM QUIGLEY
B.Sc., LL.B., LL.M.

*College of Law,
University of Saskatchewan*

DEDICATION

This edition is dedicated to the memory of Ron Delisle, who was co-author of the first edition.

Sadly, Ron passed away on March 12, 2013. He was an inspirational scholar and teacher to many Queen's students, judges and lawyers, and is sorely missed.

PREFACE TO THE
TWELFTH EDITION

With the entrenchment of the Canadian Charter of Rights and Freedoms in 1982, Canadian Criminal Procedure became a much more dynamic subject. The central issue in criminal procedure has always been the tension that exists between the rights of the accused and effective law enforcement. Is the proper balance being maintained? Have we satisfactorily accommodated the needs of justice and truth? These teaching materials focus largely on this tension in pre-trial procedure and that at trial. The constitutional dimension adds to the challenge and to the excitement.

Long before the arrival of the Charter, the procedural dimension of the criminal justice system was being extensively litigated. The volume of judgments on procedure has always far exceeded those on substance and evidence. Since many Charter rights relate directly to the criminal justice system, the case law on procedure has become a flood. The Supreme Court itself continues to produce many major and often highly complex and lengthy rulings. It is a real challenge to keep up with the torrent of decisions in lower courts. A basic knowledge of criminal procedure has also always required an investigation of many technical and intricately worded statutory provisions. These realities pose particular challenges to the teacher. Teaching materials aimed at being a comprehensive exposition of the very latest law on every detail of every procedure would quickly become out of date and would risk making it difficult for the reader to see the forest for the trees. Since the first edition of these materials in 1986, we have tried to be highly selective and always have the learning process in mind. Nevertheless, this is a complex subject and teaching choices should be made rather than trying to rush through everything in these materials.

In each section we address basic principles. We do this through a selection of primary sources and narrative text. We include many questions, problems and review exercises. Throughout we try to be scrupulously accurate about the present law but we also wish our readers to consider whether the law has reached the best balance. Our problems are often based on actual decisions and we provide citations. However, it is vital to our teaching method that it be understood that, for learning purposes, the actual answers provided by the courts to these problems are not critical. We are more concerned with developing the ability to reason from general principles.

Charter jurisprudence on criminal procedure must be carefully integrated into the context. The protection against unreasonable search and seizure under s. 8 of the Charter cannot, for example, be divorced from a consideration of statutory and common law powers to search. The power to exclude evidence under s. 24(2) of the Charter cannot be considered without being aware of common law traditions about excluding illegally obtained evidence. In the section on trial procedure we consider it crucial to address criticisms of the adversary system and issues of professional responsibility and ethical dilemmas facing Defence Counsel and Crown Attorneys. We also give special attention to the unique features of trial by jury and recent developments in their empanelling.

Starting with the eighth edition we added introductory notes and adopted a more chronological order of the criminal justice process. The book is divided into five parts: Jurisdiction, Investigation, Pre-Trial Procedure, Trial Process and Post-Trial Procedure. For these changes we are indebted to Gary Trotter, a co-author of the eighth edition and now Justice of the Ontario Superior Court of Justice. He also wrote a succinct section on Appellate Review and Extraordinary Remedies.

The publication of the tenth edition highlighted the judgments of the Supreme Court in *R. v. Grant*, handed down after having been on reserve for 15 months, and in the companion cases of *R. v. Harrison* and *R. v. Suberu*. These are bellwether rulings on the approach to detention for Charter purposes and to the remedy of exclusion of evidence under s. 24(2) of the Charter. The Court outlined new criteria for the determination of detention to trigger s. 9 and 10 rights. It expressly abandoned its previously entrenched *Collins/Stillman* approach to s. 24(2) that conscripted evidence affected the fairness of trial and had generally to be excluded, while the exclusion of non-conscripted depended on consideration of all the factors. The Court has arrived at a revised discretionary approach to s. 24(2) free of rigid rules that places special emphasis on the factor of seriousness of the breach rather than the seriousness of the offence or the reliability of the evidence. The same criteria are to be applied to all cases of Charter breach.

In this twelfth edition we have included full consideration of the following major rulings from the Supreme Court:

- *Fearon* — search of cell phones as incident to arrest
- *Vu* — search warrant must expressly authorise seizure of cell phones
- *Taylor* — searches at hospitals and exclusion following s. 10(b) violation
- *Chehil* and *MacKenzie* — power to use sniffer dogs on reasonable suspicion
- *MacDonald* — public safety searches
- *Hart* and *Mack* — new common law standards for Mr. Big confessions
- *Henry v. B.C.* — civil remedy against Crown for intentional non-disclosure
- *Anderson* — more limited stay as abuse of process remedy against Crown
- *St-Cloud* — public confidence ground to deny bail not to be used sparingly
- *Kokopenace* — limits on representative juries for Aboriginal offenders

It has been hard to keep up with hundreds of decisions under the new *Grant/Harrison/Côté* discretionary regime for s. 24(2) exclusion of evidence obtained in violation of the Charter. We discuss empirical studies showing that the Supreme Court has put in place a robust remedy for all types of Charter breaches and all types of evidence. The rates of exclusion across the country at the trial level are about two out every three cases. The further evidence is that Courts of Appeal defer in only 60% of appeals, and less where trial judges have admitted the evidence. We thank Elliot Herzig, a J.D. student at Queen's, for updating our comparison to the U.S. exclusionary rule to show how it has been much restricted by the U.S. Supreme Court.

We highlight many hot-button issues such as conflicting case law on police carding practices, racial profiling, limits to the right to counsel under s. 10(b) and the extent to which duty counsel can substitute for right to counsel of choice, the right to silence having been subsumed into the voluntary confession rule in *R. v. Singh*, the different disclosure rules for sexual offence and those for all other crimes, the scope and future of preliminary inquiries, the use of stays under the right to be tried in a reasonable time under s. 11(b), the latest controversies in jury trials, and new instances of wrongful convictions. We took the opportunity to add updates and clarifications throughout the book. We have added several problems reflecting recent decisions. We kept track of, and tried to assess, the torrent of technical new Criminal Code amendments. We also made deletions to make way for the new material.

We thank Professor Brent Snook and Inspector John House for permission to re-publish their article calling for Canadian police to use the United's Kingdom's PEACE method for police interrogation in preference to the much more coercive Reid method of interrogation now in widespread use in the United States and Canada. We assess the voluntary confession rule in *R. v. Oickle* and contrast the trend since *Hart* and *Mack* to admit confessions following coercive Mr. Big strategies by undercover officers simply because they have been corroborated by other evidence.

The picture on the cover of this edition is of the Saskatchewan Badlands.

Once again we thank the expert staff at Carswell. We are particularly grateful for the support of Pamela Corrigan and the usual meticulous work of our copy editor, Claire Cheverie.

Don Stuart
Tim Quigley
January 1, 2016

ACKNOWLEDGEMENTS

We gratefully thank the following authors, publishers or organizations for permission to reproduce excerpts from the material listed below.

Adversary System Excuse
Rowman and Allanheld

Annotations in Criminal Reports
Janine Benedet
Lisa Dufraimont

Arrest — The Decision to Take a Suspect Into Custody
W. La Fave
Little, Brown & Co.

Case for the Defence
E. Greenspan and Macmillan of Canada

Charge Screening, Disclosure and Resolution Discussions
Ministry of the Attorney General of Ontario

Closing Argument to the Jury for the Defence in Criminal Cases
Northwestern University School of Law
Canada Law Book

Code of Professional Conduct
Canadian Bar Association

Control of Police Arrest Practice
P. Weiler

Control of Process
Law Reform Commission of Canada

Discretionary Justice
K.C. Davis
Louisiana State University Press

Donald Marshall Jr. Prosecution
Royal Commission

Ethics in the Practice of Law
G.C. Hazard
Yale University Press

Give PEACE a Chance
Professor Brent Snook
Inspector John House

Joint Trials?
J.L.K. Vamplew
Canada Law Book

For Generations to Come; The Time is Now
Ministry of the Attorney General of Ontario

Jury in Criminal Trials
Law Reform Commission of Canada

Let's Make a Deal
Lexington Books

Limits of the Criminal Sanction
Stanford University Press

Making Crime
R. Ericson
Butterworth & Co.

Plea Bargaining
G. Ferguson
D.W. Roberts

Portia in a Different Voice
Berkeley Women's Law Journal

Prosecution of a Criminal Jury Trial
Canada Law Book

Questioning Suspects
Law Reform Commission of Canada

Role and Responsibility of the Defence Advocate
G.A. Martin
Canada Law Book

Search and Seizure in Criminal Law Enforcement
Law Reform Commission of Canada

The Prosecutor
University of Toronto Press

CONTENTS

PART I
INTRODUCTION

PART II
INVESTIGATION: POLICE POWERS AND RIGHTS OF ACCUSED

PART III
PRE-TRIAL PROCEDURE

PART IV
THE TRIAL PROCESS

PART V
POST-TRIAL REVIEW

Part I

INTRODUCTION

Chapter 1

JURISDICTION

This introductory chapter introduces a number of broad concepts critical to criminal procedure. While a good deal of this book is concerned with the impact of the Charter, the first part of this chapter considers the division of powers under the Constitution Act, 1867. This is followed by an explanation of the basic types of criminal offences prescribed by the Criminal Code. We then turn to a consideration of the extent to which criminal prosecutions are constrained by time and territoriality. These latter concepts are important pre-conditions to criminal prosecutions in Canada.

1. Legislative Division of Powers

CONSTITUTION ACT, 1867

[formerly named British North America Act]
30 and 31 Vic., c. 3

VI.—DISTRIBUTION OF LEGISLATIVE POWERS.

Powers of the Parliament.

91. It shall be lawful for the Queen, by and with the Advice and Consent of the Senate and House of Commons, to make Laws for the Peace, Order, and good Government of Canada, in relation to all Matters not coming within the Classes of Subjects by this Act assigned exclusively to the Legislatures of the Provinces; and for greater Certainty, but not so as to restrict the Generality of the foregoing Terms of this Section, it is hereby declared that (notwithstanding anything in this Act) the exclusive Legislative Authority of the Parliament of Canada extends to all Matters coming within the Classes of Subjects next herein-after enumerated; that is to say,—

. . .

27. The Criminal Law, except the Constitution of Courts of Criminal Jurisdiction, but including the Procedure in Criminal Matters.
28. The Establishment, Maintenance, and Management of Penitentiaries.

. . .

Exclusive Powers of Provincial Legislatures.

92. In each Province the Legislature may exclusively make Laws in relation to Matters coming within the Classes of Subject next herein-after enumerated; that is to say,—

. . .

6. The Establishment, Maintenance, and Management of Public and Reformatory Prisons in and for the Province.

. . .

13. Property and Civil Rights in the Province.

14. The Administration of Justice in the Province, including the Constitution, Maintenance, and Organization of Provincial Courts, both of Civil and of Criminal Jurisdiction, and including Procedure in Civil Matters in those Courts.

15. The Imposition of Punishment by Fine, Penalty, or Imprisonment for enforcing any Law of the Province made in relation to any Matter coming within any of the Classes of Subjects enumerated in this Section.

The federal Parliament has enacted the procedure to be followed for the prosecution of all crimes enacted by the Criminal Code of Canada and for all offences created by federal legislation. The procedure to be followed for provincial offences varies from province to province, though many federal provisions are there mirrored. This book is largely concerned with the procedure to be followed with respect to federal matters. Since the administration of justice, including the constitution of the courts, is a matter for the provinces, the nomenclature varies from province to province. The interpretation section of the Criminal Code, s. 2, sets out for each of the provinces the meaning of "court of appeal", "court of criminal jurisdiction", "justice", "magistrate", "territorial division", and "superior court of criminal jurisdiction".

The prosecution of federal matters will depend on whether the matter concerns the Criminal Code or other federal statutes. The interpretation section of the Code gives the following definitions:

"prosecutor" means the Attorney General or, where the Attorney General does not intervene, means the person who institutes proceedings to which this Act applies, and includes counsel acting on behalf of either of them;

"Attorney General"

(a)   subject to paragraphs (b.1) to (g), with respect to proceedings to which this Act applies, means the Attorney General or Solicitor General of the province in which those proceedings are taken and includes his or her lawful deputy,

(b)   with respect to the Yukon Territory, the Northwest Territories and Nunavut, or with respect to proceedings commenced at the instance of the Government of Canada and conducted by or on behalf of that Government in respect of a contravention of, a conspiracy or attempt to contravene, or counselling the contravention of, any Act of Parliament other than this Act or any regulation made under such an Act, means the Attorney General of Canada and includes his or her lawful deputy,

(b.1)   with respect to proceedings in relation to an offence under subsection 7(2.01), means either the Attorney General of Canada or the Attorney

General or Solicitor General of the province in which those proceedings are taken and includes the lawful deputy of any of them,

(c)   with respect to proceedings in relation to a terrorism offence or to an offence under section 57, 58, 83.12, 424.1 or 431.1 or in relation to an offence against a member of United Nations personnel or associated personnel under section 235, 236, 266, 267, 268, 269, 269.1, 271, 272, 273, 279 or 279.1, means either the Attorney General of Canada or the Attorney General or Solicitor General of the province in which those proceedings are taken and includes the lawful deputy of any of them,

(d)   with respect to proceedings in relation to an offence referred to in subsection 7(3.71), or in relation to an offence referred to in paragraph (a) of the definition "terrorist activity" in subsection 83.01(1) if the act or omission was committed outside Canada but is deemed under any of subsections 7(2), (2.1) to (2.21), (3),(3.1), (3.72) and (3.73) to have been committed in Canada, means either the Attorney General of Canada or the Attorney General or Solicitor General of the province in which those proceedings are taken and includes his or her lawful deputy,

(e)   with respect to proceedings in relation to an offence where the act or omission constituting the offence

(i)   constitutes a terrorist activity referred to in paragraph (b) of the definition "terrorist activity" in subsection 83.01(1), and

(ii)   was committed outside Canada but is deemed by virtue of subsection 7(3.74) or (3.75) to have been committed in Canada,

means either the Attorney General of Canada or the Attorney General or Solicitor General of the province in which those proceedings are taken and includes the lawful deputy of any of them,

(f)   with respect to proceedings under section 83.13, 83.14, 83.28, 83.29 or 83.3, means either the Attorney General of Canada or the Attorney General or Solicitor General of the province in which those proceedings are taken and includes the lawful deputy of any of them, and:

(g)   with respect to proceedings in relation to an offence referred to in sections 121.1, 380, 382, 382.1 and 400, means either the Attorney General of Canada or the Attorney General or Solicitor General of the province in which those proceedings are taken and includes the lawful deputy of any of them.

Notice that, by these definitions, the enforcement of the Criminal Code is normally given to the Attorney General of the province whereas the enforcement of other federal legislation, for example the Controlled Drugs and Substances Act, the Income Tax Act and the Customs Act, is given to the Attorney General of Canada. The definition was amended in 1969 by adding sub-paragraph (b) thereby empowering the Attorney General of Canada. In *R. v. Hauser*, [1979] 1 S.C.R. 984, 46 C.C.C. (2d) 481, 8 C.R. (3d) 89 (S.C.C.), there was a constitutional challenge mounted, challenging the right of the federal authorities to prosecute under what was then the Narcotic Control Act. It was argued that the prosecution of criminal matters was a matter for the provincial Attorney General since prosecution was a matter under the head of Administration of Justice, reserved to the provinces by s. 92(14) of the B.N.A. Act. The majority held that the Narcotic Control Act was not enacted pursuant to the Criminal Law head of power, s. 91(27), but rather pursuant to the federal government's residual head of power "to make Laws for the Peace, Order, and Good Government of Canada". The court left open the question of whether provincial Attorneys General had control over the prosecution of laws enacted by the federal government pursuant to s. 91(27). That question was answered by the court in *A.G. Can. v. C.N. Transportation Ltd.* (1983), 38 C.R. (3d) 97 (S.C.C.), a prosecution under the Combines Investigation Act, and *R. v. Wetmore* (1983), 7 C.C.C. (3d) 507, 38 C.R. (3d) 161 (S.C.C.), a prosecution under the Food and Drugs Act. With a variety of provincial Attorneys General joining in the challenge, the argument was made that both pieces of legislation were enacted pursuant to s. 91(27) and therefore prosecutorial competence was restricted to the provincial Attorneys General because s. 92(14) gave the provinces authority over Administration of Justice and that covered the area of investigation and prosecution of crimes. In both cases the court held that whether it was criminal legislation or not, the federal government could authorize, or define, who would prosecute. The court decided that prosecution is a matter of criminal procedure reserved to the federal government by s. 91(27) and that allocation of a substantive head of power to one legislative level carried with it the responsibility for administering any scheme enacted under that head. The court reasoned that the legislative body that has power to enact substantive law must have the power to enforce it. Otherwise, a province could negative federal legislation by failing to enforce it.

The subsequent ruling in *R. v. Malmo-Levine*, [2003] 3 S.C.R. 571, 16 C.R. (6th) 1, 114 C.R.R. (2d) 189 that the Controlled Drugs and Substances Act, which replaced the Narcotic Control Act, was passed by Parliament pursuant to its legislative authority over criminal law undoubtedly confirms that both the federal and provincial governments may prosecute any offence that is criminal in nature whether or not it is in the Criminal Code.

Regarding the constitutional division of prosecutorial activity see J. Whyte, "The Administration of Criminal Justice and the Provinces" (1984), 38 C.R. (3d) 184. Compare also *R. v. Trimarchi* (1987), 63 O.R. (2d) 515, 62 C.R. (3d) 204 (Ont. C.A.), leave to appeal refused (1988), 63 O.R. (2d) x (note), 64 C.R. (3d) xxx (S.C.C.); a judge who is appointed by a province is entitled to try offences created by the Criminal Code and other federal statutes. Respecting the ability of the federal government to delegate to a province authority over criminal law and procedure, see *R. v. S. (S.)*, [1990] 2 S.C.R. 254, 77 C.R. (3d) 273, 57 C.C.C. (3d) 115 (S.C.C.); Parliament, in enacting the Young Offenders Act, was entitled to leave the implementation of alternative measures programs to the discretion of the provincial Attorneys General.

Speaking for a unanimous Supreme Court in *R. v. S. (S.)*, above, Chief Justice Dickson agreed with Wilson J. in *R. v. Turpin*, [1989] 1 S.C.R. 1296, 48 C.C.C. (3d) 8, 69 C.R. (4th) 97 (S.C.C.), that a case-by-case approach was necessary to decide whether province-based distinctions in the application of federal law violates equality guarantees under s. 15 of the Canadian Charter of Rights and Freedoms. However, the Chief Justice went much further and held that accepting geographical discrimination challenges under s. 15 would undermine the division of powers, which he saw as rooted in the value of diversity:

> Obviously, the federal system of government itself demands that the values underlying s. 15(1) cannot be given unlimited scope. The division of powers not only permits differential treatment based upon province of residence, it mandates and encourages geographical distinction. There can be no question, then, that unequal treatment which stems solely from the exercise, by provincial legislators, of their legitimate jurisdictional powers cannot be the subject of a s. 15(1) challenge on the basis only that it creates distinctions based upon province of residence (77 C.R. (3d) at 299).

On the issue of no geographical discrimination, see further Stuart, *Charter Justice in Canadian Criminal Law* (6th. ed., 2014), ch. 11.

2. Classification of Offences

At common law a distinction was drawn between indictable offences (treasons, felonies and misdemeanours) triable only by judge and jury and offences triable only summarily by justices of the peace sitting without a jury. The distinction between felonies and misdemeanours was important in that the former (e.g., murder, burglary and rape) were punishable by death and resulted in forfeiture of the felon's property, while the latter never involved the death penalty and only rarely forfeiture. It is still maintained in the United States, but was abolished in England in 1967 and in Canada by the Criminal Code as early as the nineteenth century.

In the Canadian system, there are, broadly speaking, four types of offences: indictable, summary conviction, dual (hybrid) offences, and contraventions (regulatory) offences under the Contraventions Act, S.C. 1992, c. 47. The latter will not be discussed here. The type of offence is always expressly stipulated in the offence definition in the Criminal Code and nearly always in other federal legislation. However, this categorization is somewhat misleading since there are three types of indictable offences and the category of dual (hybrid) offences leads to an election by the Crown as to whether to proceed by indictment or by summary conviction. Adding to the confusion, the trial court is determined by the classification of the offence and the Code does not set out the classification in an orderly way. Instead, the provisions are haphazardly strewn across the Code and are less than explicit in some instances. The best way to explain them, therefore, is by a process of elimination. But, first, a definition of each of the types of offences:

(a) Offences Triable Only on Indictment

These are more serious offences. Usually the offence section or its penalty section sets out the punishment applicable to the offence. If it does not, s. 743 of the Code provides a maximum of five years imprisonment. Indictable offences are of three types and the type involved has a large bearing on the forum for trial. Where an accused is charged with an indictable offence, generally speaking, he must be personally present at all stages of the proceedings, although ss. 650, 650.01, and 650.02 of the Criminal Code now permit appearing in other ways in some circumstances.

The most serious offences are given into the exclusive jurisdiction of the superior court of criminal jurisdiction, in Ontario, the Superior Court of Justice. See ss. 468 and 469. The least serious indictable offences are absolutely within the jurisdiction of a provincial court judge, in Ontario, a judge of the Ontario Court of Justice. See s. 553. For the great bulk of the indictable offences remaining, the accused is entitled to choose his mode of trial. By s. 536(2) the accused will be put to his election and he will be asked to choose whether he wishes to be tried by a provincial court judge without a jury, a judge without a jury, or by a court composed of a judge and jury. If the accused does not elect a mode of trial, he will be deemed to have elected trial by judge and jury, s. 565(1)(c). It is important to note the difference between the *exclusive* jurisdiction of the superior court at one end of the scale and the *absolute* jurisdiction of the provincial court judge at the other. The superior court has exclusive jurisdiction: no other court can try these offences. The provincial court judge has absolute jurisdiction: the provincial court judge is absolutely entitled to try these offences in the sense that she is not dependent on the accused's electing to be so tried. Other courts of criminal jurisdiction are nevertheless entitled to try the accused for offences within the provincial court judge's absolute jurisdiction should the matter come before them: see *R. v. Holliday* (1973), 12 C.C.C. (2d) 56 (Alta. C.A.).

Notwithstanding that the accused has elected trial by provincial court judge, the provincial court judge may decide that the matter should be proceeded with by a judge or jury, s. 555, and the Attorney General may also override an accused's decision and compel a jury trial where the offence is punishable by more than five years, s. 568.

There are detailed provisions in the Criminal Code which allow an accused person to change his or her mind and to re-elect the mode of trial: see ss. 561 to 563.1 and 565. The heart of the re-election provisions is s. 561 which conditions the right to re-elect on the basis of a combination of: (a) the original election; (b) the point in time in the process when the accused wishes to re-elect; and (c) whether the Crown consents to the re-election. The labyrinthine nature of elections is described by Professor Tim Quigley in *Procedure in Canadian Criminal Law*, 2nd ed. (looseleaf) (Toronto: Carswell, 2005), Chapter 13.3.

(b) Summary Conviction Offences

Part XXVII of the Criminal Code sets out the procedure for the trial of summary conviction offences, i.e., trial before a provincial judge without a jury and without a preliminary inquiry. The maximum penalty for any summary conviction offence, unless otherwise provided, is $5,000 or six months imprisonment or both: s. 787(1).

Summary conviction offences are always tried in Provincial Court (or its equivalent) or by a justice of the peace (although superior court judges in some provinces also have the jurisdiction to do so, but rarely exercise it in practice). In theory, Parliament could establish a maximum penalty of up to five years less one day imprisonment without violating the right to a jury trial under s. 11(f) of the Charter.

An accused charged with a summary conviction offence normally need not appear personally in court but may instead choose to have a lawyer or some other agent appear for him unless the judge orders that he must appear personally: s. 800(2) of the Code.

(c) Crown Election Offences (dual, hybrid)

These are offences for which the prosecution may choose whether to proceed by way of summary conviction or by indictment. If the Crown elects summary conviction, such offences are in all respects summary conviction offences. If the Crown proceeds by indictment, the forum for the trial will depend upon the type of indictable offence involved. As with straight indictable offences, the penalty is usually specified in the enactment but, if not, is governed by s. 743. In 1994 Parliament increased the maximum penalty for several hybrid offences when proceeded against by way of summary conviction to 18 months: see, e.g., assault causing bodily harm (s. 267) and sexual assault (s. 271).

Various tactical considerations enter into the Crown election. The higher available penalty for indictable offences, a prior criminal record by the accused, or a desire to require the accused's personal presence throughout may be among the reasons. Sometimes it is a matter of judge shopping or wishing to get the matter over more quickly.

Only when the prosecutor elects to proceed by indictment does the accused have the choice under s. 536. If the Crown chooses summary conviction proceedings, the accused no longer has a choice of a preliminary inquiry, trial in superior court or a jury trial. The prosecutor should indicate the nature of the proceeding prior to trial and, if the trial proceeds in the absence of a Crown election, it will be deemed a summary conviction offence except in some narrow circumstances. See: T. Quigley, *Procedure in Canadian Criminal Law*, 2nd ed. (looseleaf edition) (Toronto: Carswell, 2005), Chapter 13.2(a).

The Interpretation Act, R.S.C. 1985, c. I-21, provides:

34.(1) Where an enactment creates an offence,

(a) the offence is deemed to be an indictable offence if the enactment provides that the offender may be prosecuted for the offence by indictment;

Section 34(1) has been applied to equate Crown election offences with indictable offences in various contexts such as arrest and for the purposes of fingerprinting under the Identification of Criminals Act, R.S.C. 1985, c. I-1.

3. Jurisdiction of Courts

From the foregoing, it can be seen that there are two trial courts: the superior court and the provincial or territorial court. In addition, however, there is an important role for justices of the peace, although their functions and uses vary from jurisdiction to jurisdiction. In the Criminal Code, justices are empowered to deal with the issuance of process such as a summons, arrest warrant, or search warrant, to conduct bail hearings on all but s. 469 offences, and to conduct preliminary inquiries. They also have the jurisdiction to try summary conviction offences. The importance of justices to our justice system and their consequent need for judicial independence was discussed in:

ELL v. ALBERTA
[2003] 1 S.C.R. 857, 11 C.R. (6th) 207 (S.C.C.)

MAJOR J.:—

. . .

In light of these bases of judicial independence — impartiality in adjudication, preservation of our constitutional order, and public confidence in the administration of justice — it is clear that the principle extends its protection to the judicial office held by the respondents. Alberta's non-sitting justices of the peace exercised judicial functions directly related to the enforcement of law in the court system. They served on the front line of the criminal justice process, and performed numerous judicial functions that significantly affected the rights and liberties of individuals. Of singular importance was their jurisdiction over bail hearings. Justices of the peace are included in the definition of "justice" under s. 2 of the *Criminal Code*, R.S.C. 1985, c. C-46, and the respondents were thereby authorized to determine judicial interim release pursuant to s. 515 of the *Code*. Decisions on judicial interim release impact upon the right to security of the person under s. 7 of the *Charter* and the right not to be denied reasonable bail without just cause under s. 11(*e*). Professor Friedland commented upon the importance of bail hearings in *Detention before Trial: A Study of Criminal Cases Tried in the Toronto Magistrates' Courts* (1965), at p. 172:

> The period before trial is too important to be left to guess-work and caprice. At stake in the process is the value of individual liberty. Custody during the period before trial not only affects the mental, social, and physical life of the accused and his family, but also may have a substantial impact on the result of the trial itself. The law should abhor any unnecessary deprivation of liberty and positive steps should be taken to ensure that detention before trial is kept to a minimum.

The respondents were required to exercise significant judicial discretion in adjudicating on these matters.

25. The respondents also had the authority to issue search warrants, which impact upon the right to be secure from unreasonable search and seizure under s. 8 of the *Charter*. Sopinka J. described the effect of search warrants on the right to privacy in *Baron v. Canada*, 1993 CanLII 154 (S.C.C.), [1993] 1 S.C.R. 416, at pp. 444-45:

> Physical search of private premises . . . is the greatest intrusion of privacy short of a violation of bodily integrity....
>
> Warrants for the search of any premises constitute a significant intrusion on the privacy of an individual that is both upsetting and disruptive.

In that case, the Court concluded at p. 439 that the issuance of search warrants constitutionally required discretion to be exercised by a judicial officer who remains independent from the state and its agents.

26. Each of the above judicial responsibilities makes clear that the respondents played an important role in assisting the provincial and superior courts in fulfilling the judiciary's constitutional mandate. The following conclusion of Professor Mewett on Ontario's justices of the peace is equally applicable to the respondents (Mewett Report, at p. 39):

> . . . the Justice of the Peace is the very person who stands between the individual and the arbitrary exercise of power by the state or its officials. It is essential that an independent person be the one to determine whether process should issue, whether a search warrant should be granted, whether and on what terms an accused should be released on bail and so on. This is a fundamental principle . . . [that] must be zealously preserved.

It is obvious the respondents were constitutionally required to be independent in the exercise of their duties.

. . .

Although, in some jurisdictions, justices may assume some of their functions, provincial or territorial courts are the workhorse courts in which virtually all charges are instituted. They are called by different names in some jurisdictions: Ontario Court of Justice, Court of Quebec, Territorial Court in Northwest Territories and Yukon Territory, and, in Nunavut which has amalgamated its courts, the Nunavut Court of Justice. In all other provinces, it is called the Provincial Court. A provincial or territorial court is often the arraignment court, the bail court for all but s. 469 offences, the trial court for summary conviction offences, s. 553 offences, and for offences where the accused has elected to be tried in provincial court, and the preliminary inquiry court. Provincial court judges are also empowered to issue process such as a summons, arrest warrant, or search warrant. In some instances where a justice is not empowered to act, such as for the issuance of a DNA warrant under s. 487.05, a provincial court judge is authorized to act.

The superior court in each province and territory is, again, sometimes styled differently. It is the Ontario Superior Court of Justice, Quebec Superior Court, Nunavut Court of Justice, and Prince Edward Island, Supreme Court. In Nova Scotia, British Columbia, and Newfoundland, it is named the Supreme Court. In New Brunswick, Alberta, Manitoba, and Saskatchewan, it is called the Court of Queen's Bench. This level of court tries the most serious offences under s. 469 of the Code or where the accused has elected to be tried in that court. Superior courts also are the appeal court from summary conviction decisions in the lower courts.

All appeals of indictable offences are taken to the court of appeal of that jurisdiction. In every province and territory, it is called the Court of Appeal.

PROBLEM 1

How are the following Criminal Code offences classified? What options for trial will an accused have in each case? What factors will you as counsel take into account in determining how to exercise your options?

1. frightening the Queen (s. 49)
2. murder (s. 235(1))
3. operating vehicle while impaired (ss. 253, 256)
4. shoplifting (s. 334)
5. robbery (ss. 343, 344)
6. assault (s. 266)
7. assault causing bodily harm (s. 267)
8. sexual assault (s. 271)
9. causing a disturbance in a public place (s. 175)
10. possession of stolen property over $5000 (s. 355(a))
11. attempted murder (s. 239)
12. conspiracy to commit murder (s. 465(1)(a))

PROBLEM 2

You are Crown counsel prosecuting a charge of assault causing bodily harm. The accused is charged with striking his wife with his fist. His blow cut her cheek. This required three sutures at the hospital. A senior Crown asks you to try hard to avoid the matter being bumped up to a court in which the accused could choose trial by jury. In the higher court, there is a huge backlog of cases. She advises you to elect to proceed by way of summary conviction. Consider carefully whether you should follow this advice.

PROBLEM 3

A person has been charged with the following three offences: (1) Possession of cocaine for the purposes of trafficking, contrary to s. 5(2) and (3) of the Controlled Drugs and Substances Act; (2) Possession of marijuana, contrary to s. 4(1), (4) and (5) of the Controlled Drugs and Substances Act; and (3) Driving while "over 80", contrary to ss. 253(b) and 255(1) of the Criminal Code. How will he be tried on each charge? What considerations should be taken into account by the Crown or defence counsel in making any election which may be available?

It has been well documented that the criminal jurisdiction of superior courts is shrinking and that the vast percentage of criminal trials now occur in provincial courts (see Webster and Doob, "The Superior/Provincial Criminal Court Distinction: Historical Anachronism or Empirical Reality?" (2004) 48 Crim. L.Q. 77). The major difference is that murder trials and all jury trials are confined to the superior courts.

The general and serious problems of systemic delays, complexity and judge-shopping could be better addressed by returning to the vision of those such as former Attorney General Ian Scott and others (see Martin Friedland, "The Provincial Court and the Criminal Law," (2004) 98 Crim. L.Q. 14) who called for just one federal trial court to handle all criminal trials with or without juries. He was pilloried for that view by many members of the superior courts, some members of the profession, and politicians wishing to retain provincial powers to appoint. The status quo is currently propped up by claims of special expertise by judges of higher status which increasingly ring hollow given the calibre and workload of current provincial court judges. The single court is already the reality in Nunavut.

4. Time Limitations

The common law knew no time limitations running against the King which would bar a criminal prosecution.

By s. 786(2) of the Criminal Code, no proceedings shall be instituted with respect to summary conviction offences "more than six months after the time when the subject-matter of the proceedings arose, unless the prosecutor and the defendant so agree". In the case of indictable offences, there is only one time limitation now to be found in the Criminal Code. This relates to a three year time bar from the time of commission of the crime of treason, s. 48(1).

In *R. v. Dudley*, 2009 SCC 58, 249 C.C.C. (3d) 421, [2009] 3 S.C.R. 570, 71 C.R. (6th) 1 (S.C.C.), the Supreme Court of Canada clarified the nature of the Crown election on dual or hybrid offences. If the Crown has elected to proceed summarily but it is later discovered that the information was sworn outside the six month limitation period in section 786(2) of the Code and the defence refuses to consent to summary conviction proceedings, the election and all subsequent proceedings are a nullity and the Crown may therefore proceed afresh by indictment. If this occurs prior to adjudication on the merits, the trial judge should order a mistrial; if discovered after a conviction has been entered, the defence may appeal on the ground that summary proceedings were statute-barred. On the other hand, if the defence consents to proceed summarily notwithstanding the limitation period, the proceedings may continue.

In the case of provincial offences, there are usually specified limitation periods.

What are the arguments for and against limitation periods? See Sanjeev Anand, "Should Parliament Enact Statutory Limitation Periods for Criminal Offences?" (2000) 44 Crim. L.Q. 8.

Any limitation period will not apply if the offence is a "continuing" one. This has proved to be a difficult distinction. In *Bell v. R.*, [1983] 2 S.C.R. 471 at 488, 36 C.R. (3d) 289, 8 C.C.C. (3d) 97 (S.C.C.), McIntyre J. defined a "continuing offence" as follows:

> A continuing offence is not simply an offence which takes or may take a long time to commit. It may be described as an offence where the conjunction of the *actus reus* and the *mens rea*, which makes the offence complete, does not, as well,

terminate the offence. The conjunction of the two essential elements for the commission of the offence continues and the accused remains in what might be described as a state of criminality while the offence continues.

In *R. v. Hernandez* (*sub nom R. v. Vu*) (2012), 94 C.R. (6th) 246 (S.C.C.), the Court decided that kidnapping is a continuing offence. It starts from the time of detention of the victim and continues until the time of release.

PROBLEM 4

The accused, an electrical contractor, is charged with two counts of neglecting to comply with regulations under the Power Corporation Act of Ontario. The counts allege the installation of an improper panel board and a failure to install proper electrical grounding on a service switch. The charges were commenced 10 months after the installation and well after the applicable 6 month limitation period under the Provincial Offences Act. Is the offence a "continuing" offence with the result that the time bar will not prevent the trial?

Compare *R. v. Rutherford* (1990), 75 C.R. (3d) 230 (Ont. C.A.).

PROBLEM 5

Teachers are charged with the provincial offence of failing to report sexual assault at their school. It is eight months after the alleged assault and the defence counsel argues that the prosecution is time barred by a six month limitation period. Can the Crown successfully argue that this is a continuing offence ?

Compare *R. v. Newton-Thompson* (2009), 67 C.R. (6th) 243, 244 C.C.C. (3d) 338 (Ont. C.A.); see annotation by Janine Benedet, C.R., *ibid.*

The issue of time arises in a different context. Section 11(b) of the Charter provides:

> 11. Any person charged with an offence has the right
>
> . . .
>
> (b) — to be tried within a reasonable time.

Section 11(b) does not relate to the timing of the laying of the charge in the same way that a limitation would apply: see *R. v. Kalanj*, [1989] 1 S.C.R. 1594, 70 C.R. (3d) 260, 48 C.C.C. (3d) 459 (S.C.C.). Instead, it governs the conduct of the prosecution once it is underway, ensuring that the matter comes to trial without undue delay. The issue is typically dealt with at the outset of the trial, during a pre-trial motion. This complicated (and sometimes controversial) area of the law is addressed later in Part IV "The Trial Process".

5. Territorial Limitations

Jurisdiction, from the Latin, meaning "to speak by the law", describes the limits of authority of a court to act. "The foundation of jurisdiction is physical power"; Holmes J. in *McDonald v. Mabee*, 243 U.S. 90 at 91 (1917). The sovereign's authority is generally limited therefore to matters occurring within his own territory. Within that territory there are good reasons for further limiting the place of the trial to the district of its occurrence.

Jury trials conducted during the thirteenth and fourteenth centuries were markedly different from today. Juries were not then informed of the facts by witnesses in open court. Jury members were selected because they had knowledge of the facts or were able to discover them by inquiry. It was natural then that a criminal trial should be conducted in the place where the incident occurred. From this historical fact flows the tradition that crime is to be treated as local in its nature and that a court's jurisdiction be limited to its own territory.

While the jury system has changed there is still a right in the community to see first hand that justice is done with respect to matters with which they are immediately concerned. Confining the trial to its immediate location is also appropriate when one considers the availability and convenience of witnesses to the alleged incident. The general common principle is restated today in the Criminal Code:

> **6.** (2) Subject to this Act or any other Act of Parliament, no person shall be convicted or discharged under section 730 of an offence committed outside Canada.

To this general principle there are certain statutory exceptions: s. 7, including offences committed in relation to aircraft, against internationally protected persons and property, to do with cultural property, hostage taking, nuclear material, war crimes, terrorist offences, and child sex tourism, discussed by Benjamin Perrin, "Taking a Vacation from the Law? Extraterritorial Criminal Jurisdiction and Section 7(4.1) of the Criminal Code", (2009) 13 *Can.Crim.L.Rev.* 175); s. 46(3), treason; s. 57, forging a passport; s. 58, using a citizenship certificate fraudulently; ss. 74 and 75, piracy; ss. 279.01-279.02, trafficking in persons; s. 290, bigamy; s. 354(1)(b), possession of property in Canada that was obtained elsewhere through the commission of an offence; and ss. 465(3)-(5), conspiracy.

The following decision turns on the question of whether an offence was committed "outside of Canada", for the purposes of s. 6(2).

R. v. GRECO
(2001), 159 C.C.C. (3d) 146 (Ont. C.A.)

MOLDAVER J.A.:—The appellant Raffaele Greco appeals from his conviction on a charge of breach of probation. He seeks to have the conviction overturned and an acquittal entered for two reasons. First, he submits that he was not required to comply with the terms and conditions of his probation order while outside of Canada. Second, he argues that even if he was required to comply with his probation order while outside of Canada, s. 6(2) of the Criminal Code prevents him from being convicted because the offence was committed in Cuba, not Canada. For reasons that follow, I would not give effect to either argument and I would dismiss the appeal.

Background Facts

On December 28, 1998, the appellant and his female companion, Trisha Smith, both residents of Ontario, travelled from Toronto to Cuba for a one-week vacation. In the early morning hours of January 4, 1999, the day of their scheduled return to Toronto, Mr. Greco viciously assaulted Ms. Smith in a fit of jealous rage. The attack left Ms. Smith with grave injuries to her face and head, including a fractured cheek bone and a deviated nose.

Manifestly, the assault was serious. If committed in Canada, it would most likely have attracted a charge of aggravated assault punishable by a term of imprisonment not exceeding fourteen years. As it is, the Cuban authorities, though duly contacted by Ms. Smith, chose not to become involved. Instead, they arranged for the police in Canada to meet the appellant and Ms. Smith upon their return to Toronto later that day.

After meeting with the police in Toronto, Ms. Smith was advised that the appellant could not be charged with assault in Canada because the physical attack upon her had occurred in Cuba. However, follow-up investigation revealed that as of January 4, 1999, the date of the alleged assault upon Ms. Smith in Cuba, the appellant was subject to a probation order issued by a judge of the Ontario Court of Justice on May 7, 1997 following his convictions for assault and threatening death. In accordance with s. 732.1(2)(a) of the Criminal Code, a term of that order required that the appellant keep the peace and be of good behaviour. Satisfied that his conduct in Cuba amounted to a breach of that provision, the police laid an information against the appellant on March 4, 1999, charging that:

> Raffaele Greco, on or about the 4 day of January 1999, at the country of Cuba, did while bound by a probation order made by Provincial Court Regional Municipality of Peel, on the 7 day of May 1997, fail without reasonable excuse to comply with such order, to wit keep the peace and be of good behaviour, contrary to the Criminal Code of Canada 733.1(1).

The Crown elected to proceed by way of summary conviction and the trial proceeded before Lampkin J. of the Ontario Court of Justice. [He held his court had jurisdiction and convicted. The accused was sentenced to nine months' imprisonment and probation for three years. An appeal to the Summary Conviction Appeal Court dismissed the appeal and Greco appealed to Court of Appeal.]

Issues

This appeal raises the following two issues:

(1) Was the appellant required to comply with the terms and conditions of the May 7, 1997 probation order while outside of Canada?

(2) If the answer to issue one is "yes", then, accepting that his assaultive conduct in Cuba constituted a breach of probation, did the Ontario Court of Justice have jurisdiction to try the offence and convict the appellant?

Issue One: Was the appellant required to comply with the terms and conditions of the May 7, 1997 probation order while outside of Canada?

. . .

The issue at hand is one of first impression. I know of no authority directly on point. In the end, I believe that Lampkin J. came to the correct conclusion.

To begin, I know of no rule or principle of international law that would deprive a judge of the Ontario or Superior Court of Justice of jurisdiction to make a probation order binding the conduct of a probationer both at home and abroad. To be sure, the principle of "extraterritoriality", which is defined by James R. Fox in *The Dictionary of International and Comparative Law* [2nd ed. (Dobbs Ferry, N.Y.: Oceana Publications] (1997), at p. 47 as the "operation of laws upon persons or rights beyond the territorial limits of the state enacting such laws", may impact on Canada's ability to enforce such orders.

For example, if a probationer commits a breach of the order while abroad and fails or refuses to voluntarily return to Canada, then, absent a right of extradition or some other co-operative arrangement with the foreign state, Canada would likely be powerless to bring the offender to justice. Likewise, if the "offensive conduct" abroad is conduct that the probationer is required to engage in or refrain from under the laws of the foreign state, prosecution in Canada could well constitute an affront to the requirements of international comity and result in our courts declining jurisdiction [see *Libman v. The Queen* (1985), 21 C.C.C. (3d) 206 (S.C.C.) at 233, La Forest J., for the court, explained that the term "comity" means "no more, nor less than 'kindly and considerate behaviour towards others'"]

But these limitations on the ability of the court to enforce its orders should not be confused with the jurisdiction of the court in the first instance to prescribe orders that bind the conduct of probationers both at home and abroad. In my view, the distinction is an important one and it is essential to a proper understanding of the principle of territoriality. That principle, sometimes referred to as the principle of "the sovereign equality of states", is succinctly summarized by Cory and Iacobucci JJ. at p. 17 of their majority opinion in *R. v. Cook* (1998), 128 C.C.C. (3d) 1 (S.C.C.):

> In essence, the principle of the sovereign equality of states generally prohibits extraterritorial application of domestic law since, in most instances, the exercise of jurisdiction beyond a state's territorial limits would constitute an interference under international law with the exclusive jurisdiction of another state.

The principle of territoriality is also discussed at some length by Bastarache J. in his concurring reasons in *Cook*. In the course of that discussion, at pp. 55 and 56, he identifies and explains the important distinction to which I have referred between "jurisdiction to enforce" and "jurisdiction to prescribe":

> Any discussion of territoriality begins with the fundamental distinction between a purported enforcement of domestic law in the territory of a foreign state (jurisdiction to enforce), and an attempt to give effect in domestic law to actions, people or things outside of the territory governed by domestic law (jurisdiction to prescribe). Attempts to enforce domestic law directly in the territory of a foreign state are prohibited in all but the most exceptional circumstances. In the words of Professor Brownlie, discussing "Extra-territorial Enforcement Measures":

"The governing principle is that a state cannot take measures on the territory of another state by way of enforcement of national laws without the consent of the latter. Persons may not be arrested, a summons may not be served, police or tax investigations may not be mounted, orders for production of documents may not be executed, on the territory of another state, except under the terms of a treaty or other consent given."

See Ian Brownlie, Principles of Public International Law (4th ed. 1990), p. 307. It was in this sense that the Permanent Court of International Justice observed in The case of the S.S. "Lotus" (1927), P.C.I.J. Ser. A, No. 9, pp. 18-19:

"Now the first and foremost restriction imposed by international law upon a State is that — failing the existence of a permissive rule to the contrary — it may not exercise its power in any form in the territory of another State. In this sense jurisdiction is certainly territorial; it cannot be exercised by a State outside its territory except by virtue of a permissive rule derived from international custom or from a convention."

But in the very next sentence, at p. 19, the International Court makes it very clear that the term "territoriality" has an entirely different meaning where a legal system merely purports to prescribe effects within its own legal system to events taking place abroad:

"It does not, however, follow that international law prohibits a State from exercising a jurisdiction in its own territory, in respect of any case which relates to acts which have taken place abroad, and in which it cannot rely on some permissive rule of international law. Such a view would only be tenable if international law contained a general prohibition to States to extend the application of their laws and their jurisdiction of their courts to persons, property and acts outside their territory, and if, as an exception to this general prohibition, it allowed States to do so in certain specific cases. But this is certainly not the case under international law as it stands at present. Far from laying down a general prohibition to the effect that States may not extend the application of their laws and the jurisdiction of their courts to persons, property and acts outside their territory, it leaves them in this respect a wide measure of discretion which is only limited in certain cases by prohibitive rules; as regards other cases, every State remains free to adopt the principles which it regards as best and most suitable."

These two passages clearly illustrate the gulf that separates the principle of territoriality with regard to the jurisdiction to enforce, and territoriality as it might constrain the prescription of juridical consequences within the domestic legal system. [Emphasis added.]

Although Bastarache J. was speaking only for himself and Gonthier J., I do not understand the majority to take exception with the general principles outlined in the passage above. Those principles make it clear that subject to certain limitations, a state can extend the application of its laws and the jurisdiction of its courts to persons, property and acts outside of its territory without offending against the principle of territoriality. That, of course, explains the various provisions of the Criminal Code in which Canada has asserted jurisdiction over persons who commit certain offences outside of Canada [see ss. 7, 46(3), 57, 74 and 465(4) of the Criminal Code]. Those provisions are necessary because without them, s. 6(2) of the Code would preclude convictions or findings of guilt for offences committed outside of Canada. But for present purposes, just as there is nothing in the principle of territoriality that prevents Canada from enacting laws enforceable in Canada that govern the conduct of persons outside of its territory, the principle of territoriality does not prevent courts from issuing orders, enforceable locally, that govern conduct outside of Canada.

Nor does anything in the Criminal Code or any other relevant statute preclude a probation order that governs conduct outside of Canada. Manifestly, in light of s. 6(2) of the Code, the fact that probationers may be bound by the terms of their probation orders while abroad will be of no consequence if it cannot otherwise be established that the offence of breach of probation was committed in Canada. That, however, is the subject of the second issue on appeal and it should not be confused with the issue at hand.

In support of his position that probation orders only bind the conduct of probationers while in Canada and not elsewhere, the appellant relies on s. 733.1(2) of the Criminal Code which reads as follows:

> 733.1(2) An accused who is charged with an offence under subsection (1) [breach of probation] may be tried and punished by any court having jurisdiction to try that offence in the place where the offence is alleged to have been committed or in the place where the accused is found, is arrested or is in custody, but where the place where the accused is found, is arrested or is in custody is outside the province in which the offence is alleged to have been committed, no proceedings in respect of that offence shall be instituted in that place without the consent of the Attorney General of that province.

The appellant submits that in enacting that provision, Parliament showed deference to the principle of territoriality by making it clear that probation orders are only meant to bind the conduct of probationers in Canada and not elsewhere. With respect, I disagree with that interpretation.

Section 733.1(2) does not speak one way or the other to the question whether probation orders bind the conduct of probationers while abroad as well as in Canada. Rather, it speaks to what court in Canada has jurisdiction over an accused charged with breach of probation. In other words, it deals with venue, not the reach of probation orders. The first part of the provision simply reaffirms the common law principle that jurisdiction is territorial and in the case of breach of probation, an offender may be tried and punished by a court of competent jurisdiction "in the place where the offence is alleged to have been committed". The second part of the provision broadens the jurisdictional ambit by providing that offenders can be tried and punished for the offence of breach of probation by a court of competent jurisdiction in any province where they are found, arrested or in custody, with the consent of that province's Attorney General, even though the offence itself was not committed in that province.

There is nothing in s. 733.1(2) to suggest that the offence is committed solely in the place where the conduct forming the breach occurred. Indeed, if anything, I read s. 733.1(2) as recognizing, at least implicitly, that the offence of breach of probation can be committed in more than one province, including the province where the order is made and the province where the conduct forming the breach occurred. For present purposes, however, suffice it to say that just as s. 6(2) of the Criminal Code is not dispositive of the issue whether probation orders bind the conduct of probationers outside of Canada, the same applies to s. 733.1(2) of the Code.

It follows, in my view, that there is no basis in international or domestic law for concluding that a judge of the Ontario or Superior Court of Justice lacks the jurisdiction to issue a probation order, enforceable in Canada, that binds the conduct of probationers both at home and abroad.

Nor, in my view, are there policy reasons for coming to a different conclusion. The notion that probationers are only bound by the terms and conditions of their probation orders while in Canada and that they can ignore or circumvent such orders with impunity by setting foot across the border is one that I refuse to accept. Apart from being illogical, I can see no justification for it once it is accepted that the requirements of comity remain sacrosanct and that Canadian courts will decline jurisdiction in cases where to do otherwise would result in a contravention of those requirements.

Policy considerations strongly favour an interpretation that makes the order binding on probationers regardless of where they happen to be. As this case vividly demonstrates, conduct outside of Canada in breach of a probation order made in Canada can have a serious and immediate impact within Canada. The treatment, protection and safety of the victim of this assault who lives in Canada are legitimate concerns of the Canadian criminal justice system. It is entirely consistent with those concerns that persons within the reach of Canadian courts be held to account for breaching an order made in Canada.

From a practical point of view, treating probation orders as if they were light bulbs that can be switched on and off depending on the location of the probationer, gives rise to logistical problems and fairness concerns. If probation orders cease to apply to probationers when they cross the border, then courts, probation officers and probationers alike would be faced with the logistical nightmare of having to keep track of the precise number of days or part days on which the order is operative and the days on which it is not. In oral argument, counsel for the appellant conceded, correctly in my view, that were a probationer only bound by a probation order when in Canada, then the clock would stop ticking and the order would cease to run when the probationer left Canada.

Even more troublesome is the unfairness this would occasion to those probationers who, for legitimate work, family or treatment related reasons, are required to be outside of Canada during the period of probation. If the appellant is right, such probationers, though in complete compliance with the terms of their probation orders while outside of Canada, would nonetheless receive no credit for such periods of time and the length of their probationary period would be extended accordingly. For my part, I see no reason why compliant probationers should be prejudiced in that way.

For these reasons, I am satisfied that the courts of this province have the authority to make probation orders, enforceable locally, that bind the conduct of probationers both at home and abroad. The only remaining question is whether to be effective abroad, the probation order must contain an express provision to that effect. In my view, it need not.

I think that a common sense inference can and should be drawn that, subject to the requirements of comity, probation orders are meant to apply to probationers at all times wherever they might be, absent a specific term to the contrary. In this respect, I agree with Lampkin J. that a probation order is an order made in respect of a particular individual and so long as it remains in force, it attaches to that individual wherever he or she may go.

The territorial reach of a probation order, like any other court order, is a matter of interpretation. The language of the order and the policies served by the order must be considered. The order in the present case contains no reference to its territorial scope. This silence provides no assistance as to the reach of the order. There is no suggestion that the question of whether the order should apply to conduct outside of Canada was canvassed when the order was made. As there is no presumption that an order applies only to conduct within Canada, the absence of any express reference in this probation order to its territorial reach is not indicative of any limitation on that reach. Certainly, there is nothing inherent in the nature of the term breached in this case (to keep the peace and be of good behaviour) that would suggest a territorial limitation.

In sum, I am satisfied that the appellant was required to comply with the terms and conditions of his May 7, 1997 probation order while in Cuba. Accordingly, I would answer issue one in the affirmative.

Issue Two: If the answer to issue one is "yes", then, accepting that his assaultive conduct in Cuba constituted a breach of probation, did the Ontario Court of Justice have jurisdiction to try the offence and convict the appellant?

The appellant submits that the Ontario Court of Justice had no jurisdiction to convict him for the offence of breach of probation because the conduct forming the breach occurred outside of Canada and s. 6(2) of the Code states that subject to Parliament legislating otherwise, no one can be convicted of an offence committed outside of Canada.

Manifestly, the appellant's submission turns on whether the offence of breach of probation was or was not committed in Canada. If it was, his appeal fails; if not, it succeeds.

. . .

In *Libman, supra,* at p. 232, La Forest J. summarized the approach to the limits of territoriality as follows:

> As I see it, all that is necessary to make an offence subject to the jurisdiction of our courts is that a significant portion of the activities constituting that offence took place in Canada. As it is put by modern academics, it is sufficient that there be a "real and substantial link" between an offence and this country, a test well known in public and private international law . . . [Citations omitted.]

. . .

In concluding, as I have, that the "real and substantial link" test has been met in this case, I begin with the observation that the requirements of comity, which La Forest J. believed might "well be coterminous" with "the outer limits of the test", are not engaged at all on the facts of this case.

From the outset, the Cuban authorities made it clear that they had no interest in investigating or prosecuting the appellant for his conduct in Cuba. Moreover, to state the obvious, there is no suggestion from anyone that the appellant's violent conduct towards Ms. Smith was justified or condoned, let alone required, under Cuban law; nor is there any evidence that Cuba has ever registered a complaint with Canada over the prospect of the appellant's prosecution in Canada for the offence of breach of probation.

That, of course, only makes sense. Whereas Canada has a vital interest in ensuring that orders made by Canadian courts are complied with, Cuba has no such comparable interest. Indeed, absent some form of reciprocal enforcement agreement, of which there is none here, I fail to see how Cuba would have jurisdiction to enforce the terms of a probation order made by a Canadian court even if of a mind to do so.

Once it is understood that Canada is the only country that has an interest in ensuring compliance with orders made by Canadian courts, little more need be said in terms of the "real and substantial link" test. The probation order in the instant case was imposed upon the appellant by an Ontario court. It required him to keep the peace and be of good behaviour both at home and abroad. Importantly, the offence in issue arises out of a breach of that order, a factor which I consider to be crucial in the application of the "real and substantial link" test. To the extent that he breached that order, Canada alone has an interest in bringing him to justice and it may do so. The requirements of international comity do not dictate otherwise.

Finally, there is no suggestion that the violent assault on Ms. Smith did not constitute a breach of the term requiring the appellant to keep the peace and be of good behaviour.

Accordingly, I have no hesitation in concluding that the offence of breach of probation was committed in Ontario and that s. 6(2) of the Code therefore has no application. It follows that the Ontario Court of Justice had jurisdiction to try and to convict the appellant.

What if the Crown decided to charge the assault in Cuba as well, claiming jurisdiction on the basis that the victim was being treated for her injuries in Canada? See *R. v. Ouellette* (1998), 126 C.C.C. (3d) 219 (Que. S.C.) in which the accused struck the victim while on holiday in the Dominican Republic. She later died in Canada. The Quebec Superior Court held that there was jurisdiction to try the accused for manslaughter in Canada. The Court relied on the fact that the accused's and victim's families were in Canada and that these individuals, as well as Canada as a country, had a greater interest in prosecuting the case. Moreover, the Dominican authorities were content to let Canada prosecute the case. The Dominican authorities stipulated that, if the case was not prosecuted in Canada, it would seek the extradition of the accused. See also *R. v. B. (O.)* (1997), 116 C.C.C. (3d) 189 (Ont. C.A.), in which the Ontario Court of Appeal held that Canada had no jurisdiction to try a grandfather for sexually assaulting his granddaughter while traveling in a Canadian vehicle in the United States. The offence was committed outside of Canada. For a discussion of *Greco* and *Ouelette*, see David King, "Jurisdiction for Offences Committed Outside Canada" (1999) 26 C.R. (5th) 58. For a general review of recent claims by Canada to extraterritorial jurisdiction, see Robert Currie and Stephen Coughlan, "Extraterritorial Criminal Jurisdiction: Bigger Picture or Smaller Frame?" (2007) 11 Can. Crim. L.R. 141.

In *Chowdhury v. Canada* (2014), 309 C.C.C. (3d) 447, 11 C.R. (7th) 134 (Ont. S.C.J.), the Court stayed charges under the Corruption of Foreign Public Officials Act, S.C. 1988, c.34 against an accused for behaviour in Bangladesh. The accused, a Bangladeshi national, had never been present in Canada. It was held that although the Court had enforcement jurisdiction by statutory exception over the offence, this did not automatically carry enforcement jurisdiction over the offender.

The following materials address the question of when an offence is properly prosecuted in one province, as opposed to another. Canada is a federal country and the locality principle is further emphasized by limiting jurisdiction to the province in which the offence was committed. The Code provides:

478. (1) Subject to this Act, a court in a province shall not try an offence committed entirely in another province.

This limitation is modified however by:

476. (*b*) where an offence is committed on the boundary of two or more territorial divisions or within five hundred metres of any such boundary, or the offence was commenced within one territorial division and completed within another, the offence shall be deemed to have been committed in any of the territorial divisions.

While there are territorial limitations on the right of a court to try an individual for a particular offence, the Code provides for the acceptance of a guilty plea, with the consent of the prosecutor, for offences committed in another province, s. 478(3), and for offences committed in the same province but in another district, s. 479.

Re BIGELOW and R.
(1982), 37 O.R. (2d) 304, 69 C.C.C. (2d) 204 (Ont. C.A.)

BY THE COURT:—The question raised by this appeal is whether Ontario courts have jurisdiction to entertain a charge of detaining an infant with intent to deprive the mother of her lawful custody of a child under s. 250(1)(*a*) of the *Criminal Code,* R.S.C. 1970, c. C-34, when the child had been taken by the appellant father from Ontario to Alberta.

The appellant was committed for trial on the charge that he

. . . on or about the 12th day of July, 1981 at the City of London in the County of Middlesex, did with intent to deprive Anne Elizabeth Bigelow, the parent having lawful care of Matthew Nelson Bigelow, a child under the age of 14 years, of the possession of Matthew Nelson Bigelow, did detain the said Matthew Nelson Bigelow, contrary to Section 250(1)(a) of the Criminal Code.

This appeal is taken from the decision of Mr. Justice Osborne who dismissed an application for *certiorari* to quash the committal.

The facts

The appellant and his wife resided in Ontario after their marriage. They separated shortly after the birth of their child who was three years of age when the events giving rise to this charge occurred. After separation, the family court gave custody of the child to the wife. The appellant was entitled to access on every second week-end from 7:00 p.m. on Friday to 7:00 p.m. on Sunday as well as for two weeks during the summer vacation and for a specified period at Christmas.

The appellant moved to Alberta. He returned to his wife's residence in London on Friday evening, July 10, 1981, and requested access for the week-end. His wife refused and the police were called. The police advised the wife to give the child to the appellant because the order granted week-end access to him. They also advised the appellant that he would be liable for contempt of court or abduction if he did not return the child by 7:00 p.m. on Sunday.

The wife next spoke to the husband by telephone at approximately 6:00 p.m. on the following day, Saturday, July 11th. He had returned to Calgary with the child. She asked when he would return the child to her on the following day. He stated that he was not going to return the child and that he intended to keep him. On July 24, 1981, the wife travelled to Calgary and returned to Ontario with the child who had been picked up by the Calgary police.

The issue

This charge was laid in London and alleges that the offence was committed in London on Sunday, July 12, 1981. Mr. Gold submitted that, if there was any offence, it had occurred in Alberta and was beyond the jurisdiction of the provincial court in London which had committed the appellant for trial. He relied on s. 434(1) of the *Criminal Code* which states that:

> **434.** (1). . . nothing in this Act authorizes a court in a province to try an offence committed entirely in another province.

He contended that the act of "detaining" had been committed entirely in Alberta. He referred to s. 250(1) under which the charge was laid which reads as follows:

> **250.** (1) Every one who, with intent to deprive a parent or guardian or any other person who has lawful care or charge of a child under the age of fourteen years of the possession of that child, or with intent to steal anything on or about the person of such a child, unlawfully
> (a) takes or entices away or detains the child, or
> (b) receives or harbours the child,
>
> is guilty of an indictable offence and is liable to imprisonment for ten years.

He pointed out that the appellant had not been charged with taking or enticing away the child under para. (*a*), which were acts that might have occurred in Ontario, but rather with detaining the child which he contended was an offence that could only have been committed in Alberta.

This argument has grave implications. If it is correct, a parent, having lawfully obtained possession of a child under the authority of an order granting access, could take the child from the other parent in one province to another province and be immune from prosecution in the first province. It would invite imitation in Canada where abduction of children from one province to another is already a major problem.

Jurisdiction over interprovincial offences

(1) *General principles*

Although Ontario courts could have no jurisdiction over the offence, if it was committed wholly within Alberta, this would not be the case if it was committed partly in Ontario and partly in Alberta. Section 432(*b*) of the *Criminal Code* provides:

> (*b*) where an offence is committed on the boundary of two or more territorial divisions or within five hundred yards of any such boundary, *or the offence was commenced within one territorial division and completed within another, the offence shall be deemed to have been committed in any of the territorial divisions;*

(Emphasis added.)

Section 432(*b*) is a necessary provision in a federal State like Canada where the Constitution gives jurisdiction over the administration of criminal law to the provinces. The establishment of concurrent jurisdiction over offences committed in Canada eliminates the difficulties encountered elsewhere by common law courts in dealing with criminal acts committed in two or more jurisdictions. The basis for common law jurisdiction over criminal offences is territorial unless otherwise provided by statute: see *Criminal Code*, s. 5(2). Authors of legal textbooks and learned articles have difficulty in rationalizing decisions of English and other common law courts dealing with jurisdiction over crimes with international ramifications and in predicting how they might apply to future cases. In some cases jurisdiction has been assumed because the criminal activities were initiated in the State claiming jurisdiction; in others because the activities concluded in that State, and in others, in response to an approach gaining greater support, because an element of the offence occurred in that State: see Williams and Castel, *Canadian Criminal Law: International and Transnational Aspects* (1981), pp. 71-84; Hirst, "Jurisdiction over Cross-Frontier Offences", 97 L.Q.R. 80 (1981).

These complex problems do not arise in Canada where courts have used s. 432(*b*) to establish a broad basis for jurisdiction over interprovincial offences. The test in reality has become whether any element of the offence has occurred in the province claiming jurisdiction.

. . .

Thus, Ontario courts would have jurisdiction over this offence if any element or part of it could be said to have been committed in this province. This requires an analysis of both the nature of the offence as described in s. 250(1) and the acts of the appellant. This analysis is assisted by a review of cases decided under s. 432(*b*) which illustrate the broad and flexible bases upon which courts have assumed jurisdiction over interprovincial offences. It would be imprudent to attempt a rigid and exclusionary categorization of cases where such jurisdiction has been or may be assumed. There are, however, three categories relevant to this case. They are offences where the province claiming jurisdiction can establish, first, a continuity of operation extending from that province to other provinces; secondly, the commission of an overt act in that province, or thirdly, the registration of effects in that province from acts committed in other provinces.

(2) *Continuity of operation*

From the earliest times, Canadian courts have held that s. 432(*b*) and its predecessors conferred jurisdiction over crime involving continuity of operation extending over more than one province in any province where a component of the offence took place. In *R. v. Hogle* (1896), 5 C.C.C. 53, 5 Que. Q.B. 59, the accused was charged with the fraudulent conversion of the proceeds of a valuable security. He had been given a promissory note in Iberville on the condition he collect the proceeds from the debtor in another district and then pay them over. He kept the proceeds for himself. The accused was tried and convicted in Iberville but on appeal alleged that the fraudulent conversion took place in Bedford, where the debt was collected and thus the court in Iberville was without jurisdiction in the matter. Würtele J. held that the court in Iberville had jurisdiction, stating at pp. 55-6:

> The offence may have begun in the District of Iberville when the accused received the promissory note for collection, and may have been completed when he received the proceeds in the District of Bedford; or it may have begun in the District of Bedford when the accused received the money, and have been completed in the District of Iberville when he omitted to account for or pay over the proceeds to the prosecutor at his residence. In both cases, under sec. 553 [now s. 432(*a*)], the offence would be considered as having been committed within the jurisdiction of the magistrate or justices in either district; and the proceedings of the district magistrate at St. Johns and the committal by him for trial in the District of Iberville were therefore regular and legal.

He then described the fraudulent conversion of the proceeds of a valuable security as [at p. 57] "a continuity of operation", consisting of the reception of the security, the collection and conversion of the proceeds and the failure to account for the proceeds. Accordingly, where the criminal action began in one district, then was continued and completed in another, the accused could be tried in either district.

. . .

(3) *The commission of an overt act*

More recently Canadian courts have focused on overt acts committed within a province as grounds for assumption of jurisdiction by that province when those acts are referable to or in furtherance of a criminal plan extending beyond that province. They are demonstrable elements of the offence occurring in that province.

. . .

An even more striking example of an overt act conferring jurisdiction because it is an element of an offence is provided by *Re Gayle and The Queen* (1981), 59 C.C.C. (2d) 127. The accused was charged in Alberta with unlawfully living off the avails of prostitution. He objected to Alberta jurisdiction because he had never lived there. He resided in Vancouver where the money was sent to him by telegraph from Edmonton. Feehan J. held that the accused could be tried in Alberta since the avails, which were an essential part of the offence, were generated in Alberta and stated at p. 131:

> It seems to me that in a charge of living off the avails of prostitution, the "avails" and the locus thereof are an integral part of the charge and it is therefore my view that the Provincial Court Judge was correct in deciding that the Alberta Courts did in fact have jurisdiction. As a result the application for prohibition is dismissed.

(4) *The generation of effects*

Where the act of an accused in one province generates effects in another, Canadian courts have applied s. 432(*b*) to confer jurisdiction on the second province. An early example of this principle is provided by the related decisions in *R. v. Gillespie* (1898), 1 C.C.C. 551, and *R. v. Gillespie (No. 2)* (1898), 2 C.C.C. 309.

Gillespie, the president of an Ontario company, was charged in Quebec with having made and published a statement of its affairs knowing the same to be false and with intent to defraud. The prospectus was prepared in Ontario and was sent by mail to a person in Quebec. Gillespie applied for a writ of *habeas corpus* and submitted that the court at Montreal had no jurisdiction because the offence had been committed in Ontario. In *R. v. Gillespie, supra,* Würtele J. rejected this argument, finding that the offence was commenced in Ontario but that it was continued and completed in Quebec. Accordingly, he held that s. 553(*b*) (now s. 432(*b*)) of the *Code* was applicable and the offence could be considered to have been committed in either province. A similar result was reached at the trial in *R. v. Gillespie (No. 2), supra,* for the reasons given by Ouimet J. in the passage quoted by Williams and Castel.

Fundamentally, it will be recognized that these three categories of cases merely provide examples of how courts have determined whether an element of an offence has been committed in a province claiming jurisdiction over it. They, nevertheless, demonstrate the determination of the courts to construe s. 432(*b*) flexibly and sensibly and to avoid restricting its operation by interpreting it narrowly or technically. They simplify the inquiry in this case into the essential legal characteristics of the offence and the acts or omissions which constitute it.

The nature of the offence

The gravamen of the offence under s. 250(1) is interference with the custodial rights of the mother by intentionally depriving her of those rights by "detaining" the child. It is not the mere keeping of the child in Calgary, as it would be, for example, if the charge was unlawful confinement or imprisonment under s. 247(2). Although s. 250 is placed in Part VI of the *Criminal Code* under the heading of "Offences Against the Person and Reputation" it is not an offence against the person of the child. The child of tender years is little more than the pawn which is the object of the offence. In reality it is an offence against the custodial rights of the mother. As a result, the principles enunciated in the jurisdictional decisions pertaining to offences against property are of assistance. Yet how infinitely more important to our society is the vital issue of custody when compared to property rights. The paramount consideration in the award of custody is the welfare of the child which is imperilled by any interference with custodial rights.

Section 250(1) does not, therefore, by its terms confine the offence to the single act of keeping the child in Alberta but rather describes a crime which could also have ramifications in Ontario. The law, therefore, does not preclude the possibility of Ontario having jurisdiction.

The acts constituting the offence

The more important question is whether anything which the appellant did or omitted to do in Ontario could be considered legally to be an intrinsic element of the offence. It was open to the provincial court judge to infer that a well-thought- out plan had been executed by the appellant with the intent of depriving the mother of her custodial rights. Some acts in pursuance of that plan occurred or registered their effects in Ontario. They are: obtaining possession of the child from the mother; boarding an aircraft bound for Calgary with the child; keeping the child in Calgary, and failing to redeliver the child into the mother's custody in Ontario. This series of events commenced and produced their final effects in Ontario. They must be carefully scrutinized in order to determine whether they are elements of the offence or merely preparatory acts or consequences.

The initiating acts

The nature of this offence and the circumstances of this case indicate that the acts of the appellant had progressed beyond the mere formulation of a criminal plan before he left Ontario. The gist of this offence is the specific intention of depriving the appellant's wife of her custodial rights. The inference can be readily drawn from the evidence that the appellant formed this intention before boarding an aircraft for Calgary with the child. At that moment he committed an overt act in furtherance of his criminal intention which in law was an element of the offence committed in Ontario.

This case is very similar to *Hogle, supra,* and [*R. v.*] *Solloway* [(1933), 61 C.C.C. 297, [1934] O.R. 31], where the offences involved a continuity of operations extending over more than one province. In those cases, the accused, who had obtained lawful custody of securities in one jurisdiction and converted them in another, were held amenable to prosecution in the first jurisdiction. The reasoning of Wright J. in the passage quoted from the *Solloway* case applies with particular force in this case where he said [at p. 299] "that the receipt of the securities and the subsequent fraudulent conversion were part of a scheme or system which had its inception at the City of Ottawa where the securities were first received or dealt with". Here, the appellant initiated the scheme of depriving the mother of custody by removing the child from Ontario. The offence did not consist only of the isolated act of holding the child in Calgary. That act was only part of a scheme intended to deprive the mother of custody and the initial elements of the offence were committed in Ontario. There can be no doubt that the initial acts of the appellant in Ontario were part of a continuing offence which extended beyond the province.

They are also overt acts which, under the authority of *R. v. Horbas* [5 C.R.N.S. 342, [1969] 3 C.C.C. 95 (*sub nom. R. v. Trudel; Ex* parte *Horbas and Myhaluk*) (Man. C.A.)] and *Bennett* [(1974), 19 C.C.C. (2d) 61], confer jurisdiction on Ontario. It is undeniable that the appellant, by boarding the aircraft with the child, committed an overt act in Ontario in pursuance of his intent to deprive the mother of her custodial rights.

The concluding acts

While the acts done by the appellant in Ontario at the commencement of the offence give Ontario jurisdiction, even more compelling reasons are afforded by the concluding actions of the appellant. The effect of the appellant's act of keeping the child in Alberta was felt in Ontario where the mother was deprived of the custody of her child.

While effects giving jurisdiction, as the *Gillespie* case, *supra*, shows, are most usually generated by the *acts* of the accused in another province, they may also rise from an *omission* to perform a legal duty: see *R. v. Vroom* (1975), 23 C.C.C. (2d) 345, 58 D.L.R. (3d) 565, [1975] 4 W.W.R. 113, *per* Clement J.A. at p. 355. In this case the appellant was obliged by the court order granting him access to return the child to his wife in London on Sunday evening. He failed to do so.

Whether this omission to perform a legal obligation in Ontario confers jurisdiction on this province depends on the meaning of the word "detain" in s. 250(1). "Detain" is a word with several meanings. It is defined in the Shorter Oxford English Dictionary as: "To keep in confinement or custody; to keep back, *withhold;* to keep, retain; to hold, hold down" (emphasis added). In Webster's New World Dictionary, 2nd College ed., it is defined as: "To keep in custody, confine; to keep from going on, hold back, to *withhold* " (emphasis added).

. . .

The mere keeping or confinement of the child in Alberta is not the gravamen of the offence. Rather it is the intentional withholding of the child from the wife which had the effect of depriving her of her custodial rights. There was evidence before the learned provincial judge sufficient to permit him to properly form an opinion that the offence alleged in the information took place in Ontario where the omission by the appellant to discharge his legal duty to return the child occurred. Accordingly, he was entitled to conclude, as he did, that he had jurisdiction to put the appellant on trial.

For the foregoing reasons the appeal is dismissed.

Appeal dismissed.

PROBLEM 6

The accused is charged that he did by telephone knowingly utter a threat to John Lawrence contrary to what was then s. 331 of the Criminal Code. John Lawrence received the phone call from the accused in British Columbia but there is no evidence of where the call originated. The defence objects to the jurisdiction of the British Columbia Provincial Court. Rule on the objection. Compare *R. v. Fournier* (1977), 35 C.C.C. (2d) 313 (B.C. S.C.).

PROBLEM 7

The accused is charged with conspiring with X to forge currency. Contemporaneous raids were made on the business premises of X, in Edmonton, and of the accused in Manitoba. At the accused's premises the police seized a parcel addressed to the accused which contained bank notes similar to those found on X's premises. The parcel contained fingerprints made by X and the accused was carrying an address book with X's name and address. The accused objects to the Manitoba Provincial Court's jurisdiction. Rule. Compare *R. v. Horbas*, 5 C.R.N.S. 342, [1969] 3 C.C.C. 95 (*sub nom. R. v. Trudel; Ex parte Horbas and Myhaluk*) (Man. C.A.) and *R. v. Martel* (1986), 55 C.R. (3d) 63 (P.E.I. S.C.).

PROBLEM 8

The accused purchased a rifle from a licensed gun dealer at a gun show in Michigan. At the time of purchase, he was prohibited from possessing firearms by three court orders made under the Criminal Code. The rifle was located in Ontario by a trespasser looking in an abandoned barn for salvageable property. The trespasser contacted the police, who investigated and determined that the accused bought the gun in Michigan. He was charged and convicted of breaching the court orders. His appeal was dismissed. Was this decision correct? Compare *R. v. Rattray* (2008), 229 C.C.C. (3d) 496 (Ont. C.A.).

The question of territoriality also arises at the level of territorial divisions within a province or territory. This was, at one time, a much bigger problem than it is today since there was previously a greater tendency to restrict the jurisdiction of courts to particular geographical areas, such as counties or districts. This was particularly so for the county and district courts that formerly existed in all provinces but Quebec, but there were often limitations on magistrates (predecessors of provincial courts) as well. Now, thankfully, with the abolition of district and county courts and the position in all provinces and territories that judges of all levels have jurisdiction throughout the province, the problems have largely been alleviated. Nevertheless, due to vague drafting in the Code and conflicting lines of judicial authority, there may still be some complexity in some provinces.

The starting point is the common law presumption that an accused should be tried in the jurisdiction or "venue" where the offence occurred. However, the Code has modified the common law position in bestowing jurisdiction. For indictable offences, this occurs in two sections: ss. 470 and 504. Section 470 states that any court with the power to try indictable offences may conduct the trial if the accused is found, arrested or in custody in that territorial division, or has been ordered to be tried there by that court or any other court with the authority to do so (in the latter case, for example, a provincial court judge hearing a preliminary inquiry).

In addition, s. 504 requires a justice to receive an information (provided it is validly sworn) if it alleges that the accused has committed an indictable offence which may be tried in that province and that the accused either is or resides (or there is a belief in either) in the territorial jurisdiction of the justice; or that the accused, wherever she is, has committed the offence in that territorial jurisdiction; or has anywhere received property obtained unlawfully within that jurisdiction; or has stolen property in that jurisdiction.

On the surface, these provisions might imply some restrictions on the territorial jurisdiction of the particular criminal courts within provinces. However, the definition of "territorial division" in s. 2 of the Code includes "any province, county, union of counties, township, city, town, parish or other judicial division or place to which the context applies". There are two lines of authority interpreting these provisions that seem to persist in spite of the abolition of county and district courts and the fact that all provinces grant authority to the judges of their courts throughout the province.

The first interpretation is the literal one that, because "province" is included within the definition, so long as the judge in question is granted authority to act throughout the province, there is jurisdiction under s. 470 to try the offence: *R. v. Roberts* (1927), 49 C.C.C. 171 (Sask. C.A.); *R. v. Falkner* (1977), 37 C.C.C. (2d) 330 (B.C. S.C.); *R. v. Rice* (1967), [1968] 3 C.C.C. 85 at 89 (Man. C.A.). Likewise, a justice has jurisdiction to receive an information under s. 504 if she has authority to act throughout the province. The practical effect of this interpretation is that, while the common law presumption that the offence be charged and tried where committed normally applies, there is nonetheless jurisdiction to do so elsewhere within the province.

The other interpretation holds that there is injustice in the first interpretation in the sense that a charge may be laid or an offence tried at a place far removed from the commission of the offence. Thus, even though provincial statutes may grant the court jurisdiction throughout the province, if there are also smaller territorial divisions established in the province, the smaller division is the operative one for a given court to exercise jurisdiction: *R. v. Simons* (1976), 30 C.C.C. (2d) 162 (Ont. C.A.); *R. v. Sarazin* (1978), 39 C.C.C. (2d) 131, 3 C.R. (3d) 97 (P.E.I. S.C.). This approach is seen to be necessary to ensure that an accused is not the subject of capricious treatment by the police, prosecution or, indeed, a preliminary inquiry judge committing for trial. Otherwise, an accused might be required to travel a great distance to appear in court, not only at great expense but frequently at some cost in justice due to the unavailability of witnesses, counsel, or other assistance. To the adherents of this approach, it is no answer that a change of venue application under s. 599 might be a safeguard against such unfairness, since the accused would bear the onus of showing the injustice and would still be subject to judicial discretion in seeking a remedy.

Nevertheless, the predominant (and likely the better) view is the simpler one: that any criminal offence may be tried anywhere in the province as long as the particular court has jurisdiction throughout the province: see *R. v. Ellis* (2009), 67 C.R. (6th) 313, 244 C.C.C. (3d) 438 (Ont. C.A.). The remedies for unfair conduct by the police or prosecution are via a change of venue application or, in an extreme case, seeking a judicial stay of the prosecution by showing it to be an abuse of process. Most of the time, however, the interests of the accused and the Crown are the same (in the sense that witnesses for both sides are likely to be where the offence was committed) and they coincide with the common law principle. At the same time, the more flexible, predominant view allows the police to permit an accused to appear in court in her home community, even where the offence was allegedly committed at another location. This is an advantage to all should the accused decide to plead guilty while, if the matter proceeds to trial, it will almost invariably take place where the crime was committed. In addition, this approach avoids unnecessary technicalities surrounding the issuance of process, committals for trial, etc.

The position is the same for summary conviction offences on essentially the same reasoning. Section 785 defines "summary conviction court" as the court having jurisdiction in that territorial division, while s. 798 gives every summary conviction court jurisdiction within that territorial division. Since provincial court judges now have authority throughout the province, any provincial court judge sitting anywhere in the province may try the offence. Notwithstanding the ability to try offences anywhere in the province, the common law presumption usually determines the place of the trial. There is, however, the ability to have the venue changed to another territorial division within the province upon application to the trial court under s. 599. That topic is addressed in Chapter 11 (Preliminary Considerations and Pre-Trial Motions).

6. Jurisdiction Under the Charter

The Canadian Charter of Rights and Freedoms, 1982, was entrenched by the Constitution Act of December 8, 1981.

For a review of the first thirty years of jurisprudence under the Charter, see: J. Benedet, S. Coughlan, L. Dufraimont, T. Nadon, T. Quigley, and D. Stuart, "30th Anniversary of the *Canadian Charter of Rights and Freedoms*: The Impact on Criminal Justice" (2012), 91 C.R. (6th) 71.

(a) Section 24

Section 24 is to be found under the heading of "Enforcement":

(1) Anyone whose rights or freedoms, as guaranteed by this Charter, have been infringed or denied may apply to a court of competent jurisdiction to obtain such remedy as the court considers appropriate and just in the circumstances.

(2) Where, in proceedings under subsection (1), a court concludes that evidence was obtained in a manner that infringed or denied any rights or freedoms guaranteed by this Charter, the evidence shall be excluded if it is established that, having regard to all the circumstances, the admission of it in the proceedings would bring the administration of justice into disrepute.

It is clear that the usual remedy against a Charter violation in the criminal law is to bring a motion to the trial court under s. 24. The scope of these remedies will be examined in a later chapter.

In *R. v. Mills*, [1986] 1 S.C.R. 863, 52 C.R. (3d) 1, 26 C.C.C. (3d) 481 (S.C.C.), the Supreme Court held that all criminal trial courts as defined by s. 2 of the Criminal Code, and thus including provincial court judges, were "courts of competent jurisdiction" for the purpose of granting s. 24 remedies. This was not because s. 24 conferred a new jurisdiction but because those courts already had

[J]urisdiction conferred by a statute over the offences and persons and power to make the orders sought.

However, the court ruled unanimously that a justice at a preliminary inquiry was *not* a court of competent jurisdiction for the purpose of granting Charter remedies under s. 24. Their jurisdiction under what is now Part XVIII of the Criminal Code was limited to considering whether there is sufficient evidence to put the accused on trial. Even though rules relating to the admissibility of evidence apply at preliminary hearings, the majority of the court further held that there is no jurisdiction for a justice at a preliminary inquiry to consider whether evidence should be excluded under s. 24(2) as having been obtained in violation of the Charter. A 5-4 majority of the Court re-asserted this position in *R. v. Hynes*, [2001] 3 S.C.R. 623, 47 C.R. (5th) 278, 159 C.C.C. (3d) 359 (S.C.C.), relying on statutory construction and reasons of cost and efficiency. Similarly, bail courts have been held to not be courts of competent jurisdiction for Charter remedies: *R. v. Menard* (2008), 63 C.R. (6th) 211, 240 C.C.C. (3d) 1 (B.C. C.A.).

In *Ward v. Vancouver (City)*, [2010] 2 S.C.R. 28, 76 C.R. (6th) 207 (S.C.C.), the Supreme Court recognized a new remedy of suing civilly for compensation for a Charter breach. However, this was only available in Superior Courts that had inherent jurisdiction. Provincial Courts (where most criminal trials are held) were determined to have no such jurisdiction.

The Supreme Court in *Mills* unanimously determined that superior courts have a jurisdiction concurrent with that of trial courts to deal with Charter issues but that they should normally decline to exercise that jurisdiction and leave the matter to the trial courts.

The Supreme Court in *Mills* also determined that s. 24 does not confer jurisdiction in the form of any new rights of appeal or new appellate remedies. The courts have clearly been concerned to avoid delays in criminal trials resulting from interlocutory applications to other courts and appeals from those motions. **Consider whether this worked out fairly in the case of Dr. Morgentaler.** Charged with conspiracy to procure an illegal abortion he brought a pre-trial motion challenging the constitutionality of the Criminal Code abortion provisions on July 20, 1984. His motion failed and he appealed. The Ontario Court of Appeal refused to hear the appeal before the trial. The accused was later acquitted following trial before judge and jury. On the Crown appeal, the Ontario Court of Appeal dismissed a cross-appeal of the Charter challenges. On January 28, 1988, the majority of the Supreme Court declared the abortion provisions unconstitutional.

The *Mills* position that the Charter gives no new standing at trial or under appeal is no longer clear. The Court has granted new appellate relief on leave to third parties relying on Charter rights: for example, newspapers appealing publication bans (*Dagenais v. Canadian Broadcasting Corp.*, [1994] 3 S.C.R. 835, 34 C.R. (4th) 269, 94 C.C.C. (3d) 289) and complainants appealing orders to disclose medical records (*A. (L.L.) v. B. (A.)*, [1995] 4 S.C.R. 536, 44 C.R. (4th) 91, 103 C.C.C. (3d) 92).

The Supreme Court has not directly pronounced on the issue of standing of complainants at trial to raise Charter rights. However the Court indirectly conferred such jurisdiction in its rulings in *A. (L.L.) v. B. (A.)*, [1995] 4 S.C.R. 536, and *R. v. O'Connor* [1995] 4 S.C.R. 411, 44 C.R. (4th) 1, 103 C.C.C. (3d) 1, that there must be a two-stage procedure before the trial judge to balance the accused's right to full answer and defence against the complainant's privacy interests which the 5-4 majority found protected in ss. 7 and 8.

The full Court later recognised in *R. v. Mills*, [1999] 3 S.C.R. 668, 28 C.R. (5th) 207, 139 C.C.C. (3d) 321 (S.C.C.) and *R. v. Shearing* (2002), 2 C.R. (6th) 213, 165 C.C.C. (3d) 225 (S.C.C.) that complainants in sexual assault cases also have enforceable s.15 equality rights to be weighed. In *Shearing*, the Court softens this language to that of "equality values". *Mills* and *Shearing* are fully considered later, under Trial Process, Discovery.

(b) Section 52

The supremacy clause in s. 52 of the Charter reads

The Constitution of Canada is the supreme law of Canada, and any law that is inconsistent with the provisions of the Constitution is, to the extent of the inconsistency, of no force or effect.

In *R. v. Big M Drug Mart*, [1985] 1 S.C.R. 295, 18 C.C.C. (3d) 385 (S.C.C.), Chief Justice Dickson for a unanimous Supreme Court established that s. 52 has a powerful remedial role in the context of criminal law quite independent to s. 24. An accused, whether corporate or individual, may defend a criminal charge by arguing that the law under which the charge has been brought was constitutionally invalid in its purpose or effect and thus inoperative under s. 52.

> Section 52 sets out the fundamental principle of constitutional law that the Constitution is supreme. The undoubted corollary to be drawn from this principle is that no one can be convicted of an offence under an unconstitutional law. (at 400)

Any judicial officer would have to decline jurisdiction if satisfied that the law, under which authority he or she is to proceed, was inconsistent with the Constitution.

The Charter normally has no direct application where the conduct of officials in question occurred outside Canada. However the Supreme Court has recognized a discretion in such cases to exclude evidence under ss. 7, 11(d) and 24(1) to ensure a fair trial in Canada: *R. v. Harrer*, [1995] 3 S.C.R. 562, 42 C.R. (4th) 269, 101 C.C.C. (3d) 193 (S.C.C.). A divided Court held in *R. v. Hape*, 47 C.R. (6th) 96, 220 C.C.C. (3d) 161, [2007] 2 S.C.R. 192 that the Charter does not apply to Canadian police acting outside Canada unless the foreign jurisdiction consents to their enforcement jurisdiction.

See critical reviews by Robert Currie, C.R. , *ibid.* 98 and Kent Roach, Editorial in (2007) 55 Crim. L.Q. 1. However in *Khadr v. Canada (Minister of Justice)*, [2008] 2 S.C.R. 125, 56 C.R. (6th) 255, 232 C.C.C. (3d) 101 the Court created an exception where actions violated Canada's international obligations not to torture.

See Benjamin Berger, "The Reach of Rights in the Security State: Reflections on *Khadr v. Canada (Minister of Justice)*" (2008) 56 C.R. (6th) 268.

PROBLEM 9

The accused was charged with theft on January 22, 1987. The preliminary inquiry was scheduled for August. The Crown was informed in June that no special sittings would be conducted by provincial judges during the months of July or August and that the investigating officer would not be available to assist with the conduct of the inquiry except in December or after April 1988. The Crown and defence counsel agreed to conduct the preliminary inquiry in December. They were informed that no judge was available at that time. They agreed to reschedule the preliminary inquiry to May 1988. Defence counsel wrote the Crown on July 6,1987, to confirm these arrangements and to express his concern about the "excessive delay". Can defence counsel do anything to speed the process? Must he wait until the preliminary? Can he ask the judge at the preliminary to stay the matter? Compare *R. v. Smith*, [1989] 2 S.C.R. 1120, 73 C.R. (3d) 1, 52 C.C.C. (3d) 97 (S.C.C.).

Part II

INVESTIGATION: POLICE POWERS AND RIGHTS OF ACCUSED

Chapter 2

SEARCH AND SEIZURE

1. Powers to Search and Seize

In Canada all powers of seach and seizure, statutory and common law, are now subject to the constitutional protection found in the Charter of Rights:

8. Everyone has the right to be secure against unreasonable search or seizure.

There can be no doubt that this provision has had a dramatic impact, forcing the courts to grapple in various contexts with the uneasy balance between the right of a citizen to be free from state intrusion and the need of the state to intervene on occasion for some legitimate purpose. Our law in the area is necessarily in a state of flux. Before we enter into the constitutional arena, we will first examine the basic features of our statutory and common law provisions.

(a) Criminal Code

The search powers conferred by the Code are usually but not always restricted to "peace officer" as defined in s. 2, which includes police officers but also mayors, jail guards, bailiffs, customs officers, pilots and certain designated members of the Canadian Forces.

(i) Without a Warrant

The only express Code powers to search and seize without warrant are in respect of certain stipulated offences: ss. 117.02(1), 117.04(2), weapons; s. 199(2), common gaming house; s. 254(2) to (4), impaired driving; s. 339(3), suspected stolen timber; s. 447(2), cockpits; s. 462, counterfeit money.

Why do you think that powers to search without a warrant were declared for these Criminal Code offences but for no other? What are the major policy considerations behind the apparent reluctance to authorize warrantless powers to search?

(ii) With a Search Warrant

Under ss. 487-489 a justice is empowered to issue a search warrant to search in relation to an offence under the Criminal Code or other federal statute. A justice is defined in s. 2 as a justice of the peace or provincial court judge.

487. (1) A justice who is satisfied by information on oath in Form 1 that there are reasonable grounds to believe that there is in a building, receptacle or place

- (a) anything on or in respect of which any offence against this Act or any other Act of Parliament has been or is suspected to have been committed,
- (b) anything that there are reasonable grounds to believe will afford evidence with respect to the commission of an offence, or will reveal the whereabouts of a person who is believed to have committed an offence, against this Act or any other Act of Parliament,
- (c) anything that there are reasonable grounds to believe is intended to be used for the purpose of committing any offence against the person for which a person may be arrested without warrant, or
- (c.1) any offence-related property,

may at any time issue a warrant authorizing a peace officer or a public officer who has been appointed or designated to administer or enforce a federal or provincial law and whose duties include the enforcement of this Act or any other Act of Parliament and who is named in the warrant

- (d) to search the building, receptacle or place for any such thing and to seize it, and
- (e) subject to any other Act of Parliament, to, as soon as practicable, bring the thing seized before, or make a report in respect thereof to, the justice or some other justice for the same territorial division in accordance with section 489.1.

. . .

487.1 (1) Where a peace officer believes that an indictable offence has been committed and that it would be impracticable to appear personally before a justice to make application for a warrant in accordance with section 256 or 487, the peace officer may submit an information on oath by telephone or other means of telecommunication to a justice designated for the purpose by the chief judge of the provincial court having jurisdiction in the matter.

[A number of detailed provisions follow regarding the perfection of the telewarrant process.]

487.11 A peace officer . . . may, in the course of his or her duties, exercise any of the powers described in subsection 487(1) . . . without a warrant if the conditions for obtaining a warrant exist but by reason of exigent circumstances it would be impracticable to obtain a warrant.

. . .

488. A warrant issued under section 487 or 487.1 shall be executed by day, unless

- (a) the justice is satisfied that there are reasonable grounds for it to be executed by night;
- (b) the reasonable grounds are included in the information; and
- (c) the warrant authorizes that it be executed by night.

. . .

489. (1) Every person who executes a warrant may seize, in addition to the things mentioned in the warrant, any thing that the person believes on reasonable grounds

- (a) has been obtained by the commission of an offence against this or any other Act of Parliament;
- (b) has been used in the commission of an offence against this or any other Act of Parliament; or

(c) will afford evidence in respect of an offence against this or any other Act of Parliament.

(2) Every peace officer, and every public officer who has been appointed or designated to administer or enforce any federal or provincial law and whose duties include the enforcement of this or any other Act of Parliament, who is lawfully present in a place pursuant to a warrant or otherwise in the execution of duties may, without a warrant, seize any thing that the officer believes on reasonable grounds

(a) has been obtained by the commission of an offence against this or any other Act of Parliament;

(b) has been used in the commission of an offence against this or any other Act of Parliament; or

(c) will afford evidence in respect of an offence against this or any other Act of Parliament.

29. (1) It is the duty of every one who executes a process or warrant to have it with him, where it is feasible to do so, and to produce it when requested to do so.

The legislation speaks of searching a "building, receptacle or place". **Can one obtain a search warrant to search a person?** Consider the wisdom of the blanket rule in the following case.

LAPORTE v. LAGANIÈRE
(1972), 18 C.R.N.S. 357, 8 C.C.C. (2d) 343
(*sub nom. Re Laporte and R.*) (Que. Q.B.)

HUGESSEN J.:—This is a writ of certiorari for the purpose of quashing and setting aside a search warrant issued by Laganie're J.S.P. on 29th July 1971. The warrant purports to authorize a search in the body of the petitioner Roger Laporte for one or more bullets which are alleged to have been fired from police revolvers in an exchange of gunfire, during a hold-up at Knowlton, Quebec, 23rd February 1970. The warrant is addressed to peace officers in general and to two named peace officers in particular and purports to authorize them to cause the bullet or bullets in question to be extracted from Laporte's body by one or more duly qualified doctors. The warrant further contains a proviso that if in the course of such search the doctors in question should determine that there is any serious danger to Laporte's life, the search must forthwith cease.

. . .

The facts are very simple and are really not in dispute. The petitioner was arrested on 26th July 1971 in connection with another matter which apparently has nothing whatever to do with the present case. The police however have reason to suspect that the petitioner was involved in a hold-up at Knowlton, which had taken place about a year and a half before. There are scars on the petitioner's neck and shoulder which resemble bullet wounds. X-rays reveal the presence in the petitioner's shoulder of a foreign body, a metallic object corresponding in size and shape to a 38-calibre slug. This foreign body is sufficiently deeply embedded in the flesh that it cannot be felt by simple tactile examination. To remove it would require more than minor or superficial surgery. The expert medical evidence before me was conflicting as to whether or not it was medically desirable from a petitioner's point of view that the foreign body should be removed. Both doctors were however in agreement that the operation, if performed, would require a general anaesthetic and ipso facto would involve a certain element of risk to the petitioner. They also agreed that they would not normally perform such an operation without the consent of the patient.

I need hardly add that the petitioner does not consent to having the object in question removed from his body.

I have stated at the outset that this matter arises by means of a writ of certiorari. Accordingly the only issue I have to decide is whether the Justice had jurisdiction to issue the search warrant. If such jurisdiction exists it is not for me to interfere with his discretion, provided his exercise of it has been judicial. If, on the other hand, such jurisdiction does not exist there is ample authority for the use of the writ of certiorari to quash and set aside an illegal search warrant.

. . .

All parties before me readily concede that there is no precedent in point that they have been able to find either in Canadian or British case law. Petitioner invites me to conclude from this that the answer to the question is so self-evident that it has never been raised. I am not prepared to accept this argument. The law does not stand still but must grow and change with the times. Simply because something has never been done before is no good reason to say that it should not be done now. I trust that the age of judicial innovation is not dead and there will always be room to extend the frontiers of jurisprudence. If the matter has not been decided before, it falls to be decided now, and the absence of precedent, while it renders my task more difficult, adds nothing to the argument one way or the other. What is more, even though there is no English or Canadian case directly in point, the matter has arisen before in the United States and, while not binding on me, the decisions of the courts of that country may always be looked to for guidance. Indeed it is upon the American jurisprudence that the main thrust of the respondent's argument is founded, and it is to that jurisprudence that I shall now turn.

First and most important is the case of *Re Crowder*, United States District Court for District of Columbia (not yet reported), referred to by the Justice in his reasons supporting the issuance of the warrant. In that case Curran C.J. authorized the issuance of a search warrant for the surgical removal of what was thought to be a bullet "lying superficially beneath the skin" of a prisoner's forearm. The same decision refused a search warrant for the removal of a similar bullet in Crowder's left thigh "because this procedure might cause the reduction of use or function of his left leg".

Crowder applied for a writ of prohibition in the United States Court of Appeals for the District of Columbia Circuit, and by an order dated 2nd March 1971 (McGowan and Loventhall JJ.) this relief was denied. I am advised by counsel that the Court of Appeals gave no reasons for its judgment but I have had made available to me copies of some of the motion papers filed on both sides. From these latter it would appear that the prosecution opposed the issuance of the writ of prohibition not only for reasons going to the merits of the search warrant itself, but also on procedural grounds. Since the decision of the Court of Appeals was not motivated, it is impossible for me to say whether they actually approved the issuance of the search warrant or simply held that they did not have jurisdiction to review the lower Court's decision.

The judgment of Curran C.J. in the District Court relies heavily upon the decision of the United States Supreme Court in the case of *Schmerber v. California* (1966), 384 U.S. 757. That case, it should be noted, did not concern a search warrant at all, but simply whether the result of a blood test, taken without the consent of the appellant and indeed over his objection, was admissible in evidence. The Supreme Court of the United States held that it was and that such blood test did not violate the self-incrimination, due process, or unreasonable search and seizure provisions of the United States Constitution.

It is to be noted that in the *Schmerber* case the majority of the United States Supreme Court repeatedly emphasized the minor nature of the "operation" performed upon the appellant and the fact that, having been carried out in a medical environment, there was an almost total lack of risk. The majority judgment delivered by Brennan J. ends with the following words which I find significant:

> The integrity of an individual's person is a cherished value of our society. That we to-day hold that the constitution does not forbid the states minor intrusions into an individual's body under stringently limited conditions in no way indicates that it permits more substantial intrusions, or intrusions under other conditions.

With all due respect for the contrary view, I confess that I have the greatest difficulty in following the road that leads from *Schmerber* to *Crowder*. It is trite to say that at some point a difference in degree becomes one of kind, but in my view the difference between, on the one hand, the admission after the fact of evidence obtained by the insertion of a needle beneath the skin and, on the other hand, the prior authorization of the performance of a surgical operation against the patient's will and involving, as it is bound to, some degree of risk, falls into the latter category.

Furthermore, it is to be noted that in *Crowder* the search warrant was authorized under the provisions of R. 41 of the Federal Criminal Rules of Practice. The following extracts from para. (c) of that Rule, entitled Issuance and Contents, are instructive:

> . . . If the judge or commissioner is satisfied that grounds for the application exist or that there is probable cause to believe that they exist, he shall issue a warrant identifying the property and naming or describing the *person or place* to be searched ... It shall command the officer to search forthwith the *person or place* named for the property specified. The warrant shall direct that it be served in the day-time, but if the affidavits are positive that the property is *on the person* or in the place to be searched, the warrant may direct that it be served at any time...

. . .

. . . Is it possible to say that a living human body is a "building, receptacle or place" into which a surgical intrusion may be justified by means of a search warrant?

Clearly it is not a "building". Nor Would I have said upon any ordinary construction of the term that it is a "receptacle". However, the Justice who issued the search warrant, basing himself on the definition of that word found in Butterworth's Words and Phrases Legally Defined, 2nd ed., held that it was, so the point must be examined.

The definition in Words and Phrases reads in full as follows:

Receptacle includes a vehicle or stall and any basket bag, box, vessel, stand, easel, board, tray or other structure or thing which is used (whether or not constructed or adapted for such use) as a container for or for the display of any article or thing; and article or thing includes any living thing.

Quite apart from the fact that on a careful reading of this definition it is clear that the "living thing" is the article or thing contained or displayed rather than the thing which contains it or is used for its display, the definition itself is taken, as the reference work clearly indicates, from a statute, namely, the London County Council (General Powers) Act, 1947. Section 15(1) of that Act contains a number of definitions including one for "receptacle", which is identical to that quoted above, down to the semicolon. There is another, and separate, definition for "article or thing" which is that part of the quotation following the semicolon. Section 15 itself falls under Pt. IV of the Act, which is entitled Regulation of Street Trading.

In my opinion, it is totally unjustified to make use of a definition of this sort, contained in a foreign statute and having a specific purpose, to aid in the construction of plain words used in the Criminal Code. In my view whatever else a receptacle may be it cannot in any normal construction of language be held to include the interior of a living human body.

There remains for consideration the word "place". This is a word of great generality. Amongst the definitions to be found in the Shorter Oxford English Dictionary, 3rd ed., are the following: "a particular part of space, of definite situation . . . the portion of space actually occupied by a person or thing . . . a particular part or spot in a body or surface".

Counsel for respondent argues, in my view rightly, that there is no room for the application of the ejusdem generis rule to the enumeration of "building, receptacle or place" contained in s. 443. Where the words used in an enumeration are all of more or less equal generality there is no genus or class which can be deduced from the specific words to which the general words can be made subject. This does not solve the respondent's problem however for it is still necessary, in order to justify the warrant, to find that the word "place", on its plain construction and in everyday language, can be held to extend to a living human body.

The word "place" is itself used frequently throughout the Criminal Code. It is defined for the specific purposes of Pt. V in s. 179. It is referred to in the definition of "territorial division" in s. 2. "Public place" is defined in s. 138, and s. 169 differentiates between public place as so defined and "any place".

Section 306 contains its own and different definition of place. A person sentenced to death shall by virtue of s. 672 be confined in "a safe place".

I do not in any way pretend that this enumeration is exhaustive. I do however think that it is indicative of the meaning intended by Parliament and indeed by ordinary persons when using the word "place". It is a geographic and not an anatomical location.

I have previously stated that the ejusdem generis rule should not be applied to the enumeration contained in s. 443. This does not mean however that one must exclude the other rules of interpretation and, in particular, that which requires that any statute should be read as a whole and its words interpreted the one by the other. Equally words may be coloured by the context in which they are found. By both these measures I think it is clear that the word "place" as it is used in s. 443 was never intended to extend to or to include the interior of a human body. Words much plainer than those used would be required to convince me that Parliament intended in this section to authorize the breaking-open of the human frame by means of a search warrant. As I pointed out during the argument, if the police are today to be authorized to probe into a man's shoulder for evidence against him, what is to prevent them tomorrow from opening his brain or other vital organs for the same purpose. The investigation of crime would no doubt be thereby rendered easier, but I do not think that we can, in the name of efficiency, justify the wholesale mutilation of suspected persons.

The criminal law has always had to strike the precarious balance between the protection of society on the one hand and the protection of the rights of the individual members of such society on the other. Both rights are equally important, but any conflict between them must wherever possible be resolved in a manner most compatible with individual human dignity. The constant preoccupation of our courts with the protection of the citizen against the state results in the Crown having always to bear the burden in any criminal prosecution. I am not the first judge, and I trust that I shall not be the last, to decide that the possibility that some guilty persons may escape the net of justice is not too high a price to pay for the right to live in freedom. If the Crown cannot prove its case against Laporte without doing physical violence to his person then it is better that the case be not proved.

In my view the Justice had no jurisdiction, either by statute or at common law, to issue this warrant and it is my duty to interfere and prevent what I can only describe as a grotesque perversion of the machinery of justice and an unwarranted invasion upon the basic inviolability of the human person. Even if the operation proposed were minor, and the evidence is that it is not, I would not be prepared to sanction it and I do not do so. *Crowder* may or may not be the law in the United States; it is not the law in Canada.

Other courts too have held that the existing Criminal Code search warrant power does not extend to a search of the person: see, for example, *R. v. Miller* (1987), 62 O.R. (2d) 97, 38 C.C.C. (3d) 252 (Ont. C.A.), *R. v.*

Tomaso (1989), 70 C.R. (3d) 152 (Ont. C.A.) and *R. v. Legere* (1988), 43 C.C.C. (3d) 502 (N.B. C.A.).

Parliament has established two special warrant powers to search the person. A carefully limited s. 256 in the Criminal Code allows for a search warrant for a blood sample where a person is reasonably believed to have caused bodily harm through impaired driving and is unable to consent to the taking of a sample. In 1995, following all parties' consent, Parliament enacted in just one day a power for provincial Court judges to issue warrants to obtain bodily substances for forensic DNA analysis in the investigation of certain listed offences such as murder, assault, sexual assault, robbery, kidnapping and arson (see ss. 487.04-487.09 of the Criminal Code, discussed by Renee Pomerance, "Bill C-104: A Practical Guide to the New DNA Warrants" (1995), 39 C.R. (4th) 224). Charter challenges to the new scheme for D.N.A. warrants were rejected in *R. v. B. (S.A.)*, [2003] 2 S.C.R. 678, 14 C.R. (6th) 205, 178 C.C.C. (3d) 193.

In 2000, the Criminal Code was amended to authorize (ss. 487.051-487.091) post-conviction DNA orders for samples for collection in a national DNA bank: Carol-Ann Bauman, "The D.N.A. Bank: Privacy Concerns and Safeguards", (2000) 34 C.R. (5th) 39 and David Rose and Lisa Goos, "From D.N.A. Databank to D.N.A. Warrant: The Declining Weight of a Cold Hit", (2002) 47 C.R. (5th) 106. The Supreme Court of Canada upheld the constitutionality of the DNA databank in *R. v. Rodgers* (*sub nom. R. v. Jackpine*) [2006] 1 S.C.R. 554, 37 C.R. (6th) 1, 207 C.C.C. (3d) 225 (S.C.C.) but only by a 4-3 majority.

―――――――――

In *MacIntyre v. A.G. N.S.,* [1982] 1 S.C.R. 175, 26 C.R. (3d) 193 at 207, 65 C.C.C. (2d) 129 (S.C.C.), Dickson J. (as he then was) for the majority of the Supreme Court of Canada offers a useful definition of the search warrant process:

> A search warrant may be broadly defined as an order issued by a justice under statutory powers, authorizing a named person to enter a specified place to search for and seize specified property which will afford evidence of the actual or intended commission of a crime. A warrant may issue upon a sworn information and proof of reasonable grounds for its issuance. The property seized must be carried before the justice who issued the warrant to be dealt with by him according to law.

> Search warrants are part of the investigative pre-trial process of the criminal law, often employed early in the investigation and before the identity of all of the suspects is known. Parliament, in furtherance of the public interest in effective investigation and prosecution of crime, and through the enactment of s. 443 of the Code, has legalized what would otherwise be an illegal entry of premises and illegal seizure of property. The issuance of a search warrant is a judicial act on the part of the justice, usually performed ex parte and in camera, by the very nature of the proceedings.

Under the scheme of s. 487(1) as judicially interpreted, there are three broad requirements of a valid search warrant:

1. The informant must present the justice with an information upon oath based on reasonable and probable grounds in Form 1 which provides her with sufficient factual details to confer jurisdiction.
2. The justice must act judicially in her independent assessment of the facts and in exercising her discretion as to whether to issue a search warrant.
3. The warrant to search must contain sufficient description of the objects of search in relation to category and offence.

Although in practice both the information and the search warrant documents may be prepared by the informant in advance and presented to the justice together for the justice's consideration, each of the three requirements have to be satisfied. The following case demonstrates how the courts sometimes scrutinize search warrants and informations to obtain search warrants.

Re GILLIS and R.
(1982), 1 C.C.C. (3d) 545 (Que. S.C.).

BOILARD J. (translation):—On June 1, 1982, Detective Sergeant Gilles Morel of the Montreal Urban Community (M.U.C.) Police Force swore out an information to obtain a search warrant under s. 443 of the *Criminal Code*. The information refers to a document entitled "annex A" for a description of the offence and the objects sought, and which I will reproduce in full:

> In Montreal, District of Montreal, between September 2, 1981 and March 1, 1982, an indictable offence was committed by Mr. J. Daniel Gillis, namely fraud by means of the issuance by Mr. Gillis of a promissory note for the sum of $25,000 to the victim Gregorios Veikos. The note was signed by the owners of Trevi Creations Co. Inc., then in bankruptcy, to cover a cash deposit of $10,000 made by Mr. Veikos and a loan from Mr. Veikos to Mr. Gillis for the sum of $15,000 without interest for two months. I have reason to believe, on reasonable and probable grounds, that documents of Trevi Creations Inc., the financial statements of the clients Veikos, Trevi Creations Inc. and the restaurant La Belle Vie, cheques, statements of account, deposit books, receipts, bank books, bank accounts, promissory notes from Trevi Creations Inc. or Veikos, bank notes, safety deposit keys, bonds, R.R.S.P. or R.H.O.S.P., term deposits, Treasury bonds, bank drafts and all other documents from the Canadian Imperial Bank of Commerce, corner of Ste-Catherine and St- Alexandre Streets concerning the Trevi Company, the complainant Veikos or the restaurant La Belle Vie found on the premises, would afford evidence of the commission of the offence.

The reasonable grounds set out in the information are the following: "the statement made by the victim, an examination of the documents and a police investigation". It should immediately be noted that the grounds set out in the information differ from those appearing in annex A mentioned above: "information from reliable persons, an examination of documents and a police investigation".

The warrant was issued the same day. The same document attached to the information is also annexed to the warrant.

On June 10th, the informant in the information prepared a report of the warrant's execution which I will reproduce in its entirety:

> I, Gilles Morel, Det Sgt. M.U.C. police office duly appointed in and for the District of Montreal certify and swear under oath that, in conformity with the search warrant which I was issued, I went to 435 Wickham St. in St-Lambert on June 9, 1982 at 7:15 a.m. and did there search and did seize the following: one metallic blue seal of Trevi Creations Inc., the C.I.B.C. statements of account No. 02-46530, cheques, promissory notes between Trevi Creations Inc. and presumed victims, deposit books investor lists, contracts of transactions between Trevi, C.I.B.C. and victims, various documents between Creation and C.I.B.C., receipts for payments.

A motion for the issuance of a writ of *certiorari* to quash the warrant was served on June 28, 1982, and heard on July 9, 1982.

. . .

II. *Issuance of a search warrant*

The issuance of a search warrant is a judicial act. The justice must decide whether there are reasonable grounds to believe that the objects described in the information are located in the place indicated by the informant and whether these objects will provide evidence of the commission of the offence set out in the information. The justice's belief, based on reasonable grounds, concerns two aspects of the steps to be taken by the informant who is seeking the search warrant under s. 443(1)(*b*) of the *Code:* the existence and the presence of certain objects in a given place, and their probative value.

The obligation of the justice to render his decision as set out in s. 443, was described by Mr. Justice Porter, then Chief Justice of Ontario, in the following terms, in *Re Worrall,* [1965] 2 C.C.C. 1 at p. 5, 48 D.L.R. (2d) 673, [1965] 1 O.R. 527 (Ont. C.A.):

> The police officer is not a judicial officer. It was not his function to decide whether the articles in question should be seized or not. It was the duty of the Justice, upon the evidence before him, to decide this question. He must determine whether there are reasonable grounds to believe that the articles in question *will afford* evidence with respect to the offence alleged. This does not mean that the articles will afford evidence sufficient to result in a conviction. It means, I think, that *the Justice must consider whether the production of the articles will afford evidence which would be relevant to the issue, and would be properly tendered as evidence in a prosecution in which the alleged fraud is in issue.*

(Emphasis added.)

Several years earlier, Chief Justice McRuer expressed the same opinion in *Re Bell Telephone Co. of Canada* (1947), 89 C.C.C. 196 at p. 200, [1947] O.W.N. 651, 4 C.R. 162 (Ont. H.C.):

> The *Cr. Code* makes no provision for seizing things "in connection with" offences for the purpose of observation in place. The words of the *Cr. Code* above set out must be strictly construed. They contemplate the issue of a warrant for the purpose of bringing the things that may afford evidence in the case before the Justice as soon as may reasonably be done. The Justice may give directions as to the safe custody of the things seized. He does not take personal charge of the things until after the trial is over. These matters have always been worked out in a practical

way, but the fundamental thing is that *the purpose of the search warrant is to secure things that will in themselves be relevant to a case to be proved, not to secure an opportunity of making observations in respect of the use of things, and thereby obtain evidence.* In this respect, I think the warrant is defective and an order will go quashing it.

(Emphasis added.)

Mr. Justice Solomon, of the Manitoba Queen's Bench, made similar comments in *Wiens et al. v. The Queen* (1973), 24 C.R.N.S. 341 at p. 347, [1973] 6 W.W.R. 757.

The conduct of the police officers in the execution of the warrant does not affect the judicial nature of the obligation imposed on the justice at the stage of the issuance of the warrant. In other words, the manner in which the warrant is executed does not affect its validity. Similarly, a warrant invalid at the outset is not rendered valid by the manner in which it is executed: *Re Worrall, supra,* pp. 5-6.

The purpose of the procedure set out in s. 443 is very simple; paraphrasing the text of s. 8 of the Charter, the citizen must be protected against unreasonable searches and seizures. This view was clearly expressed previously by Mr. Justice Brossard when he was a member of this court in *Regency Realties Inc. v. Loranger* (1961), 36 C.R. 291 at p. 295 (Que. S.C.):

> To permit a peace officer to blindly proceed to search an individual's home when neither the information nor the warrant would permit him to know in a reasonable manner the circumstances of the crime underlying the search or to be able to identify in a similarly reasonable manner the "things" to be seized, would lead to abuse and grave injustice. No one could even believe that he was safe from such a search.

III. *Statement of reasonable grounds*

The duty of the informant to reveal his "reasonable grounds" will vary depending on the particular circumstances set out in the information. In certain cases, the justice may infer certain grounds from the facts revealed by the informant; in other cases, a statement of the grounds must be specifically given. It should be remembered that the justice cannot leave the ultimate decision to the discretion of the informant without exceeding his jurisdiction: *Hicks v. McCune* (1921), 36 C.C.C. 141 at p. 150, 58 D.L.R. 431, 19 O.W.N. 423 (Ont. S.C.A.D.).

In support of the proposition, I will refer to an extract of the judgment delivered by Mr. Justice Zuber, when he was a member of the Ontario Supreme Court, in *Re Lubell and The Queen* (1973), 11 C.C.C. (2d) 188 at p. 190 (Ont. H.C.J.):

> Constable Murden states, in effect, that of his own knowledge and as a result of having viewed this financial statement, he believes that these other records will afford evidence that the offence of distributing obscene matter has taken place. I do not know what more could be asked of him. He pledges his own credit directly that the documents sought will afford evidence. He says further that from information received from a reliable source, he believes the items sought are at these premises. In my opinion, no fault whatever can be found with the information of Constable Murden with respect to spelling out reasonable grounds.

I perhaps should add that he does not detail exactly how these documents are to be related to the commission of the offence. It obviously is not a part of the Crown's case that the documents themselves are obscene; their very nature suggests to anyone with common sense that this cannot be so. Obviously they have to be related to distribution. The ordinary inference to be drawn, and one that a Justice of the Peace could easily draw, is that these financial documents contain evidence of distribution. It may be that in a given case where it would be extremely difficult to envisage why certain things should be searched for, *it might be necessary to spell out the reasons but, in my opinion, where the connection between the items sought and the offence is one that might be gathered easily by inference from the very nature of the offence and the material sought, the informant is not obliged to underline the obvious.*

(Emphasis added.)

A similar opinion was expressed recently by Mr. Justice Clarke, of the Nova Scotia Supreme Court, Trial Division, in *Chedrawy v. A.-G. Can. and Welton* (1981), 23 C.R. (3d) 30 at p. 37, 45 N.S.R. (2d) 146.

In *Regency Realties Inc. v. Loranger, supra,* Mr. Justice Brossard wrote the following, at p. 293:

Whereas the said information contains no serious information on the reasonable grounds of the informant to support his request for a warrant other than that these reasonable grounds are based on "information from a reliable source". Whereas *the information is insufficient and would not on its own enable the justice who is asked to issue a search warrant, to be satisfied with respect to the existence of reasonable grounds to believe that the things set out in the said information would provide evidence* concerning the perpetration of the alleged crimes in the general terms set out above.

(Emphasis added.)

In the present case, the statement of the reasonable grounds made by the informant is laconic despite the differences between the annex and the information. What were the documents examined by the informant? What was the scope of the police investigation? What information was learned? What information was received from reliable persons whose identity could not be revealed because they were police informers? What is in the victim's statement? What are the informant's reasonable grounds to believe that the "bank notes, safety deposit keys, bonds, R.R.S.P. or R.H.O.S.P., term deposits, Treasury bonds, bank drafts, and all other documents from the Canadian Imperial Bank of Commerce, corner of Ste-Catherine and St-Alexandre streets concerning the Trevi Company, the complainant Veikos or the restaurant La Belle Vie, found on the premises, would afford evidence of the commission of the offence"?

The fraud, it should be remembered, is described as having been committed by means of a promissory note in the amount of $25,000.

On what could the justice of the peace rely in order to be satisfied "that reasonable grounds" existed to believe that these objects were present at the place set out in the warrant and that these things, if found there, would afford evidence of the offence committed against Veikos? It is not sufficient for the justice to either rely solely on the good faith of the informant or on the good sense that the person who will execute the warrant may exhibit. The *Criminal Code* requires more from the justice before he may issue a warrant.

I therefore come to the conclusion without any hesitation that the grounds set out in the information and in the annex are insufficient. As a result, the justice exceeded his jurisdiction in authorizing the issuance of a search warrant on the basis of this information.

IV. *Description of the objects*

The objects or documents sought under the search warrant must be described with sufficient precision, not only with respect to their category, but also with respect to their relation to the offence for which they are to provide evidence: *Re Regina and Johnson & Franklin Wholesale Distributors Ltd.* (1971), 3 C.C.C. (2d) 484 at p. 489, 16 C.R.N.S. 107, [1971] 4 W.W.R. 534 (B.C. C.A.).

It is not sufficient to indicate in the information or on the warrant that one is looking for "the financial statements of the clients Veikos, Trevi Creations Inc. and the restaurant La Belle Vie, cheques, statements of account, deposit books, receipts, bank books, bank accounts, promissory notes from Trevi Creations Inc. or Veikos". It is necessary to specify which ones.

Finally, what is the relation between the fraud committed by the applicant Gillis between September 2, 1981, and March 1, 1982, against Veikos, and the "bank notes, safety deposit keys, bonds, R.R.S.P. or R.H.O.S.P., term deposits Treasury bonds, bank drafts and all other documents from the Canadian Imperial Bank of Commerce, corner of Ste-Catherine and St-Alexandre Streets concerning the Trevi Company, the complainant Veikos or the restaurant La Belle Vie"? None is given on the information and I find it impossible to deduce one as the justice must have done in this case.

But even if s. 445 of the *Criminal Code* confers a certain discretion on the person executing the search warrant to seize things not set out in the warrant, it should not be concluded that a similar discretion is conferred to search and seize things set out in the warrant. If that were the case, the text of s. 445 would be quite useless. The police officer who conducts a search only executes the authorization which is conferred on him by the warrant "to search . . . for any such thing, and to seize and carry it before the justice who issued the warrant or some other justice for the same territorial division to be dealt with by him according to law". The search is not and must not become a fishing trip: *Re Bell Telephone Co. of Canada* (1947), 89 C.C.C. 196, [1947] O.W.N. 651, 4 C.R. 162 (Ont. H.C.).

The law has not changed since I wrote the following comments in *Centre Communautaire Juridique de Montréal et al. v. Mierzwinski et al.*, [1978] Que. S.C. 792 (Que. S.C.); upheld on appeal to the Court of Appeal 16 C.R. (3d) 188, in which I referred to *Re Alder et al. and The Queen* (1977), 37 C.C.C. (2d) 234, [1977] 5 W.W.R. 132, 5 A.R. 473, *sub nom. Alder et al. v. A.-G. Alta. et al.* (Alta. S.C.T.D.) *Re PSI Mind Development Institute Ltd. et al. and The Queen* (1977), 37 C.C.C. (2d) 263, and *Re Abou-Assale and Pollack and The Queen* (1978), 39 C.C.C. (2d) 546, 1 C.R. (3d) 213 *sub nom. Abou-Assale and Pollack v. Bourdon J.S.P.; Champagne and Lockwood*, [1978] Que. S.C. 142 at p. 800 *sub nom. Abou-Assale et al. v. Bourdon et al.* (Que. S.C.):

It is evident that the search warrant, which is an exception to the principle of the inviolability of the home, must be interpreted restrictively and does not give carte blanche to the police officer executing the warrant to seize whatever he likes during the search. The search warrant must, in my view, set out with sufficient precision the nature and identity of the documents sought so that whoever conducts the search, and also whoever is subject to the search, can, upon reading the warrant, know what is being sought and what may be seized. This need for clarity is even more essential when the search warrant authorizes the search of a lawyer's office and the seizure of certain documents not protected by solicitor-client privilege.

To determine whether the objects sought are adequately described both as to their nature and their specific identity, consideration is given to these objects in the warrant as well as to the statement of the offence in the information which the police provide: *R. v. Trottier et al., Ex p. McLaughlin et al.,* [1966] 4 C.C.C. 321, [1966] Que. Q.B. 263*n, per* Mr. Justice Brossard, at p. 326.

Does this mean, however, that the general nature of the description of the things sought can always be corrected by the description of the offence which these things might afford evidence of? I do not believe so.

It is not sufficient to state that the objects or documents sought concern a fraud, rather than sedition or conspiracy to restrict trade. It is essential that they be more adequately identified by mentioning their date, if they are dated, or other characteristics such as numbers, amounts, in short, some indication which ties the thing or document to the offence for which the warrant was issued. Then the police officer executing the warrant will not have *carte blanche* to consult or read anything he finds which may appear to be within the category of documents sought, such as cheques, financial statements, bank accounts, bank-books, receipts, etc., in order to decide if it should be seized or not. The exercise of such discretionary power does not rest with him, and the justice cannot delegate this discretion to him. The execution of a search warrant can no longer be the occasion of generalized indiscretion by the police officer with respect to documents found in the person's home being searched.

In the present case, the nature of the documents sought is set out; however, there is nothing to identify them or tie them with the offence of which they afford evidence. This situation is very different from that considered by the British Columbia Court of Appeal in *Re B.X. Development Inc. and 9 others and The Queen* (1976), 31 C.C.C. (2d) 14, 70 D.L.R. (3d) 366, [1976] 4 W.W.R. 364, in which the informant, after setting out the categories of documents sought, had added 19 "long paragraphs" summarizing the evidence provided by these documents.

To appreciate the generality of the description of the documents or objects sought under the search warrant, one need only read from the report of the execution of the warrant where it states that "cheques, promissory notes between Trevi Creation Inc. and presumed victims, deposit books, investor lists, contracts of transactions between Trevi, C.I.B.C. and victims, various documents between Creation and C.I.B.C., receipts for payments".

I therefore come to the conclusion that the justice did not exercise, or exceeded, his jurisdiction in not adequately detailing the objects sought in the search warrant, and in simply contenting himself by describing them by category.

For all these reasons, the search warrant issued on June 1, 1982, must be quashed.

It is now necessary for me to decide whether the things seized, as well as the copies made thereof, must be returned to the applicant. I cannot request that the Crown or police now exercise some discretionary power which I denied them at the time of the execution of the warrant and ask them to decide, once the warrant is quashed, which documents they wish to retain: *Bergeron et al. v. Deschamps et al.* (1977), 33 C.C.C. (2d) 461, 73 D.L.R. (3d) 765, [1978] 1 S.C.R. 243 (S.C.C.).

On the other hand, it appears at least incongruous, in light of ss. 8 and 24 of the Charter, to permit the authorities to retain the things that they unlawfully seized. The only sanction that may be truly effective when faced with an illegal search is to order the return of the things unlawfully seized. Any other solution seems to me to be inadequate. This seems to be the conclusion reached by Chief Justice Laskin in *Bergeron et al. v. Deschamps et al., supra,* where he wrote, at pp. 462-3:

> Apart from the fact that there is no general statutory authority in England as there is here to issue search warrants, and that, accordingly, common law rules determine in most cases whether documents seized by the police in the course of their investigation of a criminal offence may be retained as evidence, it is apparent from the reasons of Lord Denning that it is the Courts and not the police who determine whether adequate grounds exist for retaining seized documents. Those grounds as set out by Lord Denning are largely involved in the regularity and validity of a search warrant under s. 443. Since they have not been met in this case, as indeed they were not met in *Ghani et al. v. Jones* [[1969] 3 All E.R. 1700], there is no reason to involve the Court *in any sorting of the seized materials.*

(Emphasis added.)

In light of s. 24 of the Charter and the comments of Chief Justice Laskin, I believe I am justified in not adopting the solution proposed by the Ontario Court of Appeal in *Model Power v. The Queen* (1980), 21 C.R. (3d) 195.

Conclusion

For the reasons given, the search warrant issued on June 1, 1982, is quashed, the seizure is declared unlawful and the respondents are ordered to return the things seized, as well as the copies made, to the applicant at the expiration of the delay for appeal, should one not be instituted.

Application granted.

R. v. M. (N.N.)
(2007), 223 C.C.C. (3d) 417 (Ont. S.C.J.)

HILL J:—319. In summary form, the principal requirements of a search warrant application are as follows:

(1) The application must disclose reasonable grounds or credibly-based probability regarding the essential statutory prerequisites. This standard

of reasonable probability does not equate to proof beyond a reasonable doubt or to a prima facie case: *R. v. Debot* (1989), 52 C.C.C. (3d) 193 (S.C.C.) at 213. Accordingly, reasonable grounds "are not proof absolute" though they must be more than mere suspicion: *Smith*, at 77.

(2)   In *R. v. Durling* (2006), 214 C.C.C. (3d) 49 (N.S.C.A.) at 56-7, the court set out a non-exhaustive list of the key elements of what must be shown to establish credibly-based probability:

(i)   The Information to obtain the warrant must set out sworn evidence sufficient to establish reasonable grounds for believing that an offence has been committed, that the things to be searched for will afford evidence and that the things in question will be found at a specified place: (*R. v. Sanchez* (1994), 93 C.C.C. (3d) 357 (Ont. Ct. Gen. Div.) at 365).

(ii)   The Information to obtain as a whole must be considered and peace officers, who generally will prepare these documents without legal assistance, should not be held to the "specificity and legal precision expected of pleadings at the trial stage." (*Sanchez*, supra, at 364)

(iii)   The affiant's reasonable belief does not have to be based on personal knowledge, but the Information to obtain must, in the totality of circumstances, disclose a substantial basis for the existence of the affiant's belief: *R. v. Yorke* (1992), 115 N.S.R. (2d) 426 (C.A.); aff'd [1993] 3 S.C.R. 647.

(iv)   Where the affiant relies on information obtained from a police informer, the reliability of the information must be apparent and is to be assessed in light of the totality of the circumstances. The relevant principles were stated by Sopinka J. in *R. v. Garofoli*, [1990] 2 S.C.R. 1421 at pp. 1456-1457:

(i)   Hearsay statements of an informant can provide reasonable and probable grounds to justify a search. However, evidence of a tip from an informer, by itself, is insufficient to establish reasonable and probable grounds.

(ii)   The reliability of the tip is to be assessed by recourse to "the totality of the circumstances". There is no formulaic test as to what this entails. Rather, the court must look to a variety of factors including:

(a)   the degree of detail of the "tip";

(b)   the informer's source of knowledge;

(c)   indicia of the informer's reliability such as past performance or confirmation from other investigative sources.

(iii)   The results of the search cannot, ex post facto, provide evidence of reliability of the information.

The fundamental point is that these specific propositions define the basic justification for the search: the existence of "credibly-based" probability that an offence has been committed and that there is evidence of it to be found in the place of search.

(3)   It is imperative that there exist a basis for issuance "founded on reliable information": *Araujo*, at 471.

(4)   The ITO ought to be clear and concise and "need not include every minute detail of the police investigation": *C.B.C. v. A.-G. for New Brunswick et al.*, at 562; *Araujo*, at 470.

320. Because a search warrant application is generally an ex parte application, there is a "legal obligation" to provide "full and frank disclosure of material facts" with the relevant facts set out "truthfully, fully and plainly": *Araujo*, at 469-470 (emphasis of original). A justice can only perform the judicial function of issuing a warrant if "provided with accurate and candid information": *R. v. Hosie* (1996), 107 C.C.C. (3d) 385 (Ont. C.A.) at 399; *R. v. Agensys International Inc.* (2004), 187 C.C.C. (3d) 481 (Ont. C.A.) at 491. The "requirement of candour is not difficult to understand; there is nothing technical about it": *R. v. Morris* (1998), 134 C.C.C. (3d) 539 (N.S.C.A.) at 551. An affiant for a warranted search is under a duty to avoid drafting which attempts to trick the reader, for example by the use of boiler-plate language, or which could mislead the court "by language used or strategic omissions": *Araujo*, at 470. Careless language in an ITO "deprives the judicial officer of the opportunity to fairly assess whether the requirements of a warrant have been met" and "strikes at the core of the administration of justice": *Hosie*, at 398-9.

321. An aspect of an affiant's disclosure obligation is to reveal, not to conceal, any unconstitutional investigative step by which the authorities have secured information relevant to the ongoing investigation: *Grant* (S.C.C.), at 196-7; *R. v. Creelman*, [2007] N.S.J. No. 174 (C.A.) at para. 28-36. As a general rule, it does not lie with the police to not disclose on the basis that they are confident that the misconduct is irrelevant because of an independent source for the information, inevitable discovery or attenuation. The court considering the warrant application will itself make the determination of the relevance of the pre- application behaviour. The disclosure may be relevant not only to the discretion to issue/refuse a warrant but also to whether the justice asks for more information (*Araujo*, at 464) or considers the imposition of conditions relating to execution of the warrant: *Baron*, at 526.

322. The existence of fraud, non-disclosure, misleading information, unconstitutionally obtained facts, new evidence, or the omission of facts material to the exercise of discretion to issue a warrant are all relevant to review of a warrant and relate to whether there continues to be any basis for the decision of the authorizing judge: *Garofoli*, at para. 56. Ordinarily, the reviewing court looks to the remaining grounds of belief in an ITO after redaction of the offensive text, or in the case of an omission with the addition of the relevant missing fact(s), in order to determine whether there is a basis upon which the court could have issued the warrant: *R. v. Bisson* (1994), 94 C.C.C. (3d) 94 (S.C.C.) at 95-6; *Araujo*, at 471-2; *R. v. Wiley* (1993), 84 C.C.C. (3d) 161 (S.C.C.) at 170-2; *R. v. Kesselring* (2000), 145 C.C.C. (3d) 119 (Ont. C.A.) at 123. "In this way, the state is prevented from benefitting from the illegal acts of the police officers, without being forced to sacrifice search warrants which would have been issued in any event": *Plant*, at 215; *Smith*, at 76.

323. That said, a reviewing judge is not foreclosed, in appropriate circumstances, "from concluding on the totality of the circumstances that the conduct of the police in seeking prior authorization was so subversive of that process that the resulting warrant must be set aside to protect the process and the preventive function it serves": *Morris*, at 553 (passage approved in *Araujo*, at 473); *Creelman*, at para. 36; *R. v. Colbourne* (2001), 157 C.C.C. (3d) 273 (Ont. C.A.) at para. 40; *Kesselring*, at 127-8; *R. v. Dellapenna* (1995), 62 B.C.A.C. 32 at para. 50; *R. v. Donaldson* (1990), 58 C.C.C. (3d) 294 (B.C.C.A.) at 310-312.

Most challenges to the legality of a search warrant now occur in the course of a s. 8 challenge at trial where the remedy may be exclusion of the evidence under s. 24(2).

Sometimes the execution of a search warrant may be challenged in a superior court by a prerogative writ. In such cases, where the motion is successful, it appears that evidence required by the State is not likely to be returned.

In Hill, Hutchinson and Pringle, "Search Warrants: Protection or Illusion" (2000), 28 C.R. (5th) 89, at 104, the authors refer to:

(2)   the trend of the reviewing courts in the prerogative writ area, where a warrant is quashed, not to grant the consequential relief of a return of the things unlawfully seized where the Crown establishes the items are required as evidence in a current investigation or proceeding,

(3)   following a successful *certiorari* application where the seized items have been ordered returned, the Crown habitually obtained a successive warrant, properly drafted, and reseized the objects of search . . .

In *Re R. v. Johnson & Franklin Wholesale Distributors Ltd.* (1971), 23 C.R.N.S. 238, 3 C.C.C. (2d) 484 (B.C. C.A.) it was held that the doctrine of severability can be properly applied to partially quash a search warrant where the bad part is clearly severable from the good. After objectionable portions have been severed, the question becomes whether the remaining evidence in the information to obtain the warrant is sufficient to meet the requirements to enable the issuance of a valid search warrant.

In determining the responsibility of the justice where reliance is placed, as is frequently the case on s. 487(1)(b), a considerable source of confusion has been that Forms 1 and 5 are unduly skimped and neither refer to a requirement that the informant or the justice have reasonable grounds to believe that the object to be seized "will afford evidence". This allowed the majority in *Re Worrall*, [1965] 1 O.R. 527, 44 C.R. 151, [1965] 2 C.C.C. 1 (Ont. C.A.) to conclude that a justice had acted properly although the information and the search warrant contained the words "may afford evidence". These words were held to be mere surplusage. It is unfortunate at best that the Code forms still have not been changed.

When s. 8 challenges are made to searches conducted by search warrant it is now clear that the reviewing judge can go beyond the documents and "amplify" the record of the issuance of the warrant: *R. v. Morris* (1998),

23 C.R. (5th) 354, 134 C.C.C. (3d) 539 (N.S. C.A.). However, in *R. v. Araujo*, [2000] 2 S.C.R. 992, 38 C.R. (5th) 307, 149 C.C.C. (3d) 449, the Supreme Court confined this to "minor, technical" drafting errors made in good faith. It is clear that deliberately misleading the issuing judge on a material point will render the warrant illegal and contrary to s. 8: see especially *R. v. Hosie* (1996), 49 C.R. (4th) 1, 107 C.C.C. (3d) 385 (Ont. C.A.), *R. v. Monroe* (1997), 8 C.R. (5th) 324 (B.C. C.A.) and compare *R. v. McLetchie* (2011), 84 C.R. (6th) 199 (Ont. S.C.J.) and *R. v. Campbell* (2011), 85 C.R. (6th) 229, [2011] 2 S.C.R. 549, 271 C.C.C. (3d) 193 (S.C.C.). It used to be that an officer could not shop around until a justice of the peace was found to authorize the search. In *R. v. Duchcherer* (2006), 38 C.R. (6th) 190, 208 C.C.C. (3d) 201 (B.C.C.A.) it was held that a second application for a warrant on the same information as for a previously rejected application did not render the warrant invalid.

In the light of these principles, consider whether a motion to quash a search warrant should succeed in each of the following cases.

PROBLEM 1

The information reads:

This is the information of Donald Charles Brown of Burnaby in the said County of Westminster a member of the R.C.M. Police, hereinafter called the informant, taken before me.

The informant says that he has reasonable and probable grounds to believe that obscene books are being kept for the purpose of distribution contrary to s. 150(1) of the Criminal Code of Canada and that invoices pertaining to the distribution of said books are kept and that he has reasonable grounds for believing that the said things or some part of them are in the building of Johnson & Franklin Wholesale Distributors Ltd. of 7488 Griffiths Ave., in the said District of Burnaby, County of Westminster, Province of British Columbia.

The search warrant is as follows:

Whereas it appears on the oath of Donald Charles Brown of Burnaby, that there are reasonable grounds for believing that obscene books are being kept for the purpose of distribution contrary to s. 150(1) of the Criminal Code of Canada and that company records, including invoices, are being kept and that he has reasonable grounds to believe that the said books and invoices are in the building at 7488 Griffiths Ave., Burnaby, B.C. hereinafter called the "premises".

Compare *Re R. v. Johnson & Franklin Wholesale Distributors Ltd.* (1971), 23 C.R.N.S. 238, 3 C.C.C. (2d) 484 (B.C. C.A.), *Re Canadiana Recreational Prods. and R.* (1984), 17 C.C.C. (3d) 473 (Ont. H.C.), *Re Times Square Book Store and R.* (1985), 48 C.R. (3d) 132, 21 C.C.C. (3d) 503 (*sub nom. Re Times Square Book Store*) (Ont. C.A.) and *R. v. Harris* (1987), 57 C.R. (3d) 356, 35 C.C.C. (3d) 1 (Ont. C.A.).

PROBLEM 2

The R.C.M.P. obtained two search warrants under the Narcotic Control Act to search specified premises for marihuana. The grounds of belief of the police officers swearing the information were specified as "reliable and confidential information received that the named person has been dealing heavily in narcotics from these premises and that at the present time there is a large amount of the drug at these premises". The search warrants were issued and executed but no drugs found. On the certiorari application to quash the informant filed an affidavit that he had explained orally to the justice while under oath that the source had provided reliable information in the past but that he could not name him since this would jeopardize the safety and life of the source.

Compare *Chedrawy v. A.G.* (1981), 23 C.R. (3d) 30 (N.S. T.D.), *Imperial Tobacco Sales Co. v. A.G. of Alberta* (1941), 76 C.C.C. 84 (Alta. C.A.), *R. v. Debot* (1986), 54 C.R. (3d) 120 at 132, 30 C.C.C. (3d) 207 (Ont. C.A.), adopted by S.C.C. on further appeal, [1989] 2 S.C.R. 1140, 73 C.R. (3d) 129 at 150-153, 52 C.C.C. (3d) 193 (S.C.C.), *R. v. Hosie* (1996), 49 C.R. (4th) 1, 107 C.C.C. (3d) 385 (Ont. C.A.) and *R. v. Duncan* (2004), 188 C.C.C. (3d) 17, 24 C.R. (6th) 129 (Man. C.A.).

PROBLEM 3

A police officer swears out an information stating that he has reasonable grounds to believe that a particular person has been murdered and that there was evidence of the offence to be found at the out buildings of certain premises. The information sets out the grounds for the officer's belief and facts upon which a Justice, acting judicially, could be satisfied that the offence has been committed and that there was evidence of the offence to be found at the place of the search. The search warrant was issued and the police found a knife, which forensic evidence indicated could have been the murder weapon, in the accused's drive shed. The Justice of the Peace, called on a *voir dire*, testified he had issued the search warrant by following a check list of seven items recommended at a Justice of the Peace seminar. These seven items were a general statement of the offence, code section number, name of the accused/suspect, time of occurrence or date, place of occurrence, name of victim and means or particulars of offence. The Justice testified that it was his practice to issue a search warrant if these seven items were contained in the information. The defence counsel argues that this practice did not meet the requirements of the Criminal Code. Make your ruling.

Compare *R. v. Moran* (1987), 36 C.C.C. (3d) 225 (Ont. C.A.).

PROBLEM 4

As a judge would you issue search warrants for the premises of the Canadian Broadcasting Corp., the CTV Television Network and The Globe and Mail authorizing the seizure of unpublished videos and photographs of a riot in downtown Toronto which resulted in more than 100 criminal offences, 78 of which remain unsolved? Reporters, photographers and camera operators from the major media were observed at the demonstration and subsequent riots. None of the published reports had identified demonstrators. The police swear that they have exhausted all other avenues in their efforts to identify the perpetrators. Should different considerations apply in the case of search warrants to be executed against the media?

Compare *R. v. Canadian Broadcasting Corp.* (1992), 17 C.R. (4th) 198, 77 C.C.C. (3d) 341 (Ont. Gen. Div.), *Société Radio-Canada v. Lessard*, [1991] 3 S.C.R. 421, 9 C.R. (4th) 133, 67 C.C.C. (3d) 517 (S.C.C.) and *C.B.C. v. B.C.* (1994), 32 C.R. (4th) 256 (B.C. S.C.).

See similarly *R. v. Serendip Physiotherapy Clinic* (2004), 25 C.R. (6th) 30, 189 C.C.C. (3d) 417 (Ont. C.A.), leave to appeal refused (2005), 125 C.R.R. (2d) 187 (note) (S.C.C.) (no special procedure to be applied to search warrants for hospital records in a fraud case).

PROBLEM 5

The accused was charged with possession of child pornography. A computer technician had arrived unannounced at his house to install a high-speed internet connection. The computer was located in a spare bedroom where the accused's three-year-old daughter was playing with toys on the floor. The technician observed two links among the accused's browser favourites with names suggesting that they linked to child pornography websites, and also saw a pornographic image on the computer. In addition, the technician noticed home videos and a webcam that was connected to a videotape recorder and was pointed at the toys and the child. When the technician returned the next day, the toys had been cleared away, the webcam was pointing at the desk, and the computer's hard drive had been formatted. The technician was suspicious because of these facts, and two months later, after speaking with his mother, reported these facts to social services. Social services in turn reported the matter to the RCMP. Two months after that, the RCMP obtained a search warrant to seize the accused's home computer and look for evidence of possession of child pornography. At trial, the accused challenged the constitutionality of the search on the basis that the search warrant was improperly issued.

In reviewing whether the warrant ought to have been issued, the majority of the Supreme Court found that there were erroneous statements in the ITO and non-disclosure. The ITO stated that the technician had seen "lolita porn" on the accused's computer, which implied that he had actually seen images of child pornography, when all he had in fact seen was a link to a website named "lolita porn". The ITO also failed to disclose that the pornographic image which had been seen was perfectly legal, and that the two links to child pornography websites were scattered through the favourites among additional links to regular adult material. The ITO created the misleading impression that the information from the accused's computer suggested a particular focus on child pornography. Further, the ITO juxtaposed the facts that the accused had child pornography links on his computer with the fact that the accused was alone in the house with a three-year-old child and had a webcam pointed at the child's toys. The ITO only noted later that the webcam was not connected to the computer. Further, the ITO never disclosed that the three-year-old child was the accused's daughter and that the accused's wife lived with them. The ITO also failed to mention that the child was fully clothed, that there was no evidence of abuse, that the computer room had a child gate and appeared to double as a playroom for the child, and that the child was playing with the scattered toys in the middle of the room when the technician arrived. Was the warrant procedure valid?

Compare *R. v. Morelli*, 72 C.R. (6th) 208, [2010] 1 S.C.R. 253, 252 C.C.C. (3d) 273 (S.C.C.) and see CR annotation by Stephen Coughlan.

PROBLEM 6

Police had obtained a warrant to search a house for evidence of theft of electricity, and that warrant also authorised them to search for documentation identifying ownership or occupancy of the premises. After they had entered the premises the police found a marihuana grow operation. They also found a desktop computer, a laptop computer, and a cell phone. The desktop computer was connected to a security camera which recorded the driveway, and in examining the photographs recorded the officer observed a vehicle which was later determined to be registered to the accused. An officer examined the laptop and found that it was logged in to MSN messenger and to Facebook, both to accounts in the accused's name. The officer also searched that laptop for documents and found the accused's resume. Finally an officer examined the cell phone and found a photograph of the accused, taken in a mirror while holding the cell phone. Was the search of the electronic storage devices within the scope of the warrant? Was it necessary for the warrant to expressly authorise a search of the computer and cell phone?

Compare *R. v. Vu,* [2013] 3 S.C.R. 657, 302 C.C.C. (3d) 427, 6 C.R. (7th) 1 (S.C.C.).

Frequently, of course, search warrants are obtained prior to any charges being laid. The information sworn and the search warrant obtained thereby discloses a good deal about police investigations and about persons under suspicion. Persons who are the object of searches clearly have an interest in being able to inspect these documents.

R. v. HUNTER
(1987), 59 O.R. (2d) 364, 57 C.R. (3d) 1, 34 C.C.C. (3d) 14 (Ont. C.A.)

The Ontario Court of Appeal held that an accused has the right to reasonable disclosure of information behind the issuance of a search warrant, even if such disclosure reveals the identity of an informer. However the trial judge was to consider editing to protect that identity. Mr. Justice Cory for the Court did not follow the Supreme Court of the United States which had not, in interpreting their due process provision of their Constitution, compelled such disclosure.

CORY J.:—What then should be done about the disclosure of information used to obtain a search warrant at the time of trial? I recognize the importance of the protection of informers. I recognize as well that a successful attack on a search warrant on the grounds that there were not reasonable and probable grounds for its issuance may well result in the suppression of the truth, as the evidence discovered during an illegal search may not be admissible.

Nevertheless, the right to search premises, particularly a home, is a powerful and potentially oppressive tool of the state. It should be exercised only on proper grounds. It is in the interest of all citizens that an accused should know the basis upon which the warrant was issued. The actions of the state taken against the least worthy of its citizens will eventually determine the pattern of its actions towards all its citizens. There should be reasonable disclosure made of the information which was used to obtain the search warrant, if it is needed and requested, despite the fact that it may disclose the identity of an informer. Yet the method by which the disclosure is made should take into account the importance of informers to society and strike a balance between the competing principles.

Upon receipt of such a request the trial judge should review the information with the object of deleting all references to the identity of the informer. The information so edited should then be made available to the accused. However, if at the conclusion of the editing procedure the Crown should still be of the opinion that the informer would become known to the accused upon production of the information, then a decision would have to be made by the Crown. The informer might by this time be willing to consent to being identified. Alternatively, the informer's identity might have become so notorious in the community or have become so well known to the accused that his or her identification would no longer be a significant issue.

It must be remembered that the object of the procedure is to make available to an accused enough information to enable the court to determine whether reasonable and probable grounds for the issuance of the warrant have been demonstrated. Most informations should lend themselves to careful editing. It would always be preferable to have the validity of the warrant determined on its merits.

This procedure should protect the rights both of the accused and of the informer, and ensure that in most cases the issue is determined on its merits. If the Crown is of the view that to produce the informant would be prejudicial to the administration of justice, the Crown may elect not to proceed or to proceed on the basis of a warrantless search. In those circumstances the trial judge will have to consider s. 24(2) of the Charter and determine whether the admission of the evidence would bring the administration of justice into disrepute. There is no way of knowing whether that situation will ever arise in this case, consequently nothing should be said about the possible result.

It is to be remembered that this case is not concerned with the propriety of a court order sealing an information used to obtain a search warrant, but only with the appropriate response of a trial court to a request for this information. There may well be other considerations to be taken into account in the former situation that need not be addressed in this case.

Do you agree with Mr. Justice Cory's conclusion?

———————

In *R. v. Leipert* (1997), 4 C.R. (5th) 259 (S.C.C.), the Court held that a police informer privilege prevented an accused from gaining access to a document which described a Crime Stoppers tip. The Court said that the only exception to the police informer privilege occurred when the accused established that the informer's identity was necessary to establish his innocence; for example, where the informer was an agent provocateur. There was no requirement of any editing or balancing unless and until the accused had established the necessity to his defence. The Court purported to distinguish *Hunter* on the basis that there the identity of the informer was in the information, whereas in *Leipert* it was in a separate document which had been referred to in the information. However, the stress on the absoluteness of the privilege, subject only to a narrow exception, might cause some rethinking as to the procedure described in *Hunter*.

On the day before Parliament prorogued for a general election, the Liberal Government, with all-parties' consent, rushed a Bill, S.C. 1997, c. 23, through the House of Commons and the Senate. This was commonly referred to as anti-gang legislation. The immediate context was the perceived need to deal with a violent and protracted fight between two biker gangs in Quebec: the Hell's Angels and the Rock Machine. The complex bill, with over fifty pages of detailed Criminal Code amendments, includes the following general provision for sealing orders to deny access to information behind a search warrant.

> **487.3** (1) On application made at the time an application is made for a warrant under this or any other Act of Parliament, an order under any of sections 487.013 to 487.018 or an authorization under section 529 or 529.4, or at a later time, a justice, a judge of a superior court of criminal jurisdiction or a judge of the Court of Quebec may make an order prohibiting access to, and the disclosure of, any information relating to the warrant, order or authorization on the ground that
>
> (a) the ends of justice would be subverted by the disclosure for one of the reasons referred to in subsection (2) or the information might be used for an improper purpose; and
>
> (b) the reason referred to in paragraph (a) outweighs in importance the access to the information.

(2) For the purposes of paragraph (1)(*a*), an order may be made under subsection (1) on the ground that the ends of justice would be subverted by the disclosure

(a) if disclosure of the information would

    (i) compromise the identity of a confidential informant,

    (ii) compromise the nature and extent of an ongoing investigation,

    (iii) endanger a person engaged in particular intelligence-gathering techniques and thereby prejudice future investigations in which similar techniques would be used, or

    (iv) prejudice the interests of an innocent person; and

(b) for any other sufficient reason.

The 1985 Criminal Code amendment also contained a new alternative telewarrant procedure (to be considered later), a long-awaited detailed procedure for the seizure of documents in the possession of a lawyer respecting which a solicitor-client privilege is claimed (s. 488.1). However Justice Arbour for a 6-3 majority of the Supreme Court in *R. v. Lavallee, Rackel & Heintz* (2002), 3 C.R. (6th) 209, 167 C.C.C. (3d) 1 (S.C.C.) found that the s. 488.1 provisions violated s. 8 by not sufficiently protecting solicitor-client privilege. The Court struck down the section, but declared detailed "common law" rules to reflect "constitutional imperatives". The 1985 amendments also contained an extremely detailed regime (ss. 489.1 and 490) concerning the possible restoration of property seized under a warrant or in the execution of statutory duty. The latter would not appear to apply to material illegally seized as would be the case where a warrant is quashed. In such a case there would appear to be a Charter remedy (see below).

Of course a rigorous search warrant procedure is in itself no guarantee that civil liberties will be protected. The Law Reform Commission of Canada conducted a four-month survey of the practice in seven cities. The results are reported in the following Working Paper.

LAW REFORM COMMISSION OF CANADA, WORKING PAPER 30: POLICE POWERS—SEARCH AND SEIZURE IN CRIMINAL LAW ENFORCEMENT
(1983), 83-89

E. The Gulf between Law and Practice

212. Although the conformity of police practice with applicable legal rules is an important issue in many aspects of search and seizure, it is perhaps most readily ascertained in the context of warrant issuance. This is largely due to the documentary nature of the procedure, which facilitates examination and evaluation. Accordingly, as part of our research programme, we examined practices of search warrant issuance over four-month periods in seven Canadian cities: Edmonton, Fredericton, Montréal, Saint John, Toronto, Winnipeg and Vancouver. The warrants covered by the survey only included those which could be issued by a magistrate or justice of the peace; hence, the survey was not designed to capture warrants issued pursuant to sections 160

and 281.3. Part of our purpose was to obtain a reliable assessment of the legality of search warrants issued in these cities. Accordingly, we assembled a panel of Canadian judges from superior and appellate courts to evaluate a stratified random sample of the application documents (informations or reports in writing) and warrants captured in our survey. Detailed results of these evaluations are presented elsewhere, but the conclusion may be stated in simple terms: there is a clear gap between the legal rules for issuing and obtaining search warrants and the daily realities of practice.

213. The judicial panel rated 39.4% of the warrants included in their sample as validly issued, and 58.9% as invalidly issued, leaving 1.7% which could not be conclusively rated due to obscured or incomplete documentation. The judicial panel found that fatal defects were most likely to occur in section 443 and *Narcotic Control Act* and *Food and Drugs Act* warrant documents. Only in the case of warrants issued under section 181 of the *Criminal Code,* the requirements of which are noticeably more lenient, did the valid warrants exceed the invalid ones.

214. What went wrong? The bases upon which the invalid warrants were found to be inadequate were usually more than formal. In fact, figures for both the written applications (informations or reports) and the warrants themselves were quite positive in terms of formal tests: of those which could be conclusively evaluated, 85.5% of the applications and 73.5% of the warrants were judged to be formally correct. The formal deficiencies that did appear tended to be in *Narcotic Control Act* and *Food and Drugs Act* warrants, and were fairly significant in character. While there were some purely clerical errors, such as the inadvertent omission of a justice's signature, there were also consistent failures on the part of certain police forces to adhere to existing statutory requirements. For example, *Narcotic Control Act* and *Food and Drugs Act* provisions requiring that the executing officer be named in the warrant were frequently ignored both in Winnipeg and in Montréal.

215. The results turned more negative when probative and substantive tests were applied. In the case of section 443 and *Narcotic Control Act* and *Food and Drugs Act* warrants, the critical probative test is the presentation of reasonable grounds to believe — a test that basically ensures the "judiciality" of warrant issuance. In 67.8% of the warrant applications conclusively evaluated, the judicial panel found the test satisfied; in 32.2%, it did not. If this bare maintenance of a 2:1 "judiciality" ratio is somewhat distressing, even worse is the statistical breakdown relating to the substantive requirements. These requirements, which largely maintain the "particularity" protections of the warrant, identify the search by items to be seized, premises to be searched, and offences alleged. Only 53.8% of the conclusively evaluated applications were found to comply with legal standards in this respect; the corresponding figure for the warrants was 48.7%.

216. The general failure of the warrant documents to adhere to legal standards does not mean that most searches carried out under the warrants *could not* have been legally authorized. The fact that 61.6% of the executed warrants reported in the cross-country survey resulted in a seizure of the item or type of item specified in the warrant supports the inference that in many

cases the police officers concerned had an adequate factual basis for their initiative to search. Indeed, an analysis of the documents in the judicial panel sample shows no decisive relationship between the legality of the search and the eventual seizure of the specified item. This argues against the possibility that the widespread illegality of the warrants is attributable to police decisions to search in inappropriate cases. Rather, the indication is that the problem resides with adherence to procedures. In other words, the necessary factual basis for a search may well exist, but the warrant is nonetheless being issued improperly.

217. Perhaps the most striking aspect of the results was the evidence that adherence to warrant requirements was to a large extent a product of local practice. The best record was presented by the warrants received from Vancouver, 71% of which were issued validly; at the other end of the spectrum was Montréal with 17%. In between stood Toronto with 50%, Edmonton with 36% and Winnipeg with 27%. And these variations can be traced further to particular idiosyncrasies of local origin. For example, the low figures in Winnipeg and Edmonton are attributable in part to the inadequate narcotic and drug warrant forms that were in use in 1978. At least one office in Montréal had developed the practice of not requiring any written elaboration of reasonable grounds to support the issuance of a warrant.

218. This raises a significant issue: Why is it that the various cities have been left, in effect, to decide upon their own procedures? In a legal system under which rules of criminal procedure are purportedly fixed in federal legislation, why have standards become so varied and so relaxed? The first and obvious conclusion is that there is a lack of effective mechanisms to enforce the legal rules. This is unquestionably a serious problem; we address it in detail in Chapter Ten of this paper. In the meantime, we will point to some explanatory factors disclosed by our empirical research.

219. One may discern in local improvisations some attempts to overcome deficiencies in existing legislation. For example, while section 443 requires that informations be in Form 1, this form as outlined in the *Criminal Code* itself does not satisfy the requirements of section 443. Confronted with this dilemma, different cities developed different variations on Form 1; indeed, in Winnipeg and Montréal, different court offices in the same city were found to be using radically dissimilar forms. These forms in turn were often the basis upon which documents for applications under *Narcotic Control Act* and *Food and Drugs Act* legislation (which prescribes no form) were prepared. The fluctuation in validity rates between the various cities reflects to some extent the success of such improvisational ventures.

220. There is a more profound factor that must be taken into account, however — the existence of differing local attitudes towards search warrant issuance. Despite the repeated reference in case-law to the zeal of the common law in preventing unjustified invasions of private rights, the warrant process has not uniformly been viewed as a judicial one. A recent report of a study of detective work in a jurisdiction near Toronto includes the following passage:

> The detectives had developed longstanding relationships with particular Justices of the Peace and relied on their routine co-operation to ease their tasks. Thus, one

detective said he regularly used two out of four possible Justices of the Peace available in his divisional area because he had a "good relationship" with them, which translated meant a "co-operative" relationship. Occasionallythisco-operation went well beyond the point of signing warrants without question. On one occasion, two detectives went to five addresses, mainly for the purpose of locating a suspect. Anticipating resistance from the various occupants, they took along some unsigned search warrants and "left handed" them (signed a J.P.'s name) as they went. These warrants were later logged in the divisional records, and the two Justices of the Peace whose names were used were subsequently contacted and their collaboration gained. In another situation the detectives arrived at an address to undertake a property search only to discover that the Justice of the Peace had dated the search warrant but had mistakenly not signed it. Commenting, "Just like the old days, left- handing a warrant," one detective signed the name of the Justice of the Peace and proceeded to effect the search.

221. The more common apprehension, however, remains the suspicion that the justice treats search warrant issuance as a "formality". While obtaining a warrant was by no means a formality in all of the cities surveyed, there were some instances in which the detail presented in the application to the issuer was so sketchy as to call into question whether the issuer really bothered to evaluate the documents he was given. In Montréal, for example, informations rarely included any elaborations of the officer's grounds for belief. In some cases, the applicant simply reported that reasonable grounds arose from inquiries conducted by the police. This sort of description gives an adjudicator no objective basis for making a judicial determination as to whether or not to issue a warrant. To simply concede to the officer's assertion that he has the grounds for conducting a search is to render the warrant process close to meaningless.

222. This is not to say that no issuers of warrants appreciate the significance of their function. Indeed, the survey discovered instances of local officials not only complying with *Criminal Code* standards, but imposing further safeguards of their own upon the authorized search. For example, the judges and justices in Edmonton developed the practice of imposing expiry dates upon warrants issued, despite the absence of a statutory requirement for doing so. Moreover, it is possible that the standards of some municipalities have improved since the survey. For example, in recent consultations with officials in Montréal, Commission researchers were told that local practices had been upgraded significantly through adoption of new procedures and the removal from office of a number of warrant issuers who had not been sufficiently judicial in their attitude. Ultimately, however, the variation in local standards suggests that assuming a judicial posture is in effect a discretionary local decision made with respect to individual issuers or groups of issuers.

223. To some extent, the police are also responsible for the quality of applications yielding warrants; after all, they generally fill in the documents. Police instructional materials set out the relevant standards for officers who resort to search warrant procedures. Yet there is some reluctance on the part of both police and court officials to believe that officers can realistically be expected to comply with existing tests. This reluctance, which was expressed to Commission researchers during consultations, might help to explain both the

unfavourable judicial panel results and the lenient attitude of some court officials towards badly prepared documents. Some justices quite candidly stated that they were willing to overlook certain legal niceties, particularly late at night when there was a degree of urgency to the matter.

224. Some of the complaints about the difficulties of preparing search warrants reflect problems recognized earlier about the anachronistic and incoherent state of the law. But these features stop short of making the warrant procedures impossible to follow. In Vancouver, at least, the record of compliance appeared strong. Why did officials in this city do so much better than the national average? Only tentative answers emerge from the available data. It may be attributable to the development of local traditions generally, and to the greater care taken to ensure the formal quality of the documentation in use. It is worth noting also that British Columbia's justices of the peace were selected from the ranks of court administrators by the provincial judicial council and given the benefit of extensive educational programmes.

225. It is also perhaps significant that Vancouver's sample of search warrants contained so large a proportion of commercial crime investigations. About one-third of the sets of documents in the judicial panel sample portion from Vancouver were directed towards this kind of investigation. Not all of the commercial crime documents were valid; indeed, only 69% were pronounced valid, a slightly lower figure than that for the Vancouver sample as a whole. However, the errors committed in these invalid cases tended to be isolated, such as the omission of a signature on an otherwise flawless document. On the whole, warrants related to commercial crime were extraordinarily detailed, not only from Vancouver but from other cities such as Toronto and Fredericton in which they also appeared frequently. It was not uncommon for informations to occupy three extra pages relating specifics about the offence alleged and its connection to items possessed by the individual concerned. In other words, even when invalid, the informations provided the justice with an intelligent basis upon which to decide to issue the warrant.

226. Why these documents in particular? Since the transactions involved in a conspiracy or fraud tend to be complex, perhaps it is natural that their descriptions on warrant documents would be more lengthy. More significant, however, is the perception that searches with warrant in commercial crime investigations carry a greater likelihood of being challenged. It is therefore not uncommon for Crown attorneys to assist in the preparation of the application. Whether or not a Crown attorney is called upon, however, it seems clear that the greater anticipation of a challenge to the legality of such searches has a salutary effect upon the quality of the application process.

227. The warrant is meant to offer protection to all individuals whose rights might be infringed by an intrusion authorized under it, not merely those likely to have the legal resources to challenge the intrusion. That there should be a double standard in the preparation of search warrants suggests, at the very least, that there is a considerable potential for reducing the disparities between law and practice.

These results are deeply disturbing although one can speculate that the entrenchment of the Charter with its clear remedies against illegality has since encouraged all concerned to be more conscientious and scrupulous about existing procedures, including those for obtaining search warrants.

A survey of search warrants issued out of Old City Hall in Toronto however still revealed a disturbing amount of illegality and or sloppy procedure: Hill, Hutchison and Pringle, "Search Warrants: Protection or Illusion?" (1999), 28 C.R. (5th) 89.

Ultimately the true efficacy of the search warrant procedure as a bulwark for the citizen against state intrusion will rest on the quality of those who are justices. Section 11(*d*) confirms that any person charged with an offence has the right "to be presumed innocent until proven guilty according to law in a fair and public hearing *by an independent and impartial tribunal*". The Ontario Court of Appeal held that both provincial judges (*R. v. Valente (No. 2)* (1983), 41 O.R. (2d) 187, 2 C.C.C. (3d) 417 (Ont. C.A.)) and justices of the peace are independent and impartial.

Valente was confirmed on further appeal by the Supreme Court: (1985), 49 C.R. (4th) 97 (S.C.C.). For a decision on Justices of the Peace in Quebec, see *Universal Spa Lté v. Valois* (1986), 33 C.C.C. (3d) 535 (Qué. C.A.). In *Charest v. Lippé* (1990), 80 C.R. (3d) 1 (Qué. C.A.), the Quebec Court of Appeal held, in a lengthy judgment, that the Quebec system of allowing part-time municipal court judges to hear provincial or municipal offences and also practice law or engage in other professional or business activities rendered them not independent and impartial within the meaning of s. 11(d) of the Charter. However, on December 5, 1990, the Supreme Court allowed the appeal from the Bench. Reasons followed later: (1991), 64 C.C.C. (3d) 513 (S.C.C.).

In *Ell v. Alberta*, [2003] 1 S.C.R. 857, 11 C.R. (6th) 207 (S.C.C.), the Court held that judicial independence was not compromised by provincial legislation authorizing a decision that required that justices of peace that exercise judicial functions to be members of the bar with at least five years of related experience. Paul Hong, "A Second Look at Justices of the Peace Reform in Ontario," (2006) 38 C.R. (6th) 22, calls for similar reforms in Ontario.

(b) Common Law

The common law is an important source of search powers. Of course, search powers at common law authorize searches without warrants, given that a search warrant can only be based on valid legislation. There are three types of search powers recognized at common law — search incident to arrest or investigative detention, consent searches and searches pursuant to the ancillary powers doctrine. While these search powers have existed for some time, some of them (search incident to arrest, in particular) have received attention and have undergone revision in light of the Charter.

(i) Incident to Arrest

As long ago as 1969 the Report of the Canadian Committee on Corrections (Ouimet Report) (1969) at pp. 61-63 called for codification of the right to search the person, the premises where the person is found and vehicles under control. The call has gone unheeded and this important power has been left to the courts to define. **In the following pre-Charter case why was the legality of the police search in issue?**

R. v. BREZACK
[1949] O.R. 888, 9 C.R. 73, 96 C.C.C. 97 (Ont. C.A.)

ROBERTSON C.J.O.:—This is an appeal from the conviction and sentence of the appellant by Magistrate Hopkins at Hamilton, on August 5, 1949, on the charge that the appellant, at the City of Hamilton, did unlawfully assault Police Constable James A. Macauley, a peace officer, while engaged in the lawful execution of his duty as such peace officer, making an arrest, contrary to the provisions of s. 296(*b*) of the *Cr. Code*.

As the circumstances are somewhat unusual, it will be well to give them in some detail.

On the day of the assault with which the appellant is charged, Constable Macauley of the Royal Canadian Mounted Police, on special duty on the narcotic squad at Hamilton with another constable, having made some investigations, and having reason to believe that the appellant was committing, or was about to commit, a breach of the *Opium and Narcotic Drug Act*, 1929 (Can.), c. 49, established themselves in a position where they could keep certain premises, known as the Golden Grill, under observation. While so stationed they saw the appellant come around a street corner and proceed in the direction of the Golden Grill. At the same time they observed certain persons known to them to be drug addicts also going in the direction of the Golden Grill. The appellant had a prior conviction for having in his possession a narcotic drug, in breach of the *Opium and Narcotic Drug Act*, and from information received the constables believed that at this time appellant had in his possession narcotics in breach of the statute. Their information led them to expect that they would find the capsules containing the narcotic concealed in appellant's mouth.

Acting on the information they had, the constables, as appellant approached the Golden Grill, left their place of concealment and, with two other constables, rushed upon him. One of them seized appellant by the arms, and Constable Macauley caught him by the throat, to prevent him swallowing anything he might have in his mouth. The three of them fell to the ground and a considerable struggle ensued there. Constable Macauley persistently tried to insert his finger in appellant's mouth, to recover the drug that he assumed was there, and each time he tried appellant bit his finger. A good deal of force was applied by the constables, and Constable Macauley at last succeeded in getting his fingers in appellant's mouth, and satisfied himself that there was no drug there. The appellant was allowed to stand upon his feet, and was taken away from the crowd that had gathered. The constables then searched his clothing, but did not find any narcotic on him anywhere.

The constables then took appellant over to the car which he had left parked around the corner when he was making his way to the Golden Grill. There were two other persons found in the car, and upon searching the car the police found, in various places on the floor, five capsules containing narcotics. Three capsules were found beside the floor-mat at the front seat, and two at the rear seat. Appellant was then taken into custody, and later this charge of assaulting the police was laid.

The acts of the appellant in biting the constable's finger, and in striking and kicking the constable in the struggle on the ground, while the constable was endeavouring to force his finger inside appellant's mouth, were alleged to constitute an unlawful assault upon a peace officer while engaged in the lawful execution of his duty as such peace officer making an arrest, contrary to the provisions of s. 296(b) [s. 246(1)(a)] of the *Code*.

. . .

In my opinion the evidence supports the finding of the Magistrate that the constable was engaged in the lawful execution of his duty as a peace officer making an arrest, and believing the information he had, was entitled even to search in appellant's mouth for evidence of the offence of which he believed appellant to be guilty. It is true that the appellant did not have any narcotic drug on his person at the time, but he had such drug in his motor car around the corner, and *prima facie* that is possession contrary to the provisions of the *Opium and Narcotic Drug Act*, s. 17, as amended 1938 (Can.), c. 9, s. 5. The constable was warranted in arresting the appellant, on the information he had, although his information was wrong as to where the drug would be found. It was his duty, in making the arrest, to make reasonable efforts to obtain possession of any narcotic that he believed to be illegally in the appellant's possession, both for the purpose of using it as evidence of possession against the appellant, and also to prevent him disposing of the drug in a manner that would involve perpetrating another crime.

Much was sought to be made in argument by appellant's counsel of the fact that, without any search warrant, the constable had gone the length of forcibly inserting his finger inside the appellant's mouth. The constable, on the other hand, appeared to think that he had very wide powers of search.

. . .

In my opinion, as I have already said, the evidence in this case supports the finding of the Magistrate that the constable was engaged in the lawful execution of his duty as a peace officer in making the arrest, and that the attempt to search the inside of appellant's mouth was a justifiable incident of that arrest. That the appellant was liable to arrest without warrant is, I think, beyond question, and the evidence—and particularly the evidence afforded by the capsules containing a narcotic, found in appellant's motor car a few minutes later—strongly supports the reasonableness of the constable's belief in the information he had received, that the prohibited drug would be found concealed in appellant's mouth.

It is important to observe that the search that was made is justifiable as an incident of the arrest. The constable who makes an arrest has important duties, such as to see that the prisoner does not escape by reason of being armed, and to see if any evidence of the offence for which he was arrested is to be found upon him. A constable may not always find his suspicions to be justified by the result of a search. It is sufficient if the circumstances are such as to justify the search as a reasonable precaution. In my opinion there was an arrest here when the constables seized the person of the appellant.

. . .

Constables have a task of great difficulty in their efforts to check the illegal traffic in opium and other prohibited drugs. Those who carry on the traffic are cunning, crafty and unscrupulous almost beyond belief. While, therefore, it is important that constables should be instructed that there are limits upon their right of search, including search of the person, they are not to be encumbered by technicalities in handling the situations with which they often have to deal in narcotic cases, which permit them little time for deliberation and require the stern exercise of such rights of search as they possess.

The appeal is dismissed.

Appeal dismissed.

LAPORTE v. LAGANIÈRE
(1972), 18 C.R.N.S. 357, 8 C.C.C. (2d) 343
(*sub nom. Re Laporte and R.*) (Qué. Q.B.)

The Court refused to extend the power to search incident to an arrest to include a surgical operation.

HUGESSON J.:—There would appear to be no doubt that there is at common law a right to search a prisoner at the time of his arrest. In the case of *Leigh v. Cole* (1853), 6 Cox C.C. 329, Vaughan Williams J. said (at p. 332):

> With respect to searching a prisoner, there is no doubt that a man when in custody may so conduct himself, by reason of violence of language or conduct, that a police officer may reasonably think it prudent and right to search him, in order to ascertain whether he has any weapon with which he might do mischief to the person or commit a breach of the peace.

Similarly, in a footnote to the judgment in *Bessell v. Wilson* (1853), 1 E. & B. 489, 118 E.R. 518, 20 L.T.O.S. 233, Lord Campbell C.J. said:

> It is often the duty of an officer to search a prisoner. If, for instance, a man is taken in the commission of a felony, he may be searched to see whether the stolen articles are in his possession, or whether he has any instruments of violence about him.

Finally, in the case of *Rex v. Brezack*, [1949] O.R. 888, 9 C.R. 73, 96 C.C.C. 97, [1950] 2 D.L.R. 265, the Ontario Court of Appeal maintained a conviction for assault against a person who had bitten a police officer while the latter was searching the inside of his mouth for narcotic capsules which were thought to be hidden there.

. . .

In my opinion it is clear that the common-law right of search is, as stated by the cases, limited to that search which is incidental to the making of an arrest or the continued detention of the prisoner in safe custody. The reasons for such right show clearly from the passages above quoted: it is to make the arrest effective, to ensure that evidence does not disappear and to prevent the commission of a further offence.

It is not necessary for me to decide whether the common-law right of search might extend as far as minor medical procedures such as the taking of a blood test or examination by X-rays, but I can find nothing in the cases which would justify a surgical intrusion into the body of a prisoner many months after his arrest, for the purpose of obtaining evidence against him on a charge other than that for which he is being held.

Appeal dismissed.

R. v. TOMASO
(1989), 70 C.R. (3d) 152 (Ont. C.A.)

The accused's vehicle was involved in a collision which resulted in a fatality. He appealed his conviction of dangerous driving. He had been unconscious in hospital. A police officer collected blood from his bleeding ear. Analysis showed the accused was impaired at the time of the accident. The accused was charged two weeks after the sample had been obtained. The Court decided the seizure was not incident to the arrest and allowed the appeal on the basis that evidence of the sample should not have been received.

HOWLAND C.J.O. (Brooke and Tarnopolsky JJ.A. concurring):—

Seizure as incident to a lawful arrest

At common law a police officer has the power to search a person as incident to a lawful arrest, and to take from his person any property which the officer reasonably believes is connected with the offence charged, or which may be used as evidence against the person arrested, or any weapon or instrument found upon the person arrested. It is the fact that the search of the person is made as incident to a lawful arrest which gives the peace officer the authority to search the person arrested: *R. v. Morrison* (1987), 35 C.C.C. (3d) 437 at 442 (Ont. C.A.). It was on the basis of this power that this court concluded in *R. v. Miller* (1987), 62 O.R. (2d) 97 (C.A.), that the blood-stained bandage had been validly seized within 18 to 19 hours after the arrest.

In *R. v. Debot* (1987), 30 C.C.C. (3d) 207, this court went somewhat further and held that some searches incident to arrest can precede the actual arrest. In that case the arrest followed quite closely on the search. As Martin J.A., in delivering the judgment of this court, pointed out at p. 223, "It is axiomatic that a search may not precede an arrest and serve as part of its justification . . .". However, a search preceding arrest may be incident to arrest provided that the police officer had reasonable grounds, prior to the search, for arresting the respondent under s. 450 of the Code (now s. 495).

In this case the seizure of the blood sample took place on July 14, 1985. However, the police officer decided to await the analysis of the blood sample and not to arrest the appellant on 14th July. The trial judge found that Constable Swaga had reasonable and probable grounds for believing that the appellant was impaired. Constable Swaga met again with the appellant on 15th July and 17th July 1985. Finally, the arrest was made on 29th July 1985, after the appellant went to the police station at the request of Constable Swaga. It has not been established that Constable Swaga had reasonable grounds on 14th July for the arrest of the appellant on the charge of criminal negligence which was subsequently laid, nor could it be said that the analysis of the blood sample was not part of the justification for such arrest. In all the circumstances it would be going too far to attempt to justify the seizure on 14th July on the basis that it was incident to an arrest more than two weeks later for the offences with which the appellant was charged.

It should be noted that since the offence and the seizure in question in this appeal the Criminal Code has been amended by the Criminal Law Amendment Act, S.C. 1985, c. 19, s. 36. Section 254(3) gives a peace officer, who believes, on reasonable and probable grounds, that an offence is or has been committed as a result of the consumption of alcohol, the right to require that a person have blood samples taken by or under the direction of a qualified medical practitioner. This right may be exercised only where there are reasonable and probable grounds to believe that the taking of breath samples is not possible, or is impracticable, by reason of any physical condition of the person. Section 256 similarly makes provision for the issue of a warrant for the taking of blood samples where there is an accident resulting in the death of or bodily injury to any person, and the medical practitioner is of the opinion that the person is unable to consent, but that the taking of the samples would not endanger his life or health. These amendments did not come into force until 4th December 1985, and accordingly were not applicable to this appeal.

Debot was affirmed on appeal, [1989] 2 S.C.R. 1140, 73 C.R. (3d) 129, 52 C.C.C. (3d)193 (S.C.C.).

The Supreme Court has addressed the requirements of search incident to arrest in light of s. 8: *Cloutier and Langlois, Stillman, Caslake, Golden* (strip searches) and *Fearon* (cell phones). We will postpone consideration of *Golden* and *Fearon* until we directly consider Charter standards under s. 8. *Cloutier and Langlois* is addressed in the controversial ruling in *Stillman.*

R. v. STILLMAN
[1997] 1 S.C.R. 607, 5 C.R. (5th) 1, 113 C.C.C. (3d) 321

A group of teenagers consumed drugs and alcohol at a camp in the woods. The accused, aged 17, left the group with a 14-year-old girl. When the accused arrived home that night he was obviously cold, shaken and wet from the upper thighs down. He was cut above one eye, and had mud and grass on his pants. The explanation for his condition was that he had been in a fight with five others and his account of where he had last seen the victim varied over time. The girl's body was found near where she had last been seen by the group. The cause of death was a wound or wounds to the head. Semen was found in her vagina and a human bite mark had been left on her abdomen.

A week later the accused was arrested for the murder. At the police station, police advised his lawyers that they wished to take hair samples and teeth impressions and to question the accused. The lawyers informed the police in writing that their client had been advised not to consent to providing any bodily samples or to speak to the police without a lawyer being present. Once the lawyers left, the police took bodily samples from the accused under threat of force. A sergeant took scalp hair samples by passing a gloved hand through the accused's hair, as well as by combing, clipping and plucking hairs. The accused was made to pull some of his own pubic hair. Plasticine teeth impressions were then taken. In the absence of the accused's parents or lawyers, a police officer interviewed the accused for an hour in an attempt to obtain a statement. The accused did not say anything, but sobbed throughout the interview. When he asked to see a lawyer the interview stopped and he was permitted to call his lawyer. While waiting for his lawyer the accused was permitted to use the washroom, escorted by an officer. He blew his nose with a tissue and threw it into a waste bin. The tissue containing mucous was seized by the officer and later used for DNA testing.

The accused was released from custody but was arrested again several months later after the police had received the DNA and ondontology results. Without the accused's consent, impressions of his teeth were taken by a dentist in a procedure which took two hours. More hair was taken, as well as a saliva sample and buccal swabs.

Following a *voir dire*, the trial judge found that the hair samples, teeth impressions and buccal swabs had been obtained in violation of the Charter but should nevertheless be admitted. He found that the tissue had not been obtained through a Charter violation. The accused was convicted by a jury of first degree murder. The majority of the New Brunswick Court of Appeal dismissed the appeal.

In the Supreme Court the appeal was allowed; a new trial was ordered at which hair samples, buccal swabs and dental impressions were to be excluded, but the tissue was to be admitted. We here consider the 7:2 ruling that the evidence of hair samples, buccal swabs and dental impressions could not be authorised as a search incident to arrest and had therefore been obtained in violation of section 8 of the Charter. The majority also found a violation of section 7.

CORY J.: — There are three requirements which must be met if a search is to be found reasonable: (a) it must be authorized by law; (b) the law itself must be reasonable; and (c) the manner in which the search was carried out must be reasonable: see *Collins*, supra, at p. 278. An appropriate starting point, therefore, is to determine whether there existed either a statutory or common law power that authorized the police to search and seize the appellant's scalp hairs and pubic hairs or to take dental impressions or buccal swabs.

At the time that this seizure occurred in 1991, the Criminal Code only provided a procedure for obtaining a warrant to search a "building, receptacle or place". It did not authorize the search of a person, nor the seizure of parts of the body. It is only with the recent addition of s. 487.05 that this limitation has been removed to the extent of its provisions. Therefore, the taking of hair and teeth samples was conducted without statutory authority. The respondent can justify these searches only by demonstrating that they were authorized by a common law power or that the appellant had no reasonable expectation of privacy in the things seized. To this end, the respondent asserts that the hair samples and teeth impressions were seized pursuant to the common law power of search incident to a lawful arrest.

. . .

Three conditions must be satisfied in order for a search to be validly undertaken pursuant to the common law power of search incident to a lawful arrest. First, the arrest must be lawful. No search, no matter how reasonable, may be upheld under this common law power where the arrest which gave rise to it was arbitrary or otherwise unlawful. Second, the search must have been conducted as an "incident" to the lawful arrest. To these almost self-evident conditions must be added a third, which applies to all searches undertaken by police: the manner in which the search is carried out must be reasonable. Were all three criteria satisfied in this instance?

[The Court decided that the arrest was lawful as the police subjectively believed there were reasonable grounds and, objectively measured, there in fact were.]

. . .

In *Hunter v. Southam Inc.*, [1984] 2 S.C.R. 145, it was held that a search conducted without prior authorization is presumptively unreasonable. However, the long- standing power of search incident to arrest is an exception to this general rule: see *Leigh v. Cole* (1853), 6 Cox C.C. 329, and *Bessell v. Wilson* (1853), 1 El. & Bl. 489, 118 E.R. 518 (Q.B.). The original rationale for this power was based on (i) the need for the arresting officers to prevent the escape of the person arrested and to protect themselves by removing from the person arrested any weapon or tool that might facilitate escape and (ii) the need to prevent evidence under the control of the detainee from being destroyed. The common law power is eminently sensible and is essential for the protection of police officers carrying out their all too often dangerous duties. Yet, reasonable limits of that power have been defined to avoid abuses.

In *Cloutier v. Langlois*, [1990] 1 S.C.R. 158, the scope of the common law power of search upon lawful arrest was considered by this Court for the first time. The case established that such a search does not require reasonable and probable grounds beyond the grounds that were sufficient to support the lawfulness of the arrest itself. The reasons set out three limitations to the common law power. First, the power is a discretionary one and in certain circumstances the officer may properly exercise his or her discretion not to conduct a search. Second, the search must be for a valid objective in pursuit of the ends of criminal justice. Third, the search must not be conducted in an abusive fashion.

Following *Cloutier v. Langlois*, the courts gradually broadened the common law power of search incident to arrest. In *R. v. Lim (No. 2)* (1990), 1 C.R.R. (2d) 136 (Ont. H.C.), at p. 145, the scope of the power was extended to include evidence beyond that which might be destroyed by the detainee. Doherty J. stated that, in his view:

> ... in Canada, the justification for a warrantless search as an incident of arrest goes beyond the preservation of evidence from destruction at the hands of the arrested person to include the prompt and effective discovery and preservation of evidence relevant to the guilt or innocence of the arrested person.

The common law power was further expanded in *R.v. Speid* (1991), 8 C.R.R. (2d) 383 (Ont. C.A.), leave to appeal to S.C.C. denied May 7, 1992, [1992] 1 S.C.R. xi. In that case, a justice of the peace refused to issue a warrant for a search. The police officers then arrested the accused so that they could nevertheless proceed with a search. The Ontario Court of Appeal extended *Lim*, supra, to hold that the police were entitled to search the car driven by the accused since it was still in the immediate vicinity of the arrest even though the search was not undertaken immediately upon the arrest.

. . .

In *R. v. Belnavis* (1996), 107 C.C.C. (3d) 195 (Ont. C.A.), Doherty J.A. carefully considered the powers of search incidental to arrest. He found that the arrest for outstanding traffic fines did not authorize the search of the trunk of a vehicle. I agree with his reasoning and conclusion on this issue.

It is important to recognize that these cases, which purport to expand the common law power of search incidental to arrest, involve less intrusive searches of motor vehicles and the seizure of evidence found in them. This type of search is not in issue in this case and I need not express any opinion with regard to them. Obviously, completely different concerns arise where the search and seizure infringes upon a person's bodily integrity, which may constitute the ultimate affront to human dignity.

The question of whether or not the common law power of search incident to arrest can be extended to permit the seizure of bodily substances has recently been considered by provincial appellate courts, with conflicting results. In *R. v. Alderton* (1985), 17 C.C.C. (3d) 204, the Ontario Court of Appeal held at p. 208 that the seizure of scalp hair samples from the accused did not violate s. 8 of the Charter, as:

> [i]t is settled law that following a valid arrest a police officer may search the person arrested and may seize anything that he reasonably believes will afford evidence of the commission of the offence with which the person arrested is charged and of the arrested person's connection with it.

Conversely, in the more recent case of *Legere*, supra, the point was made that since the police cannot enter a person's house to look for hairs without a warrant, they should not be entitled, as part of their investigation, to take hair from an individual they have just arrested. It was concluded that, on the facts of that case, the hair samples were not seized as an incident to arrest. Angers J.A., writing for the court, stated, at p. 379, that, "the forcible taking of parts of a person, in the absence of legislation authorizing such acts, is an infringement of the right to security of the person and constitutes an unreasonable seizure". This position was affirmed in *R. v. Paul* (1994), 155 N.B.R. (2d) 195 (C.A.), where Hoyt C.J.N.B. stated, at p. 203, that:

> Searches made incidentally to an arrest are justified so that the arresting officer can be assured that the person arrested is not armed or dangerous and seizures are justified to preserve evidence that may go out of existence or be otherwise lost. As neither circumstance existed here, the Crown cannot rely on a power that is incidental to an arrest to justify seizure of the hair samples.... In my opinion, the power to search and seize does not extend beyond those purposes.

I agree with that position. It has often been clearly and forcefully expressed that state interference with a person's bodily integrity is a breach of a person's privacy and an affront to human dignity. The invasive nature of body searches demands higher standards of justification. In *R. v. Pohoretsky*, [1987] 1 S.C.R. 945, at p. 949, Lamer J., as he then was, noted that, "a violation of the sanctity of a person's body is much more serious than that of his office or even of his home". In addition, La Forest J. observed in *R. v. Dyment*, [1988] 2 S.C.R. 417, at pp. 431-32, "the use of a person's body without his consent to obtain information about him, invades an area of personal privacy essential to the maintenance of his human dignity". Finally, in *R. v. Simmons*, [1988] 2 S.C.R. 495, at p. 517, Dickson C.J. stated:

> The third and most highly intrusive type of search is that sometimes referred to as the body cavity search, in which customs officers have recourse to medical doctors, to X-rays, to emetics, and to other highly invasive means.
>
> Searches of the third or bodily cavity type may raise entirely different constitutional issues for it is obvious that the greater the intrusion, the greater must be the justification and the greater the degree of constitutional protection.

It is certainly significant that Parliament has recently amended the Criminal Code, through the addition of s. 487.05, so as to create a warrant procedure for the seizure of certain bodily substances for the purposes of DNA testing. This suggests that Parliament has recognized the intrusive nature of seizing bodily samples. The section requires that the police have reasonable and probable grounds, as well as authorization from a judicial officer, before they can make such seizures. If this type of invasive search and seizure came within the common law power of search incident to arrest, it would not have been necessary for the government to create a parallel procedure for the police to follow. In my view, it would be contrary to authority to say that this is no more than a codification of the common law.

. . .

Counsel for the respondent argued that the taking of dental impressions was analogous to the routine practice of fingerprinting. The case of *R. v. Beare*, [1988] 2 S.C.R. 387, was cited as support for the proposition that the common law allowed for the use of such identification procedures upon arrest. In that case, La Forest J. noted that the reduced privacy expectation upon arrest justifies the fingerprinting. However, he added this important qualification at p. 413:

> While some may find [fingerprinting] distasteful, it is insubstantial, of very short duration, and leaves no lasting impression. There is no penetration into the body and no substance is removed from it.

How very different is the making of dental impressions. It is a lengthy and highly intrusive process. Further, the taking of the scalp and pubic hair samples involved the forceful removal of hair from the body over the specific objections of the accused. Significantly, in *R. v. Borden*, [1994] 3 S.C.R. 145, it was found that where there is no statutory authorization for the seizure of bodily samples, consent must be obtained if the seizure is to be lawful. Here the police knew they were dealing with a young offender. They were aware that the Young Offenders Act required that a parent or counsel should be present when a suspected young offender was being interviewed. Nonetheless, in the absence of any adult counsellor and contrary to the specific instruction of his lawyers, the police interviewed the appellant at length and by threat of force took bodily samples and dental impressions. This was the abusive exercise of raw physical authority by the police. No matter what may be the pressing temptations to obtain evidence from a person the police believe to be guilty of a terrible crime, and no matter what the past frustrations to their investigations, the police authority to search as an incident to arrest should not be exceeded. Any other conclusion could all too easily lead to police abuses in the name of the good of society as perceived by the officers. When they are carrying out their duties as highly respected and admired agents of the state they must respect the dignity and bodily integrity of all who are arrested. The treatment meted out by agents of the state to even the least deserving individual will often indicate the treatment that all citizens of the state may ultimately expect. Appropriate limits to the power of search incidental to arrest must be accepted and respected. The power to search and seize incidental to arrest was a pragmatic extension to the power of arrest. Obviously the police must be able to protect themselves from attack by the accused who has weapons concealed on his person or close at hand. The police must be able to collect and preserve evidence located at the site of the arrest or in a nearby motor vehicle.

The common law power cannot be so broad as to empower police officers to seize bodily samples. They are usually in no danger of disappearing. Here, there was no likelihood that the appellant's teeth impressions would change, nor that his hair follicles would present a different DNA profile with the passage of time. There was simply no possibility of the evidence sought being destroyed if it was not seized immediately. It should be remembered that one of the limitations to the common law power articulated in *Cloutier v. Langlois*, supra, was the discretionary aspect of the power and that it should not be abusive. The common law power of search incidental to arrest cannot be so broad as to encompass the seizure without valid statutory authority of bodily samples in the face of a refusal to provide them. If it is, then the common law rule itself is unreasonable, since it is too broad and fails to properly balance the competing rights involved.

L'HEUREUX-DUBÉ J. (Gonthier J. concurring) dissenting: —

. . .

The following guidelines, which incorporate the three general propositions outlined in *Cloutier v. Langlois*, properly weigh and safeguard the competing interests at issue where the taking of bodily samples or impressions occurs as an incident to arrest. Such guidelines, in my view, are thus "reasonable" within the meaning of s. 8 of the Charter.

1. The police must exercise their discretion, given all of the circumstances, in deciding whether to conduct a search for the purpose of obtaining bodily samples and impressions from a lawfully arrested person.

2. The search must be for a valid objective in pursuit of the ends of criminal justice, such as the discovery of evidence which might either incriminate or establish the innocence of the person under arrest, without running counter to the general objectives of the proper administration of justice.

3. Consideration must be given to the intrusiveness involved in the search: the more intrusive, the higher the threshold for finding that the taking of bodily samples or impressions is both justified and conducted in a reasonable manner in given circumstances. This is a matter of degree as well as common sense. While I agree with my colleague Cory J. that particular concerns arise where a search involves a person's bodily integrity, it must also be underscored that those concerns vary along the spectrum of possible investigative tools in respect of the person. Obviously, seriously intrusive procedures such as extracting blood or pumping the content of a person's stomach should not be permissible as a mere incident to arrest. By contrast, the state's law enforcement interests in undertaking more commonplace or routine procedures, which involve virtually no risk, trauma or pain for the person, may, exceptionally and in light of the totality of the circumstances, prevail over the privacy interests of the individual. In this respect, it must be remembered that a person who is lawfully arrested must "expect a significant loss of personal privacy" (*Beare*, supra, at p. 413 (per La Forest J.)).

4. The police must have reasonable and probable grounds to conduct a search for the purpose of obtaining bodily samples or impressions from a lawfully arrested person. In other words, the police must reasonably believe that the taking of such bodily samples or impressions is likely to yield highly relevant and probative evidence of, or in relation to, the offence for which that person is arrested.

5. The search must be predicated on sufficiently important circumstances in order to restrict the taking of bodily samples or impressions to situations where the state's significant law enforcement interests might otherwise be jeopardized. Those circumstances will generally be established where: (a) it is impracticable to obtain a warrant to secure the desired evidence; (b) such evidence cannot be obtained by a less intrusive means; (c) there is no alternative evidence available; (d) the offence for which the arrest was

made is a serious one; and (e) public policy is served by the type of search at issue.

6. The manner in which the search is conducted must not be abusive or unreasonable given the totality of the circumstances.

. . .

I would conclude that the search and seizure of the evidence at issue was legal as incidental to arrest and conducted in a reasonable manner in the circumstances of this case given the seriousness of the offence as well as the unavailability of any legal authorization procedure at the time of the appellant's arrest. I wish to re- emphasize that had there been a procedure available in which the police could have obtained a warrant, it is highly likely that, given those circumstances, the search could indeed have been found to be an unreasonable one.

On the issue of the seizure of the discarded tissue, the Court divided more narrowly with a 5:4 majority holding that the seizure violated section 8.

Per CORY J. (Lamer C.J., La Forest, Sopinka and Iacobucci JJ. concurring): — The appellant had advised the police, through the letter from his lawyers, that he refused to provide any bodily samples whatsoever. Despite this express refusal, the police seized a tissue, used by the appellant to blow his nose, from the garbage bin in the washroom of the RCMP headquarters. In other words, the police obtained surreptitiously that which the appellant had refused to provide them voluntarily; namely a sample from which his DNA profile could be obtained.

. . .

The appellant had been arrested at the time the tissue was seized, and was being detained. He had exercised his right to refuse to provide the police with bodily samples for the purposes of DNA analysis. Without that consent, the police had no right to take these samples from him. However, in the course of his five- day detention, it is reasonable to presume that, among other things, the appellant would blow his nose, use the toilet, possibly cut himself and bleed, and eat from a spoon.

. . .

In those circumstances, how can the appellant assert his right *not* to consent to the provision of bodily samples? He would be required to destroy every tissue he used, to hide every spoon he ate from, to keep cigarette butts, chewed gum or any other potentially incriminating evidence on his person at all times in order to prevent the police from retrieving this potentially useful waste.

. . .

Where an accused who is not in custody discards a kleenex or cigarette butt, the police may ordinarily collect and test these items without any concern about consent. A different situation is presented when an accused in custody discards items containing bodily fluids. Obviously an accused in custody cannot prevent the authorities from taking possession of these items. Whether the circumstances were such that the accused has abandoned the items and relinquished any privacy interest in them will have to be determined on the particular facts presented in each case.

However, in this case, the accused had announced through his lawyers that he would not consent to the taking of any samples of his bodily fluids. The police were aware of his decision. Despite this they took possession of the tissue discarded by the appellant while he was in custody. In these circumstances the seizure was unreasonable and violated the appellant's s. 8 Charter rights.

Four justices (L'Heureux-Dubé, Gonthier, McLachlin and Major JJ.) found that the tissue had not been obtained in violation of section 8. For example, McLachlin J. wrote:

In my view, the police action in taking the tissue did not violate s. 8 of the Charter. The tissue was not obtained as a result of a search of the appellant. Nor was it seized from him; he had discarded it. To put it another way, the appellant had abandoned any privacy interest in the tissue that he may have had. The police may find and use a gun thrown away by a killer as evidence against the killer. In my view, so may they find and use a tissue that he has discarded. The purpose of s. 8 is to protect the person and property of the individual from unreasonable search and seizure. This purpose is not engaged in the case of property which the accused has discarded.

R. v. CASLAKE
[1998] 1 S.C.R. 51, 13 C.R. (5th) 1, 121 C.C.C. (3d) 97 (S.C.C.)

While driving on a highway, the accused was arrested for possession of marijuana. He had earlier been seen to be in a field where a garbage bag containing marijuana was found. He was taken to the R.C.M.P. detachment and his car was towed to a garage across the street. Approximately six hours after the arrest, a R.C.M.P officer unlocked the garage and conducted an inventory search of the vehicle required by R.C.M.P. policy. He had neither a search warrant nor the accused's permission. He found $1400 in cash and two individual packages containing approximately 1/4 gram of cocaine each.

The accused was convicted of possession of marijuana for the purposes of trafficking, and possession of cocaine. He unsuccessfully appealed his conviction for cocaine possession to the Manitoba Queen's Bench and then to the Manitoba Court of Appeal on the ground that the search of his car was not reasonable under s. 8 of the Canadian Charter of Rights and Freedoms, and the cocaine should not have been admitted into evidence under s. 24(2). He appealed further.

The Supreme Court divided on the issue of whether the search was lawful and constitutional.

LAMER C.J. (Cory, McLachlin and Major JJ. concurring): —

. . .

C. THE SCOPE OF SEARCH INCIDENT TO ARREST

Since search incident to arrest is a common-law power, there are no readily ascertainable limits on its scope. It is therefore the courts' responsibility to set boundaries which allow the state to pursue its legitimate interests, while vigorously protecting individuals' right to privacy. The scope of search incident to arrest can refer to many different aspects of the search. It can refer to the items seized during the search. In *Stillman*, Cory J. for a majority of this Court held, at para. 42, that bodily samples could not be taken as incident to arrest, as a search so invasive is an "affront to human dignity". It can also refer to the place to be searched. The appellant argues that the power of search incident to arrest does not extend to automobiles. I would reject this position. Automobiles are legitimately the objects of search incident to arrest, as they attract no heightened expectation of privacy that would justify an exemption from the usual common law principles referred to above.

Scope can also refer to temporal limits on the power of search, which are at the core of the case at bar. The appellant suggests that the delay between the search and the arrest (six hours in this case) was too long to make the search "incident" to the arrest. In my opinion, the Court should be reluctant to set a strict limit on the amount of time that can elapse between the time of search and the time of arrest.

In my view, all of the limits on search incident to arrest are derived from the justification for the common law power itself: searches which derive their legal authority from the fact of arrest must be truly incidental to the arrest in question. The authority for the search does not arise as a result of a reduced expectation of privacy of the arrested individual. Rather, it arises out of a need for the law enforcement authorities to gain control of things or information which outweighs the individual's interest in privacy. See the Law Reform Commission of Canada, Report 24, *Search and Seizure* (1984), at p. 36. (For a more in-depth discussion, also see Working Paper 30, *Police Powers — Search and Seizure in Criminal Law Enforcement* (1983), at p. 160.) This means, simply put, that the search is only justifiable if the purpose of the search is related to the purpose of the arrest.

This position has been taken by a number of lower courts, and particularly well articulated by Doherty J.A. In *Lim (No. 2)*, supra, at p. 146, he stated:

> I begin with a determination of whether the search was truly an incident of the arrest. If it is not, the common law power to search as an incident of arrest cannot be relied upon. . . . In considering whether a search is in fact an incident of arrest, one must consider the police motives for the timing and place of the arrest and the relationship in time and place between the arrest and the search.

Similarly, in *R. v. Belnavis* (1996), 107 C.C.C. (3d) 195, at p. 213, Doherty J.A. held that an arrest for outstanding traffic fines did not authorize the search of the trunk of a vehicle, stating "[t]he authority to search as an incident of the arrest does not extend to searches undertaken for purposes which have no connection to the reason for the arrest." This decision was affirmed by this Court ([1997] 3 S.C.R. 341), although Cory J., who wrote for the majority, did not address this issue.

As L'Heureux-Dubé J. stated in *Cloutier*, the three main purposes of search incident to arrest are ensuring the safety of the police and public, the protection of evidence from destruction at the hands of the arrestee or others, and the discovery of evidence which can be used at the arrestee's trial. The restriction that the search must be "truly incidental" to the arrest means that the police must be attempting to achieve some valid purpose connected to the arrest. Whether such an objective exists will depend on what the police were looking for and why. There are both subjective and objective aspects to this issue. In my view, the police must have one of the purposes for a valid search incident to arrest in mind when the search is conducted. Further, the officer's belief that this purpose will be served by the search must be a reasonable one.

To be clear, this is not a standard of reasonable and probable grounds, the normal threshold that must be surpassed before a search can be conducted. Here, the only requirement is that there be some reasonable basis for doing what the police officer did. To give an example, a reasonable and probable grounds standard would require a police officer to demonstrate a reasonable belief that an arrested person was armed with a particular weapon before searching the person. By contrast, under the standard that applies here, the police would be entitled to search an arrested person for a weapon if under the circumstances it seemed reasonable to check whether the person might be armed. Obviously, there is a significant difference in the two standards. The police have considerable leeway in the circumstances of an arrest which they do not have in other situations. At the same time, in keeping with the criteria in *Cloutier*, there must be a "valid objective" served by the search. An objective cannot be valid if it is not reasonable to pursue it in the circumstances of the arrest.

In my view, it would be contrary to the spirit of the Charter's s. 8 guarantee of security against unreasonable searches or seizures to allow searches incident to arrest which do not meet both the subjective and objective criteria. This Court cannot characterize a search as being incidental to an arrest when the officer is actually acting for purposes unrelated to the arrest. That is the reason for the subjective element of the test. The objective element ensures that the police officer's belief that he or she has a legitimate reason to search is reasonable in the circumstances.

Requiring that the search be truly incidental to the arrest means that if the justification for the search is to find evidence, there must be some reasonable prospect of securing evidence of the offence for which the accused is being arrested. For example, when the arrest is for traffic violations, once the police have ensured their own safety, there is nothing that could properly justify searching any further (see *Belnavis*, supra).

As explained above, these limits will be no different for automobiles than for any other place. The right to search a car incident to arrest and the scope of that search will depend on a number of factors, including the basis for the arrest, the location of the motor vehicle in relation to the place of the arrest, and other relevant circumstances.

The temporal limits on search incident to arrest will also be derived from the same principles. There is no need to set a firm deadline on the amount of time that may elapse before the search can no longer said to be incidental to arrest. As a general rule, searches that are truly incidental to arrest will usually occur within a reasonable period of time after the arrest. A substantial delay does not mean that the search is automatically unlawful, but it may cause the court to draw an inference that the search is not sufficiently connected to the arrest. Naturally, the strength of the inference will depend on the length of the delay, and can be defeated by a reasonable explanation for the delay.

In summary, searches must be authorized by law. If the law on which the Crown is relying for authorization is the common law doctrine of search incident to arrest, then the limits of this doctrine must be respected. The most important of these limits is that the search must be truly incidental to the arrest. This means that the police must be able to explain, within the purposes articulated in *Cloutier*, supra (protecting the police, protecting the evidence, discovering evidence), or by reference to some other valid purpose, why they searched. They do not need reasonable and probable grounds. However, they must have had some reason related to the arrest for conducting the search at the time the search was carried out, and that reason must be objectively reasonable. Delay and distance do not automatically preclude a search from being incidental to arrest, but they may cause the court to draw a negative inference. However, that inference may be rebutted by a proper explanation.

D. WAS THE SEARCH IN THIS CASE TRULY INCIDENTAL TO THE ARREST?

The police arrested the appellant because they believed that he was either buying or selling the nine-pound bag of marijuana which Natural Resource Officer Kamann found. In this case, the appellant was arrested in his car, which had been observed at the place where the marijuana was discovered. Had Constable Boyle searched the car, even hours later, for the purpose of finding evidence which could be used at the appellant's trial on the charge of possessing marijuana for purpose of trafficking, this would have been well within the scope of the search incident to arrest power, as there was clearly sufficient circumstantial evidence to justify a search of the vehicle. However, by his own testimony, this is not why he searched. Rather, the sole reason for the search was to comply with an RCMP policy requiring that the contents of an impounded car be inventoried. This is not within the bounds of the legitimate purposes of search incident to arrest.

Naturally, the police cannot rely on the fact that, objectively, a legitimate purpose for the search existed when that is not the purpose for which they searched. The Charter requires that agents of the state act in accordance with the rule of law. This means that they must not only objectively search within the permissible scope, but that they must turn their mind to this scope before searching. The subjective part of the test forces the police officer to satisfy him or herself that there is a valid purpose for the search incident to arrest before the search is carried out. This accords with the ultimate purpose of s. 8, which, as Dickson J. stated in *Hunter*, supra, is to prevent unreasonable searches before they occur.

I would note that the six-hour delay in searching the vehicle is not, in and of itself, problematic in the case at bar. There were only two police officers in Gimli, and the regular policing commitments of one of them and the investigating matters undertaken by the other demonstrate that there is a reasonable explanation for the delay in searching the car. However, the delay further reinforces Officer Boyle's testimony that he was not searching for evidence, but simply conducting an "inventory search".

The fact that this search was not, in the mind of the searching party, consistent with the proper purposes of search incident to arrest means that it falls outside the scope of this power. As a result, the search cannot be said to have been authorized by the common law rule permitting search incident to arrest.

. . .

Suffice to say that an inventory search per se does not serve a "valid objective in pursuit of the ends of criminal justice" (*Cloutier*, supra, at p. 186) in the context of an arrest such that it can be justifiably carried out under this warrantless common-law power. Its purposes relate to concerns extraneous to the criminal law. If the police feel the need to inventory a car in their possession for their own purposes, that is one thing. However, if they wish to tender the fruits of that inventory search into evidence at a criminal trial, the search must be conducted under some lawful authority.

. . .

[Lamer C.J. further held, however, that the evidence should not be excluded under s. 24(2).]

BASTARACHE J. (L'Heureux-Dubé J. and Gonthier J. concurring):— While I agree with the Chief Justice that the appeal should be dismissed, I respectfully disagree with the reasons expressed by my colleague....

Regardless of Constable Boyle's subjective belief in the purpose and justification for his inventory search, the trial judge found that Constable Boyle had the right to search the vehicle pursuant to the common law power of search incidental to an arrest.

I agree with the trial judge. The power to search incidentally to an arrest draws its authority from the arrest itself. It is not necessary to independently establish reasonable and probable grounds to conduct a search incidental to an arrest. See *Cloutier*, supra, at pp. 185-86. Therefore, there was no onus on the Crown to establish at trial that Constable Boyle subjectively turned his mind to whether he was properly exercising his power to search incidentally to the arrest.

. . .

In my opinion, *Cloutier* describes a power of the common law which is, by definition, subject to interpretation on a case by case basis. The enumeration of purposes in *Cloutier* begins with the words "such as". This is consistent with the fact that the enumeration was taken from *Lindley v. Rutter*, [1981] Q.B.

128, where, at p. 134, it is followed by these words: "This list is not exhaustive, but it is sufficient for present purposes." Nowhere in *Cloutier* is it suggested that a subjective element is required to justify the search. To impose such a condition is tantamount to imposing that "reasonable and probable grounds" for the search be present. Indeed, how can the search be reasonable if the purpose of the police officer must be to find evidence and he or she conducts the search while having no reason to believe that the vehicle contains such evidence? I believe that a search conducted for the purpose of taking an inventory can be considered as a search for a "valid objective" under the proper circumstances. This type of search is less intrusive than a search conducted for the purpose of gathering evidence. In *Cloutier*, L'Heureux-Dubé J. described the condition under which a valid objective will be found where she wrote, at p. 186: "The purpose of the search must not be unrelated to the objectives of the proper administration of justice".

While an inventory search may be conducted for the purposes of securing the vehicle and protecting its contents, it may, in fact, provide evidence against the accused if such evidence can be found or is found. Since the test is not a subjective one, the intention of the officer is irrelevant and without any consequence, unless it is evidence of bad faith. In the case at bar, the search can then be justified because it is in fact related to the proper administration of justice. The arrest was legal, as was the impounding of the vehicle. The vehicle was a probable instrument in the perpetration of the crime. An inventory search was justified because its purpose was related to the arrest and consequential impounding of the vehicle.

The appellant argues that if the common law power to search incidentally to an arrest can authorize a search of his vehicle for evidence which is in no danger of being destroyed, then the common law is unreasonable and violates s. 8 of the Canadian Charter of Rights and Freedoms. According to the appellant, because Constable Boyle could have obtained a warrant in these circumstances, to do otherwise was unreasonable. But this reasoning is a distortion of the law. The existence of reasonable and probable grounds is precisely not a prerequisite to the existence of a police power to search incidentally to an arrest. The issue is therefore not whether Constable Boyle could have obtained a warrant, but rather whether the inventory search undertaken in these circumstances was truly incidental to the arrest and whether it was reasonably performed. As I have already established, in considering the purpose of the arrest in the context of the surrounding circumstances, the search of the appellant's vehicle was reasonable. It is then unnecessary to consider the issue of s. 24(2) of the Charter.

Caslake was applied to authorize the seizure of a briefcase as incident to an arrest of a person found in possession of a stolen vehicle: *R. v. Mohamad* (2004), 20 C.R. (6th) 178, 182 C.C.C. (3d) 97 (Ont. C.A.).

(ii) On Consent

PROBLEM 7

You are the trial judge and must deliver judgment in a civil suit brought by R against a Doctor A and four drug squad officers. The police were informed that R would be bringing back a quantity of heroin from Vancouver to Edmonton. At the Edmonton International Airport they approached him on the tarmac of the airport as he was deplaning, grabbed him by the throat to prevent him swallowing the drug that he might be carrying in his mouth, told him that he was under arrest for trafficking in heroin and applied handcuffs. In the ensuing struggle R and two police officers fell to the ground. The hold of R's throat was maintained and one of the police officers forced open the plaintiff's mouth while the other explored the interior of his mouth with a finger. Both sides of R's mouth were cut. The police version was this was caused by the wrist band of one of the officers. R maintained that it was by a police officer forcing a handcuff into his mouth and twisting it. R was subjected to a skin search at the police quarters at the air terminal during which it was noticed that the hair around his anal area had been greased. R was asked to go to the bathroom and remove the drugs or he would be taken to the hospital where they would be removed. His reply was "Let's go to the hospital". At the hospital the police officers informed Doctor A, on duty as resident physician, that R was under arrest and that they had reasonable grounds to believe that he was carrying drugs internally and requested that he be examined. Doctor A advised R that his mouth should be sutured but R refused to sign the consent form. R was then taken to an examining room at which time Doctor A told him that he would have to do a rectal examination which would be uncomfortable. R did not respond but co-operated in removing his clothes, putting on a gown and in positioning himself on the examining table because he believed that he had no choice. The doctor then performed a rectal examination by finger and then by sigmoidoscope, an instrument in the form of a hollow steel tube which was inserted in the anal canal to a depth of six inches. Condoms containing twenty-five capsules each were recovered. The examination took less than five minutes.

Compare *Reynen v. Antonenko* (1975), 30 C.R.N.S. 135, 20 C.C.C. (2d) 342 (Alta. S.C.) and see s. 25 of the Criminal Code. See too *R. v. Johal*, 2015 BCCA 246, 324 C.C.C. (3d) 546, 22 C.R. (7th) 286 (B.C. C.A.).

This power is important since police frequently purport to exercise search power on the basis of consent to the search.

LAW REFORM COMMISSION OF CANADA, WORKING PAPER 30: POLICE POWERS—SEARCH AND SEIZURE IN CRIMINAL LAW ENFORCEMENT

(1983), 68

B. Consent

126. The common law tolerance of search with consent is founded on different premises than the other existing powers of search and seizure. While the other powers establish exceptions to general prohibitive rules against intrusive conduct, and justify these exceptions on the basis of criminal law enforcement interests, the theory of "consent" search is founded on the proposition that the "search" performed does not in fact constitute an actionable intrusion. This proposition is an aspect of the common law doctrine of *volenti non fit injuria:*

> One who has invited or assented to an act being done towards him cannot, when he suffers from it, complain of it as a wrong.

According to this theory, once an individual consents to police action, he in effect waives the right to invoke the normal legal protections against the intrusions inherent in such actions. In effect, the giving of consent has been treated as a private transaction between individuals, thus rendering irrelevant such public law issues as the sufficiency of the peace officer's grounds for acting and the adherence to procedural prerequisites to intrusion.

127. It is noteworthy that, judging by available decisions, few cases of "consent" search appear to be litigated. This may be attributable to a number of factors, including the traditional absence of an exclusionary principle in Canadian evidence law, the possibility that in the presence of consent police activity may be less injurious than in its absence, and the improbability of the individual challenging the legality of the actions of peace officers to whom he previously has given his consent. The search cases, such as *Reynen v. Antonenko,* in which the issue of co-operation was raised, often contain little analysis on point beyond the simple conclusion as to whether the individual did or did not co-operate with the police. As a result, the law of "consent" search must be inferred from the law of consent generally. In some aspects this is unfortunate, since a number of issues are cast in a new context by virtue of the fact of a police investigation. These issues include the notions of true, limited and informed consent, the problem of proving consent, and perhaps foremost, the question of consent by a party other than the suspect himself. While these issues have been litigated extensively in American case-law on the Fourth Amendment, they have hardly been touched in Canadian search and seizure law.

128. This is not to say that there are no guidelines with which Canadian peace officers may resolve these issues in practice. Some police forces have established their own procedures to guide officers wishing to perform "consent" searches, particularly of premises. Some divisions of the R.C.M.P., for example, have instructed officers to use documentary consent forms, which both potentially alert the individual to his right to refuse consent, and provide evidence of consent if the issue is raised after the fact. The discretionary basis upon which police forces have adopted such practices, however, points out the wide gaps in existing Canadian law.

When a police officer asks a citizen for permission to search his person, vehicle or home what criteria should be considered in determining whether real consent was given?

DEDMAN v. R.

[1985] 2 S.C.R. 2, 46 C.R. (3d) 193, 20 C.C.C. (3d) 97 (S.C.C.)

The first question considered was whether the random stop by a police officer of the appellant's motor vehicle, as part of a programme to reduce impaired driving, was unlawful as having been made without statutory or common law authority, despite the appellant's compliance with the signal to stop.

LE DAIN J. (McIntyre, Lamer and Wilson JJ. concurring):—In allowing the appeal from the judgment of Maloney J. and setting aside the acquittal of the appellant, the Ontario Court of Appeal, in a unanimous judgment delivered by Martin J.A. (reported at 59 C.C.C. (2d) 97, 122 D.L.R. (3d) 655, 32 O.R. (2d) 641), held that the voluntary compliance of the appellant with the signal to stop made it immaterial whether the officer was exercising a police power for which there was statutory or common law authority, or was merely exercising a legal liberty—that is, doing something which he might do without any breach of law. The court concluded that in signalling the appellant to stop the police officer was not committing a crime or a tort, and that since the officer had reasonable suspicion at the time the s. 234.1(1) demand was made that the appellant had alcohol in his blood and had not placed himself in a position to make the demand by the commission of a crime or a tort, the demand was valid.

. . .

With great respect, I do not think that the issue of the lawfulness of the signal to stop in this case can be properly disposed of by reliance on the notion of legal liberties which a police officer as an individual enjoys in company with other citizens. For reasons which I shall indicate, I do not think that the appellant's compliance with the signal to stop altered the legal basis on which it must be justified. In my opinion, police officers, when acting or purporting to act in their official capacity as agents of the State, only act lawfully if they act in the exercise of authority which is either conferred by statute or derived as a matter of common law from their duties. The reason for this is the authoritative and coercive character of police action. An individual knows that he or she may ignore with impunity the signal to stop of another private individual. That is not true of a direction or demand by a police officer. It is for this reason, in my opinion, that the actions of police officers must find legal justification in statutory or common law authority. The ambit of their authority, as distinct from their liability, is not to be determined by the limits of criminal or civil responsibility. Police action may be unlawful for lack of statutory or common law authority although neither criminal nor tortious. The issue in the present case may be likened to one of *vires*. The contention is that the allegedly unauthorized and hence unlawful nature of the signal to stop affected the validity of the subsequent demand for a sample of breath.

This issue cannot be affected, in my opinion, by the appellant's compliance with the signal to stop. A person should not be prevented from invoking a lack of statutory or common law authority for a police demand or direction by reason of compliance with it in the absence of a clear indication from the police officer that the person is free to refuse to comply. Because of the intimidating nature of police action and uncertainty as to the extent of police powers, compliance in such circumstances cannot be regarded as voluntary in any meaningful sense. The possible criminal liability for failure to comply constitutes effective compulsion or coercion. It is, moreover, in the interest of public order that a person should comply with the signal to stop of a police officer. In some cases such a signal may be for the protection of the individual, as, for example, to give a warning of some danger. A person should not be penalized for compliance with a signal to stop by having it treated as a waiver or renunciation of rights, or as supplying a want of authority for the stop.

DICKSON C.J. (Beetz and Chouinard JJ. concurring):—I have had the opportunity of reading the reasons for judgment prepared by Mr. Justice Le Dain and I agree with him, for the reasons he has given, that police officers only act lawfully when they exercise authority conferred upon them by statute or at common law. The apparent voluntary compliance by a citizen with a police request to stop a motor vehicle cannot alter the legal basis which must justify such police action when it is challenged in later proceedings.

Having regard to the authoritative and coercive character of police requests, submission to a police officer's exercise of apparent authority, such as a demand to stop at a road-block, cannot be characterized as voluntary or consensual unless it was clear to the person at the time that he was free to refuse to comply.

This aspect of the *Dedman* ruling has now been relied upon to hold that the consent to a search must have been real and voluntary, and, further, that the person searched must have sufficient awareness to have waived the constitutional right to be protected against unreasonable search and seizure; the individual must be aware of the potential consequences of giving consent. See *R. v. Nielson* (1988), 43 C.C.C. (3d) 548 (Sask. C.A.), *R. v. Wills* (1992), 12 C.R. (4th) 58, 7 O.R. (3d) 337, 70 C.C.C. (3d) 529 (Ont. C.A.) and *R. v. Borden* (1994), 33 C.R. (4th) 147 (S.C.C.).

The concept of "consent" in the context of search and seizure has now been defined by Justice Doherty of the Ontario Court of Appeal in the following excerpts:

R. v. WILLS
(1992), 70 C.C.C. (3d) 529, 12 C.R. (4th) 58 (Ont. C.A.)

In my opinion, the application of the waiver doctrine to situations where it is said that a person has consented to what would otherwise be an unauthorized search or seizure requires that the Crown establish on the balance of probabilities that:

i. there was a consent, express or implied;

ii. the giver of the consent had the authority to give the consent in question;

iii. the consent was voluntary in the sense that that word is used in Goldman, *supra*, and was not the product of police oppression, coercion or other external conduct which negated the freedom to choose whether or not to allow the police to pursue the course of conduct requested;

iv. the giver of the consent was aware of the nature of the police conduct to which he or she was being asked to consent;

v. the giver of the consent was aware of his or her right to refuse to permit the police to engage in the conduct requested; and

vi. the giver of the consent was aware of the potential consequences of giving the consent.

R. v. LEWIS
(1998), 122 C.C.C. (3d) 481, 13 C.R. (5th) 34 (Ont. C.A.)

In my view, the police are not under a "duty" to advise a person of the right to refuse to consent to a search in the sense that the failure to do so will amount to a violation of s. 8. Unlike s. 10(b) of the Charter, s. 8 does not contain an informational component. The failure to advise a person of the right to refuse to consent to a search may, however, lead to a violation of s. 8 where the police conduct can be justified only on the basis of an informed consent. It is well established that a person cannot give an effective consent to a search unless the person is aware of their right to refuse to consent to that search: *R. v. Wills* (1992), 12 C.R. (4th) 58 at 78 (Ont. C.A.); *R. v. Borden* (1994), 33 C.R. (4th) 147 at 158 (S.C.C.). . . . If the police do not tell a person of the right to refuse to give a consent to a search, the police run the very real risk that any apparent consent given will be found to be no consent at all for the purposes of s. 8: *R. v. Wills, supra*, at 77. Where the police do not inform a person of the right to refuse to consent to a search, it is certainly open to a trial judge to conclude that the person was unaware of the right to refuse and could not, therefore, give an informed consent. The trial judge's conclusion that the consent given by the respondent to the search of the bag was an uninformed consent cannot be said to be unreasonable.

The Supreme Court in *R. v. Cole*, [2012] 3 S.C.R. 34, 290 C.C.C. (3d) 247, 96 C.R. (6th) 88 (S.C.C.) at paras. 76-78, firmly rejected the notion of third-party consent, distancing itself from United States jurisprudence.

PROBLEM 8

The police received an anonymous tip that the accused had marijuana growing in their home. The police checked criminal records and electric consumption and made a visual perimeter search of the dwelling-house from public property. These steps revealed nothing suspicious. The police decided on a "knock on" strategy whereby they would knock on the door and, if it was opened to reveal the smell of marijuana, they would have reasonable grounds to obtain a search warrant. The strategy worked: they smelled marijuana and obtained a warrant. Was the search lawful because by opening the door the occupant consented to the police search?

Compare *R. v. Evans*, [1996] 1 S.C.R. 8, 45 C.R. (4th) 210, 104 C.C.C. (3d) 23.

PROBLEM 9

In October an elderly woman was sexually assaulted in her home by an intruder. The woman was unable to identify her assailant as the room was dark and he covered his face. The police suspected that the accused, who was staying nearby, might be involved. The police seized from the victim's home a comforter, stained with semen.

In December a warrant was issued to arrest the accused for a sexual assault on an exotic dancer in a motel. That attack did not involve intercourse or ejaculation. When the accused was arrested for the second sexual assault he was advised of his right to counsel and right to remain silent. When advised that he was suspected as responsible for the sexual assault in the motel he made an oral exculpatory statement. He later reduced this to writing, although by then he had contacted a lawyer who had advised him to say nothing. The accused later agreed to provide samples of scalp and pubic hair. The police then asked the accused whether he would provide a blood sample. The accused agreed, believing that the blood sample requested had to do with the investigation of the sexual assault in the motel. The accused signed a consent form indicating his consent for the taking of a blood sample "for the purposes relating to their investigations". The use of the plural "investigations" was deliberate. The accused was not otherwise informed that the blood was to be used in connection with the sexual assault of the elderly woman. The blood sample was later matched by DNA typing to the semen on the comforter. The accused was charged with the sexual assault of the elderly woman. At the start of the trial on the second sexual assault charge the accused relied on s. 8 in an attempt to have the DNA evidence excluded. Was the search lawful because the accused consented?

Compare *R. v. Borden* (1994), 33 C.R. (4th) 147 (S.C.C.).

What if police obtained a hair sample from an accused with full consent on a particular investigation, but then want to use that sample in an unrelated case years later?

Compare *R. v. Arp*, [1998] 3 S.C.R. 339, 20 C.R. (5th) 1, 129 C.C.C. (3d) 321.

PROBLEM 10

In the course of a murder investigation, the police conducted a DNA canvass of twelve young men in a small remote community. It was held that the consent of the accused was valid. Is a DNA canvass permitted under the Charter? Compare *R. v. Osmond* (2009), 67 C.R. (6th) 380 (B.C. S.C.).

(iii) Incident to Duties of Police Officers if Reasonably Necessary (ancillary powers doctrine)

If a police officer has the duty of enforcing the law, is he necessarily equipped with all powers requisite to that duty? If not, what are the limitations?

DEDMAN v. R.
(1985), 46 C.R. (3d) 193, 20 C.C.C. (3d) 97 (S.C.C.)

The accused was acquitted of failing, without reasonable excuse, to provide a breath sample. He had been apprehended as part of a random vehicle stop programme. On appeal the acquittal was confirmed as it was held that there was neither statutory nor common law authority for the signal to stop and the accused therefore had a reasonable excuse. The Ontario Court of Appeal reversed and the accused appealed.

LE DAIN J. (McIntyre, Lamer and Wilson JJ. concurring):—Reliance was also placed on the general duties of police officers as the foundation for a common law authority to stop a motor vehicle for the purpose contemplated by the R.I.D.E. programme. A statutory statement of these duties is found in s. 55 of the *Police Act*, R.S.O. 1970, c. 351, which provides:

> 55. The members of police forces appointed under Part II, except assistants and civilian employees, are charged with the duty of preserving the peace, preventing robberies and other crimes and offences, including offences against the by-laws of the municipality, and apprehending offenders, and laying informations before the proper tribunal, and prosecuting and aiding in the prosecuting of offenders, and have generally all the powers and privileges and are liable to all the duties and responsibilities that belong to constables.

It has been held that at common law the principal duties of police officers are the preservation of the peace, the prevention of crime, and the protection of life and property, from which is derived the duty to control traffic on the public roads: see *Rice v. Connolly*, [1966] 2 Q.B. 414 at p. 419; *Johnson v. Phillips*, [1975] 3 All E.R. 682 at p. 685; Halsbury's Laws of England, 3rd ed. vol. 30, p. 129, para. 206.

The common law basis of police power has been derived from the nature and scope of police duty. Referring to the "powers associated with the duty", Ashworth J. in *R. v. Waterfield, supra*, at pp. 170-1, laid down the test for the existence of police powers at common law, as a reflection of police duties, as follows:

> In the judgment of this court it would be difficult, and in the present case it is unnecessary, to reduce within specific limits the general terms in which the duties of police constables have been expressed. In most cases it is probably more convenient to consider what the police constable was actually doing and in particular whether such conduct was prima facie an unlawful interference with a person's liberty or property. If so, it is then relevant to consider whether (a) such conduct falls within the general scope of any duty imposed by statute or recognized at common law and (b) whether such conduct, albeit within the general scope of such a duty, involved an unjustifiable use of powers associated with the duty.

> Thus, while it is no doubt right to say in general terms that police constables have a duty to prevent crime and a duty, when crime is committed, to bring the offender to justice, it is also clear from the decided cases that when the execution of these general duties involves interference with the person or property of a private person, the powers of constables are not unlimited. To cite only one example, in *Davis v. Lisle*, [1936] 2 K.B. 434, it was held that even if a police officer had a right to enter a garage to make inquiries, he became a trespasser after the appellant had told him to leave the premises, and that he was not therefore acting thenceforward in the execution of his duty, with the result that the appellant could not be convicted of assaulting or obstructing him in the execution of his duty.

The test laid down in *Waterfield*, while generally invoked in cases in which the issue is whether a police officer was acting in the execution of his duties, has been recognized as being a test for whether the officer had common law authority for what he did. In *Hoffman v. Thomas*, [1974] 2 All E.R. 233, the issue was whether a police constable had the power to direct a motorist to stop for the purpose of submitting to a traffic census. The appellant was charged with refusal to comply with a direction to stop given by a police constable in the execution of his duty. Applying the *Waterfield* test, which he referred to as being of "the greatest assistance", Lord Widgery C.J. affirmed that the power to control traffic was a power to be exercised for the protection of life and property and held that the traffic census could not be related to this purpose. The direction did not therefore fall within the general scope of a police constable's duties under the first branch of the *Waterfield* test. Speaking in terms of police powers, Lord Widgery C.J. said at p. 238: "Accordingly it seems to me that neither at common law, nor by any statutory provisions to which we have been referred, had this police officer any right to direct the appellant to leave the motorway and go into the census area", and he spoke of the direction as a "signal which he had no power to make either at common law or by virtue of statute". The test laid down in *Waterfield* was treated as authoritative and applied by this Court in *R. v. Stenning*, [1970] 3 C.C.C. 145, 10 D.L.R. (3d) 224, [1970] S.C.R. 631, and in *Knowlton v. The Queen* (1973), 10 C.C.C. (2d) 377, 33 D.L.R. (3d) 755, [1974] S.C.R. 443, both cases in which the issue was whether a police officer was in the execution of his duty. In *Knowlton*, Fauteux C.J.C., delivering the judgment of the court, said at p. 379 C.C.C., p. 758 D.L.R., p. 446 S.C.R.: Police duty and the use of powers associated with such duty are the sole matters in issue in this appeal", and he concluded at p. 381 C.C.C., pp. 759-600 D.L.R., p. 448 S.C.R.: "I cannot find in the record any evidence showing that Sergeant Grandish or other police officers resorted, on the occasion, to any unjustifiable use of the powers associated with the duty imposed upon them." Leigh, *Police Powers in England and Wales* (1975), p. 33, refers to the decision in *Knowlton* as reflecting a movement towards "an ancillary powers doctrine which would enable the police to perform such reasonable acts as are necessary for the due execution of their duties". In *Reference re an Application for an Authorization* (judgment rendered December 20, 1984) [since reported 15 C.C.C. (3d) 466, 14 D.L.R. (4th) 546, [1984] 2 S.C.R. 697], Chief Justice Dickson, dissenting, considered the *Waterfield* test under the heading "*The common law powers of the police*", which he referred to as "powers inherent in the execution of a police officer's duty" [see p. 481 C.C.C., p. 561 D.L.R.].

In applying the *Waterfield* test to the random stop of a motor vehicle for the purpose contemplated by the R.I.D.E. programme, it is convenient to refer to the right to circulate in a motor vehicle on the public highway as a "liberty". That is the way it was referred to in *Hoffman v. Thomas, supra*, and in *Johnson v. Phillips, supra*. In assessing the interference with this right by a random vehicle stop, one must bear in mind, however, that the right is not a fundamental liberty like the ordinary right of movement of the individual, but a licensed activity that is subject to regulation and control for the protection of life and property. Applying the *Waterfield* test, then, and using the word "liberty" in this qualified and special sense, it may be said that the random vehicle stop in this case was *prima facie* an unlawful interference with liberty since it was not authorized by statute. The first question, then, under the *Waterfield* test is whether the random stop fell within the general scope of the duties of a police officer under statute or common law. I do not think there can be any doubt that it fell within the general scope of the duties of a police officer to prevent crime and to protect life and property by the control of traffic. These are the very objects of the R.I.D.E. programme, which is a measure to improve the deterrence and detection of impaired driving, a notorious cause of injury and death.

Turning to the second branch of the *Waterfield* test, it must be said respectfully that neither *Waterfield* itself nor most of the cases which have applied it throw much light on the criteria for determining whether a particular interference with liberty is an unjustifiable use of a power associated with a police duty. There is a suggestion of the correct test, I think, in the use of the words "reasonably necessary" in *Johnson v. Phillips, supra*. The interference with liberty must be necessary for the carrying out of the particular police duty and it must be reasonable, having regard to the nature of the liberty interfered with and the importance of the public purpose served by the interference. Because of the seriousness of the problem of impaired driving, there can be no doubt about the importance and necessity of a programme to improve the deterrence of it. The right to circulate on the highway free from unreasonable interference is an important one, but it is, as I have said, a licensed activity subject to regulation and control in the interest of safety. The objectionable nature of a random stop is chiefly that it is made on a purely arbitrary basis, without any grounds for suspicion or belief that the particular driver has committed or is committing an offence. It is this aspect of the random stop that makes it capable of producing unpleasant psychological effects for the innocent driver. These effects, however, would tend to be minimized by the well-publicized nature of the programme, which is a necessary feature of its deterrent purpose. Moreover, the stop would be of relatively short duration and of slight inconvenience. Weighing these factors, I am of the opinion that having regard to the importance of the public purpose served, the random stop, as a police action necessary to the carrying out of that purpose, was not an unreasonable interference with the right to circulate on the public highway. It was not, therefore, an unjustifiable use of a power associated with the police duty, within the *Waterfield* test. I would accordingly hold that there was common law authority for the random vehicle stop for the purpose contemplated by the R.I.D.E. programme.

In view of this conclusion it is unnecessary for me to express an opinion as to whether, if the random vehicle stop were unlawful for lack of statutory or common law authority, its unlawful character would constitute a reasonable excuse, on the authority of the decision of the majority of this Court in *Brownridge v. The Queen* (1972), 7 C.C.C. (2d) 417, 28 D.L.R. (3d) 1, [1972] S.C.R. 926, for the failure to comply with the s. 234.1(1) demand for a sample of breath, or would render such demand invalid, on the reasoning of the House of Lords in *Morris v. Beardmore*, [1980] 3 W.L.R. 283.

I would accordingly dismiss the appeal. The appellant should have his costs in this Court on both the application for leave to appeal and on the appeal.

DICKSON C.J. (Beetz and Chouinard JJ. concurring) (dissenting):—

III. *Lawfulness of random vehicle stops*

A. *Statutory authority*

The R.I.D.E. programme was not, at the time the appellant was stopped, expressly authorized by statute, either federal or provincial. I agree with Mr. Justice Le Dain that none of the provincial statutory provisions relied upon can be interpreted to grant police officers authority to request a motorist stop for the purposes of the R.I.D.E. programme. In particular, s. 14 of the *Highway Traffic Act*, R.S.O. 1970, c. 202, as amended by 1979, c. 57, s. 2 (now R.S.O. 1980, c. 198, s. 19), does not provide statutory authority for the signal to stop. It is unnecessary to express any opinion as to the constitutional validity of s. 14. Section 14 is not being applied to confer authority to make a random vehicle stop for the purpose contemplated by the R.I.D.E. programme. The constitutional question set in this case need not therefore be answered.

B. *Common law authority*

With respect, I am unable to agree with Mr. Justice Le Dain that the general duties of police officers provide the foundation for common law authority to stop a motor vehicle for the purpose and in the manner contemplated by the R.I.D.E. programme.

It has always been a fundamental tenet of the rule of law in this country that the police, in carrying out their general duties as law enforcement officers of the State, have limited powers and are only entitled to interfere with the liberty or property of the citizen to the extent authorized by law. Chief Justice Laskin, dissenting, in *R. v. Biron* (1975), 23 C.C.C. (2d) 513, 59 D.L.R. (3d) 409, [1976] 2 S.C.R. 56, made the point at pp. 518-9 C.C.C., p. 415 D.L.R., pp. 64-5 S.C.R.:

> Far more important, however, is the social and legal, and indeed, political, principle upon which our criminal law is based, namely, the right of an individual to be left alone, to be free of private or public restraint, save as the law provides otherwise. Only to the extent to which it so provides can a person be detained or his freedom of movement arrested.

Absent explicit or implied statutory authority, the police must be able to find authority for their actions at common law. Otherwise they act unlawfully.

Martin J.A., in the case at bar, accurately summarized the rights of the citizen and the power of the police as follows, at pp. 108-9 C.C.C., pp. 667-8 D.L.R., pp. 652-3 O.R.:

> In carrying out their general duties, the police have limited powers, and they are entitled to interfere with the liberty and property of the citizen only where such interference is authorized by law. It is, of course, a constitutional principle that the citizen has a right not to be subjected to imprisonment, arrest, or physical restraint that is not justified by law, and every invasion of the property of the citizen is a trespass unless legally justified . . . On the other hand, when a police officer is trying to discover whether, or by whom, an offence has been committed, he is entitled to question any person, whether suspected or not, from whom he thinks useful information may be obtained. Although a police officer is entitled to question any person in order to obtain information with respect to a suspected offence, he has no lawful power to compel the person questioned to answer. Moreover, a police officer has no right to detain a person for questioning or for further investigation. No one is entitled to impose any physical restraint upon the citizen except as authorized by law, and this principle applies as much to police officers as to anyone else. Although a police officer may approach a person on the street and ask him questions, if the person refuses to answer the police officer must allow him to proceed on his way, unless, of course, the officer arrests him on a specific charge or arrests him pursuant to s. 450 of the *Code* where the officer has reasonable and probable grounds to believe that he is about to commit an indictable offence [Authorities omitted].

The common law duties of police have been described as the preservation of the peace, the prevention of crime and the protection of life and property; from this latter duty flows the duty to control traffic on the public roads. A statutory statement of the traditional common law duties of the police may be found in s. 57 of the *Police Act*, R.S.O. 1980, c. 381.

I do not think it is open to question that action to detect and prevent people from driving while impaired by alcohol, an offence under the *Criminal Code*, falls within the general duties of the police described above. It is, however, necessary to distinguish the duties of police officers from the power, or lawful authority, they possess to execute those duties. The fact that a police officer has a general duty to prevent crime and protect life and property does not mean that he or she can use any or all means for achieving these ends. The question raised by this appeal is whether the police have the power at common law, in other words the lawful authority, to execute their general duties by means of random stops of motorists when they have no reason to believe, prior to the stop, that the motorist has committed, is committing or will commit a criminal offence. In my opinion, they possess no such authority.

· · ·

I had occasion to review the *Waterfield, Stenning* and *Knowlton* cases recently in my dissenting reasons in *Reference re an Application for an Authorization* (1984), 15 C.C.C. (3d) 466, 14 D.L.R. (4th) 546, [1984] 2 S.C.R. 697 *sub nom. Wiretap Reference.* As I noted, at p. 482 C.C.C., pp. 562-3 D.L.R., p. 717 S.C.R., these cases all involved charges of assaulting or obstructing a police officer in the execution of his duty. Charges were laid as a result of altercations with the police and the defence was raised that the police were not acting in the execution of their duty at the time.

In the *Wiretap Reference* it was argued, in reliance upon *Waterfield*, that the common law recognizes certain powers inherent in the execution of a police officer's duty and that these powers would, in the circumstances, permit the police to engage in acts necessary to the fulfilment of their duty even though they involved an otherwise unlawful interference with a person's liberty or property. After noting that the police have never been entitled to exercise a general right of entry as part of the powers accorded them at common law, I stated, in dissenting reasons, that *Waterfield* does not stand for the proposition that the power of entry to private property for the purpose of installing a listening device can arise simply by virtue of a police officer's general duty to detect crime and enforce the law. I concluded that the *Waterfield* test provides no support for police conduct, where the conduct is unlawful at common law (at p. 483 C.C.C., p. 563 D.L.R., pp. 718-9 S.C.R.):

> I cannot accept that conduct of itself unlawful and initiated with full knowledge of its potential illegality could ever fall within the general scope of a policeman's duty.
>
> .. .
>
> The fact that police officers could be described as acting within the general scope of their duties to investigate crime cannot empower them to violate the law whenever such conduct could be justified by the public interest in law enforcement. Any such principle would be nothing short of a *fiat* for illegality on the part of the police whenever the benefit of police action appeared to outweigh the infringement of an individual's rights. *For the Waterfield principle to apply, the police must be engaged in lawful execution of their duty at the time of the conduct in question.*

A police officer is not empowered to execute his or her duty by unlawful means. The public interest in law enforcement cannot be allowed to override the fundamental principle that all public officials, including the police, are subject to the rule of law. To find that arbitrary police action is justified simply because it is directed at the fulfilment of police duties would be to sanction a dangerous exception to the supremacy of law. It is the function of the Legislature, not the courts, to authorize arbitrary police action that would otherwise be unlawful as a violation of rights traditionally protected at common law.

Since police lack legal authority to detain a person for questioning or for purposes of investigation at common law, even on suspicion, short of arrest, I am unable to find any basis for the power to stop and detain a motorist asserted in the circumstances of this case.

It is vital to characterize correctly the powers the police have exercised here and not allow them to be obscured by the desirable objective the R.I.D.E. programme is designed to attain. The police are stopping motorists on an entirely arbitrary basis to question them and determine if they have been drinking. As Professor Cohen notes in "The Investigation of Offences and Police Powers", *ibid.*, p. 562, note 47: "The exercise is no less random because it requires the procedure to be carried out in specific locations noted for alcohol-related accidents or frequent impaired driving. It is random insofar as it relates to each stopped motorist".

As stated above, the police had no grounds to reasonably suspect that the appellant had committed, was committing or was about to commit a criminal offence before he was requested to stop. Indeed, the police did not observe anything suspicious or improper about the appellant's driving or the condition of his car. The only reason for the random stop of the appellant was the fact that he happened to be passing through a location where the police believed there was a high incidence of drinking and driving. It is inescapable that, in essence, the police stopped and detained the appellant arbitrarily to investigate whether he might be committing a criminal offence.

In my opinion, the police were not authorized to stop the appellant at random for the purposes of the R.I.D.E. programme. A random stop of a motorist is indistinguishable from detention for questioning or investigation against a person's will, something the courts have long recognized that police lack the power to do at common law. The vice is increased and the invasion of individual autonomy magnified when the individual is detained, not under any suspicion directed at the driver personally, but on the simple chance of where he or she happens to be driving. To conclude that this action of the police was authorized would run contrary to the longstanding protection accorded individual liberty by the common law and erode the individual's fundamental right to be free from arbitrary interference.

With respect, the majority of the court departs firm ground for a slippery slope when they authorize an otherwise unlawful interference with individual liberty by the police, solely on the basis that it is reasonably necessary to carry out general police duties. The objection to a random stop made without any grounds for suspicion or belief that the particular driver has committed or is committing an offence goes far beyond the unpleasant psychological effects produced for the innocent driver. Even if these would tend to be minimized by the well-publicized nature of the R.I.D.E. programme, the erosion of individual liberty with its ultimately detrimental effect on the freedom of all members of society would remain.

Furthermore, the fact that driving a motor vehicle is a licensed activity subject to regulation and control in the interests of safety is irrelevant to police power if the conditions for licensing have been met and are adhered to; the curtailment of liberty by the police in no way flows from the fact of licensing or any other regulation. The right to circulate on the highway is not limited to freedom from unreasonable interference by the police; it exists unfettered except in so far as it is curtailed by law.

. . .

I conclude that, without validly enacted legislation to support them, the random stops by the police under the R.I.D.E. programme are unlawful. In striving to achieve one desirable objective, the reduction of the death and injury that occurs each year from impaired driving, we must ensure that other, equally important, social values are not sacrificed. Individual freedom from interference by the State, no matter how laudable the motive of the police, must be guarded zealously against intrusion. Ultimately, this freedom is the measure of everyone's liberty and one of the cornerstones of the quality of life in our democratic society.

The Supreme Court has sometimes not relied on the ancillary powers doctrine to create a new common law police power: see, for example, *Stillman* and *Kokesch* below. However, the Court now often resorts to it: see below *Chehil* (power to use dog sniffers), *Macdonald* (safety searches) and *Godoy* (entering to investigate a 911 call). Critics often point to the dangers of *ex post facto* reasoning and undue vagueness for police. Other commentators prefer the balancing of police powers and civil liberties to be done by the courts rather than law and order legislatures. Some commentators also argue that the creation of common law powers bypasses the question of reasonable justification under s. 1 of the Charter.

(c) Other Federal Statutes

Many other federal statutes contain powers of search without warrant. Particularly extensive powers were contained in the Customs Act, R.S.C. 1970, c. C-40, s. 133, 134; the Excise Act, R.S.C. 1970, c. E-12, s. 70, 71; the Food and Drugs Act, R.S.C. 1970, c. F-27, s. 22; and the Narcotic Control Act, R.S.C. 1970, c. N-1, s. 10. Until the Criminal Law Amendment Act of 1985 these four statutes allowed for the issuance of writs of assistance which have long been controversial, since the holder of a writ was a "walking search warrant", and are not subject to meaningful judicial control. A writ of assistance granted a police officer the power to search any place, including a dwelling house, without the need of having to obtain a search warrant or other judicial authorization.

In *R. v. Noble* (1984), 42 C.R. (3d) 209, 16 C.C.C. (3d) 146, (Ont. C.A.), writs of assistance were held to be contrary to s. 8 of the Charter and unconstitutional. The Law Reform Commission of Canada, *Report: Writs of Assistance and Telewarrants* (1983) had reached this conclusion earlier and had recommended the repeal of writs of assistance and their replacement by a telewarrant procedure. This was achieved by the Criminal Law Amendment

Act of 1985. The Criminal Code provides, in s. 487.1, for a telewarrant procedure. In 1996, broad search powers were bestowed in drug cases:

Controlled Drugs and Substances Act, S.C. 1996, c. 19

11. (1) A justice who, on *ex parte* application, is satisfied by information on oath that there are reasonable grounds to believe that

(a) a controlled substance or precursor in respect of which this Act has been contravened,

(b) any thing in which a controlled substance or precursor referred to in paragraph (*a*) is contained or concealed,

(c) offence-related property, or

(d) any thing that will afford evidence in respect of an offence under this Act or an offence, in whole or in part in relation to a contravention of this Act, under section 354 or 462.31 of the *Criminal Code*

is in a place may, at any time, issue a warrant authorizing a peace officer, at any time, to search the place for any such controlled substance, precursor, property or thing and to seize it.

(2) For the purposes of subsection (1), an information may be submitted by telephone or other means of telecommunication in accordance with section 487.1 of the Criminal Code, with such modifications as the circumstances require.

(3) A justice may, where a place referred to in subsection (1) is in a province other than that in which the justice has jurisdiction, issue the warrant referred to in that subsection and the warrant may be executed in the other province after it has been endorsed by a justice having jurisdiction in that other province.

(4) An endorsement that is made on a warrant as provided for in subsection (3) is sufficient authority to any peace officer to whom it was originally directed and to all peace officers within the jurisdiction of the justice by whom it is endorsed to execute the warrant and to deal with the things seized in accordance with the law.

(5) Where a peace officer who executes a warrant issued under subsection (1) has reasonable grounds to believe that any person found in the place set out in the warrant has on their person any controlled substance, precursor, property or thing set out in the warrant, the peace officer may search the person for the controlled substance, precursor, property or thing and seize it.

(6) A peace officer who executes a warrant issued under subsection (1) may seize, in addition to the things mentioned in the warrant,

(a) any controlled substance or precursor in respect of which the peace officer believes on reasonable grounds that this Act has been contravened;

(b) any thing that the peace officer believes on reasonable grounds to contain or conceal a controlled substance or precursor referred to in paragraph (*a*);

(c) any thing that the peace officer believes on reasonable grounds is offence-related property; or

(d) any thing that the peace officer believes on reasonable grounds will afford evidence in respect of an offence under this Act.

(7) A peace officer may exercise any of the powers described in subsection (1), (5) or (6) without a warrant if the conditions for obtaining a warrant exist but by reason of exigent circumstances it would be impracticable to obtain one.

(8) A peace officer who executes a warrant issued under subsection (1) or exercises powers under subsection (5) or (7) may seize, in addition to the things mentioned in the warrant and in subsection (6), any thing that the peace officer believes on reasonable grounds has been obtained by or used in the commission of an offence or that will afford evidence in respect of an offence.

12. For the purpose of exercising any of the powers described in section 11, a peace officer may

(a) enlist such assistance as the officer deems necessary; and

(b) use as much force as is necessary in the circumstances.

(d) Provincial Statutes

There are literally hundreds of search powers under various provincial statutes. Noticeably wide powers of stop, inspection and seizure are to be found under provincial Highway Traffic and Liquor Acts.

(e) Constitutional Minimum Standards

In October 1980 the draft s. 8 of the Charter read:

Everyone has the right not to be subjected to search or seizure except on grounds and in accordance with procedures established by law.

In response to urgings by civil libertarians that this would enshrine the status quo, s. 8 was re-drafted in February 1981 to its present wording of:

Everyone has the right to be secure against unreasonable search or seizure.

This differs from the more elaborate version of the 4th Amendment to the United States Constitution, discussed in *Rao*.

R. v. RAO
(1984), 46 O.R. (2d) 80, 40 C.R. (3d) 1, 12 C.C.C. (3d) 97 (Ont. C.A.)

The accused was charged with possession of cannabis resin for the purpose of trafficking contrary to the Narcotic Control Act. Police officers had found several vials of hashish oil on the accused's business premises when they had entered the premises without warrant. The accused had protested in vain that a search warrant was required and that he should be allowed to make a telephone call to his lawyer. His movements during the search were strictly controlled. After drugs were found, the accused was formally charged, cautioned and informed of his right to retain and instruct counsel without delay, but was still questioned by the police. Later, during further questioning, he was struck on the head. The trial judge acquitted, holding that s. 10(1)(*a*) of the Narcotic Control Act, authorizing a search without a warrant, was contrary to s. 8 of the Canadian Charter of Rights and Freedoms, and that the admission of the evidence would bring the administration of justice into disrepute and should be excluded under s. 24(2). The Attorney General of Canada appealed.

MARTIN J.A.:—The Fourth Amendment to the American Constitution provides:

> The right of the people to be secure in their persons, houses, papers, and effects, against unreasonable searches and seizures, shall not be violated, and no warrants shall issue, but upon probable cause, supported by oath or affirmation, and particularly describing the place to be searched, and the persons or things to be seized.

The Fourth Amendment has proved a fertile source of litigation, producing an immense body of case law, the volume and complexity of which is almost overwhelming. The decisions of the Supreme Court of the United States, admittedly, have not always been consistent in their interpretation of the Fourth Amendment, which is open to two different interpretations, depending largely on whether its two clauses are read together or separately. On its face the first clause merely provides that a search or seizure must meet the standard of reasonableness. The second clause merely provides that a warrant must meet the requirements specified in that clause.

An examination of the decisions of the United States Supreme Court reveals two distinct lines of approach to the interpretation of the Fourth Amendment. Some justices of the Supreme Court consider that the first clause should be read separately from the warrant clause, and that the existence of a warrant is only one factor in determining the reasonableness of a search: see *U.S. v. Rabinowitz*, [339 U.S. 56 (1950)] (Frankfurter J. dissenting). Other members of the court have insisted that the two clauses must be read together so that warrantless searches are per se unreasonable, subject only to a few well-delineated exceptions where it would be impracticable to obtain a warrant. Both Frankfurter J. and Stewart J. were strong proponents of this view: see Barnett, Goldman and Morris, "A Lawyer's Lawyer, A Judge's Judge: Justice Potter Stewart and the Fourth Amendment" (1982), 51 Univ. of Cincinnati L. Rev. 509, at pp. 517-18. Both interpretations have commanded majorities at one time or another: see Charles H. Whitebread, Criminal Procedure (1980), at pp. 102-103.

The first approach to the interpretation of the Fourth Amendment permits a broader range of warrantless searches. Under the second approach, the warrant requirement is the overriding directive of the Fourth Amendment, subject to specific exceptions.

In Professor Amsterdam's Oliver Wendell Holmes lecture "Perspectives on the Fourth Amendment", delivered in 1974, he summarized the trend of the decisions of the Supreme Court of the United States in the previous 20 years thus:

> 'Searches' and 'seizures' affecting protected interests are forbidden by the fourth amendment only if they are 'unreasonable.' In 1950, the Supreme Court took a broad and elastic view of the phrase 'unreasonable searches and seizures,' and occasional opinions expressing this view have been handed down even recently. During the past twenty years, however, the Court has increasingly emphasized that 'the definition of "reasonableness" turns, at least in part, on the more specific commands of the [fourth amendment's] warrant clause.' Under this theory, the Court has uniformly condemned searches and seizures made without a search

warrant, subject only to a few 'jealously and carefully drawn' exceptions. (*Perspectives on the Fourth Amendment,* 58 Minnesota Law Rev. 349 at 358).

There is some indication, however, that the first interpretation, namely, that the central requirement of the Fourth Amendment is that of reasonableness, is becoming the predominant approach to the interpretation of the Fourth Amendment. In *Texas v. Brown* (1983), 75 L. Ed. (2d) 502, 103 S. Ct. 1535, a police officer lawfully stopped an automobile as part of a routine licence check, shone his flashlight into the car and observed Brown withdraw his hand from his pants pocket. Caught between his fingers was a party balloon, which, when seized by the officer, was found to contain heroin. The Supreme Court of the United States held that the officer's initial intrusion was lawful and that there had been a valid seizure of the narcotic under the "plain view" doctrine. Rehnquist J. (with whom the Chief Justice and White and O'Connor JJ. concurred) said at p. 1539:

> Our cases hold that procedure by way of a warrant is preferred, although in a wide range of diverse situations we have recognized flexible, common-sense exceptions to this requirement. See, *e.g., Warden of Maryland Penitentiary v. Hayden* (1967), 387 U.S. 294, 18 L. Ed. (2d) 782, 87 S. Ct. 1642 (hot pursuit); *U.S. v. Jeffers* (1951), 342 U.S. 48 at 51-52, 96 L. Ed. 59, 72 S. Ct. 93 at 95-96 (exigent circumstances); *U.S. v. Ross* (1982), 72 L. Ed. (2d) 572, 102 S. Ct. 2157 (automobile search); *Chimel v. California* [(1969), 395 U.S. 752]; *U.S. v. Robinson* (1973), 414 U.S. 218, 38 L. Ed. (2d) 427, 94 S. Ct. 467; and *New York v. Belton* (1982), 453 U.S. 454, 69 L. Ed. (2d) 768, 101 S. Ct. 2860 (search of person and surrounding area incident to arrest); *Almeida-Sanchez v. U.S.* (1973), 413 U.S. 266, 37 L. Ed. (2d) 596, 93 S. Ct. 2535 (search at border or 'functional equivalent'); *Zap v. U.S.* (1946), 328 U.S. 624, 630, 90 L. Ed. 1477, 66 S. Ct. 1277 at 1280 (consent). We have also held to be permissible intrusions less severe than full-scale searches or seizures without the necessity of a warrant. See, *e.g., Terry v. Ohio* (1968), 392 U.S. 1, 20 L. Ed. (2d) 889, 88 S. Ct. 1868 (stop and frisk); *U.S. v. Brignoni-Ponce* (1975), 422 U.S. 873, 45 L. Ed. (2d) 607, 95 S. Ct. 2574 (seizure for questioning); *Delaware v. Prouse* (1979), 440 U.S. 648, 59 L. Ed. (2d) 660, 99 S. Ct. 1391 (roadblock). One frequently mentioned 'exception to the warrant requirement,' *Coolidge v. New Hampshire* (1971), 403 U.S. 443, 29 L. Ed. (2d) 564, 91 S. Ct. 2022, is the so-called 'plain view' doctrine, relied upon by the state in this case.

Later in his judgment, after reviewing the "plain view" doctrine, he said at p. 1541:

> This rule merely reflects an application of *the Fourth Amendment's central requirement of reasonableness* to the law governing seizures of property. (The italics are mine.)

On the other hand, Powell J. (with whom Blackmun J. concurred), although concurring in the disposition of the case by the court, considered that Rehnquist J.'s opinion accorded less significance to the warrant clause than was justified by the language and purpose of the Fourth Amendment. He said at p. 1544:

> I concur in the judgment, and also agree with much of the plurality's opinion relating to the application in this case of the plain view exception to the Warrant Clause. But I do not join the plurality's opinion because it goes well beyond the application of the exception. As I read the opinion, it appears to accord less

significance to the Warrant Clause of the Fourth Amendment than is justified by the language and purpose of that Amendment. In dissent in *U.S. v. Rabinowitz* [(1950), 339 U.S. 56], Justice Frankfurter wrote eloquently:

'One cannot wrench "unreasonable searches" from the text and context and historic content of the Fourth Amendment . . . When [that] Amendment outlawed "unreasonable searches" and then went on to define the very restricted authority that even a search warrant issued by a magistrate could give, the framers said with all the clarity of the gloss of history that a search is "unreasonable" unless a warrant authorizes it, barring only exceptions justified by absolute necessity.' *Id.,* at 70, 70 S. Ct., at 436.

To be sure, the opinions of this Court in Warrant Clause cases have not always been consistent. They have reflected disagreement among Justices as to the extent to which the Clause defines the reasonableness standard of the Amendment. In one of my earliest opinions, *U.S. v. U.S. D.C.* (1972), 407 U.S. 297, 32 L. Ed. (2d) 752, 92 S. Ct. 2125, I cited Justice Frankfurter's *Rabinowitz* dissent in emphasizing the importance of the Warrant Clause. *Id.,* at 316, 92 S. Ct., at 2136. Although I would not say that exceptions can be justified only by "absolute necessity," I stated that they were "few in number and carefully delineated." *Id.,* at 318, 92 S. Ct., at 2137. This has continued to be my view, as expressed recently in *Arkansas v. Sanders* (1979), 442 U.S. 753 at 759, 61 L. Ed. (2d) 235, 99 S. Ct. 2586 at 2590. It is a view frequently repeated by this Court.

One commentator, in a recent analysis of the current trend of the decisions of the Supreme Court of the United States, suggests that, despite the repeatedly- expressed preference for the use of search warrants, the court has in fact so expanded the opportunities for warrantless searches that its approach has been far more consistent with the reasonableness approach of Minton J., delivering the majority judgment of the Supreme Court of the United States in *U.S. v. Rabinowitz,* supra. He suggests that the inconsistency between the suggested preference for a warrant and the actual rulings of the court stems from its "disenchantment" with the exclusionary rule, and that an examination of the recent cases shows that the court has implicitly abandoned the "preference for a warrant" approach, at least in those situations not involving a "home, office or private communication", in favour of a less restrictive approach to the warrant requirement: Robert M. Bloom, "The Supreme Court and its Purported Preference for Search Warrants", 50 Tennessee L. Rev. 231, at pp. 232-33 and 235.

On the other hand, Professor Whitebread, writing in 1980, states that the Supreme Court still stands firmly behind the principle that a search conducted without a warrant issued upon probable cause is per se unreasonable subject only to a few specifically established and well-delineated exceptions: see Criminal Procedure by Charles H. Whitebread at p. 110.

It will be recalled that in *Texas v. Brown,* supra, Rehnquist J. listed a number of exceptions to the warrant requirement. It is unnecessary for present purposes to consider whether that list was intended to be exhaustive, or to examine the decisions defining the scope of those exceptions. Two of those exceptions are, however, of particular interest in the context of the present case. The first of those exceptions is the "automobile" exception. The Supreme Court of the United States has developed a broad exception to the warrant requirement in the case of the search of vehicles where it is not practicable to obtain a warrant because the vehicle can be quickly put out of reach of the jurisdiction of a police officer: see *Carroll v. U.S.* (1924), 267 U.S. 132, 69 L. Ed. 543, 45 S. Ct. 280, 39 A.L.R. 790. In the recent decision in *U.S. v. Ross* (1982), 102 S. Ct. 2157, the Supreme Court held that police officers who had legitimately stopped an automobile and who had probable cause to believe that it contained illicit drugs could conduct a warrantless search of the automobile as thorough as a magistrate could authorize by warrant and consequently were entitled to search containers, which the officers reasonably believed contained narcotics, found in the automobile. The rationale of the "automobile" exception is equally applicable to vessels and aircraft.

The second exception of interest in the present case is the "exigent circumstances" exception. The Supreme Court of the United States has authorized bodily intrusions to seize evidence without a warrant where the police have reasonable cause to believe that the evidence exists and the delay in obtaining a warrant would almost certainly result in the loss or destruction of the evidence, e.g., blood from a person whom there is reasonable grounds to believe was driving while intoxicated: *Schmerber v. California* (1966), 384 U.S. 757, 16 L. Ed. (2d) 908, 86 S. Ct. 1826; or scrapings from under the fingernails of a person suspected of strangling his wife: *Cupp v. Murphy* (1973), 412 U.S. 291, 36 L. Ed. (2d) 900, 93 S. Ct. 2000.

The Supreme Court of the United States does not appear to have been required to pass directly upon the question of whether a warrantless search of private premises to prevent the removal or destruction of prohibited drugs or evidence would fall within the "exigent circumstances" exception, although there are dicta indicating that the court might so find. However, a number of appellate courts have held that an entry and search of premises to prevent the removal or destruction of illicit drugs falls within the "exigent circumstances" exception. See *U.S. v. Edwards* (1979), 602 F. (2d) 458 (U.S. C.A., 1st Circ.); *Commonwealth v. Amaral* (1983), 450 N.E. (2d) 656 (Massachusetts C.A.).

WHETHER THE WARRANTLESS SEARCH IN THE PRESENT CASE MET THE STANDARD OF REASONABLENESS PRESCRIBED BY S. 8 OF THE CHARTER

Despite the two different lines of approach to the interpretation of the Fourth Amendment, it is, I think, apparent that the warrant clause in the Fourth Amendment has exerted an influence in creating a preference for a warrant in the United States.

Although the language of s. 8 of the Charter unmistakably shows the influence on the draftsman of the first clause of the Fourth Amendment, the second clause of the Fourth Amendment has no counterpart in the Charter. Consequently, the central issue in any case in which the validity of a search or seizure is challenged as offending s. 8 of the Charter is whether the particular search or seizure meets the constitutional requirement of reasonableness unfettered by any *constitutional* requirement of a warrant. In my view, however, for reasons which I will develop, whether a search was authorized by a warrant may be an important or even a critical factor in assessing the reasonableness of a search in a given case. However, the omission from s. 8 of the Charter of a warrant provision similar to that contained in the second clause of the Fourth Amendment signals caution in the extent of the use of the American jurisprudence under the Fourth Amendment. There is an additional reason for the exercise of caution in the use of American jurisprudence. The case law under the Fourth Amendment is replete with refined distinctions which, in my view, ought to be avoided in developing our jurisprudence under s. 8 of the Charter. Moreover, the decisions under the Fourth Amendment are not always clear or consistent, and it is evident that some American commentators consider that the state of the jurisprudence on the Fourth Amendment is far from satisfactory: see Amsterdam, Perspectives on The Fourth Amendment, at p. 349; Criminal Procedure by Charles Whitebread at p. 85. The Law Reform Commission of Canada has commented on the "bewildering" distinctions drawn by American courts between various fact situations and has stressed the importance of avoiding such "entanglements" in Canada: working paper 30, Police Powers: Search and Seizure in Criminal Law, at p. 126. On the other hand, the American experience can be valuable, particularly the articulation by the Supreme Court of the United States of the "common sense" exceptions to the warrant requirement of the Fourth Amendment, as set out in *Texas v. Brown,* supra.

Although there is no express constitutional warrant requirement under s. 8 of the Charter, it is, I think, manifest that the legal systems derived from the common law generally require a warrant to enter and search private premises, as distinct from vehicles and vessels which may rapidly move away.

. . .

CONCLUSION

Section 10(1)(*a*) of the Narcotic Control Act authorizes a warrantless search of a "place" other than a dwelling-house by a peace officer who has reasonable grounds for believing that the "place" contains a narcotic. The word "place" includes places of fixed location, such as offices or shops or gardens, as well as vehicles, vessels and aircraft. (The word "place" when found in a statute is usually associated with other words, which control its meaning. The word "place", however, may include an automobile: see *R. v. Thompson* (1920), 48 O.L.R. 163, 34 C.C.C. 101 (H.C.).) It does not, however, include public streets, or other public places: see *R. v. Stevens, supra,* at pp. 9-10.

I have, for the reasons which I have set forth, concluded that the search of an office without a warrant where the obtaining of a warrant is not impracticable is unreasonable and, to that extent, s. 10(1)(*a*) is of no force or effect. On the other hand, the search of an office without a warrant in circumstances where it is not practicable to obtain a warrant may be entirely reasonable. Further, a warrantless search of vehicles, vessels or aircraft, which may move quickly away, may be reasonable where there are reasonable grounds for believing that such contains a narcotic.

Section 10(1)(*a*) does not on its face necessarily clash with s. 8 of the Charter, although in some circumstances a warrantless search authorized by that subsection may in fact infringe the constitutional requirement of reasonableness secured by s. 8 of the Charter, depending upon the circumstances surrounding the particular search. The statute is inoperative to the extent that it authorizes an unreasonable search. Section 52(1) of the Constitution Act, 1982, reads:

> 52.(1) The Constitution of Canada is the supreme law of Canada, and any law that is inconsistent with the provisions of the Constitution is, *to the extent of the inconsistency*, of no force or effect. (The italics are mine.)

Appeal dismissed.

(i) Warrant Required

The following case of *Hunter v. Southam Inc.* is generally considered to be one of the most important cases decided under the Charter to date. It remains at the heart of the Canadian constitutional jurisprudence respecting search and seizure.

HUNTER v. SOUTHAM INC.

[1984] 2 S.C.R. 145, 41 C.R. (3d) 97 (*sub nom. Dir. of Investigation & Research, Combines Investigation Branch v. Southam*), 14 C.C.C. (3d) 97 (*sub nom. Hunter v. Southam*) (S.C.C.)

DICKSON J.:—The Constitution of Canada, which includes the Canadian Charter of Rights and Freedoms, Constitution Act, 1982, Pt. I, is the supreme law of Canada. Any law inconsistent with the provisions of the Constitution is, to the extent of the inconsistency, of no force or effect. Section 52(1) of the Constitution Act, 1982, so mandates. The constitutional question posed in this appeal [from 32 C.R. (3d) 141, [1983] 3 W.W.R. 385, 24 Alta. L.R. (2d) 307, [1983] A.W.L.D. 243, [1983] W.C.D. 275, 3 C.C.C. (3d) 497, 147 D.L.R. (3d) 420, 72 C.P.R. (2d) 145, 4 C.R.R. 368, 42 A.R. 93 (sub nom. *Southam Inc. v. Hunter*)] is whether s. 10(3), and by implication s. 10(1), of the Combines Investigation Act, R.S.C. 1970, c. C-23 ("the Act") are inconsistent with s. 8 of the Charter by reason of authorizing unreasonable searches and seizures and are therefore of no force and effect.

I. Background

Sections 10(1) and 10(3) of the Combines Investigation Act provide:

> 10.(1) Subject to subsection (3), in any inquiry under this Act the Director [of Investigation and Research of the Combines Investigation Branch] or any representative authorized by him may enter any premises on which the Director believes there may be evidence relevant to the matters being inquired into and may examine any thing on the premises and may copy or take away for further examination or copying any book, paper, record or other document that in the opinion of the Director or his authorized representative, as the case may be, may afford such evidence...

> (3) Before exercising the power conferred by subsection (1), the Director or his representative shall produce a certificate from a member of the [Restrictive Trade Practices] Commission, which may be granted on the *ex parte* application of the Director, authorizing the exercise of such power.

On 13th April 1982, in the course of an inquiry under the Act, the appellant Lawson A.W. Hunter, Director of Investigation and Research of the Combines Investigation Branch, authorized the other appellants, Messrs. Milton, Murphy, McAlpine and Marroco, all combines investigation officers, to exercise his authority under s. 10 of the Act to enter and examine documents and other things at the business premises of the Edmonton Journal, a division of the respondent corporation, Southam Inc.

On 16th April 1982, in fulfilment of the requirement in s. 10(3) of the Act, Dr. Frank Roseman, a member of the Restrictive Trade Practices commission ("the R.T.P.C."), certified his authorization of this exercise of the director's powers.

On 17th April 1982 the Constitution Act, 1982, incorporating the Canadian Charter of Rights and Freedoms, was proclaimed. Section 8 of the Charter provides:

8. Everyone has the right to be secure against unreasonable search and seizure.

On 19th April 1982 the officers presented their certified authorization at the premises of the Edmonton Journal. The English version of this certificate reads as follows:

In the matter of the Combines Investigation Act and section 33 and section 341(1)(c) thereof

and

in the matter of an Inquiry relating to the Production, Distribution and Supply of Newspapers and Related Products in Edmonton

To:

M.J. Milton

M.L. Murphy

J.A. McAlpine

A.P. Marrocco [sic]

being my representatives under section 10 of the Combines Investigation Act

You are hereby authorized to enter upon the premises hereinafter mentioned, on which I believe there may be evidence relevant to this inquiry, and examine anything thereon and copy or take away for copying any book, paper, record or other document that in your opinion may afford such evidence.

The premises referred to herein are those occupied by or on behalf of Southam Inc.

10006-101 Street Edmonton, Alberta

and elsewhere in Canada

This authorization is not valid after May 31, 1982.

Dated in Hull, in the Province of Quebec this 13th day of April, 1982. Lawson A.W. Hunter

Director D1 Investigation and Research Combines Investigation Act

I hereby certify that the above exercise of powers is authorized pursuant to Section 10 of the Combines Investigation Act.

Dated in Ottawa, in the Province of Ontario, this 16th day of April 1982.

Frank Roseman, Member,

Restrictive Trade Practices Commission

The authorization has a breathtaking sweep; it is tantamount to a licence to roam at large on the premises of Southam Inc. at the stated address "and elsewhere in Canada".

On 20th April the officers commenced the search. They said they wished to search every file of Southam Inc. at 10006 101 Street, Edmonton, except files in the newsroom but including all files of J. Patrick O'Callaghan, publisher of the Edmonton Journal. They declined to give the name of any person whose complaint had initiated the inquiry, or to say under which section of the Act the inquiry had been begun. They also declined to give more specific information as to the subject matter of the inquiry than that contained in the authorization to search.

At noon on 20th April Southam Inc. served upon the officers of the Combines Investigation Branch a notice of motion for an interim injunction. The application was heard by Cavanagh J., who held that, although Southam had raised a serious question as to whether the search was in violation of s. 8 of the Charter, the balance of convenience militated in favour of denying the interlocutory injunction pending trial of the matter. At the hearing, the appellants maintained, unsuccessfully, that the Director of Investigation and Research and his authorized representatives, acting pursuant to s. 10 of the Act, were a "federal board, commission or other tribunal" within s. 2(g) of the Federal Court Act, R.S.C. 1970, c. 10 (2nd Supp.), and that the Federal Court, not the provincial courts of Alberta, had jurisdiction.

. . .

In alleging that ss. 10(1) and 10(3) of the Combines Investigation Act are inconsistent with the right to be secure against unreasonable search and seizure, Southam Inc. relies heavily on the historic protections afforded by common law and by statute as defining the correct standard of reasonableness for purposes of s. 8 of the Charter. This was essentially the approach taken by Prowse J.A. when he said [p. 148 (C.R.)]:

> The roots of the right to be so secure are embedded in the common law and the safeguards according that right are found in the common law, in statutes subsequently enacted, and in decisions of the courts made as the society in which we live has evolved. The expression of the right in a constitutional document reminds us of those roots and the tradition associated with the right. One would be presumptuous to assume that we have attained the zenith of our development as a civilization and that the right accorded an individual is frozen for eternity. Section 8, however, requires us to be ever mindful of some of the criteria that have been applied in the past in securing the right.

Applying this approach, Prowse J.A. concluded—correctly, in Southam Inc.'s submission—that, absent exceptional circumstances, the provisions of s. 443 of the Criminal Code, R.S.C. 1970, c. C-34, which extends to investigations of Criminal Code offences the procedural safeguards the common law required for entries and searches for stolen goods, constitute the minimal prerequisites for reasonable searches and seizures in connection with the investigation of any criminal offence, including possible violations of the Combines Investigation

Act. Prowse J.A. summarized these procedural safeguards in the following propositions [p. 151 (C.R.)]:

(a)   that the power to authorize a search and seizure is given to an impartial and independent person (at common law a justice) who is bound to act judicially in discharging that function;

(b)   that evidence must satisfy the justice that the person seeking the authority has reasonable ground to suspect that an offence had been committed;

(c)   that evidence must satisfy the justice that the person seeking the authority has reasonable grounds to believe, at common law, that stolen property may be on the premises or, under s. 443(1)(b), that something that will afford evidence of an offence may be recovered; and

(d)   that there must be evidence on oath before him . . .

. . .

III.   "UNREASONABLE" SEARCH OR SEIZURE

At the outset it is important to note that the issue in this appeal concerns the constitutional validity of a statute authorizing a search and seizure. It does not concern the reasonableness or otherwise of the manner in which the appellants carried out their statutory authority. It is not the conduct of the appellants, but rather the legislation under which they acted, to which attention must be directed.

As is clear from the arguments of the parties as well as from the judgment of Prowse J.A., the crux of this case is the meaning to be given to the term "unreasonable" in the s. 8 guarantee of freedom from unreasonable search or seizure. The guarantee is vague and open. The American courts have had the advantage of a number of specific prerequisites articulated in the Fourth Amendment to the United States Constitution, as well as a history of colonial opposition to certain Crown investigatory practices, from which to draw out the nature of the interests protected by that amendment and the kinds of conduct it proscribes. There is none of this in s. 8. There is no specificity in the section beyond the bare guarantee of freedom from "unreasonable" search and seizure; nor is there any particular historical, political or philosophic context capable of providing an obvious gloss on the meaning of the guarantee.

It is clear that the meaning of "unreasonable" cannot be determined by recourse to a dictionary, nor, for that matter, by reference to the rules of statutory construction. The task of expounding a constitution is crucially different from that of construing a statute. A statute defines present rights and obligations. It is easily enacted and as easily repealed. A constitution, by contrast, is drafted with an eye to the future. Its function is to provide a continuing framework for the legitimate exercise of governmental power and, when joined by a bill or a charter of rights, for the unremitting protection of individual rights and liberties. Once enacted, its provisions cannot easily be repealed or amended. It must therefore be capable of growth and development over time to meet new social, political and historical realities often unimagined by its framers. The judiciary is the guardian of the constitution and must, in interpreting its provisions, bear these considerations in mind. Professor Paul Freund expressed this idea aptly when he admonished the American courts "not to read the provisions of the Constitution like a last will and testament lest it become one".

The need for a broad perspective in approaching constitutional documents is a familiar theme in Canadian constitutional jurisprudence. It is contained in Viscount Sankey L.C.'s classic formulation in *Edwards v. A.G. Can.,* [1930] A.C. 124 at 136-37, [1929] 3 W.W.R. 479, [1930] 1 D.L.R. 98 (P.C.), cited and applied in countless Canadian cases:

> The British North America Act planted in Canada a living tree capable of growth and expansion within its natural limits. The object of the Act was to grant a Constitution to Canada . . .

> Their Lordships do not conceive it to be the duty of this Board—it is certainly not their desire—to cut down the provisions of the Act by a narrow and technical construction, but rather to give it a large and liberal interpretation.

More recently, in *Min. of Home Affairs v. Fisher,* [1980] A.C. 319, [1979] 3 All E.R. 21 (P.C.), dealing with the Bermudian constitution, Lord Wilberforce reiterated at p. 329 that a constitution is a document "sui generis, calling for principles of interpretation of its own, suitable to its character", and that as such a constitution incorporating a bill of rights calls for [p. 328]:

> . . . a generous interpretation avoiding what has been called 'the austerity of tabulated legalism', suitable to give individuals the full measure of the fundamental rights and freedoms referred to.

Such a broad, purposive analysis, which interprets specific provisions of a constitutional document in the light of its larger objects, is also consonant with the classical principles of American constitutional construction enunciated by Marshall C.J. in *McCulloch v. Maryland,* 17 U.S. (4 Wheat.) 316, 4 L. Ed. 870 (1819). It is, as well, the approach I intend to take in the present case.

I begin with the obvious. The Canadian Charter of Rights and Freedoms is a purposive document. Its purpose is to guarantee and to protect, within the limits of reason, the enjoyment of the rights and freedoms it enshrines. It is intended to constrain governmental action inconsistent with those rights and freedoms; it is not in itself an authorization for governmental action. In the present case this means, as Prowse J.A. pointed out, that in guaranteeing the right to be secure from unreasonable searches and seizures s. 8 acts as a limitation on whatever powers of search and seizure the federal or provincial governments already and otherwise possess. It does not in itself confer any powers, even of "reasonable" search and seizure, on these governments. This leads, in my view, to the further conclusion that an assessment of the constitutionality of a search and seizure, or of a statute authorizing a search or seizure, must focus on its "reasonable" or "unreasonable" impact on the subject of the search or the seizure, and not simply on its rationality in furthering some valid government objective.

Since the proper approach to the interpretation of the Charter of Rights and Freedoms is a purposive one, before it is possible to assess the reasonableness or unreasonableness of the impact of a search or of a statute authorizing a search, it is first necessary to specify the purpose underlying s. 8: in other words, to delineate the nature of the interests it is meant to protect.

Historically, the common law protections with regard to governmental searches and seizures were based on the right to enjoy property and were linked to the law of trespass. It was on this basis that in the great case of *Entick v. Carrington* (1765), 19 State Tr. 1029, 2 Wils. K.B. 275, 95 E.R. 807, the court refused to countenance a search purportedly authorized by the executive, to discover evidence that might link the plaintiff to certain seditious libels. Lord Camden C.J. prefaced his discussion of the rights in question by saying, at p. 1066:

> The great end, for which men entered into society, was to preserve their property. That right is preserved sacred and incommunicable in all instances where it has not been taken away or abridged by some public law for the good of the whole.

The defendants argued that their oaths as Kings' messengers required them to conduct the search in question and ought to prevail over the plaintiff's property rights. Lord Camden C.J. rejected this contention, at p. 1067:

> Our law holds the property of every man so sacred, that no man can set his foot upon his neighbour's close without his leave: if he does he is a trespasser though he does no damage at all; if he will tread upon his neighbour's ground he must justify it by law.

Lord Camden C.J. could find no exception from this principle for the benefit of Kings' messengers. He held that neither the intrusions nor the purported authorizations were supportable on the basis of the existing law. That law would have countenanced such an entry only if the search were for stolen goods and if it were authorized by a justice on the basis of evidence upon oath that there was "strong cause" to believe that the goods were concealed in the place sought to be searched. In view of the lack of proper legal authorization for the governmental intrusion, the plaintiff was protected from the intended search and seizure by the ordinary law of trespass.

In my view the interests protected by s. 8 are of a wider ambit than those enunciated in *Entick v. Carrington,* supra. Section 8 is an entrenched constitutional provision. It is not therefore vulnerable to encroachment by legislative enactments in the same way as common law protections. There is, further, nothing in the language of the section to restrict it to the protection of property or to associate it with the law of trespass. It guarantees a broad and general right to be secure from unreasonable search and seizure.

The Fourth Amendment of the United States Constitution also guarantees a broad right. It provides:

> The right of the people to be secure in their persons, houses, papers, and effects, against unreasonable searches and seizures, shall not be violated and no Warrants shall issue, but upon probable cause, supported by Oath or affirmation, and particularly describing the place to be searched, and the persons or things to be seized.

Construing this provision in *Katz v. U.S.,* 389 U.S. 347, 19 L. Ed. 2d 576, 88 S. Ct. 507 (1967), Stewart J., delivering the majority opinion of the United

States Supreme Court, declared at p. 351 that "the Fourth Amendment protects people, not places". Stewart J. rejected any necessary connection between that amendment and the notion of trespass. With respect, I believe this approach is equally appropriate in construing the protections in s. 8 of the Charter of Rights and Freedoms.

In *Katz*, Stewart J. discussed the notion of a right to privacy, which he described at pp. 350-51 as "the right to be let alone by other people". Although Stewart J. was careful not to identify the Fourth Amendment exclusively with the protection of this right, nor to see the amendment as the only provision in the Bill of Rights relevant to its interpretation, it is clear that this notion played a prominent role in his construction of the nature and the limits of the American constitutional protection against unreasonable search and seizure. In the Alberta Court of Appeal, Prowse J.A. took a similar approach to s. 8, which he described [at p. 148 (C.R.)] as dealing "with one aspect of what has been referred to as the 'right of privacy', which is the right to be secure against encroachment upon the citizens' reasonable expectation of privacy in a free and democratic society".

Like the Supreme Court of the United States, I would be wary of foreclosing the possibility that the right to be secure against unreasonable search and seizure might protect interests beyond the right of privacy, but for purposes of the present appeal I am satisfied that its protections go at least that far. The guarantee of security from *unreasonable* search and seizure protects only a *reasonable* expectation. This limitation on the right guaranteed by s. 8, whether it is expressed negatively, as freedom from "unreasonable" search and seizure, or positively, as an entitlement to a "reasonable" expectation of privacy, indicates that an assessment must be made as to whether in a particular situation the public's interest in being left alone by government must give way to the government's interest in intruding on the individual's privacy in order to advance its goals, notably those of law enforcement.

The question that remains, and the one upon which the present appeal hinges, is how this assessment is to be made. When is it to be made, by whom and on what basis? Here again I think the proper approach is a purposive one.

(a)   *When is the balance of interests to be assessed?*

If the issue to be resolved in assessing the constitutionality of searches under s. 10 were whether *in fact* the governmental interest in carrying out a given search outweighed that of the individual in resisting the governmental intrusion upon his privacy, then it would be appropriate to determine the balance of the competing interests *after* the search had been conducted. Such a post facto analysis would, however, be seriously at odds with the purpose of s. 8. That purpose is, as I have said, to protect individuals from unjustified state intrusions upon their privacy. That purpose requires a means of *preventing* unjustified searches before they happen, not simply of determining, after the fact, whether they ought to have occurred in the first place. This, in my view, can be accomplished only by a system of *prior authorization,* not one of subsequent validation.

A requirement of prior authorization, usually in the form of a valid warrant, has been a consistent prerequisite for a valid search and seizure both at common law and under most statutes. Such a requirement puts the onus on the state to demonstrate the superiority of its interest to that of the individual. As such it accords with the apparent intention of the Charter to prefer, where feasible, the right of the individual to be free from state interference to the interests of the state in advancing its purposes through such interference.

I recognize that it may not be reasonable in every instance to insist on prior authorization in order to validate governmental intrusions upon individuals' expectations of privacy. Nevertheless, where it is feasible to obtain prior authorization, I would hold that such authorization is a precondition for a valid search and seizure.

Here also, the decision in *Katz,* supra, is relevant. In *U.S. v. Rabinowitz,* 339 U.S. 56, 94 L. Ed. 653, 70 S. Ct. 430 (1950), the Supreme Court of the United States had held that a search without warrant was not ipso facto unreasonable. 17 years later, however, in *Katz,* Stewart J. concluded that a warrantless search was prima facie "unreasonable" under the Fourth Amendment. The terms of the Fourth Amendment are not identical to those of s. 8 and American decisions can be transplanted to the Canadian context only with the greatest caution. Nevertheless, I would in the present instance respectfully adopt Stewart J.'s formulation as equally applicable to the concept of "unreasonableness" under s. 8, and would require the party seeking to justify a warrantless search to rebut this presumption of unreasonableness.

In the present case the appellants make no argument that it is infeasible or unnecessary to obtain prior authorization for the searches contemplated by the Combines Investigation Act, and in my view no such argument could be made. I would therefore conclude that, in the absence of a valid procedure for prior authorization, searches conducted under the Act would be unreasonable. In the event, s. 10(3) *does* purport to establish a requirement for prior authorization, specifying as it does that searches and seizures conducted under s. 10(1) must be authorized by a member of the R.T.P.C. The question then becomes whether s. 10(3) provides for an acceptable prior authorization procedure.

(b) *Who must grant the authorization?*

The purpose of a requirement of prior authorization is to provide an opportunity, before the event, for the conflicting interests of the state and the individual to be assessed, so that the individual's right to privacy will be breached only where the appropriate standard has been met, and the interests of the state are thus demonstrably superior. For such an authorization procedure to be meaningful it is necessary for the person authorizing the search to be able to assess the evidence as to whether that standard has been met in an entirely neutral and impartial manner. At common law the power to issue a search warrant was reserved for a justice. In the recent English case of *R. v. Inland Revenue Commrs.; Ex parte Rossminster,* [1980] 2 W.L.R. 1, 70 Cr. App. R. 157, [1980] 1 All E.R. 80 (sub nom. *Inland Revenue Commrs. v. Rossminster*) (H.L.), Viscount Dilhorne suggested at p. 87 that the power to authorize administrative searches and seizures be given to "a more senior judge". While it may be wise, in view of the sensitivity of the task, to assign the decision whether an authorization should be issued to a judicial officer, I agree with Prowse J.A. that this is not a necessary precondition for safeguarding the right enshrined in s. 8. The person performing this function need not be a judge, but he must at a minimum be capable of acting judicially.

In *M.N.R. v. Coopers & Lybrand*, [1979] 1 S.C.R. 495, [1978] C.T.C. 829, 78 D.T.C. 6258, 92 D.L.R. (3d) 1, 24 N.R. 163, this court had occasion to discuss the difference between an administrative and a judicial function in the authorization of a search and seizure. The Income Tax Act, 1970-71-72 (Can.), c. 63, confers upon the minister a number of powers, including, in s. 231(4), the power under certain conditions to authorize the entry and search of buildings. At p. 507 the court described the minister's powers as "fundamentally administrative", going on to explain [pp. 507-508]:

> The power he exercises under s. 231(4) is properly characterized as investigatory rather than adjudicatory. He will collect material and advice from many sources. In deciding whether to exercise the right [to authorize entry and search], he will be governed by many considerations, dominant among which is the public interest and his duty as an executive officer of the government to administer the Act to the best of his ability. The decision to seek authority to enter and search will be guided by public policy and expediency, having regard to all the circumstances.

The court contrasted these powers with the judicial powers which s. 231(4) conferred on a judge of the superior or county court to approve the minister's authorization.

Under the scheme envisaged by s. 10 of the Combines Investigation Act it is clear that the director exercises administrative powers analogous to those of the minister under s. 231(4) of the Income Tax Act. They too are investigatory rather than adjudicatory, with his decision to seek approval for an authorization to enter and search premises equally guided by considerations of expediency and public policy. But what of the member of the R.T.P.C. whom s. 10(3) empowers to approve the director's authorization? Is his function investigatory or adjudicatory? In the Alberta Court of Appeal Prowse J.A. carefully reviewed the respective powers of the director and the commission and concluded that the Act was not entirely successful in separating the role of the director as investigator and prosecutor from that of the commission as adjudicator. In his view [p. 154 (C.R.)] circumstances may arise under the Act where "the director is acting as investigator and prosecutor and the commission is acting as investigator and judge with respect to breaches of the Act". Southam Inc. summarizes and enlarges upon Prowse J.A.'s analysis, producing the following list of investigatory functions bestowed upon the commission or one of its members by the Act:

   i)   The power in s. 47 to instruct the Director to commence a s. 8 inquiry.

   ii) The power to cause evidence to be gathered pursuant to ss. 9, 10, 12 and 17.

   iii) The power to issue a s. 17 order.

   iv) the power under ss. 17, 22(2)(*b*) to seek further or better evidence after the Commission has commenced a hearing.

v)   the power under s. 22(2)(*b*) after commencing a hearing and receiving evidence to direct the Director to make further inquiry and, in effect, to go back to the investigatory stage;

vi)   the power under s. 22(2)(*c*) to compel the Director to turn over to the R.T.P.C. copies of all books, papers, records or other documents obtained by the Director in such further inquiry;

vii)   the power under s. 27.1 to order the Director to give evidence before any other federal board, commission or other tribunal;

viii)   the power under s. 45.1 to seek production of statistics for evidence in an inquiry;

ix)   the power to deliver to the Director all books, papers, records of other documents produced on a s. 17 hearing;

x)   the power under s. 13 to request the appointment and instruction of counsel to assist in the inquiry.

In my view, investing the commission or its members with significant investigatory functions has the result of vitiating the ability of a member of the commission to act in a judicial capacity when authorizing a search or seizure under s. 10(3). This is not, of course, a matter of impugning the honesty or good faith of the commission or its members. It is rather a conclusion that the administrative nature of the commission's investigatory duties (with its quite proper reference points in considerations of public policy and effective enforcement of the Act) ill accords with the neutrality and detachment necessary to assess whether the evidence reveals that the point has been reached where the interests of the individual must constitutionally give way to those of the state. A member of the R.T.P.C. passing on the appropriateness of a proposed search under the Combines Investigation Act is caught by the maxim "Nemo judex in sua causa". He simply cannot be the impartial arbiter necessary to grant an effective authorization.

On this basis alone I would conclude that the prior authorization mandated by s. 10(3) of the Combines Investigation Act is inadequate to satisfy the requirements of s. 8 of the Charter and consequently a search carried out under the authority of ss. 10(1) and 10(3) is an unreasonable one. Since, however, the Alberta Court of Appeal found other, perhaps even more serious, defects in these provisions, I pass on to consider whether, even if s. 10(3) did specify a truly neutral and detached arbiter to authorize searches, it would nevertheless remain inconsistent with s. 8 of the Charter.

(c)   *On what basis must the balance of interests be assessed?*

Section 10 is terse in the extreme on the subject of criteria for issuing an authorization for entry, search and seizure. Section 10(3) merely states that an R.T.P.C. member may grant an authorization ex parte. The only explicit criteria for granting such an authorization are those mentioned in s. 10(1), namely: (1) that an inquiry under the Act must be in progress; and (2) that the director must believe that the premises may contain relevant evidence.

In cases argued before passage of the Charter of Rights and Freedoms the courts took a narrow view of what s. 10 required or permitted the R.T.P.C. member to consider when asked to authorize search and seizure. In *Petrofina*

Can. Ltd. v. Chairman of Restrictive Trade Practices Comm. [(1979), 107 D.L.R. (3d) 319, 46 C.P.R. (2d) 1, [1980] 2 F.C. 386], the applicant challenged authorizations under ss. 9(2) and 10(3) of the Act on the grounds, inter alia, that the members who gave their authorizations did not show that they had before them sufficient information to enable them to determine the legality of the inquiry then in progress or the reasonableness of the director's belief that circumstances warranted the exercise of his powers. The Federal Court of Appeal rejected the relevance of such considerations to the members' decisions, at p. 391:

> In making the decisions that sections 9 and 10 require them to make, the Members must act judicially . . . However, that duty to act judicially applies only to the decisions that the Members are required to make under sections 9(2) and 10(3). Under those provisions, the Members are neither required nor authorized to determine the legality of the Director's decision to hold an inquiry: they are merely required to ascertain that there is, *de facto,* an inquiry in progress under the Act. The Members are not required or authorized, either to pass judgment on the reasonableness of the motives prompting the Director to exercise his powers under section 9 and 10. As the Members did not have to make decisions on those two points, they cannot, in my opinion, be blamed for not having required information on those points.

As Prowse J.A. pointed out, if the powers of a commission member are as the Federal Court of Appeal found them to be, then it follows that the decision of the director in the course of an inquiry to exercise his powers of entry, search and seizure is effectively unreviewable. The extent of the privacy of the individual would be left to the discretion of the director. A provision authorizing such an unreviewable power would clearly be inconsistent with s. 8 of the Charter.

Assuming, arguendo, that the Federal Court of Appeal was wrong, and the member *is* authorized, or even required, to satisfy himself as to (1) the legality of the inquiry, and (2) the reasonableness of the director's belief that there may be evidence relevant to the matters being inquired into, would that remove the inconsistency with s. 8?

To read ss. 10(1) and 10(3) as simply *allowing* the authorizing party to satisfy himself on these questions, without requiring him to do so, would in my view be clearly inadequate. Such an amorphous standard cannot provide a meaningful criterion for securing the right guaranteed by s. 8. The location of the constitutional balance between a justifiable expectation of privacy and the legitimate needs of the state cannot depend on the subjective appreciation of individual adjudicators. Some objective standard must be established.

Requiring the authorizing party to satisfy himself as to the legality of the inquiry and the reasonableness of the director's belief in the possible existence of relevant evidence would have the advantage of substituting an objective standard for an amorphous one, but would, in my view, still be inadequate. The problem is with the stipulation of a reasonable belief that evidence *may* be uncovered in the search. Here again it is useful, in my view, to adopt a purposive approach. The purpose of an objective criterion for granting prior authorization to conduct a search or seizure is to provide a consistent standard for identifying the point at which the interests of the state in such intrusions come to prevail over the interests of the individual in resisting them. To associate it with an applicant's reasonable belief that relevant evidence *may* be uncovered by the search would be to define the proper standard as the *possibility* of finding evidence. This is a very low standard, which would validate intrusion on the basis of suspicion, and authorize fishing expeditions of considerable latitude. It would tip the balance strongly in favour of the state, and limit the right of the individual to resist to only the most egregious intrusions. I do not believe that this is a proper standard for securing the right to be free from unreasonable search and seizure.

Anglo-Canadian legal and political traditions point to a higher standard. The common law required evidence on oath which gave "strong reason to believe" that stolen goods were concealed in the place to be searched before a warrant would issue. Section 443 of the Criminal Code authorizes a warrant only where there has been information upon oath that there is "reasonable ground to believe" that there is evidence of an offence in the place to be searched. The American Bill of Rights provides that "no warrants shall issue, but upon probable cause, supported by oath or affirmation". The phrasing is slightly different but the standard in each of these formulations is identical. The state's interest in detecting and preventing crime begins to prevail over the individual's interest in being left alone at the point where credibly-based probability replaces suspicion. History has confirmed the appropriateness of this requirement as the threshold for subordinating the expectation of privacy to the needs of law enforcement. Where the state's interest is not simply law enforcement, as, for instance, where state security is involved, or where the individual's interest is not simply his expectation of privacy, as, for instance, when the search threatens his bodily integrity, the relevant standard might well be a different one. That is not the situation in the present case. In cases like the present, reasonable and probable grounds, established upon oath, to believe that an offence has been committed and that there is evidence to be found at the place of the search constitutes the minimum standard consistent with s. 8 of the Charter for authorizing search and seizure. Insofar as ss. 10(1) and 10(3) of the Combines Investigation Act do not embody such a requirement, I would hold them to be further inconsistent with s. 8.

IV.   READING IN AND READING DOWN

The appellants submit that, even if ss. 10(1) and 10(3) do not specify a standard consistent with s. 8 for authorizing entry, search and seizure, they should not be struck down as inconsistent with the Charter, but rather the appropriate standard should be read into these provisions. An analogy is drawn to the case of *MacKay v. R.*, [1965] S.C.R. 798, 53 D.L.R. (2d) 532, in which this court held that a local ordinance regulating the use of property by prohibiting the erection of unauthorized signs, though apparently without limits, could not have been intended unconstitutionally to encroach on federal competence over elections, and should therefore be "read down" so as not to apply to election signs. In the present case, the overt inconsistency with s. 8 manifested by the lack of a neutral and detached arbiter renders the appellants' submissions on reading in appropriate standards for issuing a warrant purely academic. Even if this were not the case, however, I would be disinclined to give effect to these submissions. While the courts are guardians of the Constitution and of individuals' rights under it, it is the legislature's responsibility to enact legislation that embodies appropriate safeguards to comply with the Constitution's requirements. It should not fall to the courts to fill in the details that will render legislative lacunae constitutional. Without appropriate safeguards, legislation authorizing search and seizure is inconsistent with s. 8 of the Charter. As I have said, any law inconsistent with the provisions of the Constitution is, to the extent of the inconsistency, of no force or effect. I would hold ss. 10(1) and 10(3) of the Combines Investigation Act to be inconsistent with the Charter and of no force and effect, as much for their failure to specify an appropriate standard for the issuance of warrants as for their designation of an improper arbiter to issue them.

V.   SECTION 1

Section 1 of the Charter provides:

1. The *Canadian Charter of Rights and Freedoms* guarantees the rights and freedoms set out in it subject only to such reasonable limits prescribed by law as can be demonstrably justified in a free and democratic society.

The phrase "demonstrably justified" puts the onus of justifying a limitation on a right or freedom set out in the Charter on the party seeking to limit. In the present case the appellants have made no submissions capable of supporting a claim that, even if searches under ss. 10(1) and 10(3) are "unreasonable" within the meaning of s. 8, they are nevertheless a reasonable limit, demonstrably justified in a free and democratic society, on the right set out in s. 8. It is therefore not necessary in this case to consider the relationship between s. 8 and s. 1. I leave to another day the difficult question of the relationship between those two sections and, more particularly, what further balancing of interests, if any, may be contemplated by s. 1, beyond that envisaged by s. 8.

VI.   CONCLUSION

By order of Laskin C.J.C. the constitutional question was stated as follows:

Did the Alberta Court err in holding that subsection 10(3), and by implication subsection 10(1), of the *Combines Investigation Act*, R.S.C. 1970, c. C-23 are inconsistent with the provisions of Section 8 of the *Canadian Charter of Rights and Freedoms* and that they are therefore of no force or effect?

I would answer that question in the negative. I would dismiss the appeal with costs to the respondent.

Appeal dismissed.

The *Rao* decision that there can be no constitutional search of a business premise without a warrant, unless it is impractical to obtain one, was an important decision in favour of privacy interests of business premises. Since *Hunter* recognizes an exception to the warrant requirement, where it was not "feasible" to get one, and since feasibility can be equated with practicality, the basic ruling in *Rao* has survived. Indeed, the general approach in *Rao* was re-asserted after *Hunter* by Mr. Justice Martin in *Noble*. Some writers, however, see an important difference of emphasis between *Hunter* and *Rao*. Under *Hunter*, for any type of search of premises, the person or a vehicle, the question is whether a warrant was feasible. Under *Rao*, the focus is on reasonableness and a warrant is only a critical factor in respect of searches of premises. These writers suggest that, under the *Rao* approach, in the case of searches of persons or vehicles, courts will be far less likely to assert a warrant requirement.

A section 8 challenge can be made against a search power, as in *Rao*, *Hunter* and *Noble*, or as has proved much more common, to the manner of exercise in the particular case. Many cases involve challenges to warrantless searches. Another leading decision, *Collins*, was of the latter type.

(ii) Warrantless Searches

R. v. COLLINS
[1987] 1 S.C.R. 265, 56 C.R. (3d) 193, 33 C.C.C. (3d) 1 (S.C.C.)

Police officers were conducting a surveillance of a village pub in connection with a heroin investigation. They observed the accused and her husband at one of the tables. The accused's husband left the premises. The police followed him, searched his car and found heroin. They returned to the pub and one of the officers grabbed the accused by the throat to prevent her from swallowing any evidence that might be in her mouth. During the struggle, the officer observed something in her hand, told her to drop it, and retrieved a green balloon, which contained heroin. Mr. Justice Lamer, for the majority of the court (MacIntyre J. dissenting on a different point) held that a throat search for drugs would be contrary to s. 8 if there were no reasonable grounds for the search or if the search was conducted in an unreasonable manner because there were no reasonable grounds to believe the accused had drugs in her mouth.

LAMER J.:—The appellant, in my view, bears the burden of persuading the court that her Charter rights or freedoms have been infringed or denied. That appears from the wording of s. 24(1) and (2), and most courts which have considered the issue have come to that conclusion: see *R. v. Lundrigan* (1985), 19 C.C.C. (3d) 499, 15 C.R.R. 256, 33 Man. R. (2d) 286 (C.A.), and the cases cited therein, and Gibson, The Law of the Charter: General Principles (1986), p. 278. The appellant also bears the initial burden of presenting evidence. The standard of persuasion required is only the civil standard of the balance of probabilities and, because of this, the allocation of the burden of persuasion means only that, in a case where the evidence does not establish whether or not the appellant's rights were infringed, the court must conclude that they were not.

The courts have also developed certain presumptions. In particular, this court held in *Hunter v. Southam Inc.*, [1984] 2 S.C.R. 145 at 161, [1984] 6 W.W.R. 577 (*sub nom. Dir. of Research & Investigation, Combines Investigation Branch v. Southam Inc.*), 33 Alta. L.R. (2d) 193, 41 C.R. (3d) 97, 27 B.L.R. 297, 14 C.C.C. (3d) 97, 11 D.L.R. (4th) 641, 2 C.P.R. (3d) 1, 84 D.T.C. 6467, 9 C.R.R. 355, 55 A.R. 291, 55 N.R. 241:

> In *United States v. Rabinowitz*, 339 U.S. 56 (1950), the Supreme Court of the United States had held that a search without warrant was not *ipso facto* unreasonable. Seventeen years later, however, in *Katz*, Stewart J. concluded that a warrantless search was *prima facie* "unreasonable" under the Fourth Amendment. The terms of the Fourth Amendment are not identical to those of s. 8 and American decisions can be transplated to the Canadian context only with the greatest caution. Nevertheless, I would in the present instance respectfully adopt Stewart J.'s formulation as equally applicable to the concept of "unreasonableness" under s. 8, and would require the party seeking to justify a warrantless search to rebut this presumption of unreasonableness.

This shifts the burden of persuasion from the appellant to the Crown. As a result, once the appellant has demonstrated that the search was a warrantless one, the Crown has the burden of showing that the search was, on a balance of probabilities, reasonable.

A search will be reasonable if it is authorized by law, if the law itself is reasonable and if the manner in which the search was carried out is reasonable. In this case, the Crown argued that the search was carried out under s. 10(1) of the Narcotic Control Act, above. As the appellant has not challenged the constitutionality of s. 10(1) of the Act, the issues that remain to be decided here are whether the search was unreasonable because the officer did not come within s. 10 of the Act or whether, while being within s. 10, he carried out the search in a manner that made the search unreasonable.

For the search to be lawful under s. 10, the Crown must establish that the officer believed on reasonable grounds that there was a narcotic in the place where the person searched was found. The nature of the belief will also determine whether the manner in which the search was carried out was reasonable. For example, if a police officer is told by a reliable source that there are persons in possession of drugs in a certain place, the officer may, depending on the circumstances and the nature and precision of the information given by that source, search persons found in that place under s. 10, but surely, without very specific information, a seizure by the throat, as in this case, would be unreasonable. Of course, if he is lawfully searching a person whom he believes on reasonable gounds to be a "drug handler", then the "throat hold" would not be unreasonable.

Because of the presumption of unreasonableness, the Crown in this case had to present evidence of the officer's belief and the reasonable grounds for that belief. It may be surmised that there were reasonable grounds based on information received from the local police. However, the Crown failed to establish such reasonable grounds in the examination in chief of Constable Woods and, as set out earlier, when it attempted to do so on its re-examination, the appellant's counsel objected. As a result, the Crown never did establish the constable's reasonable grounds. Without such evidence, it is clear that the trial judge was correct in concluding that the search was unreasonable because [it was] unlawful and carried out with unnecessary violence.

However, the problem is that the objection raised by the appellant's counsel was groundless: this court had held that reasonable grounds can be based on information received from third parties without infringing the hearsay rule (*Eccles v. Bourque*, supra), and the question put to the constable in this case was not outside the ambit of the ground covered in cross-examination. A further problem is that the record does not disclose why the question was not answered: it is not clear whether the trial judge maintained the objection or whether the Crown had reacted to the objection by withdrawing the question. It is worthy of mention that, because a conviction was entered, the Crown could not in any event appeal against the decision.

This court has two options. We could resolve the doubt against the Crown, which had the burden of persuasion, and simply proceed on the basis that there was no such evidence. Alternatively, we could order a new trial. I would order a new trial on the basis that the trial judge either made an incorrect ruling or failed to make a ruling and, in any event, the appellant should not, in the particular circumstances of this case, be allowed to benefit from her counsel's unfounded objection.

The Lamer formula that a search will be reasonable if authorized by law, if the law is reasonable and if the manner in which the search was conducted is reasonable, must be applied with caution. The shorthand reference to "reasonable" may be confusing. It must be remembered that *Collins* holds that warrantless searches are *prima facie* unreasonable. This confirms that a search without a warrant may be unconstitutional because it offends the basic *Hunter* requirements for a warrant. According to *Collins*, even if there is no constitutional requirement of a warrant, there are further minimum constitutional standards. Since *Collins*, courts have grappled with trying to make these standards more concrete.

In *R. v. Grant*, [1993] 3 S.C.R. 679, the Supreme Court decided there is no blanket exception to the *Hunter* warrant requirement for motor vehicle searches.

R. v. GOLDEN
[2001] 3 S.C.R. 679, 47 C.R. (5th) 1, 159 C.C.C. (3d) 449 (S.C.C.)

In an effort to detect illegal drug activity in an area where trafficking was known to occur, police officers set up an observation post in an unoccupied building across from a sandwich shop. Using a telescope an officer observed the accused giving a white substance to persons entering the shop. Given the place and manner of the transactions, the officer believed the accused was trafficking cocaine. He instructed four "take-down" officers to make arrests. The accused and two others were arrested. During the arrests, the police found what they believed to be crack cocaine under the table where one of the suspects was arrested. The accused was observed to be crushing what appeared to be crack cocaine between his fingers.

Following the arrests, a police officer conducted a "pat down" search of the accused. He did not find any weapons or narcotics. The officer then decided to conduct a visual inspection of the accused's underwear and buttocks on the landing at the top of the stairwell leading to basement public washrooms. The officer undid the accused's pants and pulled them back and also his long underwear. The officer saw a clear plastic wrap protruding from between the accused's buttocks, as well as a white substance within the wrap. The officer testified that when he tried to retrieve the plastic wrap, the accused "hip-checked" and scratched him so that he nearly fell down the stairs. He then pushed the accused into the stairwell, face-first.

The accused was then escorted to a seating booth at the back of the shop. Patrons were asked to leave, but the other two arrested accused, five officers and a shop employee, remained inside. The officers forced the accused to bend over a table. His pants were lowered to his knees and his underwear pulled down. The officers tried to seize the package from his buttocks, but were unsuccessful as the accused continued to clench his muscles very tightly. Following these attempts, the accused accidentally defecated. The package did not dislodge. An officer then retrieved a pair of rubber dishwashing gloves used to clean the washrooms and toilets and again tried to remove the package. The accused was face-down on the floor, with another officer holding down his feet. The officers told him to relax. Once he did, the officers were able to remove a package which was found to contain 10.1 grams of crack cocaine with a street value of between $500 and $2000. The accused was placed under arrest for possession of a narcotic for the purpose of trafficking, and for police assault. He was taken to a police station, located about a two-minute drive away. There he was strip searched again, fingerprinted and detained pending a bail hearing.

On a voir dire the defence applied to have the evidence obtained from the search excluded under ss. 8 and 24 of the Canadian Charter of Rights and Freedoms. The application was denied, and the evidence was admitted. G was found guilty of possession of a narcotic for the purpose of trafficking, but acquitted on the police assault charge. The Court of Appeal dismissed his appeal from his conviction and sentence in a brief endorsement judgment. The accused had served his sentence of 14 months by the time his further appeal was heard in the Supreme Court.

A 5-4 majority of the Supreme Court held that the appeal should be allowed, the conviction overturned and an acquittal entered.

IACOBUCCI and ARBOUR JJ. (Major, Binnie and LeBel JJ., concurring):—

. . . [An] appropriate balance must be achieved between the interest of citizens to be free from unjustified, excessive and humiliating strip searches upon arrest, and the interests of the police and of society in ensuring that persons who are arrested are not armed with weapons that they may use against the police, themselves or others, and in finding and preserving relevant evidence.

The appellant submits that the term "strip search" is properly defined as follows: the removal or rearrangement of some or all of the clothing of a person so as to permit a visual inspection of a person's private areas, namely genitals, buttocks, breasts (in the case of a female), or undergarments. This definition in essence reflects the definition of a strip search that has been adopted in various statutory materials and policy manuals in Canada and other jurisdictions (see for example Toronto Police Service. Policy & Procedure Manual: Search of Persons. Arrest & Release at p. 3; Crimes Act 1914 (Austl.), Part 1AA, c. 3C, s. 1 "strip search"; Cal. Penal Code s. 4030 (West 1984); Col. Rev. Stat. Ann. s. 16-3-405 (West 1982); Wash. Rev. Code Ann. s. 10.79.070(1) (West 1983). In our view, this definition accurately captures the meaning of the term "strip search" and we adopt it for the purpose of these reasons. This definition distinguishes strip searches from less intrusive "frisk" or "pat down" searches, which do not involve the removal of clothing, and from more intrusive body cavity searches, which involve a physical inspection of the detainee's genital or anal regions. While the mouth is a body cavity, it is not encompassed by the term "body cavity search". Searches of the mouth do not involve the same privacy concerns, although they may raise other health concerns for both the detainee and for those conducting the search. Applying this definition of strip search to the facts, the appellant was subjected to three strip searches in the present case...

While the respondent and the interveners for the Crown sought to downplay the intrusiveness of strip searches, in our view it is unquestionable that they represent a significant invasion of privacy and are often a humiliating, degrading and traumatic experience for individuals subject to them. Clearly, the negative effects of a strip search can be minimized by the way in which they are carried out, but even the most sensitively conducted strip search is highly intrusive. Furthermore, we believe it is important to note the submissions of the ACLC and the ALST that African Canadians and Aboriginal people are overrepresented in the criminal justice system and are therefore likely to represent a disproportionate number of those who are arrested by police and subjected to personal searches, including strip searches (Report of the Aboriginal Justice Inquiry of Manitoba (1991), Vol. 1, at p. 107; The Cawsey Report: Justice on Trial: Report of the Task Force on the Criminal Justice System and its Impact on the Indian and Metis People of Alberta (1991), Vol. II, at 2.48 to 2.50; Royal Commission on Aboriginal Peoples, Bridging the Cultural Divide (1996) at 33-39; Commission on Systemic Racism in the Ontario Criminal Justice System, Report of the Commission on Systemic Racism in the Ontario Criminal Justice System (1995)). As a result, it is necessary to develop an appropriate framework governing strip searches in order to prevent unnecessary and unjustified strip searches before they occur.

The law is clear in Canada that warrantless searches are prima facie unreasonable under s. 8 of the Charter (*Hunter, supra*). Where a search is carried out without prior authorization in the form of a warrant, the burden is on the party seeking to justify the warrantless search to prove that it was not unreasonable (*Hunter*, at pp. 160-61). Searches of the person incident to arrest are an established exception to the general rule that warrantless searches are prima facie unreasonable. In considering the constitutionality of strip searches carried out as an incident to arrest, it is still important to bear in mind that warrantless searches are the exception and not the norm in Canadian law. While characterized as an exception to the normal rule that a search warrant is required for a lawful search, however, warrantless personal searches incident to arrest are an exception whose importance should not be underestimated. The practical reality is that warrantless searches of persons incident to arrest constitute the majority of searches conducted by police (see S. A. Cohen, "Search Incident to Arrest: How Broad an Exception to the Warrant Requirement?" (1988), 63 C.R. (3d) 182 at p. 184; LaFave, *supra*, p. 68-9; Dwight Newman, "Stripping Matters to Their Core: Intrusive Searches of the Person in Canadian Law" (1999) 4 Can. Crim. L.R. 85, at p. 94; Don Stuart, *Charter Justice in Canadian Criminal Law* (3rd ed. 2001), at pp. 206-7; and Law Reform Commission of Canada, Report on Recodifying Criminal Procedure (1991), Vol. 1 at p. 46).

Given that the purpose of s. 8 of the Charter is to protect individuals from unjustified state intrusions upon their privacy, it is necessary to have a means of preventing unjustified searches before they occur, rather than simply determining after the fact whether the search should have occurred (Hunter, *supra*, at p. 160). The importance of preventing unjustified searches before they occur is particularly acute in the context of strip searches, which involve a significant and very direct interference with personal privacy. Furthermore, strip searches can be humiliating, embarrassing and degrading for those who are subject to them, and any post facto remedies for unjustified strip searches cannot erase the arrestee's experience of being strip searched. Thus, the need to prevent unjustified searches before they occur is more acute in the case of strip searches than it is in the context of less intrusive personal searches, such as pat or frisk searches. As was pointed out in *Flintoff*, *supra*, at p. 257, "[s]trip-searching is one of the most intrusive manners of searching, and also one of the most extreme exercises of police power". Strip searches are thus inherently humiliating and degrading for detainees regardless of the manner in which they are carried out and for this reason they cannot be carried out simply as a matter of routine policy.

The adjectives used by individuals to describe their experience of being strip searched give some sense of how a strip search, even one that is carried out in a reasonable manner, can affect detainees: "humiliating" "degrading", "demeaning", "upsetting", and "devastating" (see *King*, *supra*, *R. v. Christopher*, [1994] O.J. No. 3120 (QL) (Gen. Div.); J.S. Lyons, Toronto Police Services Board Review. "The Search of Persons Policy - The Search of Persons - A Position Paper" (April 12, 1999)). Some commentators have gone as far as to describe strip searches as "visual rape" (Paul Shuldiner, "Visual Rape: A Look at the Dubious Legality of Strip Searches" (1979), 13 J. Marshall L. Rev. 273). Women and minorities in particular may have a real fear of strip searches and may experience such a search as equivalent to a sexual assault (Lyons, *supra*, at p. 4). The psychological effects of strip searches may also be particularly traumatic for individuals who have previously been subject to abuse (Commission of Inquiry into Certain Events at the Prison for Women in Kingston (1996), at pp. 86-89). Routine strip searches may also be distasteful and difficult for the police officers conducting them (Lyons, *supra*, at pp. 5-6). In order for a strip search to be justified as an incident to arrest, it is of course necessary that the arrest itself be lawful. In the present case, there is no question that the arrest was lawful. While the appellant disputes the lawfulness of arrest, the trial judge and the Court of Appeal concluded that there were reasonable and probable grounds for making the arrest, and we see no reason to dispute this conclusion. Thus, the first requirement of a valid search incident to arrest was met in this case.

The second requirement before a strip search incident to arrest may be performed is that the search must be incident to the arrest. What this means is that the search must be related to the reasons for the arrest itself. As expressed by Lamer C.J. in *Caslake*, *supra*, at para. 17, a search "is only justifiable if the purpose of the search is related to the purpose of the arrest". In the present case, the strip search was related to the purpose of the arrest. The arrest was for drug trafficking and the purpose of the search was to discover illegal drugs secreted on the appellant's person. Had the appellant been arrested for a different reason, such as for a traffic violation, the common law would not have conferred on the police the authority to conduct a strip search for drugs, even if the police had knowledge of previous involvement in drug related offences, since the reason for the search would have been unrelated to the purpose of the arrest. In the circumstances of the present case, we conclude that the search was conducted incident to the arrest.

The reasonableness of a search for evidence is governed by the need to preserve the evidence and to prevent its disposal by the arrestee. Where arresting officers suspect that evidence may have been secreted on areas of the body that can only be exposed by a strip search, the risk of disposal must be reasonably assessed in the circumstances. For instance, in the present case, it was suggested that the appellant might have dropped the drugs on the sidewalk or in the police cruiser on the way to the station and that it was therefore necessary to search him in the field. As we discuss below, however, the risk of his disposing of the evidence on the way to the police station was low and, had the evidence been dropped in the police cruiser on the way to the station, circumstantial evidence could easily link it back to the accused.

In addition to searching for evidence related to the reason for the arrest, the common law also authorizes police to search for weapons as an incident to arrest for the purpose of ensuring the safety of the police, the detainee and other persons. However, a "frisk" or "pat down" search at the point of arrest will generally suffice for the purposes of determining if the accused has secreted weapons on his person. Only if the frisk search reveals a possible weapon secreted on the detainee's person or if the particular circumstances of the case raise the risk that a weapon is concealed on the detainee's person will a strip search be justified. Whether searching for evidence or for weapons, the mere possibility that an individual may be concealing evidence or weapons upon his person is not sufficient to justify a strip search.

The requirement that the strip search be for evidence related to the grounds for the arrest or for weapons reflects the twin rationales for the common law power of search incident to arrest. Strip searches cannot be carried out as a matter of routine police department policy applicable to all arrestees, whether they are arrested for impaired driving, public drunkenness, shoplifting or trafficking in narcotics. The fact that a strip search is conducted as a matter of routine policy and is carried out in a reasonable manner does not render the search reasonable within the meaning of s. 8 of the Charter. A strip search will always be unreasonable if it is carried out abusively or for the purpose of humiliating or punishing the arrestee. Yet a "routine" strip search carried out in good faith and without violence will also violate s. 8 where there is no compelling reason for performing a strip search in the circumstances of the arrest.

It may be useful to distinguish between strip searches immediately incidental to arrest, and searches related to safety issues in a custodial setting. We acknowledge the reality that where individuals are going to be entering the prison population, there is a greater need to ensure that they are not concealing weapons or illegal drugs on their persons prior to their entry into the prison environment. However, this is not the situation in the present case.

. . .

The fact that the police have reasonable and probable grounds to carry out an arrest does not confer upon them the automatic authority to carry out a strip search, even where the strip search meets the definition of being "incident to lawful arrest" as discussed above. Rather, additional grounds pertaining to the purpose of the strip search are required. In *Cloutier, supra*, this Court concluded that a common law search incident to arrest does not require additional grounds beyond the reasonable and probable grounds necessary to justify the lawfulness of the arrest itself: *Cloutier, supra*, at pp. 185-86. However, this conclusion was reached in the context of a "frisk" search, which involved a minimal invasion of the detainee's privacy and personal integrity. In contrast, a strip search is a much more intrusive search and, accordingly, a higher degree of justification is required in order to support the higher degree of interference with individual freedom and dignity. In order to meet the constitutional standard of reasonableness that will justify a strip search, the police must establish that they have reasonable and probable grounds for concluding that a strip search is necessary in the particular circumstances of the arrest.

In light of the serious infringement of privacy and personal dignity that is an inevitable consequence of a strip search, such searches are only constitutionally valid at common law where they are conducted as an incident to a lawful arrest for the purpose of discovering weapons in the detainee's possession or evidence related to the reason for the arrest. In addition, the police must establish reasonable and probable grounds justifying the strip search in addition to reasonable and probable grounds justifying the arrest. Where these preconditions to conducting a strip search incident to arrest are met, it is also necessary that the strip search be conducted in a manner that does not infringe s. 8 of the Charter.

Parliament could require that strip searches be authorized by warrants or telewarrants, which would heighten compliance with the Charter. At a minimum, if there is no prior judicial authorization for the strip search, several factors should be considered by the authorities in deciding whether, and if so how, to conduct such a procedure. In this connection, we find the guidelines contained in the English legislation, P.A.C.E. concerning the conduct of strip searches to be in accordance with the constitutional requirements of s. 8 of the Charter. The following questions, which draw upon the common law principles as well as the statutory requirements set out in the English legislation, provide a framework for the police in deciding how best to conduct a strip search incident to arrest in compliance with the Charter:

1. Can the strip search be conducted at the police station and, if not, why not?

2. Will the strip search be conducted in a manner that ensures the health and safety of all involved?

3. Will the strip search be authorized by a police officer acting in a supervisory capacity?

4. Has it been ensured that the police officer(s) carrying out the strip search are of the same gender as the individual being searched?

5. Will the number of police officers involved in the search be no more than is reasonably necessary in the circumstances?

6. What is the minimum of force necessary to conduct the strip search?

7. Will the strip search be carried out in a private area such that no one other than the individuals engaged in the search can observe the search?

8. Will the strip search be conducted as quickly as possible and in a way that ensures that the person is not completely undressed at any one time?

9. Will the strip search involve only a visual inspection of the arrestee's genital and anal areas without any physical contact?

10. If the visual inspection reveals the presence of a weapon or evidence in a body cavity (not including the mouth), will the detainee be given the option of removing the object himself or of having the object removed by a trained medical professional?

11. Will a proper record be kept of the reasons for and the manner in which the strip search was conducted?

Strip searches should generally only be conducted at the police station except where there are exigent circumstances requiring that the detainee be searched prior to being transported to the police station. Such exigent circumstances will only be established where the police have reasonable and probable grounds to believe that it is necessary to conduct the search in the field rather than at the police station. Strip searches conducted in the field could only be justified where there is a demonstrated necessity and urgency to search for weapons or objects that could be used to threaten the safety of the accused, the arresting officers or other individuals. The police would also have to show why it would have beenunsafe to wait and conduct the strip search at the police station rather than in the field. Strip searches conducted in the field represent a much greater invasion of privacy and pose a greater threat to the detainee's bodily integrity and, for this reason, field strip searches can only be justified in exigent circumstances.

Having said all this, we believe that legislative intervention could be an important addition to the guidance set out in these reasons concerning the conduct of strip searches incident to arrest. Clear legislative prescription as to when and how strip searches should be conducted would be of assistance to the police and to the courts.

. . .

[The majority then held that in this case the arrest was lawful on reasonable and probable grounds and the strip search was related to the purpose of the arrest, but the Crown had failed to prove that the strip search was necessary and urgent. The strip search in the restaurant was also carried out in an unreasonable manner.]

. . .

There is no requirement that anyone cooperate with the violation of his or her Charter rights. In this case, the accused's refusal to relinquish the evidence did not justify or mitigate the fact that he was strip searched in a public place, and in a manner that showed considerable disregard for his dignity and his physical integrity, despite the absence of reasonable and probable grounds or exigent circumstances.

[The majority concluded that since the accused had already served his 14-month sentence in full, and because the courts below did not engage in a s. 24(2) analysis, it was neither necessary nor useful to determine whether the evidence deriving from the illegal strip search should have been excluded at trial.]

BASTARACHE J. (dissenting), (McLachlan C.J. and Gonthier J. concurring)—

. . .

The unworkability of [the majority] approach that would create distinct categories of searches rests in the fact that all of the types of searches listed above may take many forms ranging from a low degree of intrusiveness to a high degree of intrusiveness, depending on the circumstances of the case. For example, on the facts of this case, the strip search of the accused which occurred in the stairwell was possibly not more intrusive than "pat down" or frisk searches. By contrast, the search in the restaurant impacted more severely on the privacy and dignity of the accused. The standard of justification to which police will be held depends on the circumstances of the specific search in question, not upon the category into which it is placed.

An approach which would categorize searches according to the degree of intrusiveness also risks confusion. The taking of a hair or other easily obtainable bodily sample may seem no more intrusive than a full strip search. The taking of a hair sample in the absence of a warrant may nonetheless be found to violate s. 8 if police are not able to justify the search on the basis that it was for the purpose of discovering and preserving evidence or seizing weapons incident to arrest; see *R. v. Stillman*, [1997] 1 S.C.R. 607. By contrast, a strip search conducted in the absence of prior authorization may be lawful if it meets the common law requirements of a search incident to arrest even if the search was very intrusive. In all cases, providing the arrest is lawful and the object of the search is related to the crime, the sole issue is the reasonability of the search. My colleagues assert that the fact that police have reasonable and probable grounds to carry out an arrest does not confer on them the authority to carry out a strip search, even where the strip search is related to the purpose of the arrest. They add an additional requirement in the case of strip searches that the police must establish reasonable and probable grounds justifying the conduct of the strip search itself. By placing strip searches in a category distinct from other types of searches, my colleagues have bypassed this Court's decision in *Cloutier, supra*, at pp.185-186, that the existence of reasonable and probable grounds is not a prerequisite to the existence of a police power to search. I agree with my colleagues that the more intrusive the search and the higher the degree of infringement of personal privacy, the higher degree of justification; however, I disagree that the common law requires police to prove that they had reasonable and probable grounds to justify the strip search. Interpreting the common law in a manner consistent with Charter principles does not require the Court to redefine the common law right by adding this additional requirement. The existing common law rule that police demonstrate an objectively valid reason for the arrest rather than for the search is consistent with s. 8 of the Charter, provided that the strip search is for a valid objective and is not conducted in an abusive fashion.

The common law right to search incidental to an arrest is justified in part by the need to discover and preserve evidence. The Courts have long acknowledged that the effectiveness and the legitimacy of the law enforcement system depends on the ability of police to find and preserve relevant evidence which may assist in the investigation and prosecution of the accused: see *Cloutier, supra*; *R. v. Lim (No.2)* (1990), 1 C.R.R. (2d) 136 (Ont. H.C.J.); *Beare, supra*. My colleagues would severely limit the availability of this justification for strip searches by requiring police officers to conduct all strip searches at the police station. I do not agree that the discovery of evidence should be postponed to a time where the search can take place at a police station. The common law requirements that the evidence sought be related to the reason for the arrest and that the search be conducted in a manner that is not abusive apply to protect accused persons from indiscriminate or unreasonable searches regardless of whether the search occurs at the station or in the field.

The fear that evidence may be destroyed or lost before arriving at the police station is genuine. The common law rules must have regard to the realities of the situation. Police officers are not always close to a station. They operate in remote areas and are often alone. In my view, the argument that the risk of the detainee getting rid of the evidence is minimal is as unrealistic as the belief that an accused can never escape during his transfer to the police station or that a detainee can never escape from a prison. Also unrealistic is the assumption that evidence dropped or left behind by an accused could "easily" be linked circumstantially back to the accused.

My colleagues refer to the English legislation, the Police and Criminal Evidence Act 1984 (U.K.), c. 60 as authority for the requirement that searches be conducted in police stations. Although foreign legislation can be useful as a source of criteria to determine the reasonableness of a search, I think it is clearly excessive to adopt foreign legislation to reinvent the common law rule in Canada. This is particularly inopportune given that the foreign legislation referred to by my colleagues was specifically adopted to supersede the common law. In my view, the proposed rule that all strip searches proceed at a police station absent exigent circumstances should be left to Parliament.

Furthermore, by stating that exigent circumstances will only exist where there is a demonstrated necessity and urgency to search for weapons or objects that could be used to threaten safety, my colleagues have in fact abolished the right to search for evidence upon arrest. In doing so, they have drawn an unprecedented and unworkable distinction between the objective of discovering and preserving evidence and the objective of searching for weapons; objectives which they recognized in their reasons as the "twin rationales for the common law power to search incident to arrest" (para. 95). There is no demonstrated need for such a radical change to the common law power. My colleagues come to the conclusion that the trial judge erred in determining that the search was reasonable in all of the circumstances principally on the basis that there were no exigent circumstances to justify a search outside the police station. I disagree with their conclusion on the basis that the police are under no obligation to defer the search. With regard to the manner in which the search was conducted, I would agree with the Crown that the three searches must be looked at individually and justified according to the circumstances applicable to each of them. In my view, the first search was perfectly justified. As provided for in *Cloutier*, *supra*, the reasonable and probable grounds for the arrest provided the authority to search for evidence related to the crime. The arresting officers had reasonable cause to believe the accused was hiding evidence. Information that the accused had been observed passing a white powdery substance to other persons and receiving cash in return was passed onto the arresting officers by the surveillance team, giving rise to a suspicion that the accused would have crack cocaine on his person. In addition, as the arresting officer approached the accused, he observed the accused crushing something between his fingers that left a white residue. During the course of the arrest, the police found what looked to be cocaine under the table where one of the suspects was arrested.

The manner in which the first search was conducted was not abusive. The search was minimally intrusive on the accused's privacy. It was conducted in a private place and by one officer of the same gender of the accused. The officer did not remove the accused's clothing but only pulled back his underwear in order to visually inspect his buttocks. The officer used minimal force until the accused hip-checked and scratched him, at which point the officer responded with force only to regain control of the situation.

With regard to the second search, I would dispute in particular the obligation that my colleagues put on the arresting officer to obtain the authorization of a senior officer at para. 113. I find no authority for such a requirement and see no value in submitting the evaluation of the situation to a person who is not present nor independent of the police. Furthermore, similar to the obligation that police conduct searches only at the station, the imposition of this requirement negates the purpose of the common law power by imposing an additional barrier to the ability of the police to immediately seize evidence or weapons. The case law has always recognized that the search power is applicable to the arresting officer, the very person who is in the position to act with the immediacy justified by the exception. Given the problems inherent in the requirement for prior authorization, the preferred approach to protecting the rights of the accused is to hold police to a higher degree of justification when a highly intrusive search has been conducted; see S. A. Cohen, "Search Incident to Arrest" (1989-90), 32 Crim.L.Q. 366.

In finding the manner of the search unreasonable, my colleagues emphasized not only the "unilateral" decision of the officers, but also the danger to the health and safety of the accused and the failure of the police to give the accused the opportunity to remove his own clothing. In my view, too much was made of the issue of the appellant's health and safety, which is but one factor to be considered in the context of the reasonableness analysis. While it may have been preferable to conduct the search in more sanitary conditions, the appellant adduced no evidence of any health risk or health effect resulting from the use of the gloves. In circumstances such as this, I believe that regard must be had to the need for a police officer at the time of arrest to make instantaneous decisions without having the luxury of reflection; see *United States v. Robinson*, 414 U.S. 218 (1973).

I also disagree with my colleagues' insistence that police must always give the accused an opportunity to remove his own clothing. In this case, the officer might have given the accused the opportunity to undo his pants during the search in the stairwell, but his failure to make such a request by no means rendered the search unreasonable. With respect to the second search in the restaurant, regard must be had to the fact that the accused struggled with the officers such that they required another officer to assist them. In circumstances where the accused resists arrest or acts violently toward police, it seems unlikely that the accused will comply with a request to remove his or her own clothing. I strongly disagree with an approach which would turn this factor or any of the other factors into hard and fast requirements that must be met each and every time a strip search is conducted, without regard to the particular circumstances of the case.

On the other hand, my colleagues give practically no importance to the lack of cooperation and resistance of the accused, stating at para. 116 that there is "no requirement . . . [to] . . . cooperate with the violation . . . [of one's rights]". I disagree with my colleagues that resistance to a lawful arrest is justified as a refusal to cooperate with a violation of s. 8. In my opinion, resistance to arrest can be met with the minimal force necessary. It is also an important consideration in determining the breach of the accused's privacy interests. All persons must be treated with dignity and respect, but the expectation of privacy of the accused in the circumstances of this case must be measured in light of his conduct.

Despite my disagreement with the emphasis my colleagues have placed on certain aspects of the second search, I agree that the second search did violate the accused's s. 8 rights. In this case, the police had actual knowledge that the accused was in possession of what was thought to be narcotics, providing a greater opportunity to ensure that the evidence would not be lost before reaching the station. In addition, the accused's refusal to give up the evidence meant that it could be seized at the scene only if the police conducted the strip search in less than private conditions and applied a degree of force which may not have been necessary had the search been conducted at the station. Given these circumstances, the police should have concluded that close custody and immediate transfer to the station were the appropriate means of pursuing the ends of justice.

. . .

[Bastarache J. would, however, not have excluded the evidence under s. 24(2). L'Heureux-Dubé J. agreed with Bastarache J. in dissent, in a short separate opinion.]

For a review of *Golden* and its implications, see Eric Gottardi, "The *Golden* Rules: Raising the Bar Regarding Strip Searches Incident to Arrest", (2002) 47 C.R. (5th) 48 and Stuart, "Zigzags on Rights of Accused: Brittle Majorities Manipulate Weasel Words of Dialogue, Deference and Charter Values", (2003) 20 Sup. Ct. L. Rev. 267.

Judging by the case law there is considerable doubt as to whether police are in fact following the rigorous *Golden* standards. See David Tanovich, "Bonds: Gendered and Racialized Violence, Strip Searches, Sexual Assault and Abuse of Prosecutorial Power" (2011) 79 C.R. (6th) 132. A young black woman charged with public intoxication was strip searched in police custody and her hair and bra were cut with scissors. The trial judge stayed the charges: (2011) 79 C.R. (6th) 119. In 2010, Metro Toronto Police reported 31,072 strip searches in which an "item" was found in 9,448 cases. See: Editorial by Kent Roach, "Strip Searches" (2011) 57 Crim. L.Q. 419.

In *R. v. Backhouse* (2005), 194 C.C.C. (3d) 1, 28 C.R. (6th) 31 (Ont. C.A.), an appeal against a double murder and attempt murder convictions, resulted in the order of a new trial on the basis that the trial judge had erred in admitting similar fact evidence. The lengthy judgment of Rosenberg J.A. (Goudge and Borins JJ.A. concurring) for the Ontario Court of Appeal is also important for its careful consideration of a number of Charter and seizure rulings respecting ss. 8 and 10(b). Of particular interest are rulings respecting seizures for forensic testing.

The Court held that the seizure of the accused's clothing for forensic testing did not technically amount to a strip search. It was a lawful search incident to arrest. The arrest was lawful, the search was related to the reasons for arrest and the search was not conducted in an abusive fashion. The police were entitled to seize the clothing to preserve evidence. No reasonable grounds were required beyond those required for the arrest.

It was then held that search did not become unreasonable when the police retained the clothing for forensic examination after the accused was released. Section 489.1 of the Criminal Code applied to the common law seizure of clothing which should have been brought before a justice. The continued detention without compliance was unlawful. However it was not necessary to decide whether this could render the initial lawful search unlawful. Even it did, violate the accused's s. 8 rights, the evidence of the analysis of the jacket ought not to be excluded.

Rosenberg J.A. also held that handwashing for gunshot residue did not violate s. 8 of the Charter. The consent provided by the accused did not provide a valid waiver as he was not told that the test could be positive even if he did not fire the gun but had merely been in the vicinity of a recently fired gun. However, the search was justified as incident to the arrest. The arrest was lawful, the procedure not intrusive, and carried out in a reasonable fashion.

R. v. FEARON
2014 SCC 77, [2014] 3 S.C.R. 621, 318 C.C.C. (3d) 182, 15 C.R. (7th) 221
(S.C.C.)

As a jewellery merchant loaded her car, two men grabbed some bags containing jewellery and left in a black vehicle. One of the men was armed with a handgun. The police were called and, some time later, located and secured the getaway vehicle. They arrested the two accused, F and C. While searching F as an incident to arrest, the police found a cell phone. They searched the phone then and again about two hours later. In those searches, they found a draft text message referring to the robbery and some photos that included one of a handgun. The police obtained a warrant to search the vehicle and recovered the handgun depicted in the photo. Some months later they also obtained a warrant to search the cell phone, although no new evidence was discovered.

At his trial on robbery and other charges, F argued that the search of the cell phone violated s. 8 of the Charter. However, the trial judge rejected the argument, admitted the photos and text message, and convicted him. His appeal to the Ontario Court of Appeal was dismissed. The accused appealed further to the Supreme Court of Canada. By a majority of 4-3 the Court dismissed the appeal.

CROMWELL J. (McLACHLIN C.J., MOLDAVER and WAGNER JJ. concurring):

[1] The police have a common law power to search incident to a lawful arrest. Does this power permit the search of cell phones and similar devices found on the suspect? That is the main question raised by this appeal.

[2] Canadian courts have so far not provided a consistent answer. At least four approaches have emerged. The first is to hold that the power to search incident to arrest generally includes the power to search cell phones, provided that the search is truly incidental to the arrest: *R. v. Giles*, 2007 BCSC 1147 (CanLII); *R. v. Otchere-Badu*, 2010 ONSC 1059 (CanLII); *Young v. Canada*, 2010 CanLII 74003 (Nfld. Prov. Ct.); *R. v. Howell*, 2011 NSSC 284, 313 N.S.R. (2d) 4; *R. v. Franko*, 2012 ABQB 282, 541 A.R. 23; *R. v. Cater*, 2014 NSCA 74 (CanLII); *R. v. D'Annunzio* (2010), 224 C.R.R. (2d) 221 (Ont. S.C.J.). The second view is that "cursory" searches are permitted: *R. v. Polius* (2009), 196 C.R.R. (2d) 288 (Ont. S.C.J.). A third is that thorough "data-dump" searches are not permitted incident to arrest: *R. v. Hiscoe*, 2013 NSCA 48, 328 N.S.R. (2d) 381; *R. v. Mann*, 2014 BCCA 231, 310 C.C.C. (3d) 143. Finally, it has also been held that searches of cell phones incident to arrest are not permitted except in exigent circumstances, in which a "cursory" search is permissible: *R. v. Liew*, 2012 ONSC 1826 (CanLII). These divergent results underline both the difficulty of the question and the need for a more consistent approach.

. . .

(3) Were the Searches Truly Incidental to a Lawful Arrest?

[27] The common law framework requires that a search incident to arrest must be founded on a lawful arrest, be truly incidental to that arrest and be conducted reasonably. In my view, the initial searches of the cell phone in this case satisfied these requirements.

[28] Mr. Fearon was lawfully arrested for robbery, and that satisfies the first requirement.

[29] There is no serious suggestion in this Court that the cell phone searches that led police to the text message and the photo of the handgun were other than truly incidental to the arrest, or, in other words that they were not conducted in pursuit of a "valid purpose connected to the arrest", as required by *Caslake*, at para. 19. To understand why, we need at this point to review the facts in more detail.

. . .

[33] In my view, the searches of the cell phone that lead to the discovery of the text message and the photos that the Crown introduced as evidence at trial were truly incidental to the arrest. It is clear from the record and the trial judge's findings that the search was directed at public safety (locating the handgun), avoiding the loss of evidence (the stolen jewellery) and obtaining evidence of the crime (information linking Mr. Fearon to the robbery and locating potential accomplices).

. . .

(4) Does the Common Law Test Need to Be Modified in Light of the *Charter*?

[53] I pause here for a moment to note that some courts have suggested that the protection s. 8 affords to individuals in the context of cell phone searches varies depending on whether an individual's phone is password-protected: see, e.g., Court of Appeal judgment, 2013 ONCA 106, 114 O.R. (3d) 81, at paras. 73 and 75; Ruling, at para. 49; *R. v. Khan*, 2013 ONSC 4587, 287 C.R.R. (2d) 192, at para. 18; *Hiscoe*, at paras. 80-81. I would not give this factor very much weight in assessing either an individual's subjective expectation of privacy or whether that expectation is reasonable. An individual's decision not to password protect his or her cell phone does not indicate any sort of abandonment of the significant privacy interests one generally will have in the contents of the phone: see, e.g., *R. v. Rochwell*, 2012 ONSC 5594, 268 C.R.R. (2d) 283, at para. 54. Cell phones — locked or unlocked — engage significant privacy interests. But we must also keep this point in perspective.

. . .

[58] All of that said, the search of a cell phone has the potential to be a much more significant invasion of privacy than the typical search incident to arrest. As a result, my view is that the general common law framework for searches incident to arrest needs to be modified in the case of cell phone searches incident to arrest. In particular, the law needs to provide the suspect with further protection against the risk of wholesale invasion of privacy which may occur if the search of a cell phone is constrained only by the requirements that the arrest be lawful and that the search be truly incidental to arrest and reasonably conducted. The case law suggests that there are three main approaches to making this sort of modification: a categorical prohibition, the introduction of a reasonable and probable grounds requirement, or a limitation of searches to exigent circumstances. I will explain why, in my view, none of these approaches is appropriate here and then outline the approach I would adopt.

(a) *Categorical Prohibition*

[60] Adopting this categorical approach would mean that, although the police may lawfully seize a cell phone found in the course of a search incident to arrest where there is reason to believe it contains evidence relevant to the offence, the phone may not be searched, at all, without a warrant. The Supreme Court of the United States essentially adopted this approach in *Riley v. California*, 134 S. Ct. 2473 (2014). I would not follow suit for two reasons.

[61] First, the only case from this Court to adopt a categorical exclusion from searches incident to arrest is *Stillman*. But the considerations that prompted the Court to take a categorical approach in that case are entirely absent in this case. The record in this case shows that important law enforcement objectives are served by the power to search cell phones promptly incident to arrest. This is unlike the *Stillman* situation, in which the Court concluded that the prompt access to the suspect's bodily samples did little to serve law enforcement objectives incidental to the arrest. Moreover, and in marked contrast to the bodily sample seizures at issue in *Stillman*, while cell phone searches have the

potential to be a significant invasion of privacy, they are neither inevitably a major invasion of privacy nor *inherently* degrading. Looking at a few recent text messages or a couple of recent pictures is hardly a massive invasion of privacy, let alone an affront to human dignity.

[62] Second, I am not as pessimistic as some about the possibility of placing meaningful limits on the manner and extent of cell phone searches incident to arrest.

(b)   *Imposing a Reasonable and Probable Grounds Requirement*

[66] One possibility is to require reasonable and probable grounds for the search, as the Court did in *Golden*. This Court has described the higher threshold of "reasonable and probable grounds" as requiring "reasonable probability" or "credibly-based probability": *Debot*, at p. 1166; *Hunter v. Southam Inc.*, at p. 167. In my respectful opinion, imposing that threshold here would significantly undermine the important law enforcement objectives in this context.

(c)   *Exigent Circumstances*

[69] Another possibility is to allow cell phone searches only in exigent circumstances, as the appellant urges us to do: A.F., at paras. 41 and 53. The Ontario Superior Court of Justice adopted this approach in *Liew*, but, so far as I have been able to determine, it has not been followed in any other Canadian case. As I see it, that standard requires too much knowledge on the part of the police, given the very early point in an investigation at which a search incident to arrest will often occur. It shares the pitfalls of imposing a standard of reasonable and probable grounds and, if applied in the manner proposed by my colleague, Karakatsanis J., would go even further to prohibit a cell phone search in all but the most exceptional circumstances.

[70] This approach, in my view, gives almost no weight to the law enforcement objectives served by the ability to promptly search a cell phone incidental to a lawful arrest. If, as is my view, importing a standard of reasonable and probable grounds would significantly undermine these objectives, then imposing a requirement of urgency and restricting the purposes for which the search may be conducted would effectively gut them. This standard, in my respectful view, fails to strike the balance required by s. 8 between the privacy interests of the individual and the state's interest in protecting the public.

(5) Other Steps

[74] The focus of our attention, in my view, should not be on steps that effectively gut the usefulness of searches incident to arrest. Rather, we should concentrate on measures to limit the potential invasion of privacy that may, but does not inevitably result from a cell phone search. This may be done by making some modifications to the common law power to search cell phones incidental to arrest. Ultimately, the purpose of the exercise is to strike a balance that gives due weight, on the one hand, to the important law enforcement objectives served by searches incident to arrest and, on the other, to the very significant privacy interests at stake in cell phone searches.

[75] The requirement that the search of the cell phone be truly incidental to the arrest should be strictly applied to permit searches that are required to be done promptly upon arrest in order to effectively serve the purposes of officer and public safety, loss or destruction of evidence, or discovery of evidence. Three modifications to the general rules would give effect to this approach.

[76] First, the scope of the search must be tailored to the purpose for which it may lawfully be conducted. In other words, it is not enough that a cell phone search in general terms is truly incidental to the arrest. Both the nature and the extent of the search performed on the cell phone must be truly incidental to the particular arrest for the particular offence. In practice, this will mean that, generally, even when a cell phone search is permitted because it is truly incidental to the arrest, only recently sent or drafted emails, texts, photos and the call log may be examined as in most cases only those sorts of items will have the necessary link to the purposes for which prompt examination of the device is permitted. But these are not rules, and other searches may in some circumstances be justified. The test is whether the nature and extent of the search are tailored to the purpose for which the search may lawfully be conducted. To paraphrase *Caslake*, the police must be able to explain, within the permitted purposes, what they searched and why: see para. 25.

[77] This approach responds to the privacy concerns posed by the virtually infinite storage capacity of cell phones by, in general, excluding resort to that capacity in a search incident to arrest. It would also provide these protections while preserving the ability of the police to have resort to basic cell phone data where this serves the purposes for which searches incident to arrest are permitted.

[79] The law enforcement objectives served by searches incident to arrest will generally be most compelling in the course of the investigation of crimes that involve, for example, violence or threats of violence, or that in some other way put public safety at risk, such as the robbery in this case, or serious property offences that involve readily disposable property, or drug trafficking. Generally speaking, these types of crimes are most likely to justify some limited search of a cell phone incident to arrest, given the law enforcement objectives. Conversely, a search of a cell phone incident to arrest will generally not be justified in relation to minor offences.

[80] A further modification is that the third purpose for which searches incident to arrest are permitted — the discovery of evidence — must be treated restrictively in this context. The discovery of evidence, in the context of a cell phone search incident to arrest, will only be a valid law enforcement objective when the investigation will be stymied or significantly hampered absent the ability to promptly search the cell phone incident to arrest. Only in those types of situations does the law enforcement objective in relation to the discovery of evidence clearly outweigh the potentially significant intrusion on privacy. For example, if, as in this case, there is reason to think that there is another perpetrator who has not been located, the search of a cell phone for that purpose will be truly incidental to the arrest of the other suspects. As Det. Nicol testified, there were matters that needed to be followed up immediately in this case. If, on the other hand, all suspects are in custody and any firearms

and stolen property have been recovered, it is hard to see how police could show that the prompt search of a suspect's cell phone could be considered truly incidental to the arrest as it serves no immediate investigative purpose. This will mean, in practice, that cell phone searches are not routinely permitted simply for the purpose of discovering additional evidence. The search power must be used with great circumspection. It also means, in practice, that the police will have to be prepared to explain why it was not practical (and I emphasize that this does *not* mean impossible), in all the circumstances of the investigation, to postpone the search until they could obtain a warrant.

. . .

[82] Finally, officers must make detailed notes of what they have examined on the cell phone. The Court encouraged this sort of note keeping in *Vu* in the context of a warranted search: para. 70. It also encouraged that notes be kept in the context of strip searches: *Golden*, at para. 101. In my view, given that we are dealing here with an extraordinary search power that requires neither a warrant nor reasonable and probable grounds, the obligation to keep a careful record of what is searched and how it was searched should be imposed as a matter of constitutional imperative. The record should generally include the applications searched, the extent of the search, the time of the search, its purpose and its duration. After-the-fact judicial review is especially important where, as in the case of searches incident to arrest, there is no prior authorization. Having a clear picture of what was done is important to such review being effective. In addition, the record keeping requirement is likely to have the incidental effect of helping police officers focus on the question of whether their conduct in relation to the phone falls squarely within the parameters of a lawful search incident to arrest.

[83] To summarize, police officers will not be justified in searching a cell phone or similar device incident to every arrest. Rather, such a search will comply with s. 8 where:

(1)   The arrest was lawful;

(2)   The search is truly incidental to the arrest in that the police have a reason based on a valid law enforcement purpose to conduct the search, and that reason is objectively reasonable. The valid law enforcement purposes in this context are:

(a)   Protecting the police, the accused, or the public;

(b)   Preserving evidence; or

(c)   Discovering evidence, including locating additional suspects, in situations in which the investigation will be stymied or significantly hampered absent the ability to promptly search the cell phone incident to arrest;

(3)   The nature and the extent of the search are tailored to the purpose of the search; and

(4)   The police take detailed notes of what they have examined on the device and how it was searched.

[84] In setting out these requirements for the common law police power, I do not suggest that these measures represent the only way to make searches of cell phones incident to arrest constitutionally compliant. This may be an area, as the Court concluded was the case in *Golden*, in which legislation may well be desirable. The law enforcement and privacy concerns may be balanced in many ways and my reasons are not intended to restrict the acceptable options.

B. *Second Issue: Application of the Framework to the Present Case*

[85] The initial search of the appellant's cell phone incidental to his arrest revealed a relevant draft text message and photographs. Although there were subsequent searches, no additional evidence was found and the evidence from the cell phone tendered by the Crown at trial was that originally viewed by Sgt. Hicks: Ruling, at para. 30. It is therefore only necessary to rule on the legality of his initial searches of the cell phone.

[86] As I discussed in detail earlier in my reasons, there were important law enforcement objectives to be served by a prompt search of aspects of the phone. The police believed that to be the case, and their belief was reasonable. However, the officers' evidence about the extent of the cell phone search was not satisfactory. Sergeant Hicks said that he "had a look through the cell phone" but could not recall specifics: Ruling, at para. 20. Detective Constable Abdel-Malik said that he later did "some quick checks" for about two minutes, but, again, his evidence is not very specific: Ruling, at para. 24. There were subsequent examinations of the phone by Sgt. Hicks, Det. Const. Abdel-Malik and Det. Nicol, but they were not able to provide many specifics of exactly what was examined.

[87] The Crown bears the burden of establishing that the search incident to arrest was lawful. In my view, that burden is not met, absent detailed evidence about precisely what was searched, how and why. That sort of evidence was lacking in this case, and the lack of evidence, in turn, impedes meaningful judicial review of the legality of the search. As I mentioned earlier, this after-the-fact review is particularly important in the case of warrantless searches where there has been no prior judicial screening as occurs when a warrant is required.

[88] I conclude that the initial search was not reasonable and it therefore breached Mr. Fearon's s. 8 rights.

[The majority decided not to exclude the evidence in this case in part because the police had made an honest and reasonable mistake in relying on the law in existence at the time of the investigation]

KARAKATSANIS J. (LEBEL and ABELLA JJ. concurring) (dissenting):

I. Introduction

[100] We live in a time of profound technological change and innovation. Developments in mobile communications and computing technology have revolutionized our daily lives. Individuals can, while walking down the street,

converse with family on the other side of the world, browse vast stores of human knowledge and information over the Internet, or share a video, photograph or comment about their experiences with a legion of friends and followers.

[101] The devices which give us this freedom also generate immense stores of data about our movements and our lives. Ever-improving GPS technology even allows these devices to track the locations of their owners. Private digital devices record not only our core biographical information but our conversations, photos, browsing interests, purchase records, and leisure pursuits. Our digital footprint is often enough to reconstruct the events of our lives, our relationships with others, our likes and dislikes, our fears, hopes, opinions, beliefs and ideas. Our digital devices are windows to our inner private lives.

[102] Therefore, as technology changes, our law must also evolve so that modern mobile devices do not become the telescreens of George Orwell's *1984*. In this appeal, we are asked to decide when police officers are entitled to search a mobile phone found in the possession or vicinity of an accused person upon arrest. Because this new technology poses unique threats to peoples' privacy, we must turn to first principles to determine the appropriate response.

[103] An individual's right to a private sphere is a hallmark of our free and democratic society. This Court has recognized that privacy is essential to human dignity, to democracy, and to self-determination. Section 8 of the *Canadian Charter of Rights and Freedoms* protects the right to be free from *unreasonable* search and seizure. In defining the contours of a *reasonable* search, the law balances legitimate state interests, including safety and securing evidence in law enforcement, with the privacy interests of individuals. This balance generally requires judicial pre-authorization for a search, and a warrantless search is *prima facie* unreasonable.

[104] Nonetheless, our law recognizes that pre-authorization is not always feasible, such as when a search is reasonably necessary to effect an arrest. For this reason, the police have a limited power to search lawfully arrested individuals and their immediate vicinity. However, this police power does not extend to searches which encroach on the arrested person's most private spheres — searches of the home, or the taking of bodily samples. In my view, searches of personal digital devices risk similarly serious encroachments on privacy and are therefore not authorized under the common law power to search incident to arrest.

[105] The intensely personal and uniquely pervasive sphere of privacy in our personal computers requires protection that is clear, practical and effective. An overly complicated template, such as the one proposed by the majority, does not ensure sufficient protection. Only judicial pre-authorization can provide the effective and impartial balancing of the state's law enforcement objectives with the privacy interests in our personal computers. Thus, I conclude that the police must obtain a warrant before they can search an arrested person's phone or other personal digital communications device. Our common law already provides flexibility where there are exigent circumstances

— when the safety of the officer or the public is at stake, or when a search is necessary to prevent the destruction of evidence.

[106] In this case, the appellant was arrested in connection with an armed robbery. Upon arrest, the police searched his cell phone and discovered incriminating evidence. The police had no grounds to suspect there was an imminent threat to safety and no grounds to believe there was an imminent risk of the destruction of evidence. Consequently, I conclude that the search was unreasonable and unconstitutional. The police were required to obtain a warrant before searching the phone, although they were entitled to seize the phone pending an application for a warrant. I would exclude the evidence so obtained.

Tim Quigley "*R. v. Fearon*: A Problematic Decision"
(2014), 15 C.R. (7th) 281

. . .

It is against the backdrop of *Stillman* and *Golden* and the recognition in *Morelli*, *TELUS Communications*, and *Spencer* of the extensive privacy protection afforded digital devices in other contexts that *Fearon* should be assessed. Instead of requiring a warrant or, at the least, enhanced grounds à la *Golden*, the majority has devised a new common law regime that permits the search of a cell phone as an incident of arrest. There are four requirements but only two are them are really new. The first two—that the arrest must have been lawful and that the search must be truly incidental to that arrest—have previously applied, although Justice Cromwell is at pains to insist that they be adhered to. Yes, they should be adhered to but those requirements add nothing to the analysis. The third requirement is that the nature and extent of a cell phone search may well be limited by its purpose such that, in general, only recent items should be viewed. This criterion has, however, been left rather flexible. Finally, the police are required to make detailed notes of the examination of the cell phone. Let me comment on these latter two requirements since they are critical to the majority decision.

The third requirement is extremely loose. Even a clear rule stipulating that only recent items may be examined begs the question of what is recent—and the police have been given the role of deciding that question. However, the additional qualification, at paragraph 76, that more extensive searches may sometimes be justified is more distressing. No guidance has been given for when a cell phone search may be more intrusive. This places the police in the predicament of attempting to predict when they may search more extensively but it also invites, rather than constrains, these further searches because the Court has explicitly said that it may approve them. In contrast, Justice Karakatsanis was very alive to the difficulties of even a cursory examination:

> Moreover, it is very difficult — if not impossible — to perform a meaningfully constrained targeted or cursory inspection of a cell phone or other personal digital device. For example, recent communications could have been transmitted via a text message, an email, an instant messaging application, a social networking application, a conventional voice call or a "data" voice call, a message board, through a shared calendar or cloud

folder, a picture messaging application, or any number of websites. In short, a cursory inspection for recent communications will need to search a host of applications — the privacy infringement may be far from minimal and the inspection far from quick. Similarly, a cursory inspection of photos may involve any number of private and personal photographs of the individual — and of third parties. [para. 164]

The fourth requirement will almost certainly lead to confusion, debate, and protracted litigation to determine what is adequate note-taking. It must be kept in mind that the police make their notes after an event has occurred. A frequent line of cross-examination is to determine the accuracy and veracity of police notes. We can fully expect this to be accentuated in this context since it is a requirement imposed by our highest court. Some guidance has been provided at paragraph 82 but this is necessarily general. There will be ongoing controversy about whether the police have complied and about what is required in these circumstances. Although Justice Cromwell likened this process to the encouragement the Court has given to note-making in other contexts, encouragement is not the same as a requirement—and a requirement that is, at the moment, reasonably nebulous.

In coming to this position and in rejecting either a warrant requirement or, at the least, standards for the exercise of a warrantless or exigent search power, Justice Cromwell has downplayed the privacy interest in cell phone contents. Justice Karakatsanis is much more attentive to this concern and much more consistent with the Court's own recognition of this interest in *Morelli, TELUS Communications*, and *Spencer*. Considering this issue in the context of a factually guilty accused does not do justice to the privacy concern. In other circumstances, a citizen might be arrested on reasonable and probable grounds but subsequently found to be factually innocent. Nevertheless, the majority reasoning would permit a search of that citizen's digital device simply because it was there when the person was arrested. It may be telling that the often very conservative United States Supreme Court unanimously upheld the warrant requirement in this context in *Riley v. California*, 134 S.Ct. 2473 (2014). Justice Cromwell cited the decision but provided no convincing reason why Canada should not take the same course.

In rejecting either a warrant or objective/subjective standards, Justice Cromwell has also seemingly overlooked an important part of the evidence in this case. At paragraphs 34 and 35, he noted that the trial judge found as a fact that the police had a reasonable belief that the cell phone could provide evidence. Thus, the factual foundation in this case provided support for a warrant requirement or, at the very least, if exigent circumstances existed, a warrantless search premised on reasonable grounds. At paragraph 48, the judgment outlines the importance of a cell phone search to law enforcement. While that may well be true, especially in the context of criminal organizations and the drug trade, it is not clear why the same findings of fact as occurred in *Fearon* would not also occur in such cases. In other words, the grounds for a search may often be present. If they are, a warrant should be preferred but, as in other circumstances, in exigent circumstances a warrantless search may be acceptable.

. . .

The creation of common law police powers also takes Parliament off the hook and denies litigants the opportunity to require the state to justify its powers. Viewed in this way and in light of the other concerns discussed, *Fearon* is a highly problematic decision. Let us hope that if it proves to be unworkable or unjust, the Court will reconsider the question at a later time.

(iii) Unlawful Searches Violate s. 8

Provincial Courts of Appeal had been resistant to the view that an illegal search is necessarily unreasonable. In an often-quoted dictum in *R. v. Heisler* (1984), 11 C.C.C. (3d) 475 (Alta. C.A.), the Alberta Court of Appeal held that "it does not follow that because a search is illegal it must therefore be unreasonable". In that case, the accused's purse had been searched prior to entering a rock concert without there having been prior reasonable grounds. In a leading post-*Collins* decision on search warrants, Mr. Justice Martin for the Ontario Court of Appeal in *R. v. Harris* (1987), 57 C.R. (3d) 356, 35 C.C.C. (3d) 1 (Ont. C.A.) accepted that a search or seizure under a search warrant "invalid in substance" would be unreasonable under s. 8. His Lordship however added that

I find it difficult to think, however, that minor or technical defects in the warrant automatically make an ensuing search or seizure unreasonable under s. 8 of the Charter (at 23).

Since the decision of the Supreme Court of Canada in *Collins* and *Kokesch*, it now seems clear that a search that is not legal either under statute or at common law is necessarily unreasonable under s. 8. The question of whether the legal violation is trivial or serious is only relevant to the s. 24(2) inquiry.

KOKESCH v. R.

[1990] 3 S.C.R. 3, 1 C.R. (4th) 62, 61 C.C.C. (3d) 207 (S.C.C.)

DICKSON C.J.C.:—

The Facts

The appellant was charged on an indictment that, on or about 5th November 1986, at or near Shawnigan Lake, British Columbia, he unlawfully had in his possession a narcotic, cannabis (marijuana), for the purpose of trafficking contrary to s. 4(2) of the *Narcotic Control Act*; and that he was unlawfully cultivating marijuana contrary to s. 6(1) of the Act.

On 5th November 1986 R.C.M.P. officers entered the appellant's residence, pursuant to a search warrant dated 4th November 1986, and seized marijuana plants. This evidence formed the basis of the two charges. Prior to the commencement of trial before Cashman Co. Ct. J., counsel agreed to a *voir dire* in order for the trial judge to consider the admissibility of the seized evidence. For the purposes of the *voir dire*, counsel relied on the testimony which had been adduced at the preliminary hearing. The reasons of Cashman Co. Ct. J. on the *voir dire* provide a thorough summary of the events leading up to the seizure of the evidence [pp. 2-4]:

> The events commenced on 30th October 1986 and what occurred is best described in the evidence of Constable Povarchook. He said that his first involvement with the matter was on 30th October 1986, and on that day he and other members of the Drug Section were performing surveillance as a result of information which they had received from the Surrey Detachment [of the R.C.M.P. The information they received was that the driver of a truck on the ferry to Vancouver Island was suspected of being involved in the cultivation of marijuana]. They went out to the Swartze Bay ferry terminal in Sidney. At approximately 14:40 hours they observed a green Toyota pickup with a white canopy come out of the ferry terminal and head south on the Pat Bay Highway. They were unable to follow this vehicle directly due to traffic, but caught up to it as it was travelling up the Malahat north of Victoria. He then observed it turn onto the South Shawnigan Lake turnoff. At no time did he have an opportunity to observe the driver of that vehicle. At approximately 15:34 hours he drove by the residence of 1985 West Shawnigan Lake Road and observed the pickup which he had seen earlier parked near the house on that lot.

> The following day, 31st October, he drove by the residence at approximately 7:30 in the morning and saw that the pickup truck was still there. Later in the afternoon he went up in the forces helicopter and took aerial photographs of the residence and the general area, and observed what appeared to be a white vehicle, but he was unable to make out just what vehicle it was.

> On 4th November 1986, at approximately 2 o'clock in the morning, he went to this house with Constable Handy and they conducted what he referred to in his evidence as a perimeter search of the residence. While doing so, he noticed that the residence was a two-storey structure, basement and upper level. The basement windows were curtained off and appeared to be sealed with something behind the curtain. He observed heavy condensation on the patio door window and heard electrical humming from the basement level near the carport around the rear of the residence. He saw a piece of plywood nailed to the wall of the residence, and observed it actually covered what appeared to be a louvered metal vent. From the side of the plywood, he detected a slight odour of marijuana, and on the top of the plywood, the odour was much stronger, and as well he could detect heat coming from the area.

> . . .

> Quite clearly from that evidence, one can see that the officer went right up to this dwelling-house, and observed it closely, and it appears from questions and answers from the cross-examination by Mr. Rosenberg that he, in fact, attempted to peer into the window. He conceded in order to get to the house he had to go down a long driveway, some 75 to 100 yards long. He said he had not had any direct dealings with the accused, and his source of information came solely from the R.C.M.P. in Surrey and not from any informant.

The search of the area immediately surrounding the dwelling house was conducted without prior judicial authorization. Moreover, when asked whether he had reasonable and probable grounds to believe that an offence had been or was being committed on the property contrary to the provisions of the *Narcotic Control Act*—a circumstance which under s. 10(1)(*a*) of the *Act* would permit a warrantless search of the perimeter—Constable Povarchook of the Royal Canadian Mounted Police, Victoria Drug Section, on cross-examination during the preliminary inquiry replied:

> A. I did not have reasonable and probable grounds to believe that there was an offence being committed. I had a suspicion.
>
> Q. Surely, you must have suspected something to go there?
>
> A. Well, I had more than just suspicion. I had solid grounds, but not enough for a search warrant.

In response to further questioning, he stated that it had not been necessary to enter the property either to preserve evidence or to apprehend a felon. The constable agreed in cross-examination that his visual, olfactory and aural observations could not have been made without going to the property and coming very close to the house.

Pursuant to a search warrant dated 4th November 1986, the police entered the appellant's residence and seized a number of marijuana plants. They also conducted a search of a vehicle that was on the property. The search warrant only authorized a search of the dwelling-house. The lawfulness of the vehicle search was not pursued at trial.

After considering the evidence, the trial judge held that the evidence upon which the Crown relied in support of the charges had been obtained in violation of s. 8 of the *Canadian Charter of Rights and Freedoms*. He ruled that the evidence was inadmissible pursuant to s. 24(2) of the *Charter*. The respondent appealed the decision to the British Columbia Court of Appeal. In a unanimous judgment, the Court allowed the appeal and ordered a new trial. The appellant now appeals from that decision to this Court.

. . .

The first issue raised in this appeal is whether the warrantless perimeter search of the dwelling house of the appellant, conducted on 4th November 1986, was an unreasonable search or seizure pursuant to s. 8 of the *Charter*. At the outset, I would reiterate the dictum of this court in *Hunter v. Southam, Inc.*, supra, regarding the interpretation of s. 8 and, specifically, the role which s. 8 plays in limiting the pre-existing search powers of the state (at pp. 156-57):

> The *Canadian Charter of Rights and Freedoms* is a purposive document. Its purpose is to guarantee and to protect, within the limits of reason, the enjoyment of the rights and freedoms it enshrines. It is intended to constrain governmental action inconsistent with those rights and freedoms; it is not in itself an authorization for governmental action . . . in guaranteeing the right to be secure from unreasonable searches and seizures, s. 8 acts as a limitation on whatever powers of search and seizure the federal or provincial governments already and otherwise possess. It does not in itself confer any powers, even of "reasonable" search and seizure, on these governments.

In the case at bar, the respondent concedes that what occurred outside of the dwelling-house of the appellant on the night of 4th November 1986 was a search for the purposes of s. 8 of the *Charter*. Moreover, the search was conducted without prior judicial authorization in the form of a search warrant. Of direct relevance, then, is the dictum of this Court in *Hunter v. Southam Inc.*, *supra*, wherein it was recognized that the absence of prior authorization raises a presumption of unreasonableness which must be rebutted by the party seeking to justify the warrantless search (p. 161).

The first hurdle which must be overcome by the respondent in that attempt at justification is readily apparent. In *R. v. Collins, supra*, this court reiterated the presumption against warrantless searches and described the burden that rests on a party attempting to establish reasonableness (at p. 278):

> . . . once the appellant has demonstrated that the search was a warrantless one, the Crown has the burden of showing that the search was, on a balance of probabilities, reasonable.
>
> A search will be reasonable if it is authorized by law, if the law itself is reasonable and if the manner in which the search was carried out is reasonable.

In order to show reasonableness, then, it is first necessary for the respondent to establish that the search was authorized by law. The trial judge undertook this analysis and, quite rightly, focussed his attention on s. 10(1) [now s. 10] of the *Narcotic Control Act*.

. . .

In ruling on the *voir dire*, Cashman Co. Ct. J. had little difficulty in reaching the conclusion that the police officers involved in the perimeter search lacked the requisite reasonable grounds for compliance with s. 10(1) of the Act. Given the concession by Officer Povarchook at the preliminary hearing that he did not have reasonable and probable grounds sufficient to obtain a search warrant, the inevitable conclusion is that the police lacked statutory authority to conduct the perimeter search. Indeed, the respondent conceded before this court that the police lacked reasonable and probable grounds.

. . .

The respondent also submitted that the "perimeter search" was carried out under lawful authority pursuant to the common law powers of the police and was not a trespass on private property. In my view, this argument is without foundation. This court consistently has held that the common law rights of the property holder to be free of police intrusion can be restricted only by powers granted in clear statutory language.

. . .

For these reasons, I would conclude that the warrantless perimeter search of the dwelling house of the appellant was conducted without lawful authority under statute or the common law. In the absence of lawful authority, the perimeter search must be found unreasonable: *R. v. Debot*, [1989] 2 S.C.R. 1140, at p. 1147, *per* Lamer J. Having made this determination, it is unnecessary, strictly speaking, to consider the second and third criteria of reasonableness established in *Collins, supra*. It does seem to me, however, apart from the question of lawful authority, that the police do not have a constitutionally unrestricted right to trespass upon private property. In my view, then, the Court of Appeal of British Columbia erred in its determination that the search, although not conducted under lawful authority, was nevertheless reasonable. Consequently, I would find that the s. 8 *Charter* rights of the appellant were violated by the warrantless search conducted by the police of the perimeter of his dwelling-house.

Chief Justice Dickson spoke for the court on the s. 8 issue. He was however in the minority on the further 4-3 decision to exclude the evidence under s. 24(2).

Later, in *R. v. Grant*, [1993] 3 S.C.R. 223, 24 C.R. (4th) 1, 84 C.C.C. (3d) 173 (S.C.C.), the Court found section 10 of the Narcotic Control Act unconstitutional because it authorized warrantless searches without insisting on an exigent circumstances requirement. The Court decided to save the section by reading in such a requirement. On the facts of the case there were no exigent circumstances and the warrantless perimeter searches in *Grant* were held to be unreasonable. Note the express exigent circumstances exception in section 11(7) of the Controlled Drugs and Substances Act, supra.

(iv) Reasonable expectation of privacy

Hunter makes it clear that the constitutional standards under s. 8 only apply where there is a *reasonable* expectation of privacy. Lower courts have held that there was no reasonable expectation of privacy and no *Hunter* standards applicable where gamblers had been invited to a hotel room in which illegal gambling was to take place (*R. v. Wong* (1987), 56 C.R. (3d) 352, 34 C.C.C. (3d) 51 (Ont. C.A.)), where a public washroom had become the meeting place for a group of men involved in homosexual acts (*R. v. Lebeau* (1988), 62 C.R. (3d) 157, 41 C.C.C. (3d) 163 (Ont. C.A.)) and in the case of a garage being used to cultivate drugs (*R. v. Nicholson* (1990), 53 C.C.C. (3d) 403 (B.C. C.A.)). **Do you agree with these decisions?**

In *R. v. Wong* [1990] 3 S.C.R. 36, 1 C.R. (4th) 1, 60 C.C.C. (3d) 460, the Ontario Court of Appeal had held that the protection of section 8 was not available to the accused as these people had been invited to that room for illegal gambling and were not entitled to any reasonable expectation of privacy. La Forest J. rejected this reasoning in the Supreme Court. The question was not whether people engaged in illegal activity behind a locked hotel door had a reasonable expectation of privacy. The question had to be "framed in broad and neutral terms" and was "whether in a society like ours persons who retire to a hotel room and closed the door behind them have a reasonable expectation of privacy".

In *R. v. Simmons*, [1988] 2 S.C.R. 495, 66 C.R. (3d) 297, 45 C.C.C. (3d) 296 (S.C.C.), involving a s. 8 challenge to the powers of customs officers to search at the border under the Customs Act, Chief Justice Dickson for the majority strongly urged the need to follow *Hunter*, suggesting that regardless of the constraints inherent in the circumstances, the *Hunter* safeguards should "not be lightly rejected". However, in the particular context of customs searches, Chief Justice Dickson did decide to relax the *Hunter* standards. It was held that the degree of personal privacy reasonably to be expected at customs was lower than in most other situations. Sovereign states had the right to control both who and what enters their borders. The Court distinguished three types of border searches. The first, least intrusive, type of routine questioning by customs officers, searches of luggage, frisk or pat searches, and the second type of strip or skin searches permitted under the Customs Act on "reasonable cause to suppose", were held to be reasonable within the meaning of s. 8. The Court left open the constitutionality of the third and most intrusive type — body cavity searches, in which customs officers might resort to medical doctors, X-rays, emetics or other highly invasive procedures.

In *R. v. Monney*, [1999] 1 S.C.R. 652, 24 C.R. (5th) 97, 133 C.C.C. (3d) 129 (S.C.C.), the Court upheld the constitutionality of a "drug loo facility" used by customs officers at Pearson International Airport. A majority of the Ontario Court of Appeal had narrowly interpreted the Customs Act to not authorize such searches, and they were in violation of sections 8 and 9 of the Charter. The Supreme Court would have none of this. Parliament must have envisaged such searches on reasonable suspicion. Furthermore, the compelled production of a urine sample or a bowel movement were searches conducted in a reasonable manner and not contrary to section 8 of the Charter. While the passive "bedpan vigil" was an embarrassing process, it did not interfere with a person's bodily integrity, either in terms of an interference with the "outward manifestation" of an individual's identity, or in relation to the intentional application of force. As is the case with other investigation techniques in the second category of customs searches previously recognized as constitutional in *Simmons*, such as a strip search, subjecting travellers crossing the Canadian border to potential embarrassment was the price to be paid in order to achieve the necessary balance between an individual's privacy interest and the compelling countervailing state interest in protecting the integrity of Canada's borders from the flow of dangerous contraband materials. The constitutionality of more invasive forms of collection, such as surgery or inducing a bowel movement, was left for another day.

On the other hand, in *R. v. Buhay*, [2003] 1 S.C.R. 631, 174 C.C.C. (3d) 97, 10 C.R. (6th) 205 (S.C.C.), the full Court held that an accused person had a reasonable expectation of privacy in a locker rented at a bus station. The discovery of drugs in the locker pursuant to a warrantless search was held to violate s. 8 of the Charter and the evidence was excluded, leading to the accused's acquittal.

The Supreme Court has now clearly departed from the warning of Chief Justice Dickson that departures from the *Hunter* standards should be exceedingly rare. The present Court is now unanimous that the *Hunter* criteria are best reserved for criminal or "quasi-criminal" matters and can be departed from in some "administrative" or "regulatory" matters. The leading pronouncement is that of Sopinka and Iacobucci JJ. in *B.C. (Securities Commission) v. Branch* (1995), 38 C.R. (4th) 133 (S.C.C.) where their Lordships determined that it is clear that the standard of reasonableness which prevails in the case of a search and seizure made in the course of enforcement in the criminal context will not usually be the appropriate standard for a determination made in an administrative or regulatory context. . . . The greater the departure from the realm of criminal law, the more flexible will be the approach to the standard of reasonableness (at 158).

Sopinka J. and Iacobucci J. also adopted a previous comment of Wilson J. in *R. v. McKinlay Transport Ltd* (1990), 76 C.R. (3d) 283 (S.C.C.):

Since individuals have different expectations of privacy in different contexts and with regard to different kinds of information and documents, it follows that the standard of review of what is "reasonable" in a given context must be flexible if it is to be realistic and meaningful (at 298, cited in *Branch* at 158).

In *Baron v. R.* (1993), 18 C.R. (4th) 374 (S.C.C.) Sopinka J., speaking for a unanimous panel of six justices of the Supreme Court, held that section 231.3 of the Income Tax Act violated s. 8. Under s. 231.3 the judge hearing the application "shall issue the warrant" where satisfied that there are reasonable grounds to believe that an offence under the Income Tax Act has been committed, a document or thing that may afford evidence of the commission of the offence is likely to be found and the building, receptacle or place specified is likely to contain such a document or thing. The Court found the violation in the words "shall issue" which were incompatible with the discretion recognized in *Hunter* to balance the interests of the taxpayer to be free of state intrusion on privacy and the state interest in law enforcement. Although the Income Tax Act was regulatory what was important was not a label but the intrusiveness of the search and the purpose of gathering evidence for a tax evasion prosecution. The appropriate remedy was to strike out s. 231.3. Issuing the warrant was the linchpin of the whole scheme. The Court rejected the argument that the use of "reasonable grounds" in s. 231.3 rather than "reasonable and probable grounds" did not meet the requirements of s. 8 of the Charter. The *Hunter* standard was one of credibly based probability. The standard to be met in order to establish reasonable grounds for a search was "reasonable probability". The Court also rejected the argument that the section's requirement that the authorizing judge be satisfied that a document or thing which "may afford evidence of the commission of the offence" is "likely to be found" violated s. 8. This formulation did not make the standard the possibility of finding evidence and met the "credibly based probability" standard required by s. 8. The use of the word "may" regarding the use of the thing found as evidence in a prosecution simply reflected one of the realities of the investigation of offences. It was impossible to know with certainly at an early stage in any investigation what particular items will provide evidence in a trial. Although the Court purports not to be weakening the *Hunter* standard, it may well have done so.

In *R. v. Jarvis*, [2002] 3 S.C.R. 757, 6 C.R. (6th) 23, 169 C.C.C. (3d) 1 (S.C.C.), a case of income tax evasion contrary to the Income Tax Act, Justices Iacobucci and Major held for the Court that an inquiry by an auditor "crossed the Rubicon" when the predominant purpose became that of a prosecution. From that point, the full Charter protections were to be applied.

See David Stratas, "Crossing the Rubicon: The Supreme Court and Regulatory Investigations", (2003) 6 C.R. (6th) 74.

In the following four decisions the Supreme Court decided that there was no reasonable expectation of privacy and therefore no s. 8 protection, or, in the school search case of *R. v. M. (M.R.)*, reduced expectation of privacy leading to reduced s. 8 protection. In each case consider whether you agree with the Court's approach.

R. v. EDWARDS
[1996] 1 S.C.R. 128, 45 C.R. (4th) 307, 104 C.C.C. (3d) 136 (S.C.C.)

The accused had been convicted of possessing cocaine for the purposes of trafficking. The police had been told that he was a drug dealer operating out of his car using a cellular phone and a pager, and that he had the drugs on his person, at his residence or at his girlfriend's, S.E.'s, apartment. The police saw the accused drive S.E.'s vehicle to her apartment, enter and leave after a brief stay. The police knew his licence was under suspension and arrested him for this offence. When they approached the vehicle they saw the accused swallow an object wrapped in cellophane about the size of a golf ball. The police suspected that there might be cocaine in S.E.'s apartment but did not consider that they had reasonable grounds for a warrant. Two officers later called on her and gained her cooperation through a number of statements, some of which were lies and half-truths. Once inside, the accused's girlfriend directed them to the location of a significant cache of drugs. She was arrested a short time later but the charges against her were later dropped. At no time prior to being taken into custody was she advised of her right to refuse entry to the police or of her right to counsel. At the police station, she gave a statement naming the accused as the person who put the drugs in her apartment. At trial and on appeal, the accused denied being the owner of the drugs. The accused's appeal from conviction was dismissed with a dissenting opinion by Abella J.A. which found a reasonable expectation of privacy giving rise to the possibility of an infringement of his s. 8 Charter rights against unreasonable search or seizure. The majority of the Supreme Court dismissed the further appeal.

CORY J. (Lamer C.J., Sopinka, McLachlin, Iacobucci and Major JJ. concurring):

. . .

The Appellant's Reasonable Expectation of Privacy in Relation to Ms. Evers' Apartment

In *Hunter v. Southam Inc.*, [1984] 2 S.C.R. 145, Dickson J. writing for the Court, emphatically rejected any requirement of a connection between the rights protected by s. 8 and a property interest in the premises searched. He quoted with approval at pp. 158-59 the statement of Stewart J., delivering the majority opinion of the United States Supreme Court in *Katz v. United States*,

389 U.S. 347 (1967), at p. 351, that "the Fourth Amendment protects people, not places". Dickson J. held that this applied equally to construing s. 8.

While Dickson J. advocated a broad general right to be secure from unreasonable search and seizure, he stressed that it only protected a "reasonable expectation of privacy". He stated at pp. 159-60 that the limiting term "reasonable" implied that:

> an assessment must be made as to whether in a particular situation the public's interest in being left alone by government must give way to the government's interest in intruding on the individual's privacy in order to advance its goals, notably those of law enforcement.

It has since been determined that this assessment must be made in light of the totality of the circumstances of a particular case. I would, as well, observe that in *R. v. Plant*, [1993] 3 S.C.R. 281, at p. 291, it was held that it is not necessary for an accused to establish a possessory interest in the goods seized before seeking to enforce rights guaranteed under s. 8.

It is important to emphasize that generally, the decision as to whether an accused had a reasonable expectation of privacy must be made without reference to the conduct of the police during the impugned search. There are two distinct questions which must be answered in any s. 8 challenge. The first is whether the accused had a reasonable expectation of privacy. The second is whether the search was an unreasonable intrusion on that right to privacy. Usually, the conduct of the police will only be relevant when consideration is given to this second stage. In any determination of a s. 8 challenge, it is of fundamental importance to remember that the privacy right allegedly infringed must, as a general rule, be that of the accused person who makes the challenge. This has been stressed by the United States Supreme Court in several cases dealing with searches that allegedly violated the Fourth Amendment guarantee. In *Alderman v. United States*, 394 U.S.165 (1969), for example, White J., delivering the judgment of the majority, stated at pp. 171-72 that:

> [the] suppression of the product of a Fourth Amendment violation can be successfully *urged only by those whose rights were violated by the search itself, not by those who are aggrieved solely by the introduction of damaging evidence.* [Emphasis added.]

. . .

The intrusion on the privacy rights of a third party may however be relevant in the second stage of the s. 8 analysis, namely whether the search was conducted in a reasonable manner. The reasons in *R. v. Thompson*, [1990] 2 S.C.R. 1111, considered this question. At issue was a wiretap authorization which allowed the police to eavesdrop on several public pay telephones that were often used by the appellant as well as other members of the public. The appellants argued that the failure of the authorizing judge to limit the intrusion on those third-party users rendered the search unreasonable. Sopinka J. agreed and stated at p. 1143:

> In my view, the extent of invasion into the privacy of these third parties is constitutionally relevant to the issue of whether there has been an "unreasonable" search or seizure. To hold otherwise would be to ignore the purpose of s. 8 of the Charter which is to restrain invasion of privacy within reasonable limits. A

potentially massive invasion of the privacy of persons not involved in the activity being investigated cannot be ignored simply because it is not brought to the attention of the court by one of those persons. Since those persons are unlikely to know of the invasion of their privacy, such invasions would escape scrutiny, and s. 8 would not fulfil its purpose.

It is important to observe that Sopinka J. was careful to point out that the invasion of third-party privacy rights is not determinative of the reasonableness of the search. He put it in this way at pp. 1143-44:

> In any authorization there is the possibility of invasion of privacy of innocent third parties. For instance a wiretap placed on the home telephone of a target will record communications by other members of the household. This is an unfortunate cost of electronic surveillance. But it is one which Parliament has obviously judged is justified in appropriate circumstances in the investigation of serious crime.

In what may be somewhat rare circumstances, the extent of the invasion of privacy may be constitutionally relevant. This was the case in *Thompson*, supra, where the actions of the police were judged at p. 1143 as a "potentially massive invasion of . . . privacy" of members of the general public who were not involved in the suspected criminal activity. In the case at bar, there is no need to consider the reasonableness of the search since the appellant has not established the requisite expectation of privacy. Even if it were necessary to consider the invasion of the privacy of Ms. Evers, I would conclude that there was neither a potentially massive invasion of property nor a flagrant abuse of individual's right to privacy.

. . .

In the case at bar, one of the bases upon which the appellant asserted his right to privacy in Ms. Evers' apartment was his interest in the drugs. It is possible, in certain circumstances, to establish an expectation of privacy in the goods that are seized. . . . However, this contention cannot be raised in the circumstances of this case. At trial, the appellant denied that the drugs were his and Ms. Evers testified that they might have belonged to someone else. The appellant maintained in the Court of Appeal that the drugs were not his. It was only in this Court that he acknowledged for the first time that the drugs were his. He should not now be permitted to change his position with regard to a fundamentally important aspect of the evidence in order to put forward a fresh argument which could not be considered in the courts below. The result in this appeal must turn solely on the appellant's privacy interest in Ms. Evers' apartment.

A review of the recent decisions of this Court and those of the U.S. Supreme Court, which I find convincing and properly applicable to the situation presented in the case at bar, indicates that certain principles pertaining to the nature of the s. 8 right to be secure against unreasonable search or seizure can be derived. In my view, they may be summarized in the following manner:

1.   A claim for relief under s. 24(2) can only be made by the person whose Charter rights have been infringed. See *R. v. Rahey*, [1987] 1 S.C.R. 588, at p. 619.

2.   Like all Charter rights, s. 8 is a personal right. It protects people and not places. See *Hunter*, supra.

3.   The right to challenge the legality of a search depends upon the accused establishing that his personal rights to privacy have been violated. See *Pugliese*, supra.

4.   As a general rule, two distinct inquiries must be made in relation to s. 8. First, has the accused a reasonable expectation of privacy. Second, if he has such an expectation, was the search by the police conducted reasonably. See *Rawlings*, supra.

5.   A reasonable expectation of privacy is to be determined on the basis of the totality of the circumstances. See *Colarusso*, supra, at p. 54, and *Wong*, supra, at p. 62.

6.   The factors to be considered in assessing the totality of the circumstances may include, but are not restricted to, the following:
   (i)   presence at the time of the search;
   (ii)   possession or control of the property or place searched;
   (iii) ownership of the property or place;
   (iv)   historical use of the property or item;
   (v)   the ability to regulate access, including the right to admit or exclude others from the place;
   (vi)   the existence of a subjective expectation of privacy; and (vii)the objective reasonableness of the expectation.

See *United States v. Gomez*, 16 F.3d 254 (8th Cir. 1994), at p. 256.

7.   If an accused person establishes a reasonable expectation of privacy, the inquiry must proceed to the second stage to determine whether the search was conducted in a reasonable manner.

Taking all the circumstances of this case into account, it is my view that the appellant has not demonstrated that he had an expectation of privacy in Ms. Evers' apartment. While the factors set out in *Gomez*, supra, are helpful, they are certainly not exhaustive and indeed other factors may be determinative in a particular case. Nonetheless, it is significant that, apart from a history of use of Ms. Evers' apartment, the appellant cannot comply with any of the other factors listed in *Gomez*, supra.

There are, as well, several factors which specifically militate against a finding that the appellant had any reasonable expectation of privacy in the apartment. First, Ms. Evers stated in her testimony that the appellant was "just a visitor" who stayed over occasionally. As McKinlay J.A. found (in the Court below) "he was no more than an especially privileged guest" who "took advantage of Ms. Evers by making use of her premises to conceal a substantial quantity of illegal drugs". Second, although the appellant kept a few personal belongings at the apartment, he did not contribute to the rent or household expenses save for his alleged assistance of Ms. Evers in the purchase of a couch.

Third, although only he and Ms. Evers had keys to the apartment, the appellant lacked the authority to regulate access to the premises. In the words of McKinlay J.A., "Ms. Evers could admit anyone to the apartment whom the appellant wished to exclude, and could exclude anyone he wished to admit". An important aspect of privacy is the ability to exclude others from the premises. This is apparent from one of the definitions of the word "privacy" found in The Oxford English Dictionary (2nd ed. 1989). It is set out in these terms:

> The state or condition of being alone, undisturbed, or free from public attention, as a matter of choice or right; freedom from interference or intrusion.

The right to be free from intrusion or interference is a key element of privacy. It follows that the fact that the appellant could not be free from intrusion or interference in Ms. Evers' apartment is a very important factor in confirming the finding that he did not have a reasonable expectation of privacy. He was no more than a privileged guest.

Since no personal right of the appellant was affected by the police conduct at the apartment, the appellant could not contest the admissibility of the evidence pursuant to s. 24(2) of the Charter. It is therefore not necessary to consider either this aspect of the case or whether Ms. Evers did in fact consent to the search of her apartment. This is, in itself, a sufficient basis for dismissing the appeal.

However, the appellant has argued that automatic standing should be granted to challenge the search of a third party's premises in those circumstances where the Crown alleges that the accused is in possession of the property which was discovered and seized. The United States Supreme Court has resiled from its earlier position on this issue. See *Jones v. United States*, 362 U.S. 257 (1960). In *Salvucci*, supra, and in *Rawlings*, supra, it was determined that the correct approach to asserting Fourth Amendment rights was to satisfy the "legitimate expectation of privacy test".

Not only has the United States Supreme Court rejected the automatic standing rule, but so too have the great majority of state courts. Further, the adaptation of the automatic standing rule would seem to fly in the face the wording of s. 24 of the Charter.

As I noted earlier, s. 24(2) provides remedies only to applicants whose *own* Charter rights have been infringed. . . . The reasonable expectation of privacy concept has worked well in Canada. It has proved to be reasonable, flexible, and viable. I can see no reason for abandoning it in favour of the discredited rule of automatic standing.

In the result, I would dismiss the appeal and confirm the order of the Court of Appeal upholding the conviction of the appellant.

LA FOREST J.: — While I agree with the conclusion arrived at by my colleagues, I do so for quite different reasons than those espoused by the majority. With these I am in profound disagreement. I am deeply concerned with the implications of these reasons which, I think, result in a drastic diminution of the protection to the public s. 8 of the Canadian Charter of Rights and Freedoms was intended to ensure.

. . .

As I see it, the protection accorded by s. 8 is not in its terms limited to searches of premises over which an accused has a personal right to privacy in the sense of some direct control or property. Rather the provision is intended to afford protection to all of us to be secure against intrusion by the state or its agents by unreasonable searches or seizures, and is not solely for the protection of criminals even though the most effective remedy will inevitably protect the criminal as the price of liberty for all. The section, it must be remembered, reads: "*Everyone has the right to be secure* against unreasonable search or seizure" (emphasis added). It is a right enuring to all the public. . . . It is important for everyone, not only an accused, that police (or what is even more dangerous for the public, other agents of the state) do not break into private premises without warrant.

. . .

From this, it seems, the majority agrees, that at least in "somewhat rare circumstances" the extent of invasion of privacy of members of the public may be constitutionally relevant. I have no doubt that it is relevant and, in my view, the cases are not confined to massive invasions of privacy but to other situations where one can reasonably conclude that the public right to be secure against unreasonable search and seizure has been infringed. The wilful and forcible breaking in of the home of a person other than the accused would appear to me to be a candidate for consideration. A stronger case would be a break-in by state agents for less compelling reasons than criminal law enforcement. Not to accept this point of view is to accord greater protection to the right of privacy to the accused or other wrongdoer than to a person against whom there may be no reasonable suspicion of wrongdoing. That seems to me to turn the citizen's Charter right to be left alone on its head. We exercise discretion to exclude evidence obtained by unconstitutional searches from being used against an accused, even when it would clearly establish guilt, not to protect criminals but because the only really effective safeguard for the protection of the constitutional right we all share is not to allow use of evidence obtained in violation of this public right when doing so would bring the administration of justice into disrepute. There are other remedies such as trespass, it is true, but these are not constitutional remedies and they are not equal to the task.

L'HEUREUX-DUBÉ J.: — Although I substantially agree with Justice Cory's reasons and the result he reaches, I have some concern about the issue of the relevance of a breach of a third-party Charter right in the context of this case. Since this is an appeal as of right, that issue, in my view, does not arise.

GONTHIER J.: — I concur with Justice La Forest that the appeal be dismissed as not properly before us as of right. The dissent in the Court of Appeal was as to whether the accused had a reasonable expectation of privacy. I share the views of Justice Cory that he did not. I refrain from commenting on the other issues referred to by my colleagues.

For a comment see Ursula Hendel and Peter Sankoff, "When Two Wrongs Might Make A Right", (1996) 45 C.R. (4th) 330.

R. v. M. (M.R.)
[1998] 3 S.C.R. 393, 20 C.R. (5th) 197, 129 C.C.C. (3d) 361 (S.C.C.)

C, the vice-principal of a high school, was in charge of enforcing school policies mandated by the school and county school board. According to these policies, a student in possession of drugs on school property was to be suspended and the police called. Prior to a school dance, C received information from a number of students that M, a 13-year-old junior high school student, was selling drugs on school property and that it was believed that he would be carrying drugs to the dance. When C saw M arrive at the dance he called a police officer to come to the school. Before the officer arrived, C asked M to come to his office. He closed the office door and asked the student whether he had drugs. He said he would search him. At that point the plain clothes officer arrived and spoke briefly with C outside the office. He entered the office with C and identified himself. M stood up and turned out the inside lining of his pants pocket. C noticed a bulge in M's sock. He removed a cellophane bag and gave it to the officer who identified the contents as marijuana. The officer then arrested him for possession of a narcotic and advised him of his rights.

CORY J. (Lamer C.J. and L'Heureux-Dubé, Gonthier, McLachlin, Iacobucci, Bastarache and Binnie JJ. concurring): —

Analysis

A. APPLICATION OF THE CHARTER

(1) Application of the Charter to Public School Authorities

At the outset it must be determined whether the Charter applies to the actions of the vice-principal. The courts below assumed that it does, as have other courts in similar circumstances. The respondent in this appeal did not dispute that the Charter should apply, arguing only that the Charter analysis should take into account the school context. The appellant submitted that the Charter applies because the school board, schools and their employees are part of the apparatus of government, according to the test set out by this Court in *McKinney v. University of Guelph*, [1990] 3 S.C.R. 229. . . . In light of the concession made by the respondent it would be best to assume simply, for the purposes of this case, that schools constitute part of government and as a result the Charter applies to the actions of the vice-principal.

(2) Was the Vice-Principal Acting as an Agent of the Police?

The trial judge in this case also found that the vice-principal was acting as an agent of the police. This finding, if accepted, would not only provide an alternative basis for the application of the Charter but would also affect the analysis of the alleged violations. The appellant submits that the finding of the trial judge on this issue should not be disturbed. Generally, a finding such as this would not be interfered with by an appellate court. However, in this case, the evidence adduced cannot support that finding and it should not be accepted.

It is clear that Mr. Cadue cooperated with the police. He was aware that if drugs were found it would be a criminal matter as well as a matter of school discipline, and that it was the policy of the school to contact the police in such a case. He called the police before beginning the search and permitted an officer to observe as he conducted the search. When the marijuana was found, it was handed over to Constable Siepierski, who arrested the appellant and conducted a further search of the appellant's locker.

The mere fact that there was cooperation between the vice-principal and the police and that an officer was present during the search is not sufficient to indicate that the vice-principal was acting as an agent of the police. The trial judge stated that there was an "agreed strategy" between Mr. Cadue and Constable Siepierski that resulted in Mr. Cadue's acting as a police agent. With respect, there is no evidence to support this conclusion. There is no evidence of an agreement or of police instructions to Mr. Cadue that could create an agency relationship.

. . .

B. WERE THE RIGHTS OF THE APPELLANT UNDER SECTION 8 OF THE CHARTER VIOLATED?

(1) Reasonable Expectation of Privacy

Did the appellant have, in the circumstances presented, a reasonable expectation of privacy, and if he did, what was the extent of that expectation?... The factors to be considered in assessing the circumstances may include the accused's presence at the time of the search, possession or control of the property or place searched, ownership of the property or place, historical use of the property or item, ability to regulate access, existence of a subjective expectation of privacy, and the objective reasonableness of the expectation.

Here the search was of the appellant's person. In the circumstances it is obvious that some of the factors referred to in *Edwards* are not applicable. However, the existence of a subjective expectation of privacy and the objective reasonableness of that expectation remain important. It is also necessary to consider the context in which the search took place. Here the appellant was a student at the school, attending a school function held on school property. The search was carried out by the school authority responsible for supervision of that function. Considering all these factors, did the appellant have a reasonable expectation of privacy with respect to his person and the items he carried on his person? In my view he did. A student attending school would have a subjective expectation that his privacy, at least with respect to his body, would be respected. In light of the heightened privacy interest that has historically been recognized in one's person, a subjective expectation of privacy in that respect is reasonable. I do not think that this expectation is rendered unreasonable merely by virtue of a student's presence in a school. It follows that the appellant did have a reasonable expectation of privacy in that regard, with the result that s. 8 is engaged.

However, the reasonable expectation of privacy, although it exists, may be diminished in some circumstances, and this will influence the analysis of s. 8 and a consideration of what constitutes an unreasonable search or seizure. For example, it has been found that individuals have a lesser expectation of privacy at border crossings, because they know they may be subject to questioning and searches to enforce customs laws (see *Simmons*). It was because of this lesser expectation of privacy, that a customs search did not have to meet the standards in *Hunter v. Southam Inc.*, [1984] 2 S.C.R. 145, in order to be reasonable. Similarly, the reasonable expectation of privacy of a student in attendance at a school is certainly less than it would be in other circumstances. Students know that their teachers and other school authorities are responsible for providing a safe environment and maintaining order and discipline in the school. They must know that this may sometimes require searches of students and their personal effects and the seizure of prohibited items. It would not be reasonable for a student to expect to be free from such searches. A student's reasonable expectation of privacy in the school environment is therefore significantly diminished.

(2) Standard to Be Applied to Searches by School Authorities

(a) Is a Different Standard Required?

Teachers and principals are placed in a position of trust that carries with it onerous responsibilities. When children attend school or school functions, it is they who must care for the children's safety and well-being. It is they who must carry out the fundamentally important task of teaching children so that they can function in our society and fulfil their potential. In order to teach, school officials must provide an atmosphere that encourages learning. During the school day they must protect and teach our children. In no small way, teachers and principals are responsible for the future of the country.

It is essential that our children be taught and that they learn. Yet, without an orderly environment learning will be difficult if not impossible. In recent years, problems which threaten the safety of students and the fundamentally important task of teaching have increased in their numbers and gravity. The possession of illicit drugs and dangerous weapons in the schools has increased to the extent that they challenge the ability of school officials to fulfil their responsibility to maintain a safe and orderly environment. Current conditions make it necessary to provide teachers and school administrators with the flexibility required to deal with discipline problems in schools. They must be able to act quickly and effectively to ensure the safety of students and to prevent serious violations of school rules.

One of the ways in which school authorities may be required to react reasonably to discipline problems is by conducting searches of students and to seize prohibited items. Possession of items which are prohibited by school policy may, in some cases, also constitute or provide evidence of a criminal offence. As a result items found in a search by a school authority may be sought to be used as evidence in a criminal trial. The question then arises whether evidence found by a teacher or principal should potentially be excluded because the search would have been unreasonable if it had been conducted by police.

. . .

(b) What Standard Should Be Applied?

The general rule, established by this Court in *Hunter*, supra, is that in order to be reasonable, a search requires prior authorization, usually in the form of a warrant, from a neutral arbiter. According to this rule, a search conducted without prior authorization is prima facie unreasonable. However, the Court recognized in *Hunter* that "it may not be reasonable in every instance to insist on prior authorization". It was acknowledged that it might be appropriate to dispense with the warrant requirement in situations where it is not feasible to obtain prior authorization.

In my opinion the search of a student by a school authority is just such a situation where it would not be feasible to require that a warrant or any other prior authorization be obtained for the search. To require a warrant would clearly be impractical and unworkable in the school environment. Teachers and administrators must be able to respond quickly and effectively to problems that arise in their school. When a school official conducts a search of or seizure from a student, a warrant is not required. The absence of a warrant in these circumstances will not lead to a presumption that the search was unreasonable.

The other basic principle enunciated in the Hunter decision was that a reasonable search must be based on reasonable and probable grounds. It was held that "[t]he state's interest in detecting and preventing crime begins to prevail over the individual's interest in being left alone at the point where credibly-based probability replaces suspicion". Therefore, "reasonable and probable grounds . . . to believe that an offence has been committed and that there is evidence to be found at the place of the search, constitutes the minimum standard, consistent with s. 8 of the Charter, for authorizing search and seizure". The requirement of reasonable and probable grounds has been maintained subject only to very limited exceptions (e.g., search incident to arrest; see *Cloutier v. Langlois*, [1990] 1 S.C.R. 158.

Yet teachers and principals must be able to act quickly to protect their students and to provide the orderly atmosphere required for learning. If a teacher were told that a student was carrying a dangerous weapon or sharing a dangerous prohibited drug the parents of all the other students at the school would expect the teacher to search that student. The role of teachers is such that they must have the power to search. Indeed students should be aware that they must comply with school regulations and as a result that they will be subject to reasonable searches. It follows that their expectation of privacy will be lessened while they attend school or a school function. This reduced expectation of privacy coupled with the need to protect students and provide a positive atmosphere for learning clearly indicate that a more lenient and flexible approach should be taken to searches conducted by teachers and principals than would apply to searches conducted by the police.

A search by school officials of a student under their authority may be undertaken if there are reasonable grounds to believe that a school rule has been or is being violated, and that evidence of the violation will be found in the location or on the person of the student searched. Searches undertaken in situations where the health and safety of students is involved may well require different considerations. All the circumstances surrounding a search must be taken into account in determining if the search is reasonable.

School authorities must be accorded a reasonable degree of discretion and flexibility to enable them to ensure the safety of their students and to enforce school regulations. Ordinarily, school authorities will be in the best position to evaluate the information they receive. As a result of their training, background and experience, they will be in the best possible position to assess both the propensity and credibility of their students and to relate the information they receive to the situation existing in their particular school. For these reasons, courts should recognize the preferred position of school authorities to determine whether reasonable grounds existed for the search.

. . .

The approach to be taken in considering searches by teachers may be summarized in this manner:

(1)   A warrant is not essential in order to conduct a search of a student by a school authority.

(2)   The school authority must have reasonable grounds to believe that there has been a breach of school regulations or discipline and that a search of a student would reveal evidence of that breach.

(3)   School authorities will be in the best position to assess information given to them and relate it to the situation existing in their school. Courts should recognize the preferred position of school authorities to determine if reasonable grounds existed for the search.

(4)   The following may constitute reasonable grounds in this context: information received from one student considered to be credible, information received from more than one student, a teacher's or principal's own observations, or any combination of these pieces of information which the relevant authority considers to be credible. The compelling nature of the information and the credibility of these or other sources must be assessed by the school authority in the context of the circumstances existing at the particular school.

If this approach is followed it will permit school authorities to fashion remedies that are efficacious and flexible.

(c)   The Search Must Be Reasonable

If it is to be reasonable the search must be conducted reasonably and must be authorized by a statutory provision which is itself reasonable. There is no specific authorization to search provided in the Education Act, R.S.N.S. 1989, or its regulations. Nonetheless, the responsibility placed upon teachers, and principals to maintain proper order and discipline in the school and to attend to the health and comfort of students by necessary implication authorizes searches of students. See s. 54(b) and Regulation 3(7) and (9). Teachers must be able to search students if they are to fulfil the statutory duties imposed upon them. It is reasonable, if not essential to provide teachers and principals with this authorization to search. It is now necessary to consider the circumstances in which the search itself may be considered to be reasonable.

. . .

The factors to be considered in determining whether a search conducted by a teacher or principal in the school environment was reasonable can be summarized in this manner:

(1)   The first step is to determine whether it can be inferred from the provisions of the relevant Education Act that teachers and principals are authorized to conduct searches of their students in appropriate circumstances. In the school environment such a statutory authorization would be reasonable.

(2)   The search itself must be carried out in a reasonable manner. It should be conducted in a sensitive manner and be minimally intrusive.

(3)   In order to determine whether a search was reasonable, all the surrounding circumstances will have to be considered.

(d)   When and to Whom Does This Standard Apply?

This modified standard for reasonable searches should apply to searches of students on school property conducted by teachers or school officials within the scope of their responsibility and authority to maintain order, discipline and safety within the school. This standard will not apply to any actions taken which are beyond the scope of the authority of teachers or principals.

. . .

(3) Application to This Case

Was the search conducted in this case unreasonable? In my view it was not. As a result, there was no infringement of the appellant's rights under s. 8 of the Charter.

MAJOR J. (dissenting):—I agree with many of the conclusions reached by Cory J.

In particular, I agree that the actions of school officials as an extension of government are subject to the Canadian Charter of Rights and Freedoms. I agree that a student on school property has an expectation of privacy sufficient to engage s. 8 but that expectation is and should be lower than a member of the general public. . .

I do not agree with Cory J. in his conclusion that the Nova Scotia Court of Appeal was correct in reversing the trial judge and concluding that the vice-principal in this appeal was not acting as an agent of the police at the time he conducted the search of the appellant. The trial judge had found that the vice-principal at the critical time was acting as an agent of the police. There was evidence upon which the trial judge could reach that conclusion and neither the Court of Appeal of Nova Scotia or this Court should interfere with that finding. In the result, it is my opinion that the vice-principal, if acting as vice-principal, could have lawfully conducted the search he did. However, as he was acting as an agent of the police, the search as conducted required the appellant to be given his Charter protections.

These reasons will not interfere with the safe and orderly operation of schools. The risk of physical harm and the prevalence of alcohol and illegal drugs at some schools is a sad but well-known fact. The school staff have the ability to deal with these problems. If they elect to involve the police, which in many cases would be prudent, and if in doing so they elect to become agents of the police then the procedures prescribed for police investigations have to be followed.

. . .

———————

For a review of *M. (M.R.)*, see Stuart, "Reducing Charter Rights of Children", (1999) 20 C.R. (5th) 230. Applying *M.(M.R.)*, Himel J. in *Gillies (Litigation guardian of) v. Toronto District School Board*, 2015 ONSC 1038, 23 C.R. (7th) 400 (Ont. S.C.J.), decided that a school principal violated s. 8 in setting up a mandatory breathalyser test as a pre-condition of entry to a high school prom. There was no lawful authority, no consent by the individual in question, and the search had been conducted in an unreasonable manner.

R. v. TESSLING
[2004] 3 S.C.R. 432, 23 C.R. (6th) 207, 189 C.C.C. (3d) 129 (S.C.C.)

The R.C.M.P., relying on information from two confidential sources, investigated whether the accused and another, "I", were involved in a marijuana growing operation. Information provided by Hydro Ontario did not point to any unusual hydro usage at any of the properties owned by the suspects. Visual surveillance of their residences also revealed nothing.

The police then used an airplane equipped with a Forward Looking Infra-Red ("FLIR") camera to conduct a "structure profile" of the properties owned by the suspects to detect heat emanating from buildings. The FLIR takes a picture or image of the thermal energy or heat radiating from the exterior of a building. It can detect heat sources within a home depending on the location of the source, and how well the house is insulated, but it cannot identify the exact nature of that source or see through the external surfaces of the building. The use of FLIR technology is based on the operative theory that while heat usually emanates evenly from a building, the lights used in marijuana growing operations give off an unusual amount of heat. The FLIR camera in this case indicated that the accused's property and one of the properties owned by I had the heat emanations potentially indicative of a marijuana growing operation. Based on this information and that of the informants, the police obtained a search warrant for the accused's home. The search found a large quantity of marijuana, two sets of scales, and freezer bags and some weapons.

At trial the accused was convicted of drug trafficking and weapons charges. A motion to exclude the evidence on the basis that the warrant was unlawful and violated s. 8 of the Charter of Rights and Freedoms was dismissed.

The Ontario Court of Appeal allowed the appeal and substituted an acquittal. For the Court, Abella J.A. held (O'Connor A.C.J. and Sharpe J.A. concurring) that the use of FLIR technology to detect heat emanations from a private home constitutes a search and requires prior judicial authorization under s. 8 of the Charter, absent exigent circumstances. There had been a serious violation of s. 8 of the Charter and furthermore the evidence should be excluded under s. 24(2). The Crown appealed.

Seven justices of the Supreme Court of Canada allowed the appeal and restored the conviction.

BINNIE J.:—

. . .

The midnight knock on the door is the nightmare image of the police State. Thus it was in 1763 that in a speech before the British Parliament, William Pitt (the Elder) famously extolled the right of everyone to exclude from his private domain the forces of the King:

> The poorest man may in his cottage bid defiance to all the forces of the crown. It may be frail - its roof may shake - the wind may blow through it - the storm may enter - the rain may enter - but the King of England cannot enter! - all his force dares not cross the threshold of the ruined tenement! (Lord H. Brougham, Historical Sketches of Statesmen Who Flourished in the Time of George III (1855), vol. I, at p. 42).

It is perhaps a long spiritual journey from Pitt's ringing pronouncements to the respondent's attempt to shelter a marijuana grow-op in the basement of his home in Kingsville, Ontario, but the principle is the same. Building upon the foundation laid by the common law, s. 8 of the Charter creates for "[e]veryone" certain areas of personal autonomy where "all the forces of the Crown" cannot enter. These areas we have now gathered up under the general heading of privacy, although in *Hunter v. Southam Inc.*, [1984] 2 S.C.R. 145, at p. 159, Dickson J., as he then was, was careful not to foreclose the existence of s. 8 "interests beyond the right of privacy", saying:

> Like the Supreme Court of the United States, I would be wary of foreclosing the possibility that the right to be secure against unreasonable search and seizure might protect interests beyond the right of privacy, but for purposes of the present appeal I am satisfied that its protections go at least that far.

Much of the law in this area betrays its early roots in the law of trespass. In an earlier era, privacy was associated with private property, whose possession protected against intruders. If the rights of private property were respected, and the curtains of the home (or the drawbridge of the castle) were pulled, the King's agents could watch from a distance but would have no way of finding out what was going on inside. As technology developed, the protection offered by property rights diminished. Wiretaps, for example, require no physical intrusion, but can be implemented at a distance. FLIR images can be taken from an airplane. The courts were reluctant to accept the idea that, as technology developed, the sphere of protection for private life must shrink. Instead, it was recognized that the rights of private property were to some extent a proxy for the privacy that ownership of property originally conferred, and therefore, as the State's technical capacity for peeking and snooping increased, the idea of a protected sphere of privacy was refined and developed. The perspective adopted by the Court in *Hunter v. Southam, supra,* accordingly, is that s. 8 "protects people, not places" (at p. 159). See also *R. v. Thompson,* [1990] 2 S.C.R. 1111, at p. 1142.

A. Striking the Balance

At the same time, social and economic life creates competing demands. The community wants privacy but it also insists on protection. Safety, security and the suppression of crime are legitimate countervailing concerns. Thus s. 8 of the Charter accepts the validity of reasonable searches and seizures. A balance must be struck, as held in *Hunter v. Southam, supra* , at pp. 159-60 . . .

The notion of the "balance" was also canvassed by Sopinka J. in advocating "a contextual approach" in *R. v. Plant,* [1993] 3 S.C.R. 281, at p. 293:

> Consideration of such factors as the nature of the information itself, the nature of the relationship between the party releasing the information and the party claiming its confidentiality, the place where the information was obtained, the manner in which it was obtained and the seriousness of the crime being investigated allows for a balancing of the societal interests in protecting individual dignity, integrity and autonomy with effective law enforcement.

In the result the right to be free from examination by the State is subject to constitutionally permissible limitations. First, "not every form of examination conducted by the government will constitute a 'search' for constitutional purposes. On the contrary, only where those state examinations constitute an intrusion upon some reasonable privacy interest of individuals does the government action in question constitute a 'search' within the meaning of s. 8"; *Evans, supra,* at para. 11. It is only "[i]f the police activity invades a reasonable expectation of privacy, [that] the activity is a search"; *R. v. Wise,* [1992] 1 S.C.R. 527, at p. 533. Second, as the language of s. 8 implies, even those investigations that are "searches" are permissible if they are "reasonable". A search will not offend s. 8 if it is authorized by a reasonable law and carried out in a reasonable manner: *R. v. Caslake,* [1998] 1 S.C.R. 51; *R. v. Collins,* [1987] 1 S.C.R. 265.

B. The Reasonable Expectation of Privacy

Accordingly, the Court early on established a purposive approach to s. 8 in which privacy became the dominant organizing principle. "The guarantee of security from unreasonable search and seizure only protects a <u>reasonable</u> expectation": *Hunter v. Southam, supra,* at p. 159 (emphasis in original). Given the bewildering array of different techniques available to the police (either existing or under development), the alternative approach of a judicial "catalogue" of what is or is not permitted by s. 8 is scarcely feasible. The principled approach was carried forward in *R. v. Edwards,* [1996] 1 S.C.R. 128, at para. 45, where Cory J., referring to the need to consider "the totality of the circumstances", laid particular emphasis on (1) the existence of a subjective expectation of privacy; and (2) the objective reasonableness of the expectation.

Within the general principle thus stated, the cases have come to distinguish among a number of privacy interests protected by s. 8. These include personal privacy, territorial privacy and informational privacy.

Privacy of the person perhaps has the strongest claim to constitutional shelter because it protects bodily integrity, and in particular the right not to have our bodies touched or explored to disclose objects or matters we wish to conceal. The State cannot conduct warrantless strip searches unless they are incident to a lawful arrest and performed in a reasonable manner *R. v. Golden*, [2001] 3 S.C.R. 679, 2001 SCC 83, at paras. 90-92) in circumstances where the police have reasonable and probable grounds for concluding that a strip search is necessary in the particular circumstances of the arrest (para. 98). Nor may the police take bodily samples without authorization; *R. v. Stillman*, [1997] 1 S.C.R. 607.

The original notion of territorial privacy ("the house of everyone is to him as his castle and fortress": *Semayne's Case* (1604), [1558-1774] All E.R. Rep. 62, at p. 63) developed into a more nuanced hierarchy protecting privacy in the home, being the place where our most intimate and private activities are most likely to take place [*Evans, supra*], at para. 42; *R. v. Silveira*, [1995] 2 S.C.R. 297, at para. 140, per Cory J.: "There is no place on earth where persons can have a greater expectation of privacy than within their 'dwelling-house'": *R. v. Feeney*, [1997] 2 S.C.R. 13, at para. 43), in diluted measure, in the perimeter space around the home (*R. v. Kokesch*, [1990] 3 S.C.R. 3; *R. v. Grant*, [1993] 3 S.C.R. 223, at pp. 237 and 241; *R. v. Wiley*, [1993] 3 S.C.R. 263, at p. 273), in commercial space *Thomson Newspapers Ltd. v. Canada (Director of Investigation and Research, Restrictive Trade Practices Commission)*, [1990] 1 S.C.R. 425, at p. 517-519 . . . in private cars (*Wise, supra*, at p. 533; *R. v. Mellenthin*, [1992] 3 S.C.R. 615), in a school (*R. v. M. (M.R.)*, [1998] 3 S.C.R. 393, at para. 32), and even, at the bottom of the spectrum, a prison (*Weatherall v. Canada (Attorney General)*, [1993] 2 S.C.R. 872, at p. 877). Such a hierarchy of places does not contradict the underlying principle that s. 8 protects "people, not places", but uses the notion of place as an analytical tool to evaluate the <u>reasonableness</u> of a person's expectation of privacy. Beyond our bodies and the places where we live and work, however, lies the thorny question of how much information about ourselves and activities we are entitled to shield from the curious eyes of the State (*R. v. S.A.B.*, [2003] 2 S.C.R. 678, 2003 SCC 60). This includes commercial information locked in a safe kept in a restaurant owned by the accused (*R. v. Law*, [2002] 1 S.C.R. 227, 2002 SCC 10, at para. 16). Informational privacy has been defined as "the claim of individuals, groups, or institutions to determine for themselves when, how, and to what extent information about them is communicated to others": A. F. Westin, *Privacy and Freedom* [New York: Atheneum] (1970), at p. 7. Its protection is predicated on:

> [T]he assumption that all information about a person is in a fundamental way his own, for him to communicate or retain . . . as he sees fit. (Report of a Task Force

established jointly by Department of Communications/Department of Justice, Privacy and Computers (1972), at p. 13)

The distinction between personal, territorial and informational privacy provides useful analytical tools, but of course in a given case, the privacy interest may overlap the categories. Here, for example, the privacy interest is essentially informational (i.e. about the respondent's activities) but it also implicates his territorial privacy because although the police did not actually enter his house, that is where the activities of interest to them took place.

C. Drawing the "Reasonableness" Line

Privacy is a protean concept, and the difficult issue is where the "reasonableness" line should be drawn. Sopinka J. offered a response to this question in the context of informational privacy in *Plant, supra*, at p. 293, as follows:

> In fostering the underlying values of dignity, integrity and autonomy, it is fitting that s. 8 of the Charter should seek to protect a biographical core of personal information which individuals in a free and democratic society would wish to maintain and control from dissemination to the state. This would include information which tends to reveal intimate details of the lifestyle and personal choices of the individual. [Emphasis added.]

I emphasize the word "include" because Sopinka J. was clear that his illustration ("intimate details of the lifestyle and personal choices") was not meant to be exhaustive, and should not be treated as such. Nevertheless, *Plant* clearly establishes that not all information an individual may wish to keep confidential necessarily enjoys s. 8 protection.

The distinction between informational and territorial privacy is of some assistance in drawing the "reasonableness" line in the factual situation before the Court. Whereas Abella J.A. treated the FLIR imaging as equivalent to a search of the home, and thus "worthy of the state's highest respect" (at para. 33), I think it is more accurately characterized as an external search for information about the home which may or may not be capable of giving rise to an inference about what was actually going on inside, depending on what other information is available.

Moreover, because I emphasize the informational aspect, my focus is on the quality of information that FLIR imaging can actually deliver, whereas Abella J.A., looking to safeguard the home, looked more to the "theoretical capacity" (at para. 79) of the FLIR technology. For example, her reasons include the prediction that "[t]he nature of the intrusiveness is subtle but almost Orwellian in its theoretical capacity" (at para. 79).

In my view, with respect, the reasonableness line has to be determined by looking at the information generated by existing FLIR technology, and then evaluating its impact on a reasonable privacy interest. If, as expected, the capability of FLIR and other technologies will improve and the nature and quality of the information hereafter changes, it will be a different case, and the courts will have to deal with its privacy implications at that time in light of the facts as they then exist.

. . .

It seems to me that Abella J.A. put her finger on the key to this case when she observed with respect to FLIR's present utility that "[t]he surface emanations are, on their own, mearningless" (at para. 66) (emphasis added). The information obtained via a FLIR image, by itself cannot provide sufficient grounds to obtain a search warrant. This is because, as the Crown acknowledges, the relative crudity of the present technology does not, in itself, permit any inferences about the precise activity giving rise to the heat. For that, other evidence is required to determine if there is any reason to believe the source of the heat is a marijuana grow-op. As Crown counsel put the point in oral argument, the process of obtaining a search warrant sits "on a fulcrum. And you pile straws on one side. And this [FLIR image] is one of the straws." Moreover, "if you don't have a number of other cogent items of evidence, [FLIR] isn't going to help you greatly". Based on *current* FLIR technology, this is correct.

. . .

The United States Supreme Court declared the use of FLIR technology to image the outside of a house to be unconstitutional in *Kyllo v. United States*, 533 U.S. 27 (U.S. S.C. 2001), based largely on the "sanctity of the home" (at p. 37). We do not go so far. The fact that it was the respondent's home that was imaged using FLIR technology is an important factor but it is not controlling and must be looked at in context and in particular, in this case, in relation to the nature and quality of the information made accessible by FLIR technology to the police.

. . .

I agree with Abella J.A. that the spectre of the State placing our homes under technological surveillance raises extremely serious concerns. Where we differ, perhaps, is that in my view such technology must be evaluated according to its present capability. Whatever evolution occurs in future will have to be dealt with by the courts step by step. Concerns should be addressed as they truly arise. FLIR technology at this stage of its development is both non-intrusive in its operations and mundane in the data it is capable of producing. It is clear, to repeat, that at present no warrant could ever properly be granted solely on the basis of a FLIR image.

(f) Was the Use of Surveillance Technology Itself Objectively Unreasonable?

A justified concern about the advance of surveillance technology was expressed by Abella J.A., at para. 63, of her reasons:

> In my view, there is an important distinction between observations that are made by the naked eye or even by the use of enhanced aids, such as binoculars, which are in common use, and observations which are the product of technology.

This was also a key element in the decision of the U.S. Supreme Court in *Kyllo* in which the majority judgment, written by Scalia J., concluded (at p. 40):

> Where, as here, the Government uses a device that is not in general public use, to explore details of the home that would previously have been unknowable without physical intrusion, the surveillance is a "search" and is presumptively unreasonable without a warrant. [Emphasis added.]

Scalia J. does not elaborate on what he means by "a device that is not in general public use" and the dissenters suggested such a standard is unworkable (*Kyllo, supra*, at p. 47). On the evidence here, FLIR imaging does not disclose "details of the home", as has already been discussed. The terms "technology" or "a device that is not in general public use" (or Abella J.A.'s reference to "enhanced aids . . . which are in common use", at para. 63) are vague and take in a lot of territory. The argument, presumably, is that if an area of our lives is already exposed to surveillance by commonly available "technology" such as binoculars, we can have no reasonable continuing expectation of privacy in that respect. This may be true, but what is the test for "general public use"? In my view, the issue is not whether FLIR technology puts the police inside the home, because it does not, or whether FLIR is in general public use, (it is not) but rather the nature and quality of the information about activities in the home that the police are able to obtain. The evidence is that a FLIR image of heat emanations is, on its own, as Abella J.A. acknowledged, "meaningless". That is the bottom line.

. . .

On this point, as well, we part company with the U.S. Supreme Court majority in *Kyllo* insofar as Scalia J. declined to distinguish among types of information relating to the home. He declares that "[i]n the home, our cases show, all details are intimate details, because the entire area is held safe from prying government eyes" (at p. 37). This view seems to be predicated on the "originalism" philosophy of Scalia J. for he writes (at pp. 34-35):

> We think that obtaining by sense-enhancing technology any information regarding the interior of the home that could not otherwise have been obtained without physical "intrusion into a constituionally protected area," Silverman, 365 U.S., at 512, constitutes a search - at least where (as here) the technology in question is not in general public use. This assures preservation of that degree of privacy against government that existed when the Fourth Amendment was adopted [in 1791]. On the basis of this criterion, the information obtained by the thermal imager in this case was the product of a search. [Emphasis added.]

For reasons already stated, I do not regard the use of current FLIR technology as the functional equivalent of placing the police inside the home. Nor is it helpful in the Canadian context to compare the state of technology in 2004 with that which existed at Confederation in 1867, or in 1982 when s. 8 of the Charter was adopted. Having regard to its *purpose*, I do not accept that s. 8 is triggered by a FLIR image that discloses that heat sources of some unknown description are present inside the structure, or that the heat distribution is uneven. Certainly FLIR imaging generates information about the home but s. 8 protects people, not places. The information generated by FLIR imaging about the respondent does not touch on "a biographical core of personal information", nor does it "ten[d] to reveal intimate details of [his] lifestyle" (*Plant*, at p. 293). It shows that some of the activities in the house generate heat. That is not enough to get the respondent over the constitutional threshold.

(h) Conclusion With Respect to the Reasonable Expectation

External patterns of heat distribution on the external surfaces of a house is not information in which the respondent had a reasonable expectation of privacy. The heat distribution, as stated, offers no insight into his private life, and reveals nothing of his "biographical core of personal information". Its disclosure scarcely affects the "dignity, integrity and autonomy" of the person whose house is subject of the FLIR image (*Plant*, at p. 293).

I wish to add one further observation. In *Plant*, Sopinka J. listed the seriousness of the offence as a factor in the "balance" sought to be achieved in s. 8 of the Charter (p. 295). Undoubtedly the "seriousness of the offence" has a role to play in striking "the balance", but I do not think that it is a factor in determining whether the respondent did or did not have a reasonable expectation of privacy in the heat distribution patterns on the outside of his house. Rather, it may more logically arise at the stage the court considers whether a particular search was reasonable, or whether the evidence obtained by an unreasonable search may be admitted into evidence under s. 24(2) of the Charter.

. . .

The Supreme Court in *Tessling* has clearly decided that police use of existing F.L.I.R. technology does not offend s. 8 of the Charter. Justice Binnie decided that there was no reasonable expectation of privacy against rudimentary F.L.I.R. imaging of the outside of houses as this did not go to the biographical core or lifestyle and was rudimentary information. The Court distances Canada from the decision of the United States Supreme Court in *Kyllo v. United States*, 533 U.S. 27 (U.C. S.C., 2001) that F.L.I.R. imaging of the outside of houses is unconstitutional. Our highest Court does expressly enter two caveats:

1. F.L.I.R. information alone is insufficient ground to obtain a search warrant; and

2. If, as the Court expects, F.L.I.R. technology gets better, the constitutional issue will have to be re-considered.

Judging from a recent Canadian Forces' video *http://www.gs.flir.com/videos/Land TV3000.wmv* which shows FLIR technology swooping down to highlight details of an individual's conduct otherwise completely out of human sight, *Tessling* already looks to be obsolete.

What of aerial surveillance using binoculars? Such search for a grow operation on suspicion was held to violate s. 8 in *R. v. Kelly* (1999), 22 C.R. (5th) 248, 132 C.C.C. (3d) 122 (N.B. C.A.). **Is that different because that method is more intrusive?** However, the Court in *R. v. Kwiatkowski* (2010), 252 C.C.C. (3d) 426, 73 C.R. (6th) 244 (B.C. C.A.), found no s. 8 violation in police aerial surveillance of greenhouses in a remote part of a rural property as there was no reasonable expectation of privacy. See criticism of Steve Coughlan. "*Kwiatowski*: Privacy Protection and Risk Analysis: Losing the

Forest in the Telephoto Shots of the Trees" C.R. *ibid.*, p. 260. The Court in *Tessling* recognizes its earlier ruling in *R. v. Kokesch*, [1990] 3 S.C.R. 3, 61 C.C.C. (3d) 207, 1 C.R. (4th) 62 (S.C.C.) where the Court decided it was a serious breach of s. 8 for a police officer to walk up a driveway without a warrant to check from the outside as to a possible grow operation. *Tessling* rests uneasily with *Kokesch*. It is difficult to understand how flying over a house with F.L.I.R. technology is constitutional whereas walking up the driveway and feeling the wall for heat is not.

Overall the ruling in *Tessling* appears to tilt s. 8 principles markedly in favour of the interests of law enforcement rather than protecting privacy. **Do you agree with it?**

The Court says there was no search because there was no reasonable expectation of privacy. It is one thing to decide there was no reasonable expectation of privacy and therefore no s. 8 protection engaged. To go further and deny that there was a search would be hard to justify to a house owner watching a police helicopter flying overhead with F.L.I.R. technology or to someone whose luggage is sniffed by a police dog.

The Court's focus on the reasonableness of the search allows it to bypass the fundamental warrant requirement put in place by *Canada (Director of Investigation & Research, Combines Investigation Branch) v. Southam Inc.*, *(sub nom. Hunter v. Southam Inc.)* [1984] 2 S.C.R. 145, 14 C.C.C. (3d) 97, 41 C.R. (3d) 97 (S.C.C.) and asserted by Justice Abella in the Court below.

Justice Binnie speaks of the "perhaps a long spiritual journey" from famous pronouncements protecting one's home from the power of the King to the accused's attempt to shelter a marijuana grow-op (para. 15). **Does this remark undercut the key pronouncement of La Forest J. for the Court in *R. v. Wong*, [1990] 3 S.C.R. 36, 1 C.R. (4th) 1, 60 C.C.C. (3d) 460 (S.C.C.) as to the importance of asking the question in a neutral way?** Here the question should not have been whether grow operators have a reasonable expectation of privacy, but whether occupants of houses have a reasonable expectation of privacy from police inspection from aircraft using technology devices, however crude they may be.

For further comments on *Tessling*, see Renee Pomerance, "Shedding Light on the Nature of Heat: Defining Privacy in the wake of *R. v. Tessling*", (2005) 23 C.R. (6th) 229; Steve Coughlan and Marc Gorbet, "Nothing Plus Nothing Equals . . . Something? A Proposal for FLIR Warrants on Reasonable Suspicion", (2005) 23 C.R. (6th) 239; James Stringham, "Reasonable Expectations Revisited: A Return to the Search for a Normative Core for Section 8?", (2005) 23 C.R. (6th) 245; and, on the ruling in the Ontario Court of Appeal, see Lisa Austin, "One Step Forward or Two Steps Back?", (2004) 49 Crim. L.Q. 22. See too, Steve Coughlan, "Privacy Goes to the Dogs" (2006) 40 C.R. (6th) 31, Jonathan Shapiro, "Narcotics Dogs And the Search for Illegality: American Law in Canadian Courts" (2007) 43 C.R. (6th) 299, Ian Kerr and Jena McGill, "Emanations, Snoop Dogs and Reasonable Expectation of Privacy", (2007) 32 Crim. L.Q. 392 and Sherri Davis-Barron, "The Lawful Use of Drug Detector Dogs",

(2007) 52 Crim. L.Q. 345. For a more supportive view, see Arthur J. Cockfield, "Protecting the Social Value of Privacy in the Context of State Investigations Using New Technologies" (2007) 40 *U.B.C. L.Rev.* 41.

In a series of police sniffer dog cases, most Courts of Appeal (such as the majority of the Alberta Court of Appeal in *R. v. Kang-Brown*) applied *Tessling* to hold that there was in such cases no section 8 protection as dog searches reveal very little as to core biographical details, lifestyle or private choices. These decisions attracted much academic criticism. In *A.M.*, the Ontario Court of Appeal disagreed with the analogy to *Tessling* and held that section 8 offered protection against random search for drugs in a school.

On the appeals in *R. v. Brown* (*sub nom. R. v. Kang-Brown*), [2008] 1 S.C.R. 456, 230 C.C.C. (3d) 289, 55 C.R. (6th) 240 (S.C.C.) and *R. v. M. (A.)*, [2008] 1 S.C.R. 569, 230 C.C.C. (3d) 377, 55 C.R. (6th) 314 (S.C.C.), the Supreme Court of Canada, after reserving for 11 months, generally sided with the Ontario Court of Appeal. The Court was however deeply divided with four sets of reasons delivered in each case. In the result, a 6-3 majority held that the police use of a sniffer dog in *Kang-Brown* to find drugs in the bag of someone getting off a bus and in *A.M.* in a knapsack after a search of an entire school violated section 8 and should be excluded.

Four justices — Justice LeBel (Fish, Abella and Charron JJ. concurring) — held that there was no common law power to use sniffer dogs and that the matter should be left to Parliament. The Court should not use the ancillary powers doctrine to lower the *Hunter* standard of reasonable and probable grounds for a search.

Four justices — Justice Binnie (McLachlin C.J., Deschamps and Rothstein JJ.A. concurring) — resorted to the ancillary powers doctrine to hold that the police have a common law power to conduct a warrantless search using sniffer dogs on the basis of reasonable suspicion. They also held that these standards complied with section 8 although they were less than the *Hunter* standards. Bastarache J. agreed but he favoured a generalised suspicion standard rather than that of reasonable suspicion.

For divergent views on these complex dog sniffer rulings see Tim Quigley, "Welcome Charter Scrutiny of Dog Sniffer Use: Time for Parliament to Act" (2008) 55 C.R. (6th) 373, Don Stuart, "Revitalising Section 8: Individualised Reasonable Suspicion is a Sound Compromise for Routine Dog Sniffer Use" (2008) 55 C.R. (6th) 376, David Tanovich, "A Powerful Blow Against Police Use of Drug Courier Profiles" (2008) 55 C.R. (6th) 379, Steve Coughlan, "Improving Privacy Protection, But By How Much?", (2008) 55 C.R. (6th) 394 and Jonathan Shapiro, "Confusion and Dangers in Lowering the Hunter Standards" (2008) 55 C.R. (6th) 396.

The Supreme Court later unanimously decided that police use of dog sniffers could be authorised on individualised reasonable suspicion:

R. v. CHEHIL
2013 SCC 49, [2013] 3 S.C.R. 220, 301 C.C.C. (3d) 157, 4 C.R. (7th) 219
(S.C.C.)

Police officers examined the passenger manifest for an overnight flight from Vancouver to Halifax and observed that the accused was one of the last passengers to purchase a ticket, paid for his ticket in cash, and checked one bag. The officers testified that in their experience these characteristics were indicators of the illegal traffic of narcotics. They had the accused's bag placed with nine other items from the flight and searched them with a sniffer dog: the dog indicated the presence of narcotics in the accused's bag and also in the cooler next to it. The cooler was searched with the consent of the owner and was found not to contain narcotics. When the accused came to collect his bag he was arrested for possession of narcotics and searched incident to arrest: his bag was found to contain three kilograms of cocaine.

The trial judge concluded that the factors relied on by the police were not sufficient to establish reasonable suspicion because several of them were open to neutral explanations that were not explored. The trial judge also found that yearly validation performance was not an adequate indicator of a sniffer dog's reliability, and that the dog's performance in the field was not sufficiently reliable for the search to be reasonable. The Nova Scotia Court of Appeal overturned that decision, holding that the trial judge had erred by considering the factors in isolation rather than determining whether they coalesced to form a reasonable suspicion despite potential innocent explanations for each. The Court of Appeal also held that the trial judge had erred by rejecting the officer's testimony that the false indication on the cooler likely resulted from the scent emanating from the accused's adjacent bag. The accused appealed.

KARAKATSANIS J.:—

(1) Nature of Reasonable Suspicion

[26] Reasonable suspicion derives its rigour from the requirement that it be based on objectively discernible facts, which can then be subjected to independent judicial scrutiny. This scrutiny is exacting, and must account for the totality of the circumstances. In *Kang-Brown*, Binnie J. provided the following definition of reasonable suspicion, at para. 75:

> The "reasonable suspicion" standard is not a new juridical standard called into existence for the purposes of this case. "Suspicion" is an expectation that the targeted individual is possibly engaged in some criminal activity. A "reasonable" suspicion means something more than a mere suspicion and something less than a belief based upon reasonable and probable grounds.

[27] Thus, while reasonable grounds to suspect and reasonable and probable grounds to believe are similar in that they both must be grounded in objective facts, reasonable suspicion is a lower standard, as it engages the reasonable possibility, rather than probability, of crime. As a result, when applying the reasonable suspicion standard, reviewing judges must be cautious not to

conflate it with the more demanding reasonable and probable grounds standard.

[28] The fact that reasonable suspicion deals with possibilities, rather than probabilities, necessarily means that in some cases the police will reasonably suspect that innocent people are involved in crime. In spite of this reality, properly conducted sniff searches that are based on reasonable suspicion are *Charter*-compliant in light of their minimally intrusive, narrowly targeted, and highly accurate nature: see *Kang-Brown*, at para. 60, *per* Binnie J., and *A.M.*, at paras. 81-84, *per* Binnie J. However, the suspicion held by the police cannot be so broad that it descends to the level of generalized suspicion, which was described by Bastarache J., at para. 151 of *A.M.*, as suspicion "that attaches to a particular activity or location rather than to a specific person".

[29] Reasonable suspicion must be assessed against the totality of the circumstances. The inquiry must consider the constellation of objectively discernible facts that are said to give the investigating officer reasonable cause to suspect that an individual is involved in the type of criminal activity under investigation. This inquiry must be fact-based, flexible, and grounded in common sense and practical, everyday experience: see *R. v. Bramley*, 2009 SKCA 49, 324 Sask. R. 286, at para. 60. A police officer's grounds for reasonable suspicion cannot be assessed in isolation: see *Monney*, at para. 50.

[30] A constellation of factors will not be sufficient to ground reasonable suspicion where it amounts merely to a "generalized" suspicion because it "would include such a number of presumably innocent persons as to approach a subjectively administered, random basis" for a search: *United States v. Gooding*, 695 F.2d 78 (4th Cir. 1982), at p. 83. The American jurisprudence supports the need for a sufficiently particularized constellation of factors. See *Reid v. Georgia*, 448 U.S. 438 (1980), and *Terry v. Ohio*, 392 U.S. 1 (1968). Indeed, the reasonable suspicion standard is designed to avoid indiscriminate and discriminatory searches.

[31] While some factors, such as travelling under a false name, or flight from the police, may give rise to reasonable suspicion on their own (*Kang-Brown*, at para. 87, *per* Binnie J.), other elements of a constellation will not support reasonable suspicion, except in combination with other factors. Generally, characteristics that apply broadly to innocent people are insufficient, as they are markers only of generalized suspicion. The same is true of factors that may "go both ways", such as an individual's making or failing to make eye contact. On their own, such factors cannot support reasonable suspicion; however, this does not preclude reasonable suspicion arising when the same factor is simply one part of a constellation of factors.

[32] Further, reasonable suspicion need not be the only inference that can be drawn from a particular constellation of factors. Much as the seven stars that form the Big Dipper have also been interpreted as a bear, a saucepan, and a plough, factors that give rise to a reasonable suspicion may also support completely innocent explanations. This is acceptable, as the reasonable suspicion standard addresses the *possibility* of uncovering criminality, and not a *probability* of doing so.

[33] Exculpatory, neutral, or equivocal information cannot be disregarded when assessing a constellation of factors. The totality of the circumstances, including favourable and unfavourable factors, must be weighed in the course of arriving at any conclusion regarding reasonable suspicion. As Doherty J.A. found in *R. v. Golub* (1997), 34 O.R. (3d) 743 (C.A.), at p. 751, "[t]he officer must take into account all information available to him and is entitled to disregard only information which he has good reason to believe is unreliable". This is self-evident.

. . .

[35] Finally, the objective facts must be indicative of the possibility of criminal behaviour. While I agree with the appellant's submission that police must point to particularized conduct or particularized evidence of criminal activity in order to ground reasonable suspicion, I do not accept that the evidence must itself consist of unlawful behaviour, or must necessarily be evidence of a specific known criminal act.

. . .

[37] In sum, when single-profile narcotic dogs are deployed on the basis of reasonable suspicion, the police intrusion must be connected to factors indicating a drug-related offence. Reasonable suspicion does not, however, require the police to point to a specific ongoing crime, nor does it entail the identification of the precise illegal substance being searched for. The reasonable suspicion held by the police need only be linked to the possession, traffic, or production of drugs or other drug-related contraband.

(2) Profiling and Reasonable Suspicion

[38] The appellants in this case and in the companion appeal, *MacKenzie*, as well as the interveners the Canadian Civil Liberties Association ("CCLA") and the Samuelson-Glushko Canadian Internet Policy and Public Interest Clinic ("CIPPIC") ask this Court to rule that drug courier profiles cannot ground reasonable suspicion in and of themselves. They say that reliance on profiles replaces rigorous judicial scrutiny with the police view of the circumstances. The CCLA highlights various dangers related to the use of profiles, even as an investigative tool to identify persons of interest, such as inconsistent application or after-the-fact modification by the police, unanticipated impacts on bystanders, disproportionate harm to visible minorities, and stereotyping.

[39] In my view, it is unhelpful to speak of profiling as generating reasonable suspicion. The term itself suggests an assessment based on stereotyping and discriminatory factors, which have no place in the reasonable suspicion analysis. Rather, the analysis must remain focused on one central question: Is the totality of the circumstances, including the specific characteristics of the suspect, the contextual factors, and the offence suspected, sufficient to reach the threshold of reasonable suspicion?

[40] The application of the reasonable suspicion standard cannot be mechanical and formulaic. It must be sensitive to the particular circumstances of each case. Characteristics identified by a police profile can

be considered when evaluating reasonable suspicion; however, profile characteristics are not a substitute for objective facts that raise a reasonable suspicion of criminal activity. Profile characteristics must be approached with caution precisely because they risk undermining a careful individualized assessment of the totality of the circumstances.

[41] In this case, the profiling alleged consisted of a set of factors that the officers had been taught to look for and had learned through experience to look for in order to detect drug couriers. Whether or not these factors give rise to reasonable suspicion will depend upon a police officer's reasons for relying on specific factors, the evidence connecting these factors to criminal activity, and the entirety of the circumstances of the case.

[42] It is not alleged in this case, or in the companion appeal, that any form of discriminatory profiling took place. Even though we are not concerned with these issues here, I caution that courts must be wary that factors arising out of police experience are not in fact stereotypical or discriminatory.

[43] Furthermore, the elements considered as part of the reasonable suspicion analysis must respect *Charter* principles. The factors considered under the reasonable suspicion analysis must relate to the actions of the subject of an investigation, and not his or her immutable characteristics.

[44] Nor should the exercise of *Charter* rights, such as the right to remain silent or to walk away from questioning made outside the context of a detention, provide grounds for reasonable suspicion. These rights become meaningless to the extent that they are capable of forming the basis of reasonable suspicion. Individuals should not have to sacrifice privacy to exercise Charter rights.

(3) Nature of Judicial Scrutiny

[45] The requirement for objective and ascertainable facts as the basis for reasonable suspicion permits an independent after-the-fact review by the court and protects against arbitrary state action. Under the *Collins* framework, the onus is on the Crown to show that the objective facts rise to the level of reasonable suspicion, such that a reasonable person, standing in the shoes of the police officer, would have held a reasonable suspicion of criminal activity.

[46] Rigorous judicial scrutiny is an independent review that ensures that the suspicion relied on by the police is supported by factors that are objectively ascertainable, meaning that the suspicion is based on "factual elements which can be adduced in evidence and permit an independent judicial assessment": P. Sankoff and S. Perrault, "Suspicious Searches: What's so Reasonable About Them?" (1999), 24 C.R. (5th) 123, at p. 125. The constellation of facts must be based in the evidence, tied to the individual, and capable of supporting a logical inference of criminal behaviour. If the link between the constellation and criminality cannot be established by way of a logical inference, the Crown must lead evidence to connect the circumstances to criminality. This evidence may be empirical or statistical, or it may be based upon the investigating officer's training and experience.

[47] An officer's training and experience may provide an objective experiential, as opposed to empirical, basis for grounding reasonable suspicion. However,

this is not to say that hunches or intuition grounded in an officer's experience will suffice, or that deference is owed to a police officer's view of the circumstances based on her training or experience in the field: see *Payette*, at para. 25. A police officer's educated guess must not supplant the rigorous and independent scrutiny demanded by the reasonable suspicion standard. Evidence as to the specific nature and extent of such experience and training is required so that the court may make an objective assessment of the probative link between the constellation of factors relied on by the police and criminality. The more general the constellation relied on by the police, the more there will be a need for specific evidence regarding police experience and training. To the extent that specific evidence of the investigating officer's experience and training supports the link the Crown asks the court to draw, the more compelling that link will be.

(4) Reliability of Individual Dogs

[48] Concerns about the reliability and accuracy of a drug detection dog may arise at each level of the *Collins* inquiry. In *Kang-Brown*, the high accuracy of sniffer dogs that were properly trained and deployed was key to endorsing a reasonable suspicion standard for sniff searches. Further, in light of the consequences of a false indication, the reliability of a particular dog is also relevant to determining whether a particular sniff search was conducted reasonably in the circumstances: see *Kang-Brown*, at paras. 63-65.

[49] The consequences of a false indication by a sniffer dog can be severe. As discussed below, a positive indication for the presence of the smell of narcotics by a reliable dog may, depending on the circumstances, lead to reasonable and probable grounds for an arrest. If the police make use of a dog whose indications cannot be taken as a reliable sign of the presence of the smell of drugs, the false positive resulting from the dog's unreliable nose could lead to unnecessary arrests. Because dogs are trained to indicate for smell and thus may indicate even in the absence of drugs, validations in controlled settings are important, as it is only in such environments that a false positive can truly be identified.

[50] However, evidence of the searching dog's performance during past deployments is also relevant. Because the dog's ability is to detect the *smell* of drugs, a sniffer dog will be unable to distinguish between a smell emanating from contaminated items rather than actual drugs. If the smell of drugs from contaminated property becomes pervasive, the utility of an indication by smell is diminished. In environments with high contamination rates, a dog may be inherently unreliable; however, this should not count against a dog's performance record in general. Information about deployment may also demonstrate whether a particular dog is exceptionally prone to false alerts or detecting residual odours.

[51] A method of searching that captures an inordinate number of innocent individuals cannot be reasonable, due to the unnecessary infringement of privacy and personal dignity that an arrest would bring. Accordingly, both the capacity of the individual dog and the potential for the dog to be less accurate in certain settings due to environmental cross-contamination must factor into

the contextual analysis of reliability. In order to assist in analyzing an individual dog's susceptibility for providing false positives, handlers should keep records of the dog and team's performance. Both the results of testing in a controlled setting and the results of deployment in the field are helpful in assessing the reliability of a positive indication as a sign of the actual presence of drugs.

[52] The appellant urges the Court to insist on national testing standards in order to ensure consistent reliability of sniffer dogs. However, while standards to regulate the use of sniffer dogs would be desirable, they must be implemented through legislative action by Parliament.

[53] In the absence of legislated standards, trial judges must continue to scrutinize the evidence before them in order to determine whether the particular sniff search meets the *Collins* criteria. Thus, even though *indicia* like a dog's past performance and the risk of cross-contamination can be relevant to determining a dog's reliability, no specific evidentiary requirements will apply mechanically to every case. The prosecution does not have to prove that the dog is infallible, just as it does not have to prove that an informer's tip is infallible.

[54] Dog reliability is also important to determining whether a positive indication provides the reasonable and probable grounds required to justify further police action. The reviewing court will make this determination armed with the results of the sniff search and evidence regarding the reliability of the dog. If a sniff search is conducted lawfully, the officer already has reasonable grounds to suspect criminal conduct based on the totality of the circumstances that existed prior to the sniff search. With all these elements in mind, the court must determine whether the *totality* of the circumstances reached the reasonable and probable grounds threshold. I note that a similar approach was recently endorsed by the Supreme Court of the United States in *Florida v. Harris*, 133 S.Ct. 1050 (2013), albeit in the context of the "probable cause" test, which is specific to American law.

(5) Actions Following Positive Indication

[55] Once a sniffer dog has delivered a positive indication, the police often seek consent for a verification search. Provided that the consent is properly sought and obtained, the search will respect s. 8 of the *Charter*: see *R. v. Borden*, [1994] 3 S.C.R. 145. Alternately, the police may determine that they have the grounds required under the *Charter* to proceed with a warrantless arrest, namely reasonable and probable grounds to believe that the accused has committed an offence: see *R. v. Storrey*, [1990] 1 S.C.R. 241, at pp. 249-51. If the arrest is validly made, the police may conduct a search incident to arrest in order to secure evidence that could be used at the accused's trial: see *Caslake*. That is what occurred in this case, and in the majority of reported cases dealing with sniff searches occurring post-*Kang-Brown* in which the police conducted a search to confirm the presence of drugs.

. . .

B *Application to This Case*

(1) Reasonable Suspicion of the Police

[64] The presence of reasonable suspicion must be assessed in the context of a specific case. The officers testified that no indicator by itself was determinative, that the decision to deploy a sniffer dog was made based on the following factors: (1) the travel was on a one-way ticket; (2) the flight originated in Vancouver; (3) the appellant was travelling alone; (4) the ticket was purchased with cash; (5) the ticket was the last one purchased before the flight departed; (6) the appellant checked one piece of luggage; (7) the flight was overnight; (8) the flight took place mid- to late-week; and (9) drug couriers prefer less expensive airlines, such as WestJet...

The officers testified they had seen this constellation in Halifax, and knew that it was common to drug couriers. The constellation had been noted in their training and observed by them in their prior investigations. It was not common to innocent travellers. This assertion was not challenged on cross-examination.

[65] In some cases, evidence has been adduced that challenges the probative value of the factors relied upon by the police: see *R. v. Wong*, 2005 BCPC 24, 127 C.R.R. (2d) 342, or *R. v. Calderon* (2004), 188 C.C.C. (3d) 481 (Ont. C.A.). In those cases, a poor track record undermined the police's reliance on the particular constellations involved. As Professor Tanovich has noted, "evidence of an unreasonably high false positive rate can impact on the ability of the police to rely on a profile, for example, in establishing the requisite constitutional threshold for an investigative detention or search": "A Powerful Blow Against Police Use of Drug Courier Profiles" (2008), 55 C.R. (6th) 379, at p. 391. No such evidence was adduced in this case.

. . .

(2) Reasonableness of the Search

[70] The trial judge found that the search was unreasonable, as the sniffer dog used was not reliable. He focused on the fact that in this case, Boris indicated on a cooler containing no drugs, as well as the appellant's bag, finding this gave a reliability rating of 50 percent on the day in question. He also looked to actual deployments, including Boris's indications where no drugs were found. The trial judge concluded that the RCMP training assessment was unreliable, as it was not conducted by an independent agency and was not based on national standards. He was also of the view that the lack of instruction given by the RCMP to dog handlers with regard to the way in which a sniffer dog's reliability should be evaluated led to highly subjective accuracy assessments.

[71] The Court of Appeal overturned these findings, saying that they were based on speculation and misapprehension of the evidence.

[72] Corporal Daigle provided detailed evidence of Boris's validation performance and records of 178 deployments in the field from May 2003 to November 2005. As well, his evidence established that Boris had never given a

"false sit" in a controlled environment. Through four validation exercises Boris was 99 percent accurate in detecting hidden drugs.

[73] Further, the evidence established that 87.6 percent of Boris's indications for the smell of drugs led to the discovery of drugs or drug residue or involved circumstances that demonstrated the likely recent presence of drugs, such as admitted recent drug use by the owner of the luggage, the discovery of drug-related paraphernalia in the luggage, or the discovery of large amounts of cash (in amounts varying between $9,000 and $84,775).

[74] In my view, the trial judge erred in principle by discounting the RCMP's controlled yearly validations and by failing to consider evidence of contamination from the recent presence of drugs that explained indications where no drugs were found, an explanation that would equally apply to the indication on the cooler in this case. As a result, and based on the record, the trial judge committed a palpable and overriding error in finding that Boris was only 50 percent reliable.

[75] I agree with the Court of Appeal that the trial judge erred and that Boris was reliable. Given the reliability of the dog, the sniff search was reasonable in these circumstances.

(3) Arrest Subsequent to Positive Indication

[76] The appellant was arrested following Boris's positive indication on his bag. When the police officer arrested the appellant, he knew of the constellation of factors that led to the decision to deploy Boris, and that Boris had in fact indicated on the appellant's bag. In this case, given the strength of the constellation, the reliability of the dog, and the absence of exculpatory explanations, the positive indication raised the reasonable suspicion generated by the constellation to the level of reasonable and probable grounds to arrest the appellant.

V. Conclusion

[77] The police had a reasonable suspicion that they would discover evidence of a drug-related crime in Mr. Chehil's luggage. The sniff search was conducted reasonably. It is unnecessary to consider the fresh evidence tendered by the Crown in light of my conclusion and I would dismiss the appeal.

The Court in *Chehil* does a commendable job in carefully setting out the approach to be followed for determining reasonable suspicion and in requiring rigorous judicial scrutiny of all the circumstances to determine the objective reasonableness of the suspicion. There is, however, cause for concern on two fronts. Justice Karakatsanis too easily dismisses the utility of the term profiling. She is alive to the dangers of racial profiling. But non-racial profiling developed from police training and experience can also be unreliable and lead to injustice. For example, David Tanovich "A Powerful Blow Against Police Use of Drug Courier Profiles" (2008), 55 CR (6th) 379 at 389, points to evidence that detention at the Pearson "super loo" facility (where suspects were held until they had bowel movements) based on drug importer profiles has detained innocent suspects over 75% of the time. Defence counsel can and should under *Chehil* rigorously cross-examine and sometimes lead evidence as to the unreliability of police profiling and experience. Secondly, although the Court has now clearly established the relevance of police training and experience without expert evidence being necessary there is a real danger that that testimony as to experience may overwhelm the objective criterion for reasonable suspicion. Steve Coughlan in C.R. comment on *Chehil* suggested that the experience of the officer should always be judged against the experience of the ordinary officer in that situation. In his view, an approach needs to be adopted which allows for appropriate experience to be taken into account but which does not send to police the unspoken message "claiming your experience supports your belief is a trump card". He sees a danger of confirmation bias and draws a useful analogy to eyewitness identification. In that context, judges have over the years learned to be cautious about the reliability of sincerely held beliefs.

It will be interesting to see how far defence counsel are permitted to go in challenging evidence of police knowledge and experience. In an odd way the Court has made it easier to effectively challenge the experience and reliability of the dog than the officer!

These concerns are sharpened by the 5-4 ruling on the facts in the companion case of *R. v. MacKenzie*, [2013] 3 S.C.R. 250, 303 C.C.C. (3d) 281, 4 C.R. (7th) 260 (S.C.C.). Justice Moldaver (Abella, Rothstein, Karakatsanis and Wagner JJ. concurring) held that there had been reasonable suspicion for employing a sniffer dog when the police observed the driver of a vehicle was extremely nervous when told he was stopped for a minor speeding offence, was trembling and sweating, his carotid artery was throbbing, and his eyes were of a pinkish colour. The officer testified that these factors, from his experience, were consistent with drug trafficking. Lebel J. (McLachlin C.J., Fish and Cromwell JJ., concurring) wrote a strong dissent. The evidence did not amount to reasonable suspicion. The police could simply draw on their experience in the field to create broad categories of suspicious behaviour into which almost anyone could fall, which would risk transforming the standard of reasonable suspicion into the generalized suspicion standard that had been rejected by the Court. **With which judgment do you agree?**

In *R. v. Gomboc*, 79 C.R. (6th) 199, [2010] 3 S.C.R. 211, 263 C.C.C. (3d) 383 (S.C.C.) a 7-2 majority of the Supreme Court upheld the constitutionality of a warrantless request by police to an electric utility company for installation of a digital recording ammeter to measure flow of electricity into a residence suspected of housing a marihuana grow operation. The information from the digital recording ammeter over an 18-hour period indicated a pattern consistent with a grow operation. Based on their observation and the DRA result, the police obtained a warrant and found a marihuana grow operation.

Four justices (per Deschamps J., Charron, Rothstein and Cromwell JJ. concurring) decided that s. 8 does not offer any protection because the consumption graph of electrical use does not go to the core of biographical information and because of the regulation and absence of withdrawal of consent. Three justices (per Abella J., Binnie and LeBel JJ. concurring) held that their privacy issues were engaged but that s. 8 did not apply because there was an Alberta government regulation allowing for disclosure by utilities companies of such information if not contrary to the express request of the consumer. They note the absence of a Charter challenge to that regulation. The two dissenters, McLachlin C.J.C. and Fish J., decided that privacy interests in the house were sufficiently engaged to trigger s. 8 and that it was not reasonable to have this trumped by a regulation allowing warrantless police access whether or not the householder was aware of the regulation or of the need to expressly refuse access to the police.

The Abella cohort of three plus the two dissenters constitute a differently composed 5-4 majority ruling against the *Tessling* test of biographical core of information. The warrantless ammeter use by police should be challenged again. It seems extremely technical and certainly not a purposeful interpretation to have made the lack of a formal challenge to the regulation a reason to avoid Charter review. Also, the reliance on the regulation seems inconsistent with established case law that consent searches can only be constitutional where the consent is meaningful and amounting to unequivocal waiver of Charter rights (see *Dedman*, *Borden* and *Wills* above.)

A wider danger of *Gomboc* is that it could result in regulations in other contexts being passed or even just contractual terms being imposed in the fine print , for example by landlords or operators of homeless shelters, to get around s. 8 standards. Concern has been expressed that the Court in *Tessling* and *Gomboc* has not been sufficiently attentive to privacy concerns with invasive surveillance technologies: Matthew Johnson, "Privacy in the Balance-Novel Search Technologies, Reasonable Expectations, and Recalibrating Section 8" (2012) 58 Crim. L.Q. 442.

R. v. PATRICK

64 C.R. (6th) 1, 242 C.C.C. (3d) 158, [2009] 1 S.C.R. 579 (S.C.C.)

The police suspected that P was operating an ecstasy lab in his home. On several occasions, they seized bags of garbage that P had placed for collection from a stand indented into the back fence at the rear of his home adjacent to a public alleyway. The police did not have to step onto P's property to retrieve the bags but they did have to reach through the airspace over his property line. The police used evidence of criminal activity taken from the contents of P's garbage to obtain a warrant to search P's house and garage. More evidence was seized during the search.

The trial judge held that P did not have a reasonable expectation of privacy in the items taken from his garbage and, therefore, the seizure of the garbage bags, the search warrant and the search of P's dwelling were lawful and not in violation of section 8. A majority of the Alberta Court of Appeal and a 6-1 majority of the Supreme Court agreed, dismissing the further appeals.

Justice Binnie J. (McLachlin C.J., LeBel, Fish, Charron and Rothstein JJ. concurring) found that the accused had abandoned any constitutionally protected privacy interest in the contents of his garbage when he placed bags in the garbage alcove open to the laneway for collection. There was no reasonable expectation of privacy. The taking by the police did not constitute a search and seizure within the scope of s. 8. Neither the search of the contents of P's garbage nor the subsequent search of P's dwelling breached s. 8 of the Charter. The evidence seized in both searches had been properly admitted.

BINNIE J.:—

IV. Analysis

[14] "Expectation of privacy is a normative rather than a descriptive standard" (*Tessling*, at para. 42). A government that increases its snooping on the lives of citizens, and thereby makes them suspicious and reduces their expectation of privacy, will not thereby succeed in unilaterally reducing their constitutional entitlement to privacy protection. Equally, however, while a disembarking passenger at the Toronto airport might feel entitled to privacy when emptying his bowels after an intercontinental flight, the obligation to make use of a "drug loo facility" under the supervision of the authorities was upheld in the context of border formalities in *R. v. Monney*, [1999] 1 S.C.R. 652. Privacy analysis is laden with value judgments which are made from the independent perspective of the reasonable and informed person who is concerned about the long-term consequences of government action for the protection of privacy.

[20] The concept of abandonment is about whether a presumed subjective privacy interest of the householder in trash put out for collection is one that an independent and informed observer, viewing the matter objectively, would consider reasonable in the totality of the circumstances (*Edwards*, at para. 45, and *Tessling*, at para. 19) having regard firstly to the need to balance "societal interests in protecting individual dignity, integrity and autonomy with effective law enforcement" (*R. v. Plant*, [1993] 3 S.C.R. 281, at p. 293); secondly, whether an accused has conducted himself in a manner that is inconsistent with the reasonable continued assertion of a privacy interest and, thirdly, the long-term consequences for the due protection of privacy interests in our society.

[21] As emphasized by the Attorney General of Ontario, the police practice of looking through garbage has in the past been an important source of probative evidence for the courts in the search for truth, including documents related to a murder found in garbage bags left out front of an apartment building and commingled with other residents' bags (*R. v. Kennedy*, [1992] O.J. No. 1163 (QL) (Gen. Div.), aff'd (1996), 95 O.A.C. 321 (sub nom. *R. v. Joyce and Kennedy*)); a burned baseball bat used to beat a person to death found in a dumpster located on a residential property (*R. v. Papadopoulos*, [2006] O.J. No. 5407 (QL) (S.C.J.), at paras. 4 and 62-63); cans, cups and straws tossed into garbage bins and onto the ground in the public domain from which DNA has been extracted (*R. v. Paul* (2004), 117 C.R.R. (2d) 319 (Ont. S.C.J.), at p. 323; *R. v. Briere*, [2004] O.J. No. 5611 (QL) (S.C.J.), at paras. 179-97, and *R. v. Marini*, [2005] O.J. No. 6197 (QL) (S.C.J.)); a deceased's gloves found in garbage behind a residential address (*R. v. Rodney*, [1990] 2 S.C.R.

687); a body placed in a commercial dumpster and later located in a landfill site (*R. v. Sherratt* (1989), 49 C.C.C. (3d) 237 (Man. C.A.), at p. 245, aff'd [1991] 1 S.C.R. 509, at pp. 513- 14); a sweatshirt found in the garbage close to the scenes of a murder and sexual assaults that contained important DNA evidence (*R. v. Kinkead*, [1999] O.J. No. 1458 (QL) (S.C.J.), at para. 32, aff'd (2003), 67 O.R. (3d) 57 (C.A.); a tissue left in a garbage pail in a motel room that the accused had checked out of (*R. v. Love* (1995), 102 C.C.C. (3d) 393 (Alta. C.A.), at p. 409); and boxes found in a garbage pail in a common laundry room adjacent to an accused's suite that connected the accused to a robbery (*R. v. Leaney*, [1989] 2 S.C.R. 393, at p. 401).

A. *The Issue of Abandonment*

[22] In *R. v. Dyment*, [1988] 2 S.C.R. 417, La Forest J. treated abandonment as fatal to a reasonable expectation of privacy. He held that when an accused abandons something, it is "best to put it in Charter terms by saying that he [has] ceased to have a reasonable expectation of privacy with regard to it" (p. 435).

[23] In *R. v. Stillman*, [1997] 1 S.C.R. 607, McLachlin J., in dissent, but not on this point, stated that "[t]he purpose of s. 8 is to protect the person and property of the individual from unreasonable search and seizure. This purpose is not engaged in the case of property which the accused has discarded" (para. 223). (To the same effect see Cory J. for the majority at para. 62, and Major J., concurring in part, at para. 274).

[24] This may be contrasted with the situation in *R. v. Law*, 2002 SCC 10, [2002] 1 S.C.R. 227, where a locked safe containing confidential documents had been stolen (not discarded) and the accused had never acted in a manner inconsistent with the continued assertion of a privacy interest in the information contained therein. When the police, after recovering the stolen safe, decided to scrutinize the documents inside (and the accused subsequently was charged with tax offences), they infringed the s. 8 reasonableness line.

[25] Abandonment is therefore an issue of fact. The question is whether the claimant to s. 8 protection has acted in relation to the subject matter of his privacy claim in such a manner as to lead a reasonable and independent observer to conclude that his continued assertion of a privacy interest is unreasonable in the totality of the circumstances.

C. *Did the Appellant Have a Reasonable Expectation of Privacy in this Case?*

(1) The Subject Matter of the Alleged "Search"

[29] It is essential at the outset to identify the subject matter of the alleged search: *Tessling* (at paras. 34 and 58). In *R. v. Kang-Brown*, 2006 ABCA 199, 60 Alta. L.R. (4th) 223, the Alberta Court of Appeal accepted the Crown's argument that the subject matter of the sniffer-dog search was the public airspace surrounding a traveller's bag. In this Court, the subject matter was found to be the contents within, and specifically the existence of narcotics (2008 SCC 18, [2008] 1 S.C.R. 456). The differing perspectives made a major contribution to a different result.

[30] The Attorneys General characterize the subject matter here as "garbage" but, without more, this oversimplification misses (or assumes away) the point in issue. Residential waste includes an enormous amount of personal information about what is going on in our homes, including a lot of DNA on household tissues, highly personal records (e.g., love letters, overdue bills and tax returns) and hidden vices (pill bottles, syringes, sexual paraphernalia, etc.). As it was put by counsel for the Canadian Civil Liberties Association, a garbage bag may more accurately be described as a bag of "information" whose contents, viewed in their entirety, paint a fairly accurate and complete picture of the householder's activities and lifestyle. Many of us may not wish to disclose these things to the public generally or to the police in particular.

[31] The appellant had a direct interest not only in the garbage itself but, in particular, its informational content.

(2) Concealing Illegal Objects

[32] The majority in the Alberta Court of Appeal seems to state, in para. 35, that because the items of interest located by the police revealed involvement in criminal activity they cannot "constitute intimate details of lifestyle or core biographical details to which privacy protection ought to be extended". I would have thought, with respect, that the criminal "lifestyle" of the appellant was at the epicentre of what the police wanted to know and what the appellant wished to conceal. The question is not whether the appellant had a lifestyle which society values, but whether and at what point in the disposal process innocent citizens cease to have a reasonable expectation that the contents of their garbage will remain private. The issue ought to be framed in terms of the privacy of the area or thing being searched and the potential impact of the search on the person being searched, not the nature or identity of the concealed items (*A.M.*, at para. 72). In *Kang-Brown*, we held that a traveller had a privacy interest in his carry-on bag despite the fact that the bag turned out to contain drugs. In *A.M.*, we held that a student did not forfeit his privacy interest in a backpack despite the fact that it was left unattended in a school gymnasium and that its contents included marijuana. In *Wong*, as stated, the Court held that people who "retire to a hotel room and close the door behind them have a reasonable expectation of privacy" (p. 50), despite engaging in illegal activity once inside. The issue is not whether the appellant had a legitimate privacy interest in the concealment of drug paraphernalia, but whether people generally have a privacy interest in the concealed contents of an opaque and sealed "bag of information". I believe that they do. The focus is on "the person, place or thing searched and the purpose for which the search is undertaken" (*A.M.*, at para. 72). A warrantless search of a private place cannot be justified by the after-the-fact discovery of evidence of a crime.

[33] In the cases of searches and seizures that come before the courts, the warrantless search has almost always produced useful evidence (otherwise the matter is unlikely to be before the courts), but our concern has to take into account the spectre of random and warrantless searches which produce nothing except embarrassment and perhaps humiliation for the innocent persons who happen to be searched.

[34] A physical search (unlike the sniffer-dog searches in *Kang-Brown* and *A.M.*) is not confined to evidence of criminal activity. The seized garbage bags contained a lot of personal items other than drug-making paraphernalia. Here the police went through several bags of personal information to find what they wanted. [35] Unlike the FLIR technology at issue in *Tessling*, the police activity in this case provided very accurate and persuasive evidence of illegal activity in the house.

(3) A Subjective Expectation of Privacy

[37] At the subjective stage of the test, I do not think "reasonableness" is the issue. The question is whether the appellant had, or is presumed to have had, an expectation of privacy in the information content of the bags. This is not a high hurdle. As mentioned, in the case of information about activities taking place in the home, such an expectation is presumed in the appellant's favour. It is possible that the appellant (who did not testify on this point) may never have ceased to have a subjective expectation, reasonable or not. The "reasonableness" of an individual's belief in the totality of the circumstances of a particular case is to be tested at the second objective branch of the privacy analysis.

(4) Was the Appellant's Expectation of Privacy Objectively Reasonable?

[39] Four factual elements are of prime importance in the appeal: (i) the garbage was put out by the appellant for collection in the customary location for removal, (ii) that location was at or near the property line, (iii) there was no manifestation (such as a locked receptacle) of any continuing assertion of privacy or control, and (iv) the police took the bags to search for information about activities within the home as part of a continuing criminal investigation.

[40] I acknowledge, however, that apart from the key issue of abandonment, the circumstances in this case favour the appellant. The police were trying to find out what was "happening inside a private dwelling, the most private of places" (*Plant*, at p. 302). The contents of the opaque sealed bags were not in public view. There is no evidence that the information was already in the hands of third parties. The gathering up of the contents of the bags by the police provided them with a window into the appellant's private life.

(5) The Place Where the Alleged "Search" Occurred

[41] In this case, the long arm of the law reached across the property line and collected the bags. On the basis of their examination of the contents of four of the bags and other evidence, the police obtained a search warrant. Conrad J.A., noting that the prosecution was built on the initial garbage seizure, emphasized territorial privacy.

[42] The distinctions between personal, territorial and informational privacy provide a useful analytical tool but, as noted, in many instances the categories overlap. I would not draw as strict a distinction as Conrad J.A. did between territorial privacy and informational privacy. I regard the gravamen of the appellant's complaint as the intrusion by the police into activities taking place inside his home rather than the fact that the police invaded the airspace at the foot of his garden by reaching across the lot line for the bags. If, for

example, the appellant had been unloading sealed bags from his truck in the back alley, temporarily placing them on public property, I do not think the police could grab the bags on the basis that the bags had not yet reached the sanctuary of a residential lot. That is the implication of focussing privacy protection on "people, not places". In the circumstances of unloading a vehicle, there could be no suggestion of abandonment.

[43] I also do not think constitutional protection should turn on whether the bags were placed a few inches inside the property line or a few inches outside it. The point is that the garbage was at the property line, accessible to passers-by.

(6) This was not a Perimeter Search

[52] Nothing said in these reasons should throw any doubt on the rulings on perimeter searches in *Kokesch*; *Grant*; *Wiley*; *Evans* and *Plant*. I do not believe that what we have in this case amounts to a "perimeter search". The prohibition laid down in those cases is simply inapplicable to the facts of this case.

(7) Whether the Subject Matter of the Alleged Search Was in Public View

[53] Of course the garbage bags were in plain view but the appellant asserts no privacy interest in the outside surface of the bags. His concern, as was the concern of the police, was with the concealed contents of the bags, which were clearly not in public view.

(8) Whether the Subject Matter of the Alleged "Search" Had Been Abandoned

[54] Clearly, the appellant intended to abandon his proprietary interest in the physical objects themselves. The question is whether he had a reasonable continuing privacy interest in the information which the contents revealed to the police. There was some discussion at the bar that a privacy interest does not cease until garbage becomes "anonymous", but as Conrad J.A. noted, much garbage never becomes anonymous, e.g. addressed envelopes, personal letters and so on. In this case, the garbage included invoices for the purchase of chemicals used in the preparation of the drug Ecstasy. The idea that s. 8 protects an individuals' privacy in garbage until the last unpaid bill rots into dust, or the incriminating letters turn into muck and are no longer decipherable, is to my mind too extravagant to contemplate. It would require the entire municipal disposal system to be regarded as an extension, in terms of privacy, of the dwelling-house. Yet if there is to be a reasonable cut-off point, where is it to be located? The line must be easily intelligible to both police and homeowners. Logically, because abandonment is a conclusion inferred from the conduct of the individual claiming the s. 8 right, the reasonableness line must relate to the conduct of that individual and not to anything done or not done by the garbage collectors, the police or anyone else involved in the subsequent collection and treatment of the "bag of information".

[55] *Stillman* (at para. 62) and *Tessling* (at paras. 40-41) identified garbage as a "classic" instance of abandonment. Here, I believe, abandonment occurred when the appellant placed his garbage bags for collection in the

open container at the back of his property adjacent to the lot line. He had done everything required of him to commit his rubbish to the municipal collection system. The bags were unprotected and within easy reach of anyone walking by in a public alleyway, including street people, bottle pickers, urban foragers, nosey neighbours and mischievous children, not to mention dogs and assorted wildlife, as well as the garbage collectors and the police. This conclusion is in general accord with the jurisprudence.

[62] Nevertheless, until the garbage is placed at or within reach of the lot line, the householder retains an element of control over its disposition and cannot be said to have unequivocally abandoned it, particularly if it is placed on a porch or in a garage or within the immediate vicinity of the dwelling where the principles set out in the "perimeter" cases such as *Kokesch*, *Grant* and *Wiley* apply.

[63] In municipalities (if there are any left) where garbage collectors come to the garage or porch and carry the garbage to the street, they are operating under (at least) an implied licence from the householder to come onto the property. The licence does not extend to the police. However, when the garbage is placed at the lot line for collection, I believe the householder has sufficiently abandoned his interest and control to eliminate any objectively reasonable privacy interest.

[64] Given the "totality of the circumstances" test, little would be gained by an essay on different variations of garbage disposal. To take a few common examples, however, the rural people who take their garbage to a dump and abandon it to the pickers and the seagulls, the apartment dweller who unloads garbage down a chute to the potential scrutiny of a curious building superintendent, and the householder who takes surreptitious advantage of a conveniently located dumpster to rid himself or herself of the "bag of information" are all acting in a manner inconsistent with the reasonable assertion of a continuing privacy interest, in my view.

(9) Whether the Information Was Already in the Hands of Third Parties; if so, Was it Subject to an Obligation of Confidentiality

[67] The Criminal Lawyers' Association seeks to bring garbage collection within the proposition that private information should remain confidential to the persons (i.e. the garbage collectors) to whom it was intended to be divulged, and for the purpose for which it was divulged, citing *R. v. Mills*, [1999] 3 S.C.R. 668, at para. 108, and *Dyment*, at pp. 431-32. One can readily accept this proposition in the context, for example, of the doctor/patient relationship. However, to extend it to the garbage collector/householder relationship, such as it is, is a step too far. Not only does the garbage collector not undertake to keep the trash confidential, any expectation by a householder of any such undertaking would be plainly unreasonable.

(10) Was the Police Conduct Intrusive in Relation to the Privacy Interest?

[69] Given that the act of abandonment occurred prior to the police gathering the garbage bags, there was no privacy interest in existence at the time of the police intervention, which therefore did not constitute an intrusion into a subsisting privacy interest.

(11) Was the Policy Technique Objectively Unreasonable?

[70] Much has been written in the privacy cases about police techniques that undermine privacy and have the potential to make social life in this country intolerable (e.g. the use of electronic recordings of private conversations in *R. v. Duarte*, [1990] 1 S.C.R. 30). This is not one of those cases. There is always, as *Hunter v. Southam* established, a realistic balance that must be struck between privacy and the legitimate demands of law enforcement and criminal investigation. In this case, the appellant's conduct was, in my view, inconsistent with preservation of the former and tipped the balance in favour of the latter.

(12) Whether the Gathering of this Evidence Exposed Intimate Details of the Appellant's Lifestyle or Information of a Biographical Nature

[71] Lifestyle and biographical information was exposed but the effective cause of the exposure was the act of abandonment by the appellant, not an intrusion by the police into a subsisting privacy interest.

V. Conclusion

[73] In summary, I agree with the trial judge and the Court of Appeal majority in this case that the appellant had abandoned his privacy interest in the contents of the garbage bags gathered up by the police when he placed them in the garbage alcove open to the laneway ready for collection. The taking by the police did not constitute a search and seizure within the scope of s. 8, and the evidence (as well as the fruits of the search warrant obtained in reliance on such evidence) was properly admissible.

Appeal dismissed

ABELLA J. —

[76] What we inelegantly call "garbage" may contain the most intensely personal and private information about ourselves. Brennan J., in his dissent in *California v. Greenwood*, 486 U.S. 35 (1988), illuminated the issue as follows:

> A single bag of trash testifies eloquently to the eating, reading, and recreational habits of the person who produced it. A search of trash, like a search of the bedroom, can relate intimate details about sexual practices, health, and personal hygiene. Like rifling through desk drawers or intercepting phone calls, rummaging through trash can divulge the target's financial and professional status, political affiliations and inclinations, private thoughts, personal relationships, and romantic interests. [p. 50]

[77] As Binnie J. emphasizes, the main question in this appeal is whether there exists an objectively reasonable expectation of privacy in household waste put out for collection near one's home. While I agree with him that there is no Charter violation in this case, in my view, with respect, the privacy of personal information emanating from the home, which has been transformed into household waste and put out for disposal, is entitled to protection from indiscriminate state intrusion. Such information should not be seen to automatically lose its "private" character simply because it is put outside for garbage disposal. Before the state can rummage through the personal

information from this ultimate zone of privacy, there should be, at the very least, a reasonable suspicion that a crime has been or is likely to be committed.

[78] The protection of privacy is a central feature of the Canadian constitutional system. In *R. v. Dyment*, [1988] 2 S.C.R. 417, La Forest J. wrote:

> Grounded in man's physical and moral autonomy, privacy is essential for the well being of the individual. For this reason alone, it is worthy of constitutional protection, but it also has profound significance for the public order. The restraints imposed on government to pry into the lives of the citizen go to the essence of a democratic state. [pp. 427-28]

[79] This Court has consistently observed that the home is the most private of places. In *R. v. Silveira*, [1995] 2 S.C.R. 297, Cory J. wrote: "There is no place on earth where persons can have a greater expectation of privacy than within their 'dwelling house'" (para. 140). And in *R. v. Tessling*, 2004 SCC 67, [2004] 3 S.C.R. 432, Binnie J. referred to the home as "being the place where our most intimate and private activities are most likely to take place" (para. 22).

[80] Does the state have the right to appropriate what is otherwise intensely private information from the home when it is left out for collection and disposal? My concern with allowing such an invasion of privacy is that it permits unobstructed access to information most people would never expect to be publicly accessible.

[83] What, then, are the reasonable expectations of an individual regarding the information that emanates from the home? Do individuals knowingly and voluntarily choose to part with private information when it is left out for collection? I think that when one considers the kind of medical, financial or other personal information that is potentially exposed, the answer is that most people retain an intention that the information stay private.

[85] Abandonment is merely one factor under the *Tessling* analysis. In my view, other factors, including whether the search exposed intimate details of an individual's life and the location of the search at or in close proximity to the property line, militate in favour of finding a reasonable expectation of privacy in such information. Abandonment can be seen more as relating to the objects contained in the waste, rather than to the information they reveal or to one's privacy interest in that information. It seems to me to be reasonable to infer that most individuals do not intend that that personal information will ever be disclosed without a countervailing legitimate state interest.

[90] While personal information may be obtained by searching through household waste that is left at or in close proximity to the property line for collection, on the other hand the individual disposing of the waste has indicated an intention to part with the objects contained in it. From a balancing of the *Tessling* factors, this leads to a conclusion that we are dealing with a diminished expectation of privacy, not unlike the reduced expectation at border crossings (see, for example, *R. v. Simmons*, [1988] 2 S.C.R. 495, and *R. v. Monney*, [1999] 1 S.C.R. 652). This does not mean that the state can arbitrarily search through the information. Barring exigent circumstances, there should at least be a threshold of reasonable suspicion about the

possibility of a criminal offence before household waste left for collection is searched. (See *Litchfield v. State*, 824 N.E.2d 356 (Ind. 2005)).

[91] In this case, the police had ample evidence on which to base a reasonable suspicion that a crime had been committed by Mr. Patrick. They were therefore entitled to search the household waste left for disposal.

[92] I therefore agree with Binnie J. that there is no Charter violation and would, like him, dismiss the appeal.

Do you favour the approach of the majority or that of Abella J? For a critical review of the majority see H. Archibald Kaiser, "Interest in Garbage; A Step Too Far for the Supreme Court", (2009) 64 C.R. (6th) 30. Note the caveats to the majority ruling. Section 8 still protects against searches of garbage where the public has no access to it or where the garbage disposer shows an intent to limit access, for example by locking up the garbage. These limits are likely to be relied on in the future by defence counsel attempting to distinguish the reach of *Patrick*. The majority approach does leave no Charter protection against random searches by police of garbage set out for collection. Since the Charter does not apply in this context presumably the police could use sniffer dogs for such searches (in marked contrast to the Court's reasonable suspicion standard it insisted on for police dog sniffers in buses and schools).

The majority make it express that nothing in *Patrick* is to be read as affecting the section 8 protection as it has previously put in place for perimeter searches in *Kokesch* and "knock on" searches in *Evans*. This is important as some lower courts have appeared reluctant to apply the full rigour of such rulings. The Supreme Court also implicitly returns to the approach of Justice La Forest in *Wong* who required the question of whether there was a reasonable expectation of privacy to be asked in a neutral way. In *Patrick*, the majority of the Alberta Court of Appeal is rebuked for simply asserting that drug dealers can have no reasonable expectation of privacy. The proper question was whether householders putting out garbage for collection have a reasonable expectation of privacy in the contents of those bags.

At para. 23, Binnie J. makes an enigmatic reference to the abandonment ruling in *Stillman*:

> In *R. v. Stillman*, [1997] 1 S.C.R. 607, McLachlin J., in dissent, but not on this point, stated that "[t]he purpose of s. 8 is to protect the person and property of the individual from unreasonable search and seizure. This purpose is not engaged in the case of property which the accused has discarded" (para. 223). (To the same effect see Cory J. for the majority at para. 62, and Major J., concurring in part, at para. 274.) [para. 23 in *Patrick*]

In fact in *Stillman* Justice Cory for a 5-4 majority of the Court held that abandonment had no application to an accused throwing away a tissue after he blew his nose in police custody as there was no way for the accused to assert his right not to consent to the seizure. McLachlin J. and Major J. both dissented on this point. Binnie J. may be indicating that the present Supreme Court has changed direction on this point.

Consider s. 8 challenges in the following criminal or quasi-criminal cases. Given the authorities reviewed above, you should, depending on the circumstances, ask:

1. Was there a reasonable expectation of privacy?
2. Was the search (or seizure) legal under statute or common law?
3. Was a warrant constitutonally required?
4. Were the *Hunter standards for a warrant satisfied?*
5. Were the constitutional standards for warrantless searches satisfied? and
6. Was the search conducted in a reasonable manner?

PROBLEM 11

The police stopped a car for speeding and ran a computer check after the driver, B, could produce no documentation. The police officer asked B who owned the vehicle and she told him it belonged to a friend. While he was waiting for information on the vehicle, the officer opened the back door on the passenger side, and stuck his head inside the vehicle so he could speak with L, a passenger. He asked L to identify herself and she provided her name and birth date. As they were speaking, he noticed two garbage bags on the driver's side of the back seat. They were open and appeared to be full of clothing. He could also see price tags on some of the garments hanging out of the garbage bags. He asked L who owned the bags and she replied that they each owned one bag. She did not indicate which bag belonged to her. The officer looked in the trunk and discovered five more garbage bags filled with clothing. Did the driver have a reasonable expectation of privacy? What of the passenger?

Compare *R. v. Lawrence and Belnavis* (1997), 34 O.R. (3d) 806, 10 C.R. (5th) 65, 118 C.C.C. (3d) 405 (S.C.C.). See comment by David Schwartz, "Edwards and Belnavis: Front and Rear Door Exceptions to the Right to be Secure from Unreasonable Search and Seizure," C.R., ibid. at 100.

PROBLEM 12

The accused rented a locker at the Winnipeg bus depot. Security guards saw two individuals place a duffel bag in the locker. Ninety minutes later one of the security guards smelled a strong odour of marijuana coming from the vent of the locker. The security guards had a Greyhound agent open the locker with a master key. Inside the duffel bag they found marijuana. The security guards placed the items back in the locker, locked it, and contacted the police. The police officers smelled marijuana and the Greyhound agent opened the locker for them. One of the officers seized the bag of marijuana, and placed it in a cruiser. The police officers did not have a search warrant. One of the officers testified that the idea of obtaining a warrant did not cross his mind. The other officer mentioned that he considered obtaining a warrant, but did not think the accused had a reasonable expectation of privacy in the locker and that, further, he did not think he had sufficient grounds to obtain a warrant. The next day an individual opened the locker with a key. The accused was later arrested and charged with possession of marijuana for the purpose of trafficking. Did the accused have a reasonable expectation of privacy in the locker to trigger s. 8? Was s. 8 violated by the guards? By the police?

Compare *R. v. Buhay*, [2003] 1 S.C.R. 631, 10 C.R. (6th) 205, 174 C.C.C. (3d) 97 (S.C.C.) (considered later as a leading authority of the exclusion of evidence under s. 24(2)).

What if the locker had been a school locker where the school also had a key? Compare *R. v. Z. (S.M.)* (1998), 21 C.R. (5th) 170, 131 C.C.C. (3d) 436 (Man. C.A.).

PROBLEM 13

A high-school teacher had a work-issued laptop which he was entitled to use for personal purposes. A school technician discovered nude and partly nude photographs of an underage female student on the teacher's laptop while performing maintenance activities. The technician reported this discovery to the principal, who directed the technician to copy the photographs to a CD. The principal seized the laptop from the teacher and school board technicians copied the temporary Internet files onto a second CD. The laptop and both CDs were handed over to the police who, without a warrant, reviewed their contents and then created a mirror image of the hard drive for forensic purposes. Did the teacher have a reasonable expectation of privacy in the contents of the laptop? Did the police violate his s. 8 rights? Did the school principal?

Compare: *R. v. Cole*, 2012 SCC 53, 96 C.R. (6th) 88 (S.C.C.) and CR annotation by Stephen Coughlan.

PROBLEM 14

The accused is charged with possession of a narcotic for the purpose of trafficking. The accused had been a registered guest in a hotel suite. Ignoring a "do not disturb" sign, a chambermaid entered the room and discovered a pillowcase full of money in a storage closet. She notified the hotel manager. He went to the room and found a brown, waxy brick in addition to the cash. The police were called. The police officers entered the room accompanied by the manager but without a search warrant.

Compare *R. v. Kenny* (1992), 11 C.R. (4th) 325 (*sub nom. R. v. Mercer*), 7 O.R. (3d) 9, 70 C.C.C. (3d) 180 (Ont. C.A.) and *R. v. Wong*, [1990] 3 S.C.R. 36, 1 C.R. (4th) 1, 60 C.C.C. (3d) 460 (S.C.C.), below under Electronic Surveillance.

PROBLEM 15

The accused is charged with possession of cocaine for the purpose of trafficking. The cocaine was discovered while the police were engaged in enforcing the Liquor License Act. They attended at what is commonly known as a "booze can"; an establishment wherein liquor is sold without a permit, and after hours. A search warrant was not obtained, because the Act permits a search without a warrant except in the case of dwellings. For that reason, the only Justice of the Peace on duty all night in Ontario will not issue warrants for searches of "booze cans". During the search of the premises the accused was observed putting something into a plastic bag and putting the bag down. Upon looking into the bag the police officer found a baggie containing several small packages of cocaine.

The accused brings a motion for exclusion of evidence arguing that, in searching her bag during an investigation of an illegal drinking establishment, police violated her section 8 rights. The Crown argues that the accused had no reasonable expectation of privacy while she was in the premises, and therefore could not argue that the search was unreasonable. Rule on the Crown's argument.

Compare *R. v. Sauvé* (1998), 22 C.R. (5th) 152 (Ont. Prov. Div.).

PROBLEM 16

The accused is charged with possession of cocaine for the purpose of trafficking. The drugs were found in the accused's apartment by a police officer who was acting on information provided by an informant. The police officer had intended to seek a search warrant or a telewarrant but, in checking out that the apartment was occupied by a person with the name provided to him, he encountered the apartment manager whom, the police officer felt, would alert the suspect unless the police officer raided the apartment at once. The police officer broke down the door of the apartment, finding three sleeping occupants and a large quantity of cocaine.

Compare *R. v. Duong* (2002), 49 C.R. (5th) 165, 162 C.C.C. (3d) 242 (B.C. C.A.), leave to appeal refused (2002), 302 N.R. 198 (note) (S.C.C.) and *R. v. Pichette* (2003), 11 C.R. (6th) 301, 175 C.C.C. (3d) 73 (Que. C.A.).

PROBLEM 17

Drug squad officers receive a judicial authorization to intercept the telephone communications of two persons suspected of drug trafficking in Newfoundland. They learn through these intercepts that a package of drugs is to be sent to a certain post office box in Newfoundland and also to a certain dwelling house. With the cooperation of the post office security personnel the police intercept both packages, retaining in each case a sample of the contents which turn out to be cocaine. It is an offence under the appropriate Federal Act for anyone to tamper with the mail in Canada unless expressly authorized by the Act, which did not occur in this case. What if the tampering had been authorized under the Act. Would a warrant have been required for the dwelling house and the mail box?

Compare *R. v. Crane* (1985), 45 C.R. (3d) 368 (Nfld. Dist. Ct.).

PROBLEM 18

In *R. v. Stevens* (1983), 35 C.R. (3d) 1 (N.S. C.A.), Hart J.A. summarized the evidence as follows:

> Constable Daniel Duffy, a plainclothes member of the Drug Section of the R.C.M.P. stationed at New Minas, Nova Scotia, on 1st June 1982 at 10:50 a.m. saw the respondent sitting on the railing of a bridge on Main Street in Kentville. He stopped his unmarked car and asked the respondent to come over to his vehicle. The police officer then invited him to sit in the front seat, as he wished to talk to him. The two men were known to each other, and Constable Duffy describes their conversation when they were both seated in the car as follows:
>
> A. I asked him if he had any drugs on him.
>
> Q. What did he say? A. 'No.' I then asked him if he was making any money at it and he said he quit selling drugs two weeks ago. I then asked him if he would mind emptying his pockets.
>
> Q. And what did he do? A. He did start to empty his pockets.
>
> Q. And what pockets did he empty? A. The right pants pocket, for sure. I know he did pull something out of there. I don't recall if he pulled anything out of the other pockets or not.
>
> Q. And what were you doing while he was going through his pockets? A. I was watching [not audible].
>
> Q. What did you then do? A. When he—I believe he had finished, or it appeared to me he had, and I reached into his left jean jacket pocket and pulled out material which I felt was a narcotic.
>
> [The examination continued.]
>
> Q. Now first of all, constable, what was your purpose in approaching this particular individual on the bridge? A. I knew him from working in this area for six years. I knew Mr. Stevens as recent as the 27th April 1982; I had personal contact with Mr. Stevens and information I received along that way indicated that Mr. Stevens was involved in the drug trade in the Kentville area.
>
> Q. That contact in April: did that lead to any charges? A. That led to a charge under s. 3(1) of the Narcotic Control Act. At that time I was dressed in civilian dress and I was in the same vehicle that was used on the 1st of June 1982.
>
> Q. And the substance that was received back on April 27th—or was there anything taken that day? A. Yes, there was.
>
> Q. Was it subsequently analyzed? A. Yes, it was.

As a result of the 27th April seizure the respondent pled guilty to an offence against s. 3(1) of the Narcotic Control Act. Constable Duffy explained that he had obtained information about the activities of the respondent from many sources, including informants. His testimony continued.

Q. And what did the information pertain to with respect to Mr. Stevens? A. That he was actively involved in the so-called 'drug- trade' in the Kentville area. . . .

Q. When you first saw Mr. Stevens what was your purpose in asking him to come over to the vehicle? A. I just wanted to talk to him.

Q. As a result of that conversation, what was your purpose after you had your talk with him that you related to the court? A. Well, after I had my talk with him I felt he may have narcotics on his person.

Q. And what led you to believe that? A. Well, previous to my talk I felt that he might have had narcotics when I first—

Q. What did the talk have to do with it? A. Well, the talk reaffirmed it, in that he certainly was still using drugs.

Q. How did you determine that? A. Well, he advised me that he was still using drugs but he was not selling them . . .

A. At the time, when I asked him if he was still—if he was making any money at it, he said that he stopped selling drugs two weeks ago, and I did not state previously in evidence, however, it was asked if he was still using them.

Q. What point was that, now? A. That was done directly after he had stated to me that he had stopped selling drugs two weeks ago.

Q. What was the question? A. I asked him if he was still using narcotics or drugs.

Q. Did you receive an answer? A. Yes, he said he was.

Q. And as a result of that what did you do? A. As a result of that I asked him if he would mind emptying his pockets.

Q. Now, during this period of time had Mr. Stevens been advised he was under arrest? A. No.

Q. During this period of time until you found the item in his possession did you have any reason to arrest him? A. No, I did not.

Q. And upon finding the substance what was he told? A. He was told at that point that he had the right to obtain and instruct counsel without delay and that he was going to be charged under the Narcotic Control Act. . . .

Q. And I believe one question I had asked, or intended to ask you, was: Did you have any reason to arrest him prior to finding the substance? A. No, I did not.

Q. Why did you reach into the pocket after he had gone through his pockets? A. I still wondered if there was narcotics in his pocket.

Q. Do you recall today whether he had gone into that pocket or not?

A. No, I don't recall.

[On cross examination Constable Duffy explained further his reasons for the search.]

Q. Now, you indicated that up until the point in time you found something in his left top pocket—was it left jacket pocket? A. Yes.

Q. Up until that time you had no reason for arrest? A. No, sir.

Q. You did indicate—it's fair to say you stopped to check him out for drugs, or you had some suspicions? A. Yes, sir, I had some suspicions.

Q. You indicated to my learned friend those were based on a number of things, including police station rumours and gossip, I suppose?

A. No, sir, I wouldn't say it was that.

Q. What was it based on? A. It was based on information I had received from various sources and also based on the contact I had with Mr. Stevens one month previous to that.

Q. You figured, then, if he had drugs on him before he might have drugs now; is that correct? A. That was part of it, yes."

PROBLEM 19

Drug squad police officers are told by a trusted informant/addict that Jane is going to purchase heroin. At a distance of 100 metres they observe her meeting a man known by them to be a drugs user. Shortly after this Jane enters a public washroom. Ten minutes later she re-appears and is followed to the cocktail lounge in a hotel. There the police officers move in, shouting "Police officers. This is a drugs bust". She is seized by her arms, her throat grabbed and a choke hold is applied, forcing her mouth open. While this is happening three caps of heroin drop out of her right hand. During the search Jane is rendered semi-conscious and loses control of her bladder. She had no drugs in her mouth. Officers are trained as to the difference between a throat hold, which is to prevent swallowing, and a choke hold, which stops breathing and obstructs the flow of blood to the brain.

Compare *R. v. Collins* (1983), 33 C.R. (3d) 130, 5 C.C.C. (3d) 141 (B.C. C.A.), *R. v. Cohen* (1983) 33 C.R. (3d) 151, 5 C.C.C. (3d) 156 (B.C. C.A.), *R. v. Truchanek* (1984), 39 C.R. (3d) 137 (B.C. C.A.), *R. v. Garcia-Guiterrez* (1991), 5 C.R. (4th) 1, 65 C.C.C. (3d) 15 (B.C. C.A.) and *R. v. Greffe*, [1990] 1 S.C.R. 755, 75 C.R. (3d) 257, 55 C.C.C. (3d) 161 (S.C.C.).

PROBLEM 20

The accused owned and occupied a condominium unit in a small 10-unit building. The police suspected that the accused was involved with dealing drugs from the condominium and made three surreptitious entries into common areas of his building. The entries were without knowledge of any residents and without any prior consent. Once inside, a detective walked through the hallways, entered an unlocked storage area in the lower level, and viewed the contents of the accused's storage locker, which contained material that could be used in a grow-op. The detective also hid in the stairwell, where he observed the accused's unit and listened to what was going on inside, and saw a known drug dealer leave with a packet. Using the information gathered from these entries the police obtained a warrant. The ITO mentioned that the detective had made observations from within the condominium but not that he had entered a locked building without permission. When the warrant was executed the police found marihuana and cocaine in the unit. The accused was later arrested on drug trafficking charges and possession of property obtained by crime.

See *R. v. White* (2015), 325 C.C.C. (3d) 171, 21 C.R. (7th) 389 (Ont. C.A.).

PROBLEM 21

Airport police observed an open six-pack of Molson Canadian beer in a motor vehicle in the cargo area of an airport, which motor vehicle belonged to an airport ramp employee. The six-pack was on the front passenger floor of the vehicle. One bottle had its cap removed and appeared to have been partially consumed. A blue parka was observed on the rear floor of the car. As soon as the employee entered the vehicle the police searched the vehicle relying on their authority under a provincial Liquor Control Act to search a vehicle without a warrant on reasonable grounds to believe that it contained unlawful liquor. It is an offence under that Act to drive with liquor accessible to the driver. The search was for liquor although the officers realized that they could also find drugs since they knew that the owner had an outstanding charge of possession of a narcotic for the purpose of trafficking. Sixty grams of cocaine were found in the parka which belonged to the accused and also one hundred and ninety-five grams of cocaine where found in a plastic bag in the trunk, which bag had the accused's name on it. The wholesale value of the cocaine was $30,000 and the street value $183,000.

Compare *R. v. Annett* (1984), 43 C.R. (3d) 350, 17 C.C.C. (3d) 332 (Ont. C.A.).

Contrast *R. v. Belliveau* (1987), 54 C.R. (3d) 144, 30 C.C.C. (3d) 163 (N.B. C.A.), *R. v. I.D.D.* (1987), 61 C.R. (3d) 292 (Sask. C.A.) and *R. v. Klimchuk* (1991), 8 C.R. (4th) 327 (B.C. C.A.). See generally G. Luther, "The Search and Seizure of Motor Vehicles: Learning from an American Mistake" (1987), 12 Q.L.J. 239.

PROBLEM 22

Canadian courts have consistently held that the common law plain view doctrine does not itself authorise new police power to search and seize. It only applies to extend an existing lawful power to justify the seizure of objects in immediate vision and found inadvertently: see most recently, *R. v. Law* (2002), 48 C.R. (5th) 199, 160 C.C.C. (3d) 449 (S.C.C.), *R. v. Spindloe* (2001), 42 C.R. (5th) 58, 154 C.C.C. (3d) 8 (Sask. C.A.) at 29-37 [C.C.C.] and discussion by Stuart, *Charter Justice*, pp. 284-285. With this doctrine in mind and the provisions in ss. 489(1) and (2), consider whether the seizure of pornographic material was lawful in the following circumstances.

A police officer received a complaint from a 9-year-old girl, A.Y., that the accused, a family friend, had engaged in improper sexual conduct with her at his home and had taken two Polaroid photographs of her naked private areas. The officer formed the opinion that the accused might be a pedophile and might be in possession of child pornography. To confirm her suspicion, she consulted a psychiatrist with expertise in pedophilia who confirmed that pedophiles tend to collect and retain child pornography. On the basis of this information the officer obtained a search warrant to search for the two photographs of the complainant A.Y. and three additional items related to the photographs, as well as a list of other materials which a pedophile would be expected to have in his possession. In executing the warrant, the only item located and seized relative to the complainant A.Y. was a Polaroid camera. However, the police located and seized a quantity of material which, at his trial, the accused conceded constituted child pornography within the meaning of s.163.1(1) of the Criminal Code.

The accused was charged with an offence arising from A.Y.'s complaint, but this charge was withdrawn. However, he was charged and convicted of possession of child pornography contrary to s. 161.1(4).

Compare *R. v. Fawthrop* (2002), 4 C.R. (6th) 52, 166 C.C.C. (3d) 97 (Ont. C.A.). What if the police had brought the media along to televise the execution of the warrant? Compare *R. v. West* (1997), 12 C.R. (5th) 106, 122 C.C.C. (3d) 218 (B.C. C.A.).

PROBLEM 23

A prisoner complained of the general practices at a penitentiary whereby female guards entered the living area of male prisoners and also routinely frisk-searched male prisoners. In the prison at the time, 14.5 per cent of the guards were women. Most of the women were classifed at the lowest job classification, which required routine searching as part of its responsibilities, including frisk-searching when a prisoner passed certain points in the institution. As well, guards entered living areas for regular counts and for unscheduled surveillance patrols known as "winds". Is there a s. 15 equality issue? Which groups are to be compared? Male and female inmates and/or male and female guards?

Compare *Weatherall v. Can. A.G.* (1990), 78 C.R. (3d) 257, 58 C.C.C. (3d) 424 (Fed. C.A.), discussed by Elizabeth Thomas in "Annotation" (1990), 78 C.R. (3d) 258-261. Weatherall was confirmed by the Supreme Court in *R. v. Conway*, [1993] 2 S.C.R. 872, 23 C.R. (4th) 1, 83 C.C.C. (3d) 1 (S.C.C.), considered in an annotation by Allan Manson, 23 C.R. (4th) 2-6. See too *R. v. Major* (2004), 186 C.C.C. (3d) 513, 23 C.R. (6th) 294 (Ont. C.A.), leave to appeal refused (2005), 2005 CarswellOnt 2774 (S.C.C.) (accused having reasonable expectation of privacy in family-visit trailer in penitentiary, but warrantless search not violating s. 8).

2. Electronic Surveillance

Is there a real difference between physical search and seizure and electronic surveillance? Consider the following:

> There was of course no way of knowing whether you were being watched at any given moment. How often, or on what system, the Thought Police plugged in on any individual wire was guesswork. It was even conceivable that they watched everybody all the time. But at any rate they could plug in your wire whenever they wanted to. You had to live—did live, from habit that became instinct—in the assumption that every sound you made was overheard, and, except in darkness, every movement scrutinized.(George Orwell, *1984*).

> [T]he electronic bug is a marvellously egalitarian instrument. It does not discriminate on basis of race, creed, colour or suspicion of criminal activity. It catches everybody alike, equally; everybody within earshot of the bug, no matter how guilty or innocent. (A. Borovoy, General Counsel to the Canadian Civil Liberties Association, *Minutes of Proceedings and Evidence of the Standing Committee on Justice and Legal Affairs* (29th Parl., 1st Sess.) 16:5).

The legislation which we now find in Part VI of the Criminal Code under the heading Invasion of Privacy, was enacted in 1974 as the Protection of Privacy Act. The anomaly was recognized by Justice McIntyre in *Goldman v. R.*, [1980] 1 S.C.R. 976, 13 C.R. (3d) 228, 16 C.R. (3d) 330, 51 C.C.C. (2d) at 15 (S.C.C.):

> The purpose, it has been frequently said, of Part IV.I of the Code was to protect the right to privacy. It may be more realistic to say that the purpose or effect of Part IV.I has been to regulate the method of breach of any such right.

The legislation did create certain offences: intercepting private communications; s. 184; possessing equipment primarily useful for surreptitious interception; s. 191; disclosing intercepted private communications; s. 193(1). There are also provisions for forfeiture of equipment; s. 192; and for damages to aggrieved persons; s. 194. The legislation however also provides a procedure for the judicial authorizing of interception of private communications and the use of evidence obtained thereby. There have been a few prosecutions for the offences noted. There have been thousands of authorized intercepts. An interception is also lawful if a party consented; s. 184(2)(*a*). The numbers of consent intercepts is unknown. It is the jurisprudence emanating from judicially authorized and consent intercepts that we will be examining.

Applications for judicial authorization are made *ex parte* to a federally appointed judge; s. 185. The list of offences for which an authorization can be obtained has grown over the years; s. 183. An authorization may be granted if the judge is satisfied that it would be in the best interests of the administration of justice and that other investigative procedures have been tried and have failed, other investigative procedures are unlikely to succeed or the urgency of the situation is such that it would be impractical to use only other investigative procedures; s. 186. The legislation appears to contemplate that intercepting private communications will be exceptional. In *R. v. Araujo*, [2000] 2 S.C.R. 992, 38 C.R. (5th) 307, 149 C.C.C. (3d) 449

(S.C.C.) Justice LeBel determined for the Court that the test was not one of "last resort" which would be too restrictive but a test of "no reasonable practical alternative". A survey has indicated that Canadian police were seven times more likely to use wiretaps and bugs in criminal investigations than police in the twenty- four states of the United States where law enforcers can wiretap or bug with a court order: *Globe and Mail*, December 30, 1978. Several critics have suggested that our protection of privacy legislation, rather than protecting our privacy, has in fact authorized and encouraged its invasion.

In 1993 Parliament enacted major changes to the electronic surveillance provisions of the Criminal Code: S.C. 1993, c. 40. These amendments were in response to concerns expressed by police and prosecutors that various Charter decisions, striking down several powers to use electronic surveillance, had left police without the necessary power and had put police officers and informers at risk. To better assess these decisions and the 1993 legislative response we will first consider the law as it existed prior to the new laws.

(a) The Debate

In *The Limits of the Criminal Sanction* (1968), at pp. 195-196, Professor Packer presents the competing claims of two value systems by fashioning two models. In the electronic surveillance area they are pictured as follows:

> *The Crime Control Model.* The war on organized crime demands the use of electronic surveillance. High-ranking members of organized crime syndicates are insulated by layers of structure from direct participation in the crimes committed by their underlings. If they are to be implicated, it must be by showing that they have directed a conspiracy. Since their role may not even be known to the immediate participants in any given illegal transaction of gambling or narcotics, the only way in which evidence can be secured against them is by listening in on their telephone conversations and otherwise monitoring their discussions. Almost without exception, the conviction of top underworld figures has depended on the use of evidence or evidential leads obtained through electronic surveillance.

> It is undeniable that abuses may occur, but their danger is greatly outweighed by the necessity for using these devices. Judicial control of the use of surveillance devices will probably not do much to protect against excesses of enforcement zeal because it is impossible for the judge to whom application is made for an authorizing order to do more than generally satisfy himself that the police have reasonable grounds for wishing to use the devices to overhear conversations on a particular telephone line or in a particular place. Judges cannot exercise continuous and detailed supervision over the monitoring. And the nature of the business is such that there is going to be a high ratio of chaff to wheat. However, we do not object in principle to having to obtain a court order, so long as judges do not require an impossible degree of specificity about what we are looking for. After all, if we knew precisely what we were looking for, we wouldn't have to look.

> There should be no limitations on the kinds of criminal activity police are allowed to investigate using surveillance devices. Sometimes an important underworld figure can be tripped up on the basis of a relatively minor criminal charge. By the same token, we should be free to use what turns up whether it is what we were looking for

or not. Law-abiding citizens have nothing to fear. If conversations that we overhear produce no leads to evidence of criminal activity, we are not interested in them. Law enforcement has neither the time nor the inclination to build up files of information about activity that is not criminal.

The Due Process Model. The right of privacy, as implied by the Fourth Amendment to the Constitution, cannot be forced to give way to the asserted exigencies of law enforcement. The use of electronic surveillance constitutes just the kind of indiscriminate general search that helped to bring on the American Revolution and that the framers of the Constitution were alert to guard against. In the name of necessity this grant of power would permit an unscrupulous policeman or prosecutor to pry into the private lives of people almost at will. Knowledge that this was so would certainly inhibit the free expression of thoughts and feelings that makes life in our society worth living. Electronic surveillance by anyone under any circumstances should be outlawed.

That is the optimal position. If it cannot be established, certainly it is essential that police authority for electronic surveillance be strictly limited to a small class of very serious cases. "The fight against organized crime" is far too vague and sweeping a rubric to provide adequate protection. And the offenses allegedly committed by organized criminals are committed by many others as well. The most that should be authorized is the use of electronic surveillance in cases of espionage, treason, or other crimes directly affecting national security. And even in such cases as these, there should be judicial control comparable to what would be exercised in deciding whether to issue a search warrant.

As we examine the following jurisprudence it will be worthwhile to ask to which model of the criminal process our Canadian legislation, as interpreted by our Canadian courts, most closely approximates.

The Canadian legislation followed the example of the American Omnibus Crime Control and Safe Streets Act of 1968. It is instructive then to read some of the remarks of Ramsay Clark, former U.S. Attorney-General, testifying before the Standing Committee on Justice and Legal Affairs when the new Canadian legislation was being reviewed:

Mr. Wagner: That, of course, is being idealistic, but when you start with the premise, Mr. Clark, that wiretapping is inherently immoral, of course that jolts everybody and that is shocking—wiretapping is inherently immoral. I put it to you that killing is immoral; that stealing, bribery, conspiracy for subversive activity, conspiracy for organized crime are immoral. What are you going to do about this?

Do you not believe that wiretapping could be one weapon, one tool—not a trick as you say but a tool—which, controlled for certain purposes with judicial authority, could be used in certain cases such as against organized crime? Do you not believe that since the underworld is using wiretapping against honest people that it might be a good idea to have electronic surveillance under certain conditions in certain cases? Or do you believe that all these weapons may be used by people who live outside the law, but as far as honest people are concerned they should simply sit back and say: "We are sorry, this would not be right. Really we should not use these weapons."

You say that in the United States there are about 26 large cities where organized crime flourishes. I would say that in Canada there are probably five or six large cities where these means could be used effectively. What would your comment be?

Mr. Clark: The last place I would look for my standard of conduct would be the criminal community. They murder. I do not think police should murder. They steal. I do not think police should steal. If they wiretap, police should wiretap—who needs it? I should think they would have found out before now, if they are really doing it, that it is not very efficient, it is very wasteful and very expensive, and found some other way to accomplish their immoral meanings. I have not heard, and I thought maybe I was going to hear you defend wiretapping as being moral. Perhaps it is the sort of immoral thing we have to do to get bad people but once we break that barrier there are very few restraints on us. I think it is imperative, if we are going to have respect for law, that law be respectable. I work with police constantly . . .

Mr. Wagner: So did I.

Mr. Clark: I believe in the policemen. I want honest, effective professional policemen and I do not want to have to look them in the eye and say, "Who are you wire-tapping now?" Is that the best we can do? Is this society so helpless that there is no other way we can control crime except doing it because they do it or because we think we can be effective that way?

I do not know what is happening in your cities right now, but I do not think you would be doing the police any favour if you diverted some of their manpower, assigned two to six men—that is what Frank Hogan says it takes in New York City—to handle a tap to see what you can pick up.

Mr. Wagner: Obviously, when you give the example of people sitting night and day for two years on a tap, that certainly is exaggerated.

Mr. Clark: It has happened.

Mr. Wagner: Yes, it has happened, but that is the extreme case. Our law provides for 30 days. Of course 30 days is a very limited amount of time.

An Hon. Member: With renewals.

Mr. Wagner: Yes.

. . .

Mr. Poulin: I will refer you briefly, Mr. Clark, to the Congressional Record of Monday, April 30, 1973, and a statement by Mr. McClelland who is the Chairman, I understand of the subcommittee on criminal laws. He quotes from a statement made by the Attorney General and by the Deputy Attorney General, the Assistant Attorney General for narcotics, with respect to Title 3. He says as follows:

> The Crime Control and Safe Streets Act of 1968 is playing a key role in the war against crime. As the Attorney General testified on April 5 before the Senate Committee on Appropriations, the provision for wiretapping by Congress has been the most significant, most important weapon that our country has had to deal effectively with the problem of organized crime. Now, after four-and-a-half years, we have more than one-half of the leadership of organized crime in the country under indictment.

Would you comment on that statement and indicate how you disagree with the Attorney General's statement of April 5 of this year?

Mr. Clark: First let me say that, from the beginning, the Nixon administration, if I may call it that, has politicized the role of wiretapping. If you go back to the very beginning, to John Mitchell's confirmation hearing as Attorney General of the United States, he was asked by Senator Phil Hart; "What would you do differently to what was done by your predecessor, Ramsey Clark, if you are confirmed?" He said "The only thing I can think of right now is wiretapping." It has been that way right on down the road. What you find is that we do not know how many newspaper reporters he has wiretapped, but we know that there are some.

Mr. Poulin: We know that there are some here, too, Mr. Clark, but I . . .

Mr. Clark: But he is authorized . . .

Mr. Poulin: . . . was asking you about its effectiveness with respect to organized crime, not with respect to politicizing.

Mr. Clark: I just do not believe it.

Mr. Poulin: You do not believe the Attorney General?

Mr. Clark: If they want to show me the evidence, I will examine the evidence, if they want to state a conclusion, I think that it is a political statement and I am not prepared to accept it because it is contrary to my experience.

If you just want to count the prosecutions that have been lost because of their inadequate compliance with that law, it is terribly, terribly wasteful. I described some of the cases that have been reversed on that ground already. And who needed it? They could have prosecuted those cases without this wiretapping.

(b) The Legislation

The legislation is only concerned with the interception by "electro-magnetic, acoustic, mechanical or other device" of a "private communication". A "private communication" was originally defined as "any oral communication or any telecommunication made under circumstances in which it is reasonable for the originator thereof to expect that it will not be intercepted by any person other than the person intended by the originator thereof to receive it". In 1993 the definition section 183 was amended to require that the originator or the receiver be in Canada and to expressly include radio- based telephone communications but only where there has been an attempt to scramble the communication to prevent intelligible reception. The latter amendment responded to a decision in *R. v. Solomon* (1992), 16 C.R. (4th) 193, 77 C.C.C. (3d) 264 (C.M.Q.) that communications over cellular phones were not private communications. **Do you agree with that decision and the amendment?**

In *R. v. Wong* (1991), 1 C.R. (4th) 1 (S.C.C.), the Supreme Court found that video surveillance could not be authorized by Part VI. See generally E. Goldstein, "Surreptitious Video Surveillance and the Protection of Privacy" (1987), 56 C.R. (3d) 368 and S.C. MacLean, "Video Surveillance and the Charter of Rights" (1987), 30 Crim. L.Q. 88.

In *R. v. Wise*, [1992] 1 S.C.R. 527, 11 C.R. (4th) 253, 70 C.C.C. (3d) 193 (S.C.C.) it was held that there was no legal power for police to install a beeper in the interior of a vehicle. The police suspected that the accused was linked to several rural murders. After the expiry of a search warrant for the accused's house and vehicle had produced no evidence, the police installed a beeper in his vehicle to keep track of his movements. This enabled the officers to arrest him shortly after he had blown up a telecommunications tower, causing thousands of dollars of damage. He was charged with wilful damage to property. The Supreme Court agreed with the trial judge that the accused's s. 8 rights had been violated.

In the following problems, has there been an interception of a "private communication" such as to attract the protection of the Criminal Code?

PROBLEM 24

The accused, charged with arson in relation to forest fires, was placed in an R.C.M.P. polygraph room. The room contained a concealed microphone and a television camera. While being watched with the camera, he slid out of his chair, got down on his hands and knees, put his arms into the air and said, "Oh God, let me get away with it just this once".

Compare *R. v. Davie* (1980), 54 C.C.C. (2d) 216 (B.C. C.A.).

PROBLEM 25

The accused is an inmate in a reception centre awaiting his trial on a charge of first degree murder. His telephone conversation from the range with a woman on the outside is intercepted. Above the telephone in the prison was a sign reading "All personal calls may be monitored".

Compare *R. v. Rodney* (1984), 40 C.R. (3d) 256, 12 C.C.C. (3d) 195 (B.C. S.C.) and *R. v. Arradi* (2001), 48 C.R. (5th) 83 (Que. C.A.).

PROBLEM 26

Kidnappers call the victim's father to arrange for payment of ransom. The police listen in.

Compare *R. v. Tam* (1993), 80 C.C.C. (3d) 476 (B.C. S.C.).

(i) Exclusion of Evidence: s. 189

In 1974, after a protracted debate in the House of Commons at a time of minority government, Parliament broke with the common law position that it did not affect the admissibility of evidence that the evidence had been illegally obtained: *R. v. Wray*, [1971] S.C.R. 272, 11 C.R.N.S. 235, [1970] 4 C.C.C. 1 (S.C.C.). It enacted a special provision for the exclusion of evidence obtained contrary to Part VI:

189. (1) A private communication that has been intercepted is inadmissible as evidence against the originator of the communication or the person intended by the originator to receive it unless

(a) the interception was lawfully made; or

(b) the originator thereof or the person intended by the originator to receive it has expressly consented to the admission thereof;

but evidence obtained directly or indirectly as a result of information acquired by interception of a private communication is not inadmissible by reason only that the private communication is itself inadmissible as evidence.

(2) Notwithstanding subsection (1), the judge or provincial court judge presiding at any proceedings may refuse to admit evidence obtained directly or indirectly as

a result of information acquired by interception of a private communication that is itself inadmissible as evidence where he is of the opinion that the admission thereof would bring the administration of justice into disrepute.

(3) Where the judge or provincial court judge presiding at any proceedings is of the opinion that a private communication that, by virtue of subsection (1), is inadmissible as evidence in the proceedings

   (a) is relevant to a matter at issue in the proceedings, and

   (b) is inadmissible as evidence therein by reason only of a defect of form or an irregularity in procedure, not being a substantive defect or irregularity, in the application for or the giving of the authorization under which such private communication was intercepted,

he may, notwithstanding subsection (1), admit such private communication as evidence in the proceedings.

Under subs. 1, the communication itself shall not be received into evidence unless the interception was lawfully made or a party to the communication consents. However the judge may nevertheless receive the communication if the defect or irregularity is not substantive (subs. 3). Derivative evidence obtained as the result of an improper intercept is receivable under subs. 1 but may be excluded if the presiding judge believes that its receipt would bring the administration of justice into disrepute (subs. 2).

The guideline for the judge in determining the admissibility of the derivative evidence is whether "the admission thereof would bring the administration of justice into disrepute". What is the meaning of justice? Consider the following statements in the House of Commons debates when the privacy legislation was introduced:

OTTO LANG (Minister of Justice): Let us suppose a person is accused of murder and there is a murder weapon—the most relevant of evidence in relation to that crime—with ballistics matching the bullet which was found in the victim, with fingerprints on the weapon which matched the fingerprints of the accused in the dock. If the law were to stay as it has been reported from the committee, that murder weapon could not be admitted in evidence if it was found as a result of information which in any way came from the use of an illegal electronic intrusion or wiretap . . . We ought not to allow a rule which might keep from a court evidence which is relevant and whose absence might prevent justice from being done.

MARK MACGUIGAN (Future Minister of Justice): In my view, Mr. Speaker, justice is not to be so narrowly construed as to be confined to what takes place in the courtroom. Justice, rather, refers broadly to rectitude in the whole legal process, ranging from the time of apprehension and arrest, through trial and conviction to final release from parole. The general rectitude of the legal system includes the good faith of those who administer and enforce the law. Above all, the public must always be consciously assured of the good faith of those who enforce the law, especially of the police forces in our country. It is for this reason that I supported in committee the amended form of the bill, and that is still the direction in which I wish to see the final form of the law move.

Hansard, November 27, 1973 at 8204, 8205, 8212.

In 1993 Parliament abolished s. 189 leaving any remedy of exclusion of evidence obtained in violation of Part VI to s. 24(2) of the Charter. **Do you agree with this change?**

Since an illegal search is necessarily contrary to s. 8 (see *Collins* and *Kokesch*, above) it is still important to determine whether the electronic surveillance was lawful.

GOLDMAN v. R.

[1980] 1 S.C.R. 976, 13 C.R. (3d) 228, 16 C.R. (3d) 330 (S.C.C.)

The accused was charged with conspiring with one Dwyer and others to possess counterfeit money. The Crown's case depended on recordings made by the police of two conversations between the accused and Dwyer. The first was a telephone conversation and the second a direct conversation between the two during which Dwyer was fitted with a concealed body pack, transmissions of which were recorded by the police some distance away. Dwyer was not called at trial to give evidence. The Crown argued that the recordings were "lawfully made" within the meaning of s. 178.16(1)(*a*) [since repealed] since s. 178.11(2)(*a*) [now 184(2)(*a*)] excepted from criminal liability persons who had the consent of the originator or recipient of a private communication.

LASKIN, C.J.C. (dissenting):—In my opinion, s. 178.16, in the light of the elaborate controls set up under ss. 178.11 to 178.14 was designed to protect privacy of communication by altering the common law rule as to admission of illegally obtained evidence, so that even if collaboration with the police resulted under s. 178.11(2)(*a*), this did not *ipso facto* make the evidence obtained by a consensual interception admissible without a further consent under s. 178.16(1)(*b*). I do not agree that the legislation under examination is sufficiently clear to warrant the conclusion that a consent under s. 178.11(2)(*a*) dispenses with any further consent in relation to admissibility. Indeed, s. 178.16(2) reinforces this position.

In principle, I see a vast difference between a judicial authorization for an interception which, at the same time, would make its fruits admissible in evidence and a prior consent by a private person to an interception destroying another's expected privacy. Of course, Parliament could prescribe that for the purpose of admissibility in evidence both situations be treated the same way. It has not, however, done so with the clarity that should be present to enable A, by consenting to an interception of private communications with B, to make those communications admissible without more against B.

McINTYRE, J. (for eight judges):—Section 178.11(1) makes it an indictable offence to interpret a private communication by means of the devices described and in s-s. (2) provides that s-s. (1) which created the offence will not apply to a person who has the consent, express or implied, of the originator of the private communication or of the person intended to receive it. This consent is a consent to interception and its effect is to preserve from illegality, in other words, to render lawful, an interception of a private communication made with consent. It is important to note as well that the consent may be express or implied and may be given by either the originator of the private communication or the intended recipient. Section 178.16 is complementary to s. 178.11. It deals with admissibility of evidence which has been obtained by interceptions of private communications. It provides that an intercepted private communication is inadmissible as evidence against its originator or the person intended to receive it unless it was lawfully made or unless the originator or the person intended to receive it has expressly consented to the admission. The Crown does not allege that any such consent as that envisaged in s. 178.16(1)(b) was given in the case at bar. Therefore, that subsection is not relevant to the case. However, it is worthwhile to note that the s. 178.16(1)(b) consent differs from the consent in s. 178.11(2)(a) in that it is a consent to admit evidence not to intercept. The Crown's position here is simply this, by virtue of Dwyer's consent given under s. 178.11(2)(a), the interceptions were lawfully made within the meaning of s. 178.16(1)(a) and evidence thereof was admissible notwithstanding the absence of any further consent under s. 178.16(1)(b).

R. v. DUARTE
[1990] 1 S.C.R. 30, 74 C.R. (3d) 281, 53 C.C.C. (3d) 1 (S.C.C.)

As part of an investigation into drug trafficking, the police rented an apartment to be occupied by a police informer, who was working with an undercover police officer. The police installed audio-visual recording equipment in a wall of the apartment. Prior to the installation, the informer and the undercover officer consented to the interception of their conversations under s. 178.11(2)(a) [now s. 184(2)(a)] of the Criminal Code. The accused later discussed a cocaine transaction with the undercover officer and the informer at the apartment. Charged with the offence of conspiracy to import a narcotic, the accused challenged the validity of s. 178.11(2)(a), which excepts from the prohibition of unauthorized electronic surveillance the interception of conversations to which one of the parties consents. The trial judge found a violation of the accused's rights under s. 8 and excluded the evidence. The Ontario Court of Appeal allowed the Crown's appeal, holding that s. 8 could not be applied as there could not be a reasonable expectation of privacy in the case of a conversation where one party had consented to it being intercepted and recorded. The accused appealed.

LA FOREST J. (Dickson, C.J. and L'Heureux-Dubé, Sopinka, Gonthier and McLachlin JJ. concurring):—Notice of appeal was then filed in this court, and the following constitutional questions were stated:

1. Does s. 178.11(2)(a) of the Criminal Code, legalizing the interception of private communications with the consent of the originator or intended recipient thereof, without the need for judicial authorization, infringe or deny the rights and freedoms guaranteed by s. 8 of the Canadian Charter of Rights and Freedoms?

2. If s. 178.11(2)(*a*) of the Criminal Code does infringe or deny the rights and freedoms guaranteed by s. 8 of the Charter, is it justified by s. 1 of the Charter and therefore not inconsistent with the Constitution Act 1982?

The Attorneys General for Ontario and Quebec intervened to support the constitutionality of s. 178.11(2)(*a*).

During the argument, counsel for the appellant, however, advanced the position that the constitutionality of s. 178.11(2)(*a*) might not really arise. That provision, he noted, was really an exception to the criminal prohibition against the interception of private communications set forth in s. 178.11(1) [now s. 184(1)], an exception applicable both to the police and members of the public. Action contemplated by that exception could not be made criminal by a Charter attack on its validity. The real question, then, becomes whether, even though such action may not constitute a criminal offence, it would nonetheless, when undertaken by an instrumentality of the state, such as the police, violate s. 8 of the Charter. In my view, that is the correct approach to the matter and I shall deal with it on this basis.

The Issues

The principal issue in this apppeal is whether the commonly styled "consent" or "participant" surveillance—i.e., conversation, usually an undercover police officer or a police informer, surreptitiously records it—infringes the right under s. 8 of the Charter to be secure against unreasonable search and seizure. This raises the subsidiary issues of whether such infringement is justifiable under s. 1 of the Charter and whether the recorded conversation can nonetheless be admitted into evidence against an accused. I should at the outset note that "consent surveillance" is an unhappy term to describe a practice where only one party to a conversation has agreed to have it recorded. As put by the United States Supreme Court in *Katz v. U.S.*, 389 U.S. 347 (1967), at p. 358: "[t]he very nature of electronic surveillance precludes its use pursuant to the suspect's consent." I shall, therefore, use the term "particpant surveillance".

The importance of the issues can hardly be gainsaid. James Carr, The Law of Electronic Surveillance (1977), points out, at pp. 3-61, that in the United States this mode of surveillance is without question "the most widely used and most frequently practiced [sic] mode of eavesdropping". Though I have found no data on the relative frequency of this practice in Canada, the cases would indicate that it is also widespread here. The extensive use of electronic surveillance in this country is documented. The Law Reform Commission of Canada's working paper 47, Electronic Surveillance (1986), reports that, on a relative basis, Canadian law enforcement authorities request 20 times more authorization to conduct electronic surveillance than their American counterparts (p. 10).

. . .

The Risk Analysis of the Court of Appeal

In upholding the legality of participant surveillance, the Court of Appeal relied heavily on American authorities, citing several decisions of that country's Supreme Court, notably *U.S. v. White*, 401 U.S. 745 (1971), a plurality decision which has been interpreted as giving that court's imprimatur to the practice, though the specific legislative provisions authorizing it were not directly placed in issue; see Carr at pp. 3-62. Cory J.A., at p. 390, accurately summarized the logic of those decisions as resting on the notion that "the consent to the intreception by the recipient may be looked upon as no more than an extension of the powers of recollection of the recipient of the communication". In essence, the starting point for the analysis is the proposition that the person who divulges any confidence always runs the risk that his interlocutor will betray the confidence. As Cory J.A. put it, at p. 393: "The expression of the idea and the assumption of the risk of disclosure are therefore concomitant."

The argument is then developed by pointing out that disclosures of this nature have always been admissible in a court of law. It is but a small step to the conclusion that constitutional expectations of privacy would therefore not operate to prohibit the interception of conversations which one of the participants is surreptitiously recording. As Cory J.A. put it, at pp. 393-94:

> Given that it is accepted that the informant may testify in this manner as to pertinent conversations, the admission of electronic recordings of those conversations would seem to be a reasonable, logical and sequential step in trial proceedings. In this regard, the accurate transcript of the conversation should so often benefit the accused as the informant.
>
> . . .

Thus, for the Court of Appeal, inasmuch as the police are subjected to no warrant requirement in their use of informers or in their efforts to insinuate themselves into the confidence of a suspect, the use of electronic surveillance as an adjunct to that process is of no constitutional significance. In other words, if there has been a violation of privacy on the part of the state, it is complete when the confidence of the person under suspicion is gained. The Charter cannot purport to protect us if we don't know how to choose our "friends".

In summary, the risk analysis that is at the heart of the Court of Appeal's judgment rejects the notion that any distinction grounded on constitutional concerns should be drawn between evidence gained through the testimony of a participant to a conversation and evidence gained through a surreptitious electronic recording of that conversation. A person who has voluntarily chosen to confide his wrongdoing to another and who, by happenstance, has had the misfortune (from his perspective) of doing so in the presence of a microphone should not be able to invoke the Charter to prevent divulgation of the confidence in a court of law. Incriminating statements and confessions of wrongdoing are not per se constitutionally-protected communications; provided the accused spoke of his own free will, there is no constitutional significance to be accorded to the manner in which the evidence was gained. In effect, the court chose to treat the risk that an interlocutor will divulge one's words and the risk that he will make a permanent electronic record of them at the behest of the state as being of the same order of magnitude.

This argument is not without weight: the fact that it counts among its adherents the Supreme Court of the United States and many state appellate courts testifies to that.

The Opposing Approach

With respect, it seems to me, the Court of Appeal failed to deal with the true issue raised in this appeal. The real question, as I see it, is whether our constitutional right to be secure against unreasonable search and seizure should be seen as imposing on the police the obligation to seek prior judicial authorization before engaging in participant surveillance, or whether the police should be entirely free to determine whether circumstances justify recourse to participant surveillance and, having so determined, be allowed an unlimited discretion in defining the scope and duration of participant surveillance. This Court is accordingly called on to decide whether the risk of warrantless surveillance may be imposed on all members of society at the sole direction of the police.

I begin by stating what seems to me to be obvious: that, as a general proposition, surreptitious electronic surveillance of the individual by an agency of the state constitutes an unreasonable search or seizure under s. 8 of the Charter. The Ontario Court of Appeal has so held on at least two occasions; *R. v. Finlay* (1985), 23 C.C.C. (3d) 48, at p. 61 (leave to appeal refused, [1986] 1 S.C.R. ix); *R. v. Wong* (1987), 34 C.C.C. (3d) 51, at p. 58. Accordingly, the Crown conceded this point in the courts below and did not seriously press the matter here. The Attorney General for Ontario, for its part, assumed, though it did not concede, the point, and the Attorney General of Quebec did not deal with it at all.

It should come as no surprise that these parties shied away from engaging in such an unequal contest. *Hunter v. Southam Inc.*, [1984] 2 S.C.R. 145, instructs us that the primary value served by s. 8 is privacy, and, as I noted in *R. v. Dyment*, [1988] 2 S.C.R. 417, at p. 426, the spirit of s. 8 must not be constrained by narrow legalistic classifications. If one is to give s. 8 the purposive meaning attributed to it by *Hunter v. Southam Inc.*, one can scarcely imagine a state activity more dangerous to individual privacy than electronic surveillance and to which, in consequence, the protection accorded by s. 8 should be more directly aimed, an issue I shall more fully develop as I go along.

Not surprisingly, then, the Crown sought to focus more sharply on participant surveillance and to draw a distinction between it and other types of electronic surveillance. If that endeavour is to succeed, however, one must proceed on the assumption that the factors that support the imposition of a requirement for an authorization in the third-party interception (i.e. non-participatory surveillance) of private communications hold no currency where participant surveillance is concerned. This proposition takes one back to the rationale for the regulation of electronic surveillance generally, and I shall now deal with it at greater length.

The rationale for regulating the power of the state to record communications that their originator expects will not be intercepted by anyone other than the person intended by the originator to receive it (see definition section of Part IV.1 of the Code) has nothing to do with protecting individuals from the threat that their interlocutors will divulge communications that are meant to be private. No set of laws could immunize us from that risk. Rather, the regulation of electronic surveillance protects us from a risk of a different order, i.e., not the risk that someone will repeat our words but the much more insidious danger inherent in allowing the state, in its unfettered discretion, to record and transmit our words.

The reason for this protection is the realization that, if the state were free, at its sole discretion, to make permanent electronic recordings of our private communications, there would be no meaningful residuum to our right to live our lives free from surveillance. The very efficacy of electronic surveillance is such that it has the potential, if left unregulated, to annihilate any expectation that our communications will remain private. A society which exposed us, at the whim of the state, to the risk of having a permanent electronic recording made of our words every time we opened our mouths might be superbly equipped to fight crime, but would be one in which privacy no longer had any meaning. As Douglas J., dissenting in *U.S. v. White*, supra, put it, at p. 756: "Electronic surveillance is the greatest leveler of human privacy ever known." If the state may arbitrarily record and transmit our private communications, it is no longer possible to strike an appropriate balance between the right of the individual to be left alone and the right of the state to intrude on privacy in the furtherance of its goals, notably the need to investigate and combat crime.

This is not to deny that it is of vital importance that law enforcement agencies be able to employ electronic surveillance in their investigation of crime. Electronic surveillance plays an indispensable role in the detection of sophisticated criminal enterprises. Its utility in the investigation of drug-related crimes, for example, has been proven time and again. But, for the reasons I have touched on, it is unacceptable in a free society that the agencies of the state be free to use this technology at their sole discretion. The threat this would pose to privacy is wholly unacceptable.

It thus becomes necessary to strike a reasonable balance between the right of individuals to be left alone and the right of the state to intrude on privacy in the furtherance of its responsibilities for law enforcement. Parliament has attempted to do this by enacting Part IV.1 of the Code. An examination of Part IV.1 reveals that Parliament has sought to reconcile these competing interests by providing that the police must always seek prior judicial authorization before using electronic surveillance. Only a superior court judge can authorize electronic surveillance, and the legislative scheme sets a high standard for obtaining these authorizations. A judge must be satisfied that other investigative methods would fail, or have little likelihood of success, and that the granting of the authorization is in the best interest of the administration of justice. I share the approach of Martin J.A. in *R. v. Finlay*, supra, at pp. 70 et seq., that this latter prerequisite imports as a minimum requirement that the issuing judge must be satisfied that there are reasonable and probable grounds to believe that an offence has been or is being committed and that the authorization sought will afford evidence of that offence. It can, I think, be seen that the provisions and safeguards of Part IV.1 of the Code have been designed to prevent the agencies of the state from intercepting private communications on the basis of mere suspicion.

In proceeding in this fashion, Parliament has, in my view, succeeded in striking an appropriate balance. It meets the high standard of the Charter, which guarantees the right to be secure against unreasonable search and seizure, by subjecting the power of the state to record our private communicaitons to external restraint and requiring it to be justified by application of an objective criterion. The reason this represents an acceptable balance is that the imposition of an external and objective criterion affords a measure of protection to any citizen whose private communications have been intercepted. It becomes possible for the individual to call the state to account if he can establish that a given interception was not authorized in accordance with the requisite standard. If "privacy" may be defined as the right of the individual to determine for himself when, how, and to what extent he will release personal information about himself, a reasonable expectation of privacy would seem to demand that an individual may proceed on the assumption that the state may violate this right by recording private communications on a clandestine basis only when it has established to the satisfaction of a detached judicial officer that an offence has been or is being committed and that interception of private communications stands to afford evidence of the offence.

This, it seems to me, flows inexorably from the principles enunciated in *Hunter v. Southam Inc.*, supra. In that case, this Court (p. 157) made the important point that the "assessment of the constitutionality of a search and seizure . . . must focus on its 'reasonable' or 'unreasonable' impact on the subject of the search or the seizure, and not simply on its rationality in furthering some valid government objective". Applying this standard, it is fair to conclude that if the surreptitious recording of private communications is a search and seizure within the meaning of s. 8 of the Charter, it is because the law recognizes that a person's privacy is intruded on in an unreasonable manner whenever the state, without a prior showing of reasonable cause before a neutral judicial officer, arrogates to itself the right surreptitiously to *record* communications that the originator expects will not be intercepted by anyone other than the person intended by its originator to receive them, to use the language of the Code.

By contrast to the general provisions on electronic surveillance, the Code places no restriction on participant surveillance. The police may employ this practice in their absolute discretion, against whom they wish and for whatever reasons they wish, without any limit as to place or duration. There is a total absence of prior judicial supervision of this practice.

I am unable to see any logic to this distinction between third-party electronic surveillance and participant surveillance. The question whether *unauthorized* electronic surveillance of private communications violates a reasonable expectation of privacy cannot, in my view, turn on the location of the hidden microphone. Whether the microphone is hidden in the wall or concealed on the body of a participant to the conversation, the assessment whether the surreptitious recording trenches on a reasonable expectation of privacy must turn on whether the person whose words were recorded spoke in circumstances in which it was reasonable for that person to expect that his or her words would be heard only by the persons he or she was addressing. As I see it, where persons have reasonable grounds to believe their communications are private communications in the sense defined above, the *unauthorized* surreptitious electronic recording of those communications cannot fail to be perceived as an intrusion on a reasonable expectation of privacy.

The Charter standard just described must, in my view, apply on a uniform basis. To have any meaning, it must be taken to afford protection against the arbitrary recording of private communications every time we speak in the expectation that our words will be heard only by the person or persons to whom we direct our remarks. Section 8 of the Charter guarantees the right *to be secure* against unreasonable search or seizure. Our perception that we are protected against arbitrary interceptions of private communications ceases to have any real basis once it is accepted that the state is free to record private communications, without constraint, provided only that it has secured the agreement of one of the parties to the communication. Since we can never know if our listener is an informer, and since, if he proves to be one, we are to be taken to be tacitly consenting to the risk that the state may be listening to and recording our conversations, we should be prepared to run this risk every time we speak. I conclude that the risk analysis relied on by the Court of Appeal, when taken to its logical conclusion, must destroy all expectations of privacy.

I am unable to see any similarity between the risk that someone will listen to one's words with the intention of repeating them and the risk involved when someone listens to them while simultaneously making a permanent electronic record of them. These risks are of a different order of magnitude. The one risk may, in the context of law enforcement, be viewed as a reasonable invasion of privacy, the other unreasonable. They involve different risks to the individual and the body politic. In other words, the law recognizes that we inherently have to bear the risk of the "tattletale" but draws the line at concluding that we must also bear, as the price of choosing to speak to another human being, the risk of having a permanent electronic recording made of our words.

The risk analysis relied on by the Court of Appeal fails to take due account of this key fact that our right under s. 8 of the Charter extends to a right to be free from unreasonable invasions of our right to privacy. The Court of Appeal was correct in stating that the expression of an idea and the assumption of the risk of disclosure are concomitant. However, it does not follow that, because in any conversation we run the risk that our interlocutor may in fact be bent on divulging our confidences, it is therefore constitutionally proper for the person to whom we speak to make a permanent electronic recording of that conversation. The Charter, it is accepted, proscribes the surreptitious recording by third parties of our private communications on the basis of mere suspicion alone. It would be strange indeed if, in the absence of a warrant requirement, instrumentalities of the state, through the medium of participant surveillance, were free to conduct just such random fishing expeditions in the hope of uncovering evidence of crime or, by the same token, to satisfy any curiosity they may have as to a person's views on any matter whatsoever.

In summary, the question whether to regulate participant surveillance cannot logically be made to turn on the expectations of individuals as to whether their interlocutor will betray their confidence. No justification for the arbitrary exercise of state power can be made to rest on the simple fact that persons often prove to be poor judges of whom to trust when divulging confidences or on the fact that the risk of divulgation is a given in the decision to speak to another human being. On the other hand, the question whether we should countenance participant surveillance has everything to do with the need to strike a fair balance between the right of the state to intrude on the private lives of its citizens and the right of those citizens to be left alone.

. . .

Section 1 Justification

It is necessary to make only brief mention of possible justification under s. 1 of the police action in this case. The question whether participant surveillance constitutes a reasonable limit on the right to be secure against unreasonable search or seizure takes one back to the point that the appellant is in no way arguing that the police should be denied the right to use informers or to intercept communications themselves once they have gained the confidence of a suspect. The sole thrust of his argument is that judicial supervision of the practice should exist, just as it exists in the case of third-party surveillance. In a word, there is no justification for warrantless searches once it is accepted that the police could employ the same investigatory tool with or without a warrant. This simple fact (and I find no argument by the respondent refuting the notion that the police could have attended before a judge to secure an authorization for participant surveillance) destroys, in my view, any argument that participant surveillance can be upheld as a reasonable limit to the right to be secure from unreasonable search and seizure.

To conclude, the Charter is not meant to protect us against a poor choice of friends. If our "friend" turns out to be an informer and we are convicted on the strength of his testimony, that may be unfortunate for us. But the Charter is meant to guarantee the right to be secure against unreasonable search and seizure. A conversation with an informer does not amount to a search and seizure within the meaning of the Charter. Surreptitious electronic interception and recording of a private communication does. Such recording, moreover, should be viewed as a search and seizure in all circumstances save where *all* parties to the conversation have expressly consented to its being recorded. Accordingly, the constitutionality of "participant surveillance" should fall to be determined by application of the same standard as that employed in third-party surveillance, i.e., by application of the standard of reasonableness enunciated in *Hunter v. Southam Inc.*, supra. By application of that standard, the warrantless participant surveillance engaged in by the police here was clearly unconstitutional.

[Having decided that the participant surveillance engaged in by the police was unconsitutional, the majority went on to consider the admissibility of the evidence so obtained.]

Admissibility in Evidence

. . .

Undoubtedly, the breach infringed upon an important Charter right, and the evidence could have been obtained without breaching the Charter. But what strikes one here is that the breach was in no way deliberate, wilful or flagrant. The police officers acted entirely in good faith. They were acting in accordance with what they had good reason to believe was the law—as it had been for many years before the advent of the Charter. The reasonableness of their action is underscored by the seriousness of the offence. They had reasonable and probable cause to believe the offence had been committed, and, had they properly understood the law, they could have obtained an authorization under the Code to intercept the communication. Indeed, they could have proceeded without resorting to electronic surveillance and relied solely on the evidence of the undercover officer or the informer. In short, the Charter breach stemmed from an entirely reasonable misunderstanding of the law by the police officers who would otherwise have obtained the necessary evidence to convict the accused in any event. Under these circumstances, I hold that the appellant has not established that the admission of the evidence would bring the administration of justice into disrepute.

Disposition

I would dismiss the appeal. I would answer the constitutional questions as follows:

1. Does s. 178.11(2)(*a*) of the Criminal Code, legalizing the interception of private communications with the consent of the originator or intended recipient thereof, without the need for judicial authorization, infringe or deny the rights and freedoms guaranteed by s. 8 of the Canadian Charter of Rights and Freedoms?

Section 178.11(2)(*a*) of the Code does not infringe or deny the rights and freedoms guaranteed by s. 8 of the Charter, but the interception of private communications by an instrumentality of the state with the consent of the originator or intended recipient thereof, without prior judicial authorization, does infringe the rights and freedoms guaranteed by s. 8.

2. If s. 178.11(2)(*a*) of the Criminal Code does infringe or deny the rights and freedoms guaranteed by s. 8 of the Charter, is it justifed by s. 1 of the Charter and therefore not inconsistent with the Constitution Act, 1982?

It is not necessary to answer this question.

LAMER J.:—My colleague, Justice La Forest, has set out the facts, the law, the judgments below and the positions of the parties before this Court. I am of the view that this appeal fails. I have read the unanimous judgment of the

Court of Appeal for Ontario, written by Cory J.A. (as he then was). I am in complete agreement with those reasons and I feel I cannot improve upon them. They are conveniently reported at (1987) 60 C.R. (3d) 142, 38 C.C.C. (3d) 1.

Consequently, I need not address the issue as to whether the evidence should be excluded under s. 24(2) of the Canadian Charter of Rights and Freedoms, and I would dismiss this appeal.

R. v. WONG
[1990] 3 S.C.R. 36, 1 C.R. (4th) 1, 60 C.C.C. (3d) 460 (S.C.C.)

The issue was the admissibility of police video surveillance evidence. The police had obtained evidence of large-scale illegal gambling in a hotel room by setting up a video surveillance camera and observing the gambling for several nights. The Ontario Court of Appeal had held ((1987) 56 C.R. (3d) 352) that the protection of s. 8 of the Charter was not available as there was no reasonable expectation of privacy, given that 30 to 35 people had been invited to gamble illegally for high stakes in the room. The four to three majority held that this reasoning could not be reconciled with *Duarte*.

LA FOREST J.:—

. . .

Accordingly, it follows logically from what was held in *R. v. Duarte* that it would be an error to suppose that the question that must be asked in these circumstances is whether persons who engage in illegal activity behind the locked door of a hotel room have a reasonable expectation of privacy. Rather, the question must be framed in broad and neutral terms so as to become whether in a society such as ours persons who retire to a hotel room and close the door behind them have a reasonable expectation to privacy.

Viewed in this light, it becomes obvious that the protections of s. 8 of the *Charter* are meant to shield us from warrantless video surveillance when we occupy hotel rooms. Clearly, our homes are places in which we will be entitled, in virtually all conceivable circumstances, to affirm that unauthorized video surveillance by the state encroaches on a reasonable expectation of privacy. It would be passing strange if the situation should be any different in hotel or motel rooms. Normally, the very reason we rent such rooms is to obtain a private enclave where we may conduct our activities free of uninvited scrutiny. Accordingly, I can see no conceivable reason why we should be shorn of our right to be *secure* from unreasonable searches in these locations which may be aptly considered to be our homes away from home. Moreover, *R. v. Duarte* reminds us that unless the question posed in the preceding paragraph is answered in neutral terms as I have suggested, it follows not only that those who engage in illegal activity in their hotel rooms must bear the risk of warrantless video surveillance, but also that all members of society when renting rooms must be prepared to court the risk that agents of the state may choose, at their sole discretion, to subject them to surreptitious surveillance; see again at pp. 51-52.

[La Forest J. also held that it was not appropriate for courts to authorize video surveillance.]

Part IV.1 of the *Code* is designed to set strict limits on the ability of the agents of the state to intercept private *oral* communications. It does not speak to the very different, and I might add, more pernicious threat to privacy constituted by surreptitious video surveillance. On my view of the matter, the courts would be forgetting their role as guardians of our fundamental liberties if they were to usurp the role of Parliament and purport to give their sanction to video surveillance by adapting for that purpose a code of procedure dealing with an altogether different surveillance technology. It is for Parliament, and Parliament alone, to set out the conditions under which law enforcement agencies may employ video surveillance technology in their fight against crime. Moreover the same holds true for any other technology which the progress of science places at the disposal of the state in the years to come. Until such time as Parliament, in its wisdom, specifically provides for a code of conduct for a particular invasive technology, the courts should forebear from crafting procedures authorizing the deployment of the technology in question. The role of the courts should be limited to assessing the constitutionality of any legislation passed by Parliament which bears on the matter.

By Criminal Code amendments in 1993 Parliament enacted a General Warrant power. Section 487.01 allows provincial court judges and other judges to authorise the use of any device or investigative technique or procedure or do anything described in the warrant that would, if authorised, constitute an unreasonable search or seizure in respect of a person or a person's property.

Section 487.01(4) expressly authorises video surveillance but clearly s. 487.01 goes much wider in allowing a judge to authorise any investigative technique The only real limit is that in s. 487.01(2) that nothing can be construed to authorise permit interference with the bodily integrity of any person.

The provision is a dangerously wide and somewhat intemperate "in your face" response to *Wong* and other Supreme Court rulings setting out search standards. One might have expected courts to subject the provision to rigorous Charter review. However, such arguments as void for vagueness or overbreadth have thus far been rejected. In *R. v. Telus Communications Co.*, [2013] 2 S.C.R. 3, 294 C.C.C. (3d) 498, 100 C.R. (6th) 221 (S.C.C.), a majority of the Supreme Court held that a general warrant should be used sparingly and was not available where the technique could be authorised by another substantively equivalent provision. The Court quashed a general warrant to produce text messages received or sent in a future period of two weeks. The provisions for electronic surveillance authorisation should have been followed. See analysis of the complex divisions in the Court by Stephen Coughlan, "Telus: Asking the Right Questions About General Warrants" (2013), 100 C.R. (7th) 221.

Parliament also declared two distinct powers to electronically intercept on consent of one of the parties to the private communication: one without prior authorization where there are reasonable grounds to fear the risk of bodily harm (s. 184.1) and the other by obtaining an authorization from a provincial court judge or other judge (s. 184.2). It also enacted a power for a police officer to intercept in exceptional circumstances where an authorization "could not, with reasonable diligence, be obtained" (s. 184.4), and also powers for a justice to issue warrants for a tracking device (s. 492.1) or to install and monitor a telephone number recorder (s. 492.2). **Were these new powers necessary and are they constitutional?**

In *R. v. Tse* (2012), 280 C.C.C. (3d) 423, [2012] 1 S.C.R. 531, 91 C.R. (6th) 223 (S.C.C.), s. 184.4 was declared unconstitutional because it did not have an after-the-fact notice provision to those whose communications are intercepted.

In 1997 Parliament granted police much wider powers respecting gangs. Where police suspect that a person has committed the new s. 467.1 offence of participation in criminal organizations or an offence committed for the benefit of, at the direction of or in association with a criminal organization, Bill C-95 confers special and wider powers to use electronic surveillance. Police have the option of applying for a judicial authorization, (s. 183), the authorising judge does not have to be satisfied that electronic surveillance was necessary, ss. 185(1.1) and 186(1.1), authorizations and renewals can be for periods of up to a year, s. 186.1, and the notification period may be extended for up to three years, s. 196(5).

In 2001 Parliament extended the special electronic surveillance provisions to investigation of suspected terrorists under the wide definition in Bill C-36. It has been suggested that the deletion of the s.186 investigative necessity requirement (as defined in *Araujo*) renders these special powers unconstitutional: N.J. Whiting, "Wiretapping, Investigative Necessity, and the Charter", (2002) 46 Crim. L.Q. 89. This view was rejected in *R. v. Lucas* (2014), 313 C.C.C. (3d) 159 (Ont. C.A.), leave to appeal refused 2015 CarswellOnt 638, 2015 CarswellOnt 639 (S.C.C.), leave to appeal refused 2015 CarswellOnt 652, 2015 CarswellOnt 653 (S.C.C.).

See further Morris, "A New Frontier for Judicial Authorization of Electronic Surveillance" (1985), 43 C.R. (3d) 180. For an argument that Canada's electronic surveillance laws need to be revised to keep up with wireless and digital technologies see Steven Penney, "Updating Canada's Communications Surveillance Laws: Privacy and Security in the Digital age" (2008) 12 *Can.Crim.L.R.* 115.

In *R. v. Thompson* (1990), 80 C.R. (3d) 129, 59 C.C.C. (3d) 225 (S.C.C.), the Supreme Court held that interceptions obtained by means of surreptitious entry into residential premises, which were not specifically mentioned on the face of the authorizations in question, violated s. 8 of the Charter.

An applicant for judicial authorization is required to set out in the application the names, if known, of all persons whose communications he seeks to intercept: s. 185(1)(*e*). The authorization, in turn, must state the identity of the persons, if known, whose private communications may be intercepted: s. 178.13(2)(*c*). In *R. v. Welsh and Iannuzzi (No. 6)* (1977), 15 O.R. (2d) 1, 32 C.C.C. (2d) 363 (Ont. C.A.), the authorization named four individuals. Pursuant to that authorization, while monitoring the telephone of one of the named individuals, the police intercepted and recorded a conversation originating from Welsh, a police officer, and directed to Iannuzzi, neither of whom were named in the authorization. Evidence of the interception was held to be inadmissible. In dismissing the Crown's appeal, Zuber J.A. wrote:

> An examination of the authorization in the case reveals the obvious fact that four persons were named; none of them was a party to any of the communications that were intercepted. It is clear as well that *the authorization does not go on, as it might have done, depending on the material filed, to include unknown persons,* designating the place of interception, or, failing that, the method of interception. . . . An attempt to extend the authorization to include persons, *none of whom is specified or included as unknown persons,* collides directly with the declared purpose of this legislation, i.e., the protection of private communications. If an authorization naming specific persons could be used to authorize the interception of the communication of others on the grounds that they simply flowed from, or were connected to an initial lawful interception, there might well be no end to the process and the judicial supervision envisaged by this legislation would be nullified. A single authorization would enable the authorities to proceed from interception to interception, and Part IV.I of the Code would become a very illusory protection of privacy.

Following this case it became very common for authorizations to include a so-called "basket clause" authorizing the interception of communications between unknown persons at designated premises. For a Supreme Court review of this area, see *R. v. Chesson*, [1988] 2 S.C.R. 148, 65 C.R. (3d) 193, 43 C.C.C. (3d) 353 (S.C.C.).

The application for an authorization must state the particulars of the offence being investigated: s. 185(1)(*c*). The authorization is then required to state the offence in respect of which private communications may be intercepted: s. 186(4)(*a*). Section 189(4) however, states that an intercepted private communication may be admitted in any criminal or civil proceeding whether or not the same relates to the offence specified in the authorization. For a Supreme Court review of this area, see *R. v. Commisso*, [1983] 2 S.C.R. 121, 36 C.R. (3d) 105, 7 C.C.C. (3d) 1 (S.C.C.).

We have seen above, e.g., *Re Gillis and R.* (1982), 1 C.C.C. (3d) 545 (Que. S.C.), painstaking judicial review of the issuance of a search warrant. We noted the access that a person, the object of a search, had to the underlying material that gave rise to the issuance of a warrant by a justice of the peace. With respect to the issuance of warrants for electronic searches, however, the law placed a major stumbling block in the way of review. Section 187 of the Code provides that all documents relating to an application for authorization for electronic surveillance are confidential and, following the determination of the application, are to be placed in a packet and sealed by the judge who heard the application. A line of authority required the accused to show *prima facie* evidence of misconduct before an order to open the packet could be granted. Other courts, however, held that this caught the accused in a "Catch-22" situation and that access should normally be granted an accused as part of the right to make full answer and defence under s. 7 of the Charter. This latter view was adopted by the Supreme Court in *R. v. Dersch* (1990), 80 C.R. (3d) 299 (S.C.C.). The Supreme Court also considered several technical issues respecting the scope, jurisdiction and procedure for review: see *R. v. Garofoli* (1991), 80 C.R. (3d) 317 (S.C.C.), discussed by James O'Reilly, "Reviewing Wiretap Authorizations—The Supreme Court Goes Through the Motions", 80 C.R. (3d) 386. A revised procedure was declared by Parliament in 1993 with the enactment of a new s. 187 concerning the sealed packet and access to it.

Section 187 requires that the application for authorization and the authorization itself are to be sealed in a packet and kept in the custody of the court. The packet may be opened to seek to renew an authorization or on the order of a superior court judge or a provincial court judge.

In addition, s. 187(1.1)-(1.5) now sets out a much-simplified process for enabling an accused to have access to the packet in order to make full answer and defence. In this instance, Parliament paid some attention to the approach advocated by Sopinka J. in *Garofoli*. The accused must apply to the trial judge for an order to examine the sealed packet. The prosecutor is given an opportunity to edit the packet to remove information concerning the identity of confidential informers, or information that would compromise ongoing investigations, endanger persons involved in intelligence-gathering, or prejudice the interests of innocent persons. The accused is then entitled to an edited copy of the documents. If the accused then applies for a copy of the edited portions, the trial judge must determine whether or not it is necessary to full answer and defence for him to receive it.

In some circumstances, the defence may wish to cross-examine the person who swore the affidavit to obtain the authorization. In *Garofoli*, the Supreme Court stipulated that to do so required the leave of the trial judge. This position was challenged in *R. v. Lising*, [2005] 3 S.C.R. 343, 33 C.R. (6th) 241, 201 C.C.C. (3d) 449 (S.C.C.), but the Court held that the leave requirement was consistent with Charter requirements. Thus, in order to obtain leave to cross-examine, the defence must show a reasonable likelihood that the cross-examination would elicit testimony that was relevant and material to the issue of the validity of the authorization. The leave requirement was seen not to infringe on the right to make full answer and defence but as a means of preventing unduly long proceedings and protecting the identity of informants.

Chapter 3

CHARGING, ARREST AND DETENTION

This chapter addresses who can charge before a justice, powers of arrest, and duties of police to bring an individual to court. Once again the Charter figures prominently, particularly s. 9, which protects against arbitrary detention or imprisonment. In the context of stop powers we consider the controversial topic of racial profiling.

1. Powers of Any Individual

(a) Information Before a Justice: Summons or Arrest Warrant

Any individual can attempt to initiate a criminal prosecution by laying an information in writing and on oath before a justice who must receive the information but has a discretion to decide whether a case is made out for compelling the accused to attend to answer the charge by issuing a summons or an arrest warrant. In the case of indictable offences there are detailed Criminal Code provisions which, by virtue of s. 795, apply also "insofar as they are not inconsistent" and "with such modification as the circumstances require" to summary conviction proceedings under Part XXVII. See the general provisions respecting informations (s. 504), the form of the information (s. 506 and Form 2), the duty of the justice in receiving the information (s. 507), the content and service of a summons (s. 509 and Form 6), the form and execution of an arrest warrant (ss. 511-514 and Form 7) and a provision relating to the backing of a warrant (s. 528).

The requirements of a valid information were reviewed in *R. v. Pilcher*.

R. v. PILCHER
(1981), 58 C.C.C. (2d) 435 (Man. Prov. Ct.)

MINUK PROV. CT. J. (orally):—This is a motion by the accused, both members of the City of Winnipeg Police Force to quash an information sworn by Arthur Lobson on September 30, 1980, alleging 11 counts of theft of firearms, each to a value not exceeding $200, the property of the Province of Manitoba.

The accused are jointly charged on two counts, and the accused Pilcher on the remaining nine counts. In the information the informant swears that: ' "He has reasonable and probable grounds to believe and does believe the allegations contained therein".

Counsel for the accused contend that the informant did not in fact have reasonable and probable grounds to believe the allegations, and that such lack of grounds for belief constitutes a latent defect in the information requiring it to be quashed.

In other words, counsel allege that there was a failure to observe s. 455 of the *Criminal Code*, R.S.C. 1970, c. 34; and that such failure was a jurisdictional defect which has the effect of voiding the information.

The relevant parts of s. 455 [now s. 504] states:

455. Any one who, *on reasonable and probable grounds*, believes that a person has committed an indictable offence may lay an information in writing and under oath before a justice. (Emphasis added.)

[The words "and probable" have since been deleted from the section.]

Section 455.2 states:

455.2. An information laid under section 455 or 455.1 may be in Form 2.

The relevant part of Form 2 states:

The informant says that (if the informant has not personal knowledge state that he has reasonable and probable grounds to believe and does believe and state the offence).

The issue in this case is therefore whether the informant had reasonable and probable grounds to believe and did believe that the accused committed the offences charged.

. . .

At the close of the Crown's case, the defence called as its witness, the informant Arthur Lobson.

He holds the rank of a detective, and has worked in the Court Unit at the Public Safety Building for approximately 15 months. One of his main duties is the swearing of informations. He was asked to explain the events leading up to the laying of the information on September 30th. He stated that on that day he was instructed by Crime Superintendent Ed Ogelski to attend at the office of Wayne Myshkowsky, the senior Crown Attorney, and obtain from him a draft information. He was then to attend at the Clerk of the Court's office, and have the draft typed out and the information sworn. Superintendent Ogelski did not discuss the case with Lobson, nor did he give Lobson any details regarding the investigation. Lobson attended at Mr. Myshkowsky's office where he was shown a foolscap sheet of paper containing the charges in handwritten form. Mr. Myshkowsky also had a supplementary police report from which he filled in the serial numbers of the firearms in question on to the foolscap. Myshkowsky did not discuss the case with Lobson, nor did he inform him of any of the details surrounding the investigation. The detective then went directly to the Clerk of the Court's office where he handed the sheet to Magistrate Dowbenko, and had him type out the charges on Form 2, after which Lobson swore same.

It is germane to point out that Lobson did not discuss the case with any of the investigating officers, nor was he given any of the police reports on the case.

In short, Lobson admitted that all he knew about the case was what he read in the information itself, an admission not unlike that of the American folk hero Will Rogers, who once said: "All I know is what I read in the newspapers!"

Lobson stated that he laid the information because he was instructed to do so by a superior officer and by the senior Crown Attorney. He further stated that this was a departure from the usual practice. He had laid many informations while working in the Court Unit, and usually prior to the laying of an information, he would read the police reports and summaries of the investigation. It was a consideration of these reports that gave him the reasonable and probable grounds to believe that the offence had probably been committed by the accused.

Detective Lobson further testified that he was unhappy because in the instant case he had been put in the awkward position of swearing an information when he knew nothing about the case.

. . .

The solution to this issue depends upon the meaning of the expression "reasonable and probable grounds believes".

The phrase occurs in many sections of the *Code*; for example ss. 25(3), 27(*b*), 31(1) and (2), 34(2), 35(*a*)(ii), 235(1) [rep. & sub. 1974-75-76, c. 93, s. 16(1)] 449, 450(1)(1)(*a*), (*c*) and 2(*e*), and 452(1)(*f*) and (*g*).

Some of these sections apply to Judges or Justices of the Peace, some to peace officers and other persons enforcing the law, and some to accused persons. A useful definition of the term may be found in the case of *Herniman v. Smith*, [1938] A.C. 305 at p. 316, where the House of Lords defined reasonable and probable grounds as follows:

> . . . an honest belief in the guilt of the accused based upon a full conviction, founded upon reasonable grounds, of the existence of a state of circumstances, which, assuming them to be true, would reasonably lead any ordinarily prudent and cautious man, placed in the position of the accuser, to the conclusion that the person charged was probably guilty of the crime imputed.

It will be noted that the Court emphasized the element of *"belief "* in the above definition (emphasis added).

. . .

In *R. v. Sanderson* (1977), 11 Nfld. & P.E.I.R. 223, a decision of the Prince Edward Island Supreme Court, the accused was charged with refusal, contrary to s. 235 [rep. & sub. 1974-75-76, c. 93, s. 16] of the *Code*. The information was sworn by an R.C.M.P. officer on reasonable and probable grounds. It was proven that the informant did not discuss the case with the two arresting officers. The informant was not called as a witness by either the Crown or by the defence. An application to quash the information as being defective was rejected by McQuaid J. who in his reasons stated at p. 228:

> In the case at bar the Informant does not allege personal knowledge but only reasonable and probable grounds, and the reasonable and probable grounds Officer Ralph [the informant] had for believing that an offence had been committed would be the *records kept by the Royal Canadian Mounted Police* and in *my opinion these records could be relied upon by the Informant and would be sufficient on which to base an Information.* (Emphasis added.)

It appears that McQuaid J. based his judgment on the reasoning of Henry J. in *R. v. Peavoy* (1974), 15 C.C.C. (2d) 97, who held that the accused must discharge the onus of proving by a preponderance of evidence that the informant did not have reasonable and probable grounds. It is submitted that had the informant been called as a witness, and had it been shown that he had not read any of the crime reports, the result might have been different.

The duties and responsibilities of a person swearing an information and clearly set out by Henry J. in *Peavoy, supra,* at p. 106, where he said:

> Recognizing that the pressure of duties and administration upon police forces may quite naturally cause them, when under pressure, to manage the laying of informations as a form of routine "paperwork", I feel obliged to add the following comments. A person swearing an information, particularly a law enforcement officer, is not at liberty to swear the information in a perfunctory or irresponsible manner with a reckless disregard as to the truth of his assertion. To do so is clearly an affront to the Courts and is at variance with the right of the citizen to be left alone by the authorities unless there is reasonable and probable grounds for invading his liberty by compelling his attendance before the Courts. The police officer who does not satisfy himself that he can personally swear to the truth of the information according to its terms, (i.e. personal knowledge or reasonable and probablegrounds), yet does so, jeopardizes his personal position and also does a disservice to the upholding of law in the community. His oath must be beyond reproach. He need not, of course, have personal knowledge of all the facts or even most of the facts that support the allegation; indeed much of what would be available to him will, so far as he is concerned, be hearsay. He must however, be satisfied, even if it be on the basis of reliable reports made by other persons in the course of an investigation, that there is some evidence to support the charge, that that evidence in fact constitutes reasonable and probable grounds for believing that the accused committed the offence and that he believes that the accused did so. Moreover, he must be prepared to satisfy the Justice of the Peace who, in turn, has an obligation judicially, and not arbitrarily, to hear and consider the allegations before endorsing the information.
>
> If it should transpire that the person swearing the information has done so falsely or had misled the Justice of the Peace, then he risks the possibility of both criminal and civil proceedings against him personally for his misconduct.

After considering the evidence of Arthur Lobson, I am satisfied that the defence has discharged the onus of proving by a preponderance of evidence that Lobson did not have reasonable and probable grounds for believing that the offences had been committed.

Now I have no doubt that Mr. Myshkowsky is a fine fellow, and likewise I acknowledge without hesitation that Superintendant Ogelski is an experienced and competent police officer; however, I am of the view that the informant Lobson was not entitled to lay the charges on the mere say so of these two gentlemen, without anything more.

The authorities to which I have alluded lead me to the conclusion that s. 455 of the *Code* contemplates a situation where an informant acting in a prudent and cautious manner, apprises himself of the relevant circumstances surrounding the case which he reasonably and in good faith believes to be true and concludes with a genuine conviction that the person to be charged is probably guilty of the crime. By merely reading what appears in an information given to him by others, an informant could not be informed in such a manner in which he is obliged to be informed, in order to protect an accused person from frivolous or foundationless accusations.

I find that there has been a failure to comply with the mandatory requirements of s. 455 of the *Criminal Code* and as a result, the information is invalid, and I do hereby declare it to be a nullity. The information is therefore quashed for want of jurisdiction.

Application granted.

Under s. 506 an information "may be" in Form 2. However, in the case of summary conviction proceedings, s. 788 declares that proceedings "shall be commenced by laying an information in Form 2".

It is well established that an information may be presented to another justice if the first one does not act: *R. v. Allen* (1975), 20 C.C.C. (2d) 447 (Ont. C.A.).

It was held in *R. v. Jeffrey* that a justice receiving an information must perform a ministerial function and also a separate judicial one in determining whether to issue process. For a helpful review of these different functions of a justice and the process by which a summons is to be issued, see: *R. v. Whitmore* (1987), 41 C.C.C. (3d) 555 (Ont. H.C.), affirmed (1989), 51 C.C.C. (3d) 294 (Ont. C.A.).

R. v. JEFFREY
(1976), 34 C.R.N.S. 283 (Ont. Prov. Ct.)

DELISLE PROV. J.:—In the cases before the Court it would not appear that there is any dispute regarding the facts. Each accused is charged with unlawfully keeping liquor for sale, Neal under s. 60(1) of The Liquor Control Act, R.S.O. 1970, c. 249, and Martin and Jeffrey under s. 4(1) of The Liquor Licence Act, R.S.O. 1970, c. 250. The reason for the charges being laid under different statutes is the amendments to those Acts effective January 1976 and the dates of the alleged offences. In each case counsel for the accused made a preliminary objection respecting my jurisdiction to deal with the charges before the Court by reason of the manner in which process had issued. This Court recognizes the wisdom of the remarks of Henry J. in *Regina v. Peavoy* (1974), 15 C.C.C. (2d) 97 at 105 (Ont.), that:

> There is no obligation on the Crown to go behind the information and to demonstrate to the Court having jurisdiction that the proceedings were regular . . . the onus of showing that it is subject to a latent defect is on the person challenging it, namely, the accused.

This Court further recognizes that s. 732(1) of the Criminal Code, R.S.C. 1970, c. C-34, commands that objections for patent defects must be taken prior to plea unless the court later grants leave. That command, however, does not deny the ability to object prior to plea with respect to latent defects which go to jurisdiction. If a jurisdictional defect is alleged it seems eminently reasonable to deal with it prior to plea.

In each case Detective James Sheridan was the informant and he was called by the accused to testify, prior to plea, respecting the manner in which the informations were laid and the summonses were issued. In each case Mr. Sheridan attended on the Justice of the Peace and requested that informations be prepared. The informant provided the name of the defendant, the relevant section of The Liquor Licence Act and the date of the offence, and the informations were then typed by the secretary of the Justice of the Peace. Mr. Sheridan then signed the informations, swore on the Bible that they were true and the Justice of the Peace then endorsed them. Nothing further occurred before summonses were issued by the Justice of the Peace compelling the attendance of the defendants to answer to the charges.

Counsel for the accused submit that the defendants who have responded to the summonses are not lawfully before the Court and that I accordingly have no jurisdiction over their persons. They base their argument on the wording of ss. 455 [re-en. R.S.C. 1970, c. 2 (2nd Supp.), s. 5] and 455.3(1) [en. R.S.C. 1970, c. 2 (2nd Supp.), s. 5] of the Criminal Code.

. . .

These sections govern the manner in which an information charging an offence under an Ontario statute is to be received by a justice and the manner in which a summons is to be issued compelling the attendance of a person to answer such a charge by virtue of ss. 2 and 3 of The Summary Convictions Act, R.S.O. 1970, c. 450, and ss. 720(1), 723(1) and 728(1) of the Criminal Code. Counsel for the defendants submit that receiving an information is one action which the Justice of the Peace is commanded to do by the legislation on an informant's swearing the contents of the same to be true. They submit that on the evidence of Mr. Sheridan of what occurred, the Justice of the Peace in these cases was permitted to do nothing more than to receive the informations. They submit that he could do no more unless he afterwards complied with the provisions of s. 455.3(1). They submit that the Justice is not authorized in law to issue either a summons or a warrant for the arrest of the accused to compel the accused to attend before him to answer to the charges unless he first complies with s. 455.3(1)(a). They note that that paragraph commands a justice who receives an information to then "hear and consider, *ex parte*, the allegations of the informant". They note that the justice may, where he considers it desirable or necessary to do so, hear and consider the evidence of witnesses but that he is not obliged so to do. They submit that in these cases the Justice of the Peace did not hear and consider the allegations of the informant. The prosecutor argues that it is not necessary for the informant to actually say anything for the Justice of the Peace to hear him but that rather the word "hear" can be broadly interpreted to include the mere reading of the "allegation" appearing in the information. It appears to me that there are two difficulties with the Crown's position. First, it appears to fly in the face of the normal rule of statutory interpretation that penal statutes ought to be strictly construed, and if I am to give effect to this rule of statutory interpretation. I cannot interpret "hear" to mean "see" or "read". Second, the position appears to disregard the fact that the Justice of the Peace has already seen and read the "allegation" in the information when he received it under s. 455 and the Crown's interpretation accordingly would make the mandatory requirement in 455.3(1)(*a*) largely redundant. The prosecutor argues that if the Court is to insist on auditory perception the same is satisfied by the informant saying "I swear" to the administration of the oath by the Justice, but again my second response above appears to be applicable. The Justice of the Peace is required by s. 455 to perform one function, a ministerial function, and is required by s. 455.3(1) to perform a second separate function. Dryer J. in *MacLean v. The Queen*, 21 C.R.N.S. 354, [1972] 1 W.W.R. 159 (B.C.), commenting on similar legislation in The Summary Convictions Act of British Columbia, R.S.B.C. 1960, c. 373, makes it clear that there are two separate functions involved. In that case the Crown contended [pp. 354-55]:

> ... that it was not necessary for him [the Justice] to hear these allegations after the information was laid because he had heard them before [on the receipt of the information], but I am not satisfied that that is so since, as in this case, the Justice might, rightly or wrongly, feel that he was obliged to permit the information to be laid before him and if so he would not necessarily, at that time, weigh and consider the allegations to the same extent as he would if he were engaged in a proceeding in which *he knew he had a decision to make.* (The italics are mine.)

Dryer J. further noted that the informant "is entitled to insist on strict compliance with the provisions of the statute if he is so minded". If the informant can insist on strict compliance I would hope that the accused can as well. The Court in *MacLean* relied on the decision of *Regina v. Southwick; Ex parte Gilbert Steel Ltd.,* 2 C.R.N.S. 46, [1967] 2 O.R. 428 (C.A.), where the Court considered the then existing counterparts to ss. 455 and 455.3(1) and described them as follows [p. 48]:

> *The laying of an information* which is really the completion of the complaint under s. 439 *is separate and distinct from the inquiry contemplated by s. 440.* The former deals with jurisdictional requirements while the latter is concerned with the issuance of a judicial process to compel the attendance of the alleged offender . . . in s. 439 the word 'receive' means that the justice shall not reject a complaint which is in writing and which complies with the conditions set out in that section. The complaint or details of the alleged offence are reduced to writing and when sworn to by the justice of the peace constitute an information. On the swearing of the written complaint the information is 'laid' and becomes the first step or commencement of criminal proceedings...
> Section 440 contemplates *the next step* in the criminal proceedings and *requires* that a justice to whom an information is presented *conduct an inquiry* for the purpose of determining whether a summons or a warrant shall issue. *The two steps are separate and distinct.* They are related only in the sense that they are successive but they involve the determination of entirely different considerations. (The italics are mine.)

. . .

Parliament clearly intended by s. 455.3(1) to place a judicial officer between the informant and the defendant to ensure that the liberty of the subject was secure from unwarranted intrusion. It may possibly be that we could now trust the decision of a professional policeman and leave it to him alone to decide whether a person must attend in court but the present legislation reserves that decision to a judicial officer.

In *Regina v. Allen* (1974), 20 C.C.C. (2d) 447, the Ontario Court of Appeal said [p. 448]:

> In our view the determination which is made by the Justice under s. 455.3(1) is a determination, to be made judicially, whether on the *evidence* which is placed before him upon that hearing a case for the issue of a summons has been made out. (The italics are mine.)

In *Regina v. Brown*, August Prov. J. [(1976) 28 C.C.C. (2d) 398 (Ont. Prov. Ct.) the learned Provincial Judge has this to say:

> If Parliament did not intend to make the procedures set out in ss. 455.3 and 455.4 of the Criminal Code mandatory before a justice issues a summons or a warrant or confirms the appearance notice, why is the word 'shall' used in these sections? It would appear that Parliament had reason to make the procedure mandatory and the reason is that this procedure is the first step in the protection of people accused of committing criminal offences. This is a simple procedure in determining if the charge against the accused is frivolous and without foundation. There is only one way to accomplish this intention as set out in s. 455.4 and that is for the justice who receives an information to actually hear and listen to the allegations of the informant. By merely reading the information the justice could not be informed in a manner which he is obliged to be informed by these sections in order to protect the accused person and he would not be acting 'judiciously'."

I note as well that s. 455.3(1)(a)(ii) commands the justice to hear and consider "the evidence of witnesses, *where* he considers it desirable or necessary to do so". It is clear that the justice has been given a discretion as to whether witnesses need to be called; it is clear by the absence of such words in s. 455.3(1)(a)(i) that Parliament has given him no such discretion respecting whether he shall hear and consider "the allegations of the informant."

The closing remarks of Henry J. in *Regina v. Peavoy*, supra, while addressed to the police constable's duties, are equally pertinent to the duties of the justice of the peace. At p. 106 he noted:

> Recognizing that the pressure of duties and administration upon police forces may quite naturally cause them, when under pressure to manage the laying of informations as a form of routine 'paperwork', I feel obliged to add the following comments. A person swearing an information, particularly a law enforcement officer, is not at liberty to swear the information in a perfunctory or irresponsible manner with a reckless disregard as to the truth of his assertion. To do so is clearly an affront to the Courts and is at variance with the right of the citizen to be left alone by the authorities unless there is reasonable and probable grounds for invading his liberty by compelling his attendance before the Courts . . . Moreover, he must be prepared to so satisfy the Justice of the Peace who, in turn, has an obligation judicially, not arbitrarily, to hear and consider the allegations before endorsing the information.

The present legislation states that the judicial officer can only compel the attendance of the defendant if he first hears and considers the allegations of the informant. In none of the cases before the Court was this done and accordingly this Court holds that the process which issued is defective.

In the case before the Court the defendants appeared in response to summonses. By s. 133(4) [re-en. R.S.C. 1970, c. 2 (2nd Supp.), s. 4] of the Criminal Code it is an offence to fail to attend court in accordance with a summons and the defendants might have faced prosecution if they did not appear. I cannot hold therefore that their appearance has conferred on me jurisdiction over their persons. In the result I cannot deal with any of these accused persons respecting their alleged involvement in the informations before the Court.

RE BUCHBINDER and VENNER
(1985), 47 C.R. (3d) 135, 20 C.C.C. (3d) 481 (Ont. C.A.)

The justice received an information sworn by Buchbinder against "unknown persons that can be pointed out". Pursuant to s. 455.3 (now s. 507) the justice issued a subpoena commanding the attendance of Venner to give evidence. Venner applied for a writ of prohibition prohibiting the hearing before the justice. The application was dismissed and Venner appealed. Buchbinder conceded that the information was defective in failing to name a person, or sufficiently describe him so that he could be identified, and that a summons or warrant could not issue thereon. He maintained, however, that it was still adequate to clothe the justice of the peace with jurisdiction to conduct a hearing and to compel witnesses to attend. The witnesses then would identify the accused, the information would be amended to name him and process could issue. The Court disagreed.

This is to give him investigative jurisdiction, whereas, in my view, it is apparent that his function is a judicial one, to test the quality and sufficiency of the evidence of the complainant and satisfy himself as to whether or not there are reasonable and probable grounds to believe that a certain person or persons has committed the offence set out in the information. The information might well be amended on the basis of the evidence adduced before the justice of the peace or (absent any limitation restrictions) a fresh information laid, but certainly the justice of the peace must at least be confident that he is dealing with a particular person who has either been named or is described with sufficient specificity that he could be recognized or identified. He is in no sense charged with the responsibility of investigating alleged crimes and determining who may be responsible for their commission; that is the role of the police.

(b) Arrest Without Warrant

The power of citizen arrest is expressed in the Criminal Code and carefully circumscribed.

494.(1) Any one may arrest without warrant

(a) a person whom he finds committing an indictable offence; or

(b) a person who, on reasonable grounds, he believes

(i) has committed a criminal offence, and

(ii) is escaping from and freshly pursued by persons who have lawful authority to arrest that person.

. . .

(3) Any one other than a peace officer who arrests a person without warrant shall forthwith deliver the person to a peace officer.

Crown election offences are treated as indictable for the purpose of the law of arrest by virtue of Interpretation Act, R.S.C. 1985, c. I-27, s. 34(1) as interpreted, for example in *R. v. Seward,* 48 C.R. 220, [1966] 4 C.C.C. 166 (N.W.T. Mag. Ct.) and *R. v. Reed* (1975), 23 C.C.C. (2d) 121 (B.C. S.C.).

PROBLEM 1

A passenger leaves a taxi without paying the fare of six dollars. The cab driver follows him and tries unsuccessfully to stop him running off into a park. The cab driver then calls the police who arrive within five minutes. Can the cab driver and/or the police validly arrest the passenger under s. 494(1)?

Compare *R. v. Lawson* (1973), 22 C.R.N.S. 215 (Ont. Prov. Ct.).

2. Special Power of Arrest of Owners, Possessors and Those They Authorize

The Criminal Code confers an extended power:

494.(2) The owner or a person in lawful possession of property, or a person authorized by the owner or by a person in lawful possession of property, may arrest a person without a warrant if they find them committing a criminal offence on or in relation to that property and

(a) they make the arrest at that time; or

(b) they make the arrest within a reasonable time after the offence is committed and they believe on reasonable grounds that it is not feasible in the circumstances for a peace officer to make the arrest.

(3) Any one other than a peace officer who arrests a person without warrant shall forthwith deliver the person to a peace officer.

(4) For greater certainty, a person who is authorized to make an arrest under this section is a person who is authorized by law to do so for the purposes of section 25.

This power was broadened by Parliament in 2012 after a Toronto grocer was charged with assault after he ran after and arrested a man he recognized as one who had stolen from him before. Parliament also enacted simpler and broader defences of self-defence and defence of property. The Government did not take the opportunity to revisit the general power of citizen arrest in s. 494(1).

3. Powers of Peace Officers

Peace officers as defined in s. 2 of the Criminal Code have special, more extensive powers.

(a) Breach of the Peace

Section 31 of the Criminal Code contains a special power of arrest:

31. (1) Every peace officer who witnesses a breach of the peace and every one who lawfully assists him is justified in arresting any person whom he finds committing the breach of the peace or who, on reasonable grounds, the police officer believes is about to join in or renew the breach of the peace.

(2) Every peace officer is justified in receiving into custody any person who is given into his charge as having been a party to a breach of the peace by one who has, or who on reasonable grounds the police officer believes has, witnessed the breach of the peace.

(b) Arrest Without Warrant

Arrest without warrant is now subject to the limitation of the appearance notice situation (see below).

Section 495(1) of the Criminal Code clearly envisages three distinct powers of arrest:

495. (1) A peace officer may arrest without warrant

(a) a person who has committed an indictable offence or who, on reasonable grounds, he believes has committed or is about to commit an indictable offence,

(b) a person whom he finds committing a criminal offence, or

(c) a person in respect of whom he has reasonable grounds to believe that a warrant of arrest or committal, in any form set out in Part XXVIII in relation thereto, is in force within the territorial jurisdiction in which the person is found.

What standard do you think is appropriate for a valid arrest?

Recall the constitutional minimum standards for the issuance of a search warrant in *Hunter v. Southam*, [1984] 2 S.C.R. 145 (S.C.C.). Chief Justice Dickson wrote that to issue a search warrant it would not be sufficient to believe that there may possibly be evidence to be found. Possibilities were not enough.

The state's interest in detecting and preventing crime begins to prevail over the individual's interest in being left alone at the point where credibly-based probability replaced suspicion.

Is the same standard appropriate to condition a lawful arrest?

R. v. STORREY
[1990] 1 S.C.R. 241, 75 C.R. (3d) 1, 53 C.C.C. (3d) 316 (S.C.C.)

The accused argued that his arrest was unlawful and arbitrary. The court decided that was not the case, since there were reasonable and probable grounds for the arrest. Justice Cory, speaking for the Court, gave valuable instruction on the meaning of that requirement.

CORY J.:—Section 450(1) [now s. 495(1)] makes it clear that the police were required to have reasonable and probable grounds to believe that the appellant had committed the offence of aggravated assault before they could arrest him. Without such an important protection, even the most democratic society could all too easily fall prey to the abuses and excesses of a police state. In order to safeguard the liberty of citizens, the Criminal Code requires the police, when attempting to obtain a warrant for an arrest, to demonstrate to a judicial officer that they have reasonable and probable grounds to believe that the person to be arrested has committed the offence. In the case of an arrest made without a warrant, it is even more important for the police to demonstrate that they have those same reasonable and probable grounds upon which they base the arrest.

The importance of this requirement to citizens of a democracy is self-evident. Yet society also needs protection from crime. This need requires that there be a reasonable balance achieved between the individual's right to liberty and the need for society to be protected from crime. Thus the police need not establish more than reasonable and probable grounds for an arrest.

· · ·

It is not sufficient for the police officer to personally believe that he or she has reasonable and probable grounds to make an arrest. Rather, it must be objectively established that those reasonable and probable grounds did in fact exist, that is to say, a reasonable person, standing in the shoes of the police officer, would have believed that reasonable and probable grounds existed to make the arrest.

In summary then, the Criminal Code requires that an arresting officer must subjectively have reasonable and probable grounds on which to base the arrest. Those grounds must, in addition, be justifiable from an objective point of view. That is to say, a reasonable person placed in the position of the officer must be able to conclude that there were indeed reasonable and probable grounds for the arrest. On the other hand, the police need not demonstrate anything more than reasonable and probable grounds. Specifically they are not required to establish a prima facie case for conviction before making the arrest.

The Court in *Storrey* appears to be unaware that Parliament had deleted the words "and probable" from what is now s. 495. In *R. v. Loewen* (2011), 273 C.C.C. (3d) 1, [2011] 2 S.C.R. 167, 84 C.R. (6th) 215 (S.C.C.) the Supreme Court confirmed that "reasonable grounds" in s. 495(1)(a) requires reasonable and probable grounds. Lower courts have determined that the objective aspect of the test can be individualised to take into account the experience of the officer: see, for example, *R. v. Wilson*, 2012 BCCA 517 (B.C. C.A.), leave to appeal refused [2013] 3 S.C.R. xi (note) (S.C.C.). See, too, *Chehil* in Chapter 2 concerning a test of reasonable suspicion. For criticism of recent rulings on the standard of arrest see Stephen Coughlan, "Keeping "Reasonable grounds" Meaningful" (2011), 80 C.R. (6th) 73. In *R. v. Besharah* (2010), 251 C.C.C. (3d) 516, 72 C.R. (6th) 277 (Sask. C.A.), the Court confirmed that the onus of proving reasonable and probable grounds for arrest is on the Crown.

The peace officers' power to arrest anyone found committing a criminal offence in s. 495(1)(*b*) was interpreted by the majority of the Supreme Court in *R. v. Biron*, below, to mean "apparently" committing an offence.

R. v. BIRON
[1976] 2 S.C.R. 56, 30 C.R.N.S. 109, 23 C.C.C. (2d) 513 (S.C.C.)

MARTLAND J. (Judson, Ritchie and Pigeon JJ. concurring):—This is an appeal, by leave of this Court, from the judgment of the Court of Appeal of the Province of Quebec, which, by a majority of two to one, allowed the appeal of the respondent, hereinafter referred to as "Biron", from his conviction on a charge of resisting a peace officer, contrary to what is now s. 118(*a*) (then 1953-54 (Can.), c. 51, s. 110(*a*)) of the Criminal Code, R.S.C. 1970, c. C-34,

. . .

The charge related to resistance to an officer of the Montreal police force, Constable Dorion.

The facts which gave rise to this charge were as follows:

The Montreal police made an authorized raid on a Montreal bar on 24th October 1970. The raid was in search of illegal firearms and liquor. Biron was at the bar while the raid was taking place. He had been drinking. He refused to co-operate with the police, verbally abusing them and refusing to give his name.

Biron was arrested inside the restaurant by Constable Maisonneuve. He was led outside by Constable Gauthier for questioning. He was handed over by Constable Gauthier to Constables Dorion and Marquis, who took him to a police car. Subsequently, Constable Dorion tried to take him to the police wagon. Biron protested his arrest at this point and a scuffle with Constable Dorion occurred.

Biron was charged with creating a disturbance in a public place by shouting, contrary to s. 171(*a*)(i) of the Code (then s. 160(*a*)(i)). He was also charged with resisting a peace officer, as previously mentioned.

. . .

Biron was convicted of both offences before a Judge of the Municipal Court. A trial de novo was held in respect of the s. 171(*a*)(i) offence. He was acquitted of "creating a disturbance by shouting" on the ground that there was no evidence he had been shouting as was alleged in the information.

Biron appealed the s. 118(*a*) conviction to the Quebec Court of Appeal. By a two to one majority, the appeal was allowed and Biron was acquitted.

. . .

The question in issue is as to whether the charge against Biron of resisting Dorion in the execution of his duty must fail because of his successful appeal from his conviction under s. 171(*a*)(i) for causing a disturbance.

It is contended on behalf of Biron that he could not be so convicted because he was not under lawful arrest, and so was entitled to resist Dorion's efforts to take him to the patrol wagon. It is argued that he had not been lawfully arrested because Maisonneuve's right to arrest him for a summary conviction offence had to be based on s. 450(1)(*b*) [re-en. R.S.C. 1970, c. 2 (2nd Supp.), s. 5] of the Code.

. . .

It is submitted by the respondent that Maisonneuve did not find him committing a criminal offence because he was acquitted on the charge laid against him. Reliance is placed on the judgment of the Court of Appeal for Saskatchewan in *A.G. Sask. v. Pritchard* (1961), 35 C.R. 150, 34 W.W.R. 458, 130 C.C.C. 61.

Paragraph (*a*) of s. 450(1) permits a peace officer to arrest without a warrant:

"(*a*) a person who has committed an indictable offence or who, on reasonable and probable grounds, he believes has committed or is about to commit an indictable offence".

This paragraph, limited in its application to indictable offences, deals with the situation in which an offence has already been committed or is expected to be committed. The peace officer is not present at its commission. He may have to rely upon information received from others. The paragraph therefore enables him to act on his belief, if based on reasonable and probable grounds.

Paragraph (*b*) applies in relation to any criminal offence and it deals with the situation in which the peace officer himself finds an offence being committed. His power to arrest is based upon his own observation. Because it is based on his own discovery of an offence actually being committed there is no reason to refer to a belief based upon reasonable and probable grounds.

If the reasoning in the *Pritchard* case, supra, is sound, the validity of an arrest under s. 450(1)(*b*) can only be determined after the trial of the person arrested and after the determination of any subsequent appeals. My view is that the validity of an arrest under this paragraph must be determined in relation to the circumstances which were apparent to the peace officer at the time the arrest was made.

. . .

If the words "committing a criminal offence" are to be construed in the manner indicated in the *Pritchard* case, para. (*b*) becomes impossible to apply. The power of arrest which that paragraph gives has to be exercised promptly, yet, strictly speaking, it is impossible to say that an offence is committed until the party arrested has been found guilty by the courts. If this is the way in which this provision is to be construed, no peace officer can ever decide, when making an arrest without a warrant, that the person arrested is "committing a criminal offence". In my opinion the wording used in para. (*b*), which is over-simplified, means that the power to arrest without a warrant is given where the peace officer himself finds a situation in which a person is apparently committing an offence.

In the present case Constable Maisonneuve observed an apparent offence being committed by Biron. That he was justified in so thinking is shown by the fact that, at trial, Biron was convicted of the offence of causing a disturbance, and that his appeal from conviction resulted from the fact that the information charged only causing a disturbance "by shouting", which "shouting" the Judge on appeal found was not established by the evidence.

In my opinion the arrest of Biron by Maisonneuve was lawful, and, consequently, the resistance offered by Biron to Dorion constituted an offence.

. . .

I would allow the appeal and restore the conviction.

[De Grandpré J. gave a short concurring judgment but Laskin C.J. (Spence and Dickson JJ. concurring) dissented, saying inter alia:]

We are not concerned in this case with a constable's own responsibility or liability for effecting an allegedly unlawful arrest. It is to that that provisions such as s. 25 of the Criminal Code are addressed. I would find it astonishing that a provision concerned with a constable's criminal or other responsibility, and which immunizes him in specified circumstances in respect of an arrest that he has made, should become the vehicle for providing a basis upon which an accused may himself be convicted of resisting the arrest. To do that is to turn a protective provision, a shield, for the constable into a sword against an accused by treating the protection as an expansion of the powers of arrest given by what is now s. 450 [re-en. R.S.C. 1970, c. 2 (2nd Supp.), s. 5] of the Criminal Code.

. . .

There is a further point that merits emphasis. If the word "apparently" is to be read into s. 450(1)(b), logical consistency, if not also ordinary canons of construction, demand that the word be read into s. 449(1)(a) [re-en. R.S.C. 1970, c. 2 (2nd Supp.), s. 5] which empowers any person to arrest without warrant a person whom he "finds committing" an indictable offence. Moreover, it is plain to me, on grounds of context in aid of construction, that when s. 449(1)(a) is read with s. 449(1)(b), the former could not possibly embrace arrest without warrant on apparency or on reasonable and probable grounds. Further, reasonable and probable grounds for an arrest without warrant govern s. 450(1)(a) and 450(1)(c) but the words are excluded from s. 450(1)(b), and I see no textual or policy justification for reading them or the equivalent term "apparently" into s. 450(1)(b). Of course, as Kaufman J.A. points out in his reasons, a constable's lot is a heavy and even unenviable one when he has to make an on-the-spot decision as to an arrest. But he may be over-zealous as well as mistaken, and it may be too that when a charge or charges come to be laid the Crown attorney or other advising counsel may mistake the grounds and thus lay a charge which does not support the arrest. We cannot go on a guessing expedition out of regret for an innocent mistake or a wrong-headed assessment. Far more important, however, is the social and legal, and indeed political, principle upon which our criminal law is based, namely, the right of an individual to be left alone, to be free of private or public restraint, save as the law provides otherwise. Only to the extent to which it so provides can a person be detained or his freedom of movement arrested.

The position as it relates to resistance to unlawful arrest was established at common law as early as 1709 in *Regina v. Tooley* (1709), 2 Ld. Raym. 1296, 92

E.R. 349, and has been reaffirmed time and again: see, for example, *Rex v. Curvan* (1826), 1 Mood. C.C. 132, 168 E.R. 1213; *Regina v. Wilson,* [1955] 1 W.L.R. 493, 39 Cr. App. R. 12, [1955] 1 All E.R. 744 at 745, referring also to the qualification of the use of excessive force in resisting. It has been part of our criminal law from the beginning and is reflected in the provisions of the Criminal Code, which has sought to balance the competing interests in freedom and order by giving the peace officer protection in specified circumstances where he has exceeded his authority to make an arrest. Our law has not, as I understand it, deprived the citizen of his right to resist unlawful arrest. His resistance may be at his own risk if the arrest proves to be lawful, but so too must the police officer accept the risk of having effected a lawful arrest. Of course, even if the resisted arrest is unlawful, the person resisting may still become culpable if he uses excessive force.

Which judgment do you prefer?

In *Roberge v. R.,* [1983] 1 S.C.R. 312, 33 C.R. (3d) 289, 300 (S.C.C.), Lamer J., for the Court, interpreted Biron to mean that "apparently committing" was the same as having reasonable and probable grounds for believing an offence has been committed. The effect of this gloss is that a requirement of reasonable and probable grounds is now to be read into all forms of arrest powers. It is high time that Parliament simplified powers of arrest.

The Lamer gloss was not followed by the Saskatchewan Court of Appeal in *R. v. Janvier* (2007), 54 C.R. (6th) 253, 227 C.C.C. (3d) 294 (Sask. C.A.). A police officer stopping a truck with a broken front headlight that was driven by the accused, smelled burned marihuana and concluded that someone had been smoking marihuana in the truck within the previous twenty minutes. He arrested the accused for possession and searched him and the truck, finding eight grams of marihuana and what he believed to be a list of contacts and money. The accused was then charged with possession for the purposes of trafficking. The Saskatchewan Court of Appeal upheld the trial judge's finding that the smell of burned marihuana alone was not sufficient to justify the arrest and therefore the search of the accused. The trial judge did not err in finding a violation of section 8 of the Charter and in excluding the evidence.

Speaking through Justice Jackson, the Court reasoned that because the reason for the arrest of the accused was possession of marihuana of an amount less than thirty grams, the offence was a summary conviction offence and it was therefore necessary under s. 495(1) (b) for the police officer to have found the accused committing the offence. However, because the officer did not see, hear, or smell the accused committing the offence of possession, he did not find him committing that offence. The officer's belief that an offence was being committed had to be based on his observation of the offence being committed or apparently committed, and not merely an inference from what he smelled. The smell of recently smoked marihuana might have led to an inference of the presence of additional unsmoked marihuana but it was not an observation of current possession. An arrest was not permitted when made on an inference derived from the smell of burned marihuana alone.

Justice Jackson went on to hold that, even if such an inference was permitted to justify an arrest, the evidence was not sufficient for a reasonable person in the shoes of the police officer to conclude that more unsmoked marihuana was present. Such inference would rest on the assumptions that the accused was the person who smoked the marihuana and that a person who had recently smoked marihuana probably possessed more unsmoked marihuana. The truck had not been under observation during the previous twenty minutes and therefore there was no basis to determine the person who consumed the marihuana in the vehicle. No evidence was offered in support of the second assumption and it was speculative at best.

She also held that the arrest also could not be justified under section 11(7) of the *Controlled Drugs and Substances Act*, which would have permitted an arrest on reasonable grounds. This was because it was not objectively reasonable to conclude that more unsmoked marihuana was present based on the smell of burned marihuana alone.

Janvier was distinguished in *R. v. Harding* (2010), 256 C.C.C. (3d) 284 (Alta. C.A.). The Court held that the odour of raw marihuana, detected by an experienced officer, was sufficient grounds to arrest the accused for the summary conviction offence of possession of marihuana.

(c) Constitutional Minimum Standards (Charter ss. 9, 10(a))

There is also a constitutional dimension to the law of arrest. Under s. 9 of the Charter everyone has the right "not to be arbitrarily detained or imprisoned", while s. 10(*a*) now establishes the right of everyone "on arrest or detention (a) to be informed promptly of the reasons therefor".

The recent re-consideration in *R. v. Grant* (2009), 66 C.R. (6th) 1 (S.C.C.) of the meaning of detention for Charter purposes will be considered in the next chapter on the right to counsel under s. 10(b).

The Court in *Grant* also made it clear for the first time that an unlawful detention is necessarily arbitrary under s. 9.

Most lower courts had held for many years that the illegality of a detention does not necessarily make it arbitrary under section 9. However in *Grant* (2009) the Supreme decided that unlawful detention was necessarily arbitrary:

> The s. 9 guarantee against arbitrary detention is a manifestation of the general principle, enunciated in s. 7, that a person's liberty is not to be curtailed except in accordance with the principles of fundamental justice. As this Court has stated: "This guarantee expresses one of the most fundamental norms of the rule of law. The state may not detain arbitrarily, but only in accordance with the law": *Charkaoui v. Canada (Citizenship and Immigration)*, 2007 SCC 9, [2007] 1 S.C.R. 350, at para. 88. Section 9 serves to protect individual liberty against unlawful state interference. A lawful detention is not arbitrary within the meaning of s. 9 (*Mann*, at para. 20), unless the law authorizing the detention is itself arbitrary. Conversely, a detention not authorized by law is arbitrary and violates s. 9. [para. 54]

The Court saw this approach as mirroring that developed for unreasonable searches and seizures under s. 8 of the Charter. Under *R. v. Collins*, [1987] 1 S.C.R. 265, 56 C.R. (3d) 193, 33 C.C.C. (3d) 1 we have seen that a search must be authorized by law , the authorizing law must itself be reasonable; and the search must be carried out in a reasonable manner. Similarly,

> it should now be understood that for a detention to be non-arbitrary, it must be authorized by a law which is itself non-arbitrary. We add that, as with other rights, the s. 9 prohibition of arbitrary detention may be limited under s. 1 by such measures "prescribed by law as can be demonstrably justified in a free and democratic society": see *R. v. Hufsky*, [1988] 1 S.C.R. 621, and *R. v. Ladouceur*, [1990] 1 S.C.R. 1257.

The Court could have been clearer in adopting the well established approach to section 8. It would appear that from now on there will be a section 9 violation where there is no lawful authority for the detention (either by statute or common law), or the law is arbitrary. These are challenges to the law and section 1 justification may be at play. However the Court makes it clear that section 9 is violated where a lawful detention or imprisonment was carried out in an arbitrary manner. In such a challenge to police conduct section 1 cannot be resorted to as the limit is not prescribed by law. This new structure for section 9 analysis has been welcomed. The approach better reflects the rule of law and the view Chief Justice Dickson in *Hunter v. Southam* that the Charter should not be a vehicle to authorise State action.

We will discover in this chapter that other established meanings of arbitrary have been held to be a police power with no criteria, express or implied (see *Hufsky* and *Ladouceur*, below) and a power exercised capriciously (as in racial profiling, see *Brown*, below).

(d) Stop Powers and Racial Profiling

(i) Vehicle Stops

In *R. v. Hufsky*, [1988] 1 S.C.R. 621, 63 C.R. (3d) 14, 40 C.C.C. (3d) 398 (S.C.C.) and *R. v. Ladouceur*, [1990] 1 S.C.R. 1257, 77 C.R. (3d) 110, 56 C.C.C. (3d) 22, the Supreme Court held that a detention in the unfettered discretion of a police officer is necessarily "arbitrary" contrary to s. 9. The issue in both cases was the constitutionality of the spot check procedure in s. 189(a) now s. 216, of the Ontario Highway Traffic Act which reads as follows:

> (1) A police officer, in the lawful execution of his duties and responsibilities, may require the driver of a motor vehicle to stop and the driver of a motor vehicle, when signalled or requested to stop by a police officer who is readily identifiable as such, shall immediately come to a safe stop.

> (2) Every person who contravenes subsection (1) is guilty of an offence and on conviction is liable to a fine of not less than $100 and not more than $2,000 or to imprisonment for a term of not more than six months, or to both.

For a unanimous Court in *Hufsky*, Mr. Justice LeDain had little difficulty in finding a contravention of s. 9:

Although authorized by statute and carried out for lawful purposes, the random stop for the purposes of the spot check procedure nevertheless resulted, in my opinion, in an arbitrary detention, because there were no criteria for the selection of the drivers to be stopped and subjected to the spot check procedure. The selection was in the absolute discretion of the police officer. A discretion is arbitrary if there are no criteria, express or implied, which govern its exercise.

He went on however:

The section 1 material that was placed before the Court by the respondent on the issue of arbitrary detention . . . reinforces the impression of the gravity of the problem of motor vehicle accidents in terms of the resulting deaths, personal injury and property damage, and the overriding importance of the effective enforcement of the motor vehicle laws and regulations in the interests of highway safety. The charts or tables prepared by the respondent from the statistical data in the government reports stress the following points: the relative importance of licence suspension and the effective enforcement of it; the relatively higher proportion of unlicensed and uninsured drivers, by comparison with the proportion of licensed and insured drivers, involved in motor vehicle accidents resulting in death or personal injury; and the relative importance of the motor vehicle offences, including driving without a licence or while under licence suspension or without insurance, which cannot be detected by observation of the driving. Again, a random stop authority is said to be justified by increasing the perceived risk of the detection of such offences. In view of the importance of highway safety and the role to be played in relation to it by a random stop authority for the purpose of increasing both the detection and the perceived risk of detection of motor vehicle offences, many of which cannot be detected by mere observation of driving, I am of the opinion that the limit imposed by s. 189a(1) of the Highway Traffic Act on the right not to be arbitrarily detained guaranteed by s. 9 of the Charter is a reasonable one that is demonstrably justified in a free and democratic society. The nature and degree of the intrusion of a random stop for the purposes of the spot check procedure in the present case, remembering that the driving of a motor vehicle is a licensed activity subject to regulation and control in the interests of safety, is proportionate to the purpose to be served.

Hufsky dealt with a fact situation where the random spot check was at a fixed location. *Ladouceur* dealt with the justification of a roving random stop. This time the Court divided 5:4. For the majority Cory J. (Lamer, L'Heureux-Dubé, Gonthier and McLachlin JJ. concurring) wrote:

The two officers had been in the area maintaining surveillance on a house. Just as they were leaving, they saw the appellant driving his car. The officers followed the appellant's car along Donald St. and then pulled him over on at the corner of St. Laurent Blvd. and Queen Mary St., across from a convenience store. The officers did not suspect that the appellant was acting unlawfully or that he was in any way connected with the house under surveillance. Constable Bell testified that the sole purpose of the stop was to ensure that the appellant's papers were in order and that he had a valid driver's licence. He said they had stopped several other vehicles in the area on the same night. When asked in cross-examination whether the stops were "at random", he replied: "Pretty well, yes."

. . .

CAN THE S.9 VIOLATION BE JUSTIFIED UNDER S.1 OF THE CHAR-
TER?

. . .

To recognize the validity of the random routine check is to recognize reality. In
rural areas it will be an impossibility to establish an effective organized program.
Yet the driving offences in these areas lead to consequences just as tragic as those
that arise in the largest urban centres. Even the large municipal police force will,
due to fiscal constraints and shortages of personnel, have difficulty establishing an
organized program that would constitute a real deterrent. From the foregoing, it is
readily apparent that there is a rational connection between the routine check and
the goal of the empowering provision of the Highway Traffic Act. . . . Licensed
activities must be carried out exclusively by licence holders who have demonstrated
their competence and of their willingness to comply with the fair and reasonable
guidelines and requirements that govern all licence holders. There would be no
point to requiring licences for those who engage in activities that are potentially
dangerous and require a demonstrated degree of skill if there were no means of
ensuring that a driver holds a valid licence. . . . Finally, it must be shown that the
routine check does not so severely trench upon the s. 9 right so as to outweigh the
legislative objective. The concern at this stage is the perceived potential for abuse
of this power by law enforcement officials. In my opinion, these fears are
unfounded. There are mechanisms already in place which prevent abuse. Officers
can stop persons only for legal reasons, in this case reasons related to driving a car
such as checking the driver's licence and insurance, the sobriety of the driver and
the mechanical fitness of the vehicle. Once stopped the only questions that may
justifiably be asked are those related to driving offences. Any further, more
intrusive procedures could only be undertaken based upon reasonable and
probable grounds. Where a stop is found to be unlawful, the evidence from the
stop could well be excluded under s. 24(2) of the Charter. . . . In the result, I have
concluded that routine checks are ajustifiable infringement on the rights conferred
by s. 9.

For the minority Sopinka J. (Dickson C.J., Wilson and La Forest JJ. concurring) wrote:

This case may be viewed as the last straw. If sanctioned, we will be agreeing that a
police officer can stop any vehicle at any time, in any place, without having any
reason to do so. For the motorist, this means a total negation of the freedom from
arbitrary detention guaranteed by s. 9 of the Charter. This is something that would
not be tolerated with respect to pedestrians in their use of the public streets and
walkways. It is in this light that the efforts of the Crown to discharge its s. 1 onus
must be viewed. Although the statistics are voluminous, there is no evidence as to
whether during the relevant period police officers were actually exercising the
"roving random stop" power. For example, was the percentage of accidents
involving unlicensed drivers realized notwithstanding the fact that police officers
were employing this method of enforcement? If it was, presumably it is only since s.
189a(1) was enacted in 1981. What were the percentages before this method was
used? How many motorists who were perfectly law-abiding were stopped for every
one that was committing some violation? On the other hand, if the police have not
been using this method and this case is an isolated incident, what is the evidence
that police officers consider that this power is essential to effective enforcement?
The record is surprisingly devoid of any reference to police practice in this regard. .
. . Random checking at a stationary, predetermined location infringes the right

much less than the unlimited right contended for. The decision to locate the check point will be made either by a superior officer or by the decision of several officers. While the decision as to which automobile will be stopped will be made by an individual officer, his conduct can be observed by other officers. Since he has limited time to observe a vehicle, his decision will be either truly random or based on some objective basis. . . . By contrast, the roving random stop would permit any individual officer to stop any vehicle, at any time, at any place. The decision may be based on any whim. Individual officers will have different reasons. Some may tend to stop younger drivers, others older cars, and so on. Indeed, as pointed out by Tarnopolsky J.A., racial considerations may be a factor too. My colleague states that in such circumstances, a Charter violation may be made out. If, however, no reason need be given nor is necessary, how will we ever know? The officer need only say, "I stopped the vehicle because I have the right to stop it for no reason. I am seeking unlicensed drivers."

According to research reported in the *Report of the Commission on Systemic Racism in the Ontario Criminal Justice System* (1995), black men [in Metro Toronto] are particularly vulnerable to being stopped by police. About 43 per cent of black male residents, but only 25 per cent of white and 19 per cent of Chinese male residents report being stopped by the police in the previous two years. Significantly more black men (29 per cent) than white (12 per cent) or Chinese (7 per cent) report two or more police stops in the previous two years (p. ix).

In *R. v. Mellenthin*, [1992] 3 S.C.R. 615, the police directed the accused's vehicle into a check stop set up as part of a program to check vehicles. An officer shone his flashlight in the interior of the vehicle. That revealed an open gym bag on the front seat. The officer asked the accused what was in the bag and the accused said there was food inside. The officer saw a reflection of glass, asked the accused about it and the accused pulled out a bag containing glass vials. The accused was charged with possession of hash oil. Justice Cory, for a unanimous five-person court, wrote:

> In those cases, [*Hufsky* and *R. v. Ladouceur*] it was deemed appropriate for the officers conducting a check stop program to pose questions as to the mechanical condition of the vehicle and to require the production of a driver's licence, certificate of ownership and proof of insurance. . . . There can be no quarrel with the visual inspection of the car by police officers. At night the inspection can only be carried out with the aid of a flashlight and it is necessarily incidental to a check stop program carried out after dark. The inspection is essential for the protection of those on duty in the check stops. There have been more than enough incidents of violence to police officers when vehicles have been stopped. . . . However, the subsequent questions pertaining to the gym bag were improper. At the moment the questions were asked, the officer had not even the slightest suspicion that drugs or alcohol were in the vehicle or in the possession of the appellant. The appellant's words, actions and manner of driving did not demonstrate any symptoms of impairment. Check stop programs result in the arbitrary detention of motorists. The programs are justified as a means aimed at reducing the terrible toll of death and injury so often occasioned by impaired drivers or by dangerous vehicles. The primary aim of the program is thus to check for sobriety, licences, ownership, insurance and the mechanical fitness of cars. The police use of check stops should

not be extended beyond these aims. Random stop programs must not be turned into a means of conducting either an unfounded general inquisition or an unreasonable search.

In the result the evidence was excluded and the accused acquitted.

_____

R. v. NOLET
76 C.R. (6th) 1, [2010] 1 S.C.R. 851, 256 C.C.C. (3d) 1 (S.C.C.)

The accused were travelling eastward along the Saskatchewan portion of the Trans-Canada Highway in an empty 53-foot commercial tractor-trailer unit licensed in Quebec. They were pulled over by an RCMP officer in a spot check, during which it emerged that the truck's registration was not pro-rated to include the province and that the appropriate fuel sticker had expired. The accused, Nolet, produced a log book that was incomplete but indicated that the truck normally operated east of the Manitoba border. The officer searched the cab of the truck, finding a duffle bag behind the driver's seat. The officer testified that when he touched the bag the contents crackled like paper, and so he opened it assuming it would contain old log books or travel documents. The officer found $115,000 in cash in the bag, and arrested the accused for the possession of proceeds of crime. A subsequent search of the truck about two hours later revealed 392 pounds of marihuana concealed in a secret compartment in the trailer. The next day the RCMP conducted an inventory search and found further documentation relating to the *Highway Traffic Act* offences. The trial judge found that the search of the duffle bag violated the Charter, excluded the evidence, and acquitted the accused. The Saskatchewan Court of Appeal found that there were no Charter violations and ordered a new trial. The accused appealed.

The Supreme Court were unanimous in dismissing the appeal.

BINNIE J. (for the full Court):—

A. The Initial Stop

[23] Random roadside stops must be limited to their intended purposes. "A check stop does not and cannot constitute a general search warrant for searching every vehicle, driver and passenger that is pulled over", per Cory J., in *Mellenthin*, at p. 629. It thus becomes necessary to examine the authority claimed by the police at each step from the original demand to the appellants to pull their truck over on the Trans-Canada Highway to the discovery of the cash and subsequently the marijuana a couple of hours later as well as the follow-up "inventory search" the next morning, to determine at what point, if at all, the police infringed the rights of the appellants under s. 8 or s. 9 of the Charter. A roadside stop is not a static event. Information as it emerges may entitle the police to proceed further, or, as the case may be, end their enquiries and allow the vehicle to resume its journey.

[24] Much of the debate on the appeal focussed on whether the search of the duffle bag was or was not covered by s. 63(5) of the H&TA. This inquiry is

important but not sufficient. A distinction must be drawn between the existence of a police power and the further issue of whether that power, otherwise legal, is exercised in violation of s. 8 of the Charter, having regard to a trucker's reasonable expectation of some privacy in the sleeping area of the cab. An exclusive focus on police powers under the H&TA may not give adequate weight to Charter concerns. Equally, restricting the Court's focus to the Charter may distract attention from the important preliminary question of whether the police possessed the power to conduct a search in the first place.

[25] The Court has ruled on a number of occasions that pursuant to statutory authority, the police officers can randomly stop persons for "reasons related to driving a car such as checking the driver's licence and insurance, the sobriety of the driver and the mechanical fitness of the vehicle": *Ladouceur* (Ont.), at p. 1287. See also *R. v. Orbanski*, 2005 SCC 37, [2005] 2 S.C.R. 3, at para. 41; *Mellenthin*, at p. 624. The courts below held that the appellants' truck was stopped for the valid purpose of carrying out an H&TA document check, and this issue is no longer seriously in dispute. The stop was valid. On this basis, the case is readily distinguishable from our Court's recent ruling in *R. v. Harrison*, 2009 SCC 34, [2009] 2 S.C.R. 494, where the accused had been pulled over for no valid purpose. The police equally exceed their powers in the Saskatchewan case of *R. v. Ladouceur*, 2002 SKCA 73, 165 C.C.C. (3d) 321 (hereinafter "*Ladouceur* (Sask.)"), where the officers set up a random stop program called "Operation Recovery" specifically to detect not only highway infractions but to "locate contraband being transported on our highways" (para. 69). For that purpose the Saskatchewan checkpoint was staffed not only with police, but on occasion customs and immigration officials, "tobacco people", wildlife officials and sniffer dogs (para. 44). The random stop program in *Ladouceur* (Sask.) was designed as a "comprehensive check for criminal activity" (para. 43) and was therefore fatally flawed from the outset.

[26] In the present case, by contrast, the random stop program was directly related to legitimate highway purposes. Commercial trucking is regulated in every aspect from loads and load safety under The Motor Carrier Act to potentially dangerous cargo under The Dangerous Goods Transportation Act, S.S. 1984-85-86, c. D-1.2. As such, the initial stop, in this case under s. 40 of The Highway Traffic Act, did not violate the s. 9 rights of the appellants: *Ladouceur* (Ont.), at p. 1287; *Orbanski*, at p. 41.

B. The Regulatory Search

[27] Section 32(1) of The Motor Carrier Act authorizes a peace officer to "order the driver or owner of a vehicle to submit the vehicle . . . or the cargo being carried on such a vehicle to any examination and tests that the peace officer considers necessary". In the same vein, s. 63(5) of the H&TA provides that if a police officer "has reasonable grounds to believe that a vehicle is being operated in contravention" of regulatory requirements, he may conduct a warrantless search of "the vehicle for evidence of an offence" and "seize anything that may be evidence of an offence". In such cases, of course, "an offence" refers to H&TA provisions that include regulation of the manner in which any part of a vehicle or its load is to be marked or labelled; the contents

of a driver's log and the manner in which a driver's log is to be kept and maintained; the number of hours a driver can be on duty or drive; and, the classes or types of vehicles for which a trip inspection report is to be completed (s. 69(1)).

C. The Highways and Transportation Act Power of Search and Seizure was Properly Invoked

[28] There is no doubt that, after the initial stop, the officer quickly obtained reasonable grounds to believe that the appellants were operating the truck in violation of the H&TA, having regard to the lack of a truck licence valid in Saskatchewan, the display of an expired fuel sticker and inconsistent entries in the driver's log-book. At the time the officer began to investigate the cab of the tractor unit, it was quite within his statutory authority to search for further evidence related to H&TA offences.

[29] In these circumstances, the continued detention of the appellants was not arbitrary and the search of the tractor-trailer rig for relevant papers was authorized by s. 63(5)(b). At least initially, they were not unreasonable.

D. The Appellants' Limited Expectation of Privacy in the Sleeping Area of the Cab

[30] I agree with the trial judge that drivers ordinarily have some expectation of privacy in the sleeping area of a cab of the tractor-trailer, including the space behind the front seats where the duffle bag with the money was found. Whether or not an individual has a subjective expectation of privacy, and whether or not that expectation is objectively reasonable, is an assessment to be made having regard to the totality of the circumstances: *R. v. Edwards*, [1996] 1 S.C.R. 128, at para. 45; *R. v. Tessling*, 2004 SCC 67, [2004] 3 S.C.R. 432; *R. v. Kang-Brown*, 2008 SCC 18, [2008] 1 S.C.R. 456, at paras. 8-10 and 48. The onus of proof of such reasonable expectation, to a probability standard, lies on the Charter claimant.

[31] While the appellants did not testify about their subjective belief, the court may presume that individuals would expect a measure of privacy in what, for a long- distance trucker, suffices as a temporary mobile home. The expectation is objectively reasonable because living quarters, however rudimentary, should not be classified as a Charter-free zone: *Johnson v. Ontario (Minister of Revenue)* (1990), 75 O.R. (2d) 558 (C.A.), and *R. v. Belnavis*, [1997] 3 S.C.R. 341. Nevertheless, the level of expectation is necessarily low because the cab of a tractor-trailer rig is not only a place of rest but a place of work, and the whole of the cab is therefore vulnerable to frequent random checks in relation to highway transport matters. As Wilkinson J.A. pointed out, "[k]nowledge of the transportation legislation is a requirement to be licensed as a driver. The [appellants] would be well aware of the possibility of mandatory inspections and searches, whether for documents or for potential violation of any one of the countless obligations imposed by the regulatory scheme" (para. 70). Accordingly, there can be little expectation of privacy, even in the sleeping area of a truck (particularly one which is travelling in violation of relevant highway

regulations). A stop may quickly precipitate a search, and the occupants either know or ought to know of that reality and govern themselves accordingly.

E. Did the Regulatory Search Authority Cease Because of Taint by an Impermissible Criminal Law Purpose?

[32] As stated, this is not a case where the random stop was constitutionally flawed from the outset. The argument of the appellants is that an investigation lawful at the outset became unlawful when the police officer, based on information lawfully obtained from the appellants and the appearance of their vehicle, began to suspect criminal activity. The trial judge found, and the appellants contend, that the policeman's search of the duffle bag should be attributed predominantly to his interest in illegal criminal activity, and as such, they say it fell outside any valid regulatory purpose.

[33] The officer made no secret at trial of his interest in finding contraband. It was part of his job to take an interest in contraband. In the nature of things, contraband is a bigger issue for police than trucking documents. However, he testified that it was only "at that point" of finding the money that he believed "there was a good possibility there was a secret compartment in the trailer" (A.R., vol. 2, at p. 204).

[34] The first question is whether the police officer, in continuing the search, exceeded his s. 63(5) authority when he reached the point of suspicion. The second question is whether what he did, despite the authority of s. 63(5) to pursue regulatory offences, was unreasonable in relation to the protected Charter privacy interests of the accused in the sleeping area of the cab. The statutory authority for the search and the reasonableness of its exercise are two distinct issues.

[35] As to the police powers issue, the trial judge agreed that notwithstanding that the officer had found "sufficient irregularities in a very short span of time to be concerned that there could be more" and that "it might be reasonable to conclude that the officer continued his investigation to check for further regulatory infractions", nevertheless, "given the totality of the circumstances, it does appear that the officer was more interested in looking for evidence of criminal activity than for contraventions of commercial trucking regulations" (para. 19 (emphasis added)). This led to a discussion about "dual purpose" searches, and whether a "dominant" criminal law purpose would invalidate an otherwise valid regulatory search or, on the contrary, a legitimate regulatory purpose could "sanitize" or "cleanse" an unlawful criminal law purpose.

[36] Wilkinson J.A., for the majority in the court below, found the dual purpose debate unhelpful and succinctly expressed the view that

> the lawful aim cannot be used as a pretext, ruse, or subterfuge to perpetuate the unlawful aim. That, ultimately, is the focal point of the inquiry. It is not a question of degree, or determining which purpose is predominate or subordinate. Rather, it is a question whether a lawful purpose is being exploited to achieve an impermissible aim. [para. 85]

What happened here, in her view, is not within the mischief contemplated by the late Chief Justice Bayda in *Ladouceur* (Sask.) that "it is important not to encourage the establishment of checkstops where a nominally lawful aim is but a plausible facade for an unlawful aim" (para. 66).

[37] It is to be expected that RCMP officers patrolling the Trans-Canada Highway are interested in any number of potential infractions including criminal offences as well as provincial matters. It could hardly be otherwise. However, as pointed out by Martin J.A., "[t]he lawful search was not converted into an unlawful or an unreasonable search because the officers, in addition, had the expectation that the search might also uncover drugs": *R. v. Annett* (1984), 17 C.C.C. (3d) 332 (Ont. C.A.), at p. 335, leave to appeal refused, [1985] 1 S.C.R. v.

[38] In *Brown v. Durham Regional Police Force* (1998), 43 O.R. (3d) 223 (C.A.), the police used the Ontario equivalent H&TA powers to stop and question bikers attending a gathering of the Paradise Riders Motorcycle Club, suspected to be a criminal organization. The police took advantage of the stop to gather information about the individuals and the gathering. Doherty J.A., for the court, while upholding as valid the police conduct in that particular case, stated:

> While I can find no sound reason for invalidating an otherwise proper stop because the police used the opportunity afforded by that stop to further some other legitimate interest, I do see strong policy reasons for invalidating a stop where the police have an additional improper purpose. Highway safety concerns are important, but they should not provide the police with a means to pursue objects which are themselves an abuse of the police power or are otherwise improper. [p. 238]

[39] Police power, whether conferred by statute or at common law, is abused when it is exercised in a manner that violates the Charter rights of an accused. This is a better framework of analysis, in my opinion, than the "predominant purpose" test applied here by the trial judge. If the Charter is violated, it makes little difference, I think, that the police had in mind multiple purposes. A valid regulatory purpose, whether predominant or not, would not sanitize or excuse a Charter violation.

[40] This position is consistent with what the Court said about Annett in *R. v. Law*, 2002 SCC 10, [2002] 1 S.C.R. 227:

> The distinguishing feature of *Annett*, however, is that the full scope of the officers' search was authorized by statute; thus, the only issue was whether their hidden intentions rendered the search unreasonable. [Emphasis added; para. 24.]

Law involved a theft investigation. The police recovered a stolen security safe, and decided to look at the contents for the totally unrelated purpose of investigating potential tax evasion by the complainant in the theft case. We held that the evidence obtained from the safe was properly excluded in the resulting tax prosecution. Of interest for present purposes, however, is the distinction noted by the Court between police powers and Charter compliance.

[41] I agree with Wilkinson J.A. that the question is not "determining which purpose is predominate or subordinate" (para. 85). As long as there is a continuing regulatory purpose on which to ground the exercise of the regulatory power, the issue is whether the officer's search of the duffle bag

infringed the reasonable expectations of privacy of the appellants. I do not think that it did, having regard to the totality of the circumstances as they had progressed to the time of that search.

F. Did Discovery of the Cash in the Duffle Bag Violate Section 8?

[42] The trial judge, with respect, set the barrier to the ongoing police investigation too high when she wrote:

> In this case, I have no difficulty in concluding that the initial stop and detention were lawful and did not infringe s. 9. Likewise, the initial search did not violate s. 8. However, once the officer became suspicious that alterations had been made to the trailer, the focus of his inquiry shifted from a regulatory inspection to a criminal investigation. Given this change in focus, he required either informed consent or reasonable and probable grounds to continue searching for evidence to support his suspicions, neither of which existed. [para. 28]

[43] I do not agree that the officer's concurrent interest in contraband (even if it was "predominant") rendered the H&TA search unlawful or unreasonable within the scope of s. 8 of the Charter. As already stated, knowledge of transportation legislation is a requirement to be licensed as a driver. Commercial drivers are well aware of the police authority to conduct random stops and to search a vehicle for evidence of infractions. Commercial trucking is a highly regulated industry. Breaching a law will not in itself reduce an individual's legitimate privacy expectations (otherwise, it would be argued that offenders would always forfeit s. 8 protection relevant to evidence of the offence), but here, as events progressed from the police stop to the initial regulatory search of the cab, there was no police invasion of the minimal privacy interest that existed. As was the case in *Annett*, "the expectation that the search might also uncover drugs" (at para. 335) did not convert a Charter-compliant regulatory search into a Charter violation: *R. v. Sewell*, 2003 SKCA 52, 175 C.C.C. (3d) 242.

[44] The trial judge did not express any doubt about the officer's evidence that relevant papers were frequently dispersed around a cab, often collected in a bag similar to the one at issue here, and that when he "pushed down on the duffel bag, [he] felt and heard paper products inside" (A.R., vol. 2, at p. 181). In other words, the officer did not proceed immediately to open the bag without some preliminary evaluation of its likely relevance to the regulatory search. The paper contents felt more like items connected to the H&TA inquiry than if the contents had felt solid in a way that might have indicated personal clothing (or drugs). In the circumstances, it was not unreasonable, given the appellants' very limited privacy interest, for the officer to open the bag. At that point, the cash was in plain view.

For a critical comment see Stephen Coughlan, "Stopping Vehicles on a Downhill Slope: *R. v. Nolet*" (2010) 76 C.R. (6th) 1 (S.C.C.).

PROBLEM 2

The accused was charged with several counts relating to a loaded firearm and quantities of cocaine and marihuana that were discovered in his car after he was stopped by the police. The police had run his license plate as he drove by them and discovered that there was a caution marked on it with regard to the driver. They stopped the car using their highway traffic powers. The police testified that but for the caution they would not have stopped the vehicle. Upon approaching the vehicle the officers smelled fresh marihuana and decided at that point that they had reasonable grounds to arrest. They asked the accused if he had been smoking marihuana. He replied that he had. The officers decided that they could smell fresh rather than burnt marihuana and arrested the accused. They then searched the vehicle and found the firearm and drugs. The accused argued that the stop had violated his rights under ss. 9 and 10 of the Charter. Rule on his application.

Compare *R. v. Morris* (2011), 87 C.R. (6th) 362 (Ont. S.C.J.). See CR comment by Stephen Coughlan.

In *R. v. Orbanski*, [2005] 2 S.C.R. 3, 29 C.R. (6th) 205 a 7-2 majority decided that implied in the operation requirements of our drunk driving provincial and federal legislation were police powers to ask motorists whether they had anything to drink and also to administer sobriety tests. We will consider the Charter rulings later. **Do you think these powers are implied and are they reasonable?**

Parliament has now enacted detailed powers to conduct sobriety tests, mostly out of a concern to be able to detect driving under the influence of marihuana.

Police now have express Criminal Code powers to demand:

(a) — forthwith a breath sample in an approved screening device or physical coordination tests on reasonable suspicion grounds to suspect impaired driving or having care and control while impaired by drugs or alcohol (s. 254(2));

(b) — as soon as practicable a breathalyzer or blood sample demand on "reasonable grounds" (interpreted as reasonable and probable grounds but not a high standard in *R. v. Bush* (2010), 80 C.R. (6th) 29, 259 C.C.C. (3d) 127 (Ont. C.A.)) (s. 254(3)); and

(c) — as soon as practicable an evaluation conducted by an evaluation officer on "reasonable grounds" (s. 254(3.1)) (aimed at driving while under the influence of marihuana or other drugs and leading to demands for urine and blood samples).

Where the specified ground for a demand is not established the search is illegal and contrary to s. 8 of the Charter.

PROBLEM 3

The accused was observed to be unsteady on his feet and to be having difficulty as he tried to back his car down a boat launch to take his boat out of the water by a person who concluded that he had been drinking and called 911. The accused was stopped about ten minutes later by an officer who had been dispatched on the call. That officer asked the accused what he had been doing, and the accused replied that he had been on his boat since noon and was a bit out of it. The accused was described as lethargic and "out of it" as he obtained his license and insurance for the officer. The officer noticed that the accused had a bad sunburn and asked whether the accused had had anything to drink, to which he replied that he had had a vodka in the morning but nothing else. The officer was unsure whether the accused's lethargy was due to alcohol or due to the effects of the sun, and so made an approved screening device demand to the accused. Was the demand legal?

Compare *R. v. Staples* (2010), 84 C.R. (6th) 71 (Ont. C.J.). What of an admission of having had two beers and the smell of alcohol in the car: see *R. v. Mitchell* (2013), 298 C.C.C. (3d) 525, 3 C.R. (7th) 297 (Man. C.A.)?

In *R. v. Quansah* (2012), 286 C.C.C. (3d) 307, 92 C.R. (6th) 1 (Ont. C.A.), the Court interpreted the "forthwith" requirement for an ASD demand as a flexible approach, in this case permitting a 17-minute delay in the ASD demand. In *R. v. Evans* (2015), 21 C.R. (7th) 133 (Ont. C.J.), in contrast, Stribopoulos J. held that a breath sample demand was not lawful and contrary to s. 8 because a 17-minute delay did not meet the test of "as soon as practicable".

(ii) Investigative Detention

R. v. SIMPSON
(1993), 20 C.R. (4th) 1, 12 O.R. (3d) 182, 79 C.C.C. (3d) 482 (Ont. C.A.)

The accused was charged with possession of cocaine for the purpose of trafficking. He was a passenger in a motor vehicle stopped by a police constable. After the vehicle was stopped, the constable searched the accused and seized 10g of cocaine.

The constable testified that shortly before the stop he had read an internal police memo describing a particular residence as a suspected "crack house." He patrolled the area and observed a woman leave a car parked in the driveway of the house, enter the residence, and leave a short time later accompanied by the accused. The police officer, who had no information about either person, followed them and stopped the vehicle. The police officer noticed a bulge in the accused's front pant pocket. He touched it and felt a hard lump. At that point the officer did not have reasonable grounds to arrest the accused. He asked the accused to remove the object, which turned out to be a baggie containing cocaine. The trial judge rejected the accused's argument that his rights under ss. 8 and 9 of the Canadian Charter of Rights and Freedoms had been infringed. The accused was convicted and appealed.

DOHERTY J.A. (Krever, McKinlay JJ.A., concurring):—

. . .

The appellant was clearly detained when the motor vehicle in which he was riding was pulled over by Constable Wilkin. . . . Section 9 of the *Charter* limits the power of the police to detain individuals. It draws the line, subject to s. 1 of the *Charter*, at detentions which are arbitrary. The words "arbitrary" and "unlawful" are not synonymous. . . . Although an assessment of the lawfulness of a detention is not dispositive of the s. 9 claim, it is appropriate to begin by addressing the lawfulness of the detention. If the detention is lawful, it is not arbitrary unless the law authorizing the detention is arbitrary. If the detention is found to be unlawful, that finding will play a central role in determining whether the detention is also arbitrary.

[The Court considered the statutory authority under the Highway Traffic Act to stop motor vehicles, s. 216(1), and concluded that this stop could not be justified under that head of power as the stop was not made for the purposes of enforcing driving related laws and promoting the safe use of motor vehicles.]

. . .

The search for a legal authority for this stop and detention must go beyond s. 216(1) of the *Highway Traffic Act*.

The law imposes broad general duties on the police but it provides them with only limited powers to perform those duties. Police duties and their authority to act in the performance of those duties are not co-extensive. Police conduct is not rendered lawful merely because it assisted in the performance of the duties assigned to the police. Where police conduct interferes with the liberty or freedom of the individual, that conduct will be lawful only if it is authorized by law. That law may be a specific statutory power or it may be the common law. As I have rejected the only statutory authority put forward to support this detention (s. 216(1) of the *Highway Traffic Act*), I will now consider whether the common law authorized this detention.

. . .

As the authorities plainly show, judicial efforts to define the police common law power have generated considerable disagreement. The appellant submits that, whatever uncertainties may exist concerning the reach of police common law powers, this court has held that a detention for investigative purposes, absent proper grounds for an arrest, is an unauthorized and potentially arbitrary detention. In *Duguay*, supra, at p. 383 O.R., p. 296 C.C.C. [p. 148 C.R.], MacKinnon A.C.J.O. said:

> In my view, on the facts as found by the trial judge, the arrest or detention was arbitrary, being for quite an improper purpose — namely, to assist in the investigation.

The facts which precipitated this statement were, however, significantly different than those present in this case. In *Duguay*, the police formally arrested the suspects near the scene of the alleged crime, placed them in a police cruiser, transported them to the police station and held them in locked interview rooms for a considerable period of time during which the suspects were interrogated at some length. It was that prolonged and highly intrusive detention, premised only on a suspicion short of reasonable and probable grounds for an arrest, that was held to be arbitrary. In my view, it does not follow from *Duguay* that any and all detentions for investigative purposes constitute a violation of s. 9 of the *Charter*; Young, "All Along the Watch Tower", supra at p. 367.

The appellant also relies on this court's judgment in *R. v. Dedman* (1981), 32 O.R. (2d) 641 at 652-53, 59 C.C.C. (2d) 97 at 108-09 [23 C.R. (3d) 228 at 242] where Martin J.A. for the court said:

> In carrying out their general duties, the police have limited powers, and they are entitled to interfere with the liberty and property of the citizen only where such interference is authorized by law. It is, of course, a constitutional principle that the citizen has a right not to be subjected to imprisonment, arrest or physical restraint that is not justified by law, and every invasion of the property of the citizen is a trespass unless legally justified . . . Although a police officer is entitled to question any person in order to obtain information with respect to a suspected offence, he has no lawful power to compel the person questioned to answer. Moreover, *a police officer has no right to detain a person for questioning or for further investigation. No one is entitled to impose any physical restraint upon the citizen except as authorized by law, and this principle applies as much to police officers as to anyone else.* [Emphasis added.]

The appellant argues that this passage limits the police power to detain to those situations where there are reasonable and probable grounds to arrest the individual detained. There is certainly support for this contention: *Report of the Canadian Committee on Corrections, Towards Unity: Criminal Justice and Corrections* (Ottawa: The Queen's Printer, 1969) (Chair, R. Ouimet), at pp. 56-57; Hogg, *Constitutional Law of Canada*, 3rd ed. (Toronto: Carswell, 1992) at p. 1072; *Dedman*, supra, per Dickson C.J.C. in dissent at p. 13 S.C.R., p. 104 C.C.C. [p. 202 C.R.].

I have no doubt that the passage from *Dedman*, supra, accurately states the law. It has been approved in numerous subsequent judgments including *Duguay*, supra, at p. 385 O.R.

. . .

I do not, however, read the words of Martin J.A. in *Dedman* as holding that the common law power of the police never extends to the power to detain an individual in the course of a criminal investigation unless the police have the power to arrest that individual. I understand the passage to state that the desire to question or otherwise investigate an individual does not, in and of itself, authorize the detention of that individual. In other words, there is no general power to detain whenever that detention will assist a police officer in the execution of his or her duty. To deny that general power is not, however, to deny the authority to detain short of arrest in all circumstances where the detention has an investigative purpose.

[The Court then considered the Supreme Court's decision in *Dedman*.]

. . .

Especially in light of the definition of "detention" adopted in *R. v. Therens*, [1985] 1 S.C.R. 613, 18 C.C.C. (3d) 481 [45 C.R. (3d) 97] and *R. v. Thomsen*, [1988] 1 S.C.R. 640, 40 C.C.C. (3d) 411 [63 C.R. (3d) 1], I have no doubt that the police detain individuals for investigative purposes when they have no basis to arrest them. In some situations the police would be regarded as derelict in their duties if they did not do so. I agree with Professor Young, "All Along the Watch Tower", supra, at p. 367, when he asserts:

> The courts must recognize the reality of investigatory detention and begin the process of regulating the practice so that street detentions do not end up being non- stationhouse incommunicado arrests.

Unless and until Parliament or the Legislature acts, the common law and specifically the criteria formulated in *Waterfield*, supra, must provide the means whereby the courts regulate the police power to detain for investigatory purposes.

In deciding whether an interference with an individual's liberty is authorized under the common law, one must first decide whether the police were acting in the course of their duty when they effected that interference. In this case, Constable Wilkin indicated that he was investigating the possible commission of drug- related criminal offences at the suspected "crack house". While a police officer's stated purpose is not determinative when deciding whether the officer was acting in the course of his or her duty, there is no suggestion here that Constable Wilkin was not pursuing an investigation into the possible commission of drug-related crimes when he stopped and detained the appellant. The wide duties placed on police officers in relation to the prevention of crime and the enforcement of criminal laws encompass investigations to determine whether criminal activities are occurring at a particular location as well as efforts to substantiate police intelligence. I am satisfied that Constable Wilkin was engaged in the execution of his duty when he stopped and detained the appellant. The lawfulness of that conduct will depend on whether the stop and detention involved an unjustifiable use of the powers associated with Constable Wilkin's duty.

. . .

In my opinion, where an individual is detained by the police in the course of efforts to determine whether that individual is involved in criminal activity being investigated by the police, that detention can only be justified if the detaining officer has some "articulable cause" for the detention.

The phrase "articulable cause" appears in American jurisprudence concerned with the constitutionality of investigative detentions. In *Terry v. Ohio*, 392 U.S. 1, 88 S. Ct. 1868 (1968) the court considered whether a police officer could "stop and frisk" a suspect whom he did not have reasonable cause to arrest. In an analysis that bears a similarity to the *Waterfield* description of the common law ancillary police power doctrine, the court held at pp. 20-21 U.S., p. 1880 S. Ct., that no interference with the individual's right to move about could be justified absent articulable cause for that interference.

. . .

These cases require a constellation of objectively discernible facts which give the detaining officer reasonable cause to suspect that the detainee is criminally implicated in the activity under investigation. The requirement that the facts must meet an objectivity [sic] discernible standard is recognized in connection with the arrest power: *R. v. Storrey*, [1990] 1 S.C.R. 241 at 251, 53 C.C.C. (3d) 316 at 324 [75 C.R. (3d) 1 at 9], and serves to avoid indiscriminate and discriminatory exercises of the police power. A "hunch" based entirely on intuition gained by experience cannot suffice, no matter how accurate that "hunch" might prove to be. Such subjectively based assessments can too easily mask discriminatory conduct based on such irrelevant factors as the detainee's sex, colour, age, ethnic origin or sexual orientation. Equally, without objective criteria detentions could be based on mere speculation. A guess which proves accurate becomes in hindsight a "hunch".

. . .

I should not be taken as holding that the presence of an articulable cause renders any detention for investigative purposes a justifiable exercise of a police officer's common law powers. The inquiry into the existence of an articulable cause is only the first step in the determination of whether the detention was justified in the totality of the circumstances and consequently a lawful exercise of the officer's common law powers as described in *Waterfield*, supra, and approved in *Dedman*, supra. Without articulable cause, no detention to investigate the detainee for possible criminal activity could be viewed as a proper exercise of the common law power. If articulable cause exists, the detention may or may not be justified. For example, a reasonably based suspicion that a person committed some property—related offence at a distant point in the past while an articulable cause, would not, standing alone, justify the detention of that person on a public street to question him or her about that offence. On the other hand, a reasonable suspicion that a person had just committed a violent crime and was in flight from the scene of that crime could well justify some detention of that individual in an effort to quickly confirm or refute the suspicion. Similarly, the existence of an articulable cause that justified a brief detention, perhaps to ask the person detained for identification, would not necessarily justify a more intrusive detention complete with physical restraint and a more extensive interrogation.

In summary, I do not consider the articulable cause inquiry as providing the answer to the lawfulness of the police conduct but rather as the first step in the broader inquiry described in *Waterfield*, supra, and *Dedman*, supra.

Turning to this case, I can find no articulable cause justifying the detention. Constable Wilkin had information of unknown age that another police officer had been told that the residence was believed to be a "crack house". Constable Wilkin did not know the primary source of the information and he had no reason to believe that the source in general, or this particular piece of information, was reliable. It is doubtful that this information standing alone could provide a reasonable suspicion that the suspect residence was the scene of criminal activity.

Any glimmer of an articulable cause disappears, however, when one considers whether Constable Wilkin had reason to suspect that the appellant or the driver of the car was involved in criminal activity. He knew nothing about either person and he did not suggest that anything either had done, apart from being at the house, aroused his suspicion or suggested criminal activity. Attendance at a location believed to be the site of ongoing criminal activity is a factor which may contribute to the existence of "articulable cause". Where that is the sole factor, however, and the information concerning the location is itself of unknown age and reliability, no articulable cause exists. Were it otherwise, the police would have a general warrant to stop anyone who happened to attend at any place which the police had a reason to believe could be the site of ongoing criminal activity.

As Constable Wilkin had no articulable cause for the detention, the common law police power did not authorize his conduct. It was unlawful. Following *Duguay*, supra, it may be that a detention although unlawful would not be arbitrary if the officer erroneously believed on reasonable grounds that he had an articulable cause. I need not decide whether such a belief could avoid an infringement of s. 9 of the *Charter*. Constable Wilkin clearly had no belief that the facts, as he believed them to be, constituted an articulable cause as I have defined it. The detention was both unlawful and arbitrary as that word has been defined in the jurisprudence: *Duguay*, supra; *Cayer*, supra. As the detention was not authorized by law, s. 1 of the *Charter* has no application. The appellant's right not to be arbitrarily detained was infringed by Constable Wilkin.

[The evidence of the cocaine found on the accused's person was excluded, the conviction quashed and an acquittal entered. For a criticism see Delisle, "Judicial Creation of Police Powers" (1993), 20 C.R. (4th) 29. See too David Tanovich, "The Constitutionality of Searches Incident to Vehicle Stops and *Mellenthin*", later under s. 24(2).]

Simpson and other decisions interpret *Ladouceur* to only allow vehicle stops under Highway Traffic Act provisions to be for vehicle-related reasons. *Simpson* does utilise the ancillary powers doctrine to create a limited stop power on articulable cause which can authorise stops of vehicles or pedestrians. A highly contentious issue is whether *Simpson* is an adequate response to issues of racial profiling. David Tanovich, "Operation Pipeline and Racial Profiling", (2002) 1 C.R. (6th) 52, "Using the Charter to Stop Racial Profiling: The Development of an Equality Based Conception of Arbitrary Detention", (2002) 40 Osgoode Hall. L.J. 145; and "Res Ipsa Loquitur and Racial Profiling", (2002) 46 Crim. L.Q. 329 suggests that racial profiling is pervasive and that further resort must be had to s. 15 guarantees and reverse onuses where stops involve racial minorities. In contrast, University of Toronto law professor Ed Morgan, "Racial Profiling as an Investigative Tool", Law Times, Oct. 15, 2002, is quoted as suggesting that, depending on the context, sex, age, ethnic origin and sexual orientation are relevant grounds of investigation. He suggests that the *Simpson* principles may well not be applied in other contexts such as immigration and border crossing, given the "ubiquitous threat of mass violence" since the September

11, 2001 attack on the World Trade Centre Towers. **Is this distinction persuasive?**

The leading pronouncement on racial profiling is now that of Morden J.A. of the Ontario Court of Appeal in *Brown*.

R. v. BROWN
(2003), 9 C.R. (6th) 240, 173 C.C.C. (3d) 23 (Ont. C.A.)

MORDEN J.A. (Laskin and Feldman JJ.A. concurring):

There is no dispute about what racial profiling means. In its factum, the appellant defined it compendiously:

> "Racial profiling involves the targeting of individual members of a particular racial group, on the basis of the supposed criminal propensity of the entire group"

and then quoted a longer definition offered by the African Canadian Legal Clinic in an earlier case, *R. v. Richards* (1999), 26 C.R. (5th) 286 (Ont. C.A.), as set forth in the reasons of Rosenberg J.A. at p. 295:

> Racial profiling is criminal profiling based on race. Racial or colour profiling refers to that phenomenon whereby certain criminal activity is attributed to an identified group in society on the basis of race or colour resulting in the targeting of individual members of that group. In this context, race is illegitimately used as a proxy for the criminality or general criminal propensity of an entire racial group.

The attitude underlying racial profiling is one that may be consciously or unconsciously held. That is, the police officer need not be an overt racist. His or her conduct may be based on subconscious racial stereotyping.

In the opening part of his submission before this court, counsel for the appellant said that he did not challenge the fact that the phenomenon of racial profiling by the police existed. This was a responsible position to take because, as counsel said, this conclusion is supported by significant social science research. I quote from the Report of The Commission on Systemic Racism in the Ontario Criminal Justice System (Toronto: Queen's Printer for Ontario, 1995) (Co-chairs: M. Gittens and D. Cole) at 358:

> The Commission's findings suggest that racialized characteristics, especially those of black people, in combination with other factors, provoke police suspicion, at least in Metro Toronto. Other factors that may attract police attention include sex (male), youth, make and condition of car (if any), location, dress, and perceived lifestyle. Black persons perceived to have many of these attributes are at high risk of being stopped on foot or in cars. This explanation is consistent with our findings that, overall, black people are more likely than others to experience the unwelcome intrusion of being stopped by the police, but black people are not equally vulnerable to such stops.

There is no dispute respecting the test to be applied under s. 9 of the Charter. The question is whether the police officer who stopped the motorist had articulable cause for the stop. Articulable cause exists where the grounds for stopping the motorist are reasonable and can be clearly expressed: *R. v. Wilson* (1990), 56 C.C.C. (3d) 142 (S.C.C.) at 144. If a police officer stops a person based on his or her colour (or on any other discriminatory ground) the purpose is improper (*Brown v. Durham Regional Police Force* (1998), 131 C.C.C. (3d) 1 (Ont. C.A.) at 17) and clearly would not be an articulable cause.

Accordingly, to succeed on the application before the trial judge, the respondent had to prove that it was more probable than not that there was no articulable cause for the stop, specifically, on the evidence in this case, that the real reason for the stop was the fact that he was black.

Are you satisfied with this definition of racial profiling? Is it too wide? Section 8 and 9 Charter arguments based on racial profiling succeeded in a cocaine case of *R. v. Khan* (2004), 24 C.R. (6th) 48, 189 C.C.C. (3d) 49 (Ont. S.C.J.) where the judge disbelieved the police testimony and found that the accused had been singled out because he was a young black man driving a Mercedes. Such arguments have, however, more often failed; see, for example, *R. v. Greaves* (2004), 24 C.R. (6th) 15, 189 C.C.C. (3d) 305 (B.C. C.A.), leave to appeal refused (2005), 125 C.R.R. (2d) 187 (note) (S.C.C.) criticized by Tim Quigley, Annotation, C.R., *ibid.* p. 17. See further David Tanovich, "E-Racing Racial Profiling", (2004) 41 Alberta L. Rev. 905.

Courts tend to reject racial profiling arguments where race was only part of the reason for police intervention. Police assessment of suspicion depends on experience and interpretation. The problem, suggests Tanovich, in "The Colourless World of Mann", above at p. 53, is that this can be influenced or distorted by unconscious racism.

> For example, an officer may see a Black man in a white neighbourhood carrying a Plasma television and decide to stop him to investigate because, in the officer's mind, he appears "out of place". Alternatively, an officer may interpret a handshake between two Black men in a high crime area as a drug transaction. Such innocent behaviour might not be interpreted in such an incriminating manner if the men were White. Evasive action is another example. An African Canadian who has historically been harassed by the police or who is aware of a history of community harassment may understandably avoid a police officer who is approaching, not out of a case of consciousness of guilt, but to avoid being harassed, or in some cases, out of a sense of self-preservation.

Some lower court judges have favoured a reverse onus for racial profiling. However Doherty J.A for the Ontario Court of Appeal in *Peart v. Peel (Regional Municipality) Police Services Board* (2006), 43 C.R. (6th) 175 (Ont. C.A.), concerning an unsuccessful civil suit alleging racial profiling, refused to reverse the ultimate burden. The reality of racial profiling cannot be denied but the Court could not accept that "racial profiling is the rule rather than the exception where the police detain black men" (at 209). Justice Doherty did hold that there would be a "significant tactical burden" on the defendant (*ibid.*).

Professor Tanovich's major study of race issues in the Canadian justice system, *The Colour of Justice. Policing Race in Canada* (Irwin Law, 2006), certainly provides a strong basis for suggesting defence counsel and our courts are too reticent to address such concerns. There is a disturbing pattern of trial counsel and judges ignoring the admittedly difficult and sensitive issue of race, despite considerable evidence of systemic discrimination in stops. It may be that counsel have found by experience that directly playing the race card is an unwise strategy, in practice hard to establish and also time- consuming and expensive. The problem is that if race is not raised at trial, courts of appeal will not be able to take judicial notice of this adjudicative fact on appeal (*R. v. Spence*, [2005] 3 S.C.R. 458, 33 C.R. (6th) 1, 202 C.C.C. (3d) 1 (S.C.C.)).

Racial profiling has yet to be addressed by the Supreme Court.

Following *Simpson* lower courts were in disarray as to whether, once the Court is satisfied that there is articulable cause for detention, there can be a search incident to that detention for weapons AND evidence. The matter reached the Supreme Court in *Mann*.

R. v. MANN
[2004] 3 S.C.R. 59, 21 C.R. (6th) 1, 185 C.C.C. (3d) 308 (S.C.C.)

Shortly before midnight, two police officers received a radio dispatch message detailing a break and enter in progress in a neighbouring district of downtown Winnipeg. The suspect was described as a 21-year-old aboriginal male, approximately five feet eight inches tall, weighing about 165 pounds, clad in a black jacket with white sleeves, and thought to be one "Zachary Parisienne". As the officers approached the scene of the reported crime, they observed an individual walking casually along the sidewalk. They testified that this individual matched the description of the suspect "to the tee". The officers stopped the accused and asked him to identify himself. He stated his name and provided his date of birth to the officers. He also complied with a pat-down search of his person for concealed weapons. The accused was wearing a pullover sweater with a kangaroo pouch pocket in the front. During the pat-down search, one officer felt a soft object in this pocket. The officer reached into the accused's pocket and found a small plastic bag containing 27.55 grams of marijuana. In another pocket, the officer found a number of small plastic baggies, two Valium pills and a treaty status card confirming the accused's identity.

The accused was arrested and charged with possession of marijuana for the purpose of trafficking. The trial judge found that the search of M's pocket contravened s. 8 of the Charter of Rights and Freedoms. The police officer was justified in his search of the accused for security reasons, but that there was no basis to infer that it was reasonable to look inside M's pocket for security reasons. The evidence was excluded under s. 24(2) as its admission would interfere with the fairness of the trial. The accused was acquitted.

The Manitoba Court of Appeal set aside the acquittal and ordered a new trial. The detention and the pat-down search were authorized by law and were reasonable in the circumstances. The accused appealed.

The majority of the Supreme Court allowed the appeal and restored the acquittal. Section 8 had been breached. A 5-2 majority further decided that the evidence had been properly excluded by the trial judge.

IACOBUCCI J. (Major, Binnie, LeBel and Fish JJ. concurring):

. . .

A. Introduction

As stated earlier, the issues in this case require the Court to balance individual liberty rights and privacy interests with a societal interest in effective policing. Absent a law to the contrary, individuals are free to do as they please. By contrast, the police (and more broadly, the state) may act only to the extent that they are empowered to do so by law. The vibrancy of a democracy is apparent by how wisely it navigates through those critical junctures where state action intersects with, and threatens to impinge upon, individual liberties.

Nowhere do these interests collide more frequently than in the area of criminal investigation. Charter rights do not exist in a vacuum; they are animated at virtually every stage of police action. Given their mandate to investigate crime and keep the peace, police officers must be empowered to respond quickly, effectively, and flexibly to the diversity of encounters experienced daily on the front lines of policing. Despite there being no formal consensus about the existence of a police power to detain for investigative purposes, several commentators note its long-standing use in Canadian policing practice: see A. Young, "All Along the Watchtower: Arbitrary Detention and the Police Function" (1991) 29 Osgoode Hall L.J. 329, at p. 330; and J. Stribopoulos, "A Failed Experiment? Investigative Detention: Ten Years Later" (2003) 41 Alta. L. Rev. 335, at p. 339. At the same time, this Court must tread softly where complex legal developments are best left to the experience and expertise of legislators. As McLachlin J. (as she then was) noted in *Watkins v. Olafson*, [1989] 2 S.C.R. 750, at p. 760, major changes requiring the development of subsidiary rules and procedures relevant to their implementation are better accomplished through legislative deliberation than by judicial decree. It is for that very reason that I do not believe it appropriate for this Court to recognize a general power of detention for investigative purposes. The Court cannot, however, shy away from the task where common law rules are required to be incrementally adapted to reflect societal change. Courts, as its custodians, share responsibility for ensuring that the common law reflects current and emerging societal needs and values: *R. v. Salituro*, [1991] 3 S.C.R. 654, at p. 670. Here, our duty is to lay down the common law governing police powers of investigative detention in the particular context of this case. Where, as in this case, the relevant common law rule has evolved gradually through jurisprudential treatment, the judiciary is the proper forum for the recognition and ordering of further legal developments, absent legislative intervention. Over time, the common law has moved cautiously to carve out a limited sphere for state intrusions on individual liberties in the context of policing. The recognition of a limited police power of investigative detention marks another step in that measured development. It is, of course, open to Parliament to enact legislation in line with what it deems the best approach to the matter, subject to overarching requirements of constitutional compliance. As well, Parliament may seek to legislate appropriate practice and procedural techniques to ensure that respect for individual liberty is adequately balanced against the interest of officer safety. In the meantime, however, the unregulated use of investigative detentions in policing, their uncertain legal status, and the potential for abuse inherent in such low-visibility exercises of discretionary power are all pressing reasons why the Court must exercise its custodial role.

"Detention" has been held to cover, in Canada, a broad range of encounters between police officers and members of the public. Even so, the police cannot be said to "detain", within the meaning of ss. 9 and 10 of the Charter, every suspect they stop for purposes of identification, or even interview. The person who is stopped will in all cases be "detained" in the sense of "delayed", or "kept waiting". But the constitutional rights recognized by ss. 9 and 10 of the Charter are not engaged by delays that involve no significant physical or psychological restraint. In this case, the trial judge concluded that the appellant was detained by the police when they searched him. We have not been urged to revisit that conclusion and, in the circumstances, I would decline to do so.

A detention for investigative purposes is, like any other detention, subject to Charter scrutiny. Section 9 of the Charter, for example, provides that everyone has the right "not to be arbitrarily detained". It is well recognized that a lawful detention is not "arbitrary" within the meaning of that provision. Consequently, an investigative detention that is carried out in accordance with the common law power recognized in this case will not infringe the detainee's rights under s. 9 of the Charter. Section 10(a) of the Charter provides that "[e]veryone has the right on arrest or detention to be informed promptly of the reasons therefor". At a minimum, individuals who are detained for investigative purposes must therefore be advised, in clear and simple language, of the reasons for the detention.

Section 10(b) of the Charter raises more difficult issues. It enshrines the right of detainees "to retain and instruct counsel without delay and to be informed of that right". Like every other provision of the Charter, s. 10(b) must be purposively interpreted. Mandatory compliance with its requirements cannot be transformed into an excuse for prolonging, unduly and artificially, a detention that, as I later mention, must be of brief duration. Other aspects of s. 10(b), as they arise in the context of investigative detentions, will in my view be left to another day. They should not be considered and settled without the benefit of full consideration in the lower courts, which we do not have in this case.

B. The Common Law Development of Investigative Detention

A number of cases occurring over the years have culminated in the recognition of a limited power of officers to detain for investigative purposes.

The test for whether a police officer has acted within his or her common law powers was first expressed by the English Court of Criminal Appeals in *Waterfield, supra*, at pp. 660-661. From the decision emerged a two-pronged analysis where the officer's conduct is *prima facie* an unlawful interference with an individual's liberty or property. In those situations, courts must first consider whether the police conduct giving rise to the interference falls within the general scope of any duty imposed on the officer by statute or at common law. If this threshold is met, the analysis continues to consider secondly whether such conduct, albeit within the general scope of such a duty, involved an unjustifiable use of powers associated with the duty.

This Court has adopted, refined and incrementally applied the *Waterfield* test in several contexts, including the pre-Charter lawfulness of random automobile stops under the Reduced Impaired Driving Everywhere (R.I.D.E.) Program (*Dedman v. The Queen* . . .); the scope of police power to search incident to lawful arrest (*Cloutier v. Langlois* . . .); and the scope of police authority to investigate 911 calls (*R. v. Godoy* .. .).

At the first stage of the *Waterfield* test, police powers are recognized as deriving from the nature and scope of police duties, including, at common law, "the preservation of the peace, the prevention of crime, and the protection of life and property" (*Dedman, supra*, at p. 32). The second stage of the test requires a balance between the competing interests of the police duty and of the liberty interests at stake. This aspect of the test requires a consideration of:

> . . . whether an invasion of individual rights is necessary in order for the peace officers to perform their duty, and whether such invasion is reasonable in light of the public purposes served by effective control of criminal acts on the one hand and on the other respect for the liberty and fundamental dignity of individuals. (*Cloutier, supra*, at pp. 181-82)

The reasonable necessity or justification of the police conduct in the specific circumstances is highlighted at this stage. Specifically, in *Dedman, supra*, at p. 35, Le Dain J. provided that the necessity and reasonableness for the interference with liberty was to be assessed with regard to the nature of the liberty interfered with and the importance of the public purpose served.

The Court of Appeal for Ontario helpfully added a further gloss to this second stage of the *Waterfield* test in *R. v. Simpson* . . . by holding that investigative detentions are only justified at common law "if the detaining officer has some 'articulable cause' for the detention", a concept borrowed from U.S. jurisprudence. Articulable cause was defined by Doherty J.A., at p. 202, as:

> . . . a constellation of objectively discernible facts which give the detaining officer reasonable cause to suspect that the detainee is criminally implicated in the activity under investigation.

Articulable cause, while clearly a threshold somewhat lower than the reasonable and probable grounds required for lawful arrest (*Simpson, supra*, at p. 203), is likewise both an objective and subjective standard (*R. v. Storrey* ... Doherty J.A. limited the scope of common law investigative detention by explaining that the articulable cause requirement was only an initial step in the ultimate determination of "whether the detention was justified in the totality of the circumstances", and was thus a lawful exercise of the officer's common law powers under *Waterfield* (*Simpson, supra*, at p. 203). The court did not, however, set concrete guidelines concerning investigative detentions, leaving the matter to be resolved on a case by case approach to the power.

The Court of Appeal of Quebec did not find it necessary to apply the articulable cause doctrine in *R. v. Murray* (1999), 136 C.C.C. (3d) 197. Relying upon the *Waterfield* test, Fish J.A. (as he then was) recognized a narrow police power at common law to set up immediate road blocks along an obvious avenue of escape from the scene of a serious crime. Fish J.A.'s comments on the exercise of this power focus specifically on its reasonable necessity in the totality of the circumstances (p. 205). The road block in *Murray* was set up immediately after the commission of a crime and was limited to an obvious escape route for the sole purpose of apprehending the fleeing perpetrators.

. . .

As mentioned above, the articulable cause standard discussed in *Simpson* has been adopted from American Fourth Amendment jurisprudence, namely the "stop and frisk" doctrine with its genesis in *Terry v. Ohio*, 392 U.S. 1 (1968). The doctrine developed as an exception to the Fourth Amendment right to be free from unreasonable search and seizure, where detention is viewed as a "seizure" of the person. The United States Supreme Court held in *Terry* that a police officer may seize an individual reasonably suspected of imminent or on-going criminal activity, ask questions of him or her, and perform a limited frisk search for weapons. Subsequent jurisprudence requires the totality of the circumstances to be taken into account when determining that sufficient reasonable articulable suspicion of criminal activity exists to justify the seizure (see *United States v. Cortez*, 449 U.S. 411 (1981)).

The U.S. case law has evolved significantly since *Terry*. Police authority was expanded in *Adams v. Williams*, 407 U.S. 143 (1972) beyond imminent violent offences to possessory offences reported by reliable informants. In 1980, *United States v. Mendenhall*, 446 U.S. 544 (1980), the U.S. Supreme Court developed a no-seizure rule permitting brief detentions of individuals where reasonable suspicion is lacking. Five years later, in *United States v. Hensley*, 469 U.S. 221 (1985), the U.S. Supreme Court extended *Terry* and *Adams* to permit detention and questioning of persons suspected of involvement in completed felonies, where the suspicion was grounded in specific and articulable facts, on the basis of a public interest in investigating crime and safeguarding the public.

With respect to terminology, I prefer to use the term "reasonable grounds to detain" rather than the U.S. phrase "articulable cause" since Canadian jurisprudence has employed reasonable grounds in analogous circumstances and has provided useful guidance to decide the issues in question. As I discuss below, the reasonable grounds are related to the police action involved, namely, detention, search or arrest.

The case law raises several guiding principles governing the use of a police power to detain for investigative purposes. The evolution of the *Waterfield* test, along with the *Simpson* articulable cause requirement, calls for investigative detentions to be premised upon reasonable grounds. The detention must be viewed as reasonably necessary on an objective view of the totality of the circumstances, informing the officer's suspicion that there is a clear nexus between the individual to be detained and a recent or on-going criminal offence. Reasonable grounds figures at the front-end of such an assessment, underlying the officer's reasonable suspicion that the particular individual is implicated in the criminal activity under investigation. The overall reasonableness of the decision to detain, however, must further be assessed against all of the circumstances, most notably the extent to which the interference with individual liberty is necessary to perform the officer's duty, the liberty interfered with, and the nature and extent of that interference, in order to meet the second prong of the *Waterfield* test.

Police powers and police duties are not necessarily correlative. While the police have a common law duty to investigate crime, they are not empowered to undertake any and all action in the exercise of that duty. Individual liberty interests are fundamental to the Canadian constitutional order. Consequently, any intrusion upon them must not be taken lightly and, as a result, police officers do not have carte blanche to detain. The power to detain cannot be exercised on the basis of a hunch, nor can it become a de facto arrest.

C. Search Powers Incident to Investigative Detention

. . .

This appeal marks the first opportunity for the Court to discuss whether a search incident to an investigative detention is authorized by law. Underlying this discussion is the need to balance the competing interests of an individual's reasonable expectation of privacy with the interests of police officer safety. In the context of an arrest, this Court has held that, in the absence of a warrant, police officers are empowered to search for weapons or to preserve evidence: *R. v. Golden* . . . In the reasons following, I consider whether and to what extent a power to search incidental to investigative detention exists at common law. I note at the outset the importance of maintaining a distinction between search incidental to arrest and search incidental to an investigative detention. The latter does not give license to officers to reap the seeds of a warrantless search without the need to effect a lawful arrest based on reasonable and probable grounds, nor does it erode the obligation to obtain search warrants where possible.

I rely upon the *Waterfield* test discussed above to recognize that a power of search incidental to investigative detention does exist at common law. Under the first prong of the *Waterfield* test, the interference clearly falls within the general scope of a duty imposed by statute or recognized at common law. The duty at issue here is the protection of life and property, which was also at issue in *Dedman, supra*, at p. 32.

To continue in the *Waterfield* analysis, the conduct giving rise to the interference must involve a justified use of a police power associated with a general duty to search in relation to the protection of life and property. Put differently, the search must be reasonably necessary. The relevant considerations here include the duty being performed, the extent to which some interference with individual liberty is necessary in the performance of that duty, the importance of the performance of the duty to the public good, the nature of the liberty being interfered with, and the nature and extent of the interference: *Dedman, supra*, at pp. 35-36.

The general duty of officers to protect life may, in some circumstances, give rise to the power to conduct a pat-down search incident to an investigative detention. Such a search power does not exist as a matter of course; the officer must believe on reasonable grounds that his or her own safety or the safety of others, is at risk. I disagree with the suggestion that the power to detain for investigative searches endorses an incidental search in all circumstances: see S. Coughlan, "Search Based on Articulable Cause: Proceed with Caution or Full Stop?" (2003), 2 C.R. (6th) 49, at p. 63. The officer's decision to search must also be reasonably necessary in light of the totality of the circumstances. It cannot be justified on the basis of a vague or non-existent concern for safety, nor can the search be premised upon hunches or mere intuition.

The determination as to when a protective search may be merited has been addressed in the United States through several decades of jurisprudence. In *Terry, supra*, at p. 27, the United States Supreme Court carefully circumscribed the search power, by holding that:

> . . . there must be a narrowly drawn authority to permit a reasonable search for weapons for the protection of the police officer, where he has reason to believe that he is dealing with an armed and dangerous individual, regardless of whether he has probable cause to arrest the individual for a crime.

In exercising this authority, the officer must not be acting solely on a hunch, but rather is required to act on reasonable and specific inferences drawn from the known facts of the situation. The search must also be confined in scope to an intrusion reasonably designed to locate weapons (p. 29).

. . .

The importance of ensuring officer safety has been recognized in *obiter* by this Court in *R. v Mellenthin*, [1992] 3 S.C.R. 615. Police officers face any number of risks everyday in the carrying out of their policing function, and are entitled to go about their work secure in the knowledge that risks are minimized to the greatest extent possible. As noted by L'Heureux-Dubé J., in *Cloutier, supra*, at p. 185, a frisk search is a "relatively non-intrusive procedure", the duration of which is "only a few seconds". Where an officer has reasonable grounds to believe that his or her safety is at risk, the officer may engage in a protective pat-down search of the detained individual. The search must be grounded in objectively discernible facts to prevent "fishing expeditions" on the basis of irrelevant or discriminatory factors.

A finding that a limited power of protective search exists at common law does not obviate the need to apply the *Collins* test for determining whether a warrantless search passes constitutional muster under s. 8 of the Charter. To recall, the search must be authorized by a reasonable law, and be carried out in a reasonable manner. The reasonableness of the search necessarily overlaps the second-prong of the *Waterfield* test, with the third factor under *Collins*. The officer must have reasonable grounds to search before the overall reasonableness of the search is considered on the totality of the circumstances.

To summarize, as discussed above, police officers may detain an individual for investigative purposes if there are reasonable grounds to suspect in all the circumstances that the individual is connected to a particular crime and that such a detention is necessary. In addition, where a police officer has reasonable grounds to believe that his or her safety or that of others is at risk, the officer may engage in a protective pat-down search of the detained individual. Both the detention and the pat-down search must be conducted in a reasonable manner. In this connection, I note that the investigative detention should be brief in duration and does not impose an obligation on the detained individual to answer questions posed by the police. The investigative detention and protective search power are to be distinguished from an arrest and the incidental power to search on arrest, which do not arise in this case.

VI. Application to the Facts

. . .

The officers had reasonable grounds to detain the appellant. He closely matched the description of the suspect given by radio dispatch, and was only two or three blocks from the scene of the reported crime. These factors led the officers to reasonably suspect that the appellant was involved in recent criminal activity, and at the very least ought to be investigated further. The presence of an individual in a so-called high crime area is relevant only so far as it reflects his or her proximity to a particular crime. The high crime nature of a neighbourhood is not by itself a basis for detaining individuals.

Furthermore, there were reasonable grounds for a protective search of the appellant. There was a logical possibility that the appellant, suspected on reasonable grounds of having recently committed a break-and-enter, was in possession of break-and-enter tools, which could be used as weapons. The encounter also occurred just after midnight and there were no other people in the area. On balance, the officer was justified in conducting a pat-down search for protective purposes.

The officer's decision to go beyond this initial pat-down and reach into the appellant's pocket after feeling an admittedly soft object therein is problematic. The trial judge found that the officer had no reasonable basis for reaching into the pocket. This more intrusive part of the search was an unreasonable violation of the appellant's reasonable expectation of privacy in the contents of his pockets. The trial judge found as a fact that "there was nothing from which [he could] infer that it was reasonable to proceed beyond a pat down search for security reasons". The Court of Appeal did not give due deference to this important finding, which was largely based on the credibility of witnesses, an area strictly in the domain of the trial judge absent palpable and overriding error: *Housen v. Nikolaisen*, [2002] 2 S.C.R. 235, 2002 SCC 33. Moreover, the Crown has not discharged its burden to show on the balance of probabilities that the third aspect of the Collins test has been satisfied, namely that the search was carried out in a reasonable manner.

The seizure of the marijuana from the appellant was unlawful in this case.

[The majority decided that the violation of s. 8 was serious and the evidence had been properly excluded by the trial judge.]

DESCHAMPS J. (Bastarache J. concurring) (dissenting):

. . . I concur in principle with [Iacobucci J's] analysis on the issue of the existence of a power to detain at common law. However, I express certain reservations as regards the terminology which he adopts in setting out the conditions necessary to give rise to that power and the precise scope of the search which is incidental to it. In addition, while I conclude, as he does, that the search of the appellant violated s. 8 of the Canadian Charter of Rights and Freedoms, I cannot accept that the violation is such that the admission of the evidence which was obtained by the police in the present case would "bring the administration of justice into disrepute". As such, I cannot agree with his disposition in the present appeal.

II. Articulable Cause and Reasonable Grounds to Detain

Iacobucci J. is of the view that in formulating in the standard which must be met in order to give rise to the common law power to detain, the term "reasonable grounds to detain" is preferable to the term "articulable cause" (para. 33). I disagree. "Articulable cause" is a criterion which Canadian courts are familiar with and which they have had little difficulty applying. In the years since *R. v. Simpson* (1993), 12 O.R. (3d) 182, was decided by the Ontario Court of Appeal, it has been adopted by many lower courts across the country, including the courts of appeal of three provinces besides Ontario . . . Furthermore, as my colleague points out, it has been in use in the United States for nearly 40 years (see *Terry v. Ohio*, 392 U.S. 1 (1968)), a fact which lends further support to the view that it is a useful and workable standard.

More important, however, than the merits of the phrase "articulable cause" are the problems associated with the alternative which the majority has adopted. "Reasonable grounds" has traditionally been employed to describe the standard which must be met in order to give rise to the power to arrest a suspect (see, e.g., ss. 494, 495 and 504 of the Criminal Code, R.S.C. 1985, c. C-46). Using this term in the present context could lead to the erroneous conclusion that the same degree of justification is required for a detention as is required in order to carry out an arrest. This cannot be the case. It would undermine the very purpose of the common law power to detain, which is to provide police with a less extensive and intrusive means of carrying out their duties where they do not have sufficient grounds for arrest, i.e. where there are no "reasonable grounds".

III. The Scope of the Power of Search Incidental to Detention

I agree with the majority that there is a power to search incidental to detention at common law, stemming from the test set out in *R. v. Waterfield*, [1963] 3 All E.R. 659 (C.C.A.). I wish to add, however, that I do not believe that such a search must always be restricted to concerns for the safety of a police officer. In the case at bar, security was the only ground raised by the respondent. However, other circumstances may justify resorting to a search incidental to detention.

A good example of a lawful search incidental to detention which was not motivated by safety concerns is provided by the decision of the Quebec Court of Appeal in *R. v. Murray* (1999), 136 C.C.C. (3d) 197. In that case, a robbery had been committed by three individuals. The police had set up a road block on a bridge which would have been a likely avenue of flight from the scene of the crime, and were stopping all vehicles which could hide three people. One of the individuals stopped and questioned was the respondent, who was driving a pickup truck. A taut piece of canvass blocked the view of the vehicle's cargo area. Thinking that the suspects in the robbery could be hiding beneath the canvass, a police officer removed it and discovered smuggled cigarettes. Fish J.A. (as he then was), applied the *Waterfield* test, and concluded that the search was a valid exercise of the common law power of search incidental to detention. He wrote (at p. 212):

> A search incident to detention is a valid exercise of police powers at common law only if the detention is itself lawful. . .
>
> The search must be for a valid purpose that is rationally connected to the purposes of the initial detention. It must also be reasonably necessary: (1) to secure non-conscriptive evidence of a crime; (2) to protect the police or any member of the public from imminent danger; or (3) to discover and secure anything that could endanger the police, the person detained or any member of the public, or facilitate escape.

I agree with these statements. In my view, any search incidental to detention would have to be both rationally connected to the purpose of the initial detention and reasonably necessary to ensure the security of police officers or the public, to preserve evidence or to prevent the escape of an offender. I do not rule out the possibility that other goals might be permissible, under appropriate circumstances.

That being said, I wish to reiterate the view I have espoused above, that given the lower threshold for justifying a detention as opposed to an arrest, the power of search in the former case is less extensive than in the latter. Thus, for example, the objective of discovering (as opposed to preserving) evidence of a crime could not be used to justify a search incidental to investigative detention. Such searches may only be conducted with a warrant, or pursuant to the common law power of search incidental to arrest (see *Cloutier v. Langlois* ... *R. v. Stillman* ... *R. v. Caslake* . . .). In addition, as I mentioned above, searches incidental to detention must be reasonably necessary to the investigation, and not just rationally connected to it (as is the norm for searches incidental to arrest: *Caslake, supra*, at para. 19). Finally, it bears mentioning that a degree of intrusiveness which may be permitted in the context of an arrest may be disproportionate in the context of detention.

The respondent has not demonstrated that the search conducted in the present case was motivated by a need to ensure the safety of the police or the public, to preserve evidence or to prevent the appellant from escaping. Rather, Conner Prov. Ct. J. seems to have been of the view that the search of the appellant's pocket was the result of mere "curiosity". As such, I have no problem concluding, as the majority does, that the search of the appellant in the present case was illegal.

. . .

For comments on *Mann* see Eric Gottardi, "*R. v. Mann*: Regulating State Intrusions in the context of Investigative Detentions",(2004) 21 C.R. (6th) 27, Tim Quigley, "*Mann*, It's a Disappointing Decision", (2004) 21 C.R. (6th) 41, David Tanovich, "The Colourless World of *Mann*", (2004) 21 C.R. (6th) 47 and Benjamin Berger, "Race and Erasure in *R. v. Mann*", (2004) 21 C.R. (6th) 58. See too Lesley McCoy, "Some Answers from the Supreme Court on Investigative Detention . . . and Some More Questions", (2004) 49 Crim. L.Q. 268; James Stribopoulos, "The Limits of Judicially Created Police Powers: Investigative Detention after *Mann*", (2007) 52 Crim. L.Q. 299; Alec Fiszauf, "Articulating Cause — Investigative Detention and its Implications", (2007) 52 Crim. L.Q. 327 and Christina Skibinsky, "Regulating *Mann* in Canada", (2006) 69 Sask. L. Rev. 197.

In *R. v. Yeh* (2009), 69 C.R. (6th) 197, 248 C.C.C. (3d) 125 (Sask. C.A.) a Court of seven justices unanimously held that the police cannot lawfully employ a sniffer dog to search for drugs in conjunction with a brief investigative detention. The Court is unanimous in holding that the two investigative procedures must be kept analytically distinct. In *Mann*, the Court held that the only search power available during an investigative detention is a search for safety reasons where there are reasonable grounds to believe that the accused may have a weapon. To justify a sniffer dog search, the cumulative effect of the various judgments in *Kang-Brown* and *R. v. A.M.* is that a reasonable suspicion of criminal activity, usually involving drugs, is required.

It is indeed important to keep them analytically distinct for two reasons. First, they concern quite different police powers. An investigative detention is a detention power while the use of a sniffer dog is a search. Second, and more important, it is essential that the two powers not be conflated because otherwise the police might be entitled to search a detainee on grounds other than the narrow basis provided for in *Mann*.

The second issue in *Yeh* concerned an aspect of *Mann* that has thus far not drawn a great deal of attention. In *Mann*, the Court was careful not to permit investigative detentions on mere hunches of whether criminal activity was afoot but was not especially clear on the extent to which criminality must be certain. The Supreme Court did not use the terms "known offence" or "suspected offence" as the entire Court in this case acknowledges. However, the Supreme Court did refer to "a recent or on-going criminal offence" (para. 34) and "a particular crime" (para. 45), thus indicating a restriction on the use of this investigative power in order to avoid its overuse. The 5-2 majority in *Yeh* determined that, in addition to a reasonable suspicion that the individual was engaged in criminal activity, the criminal activity in question should only be merely reasonably suspected.

On the other hand, Justice Jackson, dissenting on this point, decided that the standard should be higher, although she acknowledges that certainty is an impossibly high standard. She settled on a standard under which a reviewing judge must be able to determine that a crime had been recently committed or was apparently being committed at the time of the detention. If not, the detention would be arbitrary contrary to section 9. Her argument is that the reduced standard of a reasonable suspicion of a criminal offence comes too close to the generalized suspicion standard in vogue in the United States in this context (and that was rejected by eight of nine justices of the Supreme Court as the standard for a sniffer dog search in *Kang-Brown* and *A.M.*). She also rejects an incremental extension of police powers without the democratic input of Parliament and the opportunity for overview by the courts.

For further analysis of *Yeh* see Tim Quigley, "Investigative Detentions. Some Loose Ends Remain" (2010) 69 C.R. (6th) 247.

PROBLEM 4

Two police officers were on patrol in a police vehicle when they saw a car parked the wrong way in a no parking zone in an area known to them to be used for drug buys. As they drove by, they saw the accused with a surprised look on his face bent over in a manner appearing as though he were hiding something. They came to the car and asked the occupants to identify themselves. When the accused did so, one of the officers recognized his name from a weapons alert and, out of earshot of the accused, informed the other officer. The alert had information about the accused being in possession of a handgun and a bulletproof vest, that he was concerned about avenging a shooting, and that he should be approached with caution since he was armed and dangerous. The officers asked the accused to get out of the car and conducted a pat-down search, where he discovered that the accused was wearing a bulletproof vest. The car was then searched and, although one of the officers testified that a handgun was in plain view, the trial judge found as a fact that it was hidden in the accused's girlfriend's overnight bag. The accused fled the scene but was subsequently charged with various firearms and related offences.

At trial, the accused argued that his rights under ss. 8 and 9 of the Charter had been violated and that the evidence should be excluded from evidence. Rule.

See *R. v. Plummer* (2011), 85 C.R. (6th) 41, 272 C.C.C. (3d) 172 (Ont. C.A.) and see C.R. annotation by Tim Quigley.

PROBLEM 5

Police stopped five black youths running in a lane without sidewalks near a construction zone. The police prevented the youths from leaving the scene in their BMW vehicle parked in that lane. The accused, A.K., a black youth, was charged with eight counts relating to the possession of an unregistered loaded handgun found in his coat pocket. The police employed the "carding" practice of a Toronto Anti-Violence Intervention Strategy Unit. This practice involved stops of citizens by the police, whether there was an offense being committed or not, and recording the contact and personal information about the citizen on a "208" card. This case involves the practice at the time of the alleged offense. The Toronto Police Board later passed a new policy restricting the use of carding. In this case the police threw the accused to the ground when he refused to be searched. This fractured his jaw. The trial judge evidence included the oral testimony called by the Crown, in-car police videos, and an audio recording of the testimony of officers who appeared at the Special Investigative Unit for questioning. Did carding here violate s. 8 Charter standards for investigative detention?

See *R. v. K. (A.)* (2014), 13 C.R. (7th) 75 (Ont. C.J.) and C.R. comment by Stuart and Tanovich.

PROBLEM 6

The accused, who is black, was convicted of possession of a firearm. He had been singled out in a carding operation by Toronto police. The officer clarified his identity and that he had asked whether he had outstanding warrants. Satisfied, the officer turned to filling out a 208 card. The trial judge determined that this was an unlawful detention. As this occurred, a third party approached and the accused turned sideways, refusing to show his hands when the officer requested him to do so. The officer reached out to pat the accused's side, felt a hard object and yelled "gun", at which point the accused fled, with a handgun falling out of his jacket as he did so. The accused appealed his conviction on the basis that he had been unreasonably searched and that the evidence of the gun should be excluded as a result.

See *R. v. Fountain* (2015), 324 C.C.C. (3d) 425, 20 C.R. (7th) 371 (Ont. C.A.). See C.R. comment by Steve Coughlan.

PROBLEM 7

An off-duty police officer saw the accused driving his vehicle in an erratic manner. A different officer stopped him and administered a roadside breath test. He registered a "pass." In the course of checking him on CPIC and related databases, the police officer received information about a possible connection he had to drugs. The officer decided to ask him if he would consent to a search of his vehicle. The officer readily acknowledged that he did not have reasonable grounds to conduct a search.

The trial judge accepted the police officer's version of the relevant events. He testified:

> I basically just spoke to Mr. Sebben and asked if he would consent to me searching his vehicle, and Mr. Sebben replied quickly that he didn't think he needed to. He began to roll his rear window down and he said all he had were — he's — he said you can look in the back if you want "cause all I had were tools and Christmas presents." And I then indicated to Mr. Sebben that a — a consent search wouldn't be for Christmas presents and such it would be for things like drugs or marihuana. And immediately, as soon as I said the word marihuana, he reached the centre console area and — and indicated he had

marihuana and showed me a bag of — like — a clear Ziploc bag of what appeared to be marihuana and turned it over to me.

The accused was arrested and a further search resulted in more marihuana found in his vehicle. Was the initial search lawful?

See *R. v. Sebben* (2015), 322 C.C.C. (3d) 474 (Ont. C.A.), leave to appeal refused 2015 CarswellOnt 16495, 2015 CarswellOnt 16496 (S.C.C.)

(iii) Roadblock Stops

R. v. CLAYTON and FARMER
[2007] S.C.R. 725, 47 C.R. (6th) 219, 220 C.C.C. (3d) 449 (S.C.C.)

In *R. v. Clayton and Farmer* (2005), 27 C.R. (6th) 197, 194 C.C.C. (3d) 289 (Ont. C.A.), Justice Doherty, speaking for the Ontario Court of Appeal, McMurtry C.J.O. and Lang J.A. concurring, turned again to the ancillary powers doctrine to create roadblock stop powers distinct from the investigative detention power recognised in *Mann*.

At about 1:25 a.m. on September 24, 1999, an individual made a 911 call from a coffee shop located across from a strip club indicating that about ten black men were congregated outside the club and that four had handguns. He described by model and colour four vehicles that he associated with the group of individuals in the parking area. A number of police vehicles converged on the scene. Two officers arrived at the rear exit to the parking lot at 1:26 a.m. and parked near that exit. They intended to stop any vehicle attempting to exit the parking lot and to investigate the "gun call". The first car they stopped was a sporty black Jaguar driven by a black man, Farmer, with another black man, Clayton, in the passenger seat. The Jaguar did not match, or even come close to, the description of any of the four vehicles provided by the 911 caller. One officer advised Clayton that he was investigating a gun call and told him to step out of the vehicle. As soon as the officer touched Clayton, a struggle ensued and Clayton ran towards the front of the strip club. Robson and Dickson gave chase. On his arrest he acknowledged he had a gun in his pocket. It was removed and he was arrested. Farmer was also arrested and found to be in possession of a gun. Both accused were charged with a number of firearms offences.

The Ontario Court of Appeal allowed the appeals, quashed the convictions and substituted acquittals. The Court held that the initial roadblock stop was unlawful. Justice Doherty held that as the police did not have reasonable grounds to suspect that either accused was implicated in criminal activity, the detention could not be justified as investigative detention under *Mann*. There was no reasonable individualised suspicion. There were also no specific statutory powers to establish roadblocks. Justice Doherty then held that the ancillary police power can justify the use of a roadblock stop to investigate and prevent crime as well as apprehend offenders. However where the police do not have grounds to suspect any specific person or persons, the use of a roadblock stop could not, he held, be justified in furtherance of the police duty to investigate and prevent crime unless the police have reasonable grounds to believe both that a serious crime has been committed and that the roadblock stop may apprehend the perpetrator. Doherty J. added that the existence of those reasonable grounds would not necessarily justify the use of a roadblock stop. If those prerequisites exist, then other factors, like the availability of other less intrusive investigative alternatives, have to be taken into account. The Court of Appeal concluded that the "roadblock" was unlawful because there was no imminent danger and because the police did not tailor their intervention to stop only the four vehicles identified in the 911 call. Had they properly tailored their response, Farmer and Clayton's vehicle would not have been detained. As a result, their detention and subsequent searches violated ss. 9 and 8 of the Charter. The evidence was furthermore excluded under s. 24(2).

In the Supreme Court, all nine justices decided that on these facts there had been no section 8 or 9 breaches and therefore no need for any remedy. Like Justice Doherty, the Court saw the need for a roadblock stop powers wider than *Mann*. The Court divided 6-3 as to how that power should be recognised. Justice Abella spoke for the majority.

ABELLA J. (McLachlin C.J., Bastarache, Deschamps, Charron and Rothstein JJ. Concurring):—

. . .

If the police conduct in detaining and searching Clayton and Farmer amounted to a lawful exercise of their common law powers, there was no violation of their Charter rights. If, on the other hand, the conduct fell outside the scope of these powers, it represented an infringement of the right under the Charter not to be arbitrarily detained or subjected to an unreasonable search or seizure.

The following passages from *Mann* are instructive:

A detention for investigative purposes is, like any other detention, subject to Charter scrutiny. Section 9 of the Charter, for example, provides that everyone has the right "not to be arbitrarily detained". It is well recognized that a lawful detention is not "arbitrary" within the meaning of that provision. Consequently, an investigative detention that is carried out in accordance with the common law power recognized in this case will not infringe the detainee's rights under s. 9 of the Charter. . . . . .The general duty of officers to protect life may, in some circumstances, give rise to the power to conduct a pat-down search incident to an investigative detention. Such a search power does not exist as a matter of course; the officer must believe on reasonable grounds that his or her own safety, or the safety of others, is at risk. [paras. 20 and 40.]

Thus, a detention which is found to be lawful at common law is, necessarily, not arbitrary under s. 9 of the Charter. A search done incidentally to that lawful detention will, similarly, not be found to infringe s. 8 if the search is carried out in a reasonable manner and there are reasonable grounds to believe that police or public safety issues exist.

The statement that a detention which is lawful is not arbitrary should not be understood as exempting the authorizing law, whether it is common law or statutory, from Charter scrutiny. Previous decisions of this Court are clear that where a detention by police is authorized by law, the law authorizing detention is also subject to Charter scrutiny: *R. v. Hufsky*, [1988] 1 S.C.R. 621 (S.C.C.); *R. v. Ladouceur*, [1990] 1 S.C.R. 125 (S.C.C.). The courts can and should develop the common law in a manner consistent with the Charter: *Dagenais v. Canadian Broadcasting Corp.*, [1994] 3 S.C.R. 835 (S.C.C.), at pp. 875-78. The common law regarding police powers of detention, developed building on *R. v. Waterfield*, [1963] 3 All E.R. 659 (Eng. C.A.) and *Dedman*, is consistent with Charter values because it requires the state to justify the interference with liberty based on criteria which focus on whether the interference with liberty is necessary given the extent of the risk and the liberty at stake, and no more intrusive to liberty than reasonably necessary to address the risk. The standard of justification must be commensurate with the fundamental rights at stake.

The justification for a police officer's decision to detain, as developed in *Dedman* and most recently interpreted in *Mann*, will depend on the "totality of the circumstances" underlying the officer's suspicion that the detention of a particular individual is "reasonably necessary". If, for example, the police have particulars about the individuals said to be endangering the public, their right to further detain will flow accordingly. As explained in *Mann*, searches will only be permitted where the officer believes on reasonable grounds that his or her safety, or that of others, is at risk.

The determination will focus on the nature of the situation, including the seriousness of the offence, as well as on the information known to the police about the suspect or the crime, and the extent to which the detention was reasonably responsive or tailored to these circumstances, including its geographic and temporal scope. This means balancing the seriousness of the risk to public or individual safety with the liberty interests of members of the public to determine whether, given the extent of the risk, the nature of the stop is no more intrusive of liberty interests than is reasonably necessary to address the risk.

In my view, both the initial and the continuing detentions of Clayton and Farmer's car were justified based on the information the police had, the nature of the offence, and the timing and location of the detention.

The police set up the initial stop in response to a 911 call identifying the presence of about ten "black guys", four of them with guns. The police described what they were doing as setting up perimeter surveillance posts to secure the confined geographical area where the offence they were investigating had reportedly taken place. The police had reasonable grounds to believe that there were several handguns in a public place. This represented a serious offence, accompanied by a genuine risk of serious bodily harm to the public. The police were entitled to take reasonable measures to investigate the offence without waiting for the harm to materialize and had reasonable grounds for believing that stopping cars emerging from this parking lot would be an effective way to apprehend the perpetrators of the serious crime being investigated.

Like Doherty J.A., I am of the view that, as he indicated at para. 56 of his reasons, the information conveyed by the 911 call provided reasonable grounds for the police to believe that "several individuals were committing serious firearms-related criminal offences in front of the club" and that "those individuals who had vehicles would leave the parking area through one of the two available exits". As Doherty J.A. pointed out, the 911 system assumes that the police will react in a timely fashion to the information provided and that the police should be entitled to rely on such information.

The seriousness of the offences being investigated and the potential risk to public safety were also relied upon by Durno J. to conclude that the initial detention was a justifiable use of police powers. Additionally, he noted that the detention took place within minutes of the 911 call; that only those leaving the parking area were restricted in their movement; and that the exits from the parking area were the principal escape routes for those seen with guns.

Doherty J.A. acknowledged that the purpose of stopping the car was "to apprehend individuals in possession of dangerous weapons and seize those weapons before they could be used in criminal activity to harm others". Significantly, he also accepted that the information received by the police represented "a significant and undeniable danger":

> Criminal conduct involving the use of firearms, especially handguns, is a serious and growing societal danger. The law abiding segment of the community expects the police to react swiftly and decisively to seize illegal firearms and arrest those in possession of them. The risk posed to the community by those in possession of handguns gives an added significance to police efforts to seize those weapons and apprehend those in possession of them beyond the always important police duty to investigate and prevent criminal activity. [para. 41] (See also *Reference re Firearms Act (Canada)*, [2000] 1 S.C.R. 783, 2000 SCC 31 (S.C.C.), at para. 45; *R. v. Felawka*, [1993] 4 S.C.R. 199 (S.C.C.), at p. 211.)

I part company with him, however, when he concludes that notwithstanding the seriousness of the crimes and the inevitability that the perpetrators would use one of the exits, the police were not entitled to stop a car leaving the area unless it and the occupants matched exactly the information provided by the 911 caller as to the make of the vehicles or the casual clothing of the men in the parking lot. The detention of Clayton and Farmer's car was, as a result, found by him not to be sufficiently tailored to the circumstances because the police had decided to detain every car leaving the parking lot instead of just the four vehicles specifically described in the 911 call. With great respect, in my view requiring the police to stop only those vehicles described in the 911 call imposes an unrealistic burden on the police in this case, and one inconsistent with their duty to respond in a timely manner, at least initially, to the seriousness of the circumstances.

It is true that the caller described only four cars of the several in the parking lot, but the four vehicles described in the call were part of a larger scenario: four men with guns, part of a larger group of about ten men, all of whom were standing outside in the parking lot at the front of the strip club, none inside their vehicles, and any one of whom may have used a car other than those specifically described. The police set up their vehicles at the exit of the club's parking lot so as to detain only those vehicles in the parking lot at the time. Stopping a car emerging from this site was, with respect, an eminently reasonable response to the safety issues at stake.

The police timing was also responsive to the circumstances. They received the 911 call at 1:22 a.m. The officers in the area were notified at 1:24 a.m. and P.C. Robson and P.C. Dickson arrived at the rear exit of the parking lot at 1:26 a.m. By 1:27 a.m., within five minutes of the 911 call and one minute of their own arrival at the strip club, they had detained Farmer's vehicle.

The police had reasonable grounds to believe that public safety was at risk, that handguns could be in the possession of those leaving the parking area, and that stopping cars leaving that area could result in their apprehension. The steps taken by the police in this case in stopping the car, based on the information they had, were reasonable and reasonably tailored to the information they had.

In the totality of the circumstances, therefore, the initial detention in this case was reasonably necessary to respond to the seriousness of the offence and the threat to the police's and public's safety inherent in the presence of prohibited weapons in a public place, and was temporally, geographically and logistically responsive to the circumstances known by the police when it was set up. The initial stop was consequently a justifiable use of police powers associated with the police duty to investigate the offences described by the 911 caller and did not represent an arbitrary detention contrary to s. 9 of the Charter.

Having concluded that their initial detention was constitutionally permissible, the next issue is whether the conduct of the police in further detaining and searching Clayton and Farmer was justified.

. . .

I accept Doherty J.A.'s conclusion that had the police stopped the vehicle and discovered that the occupants did not correspond to the description given by the 911 caller, they would have had no reasonable grounds for the continued detention of the occupants. For example, had the caller described individuals who were white, the police would not have had reasonable grounds for the continued detention of non-white occupants. On the particular facts of this case, however, based on their subsequent observations, there were reasonable grounds, as required by *R. v. Mann*, for the police to conclude that the two occupants of the car they had stopped were implicated in the crime being investigated.

The officers' safety concerns also justified the searches incidental to the detention. The trial judge based his finding that Farmer's and Clayton's s. 8 rights were violated on his conclusion that the decision to search them was made before the officer had the objective grounds to do so. This, it seems to me, ignores the fact that the relevant time is the time of the actual search and seizure. By that time, the officers had the requisite subjective and objective grounds. Intention alone does not attract a finding of unconstitutionality. It is not until that subjective intent is accompanied by actual conduct that it becomes relevant. We would otherwise have the Orwellian result that Charter breaches are determined on the basis of what police officers intend to do, or think they can do, not on what they actually do. The Charter protects us from conduct, not imagination, and even a benign motive may not justify objectively unreasonable police conduct.

. . .

I would therefore allow the appeal and restore the respondents' convictions.

Justice Binnie (Lebel and Fish JJ. concurring) would have preferred to build this emergency stop power around the issue of reasonable grounds to believe that a firearms offence has been committed, encouraging Parliament to address any need for wider emergency powers. In their view, the following new common law police power should be recognised:

(1) to form a blockade (2) on receipt of information the police consider reliable (3) about serious firearms offences underway or recently committed (4) limited to the premises where the offence allegedly occurred (5) sufficiently soon after the alleged incident to give police reasonable grounds for belief that the perpetrators may be caught.

Was the Supreme Court right to reverse Doherty J.A. on the facts? Which approach to roadblock stops do you prefer — that of Doherty J.A., Abella J. or Binnie J.?

There is a profound and mind-boggling disagreement between Justices Abella and Binnie as to the proper approach to justification under section 9. The Binnie cohort called for a more meaningful standard of Charter scrutiny under which justification must be determined under section 1. "Reasonably necessary" was no substitute for Charter review. The more specific power they would have adopted could be justified under the *Oakes* test for section 1 as it was carefully tailored and minimally intrusive. **Which approach is preferable?**

PROBLEM 8

Police learn of a biker gang meeting and set up a roadblock. They stop and search every motorcycle driven by someone wearing biker gear.

Compare *Brown v. Durham Regional Police Force* (1998), 21 C.R. (5th) 1, 131 C.C.C. (3d) 1 (Ont. C.A.) and Nolet, see above.

PROBLEM 9

Police set up a roadblock to stop and check all vehicles to try to apprehend escaping bank robbers.

Compare *R. v. Murray* (1999), 32 C.R. (5th) 253, 136 C.C.C. (3d) 197 (Que. C.A.).

PROBLEM 10

Two undercover officers saw the accused engage in hand contact with a male person in an area believed by the police to be frequented by

drug traffickers. These observations aroused their suspicions although they had no grounds for an arrest. The undercover officers approached the accused who struck one of them in the face as the officers were starting to identify themselves. The officer, however, decided to give him the benefit of the doubt and not to arrest him for assault. The officer told the appellant to settle down, put his arm on him and told him, "We are going to have a chat." One of the officers ushered the accused off the sidewalk towards a building and questioned him with respect to his identification and immigration status. The officer had a policing function respecting immigration status pursuant to s. 103 of the Immigration Act. The officer's stated purpose in asking questions about immigration status was to ascertain if he could obtain some basis for holding him in order to search him. After the accused gave the officers a name, one of them radioed the police Street Crime Unit to obtain immigration information concerning the name the accused had given. When the information came back that the accused was not a person known to the immigration authorities, he was arrested on a purported violation of the Immigration Act. During the search in connection with his arrest, crack cocaine was found on the accused.

He was charged with possession of cocaine for the purpose of trafficking.

Compare *R. v. Nicely* (2000), 39 C.R. (5th) 340 (Ont. C.A.) and *R. v. Powell* (2000), 35 C.R. (5th) 89 (Ont. C.J.).

PROBLEM 11

The accused was arrested under s. 253 of the Code for driving a motor vehicle on the Don Valley Parkway in Toronto, having consumed alcohol in such a quantity that its concentration in his blood exceeded the proscribed limit. Before he was stopped by the arresting officer, he was driving at a speed slightly in excess of the posted limit in the area. Traffic was moderate at the time. Speeding is common on this freeway. The motor vehicle driven was an expensive one, a Ford Expedition. The accused is a young black man, a member of the Raptors of the National Basketball Association. At the time of the incident he was wearing a baseball cap and an athletic suit. He was polite and courteous to the police throughout the investigation of the incident including when he gave samples of his breath.

The trial judge dismissed the defence application to exclude evidence based on racial profiling without calling upon the Crown Attorney for submissions. An impaired driving conviction was entered. At sentencing the trial judge indicated that it was distasteful for the defence to have raised the racial profiling issue on the facts and that the officer deserved an apology.

Was there evidence of racial profiling? Should there be a new trial ordered on the basis of a reasonable apprehension of bias by the trial judge?

Compare *R. v. Brown* (2002), 48 C.R. (5th) 291, 162 C.C.C. (3d) 27
(Ont. S.C.J.); affirmed (2003), 9 C.R. (6th) 240 (Ont. C.A.).

PROBLEM 12

The two accused were charged with possession of marijuana for
the purpose of trafficking. The police had stopped a vehicle being
driven by the accused in the early morning hours. The police stopped
the car because it was a rental vehicle with out of province plates which
looked too expensive for the occupants, and they suspected that the
occupants were drug couriers. Looking into the car the police saw cell
phones, a pager, a road map, fast food wrappers and two duffel bags.
They asked the driver whether they could search the car, but the driver
refused. The police then asked the passenger, in whose name the car
had been rented, the same question. He consented and stepped out of
the car, at which point an officer testified that he detected the scent of
marijuana. A few seconds after consenting to the search the passenger
withdrew his consent. The officers searched the vehicle nonetheless,
finding two duffel bags in the trunk containing marijuana. They then
arrested the accused and advised them of their right to counsel. At trial
the accused applied for exclusion of the evidence, based on violations
of their s. 8, 9 and 10 (b) Charter rights.

Compare *R. v. Calderon* (2004), 23 C.R. (6th) 1, 188 C.C.C. (3d) 481
(Ont. C.A.). See annotation by Steve Coughlan, C.R., *ibid.*, at p. 3.

PROBLEM 13

You are the trial judge presiding over the trial of an accused
charged with possession of cocaine for the purposes of trafficking and
possession of proceeds of crime. At trial the main issue is the
constitutionality of the stop and search.

Two plainclothes officers concluded that a white woman under
their observation was working as a prostitute. She was hitchhiking and
seemed to be attempting to catch the eye of male drivers. They saw her
get into a van and return to the area about ten minutes later. She
entered a variety store and was seen near a telephone. About five
minutes later she was picked up by a black man driving a Honda
Accord. One of the officers had worked on the prostitution squad in the
past and knew that it is common for prostitutes to purchase drugs after
turning a trick. On cross-examination the officer admitted that in his
experience drug traffickers are often persons of colour. While they
quietly followed the vehicle they learned from police headquarters that
the registered driver was before the courts on a number of criminal
charges. They saw the woman leave the vehicle. They decided to stop
the vehicle. After a brief chase they got the driver, the accused, to stop.
He jumped out of the vehicle with his hands up. One of the officers
noticed a bulge on the accused's front pocket. He touched the outside
of the pocket with his hand and felt around towards the accused's

crotch area. **The officer asked him what was in his pocket and the accused pulled out a bundle of money. The officer then asked the man to step into a laneway, where no passersby could see them, and then asked him to drop his pants. As he did so a baggie later found to contain crack cocaine fell out. At this point the officer placed the man under arrest under the Controlled Drugs and Substances Act. Before putting him into the cruiser the officer asked him where he kept his supply, at which the accused answered "in a cupboard in my apartment". Based on this information the police later obtained a search warrant for the apartment and there found a large quantity of cocaine in the cupboard. With reference to authority consider whether ss. 8 and 9 of the Charter have been violated. Compare *R. v. Byfield* (2005), 193 C.C.C. (3d) 139, 26 C.R. (6th) 61 (Ont. C.A.).**

(e) Reasons for Arrest

Common law requirements respecting the duty to provide the reason for an arrest were laid down by the House of Lords in *Christie v. Leachinsky*, [1947] A.C. 573, [1947] 1 All E.R. 567 at 572-573 (H.L.):

These citations . . . seem to me to establish the following propositions:

1. If a policeman arrests without warrant on reasonable suspicion of felony, or of other crime of a sort which does not require a warrant, he must in ordinary circumstances inform the person arrested of the true ground of arrest. He is not entitled to keep the reason to himself or to give a reason which is not the true reason. In other words, a citizen is entitled to know on what charge or on suspicion of what crime he is seized.

2. If the citizen is not so informed, but is nevertheless seized, the policeman, apart from certain exceptions, is liable for false imprisonment.

3. The requirement that the person arrested should be informed of the reason why he is seized naturally does not exist if the circumstances are such that he must know the general nature of the alleged offence for which he is detained.

4. The requirement that he should be so informed does not mean that technical or precise language need be used. The matter is a matter of substance, and turns on the elementary proposition that in this country a person is, *prima facie*, entitled to his freedom and is only required to submit to restraint on his freedom if he knows in substance the reason why it is claimed that this restraint should be imposed.

5. The person arrested cannot complain that he has not been supplied with the above information as and when he should be, if he himself produces the situation which makes it practically impossible to inform him, *e.g.,* by immediate counter-attack or by running away.

There may well be other exceptions to the general rule in addition to those I have indicated, and the above propositions are not intended to constitute a formal or complete code, but to indicate the general principles of our law on a very important matter. These principles equally apply to a private person who arrests on suspicion. If a policeman who entertained a reasonable suspicion that X had committed a felony were at liberty to arrest him and march him off to a police station without giving any explanation of why he was doing this, the *prima facie* right of personal liberty would be gravely infringed. No one, I think, would approve a situation in which, when the person arrested asked for the reason, the policeman replied: 'That has nothing to do with you. Come along with me.'Such a situation may be tolerated under other systems of law, as for instance, in the time of *lettres de cachet* in the eighteenth century in France, or in more recent days when the Gestapo swept people off to confinement under an overriding authority which the executive in this country happily does not in ordinary times possess. This would be quite contrary to our conceptions of individual liberty.

This classic pronouncement was widely followed by Canadian courts until a majority of the Supreme Court of Canada in *Gamracy v. R.,* [1974] S.C.R. 640, 22 C.R.N.S. 224, 12 C.C.C. (2d) 209 (S.C.C.) held that the duty was exhaustively codified in s. 29(2) of the Criminal Code.

29. (2) It is the duty of everyone who arrests a person, whether with or without warrant, to give notice to that person, where it is feasible to do so, of

(a) the process or warrant under which he makes the arrest, or

(b) the reason for the arrest.

Section 10(a) of the Charter now establishes the right of everyone "on arrest or detention (a) to be informed promptly of the reasons therefor". The leading decision is that in

R. v. EVANS

[1991] 1 S.C.R. 869, 4 C.R. (4th) 144, 63 C.C.C. (3d) 289 (S.C.C.)

The accused, a mentally challenged youth, was convicted of first degree murder in the brutal killings of two women. Initially, the police thought his brother had committed the murders and arrested the accused on a marijuana charge. During the course of an interrogation that followed, the accused became the prime suspect in the two murders. The police did not formally advise the accused that he was then being detained for murder. The police investigation was aggressive and marked by their lying about finding the accused's fingerprint at one of the murder scenes. Eventually incriminating statements were obtained. These statements formed virtually the entire basis of his conviction. An appeal to the Court of Appeal was dismissed.

The Supreme Court held that the police had violated the accused's s. 10(b) rights by not explaining them to the accused where it was clear that the accused did not understand his rights. The statements were excluded under s. 24(2). However the majority of the Court found no violation of s. 10(a):

McLACHLIN J. (Gonthier and Cory JJ. concurring):—

. . .

The right to be promptly advised of the reason for one's detention embodied in s. 10(a) of the Charter is founded most fundamentally on the notion that one is not obliged to submit to an arrest if one does not know the reasons for it: *R. v. Kelly* (1985), 17 C.C.C. (3d) 419 (Ont. C.A.), at p. 424. A second aspect of the right lies in its role as an adjunct to the right to counsel conferred by s. 10(b) of the Charter. As Wilson J. stated for the Court in *R. v. Black*, [1989] 2 S.C.R. 138, at pp. 152-53, "[a]n individual can only exercise his

s. 10(b) right in a meaningful way if he knows the extent of his jeopardy". In interpreting s. 10(a) in a purposive manner, regard must be had to the double rationale underlying the right.

The majority of the Court of Appeal inclined to the view that the accused's right to be advised of the reasons for his detention was violated by the failure of the police to advise him when the focus of the investigation changed that he was then suspected of murder. While serious issue was not taken with this conclusion, I am hesitant to let it pass without comment lest the inference be drawn that police conduct, such as that found in this case, necessarily results in a breach of s. 10(a). In fact the police informed the appellant that he was a suspect in the killings shortly after their suspicion of him formed, as the following portion of the interview discloses:

> JS: (LONG PAUSE) To traffic marijuana, that was originally why we're here. But now that things have taken quite a change.

> WE: Yeah but . . . why are you asking me this? I never killed no one . . . I don't know who did. It's none of my business.

This passage suggests to me that both parties, the police and the appellant, were aware that the appellant was at that point under investigation for murder. Any doubt about that fact is resolved at the beginning of the second interview when Detective Spring states the following:

> JS: And we've come up with a few little things which ah . . . I feel are um . . . important in this case and that um . . . ah . . . they also um . . . point to . . . towards you as possibly being the person who committed that crime that night that we were discussing.

Thus, very shortly after the point where the appellant became the prime suspect in the killings, the police indicated that they were investigating the appellant for that purpose, and the appellant in turn seemed to recognize that the nature of the questioning had altered.

When considering whether there has been a breach of s. 10(a) of the Charter, it is the substance of what the accused can reasonably be supposed to have understood, rather than the formalism of the precise words used, which must govern. The question is whether what the accused was told, viewed reasonably in all the circumstances of the case, was sufficient to permit him to make a reasonable decision to decline to submit to arrest, or alternatively, to undermine his right to counsel under s. 10(b).

The appellant's response to the officer's statement that, while he had originally been arrested on marijuana charges, things had now taken "quite a change", indicates that the appellant was aware that the focus of the questioning had changed and that he was then being questioned with respect to the killings. It might, therefore, be argued that he was given the facts relevant to determining whether he should continue to submit to the detention. Nor can any failure to comply with s. 10(b) be attributed to failure to advise the accused of the reasons why his detention and questioning was continuing.

These considerations suggest that the requirements of s. 10(a) were met in the case at bar.

. . .

STEVENSON J.:— I have had the advantage of reading the judgment of my colleague, Justice McLachlin, and agree with her disposition of the appeal.

I restrict my agreement to the principal ground, namely that the police violated s. 10(b) of the Canadian Charter of Rights and Freedoms in failing to make a reasonable effort to explain to the accused his right to counsel.

SOPINKA J.:—I agree with the conclusion reached by Justice McLachlin with respect to s. 10(b) of the Canadian Charter of Rights and Freedoms and that the admission of the statements would bring the administration of justice into disrepute. I also agree with her disposition of the appeal. As was Southin J.A., however, I am of the opinion that s. 10(a) was violated as well. Section 10(a) and (b) set out very fundamental rights of a person arrested or detained. The instructions to the authorities which they contain are relatively simple. In each case, the detainee is to be "informed". In the case of s. 10(a), the right is to be informed of the reasons for the arrest or detention. The right to be informed of the true grounds for the arrest or detention is firmly rooted in the common law which required that the detainee be informed in sufficient detail that he or she "knows in substance the reason why it is claimed that this restraint should be imposed" (Christie v. Leachinsky, [1947] A.C. 573, at pp. 587-88). When an arrest is made pursuant to a warrant, this is set out in writing in the warrant. An arrest without warrant is only lawful if the type of information which would have been contained in the warrant is conveyed orally. The purpose of communicating this information to the accused in either case is, inter alia, to enable the person under arrest or detention to immediately undertake his or her defence, including a decision as to what response, if any, to make to the accusation. It seems axiomatic, therefore, that this information should be conveyed prior to questioning and obtaining a response from the person under arrest or detention. These basic and important values are included in s. 10(a) of the Charter.

In this case, the arresting officers were forewarned that they were dealing with a person of subnormal intelligence. In these circumstances, it was incumbent on them to be scrupulous in ensuring that his rights were respected. Instead, they concocted a ground for the arrest in order to question him about the involvement of his brother in the murders. In my opinion, having explicitly advised the appellant that he was in jeopardy for trafficking in narcotics, the arresting officers were obliged to disabuse him of this false information before seeking to elicit incriminatory evidence from him. This could only be accomplished by an equally explicit statement of the true ground for his arrest.

While in some circumstances the initial questions, which are put before an incriminatory response is obtained, may disclose the true ground for an arrest, in my opinion this is not such a case. The appellant, whose mental development was equated to that of a 14-year-old, should not have been required to deduce from the content of questions that the initial explicit reason for his arrest had shifted to a far more serious ground.

I have agreed that the statements referred to in the reasons of McLachlin J. should be excluded by reason of the violation of s. 10(b). The violation of s. 10(a) gives added support to the reasons for such exclusion.

However in *R. v. Mann* we have seen that Iacobucci J. decided that "At a minimum, individuals who are detained for investigative purposes must therefore be advised, in clear and simple language, of the reasons for the detention." There is a strong tendency, especially among trial judges, to follow *Mann* rather than *Evans*. In *R. v. Mian*, [2014] 2 S.C.R. 689, 315 C.C.C. (3d) 453, 13 C.R. (7th) 1 (S.C.C.), the Supreme Court held without reference to either *Evans* or *Mann* that a 22-minute delay in advising of the reason for a vehicle stop and arrest violated s. 10(a) "absent exceptional circumstances"

PROBLEM 14

Customs officials at an airport were alerted by the R.C.M.P. that they had confidential information that the accused was entering Canada with a quantity of heroin. On his arrival, customs officers searched his luggage and found nothing. They then conducted a visual personal search. The accused was not informed of his right to counsel and was not told of his right under the Customs Act to have the proposed search reviewed by a senior official or a justice of the peace. No drugs were found. The accused was then handed over to R.C.M.P. officers, who arrested him and advised him of his right to retain and instruct counsel without delay and advised him that he was not obliged to say anything unless he wished to do so. He was told that he would be the subject of a body search by a doctor at a hospital. The rectal examination by the doctor at the hospital, using a sigmoidoscope, resulted in the recovery of two condoms containing heroin of a street value of approximately $225,000. At his subsequent trial on charges of importing heroin and being in possession of heroin for the purpose of trafficking, the accused was acquitted. The trial judge found that the officers had reasonable and probable grounds to believe that the accused was importing heroin, but found, basing his ruling on discrepancies in the testimony and notes taken by the officers, that the accused had been arrested at the airport on the spurious reason of outstanding traffic warrants, although unexecuted warrants for arrest on minor matters did exist.

Have the accused's rights, under s. 10(*a*), been violated? *Compare R. v. Greffe*, [1990] 1 S.C.R. 755, 75 C.R. (3d) 257, 55 C.C.C. (3d) 161 (S.C.C.).

PROBLEM 15

The accused, aged 26, was a daycare worker at a child care centre that the three-year-old complainant attended. The complainant told her mother that the accused put his finger in her "peepee" and in her mouth. After police interviewed the complainant and her mother, they asked the accused to come to the police station. When he arrived he was arrested for sexual assault and sexual interference, read his rights, and cautioned. The accused spoke with duty counsel for nine minutes and was then interrogated. The accused was informed that he was alleged to have assaulted a child at the daycare but he was not at first advised of the details of the alleged offence, and indicated on several occasions that he had no idea of the allegations or of what was going on. Has s. 10(a) been breached?

See *R. v. Koivisto* (2011), 87 C.R. (6th) 285 (Ont. C.J.).

(f) Entry into Premises

The majority of the Supreme Court in *R. v. Feeney*, [1997] 2 S.C.R. 13 decided that the *Hunter v. Southam* warrant standard for searches should be applied to entries to arrest. In response, on December 18, 1997, Parliament enacted new entry powers. See ss. 529-529.3.

Parliament enacted an exigent circumstances exception for warrantless entry as follows:

s. 529.3 . . . exigent circumstances include circumstances in which the peace officer

(a) has reasonable grounds to suspect that entry into the dwelling-house is necessary to prevent imminent bodily harm or death to any person; or

(b) has reasonable grounds to believe that evidence relating to the commission of an indictable offence is present in the dwelling-house and that entry into the dwelling-house is necessary to prevent the imminent loss or imminent destruction of the evidence.

See Renee Pomerance, "Parliament's Response to *R. v. Feeney*: A New Regime for Entry and Arrest in Dwelling Houses" (1998), 13 C.R. (5th) 84.

R. v. CORNELL
76 C.R. (6th) 228, [2010] 2 S.C.R. 142, 258 C.C.C. (3d) 429 (S.C.C.)

The police executed a search warrant at the accused's house and found cocaine in his bedroom. The subject of the search had not been the accused, but rather two members of a criminal gang who were suspected of running a "dial-a-dope" operation to sell cocaine. Neither of those suspects lived in the house, but they were thought to be using it as a place to store the drugs. The police executed the warrant by means of a "hard entry", which involved the use of a battering ram and an entry by nine masked officers wearing body armour and with guns drawn. The house was not being used as a storage facility for a "dial-a-dope" operation, and the only person present at the time of the search was the accused's mentally challenged brother. The accused argued that there was a violation of his s. 8 rights because the manner in which the search was conducted was unreasonable. At trial, no violation was found, and this decision was upheld on appeal by a majority of the Alberta Court of Appeal.

A 4-3 majority of the Supreme Court found that there was no violation.

CROMWELL J. (McLACHLIN C.J.C., CHARRON and ROTHSTEIN JJ. concurring):—

[13] The appellant submits that the critical issue on appeal is whether the manner of entry by the members of the police tactical team was reasonable in the circumstances. The focus is on the decision to use a forced, unannounced entry with masked officers who did not have a copy of the search warrant with them. In the appellant's submission, the most aggravating component of the search flows from choices made by the police with respect to the manner of entry.

B. Legal Principles

(1) Reasonable Search and Seizure

[16] To be reasonable under s. 8 of the Charter, a search must be authorized by law, the authorizing law must itself be reasonable, and the search must be conducted in a reasonable manner: *R. v. Collins*, [1987] 1 S.C.R. 265, at p. 278. There is now no dispute that the first two of these conditions are met; the only issue is whether the lawfully authorized search was conducted reasonably.

[17] The onus is on the appellant, as the party alleging a breach of his Charter rights, to prove that the search contravened s. 8 of the Charter.

(2) Knock and Announce

[18] Except in exigent circumstances, police officers must make an announcement before forcing entry into a dwelling house. In the ordinary case, they should give: "(i) notice of presence by knocking or ringing the door bell; (ii) notice of authority, by identifying themselves as law enforcement officers and (iii) notice of purpose, by stating a lawful reason for entry: *Eccles v. Bourque*, [1975] 2 S.C.R. 739, at p. 747.

[19] Neither the wisdom nor the vitality of the knock and announce principle is in issue on this appeal. Experience has shown that it not only protects the dignity and privacy interests of the occupants of dwellings, but it may also enhance the safety of the police and the public: Commission of Inquiry into Policing in British Columbia, Closing the Gap: Policing and the Community — The Report (1994), vol. 2, at pp. H-50 to H-53. However, the principle, while salutary and well established, is not absolute: *Eccles v. Bourque*, at pp. 743 47.

[20] Where the police depart from this approach, there is an onus on them to explain why they thought it necessary to do so. If challenged, the Crown must lay an evidentiary framework to support the conclusion that the police had reasonable grounds to be concerned about the possibility of harm to themselves or occupants, or about the destruction of evidence. The greater the departure from the principles of announced entry, the heavier the onus on the police to justify their approach. The evidence to justify such behaviour must be apparent in the record and available to the police at the time they acted. The Crown cannot rely on ex post facto justifications: see *R. v. Genest*, [1989] 1 S.C.R. 59, at pp. 89-91; *R. v. Gimson*, [1991] 3 S.C.R. 692, at p. 693. I would underline the words Chief Justice Dickson used in *Genest*: what must be

present is evidence to support the conclusion that "there were grounds to be concerned about the possibility of violence": p. 90. I respectfully agree with Slatter J.A. when he said in the present case that "[s]ection 8 of the Charter does not require the police to put their lives or safety on the line if there is even a low risk of weapons being present": para. 24.

[21] Although *Genest* sets out the correct legal test, it is important to note that the facts in *Genest* are not similar to those in this case. Whereas in this case, the search was conducted pursuant to a valid search warrant, in *Genest*, the evidence did not support the issuance of a search warrant. Accordingly, the search in *Genest*, regardless of how it was conducted, was unreasonable because it was not authorized by law. Furthermore, there was no factual foundation presented to account for the means used by the police during the search. In the case before us, there was a valid warrant and an extensive evidentiary basis for the manner of search.

(3) Judicial Review

[22] The main question is whether the police had reasonable grounds for concern to justify use of an unannounced, forced entry while masked in this case. The trial judge is required to assess the decision of the police to act as they did and the appellate court is required to review the trial judge's conclusions. Three things must be kept in mind throughout these reviews.

[23] First, the decision by the police must be judged by what was or should reasonably have been known to them at the time, not in light of how things turned out to be. Just as the Crown cannot rely on after-the-fact justifications for the search, the decision about how to conduct it cannot be attacked on the basis of circumstances that were not reasonably known to the police at the time: *R. v. DeWolfe*, 2007 NSCA 79, 256 N.S.R. (2d) 221, at para. 46. Whether there existed reasonable grounds for concern about safety or destruction of evidence must not be viewed "through the 'lens of hindsight' ": *Crampton v. Walton*, 2005 ABCA 81, 40 Alta. L.R. (4th) 28, at para. 45.

[24] Second, the police must be allowed a certain amount of latitude in the manner in which they decide to enter premises. They cannot be expected to measure in advance with nuanced precision the amount of force the situation will require: *R. v. Asante-Mensah*, 2003 SCC 38, [2003] 2 S.C.R. 3, at para. 73; *Crampton*, at para. 45. It is often said of security measures that, if something happens, the measures were inadequate but that if nothing happens, they were excessive. These sorts of after-the-fact assessments are unfair and inappropriate when applied to situations like this where the officers must exercise discretion and judgment in difficult and fluid circumstances. The role of the reviewing court in assessing the manner in which a search has been conducted is to appropriately balance the rights of suspects with the requirements of safe and effective law enforcement, not to become a Monday morning quarterback.

[25] Third, the trial judge's assessment of the evidence and findings of fact must be accorded substantial deference on appellate review.

C. The Police Decision to Depart From Knock and Announce in This Case

[26] The appellant's position is that the police had inadequate information to support the decision to use a hard entry, that they ought to have taken further investigative steps and that their internal decision-making processes were either inadequate or not followed. I will examine these points in turn.

(1) Sufficiency of Information

[27] The appellant submits that the police had no reason to suspect violence in the residence and had no evidence to support the conclusion that any occupant had made provisions for destruction of evidence. Therefore, says the appellant, there was no information to support any grounds or necessity to deviate from the standard knock and announce principle. Respectfully, the trial judge's reasons for decision provide a complete answer to this submission. He correctly set out the applicable legal principles. In finding the police conduct of the search met the required standard, the judge made the following findings of fact which support his conclusion:

- It was reasonable for the police to be concerned about their safety and the safety of other occupants given their experience that those who traffic in cocaine frequently are violent and the fact that a cocaine trafficker who associated with violent people was welcome in the residence. The ITO also disclosed that in a dial-a-dope operation, the dealer usually has a place from which to operate which could contain drugs, money, weapons and score sheets. As detailed in the ITO, the whole point of having a location such as the Cornell residence at which to "reload" is to reduce the risk of losing large amounts of drugs or money in the event of a police stop while making deliveries. The Cornell residence was suspected of being such a place.

- The police had reasonable grounds to be concerned that the evidence to be found would be destroyed having regard to the fact that there were reasonable grounds to believe that cocaine would be found in the premises and that it is a substance that may be easily destroyed.

- No circumstances arose before the search warrant was executed which might remove the exigency of the situation.

- Notwithstanding that, by the time of the search, Nguyen was in custody and the police had observed Lorraine Cornell and her daughter leave the house, the police had no means of knowing who, if anybody, was in the residence or whether there was any person in the residence who would destroy the cocaine evidence upon learning of the presence of the police at the door. As the trial judge noted, the evidence showed that the police had reasonable grounds to believe that a cocaine trafficker who associated with violent people ... was welcome in the residence": A.R., vol. I, at p. 18.

- The fact that Lorraine Cornell and Jason Cornell, who were thought by police to be occupants of the house, had no prior criminal record did not affect the reasonableness of the police concern that evidence could be destroyed; as the trial judge observed, "[a] person without a criminal record could destroy evidence as easily as a person with a criminal record": A.R., vol. I, at p. 18.

[28] Having correctly stated the legal principles and made findings of fact untainted by clear and determinative error, the judge concluded that

the evidence demonstrated a reasonable explanation by the police for conducting a forceful entry to ensure the cocaine was not destroyed and ensure the safety of the police and the public in all of the circumstances. [A.R., vol. I, at p. 18]

[29] In addition to this finding, the judge also concluded, on the basis of the testimony of many of the police participants, that both the investigative team and the tactical team "possessed a genuine belief that only a forced tactical entry into the residence would lessen the possibility of the illicit substance being destroyed and would enhance the possible safety of the police and the possible occupants of the house": A.R., vol. I, at p. 19.

[30] I see no reviewable error in these conclusions that the police view of the need for a hard entry was both reasonably based and genuinely held. These conclusions are also supported, in my view, by other evidence in the record to which the trial judge does not specifically refer but relates to matters known to the police at the time of entry. The day before entry, the vehicle often driven by Nguyen was observed with Hans Eastgaard as a passenger. Eastgaard had an extensive criminal record which included weapons and drug charges. About two hours before entry, the vehicle often driven by Nguyen was observed to pull up to the rear of the Cornell residence. The driver, described by an officer conducting surveillance as an Asian male, left the vehicle and appeared to retrieve something from the yard of the residence near the fence. The car was stopped about an hour later. At the time, it was driven by Nguyen, who was wearing body armour. His passenger was Eastgaard. Nguyen was in possession of cocaine and cash. There was good reason to be concerned about violence on the part of Nguyen, Tran and Eastgaard. As Slatter J.A. observed, if Nguyen thought his business was dangerous enough to justify wearing body armour, it can hardly have been unreasonable for the police to think the same thing: C.A., at para. 23. At the time of the entry into the Cornell residence, Nguyen and Eastgaard were in custody, but Tran's whereabouts were unknown. These additional facts strengthen the grounds to believe that cocaine would be in the residence (and therefore liable to be easily destroyed) and that a violent reaction to entry might be encountered.

[31] The appellant objects to the use of masks by the police. My view, however, is that the question for the reviewing judge is not whether every detail of the search, viewed in isolation, was appropriate. The question for the judge, and the question the judge in this case answered, is whether the search overall, in light of the facts reasonably known to the police, was reasonable. Having determined that a hard entry was justified, I do not think that the court should attempt to micromanage the police's choice of equipment. I should add that *R. v. Lau*, 2003 BCCA 337, 175 C.C.C. (3d) 273, and *R. v. Schedel*, 2003 BCCA 364, 175 C.C.C. (3d) 193, are of no assistance to the appellant. In neither case was there any mention of the police wearing balaclavas. Both cases concerned

police reliance on a blanket policy (one that did not involve balaclavas), of which there was evidence in those cases, always to use a hard entry for the search of suspected marijuana grow operations even in the complete absence of evidence of risk of violence or destruction of evidence. There is no such "blanket policy" in evidence here and the record shows that there were ample grounds for the police to be concerned about violence and destruction of evidence in this case.

(2) The Need for Additional Investigation

[32] The appellant submits that the police should have known more about the residence and its occupants and that, if they had, they would have made a different decision concerning the type of entry to be made. I cannot accept this contention.

[33] The trial judge found as a fact that the police had no means of knowing before executing the warrant who, if anybody, was in the residence or whether there was anyone in the residence who might destroy the cocaine, if there was any, upon learning of the police presence at the door. The judge also found that the police had done what could reasonably be expected in formulating their decision to use a forced entry. These conclusions, which are mainly concerning matters of fact, are well-supported by the record.

D. Failure of Tactical Team to Have the Warrant With Them

[38] The appellant makes very brief submissions, without reference to authority, in support of his contention that the search was unreasonable because the tactical team did not have a copy of the warrant with it when it made the entry. This position is based on s. 29(1) of the Criminal Code, R.S.C. 1985, c. C-46, which reads:

> It is the duty of every one who executes a process or warrant to have it with him, where it is feasible to do so, and to produce it when requested to do so.

[41] The trial judge, relying on *R. v. Patrick*, 2007 ABCA 308, 81 Alta. L.R. (4th) 212, at paras. 49-51, aff'd on other grounds, 2009 SCC 17, [2009] 1 S.C.R. 579, held that s. 29 had been complied with. The judge reasoned that the warrant was present at the scene and that it was reasonable in the case of a hard entry for the tactical team to secure the premises — something that took only a very few minutes in this case — and for the primary investigator, who was in possession of the warrant, to wait outside with it until informed that it was safe to enter.

[42] As noted, s. 29(1) of the Code requires "every one who executes a . . . warrant to have it with him, where it is feasible to do so, and to produce it when requested to do so". The trial judge found as a fact that no one requested that the warrant be produced and that finding of fact is not challenged. There is no issue therefore as to any failure on the part of the police to produce the warrant when requested to do so. The question, therefore, is the meaning of the requirement that "every one" have the warrant "with him, where it is feasible to do so". The trial judge concluded that the section did not require that each member of the police team executing the warrant have a copy on his or her

person. This, in my view, is a sensible interpretation of the provision. Otherwise, it would be read as requiring all 15 members of the team executing this warrant to have a copy. The trial judge found that it was sufficient that, as he found to be the case, "the police team had it with them when executing the warrant". This seems to me to be a purposive and appropriate interpretation of the provision in the context of a search conducted by multiple officers.

[43] I agree with the authors of Search and Seizure Law in Canada (loose-leaf), at p. 17-5, that the purpose of s. 29(1) is to allow the occupant of the premises to be searched to know why the search is being carried out, to allow assessment of his or her legal position and to know as well that there is a colour of authority for the search, making forcible resistance improper. These purposes, in my view, are fully achieved by insisting that the warrant be in the possession of at least one member of the team of officers executing the warrant. While I think it is a better practice for someone among the first group of officers in the door to have a copy on his or her person, I would not conclude that the officers failed to have the warrant with them when a copy was in the possession of the primary investigator who was in charge of the search and immediately at hand. Moreover, it cannot in my view be said that the police conduct in relation to the warrant contributed in any respect to making this search unreasonable.

IV. Disposition

[44] In view of my conclusion that the search was not unreasonable, it is not necessary for me to address whether, if it had been, the evidence should have been excluded by virtue of s. 24(2) of the Charter.

FISH J. (BINNIE and LEBEL JJ. concurring) (dissenting):—

[46] Loaded weapons in hand, nine masked members of a police tactical unit smashed their way into the appellant's home in a residential Calgary neighbourhood. They forced the appellant's brother, who has a mental disability, face-down to the floor and cuffed his hands behind his back. They dented the front door with their battering ram and broke the door frame, destroyed some of the interior doors, pried locks off a garage door and rendered the garage door itself inoperable.

[47] The police were acting under a search warrant issued pursuant to s. 11 of the Controlled Drugs and Substances Act, S.C. 1996, c. 19 ("CDSA"). In virtue of s. 12 of the CDSA, the police were authorized to use only "as much force as is necessary in the circumstances". Nothing in the record indicates that the force used in this case was necessary in the circumstances.

[48] I hasten to make clear from the outset that officers conducting a search for drugs must be afforded considerable latitude in adopting appropriate procedures to ensure their own safety and to secure the evidence sought. Courts will not lightly interfere in operational decisions of this sort. But those decisions must be reasonable, and to be reasonable they must be informed by a fact-based assessment of the particular circumstances of the search and the force necessary to preserve evidence and to neutralize perceived threats to their safety. No such assessment was made in respect of the unannounced and violent entry into the Cornell residence.

[49] Neither the appellant nor any member of his family had a history of violence or a criminal record of any sort. No one else lived in their home. From their extensive surveillance of the premises, the police were well aware that the Cornell home was neither a gang house nor a drug house frequented by addicts or users.

[50] The police had no reason to believe that anyone at all who might be a threat to their safety was then in or near the dwelling. More specifically, they had no reason to believe that anyone in the house was armed or dangerous. They made no mention of weapons in their Information to obtain the search warrant. They alleged no grounds to believe that any would be found on the premises.

[51] Nor did the police have any basis for a particularized and reasonable belief that, in the absence of a swift and violent entry, evidence would be concealed or destroyed by anyone present or likely to be present at the time. Generic assertions in this regard are plainly insufficient to justify a violent entry of the kind that occurred here.

[52] Indeed, in the particular circumstances of the present search, the only anticipated violence related to the manner in which it was to be conducted by the police — euphemistically described as a "hard" or "dynamic" entry. It is undisputed that the police, before battering their way into the home, made no inquiry as to the character or background of its inhabitants. Nor has the Crown adduced any evidence whatever to suggest that it would have been difficult to do so, or that the urgency of the matter justified the failure of the police to conduct even a rudimentary investigation in this regard.

[53] The members of the tactical squad were bound by s. 29 of the Criminal Code, R.S.C. 1985, c. C-46, to have with them, where feasible, the search warrant under which they were acting. The Crown led no evidence that it was not feasible in this case. This is not a technical or insignificant breach of the law. It is a violation of a venerable principle of historic and constitutional importance.

. . .

[133] Finally... I agree with Justice Cromwell that the police must be granted appropriate latitude in adopting necessary procedures to ensure their own safety and to secure the evidence sought. But in affording police officers the flexibility to which they are entitled, courts are not relieved of their duty to ensure that the police respect the legal and constitutional restraints by which they are bound in virtue of the CDSA, the Charter and the common law. This is not a matter of judicial micromanagement of police operations (Justice Cromwell's reasons, at para. 31). It is about judicial enforcement of the rule of law.

Fish J. decided that the violation of s. 8 was serious and should result in exclusion of the evidence.

Do you agree with the majority or the minority?

For criticisms of the majority judgment see H. Archibald Kaiser, "Cornell: A Divided Court Accords Too Much Latitude to the Police- 'Canada is not a police state'" (2010) C.R. (6th) 228 and Michael Johnson, "Knockin' On Feeney's Door? A Case Comment on *R. v. Cornell*' (2012), 58 Crim. L.Q. 379.

The Supreme Court in *Godoy* has also recognized a common law power to enter premises to investigate a disconnected 911 call.

R. v. GODOY

(1998), [1999] 1 S.C.R. 311, 21 C.R. (5th) 205, 131 C.C.C. (3d) 129 (S.C.C.)

Two police officers received a call from radio dispatch concerning a 911 emergency call originating from the accused's apartment. The line had been disconnected before the caller spoke. The police arrived at the accused's apartment and knocked on the door. The accused partially opened the door. He told the police that everything was all right inside. One of the officers asked if they could enter the apartment to investigate but the accused tried to close the door. The officer prevented him from shutting the door and the four officers entered the dwelling. As soon as they got inside, an officer heard a woman crying. The accused's common law wife was found in the bedroom, curled in a fetal position and sobbing. The officer observed considerable swelling above her left eye. She stated the accused had hit her. The accused was placed under arrest for assaulting his wife. He resisted the arrest and in the ensuing struggle, an officer's finger was broken. The accused was charged with assaulting a police officer with the intent of resisting arrest.

The trial judge dismissed the charge, holding that the officers' entry into the accused's apartment was unauthorized and that therefore all subsequent actions of the police, including the arrest of the accused, were illegal.

The Ontario Court (General Division) allowed the Crown's appeal and ordered a new trial.The Court of Appeal upheld that decision. The accused appealed to the Supreme Court.

LAMER C.J.:—In my view, public policy clearly requires that the police ab initio have the authority to investigate 911 calls, but whether they may enter dwelling houses in the course of such an investigation depends on the circumstances of each case.

The accepted test for evaluating the common law powers and duties of the police was set out in *Waterfield*, [[1964] 1 Q.B. 164 (Eng. C.A.)] (followed by this Court in *R. v. Stenning*, [1970] S.C.R. 631; *Knowlton v. The Queen*, [1974] S.C.R. 443; and *Dedman v. The Queen*, [1985] 2 S.C.R. 2). If police conduct constitutes a prima facie interference with a person's liberty or property, the court must consider two questions: first, does the conduct fall within the general scope of any duty imposed by statute or recognized at common law; and second, does the conduct, albeit within the general scope of such a duty, involve an unjustifiable use of powers associated with the duty.

There is no doubt that the forcible entry by police into a private dwelling home constitutes a prima facie interference with a person's liberty and property. It is therefore incumbent upon the Court to consider the two questions posed in *Waterfield*, supra.

(1) *The general statutory and common law duties of the police*

Section 42 of the Police Services Act, R.S.O. 1990, c. P.15 (the "Act") read as follows at the relevant time:

> 42.—(1) The duties of a police officer include,
>   (a) preserving the peace;
>   (b) preventing crimes and other offences and providing assistance and encouragement to other persons in their prevention;
>   (c) assisting victims of crime;
>   (d) apprehending criminals and other offenders and others who may lawfully be taken into custody;
>   (e) laying charges, prosecuting and participating in prosecutions;
>   (f) executing warrants that are to be executed by police officers and performing related duties;
>   (g) performing the lawful duties that the chief of police assigns;
>   (h) in the case of a municipal police force and in the case of an agreement under section 10 (agreement for provision of police services by O.P.P.), enforcing municipal by-laws;
>   (i) completing the prescribed training.
> (2) A police officer has authority to act as such throughout Ontario.
> (3) *A police officer has the powers and duties ascribed to a constable at common law.* [Emphasis added.]

In *Dedman*, supra, at pp. 11-12, this Court held that the common law duties of the police (statutorily incorporated in s. 42(3)) include the "preservation of the peace, the prevention of crime, and *the protection of life and property*" (emphasis added). As Finlayson J.A. noted in the Court of Appeal, the common law duties of the police have yet to be judicially circumscribed. Furthermore, the duty to protect life is a "general duty" as described by Finlayson J.A., and is thus not limited to protecting the lives of victims of crime.

A 911 call is a distress call — a cry for help. It may indeed be precipitated by criminal events, but criminal activity is not a prerequisite for assistance. The duties specifically enumerated in s. 42(1) of the Act may or may not be engaged. The point of the 911 emergency response system is to provide whatever assistance is required under the circumstances of the call. In the context of a disconnected 911 call, the nature of the distress is unknown. However, in my view, it is reasonable, indeed imperative, that the police assume that the caller is in some distress and requires immediate assistance. To act otherwise would seriously impair the effectiveness of the system and undermine its very purpose. The police duty to protect life is therefore engaged whenever it can be inferred that the 911 caller is or may be in some distress, including cases where the call is disconnected before the nature of the emergency can be determined.

Before this Court, the parties did not seriously debate whether the police have a common law duty to respond to distress calls. Rather, the real question is whether the discharge of this common law duty entitles the police to forcibly enter a dwelling. In other words, the central issue concerns the second branch of the *Waterfield* test.

(2) Does the conduct in question involve an unjustifiable use of police powers in the circumstances?

In *Simpson*, supra, Doherty J.A. applied both *Waterfield*, supra, and *Dedman*, supra, and described what is meant by a "justifiable" use of police power as follows (at p. 499):

> . . . the justifiability of an officer's conduct depends on a number of factors including the duty being performed, the extent to which some interference with individual liberty is necessitated in order to perform that duty, the importance of the performance of that duty to the public good, the liberty interfered with, and the nature and extent of the interference.

I agree that these considerations should form the basis of analysis. In the case at bar, it was necessary for the police to enter the appellant's apartment in order to determine the nature of the distress call. There was no other reasonable alternative to ensure that the disconnected caller received the necessary assistance in a timely manner. While the appellant suggested that the police could knock on the neighbours' doors and question them, or wait in the apartment corridor for further signs of distress, in my view these suggestions are not only impractical but dangerous. If a 911 caller is in serious danger and is unable either to communicate with the 911 dispatcher or answer the door upon police arrival, the caller's only hope is that the police physically locate him or her within the apartment and come to his or her aid.

. . .

One can imagine, for example, a person having a heart attack who dials 911 but cannot speak. Perhaps there is no one home to answer the door. Would a reasonable person expect that the police would take steps to ensure that the 911 caller was alright? I believe so. A further example might be a situation where a home is burglarized and a resident is being held at gunpoint. Assuming a resident can actually make the 911 call, he or she might answer the door to the police under a threat of bodily injury should the police be allowed to enter. On the other hand, the person who answers the door might well be the intruder. I see no other use for an emergency response system if those persons who are dispatched to the scene cannot actually respond to the individual caller. I certainly cannot accept that the police should simply take the word of the person who answers the door that there is "no problem" inside.

Further, the courts, legislators, police and social service workers have all engaged in a serious and important campaign to educate themselves and the public on the nature and prevalence of domestic violence. One of the hallmarks of this crime is its private nature. Familial abuse occurs within the supposed sanctity of the home. While there is no question that one's privacy at home is a value to be preserved and promoted, privacy cannot trump the safety of all members of the household. If our society is to provide an effective means of dealing with domestic violence, it must have a form of crisis response. The 911 system provides such a response. Given the wealth of experience the police have in such matters, it is unthinkable that they would take the word of the person who answers the door without further investigation. Without making any comment on the specific facts of this case, it takes only a modicum of common sense to realize that if a person is unable to speak to a 911 dispatcher when making a call, he or she may likewise be unable to answer the door when help arrives. Should the police then take the word of the person who does answer the door, who might well be an abuser and who, if so, would no doubt pronounce that all is well inside? I think not.

The importance of the police duty to protect life warrants and justifies a forced entry into a dwelling in order to ascertain the health and safety of a 911 caller. The public interest in maintaining an effective emergency response system is obvious and significant enough to merit some intrusion on a resident's privacy interest. However, I emphasize that the intrusion must be limited to the protection of life and safety. The police have authority to investigate the 911 call and, in particular, to locate the caller and determine his or her reasons for making the call and provide such assistance as may be required. The police authority for being on private property in response to a 911 call ends there. They do not have further permission to search premises or otherwise intrude on a resident's privacy or property. In *Dedman*, supra, at p. 35, Le Dain J. stated that the interference with liberty must be necessary for carrying out the police duty and it must be reasonable. A reasonable interference in circumstances such as an unknown trouble call would be to locate the 911 caller in the home. If this can be done without entering the home with force, obviously such a course of action is mandated. Each case will be considered in its own context, keeping in mind all of the surrounding circumstances. (I specifically refrain from pronouncing on whether an entry in response to a 911 call affects the applicability of the "plain view doctrine" as it is not at issue on the facts of the case at bar.)

. . .

(3) *The impact of the decision in R. v. Feeney*, [1997] 2 S.C.R. 13

... *Feeney* was concerned solely with when the police can enter a dwelling without a warrant to make an arrest. Thus, in my view, the reasoning in *Feeney* does not apply to the case at bar, which is unconcerned with powers of arrest.

. . .

In summary, emergency response systems are established by municipalities to provide effective and immediate assistance to citizens in need. The 911 system is promoted as a system available to handle all manner of crises, including situations which have no criminal involvement whatsoever. When the police are dispatched to aid a 911 caller, they are carrying out their duty to protect life and prevent serious injury. This is especially true where the call is disconnected and the nature of the emergency unknown. When a caller uses a 911 system, he or she has requested direct and immediate intervention and has the right to expect emergency services will arrive and locate the caller. The public interest in maintaining this system may result in a limited intrusion in one's privacy interests while at home. This interference is authorized at common law as it falls within the scope of the police duty to protect life and safety and does not involve an unjustifiable use of the powers associated with this duty.

––––––––––

For criticism of *Godoy*, see Heather Pringle, "The Smoke and Mirrors of *Godoy*: Creating Common Law Authority While Making *Feeney* Disappear" (1999), 21 C.R. (5th) 227, and Stuart, "*Godoy*: The Supreme Court Reverts to the Ancillary Powers Doctrine to Fill a Gap in Power" (1999), 21 C.R. (5th) 225.

In *R. v. MacDonald*, 2014 SCC 3, [2014] 1 S.C.R. 37, 303 C.C.C. (3d) 113, 7 C.R. (7th) 229 (S.C.C.), police responded to a noise complaint at the accused's home. He opened the door only partially and the officer saw that he had something black and shiny in his hand, hidden behind his leg. The officer asked twice what the accused was holding but the accused did not answer. Thinking it might be a knife, the officer pushed the door open a few more inches and saw that it was a gun. A struggle followed and the accused was arrested and later convicted on firearm charges. When the matter reached the Supreme Court, the Court decided that the accused had an implied licence to come to the door and knock. However, the Court unanimously held that pushing the door open to explore the object was lawful under a common law power to search for public safety. The Court divided 4-3 on the test for that search. For the majority, Lebel J. (McLachlin C.J., Fish and Abella JJ. concurring) insisted that such a power is not "unbridled" and decided that:

> The principles laid down in *Mann* and reaffirmed in *Clayton* require the existence of circumstances establishing the necessity of safety searches, reasonable and objectively considered, to address an imminent threat to the safety of the public or the police [para 41]

There was a vehement and lengthy dissent on the law by Justices Moldaver and Wagner (Rothstein J. concurring), who maintained that a reasonable suspicion test for a valid safety search would better protect police had in their view already been adopted in *R. v. Mann*, [2004] 3 S.C.R. 59, 185 C.C.C. (3d) 308, 21 C.R. (6th) 1 (S.C.C.) and recently for dog sniffer searches in *R. v. Chehil*, 2013 SCC 49, [2013] 3 S.C.R. 220, 301 C.C.C. (3d) 157, 4 C.R. (7th) 219 (S.C.C.). See, too, criticism of the majority view by Terry Skolnik, "*R. v. Macdonald* and the Illogicality of the Reasonable Belief Requirement for Safety Searches" (2015), 62 Crim.L.Q. 43.

In his comment on *MacDonald*, Steve Coughlan, "The Need for Clarity in Creating Common Law Police Powers" (2014), 7 C.R. (7th) 263 traces how the Supreme Court, in creating various ancillary powers for police, has often been less than clear. In *MacDonald*, as in *Mann* and *Clayton*, the majority insisted on "reasonable grounds" but did not expressly say "reasonable and probable grounds" or use the *Hunter* language of "credibly-based probabilities replacing suspicion".

Decisions applying *MacDonald* in *R. v. Ahmed-Kadir*, 2015 BCCA 346, 327 C.C.C. (3d) 33, 22 C.R. (7th) 1 (B.C. C.A.) and *R. v. Schwab*, 2015 ABPC 180, 22 C.R. (7th) 36 (Alta. Prov. Ct.), are of particular significance for demonstrating that on either the test of reasonable and probable grounds or reasonable suspicion, automatic safety searches based simply on following police routines and/ or training must be held to violate s. 8 protections. The Supreme Court make it clear in *Chehil* that even a standard of individualized reasonable suspicion cannot be based on police routine, a subjective hunch or a generalised suspicion.

In *R. v. Fountain* (2015), 324 C.C.C. (3d) 425, 20 C.R. (7th) 371 (Ont. C.A.), the Court confirmed that since *MacDonald*, for a safety search to be lawful an officer must have reasonable grounds to believe that there is an imminent threat to police or public safety. The Court also held that such a safety search need not be limited to a lawful investigative detention under *Mann*. The latter ruling has been strongly criticized by Steve Coughlan in his C.R. comment.

PROBLEM 16

The accused was charged with unlawful possession of cocaine and possession of marihuana for the purposes of trafficking after police searched his home. The accused's girlfriend had phoned her mother to say that she had had a fight with the accused and wanted to be picked up. The girlfriend's mother called the RCMP, saying that her daughter was being abused and needed to be picked up. The police were aware of the accused, considered him to be violent, and believed him to be a major drug trafficker. The police were unable to find the residence and called the mother again, at which point they obtained the girlfriend's cell phone number. When they called the girlfriend she insisted that she was fine, had only wanted a lift, and that she had arranged for a ride; she refused to tell the RCMP where she was located. The police then phoned the home of the person who was supposed to pick the girlfriend up and were told that he had received the phone call and had just left. The police were also able to find the accused's address in this call.

The police did finally appear at the residence, two hours after they had initially been called. The girlfriend answered the door and said that everything was fine, that there had been no assault, simply a verbal disagreement. The police could see a bedroom from where they had entered and the accused lying on the bed. One officer went straight there and asked the accused to get up and be searched for officer safety reasons. Other officers then went through each room and space in the house that could hold a person to ensure that no one was concealed there and that there were no firearms. After observing a number of items relating to controlled substances the police decided to obtain a search warrant, and waited at the house until it arrived and was executed.

The accused sought to have the evidence excluded based on the warrantless entry and search of his premises. The trial judge found that there was no Charter violation and convicted the accused. The accused appealed. Rule.

Compare **R. v. Timmons (2011), 86 C.R. (6th) 48, 275 C.C.C. (3d) 59 (N.S. C.A.) and see CR annotation by Stephen Coughlan.**

(g) Meaning of Arrest

Of course the legality of an arrest will only arise if there is an arrest. The leading case of what constitutes an arrest is now *R. v. Latimer.*

R. v. LATIMER
[1997] 1 S.C.R. 217, 4 C.R. (5th) 1, 112 C.C.C. (3d) 193 (S.C.C.)

The accused was the father of T, a severely disabled child, who suffered from extreme cerebral palsy and was quadriplegic. T was in constant pain, and despite the administration of medication, experienced five or six seizures a day. T died while in the care of the accused, who advised the RCMP by telephone that she had passed away in her sleep. An autopsy found signs consistent with poisoning, and tests then indicated that T's blood was saturated with carbon monoxide. The RCMP then began to treat the matter as a homicide investigation. The accused was convicted of second degree murder. The Court of Appeal dismissed his appeal. The accused appealed further alleging, *inter alia*, that he had been arbitrarily detained and that his confession should have been excluded.

The judgment of the Court was delivered by Lamer C.J.C.:

. . .

The members of the Wilkie detachment of the RCMP inferred the possibility of motive and opportunity from the facts before them - the appellant was alone with Tracy at the time of her death, and Tracy was bedridden and in constant pain. They then decided to seek the assistance of the General Investigation Section at North Battleford, representatives of which they met with on Wednesday, November 3, 1993. As a result of that meeting, members of the North Battleford detachment decided to attend at the Latimer farm, take Mr. Latimer into custody, interview his wife and execute a search warrant.

This plan was put into effect the next day, on Thursday, November 4, 1993. The events are described in the uncontradicted testimony of one of the principal investigators, Corporal Lyons, which is quoted in the trial judgment. Important portions of that testimony, which are central to the disposition of this appeal, are underlined for emphasis:

At 8:28 that morning, Sergeant Conlon and I went to the residence. We went to the door, we rapped on it, waited a couple of minutes. Robert Latimer came to the door. He was appeared to have just been in the process of getting up, he was in a housecoat, hair messed a little bit. Sergeant Conlon introduced ourselves to him, identified us, of course. We shook hands. Sergeant Conlon told him that we were from North Battleford and were assisting Wilkie in the investigation of Tracy's death, being his daughter, and told Mr. Latimer that we'd like to speak to him. He went into a bedroom and got dressed, came out a couple of minutes later. We were waiting in the kitchen. Sergeant Conlon said that we'd like to speak to him outside. There was no response. He put on his rubber boots and a jacket and went outside to the car with us. We had an unmarked police vehicle. I went into the driver's seat, Sergeant Conlon the passenger side, and Mr. Latimer in the back seat behind me. At 8:32 [a.m.] I turned in the bucket seats [sic] of the car and looked directly at him. I said, as Sergeant Conlon explained, we are assisting Wilkie detachment in the investigation of his daughter's death. I said I realize that this is a very trying time for him and his family and I said what I am about to say has very serious consequences and he should listen very closely. He nodded to me. I said, "You are being detained for investigation into the death of your daughter Tracy." I then said, "You have the right to retain and instruct counsel without delay. You may call any lawyer you wish. Legal Aid duty counsel is available to provide legal advice to you without any charge and can explain the Legal Aid plan to you." I asked, "Do you understand?" He replied, "Yes." I asked, "Do you wish to call a lawyer now?" He replied, "Not really, no." I then warned him the standard police warning, "You need not say anything. You have nothing to hope from any promise of favour, nothing to fear from any threat, whether or not you say anything. Anything you do say may be used as evidence." I asked, "Do you understand?" And he replied, "Yes." At that point, Sergeant Conlon told him that we would be going to North Battleford for the purpose of speaking to him. Mr. Latimer raised no objection.

[At the police station Mr. Latimer went on to make a full confession. That afternoon, Mr. Latimer returned with the officers where he pointed out the equipment he claimed to have used to end Tracy's life.]

. . .

ANALYSIS

1. *Was the appellant arbitrarily detained in contravention of s. 9 of the Charter?*

The appellant alleges that his right under s. 9 against arbitrary detention was violated when he was detained at his farm on the morning of November 4, 1993. There is no doubt in my mind that the appellant was detained, and the parties agree on this point. However, I am equally certain that Mr. Latimer's detention was not arbitrary. The RCMP officers who attended at the Latimer farm put Mr. Latimer under *de facto* arrest. Moreover, on the facts of this case, that *de facto* arrest was entirely lawful because it was based on reasonable and probable grounds that Mr. Latimer had taken his daughter's life. A de facto arrest which is lawful, in my opinion, cannot be an arbitrary detention for the purposes of s. 9.

The appellant's strongest argument is that no arrest occurred because the officers deliberately chose not to arrest Mr. Latimer. He points to testimony by officers Lyon and Conlon at trial, in which they indicated that they decided prior to appearing at the farm they did not wish to arrest Mr. Latimer. As well, he also points to the use of the word "detention", instead of the word "arrest", as proof of that intention.

However, notwithstanding what the intention of the officers may have been, their conduct had the effect of putting Mr. Latimer under arrest. To understand why, we need only turn to the definition of arrest offered by this Court in *R. v. Whitfield*, [1970] S.C.R. 46. Judson J., speaking for the majority of the Court, held that an arrest consists either of (i) the actual seizure or touching of a person's body with a view to his detention, or (ii) the pronouncing of "words of arrest" to a person who submits to the arresting officer. The term "words of arrest" was not defined in that judgment. However, in my mind we should decline the invitation to adopt the narrow view of that term proposed by the appellant, i.e. that only the word "arrest" will suffice. As this Court has held with respect to s. 10(a) of the Charter (*R. v. Evans*, [1991] 1 S.C.R. 869, at p. 888), what counts is

> the substance of what the accused can reasonably be supposed to have understood, rather than the formalism of the precise words used. The question is what the accused was told, viewed reasonably in all the circumstances of the case.

On the facts of this case, a *de facto* arrest occurred through the use of words that conveyed clearly that Latimer was under arrest, the conduct of the officers, and Mr. Latimer's submission to the authority of officers Conlon and Lyons. Mr. Latimer was told that he was being detained, and that he would be taken back to North Battleford to be interviewed. The police officers informed him of his right to silence and his right to counsel. They accompanied him back into his house while he changed his clothes, telling him that they were doing so because he was now in their custody. Finally, at no point did Mr. Latimer protest or resist the police — he submitted to the authority of the arresting officers.

The fact that a *de facto* arrest occurred, however, is not sufficient to dispose of the matter, because of the potential that his arrest was unlawful. Unlawful arrests may be inherently arbitrary: see P. W. Hogg, *Constitutional Law of Canada* (3rd ed., 1992), at p. 1073. However, it is not necessary to address that question, because Mr. Latimer's arrest was entirely lawful, and failing an attack against the legislative provision which authorized the arrest, I do not see how a lawful arrest can contravene s. 9 of the Charter for being arbitrary. The arresting power of police officers is set down by s. 495 of the Criminal Code. What counts as reasonable grounds was laid down by Cory J. in *R. v. Storrey*, [1990] 1 S.C.R. 241, at pp. 250-51. . . . The trial judge made a specific finding that reasonable grounds for the arrest of Mr. Latimer existed, and I see no reason to disturb that finding. Subjectively, despite the fact that the officers decided not to arrest Mr. Latimer, it is clear that they believed that they had reasonable grounds to arrest him. They chose not to because at the time of the arrest, they believed that they did not have enough evidence to obtain a conviction. This is most evident from the testimony of Constable Lyons, who stated that "certainly the grounds to arrest were present" and "[c]ertainly there were reasonable and probable grounds to arrest him". Objectively, the reasonable person in the position of the arresting officer would have concluded there were reasonable grounds for arrest. Those grounds included: the carbon monoxide in Tracy's blood, strongly suggesting that she had been poisoned; the fact that it was extremely unlikely that Tracy's death had been accidental; the fact that, because of Tracy's physical condition, her death could not have been suicide; and finally, the fact that the accused had both opportunity and motive. I therefore conclude that the trial judge was correct in deciding that there were reasonable and probable grounds for an arrest.

2. *Did the failure to inform the appellant that he had been "arrested" and that he could be charged with murder violate s. 10(a) of the Charter?*

Section 10(a) of the Charter provides the right to be informed promptly of the reasons for one's arrest or detention. The purpose of this provision is to ensure that a person "understand generally the jeopardy" in which he or she finds himself or herself: *R. v. Smith*, [1991] 1 S.C.R. 714, at p. 728. There are two reasons why the Charter lays down this requirement: first, because it would be a gross interference with individual liberty for persons to have to submit to arrest without knowing the reasons for that arrest, and second, because it would be difficult to exercise the right to counsel protected by s. 10(b) in a meaningful way if one were not aware of the extent of one's jeopardy. . . . There is no doubt that Mr. Latimer was not told that he was under "arrest"; he was told that he was being "detained". Nor was he explicitly told that he could be charged with murder. However, as with determining whether there has been a *de facto* arrest, when considering whether there has been a violation of s. 10(a), one must look beyond the exact words used. . . . On the facts of this case, I have no doubt that the trial judge was right in finding that Mr. Latimer understood the basis for his apprehension by the police and hence the extent of his jeopardy. He knew that his daughter had died, and that he was being detained for investigation into that death. Constable Lyons prefaced his comments in the car by saying "what I am about to say has very serious consequences". Mr. Latimer was then informed of his right to counsel and his right to silence, which clearly conveyed that he was being placed under arrest. Finally, he was told that he could not go into his own house by himself to change his clothes. It is clear on these facts that Mr. Latimer knew that he was in an extremely grave situation as regards his daughter's death, and that s. 10(a) cannot be said to have been violated.

PROBLEM 17

At their morning briefing police officers were told that a robbery had occurred at 6:45 a.m. that morning and that the suspect was "male, black, 5'8" to 5'11", with a short afro, wearing a dark jacket, armed with a knife and a gun". About three and one half hours after the robbery the officers saw a man matching this description walking through a shopping mall near the scene of the robbery. He was not acting suspiciously but they arrested him when he refused to answer their questions. They advised him he was charged with robbery. That charge was not proceeded with. However, the police found on the arrest that the accused had a revolver. He was later charged with carrying a concealed weapon. Was the arrest lawful and did it violate s. 9?

Compare *R. v. Charley* (1993), 22 C.R. (4th) 297 (Ont. C.A.) and *R. v. Johnson* (1995), 39 C.R. (4th) 78 (Ont. C.A.). For pre-Charter rulings see *Koechlin v. Waugh* (1957), 118 C.C.C. 24 (Ont. C.A.), and *R. v. Evans* (1991), 10 C.R. (4th) 192 (Ont. Prov. Div.). For *obiter* recognition that racial discrimination in law enforcement may lead to a successful section 15 challenge see *R. v. Smith* (1993), 23 C.R. (4th) 164 (N.S. C.A.)

and, similarly, for gender discrimination see *R. v. White* (1994), 35 C.R. (4th) 88 (N.S. C.A.).

(h) Appearance Notice

Professor Martin Friedland's empirical study, *Detention Before Trial* (1963), investigated in detail the pre-trial disposition of all criminal offences (almost six thousand cases) tried in the Toronto Magistrate's Courts over a six-month period from September, 1961 to February, 1962. He found that in over ninety per cent of the cases the criminal proceeding had been initiated by an arrest and of those arrested about eighty five per cent had been kept in police custody until their first court appearance, many for a substantial period of time. He concluded that the release practices operated in "an ineffective, inequitable and inconsistent manner" and that a "complete re-thinking" was required (at 172). On March 22, 1971, the House of Commons passed major amendments to the Criminal Code contained in the Bail Reform Bill which had considerable impact on powers to initiate the criminal proceedings, not only in respect of the law of bail. Before we examine these various powers it will be helpful to first examine the philosophy behind the 1971 amendments. On June 8, 1970 the then Minister of Justice, Mr. John Turner, issued the following press release:

The objectives of the Bail Reform Bill, then, are four-fold:

1. To avoid unnecessary pre-trial arrest and detention; for the initial decision to arrest is the decision which activates the criminal law process. It sets the administrative machinery in motion, and is the citizen's first confrontation with the criminal law process. It may well have a determining influence on that citizen's reaction to the law generally and the criminal law in particular.

2. To ensure that, in cases where arrest with or without warrant has taken place, the person accused, whatever his means, is not unnecessarily held in custody until his trial.

3. To ensure an early trial for those who have been detained in custody pending trial.

4. To provide statutory guidelines for decision-making in this part of the Criminal law process and thereby mitigate against the possibilities for "discretionary injustice" in the decision to arrest, hold for custody, admit to bail, etc.

"The Bail Reform Bill", said Mr. Turner, "will continue to humanize the administration of criminal justice in Canada. The right to bail should not be the prerogative of the rich and detention the plight of the poor. If we are to have equal justice before the law, the law must protect all equally."

Mr. Turner further observed that, "an accused person should not be subjected to detention without good reason, at least until he is convicted and sentenced by due process before a court of law. The Bail Reform Bill is designed to harmonize the protection of individual liberty with the requirement of public order."

One of the techniques for discouraging arrests adopted was a new provision for appearance notices.

495. (2) A peace officer shall not arrest a person without warrant for

(a) an indictable offence mentioned in section 553,

(b) an offence for which the person may be prosecuted by indictment or for which he is punishable on summary conviction, or

(c) an offence punishable on summary conviction, in any case where

(d) he believes on reasonable grounds that the public interest, having regard to all the circumstances including the need to

    (i) establish the identity of the person,

    (ii) secure or preserve evidence of or relating to the offence, or

    (iii) prevent the continuation or repetition of the offence or the commission of another offence,

may be satisfied without so arresting the person, and

(e) he has no reasonable grounds to believe that, if he does not so arrest the person, the person will fail to attend in court in order to be dealt with according to law.

One of the strategies adopted in the Bail Reform Act to reduce the number of accused detained before trial was to declare in s. 495(2) that a power of arrest under s. 495(1) for stipulated types of less serious offences—offences in the absolute jurisdiction of provincial judges, those hybrid and those punishable on summary conviction—*shall not* be exercised (an appearance notice being possible) if certain conditions are met. An appearance notice is very much like a summons except that it is issued by a peace officer and not a justice. Unfortunately s. 495(2) is characterized by bewildering complexity. The correct interpretation is that a police officer may still arrest for "an appearance notice offence" when he has reasonable grounds for believing that an arrest is in the public interest (s. 495(2)(*d*)) *or* where he has reasonable grounds for believing that the accused will fail to attend court (s. 495(2)(*e*)). Courts have battled to interpret this section. Pity the police officer making a decision on the spot. The appearance notice must be in the proper form (s. 501) supported by an information laid before a justice as soon as practicable (s. 505(*a*) and s. 508). The justice must cancel or confirm the appearance notice.

Technical errors in an appearance notice, or a delay in its confirmation by an information, are no longer being held sufficient to render the notice a nullity. Errors may be cured by a valid information (*R. v. Littlejohn* (1981), 27 C.R. (3d) 263 (B.C. C.A.) and *Re Thompson and R.* (1984), 11 C.C.C. (3d) 435 (Alta. C.A.)). Lack of a timely supporting information can be cured by the accused attorning to the jurisdiction by his appearance (*R. v. Naylor* (1978), 42 C.C.C. (2d) 12 (Ont. C.A.)). Even after an appearance notice has lapsed, a valid information can still be sworn and the accused's appearance compelled by way of summons (*R. v. Tremblay* (1982), 28 C.R. (3d) 262, 68 C.C.C. (2d) 273 (B.C. C.A.).

The Bail Reform Act, having limited the power of arrest in s. 495(2), however enacted a wide justification in s. 495(3):

495. (3) Notwithstanding subsection (2), a peace officer acting under subsection (1) is deemed to be acting lawfully and in the execution of his duty for the purposes of

(a) any proceedings under this or any other Act of Parliament, and

(b) any other proceedings, unless in any such proceedings it is alleged and established by the person making the allegation that the peace officer did not comply with the requirements of subsection (2).

Appeal courts have construed s. 495(3)(*a*) literally, to conclusively deem an arrest contrary to s. 495(2) as legal for all purposes connected with criminal proceedings: see *R. v. Adams* (1973), 21 C.R.N.S. 257 (Sask. C.A.) (obstructing peace officer); *R. v. McKibbon* (1973), 12 C.C.C. (2d) 66 (B.C. C.A.) (assault with intent to resist arrest) and *R. v. Tully* (1984), 41 C.R. (3d) 182 (Ont. Co. Ct.) (assaulting peace officer).

Some trial judges have sought to interpret s. 495(3)(*a*) restrictively. In *R. v. Prince* (1981), 61 C.C.C. (2d) 73 at 79 (Man. Prov. Ct.) (obstructing peace officer), Kopstein Prov. J. observed that, on the *Adams* and *McKibbon* view, "s. 450(3) [now 495(3)] effectively and totally emasculates any restriction placed upon peace officers by virtue of s. 450(2) [now 495(2)], rendering the latter a mere paper restriction". In the now overruled judgment in the court below in *Tully,* Harris Prov. J. rejects *McKibbon.* Instead, s. 495(3) is viewed as a shield for police officers against civil or criminal proceedings *against themselves.* However, it is not to be used as a sword for criminal prosecution of others. So, where s. 495(2) has been breached, the officer, although personally protected from liability, is acting unlawfully, and an accused cannot be convicted of an offence an essential element of which is lawful conduct by the police. Is this view preferable?

In the case of a civil suit against the police, s. 495(3)(*b*) would apply: see *Mason v. Basse,* Ont. Co. Ct., Salhany Co. Ct. J., September 20, 1983. It casts the onus on the plaintiff of proving on a balance of probabilities that the officer did not comply with s. 495(2).

PROBLEM 18

Jim Smith has been a police constable for four years with the City Police Department. Owing to the manpower shortage, he is on patrol in a motor vehicle alone on the west side of the City. At 2 a.m. he is proceeding in a northerly direction up a residential street, where he meets a truck coming from the opposite direction. The snow banks have narrowed the road. He does not give way and stops with the lights still on. On his approach to the open truck he notices that there is a 20" T.V. set in the back. He asks the driver, a man of about 20 who is scruffily dressed, if he owns the T.V. set. With an apparent hesitation, he says "Yes". Jim asks him for his name and address, which is given as "John Piper, 510 Montreal Street". Jim himself has no personal knowledge of this address. Jim asks him further how old the T.V. set is. He replies that he doesn't know, as a friend gave it to him about a year ago in return for a favour he did. He adds that it is due for repairs and that is why he has it in his truck, to save him the bother of loading it into the truck in the morning when he starts work. He also adds that he goes on shift work at 6 a.m. When Jim asks him where he has come from he says, and his breath indeed smells of alcohol, although he is not drunk,

that he is just returning from a friend's house and was taking a short-cut home. Jim says he would like John to take him to his friend, at which he becomes belligerent and swears. He says, "Piss off, Cop, I'm going".

Jim lets him go but, as similar incidents have left him in a quandary before, he reports the incident to his sergeant. He in turn asks you, a practising lawyer, for a brief, discussing the appropriate sections and cases, as to whether or not Jim could have lawfully made an arrest.

PROBLEM 19

A plainclothes police officer made initial contact with a person who offered her services as a prostitute. She was arrested and detained overnight for court appearances in the morning, pursuant to a blanket policy to arrest all street prostitutes. Is this arbitrary detention contrary to s. 9? What of a blanket policy to arrest all impaired drivers?

Compare *R. v. Pithart* (1987), 57 C.R. (3d) 144, 34 C.C.C. (3d) 150 (B.C. Co. Ct.); *R. v. Cayer* (1988), 66 C.R. (3d) 30 (Ont. C.A.) and *R. v. Sieben* (1989), 51 C.C.C. (3d) 343 (B.C. C.A.).

Chapter 4

INTERROGATION

This chapter addresses the limits placed on the police when they interrogate a suspect. The law respecting interrogation is a complicated amalgam of three related bodies of law — the common law confessions rule, the right to counsel in s. 10(*b*) of the Charter and the right to silence in s. 7 of the Charter.

1. Right to Counsel (Charter, s. 10(*b*))

Section 2(*c*) of the Canadian Bill of Rights provides:

2. Every law of Canada shall, unless it is expressly declared by an Act of the Parliament of Canada that it shall operate notwithstanding the *Canadian Bill of Rights,* be so construed and applied as not to abrogate, abridge or infringe or to authorize the abrogation, abridgment or infringement of any of the rights or freedoms herein recognized and declared, and in particular, no law of Canada shall be construed or applied so as to . . .

(c) deprive a person who has been arrested or detained

   (i) of the right to be informed promptly of the reason for his arrest or detention,

   (ii) of the right to retain and instruct counsel without delay, or

   (iii) of the remedy by way of *habeas corpus* for the determination of the validity of his detention and for his release if the detention is not lawful;

. . .

Under s. 10 of the Canadian Charter of Rights and Freedoms everyone has the right on arrest or detention

(a) to be informed promptly of the reasons therefor;

(b) to retain and instruct counsel without delay and to be informed of that right; and

(c) to have the validity of the detention determined by way of *habeas corpus*

and to be released if the detention is not lawful.

(a) Triggering Mechanism

For many years the leading pronouncements on the meaning of detentions were those of Justice Le Dain first for half the court in *R. v. Therens*, [1985] 1 S.C.R. 613, 18 C.C.C. (3d) 481, 45 C.R. (3d) 97 (S.C.C.) and then for the full court in *R. v. Thomsen*, [1988] 1 S.C.R. 640, 40 C.C.C. (3d) 411, 63 C.R. (3d) 1 (S.C.C.). Justice Le Dain decided that a purposeful interpretation of the Charter required a holding that both someone subject to a breathalyzer demand under what is now s. 254(3) (*Therens*) and one subject to an alert test demand at the roadside under what is now s. 254(2) was detained. This triggered the right to counsel under s. 10(b). However, in *Thomsen* the Court held that there was no right to counsel in the case of alert test demands since the provision for preliminary testing for impaired drivers constituted a demonstrably justified reasonable limit under s. 1. In *R. v. Jaycox*, 2012 BCCA 365, 292 C.C.C. (3d) 379 (B.C. C.A.), the Court held *Thomsen* still applied despite the expanded Code powers to deny the application of s. 10(b) rights under the expanded alert, and physical co-ordination test demands. Section 10(b) still has full application to breathalyzer demand cases. In *Thomsen* the Court decided on the following approach to the meaning of detention:

LE DAIN J.:—I venture to restate what I perceive to be the essentials of those reasons, as they appear in my judgment in *Therens*, as follows:

1. In its use of the word "detention", s. 10 of the *Charter* is directed to a restraint of liberty other than arrest in which a person may reasonably require the assistance of counsel but might be prevented or impeded from retaining and instructing counsel without delay but for the constitutional guarantee.

2. In addition to the case of deprivation of liberty by physical constraint, there is a detention within s. 10 of the *Charter*, when a police officer or other agent of the state assumes control over the movement of a person by a demand or direction which may have significant legal consequence and which prevents or impedes access to counsel.

3. The necessary element of compulsion or coercion to constitute a detention may arise from criminal liability for refusal to comply with a demand or direction, or from a reasonable belief that one does not have a choice as to whether or not to comply.

4. Section 10 of the *Charter* applies to a great variety of detentions of varying duration and is not confined to those of such duration as to make the effective use of *habeas corpus* possible.

Principle 3 embraced, *obiter*, a notion of psychological detention also triggering s. 10(b) rights. This notion has for years been controversial and, for some, too wide.

In *R. v. Mann* we saw that Iacobucci J. remarked that

"Detention" has been held to cover, in Canada, a broad range of encounters between police officers and members of the public. Even so, the police cannot be said to "detain", within the meaning of ss. 9 and 10 of the *Charter*, every suspect they stop for purposes of identification, or even interview. The person who is stopped will in all cases be "detained" in the sense of "delayed", or "kept waiting". But the constitutional rights recognized by ss. 9 and 10 of the *Charter* are not engaged by delays that involve no significant physical or psychological restraint. In this case, the trial judge concluded that the appellant was detained by the police when they searched him. We have not been urged to revisit that conclusion and, in the circumstances, I would decline to do so.

This obiter leads to further disarray in lower courts. See Stuart, "The Ontario Court of Appeal Blinks and Flutters: Less Exclusion and Inconsistency in Stop Cases", (2007) 49 C.R. (6th) 282, Ken Lockhart, "The Urgent Need for the Supreme Court to Reconsider the Meaning of Detention for Charter Purposes", (2008) 58 C.R. (6th) 222 and Mathew Oleynik, "What Makes or Breaks a Charter Argument on a Pedestrian Youth Stop" (2008) 54 Crim. L.Q. 79. Thankfully the Supreme Court comprehensively re-considered its approach to detention in *Grant*.

R. v. GRANT

66 C.R. (6th) 1, 245 C.C.C. (3d) 1, [2009] 2 S.C.R. 353 (S.C.C.)

Three officers were on patrol at mid-day in the Greenwood and Danforth area of Toronto where four schools had a history of student assaults, robberies and drug offences occurring over the lunch hour. Two plainclothes officers driving an unmarked car noticed the accused, an 18-year-old black man, walk by them in a manner they considered suspicious. He stared at them and fidgeted with his coat and pants. They asked a uniformed officer to have a chat with him. That officer was on directed patrol to maintain high visibility presence to provide student reassurance and to deter crime. The uniformed officer stood in his path, told him to keep his hands in front, and began to question him. He was first asked "what was going on" and for his name and address. The plainclothes officers arrived and stood behind the uniformed officer. The questioning turned to whether or not he had ever been arrested and whether "he had anything on him he that he shouldn't". He responded that he had a small amount of marijuana. When the officer asked if there was anything else, he admitted he had a firearm. The officer arrested him and searched him, finding marihuana and a loaded revolver. Grant was charged with five firearms offences.

At trial, the defence motion to exclude the revolver from evidence because of violations of s.8, 9 and 10(b) of the Charter was dismissed. The judge found neither a detention nor a search to trigger Charter rights. The Ontario Court of Appeal dismissed the accused's appeal on the basis the evidence should not be excluded. However, Justice Laskin (McMurtry C.J.O. and Lang J.A. concurring), the trial judge had erred in deciding that the accused had not been detained. The accused was psychologically detained from the time he was asked about his criminal record and when his path was blocked by the officers. The detention had been arbitrary, contrary to section 9 of the Charter.

The Supreme Court of Canada dismissed the appeal. The Court of seven justices were unanimous in deciding that the accused was detained and Charter rights violated but held that the evidence of the firearm should not be excluded under s.24(2). This major aspect of the judgment will be considered later in these materials under *Remedy*.

A lengthy and detailed joint opinion of McLachlin C.J. and Charron J. (LeBel, Fish and Abella JJ. concurring, but with Binnie and Deschamps J. dissenting), concluded that the following should be the approach to detention:—

[17] While the twin principles of purposive and generous interpretation are related and sometimes conflated, they are not the same. The purpose of a right must always be the dominant concern in its interpretation; generosity of interpretation is subordinate to and constrained by that purpose (P. W. Hogg, Constitutional Law of Canada (5th ed. Supp.), vol. 2, at pp. 36-30 and 36-31). While a narrow approach risks impoverishing a Charter right, an overly generous approach risks expanding its protection beyond its intended purposes. In brief, we must construe the language of ss. 9 and 10 in a

generous way that furthers, without overshooting, its purpose: *Big M Drug Mart*, at p. 344.

[18] To interpret "detention" in ss. 9 and 10 generously, yet purposively, we must consider the context in which it is embedded — in other words, the role it plays in conjunction with related protections in the Charter.

(c) The Purpose of the Rights Linked to Detention

[19] Detention represents a limit on the broad right to liberty enjoyed by everyone in Canada at common law and by virtue of s. 7 of the Charter, which guarantees that liberty will only be curtailed in accordance with the principles of fundamental justice. Section 9 of the Charter establishes that "[e]veryone has the right not to be arbitrarily detained or imprisoned." Section 10 accords certain rights to people who are arrested or detained, including the right to retain and instruct counsel.

[20] The purpose of s. 9, broadly put, is to protect individual liberty from unjustified state interference. As recognized by this Court in *Blencoe v. British Columbia (Human Rights Commission)*, 2000 SCC 44, [2000] 2 S.C.R. 307, "liberty", for Charter purposes, is not "restricted to mere freedom from physical restraint", but encompasses a broader entitlement "to make decisions of fundamental importance free from state interference" (para. 49). Thus, s. 9 guards not only against unjustified state intrusions upon physical liberty, but also against incursions on mental liberty by prohibiting the coercive pressures of detention and imprisonment from being applied to people without adequate justification. The detainee's interest in being able to make an informed choice whether to walk away or speak to the police is unaffected by the manner in which the detention is brought about.

[21] More specifically, an individual confronted by state authority ordinarily has the option to choose simply to walk away: *R. v. Esposito* (1985), 24 C.C.C. (3d) 88 (Ont. C.A.), at p. 94; *Dedman v. The Queen*, [1985] 2 S.C.R. 2, at p. 11, citing Martin J.A. in the Ontario Court of Appeal ((1981), 32 O.R. (2d) 641, at p. 653):

> Although a police officer may approach a person on the street and ask him questions, if the person refuses to answer the police officer must allow him to proceed on his way, unless . . . [he] arrests him. . . .

See also Application under s. 83.28 of the Criminal Code (Re), 2004 SCC 42, [2004] 2 S.C.R. 248, at para. 131. Where this choice has been removed — whether by physical or psychological compulsion — the individual is detained. Section 9 guarantees that the state's ability to interfere with personal autonomy will not be exercised arbitrarily. Once detained, the individual's choice whether to speak to the authorities remains, and is protected by the s. 10 informational requirements and the s. 7 right to silence.

[22] "Detention" also identifies the point at which rights subsidiary to detention, such as the right to counsel, are triggered. These rights are engaged by the vulnerable position of the person who has been taken into the effective control of the state authorities. They are principally concerned with addressing the imbalance of power between the state and the person under its control.

More specifically, they are designed to ensure that the person whose liberty has been curtailed retains an informed and effective choice whether to speak to state authorities, consistent with the overarching principle against self-incrimination. They also ensure that the person who is under the control of the state be afforded the opportunity to seek legal advice in order to assist in regaining his or her liberty. As this Court observed in *R. v. Hebert*, [1990] 2 S.C.R. 151:

> In a broad sense, the purpose of ss. 7 to 14 is two-fold to preserve the rights of the detained individual, and to maintain the repute and integrity of our system of justice. More particularly, it is to the control of the superior power of the state vis-à-vis the individual who has been detained by the state, and thus placed in its power, that s. 7 and the related provisions that follow are primarily directed. The state has the power to intrude on the individual's physical freedom by detaining him or her. The individual cannot walk away. This physical intrusion on the individual's mental liberty in turn may enable the state to infringe the individual's mental liberty by techniques made possible by its superior resources and power. [Emphasis added; pp. 179-80.]

[23] By setting limits on the power of the state and imposing obligations with regard to the detained person through the concept of detention, the Charter seeks to effect a balance between the interests of the detained individual and those of the state. The power of the state to curtail an individual's liberty by way of detention cannot be exercised arbitrarily and attracts a reciprocal obligation to accord the individual legal protection against the state's superior power.

(d) Defining Detention

[24] The word "detention" admits of many meanings. Read narrowly, "detention" can be seen as indicating situations where the police take explicit control over the person and command obedience. Read expansively, "detention" can be read as extending to even a fleeting interference or delay. Neither of these extremes offers an acceptable definition of "detention" as used in ss. 9 and 10 of the Charter.

[25] The first extreme was rejected by this Court in *R. v. Therens*, [1985] 1 S.C.R. 613, which held that detention for Charter purposes occurs when a state agent, by way of physical or psychological restraint, takes away an individual's choice simply to walk away. This encompasses not only explicit interference with the subject's liberty by way of physical interference or express command, but any form of "compulsory restraint". A person is detained where he or she "submits or acquiesces in the deprivation of liberty and reasonably believes that the choice to do otherwise does not exist" (*Therens*, at p. 644). It is clear that a person may reasonably believe he or she has no choice in circumstances where there has been no formal assertion of police control. Thus the first interpretation must be rejected. This comports with the principle that a generous rather than legalistic approach must be applied to the interpretation of Charter principles and avoids cramping the purpose of the protections conferred by ss. 9 and 10 of the Charter.

[26] The second interpretation of "detention", reducing it to any interference, however slight, must also be rejected. As held in *Mann*, at para. 19, per Iacobucci J.:

> . . . the police cannot be said to "detain", within the meaning of ss. 9 and 10 of the Charter, every suspect they stop for purposes of identification, or even interview. The person who is stopped will in all cases be "detained" in the sense of "delayed", or "kept waiting". But the constitutional rights recognized by ss. 9 and 10 of the Charter are not engaged by delays that involve no significant physical or psychological restraint.

It is clear that, while the forms of interference s. 9 guards against are broadly defined to include interferences with both physical and mental liberty, not every trivial or insignificant interference with this liberty attracts Charter scrutiny. To interpret detention this broadly would trivialize the applicable Charter rights and overshoot their purpose. Only the individual whose liberty is meaningfully constrained has genuine need of the additional rights accorded by the Charter to people in that situation.

[27] Having rejected the extreme positions advanced, the question is where between them the line that marks detention under ss. 9 and 10 is to be traced. This is a question that is not easily answered in the abstract; as in so many areas of the law, the most useful guidance derives from the decided cases. In what follows, we set out the general principle of choice that underlies the determination. We then discuss situations which illustrate where the line should be drawn.

[28] The general principle that determines detention for Charter purposes was set out in *Therens*: a person is detained where he or she "submits or acquiesces in the deprivation of liberty and reasonably believes that the choice to do otherwise does not exist" (per Le Dain J., at p. 644). This principle is consistent with the notion of choice that underlies our conception of liberty and, as such, shapes our interpretation of ss. 9 and 10 of the Charter. When detention removes the "choice to do otherwise" but comply with a police direction, s. 10(b) serves an indispensable purpose. It protects, among other interests, the detainee's ability to choose whether to cooperate with the investigation by giving a statement. The ambit of detention for constitutional purposes is informed by the need to safeguard this choice without impairing effective law enforcement. This explains why the extremes of formally asserted control on the one hand and a passing encounter on the other have been rejected; the former restricts detention in a way that denies the accused rights he or she needs and should have, while the latter would confer rights where they are neither necessary or appropriate.

[29] The language of ss. 9 and 10 is consistent with this purpose-based approach to detention. The pairing of "detained" and "imprisoned" in s. 9 provides textual guidance for determining where the constitutional line between justifiable and unjustifiable interference should be drawn. "Imprisonment" connotes total or near-total loss of liberty. The juxtaposition of "imprisoned" with "detained" suggests that a "detention" requires significant deprivation of liberty. Similarly, the words "arrest or detention" in s. 10 suggest that a "detention" exists when the deprivation of

liberty may have legal consequences. This linguistic context requires exclusion of police stops where the subject's rights are not seriously in issue.

[30] Moving on from the fundamental principle of the right to choose, we find that psychological constraint amounting to detention has been recognized in two situations. The first is where the subject is legally required to comply with a direction or demand, as in the case of a roadside breath sample. The second is where there is no legal obligation to comply with a restrictive or coercive demand, but a reasonable person in the subject's position would feel so obligated. The rationale for this second form of psychological detention was explained by Le Dain J. in *Therens* as follows:

> In my opinion, it is not realistic, as a general rule, to regard compliance with a demand or direction by a police officer as truly voluntary, in the sense that the citizen feels that he or she has the choice to obey or not, even where there is in fact a lack of statutory or common law authority for the demand or direction and therefore an absence of criminal liability for failure to comply with it. Most citizens are not aware of the precise legal limits of police authority. Rather than risk the application of physical force or prosecution for wilful obstruction, the reasonable person is likely to err on the side of caution, assume lawful authority and comply with the demand. The element of psychological compulsion, in the form of a reasonable perception of suspension of freedom of choice, is enough to make the restraint of liberty involuntary. Detention may be effected without the application or threat of application of physical restraint if the person concerned submits or acquiesces in the deprivation of liberty and reasonably believes that the choice to do otherwise does not exist. [Emphasis added; p. 644.]

[31] This second form of psychological detention — where no legal compulsion exists — has proven difficult to define consistently. The question is whether the police conduct would cause a reasonable person to conclude that he or she was not free to go and had to comply with the police direction or demand. As held in *Therens*, this must be determined objectively, having regard to all the circumstances of the particular situation, including the conduct of the police. As discussed in more detail below and summarized at para. 44, the focus must be on the state conduct in the context of the surrounding legal and factual situation, and how that conduct would be perceived by a reasonable person in the situation as it develops.

[32] The objective nature of this inquiry recognizes that the police must be able to know when a detention occurs, in order to allow them to fulfill their attendant obligations under the Charter and afford the individual its added protections. However, the subjective intentions of the police are not determinative. (Questions such as police "good faith" may become relevant when the test for exclusion of evidence under s. 24(2) is applied, in cases where a Charter breach is found.) While the test is objective, the individual's particular circumstances and perceptions at the time may be relevant in assessing the reasonableness of any perceived power imbalance between the individual and the police, and thus the reasonableness of any perception that he or she had no choice but to comply with the police directive. To answer the question whether there is a detention involves a realistic appraisal of the entire interaction as it developed, not a minute parsing of words and movements. In

those situations where the police may be uncertain whether their conduct is having a coercive effect on the individual, it is open to them to inform the subject in unambiguous terms that he or she is under no obligation to answer questions and is free to go. It is for the trial judge, applying the proper legal principles to the particular facts of the case, to determine whether the line has been crossed between police conduct that respects liberty and the individual's right to choose, and conduct that does not.

[33] In most cases, it will be readily apparent whether or not an encounter between the police and an individual results in a detention. Making the task easier is the fact that what would reasonably be understood by all concerned is often informed by generally understood legal rights and duties, as a few examples illustrate.

[34] At one end of the spectrum of possibilities, detention overlaps with arrest or imprisonment and the Charter will clearly apply. Similarly, a legal obligation to comply with a police demand or direction, such as a breath sample demand at the roadside, clearly denotes s. 9 detention. As Le Dain J. observed in *Therens*, "[i]t is not realistic to speak of a person who is liable to arrest and prosecution for refusal to comply with a demand which a peace officer is empowered by statute to make as being free to refuse to comply" (p. 643).

[35] At the other end of the spectrum lie encounters between individual and police where it would be clear to a reasonable person that the individual is not being deprived of a meaningful choice whether or not to cooperate with a police demand or directive and hence not detained.

[36] We may rule out at the outset situations where the police are acting in a non-adversarial role and assisting members of the public in circumstances commonly accepted as lacking the essential character of a detention. In many common situations, reasonable people understand that the police are not constraining individual choices, but rather helping people or gathering information. For instance, the reasonable person would understand that a police officer who attends at a medical emergency on a 911 call is not detaining the individuals he or she encounters. This is so even if the police in taking control of the situation, effectively interfere with an individual's freedom of movement. Such deprivations of liberty will not be significant enough to attract Charter scrutiny because they do not attract legal consequences for the concerned individuals.

[37] Another often-discussed situation is when police officers approach bystanders in the wake of an accident or crime, to determine if they witnessed the event and obtain information that may assist in their investigation. While many people may be happy to assist the police, the law is clear that, subject to specific provisions that may exceptionally govern, the citizen is free to walk away: *R. v. Grafe* (1987), 36 C.C.C. (3d) 267 (Ont. C.A.). Given the existence of such a generally understood right in such circumstances, a reasonable person would not conclude that his or her right to choose whether to cooperate with them has been taken away. This conclusion holds true even if the person may feel compelled to cooperate with the police out of a sense of moral or civic

duty. The Ontario Court of Appeal adverted to this concept in *Grafe*, where Krever J.A. wrote, at p.271:

> The law has long recognized that although there is no legal duty, there is a moral or social duty on the part of every citizen to answer questions put to him or her by the police and, in that way to assist the police: see, for example, *Rice v. Connolly*, [1966] 2 All E.R. 649 at p. 652, per Lord Parker C.J. Implicit in that moral or social duty is the right of a police officer to ask questions even, in my opinion, when he or she has no belief that an offence has been committed. To be asked questions, in these circumstances, cannot be said to be a deprivation of liberty or security.

[38] In the context of investigating an accident or a crime, the police, unbeknownst to them at that point in time, may find themselves asking questions of a person who is implicated in the occurrence and, consequently, is at risk of self-incrimination. This does not preclude the police from continuing to question the person in the pursuit of their investigation. Section 9 of the Charter does not require that police abstain from interacting with members of the public until they have specific grounds to connect the individual to the commission of a crime. Nor does s. 10 require that the police advise everyone at the outset of any encounter that they have no obligation to speak to them and are entitled to legal counsel.

[39] Effective law enforcement is highly dependent on the cooperation of members of the public. The police must be able to act in a manner that fosters this cooperation, not discourage it. However, police investigative powers are not without limits. The notion of psychological detention recognizes the reality that police tactics, even in the absence of exercising actual physical restraint, may be coercive enough to effectively remove the individual's choice to walk away from the police. This creates the risk that the person may reasonably feel compelled to incriminate himself or herself. Where that is the case, the police are no longer entitled simply to expect cooperation from an individual. Unless, as stated earlier, the police inform the person that he or she is under no obligation to answer questions and is free to go, a detention may well crystallize and, when it does, the police must provide the subject with his or her s. 10(b) rights. That the obligation arises only on detention represents part of the balance between, on the one hand, the individual rights protected by ss. 9 and 10 and enjoyed by all members of society, and on the other, the collective interest of all members of society in the ability of the police to act on their behalf to investigate and prevent crime.

[40] A more complex situation may arise in the context of neighbourhood policing where the police are not responding to any specific occurrence, but where the non-coercive police role of assisting in meeting needs or maintaining basic order can subtly merge with the potentially coercive police role of investigating crime and arresting suspects so that they may be brought to justice. This is the situation that arises in this case.

[41] As discussed earlier, general inquiries by a patrolling officer present no threat to freedom of choice. On the other hand, such inquiries can escalate into situations where the focus shifts from general community-oriented concern to suspicion of a particular individual. Focussed suspicion, in and of itself, does not turn the encounter in a detention. What matters is how the

police, based on that suspicion, interacted with the subject. The language of the Charter does not confine detention to situations where a person is in potential jeopardy of arrest. However, this is a factor that may help to determine whether, in a particular circumstance, a reasonable person would conclude he or she had no choice but to comply with a police officer's request. The police must be mindful that, depending on how they act and what they say, the point may be reached where a reasonable person, in the position of that individual, would conclude he or she is not free to choose to walk away or decline to answer questions.

[42] The length of the encounter said to give rise to the detention may be a relevant consideration. Consider the act of a police officer placing his or her hand on an individual's arm. If sustained, it might well lead a reasonable person to conclude that his or her freedom to choose whether to cooperate or not has been removed. On the other hand, a fleeting touch may not, depending on the circumstances, give rise to a reasonable conclusion that one's liberty has been curtailed. At the same time, it must be remembered that situations can move quickly, and a single forceful act or word may be enough to cause a reasonable person to conclude that his or her right to choose how to respond has been removed.

[43] Whether the individual has been deprived of the right to choose simply to walk away will depend, to reiterate, on all the circumstances of the case. It will be for the trial judge to determine on all the evidence. Deference is owed to the trial judge's findings of fact, although application of the law to the facts is a question of law.

[44] In summary, we conclude as follows:

1. Detention under ss. 9 and 10 of the Charter refers to a suspension of the individual's liberty interest by a significant physical or psychological restraint. Psychological detention is established either where the individual has a legal obligation to comply with the restrictive request or demand, or a reasonable person would conclude by reason of the state conduct that he or she had no choice but to comply.

2. In cases where there is no physical restraint or legal obligation, it may not be clear whether a person has been detained. To determine whether the reasonable person in the individual's circumstances would conclude that he or she had been deprived by the state of the liberty of choice, the court may consider, inter alia, the following factors:

a) The circumstances giving rise to the encounter as would reasonably be perceived by the individual: whether the police were providing general assistance; maintaining general order; making general inquiries regarding a particular occurrence; or, singling out the individual for focussed investigation.

b) The nature of the police conduct, including the language used; the use of physical contact; the place where the interaction occurred; the presence of others; and the duration of the encounter.

c) The particular characteristics or circumstances of the individual where relevant, including age; physical stature; minority status; level of sophistication.

2. Was the Appellant Detained Prior to Incriminating Himself?

[45] Against this background, we return to the question at hand: was Mr. Grant detained within the meaning of ss. 9 and 10 of the Charter before the questions that led him to disclose his firearm? The trial judge held that he was not. An appellate court must approach a trial judge's decision on this issue with appropriate deference. However, we agree with Laskin J.A. that the trial judge's conclusion on the question of detention is undermined by certain key findings of fact that cannot reasonably be supported by the evidence. In the circumstances, it is necessary to revisit the issue.

[46] This is not a clear case of physical restraint or compulsion by operation of law. Accordingly, we must consider all relevant circumstances to determine if a reasonable person in Mr. Grant's position would have concluded that his or her right to choose how to interact with the police (i.e. whether to leave or comply) had been removed.

[47] The encounter began with Cst. Gomes approaching Mr. Grant (stepping in his path) and making general inquiries. Such preliminary questioning is a legitimate exercise of police powers. At this stage, a reasonable person would not have concluded he or she was being deprived of the right to choose how to act, and for that reason there was no detention.

[48] Cst. Gomes then told the appellant to "keep his hands in front of him". This act, viewed in isolation, might be insufficient to indicate detention, on the ground that it was simply a precautionary directive. However, consideration of the entire context of what transpired from this point forward leads to the conclusion that Mr. Grant was detained.

[49] Two other officers approached, flashing their badges and taking tactical adversarial positions behind Cst. Gomes. The encounter developed into one where Mr. Grant was singled out as the object of particularized suspicion, as evidenced by the conduct of the officers. The nature of the questioning changed from ascertaining the appellant's identity to determining whether he "had anything that he shouldn't". At this point the encounter took on the character of an interrogation, going from general neighbourhood policing to a situation where the police had effectively taken control over the appellant and were attempting to elicit incriminating information.

[50] Although Cst. Gomes was respectful in his questioning, the encounter was inherently intimidating. The power imbalance was obviously exacerbated by Mr. Grant's youth and inexperience. Mr. Grant did not testify, so we do not know what his perceptions of the interaction actually were. However, because the test is an objective one, this is not fatal to his argument that there was a detention. We agree with Laskin J.A.'s conclusion that Mr. Grant was detained. In our view, the evidence supports Mr. Grant's contention that a reasonable person in his position (18-years-old, alone, faced by three physically larger policemen in adversarial positions) would conclude that his or her right to choose how to act had been removed by the police, given their conduct.

[51] The police conduct that gave rise to an impression of control was not fleeting. The direction to Mr. Grant to keep his hands in front, in itself

inconclusive, was followed by the appearance of two other officers flashing their badges and by questioning driven by focussed suspicion of Mr. Grant. The sustained and restrictive tenor of the conduct after the direction to Mr. Grant to keep his hands in front of him reasonably supports the conclusion that the officers were putting him under their control and depriving him of his choice as to how to respond.

[52] We conclude that Mr. Grant was detained when Cst. Gomes told him to keep his hands in front of him, the other two officers moved into position behind Cst. Gomes, and Cst. Gomes embarked on a pointed line of questioning. At this point, Mr. Grant's liberty was clearly constrained and he was in need of the Charter protections associated with detention.

The majority found that the detention was arbitrary contrary to s. 9 because the officers did not have legal grounds or reasonable suspicion to detain the accused prior to his incriminating statements .There had also been a breach of Grant's right to counsel under s. 10(b). As determined in *R. v. Suberu*, the s. 10(b) right to counsel arises immediately upon detention, whether or not the detention is for solely for investigative purposes. The officers had not complied with s. 10(b) as they did not believe they had detained him.

In dissent, Justice Binnie voiced concerns as to the majority's approach to detention under ss. 9 and 10 of the Charter. They had laid too much emphasis on the claimant's perception of psychological pressure, albeit as filtered through the eyes of the hypothetical reasonable person in the claimant's situation. A better and broader approach to detention would explicitly take into account (i) the objective facts of such encounters, whether or not evident to the person stopped, as well as (ii) the perception of the police in initiating the encounter, whether or not evident to the person stopped, and (iii) whatever information the police possess at the time, which may or may not be known to the person stopped, as well as whatever change in the police perception occurs as the encounter develops (para. 180).

Binnie J. identifies a number of problems with the Court's reasonable person test for the purpose of determining when a simple interaction crystallizes into a detention. A problem in calibrating the "reasonable person" is to define exactly what information this fictional person possesses and what experience he or she brings to the assessment of the encounter. This was of particular relevance to visible minorities who may, because of their background and experience, feel especially unable to disregard police directions, and feel that assertion of their right to walk away will itself be taken as evasive and subsequently argued by the police to be sufficient grounds of suspicion to justify a *Mann* detention.

Which approach is preferable? For differing views see Stephen Coughlan "Great Strides in Section 9 Jurisprudence" (2009) C.R. (6th) 75 and Tim Quigley, "Was It Worth the Wait? The Supreme Court's New Approaches to Detention and Exclusion of Evidence" (2009) C.R. (6th) 88. It is salutary that the majority confirmed the Ontario Court of Appeal's ruling in

Grant that the concept of psychological detention applies to both vehicle and pedestrian stops where there is a reasonable belief that there is no choice but to comply with a police request. Courts should not play down the coercive realities of all exchanges with police.

The problem with a sole focus on psychological detention from the point of view of suspect is that one who naively or ignorantly thinks he or she is free to go is not detained and is therefore without Charter protection. The test also encourages police to avoid section 9 and 10 rights by delaying arrest, and resorting to such strategies as telling the detainee he or she is free to leave when in fact they are not and are suspected of criminal activity. These concerns would been addressed had the majority adopted as an alternative test that detention also occurs where police have a suspicion which has reached the point that they are attempting to obtain incriminating evidence, whether or not the person was aware of this reality. That was the compromise test carefully articulated by a majority of the Newfoundland Court of Appeal in *R. v. Hawkins* (1992), 14 C.R. (4th) 286 (N.L. C.A.). The Supreme Court certainly gives little justification for rejection the wisdom of lower courts such as the Ontario Court of Appeal in *Moran* (1987), 36 C.C.C. (3d) 225 (Ont. C.A.) that the perceptions of the police are important factors. It is doubtful whether the perceptions of the police will as a practical matter be able to be kept out of the *Grant* inquiry. These general concerns as to the new *Grant* approach are exacerbated by the majority ruling of the Supreme Court in the companion case of *Suberu* that in the circumstances *Suberu* was NOT detained.

R. v. SUBERU
66 C.R. (6th) 127, 245 C.C.C. (3d) 112, [2009] 2 S.C.R. 460 (S.C.C.)

The police received a call that a male was attempting to use a stolen credit card at a liquor store in Cobourg and that the clerk was trying to stall the suspect. Officer R arrived on the scene and saw that another officer was speaking to an individual at the cash register. Another individual, the accused, walked by him saying "he did this, not me, so I guess I can go". The officer replied "wait a minute, I need to talk to you before you go anywhere" and followed the accused outside to a parking lot. The accused sat in the driver's seat of a minivan and the officer engaged him in conversation, asking him questions about his connection to the events in the store. The accused indicated that the man in the shop was his friend and that the van belonged to the accused's girlfriend. Officer R then received information over the radio that two suspects who had used a stolen credit card in Belleville were driving a van. The description of the van and license number matched the van in the parking lot and the officer saw shopping bags in the van. Officer R arrested the accused, advised him of his right to counsel, questioned him, and searched his person and his purse. The accused was found guilty of possession of property obtained by crime and possession of stolen credit and debit cards. On the appeal against conviction, it was argued that his right to counsel under section 10(b) of the Charter had been breached, in that, he had not been advised of his right to counsel immediately upon detaining him for investigative purposes and before asking him any questions that could possibly elicit incriminating answers.

The Ontario Court of Appeal held that a proper interpretation of s. 10(b) in the context of investigative detentions must bear in mind not only the purposes underlying s. 10(b), but the practical realities of the nature, length, and purpose of investigative detentions. A brief interlude between the commencement of an investigative detention and the advising of the detained person's right to counsel under s. 10(b) during which the officer makes a quick assessment of the situation to decide whether anything more than a brief detention of the individual may be warranted, was not inconsistent with the requirement that a detained person be advised of his or her right to counsel "without delay". Here there had been no section 10(b) violation.

The Supreme Court however refused to accept that the right to be advised of counsel under s. 10(b) "without delay" could be tempered as the Court of Appeal had suggested. The phrase had to be interpreted purposively, in order to ensure that individuals know of their right to counsel and have access to it in situations where they suffer a significant deprivation of liberty due to state coercion which leaves them vulnerable to the exercise of state power and in a position of legal jeopardy. Specifically, the right to counsel was meant to assist detainees regain their liberty, and to guard against the risk of involuntary self-incrimination. That risk was created at the outset of a detention, and so it was logical to interpret "without delay" to mean "immediately". To allow for a delay between the outset of a detention and the engagement of the police duties under section 10(b), the Court held, would create an ill-defined and unworkable test for the application of the section 10(b) right.

However the Supreme Court decided 5-2 that Suberu had, applying the new *Grant* criteria, not been detained and there was no s. 10(b) breach.

Chief Justice McLACHLIN and Justice CHARRON (Justices LeBel, Deschamps and Abella concurring):—

[28] As discussed more fully in *Grant*, in a situation where the police believe a crime has recently been committed, the police may engage in preliminary questioning of bystanders without giving rise to a detention under ss. 9 and 10 of the Charter. Despite a police request for information or assistance, a bystander is under no legal obligation to comply. This legal proposition must inform the perspective of the reasonable person in the circumstances of the person being questioned. The onus is on the applicant to show that in the circumstances he or she was effectively deprived of his or her liberty of choice. The test is an objective one and the failure of the applicant to testify as to his or her perceptions of the encounter is not fatal to the application. However, the applicant's contention that the police by their conduct effected a significant deprivation of his or her liberty must find support in the evidence.

[29] The line between general questioning and focussed interrogation amounting to detention may be difficult to draw in particular cases. It is the task of the trial judge on a Charter application to assess the circumstances and determine whether the line between general questioning and detention has been crossed. While the trial judge in this case did not have the benefit of the test refined in *Grant*, his findings on the facts, supported by the evidence, lead to the view that a reasonable person in the circumstances would have concluded that the initial encounter was preliminary investigative questioning falling short of detention.

[30] The trial judge characterized the factual situation at issue as "an exploratory investigation in which Constable Roughley was fully justified and duly [sic] bound to pursue a cursory questioning of Suberu". He went on to observe that "the introductory and preliminary questions were merely to determine if there was any involvement by this person before him". As the trial judge put it: "One must ask a number of preliminary questions to determine how to proceed thereafter. Until that information was obtained as to a possible criminal offence and who the party was, no detention or arrest or rights to caution, in my view, were required."

[31] The trial judge's finding that the initial part of the encounter was of a preliminary or exploratory nature on its face does not support the contention that Mr. Suberu was under detention within the meaning of the Charter at this point. It suggests rather that Constable Roughley's conduct indicated that he was engaged in a general inquiry and had not yet zeroed in on the individual as someone whose movements must be controlled. Looking at the matter through the lens of the detention analysis proposed in *Grant*, the trial judge's conclusion that the circumstances did not trigger the right to counsel cannot be said to be in error. There was no right to counsel because there was no detention.

[32] The first factor directs us to the circumstances giving rise to the encounter, as reasonably perceived by an individual in Mr. Suberu's position. The evidence indicates that Constable Roughley engaged Mr. Suberu in an attempt to orient himself to the situation as it was unfolding in front of him. A possible crime had just occurred, and the police had arrived to investigate the matter. However, as Binnie J. aptly observes (para. 62), it would be absurd to suggest that Constable Roughley should give everyone present their right to counsel before proceeding to sort out the situation. In our view, it would also be unreasonable to require that the right to counsel be given the moment the police approach any suspect in the process of sorting out the situation. In the circumstances here, one man appeared to be involved in the matter under investigation and another, Mr. Suberu, had attracted attention. Constable Roughley was engaging him to determine, in the trial judge's words, "if there was any involvement by this person". The evidence was that it occurred to Constable Roughley that this man might be involved. However, on the officer's evidence, he did not at that time believe he had sufficient information to act on his suspicion by detaining Mr. Suberu. It was only after he received additional information over the radio linking the appellant, the van, and the contents of the van to an offence that he believed the appellant was involved in a criminal act such that he could not allow the appellant to leave the scene. As a whole,

the circumstances of the encounter support a reasonable perception that Constable Roughley was orienting himself to the situation rather than intending to deprive Mr. Suberu of his liberty. Further, as noted, Mr. Suberu did not testify or call evidence on that matter. In summary, the circumstances, as revealed by the evidence, do not suggest detention.

[33] Further light is shed by considering the police conduct, the second factor in the *Grant* detention analysis. The question is whether the police conduct, taken as a whole, supported a reasonable conclusion that Mr. Suberu had no choice but to comply. As Mr. Suberu walked past Constable Roughley, he said, "He did this, not me, so I guess I can go." Constable Roughley followed him to his van and as Mr. Suberu entered it, said, "Wait a minute, I need to talk to you before you go anywhere." In the context, these words admit more than one interpretation. They might be understood as, "I need to talk to you to get more information". They might also be construed as an order not to leave, suggestive of putting Mr. Suberu under police control. In interpreting these words, it is relevant to note that Constable Roughley made no move to obstruct Mr. Suberu's movement. He simply spoke to him as he sat in his van. Further, while the exact duration of the encounter is not clear on the record, it was characterized by the Court of Appeal as a "very brief dialogue" (para. 17). Taken as a whole, the conduct of the officer viewed objectively supports the trial judge's view that what was happening at this point was preliminary questioning to find out whether to proceed further.

[34] The third factor to consider is the individual's personal circumstances as they bear on the dynamics of the encounter. As already indicated, the test is objective, incorporating the perspectives of the person spoken to in the dynamic context of the evolving situation. The question is whether a reasonable person in the circumstances thus viewed would have concluded by reason of the state conduct that he or she had no choice but to comply. As discussed above, the fact that a person is delayed by the police is insufficient to ground a reasonable conclusion that he or she was not free to go, or that he or she was bound to comply with the officer's request for information. Mr. Suberu did not testify on the application, and there was no evidence as to whether he subjectively believed that he could not leave. Nor was there evidence of his personal circumstances, feelings or knowledge. The only evidence came from Constable Roughley, who testified that he was merely "exploring the situation". The Officer testified that Mr. Suberu never told him that he did not wish to speak with him, and that the conversation was not "strained".

[35] We conclude that, viewed through the lens of *Grant*, the trial judge cannot be said to have erred in effectively finding that Mr. Suberu was not detained within the meaning of the Charter when Constable Roughley spoke to him in his van. It follows that there was no violation of the appellant's right under s. 10(b) of the Charter.

Justices Binnie and Fish, in separate reasons, disagreed with this conclusion. It would be clear to a reasonable person in the accused's situation that he had been stopped at an alleged crime scene and was not free to walk away. In context the accused's words to the officer amounted to the question "can I leave" and the officer's response amounted to "no". In that event there was at that point a detention. No rational person in Suberu's shoes would have thought he was free to walk away or that the police would have let him go, had he tried. There was therefore a violation of section 10(b) and the evidence ought to have been excluded and a new trial ordered.

It is indeed hard to accept that Suberu was not detained as was the consensus in the courts below. The discrepancy between the ruling on the facts in *Grant* and that in *Suberu* will undoubtedly lead to uncertainty and protracted litigation. The concern about *Suberu* is that since the Court has determined that s. 10(b) rights apply immediately to investigative detention some courts will bend over backwards to find that there was no detention, as in *Suberu*. On the other hand, the ruling in *Grant* seems to find that detention arises the moment aggressive police questioning has crystallised in to trying to obtain incrimination evidence.

Surely, contrary to some recent pre *Grant* rulings suspects are detained when police start to ask a person for identification to facilitate a criminal records search and/or search back packs whether the person is in a vehicle, place of public transit or in the street. See *R. v. Rajaratnam* (2006), 43 C.R. (6th) 280, 214 C.C.C. (3d) 547 (Alta. C.A.), *R. v. Lewis* (2007), 217 C.C.C. (3d) 82 (N.S. C.A.) and *R. v. B. (L.)* (2007), 49 C.R. (6th) 245, 227 C.C.C. (3d) 70 (Ont. C.A.). Compare *R. v. Harris* (2007), 49 C.R. (6th) 220, 225 C.C.C. (3d) 193 (Ont. C.A.) (majority holding no power to compel identification other than for traffic offences leading to s. 8 breach). See also the persuasive analyses of Lane J. in *R. v. Powell* (2000), 35 C.R. (5th) 89 (Ont. C.J.) (pedestrian stopped for identification and records check arbitrarily detained), Jones J. in *R. v. D. (J.)* (2007), 45 C.R. (6th) 292 (Ont. C.J.) and LaForme J. (as he then was) in *R. v. Ferdinand* (2004), 21 C.R. (6th) 65 (Ont. S.C.J.), who said:

> It needs repeating once again: stopping and investigating people merely because of some "Spidey sense" being engaged goes far beyond the standards our society demands and expects of our police. Young people have the right to "just hang out" especially in their neighbourhood and to move freely without fear of being detained and searched on mere whim, and without being being advised of their rights, and without their consent. Mere hunches do not give the police the grounds to "surprise" a group of young people or to "get right on them" for investigative purposes without something further that provides a lawful basis for doing so.

In view of *Grant* and *Suberu*, has there been a detention within the meaning of s. 10 in the following cases? At what point?

PROBLEM 1

The police have a suspect in a sexual assault case. They telephone him and ask him if he would not mind coming down to the police station to assist them in their inquiries. He does so and is taken to an interrogation room where the police begin to question him. What if the

questioning had taken place in the suspect's living room? What if he submitted to a polygraph test? What if he failed?

Compare *R. v. Esposito* (1985), 53 O.R. (2d) 356, 49 C.R. (3d) 193, 24 C.C.C. (3d) 88, leave to appeal to S.C.C. refused, 53 O.R. (2d) 356n, 50 C.R. (3d) xxvn, 24 C.C.C. (3d) 88n, *R. v. Smith* (1986), 49 C.R. (3d) 210, 25 C.C.C. (3d) 361 (Man. C.A.), *R. v. Belliveau* (1986), 54 C.R. (3d) 144, 25 C.C.C. (3d) 361 (N.B. C.A.), *R. v. Jacobs* (1987), 54 C.R. (3d) 352, 30 C.C.C. (3d) 163, 31 C.C.C. (3d) 40 (Alta. C.A.), *R. v. Voss* (1989), 71 C.R. (3d) 178, 50 C.C.C. (3d) 58 (Ont. C.A.), *R. v. Lawrence* (1990), 80 C.R. (3d) 289 (Ont. C.A.), *R. v. Amyot* (1990), 78 C.R. (3d) 129, 58 C.C.C. (3d) 312 (Qué. C.A.), *R. v. Caputo* (1997), 114 C.C.C. (3d) 1 (Ont. C.A.) and *R. v. Johns* (1998), 14 C.R. (5th) 302, 123 C.C.C. (3d) 190 (Ont. C.A.).

PROBLEM 2

Following a motor vehicle accident, the accused was invited to sit in the police car where he was asked to show his driving licence and car registration to explain how the accident occurred. He was later taken by ambulance to a hospital. When he came out of the x-ray room, an officer told him he was detained on a charge of drunk driving, advising him of his right to counsel. The officer knew that a person injured in the accident had died but did not inform the accused of this fact. The accused is later charged with causing death by criminal negligence.

Compare *R. v. Black*, [1989] 2 S.C.R. 138, 70 C.R. (3d) 47, 50 C.C.C. (3d) 1 (S.C.C.), *R. v. Nelson* (1982), 32 C.R. (3d) 256, 3 C.C.C. (3d) 147 (Man. Q.B.), *R. v. Chartrand* (1992), 15 C.R. (4th) 231, 74 C.C.C. (3d) 409 (Man. C.A.), *R. v. Sawatsky* (1997), 9 C.R. (5th) 23, 118 C.C.C. (3d) 17 (Ont. C.A.) and *R. v. Evans*, [1991] 1 S.C.R. 869, 4 C.R. (4th) 144, 63 C.C.C. (3d) 289 (S.C.C.). The leading authority is now *R. v. Sinclair*, [2010] 2 S.C.R. 310, 259 C.C.C. (3d) 443, 77 C.R. (6th) 203 (S.C.C.), considered later in this chapter.

PROBLEM 3

Police officers on a routine patrol in their cruiser noticed two pedestrians on a sidewalk staring at them, in their view, suspiciously. The officers stopped and asked the pedestrians' names. There was conflict in the evidence as to whether the police officers made the request from inside or outside the cruiser. One of the pedestrians, the accused, wrongly gave the name of his brother, since he knew he had not yet paid a fine for trespassing. When the police later discovered the misidentification, they charged the accused with fraudulent personation contrary to s. 361(1) of the Criminal Code.

Compare *R. v. Grafe* (1987), 60 C.R. (3d) 242, 36 C.C.C. (3d) 267 (Ont. C.A.).

PROBLEM 4

The police were investigating a shortage of funds involving a community recreation committee. An examination of a number of committee documents and records lead them to the treasurer, the accused. A police officer visited her at her place of employment and said he wanted to talk to her about the shortages of money. He told her that he would pick her up an hour later and take her down to the police station for an interview. He did so, there questioned her, and obtained a statement. The accused was frightened and felt that she was obliged to accompany him.

Compare *R. v. Keats* (1987), 60 C.R. (3d) 250 (Nfld. C.A.).

PROBLEM 5

The accused arrived at Toronto International Airport from Jamaica. A customs inspector observed that she was nervous and referred her for a secondary inspection. Another inspector's suspicions were further aroused by the accused presenting unsatisfactory identification and because she appeared slightly heavy and bulging in the area of her upper abdomen. She was taken to a search room where a body search was conducted under the authority of the Customs Act. Six plastic bags of hash oil were found wrapped in bandages around the accused's body. At this point she was arrested, charged with importing a narcotic and read her Charter rights. Compare *R. v. Simmons* (1984), 45 O.R. (2d) 609, 39 C.R. (3d) 223 (Ont. C.A.), overruled on this point, [1988] 2 S.C.R. 495, 66 C.R. (3d) 297, 45 C.C.C. (3d) 296 (S.C.C.).

The Supreme Court's interpretation of the content of the section 10(*b*) guarantee has been dominated by the majority judgments of Chief Justice Lamer. He summarized his approach distinguishing between informational and implementational duties:

R. v. BARTLE
[1994] 3 S.C.R. 173, 33 C.R. (4th) 1, 92 C.C.C. (3d) 289 (S.C.C.)

LAMER C.J. (La Forest, Sopinka, Gonthier, Cory, McLachlin, Iacobucci and Major JJ. concurring):—

(a) *The Purpose of Section 10(b)*

The purpose of the right to counsel guaranteed by s. 10(*b*) of the Charter is to provide detainees with an opportunity to be informed of their rights and obligations under the law and, most importantly, to obtain advice on how to exercise those rights and fulfil those obligations. This opportunity is made available because, when an individual is detained by state authorities, he or she is put in a position of disadvantage relative to the state. Not only has this person suffered a deprivation of liberty, but also this person may be at risk of incriminating him- or herself. Accordingly, a person who is "detained" within the meaning of s. 10 of the Charter is in immediate need of legal advice in order to protect his or her right against self-incrimination and to assist him or her in regaining his or her liberty. Under s. 10(b), a detainee is entitled as of right to seek such legal advice "without delay" and upon request.

(b) *The Duties Under Section 10(b)*

This Court has said on numerous previous occasions that s. 10(*b*) of the Charter imposes the following duties on state authorities who arrest or detain a person:

(1)   to inform the detainee of his or her right to retain and instruct counsel without delay and of the existence and availability of legal aid and duty counsel;

(2)   if a detainee has indicated a desire to exercise this right, to provide the detainee with a reasonable opportunity to exercise the right (except in urgent and dangerous circumstances); and

(3)   to refrain from eliciting evidence from the detainee until he or she has had that reasonable opportunity, again, except in cases of urgency or danger.

The first duty is an informational one which is directly in issue here. The second and third duties are more in the nature of implementation duties and are not triggered unless and until a detainee indicates a desire to exercise his or her right to counsel.

Importantly, the right to counsel under s. 10(*b*) is not absolute. Unless a detainee invokes the right and is reasonably diligent in exercising it, the correlative duty on the police to provide a reasonable opportunity and to refrain from eliciting evidence will either not arise in the first place or will be suspended. Furthermore, the rights guaranteed by s. 10(b) may be waived by the detainee, although the standard for waiver will be high, especially in circumstances where the alleged waiver has been implicit.

(b) Informational Duties

Unlike the Bill of Rights, s. 10(*b*) of the Charter expressly confers the right to be informed of the right to retain and instruct counsel. It is clearly mandatory on arrest or detention "without delay", which under *Suberu* means "immediately". A failure to so inform will, by itself, constitute a violation of s. 10(*b*).

R. v. BRYDGES

[1990] 1 S.C.R. 190, 74 C.R. (3d) 129, 53 C.C.C. (3d) 330 (S.C.C.)

The accused, a resident of Alberta, was arrested in Manitoba on a charge of murder which had occurred in Edmonton 6 years previously. He was informed without delay of his right to retain and instruct counsel. Upon arrival at the police station, the accused was placed in an interview room and, at the beginning of the interrogation, given another opportunity to call a lawyer. The accused asked the officer if they had Legal Aid in Manitoba because he could not afford a private lawyer. The officer, who was from Edmonton, answered that he imagined that they had such a system in Manitoba. The officer then asked whether there was a reason for him to want to talk to a lawyer right then. The accused answered "Not right now no". The accused made a number of statements. He later interrupted the questioning and requested a Legal Aid lawyer. The Legal Aid lawyer contacted by the police advised the accused not to say anything more and the interrogation ended. At trial, the judge found that, at the beginning of the interrogation, the accused essentially requested the assistance of counsel but that he was unsure if he could afford one. He held that the police should have assisted the accused by determining the availability of Legal Aid at that time. He found the accused's rights under s. 10(*b*) violated and excluded the statements. The accused was acquitted. A majority of the Court of Appeal set aside the acquittal and ordered a new trial.

LAMER J. (Wilson, Gonthier and Cory JJ. concurring):—

. . .

Once the appellant in effect requested the assistance of counsel it was incumbent on the police officer to facilitate contact with counsel by giving the appellant a reasonable opportunity to exercise his right to counsel. On the specific facts of this case, the court is faced with the following question: when an accused expresses a concern that his inability to afford a lawyer is an impediment to the exercise of the right to counsel, is there a duty on the police to inform him of the existence of duty counsel and the ability to apply for Legal Aid? In my view there is. I say this because imposing this duty on the police in these circumstances is consistent with the purpose underlying the right to retain and instruct counsel. A detainee is advised of the right to retain and instruct counsel without delay because it is upon arrest or detention that an accused is in *immediate need of legal advice*. As I stated in *Manninen*, supra, at p. 1243, one of the main functions of counsel at this early stage of detention is to confirm the existence of the right to remain silent and to advise the detainee about how to exercise that right. It is not always the case that immediately upon detention an accused will be concerned about retaining the lawyer that will eventually represent him at a trial, if there is one. Rather, one of the important reasons for retaining legal advice without delay upon being detained is linked to the protection of the right against self-incrimination. This is precisely the reason that there is a duty on the police to cease questioning the detainee until he has had a reasonable opportunity to retain and instruct counsel.

On the facts of the case at bar, it is clear that the advice the appellant received from the Legal Aid lawyer he spoke to was to the effect that, and this was a situation which is not always the case, he should rest on his right not to make any more statements until he spoke to a lawyer in Edmonton. In retrospect, had the appellant been informed of the availability of duty counsel or Legal Aid at the time that he first raised a concern about affordability, the subsequent interrogation may never have taken place.

. . .

The failure of the police to inform the appellant of the existence of Legal Aid or duty counsel at the time that he first indicated a concern about his ability to pay a lawyer, was a restriction on the appellant's right to counsel, insofar as the appellant was left with an erroneous impression of the nature and extent of his s. 10(*b*) rights. As a result, I would conclude, along with the trial judge and Harradence J.A. in dissent at the Court of Appeal, that the appellant's s. 10(*b*) rights were violated.

. . .

Although my reasons thus far are sufficient to dispose of this appeal in favour of the appellant, I feel compelled to make certain comments on the broader question raised by Watt J. in *Parks*, supra, namely whether it should be part of the information component of the constitutional guarantee under s. 10(*b*) that accused persons should be told as a matter of routine *in all cases* of arrest or detention of the existence and availability of duty counsel and Legal Aid plans. In my view, it is consistent with the purpose underlying s. 10(*b*) of the Charter to impose that duty on the police in all cases of detention. I find it necessary to address this issue because otherwise, among other reasons, there is an element of uncertainty facing law enforcement officials as a result of the disposition of this appeal. Although, in a case like *Parks* or the case at bar, it is clear that the accused expressed a concern about the inability to afford counsel acting as an impediment to the exercise of the right to counsel, that will not be the case in all situations. For example, there may be cases where the detainee does not explicitly ask for or about Legal Aid, but still expresses a concern about affordability of counsel. Additionally, there may be cases where a detainee says nothing about his inability to afford counsel because he believes it is a forgone conclusion that unless he can afford a lawyer, there is no other way to exercise the right to retain and instruct counsel. Thus, police officers would be put in the difficult position of having to judge, on the spot, whether a person has expressed concerns about affordability or whether there should be further inquiries made of a detainee who does not express concerns about affordability but whom the police officer suspects may be indigent and in need of duty counsel or Legal Aid. In fact, it is most often the indigent and the disadvantaged in our society that are not as aware of the schemes that the state has set up on their behalf. In this respect I quote from the landmark decision of the United States Supreme Court in *Miranda v. Arizona*, 384 U.S. 426 (1965), at p. 473:

> The warning of a right to counsel would be hollow if not couched in terms that would convey to the indigent—the person most often subjected to interrogation—the knowledge that he too has a right to have counsel present. As with the warning of the right to remain silent and of the general right to counsel, only by effective and express explanation to the indigent of this right can there be assurance that he was truly in a position to exercise it.

In my view then, these policy concerns in respect of making police officers' duties under the Charter clear and of ensuring that all detainees are made aware of the existence of duty counsel and Legal Aid complement each other, and support the view that information about the existence and availability of duty counsel and Legal Aid plans should be part of the standard s. 10(*b*) caution upon arrest or detention.

. . .

Before concluding, it is my view that in light of the imposition of the additional duty on the police as part of the information component of s. 10(*b*) caution, a transition period is appropriate. This transition period is needed to enable the police to properly discharge their new burden, more specifically to take into account the reality that police officers often use printed cards from which they read the caution given to detainees. In my view a period of 30 days from the date of this judgment is sufficient time for the police forces to react, and to prepare new cautions. I note, in passing, that the imposition of a transition period is not unusual. In *Mills v. R.*, [1986] 1 S.C.R. 863, for example, I stated that a transitional period was appropriate in the context of the application of the principles developed under s. 11(*b*) of the Charter. In addition, in *Reference Re Manitoba Language Rights*, [1985] 1 S.C.R. 721, this court established a period of temporary validity for the Acts of the Manitoba legislature, in order to allow for the translation, re-enactment, printing and publishing of previously unilingual legislation.

I would, accordingly, allow the appeal and restore the acquittal of the appellant at trial.

LA FOREST J. (L'Heureux-Dubé and McLachlin, JJ. concurring):—I agree with Lamer J. that on the facts of this case the appeal should be allowed and the acquittal restored, but I find it unnecessary to consider the broader issues raised by my colleague in the latter part of his reasons.

See Peter B. Michalyshyn, "*Brydges*: Should the Police be Advising of the Right to Counsel?" (1990) 74 C.R. (3d) 151.

PROBLEM 6

After *Brydges*, the standard caution carried by police officers in Ontario was changed to the following:

1. It is my duty to inform you that you have a right to retain and instruct counsel without delay.
2. You have the right to telephone any lawyer you wish.
3. You also have the right to free advice from a legal aid lawyer.
4. If you are charged with an offence, you may apply to the Ontario Legal Aid Plan for assistance.
5. Do you understand?
6. Do you wish to call a lawyer now?

In Ontario there is immediate and free access to duty counsel available throughout the province on a 1-800 (toll-free) telephone number at all times of the day and night. The number is well known at all police stations. Do you think that the right to be informed of the right to

counsel has been violated if officers read the standard caution but do not inform the detainee of the 1-800 number?

The Supreme Court held that this would be a breach, reversing the contrary opinion of the Ontario Court of Appeal.

R. v. BARTLE
(1994), 33 C.R. (4th) 1 (S.C.C.)

The accused was arrested for impaired driving after he failed a roadside breath test in the early hours of a Saturday morning. The arresting officer read the accused his rights under s. 10(*b*) of the Charter from a pre-printed caution card that mentioned the availability of legal aid. The officer did not, however, refer to the fact that free and immediate preliminary legal advice was available from duty counsel, who could be reached by calling a toll-free number printed on the caution card. After being taken to the police station, the appellant was twice asked whether he wanted to call a lawyer. Again, no mention was made of the toll-free number for free duty counsel. On both occasions the accused declined.

LAMER C.J. (La Forest, Sopinka, Gonthier, Cory, McLachlin, Iacobucci and Major JJ. concurring):—

. . .

[It] is critical that the information component of the right to counsel be comprehensive in scope and that it be presented by police authorities in a "timely and comprehensible manner: *R. v. Dubois*. . . . Unless they are clearly and fully informed of their rights *at the outset*, detainees cannot be expected to make informed choices and decisions about whether or not to contact counsel and, in turn, whether to exercise other rights, such as their right to silence: *Hebert*. Moreover, in light of the rule that, absent special circumstances, indicating that a detainee may not understand the s. 10(*b*) caution, such a language difficulties or a known or obvious mental disability, police are not required to assure themselves that a detainee fully understands the s. 10(*b*) caution, it is important that the standard caution given to detainees be as instructive and clear as possible: *R. v. Baig* ... and *Evans* ...

Indeed, the pivotal function of the information component under s. 10(*b*) has already been recognized by this court. For instance, in *Evans*, McLachlin J. for the majority, stated . . . that a "person who does not understand his or her right cannot be expected to assert it". In that case, it was held that, in circumstances which suggest that a particular detainee may not understand the information being communicated to him or her by state authorities, a mere recitation of the right to counsel will not suffice. Authorities will have to take additional steps to ensure that the detainee comprehends his or her s. 10(*b*) rights. Likewise, this court has stressed on previous occasions that, before an accused can be said to have waived his or her right to counsel, he or she must be possessed of sufficient information to allow him or her to make an informed choice as regards exercising the right: *R. v. Smith* ... and *Brydges* ...

To conclude, because the purpose of the right to counsel under s. 10(*b*) is about providing detainees with meaningful choices, it follows that a detainee should be fully advised of available services *before* being expected to assert that right, particularly given that subsequent duties on the state are not triggered unless and until a detainee expresses a desire to contact counsel. In my opinion, the purpose of the right to counsel would be defeated if police were only required to advise detainees of the existence and availability of Legal Aid and duty counsel *after* some triggering assertion of the right by the detainee.

. . .

A detainee is entitled under the information component of s. 10(*b*) of the Charter to be advised of whatever system for free, preliminary legal advice exists in the jurisdiction and of how such advice can be accessed (e.g., by calling a 1-800 number, or being provided with a list of telephone numbers for lawyers acting as duty counsel). What remains to be decided, then, is whether the caution given to the appellant by the police in this case complied with the informational requirements under s. 10(*b*), or whether the appellant waived his informational s. 10(*b*) rights. It is to this question that I now turn.

(f) *Application*

At the time when the appellant was arrested and detained, there was in place in Ontario a 24-hour duty counsel service accessible by dialling a toll-free number. This service was known to the police and, indeed, the 1-800 number was printed on their caution cards. Section 10(*b*) required that the existence and availability of this duty counsel system and how to access it be routinely communicated by police in a timely and comprehensible manner to detainees. In reviewing what was said to the appellant, both at the roadside where he was arrested and later, at the police station, I am of the opinion that the appellant was not properly informed of his rights under s. 10(*b*). As a result, he may have been misled about the nature and extent of his right to counsel, particularly given that he was detained during the early hours of a Saturday, a time when a person might reasonably expect that immediate legal assistance would not be available.

On its face, the caution extended to the appellant both at the roadside and at the police station did not advise him of the existence and availability of any "duty counsel" service, nor did it provide him with the toll-free telephone number by which the service could be accessed. However, what must be considered is whether, despite the absence of precise words to this effect, the essence of the appellant's right to immediate and temporary free legal advice was adequately communicated to him, or, alternatively, whether the appellant fully understood his rights and waived the right to be expressly informed of them by the authorities. In my opinion, the s. 10(*b*) caution that the appellant received, both at the roadside and at the police station, failed to convey the necessary sense of immediacy and universal availability of legal assistance. First, when the appellant was arrested at the roadside, he was not told of the existence of the 1-800 number for duty counsel and that he would be allowed to call a lawyer as soon as he arrived at the police station where there were telephones. Although it was subsequently made clear upon arrival at the station that he could call "now", the appellant had, in the intervening period between detention at the roadside and arrival at the station, made a self-incriminating statement. Second, reference to Legal Aid was confusing in so far as it implied that free legal advice, while available, was contingent on applying for it once charged—a process which takes time and for which there are qualifying financial requirements. The caution he received failed to communicate the fact that, at the pre-charge stage, a detainee has the opportunity by virtue of the scheme for immediate legal assistance set up by Ontario to speak to duty counsel and to obtain preliminary legal advice before incriminating him- or herself.

The 1-800 number, or at least the existence of a toll-free telephone number, should have been conveyed to the appellant upon his arrest at the roadside even though there were no telephones available. Indeed, the police should have explained to the appellant that, as soon as they reached the police station, he would be permitted to use a telephone for the purpose of calling a lawyer, including duty counsel which was available to give him immediate, free legal advice. It can hardly be described as an undue hardship on police to require them to provide detainees with this basic information, especially when the toll-free number is already printed on their caution cards. I am satisfied that the 1-800 number was part of the informational requirement under s. 10(*b*) of the Charter. I agree with counsel for the appellant that, in today's highly technological and computerized world, 1-800 numbers are simple and effective means of conveying the sense of immediacy and universal availability of legal assistance which the majority of this Court in *Brydges* said must be conveyed as part of the standard s. 10(*b*) warning in jurisdictions where such a service exists.

Furthermore, the appellant did not waive his right to receive a caution that fully informed him of his right to counsel. Although detainees can waive their s. 10(*b*) rights, valid waivers of the informational component of s. 10(*b*) will, in my view, be rare. As I stated in *Korponay v. Attorney General of Canada*, [1982] 1 S.C.R. 41 at p. 49, the validity of a waiver of a procedural right ". . . is dependent upon it being clear and unequivocal that the person is waiving the procedural safeguard and is doing so with full knowledge of the rights the procedure was enacted to protect. This standard applies equally to waivers of Charter rights, including the rights guaranteed by s. 10(*b*): *Evans*, supra, at p. 894. In the case of s. 10(*b*)'s informational component, requiring that a person waiving the right have "full knowledge" of it means that he or she must already be fully apprised of the information that he or she has the right to receive. A person who waives the right to be informed of something without knowing what it was that he or she had the right to be informed of can hardly be said to be possessed of "full knowledge" of his or her rights. For this reason, the fact that a detainee indicates that he or she does not wish to hear the information conveyed by the standard police "caution" mandated by s. 10(*b*) will not, by itself, be enough to constitute a valid waiver of s. 10(*b*)'s informational component.

(c) Implementation Duties

The following passage of Laskin J. in his minority concurring judgment in *Brownridge* under the Bill is still referred to (1972), 18 C.R.N.S. 308 at 328:

> The right to retain and instruct counsel without delay can only have meaning to an arrested or detained person if it is taken as raising a correlative obligation upon the police authorities to facilitate contact with counsel. This means allowing him upon his request to use the telephone for that purpose if one is available. I am not concerned in this case with determining how many calls must be permitted. Here, on the facts, the accused was prevented from making even one. I am content to say for the purposes of this case that the accused's right under s. 2(c)(ii) would have been sufficiently recognized if, having been permitted to telephone, he had reached his counsel and had spoken with him over the telephone. I would not construe the right given by s. 2(c)(ii), when invoked by an accused upon whom a demand is made under s. 223(1), as entitling him to insist on the personal attendance of his counsel if he can reach him by telephone.

In *R. v. Louttit* (1974), 21 C.C.C. (2d) 84 at 86 (Man. C.A.) Freedman C.J. remarked that:

> The "one phone call" rule is a fiction propagated by Hollywood. Reasonable conduct by the police is always required, and that may in the appropriate circumstances require that a plurality of telephone calls be permitted.

Some courts held that privacy should be afforded in all cases and others only when it was requested. In *Jumaga v. R.*, [1977] 1 S.C.R. 486, 34 C.R.N.S. 172, 29 C.C.C. (2d) 269 (S.C.C.), the majority of the Supreme Court held that there was no obligation on the police to afford privacy at least in the absence of a request by the accused.

These are decisions under the Bill of Rights. In *R. v. Pavel* (1989), 74 C.R. (3d) 195, 53 C.C.C. (3d) 296 (Ont. C.A.) the Ontario Court expressly adopted *Louttit* in holding that an abortive telephone call to a lawyer following the advice that he could only make one call violated s. 10(*b*). The positive wording of s. 10(*b*) has been relied upon to distinguish *Jumaga* to hold that privacy must be afforded whether or not it is requested: see *R. v. Playford* (1987), 61 C.R. (3d) 101, 40 C.C.C. (3d) 142, 63 O.R. (2d) 289 (Ont. C.A.). Of course the accused has to establish that privacy was in fact breached and whether he asked for privacy may be a factor in the inquiry: *R. v. Burley* (2004), 181 C.C.C. (3d) 463 (Ont. C.A.) and *R. v. O'Donnell* (2004), 19 C.R. (6th) 354, 185 C.C.C. (3d) 367 (N.B. C.A.).

R. v. MANNINEN
[1987] 1 S.C.R. 1233, 58 C.R. (3d) 97, 34 C.C.C. (3d) 385 (S.C.C.)

LAMER J.:—This appeal raises once again the difficult question of the exclusion of evidence under s. 24(2) of the Canadian Charter of Rights and Freedoms, this time in the context of the right to counsel in s. 10(*b*).

FACTS

On 26th October 1982 there was a robbery at a Mac's Milk store in Toronto. According to the store owner and an employee, the robber was armed with a gun and a knife and he wore a grey sweatshirt with a hood. The store owner and the employee could not positively identify the gun, the knife or the sweatshirt found in the car driven by the respondent at the time of his arrest, except to say that the sweatshirt was similar in colour. An eyewitness saw a man running from the store to a car, and he noted the licence number of the car. The car had been stolen a few hours previously.

On 28th October, two days after the robbery, police officers MacIver and Train, acting on information received, attended at E & R. Simonizing on Caledonia Road in Toronto at around 1:30 p.m. Both officers were in plain clothes. At approximately 2:33 p.m., the respondent drove up to the premises in a car which answered the description of the stolen car used in the armed robbery.

The respondent left the car and proceeded to the office premises, where Constable Train was waiting. Constable MacIver, who had been waiting in the parking lot, investigated the car. He saw a gun butt protruding from under the driver's seat. He put the gun into his hip pocket, and he then followed the respondent into the office. When the respondent entered the office, Constable Train greeted him with "Hi, Ron." The respondent asked "Do I know you?" At that stage both officers identified themselves as police officers and showed the respondent their badges. They searched and handcuffed the respondent.

At 2:40 p.m., Constable Train arrested the respondent for theft and possession of the stolen car and for armed robbery at the Mac's Milk store. He read him his rights from a card which was issued to all police officers when the Charter was proclaimed. The card from which the constable read stated as follows:

Charter of Rights

1. *Notice Upon Arrest*
I am arresting you for . . . (briefly describe reasons for arrest)
2. *Right to Counsel*
It is my duty to inform you that you have the right to retain and instruct counsel without delay.
Do you understand?
Caution to Charged Person
You (are charged, will be charged) with . . . Do you wish to say anything in answer to the charge? You are not obliged to say anything unless you wish to do so, but whatever you say may be given in evidence.
Secondary Caution to Charged Person
If you have spoken to any police officer or to anyone with authority or if any such person has spoken to you in connection with this case, I want it clearly understood that I do not want it to influence you in making any statement.

The respondent made a flippant remark at the reading of the caution and the right to counsel to the effect that "It sounds like an American T.V. program." Constable Train reread the whole card to the respondent, and at that time the respondent said:

Prove it. I ain't saying anything until I see my lawyer. I want to see my lawyer.

Constable MacIver then questioned the respondent as follows:

Q. What is your full name? A. Ronald Charles Manninen.

Q. Where is your address? A. Ain't got one.

Q. Where is the knife that you had along with this [showing the respondent the CO2 gun found in the car] when you ripped off the Mac's Milk on Wilson Avenue? A. He's lying. When I was in the store I only had the gun. The knife was in the tool box in the car.

This last answer was relied on by the trial judge in convicting the respondent on the charge of armed robbery.

Constable MacIver then returned to the car, where he found two knives and the grey sweatshirt. While Constable MacIver was out of the room, Constable Train asked the respondent the following questions:

Q. What is your business here, Ron? A. [No response.]

Q. Do you know someone that works here? A. No. Why?

Q. Why did you come to this place? A. [No response.]

Constable MacIver returned to the office, showed the respondent the two knives he had found in the car and had the following conversation with the respondent:

Q. What are these for?

A. What the fuck do you think they are for? Are you fucking stupid?

Q. You tell me what they are for, and is this yours? [showing the grey sweatshirt]

A. Of course it's mine. You fuckers are really stupid. Don't bother me any more. I'm not saying anything until I see my lawyer. Just fuck off. You fuckers have to prove it.

Constable Train had gone out on Constable MacIver's return to check the trunk of the car and he stated that he had not heard the respondent repeat that he was not saying anything until he saw his lawyer.

There was an operating telephone in the small office where the respondent was arrested and the police officers used it in the course of the afternoon. The respondent did not make a direct request to use the telephone and the police officers did not volunteer the use of the telephone to the respondent. The trial judge made the following finding:

I find that the police had no desire to have him call a lawyer, and intended to call a lawyer back at the station when the arrest was completed.

The respondent did not speak to his lawyer until the lawyer called him at the police station, at 8:35 p.m.

It is not disputed that the respondent was informed of his right to retain and instruct counsel without delay. Further, the sufficiency of the communication is not challenged.

The respondent's comment on being informed of his right to counsel was:

Prove it. I ain't saying anything until I see my lawyer. I want to see my lawyer.

Since there could hardly be a clearer assertion of the desire to exercise the right to counsel, it is not necessary in this appeal to decide whether an arrested or detained person is required to positively assert his right to counsel before a correlative obligation is imposed on the police.

In my view, s. 10(*b*) imposes at least two duties on the police in addition to the duty to inform the detainee of his rights. First, the police must provide the detainee with a reasonable opportunity to exercise the right to retain and instruct counsel without delay. The detainee is in the control of the police and he cannot exercise his right to counsel unless the police provide him with a reasonable opportunity to do so. This aspect of the right to counsel was recognized in Canadian law well before the advent of the Charter. In *Brownridge v. R.*, [1972] S.C.R. 926, 18 C.R.N.S. 308, 7 C.C.C. (2d) 417, 28 D.L.R. (3d) 1 [Ont.], a case decided under the Canadian Bill of Rights, Laskin J. (as he then was) wrote at 952-53:

> The right to retain and instruct counsel without delay can only have meaning to an arrested or detained person if it is taken as raising a correlative obligation upon the police authorities to facilitate contact with counsel. This means allowing him upon his request to use the telephone for that purpose if one is available.

The duty to facilitate contact with counsel has been consistently acknowledged under s. 10(*b*) of the Charter by the lower courts: *R. v. Nelson* (1982), 32 C.R. (3d) 256, 3 C.C.C. (3d) 147, 4 C.R.R. 88 (Man. Q.B.); *R. v. Anderson* (1984), 45 O.R. (2d) 225, 39 C.R. (3d) 193, 10 C.C.C. (3d) 417, 7 D.L.R. (4th) 306, 9 C.R.R. 161, 2 O.A.C. 258 (C.A.); *R. v. Dombrowski* (1985), 44 C.R. (3d) 1, 18 C.C.C. (3d) 164, 14 C.R.R. 165, 37 Sask. R. 259 (C.A.); and the Ontario Court of Appeal in this case. In *Dombrowski*, the court held that, where a telephone is available at an earlier occasion, there is no justification for delaying the opportunity to contact counsel until arrival at the police station.

In my view, this aspect of the right to counsel was clearly infringed in this case. The respondent clearly asserted his right to remain silent and his desire to consult his lawyer. There was a telephone immediately at hand in the office, which the officers used for their own purposes. It was not necessary for the respondent to make an express request to use the telephone. The duty to facilitate contact with counsel included the duty to offer the respondent the use of the telephone. Of course, there may be circumstances in which it is particularly urgent that the police continue with an investigation before it is possible to facilitate a detainee's communication with counsel. There was no urgency in the circumstances surrounding the offences in this case.

Further, s. 10(*b*) imposes on the police the duty to cease questioning or otherwise attempting to elicit evidence from the detainee until he has had a reasonable opportunity to retain and instruct counsel. The purpose of the right to counsel is to allow the detainee not only to be informed of his rights and obligations under the law but, equally if not more important, to obtain advice as to how to exercise those rights. In this case, the police officers correctly informed the respondent of his right to remain silent and the main function of counsel would be to confirm the existence of that right and then to advise him as to how to exercise it. For the right to counsel to be effective, the detainee must have access to this advice before he is questioned or otherwise required to provide evidence. I discussed the duty imposed on the police in the context of a breathalyzer demand in *R. v. Therens*, [1985] 1 S.C.R. 613 at 624, 45 C.R. (3d) 97, [1985] 4 W.W.R. 286, 32 M.V.R. 153, 18 C.C.C. (3d) 481, 18 D.L.R. (4th) 655, 13 C.R.R. 193, 40 Sask. R. 122, 59 N.R. 122:

I do not want to be taken here as giving an exhaustive definition of the s. 10(*b*) rights and will limit my comments in that respect to what is strictly required for the disposition of this case. In my view, s. 10(*b*) requires at least that the authorities inform the detainee of his rights, not prevent him in any way from exercising them and, where a detainee is required to provide evidence which may be incriminating and refusal to comply is punishable as a criminal offence, as is the case under s. 235 of the *Code, s. 10(b) also imposes a duty not to call upon the detainee to provide that evidence without first informing him of his s. 10(b) rights and providing him with a reasonable opportunity and time to retain and instruct counsel.* [Emphasis added.]

This passage was cited by Wilson J. in *Clarkson v. R.*, [1986] 1 S.C.R. 383 at 394, 50 C.R. (3d) 289, 25 C.C.C. (3d) 207, 26 D.L.R. (4th) 493, 19 C.R.R. 209, 69 N.B.R. (2d) 40, 177 A.P.R. 40, 66 N.R. 114, in the context of confessions, and I agree that this duty is equally applicable in that context. The Ontario Court of Appeal came to the same conclusion in *Anderson*, supra and in *R. v. Esposito* (1985), 53 O.R. (2d) 356, 49 C.R. (3d) 193, 24 C.C.C. (3d) 88 at 97, 20 C.R.R. 102, 12 O.A.C. 350:

> If the suspect states that he wishes to retain counsel all questioning must cease until he has been afforded the opportunity of consulting counsel . . .

This aspect of the respondent's right to counsel was clearly infringed in the circumstances of this case. Immediately after the respondent's clear assertion of his right to remain silent and his desire to consult his lawyer, the police officer commenced his questioning as if the respondent had expressed no such desire. Again, there may be circumstances in which it is particularly urgent that the police proceed with their questioning of the detainee before providing him with a reasonable opportunity to retain and instruct counsel, but there was no such urgency in this case.

The Crown contends that there was no infringement of the right to counsel because the respondent has waived his right by answering the police officer's questions. While a person may implicitly waive his rights under s. 10(*b*), the standard will be very high: *Clarkson*, supra, at pp. 394-95. In my view, the respondent's conduct did not intend to waive his right, as he clearly asserted it at the beginning and at the end of the questioning. Rather, the form of the questioning was such as to elicit involuntary answers. The police officer asked two innocuous questions followed by a baiting question which led the respondent to incriminate himself. In addition, where a detainee has positively asserted his desire to exercise his right to counsel and the police have ignored his request and have proceeded to question him, he is likely to feel that his right has no effect and that he must answer. Finally, the respondent had the right not to be asked questions, and he must not be held to have implicitly waived that right simply because he answered the questions. Otherwise, the right not to be asked questions would exist only where the detainee refused to answer and thus where there is no need for any remedy or exclusionary rule.

For these reasons, I would conclude that the respondent's rights under s. 10(*b*) were infringed.

In *Manninen* the accused had clearly asserted his right to counsel so it was not necessary to decide whether the correlative duties on the police arise only where there is such an assertion. *R. v. Anderson* (1984), 45 O.R. (2d) 225 (Ont. C.A.) holds that an assertion *is* required. The language of obligation throughout *Manninen* suggested that the Supreme Court might well reverse *Anderson*. However, the Supreme Court later endorsed part of *Anderson*.

BAIG v. R.
[1987] 2 S.C.R. 537, 61 C.R. (3d) 97, 37 C.C.C. (3d) 181 (S.C.C.)

Per curiam:—This appeal comes to us as of right. The appellant was charged with murder and tried in the Supreme Court of Ontario before a jury. He was acquitted following a directed verdict. This verdict was pursuant to the exclusion from the evidence of a statement given by the accused. The statement was excluded under s. 24(2) of the Canadian Charter of Rights and Freedoms following a finding by the trial judge that the accused's right to counsel and to be informed thereof, guaranteed by s. 10(*b*) of the Charter, had been violated. The Court of Appeal quashed the acquittal and ordered a new trial, finding that the accused's rights under the Charter had not been violated.

The relevant facts, to state them succinctly, are as follows:

FACTS

The accused, Mohsin Majeed Baig, was arrested at approximately 1:50 p.m. on 20th September 1982 and was charged with murder. The police had met the accused outside his house. The accused entered the police vehicle. The following exchange then took place between Constable Kelly and the accused:

KELLY: Okay, Mohsin, You are under arrest for the murder of Navneet Uppal ... Now, before you say anything, just listen to this. You are not obliged to say anything unless you wish to do so, but whatever you say will be taken down in writing and may be given in evidence . . . It is my duty to inform you that you have the right to retain and instruct counsel without delay; do you understand?

BAIG: How can you prove this thing?

KELLY: We can prove it, okay.

The accused was then taken to the police headquarters. No conversation took place en route. Upon arrival, the accused was taken to an interview room, where the following exchange took place:

KELLY: Okay, Mohsin, you have had a chance to think things out on the way here. Anees and Raza have been arrested, and we know exactly what happened, so you may as well tell us about it.

BAIG: You have Anees and Raza here?

KELLY: Yes, we have. We may as well tell you, we have also arrested Kumerjeet. You're the last one we had to get.

BAIG: Okay, okay, I'll tell you.

KELLY: Just a second. You understand, that caution that I told you when you were arrested, that still applies.

BAIG: Yes, I know.

The accused then made an oral statement concerning his knowledge of and involvement in the murder of Uppal. The statement was taken down in writing by Constable Kelly.

Kelly then typed the written statement on a statement form. The form contained the following three questions.

1. Do you understand the charge?
2. Do you understand the caution?
3. I have to inform you that you have the right to retain and instruct counsel without delay. Do you understand that?

The form was read to the accused and the accused answered "Yes" to each of the three questions. The accused then read and signed the statement.

We are in substantial agreement with the Court of Appeal. As there was and is no need to determine whether, under the circumstances of this case, the accused's conduct amounted to a waiver of his right to counsel, we prefer not to pronounce upon that matter. We agree with Tarnopolsky J.A. in *R. v. Anderson* (1984), 45 O.R. (2d) 225, 39 C.R. (3d) 193, 10 C.C.C. (3d) 417, 7 D.L.R. (4th) 306, 9 C.R.R. 161, 2 O.A.C. 258 (C.A.), wherein he said, at p. 431:

> . . . I am of the view that, absent proof of circumstances indicating that the accused did not understand his right to retain counsel when he was informed of it, the onus has to be on him to prove that he asked for the right but it was denied or he was denied any opportunity to even ask for it. No such evidence was put forth in this case.

In the present case, the accused did not put forward, nor does the record reveal, any evidence suggesting that he was denied an opportunity to ask for counsel. Absent such circumstances as that referred to by Tarnopolsky J.A., once the police have complied with s. 10(*b*) by advising the accused without delay of his right to counsel without delay, there are no correlative duties triggered and cast upon them until the accused, if he so chooses, has indicated his desire to exercise his right to counsel.

The appeal is dismissed.

LECLAIR and ROSS v. R.
[1989] 1 S.C.R. 3, 67 C.R. (3d) 209, 46 C.C.C. (3d) 129 (S.C.C.)

Three youths were arrested in the middle of the night and charged with break, enter and theft. They were advised of their right to counsel and tried unsuccessfully to contact their counsel by telephone at about 2:00 a.m. Leclair was asked if he wished to call another lawyer and he indicated that he did not. The police conducted a line-up an hour later. The boys were not advised that they were under no obligation to participate.

LAMER J.:—

(1) *A reasonable and effective opportunity to retain and instruct counsel*

The appellants were obviously detained, and that they had the right to retain and instruct counsel is not in dispute. Moreover, the police complied initially with s. 10(*b*) and advised Ross and Leclair of their right to retain and instruct counsel without delay. As this court held in *R. v. Manninen*, [1987] 1 S.C.R. 1233, 58 C.R. (3d) 97, 34 C.C.C. (3d) 385, 41 D.L.R. (4th) 301, 21 O.A.C. 192, 76 N.R. 198, s. 10(*b*) imposes at least two duties on the police in addition to the duty to inform detainees of their rights. The first is that the police must give the accused or detained person who so wishes a *reasonable* opportunity to exercise the right to retain and instruct counsel without delay. The second is that the police must refrain from attempting to elicit evidence from the detainee until the detainee has had a reasonable opportunity to retain and instruct counsel. I am of the view that in this case the police fulfilled neither duty.

The first duty: affording a reasonable opportunity

Having been informed of their right to counsel and having clearly indicated their desire to assert that right, both appellants were permitted to telephone lawyers of their choice but were unable to make contact with them. This is hardly surprising, since the calls were made at approximately 2:00 a.m. In the circumstances, it was highly unlikely that they would be able to contact their counsel before normal office operating hours.

At this juncture, I would underline the fact that the appellant Leclair was asked if he wanted to call another lawyer, and his answer was "No". The Crown's submission was that by giving this answer Leclair waived his right to counsel. I do not agree. Leclair had clearly indicated that he wished to contact *his* lawyer. The mere fact that he did not want to call *another* lawyer cannot fairly be viewed as a waiver of his right to retain counsel. Quite the contrary: he merely asserted his right to counsel and to counsel of his choice. Although an accused or detained person has the right to choose counsel, it must be noted that, as this court said in *R. v Tremblay*, [1987] 2 S.C.R. 435, 60 C.R. (3d) 59, 2 M.V.R. (2d) 289, 37 C.C.C. (3d) 565, 45 D.L.R. (4th) 445, 32 C.R.R. 381, 25 O.A.C. 93, 79 N.R. 153, a detainee must be reasonably diligent in the exercise of these rights, and if he is not, the correlative duties imposed on the police and set out in *Manninen*, supra, are suspended. Reasonable diligence in the exercise of the right to choose one's counsel depends upon the context facing the accused or detained person. On being arrested, for example, the detained person is faced with an immediate need for legal advice and must exercise reasonable diligence accordingly. By contrast, when seeking the best lawyer to conduct a trial, the accused person faces no such immediacy. Nevertheless, accused or detained persons have a right to choose their counsel and it is only if the lawyer chosen cannot be available within a reasonable time that the detainee or the accused should be expected to exercise the right to counsel by calling another lawyer.

Moreover, once the appellant asserted his right to instruct counsel, and absent a clear indication that he had changed his mind, it was unreasonable for the police to proceed as if Leclair had waived his right to counsel. As a majority of this court held in *Clarkson v. R.*, [1986] 1 S.C.R. 383 at 394-95, 50 C.R. (3d) 289, 25 C.C.C. (3d) 207, 26 D.L.R. (4th) 493, 19 C.R.R. 209, 69 N.B.R. (2d) 40, 177 A.P.R. 40, 66 N.R. 114:

> Given the concern for fair treatment of an accused person which underlies such constitutional civil liberties as the right to counsel in s. 10(*b*) of the Charter, it is evident that any alleged waiver of this right by an accused must be carefully considered and that the accused's awareness of the consequences of what he or she was saying is crucial. Indeed, the Court stated with respect to the waiver of statutory procedural guarantees in *Korponay v. Attorney General of Canada*, [1982] 1 S.C.R. 41, at p. 49, that any waiver ". . . is dependent upon it being *clear and unequivocal that the person is waiving the procedural safeguard and is doing so with full knowledge of the rights the procedure was enacted to protect and of the effect the waiver will have on those rights in the process*" (emphasis in original).

Since the evidence reveals that Leclair asserted his right to counsel, the burden of establishing an unequivocal waiver is on the Crown. Here, the Crown has failed to discharge the onus.

In the case of the appellant Ross, there is no evidence that the police even asked whether he wanted to call another lawyer. Once Ross had tried and failed to reach his lawyer, it would appear that the police assumed that their obligation to provide a reasonable opportunity to retain counsel was at an end. One can reasonably infer that they also misconstrued the nature of their obligation as concerned the appellant Leclair. Obviously, there was no urgency or other reason justifying that the police proceed forthwith, and it cannot be said that the appellants had a real opportunity to retain and instruct counsel. This therefore leads us to consider the second duty.

The second duty: refraining from taking further steps

Having seen the appellants got no answer to their telephone calls, the police officers placed them in police cells, and a few minutes later the appellants were told to participate in a line-up, which they did.

The police were mistaken to follow such a procedure. As this court held in *Manninen, supra*, the police have at least a duty to cease questioning or otherwise attempting to elicit evidence from the detainee until he has had a reasonable opportunity to retain and instruct counsel. In my view, the right to counsel also means that, once an accused or detained person has asserted that right, the police cannot in any way compel the detainee or accused person to make a decision or participate in a process which could ultimately have an adverse effect in the conduct of an eventual trial until that person has had a reasonable opportunity to exercise that right. In the case at bar, it cannot be said that the appellants had a real opportunity to retain and instruct counsel before the line-up was held. Nor can it be said that there was any urgency or other compelling reason which justified proceeding with the line-up so precipitously.

The Crown urged upon us that it was necessary to hold the line-up immediately, while the memories of the witnesses were fresh and undisturbed. I cannot accept this submission. While it may be desirable to hold a line-up as soon as possible, this concern must generally yield to the right of the suspect to retain counsel, which right must, of course, be exercised with reasonable diligence. Here, the line-up was held with utmost, indeed highly unusual, dispatch. There is nothing to suggest that the line-up could not have been held a few hours later, after the appellants had again attempted to contact their lawyers during normal business hours.

The respondent also submitted that there was no violation of the right to counsel because the appellants did not have the right to have their lawyers present during the line-up. This submission is without merit. Even if the appellants could not have their lawyers present during the line-up, this does not imply that counsel is of no assistance to a suspect. Identification evidence obtained through a line- up is usually strong evidence susceptible of influencing trial deliberations. The question as to whether a suspect has a positive right to refuse to participate in a line-up has not been decided in our law and was not raised in the courts below or by counsel before this court. It would thus be inappropriate to resolve this question here. However, it is clear that there is no legal obligation to participate in a line-up. There is certainly no statutory obligation to participate in a line-up equivalent to s. 453.4 [now s. 502] of the Criminal Code, which, together with the Identification of Criminals Act, R.S.C. 1970, c. I-1, obliges an accused person to appear before a police officer for the purposes of fingerprinting. Nor have the courts ever imposed an obligation to participate in a line-up. Since there is no such legal obligation, it is clear that counsel has an important role in advising a client about participating voluntarily in a line-up. In *Marcoux v. R.*, supra, this court considered the case of an accused who refused to participate in a line-up. The police subsequently had a witness confront the accused directly and the witness made a positive identification. Evidence that the accused refused to participate in the line-up was admitted to meet the contention that the police failed to conduct a proper line-up. This case illustrates that, while an accused or detained person has no obligation to participate in a line-up, failure to do so can have legal consequences respecting the evidence that might be admitted at trial. In the case at bar, had the appellants been allowed access to their lawyers, they could have been advised that they were under no statutory obligation to participate in the line-up, although failure to do so might have certain prejudicial consequences. They could have been advised, for example, not to participate unless they were given a photograph of the line-up, or not to participate if the others in the line-up were obviously older than themselves. In short, they could have been told how a well-run line-up is conducted, even though there is no statutory framework governing the line-up process. It was this advice, not the presence of their lawyers at the line-up, of which the appellants were deprived.

Furthermore, that the accused did not refuse to participate in the line-up cannot by itself amount to a waiver of right to counsel. The very purpose of the right to counsel is to ensure that those who are accused or detained are advised of their legal rights and how to exercise them when dealing with the authorities. It would contradict this purpose to conclude that a detained or accused person has waived the right to counsel simply by submitting, before being instructed by counsel, to precisely those attempts to secure the detainee's participation from which the police should refrain. Here, the appellants were unable to make an informed decision about participating in the line-up because they were ignorant of their legal position, not having been advised by their lawyers. Nor did the police even give them the choice as to whether they should participate. In the circumstances, therefore, to conclude that the appellants had waived their rights by participating in the line-up would render the right to counsel nugatory.

R. v. Taylor, [2014] 2 S.C.R. 495, 311 C.C.C. (3d) 285, 12 C.R. (7th) 1 (S.C.C.) is a significant ruling on how s. 10(b) of the Charter is to operate in the commonly occurring situation where suspects are first taken by police to hospital for medical attention. Justice Abella, speaking for Supreme Court, ruled in the context of an impaired driving case:

1. Section 10(b) of the Charter requires police to provide phone access to counsel immediately on arrest or detention where requested, where reasonable practical and prior to any effort to elicit evidence. The Court does not impose a duty on the police to provide access to an officer's cell phone given privacy and safety considerations.

2. This applies equally in the hospital situation where proof that this access was not reasonably practical has to be provided by the Crown.

3. Getting a warrant to seize medical blood samples cannot cure a section 10(b) breach.

R. v. BURLINGHAM
[1995] 2 S.C.R. 206, 38 C.R. (4th) 265, 97 C.C.C. (3d) 385 (S.C.C.)

The accused was arrested on a charge of murder of B.H. He confessed. The police suspected him of an earlier murder of D.W., committed in the same time in a similar manner. Over a three day period the police subjected the accused to an intensive and often manipulative interrogation about the D.W. murder. He was systematically questioned although he repeatedly stated that he would not speak unless he could consult a lawyer. The police urged him to reveal what he knew about the crime, suggesting that any delay would hurt his parents who would be doubly hurt by a second murder charge just as they were getting over the shock of the first murder. The police also constantly denigrated the integrity of defence counsel suggesting that they were more trustworthy.

On the fourth day the police offered the accused a "deal". They indicated their "boss" and Crown counsel had instructed them to tell him that he would only be charged with second degree murder in the D.W. case in exchange for providing the police with the location of the gun and other information. When the accused refused to accept the deal without consulting his lawyer, the officers continued to express doubts about the usefulness of the lawyer, emphasizing that he was taking the weekend off. They then made it clear that the deal was a "one-time chance" only open during that weekend when the lawyer was not available. The accused eventually acquiesced despite advice from another lawyer not to talk to the police. He fulfilled his part of the bargain: he confessed, brought the police to the murder site and told them where the murder weapon had been thrown. The next morning he also told his girlfriend, J.H., that he had taken the police to where he had left the gun months earlier and that he knew something about the death of D.W. Later that day the police told him the deal did not consist in accepting a plea of second degree murder just that he could plead not guilty on a charge of first degree murder. The trial judge found that the police had made an honest mistake.

At trial for first degree murder of D.W. the trial judge found a breach of the accused's right to counsel under s. 10(*b*) of the Canadian Charter of Rights and Freedoms and excluded the evidence of the confession and disclosure of the location of the gun. However the trial judge admitted the fact of finding the gun and the girlfriend's evidence of his statements made to her after the deal. The accused was convicted of first degree murder in both cases. His appeal against conviction in the B.H. case was dismissed. His appeal against conviction in the D.W. case was also dismissed by a majority of the British Columbia Court of Appeal. McEachern C.J.B.C. dissenting on the basis that all the derivative evidence should have been excluded under s. 24(2).

On further appeal the Supreme Court unanimously held that section 10(*b*) had been violated. We shall later consider their divided opinion on the issue of exclusion under s. 24(2).

IACOBUCCI J.:—

. . .

Was there a denial of the accused's right to counsel?

Section 10(*b*) of the *Charter* guarantees an accused the right, upon arrest and detention, to retain and instruct counsel without delay and to be informed of that right. This Court has consistently given a broad interpretation to s. 10(*b*). In the case at bar, there were several ways in which the appellant's right to counsel was denied.

First, the police continually questioned him despite his repeated statements that he would say nothing absent consultation with his lawyer. Section 10(*b*) requires, barring urgent circumstances, that the police refrain from attempting to elicit incriminatory evidence once a detainee has asserted his or her right to counsel: *R. v. Prosper*, [1994] 3 S.C.R. 236; *R. v. Matheson*, [1994] 3 S.C.R. 328; *R. v. Brydges*, [1990] 1 S.C.R. 190.

Second, s. 10(*b*) specifically prohibits the police, as they did in this case, from belittling an accused's lawyer with the express goal or effect of undermining the accused's confidence in and relationship with defence counsel. It makes no sense for s. 10(*b*) of the *Charter* to provide for the right to retain and instruct counsel if law enforcement authorities are able to undermine either an accused's confidence in his or her lawyer or the solicitor-client relationship.

Third, the improper conduct by the police regarding the plea bargain also amounted to an infringement of s. 10(*b*). On this issue, I would affirm the conclusion of Toy J. at trial and McEachern C.J. on appeal that s. 10(*b*) was violated when the officers pressured the appellant into accepting the "deal" without first having the opportunity to consult with his lawyer.

An argument could be made that, at the moment the plea bargain was offered, no s. 10(*b*) violation arose since the accused had an opportunity to call a lawyer, albeit not his particular lawyer, whom the police knew to be unavailable for the one night the offer was left open. However, I am not persuaded by such an argument. Allowing the appellant to call a random lawyer is, given the seriousness of the situation he faced and the circumstances of this case, insufficient for the officers to discharge their responsibilities under s. 10(*b*). This is especially so when the call to this unknown lawyer is placed within the context of the general trickery and subterfuge used by the police in arranging matters so that the appellant himself had to decide on the plea in the absence of his own counsel. Although it is clear that s. 10(*b*) does not guarantee an accused the right to the counsel of his or her choice at all times, in a situation such as the appellant's I believe that either the offer should have been made at a point in time when the accused's lawyer (who was entirely familiar with the facts of his case) was available or the police should have kept it open to a point in time when the accused's counsel would reasonably be considered to be available.

. . .

When, at first, the appellant refused to accept the deal without consulting with a lawyer, the officers resumed their attempts to discourage the appellant from meeting with his lawyer by observing that the appellant's lawyer was taking the weekend off, by stressing that any delays in accepting the deal would prove painful for the appellant's family, and by underscoring that the deal was being offered for that night only. The end result of this badgering was that the accused did not understand the full content of his right to counsel. When it is evident that there is such a misunderstanding, the police cannot rely on a mechanical recitation of the right to counsel in order to discharge their responsibilities under s. 10(*b*): *R. v. Evans*, [1991] 1 S.C.R. 869, at p. 891. They must take positive steps to facilitate that understanding. In the case at bar, not only did the police fail to take affirmative steps to clear up the appellant's confusion, but they also in fact created this confusion in the first place.

. . .

It is thus apparent from the transcripts that the accused would not have made the deal with police if it were not for the concerted effort by the police to convince the accused not to consult with his counsel.

I underscore that, in *R. v. Evans*, supra, McLachlin J. held that the police have the duty to advise a suspect of the right to counsel where there is a fundamental and discrete change in the purpose of an investigation which involves a different and unrelated offence or a significantly more serious offence than that contemplated at the time of the original instruction of the right to counsel. Such a situation arose in the case at bar. The deal offered by the police involved a different offence and was of such material importance to the appellant that it constituted a fundamental change in the course of his prosecution. For the reasons discussed earlier, a genuine effort should have been made to contact the accused's own lawyer.

Furthermore, I conclude that s. 10(b) mandates the Crown or police, whenever offering a plea bargain, to tender that offer either to accused's counsel or to the accused while in the presence of his or her counsel, unless the accused has expressly waived the right to counsel. It is consequently a constitutional infringement to place such an offer directly to an accused, especially (as in the present appeal) when the police coercively leave it open only for the short period of time during which they know defence counsel to be unavailable. In the case at bar, the police should have negotiated the "deal" with the appellant's counsel or, at a minimum, with the appellant while accompanied by his lawyer.

I emphasize that, in the case at bar, there was no urgency to the matter. Mere expediency or efficiency is not sufficient to create enough "urgency" to permit a s. 10(b) breach: *Prosper*, supra. Neither the precipitous issuing of the plea bargain by the police nor their conscious undermining of the accused's relationship with his counsel can be justified on the basis that such conduct allegedly facilitated the investigatory process.

In closing, given the appellant's success on the other questions he raises, I need not deal with his submission that the breach by the Crown of the plea bargain deal also triggered constitutional violations. However, I should mention that, to the extent that the plea bargain is an integral element of the Canadian criminal process, the Crown and its officers engaged in the plea bargaining process must act honourably and forthrightly.

In *R. v. Prosper* (1994), 33 C.R. (4th) 85 (S.C.C.) the Court was unanimous in holding that there is no constitutional obligation on governments to provide a free duty counsel system on arrest or detention. Chief Justice Lamer for a 6-3 majority further determined that, where a detainee asserts the right to this counsel, there is a violation of s. 10(b) where the accused is not given a reasonable opportunity to consult counsel and that the lack of availability of duty counsel in a particular jurisdiction is a factor to be considered in the determination of reasonableness. Chief Justice Lamer makes it express that in such circumstances the police must "hold off" eliciting incriminating evidence until the opportunity has been provided. The majority warns that in jurisdictions without a duty counsel system the delay may have to be longer even if this means that the breathalyzer test cannot be taken within the two-hour limit (Parliament has now extended the limit to three hours). This ruling produced a strong dissent by L'Heureux-Dubé J. (with La

Forest J. and Gonthier J. concurring): the "holding off" proposal was neither warranted nor appropriate. **Which view do you prefer?**

(d) Waiver and Duty to be Reasonably Diligent in Exercise of Right

It would appear in the cases that follow that the Supreme Court is generous to accused when the Court characterizes the issue as one of waiver. It is far less generous when insisting on the duty to assert the s. 10(*b*) right with reasonable diligence. It is unfortunately unclear which emphasis will be adopted in any case and the rulings appear inconsistent.

R. v. CLARKSON
[1986] 1 S.C.R. 383, 50 C.R. (3d) 289, 25 C.C.C. (3d) 207 (S.C.C.)

The accused was very intoxicated when she was charged with her husband's murder. She was given the customary police warning and informed of her right to counsel. She said there was "no point" in having counsel and underwent police questioning while still drunk and very emotional. The questioning continued in spite of the efforts of an aunt to have it postponed and to convince the accused to stop talking until counsel was present. The trial judge excluded her statements, finding that she did not appreciate the consequences of making the statements. The Court of Appeal found this to be error and ordered a new trial. The accused appealed.

WILSON J. (Estey, Lamer, LeDain and LaForest JJ., concurring):—

. . .

4. Waiver of the Right to Counsel

The question of whether the appellant's right to counsel has been violated may well provide an acceptable alternative approach to the problem posed by the police extraction of an intoxicated confession. This right, as entrenched in s. 10(*b*) of the Canadian Charter of Rights and Freedoms is clearly aimed at fostering the principles of adjudicative fairness. As Lamer J. indicated in *R. v. Therens*, [1985] 1 S.C.R. 613, at p. 624,

> where a detainee is required to provide evidence which may be incriminating . . . s. 10(*b*) also imposes a duty not to call upon the detainee to provide that evidence without first informing him of his s. 10(*b*) rights and providing him with a reasonable opportunity and time to retain and instruct counsel.

This constitutional provision is clearly unconcerned with the probative value of any evidence obtained by the police but rather, in the words of Le Dain J. in *Therens*, supra, at pp. 641-42, its aim is "to ensure that in certain situations a person is made aware of the right to counsel" where he or she is detained by the police in a situation which may give rise to a "significant legal consequence".

Given the concern for fair treatment of an accused person which underlies such constitutional civil liberties as the right to counsel in s. 10(*b*) of the Charter, it is evident that any alleged waiver of this right by an accused must be carefully considered and that the accused's awareness of the consequences of what he or she was saying is crucial. Indeed, this Court stated with respect to the waiver of statutory procedural guarantees in *Korponay v. Attorney General of Canada*, [1982] 1 S.C.R. 41, at p. 49, that any waiver

> . . . is dependent upon it being *clear and unequivocal that the person is waiving the procedural safeguard and is doing so with full knowledge of the rights the procedure was enacted to protect and of the effect the waiver will have on those rights in the process.* (emphasis in original).

There is also a wealth of case law in the United States to the effect that an accused may waive his constitutional right to counsel only "if he knows what he is doing and his choice is made with eyes open": *Adams v. United States*, 317 U.S. 269 (1942), at p. 279. Thus, an accused must "knowingly intelligently and with a full understanding of the implications, waive his constitutional rights to counsel": *Minor v. United States*, 375 F.2d 170 (8th Cir. 1967), at p. 179 certiorari denied 389 U.S. 882 (1967). Indeed, the Supreme Court of the United States had gone so far as to indicate that not only must an accused person be cognizant of the consequences of waiving the constitutional right to counsel in a general way, but he or she must be aware of the legal specificities of his or her own case such that there is a presumption against a valid waiver where the accused is not perceived at the time of the waiver to be capable of comprehending its full implications. For instance, it was stated in *Von Moltke v. Gillies*, 332 U.S. 708 (1947), at p. 724:

> To be valid such waiver must be made with an apprehension of the nature of the charges, the statutory offenses included within them, the range of allowable punishments thereunder, possible defenses to the charges and circumstances in mitigation thereof, and all other facts essential to a broad understanding of the whole matter.

Whether or not one goes as far as requiring an accused to be tuned in to the legal intricacies of the case before accepting as valid a waiver of the right to counsel, it is clear that the waiver of the s. 10(*b*) right by an intoxicated accused must pass some form of "awareness of the consequences" test. Unlike the confession itself, there is no room for an argument that the court in assessing such a waiver should only be concerned with the probative value of the evidence so as to restrict the test to the accused's mere comprehension of his or her own words. Rather, the purpose of the right, as indicated by each of the members of this court writing in *Therens*, supra, is to ensure that the accused is treated fairly in the criminal process. While this constitutional guarantee cannot be forced upon an unwilling accused, any voluntary waiver, in order to be valid and effective, must be premised on a true appreciation of the consequences of giving up the right.

5. Conclusion

The trial judge found as a fact that the appellant's confession could not pass the "awareness of the consequences" test and, if such is the case, then presumably neither could the waiver of the s. 10(*b*) right to counsel. Accordingly, the test for a valid and effective waiver of the right was not met and the continued questioning of the appellant constituted a violation of s. 10(*b*) of the Charter. At the very minimum it was incumbent upon the police to delay their questioning and the taking of the appellant's statement until she was in a sufficiently sober state to properly exercise her right to retain and instruct counsel or to be fully aware of the consequences of waiving this right. Accordingly, regardless of the view one takes of the admissibility of the intoxicated confession per se, the conclusion that the appellant's confession was improperly obtained is inescapable.

Justices McIntyre and Chouinard would have allowed the appeal on the basis that the trial judge's finding of fact should not have been disturbed, and decided there was no need to deal with the Charter.

Bartle and the companion cases also hold that a waiver of the informational component of the right to counsel will have to be explicit and will require a reasonable belief that the detainee knew about the right to counsel and how to exercise it. These rulings and that in *Tran* (1994), 32 C.R. (4th) 34 (S.C.C.) (respecting waiver of the s. 14 right to an interpreter) appear to supersede the unanimous judgment of the Supreme Court in *Whittle* (1994), 32 C.R. (4th) 1 (S.C.C.), handed down only one month earlier. In *Whittle* the Court determined that the trial judge had erred in holding that any waiver of the right to counsel required an "awareness of consequences" test. *Whittle* has been criticized as drawing a false analogy to tests for fitness to stand trial and for ignoring the authority of *Clarkson* (1986), 50 C.R. (3d) 289 (S.C.C.): see R.J. Delisle, "*Whittle* or *Tran*: Conflicting Messages on How Much an Accused Must Understand", (1994) 32 C.R. (4th) 29 (S.C.C.). The authority of *Clarkson* is fully restored in *Bartle* and *Tran*.

R. v. SMITH
[1989] 2 S.C.R. 368, 71 C.R. (3d) 129, 50 C.C.C. (3d) 308 (S.C.C.)

The accused was arrested at his home around 7:00 p.m. on a charge of robbery and informed of his right to retain and instruct counsel. The robbery had occurred five months previously. After various stops made to accommodate personal requests of the accused, the police officers and the accused arrived at the police station at approximately 9:00 p.m. The accused requested the opportunity to communicate with his lawyer and the police gave him access to a telephone and a telephone book. Because of the hour and because the only telephone number appearing in the telephone book was his lawyer's office number, the accused decided not to call. He would contact his lawyer in the morning. The police suggested that he try to make the call, but he refused. He was placed in a police cell and was questioned approximately one hour later in an interview room. The accused told the police that he would not answer questions concerning the robbery until he could speak with his lawyer. The police continued their questioning and tried to obtain a statement from him. The accused indicated on two other occasions that he wanted to speak to his lawyer. Finally, he made a statement, specifying that it was made "off the record". At trial, a voir dire was held to determine the admissibility of this statement. The trial judge ruled that the accused's rights under s. 10(*b*) of the Canadian Charter of Rights and

Freedoms had not been violated and admitted the statement. The accused was convicted. The majority of the British Columbia Court of Appeal upheld the conviction.

LAMER J. (Gonthier J., concurring):—The police officers, in these circumstances, were justified to continue their questioning and to act as they did. This court, in *R. v. Tremblay*, [1987] 2 S.C.R. 435 at p. 439, clearly indicated that the duties imposed on the police as stated in *Manninen*, [1987] 1 S.C.R. 1233, were suspended when the arrested or detained person is not reasonably diligent in the exercise of his rights:

> Generally speaking, if a detainee is not being reasonably diligent in the exercise of his rights, the correlative duties set out in this Court's decision in *R. v. Manninen*, [1987] 1 S.C.R. 1233, imposed on the police in a situation where a detainee has requested the assistance of counsel are suspended and are not a bar to their continuing their investigation and calling upon him to give a sample of his breath.

This limit on the rights of an arrested or detained person is essential because without it, it would be possible to delay needlessly and with impunity an investigation and even, in certain cases, to allow for an essential piece of evidence to be lost, destroyed or rendered impossible to obtain. The rights set out in the Charter, and in particular the right to retain and instruct counsel, are not absolute and unlimited rights. They must be exercised in a way that is reconcilable with the needs of society. An arrested or detained person cannot be permitted to hinder the work of the police by acting in a manner such that the police cannot adequately carry out their tasks.

. . .

The situation would be very different if, as in the case of *R. v. Ross*, [1989] 1 S.C.R. 3, the appellant had tried to contact his lawyer but had failed in his attempt. The appellant, in these circumstances, would have been justified to ask for a delay until the opening of offices in the morning. However, his decision to not even try to contact his lawyer is fatal, in my view, and prevents him from establishing that he was reasonably diligent in the exercise of his rights. The burden of proving that it was impossible for him to communicate with his lawyer when the police offered him the opportunity to do so was on the appellant.

The fact that the appellant subsequently, during the questioning, reiterated his intention to speak with his lawyer before saying anything with respect to the robbery for which he was charged does not change my conclusion. An arrested or detained person who has had a reasonable opportunity to communicate with counsel but who was not diligent in the exercise of this right cannot, subsequently, require the police to suspend, one more time, the investigation or the questioning. This principle, however, does not apply when the circumstances that exist when he asks subsequently to exercise the right are substantially different from those which existed when he had the opportunity to communicate with a lawyer. Such would be the case, for example, where a person believes he is being accused of having disturbed the public peace but learns, during the questioning, that he will possibly be accused of murder.

. . .

Consequently, I am of the opinion that the appeal be dismissed.

L'HEUREUX-DUBÉ J. (concurring):—I agree with my colleague Justice Lamer that this appeal should be dismissed.

. . .

In my view, s. 10(b) of the Charter was not infringed in the present case. The circumstances of time and place as well as the responsible behaviour of the police officers, as set out in Justice Lamer's judgment, clearly gave the appellant more than a reasonable opportunity to communicate with counsel of his choice, or at the very least, to obtain legal advice before answering the questions. The appellant elected not to avail himself of this opportunity.

Moreover, the appellant did not contend that his statements had not been made freely and voluntarily. The legality of the subsequent conduct of the police, in resuming the questioning after the appellant had passed up the reasonable opportunity to contact counsel, is accordingly not at issue here.

SOPINKA J. (concurring):—I have had the opportunity of reading the reasons proposed for delivery herein by my colleagues Justices Lamer and La Forest and Madame Justice L'Heureux-Dubé. I am respectfully of the opinion that the conclusion reached by Justice Lamer, concurred in by Madame Justice L'Heureux-Dubé, is the correct one. This is, however, a case close to the line and, in view of the cogency of the reasons delivered by my colleague La Forest J., I wish to explain briefly why I have decided as I have.

The right to counsel provided by s. 10(b) is a most important right for a person accused of crime. Its importance is underscored by the inroads that it makes on what was standard police practice before the Charter of Rights and Freedoms, namely proceeding without delay after arrest to interrogate the person charged. The importance of this right with its correlative restraint on police action demands from the accused that he or she recognize the importance of the right and act accordingly.

In this case the appellant was most casual in asserting his right. He frittered away about two hours worrying about comparatively trivial matters at a time when counsel was more likely to be available. Despite police urging, he would not place a phone call to determine if counsel could be contacted at about 9 p.m. In these circumstances the courts below concluded that the appellant had been afforded a resonable opportunity to retain and instruct counsel.

In my opinion, this determination is largely a question of fact. The law is clear that the person under detention is to be advised promptly of the right to counsel and must be given a reasonable opportunity to retain and instruct counsel. During this period, police questioning is to be suspended. What is a reasonable opportunity is determined by reference to all the circumstances of the case, including the action of the accused. Whether an opportunity is reasonable must be judge in part in light of the diligence with which the accused seeks to avail himself or herself of the right.

The courts below took these matters into account, applied the law correctly and as a matter of fact concluded that the opportunity afforded to the appellant was reasonable. I see no reason to interfere in that determination and would dismiss the appeal.

LA FOREST J. (dissenting) (Dickson, C.J. and Wilson J. concurring):—The appellant was arrested at home at 7:13 p.m. on 22nd May 1986 in connection with a robbery that had occurred some five months before. After various stops, some at the appellant's request, he arrived at the police station at approximately 9:00 p.m. He had been informed on arrest of his right to counsel and was not questioned en route to the police station, the arresting officers having advised the appellant that they did not wish to discuss the robbery before arriving at the station. On arrival there, the accused made a request to communicate with his lawyer and was handed a telephone and telephone book and given the opportunity to call him. He wanted to speak with George Brown. However, he was unable to locate a home telephone number for Mr. Brown, and, it being at 9:00 p.m., he declined the opportunity to telephone the lawyer's office in the event that there might be an answering service. Rather, he advised the police he would contact his lawyer in the morning.

An hour later, the appellant was taken to an interview room for interrogation. He agreed to talk about himself but would not talk about the robbery. What then transpired is fully set out in the following excerpt from the reasons of McLachlin J.A., as she then was, beginning with an exchange between the appellant and the police at 11:40 p.m. [pp. 388-89]:

"Smith: I would like my lawyer present.

"Johnson: No problem, but with your lawyer you won't say anything. I need to hear this from you. You can understand, but I need to hear from you."

Further questioning ensued with the second police officer, Constable Dahl, taking over. At one point the subject of Smith's mother was raised and he became emotional and cried. After further questioning which once again introduced the subject of robbery, the following exchange took place:

"Dahl: What is your reason for the robbery?

"Smith: I really don't want to say anything. I will talk to you guys, but I will wait for a lawyer.

"Dahl: What can a lawyer do for you? "Smith: I can explain to him what went on.

"Dahl: Your lawyer is going to tell you not to talk to the police like they always do. "Smith: Yes.

"Dahl: What is that going to get you? You have to be honest with yourself if you want your kids to be honest.

"Smith: Yeah.

"Dahl: If the kids steal something, you would want your kids to be honest? "Smith: Yes."

A short while later, Smith made a statement, stating that it was "off the record".

On the *voir dire* into the admissibility of this statement, Constable Johnson agreed that the officers had entertained no doubt that Smith wanted to consult his lawyer before discussing the robbery. The officers made a conscious effort to dissuade him from this course, as the following excerpt from Constable Johnson's cross-examination discloses:

"Q. Well officer, you agreed with me that you made a conscious effort to persuade him not to involve his lawyer at that point.

"A. Yes.

"Q. Okay. And you did that because you thought that if this man talked to his lawyer he isn't going to say anything to us?

"A. Quite possible, yes.

"Q. Well, it was more than possible. It was what you feared, was it not?

"A. Well, again he was saying he would like his lawyer present before offering his explanation. It's been my experience that most often a lawyer will counsel their client to say nothing.

"Q. And that is what you wanted to avoid, is it not? "A. Yes."

The appellant argues that he did not waive his right to counsel. Following *Clarkson*, [1986] 1 S.C.R. 383, this cannot be successfully disputed. The accused positively and repeatedly asserted his desire to exercise his right to counsel. Answering the questions put to him does not constitute a waiver of his right to counsel in these circumstances. It is clear that these answers were given after he had asserted his desire to speak with his lawyer. It is also clear that he believed they were given "off the record", and the police did nothing to disabuse him of that notion. In these circumstances, it could not be said that there was an awareness of the consequences of speaking in the absence of his lawyer.

The case, as I see it, really turns on whether the appellant had a reasonable opportunity to contact counsel. In my view, the appellant did not have that opportunity. What the evidence discloses is that the appellant was advised of his right to retain and instruct counsel and that he initially requested a telephone to speak with his lawyer. He decided not to make the call thinking, quite reasonably in the view of McLachlin J.A., that at that time of night there would be no one in the lawyer's office. He said he would call his lawyer in the morning. From that point on, he continually asserted his intention not to speak about the robbery in the absence of his lawyer. The evidence also discloses that the police actively dissuaded the accused from his resolve not to speak until he had talked with his lawyer.

The Crown submits, however, that the appellant did not diligently pursue his s. 10(b) rights. I cannot accept this position. The appellant wanted his lawyer, George Brown. It is true that he did not telephone Mr. Brown's office at 9:00 p.m. to get in touch with him, but that does not persuade me that the appellant was not diligently pursuing his rights. An individual in the appellant's position might quite realistically think that he could not reach a lawyer at his office at that time of night and that, even if he did, the lawyer would postpone any meeting to the next day.

I should add that the appellant should be able to wait and get in touch with his lawyer, rather than with any lawyer. If the investigation needed urgently to be pursued, the position might be different, but it cannot be said that there was any urgency in this case. There was nothing that would preclude the investigation from proceeding just as effectively the following morning. The alleged crime had taken place five months before.

The Crown attempted to distinguish *Manninen*, [1987] 1 S.C.R. 1233, from this case on the ground that here the police did not question the accused until after he had made the decision not to telephone his lawyer. The distinction, however, is irrelevant. The essential point in both cases is that the accused asserted and continued to assert his right to counsel. The Crown also attempted to distinguish *Ross*, [1989] 1 S.C.R. 3, on the basis that the arrest in this case took place at 9:00 p.m., whereas that in *Ross* occurred at 2:00 a.m. I do not find this distinction persuasive either. It may be harder to obtain the services of a lawyer at 2:00 a.m., but it is by no means easy to get a specific lawyer at 9:00 p.m. either. To make a distinction such as this is at once to interpret the Charter in a grudging way and to give the police, who must administer the law, very unclear guidelines.

In my view, this case is governed by *Ross*.

. . .

There was no reason to proceed before the appellant had the opportunity to speak with counsel the next morning. As well, as the portions of the transcript set forth in the excerpt from McLachlin J.A.'s judgment cited earlier demonstrate, the police, in questioning the appellant following his insistence on speaking to his lawyer, completely disregarded the appellant's rights.

The only factor I can find in the police's favour in this case is that the appellant did not attempt to call his lawyer. However, I cannot hold it against the appellant that he was willing to spend the night in jail when the likelihood was that he would not have been able to talk to his lawyer that night anyway. All in all, I have no difficulty in holding that the police did not, in the circumstances, give the appellant a reasonable opportunity to retain and instruct counsel. I would go further and say that their conduct constituted a wilful violation of the appellant's rights.

The ruling of the majority has been criticised: see Stanley A. Cohen, "Police Interrogation of the Wavering Suspect", (1989) 71 C.R. (3d) 148 and Patrick Healy, "The Value of Silence", (1990) 74 C.R. (3d) 176.

Has s. 10(*b*) of the Charter been violated in the following cases?

PROBLEM 7

Called to the scene of a minor accident, the police request the driver to submit to a breathalyzer demand at the police station. Before the breathalyzer test is administered the police do not read the accused his rights, but he actually reads for himself a sign containing the words of s. 10(*b*) on the wall. Compare *R. v. Ahearn* (1983), 8 C.C.C. (3d) 257 (P.E.I. C.A.).

PROBLEM 8

The accused, a mechanic, resided in a motorhome parked beside his place of work. Police searched his motorhome acting under a search warrant granted on reasonable grounds for believing that the trailer contained two batteries that were the property of his employer. Batteries were found and the accused was arrested for theft and advised that he had the right to retain and instruct counsel and that he would be permitted to do so at the police station. There was no telephone in the motorhome but there was one at the accused's place of work where he had been when the police arrived. The police officers then warned the accused that he had the right to remain silent but they proceeded to elicit oral statements which they recorded. At the police station the accused tried at the first opportunity to telephone counsel and refused to give a written statement. Compare *R. v. Dombrowski* (1985), 44 C.R. (3d) 1 (Sask. C.A.).

PROBLEM 9

You are retained by Steve, who has been arrested and charged with income tax evasion. You arrange with the sergeant in charge of the lock-up to interview Steve alone in a detective's office. Your previous dealings with the police leave you confident that the room will not be bugged. (It is not.) Your practice is never to ask a client whether he or she is guilty but rather to concentrate on ascertaining what evidence the Crown has obtained. The interview is lengthy and the information Steve is providing is technical and boring. At one point a janitor enters to collect a wastebin and to sweep. "Don't mind me," he says. You don't. At this point Steve is telling you that his "Gold accounts" have not been seized by the police and are in the custody of his girlfriend. A little later you take a break and discover to your horror that the "janitor" is a disguised detective, who is now arranging for a search warrant to seize the "Gold accounts". It turns out that these will be the key Crown evidence.

In decisions in *Sinclair*, *McCrimmon* and *Willier* in 2010 the Supreme Court refused to extend s. 10(b) and appears furthermore to have markedly weakened its protections.

R. v. SINCLAIR

77 C.R. (6th) 203, [2010] 2 S.C.R. 310, 259 C.C.C. (3d) 443 (S.C.C.)

On his arrest for murder, Sinclair was advised of his right to counsel. He had two three-minute conversations with a lawyer of his choice. Seven hours later he was interviewed by a police officer for five hours. S stated on a number of occasions during the interview that he had nothing to say and that he wished to have his lawyer present or to speak with him again. The officer confirmed that S had the right to choose whether to speak. However, he refused to allow S to consult with his lawyer again and advised that he did not have the right to have his lawyer present during questioning. The officer continued the conversation. S finally confessed when the officer told him they had found blood on the hotel bead and (falsely) that the DNA implicated him. The police placed S into a cell with an undercover officer. While in the cell, S made further incriminating statements to that officer. S later accompanied the police to the location where the victim had been killed and participated in a re-enactment. Following a voir dire, the trial judge ruled that the interview, the statements to the undercover officer, and the re-enactment were admissible. The trial judge found that the Crown had proven their voluntariness beyond a reasonable doubt, and that the police had not infringed S's rights as guaranteed by s. 10(b) of the Charter. The B.C. Court of Appeal agreed. The accused appealed.

A 5-4 majority of the Supreme Court dismissed the appeal.

Section 10(b) does not give the right to have a lawyer present during interrogation

According to McLachlin C.J.C. and Charron J. (Deschamps, Rothstein and Cromwell JJ. concurring) s. 10(b) of the Charter does not mandate the presence of defence counsel throughout a custodial interrogation. Precedent was against this interpretation and the language of s. 10(b) did not appear to contemplate this requirement. Moreover, the purpose of s. 10(b) is to inform the detainee of his or her rights and to get legal advice on how to exercise them. These purposes do not demand the continued presence of counsel throughout the interview process. This aspect of the Miranda rule should not be transplanted into Canadian soil. The scope of s. 10(b) of the Charter must be defined by reference to its language; the right to silence; the common law confessions rule; and the public interest in effective law enforcement in the Canadian context. Adopting procedural protections from other jurisdictions in a piecemeal fashion would risk upsetting the balance struck by Canadian courts and legislatures. There was, the majority added, nothing to prevent counsel from being present at an interrogation where all sides consent, as already occurs. The police remain free to facilitate such an arrangement if they so choose, and the detainee may wish to make counsel's presence a precondition of giving a statement [para. 42].

Even the dissenters do not adopt the position that counsel has a right to be present. LeBel and Fish (Abella J. concurring) do not find it necessary for their decision. Binnie J. is of the view that that interpretation would overshoot the s. 10(b) right and he doubts the rule's wisdom and practicability.

> No doubt a defence counsel sitting mute in the interrogation room would be better informed than one who is excluded, but the potential "to delay needlessly and with impunity" cannot be doubted. [para. 101]

5-4 No right to further consultation with counsel unless circumstances objectively change

Majority

The real heat of the very strong divisions in the Court stem from the further decision of the 5-4 majority that the right to counsel normally ends with the initial consultation with counsel. The majority decide that in most cases an initial warning, coupled with a reasonable opportunity to consult counsel when the detainee invokes the right, satisfies s. 10(b). However, the police must give the detainee an additional opportunity to receive advice from counsel where developments in the course of the investigation make this necessary to serve the purpose underlying s. 10(b) of providing the detainee with legal advice relevant to his s. 7 right to choose whether to cooperate with the police interrogation. The majority recognises existing jurisprudence that a second consultation should occur when there is a change of circumstance such as a new procedure for the detainee (e.g. the identification parade in *R. v. Leclair*, [1989] 1 S.C.R. 3, 46 C.C.C. (3d) 129, 67 C.R. (3d) 209 (S.C.C.), or a new jeopardy, where the victim dies, as in *R. v. Black*, [1989] 2 S.C.R. 138, 50 C.C.C. (3d) 1, 70 C.R. (3d) 97 (S.C.C.)) and where the "detainee may not have understood the initial advice" [para. 52]. The wording of the latter category may crack open the door a little for new defence arguments and the majority indicates these categories are not closed [para. 54]. However, the majority quickly adds:

> [55] The change of circumstances, the cases suggest, must be objectively observable in order to trigger additional implementational duties for the police. It is not enough for the accused to assert, after the fact, that he was confused or needed help, absent objective indicators that renewed legal consultation was required to permit him to make a meaningful choice as to whether to cooperate with the police investigation or refuse to do so.

According to the majority, their interpretation of s. 10(b) does not give carte blanche to the police as contended by the dissenters. This argument overlooked the requirement that confessions must be voluntary in the "broad sense" now recognized by the law. The police must not only fulfill their obligations under s. 10(b), they must conduct the interview in strict conformity with the confessions rule.

In this case, the majority found no s. 10(b) breach. The test for a second legal consultation was not met. Before the interview took place, Mr. Sinclair was advised of his right to counsel and twice spoke with counsel of his choice. At the beginning of the interview, he said to the officer that he had been told about some of the devices the police might use to obtain information from him, including lying to him, and that he had been advised not to discuss anything important with anyone. Later in the course of the interview, the police repeatedly confirmed that it was his choice whether he wished to speak with them or not. There were no changed circumstances requiring renewed consultation with a lawyer.

Dissenters

Justices LeBel and Fish (Abella J. concurring) dissented. The words of s. 10(b), and particularly the term "l'assistance" in the French version, connoted a broader role for legal counsel than simply providing the advice to keep quiet. Accordingly, the "assistance" of counsel could not be confined to a single consultation followed by a lengthy interrogation during which the detainee is held virtually incommunicado.

According to these dissenters the right to silence, the right against self-incrimination, and the presumption of innocence work together to ensure that suspects are never obligated to participate in building the case against them. The assistance of counsel is a right granted not only to detainees under s. 10(b) of the Charter, but a right granted to every accused by the common law, the Criminal Code and ss. 7 and 11(d) of the Charter. It is not just a right to the assistance of counsel, but to the effective assistance of counsel, and one that this Court has characterized "as a principle of fundamental justice". Like the right to silence, this right has not been granted to suspects and to persons accused of a crime on the condition that it not be exercised when they are most in need of its protection — notably at the stage of custodial interrogation, when they are particularly vulnerable and in an acute state of jeopardy.

In this case, in the view of these dissenters, S's right to counsel was infringed because the police prevented him from obtaining the legal advice to which he was entitled. His access to legal advice would have mitigated the impact of the police's relentless and skilful efforts to obtain a confession from him. This breach of S's right to counsel went to the core of the self-incrimination interest that s. 10(b) is meant to protect. S's statement to the undercover officer and his participation in the re-enactment were inextricably linked to his original confession and were therefore obtained in violation of s. 10(b) as well. That evidence should be excluded pursuant to s. 24(2) of the Charter. The violation of S's constitutionally guaranteed right to counsel was particularly serious and not merely technical.

Binnie J. dissented on a different basis. An intermediate position should be adopted which would entitle a detainee to a further opportunity or opportunities to receive advice from counsel during a custodial interview where his or her request falls within the purpose of the s. 10(b) right (i.e. related to the need for legal assistance not simply to delay or distract), and such request is reasonably justified by the objective circumstances that were or ought to have been apparent to the police during the interrogation. These factors would include the extent of prior contact with counsel; the length of the interview at the time of the request; the extent of other information (true or false) provided by the police to the detainee about the case during the interrogation, which may reasonably suggest to the detainee that the advice in the initial consultation may have been overtaken by events; the existence of exigent or urgent circumstances that militate against any delay in the interrogation; whether an issue of a legal nature has arisen in the course of the interrogation; and the mental and physical condition of the detainee to the extent that this is or ought to be apparent to the interrogator.

In this case, according to Binnie J., the initial refusal to allow S to consult further with his counsel did not constitute a Charter breach. The breach occurred when after several hours or so of suggestions (subtle and not so subtle) and argument the officer confronted S with what he said was overwhelming evidence linking the accused to the crime and the accused repeated his desire to consult with his counsel. The accused's subsequent admission to the undercover officer in the cell and the re-enactment were causally linked to the Charter breach and should be excluded under s. 24(2).

With which opinion do you agree?

In the companion cases of *R. v. McCrimmon*, 77 C.R. (6th) 266, [2010] 2 S.C.R. 402, 259 C.C.C. (3d) 515 (S.C.C.) and *R. v. Willier*, 77 C.R. (6th) 283, [2010] 2 S.C.R. 429, 259 C.C.C. (3d) 536 (S.C.C.), the Supreme Court justices repeat and apply their *Sinclair* positions in cases where the detainee had only brief access to duty counsel but not to the counsel of their choice. In *McCrimmon* a 6-3 majority found no s. 10(b) violation but in *Willier* the Court was unanimous in finding no violation. In *Willier* each judgement noted that the detainee expressed satisfaction with the advice received from duty counsel and did not assert his right to counsel of his choice with reasonable diligence. The Court rejected the view of the trial judge that W's two conversations with duty counsel were inadequate given their brevity to amount to a meaningful exercise of his right to counsel in this murder case. The police had been entitled to interrogate on a Sunday before the detainee could speak to his lawyer of choice.

In most cases under the *Sinclair* regime the detainee will now get just one chance to speak to a lawyer, who could just be a busy duty counsel. Of course even that will only occur if the detainee is confident enough to assert his right to counsel and to keep asserting it with reasonable diligence, factors key to the companion case rulings. A naive, frightened and timid detainee will get no rights at all. Hopefully the detainee who gets advice will always be advised to keep silent at all costs and should receive detailed instructions as to likely police tactics to wear out any resistance in the coming hours of interrogation. "Lie on the floor and assume the fetal position" suggested one experienced Ottawa defence counsel, Rod Sellars, at a recent conference. Duty counsel need to be quickly re-educated as to their now more crucial role. As Justice Binnie points out, advice to remain silent could actually turn out to be bad advice, for example where there are several accused. However, under *Sinclair* the lawyer will very seldom have another chance to re-consider the initial advice. The majority suggest the lawyer can bargain with the police that the client will only talk if the lawyer is present. Of course the unfettered power to refuse will remain with the police.

We will return to the vehement splits in the Court once we have considered the Court's rulings in *Oickle* and *Singh*.

PROBLEM 10

The accused was arrested and informed of her rights to counsel, including the toll-free number for duty counsel. She indicated she wished to call a specific lawyer, Billy. She repeated this request at the police station. The officer was unable to locate Billy's telephone number and suggested, as a precaution, that he place a call to duty counsel for her. He left a message with duty counsel to call back. The accused found Billy's number. The officer called that number. Billy indicated he was not a lawyer but worked in a law firm and would have someone return the call. Within a minute, duty counsel called back and the accused spoke to that counsel. When the police found that that conversation was over she was turned over to the breath technician. Once in the breath room, the accused reiterated she wanted a lawyer. That request was refused. As she continued to insist on speaking with counsel of her choice before proving a breath sample she was charged with refusal to provide a breath sample. Have her s. 10(b) rights been violated?

See *R. v. Soomal* (2014), 10 C.R. (7th) 279 (Ont. C.J.).

PROBLEM 11

The accused was arrested and charged with operating a vehicle while over 80. On arrest the accused was read his rights to counsel and asked "Do you wish to call a lawyer now?" He replied "Maybe duty counsel later, please give me a break". At 6:36 p.m. the accused was in the booking room. At 6:40 p.m. the arresting officer placed a call for duty counsel. The police had no notes or recall as to why that call was made. At 6:56 the accused had a four-minute conversation with duty counsel. Has there been a breach of the right to consult with counsel of choice?

R. v. Hegedus (2015), 17 C.R. (7th) 368 (Ont. C.J.).

2. Right to Silence

(a) Voluntary Confession Rule prior to *R. v. Oickle*

Confessions are necessary, or at least are perceived by many to be necessary, to effective police enforcement. In *Culombe v. Connecticut,* 367 U.S. 568 (1961), Justice Frankfurter wrote "despite modern advances in the technology of crime detection, offences frequently occur about which things cannot be made to speak". The suspect is seen as a prime source of information concerning the crime and the police believe it essential to question him early and record his position. It is obviously necessary and proper that the police ask questions of those who might have information about a supposed crime. Should the rules be different, however, when the person being questioned becomes, in the eyes of the questioner, not just a source of information but the prime suspect? Should the police behave differently when their investigation has become specific and focusses on the individual as an accused? An accused is not obliged to answer any questions by a judicial officer; should he be required to answer the police officer?

From an early period, our courts have insisted that before an accused's out-of-court statement to a person in authority can be received into evidence it must be proved to be voluntary. In Canada such persuasion needs to be beyond a reasonable doubt; see *R. v. Pickett* (1975), 31 C.R.N.S. 239 (Ont. C.A.).

Prior to the enactment of the Charter in 1982, the Supreme Court insisted that the sole reason for the voluntariness requirement is to promote trustworthiness; a voluntary statement is more deserving of credit. This is evident in the celebrated ruling in *R. v. Wray*, [1971] S.C.R. 272, where the Court held receivable part of an involuntary statement because its truth had been confirmed by facts found as a result. A robbery of a gas station in Peterborough had resulted in the shooting of an attendant. The accused was later arrested, denied access to counsel and then taken to Toronto for a polygraph test. This was followed by an interrogation by the polygraph operator, Jurems:

JUREMS: John, now listen to me good. Now I was through the war, see, and I've been around. Now remember this and remember it good. Have you ever seen rubby dubbies, winos?

WRAY: Yes.

JUREMS: Have you ever seen the alcoholics? WRAY: Yes.

JUREMS: Do you know why they got that way. Have you got a clue? WRAY: No. I have an idea.

JUREMS: I'll explain you something. You have the cerebreal [sic], cerebreal [sic] and then you have the tholmus [sic] and the hipatholmus [sic]. Now a person is going to blot out something he doesn't like, see, but you just can't do it, John. You just no can do, because the subconscious mind takes over and you never live it down. Every time you want to do something you think of it. Now here's this poor joker, he's in the grave, oh, yes, now you can never go to him and explain to him, say I'm sorry I did it. He won't understand you. Do you believe in E.S.P., Extra Sensory Perception?

WRAY: I don't understand it too much, but I know it exists.

JUREMS: All right. All right, do you know what happens when they're dead. The spirit takes off.

WRAY: Yes.

JUREMS: The body's spirit takes off. Now his body's lying there in the grave. Now for Christ sake, John, if you did it, see, if you did it and if you think for one goddamn minute you can live with this all your life without telling you'll never make it. You'll never make it. It will haunt you and in about five years time you will be in the goddamn with the rubby dubs trying to hide it, you'll be trying to get in behind some curtains, you'll be trying to pull a shroud around you but you'll never make it, see. You get half a dozen of those rubby dubs and you bring them in here and I'll put them on the machine and they tell me why they're like that. You know why? They're trying to forget something. They're trying to forget something they did that was very goddamn serious, very bad, see, but they never make it. They go rubby dub, they go here, they steal here, they do every goddamn thing wrong, all their life, eh. Now, if you committed this goddamn thing, see, tell them, tell the cops. What the hell can you get? They're not going to hang you. That's out. There is no capital murder. They're not going to hang you. What do you do. You get in there for seven or eight years and you're out. But at least you've got it and after that you can live with your conscience. But how the hell are you going to go to the grave and explain? You can't, and if you think for one minute, John, remember this that that boy has relatives, that boy has mother and brothers and sisters and do you know what a vindictive person is? Eh? They'll go for you and maybe a year, maybe five years from now you'll be going down the road and some son of a bitch will run you off the road. You'll never know why, but you'll guess why. See. Now, you were there, see.

You were in the goddamn service station. Now when I asked you whether it was an accident you said, yes, and it was an accident, see. There's extenuating circumstances because a person goes in there you didn't go in — you don't go in the — there to shoot the fellow. When a fellow goes in there, sure, what happened to this — look at that goofy one that came here from Montreal, he shot three people in a bank robbery, what did he get, he's out now. He didn't even serve ten years. Three people in a bank robbery. See. So you went in there. You didn't go in there to shoot the guy, but the gun went off. It was at close range. What did he do, grab the gun from you. Did he grab the rifle from you? Eh?

WRAY: No.

JUREMS: What happened? Well, get it off your chest man, you're young, but in a few years you'll be out. But if you think that you're going to live with this, laddie, you'll never ever make it. It's going to bug you for the rest of your goddamn life. And you try and sleep, that's the kicker, you try and lay down and go to sleep. Now what the hell happened there. Did you get in a tussle with him — what happened. Well, spit it out. Your mother knows, your brother knows, your sisters know, your uncle knows. Do you think you can kid your mother for one minute — never! Your mother knows. That's why she tried to protect you. You know. Now what the hell happened, eh? Will you tell us what happened?

WRAY: Yes.

JUREMS: Okay, tell us what happened. WRAY: I went in.

JUREMS: You went in, talk a little louder, John. WRAY: I went in there.

JUREMS: Yeah.

WRAY: To Knoll's.

JUREMS: Yeah, you went in to Knoll's, yeah.

WRAY: And the boy — JUREMS: Which boy? WRAY: There's only one boy.

JUREMS: Just the boy that was shot. Yea, what happened? WRAY: He came out.

JUREMS: Talk a little louder, John. WRAY: He came out.

JUREMS: Yeah.

WRAY: And asked me what I wanted. JUREMS: He asked you what you wanted. WRAY: And I told him to open the till.

JUREMS: And told him to open the till. Was it closed? WRAY: Yes.

JUREMS: And what did he say? WRAY: He said, all right.

JUREMS: He opened the till, yeah

WRAY: And then he — he gave me the money.

JUREMS: He gave you the money. Well, what the hell did you shoot him for? WRAY: It was an accident.

JUREMS: What?

WRAY: It was an accident.

JUREMS: It was an accident. Sure, you showed it on your check it was an accident. All the reactions you gave me when I asked you was the shooting an accident. Well, what the hell is wrong with that. All they are going to charge you with. You went in there, your intentions weren't to do any harm to the man. Where is the gun now?

WRAY: I don't know exactly.

JUREMS: Well, where did you drop it, on the way home? WRAY: No, eh?

JUREMS: On the way to Toronto? WRAY: Yes.

JUREMS: Around Oshawa? WRAY: No.

JUREMS: Where?

WRAY: Near Omemee someplace. JUREMS: Where?

WRAY: Omemee.

JUREMS: Omemee, in the ditch? WRAY: No.

JUREMS: Where? WRAY: In the swamp.

JUREMS: In the swamp. Could you, could you show the police where it is? WRAY: Yes.

JUREMS: Now you're talking like a man. Jesus Christ, John, because you got to live with it all your life, man, oh man, you'll never make it if you a person sleeps, hasn't it been bothering you?

WRAY: Yes.

JUREMS: Have you been sleeping well? WRAY: Yes, fairly well.

JUREMS: But it bothers you. A person never lives it down. Now then, now I'll call in the — the inspector there and you tell him what happened, okay. Will you tell him?

WRAY: Yes.

LIDSTONE: Now, John, you will be charged with the non-capital murder of Donald Comrie on the 23rd day of March, 1968, at Otonabee Township. You are not required to say anything in answer to the charge, but what you do say will be given in evidence. Do you understand that?

WRAY: Yes.

The accused directed the police to the area where the rifle was found and ballistic evidence matched the bullet from the victim's body to the gun. After a lengthy *voir dire*, the trial judge ruled the accused's statement was involuntary and hence legally inadmissible. The prosecution then wished to introduce into evidence the accused's involvement in finding the murder weapon and relied on *R. v. St. Lawrence*, [1949] O.R. 215, 7 C.R. 464, 93 C.C.C. 376 (Ont. H.C.) where McRuer C.J.H.C. had said:

> Where the discovery of the fact confirms the confession—that is, where the confession must be taken to be true by reason of the discovery of the fact—then that part of the confession that is confirmed by the discovery of the fact is admissible, but further than that no part of the confession is admissible.

The trial judge purported to exercise a discretion to disallow this evidence and directed a verdict of acquittal. The Ontario Court of Appeal, while recognizing the validity of the *St. Lawrence* rule, declined to disturb his decision, saying:

> In our view, a trial Judge has a discretion to reject evidence, even of substantial weight, if he considers that its admission would be unjust or unfair to the accused or calculated to bring the administration of justice into disrepute, the exercise of such discretion, of course, to depend upon the particular facts before him. Cases where to admit certain evidence would be calculated to bring the adminisration of justice into disrepute will be rare, but we think the discretion of a trial Judge extends to such cases.

The Supreme Court of Canada reversed and directed a new trial. Martland J. reasoned:

> This development of the idea of a general discretion to exclude admissible evidence is not warranted by the authority on which it purports to be based . . . the exercise of a discretion by the trial Judge arises only if the admission of the evidence would operate unfairly. The allowance of admissible evidence relevant to the issue before the Court and of substantial probative value may operate unfortunately for the accused, but not unfairly. It is only the allowance of evidence gravely prejudicial to the accused, the admissibility of which is tenuous, and whose probative force in relation to the main issue before the court is trifling, which can be said to operate unfairly.

At other times the courts advanced the privilege against self-incrimination as another reason for insisting on voluntariness; the accused's right to silence is made effective by rejecting any statement obtained when that right was overborne. See *R. v. Piche*, [1971] S.C.R. 23, 12 C.R.N.S. 222 (S.C.C.), delivered on the same day as *R. v. Wray*. In *R. v. Piche* the Court held that an accused's out-of-court statement must be proved voluntary though the Crown was not seeking to prove the statement was true but only to show that her evidence at trial was inconsistent with her earlier position.

This debate seems always to have been with us. Regarded by many as the fount of authority in confessions, *Ibrahim v. R.*, [1914] A.C. 599 (P.C.), is itself a prime example of the controversy. In that case Lord Sumner articulated the oft-quoted classic formula:

> It has long been established as a possible rule of English criminal law, that no statement by an accused is admissible in evidence against him unless it is shown by the prosecution to have been *a voluntary statement, in the sense that it has not been obtained from him either by fear of prejudice or hope of advantage exercised or held out by a person in authority.* (Emphasis added).

The bulk of his judgment, however, was spent considering whether there was, apart from this rule, a discretion to exclude when the trial judge viewed the questioning as improper. He recognized that:

> Many judges, in their discretion, exclude such evidence, for they fear that nothing less than the exclusion of all such statements can prevent improper questioning of prisoners by removing the inducement to resort to it.

The Privy Council decided they were unable to settle the matter and that such would have to be done by a court which exercised, as it did not, the revising functions of a general Court of Criminal Appeal.

In 1966, in *Commrs. of Customs and Excise v. Harz,* [1967] 1 A.C. 760 at 820, [1967] 1 All E.R. 177 (H.L.), Lord Reid reviewed the authorities and concluded:

> I do not think that it is possible to reconcile all the very numerous judicial statements on rejection of confessions but two lines of thought appear to underline them: first, that a statement made in response to a threat or promise may be untrue or at least untrustworthy: and, secondly, that nemo tenetur seipsum prodere. It is true that many of the so-called inducements have been so vague that no

reasonable man would have been influenced by them, but one must remember that not all accused are reasonable men or women: they may be very ignorant and terrified by the predicament in which they find themselves. So it may have been right to err on the safe side.

In *Rothman v. R.*, [1981] 1 S.C.R. 640, 20 C.R. (3d) 97 (S.C.C.) the accused was charged with possession of narcotics for the purpose of trafficking. While the accused was lodged in the cells he described his involvement in the trafficking to a person who he believed to be a fellow prisoner. The "fellow prisoner" was in fact a policeman. The Ontario Court of Appeal divided. The majority found the confession rule to be inapplicable as the accused did not regard the undercover officer as a "person in authority" within the meaning of the *Ibrahim* rule. Dubin J.A. dissented:

> In my respectful opinion, the rules respecting confessions and privilege against self-incrimination are related. I use that term in the sense of the right of a person under arrest to remain silent when questioned by law enforcement officers.

On appeal to the Supreme Court of Canada the majority ruled that the privilege against self-incrimination was not relevant to the circumstances presented and Lord Sumner's classic statement of the rule was seemingly exhaustive. Speaking for the majority, Martland J. did allow, however, that even though the Crown meets the requirements there stipulated:

> . . . there may be circumstances involved in connection with the obtaining of the confession from which the Court may conclude that the confession was not free and voluntary, e.g., as in *Horvath* [(1979), 7 C.R. (3d) 97 (S.C.C.)] and *Ward* [[1979] 2 S.C.R. 30, 7 C.R. (3d) 153 (S.C.C.)], where there is a reasonable doubt as to whether the statement was the utterance of an operating mind. In such a case, the confession is not admissible.

In *Ward v. R.*, [1979] 2 S.C.R. 30, 7 C.R. (3d) 153 (S.C.C.), the accused was charged with criminal negligence in the operation of a motor vehicle. He was interviewed by the police shortly after the accident while he was still in a state of shock from its effects. No fear of prejudice or hope of advantage had been held out by any person in authority but still the Court found the trial judge had acted properly in excluding the confession. Embracing this idea see further, *Horvath v. R.* (1979), 7 C.R. (3d) 97 (S.C.C.); *Nagotcha v. R.*, [1980] 1 S.C.R. 714 (S.C.C.), and *Hobbins v. R.* (1982), 27 C.R. (3d) 289 (S.C.C.).

In evaluating the voluntariness of a confession it is commonly understood that the presence or absence of a caution is only one factor to be taken into account with all the other circumstances: see *Boudreau v. R.*, [1949] S.C.R. 262, 7 C.R. 427 (S.C.C.). The existing practice is to give the caution regarding the person's right to remain silent only after the officer has decided to charge the person. Should the officer be obliged to warn the person at an earlier stage, when the person is suspected, but there are not reasonable and probable grounds to arrest and charge? Consider the proposed section by the Law Reform Commission:

A police officer shall not question a suspect with regard to any offence for which that person is a suspect unless he has given that person a warning in the following terms:

You have a right to remain silent, and you are free to exercise that right at any time. If you wish to make a statement or answer questions, anything you say may be introduced as evidence in court. Before you make a statement or answer any questions you may contact a lawyer.

This warning shall be given orally and may also be given in writing.

(*Report No. 23 Questioning Suspects* (1985) 12-13).

SALHANY AND CARTER, FUTURE OF THE LAW OF EVIDENCE—THE RIGHT TO REMAIN SILENT

Studies in Canadian Criminal Evidence (1972)

THE HONOURABLE EDSON HAINES:—I will deal with these matters in the order raised, but first what is this right to remain silent and how did it come about? It is the right of a suspect to refuse to identify himself even to a police officer, to answer his reasonable questions, the right to remain silent at his trial, and the additional right to compel the judge and the prosecution to refrain from any comment to a jury upon the failure of the accused or his wife to testify. There are a few exceptions. For example, a motorist suspected of breach of the traffic laws, or who is involved in an accident, must identify himself, but the suspected murderer, rapist, robber and thief can thumb his nose at a constable, saying, "Prove it if you can, but don't ask me."

That great English jurist and philosopher Jeremy Bentham's criticism of the right to remain silent is still the fullest and best in our literature. He calls the rule:

One of the most pernicious and irrational rules that ever found its way into the human mind... If all criminals of every class had assembled and framed a system after their own wishes, is not this rule the very first they would have established for their security? Innocence never takes advantage of it; innocence claims the right of speaking as guilt invokes the privilege of silence.

Great criminal judges like the famous Mr. Justice Stephen opposed it. Still we retain it, and these are the rules by which we fight the most dangerous criminals. In modern metaphor a member of the Toronto Homicide Squad described it as "a set of Queensberry Rules requiring a police officer to fight with one arm tied behind his back".

The rules about admissibility of statements by accused persons are very ancient. They arose in medieval time when illiterate prisoners often were subject to torture in order to extort confessions. The statements thus obtained were made in the hope of escaping further suffering, so were untrue and not to be relied upon. It must also be remembered that in those days the accused could not testify, call witnesses or be defended by a lawyer. Equally important were the large number of offences punishable by death. A man could be hanged for stealing a sheep. But today there are no such reasons. Adequate safeguards usually exist to prevent the extortion of statements which are false. Our society is literate. The accused is defended by a lawyer (in Ontario at the expense of the province if he cannot afford one), capital punishment has been abolished substantially. The accused can testify, cross-examine, call witnesses and make the fullest defence. His guilt must be proven beyond all reasonable doubt. Trials are in public.

In the middle of this twentieth century what possible reason can exist for not asking the accused in a public court all reasonable questions pertaining to the offence?

Can you justify a pre-trial right to silence? Is there anything wrong with training police interrogators to "Keep control, never provide the suspect with information he is not in possession of" and "Ask questions where the suspect has two answers, both incriminating, such as 'Did you do it on purpose or was it an accident' and 'Did you plan this for a long time or did it happen on the spur of the moment?'"

(b) Principles of Fundamental Justice (Charter, s. 7)

REFERENCE Re SECTION 94(2) OF THE MOTOR VEHICLE ACT
[1985] 2 S.C.R. 486, 48 C.R. (3d) 289, 23 C.C.C. (3d) 289 (S.C.C.)

LAMER J. (Dickson C.J.C., Beetz, Chouinard and Le Dain JJ. concurring):—The concerns with the bounds of constitutional adjudication explain the characterization of the issue in a narrow and restrictive fashion, *i.e.*, whether the terms "principles of fundamental justice" have a substantive or merely procedural content. In my view, the characterization of the issue in such fashion preempts an open-minded approach to determining the meaning of "principles of fundamental justice".

The substantive/procedural dichotomy narrows the issue almost to an all-or-nothing proposition. Moreover, it is largely bound up in the American experience with substantive and procedural due process. It imports into the Canadian context American concepts, terminology and jurisprudence, all of which are inextricably linked to problems concerning the nature and legitimacy of adjudication under the U.S. Constitution. That Constitution, it must be remembered, has no s. 52 nor has it the internal checks and balances of sections 1 and 33. We would, in my view, do our own Constitution a disservice to simply allow the American debate to define the issue for us, all the while ignoring the truly fundamental structural differences between the two constitutions. Finally, the dichotomy creates its own set of difficulties by the attempt to distinguish between two concepts whose outer boundaries are not always clear and often tend to overlap. Such difficulties can and should, when possible, be avoided.

. . .

The task of the Court is not to choose between substantive or procedural content *per se* but to secure for persons "the full benefit of the *Charter's* protection" (Dickson C.J.C. in *R. v. Big M Drug Mart Ltd.*, [1985] 1 S.C.R. 295 at 344 (S.C.C.)), under s. 7, while avoiding adjudication of the merits of public policy. This can only be accomplished by a purposive analysis and the articulation (to use the words in *Curr v. The Queen*, [1972] S.C.R. 889, at p. 899) of "objective and manageable standards" for the operation of the section within such a framework.

. . .

4. *Proceedings and Evidence of the Special Joint Committee of the Senate and of the House of Commons on the Constitution of Canada*

A number of courts have placed emphasis upon the Minutes of the Proceedings and Evidence of the Special Joint Committee of the Senate and of the House of Commons on the Constitution in the interpretation of "principles of fundamental justice". . . .

In particular, the following passages dealing with the testimony of federal civil servants from the Department of Justice have been relied upon:

Mr. Strayer (Assistant Deputy Minister, Public Law):

> Mr. Chairman, it was our belief that the words "fundamental justice" would cover the same thing as what is called procedural due process, that is the meaning of due process in relation to requiring fair procedure. However, it in our view does not cover the concept of what is called substantive due process, which would impose substantive requirements as to policy of the law in question.
>
> This has been most clearly demonstrated in the United States in the area of property, but also in other areas such as the right to life. The term due process has been given the broader concept of meaning both the procedure and substance. Natural justice or fundamental justice in our view does not go beyond the procedural requirements of fairness....
>
> Mr. Strayer: The term "fundamental justice" appears to us to be essentially the same thing as natural justice.

Mr. Tassé (Deputy Minister) also said of the phrase "principles of fundamental justice" in testimony before the Committee:

> We assume that the Court would look at that much like a Court would look at the requirements of natural justice, and the concept of natural justice is quite familiar to courts and they have given a good deal of specific meaning to the concept of natural justice. We would think that the Court would find in that phraseology principles of fundamental justice a meaning somewhat like natural justice or inherent fairness.
>
> Courts have been developing the concept of administrative fairness in recent years and they have been able to give a good deal of consideration, certainly to these sorts of concepts and we would expect they could do the same with this.

The Honourable Jean Chrétien, then federal Minister of Justice, also indicated to the Committee that, while he thought "fundamental justice marginally more appropriate than natural justice" in s. 7, either term was acceptable to the government.

. . .

The main sources of support for the argument that "fundamental justice" is simply synonymous with natural justice have been the Minutes of the Proceedings and Evidence of the Special Joint Committee on the Constitution and the *Bill of Rights* jurisprudence. In my view, neither the Minutes nor the *Bill of Rights* jurisprudence are persuasive or of any great force. The historical usage of the term "fundamental justice" is, on the other hand, shrouded in ambiguity. Moreover, not any one of these arguments, taken singly or as a whole, manages to overcome in my respectful view the textual and contextual analyses.

Consequently, my conclusion may be summarized as follows:

The term "principles of fundamental justice" is not a right, but a qualifier of the right not to be deprived of life, liberty and security of the person; its function is to set the parameters of that right.

Sections 8 to 14 address specific deprivations of the "right" to life, liberty and security of the person in breach of the principles of fundamental justice, and as such, violations of s. 7. They are therefore illustrative of the meaning, in criminal or penal law, of "principles of fundamental justice"; they represent principles which have been recognized by the common law, the international conventions and by the very fact of entrenchment in the Charter, as essential elements of a system for the administration of justice which is founded upon a belief in the dignity and worth of the human person and the rule of law.

Consequently, the principles of fundamental justice are to be found in the basic tenets and principles, not only of our judicial process, but also of the other components of our legal system.

We should not be surprised to find that many of the principles of fundamental justice are procedural in nature. Our common law has largely been a law of remedies and procedures and, as Frankfurter J. wrote in *McNabb v. U.S.* 318 U.S. 332 (1942) at p. 347, "the history of liberty has largely been the history of observance of procedural safeguards". This is not to say, however, that the principles of fundamental justice are limited solely to procedural guarantees. Rather, the proper approach to the determination of the principles of fundamental justice is quite simply one in which, as Professor Tremblay has written, "future growth will be based on historical roots". ((1984) 18 U.B.C.L. Rev. 201 at 254).

Whether any given principle may be said to be a principle of fundamental justice within the meaning of s. 7 will rest upon an analysis of the nature, sources, rationale and essential role of that principle within the judicial process and in our legal system, as it evolves.

Consequently, those words cannot be given any exhaustive content or simple enumerative definition, but will take on concrete meaning as the courts address alleged violations of s. 7.

R. v. HEBERT
[1990] 2 S.C.R. 151, 77 C.R. (3d) 145, 57 C.C.C. (3d) 1 (S.C.C.)

The accused was arrested for robbery. He was advised of his right to retain and instruct counsel and was taken to the police station. He contacted counsel, was advised regarding his right to refuse to give a statement, and was taken to an interview room. He was given the usual police caution and was asked why he had committed the robbery. The accused indicated that he did not wish to make a statement. He was then placed in a cell. An officer, disguised in plain clothes, posed as a suspect under arrest. While in the cell, the officer engaged the accused in conversation, and the accused made incriminating statements which implicated him in the robbery.

The trial judge held that the accused's right to counsel and his right to remain silent had been violated, and excluded the statement. The Crown offered no other evidence, and the accused was acquitted. On appeal, the Court of Appeal held that the trial judge had erred in rejecting the statement, and ordered a new trial. The accused appealed further.

McLACHLIN J. (Dickson C.J.C. and Lamer, La Forest, L'Heureux-Dubé, Gonthier and Cory JJ. concurring):—This case raises the issue of whether a statement made by a detained person to an undercover police officer violates the rights of the accused under the Canadian Charter of Rights and Freedoms.

. . .

The parties agree that s. 7 of the Charter accords a right to silence to a detained person. As Cory J.A. (as he then was) stated in *R. v. Woolley* (1988), 40 C.C.C. (3d) 531 at 539 (Ont. C.A.): "The right to remain silent is a well-settled principle that has for generations been part of the basic tenets of our law." The parties disagree, however, over the extent of the right to silence of a detained person accorded by s. 7 of the Charter.

The Crown submits that the right to silence is defined by the ambit of the confessions rule as it stood at the time the Charter was adopted. It would follow from this that statements obtained by tricks such as the one practised here would be admissible: *Rothman*, [1981] 1 S.C.R. 640.

The accused submits that the right to silence guaranteed by s. 7 of the Charter is broader than the confessions rule as it stood in 1982, and that the use of tricks to obtain a confession after the suspect has chosen not to give a statement violates the Charter.

The parties also agree that s. 10(*b*) of the Charter creates a right to counsel. The disagreement, once again, is as to the extent of that right. Is it confined to s. 10(*b*)? Or is there a broader right to counsel under s. 7?

I see the issues of the right of a detained person to remain silent and the right to counsel as intertwined. The question, as I view it, is whether, bearing in mind the Charter guarantee of the right to counsel and other provisions of the Charter, the accused's right to remain silent has been infringed.

ANALYSIS

I. *Have the appellant's Charter rights been violated?*

(a) General Considerations

The appellant's liberty is at stake. Under s. 7 of the Charter, he can be deprived of that liberty only in accordance with the principles of fundamental justice. The question is whether the manner in which the police obtained a statement from him violates that right. The answer to this question lies in an exploration of the underlying legal principles of our system of justice relevant to a detained person's right to silence. As Lamer J. stated in *Re B.C. Motor Vehicle Act*, [1985] 2 S.C.R. 486 at 503 "the principles of fundamental justice are to be found in the basic tenets of our legal system".

How do we discover the "basic tenets of our legal system" in a case such as this? Initially, it must be by reference to the legal rules relating to the right which our legal system has adopted. As D.J. Galligan points out in "The Right to Silence Reconsidered" (1988), 41 Current Legal Problems 69, at pp. 76-77: "The right . . . is general and abstract, concealing a bundle of more specific legal relationships. It is only by an analysis of the surrounding legal rules that those more precise elements of the right can be identified." Thus rules such as the common law confessions rule, the privilege against self-incrimination and the right to counsel may assist in determining the scope of a detained person's right to silence under s. 7.

At the same time, existing common law rules may not be conclusive. It would be wrong to assume that the fundamental rights guaranteed by the Charter are cast forever in the strait-jacket of the law as it stood in 1982. The reference in s. 7 of the Charter is broadly to "principles of fundamental justice", not to this rule or that. Thus Le Dain J. wrote in *R. v. Therens*, [1985] 1 S.C.R. 613 at 638:

> In my opinion the premise that the framers of the *Charter* must be presumed to have intended that the words used by it should be given the meaning which had been given to them by judicial decisions at the time the *Charter* was enacted is not a reliable guide to its interpretation and application. By its very nature a constitutional charter of rights and freedoms must use general language which is capable of development and adaptation by the courts.

For this reason, a fundamental principle of justice under s. 7 of the Charter may be broader and more general than the particular rules which exemplify it.

A second reason why a fundemantal principle of justice under s. 7 may be broader in scope than a particular legal rule such as the confessions rule is that it must be capable of embracing more than one rule and reconciling diverse but related principles. Thus the right of a detained person to silence should be philosophically compatible with related rights, such as the right against self-incrimination at trial and the right to counsel.

The final reason why a principle of fundamental justice under s. 7 may be broader than a particular rule exemplifying it lies in considerations relating to the philosophy of the Charter and the purpose of the fundamental right in question in that context. The Charter has fundamenally changed our legal landscape. A legal rule relevant to a fundamental right may be too narrow to be reconciled with the philosophy and approach of the Charter and the purpose of the Charter guarantee.

These considerations suggest that the task of defining the scope of the right of a detained person to silence under s. 7 of the Charter must focus initially on the related rules which our legal system has developed—in this case the confessions rule and the privilege against self-incrimination. However, that is not the end of the inquiry. The scope of a fundamental principle of justice will also depend on the general philosophy and purpose of the Charter, the purpose of the right in question, and the need to reconcile that right with others guaranteed by the Charter.

(b) The Scope of the Pre-Trial Right to Silence Suggested by Related Rules

A detained person's right to silence under s. 7 of the Charter is general and abstract, subsuming a bundle of more specific legal relationships. The first step in defining the ambit of the right to silence is to consider these specific relationships and the rules which arise from them, with a view to identifying a common substratum of principle.

The right to silence conferred by s. 7 of the Charter is rooted in two common law concepts. The first is the confessions rule, which makes a confession which the authorities improperly obtain from a detained person inadmissible in evidence. The second is the privilege against self-incrimination, which precludes a person from being required to testify against himself at trial. While the exact scope of the confessions rule has been the subject of debate over the past century, a common theme can be said to unite these two quite separate rules—the idea that a person in the power of the state in the course of the criminal process has the right to choose whether to speak to the police or remain silent.

(i) The Confessions Rule

. . .

The traditional confessions rule set out in *Ibrahim v. R.*, [1914] A.C. 599 (P.C.) [Hong Kong], defines the choice negatively, in terms of the absence of threats or promises by the authorities inducing the statement, and objectively, in terms of the physical acts and words of the parties. The awareness of the detained person of his alternatives is irrelevant. He need not be told that he has the right to remain silent. He need not be told that he has the right to cousult counsel to determine what his options are. The only right he has is a negative right—the right not to be tortured or coerced into making a statement by threats or promises held out by a person who is and whom he subjectively believes to be a person in authority. The act of choosing is viewed objectively, and the mental state of the suspect, apart from his belief that he is speaking to a person in authority, is irrelevant. Were it not for the insistence in the cases that the absence of threats and promises establishes the voluntariness of the statement and that voluntariness is the ultimate requirement for an admissible confession, one would be tempted to say that choice in the usual sense of deciding between altneratives plays little role in the traditional narrow formulation of the confessions rule.

Allied with this narrow concept of choice in the traditional confessions rule is the view that the rationale for the rule is the rejection of unreliable statements. The questions of the suspect's actual state of mind and whether, given that state of mind, it is unfair to use the statement against him do not arise.

The second approach to choice in the confessions rule is much broader. It starts from the proposition that choice involves not only an act but a mental element. On this view, the act of choosing whether to remain silent or speak to the police necessarily comprehends the mental act of selecting one alternative over another. The absence of violence, threats and promises by the authorities does not necessarily mean that the resulting statement is voluntary, if the necessary mental element of deciding between alternatives is absent. On this view, the fact that the accused may not have realized he had a right to remain silent (e.g., where he has not been given the standard warning) or has been tricked into making the statement is relevant to the question of whether the statement is voluntary.

The modern Canadian confessions rule accepts some aspects of this approach. Thus a voluntary choice to confess presupposes an "operating mind": *Horvath v. R.*, [1979] 2 S.C.R. 376 [B.C.]; and *Ward v. R.*, [1979] 2 S.C.R. 30. Beyond this basic requirement, however, the mainstream of contemporary Canadian confessions law has not, by and large, acknowledged the mental element involved in choice. Nevertheless, the second, broader concept of choice persists as part of our fundamental notion of procedural fairness. Older Canadian cases acknowledge it, as does the law in other jurisdictions. And it recurs like a leitmotif through the dissenting judgments of distinguished Canadian jurists and in the work of scholars.

Allied with this second, broader approach to voluntariness or choice under the confessions rule is the view that the rule's rationale goes beyond the exclusion of unreliable statements and extends to considerations of whether reception of the statement will be unfair or tend to bring the administration of justice into disrepute.

Until the case of *R. v. Wray*, [1971] S.C.R. 272 [Ont.], the confessions rule in Canada, as in England and elsewhere in the Commonwealth, may be characterized as an uneasy and to some extent illogical amalgam of these two quite different views of choice. It was said that the test for admissibility was whether the confession was voluntary, which carries with it the idea of an active choice between alternatives. At the same time, voluntariness was said to be established objectively by the simple absence of threats and promises: *Ibrahim*, [1914] A.C. 599 (P.C.).

. . .

Nevertheless, until the decision in *Wray*, supra, it was generally thought to be open to judges in Canada to reject statements which met the *Ibrahim* test but which had been obtained unfairly. As Kaufman J.A. puts it (F. Kaufman, The Admissibility of Confessions, 3rd ed. (1979), at p. 236):

> It was generally believed, and not without reason, that a judge was entitled to exercise his discretion in cases such as these, and that appellate courts would not lightly interfere.

. . .

Wray changed this. The issue in that case was the admissiblity, not of a confession, but rather of real evidence obtained as a result of a statement. Nevertheless, the principle enunciated had a profound effect on the power of a trial judge to exclude a confession which was, strictly speaking, admissible on the *Ibrahim* test. The ruling was simple: a court did not have the power to exclude admissible and relevant evidence merely because its admission would bring the administration of justice into disrepute. This represented a divergence from the approach to confessions elsewhere in the Commonwealth. Instead of a two-pronged approach to confessions—the basic rule supplemented by a residual discretion to exclude on grounds of unfairness or the repute of the administration of justice—Canada was left with the narrow *Ibrahim* rule. Reliability was the only concern. All statements were admissible unless induced by threats, promises or violence.

It was in this context that the majority of this court ruled in *Rothman*, supra, that a statement obtained by a trick after the accused had indicated his wish not to speak to the authorities was admissible. As Martland J., speaking for five of the nine judges, succinctly put it at p. 666:

> It was not, in my opinion, a sufficient basis for the refusal of the trial judge to receive the confession in evidence solely because he disapproved of the method by which it was obtained.

Not all judges found it easy to accept the strictures of *Wray* and the departure it represented from a more liberal jurisprudence elsewhere in the Commonwealth. In *Rothman*, Lamer J., after an extensive review of the authorities, concluded that the rule governing the reception of confessions was twofold: such statements might be excluded either where the conduct of the persons in authority to whom they were made might have rendered them untrue, or where the conduct of the authorities in obtaining the statement would tend to bring the administration of justice into disrepute. Lamer J. (who agreed with the majority in the result) also affirmed that the suspect's right of silence—the right to choose whether to make a statement to the authorities or to remain silent—was fundamental to the confessions rule.

Estey J., dissenting (Laskin C.J.C. concurring), similarly emphasized the connection between the confessions rule and the fairness and repute of the judicial process, basing his dissent on his conclusion that the use of an undercover agent to obtain a statement would bring into disrepute the administration of justice.

The reasons of Estey J. and Lamer J. disclose an array of distinguished Canadian jurists who recognized the importance of the suspect's freedom to choose whether to give a statement to the police or not, and emphasized the fairness and repute of the administration of justice as an underlying reationale for the confessions rule, both before and after *Wray*. Among them is Chief Justice Freedman, "Admissions and Confessions", reproduced in R.E. Salhany and R.J. Carter (eds.), Studies in Canadian Criminal Evidence (1972), at p. 99, who emphasized the centrality to the confessions rule of individual freedom and the integrity of the judicial system:

> It is justice then that we seek, and within its broad framework we may find the true reasons for the rule excluding induced confessions. Undoubtedly . . . the main reason for excluding them is the danger that they may be untrue. But there are other reasons, stoutly disclaimed by some judges, openly professed by others, and silently acknowledged by still others—the last perhaps being an instance of an "inarticulate major premise" playing its role in decision-making. These reasons, all of them, are rooted in history. They are touched with memories of torture and the rack, they are bound up with the cause of individual freedom, and they reflect a deep concern for the integrity of the judicial process.

. . .

(ii) The Privilege Against Self-Incrimination

The second rule which is closely concerned with the right to silence of a person in jeopardy in the criminal process is the privilege against self-incrimination. It is distinct from the confessions rule, applying at trial rather than at the investigational phase of the criminal process: see *Marcoux v. R.*, [1976] 1 S.C.R. 763 at 768-69 [Ont.]. Yet it is related to the confessions rule, both philosophically and practically.

Philosophically, courts have frequently justified both the confessions rule and the privilege against self-incrimination by reference to the right of every person not to be required to produce evidence against himself—nemo tenetur seipsum accusare. The privilege against self-incrimination, like the confessions rule, is rooted in an abhorrence of the interrogation practised by the old ecclesiastical courts and the Star Chamber and the notion, which grew out of that abhorrence, that the citizen involved in the criminal process must be given procedural protections against the over-weening power of the state. While the privilege against self-incrimination relies in part on a notion which does not find place in the confessions rule—the obligation of the Crown to prove its case—it shares with that rule the notion that an accused person has no obligation to give evidence against himself, that he or she has the right to choose. This, it may be postulated, is the shared conceptual core of the two rules fundamental to the more general right to silence.

From a practical point of view, the relationship between the privilege against self-incrimination and right to silence at the investigatorial phase is equally clear. The protection conferred by a legal system which grants the accused immunity from incriminating himself at trial but offers no protection with respect to pre-trial statements would be illusory. As Ratushny writes (Self-Incrimination in the Canadian Criminal Process (1979), at p. 253):

> Furthermore, our system meticulously provides for a public trial only after a specific accusation and where the accused is protected by detailed procedures and strict evidentiary rules. Ordinarily he is represented by a lawyer to ensure that he in fact receives all of the protections to which he is entitled. The accused is under no legal or practical obligation to respond to the accusation until there is an evidentiary case to meet. There is a hypocrisy to a system which provides such protections but allows them all to be ignored at the pre-trial stage where interrogation frequently occurs in secret, after counsel has been denied, with no rules at all and often where the suspect or accused is deliberately misled about the evidence against him.

The privilege against self-incrimination clearly imports the right to choose whether to testify or to remain silent. The accused is usually advised by counsel. The presence of the presiding judge precludes undue pressure by the Crown. The consequences of testifying or not are clear. The philosophic and practical relationship between the privilege against self-incrimination and the right of the suspect to silence prior to trial suggests that the same right of choice should prevail at the earlier phase of the criminal process.

(iii) Summary of Implications to be Drawn From the Rules Relating to the Right to Silence

Despite their differences, the common law confessions rule and the privilege against self-incrimination share a common theme—the right of the individual to choose whether to make a statement to the authorities or to remain silent, coupled with concern with the repute and integrity of the judicial process. If the measure of a fundamental principle of justice under s. 7 is to be found, at least in part, in the underlying themes common to the various rules related to it, then the measure of the right to silence may be postulated to reside in the notion that a person whose liberty is placed in jeopardy by the criminal process cannot be required to give evidence against himself or herself, but rather has the right to choose whether to speak or to remain silent. This suggests that the scope of the right of a detained person to silence prior to trial under s. 7 of the Charter must extend beyond the narrow view of the confessions rule which formed the basis of the decision of the majority of this court in *Rothman*, supra.

(c) The Scope of the Right of a Detained Person to Silence Suggested by Other Provisions of the Charter

The common law rules relating to the right to silence suggest that the essence of the right is the notion that the person whose freedom is placed in question by the judicial process must be given the choice of whether to speak to the authorities or not. The next question is whether this hypothesis is confirmed by consideration of the right to silence in the context of other Charter provisions.

. . .

(i) Related Rights

. . .

The most important function of legal advice upon detention is to ensure that the accused understands his rights, chief among which is his right to silence. The detained suspect, potentially at a disadvantage in relation to the informed and sophisticated powers at the disposal of the state, is entitled to rectify the disadvantage by speaking to legal counsel at the outset, so that he is aware of his right not to speak to the police and obtains appropriate advice with respect to the choice he faces. Read together, ss. 7 and 10(*b*) confirm the right to silence in s. 7 and shed light on its nature.

The guarantee of the right to consult counsel confirms that the essence of the right is the accused's freedom to choose whether to make a statement or not. The state is not obliged to protect the suspect against making a statement; indeed, it is open to the state to use legitimate means of persuasion to encourage the suspect to do so. The state is, however, obliged to allow the suspect to make an informed choice about whether or not he will speak to the authorities. To assist in that choice, the suspect is given the right to counsel.

This suggests that the drafters of the Charter viewed the ambit of the right to silence embodied in s. 7 as extending beyond the narrow formulation of the confessions rule, comprehending not only the negative right to be free of coercion induced by threats, promises or violence, but a positive right to make a free choice as to whether to remain silent or speak to the authorities.

. . .

(ii) The Philosophy of the Charter with Respect to Improperly-Obtained Evidence

The narrow view of the confessions rule adopted in Canada in recent years stems primarily from the *Wray* approach, which emphasized reliability of evidence and virtually removed the discretion of the courts to reject statements on the ground that they had been obtained unfairly.

The Charter introduced a marked change in philosophy with respect to the reception of improperly- or illegally-obtained evidence. Section 24(2) stipulates that evidence obtained in violation of rights may be excluded if it would tend to bring the administration of justice into disrepute, regardless of how probative it may be. No longer is reliability determinative. The Charter has made the rights of the individual and the fairness and integrity of the judicial system paramount. The logic upon which *Wray*, supra, was based and which led the majority in *Rothman*, supra, to conclude that a confession obtained by a police trick could not be excluded, finds no place in the Charter. To say there is no discretion to exclude a statement on grounds of unfairness to the suspect and the integrity of the judicial system, as did the majority in *Rothman*, runs counter to the fundamental philosophy of the Charter.

This suggests that the right of a detained person to silence under s. 7 of the Charter should be viewed as broader in scope than the confessions rule as it stood in Canada at the time of the adoption of the Charter. The right must reflect the Charter's concerns with individual freedom and the integrity of the judicial process, and permit the exclusion of evidence which offends these values.

(iii) The Purpose of the Right to Silence under the Charter

. . .

In a broad sense, the purpose of ss. 7 to 14 is twofold: to preserve the rights of the detained individual, and to maintain the repute and integrity of our system of justice. More particularly, it is to the control of the superior power of the state vis-à-vis the individual who has been detained by the state, and thus placed in its power, that s. 7 and the related provisions that follow are primarily directed. The state has the power to intrude on the individual's physical freedom by detaining him or her. The individual cannot walk away. This physical intrusion on the individual's mental liberty in turn may enable the state to infringe the individual's mental liberty by techniques made possible by its superior resources and powers.

The Charter, through s. 7, seeks to impose limits on the power of the state over the detained person.

. . .

The scope of the right to silence must be defined broadly enough to preserve for the detained person the right to choose whether to speak to the authorities or to remain silent, notwithstanding the fact that he or she is in the superior power of the state. On this view, the scope of the right must extend to exclude tricks which would effectively deprive the suspect of his choice. To permit the authorities to trick the suspect into making a confession to them after he or she has exercised the right of conferring with counsel and declined to make a statement is to permit the authorites to do indirectly what the Charter does not permit them to do directly. This cannot be in accordance with the purpose of the Charter.

. . .

(d) Conclusion of the Scope of the Right to Silence

. . .

The right to choose whether or not to speak to the authorities is defined objectively rather than subjectively. The basic requirement that the suspect possess an operating mind has a subjective element. But, this established, the focus under the Charter shifts to the conduct of the authorities vis-à-vis the suspect. Was the suspect accorded the right to consult counsel? Was there other police conduct which effectively and unfairly deprived the suspect of the right to choose whether to speak to the authorities or not?

Such a change, while important, is far from radical. It retains the essentially objective approach of the traditional confessions rule, while increasing the range of police conduct which may be considered in determining the admissibility of a suspect's statement, and it conforms to current trends in the law. Even before the Charter, this court had taken a step away from the traditional "threat-promise" formula by recognizing that the decision to speak to the police must be the product of an operating mind. Moreover, experience in other jurisdictions—and in ours, I venture to suggest—has proven the traditional *Ibrahim* formulation of the confessions rule too narrow. The idea that judges can reject confessions on grounds of unfairness and concerns for the repute and integrity of the judicial process has long been accepted in other democratic countries without apparent adverse consequences. Thus in England, Australia and New Zealand the traditional confessions rule has been supplemented by judicial discretion. In the United States it has been abandoned. In Canada, its retention has been marked by continual tension between minority and majority viewpoints, between what trial judges feel they should do in justice and what they find they are compelled to do. To those tensions has now been added an evident tension with the philosophy underlying the Charter. The jurisprudence on the rights of detained persons can only benefit, in my view, from rejection of the narrow confessions formula and adoption of a rule which permits consideration of the accused's informed choice, as well as fairness to the accused and the repute of the administration of justice.

Finally, the change proposed arguably strikes a proper and justifiable balance between the interest of the state in law enforcement and the interest of the suspect. The alternative—the strict post-*Wray* application of the confessions rule—leaves courts powerless to correct abuses of power by the state against the individual, so long as the objective formalities of the "threat-promise" formula are filled and the statement is reliable. Drawing the balance where I have suggested that the Charter draws it permits the courts to correct abuses of power against the individual, while allowing them to nevertheless admit evidence under s. 24(2) where, despite a Charter violation, the admission would not bring the administration of justice into disrepute.

This approach may be distinguished from an approach which assumes an absolute right to silence in the accused, capable of being discharged only by waiver. On that approach, all statements made by a suspect to the authorities after detention would be excluded unless the accused waived his right to silence. Waiver, as defined in *Clarkson v. R.*, [1986] 1 S.C.R. 383, is a subjective concept dependent, among other things, on the accused's knowing that he is speaking to the authorities. On this approach, *all* statements made by a person in detention which were not knowingly made to a police officer would be excluded because, absent knowledge that the suspect is speaking to a police officer, the Crown cannot establish waiver. This would include statements made to undercover agents (regardless of whether the officer is merely passive or has elicited the statement) as well as conversations with fellow prisoners overheard by the police and statements overheard through mechanical listening devices on the wall. There is nothing in the rules underpinning the s. 7 right to silence or other provisions of the Charter that suggests that the scope of the right to silence should be extended this far. By contrast, the approach I advocate retains the objective approach to confessions which has always prevailed in our law, and would permit the rule to be subject to the following limits.

First, there is nothing in the rule to prohibit the police from questioning the accused in the absence of counsel after the accused has retained counsel. Presumably, counsel will inform the accused of the right to remain silent. If the police are not posing as undercover officers and the accused chooses to volunteer information, there will be no violation of the Charter. Police persuasion, short of denying the suspect the right to choose or depriving him of an operating mind, does not breach the right to silence.

Second, it applies only after detention. Undercover operations prior to detention do not raise the same considerations. The jurisprudence relating to the right to silence has never extended protection against police tricks to the pre-detention period. Nor does the Charter extend the right to counsel to pre-detention investigations. The two circumstances are quite different. In an undercover operation prior to detention, the individual from whom information is sought is not in the control of the state. There is no need to protect him from the greater power of the state. After detention, the situation is quite different: the state takes control and assumes the responsibility of ensuring that the detainee's rights are respected.

Third, the right to silence predicated on the suspect's right to choose freely whether to speak to the police or to remain silent does not affect voluntary statements made to fellow cellmates. The violation of the suspect's rights occurs only when the Crown acts to subvert the suspect's constitutional right to choose not to make a statement to the authorities. This would be the case regardless of whether the agent used to subvert the accused's right was a cellmate, acting at the time as a police informant, or an undercover police officer.

Fourth, a distinction must be made between the use of undercover agents to observe the suspect and the use of undercover agents to actively elicit information in violation of the suspect's choice to remain silent. When the police use subterfuge to interrogate an accused after he has advised them that he does not wish to speak to them, they are improperly eliciting information that they were unable to obtain by respecting the suspect's constitutional right to silence: the suspect's rights are breached, because he has been deprived of his choice. However, in the absence of eliciting behaviour on the part of the police, there is no violation of the accused's right to choose whether or not to speak to the police. If the suspects speaks, it is by his or her own choice, and he or she must be taken to have accepted the risk that the recipient may inform the police.

It may be noted that a similar distinction has been made in the United States under the Sixth Amendment, which provides that: "In all criminal prosecutions, the accused shall . . . have the Assistance of Counsel for his defense." American courts have consistently held that the use of undercover police to question an accused in prison violates this amendment, as the accused has the right to have his lawyer present when being questioned. The leading case is *Kuhlmann v. Wilson*, 477 U.S. 436 (1986). There the police paid an informer to listen to and report the accused's incriminating evidence but gave the informer explicit instructions not to elicit any information. The Supreme Court of the United States held that the evidence was admissible, concluding that "the defendant must demonstrate that the police and their informant took some action, beyond merely listening, that was designed deliberately to elicit incriminating remarks." (p. 459). Thus, even under the arbuably, more stringent American constitutional protection, the law permits the use of a police informant after detention, provided he or she does not take active and intentional steps to elicit confession.

Some Canadian police forces appear to already be following the rules implict in this approach. Thus in *R. v. Logan* (1988), 30 O.A.C. 321 (C.A.), it is stated at p. 365:

> In his evidence, P.C. Grant (testifying under the pseudonym used by him in the undercover operation) said:
>
> "(P)art of my instructions entailed—and it was made quite clear to me that *I was not to initiate any conversation, if possible, with the accused persons* and in the event that we did or were able to get in conversations with these persons, that *we would not ask leading questions or lead them on to the area in which Iwasattempting to gather information for.*
>
> "(W)e were to act as normal as possible and of course from further instructions from the official we had a very good idea of what would be an acceptable line of conversation, what questions would [sic] be acceptable, what wouldn't be acceptable."
>
> [Emphasis added.]

Moreover, even where a violation of the detainee's rights is established, the evidence may, where appropriate, be admitted. Only if the court is satisfied that its reception would be likely to bring the administration of justice into disrepute can the evidence be rejected: s. 24(2). Where the police have acted with due care for the accused's rights, it is unlikely that the statements they obtain will be held inadmissible.

(e) Application of the Right to Silence in This Case

The essence of the right to silence is that the suspect be given a choice: the right is quite simply the freedom to choose—the freedom to speak to the authorities, on the one hand, and the freedom to refuse to make a statement to them, on the other. This right of choice comprehends the notion that the suspect has been accorded the right to consult counsel and thus to be informed of the alternatives and their consequences, and that the actions of the authorities have not unfairly frustrated his or her decision on the question of whether to make a statement to the authorities.

In this case, the accused exercised his choice not to speak to the police when he advised them that he did not wish to make a statement. When he later spoke to the undercover policeman, he was not reversing that decision and choosing to speak to the police. He was choosing to speak to a fellow prisoner, which is quite a different matter. The Crown, in using a trick to negate his decision not to speak, violated his rights.

II. *Section 1 of the Charter*

Having found a violation of s. 7, the question arises of whether s. 1 of the Charter has application. In my view, it does not, since the conduct here in question is not a limit "prescribed by law" within s. 1.

In *R. v. Thomsen*, [1988] 1 S.C.R. 640 at 650-51, Le Dain J. stated for the court [quoting *Therens*, supra, at p. 645]:

> The limit will be prescribed by law within the meaning of s. 1 if it is expressly provided for by statute or regulation, or results by necessary implication from the terms of a statute or regulation or from its operating requirements. The limit may also result from the application of a common law rule.

The police conduct here at issue does not meet this test. It was not done in execution of or by necessary implication from a statutory or regulatory duty, and it was not the result of application of a common law rule. In short, it was not "prescribed by law" within s. 1 of the Charter.

. . .

CONCLUSION

I would allow the appeal and restore the acquittal.

SOPINKA J.:—This appeal raises the vexed question whether jailhouse confessions induced by deception can withstand Charter scrutiny. For the reasons that follow, I am of the view that they cannot.

. . .

I would respectfully adopt the *Clarkson* standard as appropriate in relation to waiver of the right to remain silent. The right to remain silent is, as much as the right to counsel, predicated on the fair treatment of an accused in the criminal process. Indeed, in an important respect, the right to remain silent is more fundamental. The principal effect in many cases of granting the right to counsel is that the accused is informed of the right to remain silent: *R. v. Manninen*, [1987] 1 S.C.R. 1233 at 1242-43, per Lamer J. It follows, in my view, that any waiver of the right to remain silent must, similar to a waiver of the right to counsel, pass an "awareness of the consequences" test.

This court has applied the *Clarkson* standard in relation to several different Charter rights: see, e.g., *R. v. Conway*, [1989] 1 S.C.R. 1659 at 1686 (s. 11(*b*)); and *R. v. Turpin*, [1989] 1 S.C.R. 1296 at 1315-16 (s. 11(*f*)). In my opinion, to now hold that something less than informed waiver can suffice to deprive an accused of the right to remain silent would be inconsistent with this court's previous position on waiver of these other equally important Charter rights, and could signal an errosion of the high standard we have required for waiver of the right to counsel itself. This right is, as pointed out by my colleague, similar to the right to remain silent, in that each involves making a choice. Accordingly, this course does not appeal to me, either in principle or as a matter of policy.

It is patent that the deliberate deception practiced here prevented (indeed, was designed to prevent) the appellant from being aware of the consequences of his actions, and that it operated to vitiate any waiver that might have been forthcoming otherwise. In the circumstances, there could be no waiver, and the appellant's right to remain silent, as embodied in s. 7 of the Charter, was violated.

. . .

WILSON J.:—I have had the benefit of the reasons of my colleagues Justice McLachlin and Sopinka, and wish only to address very briefly the issues on which their reasons disclose a significant difference of view. There are three of them, namely:

1. When does the right to silence arise?
2. What is the scope of the right to silence?
3. Does the doctrine of waiver apply to the right of silence?

1. *When does the right to silence arise?*

I would respectfully agree with my colleagues Sopinka J. that the right to silence, if it is to achieve the purpose that it was clearly intended to achieve, must arise whenever the coercive power of the state is brought to bear upon the citizen. I think that this could well predate detention and extend to the police interrogation of a suspect. It will of course be a question of fact in each case whether or not the coercive power of the state has been brought to bear upon the citizen. This is not an issue in the present case.

2. *What is the scope of the right to silence?*

I agree with my colleagues that the right to silence is a principle of fundamental justice within the meaning of s. 7 of the Canadian Charter of Rights and Freedoms and that a person cannot therefore be deprived of his or her right to life, liberty or security of the person by violating that right.

I believe that the right must be given "a generous rather than a legalistic [interpretation], aimed at fulfilling the purpose of the guarantee and securing for individuals the full benefit of the *Charter's* protection": see *R. v. Big M Drug Mart Ltd.*, [1985] 1 S.C.R. 295, per Dickson J. (as he then was) at p. 344 [S.C.R.]. It is accordingly inappropriate to qualify it by balancing the interests of the state against it or by applying to it the considerations relevant to the admissibility of evidence set out in s. 24(2) of the Charter.

Section 7 confers on an accused the right to life, liberty and security of the person. It then provides that the accused may not be deprived of that right except in accordance with the principles of fundamental justice. In other words, he or she may be deprived of the s. 7 right provided the deprivation is effected without offending fundamental justice. In deciding whether or not the authorities have offended fundamental justice, it is, in my view, essential to focus on the treatment of the accused and not on the objective of the state. It would, in my view, be quite contrary to a purposive approach to the s. 7 right to inject justificatory considerations for putting limits upon it into the ascertainment of its scope or content.

I believe for the same reasons that it is inappropratie to merge the question whether statements elicited in violation of the s. 7 right should be admitted into evidence with the question whether the right has in fact been violated.The repute of the justice system is, in my view, relevant only to the former. It has no bearing on whether the right to silence has been violated contrary to the principles of fundamental justice.

3. *Does the doctrine of waiver apply to the right to silence?*

Justice McLachlin finds the doctrine of waiver inapplicable to the right to silence, on the basis, as I understand it, that it is not an absolute right but must be qualified by considerations of the state interest and the repute of the justice system. It seems to me, however, that, once it is determined that an individual has a choice, as my colleague states, to either remain silent or to speak to the authorities, and he or she decides voluntarily and with full knowledge and appreciation of the consequences to speak to the authorities, then he or she must be taken to have waived (or given up) the right to silence. I see no reason why the doctrine of waiver should not apply to the right to silence as it does to other rights in the Charter.

For these reasons and for the reasons given by my colleague Justice Sopinka, I agree with his proposed disposition of the appeal.

For differing views on *Hebert*, see Michael Brown, "The American Approach to Cell Statements Makes Good Sense", (1990) 77 C.R. (3d) 194 and Patrick Healy, "The Right to Remain Silent: Value Added, But How Much?" (1990) 77 C.R. (3d) 199.

PROBLEM 12

An undercover police officer was assigned to attend the preliminary inquiry into a murder alleged to have been committed by J and D. She was instructed to pose as a student writing a paper on the judicial system and to become friendly with D's wife in the hope of overhearing conversations which might assist in the investigation. During the preliminary inquiry, Mrs. D told the officer that J was interested in her. The officer informed her superiors, who instructed her to visit J at the local gaol, still posing as a student. She visited J in the gaol 6 times over a 6-month period and exchanged correspondence. She wanted to get from J whatever information she could about the killing and tried to build a close relationship with him. J developed a strong sexual interest in her. Most of the conversations were not about the killing but the officer tried to direct the conversations to the killing and on more than one occasion put specific questions provided to her by her superiors. Were these statements obtained in violation of the accused's right to silence under s. 7?

Compare *R. v. Jackson* (1991), 9 C.R. (4th) 57, 68 C.C.C. (3d) 385 (Ont. C.A.). See also *R. v. Broyles*, [1991] 3 S.C.R. 595, 9 C.R. (4th) 1, 68 C.C.C. (3d) 308 (S.C.C.) and *R. v. Liew*, [1999] 3 S.C.R. 227, 27 C.R. (5th) 29, 137 C.C.C. (3d) 353 (S.C.C.).

R. v. TURCOTTE

[2005] 2 S.C.R. 519, 31 C.R. (6th) 197, 200 C.C.C. (3d) 289 (S.C.C.)

The accused went to a police station and asked that a car be sent to the ranch where he lived and worked. Despite repeated questions from the police, he refused to explain why a car was necessary or what would be found at the ranch. He indicated there was a rifle in his truck. Officers found three victims at the ranch. All three died from axe wounds to the head. The accused was charged with three counts of second degree murder.

At trial, the evidence against the accused was entirely circumstantial, including his conduct at the police station, fingerprints on two items at the farm and small blood stains from two of the victims found on his clothing. The accused admitted finding the victims but denied killing them. With respect to the accused's refusal to respond to police questioning as to why he told them to go to the farm, the trial judge told the jury that they could not draw inferences from the accused's silence but that this silence could be considered as relevant to his state of mind. He later instructed the jury that it could be considered "post-offence conduct", and that it was the only circumstantial evidence proving guilt. The jury returned a verdict of guilty on each count.

The B.C. Court of Appeal set aside the convictions and ordered a new trial. No adverse inference should have been drawn from the accused's silence. The Crown appealed.

. . .

ABELLA J.:

The essence of the Crown's argument is that Mr. Turcotte's refusal to respond to some of the questions from the police can be relied on as post-offence conduct from which an inference of guilt can be drawn.

"Post-offence conduct" is a legal term of art. It is not meant to be a neutral term embracing all behaviour by an accused after a crime has been committed, but only that conduct which is probative of guilt. It is, by its nature, circumstantial evidence.

The more traditional designation of such conduct, "consciousness of guilt" evidence, was changed by this Court to "post-offence conduct" evidence in *R. v. White*, [1998] 2 S.C.R. 72. Major J. held, at para. 20, that use of the phrase "consciousness of guilt" should be discouraged because it might undermine the presumption of innocence or may mislead the jury. In *White*, at para. 19, Major J. provided a non-exhaustive list of conduct that is typically admitted as post-offence conduct evidence: flight from the scene of the crime or the jurisdiction in which the crime was committed; attempts to resist arrest; failure to appear at trial; and acts of concealment such as lying, assuming a false name, changing one's appearance, and hiding or disposing of evidence. In *White*, the post-offence conduct was the accused's running from the police to avoid arrest, the attempted disposal of one of the murder weapons, and fleeing the jurisdiction following the killing.

Although the terminology has been changed, the evidentiary concept has not. As with evidence of "consciousness of guilt", only evidence after a crime has been committed that is probative of guilt can be relied on as "post-offence conduct".

The first issue, therefore, is to determine whether the trial judge erred in designating Mr. Turcotte's refusal to answer some of the police questions as "post-offence conduct" capable of supporting an inference of guilt. This in turn requires a determination of whether Mr. Turcotte had the right to refuse to answer the police's questions. The Crown's dual argument is that no right to silence was engaged in this case, but that even if it was, Mr. Turcotte's conduct in going to the police station and answering some of the police's questions, showed that it was a right he chose to waive.

Under the traditional common law rules, absent statutory compulsion, everyone has the right to be silent in the face of police questioning. This right to refuse to provide information or answer inquiries finds cogent and defining expression in *Rothman v. The Queen*, [1981] 1 S.C.R. 640, per Lamer J.:

> In Canada the right of a suspect not to say anything to the police . . . is merely the exercise by him of the general right enjoyed in this country by anyone to do whatever one pleases, saying what one pleases or choosing not to say certain things, unless obliged to do otherwise by law. It is because no law says that a suspect, save in certain circumstances, must say anything to the police that we say that he has the right to remain silent, which is a positive way of explaining that there is on his part no legal obligation to do otherwise. [Footnotes omitted; p. 683]
> [page12]

Although its temporal limits have not yet been fully defined, the right to silence has also received Charter benediction. In *R. v. Hebert*, [1990] 2 S.C.R. 151, 57 C.C.C. (3d) 1, the first ..... McLachlin J. founded the s. 7 right to silence in two common law doctrines: the confessions rule and the privilege against self-incrimination, explaining that both emerge from the following unifying theme:

The idea that a person in the power of the state in the course of the criminal process has the right to choose whether to speak to the police or remain silent. [p. 164]

It would be an illusory right if the decision not to speak to the police could be used by the Crown as evidence of guilt. As Cory J. explained in *Chambers*, where the trial judge failed to instruct the jury that the accused's silence could not be used as evidence of guilt:

> It has as well been recognized that since there is a right to silence, it would be a snare and a delusion to caution the accused that he need not say anything in response to a police officer's question but nonetheless put in evidence that the accused clearly exercised his right and remained silent in the face of a question which suggested his guilt. [p. 1316]

Although *Chambers* dealt specifically with silence after the accused had been cautioned, it would equally be "a snare and a delusion" to allow evidence of any valid exercise of the right to be used as evidence of guilt.

Moreover, as Doherty and Rosenberg JJ.A. explained in *R. v. B. (S.C.)* (1997) 119 C.C.C. (3d) 530 (Ont. C.A.), since, in most circumstances, individuals are under no obligation to assist the police, their silence cannot, on its own, be probative of guilt: [page 13]

> . . . a refusal to assist is nothing more than the exercise of a recognized liberty and, standing alone, says nothing about that person's culpability. [p. 529]

Evidence of silence is, however, admissible in limited circumstances. As Cory J. held in *Chambers*, at p. 1318, if "the Crown can establish a real relevance and a proper basis", evidence of silence can be admitted with an appropriate warning to the jury.

There are circumstances where the right to silence must bend. In *R. v. Crawford*, [1995] 1 S.C.R. 858, for example, the Court was confronted with a conflict between the right to silence and the right to full answer and defence. Two men were charged with second degree murder after a man was beaten to death. At their joint trial, each blamed the other. Crawford, one of the accused, had not given the police a statement, but he chose to testify at trial in his own defence. His co-accused's counsel cross-examined him on his failure to make a statement to the police. This failure was negatively contrasted with the fact that his co-accused had given a full statement to the police at the earliest opportunity. Sopinka J., writing for the majority, held that a balance between the two competing rights can be achieved if the evidence of silence is admitted, but used only to assess credibility and not to infer guilt. Since the jury had been invited to infer guilt from Crawford's silence, the Court ordered a new trial.

Evidence of silence may also be admissible when the defence raises an issue that renders the accused's silence relevant. Examples include circumstances where the defence seeks to emphasize the accused's cooperation with the authorities (*R. v. Lavallee*, [1980] O.J. No. 540 (QL) (C.A.)); where the accused testified that he had denied the charges against him at the time he was arrested (*R. v. Ouellette* (1997) 119 C.C.C. (3d) 30 (B.C.C.A.)); or where silence is relevant to the defence theory of mistaken identity and a flawed police investigation (*R. v. M.C.W.* (2002) 165 C.C.C. (3d) 129) (B.C.C.A.). Similarly, cases where the accused failed to disclose his or her alibi in a timely or adequate manner provide a well established exception to the prohibition on using pre-trial silence against an accused: *R. v. Cleghorn*, [1995] 3 S.C.R. 175. Silence might also be admissible if it is inextricably bound up with the narrative or other evidence and cannot easily be extricated.

The Crown argued that any right to silence is engaged only when the accused comes within "the power of the state" and that the right has no relevance when the state has done nothing to use that power against the individual. This, with respect, makes the right's borders too confining. In general, absent a statutory requirement to the contrary, individuals have the right to choose whether to speak to the police, even if they are not detained or arrested. The common law right to silence exists at all times against the state, whether or not the person asserting it is within its power or control. Like the confessions rule, an accused's right to silence applies any time he or she interacts with a person in authority, whether detained or not. It is a right premised on an individual's freedom to choose the extent of his or her cooperation with the police, and is animated by a recognition of the potentially coercive impact of the state's authority and a concern that individuals not be required to incriminate themselves. These policy considerations exist both before and after arrest or detention. There is, as a result, no principled basis for failing to extend the common law right to silence to both periods.

Nor do I share the Crown's view that by attending at the detachment and answering some of the police's questions, Mr. Turcotte waived any right he might otherwise have had. A willingness to impart some information to the police does not completely submerge an individual's right not to respond to police questioning. He or she need not be mute to reflect an intention to invoke it. An individual can provide some, none, or all of the information he or she has. A voluntary interaction with the police, even one initiated by an individual, does not constitute a waiver of the right to silence. The right to choose whether to speak is retained throughout the interaction.

At various points throughout the trial, the Crown, and the trial judge at the Crown's request, characterized Mr. Turcotte's silence in two ways: as post-offence conduct evidence (called "consciousness of guilt" evidence by the Crown), and as state of mind evidence rebutting his claim to be in shock and panic. Most troubling was the trial judge's final instructions on post-offence conduct. During this portion of his instructions, the trial judge told the jury that Mr. Turcotte's silence was post-offence conduct and zeroed in on his silence as the only relevant post-offence conduct. His invocation was: "[y]ou may decide that the only substantial evidence proving the guilt of Mr. Turcotte arises from his post-offence conduct".

Even before his detention at 10:06 a.m., Mr. Turcotte had no duty to speak to or cooperate with the police. He exercised this right by refusing to answer some of the questions put to him by the police, declining to explain why a car should be sent to the Erhorn Ranch and refusing to say what the police would find there. Although he answered some of the police's questions, when he did not answer others he was nonetheless exercising his right to silence.

This is significant in deciding whether evidence of his silence was admissible as post-offence conduct, that is, evidence that is probative of guilt. Conduct after a crime has been committed is only admissible as "post-offence conduct" when it provides circumstantial evidence of guilt. The necessary relevance is lost if there is no connection between the conduct and guilt. The law imposes no duty to speak to or cooperate with the police. This fact alone severs any link between silence and guilt. Silence in the face of police questioning will, therefore, rarely be admissible as post-offence conduct because it is rarely probative of guilt. Refusing to do what one has a right to refuse to do reveals nothing. An inference of guilt cannot logically or morally emerge from the exercise of a protected right. Using silence as evidence of guilt artificially creates a duty, despite a right to the contrary, to answer all police questions.

Since there was no duty on Mr. Turcotte's part to speak to the police, his failure to do so was irrelevant; because it was irrelevant, no rational conclusion about guilt or innocence can be drawn from it; and because it was not probative of guilt, it could not be characterized for the jury as "post-offence conduct".

Nor do I see how Mr. Turcotte's silence could be used as "state of mind" evidence from which guilt could be inferred. The Crown argued that Mr. Turcotte's silence negated his claim that his state of mind was one of shock and panic. It is clear from the Crown's closing argument that there was little difference between asking the jury to consider Mr. Turcotte's silence as evidence of his state of mind, and asking them to consider it as evidence of his guilty conscience. So, for example, during his closing argument the Crown argued:

> That may tell you something about the guilty mind of Mr. Turcotte at the time. But again, it doesn't show that he was in a state of shock or panic, but rather [page16] that he was thinking about what he said and chose to say what he wanted to say and didn't want to say.

In order to make this claim, it was necessary for the Crown to suggest that his silence was motivated by a different state of mind, namely his guilty conscience. Characterizing the silence as state of mind evidence was simply another way of arguing that the silence was post-offence conduct probative of Mr. Turcotte's guilt.

While not admissible as post-offence conduct or state of mind evidence, Mr. Turcotte's behaviour at the R.C.M.P. detachment, including his refusal to answer some of the police's questions, was, arguably, admissible as an inextricable part of the narrative. As previously indicated, no issue was raised about its admissibility either at trial or on appeal. But, having admitted his silence into evidence, the trial judge was obliged to tell the jury in the clearest of terms that it could not be used to support an inference of guilt in order to contradict an intuitive impulse to conclude that silence is incompatible with innocence. Where evidence of silence is admitted, juries must be instructed about the proper purpose for which the evidence was admitted, the impermissible inferences which must not be drawn from evidence of silence, the limited probative value of silence, and the dangers of relying on such evidence. The failure to give the jury this limiting instruction, particularly given the circumstantial nature of the Crown's case, was highly prejudicial.

Given the significance of the error, I agree with the Court of Appeal that the curative proviso is inapplicable and a new trial is required.

Appeal dismissed.

After *Turcotte* it will be especially important to distinguish between the common law right to silence, on which the judgment turns, and the s. 7 Charter pre-trial right to silence recognised in *R. v. Hebert.*

The Court decides that the common law right to silence applies whether or not the accused was cautioned as to the right to silence prior to arrest or detention and also that the doctrine of waiver applies. As to waiver, as you cannot waive something of which you are unaware, it would appear that the Court is asserting a common law right to be advised of the right to silence, although it never says this expressly. In contrast, limits imposed on the Charter right to silence recognized in *Hebert* include that the right is only triggered on detention and that the doctrine of waiver does not apply.

The gains in *Turcotte* are not all in favour of accused. The Court indicated that evidence of silence is admissible in limited circumstances with an appropriate warning where the Crown can establish a real relevance and a proper basis. Justice Abella offered six examples. The sixth is "inextricably bound up with the narrative or other evidence and cannot easily be extricated". No authority is provided for this new exception. Resort to language of "admissible as part of the narrative" is notorious as a device to avoid evidential rules and principles. In this case, Abella J. remarked that the evidence of how the accused refused to answer the police may "arguably be admissible as part of the narrative". This may suggest that the Court was not unanimous on this point. Justice Abella did say that

> juries would have to instructed about the proper purpose for which evidence was admitted, the impermissible inferences which must not be drawn from evidence of silence, the limited probative value of silence, and the dangers of relying on such evidence [para. 58].

Could a jury ever not use such evidence to draw an adverse inference from silence or lack of co-operation? If this exception is widely applied, the right to silence may be illusory, which is what the Court set out to avoid.

(c) Non-compellability (s. 11(c)) and Privilege against Self-incrimination (s. 13)

> 11. Any person charged with an offence has the right. . .
>
> (c) not to be compelled to be a witness in proceedings against that person in respect of the offence;
>
> 13. A witness who testifies in any proceedings has the right not to have any incriminating evidence so given used to incriminate that witness in any other proceedings, except in a prosecution for perjury or for the giving of contradictory evidence.

The Canada Evidence Act and the Charter appear to be very specific as to the scope of a person's privilege against self-incrimination. Non-compellability is bestowed only on those who are charged with an offence and protection is only in proceedings in respect to that offence. Subsequent use immunity is granted to those who are asked questions which tend to incriminate but the immunity is against the use of the evidence given; there is no immunity against the use of evidence discovered, or derived from the answers. Until quite recently there was not in Canada a broad principle against self-incrimination. There existed two protections: non-compellability at trial (see s. 4 of the Canada Evidence Act and s. 11(c) of the Charter) and protection against subsequent use of evidence given at a prior proceeding (see s. 5(2) of the Canada Evidence Act and s. 13 of the Charter). Justice Iacobucci wrote in S.(R.J.) (1995), 36 C.R. (4th) 1 (S.C.C.):

> Before the Charter, and, indeed, before Thomson Newspapers [(1990), 76 C.R. (3d) 129 (S.C.C.)], it was generally believed that there was no functional principle against self-incrimination, but only a collection of specific rules which might be grouped beneath such a label.

In Rothman v. R. (1981), 59 C.C.C. (2d) 30 (S.C.C.), the Court dealt with a confession obtained by an undercover officer in the accused's cell. This was a year before the Charter. Lamer, J. concurred in the result that the confession was admissible and characterized the "right to silence":

> In Canada, the right of a suspect not to say anything to the police is not the result of a right of no self-incrimination, but is merely the exercise by him of the general right enjoyed in this country by anyone to do whatever one pleases, saying what one pleases or choosing not to say certain things, unless obliged to do otherwise by law.

In Dubois v. The Queen, [1985] 2 S.C.R. 350, the Court addressed the admissibility into evidence of statements made by an accused at his first trial for murder into the second trial. The Court decided that this was a violation of s. 13 of the Charter. In doing so, the Court noted that otherwise the Crown would be able to do indirectly what it couldn't do directly by virtue of s. 11(c) of the Charter, i.e. compel the accused to testify. It also was observed that permitting receipt of his earlier testimony would permit an indirect violation of the right to be presumed innocent as guaranteed by s. 11(d) of the Charter. The Court found underlying the Charter rights in 11(c), 11(d) and s. 13 and the benefit of an initial right to silence at trial the common concept of a "case to meet".

This was extended in R. v. Mannion, [1986] 2 S.C.R. 272, 53 C.R. (3d) 193, 28 C.C.C. (3d) 544 to prevent cross-examination by the Crown on the accused's testimony from the first trial, although this ruling was on the narrow footing that the purpose of the cross-examination was to incriminate Mannion. Then, in R. v. Kuldip, [1990] 3 S.C.R. 618, 1 C.R. (4th) 285, 61 C.C.C. (3d) 385, the Supreme Court held that cross-examination on the accused's previous voluntary testimony is permitted if the purpose is to impugn her credibility, rather than to incriminate her. The policy behind Kuldip was laudable — to prevent an accused from advancing conflicting versions without being faced with the inconsistency — but the distinction between an incriminating purpose and impugning credibility was sometimes difficult to draw and to explain clearly to a jury. In *R. v. Noël*, [2002] 3 S.C.R. 433, 5 C.R. (6th) 1, 168 C.C.C. (3d) 193, the Supreme Court decided that under s.13 of the Charter, when an accused testifies at trial, he or she cannot be cross-examined on prior testimony from an earlier trial unless the trial judge is satisfied that there is no realistic danger that the prior testimony could be used to incriminate the accused.

Subsequent to *Noël*, however, in *R. v. Henry*, [2005] 3 S.C.R. 609, 33 C.R. (6th) 215, 202 C.C.C. (3d) 449, Justice Binnie, speaking for the Supreme Court of Canada, simplified the Court's interpretation of s. 13. In *Henry*, the two accused had voluntarily testified at their first trial and then, after a new trial was ordered, provided quite different testimony at their second trial. The s. 13 issue arose because the Crown cross-examined them on their prior inconsistent testimony. On the previous jurisprudence, *Mannion* would have barred the cross-examination. However, the Supreme Court departed from its previous position and overruled *Mannion* and modified *Kuldip*. The position now is that the focus has shifted to whether or not the accused voluntarily testified at the other proceeding. If so, the Crown may cross-examine on the prior testimony, regardless of whether the purpose is to impeach credibility or to incriminate. The Court declined, however, to overrule *Dubois*, with the result that the Crown may not introduce the prior testimony as a part of its case in chief, even if the accused voluntarily testified at the previous trial. On the other hand, where the accused has been compelled to testify in the previous proceeding, usually at the trial of another person, that prior testimony may not be used by the Crown for any purpose at the accused's trial. Thus, the decision leaves *Noël* intact as well. For comments on *Henry*, see: Stuart, "Annotation" (2005), 33 C.R. (6th) 215 and Hamish Stewart, "*Henry* in the Supreme Court of Canada: Reorienting the s. 13 Right against Self-incrimination" (2006), 34 C.R. (6th) 112, especially at 119.

Henry was partially reversed in the Supreme Court's complex divided ruling in *Nedelcu*. In essence the full Court first confirms the basic ruling in *Henry* that use immunity under s. 13 of the Charter only applies where an accused gave incriminating evidence under compulsion at a prior proceeding. However, Justice Moldaver for a 6-3 majority held the trial judge had not erred in permitting the Crown to cross-examine the accused on civil discovery statements because the statements were not incriminating, as "incriminating evidence" only refers to evidence the Crown could (if permitted) use in subsequent proceedings to prove or assist in proving one or more essential elements of the offence charged.

This effectively reversed the clear bright line approach under *Henry* that previously compelled testimony is always inadmissible even if tendered for credibility, a pragmatic decision widely applauded by judges and commentators. See comments of Stuart, *Charter Justice in Canadian Criminal Law* (6th ed., 2014) pp. 559-565, Paul Calarco, "*R. v. Nedelcu*: Whatever Happened to a Large and liberal Interpretation of the Charter?"

(2013), 96 C.R. (6th) 438, and Lisa Dufraimont, "Section 13 Use Immunity After *R. v. Nedelcu*" (2013), 96 C.R. (6th) 431.

R. v. NEDELCU
[2012] S.C.J. No. 59, 96 C.R. (6th) 391 (S.C.C.)

The accused took a fellow employee, P, for a motorcycle ride on company property. There was a crash. P was not wearing a helmet and suffered permanent brain damage. The accused suffered minor brain damage and was hospitalised overnight. The accused was charged with dangerous driving causing bodily harm. At trial the Crown sought to cross-examine the accused on his examination for discovery in a civil suit by P and his family. In his discovery answers on oath the accused indicated he had no memory of the accident until he woke up the next day in hospital. At the criminal trial 14 months later, he gave a detailed account of how the accident occurred. The trial judge allowed the Crown to cross-examine on the statement as to credibility on the basis that s. 13 of the Charter did not apply to compelled discovery evidence in a civil case. The accused was not afforded the protection of s. 13 of the Charter because his situation did not meet the quid pro quo rationale of compulsion. The accused had given his discovery evidence to further his own private interest in a civil action against him. The accused was convicted and appealed.

The Ontario Court of Appeal, applying *Henry*, allowed the appeal, quashed the conviction and ordered a new trial. The Court held that under s. 13 of the Charter the accused's compelled testimony on civil discovery is inadmissible at the subsequent criminal trial for purposes of incrimination or for testing credibility. The protection was not only available where the prior testimony assists the Crown. The accused had been compelled to testify on the examination for discovery solely for the benefit of the plaintiffs. Quid pro quo had a wider meaning than that given by the trial judge. Any other proceeding in s. 13 includes royal commissions, statutory boards and tribunals, bankruptcy proceedings, and other forms of judicial and quasi-judicial proceedings. The trial judge's distinction between criminal and non-criminal interrogatories was not relevant.

On further appeal a 6-3 majority allowed the Crown appeal and substituted a conviction.

MOLDAVER J. (McLACHLIN C.J.C. and DESCHAMPS, ABELLA, ROTHSTEIN, and KARAKATSANIS JJ. concurring):—

1 I have had the privilege of reading Justice LeBel's reasons for judgment and I agree with him on the issue of compulsion. In particular, I accept his conclusion, at para. 109, that Mr. Nedelcu "was statutorily compellable, and therefore 'compelled' ... for the purposes of s. 13 [of the Canadian Charter of Rights and Freedoms]" to testify at his examination for discovery in the civil action.

2 Where I part company with my colleague is on the interpretation of s. 13 and in particular, its application to the facts of this case. In my respectful view, s.

13 was never meant to apply to a case such as this—and I am convinced it does not. This Court's decision in *R. v. Henry*, 2005 SCC 76, [2005] 3 S.C.R. 609, does not provide otherwise.

. . .

4 The difficulty I have with the present case is that there was no "quid" for there to be a "quo"—and hence, in my view, s. 13 was never engaged. I would accordingly allow the appeal.

. . .

6 As I read [section 13] , the "quid" that forms the critical first branch of the historical rationale, refers to "incriminating evidence" the witness has given at a prior proceeding in which the witness could not refuse to answer. The section does not refer to all manner of evidence the witness has given at the prior proceeding. It refers to "incriminating evidence" the witness has given under compulsion.

7 The "quo" refers to the state's side of the bargain. In return for having compelled the witness to testify, to the extent the witness has provided "incriminating evidence", the state undertakes that it will not use that evidence to incriminate the witness in any other proceeding, except in a prosecution for perjury or for the giving of contradictory evidence.

8 Thus, a party seeking to invoke s. 13 must first establish that he or she gave "incriminating evidence" under compulsion at the prior proceeding. If the party fails to meet these twin requirements, s. 13 is not engaged and that ends the matter.

9 What then is "incriminating evidence"? The answer, I believe, should be straightforward. In my view, it can only mean evidence given by the witness at the prior proceeding that the Crown could use at the subsequent proceeding, if it were permitted to do so, to prove guilt, i.e. to prove or assist in proving one or more of the essential elements of the offence for which the witness is being tried.

. . .

16 The law is clear and I accept it to be so, that the time for determining whether the evidence given at the prior proceeding may properly be characterized as "incriminating evidence" is the time when the Crown seeks to use it at the subsequent hearing. (See *Dubois v. The Queen*, [1985] 2 S.C.R. 350, at pp. 363-64). That however, does not detract from my contention that the evidence to which s. 13 is directed is not "any evidence" the witness may have been compelled to give at the prior proceeding, but evidence that the Crown could use at the subsequent proceeding, if permitted to do so, to prove the witness's guilt on the charge for which he or she is being tried.

17 In so concluding, I recognize that there will be instances where evidence given at the prior proceeding, though seemingly innocuous or exculpatory at the time, may become "incriminating evidence" at the subsequent proceeding, thereby triggering the application of s. 13.

18 Take for example, the witness who, at the trial of a third party for robbery, admits to having been present at the scene of the crime but denies any

involvement in it. If the witness is subsequently charged with the same robbery and testifies that he was not present when the robbery occurred, his evidence from the prior proceeding, though innocuous at the time, will have taken on new meaning. For purposes of s. 13, it would now be treated as "incriminating evidence" because it is evidence that the Crown could use at the witness's robbery trial, if permitted to do so, to prove the essential element of identity. And that is where s. 13 comes in. It precludes the Crown from introducing it for any purpose, whether as part of its case to prove identity or as a means of impeaching the witness's testimony.

19 Manifestly, I take a different view where the evidence given by the witness at the prior proceeding could not be used by the Crown at the subsequent proceeding to prove the witness's guilt on the charge for which he or she is being tried. In such circumstances, because the prior evidence is not "incriminating evidence", there can be no "quid" for purposes of s. 13—and because there is no "quid", no "quo" is owed in return. The case at hand provides a classic example of this.

. . .

LEBEL J. (FISH and CROMWELL JJ. concurring) (dissenting):—

44 The right against self-incrimination is a principle that lies at the heart of our justice system and is enshrined in the *Canadian Charter of Rights and Freedoms*. A specific form of protection against self-incrimination is the right against testimonial self-incrimination provided for in s. 13 of the *Charter*. Section 13 protects a witness who gives evidence in any proceeding from having that evidence used against him or her in a subsequent proceeding. This *Charter* guarantee has engendered many decisions of this Court, the latest significant pronouncement being *R. v. Henry*, 2005 SCC 76, [2005] 3 S.C.R. 609.

45 The Crown asks this Court to reconsider the s. 13 principles it unanimously espoused in *Henry*. For the reasons that follow, I would decline to do so. I would therefore dismiss the appeal.

. . .

D. Compelled Testimony

101 One of the Crown's main submissions is that the respondent was not "compelled" to testify at his examination for discovery in the civil action against him in the sense described in *Henry*. The Crown argues that the respondent was not subjectively compelled, because he freely decided to attend the discovery proceeding [FAP 36], and that he was not objectively compelled, because he chose to file a statement of defence and to therefore put himself "within the grasp of procedural rules ... that would, only then, compel his evidence" (A.F., at para. 37).

102 Although Binnie J. did not fully canvass what constitutes "compelled" evidence in the *Henry* sense, he did note that an accused who chooses to testify freely at his or her first trial and then at a retrial is not "compelled" and so does not qualify for s. 13 protection (para. 43). He also stated parenthetically that "[f]or present purposes, evidence of compellable

witnesses should be treated as compelled even if their attendance was not enforced by a subpoena" (para. 34; emphasis added).

103 Binnie J.'s observation that evidence from an accused who decides to testify is "voluntary" simply means that, because accused persons have a right not to be called to testify in their own defence under s. 11(c) of the *Charter*, any accused who chooses to testify waives his or her right not to be compellable. In contrast, a witness who voluntarily gives evidence at someone else's trial is not giving evidence "voluntarily" within the meaning of *Henry* even if the witness decides to testify on his or her own volition, for example, to assist the accused. The difference is this: An accused who testifies voluntarily is waiving a constitutional right by choosing to testify. Any other witness can otherwise be compelled, meaning the witness is statutorily compellable regardless of whether he or she "volunteers" to take the stand. This view is confirmed by Binnie J.'s observation that "evidence of compellable witnesses should be treated as compelled even if their attendance was not enforced by a subpoena".

104 Therefore, whether the respondent freely decided to attend the discovery proceeding is irrelevant. Whether a witness was compelled should not be determined on a subjective standard. It would be unprincipled to give a lesser degree of *Charter* protection to a witness who testifies willingly than to a witness who must be subpoenaed or otherwise forced to give evidence, if both could have been statutorily compelled to testify in any event. Therefore, to determine whether the quid pro quo is engaged in a particular case, the court should consider whether the witness was statutorily compellable and not whether the witness felt subjectively compelled to testify. The relevant question is this: Was the respondent statutorily compelled to give evidence in the proceeding?

105 The Crown's second argument on compulsion is that the respondent was not objectively compelled because he chose to file a statement of defence, and therefore that he voluntarily put himself within the grasp of the powers of civil discovery.

106 This argument must also fail. First, as noted by the intervener Advocates' Society, the integrity of the civil discovery process could be undermined if courts considered that those who defend civil actions are not "compelled" for the purposes of s. 13. Parties facing criminal proceedings might then find it advantageous not to co-operate in any civil action, thereby forcing the other party to obtain a court order compelling their testimony on discovery.

. . .

E. Should the Court Revisit *Henry*?

110 *Henry* makes it quite clear that the distinction between using prior compelled testimony to impeach credibility and using it to incriminate the accused is unworkable. Even using so-called "innocent statements" to expose inconsistencies in the testimony of an accused will, as Martin J.A. said in *Kuldip*, "assist the Crown in its case and, in a broad sense, may help to prove guilt" (p. 23). Counsel for the respondent summarized this

concern in oral argument before this Court: "... the distinction doesn't really exist between incriminating and impeaching. If you are impeaching, you are advancing the Crown's case. There may be an inference of consciousness of guilt" (transcript, at p. 52).

111 I agree that, in the context of s. 13, there can be no such distinction in practice. Any evidence that may assist the Crown in proving its case, including evidence impeaching the credibility of the accused, will have an incriminating effect and must therefore be subject to s. 13 protection.

112 It seems evident, therefore, that this distinction is not compatible with the underlying purpose of s. 13. One need only go back to the cases in which the distinction was maintained to see just how inconsistently—and at times arbitrarily—it was applied in practice. There were undoubtedly accused persons whose s. 13 *Charter* rights were unduly diminished under this approach. It is for this reason that the Court abolished this problematic distinction in *Henry*.

113 The concerns expressed in *Henry* with respect to the difference between using prior compelled testimony to impeach credibility and using it to incriminate still exist. Should this Court nevertheless revisit *Henry* on this point?

. . .

115 In my view, there are no substantial reasons to believe *Henry* was wrongly decided. Nor are there any compelling or principled reasons to reintroduce the distinction between impeachment and incrimination, thereby reducing the scope of s. 13 of the Charter. *Henry* is a fairly recent, unanimous decision of this Court, which has largely been welcomed by the profession for providing predictability and simplifying the law in this area . . .

116 Nothing has changed since *Henry*, and it should not be revisited.

. . .

128 . . ., my colleague's approach dilutes *Henry*. As I stated earlier in these reasons, *Henry* has been lauded as a decision that brought predictability and clarity to a previously murky area of law. This interpretation of *Henry* will again send the application of s. 13 into a state of confusion. It will cause uncertainty regarding the s. 13 rights of an accused.

129 I am not aware of any decision since *Henry* in which a court has inquired into whether the statements of an accused were "innocent" or "incriminating" in order to determine whether s. 13 applied. Courts will now have to conduct voir dires to make this determination, which will both encumber the trial process and render the scope of s. 13 dubious in theory and uncertain in practice. Such uncertainty undermines the objective of the quid pro quo, which is to encourage full and frank testimony. Without knowing in advance how their evidence might be used in future proceedings, witnesses will undoubtedly be less likely to display candour, a consequence that is completely at odds with what this Court sought to accomplish in *Henry*. This will also undoubtedly reduce the scope of the s. 13 protection that previously compelled witnesses have had since *Henry*.

130 In *Henry*, Binnie J. recognized the importance of ensuring predictability in the application of s. 13. He concluded his reasons by stating that the approach he proposed would avert the "unpredictability inherent in sorting out attacks on credibility from attempts at incrimination" (para. 60). In my view, my colleague's opinion reintroduces uncertainty by resurrecting the abandoned distinction, for s. 13 purposes, between "innocuous" and "incriminating" evidence. Witnesses will be less likely to testify truthfully if they do not know, when called to testify, whether and to what extent the evidence they give will be admissible against them in future proceedings.

With whom do you agree?

(d) Principle against Self-incrimination (s. 7)

In *R. v. P. (M.B.)* (1994), 29 C.R. (4th) 209 (S.C.C.), the Court, deciding it was wrong to permit the prosecution to reopen its case after the accused had outlined its defence, repeated the thought of a "case to meet," and spoke of:

> Perhaps the single most important organizing principle in criminal law is the right of an accused not to be forced into assisting in his or her own prosecution... This means, in effect, that an accused is under no obligation to respond until the state has succeeded in making out a prima facie case against him or her. In other words, until the Crown establishes that there is a "case to meet", an accused is not compellable in a general sense (as opposed to the narrow, testimonial sense) and need not answer the allegations against him or her.

> The broad protection afforded to accused persons is perhaps best described in terms of the *overarching principle against self-incrimination*, which is firmly rooted in common law and is a fundamental principle of justice under s. 7 of the Charter. (at 226, emphasis added)

The Court recognized that apart from the *privilege* against self-incrimination, which grants the specific protections outlined above, there is also a *principle* against self-incrimination which may give greater protection than formerly contemplated. This is not merely seen as an organizing principle of existing rules and principles but one that has the capacity to introduce new protections.

In *R. v. Jones* (1994), 30 C.R. (4th) 1 (S.C.C.) the issue was the receipt into evidence of pre-trial psychiatric assessments on dangerous offender proceedings that were initiated after the finding of guilt. The accused had agreed to the assessments for the purposes of determining fitness to stand trial and the possibility of an insanity defence. The majority saw no violation of s. 7 as guilt had already been determined and the dangerous offender proceedings were sentencing provisions. The dissent saw things differently as the *principle* against self-incrimination was of broad scope. Chief Justice Lamer expanded on what he had earlier written about the *principle*:

> Any state action that coerces an individual to furnish evidence against himself in a proceeding in which the individual and the state are adversaries violates the

principle against self-incrimination. . . . The *privilege* is the narrow traditional common law rule relating only to testimonial evidence at trial. (at 41)

There has been, in the past, an ability in the state to avoid the strictures of the privilege against self-incrimination, by compelling a suspect or an accused to testify at some other proceeding prior to his criminal trial and discovering evidence usable against him at his trial. The Court may have now moved to foreclose that possibility.

The accused in *R. v. S. (R.J.)* (1995), 36 C.R. (4th) 1, 96 C.C.C. (3d) 1, [1995] 1 S.C.R. 451 (S.C.C.) was charged with break enter and theft. The charges were laid separately because of a procedure at Youth Court which called for different trials dependent on the age of the youths. M. was charged separately with the same offence. M. was subpoenaed by the Crown as its main witness at the accused's trial. The subpoena was quashed on the basis that otherwise M.'s right to silence under s. 7 would be violated. *S.(R.J.)* involves a complex series of divided opinions in the Supreme Court. Differently constituted majorities establish doctrines of derivative use immunity and a discretion to exempt witnesses from compellability. A 5/4 majority decided that in addition to the protection against the subsequent use of testimony, there is also protection under s. 7 of the Charter against the use of evidence derived from such testimony. In addition a differently constituted 5/4 majority decided that an exception to the general rule of compellability could be made in appropriate circumstances.

In *British Columbia Securities Commission v. Branch* (1995), 38 C.R. (4th) 133, 97 C.C.C. (3d) 505, [1995] 2 S.C.R. 3 (S.C.C.), the Court amplified its earlier thoughts on compellability. Two officers of a company were served with summonses from the Commission compelling their attendance for examination and requiring them to produce all records in their possession. The summonses were issued pursuant to the provincial Securities Act. When the officers failed to appear, the Commission sought an order from the Court committing the officers for contempt. The officers applied for a declaration that the Act violated ss. 7 and 8 of the Charter.

The Supreme Court decided that the principle against self-incrimination required that persons compelled to testify be provided with subsequent derivative-use immunity in addition to the use immunity guaranteed by s. 13 of the Charter. The accused would have the evidentiary burden of showing a plausible connection between the compelled testimony and the evidence later sought to be adduced. Once this was done, in order to have the evidence admitted, the Crown would have to satisfy the court on a balance of probabilities that the authorities would have discovered the impugned derivative evidence absent the compelled testimony. They also decided that in addition courts can, in certain circumstances, grant exemptions from compulsion to testify. The crucial question was whether the predominant purpose for seeking the evidence is to obtain incriminating evidence against the person compelled to testify or rather some legitimate public purpose. That test was seen to strike the appropriate balance between the interests of the state in obtaining the evidence for a valid public purpose on the one hand, and the right to silence of the person compelled to testify on the other.

In *R. v. B. (S.A.)*, [2003] 2 S.C.R. 678, 14 C.R. (6th) 205, 178 C.C.C. (3d) 193 (S.C.C.) the Court dismissed a number of Charter challenges to the D.N.A. warrant powers. In the course of this ruling, Justice Arbour, speaking for the full Court, asserted that the principle against self-incrimination developed under s. 7 of the Charter is of "limited application". Previously we saw that in *R. v. P. (M.B.)*, [1994] 1 S.C.R. 555, 29 C.R. (4th) 209, 89 C.C.C. (3d) 289 (S.C.C) the Court had described the principle as the "single most important organizing principle in criminal law" and one capable of growth. Growth is clearly now stunted. This may well come as a relief to lower court judges who have often been resistant to wide applications. Arbour J. sees the application of the principle as depending on context (that unruly horse), and hinging on consideration of factors of reliability and state abuse of no concern in the D.N.A. legislation. See further David Stratas, "*R. v. B. (S.A.)* and the Right Against Self-Incrimination: A Confusing Change of Direction" (2003), 14 C.R. (6th) 227 and Lee Stuesser, "*R. v. B. (S.A.)*: Putting Self-incrimination in Context" (2004), 42 Alberta L. Rev. 543.

The Supreme Court later rejected a principle against self-incrimination challenge to investigative hearings under anti-terrorist provisions: see *Application under s. 83.28 of the Criminal Code, Re*, [2004] 2 S.C.R. 248, 21 C.R. (6th) 82, 184 C.C.C. (3d) 449 (S.C.C.).

(e) Silence at Trial

It is very important to distinguish between inferences that might flow from silence during the investigative process and inferences from silence at trial. The appropriateness of drawing such inferences, the fairness, must be judged separately. Many protections available to an accused at trial are not present during police questioning. At trial the accused will normally be represented by counsel. He will then know the charge against him and will have listened to and been able to challenge the evidence against him. The trial is in public and an impartial judge is present to ensure the accused's rights are safeguarded and the hearing is conducted according to the rules of natural justice. There are certain procedural safeguards in place as to how he may be questioned if he decides to take the stand. Before the accused is called on to answer, the judge will have decided that there is a case to meet; the trial judge will have decided that there is evidence upon which a reasonable jury properly instructed could return a verdict of guilty. Finally, it is almost certain that judges and juries will draw adverse inferences from the accused's silence at trial as they personally witness the accused's silence in the face of accusation; there is no need for evidence to be led as to the accused's silence.

R. v. NOBLE

[1997] 1 S.C.R. 874, 6 C.R. (5th) 1, 114 C.C.C. (3d) 385 (S.C.C.)

The manager of an apartment building found two young men in the parking area, one of whom appeared to be attempting to break into a car with a screwdriver. When the manager asked the man for identification, he handed over an expired driver's licence. The manager testified that he thought the photograph on the licence accurately depicted the man in front of him. He told the man that he could retrieve the licence from the police. The accused was charged with breaking and entering and having in his possession an instrument suitable for the purpose of breaking into a motor vehicle. At trial, the manager could not identify the accused, but the trial judge concluded that he, as the trier of fact, could compare the picture in the driver's licence with the accused in the courtroom and conclude that the driver's licence accurately depicted the accused. The trial judge noted that the accused faced an overwhelming case to meet as a result of the licence, yet remained silent. In the trial judge's view, he could draw "almost an adverse inference" that "certainly may add to the weight of the Crown's case on the issue of identification". The accused was convicted on both counts. The Court of Appeal set aside the conviction and ordered a new trial. A 5:4 majority of the Supreme Court dismissed the Crown's appeal.

SOPINKA J. (L'Heureux-Dubé, Cory, Iacobucci and Major JJ. concurring):—

. . .

The right to silence is based on society's distaste for compelling a person to incriminate him- or herself with his or her own words. Following this reasoning, in my view the use of silence to help establish guilt beyond a reasonable doubt is contrary to the rationale behind the right to silence. Just as a person's words should not be conscripted and used against him or her by the state, it is equally inimical to the dignity of the accused to use his or her silence to assist in grounding a belief in guilt beyond a reasonable doubt. To use silence in this manner is to treat it as communicative evidence of guilt. To illustrate this point, suppose an accused did commit the offence for which he was charged. If he testifies and is truthful, he will be found guilty as the result of what he said. If he does not testify and is found guilty in part because of his silence, he is found guilty because of what he did not say. No matter what the non-perjuring accused decides, communicative evidence emanating from the accused is used against him. The failure to testify tends to place the accused in the same position as if he had testified and admitted his guilt. In my view, this is tantamount to conscription of self-incriminating communicative evidence and is contrary to the underlying purpose of the right to silence. In order to respect the dignity of the accused, the silence of the accused should not be used as a piece of evidence against him or her.

The presumption of innocence, enshrined at trial in s. 11(d) of the Charter, provides further support for the conclusion that silence of the accused at trial cannot be placed on the evidentiary scales against the accused. If silence may be used against the accused in establishing guilt, part of the burden of proof has shifted to the accused. In a situation where the accused exercises his or her right to silence at trial, the Crown need only prove the case to some point short of beyond a reasonable doubt, and the failure to testify takes it over the threshold. The presumption of innocence, however, indicates that it is not incumbent on the accused to present any evidence at all, rather it is for the Crown to prove him or her guilty. Thus, in order for the burden of proof to remain with the Crown, as required by the Charter, the silence of the accused should not be used against him or her in building the case for guilt. Belief in guilt beyond a reasonable doubt must be grounded on the testimony and any other tangible or demonstrative evidence admitted during the trial.

Some reference to the silence of the accused by the trier of fact may not offend the Charter principles discussed above: where in a trial by judge alone the trial judge is convinced of the guilt of the accused beyond a reasonable doubt, the silence of the accused may be referred to as evidence of the absence of an explanation which could raise a reasonable doubt. If the Crown has proved the case beyond a reasonable doubt, the accused need not testify, but if he doesn't, the Crown's case prevails and the accused will be convicted. It is only in this sense that the accused need respond once the Crown has proved its case beyond a reasonable doubt. Another permissible reference to the silence of the accused was alluded to by the Court of Appeal in this case. In its view, such a reference is permitted by a judge trying a case alone to indicate that he need not speculate about possible defences that might have been offered by the accused had he or she testified. . . . Such treatment of the silence of the accused does not offend either the right to silence or the presumption of innocence. If silence is simply taken as assuring the trier of fact that it need not speculate about unspoken explanations, then belief in guilt beyond a reasonable doubt is not in part grounded on the silence of the accused, but rather is grounded on the evidence against him or her. The right to silence and its underlying rationale are respected, in that the communication or absence of communication is not used to build the case against the accused. The principles to which I have referred which derive from ss. 7 and 11(d) of the Charter find ample support in recent case law of this Court. While earlier cases on the appropriate use of silence by the trier of fact are admittedly ambiguous, recent decisions are clear: silence may not be used by the trier of fact as a piece of inculpatory evidence. . . . In my view, these comments clearly indicate that it is not permissible to use the failure to testify as a piece of evidence contributing to a finding of guilt beyond a reasonable doubt where such a finding would not exist without considering the failure to testify. McLachlin J. stated that the failure to testify could not be used to "shore up a Crown case which otherwise does not establish guilt beyond a reasonable doubt". Major J. stated that "this lack of testimony cannot otherwise be used to strengthen the Crown's case where the Crown has fallen short of proving guilt". In my view, these statements indicate that silence cannot be used to take an unproven case to a proven case.

. . .

There may, however, be confusion over the use of the words "adverse inference" in the above cases. Professor R. J. Delisle, in an annotation to *R. v. Francois* (1994), 31 C.R. (4th) 203, asked that if an adverse inference is permitted, what inference is relevant if it can only be drawn after guilt beyond a reasonable doubt has been proved? He stated at p. 204:

> The essence of a criminal trial is whether the Crown has established its case beyond a reasonable doubt. If a jury cannot use the failure to testify to assist in its

determination of whether they are satisfied beyond a reasonable doubt, then pray tell what the permissible adverse inference does? For what else can the jury use it?

As set out above, silence is not inculpatory evidence, but nor is it exculpatory evidence. Thus, as in *Lepage*, if the trier of fact reaches a belief in guilt beyond a reasonable doubt, silence may be treated by the trier of fact as confirmatory of guilt. Silence may indicate, for example, that there is no evidence to support speculative explanations of the Crown's evidence offered by defence counsel, or it may indicate that the accused has not put forward any evidence that would require that the Crown negative an affirmative defence. In this limited sense, silence may be used by the trier of fact. If, however, there is a rational explanation which is consistent with innocence and which may raise a reasonable doubt, the silence of the accused cannot be used to remove that doubt. Thus, there are permissible uses of silence by the trier of fact. However, Delisle is correct in stating that, since these permissible uses only arise after the trier of fact has reached a belief in guilt beyond a reasonable doubt, the uses may be superfluous. I would therefore conclude that courts should generally avoid using the potentially confusing term "inference" in discussing the silence of the accused. "Inference" could be taken to indicate that the trier of fact used silence to help establish the case for guilt beyond a reasonable doubt, which is not a permissible use of silence. Indeed, because of the potential for confusion, discussion of the silence of the accused should generally be avoided. However, where silence is mentioned by the trial judge as confirmatory of guilt given the totality of the evidence, but not as a "make-weight", there is no reversible error. *Lepage* provides an example of such a situation.

. . .

The appellant submitted that *Vezeau v. The Queen*, [1977] 2 S.C.R. 277, held that silence could be treated as a "make-weight". In *Vezeau*, this Court considered the significance of the failure to testify in the context of a defence of alibi. In that case, the defence was alibi, but the accused did not testify. In giving his instructions to the jury, the judge said that they could not draw any conclusion unfavourable to the accused from the fact that he had not testified. The majority of this Court held that, aside from the prohibition of comment on the failure of the accused to testify set out in the Canada Evidence Act, it was an error of law for the trial judge to instruct the jury that they could not consider the absence of testimony by the accused in assessing the alibi. Martland J. stated on behalf of the majority at p. 292 that:

> It was part of the appellant's defence to the charge that he could not have committed the offence because he was in Montreal when the murder occurred. Proof of this alibi was tendered by a witness who claimed to have been with the appellant in Montreal. The direction of the trial judge precluded the jury, when considering this defence, from taking into consideration the fact that the appellant had failed to support his alibi by his own testimony. The failure of an accused person, who relies upon an alibi, to testify and thus to submit himself to cross-examination is a matter of importance in considering the validity of that defence. The jury, in this case, was instructed that they could not take that fact into account in reaching their verdict.

In my view, *Vezeau* set out a narrow exception to the impermissibility of using silence to build the case against the accused at trial. It has clearly been recognized in other contexts that alibi defences create exceptions to the right to silence. . . . In my view, there are two reasons supporting the alibi exception to the right to silence pre-trial which apply also to the right to silence at trial: the ease with which alibi evidence may be fabricated; and the diversion of the alibi inquiry from the central inquiry at trial. I am therefore sympathetic to the view expressed in *Vezeau* that in the limited case of alibi, the failure of the accused at trial to testify and expose him- or herself to cross-examination on the alibi defence may be used to draw an adverse inference about the credibility of the defence. A second reason to permit such a limited exception to the right to silence at trial is that the alibi defence is not directly related to the guilt of the accused; as Gooderson put it, "[a]libi evidence, by its very nature, takes the focus right away from the area of the main facts". Rejecting the alibi defence does not build the case for the Crown in the sense of proving the existence of the required elements of the offence in question, but rather negatives an affirmative defence actively put forward by the accused. Using silence to inform the trier of fact's assessment of the credibility of the accused's affirmative defence of alibi simply goes to the alibi defence itself.

. . .

On balance, it appears to me that the trial judge used the failure to testify as evidence going to identification which permitted him to reach a belief in guilt beyond a reasonable doubt. Indeed, he stated explicitly that the failure to testify "certainly may add to the weight of the Crown's case" and concluded by finding guilt on the basis of "those reasons", which appeared to include the discussion of the failure to testify. In light of these statements, when the trial judge stated that he "can be" satisfied on the identity issue prior to discussing the failure to testify, in my view he indicated that the evidence before him was consistent with proof of identity, and the failure to testify took belief in identity beyond a reasonable doubt. . . . Given my conclusion that such reasoning constituted an error of law, I would dismiss the appeal and confirm the judgment of the Court of Appeal ordering a new trial.

Per LAMER C.J.C., dissenting: — According to Sopinka J. the silence of an accused can only be used by the trier of fact in two very limited senses. The accused's silence may: (1) confirm prior findings of guilt beyond a reasonable doubt; and (2) remind triers of fact that they need not speculate about unstated defences. With greatest respect, this misinterprets the case law. This Court and others have repeatedly held that when the Crown presents a case to meet that implicates the accused in a "strong and cogent network of inculpatory facts", the trier of fact is entitled to consider the accused's failure to testify in deciding whether it is in fact satisfied of his or her guilt beyond a reasonable doubt. . . . None of these early cases suggests that the accused should be compelled to testify or that the accused is anything other than presumed innocent until proven guilty. They merely recognize that when an accused is implicated or "enveloped" in a case of unexplained inculpatory circumstances, there are consequences to silence that trial judges, juries, and appellate courts alike may consider in reaching a verdict. This does not happen in every case. A trier of fact is entitled to draw adverse inferences only where there is a "damning chain of evidence" or more aptly a "strong and cogent network of inculpatory facts". This approach to adverse inferences has been expressly adopted and refined by this Court in a number of judgments in recent years, both before and after the advent of the Charter.

. . .

Why, one might ask, has this Court commented so frequently on the effect of the accused's silence? Why has it arisen so often as an issue before this Court? The reason is simple: silence can be very probative. Consider, for example, a case of sexual assault where the victim describes her attacker as a man with a very unusual tattoo on the upper portion of his arm. Nothing allows the Crown to call the accused as its first witness, as it could do under an inquisitorial system of criminal justice. However, assuming the Crown, by adducing other evidence, establishes a case to meet (i.e. enough evidence to make a guilty verdict reasonable), would not every man wrongly accused who lacks the described tattoo roll up his sleeve in court to exonerate himself? . . . Recognizing that silence can be probative, this Court has said in the above-mentioned cases that it is a factor that both juries and appellate courts may properly consider.

. . .

My brother Sopinka disagrees. He asserts that these cases mean only that the silence of the accused can confirm verdicts or at most serve as the basis to refuse to speculate about unstated defences. Nothing, he says, provides that silence can be used as evidence itself. With respect, I find Sopinka J.'s interpretation difficult to support. For one, an inference which merely confirms prior conclusions of guilt is superfluous. As Professor R. J. Delisle has commented:

> The essence of a criminal trial is whether the Crown has established its case beyond a reasonable doubt. If a jury cannot use the failure to testify to assist in its determination of whether they are satisfied beyond a reasonable doubt, then pray tell what the permissible adverse inference does? For what else can the jury use it? (Annotation to *R. v. Francois* (1994), 31 C.R. (4th) 201 (S.C.C.) at p. 204.)

Second, I find it illogical for the Court to say that silence may be used by judges and juries but only to the extent that it highlights the fact that the Crown's evidence remains uncontradicted. Uncontradicted by whom? To allow a trial judge to instruct the jury that the evidence remains uncontradicted is just a coded message to remind the jury that the accused has not led any evidence in his or her own defence. The jurisprudence clearly establishes that, once the Crown has proffered a case to meet, the silence of an accused itself can be used in determining whether an accused is guilty beyond a reasonable doubt. I believe that we should be straightforward and say so.

. . .

With respect, I find it profoundly illogical to say that trial judges and juries must not weigh the silence of the accused on the evidentiary scales, but in reviewing whether their verdicts are reasonable appellate courts can assume that they did.... I simply cannot conceive how a trial verdict that is a miscarriage of justice can be cured by an appellate court pursuant to s. 686(1)(*b*)(iii) because we say that certain Charter rights no longer apply on appeal. I similarly cannot understand how a verdict that would ordinarily be considered unreasonable can magically become reasonable pursuant to s. 686(1)(*a*)(i) simply because the case has progressed from one level of court to another. If the role of a trier of fact is to have any meaning, appellate courts must undertake their statutory responsibility to review the fitness of verdicts and to cure trial errors on the same understanding of the silence of an accused. I cannot endorse a criminal justice system in which an accused's silence may be used to a greater extent by appellate judges than by triers of fact at the trial level. Otherwise the Court is effectively sanctioning what it says is prohibited — inviting both judges and juries to use silence as evidence, but asking them to keep it quiet.

. . .

The act of drawing adverse inferences from the silence of an accused is not contrary to the accused's right of non-compellability or the presumption of innocence. This point becomes clear upon a proper understanding of the case to meet. If the Crown establishes a case to meet, such that its case cannot be non-suited by a motion for a directed verdict of acquittal, it has put forth, by definition, sufficient evidence upon which a jury, properly instructed, could reasonably convict. Put differently, when the Crown provides a case to meet, all of the evidence to sustain a conviction has been put forth by the Crown in keeping with its burden of proof. As Professor R. J. Delisle has argued:

> Some object that permitting an inference of guilt modifies the burden of proof. But query whether this is so. The prosecution has the burden of proving the accused's guilt beyond a reasonable doubt and the Crown will not have discharged that burden, if at all, until the end of the case after all the evidence has been heard. The defendant's silence may be treated as a piece of evidence in assisting the discharge of the Crown's burden, it may constitute part of the totality of the evidence, but that does not mean the burden of proof has been shifted. "Silence at Trial: Inferences and Comments" (1997), 1 C.R. (5th) 313, at pp. 318-19.

. . .

In separate opinions La Forest, Gonthier and McLachlin JJ. agreed with Lamer C.J.C. in dissent.

R. v. PROKOFIEW
(2012), 96 C.R. (6th) 57 (S.C.C.)

The accused was charged with conspiracy to defraud. At trial, the Crown alleged that P and his co-accused, S, participated in a fraudulent scheme involving the fictitious sale of heavy equipment to generate harmonized sales tax that was then not remitted to the federal government as required. The fraudulent nature of the scheme was never challenged. The involvement of P and S in the scheme was also conceded. The question for the jury was whether either or both accused were aware of the fraudulent nature of the scheme. P did not testify, but was incriminated by S's testimony. In his closing address, S's counsel invited the jury to infer P's guilt from the latter's failure to testify. The trial judge, relying on dicta of Justice Sopinka for the Supreme Court in *R. v. Crawford* and *R. v. Noble*, concluded that s. 4(6) of the Canada Evidence Act prohibited him from telling the jury that it could not use the accused's silence at trial as evidence against him. Section 4(6) provides that: "The failure of the person charged to testify shall not be made the subject of comment by the judge or by the counsel for the prosecution". The trial judge made it clear that, but for his understanding of the prohibition in s. 4(6), he would have given a remedial instruction. The jury convicted the appellant and his co-accused. The accused appealed, *inter alia,* arguing that s. 4(6) was unconstitutional.

The appeal was dismissed by Doherty J.A on behalf of a unanimous five-person panel of the Ontario Court of Appeal ((2010), 77 C.R. (6th) 52, 256 C.C.C. (3d) 355 (Ont. C.A.)). Justices Feldman, MacPherson, Blair and Juriansz concurred. The Court held that Justice Sopinka's comments were obiter and should not be followed given earlier pronouncements from the Supreme Court that s. 4(6) did not preclude comments not prejudicial to the accused and permitted a trial judge to tell a jury that an accused who does not testify is exercising his or her constitutional right and that no adverse inference can be drawn from that failure to testify. However, the Court held on consideration of the entirety of the instructions on the presumption of innocence and reasonable doubt that this was a case for the curative proviso under s. 686(1)(b)(iii). The jury would have to understand that guilt had to be established on the evidence and that the accused's silence at trial could not be used to infer the accused's guilt. The appeal was dismissed.

A 5-4 majority of the Supreme Court dismissed the further appeal.

MOLDAVER   J. (DESCHAMPS, ABELLA, ROTHSTEIN and KARA-KATSANIS JJ. concurring):—

[1] Largely for the reasons given by Doherty J.A., I would dismiss Mr. Prokofiew's further appeal to this Court.

[2] I have had the benefit of reading the reasons of my colleague Justice Fish and I agree with much of his analysis. Where I disagree with him is in the result. I will explain our disagreement and why the appeal should be dismissed, but before doing so, I will address the matters on which my colleague and I agree — albeit with some additional observations.

I. Matters of Agreement

[3] My colleague and I agree that s. 4(6) of the *Canada Evidence Act*, R.S.C. 1985, c. C-5 ("*CEA*"), does not prohibit a trial judge from affirming an accused's right to silence. In so concluding, I should not be taken — nor do I understand my colleague to suggest — that such an instruction must be given in every case where an accused exercises his or her right to remain silent at trial. Rather, it will be for the trial judge, in the exercise of his or her discretion, to provide such an instruction where there is a realistic concern that the jury may place evidential value on an accused's decision not to testify.

[4] In cases where the jury is given an instruction on the accused's right to remain silent at trial, the trial judge should, in explaining the right, make it clear to the jury that an accused's silence is not evidence and that it cannot be used as a makeweight for the Crown in deciding whether the Crown has proved its case. In other words, if, after considering the whole of the evidence, the jury is not satisfied that the charge against the accused has been proven beyond a reasonable doubt, the jury cannot look to the accused's silence to remove that doubt and give the Crown's case the boost it needs to push it over the line.

[5] The case at hand provides an example of a situation where such an instruction would be warranted — cut-throat defences where one accused testifies and points the finger at the other, while the other exercises his right not to testify. My colleague and I agree that, in summing up to the jury, Mr. Solty's counsel could have relied on the fact that his client had testified to argue that Mr. Solty was innocent and had "nothing to hide". Moreover, he could have emphasized that Mr. Solty's testimony stood uncontradicted and that the jury could consider this in assessing whether they believed his evidence or whether it left them in a state of reasonable doubt.

[6] What Mr. Solty's counsel could not do is mislead the jury on a matter of law. He could not invite the jury to use Mr. Prokofiew's silence at trial as evidence, much less evidence of guilt.

[7] In cases where there is a risk of counsel misleading the jury on a co-accused's right to remain silent at trial, trial judges would do well to spell out the governing principles and ensure that counsel's remarks conform to those principles. That way, the potential harm can be prevented from occurring, thereby sparing the need for a remedial instruction.

[8] In the context of the charge as a whole, I think it might be helpful to explain how a jury may use a lack of contradictory evidence in deciding whether the Crown has proved its case beyond a reasonable doubt.

[9] Apart from a few notable exceptions — such as when an accused raises the defence of not criminally responsible on account of a mental disorder under s. 16 of the *Criminal Code*, R.S.C. 1985, c. C-46 — in every criminal trial, juries are instructed that an accused has no obligation to prove anything. The onus of proof rests upon the Crown from beginning to end and it never shifts.

[10] Juries are also told that in deciding whether the Crown has proved its case to the criminal standard, they are to look to the whole of the evidence — and, having done so, they may only convict if they are satisfied, on the basis of evidence they find to be both credible and reliable, that the Crown has established the accused's guilt beyond a reasonable doubt. In coming to that conclusion, a jury may not use an accused's silence at trial as evidence, much less evidence of guilt, and, where appropriate, the jury should be so instructed.

[11] That said, in assessing the credibility and reliability of evidence upon which the Crown can and does rely, a jury is entitled to take into account, among other things, the fact that the evidence stands uncontradicted, if that is the case — and the jury may be so instructed. Of course, the fact that evidence is uncontradicted does not mean that the jury must accept it, and an instruction to that effect should be given.

II. Is a New Trial Required?

A. *Failure to Instruct the Jury on the Appellant's Right to Silence*

[12] In the course of his closing address to the jury, which covered 23 pages of transcript, counsel for Mr. Solty incorporated the following rhetorical question into his remarks: "Did [Mr. Prokofiew] have something to hide or did he simply have no response that could help him since there is no point in trying to contradict the truth?" (A.R., vol. V, at p. 17). That comment was improper in that it implicitly invited the jury to treat Mr. Prokofiew's silence at trial as evidence of guilt. It should not have been made.

. . .

[26] In sum, while I agree that an explicit remedial instruction from the trial judge would have been preferable — and would have been warranted in these circumstances — I am satisfied that the instructions that were given in the instant case, when considered as a whole, were adequate. Like Doherty J.A., I am confident that the jury would have understood, in the context of the entirety of the instructions, that the Crown could prove Mr. Prokofiew's guilt only on the evidence and, as Mr. Prokofiew's silence at trial did not constitute evidence, it could not be used to prove his guilt. However, I do not fault the trial judge for concluding — wrongly but understandably — that he was prohibited by s. 4(6) of the *CEA* from making any reference at all to Mr. Prokofiew's failure to testify. My colleague has addressed that matter and it should not pose a problem in future cases.

FISH J. (McLACHLIN C.J.C. and LEBEL and CROMWELL JJ. concurring) (dissenting):—

[44] The Court of Appeal for Ontario, correctly in my view, held that s. 4(6) prohibits comments *prejudicial to the accused* — but not the remedial instruction requested by defence counsel and contemplated by the judge (2010 ONCA 423, 100 O.R. (3d) 401). The Court of Appeal held as well, again correctly, that the trial judge had erred in admitting hearsay evidence. It is undisputed in this Court that the hearsay evidence was inadmissible and ought to have been excluded.

[45] The Court of Appeal nonetheless dismissed Mr. Prokofiew's appeal on the ground that both errors were harmless. With respect, I am of a different view. For the reasons that follow, I would quash Mr. Prokofiew's conviction, allow the appeal and order a new trial.

. . .

[64] *Noble* establishes that a trier of fact may not draw an adverse inference from the accused's failure to testify and that the accused's silence at trial may not be treated as evidence of guilt. To do so would violate the presumption of innocence and the right to silence. It would to that extent and for that reason shift the burden of proof to the accused, turning the accused's constitutional right to silence into a "snare and a delusion" (*Noble*, at para. 72).

[65] We are now urged by the Crown to overrule *Noble*. Upon careful consideration of Crown counsel's full and able argument, and the helpful submissions of all counsel on this issue, I would decline to do so.

[66] I see no persuasive reason to overturn *Noble*. *Noble* is a recent and important precedent regarding a fundamental constitutional principle. The Court's decision in that case is constitutionally mandated and has not proven unworkable in practice. Nothing of significance has occurred since 1997 to cause the Court to reconsider its decision. And it is well established that the Court must exercise particular caution in contemplating the reversal of a precedent where the effect, as here, would be to diminish the protection of the *Canadian Charter of Rights and Freedoms*: *R. v. Henry*, 2005 SCC 76, [2005] 3 S.C.R. 609, at para. 44.

. . .

[79] In short, s. 4(6) of the *Canada Evidence Act* does not prohibit an affirmation by the trial judge of the accused's right to silence. And, in appropriate circumstances, an instruction that no adverse inference may be drawn from the silence of the accused at trial is not a prohibited "comment" on the accused's failure to testify within the meaning of that provision.

[80] I turn now to consider whether the trial judge in this case erred in failing to instruct the jury that no adverse inference could be drawn from the appellant's failure to testify. Unlike the Court of Appeal, and with the greatest of respect, I believe that he did. And I believe as well that this error, though understandable in light of *Crawford* and *Noble*, is fatal to the jury's verdict.

. . .

[94] Trial judges must take care to ensure that the right to silence becomes neither a snare nor a delusion (*Noble*, at para. 72). To this end, whenever there is a "significant risk" ? as the trial judge found in this case ? that the jury will otherwise treat the silence of the accused as evidence of guilt, an appropriate remedial direction ought to be given to the jury. That was not done here.

[95] Standard instructions on the definition of evidence, the presumption of innocence, the Crown's burden of proof, and the reasonable doubt standard will not suffice. That is particularly true where, as here, counsel for one accused has suggested unmistakably to the jury that the guilt of a co-accused may be inferred from that person's failure to testify.

. . .

[104] We urged by the Crown to apply the curative *proviso* of s. 686(1)(*b*)(iii) if we conclude, as I would, that the trial judge erred in law in failing to give the jury the remedial instruction requested by defence counsel and, again, in admitting the hearsay evidence that ought to have been excluded.

[105] It is now well established that the *proviso* may only be applied where the Crown satisfies the court that the evidence of the appellant's guilt is overwhelming or that the trial judge's errors of law were harmless because there is "no realistic possibility that a new trial would produce a different verdict" (*R. v. Jolivet*, 2000 SCC 29, [2000] 1 S.C.R. 751, at para. 46; *R. v. Sarrazin*, 2011 SCC 54, [2011] 3 S.C.R. 505, at paras. 23-24). I am not satisfied that the Crown has discharged its burden in this case.

Do you think the Supreme Court ought to have required a mandatory direction in every jury case where an accused does not testify that the jury should not draw an adverse inference where an accused has exercised his right to silence? Do you think that allowing instructions to the jury that Crown evidence was uncontradicted in fact allows indirect comments on the accused's failure to testify?

See C.R. annotation by Don Stuart and C.R. article by Daniel Libman, "Prokofiew: The Need for Instruction on Trial Silence in Cut Throat Defence Cases" (2012) 96 C.R. (6th) 83.

(f) Re-stated Voluntary Confession Rule: *R. v. Oickle*

R. v. OICKLE
[2000] 2 S.C.R. 3, 36 C.R. (5th) 129, 147 C.C.C. (3d) 321 (S.C.C.)

In investigating several apparent arsons the police became suspicious that Oickle, a volunteer firefighter, was at each fire. He agreed to take a polygraph test. The test, which commenced at 3 p.m., was audiotaped. The accused was informed of his rights to silence, to counsel, and his ability to leave at any time. He was also informed that while the interpretation of the polygraph results was not admissible, anything he said was admissible. At the end of the test, around 5 p.m., the officer conducting the test informed the accused that he had failed. The accused was reminded of his rights and questioned for one hour. At 6:30 p.m., a second officer questioned the accused and, after 30 to 40 minutes, the accused confessed to setting the fire to his fiancée's car and provided the police with a statement. He appeared emotionally distraught at this time. The accused was arrested and warned of his rights. At the police station, he was placed in an interview room equipped with videotaping facilities where he was questioned about the other fires. Around 8:30 p.m. and 9:15 p.m., the accused indicated that he was tired and wanted to go home. He was informed that he was under arrest and he could call a lawyer, but that he could not go home. A third officer took over the interrogation at 9:52 p.m. He questioned the accused until about 11:00 p.m., at which time the accused confessed to setting seven of the eight fires. The accused was then seen crying with his head in his hands. The police then took a written statement from the accused. He was placed in a cell to sleep at 2:45 a.m. At 6:00 a.m., a police officer noticed that the accused was awake and asked whether he would agree to a re-enactment. On the tape of the re-enactment, the accused was informed of his rights and was advised that he could stop the re-enactment at any time. The police drove the accused to the various fire scenes, where he described how he had set each fire. The accused was charged with seven counts of arson. The trial judge ruled on a voir dire that the accused's statements, including the video re-enactment, were voluntary and admissible, and subsequently convicted him on all counts. Justice Cromwell, then writing for the Nova Scotia Court of Appeal, delivered a lengthy judgment finding that the confession should be excluded because it had been obtained in circumstances of oppression. The Court entered an acquittal.

The Supreme Court, over the sole dissent of Arbour J., restored the decision of the trial judge.

IACOBUCCI J. (McLachlin, C.J., L'Heureux-Dubé, Major, Bastarache and Binnie JJ. concurring):—This appeal requires this Court to rule on the common law limits on police interrogation. Specifically, we are asked to decide whether the police improperly induced the respondent's confessions through threats or promises, an atmosphere of oppression, or any other tactics that could raise a reasonable doubt as to the voluntariness of his confessions. I conclude that they did not. The trial judge's determination that the confessions at stake in this appeal were voluntarily given should not have been disturbed on appeal, and accordingly the appeal should be allowed.

In this case, the police conducted a proper interrogation. Their questioning, while persistent and often accusatorial, was never hostile, aggressive, or intimidating. They repeatedly offered the accused food and drink. They allowed him to use the bathroom upon request. Before his first confession and subsequent arrest, they repeatedly told him that he could leave at any time. In this context, the alleged inducements offered by the police do not raise a reasonable doubt as to the confessions' voluntariness. Nor do I find any fault with the role played by the polygraph test in this case. While the police admittedly exaggerated the reliability of such devices, the tactic of inflating the reliability of incriminating evidence is a common, and generally unobjectionable one. Whether standing alone, or in combination with the other mild inducements used in this appeal, it does not render the confessions involuntary. . .

The Development of the Confessions Rule

In *Hebert, supra*, McLachlin J. interpreted the right to silence in light of existing common law protections, such as the confessions rule. However, given the focus of that decision on defining constitutional rights, it did not decide the inverse question: namely, the scope of the common law rules in light of the Charter. One possible view is that the Charter subsumes the common law rules.

But I do not believe that this view is correct, for several reasons. First, the confessions rule has a broader scope than the Charter. For example, the protections of s. 10 only apply "on arrest or detention". By contrast, the confessions rule applies whenever a person in authority questions a suspect. Second, the Charter applies a different burden and standard of proof from that under the confessions rule. Under the former, the burden is on the accused to show, on a balance of probabilities, a violation of constitutional rights. Under the latter, the burden is on the prosecution to show beyond a reasonable doubt that the confession was voluntary. Finally, the remedies are different. The Charter excludes evidence obtained in violation of its provisions under s. 24(2) only if admitting the evidence would bring the administration of justice into disrepute: see *R. v. Stillman*, [1997] 1 S.C.R. 607, R. v. Collins, [1987] 1 S.C.R. 265, and the related jurisprudence. By contrast, a violation of the confessions rule always warrants exclusion.

These various differences illustrate that the Charter is not an exhaustive catalogue of rights. Instead, it represents a bare minimum below which the law must not fall. A necessary corollary of this statement is that the law, whether by statute or common law, can offer protections beyond those guaranteed by the Charter. The common law confessions rule is one such doctrine, and it would be a mistake to confuse it with the protections given by the Charter. While obviously it may be appropriate, as in *Hebert*, to interpret one in light of the other, it would be a mistake to assume one subsumes the other entirely.

The Confessions Rule Today

. . .

In defining the confessions rule, it is important to keep in mind its twin goals of protecting the rights of the accused without unduly limiting society's need to investigate and solve crimes. Martin J.A. accurately delineated this tension in *R. v. Precourt* (1976), 18 O.R. (2d) 714 (C.A.), at p. 721:

> Although improper police questioning may in some circumstances infringe the governing [confessions] rule it is essential to bear in mind that the police are unable to investigate crime without putting questions to persons, whether or not such persons are suspected of having committed the crime being investigated. Properly conducted police questioning is a legitimate and effective aid to criminal investigation. . . . On the other hand, statements made as the result of intimidating questions, or questioning which is oppressive and calculated to overcome the freedom of will of the suspect for the purpose of extracting a confession are inadmissible. . . .

All who are involved in the administration of justice, but particularly courts applying the confessions rule, must never lose sight of either of these objectives.

1. The Problem of False Confessions

The history of police interrogations is not without its unsavoury chapters. Physical abuse, if not routine, was certainly not unknown. Today such practices are much less common. In this context, it may seem counterintuitive that people would confess to a crime that they did not commit. And indeed, research with mock juries indicates that people find it difficult to believe that someone would confess falsely. See S. M. Kassin and L. S. Wrightsman, "Coerced Confessions, Judicial Instructions, and Mock Juror Verdicts" (1981), 11 J. Applied Soc. Psychol. 489.

However, this intuition is not always correct. A large body of literature has developed documenting hundreds of cases where confessions have been proven false by DNA evidence, subsequent confessions by the true perpetrator, and other such independent sources of evidence. See, e.g., R. A. Leo and R. J. Ofshe, "The Consequences of False Confessions: Deprivations of Liberty and Miscarriages of Justice in the Age of Psychological Interrogation" (1998), 88 J. Crim. L. & Criminology 429 (hereinafter Leo & Ofshe (1998)); R. J. Ofshe and R. A. Leo, "The Social Psychology of Police Interrogation: The Theory and Classification of True and False Confessions" (1997), 16 Stud. L. Pol.&Soc. 189 (hereinafter Ofshe & Leo (1997)); R. J. Ofshe and R. A. Leo, "The Decision to Confess Falsely: Rational Choice and Irrational Action" (1997), 74

Denv. U. L. Rev. 979 (hereinafter Ofshe & Leo (1997a)); W. S. White, "False Confessions and the Constitution: Safeguards Against Untrustworthy Confessions" (1997), 32 Harv. C.R.-C.L. L. Rev. 105; G. H. Gudjonsson and J. A. C. MacKeith, "A Proven Case of False Confession: Psychological Aspects of the Coerced-Compliant Type" (1990), 30 Med. Sci.&L. 329 (hereinafter Gudjonsson & MacKeith (1990)); G. H. Gudjonsson and J. A. C. MacKeith, "Retracted Confessions: Legal, Psychological and Psychiatric Aspects" (1988), 28 Med. Sci.&L. 187 (hereinafter Gudjonsson & MacKeith (1988)); H. A. Bedau and M. L. Radelet, "Miscarriages of Justice in Potentially Capital Cases" (1987), 40 Stan. L. Rev. 21.

One of the overriding concerns of the criminal justice system is that the innocent must not be convicted: see, e.g., *R. v. Mills*, [1999] 3 S.C.R. 668, at para. 71; *R. v. Leipert*, [1997] 1 S.C.R. 281, at para. 4. Given the important role of false confessions in convicting the innocent, the confessions rule must understand why false confessions occur. Without suggesting that any confession involving elements discussed below should automatically be excluded, I hope to provide a background for my synthesis of the confessions rule in the next section.

Ofshe & Leo (1997), *supra*, at p. 210, provide a useful taxonomy of false confessions. They suggest that there are five basic kinds: voluntary, stress-compliant, coerced-compliant, non-coerced-persuaded, and coerced-persuaded. Voluntary confessions *ex hypothesi* are not the product of police interrogation. It is therefore the other four types of false confessions that are of interest.

According to Ofshe & Leo (1997), *supra*, at p. 211, stress-compliant confessions occur "when the aversive interpersonal pressures of interrogation become so intolerable that [suspects] comply in order to terminate questioning".

They are elicited by "exceptionally strong use of the aversive stressors typically present in interrogations", and are "given knowingly *in order to escape* the punishing experience of interrogation" (emphasis in original). See also Gudjonsson & MacKeith (1990), *supra*. Another important factor is confronting the suspect with fabricated evidence in order to convince him that protestations of innocence are futile: see *ibid*.; Ofshe & Leo (1997a), *supra*, at p. 1040.

Somewhat different are coerced-compliant confessions. These confessions are the product of "the classically coercive influence techniques (e.g., threats and promises)", with which the Ibrahim rule is concerned: Ofshe & Leo (1997), *supra*, at p. 214. As Gudjonsson & MacKeith (1988), *supra*, suggest at p. 191, "most cases of false confession that come before the courts are of the compliant-coerced type". See also White, *supra*, at p. 131.

A third kind of false confession is the non-coerced-persuaded confession. In this scenario, police tactics cause the innocent person to "become confused, doubt his memory, be temporarily persuaded of his guilt and confess to a crime he did not commit": Ofshe & Leo (1997), *supra*, at p. 215. For an example, see *Reilly v. State*, 355 A.2d 324 (Conn. Super. Ct. 1976); Ofshe & Leo (1997), *supra*, at pp. 231-34. The use of fabricated evidence can also help convince an innocent suspect of his or her own guilt.

A final type of false confession is the coerced-persuaded confession. This is like the non-coerced-persuaded, except that the interrogation also involves the classically coercive aspects of the coerced-compliant confession: see Ofshe & Leo (1997), *supra*, at p. 219.

From this discussion, several themes emerge. One is the need to be sensitive to the particularities of the individual suspect. For example, White, *supra*, at p. 120, notes the following:

> False confessions are particularly likely when the police interrogate particular types of suspects, including suspects who are especially vulnerable as a result of their background, special characteristics, or situation, suspects who have compliant personalities, and, in rare instances, suspects whose personalities make them prone to accept and believe police suggestions made during the course of the interrogation.

And indeed, this is consistent with the reasons of Rand J. in *Fitton, supra*, at p. 962:

> The strength of mind and will of the accused, the influence of custody or its surroundings, the effect of questions or of conversation, all call for delicacy in appreciation of the part they have played behind the admission, and to enable a Court to decide whether what was said was freely and voluntarily said, that is, was free from the influence of hope or fear aroused by them.

Ward, supra, and *Horvath, supra*, similarly recognized the particular circumstances of the suspects that rendered them unable to confess voluntarily: in *Ward*, the accused's state of shock, and in *Horvath*, the psychological fragility that precipitated his hypnosis and "complete emotional disintegration".

Another theme is the danger of using non-existent evidence. Presenting a suspect with entirely fabricated evidence has the potential either to persuade the susceptible suspect that he did indeed commit the crime, or at least to convince the suspect that any protestations of innocence are futile.

Finally, the literature bears out the common law confessions rule's emphasis on threats and promises. Coerced-compliant confessions are the most common type of false confessions. These are classically the product of threats or promises that convince a suspect that in spite of the long-term ramifications, it is in his or her best interest in the short- and intermediate-term to confess.

Fortunately, false confessions are rarely the product of proper police techniques. As Leo & Ofshe (1998), *supra*, point out at p. 492, false confession cases almost always involve "shoddy police practice and/or police criminality". Similarly, in Ofshe & Leo (1997), *supra*, at pp.193-96, they argue that in most cases, "eliciting a false confession takes strong incentives, intense pressure and prolonged questioning... . Only under the rarest of circumstances do an interrogator's ploys persuade an innocent suspect that he is in fact guilty and has been caught."

Before turning to how the confessions rule responds to these dangers, I would like to comment briefly on the growing practice of recording police interrogations, preferably by videotape. As pointed out by J. J. Furedy and J. Liss in "Countering Confessions Induced by the Polygraph: Of Confessionals and Psychological Rubber Hoses" (1986), 29 Crim. L.Q. 91, at p. 104, even if "notes were accurate concerning the *content* of what was said..., the notes cannot reflect the tone of what was said and any body language that may have been employed". White, *supra*, at pp. 153-54, similarly offers four reasons why videotaping is important:

> First, it provides a means by which courts can monitor interrogation practices and thereby enforce the other safeguards. Second, it deters the police from employing interrogation methods likely to lead to untrustworthy confessions. Third, it enables courts to make more informed judgments about whether interrogation practices were likely to lead to an untrustworthy confession. Finally, mandating this safeguard accords with sound public policy because the safeguard will have additional salutary effects besides reducing untrustworthy confessions, including more net benefits for law enforcement.

This is not to suggest that non-recorded interrogations are inherently suspect; it is simply to make the obvious point that when a recording is made, it can greatly assist the trier of fact in assessing the confession.

2. The Contemporary Confessions Rule

The common law confessions rule is well-suited to protect against false confessions. While its overriding concern is with voluntariness, this concept overlaps with reliability. A confession that is not voluntary will often (though not always) be unreliable. The application of the rule will by necessity be contextual. Hard and fast rules simply cannot account for the variety of circumstances that vitiate the voluntariness of a confession, and would inevitably result in a rule that would be both over- and under-inclusive. A trial judge should therefore consider all the relevant factors when reviewing a confession.

(a) Threats or Promises

This is of course the core of the confessions rule from *Ibrahim, supra*. It is therefore important to define precisely what types of threats or promises will raise a reasonable doubt as to the voluntariness of a confession. While obviously imminent threats of torture will render a confession inadmissible, most cases will not be so clear.

As noted above, in *Ibrahim* the Privy Council ruled that statements would be inadmissible if they were the result of "fear of prejudice or hope of advantage". The classic "hope of advantage" is the prospect of leniency from the courts. It is improper for a person in authority to suggest to a suspect that he or she will take steps to procure a reduced charge or sentence if the suspect confesses. Therefore in *Nugent, supra*, the court excluded the statement of a suspect who was told that if he confessed, the charge could be reduced from murder to manslaughter. See also *R. v. Kalashnikoff* (1981), 57 C.C.C. (2d) 481 (B.C.C.A.); *R. v. Lazure* (1959), 126 C.C.C. 331 (Ont. C.A.); R. J. Marin, *Admissibility of Statements* (9th ed. (loose-leaf)),at p. 1-15. Intuitively implausible as it may seem, both judicial precedent and academic authority confirm that the pressure of intense and prolonged questioning may convince a suspect that no one will believe his or her protestations of innocence, and that a conviction is inevitable. In these circumstances, holding out the possibility of a reduced charge or sentence in exchange for a confession would raise a reasonable doubt as to the voluntariness of any ensuing confession. An explicit offer by the police to procure lenient treatment in return for a confession is clearly a very strong inducement, and will warrant exclusion in all but exceptional circumstances.

Another type of inducement relevant to this appeal is an offer of psychiatric assistance or other counselling for the suspect in exchange for a confession. While this is clearly an inducement, it is not as strong as an offer of leniency and regard must be had to the entirety of the circumstances. A good example of this comes from *R. v. Ewert* (1991), 68 C.C.C. (3d) 207 (B.C.C.A.). In that case, the police made what Hinkson J.A. at the Court of Appeal described as a "bold offer to the accused to help him, in the sense of providing psychiatric help, if he told them what had happened" (p. 216). Reversing the Court of Appeal, this Court upheld the trial judge's conclusion that, while the police conduct was an inducement, it was not a factor in the suspect's decision to confess. *Ewert* thus recognizes the importance of a contextual approach.

Threats or promises need not be aimed directly at the suspect for them to have a coercive effect. For example, in *R. v. Jackson* (1977), 34 C.C.C. (2d) 35 (B.C.C.A.), McIntyre J.A. (as he then was) addressed a confession obtained in a case where the accused and his friend Winn had robbed and murdered a hitchhiker. The police suspected the murder was Jackson's doing, and urged him to confess, lest his friend Winn be unjustly convicted of murder. The trial judge had concluded that:

> [The police] were exerting a subtle form of pressure on Jackson, they were appealing to his concept of right and wrong. . . . They indicated that unless they got to the truth of the matter, it might be necessary to charge both, and this too was a very likely possibility. The officers were completely frank with him. The officers hoped that when Jackson was faced with what they had, and what might transpire if he didn't speak up, that he would take Winn off the hook and confess. That is exactly what he did. I can see nothing in what they said or in what they did that can be construed by Jackson as holding out the possibility of any benefit to him should he confess.

McIntyre J.A. agreed that no hope of advantage that would render a confession inadmissible had been held out to the accused. He then presented the following very helpful analysis of the law (at p. 38):

> [Cases] must be considered in relation to their own facts. It is my opinion that for a promised benefit to a person other than the accused to vitiate a confession, the benefit must be of such a nature that when considered in the light of the relationship between the person and the accused, and all the surrounding circumstances of the confession, it would tend to induce the accused to make an untrue statement, for it is the danger that a person may be induced by promises to make such a statement which lies at the root of this exclusionary rule.

McIntyre J.A. offered, as examples of improper inducements, telling a mother that her daughter would not be charged with shoplifting if the mother confessed to a similar offence (see *Commissioners of Customs and Excise v.*

Harz, [1967] 1 A.C. 760 (H.L.), at p. 821), or a sergeant-major keeping a company on parade until he learned who was responsible for a stabbing (see *R. v. Smith*, [1959] 2 Q.B. 35). In *Jackson*, by contrast, the accused had merely known Winn for a year in prison. The offence occurred a few days after their release. Neither testified to a relationship such that "the immunity of one was of such vital concern to the other that he would untruthfully confess to preserve it" (p. 39). The confession was therefore admissible.

The *Ibrahim* rule speaks not only of "hope of advantage", but also of "fear of prejudice". Obviously, any confession that is the product of outright violence is involuntary and unreliable, and therefore inadmissible. More common, and more challenging judicially, are the more subtle, veiled threats that can be used against suspects. The Honourable Fred Kaufman, in the third edition of *The Admissibility of Confessions* (1979), at p. 230, provides a useful starting point:

> Threats come in all shapes and sizes. Among the most common are words to the effect that "it would be better" to tell, implying thereby that dire consequences might flow from a refusal to talk. Maule J. recognized this fact, and said that "there can be no doubt that such words, if spoken by a competent person, have been held to exclude a confession at least 500 times" (*R. v. Garner* (1848), 3 Cox C.C. 175, at p. 177).

Courts have accordingly excluded confessions made in response to police suggestions that it would be better if they confessed. See *R. v. Desmeules*, [1971] R.L. 505 (Que. Ct. Sess. P.); *Comeau v. The Queen* (1961), 131 C.C.C. 139 (N.S.S.C.); *Lazure, supra*; *R. v. Hanlon* (1958), 28 C.R. 398 (Nfld. C.A.), at p. 401; *White, supra*, at p. 129.

However, phrases like "it would be better if you told the truth" should not automatically require exclusion. Instead, as in all cases, the trial judge must examine the entire context of the confession, and ask whether there is a reasonable doubt that the resulting confession was involuntary. Freedman C.J.M. applied this approach correctly in *R. v. Puffer* (1976), 31 C.C.C. (2d) 81 (Man. C.A.). In that case a suspect in a robbery and murder asked to meet with two police officers of his acquaintance. At this meeting, one officer said: "The best thing you can do is come in with us and tell the truth" (p. 95). Freedman C.J.M. held that while the officer's language was "unfortunate", it did not require exclusion (at p. 95): "McFall *wanted* to talk, he *wanted* to give the police his version of what had occurred, and above all he did not want Puffer and Kizyma to get away, leaving him to face the music alone" (emphasis in original).

In his reasons, Freedman C.J.M. referred to a passage from an article he had written earlier, "Admissions and Confessions", published in Salhany and Carter, eds., *Studies in Canadian Criminal Evidence* (1972), at pp. 110-11, where he stated the following:

> Risky though it be for a policeman to use words like "better tell us everything"— and an experienced and conscientious officer will shun them like the plague — their consequences will not always be fatal. There have been some instances where words of that type have been employed, and yet a confession following thereon has been admitted. That may occur when the court is satisfied that the offending

words, potentially perilous though they be, did not in fact induce the accused to speak. In other words, he would have confessed in any event, the court's enquiry on the point establishing that his statement was indeed voluntarily made. It is scarcely necessary to emphasize, however, that cases of the kind just mentioned will confront a prosecuting counsel with special difficulty. For words like "better tell the truth" carry the mark of an inducement on their very face, and a resultant confession may well find itself battling against the stream.

This Court upheld the Court of Appeal's ruling. See *McFall v. The Queen*, [1980] 1 S.C.R. 321; see also *R. v. Hayes* (1982), 65 C.C.C. (2d) 294 (Alta. C.A.), at pp. 296-97. I agree that "it would be better" comments require exclusion only where the circumstances reveal an implicit threat or promise.

A final threat or promise relevant to this appeal is the use of moral or spiritual inducements. These inducements will generally not produce an involuntary confession, for the very simple reason that the inducement offered is not in the control of the police officers. If a police officer says "If you don't confess, you'll spend the rest of your life in jail. Tell me what happened and I can get you a lighter sentence", then clearly there is a strong, and improper, inducement for the suspect to confess. The officer is offering a *quid pro quo*, and it raises the possibility that the suspect is confessing not because of any internal desire to confess, but merely in order to gain the benefit offered by the interrogator. By contrast, with most spiritual inducements the interrogator has no control over the suggested benefit. If a police officer convinces a suspect that he will feel better if he confesses, the officer has not offered anything. I therefore agree with Kaufman, *supra*, who summarized the jurisprudence as follows at p. 186:

> We may therefore conclude that, as a general rule, *confessions which result from spiritual exhortations or appeals to conscience and morality, are admissible in evidence, whether urged by a person in authority or by someone else* (emphasis in original).

In summary, courts must remember that the police may often offer some kind of inducement to the suspect to obtain a confession. Few suspects will spontaneously confess to a crime. In the vast majority of cases, the police will have to somehow convince the suspect that it is in his or her best interests to confess. This becomes improper only when the inducements, whether standing alone or in combination with other factors, are strong enough to raise a reasonable doubt about whether the will of the subject has been overborne. On this point I found the following passage from *R. v. Rennie* (1981), 74 Cr. App. R. 207 (C.A.), at p. 212, particularly apt:

> Very few confessions are inspired solely by remorse. Often the motives of an accused are mixed and include a hope that an early admission may lead to an earlier release or a lighter sentence. If it were the law that the mere presence of such a motive, even if promoted by something said or done by a person in authority, led inexorably to the exclusion of a confession, nearly every confession would be rendered inadmissible. This is not the law. In some cases the hope may be self-generated. If so, it is irrelevant, even if it provides the dominant motive for making the confession. In such a case the confession will not have been obtained by anything said or done by a person in authority. More commonly the presence of such a hope will, in part at least, owe its origin to something said or done by such a

person. There can be few prisoners who are being firmly but fairly questioned in a police station to whom it does not occur that they might be able to bring both their interrogation and their detention to an earlier end by confession.

The most important consideration in all cases is to look for a *quid pro quo* offer by interrogators, regardless of whether it comes in the form of a threat or a promise.

(b) Oppression

There was much debate among the parties, interveners, and courts below over the relevance of "oppression" to the confessions rule. Oppression clearly has the potential to produce false confessions. If the police create conditions distasteful enough, it should be no surprise that the suspect would make a stress-compliant confession to escape those conditions. Alternately, oppressive circumstances could overbear the suspect's will to the point that he or she comes to doubt his or her own memory, believes the relentless accusations made by the police, and gives an induced confession.

A compelling example of oppression comes from the Ontario Court of Appeal's recent decision in *R. v. Hoilett* (1999), 136 C.C.C. (3d) 449. The accused, charged with sexual assault, was arrested at 11:25 p.m. while under the influence of crack cocaine and alcohol. After two hours in a cell, two officers removed his clothes for forensic testing. He was left naked in a cold cell containing only a metal bunk to sit on. The bunk was so cold he had to stand up. One and one-half hours later, he was provided with some light clothes, but no underwear and ill-fitting shoes. Shortly thereafter, at about 3:00 a.m., he was awakened for the purpose of interviewing. In the course of the interrogation, the accused nodded off to sleep at least five times. He requested warmer clothes and a tissue to wipe his nose, both of which were refused. While he admitted knowing that he did not have to talk, and that the officers had made no explicit threats or promises, he hoped that if he talked to the police they would give him some warm clothes and cease the interrogation.

Under these circumstances, it is no surprise that the Court of Appeal concluded the statement was involuntary. Under inhumane conditions, one can hardly be surprised if a suspect confesses purely out of a desire to escape those conditions. Such a confession is not voluntary. For similar examples of oppressive circumstances, see *R. v. Owen* (1983), 4 C.C.C. (3d) 538 (N.S.S.C., App. Div.); *R. v. Serack*, [1974] 2 W.W.R. 377 (B.C.S.C.). Without trying to indicate all the factors that can create an atmosphere of oppression, such factors include depriving the suspect of food, clothing, water, sleep, or medical attention; denying access to counsel; and excessively aggressive, intimidating questioning for a prolonged period of time.

A final possible source of oppressive conditions is the police use of non-existent evidence. As the discussion of false confessions, *supra*, revealed, this ploy is very dangerous: see Ofshe & Leo (1997a), *supra*, at pp. 1040-41; Ofshe & Leo (1997), *supra*, at p. 202. The use of false evidence is often crucial in convincing the suspect that protestations of innocence, even if true, are futile. I do not mean to suggest in any way that, standing alone, confronting the suspect with inadmissible or even fabricated evidence is necessarily grounds for excluding a statement. However, when combined with other factors, it is certainly a relevant consideration in determining on *voir dire* whether a confession was voluntary.

England has also recognized the role of oppression. Section 76(8) of the Police and Criminal Evidence Act 1984 (U.K.), 1984, c. 60, states that a confession must not be the product of "oppression", which is defined to include "torture, inhuman or degrading treatment, and the use or threat of violence (whether or not amounting to torture)". The Code of Practice for the Detention, Treatment and Questioning of Persons by Police Officers goes on to offer examples of what may amount to oppression, which are similar to what I described above.

(c) Operating Mind

This Court recently addressed this aspect of the confessions rule in *Whittle, supra,* and I need not repeat that exercise here. Briefly stated, Sopinka J. explained that the operating mind requirement "does not imply a higher degree of awareness than knowledge of what the accused is saying and that he is saying it to police officers who can use it to his detriment" (p. 936). I agree, and would simply add that, like oppression, the operating mind doctrine should not be understood as a discrete inquiry completely divorced from the rest of the confessions rule. Indeed, in his reasons in *Horvath, supra,* at p. 408, Spence J. perceived the operating mind doctrine as but one application of the broader principle of voluntariness: statements are inadmissible if they are "not voluntary in the ordinary English sense of the word because they were induced by other circumstances such as existed in the present case".

. . .

(d) Other Police Trickery

A final consideration in determining whether a confession is voluntary or not is the police use of trickery to obtain a confession. Unlike the previous three headings, this doctrine is a distinct inquiry. While it is still related to voluntariness, its more specific objective is maintaining the integrity of the criminal justice system. Lamer J.'s concurrence in *Rothman, supra,* introduced this inquiry. In that case, the Court admitted a suspect's statement to an undercover police officer who had been placed in a cell with the accused. In concurring reasons, Lamer J. emphasized that reliability was not the only concern of the confessions rule; otherwise the rule would not be concerned with whether the inducement was given by a person in authority. He summarized the correct approach at p. 691:

> [A] statement before being left to the trier of fact for consideration of its probative value should be the object of a voir dire in order to determine, not whether the statement is or is not reliable, but whether the authorities have done or said anything that could have induced the accused to make a statement which was or might be untrue. It is of the utmost importance to keep in mind that the inquiry is not concerned with reliability but with the authorities' conduct as regards reliability.

Lamer J. was also quick to point out that courts should be wary not to unduly limit police discretion (at p. 697):

[T]he investigation of crime and the detection of criminals is not a game to be governed by the Marquess of Queensbury rules. The authorities, in dealing with shrewd and often sophisticated criminals, must sometimes of necessity resort to tricks or other forms of deceit and should not through the rule be hampered in their work. What should be repressed vigorously is conduct on their part that shocks the community.

As examples of what might "shock the community", Lamer J. suggested a police officer pretending to be a chaplain or a legal aid lawyer, or injecting truth serum into a diabetic under the pretense that it was insulin. Lamer J.'s discussion on this point was adopted by the Court in *Collins, supra*, at pp. 286-87; see also *R. v. Clot* (1982), 69 C.C.C. (2d) 349 (Que. Sup. Ct.).

In *Hebert, supra*, this Court overruled the result in *Rothman* based on the Charter's right to silence. However, I do not believe that this renders the "shocks the community" rule redundant. There may be situations in which police trickery, though neither violating the right to silence nor undermining voluntariness *per se*, is so appalling as to shock the community. I therefore believe that the test enunciated by Lamer J. in *Rothman*, and adopted by the Court in *Collins*, is still an important part of the confessions rule.

(e) Summary

While the foregoing might suggest that the confessions rule involves a panoply of different considerations and tests, in reality the basic idea is quite simple. First of all, because of the criminal justice system's overriding concern not to convict the innocent, a confession will not be admissible if it is made under circumstances that raise a reasonable doubt as to voluntariness. Both the traditional, narrow *Ibrahim* rule and the oppression doctrine recognize this danger. If the police interrogators subject the suspect to utterly intolerable conditions, or if they offer inducements strong enough to produce an unreliable confession, the trial judge should exclude it. Between these two extremes, oppressive conditions and inducements can operate together to exclude confessions. Trial judges must be alert to the entire circumstances surrounding a confession in making this decision.

The doctrines of oppression and inducements are primarily concerned with reliability. However, as the operating mind doctrine and Lamer J.'s concurrence in *Rothman, supra*, both demonstrate, the confessions rule also extends to protect a broader conception of voluntariness "that focuses on the protection of the accused's rights and fairness in the criminal process": J. Sopinka, S. N. Lederman and A.W. Bryant, *The Law of Evidence in Canada* (2nd ed. 1999), at p. 339. Voluntariness is the touchstone of the confessions rule. Whether the concern is threats or promises, the lack of an operating mind, or police trickery that unfairly denies the accused's right to silence, this Court's jurisprudence has consistently protected the accused from having involuntary confessions introduced into evidence. If a confession is involuntary for any of these reasons, it is inadmissible.

Again, I would also like to emphasize that the analysis under the confessions rule must be a contextual one. In the past, courts have excluded confessions made as a result of relatively minor inducements. At the same time, the law ignored intolerable police conduct if it did not give rise to an "inducement" as it was understood by the narrow *Ibrahim* formulation. Both results are incorrect. Instead, a court should strive to understand the circumstances surrounding the confession and ask if it gives rise to a reasonable doubt as to the confession's voluntariness, taking into account all the aspects of the rule discussed above. Therefore a relatively minor inducement, such as a tissue to wipe one's nose and warmer clothes, may amount to an impermissible inducement if the suspect is deprived of sleep, heat, and clothes for several hours in the middle of the night during an interrogation: see *Hoilett, supra*. On the other hand, where the suspect is treated properly, it will take a stronger inducement to render the confession involuntary. If a trial court properly considers all the relevant circumstances, then a finding regarding voluntariness is essentially a factual one, and should only be overturned for "some *palpable and overriding* error which affected [the trial judge's] assessment of the facts": *Schwartz v. Canada*, [1996] 1 S.C.R. 254, at p. 279 (quoting *Stein v. The Ship "Kathy K"*, [1976] 2 S.C.R. 802 at p. 808) (emphasis in *Schwartz*).

D. Application to the Present Appeal

Applying the foregoing law to the facts of this appeal, and having viewed the relevant video- and audiotapes, I find no fault with the trial judge's conclusion that the respondent's confession was voluntary and reliable. The respondent was fully apprised of his rights at all times; he was never subjected to harsh, aggressive, or overbearing interrogation; he was not deprived of sleep, food, or drink; and he was never offered any improper inducements that undermined the reliability of the confessions. As the Court of Appeal reached a contrary conclusion with respect to a number of these issues, I will address them in turn.

[The Court then analyzed the fact situation under a variety of heads: 1. Minimizing the Seriousness of the Crimes; 2. Offers of Psychiatric Help; 3. "It Would Be Better"; 4. Alleged Threats Against the Respondent's Fiancee; 5. Abuse of Trust; 6. Atmosphere of Oppression.]

E. The Relevance of the Polygraph Test

In addition to the issues addressed above, the Court of Appeal found the police use of a polygraph particularly problematic. Because of the growing frequency with which police are using the polygraph as an investigative tool, and the absence of any direction thus far from this Court regarding the proper use of polygraphs in interrogations, I will now briefly discuss how polygraphs fit into the analytical framework set out above. The Court of Appeal identified several problems with the police's use of a polygraph in this appeal. I will address each in turn.

1. Informing the Suspect of the Uses to Which the Polygraph Test Can Be Put

The Court of Appeal first stated that the police failed "to inform the accused clearly that the polygraph test was not admissible in court to show whether the accused was lying or telling the truth" (para. 156); see also *R. v. James,* Ont. Ct. (Gen. Div.), January 25, 1991; *R. v. Ollerhead* (1990), 86 Nfld.

& P.E.I.R. 38 (Nfld. S.C.T.D.); *R. v. Fowler* (1979), 23 Nfld. & P.E.I.R. 255 (Nfld. C.A.).

To the contrary is *R. v. Alexis* (1994), 35 C.R. (4th) 117 (Ont. Ct. (Gen. Div.)). As noted at para. 159 of Hill J.'s lucid reasons in that case,

> confrontation of a suspect with polygraph test results, in such circumstances, is not qualitatively dissimilar from such permissible techniques of persuasion as the police showing a detained suspect a co-accused's confession inadmissible in evidence against the suspect, or police trickery, for example, the ruse of relating to the suspect that his or her fingerprint has been discovered at the scene of the crime.

On this view, police trickery or use of inadmissible evidence is not necessarily grounds for exclusion.

I agree that merely failing to tell a suspect that the polygraph is inadmissible will not automatically produce an involuntary confession. Courts should engage in a two-step process. First, following *Rothman, supra*, and *Collins, supra*, the confession should be excluded if the police deception shocks the community. Second, even if not rising to that level, the use of deception is a relevant factor in the overall voluntariness analysis. At this stage, the approach is similar to the one used with fabricated evidence, *supra*—though of course the use of inadmissible evidence is inherently less problematic than fabricated evidence. Standing alone, simply failing to tell the suspect that the polygraph results are inadmissible will not require exclusion. The most it can do is be a factor in the overall voluntariness analysis.

Moreover, in this particular appeal, the police made it abundantly clear to the respondent just what was admissible and what was not....

2. Exaggerating the Polygraph's Validity

The Court of Appeal also noted, correctly in my opinion, that the police made "repeated assertions to the accused that the polygraph was an infallible determiner of truth" (para. 156) . . .

I agree that the police exaggerated the accuracy of the polygraph. As many sources have demonstrated, polygraphs are far from infallible: see, e.g., D. T. Lykken, A Tremor in the Blood: Uses and Abuses of the Lie Detector (1998); J. J. Furedy, "The 'control' question 'test' (CQT) polygrapher's dilemma: logico-ethical considerations for psychophysiological practitioners and researchers" (1993), 15 Int. J. Psychophysiology 263; C. J. Patrick and W. G. Iacono, "Validity of the Control Question Polygraph Test: The Problem of Sampling Bias" (1991), 76 J. App. Psych. 229. Similarly, this Court recognized in *R. v. Béland*, [1987] 2 S.C.R. 398, that the results of polygraph examinations are sufficiently unreliable that they cannot be admitted in court.

The Quebec Court of Appeal concluded in *R. v. Amyot* (1990), 58 C.C.C. (3d) 312, at p. 324, that representing the polygraph as infallible rendered a confession involuntary. In that case the polygrapher told the accused that "the test showed him that he is not telling the truth". This, the court found, was inappropriate in that it

> pushed what the examination consisted of much too far, into the absolute. The result was presented to the appellant as a certitude which obviously was going to shake him up and it made him say "but what is going to happen now?" It seems to

me that, as a result, the appellant was led into error on the infallibility of the test and this manner of proceeding could naturally induce a person to "confess".

See also *Fowler, supra.* The Court of Appeal in *Amyot* put particular emphasis on the fact that the suspect confessed almost immediately after hearing the polygraph results, suggesting that his will was overwhelmed upon being confronted with the damning, supposedly incontrovertible evidence.

Without expressing an opinion as to whether *Amyot* was correctly decided, I note that the facts of the present appeal are very different. . . .

Various lower courts have thus taken very different approaches to determining whether polygraphs create an oppressive atmosphere. The contrasting approaches in cases like *Amyot* and *Ollerhead* demonstrate that the timing of the confession vis-à-vis the polygraph cannot be determinative. Instead, it is but a piece of evidence for the trial judge to consider in determining whether the confession was voluntary.

Granted that the police misled the respondent with regards to the accuracy of the polygraph, the question remains whether, in light of the entire circumstances of the interrogation, this rendered the confessions inadmissible. In my opinion it did not. As discussed above, there was no emotional disintegration in this case. The mere fact that a suspect begins to cry when he or she finally confesses, as the respondent did, is not evidence of "complete emotional disintegration"; tears are to be expected when someone finally divulges that they committed a crime—particularly when the suspect is a generally law-abiding and upstanding citizen like the respondent.

Nor, as discussed above, do I believe that the police created an oppressive atmosphere. Simply confronting the suspect with adverse evidence, like a polygraph test, is not grounds for exclusion: see *Fitton, supra.* This holds true even for inadmissible evidence: see *Alexis, supra.* Nor does the fact that the police exaggerate the evidence's reliability or importance necessarily render a confession inadmissible. Eyewitness accounts are by no means infallible; yet in *Fitton*, this Court ruled admissible a statement taken after the police told a suspect they did not believe his denials because several eyewitnesses had come forward against him. In short, merely confronting a suspect with adverse evidence — even exaggerating its accuracy and reliability—will not, standing alone, render a confession involuntary.

3. *Misleading the Accused Regarding the Duration of the Interview*

The final ground on which the Court of Appeal challenged the use of the polygraph, at para. 156, was the police's misleading the accused about the expected duration of the test procedure, particularly concerning the interrogation to follow and immediately commencing intense questioning upon informing the accused that he had "failed" the test....

A similar argument was made in *Nugent, supra.* Since this Court has ruled that polygraph results are not admissible in evidence, *Béland, supra,* "then the administering of a test must be clearly separated from questioning for the purpose of obtaining statements" (*Nugent, supra,* at p. 212). According to the Court of Appeal, a statement directly following a polygraph should not be admissible because the defence cannot adequately explain the context of the statement—which it might wish to do in order to attack the weight of the statement before the jury—without notifying the jury that the accused failed a polygraph test.

Drawing on these arguments, the intervener, the Criminal Lawyers' Association, argued that the police have only two options when using polygraphs. One is to ensure that the suspect has consulted with counsel before consenting to the test. The other is to "clearly separate any post-test interrogation from the test itself". I do not believe that it is necessary to limit the police's discretion in this manner. It is true that the police procedures present the defence with the unpalatable choice of either trying to explain away the confession without using the polygraph, or admitting that the accused failed the test. However, this is true any time a suspect confesses after being confronted with inadmissible evidence, and it does not necessarily render the confession involuntary. Tactical disadvantage to the defence is not relevant to the voluntariness of the defendant's confession; instead, if anything, it simply suggests prejudicial effect. However, given the immense probative value of a voluntary confession, I cannot agree that exclusion is appropriate.

ARBOUR J. (dissenting):—I have had the benefit of the reasons of my colleague, Justice Iacobucci, on this appeal. With respect, I believe that there were improper inducements held out by the police officers who interrogated the respondent and that these inducements, considered cumulatively and contextually in light of the "failed" polygraph test, require the exclusion of the respondent's statements. Moreover, in my view the proximity and the causal connection between the "failed" polygraph test and the confession also compels this result. Accordingly, I would dismiss the appeal, set aside the convictions and enter acquittals on all counts. . .

Properly understood, this case involves two confessions obtained by the police following the "failure" of a polygraph test and a skillful interrogation which lasted nearly six hours. Repeated threats and promises were made. They were often subtle but in my view, against the backdrop of the polygraph procedure, they overwhelmed the free will of the respondent. These seemingly mild pressures make this case a difficult one in which to apply the confessions rule and demand an attentive appreciation of the full context in which the alleged voluntary, incriminating statements were made.

[Justice Arbour then analyzed admissibility under the headings of The Administration of the Polygraph Test, The Post-Polygraph Interrogation, Promise of Psychiatric Help, Minimization of the Seriousness of the Crimes, Threat to Interrogate the Accused's Girlfriend, and Fair Trial Considerations.]

Do you think *Oickle* has broadened police power to interrogate? Do you have any concerns about *Oickle*? Is the court too encouraging of the use of polygraphs as a coercive technique? Is *Oickle* consistent with the Supreme Court's jurisprudence on the principle against self-incrimination?

For a number of divergent views on these questions, see Stuart, *Charter Justice in Canadian Criminal Law* (6th ed., 2014) pp. 156-168; Trotter, "False Confessions and Wrongful Convictions", (2003-2004) 35 Ottawa L. Rev. 179; Christopher Sherrin, "False Confessions and Admissions in Canadian Law", (2005) 30 Queen's L.J. 601; Lisa Dufraimont, "The Common Law Confessions Rule in the Charter Era: Current Law and Future Directions" (2008) 40 *Supr.Crt. L.Rev.* (2nd) 250; Dale Ives, "Preventing False Confessions: Is Oickle Up to the Task" (2007) *San Diego L.Rev.* 1; and Edmund Thomas, "Lowering the Standard: R. v. Oickle and the Confessions Rule in Canada", (2005) 10 *Can. Crim. L .Rev.* 69.

In *R. v. Spencer*, [2007] 1 S.C.R. 500, 44 C.R. (6th) 199, 217 C.C.C. (3d) 353, a majority of the present Court makes it very clear that the police are to be given considerable leeway to offer inducements to obtain confessions without rendering a statement involuntary. Charged with robbery, the accused was very much concerned with whether his girlfriend would also be charged. The majority, in holding the confession was properly admitted, see the case as all about promises. The dissenters see the reality as an implied threat to charge the girlfriend unless Spencer confessed.

Spencer and *Oickle* will encourage police to exploit emotions about possible prosecution against partners. *Oickle* says police may use polygraphs and lie about their accuracy. *Oickle* has resulted in few judicial controls on interrogation by one known to be a police officer. Those looking for further limits through interpretations of the s. 7 pre-trial right to silence were disappointed by the majority decision in *Singh*.

R. v. SINGH
(2007), 51 C.R. (6th) 199, 225 C.C.C. (3d) 103 (S.C.C.)

The accused was charged with second degree murder after an altercation outside a pub resulted in a man's death. Several shots were fired and an innocent bystander was fatally shot by a stray bullet. There was no physical evidence linking the accused to the shooting, but the doorman and another eyewitness implicated the accused as the shooter.

The accused was arrested, properly cautioned and advised of his right to counsel, and he privately consulted with counsel. The accused was subsequently interviewed twice by a police officer while in detention. During these interviews, which were videotaped, the accused stated on numerous occasions that he did not want to talk about the incident, that he knew nothing about it, and that he wished to return to his cell. On each occasion, the officer either affirmed that the accused did not have to say anything or explained that he, the officer, had a duty or desire to place the evidence before the accused. In all cases the officer persisted in questioning the accused and confronting the accused with incriminating evidence. The officer testified that he intended to put the police case before the accused in an attempt to get him to confess, no matter what.

During the first interview, the accused did not confess but made incriminating statements, admitting that he had been in the pub on the night of the shooting and identifying himself in pictures taken from video surveillance inside the pub in question and another pub. The accused had asserted his right to silence 18 times before making these admissions.

At trial, the accused challenged the admissibility of the statements, arguing that they were involuntary and that they were obtained in violation of the accused's pre-trial right to silence under s. 7 of the Charter. The trial judge admitted the statements and the accused was convicted. The accused's appeal to the British Columbia Court of Appeal was dismissed. The accused appealed to the Supreme Court on the s. 7 issue.

A 5-4 majority dismissed the appeal.

Per CHARRON J. (McLachlin C.J., Bastarache, Deschamps, Rothstein JJ. concurring): —

. . .

Mr. Singh contends that trial and appellate courts, including the courts below, have generally misinterpreted the holding in *Hebert* as an authoritative statement which permits the police to ignore a detainee's expressed wish to remain silent and to use "legitimate means of persuasion" to break that silence (p. 177). He contends that the British Columbia Court of Appeal in the case at bar went even further and effectively extinguished the s. 7 right to silence when it questioned the utility of conducting "a double-barrelled test of admissibility", stating that "[i]n the context of an investigatory interview with an obvious person in authority" the expansive view of the common law confessions rule adopted in *Oickle* "may leave little additional room" for a separate s. 7 Charter inquiry (para. 19). Mr. Singh therefore submits that the Court of Appeal proceeded on the basis of erroneous legal principles when it affirmed the trial judge's dismissal of his s. 7 Charter application.

Further, Mr. Singh invites this Court to enhance the protection afforded to detainees under s. 7 by adopting a new approach that would require police officers to inform the detainee of his or her right to silence and, absent a signed waiver, to refrain from questioning any detainee who states that he or she does not wish to speak to the police.

First, I reject the appellant's contention that this Court should change the law relating to the pre-trial Charter right to silence. The new approach advocated by the appellant ignores the critical balancing of state and individual interests which lies at the heart of this Court's decision in *Hebert* and of subsequent s. 7 decisions. I see no reason to depart from these established principles.

Second, I find no error in law in the approach adopted by the courts below. The Court of Appeal's impugned comment on the interplay between the confessions rule and s. 7 of the Charter merely reflects the fact that, in the context of a police interrogation of a person in detention, where the detainee knows he or she is speaking to a person in authority, the two tests are functionally equivalent. It follows that, where a statement has survived a thorough inquiry into voluntariness, the accused's Charter application alleging that the statement was obtained in violation of the pre-trial right to silence under s. 7 cannot succeed. Conversely, if circumstances are such that the accused can show on a balance of probabilities that the statement was obtained in violation of his or her constitutional right to remain silent, the Crown will be unable to prove voluntariness beyond a reasonable doubt. As I will explain, however, this does not mean that the residual protection afforded to the right to silence under s. 7 of the Charter does not supplement the common law in other contexts.

Finally, I see no basis for interfering with the trial judge's factual determinations concerning Sgt. Attew's conduct and its effect on the appellant's freedom to choose whether to speak to the police. I would therefore dismiss the appeal.

. . .

Although historically the confessions rule was more concerned with the reliability of confessions than the protection against self-incrimination, this no longer holds true in the post-Charter era. Both the confessions rule and the constitutional right to silence are manifestations of the principle against self-incrimination. The principle against self-incrimination is a broad concept which has been usefully described by Lamer C.J. as "a general organizing principle of criminal law" from which a number of rules can be derived:

. . .

What the common law recognizes is the individual's right to remain silent. This does not mean, however, that a person has the right not to be spoken to by state authorities. The importance of police questioning in the fulfilment of their investigative role cannot be doubted. One can readily appreciate that the police could hardly investigate crime without putting questions to persons from whom it is thought that useful information may be obtained. The person suspected of having committed the crime being investigated is no exception. Indeed, if the suspect in fact committed the crime, he or she is likely the person who has the most information to offer about the incident. Therefore, the common law also recognizes the importance of police interrogation in the investigation of crime.

Of course, the information obtained from a suspect is only useful in the elucidation of crime if it can be relied upon for its truth — hence the primary reason for the confessions rule, the concern about the reliability of confessions. The common law confessions rule is largely informed by the problem of false confessions. As noted in *Oickle*, "[t]he history of police interrogations is not without its unsavoury chapters" (para. 34). The parameters of the rule are very much tailored to counter the dangers created by improper interrogation techniques that commonly produce false confessions: see *Oickle*, at paras. 32-46. Further, a confession is a very powerful item of evidence against an accused which, in and of itself, can ground a conviction. One of the overriding concerns of the criminal justice system is that the innocent must not be convicted. Because it is recognized that involuntary confessions are more likely to be unreliable, the confessions rule requires proof beyond a reasonable doubt of the voluntariness of any statement obtained from an accused by a person in authority before it may be admitted in evidence, so to avoid miscarriages of justice.

Of course, not every involuntary confession is false. While the confession rule's primary concern is with reliability, it is well established that voluntariness is a broader concept. As this Court stated in *Oickle* (at para. 70): "Wigmore perhaps summed up the point best when he said that voluntariness is 'shorthand for a complex of values': *Wigmore on Evidence* (Chadbourn rev. 1970), vol. 3, § 826, at p. 351." These values include respect for the individual's freedom of will, the need for law enforcement officers themselves to obey the law, and the overall fairness of the criminal justice system: see *Oickle*, at paras. 69-70, citing *Blackburn v. Alabama*, 361 U.S. 199 (1960), at p. 207.

Therefore, the notion of voluntariness is broad-based and has long included the common law principle that a person is not obliged to give information to the police or to answer questions. This component of the voluntariness rule is reflected in the usual police caution given to a suspect and the importance attached (even before the advent of the Charter) to the presence of a caution as a factor in determining the voluntariness of a statement made by a person under arrest or detention: see *Boudreau v. The King*, [1949] S.C.R. 262; *R. v. Fitton*, [1956] S.C.R. 958; and *R. v. Esposito* (1985), 24 C.C.C. (3d) 88 (Ont. C.A.). A common form of the police caution given to a person who has been charged with an offence is the following: "You are charged with... Do you wish to say anything in answer to the charge? You are not obliged to say anything but whatever you do say may be given in evidence." Therefore, the police caution, in plain language, informs the suspect of his right to remain silent. Its importance as a factor on the question of voluntariness was noted by this Court as early as 1949 in *Boudreau*:

> The fundamental question is whether a confession of an accused offered in evidence is voluntary. There mere fact that a warning was given is not necessarily decisive in favour of admissibility but, on the other hand, the absence of a warning should not bind the hands of the Court so as to compel it to rule out a statement. All the surrounding circumstances must be investigated and, if upon their review the Court is not satisfied of the voluntary nature of the admission, the statement will be rejected. Accordingly, the presence or absence of a warning will be a factor and, in many cases, an important one. [Emphasis added; p. 267.]

Although the confessions rule applies whether or not the suspect is in detention, the common law recognized, also long before the advent of the Charter, that the suspect's situation is much different after detention. (As we shall see, the residual protection afforded to the right to silence under s. 7 of the Charter is only triggered upon detention.) After detention, the state authorities are in control and the detainee, who cannot simply walk away, is in a more vulnerable position. There is a greater risk of abuse of power by the police. The fact of detention alone can have a significant impact on the suspect and cause him or her to feel compelled to give a statement. The importance of reaffirming the individual's right to choose whether to speak to the authorities after he or she is detained is reflected in the jurisprudence concerning the timing of the police caution. Rene Marin, in his text, *Admissibility of Statements* (9th ed. (looseleaf)), at pp. 2-24.2 and 2-24.3, provides a useful yardstick for the police on when they should caution a suspect:

The warning should be given when there are reasonable grounds to suspect that the person being interviewed has committed an offence. An easy yardstick to determine when the warning should be given is for a police officer to consider the question of what he or she would do if the person attempted to leave the questioning room or leave the presence of the officer where a communication or exchange is taking place. If the answer is arrest (or detain) the person, then the warning should be given.

These words of advice are sound. Even if the suspect has not formally been arrested and is not obviously under detention, police officers are well advised to give the police caution in the circumstances described by *Marin*. Of course, with the advent of the Charter, the s. 10 right to counsel is triggered upon arrest or detention. The right to counsel has both an informational and an implementational component. It seeks to ensure that persons who become subject to the coercive power of the state will know about their right to counsel and will be given the opportunity to exercise it so they can make an informed choice whether to participate in the investigation against them. Therefore, if the detainee has exercised his s. 10 Charter right to counsel, he will presumably have been informed of his right to remain silent, and the overall significance of the caution may be somewhat diminished. Where the suspect has not consulted with counsel, however, the police caution becomes all the more important as a factor in answering the ultimate question of voluntariness.

. . .

On the question of voluntariness, as under any distinct s. 7 review based on an alleged breach of the right to silence, the focus is on the conduct of the police and its effect on the suspect's ability to exercise his or her free will. The test is an objective one. However, the individual characteristics of the accused are obviously relevant considerations in applying this objective test.

Therefore, voluntariness, as it is understood today, requires that the court scrutinize whether the accused was denied his or her right to silence. The right to silence is defined in accordance with constitutional principles. A finding of voluntariness will therefore be determinative of the s. 7 issue. In other words, if the Crown proves voluntariness beyond a reasonable doubt, there can be no finding of a Charter violation of the right to silence in respect of the same statement. The converse holds true as well. If the circumstances are such that an accused is able to show on a balance of probabilities a breach of his or her right to silence, the Crown will not be in a position to meet the voluntariness test....

Mr. Singh takes particular issue with the leeway afforded to the police in questioning the detainee, even after he has retained counsel and has asserted his choice to remain silent. He submits that courts have erroneously interpreted the underlined passage above as permitting the police to ignore a detainee's expressed wish to remain silent and to use "legitimate means of persuasion". I say two things in response to this argument. First, the use of legitimate means of persuasion is indeed permitted under the present rule — it was expressly endorsed by this Court in *Hebert*. This approach is part of the critical balance that must be maintained between individual and societal interests. Second, the law as it stands does not permit the police to ignore the detainee's freedom to choose whether to speak or not, as contended. Under both common law and Charter rules, police persistence in continuing the interview, despite repeated assertions by the detainee that he wishes to remain silent, may well raise a strong argument that any subsequently obtained statement was not the product of a free will to speak to the authorities. As we shall see, the trial judge in this case was very much alive to the risk that the statement may be involuntary when a police officer engages in such conduct.

. . .

Despite Sgt. Attew's admitted intention to put parts of the police case against Mr. Singh before him in an effort to get him to confess, "no matter what", his conduct of the interview as evidenced on the videotape shows that in so describing his method his bark is much worse than his bite. In my respectful view, the trial judge's ultimate judgment call on this issue is supported by the record and is entitled to deference. Therefore, I see no reason to interfere with his ruling on admissibility.

It must again be emphasized that such situations are highly fact-specific and trial judges must take into account all the relevant factors in determining whether or not the Crown has established that the accused's confession is voluntary. In some circumstances, the evidence will support a finding that continued questioning by the police in the face of the accused's repeated assertions of the right to silence denied the accused a meaningful choice whether to speak or to remain silent: see *Otis*. The number of times the accused asserts his or her right to silence is part of the assessment of all of the circumstances, but is not in itself determinative. The ultimate question is whether the accused exercised free will by choosing to make a statement: *Otis*, at paras. 50 and 54.

Per FISH J. (Binnie, LeBel, Abella JJ. concurring) (dissenting): —

The question on this appeal is whether "no" means "yes" where a police interrogator refuses to take "no" for an answer from a detainee under his total control. As a matter of constitutional principle, I would answer that question in the negative, allow the appeal and order a new trial.

. . .

What is at stake, rather, is the Court's duty to ensure that a detainee's right to silence will be respected by interrogators once it has been unequivocally asserted, and not disregarded or insidiously undermined as an investigative "stratagem" (the trial judge's own word in this case).

The appellant, Jagrup Singh, asserted his right to silence unequivocally — not once, but eighteen times. Throughout his interrogation, Mr. Singh was imprisoned in a police lock-up. In the trial judge's words, he was "totally under the control of the police authorities", "[did] not have freedom of unescorted movement" and "relie[d] totally on his jailers for the necessaries of life" (Ruling on the voir dire, [2003] B.C.J. No. 3174 (QL), 2003 BCSC 2013, at para. 8). Powerless to end his interrogation, Mr. Singh asked, repeatedly, to be returned to his cell. Yet he was not permitted to do so until he capitulated and made the incriminating statements impugned on this appeal.

Mr. Singh's interrogator understood very well that Mr. Singh had chosen not to speak with the police. The interrogator nonetheless disregarded Mr. Singh's repeated assertions of his right to silence. It is undisputed that he did so in "an effort to get [Mr. Singh] to confess, no matter what" (Ruling on the voir dire, at para. 34 (emphasis added)).

In his relentless pursuit of this objective, the interrogator urged Mr. Singh, subtly but unmistakeably, to forsake his counsel's advice. I find this aspect of the interrogation particularly disturbing.

To the officer's knowledge, Mr. Singh had been advised by his lawyer to exercise his right to silence. The officer, with irony if not cynicism, discounted this "absolutely great advice" (his words) as something he too would say if he were Mr. Singh's lawyer. And he then pressed Mr. Singh to instead answer his questions — "to confess, no matter what".

Mr. Singh was thus deprived not only of his right to silence, but also, collaterally, of the intended benefit of his right to counsel. These rights are close companions, like glove and hand.

. . .

At the very least, the interrogator's conduct in this case "unfairly frustrated [Mr. Singh's] decision on the question of whether to make a statement to the authorities" (*Hebert*, at p. 186). Accordingly, the impugned statements, in the words of s. 24(2) of the Charter, were "obtained in a manner that infringed or denied" Mr. Singh's constitutional right to silence. And I am satisfied that authorizing their admission in the circumstances of this case would bring the administration of justice into disrepute. They should therefore have been excluded at trial.

In the trial judge's view, Mr. Singh's repeated assertions of his right to silence signify that "Mr. Singh successfully invoked his right to silence" (para. 36) ....

Where continued resistance has been made to appear futile to one person under the dominance or control of another, as it was in this case, ultimate submission proves neither true consent nor valid waiver. It proves the failure, not the success, of the disregarded assertions of the right of the powerless and the vulnerable to say "no".

. . .

I take care not to be understood to have held that eighteen (a significant number in other contexts) is of any importance at all in determining whether a detainee's right of silence has been effectively undermined. On the contrary, I favour a purposive approach and find it unnecessary to decide whether eighteen times is too many or once is too few. Constitutional rights do not have to be asserted or invoked a pre-determined number of times before the state and its agents are bound to permit them to be exercised freely and effectively. A right that need not be respected after it has been firmly and unequivocally asserted any number of times is a constitutional promise that has not been kept.

Nothing in *Hebert*, or in any other decision of this Court, permits the police to press detainees to waive the Charter rights they have firmly and unequivocally asserted, or to deliberately frustrate their effective exercise. This is true of the right to counsel and true as well of the right to silence.

Justice Charron agrees with the British Columbia Court of Appeal that "[i]n the context of an investigatory interview with an obvious person in authority, the expansive view of the confession rule in *Oickle* may leave little additional room for s. 7" ((2006), 38 C.R. (6th) 217 (B.C.C.A.), at para. 19). With respect, I am of a different view.

The rationale of the enhanced confessions rule adopted in *R. v. Oickle*, [2000] 2 S.C.R. 3, 2000 SCC 38, like the rationale of its narrower predecessor, is distinct from the purposes served by the Charter. A confession may be "voluntary" under the common law rule and yet be obtained by state action that infringes s. 7 of the Charter. And s. 7 will be infringed where, as in this case, a police interrogator has undermined a detainee's "freedom to choose whether to make a statement or not" (*Hebert*, at p. 176). Flagrantly disregarded in this way, the detainee's "positive right to make a free choice" (*Hebert*, at p. 177), is neither "positive" nor "free".

. . .

Justice Charron finds that the expansion of the confessions rule in *Oickle* leaves no additional room for the operation of s. 7 in the context of an "investigatory interview" (paras. 8, 25). I agree with her that there is considerable overlap between the Charter protection of the right to silence and the common law confessions rule. Given their different purposes, however, they should remain distinct doctrines: To overlap is not to overtake.

Even under its broader formulation in *Oickle*, the common law rule remains principally concerned with the reliability of confessions and the integrity of the criminal justice system. The purpose of the Charter, on the other hand, is "to constrain government action in conformity with certain individual rights and freedoms, the preservation of which are essential to the continuation of a democratic, functioning society in which the basic dignity of all is recognized" (*Canadian Egg Marketing Agency v. Richardson*, [1998] 3 S.C.R. 157, at para. 57).

As this case illustrates, a purposive approach makes plain that the right to pre-trial silence under s. 7 of the Charter is not eclipsed by the common law confessions rule under *Oickle*. This asymmetry should not surprise. The Court has consistently held that the two doctrines are distinct. Lower courts have continued to apply them separately. And even upon expanding the common law rule in *Oickle*, the Court took care to explain that neither rule "subsumes the other" (at para. 31).

Justice Charron finds the reasons of Proulx J.A. in *Otis* "particularly instructive" on the issue that concerns us here. I agree. In Justice Proulx's words: [Translation] "The refusal of the investigator to respect the respondent's specific insistent request to end the interrogation constitutes a violation of the right to remain silent": *R. v. Otis* (2000), 151 C.C.C. (3d) 416 (Que. C.A.), at para. 43. And I think it especially instructive that Justice Proulx [Translation] "ruled that the confession should be excluded due to the breach of a right guaranteed by the Charter" (para. 57) rather than under the common law confessions rule — even though, in the particular circumstances of *Otis* (notably the "emotional disintegration" of the accused), he would have excluded the accused's statement under the confessions rule as well.

The Court held in *Hebert*, as we have seen, that the s. 7 right to silence "must be interpreted in a manner which secures to the detained person the right to make a free and meaningful choice as to whether to speak to the authorities or to remain silent" (p. 181). Under the *Oickle* test, as noted earlier, a statement is admissible at common law where the detainee had an operating mind and the confession did not result from inducements, oppression, or police trickery that would shock the community. Clearly, however, a confession that meets these common law standards does not invariably represent a "free and meaningful choice" for the purposes of the Charter. A choice that has been disregarded, and "unfairly frustrated" (*Hebert*, at p. 186) by relentless interrogation in "an effort to get a detainee to confess, no matter what", is, once again, neither "free" nor "meaningful". And it is a choice not born of "legitimate means of persuasion" within the meaning of *Hebert* (at p. 177).

. . .

With respect, I am troubled by Justice Charron's suggestion that the ability of the police to investigate crime in Canada would be unduly impaired by the effective exercise of the pre-trial right to silence. In a similar vein, the respondent warns against its "massive and far-reaching consequences in the arena of police investigations" and the federal Director of Public Prosecutions, an intervener, submits that it would have "a devastating impact on criminal justice in Canada".

. . .

Potential witnesses are rightfully expected, as a matter of civic duty, to assist the police by answering their questions. As a matter of law, however, they may refuse to answer, and go on home. Prisoners and detainees, on the other hand, are by definition not free to leave as they please. They are powerless to end their interrogation. As explained in *Hebert*, this is why they have been given the right to counsel and its close relative, the right to silence.

Neither of these rights has been given constitutional protection on the condition that it not be exercised, lest the investigation of crime be brought to a standstill. On the contrary, the policy of the law is to facilitate, and not to frustrate, the effective exercise of both rights by those whom they are intended to protect. They are Charter rights, not constitutional placebos.

Moreover, we have no evidence to support the proposition that requiring the police to respect a detainee's right of silence, once it has been unequivocally asserted, would have a "devastating impact" on criminal investigations anywhere in this country.

For more than 40 years, it has been the law in the United States that where a suspect "indicates in any manner, at any time prior to or during questioning, that he wishes to remain silent, the interrogation must cease": *Miranda v. Arizona*, 384 U.S. 436 (1966), at pp. 473-74. And yet, as Wharton puts it, "[n]umerous studies in the years following this decision have concluded that

Miranda had little impact on the ability of the police to obtain statements": *Wharton's Criminal Procedure* (14th ed. looseleaf), at p. 19-9.

Moreover, after nearly a decade of experience with *Miranda*, the U.S. Supreme Court reaffirmed its underlying rationale in these terms:

> A reasonable and faithful interpretation of the *Miranda* opinion must rest on the intention of the Court in that case to adopt "fully effective means . . . to notify the person of his right of silence and to assure that the exercise of the right will be scrupulously honored . . . ." 384 U.S. 436, at 479. The critical safeguard identified in the passage at issue is a person's "right to cut off questioning." Id., at 474. Through the exercise of his option to terminate questioning he can control the time at which questioning occurs, the subjects discussed, and the duration of the interrogation. The requirement that law enforcement authorities must respect a person's exercise of that option counteracts the coercive pressures of the custodial setting. We therefore conclude that the admissibility of statements obtained after the person in custody has decided to remain silent depends under *Miranda* on whether his "right to cut off questioning" was "scrupulously honored."
>
> (*Michigan v. Mosley*, 423 U.S. 96 (1975), at pp. 103-4)

In *Mosley*, upon the detainee's request, "the police ... immediately ceased the interrogation, resumed questioning only after the passage of a significant period of time and the provision of a fresh set of warnings, and restricted the second interrogation to a crime that had not been a subject of the earlier interrogation" (p. 106). The Court was therefore satisfied that the detainee's "right to cut off questioning" had been "scrupulously honored", within the meaning of *Miranda*.

More recently, after an additional quarter-century under this investigatory regime, the U.S. Supreme Court affirmed that "*Miranda* and its progeny in this Court govern the admissibility of statements made during custodial interrogation in both state and federal courts." See *Dickerson v. United States*, 530 U.S. 428 (2000), at p. 432, where the Court held that Congress could not circumvent or override *Miranda* by making voluntariness the sole criterion of admissibility of a detainee's statements to the police.

Not everyone will agree with Wharton that *Miranda* appears to have had little effect on the ability of the police to obtain statements. There are, of course, conflicting assessments of the evidence as to its impact, but *Miranda* can hardly be said to have paralysed criminal investigations in the United States. And there is no evidentiary basis for suggesting that it would do so in Canada.

In any event, the success of this appeal does not depend on the importation of the *Miranda* rule into Canada. And I take care not to be misunderstood to suggest that *Miranda* either is now, or ought to be made, the law in Canada. Here, the right to silence, once asserted, is not a barrier to the admissibility of any subsequent pre-trial statement of a detainee or prisoner. Nor is there any requirement that interrogators obtain a signed waiver from detainees, as the appellant suggests there ought to be. On the other hand, in the words of Professors Delisle and Stuart, "once an accused has clearly stated he wishes to remain silent, the police cannot act as if there has been a waiver" (R.

Delisle, D. Stuart and D. Tanovich, *Evidence: Principles and Problems* (8th ed. 2007), at p. 489).

In short, detainees who have asserted their right to silence are entitled to change their minds. As I have stated elsewhere, "[a]n initial refusal can later give way to a crisis of conscience, to an 'unconscious compulsion to confess' — or, simply, to a genuine change of heart": *R. v. Timm* (1998), 131 C.C.C. (3d) 306 (Que. C.A.), at para. 145. But they cannot be compelled to do so by the persistent disregard of that choice. As mentioned earlier, that is what happened here.

Finally, even in the absence of the required evidentiary foundation, I am prepared for present purposes to recognize that the work of the police would be made easier (and less challenging) if police interrogators were permitted to undermine the constitutionally protected rights of detainees, including the right to counsel and the right to silence — either by pressing detainees to waive them, or by "unfairly frustrat[ing]" their exercise (*Hebert* at p. 186). More draconian initiatives might prove more effective still.

Nonetheless and without hesitation, I much prefer a system of justice that permits the effective exercise by detainees of the constitutional and procedural rights guaranteed to them by the law of the land. The right to silence, like the right to counsel, is in my view a constitutional promise that must be kept.

Which judgment do you prefer and why? In a C.R. annotation on *Singh*, Professor Lisa Dufraimont writes in part:

> Arguably, *Singh* provides insufficient protection for the right to silence. As long as the Charter protects the pre-trial right to silence, there is something unseemly about the Supreme Court jealously guarding the power of police interrogators to undermine a suspect's choice to remain silent. At the same time, the majority in *Singh* recognizes that persistent questioning of suspects who repeatedly assert their right to silence can result in the exclusion of the resulting statements under the voluntariness rule. Such a statement will be involuntary, and exclusion automatic, where it was not the product of the suspect's free will to speak to the authorities.
>
> Ultimately, then, there may be less separating the majority and the minority in *Singh* that one might initially suppose. Certainly the majority rejects the dissenters' suggestion that the police are obliged to stop questioning a detainee who clearly asserts the right to silence. However, the full court agrees that persistent questioning in the face of repeated assertions of the right to silence can render a statement inadmissible. The question whether the exclusionary remedy arises from the confessions rule or the s. 7 pre-trial right to silence is less important than the availability of the remedy itself.

The problem is that even *Oickle* is not just about voluntariness. Under *Oickle* there is a freestanding discretion to exclude confessions obtained by tricks that shock the community. Why wasn't such a sustained effort by the police to override an assertion of the right to silence shocking? The Supreme Court has held that adverse inferences should not be drawn against someone who is silent at the pre-trial stage as it would be a "snare and delusion" to advise about the right to silence and then to turn around and use silence as a sign of guilt (*R. v. Turcotte*). Why isn't it a snare and delusion to say a suspect has the right to silence but allow police to ignore its exercise? The s. 7 pre-trial right to silence was recognised with very strong language in *R. v. Hebert* regarding the need to move beyond the old common law's focus on reliability to allow judicial control of police interrogation abuses and forced incrimination. *Singh* has suddenly reduced this to the very little right that an undercover agent cannot elicit statements from someone detained by the functional equivalent of an interrogation. Certainly under *Singh* there is no s. 7 right to be advised of the right to silence where police are not undercover. Whether the accused receive advice from the police or a lawyer (if there was one) is just a factor to be considered on the voluntariness inquiry.

The community shock test is a very high hurdle for accused and does not apply in the current tests for the s. 24(2) remedy of exclusion for Charter breaches. In the United Kingdom, judges under s. 76(2) of the Evidence Act of 1984 have a discretion to exclude a confession where police interrogation methods are considered oppressive and not just where they shock the community. Under s. 76(5) oppression "includes torture, inhuman or degrading treatment or the use or threatened use of violence (whether or not amounting to torture)".

Trial judges in Canada who have relied on *Oickle* to exclude confessions on the basis that oppression has resulted in involuntariness have often felt it necessary to buttress their rulings by also finding a s. 7 breach. See, for example, *R. v. Hammerstrom* (2006), 43 C.R. (6th) 346 (B.C. S.C.) (police tricking the accused by claiming they had the crime videotaped on a store surveillance tape), and *R. v. N.* (2005), 28 C.R. (6th) 140 (Ont. S.C.J.) (five-hour polygraph, hostile interrogation and shocking number of tricks). Some judges appear to be excluding confessions since Oickle by giving a very wide meaning to the category of oppression resulting in involuntariness: *R. v. Taylor* (2008), 63 C.R. (6th) 142 (N.B. Q.B.) and *R. v. Choy* (2008), 239 C.C.C. (3d) 207 (Alta. Q.B.). The resort to s. 7 analysis is no longer available.

For critical comments on *Singh* see Timothy Moore and Karina Gagnier, "You can talk if you want to: Is the Police Caution on the Right to Silence Understandable?" ((2008) 51 C.R. (6th) 233 and Dale Ives and Christopher Sherrin, "R. v. Singh — A Meaningless Right to Silence with Dangerous Consequences" (2008) 51 C.R. (6th) 250 but see however Suhail Akhtar, "Whatever Happened to The Right to Silence? (2009) 62 C.R. (6th) 73.

Regulation of police interrogation is one area where Parliament may have achieved a better balance than the courts. The crime of torture in s. 269.1 was added to the Criminal Code in 1987 when Canada ratified the United Nations Convention Against Torture: see generally Donald Macdougall, "Torture in Canadian Criminal Law", (2005) 24 C.R. (6th) 74. Under s. 269.1 of the Criminal Code, torture is an indictable offence punishable to a maximum of fourteen years. Torture is widely defined in s. 269.1(2) as

> any act or omission by which severe pain or suffering, whether physical or mental, is intentionally inflicted on a person.

Further, under subsection 4, a statement obtained by torture is inadmissible in any proceedings over which Parliament has jurisdiction. This may be a vehicle for further judicial checks on police interrogation.

In *R. v. Moore-McFarlane* (2001), 47 C.R. (5th) 203, 160 C.C.C. (3d) 493 (Ont. C.A.), Charron J.A. (as she then was) gets preciously close to suggesting for the Ontario Court of Appeal that there can be no finding of voluntariness of confessions to police in the absence of a recording. However, other provincial courts of appeal have pointed out that *Oickle* does not speak of an absolute rule that confessions are inadmissible if not recorded. In fact, after pointing out the benefits of recording, Iacobucci J. says: "This is not to suggest that non-recording interrogations are inherently suspect, it is simply to make the obvious point that when a recording is made, it can greatly assist the trier of fact in assessing the confession". See also *R. v. Ducharme* (2004), 20 C.R. (6th) 332, 182 C.C.C. (3d) 243 (Man. C.A.), leave to appeal refused (2004), 330 N.R. 395 (note) (S.C.C.), relying on Professor Trotter's paper, see above.

In both *R. v. Backhouse* (2005), 194 C.C.C. (3d) 1, 28 C.R. (6th) 31 (Ont. C.A.) and *R. v. Swanek* (2005), 28 C.R. (6th) 93 (Ont. C.A.) different panels of the Ontario Court of Appeal refer to *Moore-McFarlane* but now hold that in Ontario too there is no such automatic rule. Justice Rosenberg in *Backhouse* does add an important caveat that judges must look with suspicion at police claims that the accused refused to be recorded. Doherty J.A. in *Swanek* suggests that lack of a recording may require a warning to the jury.

The Supreme Court held in *R. v. Hodgson*, [1998] 2 S.C.R. 449, 127 C.C.C. (3d) 449, 18 C.R. (5th) 135 (S.C.C.) that the definition of person in authority is subjectively determined. This means that the voluntary confession rule does not apply in the case of confessions to undercover officers. In *Hodgson*, Justice Cory called for an urgent review by Parliament and in the meantime for warning juries as follows:

> A statement obtained as a result of inhuman or degrading treatment or the use of violence or threats of violence may not be the manifestation of the exercise of a free will to confess. Rather, it may result solely from the oppressive treatment or fear of such treatment. If it does , the statement may very well be either unreliable or untrue. Therefore, if you conclude that the statement was obtained by such oppression very little if any weight should be attached to it". (paras. 29-30)

Parliament has not acted.

In *Sinclair, McCrimmon* and *Willier* (reviewed earlier on p. 361) a 5-4 majority of the Supreme Court refuse to extend s. 10 (b) or to revise earlier controversial decisions in *Singh* on the right to silence. The majority is content to stay the course of setting low Charter standards to control police interrogation and to rest content to rely on the also much criticised decision on the voluntary confession rule in *Oickle*. The concerns mouthed in *Oickle* about the danger of coerced confessions leading to wrongful convictions is no longer evident. The vehemence of the dissenters is palpable. Justice Binnie fires the most direct salvo:

What now appears to be licenced as a result of the "interrogation trilogy" — *Oickle*, *Singh*, and [now *Sinclair*] — is that an individual (presumed innocent) may be detained and isolated for questioning by the police for at least five or six hours without reasonable recourse to a lawyer, during which time the officers can brush aside assertions of the right to silence or demands to be returned to his or her cell, in an endurance contest in which the police interrogators, taking turns with one another, hold all the important legal cards. [para. 98]

When the decisions are read together the resulting latitude allowed to the police to deal with a detainee, who is to be presumed innocent, disproportionately favours the interests of the state in the investigation of crime over the rights of the individual in a free society. [para. 77]

According to LeBel and Fish JJ. (with Abella J. concurring) the suggestion of the majority that our residual concerns can be meaningfully addressed by way of the confessions rule thus ignores what we have learned about the dynamics of custodial interrogations and renders pathetically anaemic the entrenched constitutional rights to counsel and to silence [para. 184].

In the view of these three dissenters the majority opinions in both *Singh* and *Sinclair* project a view of the right to silence that hinges too closely on the voluntariness of a detainee's inculpatory statement. This approach ignores the fact that the right to silence can be breached in a manner other than the taking by the police of an involuntary statement. The majority's conclusion in *Singh* that a detainee cannot use the s. 7 right to silence to cease a custodial interview, and the majority view in this case that a detainee cannot use s. 10(b) in this same fashion, in effect creates a new right on the part of the police to the unfettered and continuing access to the detainee, for the purposes of conducting a custodial interview to the point of confession. The clear result is that custodial detainees cannot exercise their constitutional rights in order to prevent their participation in the investigation against them. These dissenters added that none of the majority's justification based on law enforcement concerns were put through the rigour of a s. 1 analysis, and were based on nothing more than speculation rather than empirical evidence, for example, as to the effect of the Miranda rules in the United States.

The majority fire back:

Our colleagues LeBel and Fish JJ. also assert that our approach is such that the detainee is effectively forced to participate in the police investigation. The suggestion is that the questioning of a suspect, in and of itself, runs counter to the presumption of innocence and the protection against self-incrimination. This is clearly contrary to settled authority and practice. In our view, in defining the contours of the s. 7 right to silence and related Charter rights, consideration must be given not only to the protection of the rights of the accused but also to the societal interest in the investigation and solving of crimes. The police are charged with the duty to investigate alleged crimes and, in performing this duty, they necessarily have to make inquiries from relevant sources of information, including persons suspected of, or even charged with, committing the alleged crime. While the police must be respectful of an individual's Charter rights, a rule that would require the police to automatically retreat upon a detainee stating that he or she has nothing to say, in our respectful view, would not strike the proper balance between the public interest in the investigation of crimes and the suspect's interest in being left alone. [para. 63]

Although there is still strong rhetoric in the majority opinion in *Sinclair* about the apparently fundamental s. 7 right to choose not to speak to known police interrogators, there is no requirement that the accused be advised of that right and no remedy contemplated if that right is breached. As pointed out by the dissenters, a major disappointment is that, as in *Singh*, the detainee repeatedly asserting the right to silence and/or right to consult counsel will not in itself lead to a Charter remedy under ss. 7 or 10(b). That is apparently not a snare and delusion. A right without a remedy is meaningless. In this context the right to remain silent does not presently exist.

Prior to *Oickle* Justice Ketchum, in *R. v. S. (M.J.)* (2000), 32 C.R. (5th) 378 (Alta. Prov. Ct.), excluded a confession in part because a videotape revealed the use of the Reid method of interrogation pioneered in the United States, which was seen to be an oppressive and brainwashing technique which should not be accepted in Canada. The Reid method involves a nine-step procedure of sustained confrontation with allegations of guilt and minimisation of the consequences of confession. Since *Oickle,* the Reid technique has been adopted by police training and practice in most parts of the country and has been seen by most courts as consistent with *Oickle.* See Thierry Nadon, "The Reid Interrogation Technique: Effective, For Some Controversial and Legal" (2012), 91 C.R. (6th) 359. However, social psychologists have increasingly pointed to the danger that the Reid method risks, and has led to, false confessions in the United States and in Canada. See especially Tim Moore and Lindsay Fitzsimmons, "Justice Imperiled: False Confessions and the Reid Technique" (2011), 57 Crim. L.Q. 509 and the CBC The National's special report "Truth, Lies and Confessions", June 24, 2012 (see the CBC website for a wealth of material and videotapes of interrogations).

Recently there has been a call from a Newfoundland psychology professor and a police Inspector to abandon the Reid method in favour of the less accusatorial PEACE used in the United Kingdom.

BRENT SNOOK AND JOHN HOUSE, "AN ALTERNATIVE INTERVIEWING METHOD. ALL WE ARE SAYING IS GIVE PEACE A CHANCE."
Blue Line Magazine November 2008 (reference list omitted)

Police interviews of suspects, accused persons, witnesses and victims are one of the most fundamental aspects of criminal investigations. The primary goals are to seek the truth, obtain information to assist a criminal investigation and elicit a true confession (see *Kassin, 1997 and Kassin & Gudjonsson, 2004* for review of the potency of confession evidence in legal proceedings).

In Canada, the Reid Technique, a social-psychological process model of interrogation, is the most routinely taught and used method to achieve those goals. This ubiquitous interrogation model was first described in-depth in 1962 in the book *Criminal interrogation and confessions,* and has subsequently been taught to hundreds of thousands of investigators around the world (*Buckley, 2006; Inbau, Reid, Buckley, & Jayne, 2004*; also see *Inbau, Reid, Buckley, & Jayne, 2005*).

"The Reid Technique is widely considered to be the most effective interrogation technique in use today," according to Buckley *(2006) (p. 190)*. Based on employing the "nine steps" approach to interrogation, it's claimed that "none of the steps is apt to make an innocent person confess and that all the steps are legally as well as morally justifiable" (*Buckley, p. 198*).

What many readers may not know is that an alternative interviewing method is used in many quarters of the world. As we will attempt to argue in this brief article, Canadian police agencies could be more progressive and consider giving PEACE (Planning and preparation, Engage and explain, Account, Closure, Evaluation) a chance.

Antiquated and coercive

Reid consists of two main phases: the interview and the nine-step interrogation. The interview is non-accusatory in nature and allows the interviewer to gather investigative and behavioral information from the suspect using a behavioural analysis interview (BAI) (*Inbau et al., 2004*). The officer uses the information obtained to assess an individual's guilt and decide if an interrogation is necessary.

Only individuals judged likely to be guilty are subsequently interrogated using Reid, according to Inbau and colleagues. The interrogation differs from the interview in that it is accusatory in nature and based on an assumption of guilt. It involves active persuasion, meant to increase the anxiety associated with denying the offence, and decreases the perceived consequences of confession (*Kassin, 1997; Ofshe, 1989; Ofshe & Leo, 1997*).

Canadian courts have deemed the Reid technique acceptable. The case of *R. v. Oickle (2000)* provides the framework for determining a confession's voluntariness. Canadian judges are directed to consider all relevant factors in making such a decision, including "threats or promises, oppression, the operating mind requirement and police trickery" (*R. v. Oickle, 2000, p. 3*). Having said that, most cases are not clear-cut.

Direct threats of physical harm render a confession inadmissible, for example, but veiled or implicit threats do not necessarily do so. Judgments regarding the admissibility of police trickery are driven by the subjective guideline of whether it "appalls or shocks the community." Thus, it appears Canadian judges have significant flexibility in deciding whether a confession was voluntary and should be admitted. In the end, Canadian police officers also have some flexibility in the strategies they are permitted to use.

Why advocate, you might ask, for another method if the courts have accepted the Reid technique. Reid has come under close scrutiny by a range of academics and police practitioners. As succinctly argued by Saul Kassin (*2008*), Inbau and his colleagues "recommend a multistep approach that is essentially reducible to an interplay of three processes: isolation, which increases anxiety and the suspect's desire to escape; confrontation, when an interrogator accuses the suspect of the crime, sometimes citing real or fictitious evidence to bolster the claim; and minimization, where a sympathetic interrogator morally justifies the crime, leading the suspect to expect leniency upon confession" (*p. 250*).

Reid is based on a series of assumptions that lack scientific support, including that interrogators can accurately determine a suspect's guilt and preventing denials leads to more confessions.

Two crucial findings have experts extremely concerned about Reid's impact on interrogation outcomes:

- Twenty five per cent of individuals exonerated by DNA in the US provided a false confession; and
- Experimental research has illustrated the link between interrogation tactics and false confessions (see *Kassin & Kiechel, 1996; Russano, Meissner, Narchet, & Kassin, 2005*)

One case that caused concern in Canada was when police officers employing Reid elicited confessions from three young men in 1992. They were subsequently charged with first-degree murder of a 14-year old Regina girl, Darelle Exner (*Legge, 2003*). Their confessions were exposed as false only after DNA evidence led to the identification of another individual (Kenneth Patton) as being responsible for the murder (he too subsequently confessed). Subsequent analysis of the transcripts showed that the interrogation was highly suggestive and coercive.

The effect of Reid on potential false confessions is rather intricate (and beyond the scope of this article). *Kassin and Gudjonnson (2003)* and *Kassin (2008)* review evidence illustrating the relationship between Reid-based interrogation tactics and false confessions (or see Kassin's web page: http://www.williams.edu/Psychology/Faculty/Kassin/index.html).

Lessons from England and Wales

Several high-profile wrongful conviction cases in England (e.g., Guilford Four, Birmingham Six) resulted in close scrutiny of investigative practices culminating in wrongful convictions. One issue that garnered a lot of attention was the tactics used to interrogate the suspects. It was determined that the overly manipulative and coercive nature of interrogation practices contributed to the wrongful convictions. In response, substantive reforms occurred, culminating in the adoption of the inquisitorial (non-manipulative or coercive) interviewing method PEACE in 1992.

Cases of wrongful conviction have also been uncovered at an increasing rate in Canada. Recognizing the need to prevent wrongful convictions, the Federal-Provincial-Territorial Heads of Prosecutions (FPT) committee set up a working group in 2002 to identify the factors contributing to justice system errors.

The committee mandate included ascertaining why wrongful convictions occur, how criminal investigations failed, how police resources could be used more efficiently and ways to ensure cases are resolved in a timely manner. It concluded that criminal investigative failures were sometimes a function of unethical conduct by investigators who blamed the wrong individuals.

Investigators sometimes failed to use best practices, it noted, such as appropriate interrogation strategies (e.g., asking open and closed-ended questions). Despite their concerns about interrogation practices and research suggesting that Reid-based interrogations can result in false confessions, changes have yet to emerge in Canada.

The PEACE model

More than 120,000 police officers in England and Wales have been trained to use PEACE, which was created to provide them with a more ethical approach to interviewing. According to *Gudjonnson (2004)* and *Milne and Bull (1999)*, it can be used to interview witnesses, suspects and accused persons. Here is an overview of the method.

1. *Preparation and planning:* Interviewers are encouraged to have intimate knowledge of case files before commencing an interview and to establish a schedule with a set of objectives and aims to be met.

2. *Engage and explain:* The interviewer explains the interview's purpose, introduces those present in the room, where applicable administers the police caution and Charter rights, establishes rapport with the interviewee and engages them in conversation.

3. *Account:* Involves obtaining an account of the event by using the cognitive interview (typically used in interviewing agreeable interviewees) and conversation management (for less agreeable interviewees). According to *Milne, Shaw, & Bull (in press)*, conversation management — the crux of PEACE — can be divided into three stages; (i) the suspect account, (ii) the police agenda and (iii) the challenge stage.

The suspect account involves listening carefully and noting points of interest that can be pursued later in the interview. Once an account has been taken, the officer should attempt to deal with specific topics or areas in a structured manner by using an appropriate questioning strategy (e.g., using open and closed-ended questions and avoiding leading questions) and checking the suspect's account of events for comprehension and understanding at the end of each question-answer session.

The process of "probing and summarizing" should be repeated until the interviewer is satisfied that all crucial aspects of the events under question have been sufficiently covered. At this stage, it is recommended that the interviewer not challenge the suspect's account. The interviewer should then pursue (by probing and summarizing) any areas not covered.

As indicated in stage one, the police agenda involves good preparation. The interviewer is encouraged to create a schedule of the topics that need to be covered, such as actual evidence against the suspect, facts that need to be established, potential lines of defence and so on.

Aspects of the suspect's account will then need to be challenged. If any contradictory facts or information remain, the interviewer is encouraged to challenge the suspect as to why such discrepancies exist. PEACE advocates recommend that challenges not be conducted in an aggressive manner but rather as a presentation of information that the interviewee is knowledgeable about. According to Milne and her colleagues (in press), the point of this section is to give the subject an opportunity to comment on the information presented which challenges their account.

4.   *Closure:* Ending the interview by summarizing the main points that emerged, giving the suspect an opportunity to correct any part of the summary or add information, and explaining what will happen in the future.

5.   *Evaluate:* Involves evaluating the information obtained from the interview and how it affects the progress of the investigation and the interviewer's performance.

If you do not find the method intuitively appealing, here are some points that might convince you to consider PEACE as a viable alternative or even a supplementary method.

1.   This method does not contain coercive or manipulative strategies, which should appeal to today's policing ethos. From an organizational perspective, every attempt should be made to weed out practices that may result in wrongful convictions and ultimately damage an agency's reputation. Moreover, removing coercive techniques will decrease the chances that a confession will be deemed inadmissible, even if it is truthful.

2.   Research has shown that, regardless of the tactics used, very few suspects (three per cent or so in the United Kingdom, according to *Baldwin, 1993*) change their story throughout an interrogation.

     Regardless of the strategy used, the same proportion of interviews end with a confession. Roughly 50 per cent of suspects in England and Wales confess to their crimes, and that figure did not change after PEACE was adopted. Given this, it seems more desirable to use a non-coercive technique that will result in positive community perceptions of the police organization.

     Using coercion in an interrogation may result in: offender resentment (especially those who have interacted with police over many years) and undermine public confidence. It can also cause a "boomerang effect," where a suspect decides not to confess because they felt manipulated or treated inappropriately (see *Gudjonnson, 2004* for further discussion of these issues).

3.   If 120,000 English and Welsh police officers can continue to conduct effective criminal investigations in the face of such substantive interviewing reform, it's highly likely that the same results can be reproduced by Canadian police officers.

4.   This method contains an attractive suite of training, supervision and monitoring tools that result in the development and maintenance of professional interviewers, including recruits, seasoned investigators and those interviewing vulnerable and special victims. Although anecdotal, officers in New Zealand have commented that PEACE was the best training they had ever received (*Grantham, 2008*).

We believe strongly that a more progressive approach to police interviewing (and interviewing witnesses, vulnerable populations and special victims) is needed in this country. Even if you are not convinced, there is also a practical element to consider. If the Supreme Court bans Reid (or associated manipulative or coercive tactics) — and we think this will happen sooner rather than later — police forces which have adopted the PEACE approach will be well prepared.

Interest?

A primary goal of this article is to provide Canadian police with a brief overview of an alternative method for interviewing suspects, accused persons, witnesses and victims. The Royal Newfoundland Constabulary (RNC), in partnership with the Bounded Rationality and the Law Laboratory at Memorial University of Newfoundland, has begun working to shift its interviewer training towards the PEACE model.

We urge Canadian law enforcement agencies interested in learning more or conducting a pilot project to contact either author so that we might gauge the level of interest in embracing PEACE.

An associate professor of psychology at Memorial University of Newfoundland, Brent Snook can be reached at bsnook@play.psych.mun.ca. John C. House is an Inspector in the RNC Criminal Investigation Division and can be reached at jhouse@mun.ca.

In the case of undercover officers the small *Hebert* right to silence right has no application to undercover activities in the field as there is no detention nor is the voluntary confession rule applicable given that there is no known person in authority. There seem to be few if any legal controls on such undercover tactics.

This has even proved true in the case of the use of the "Mr. Big" strategy where undercover agents pretend to be organised crime bosses and then allow the suspect to "join" as long as the suspect gain "respect" by admitting to a crime. Arguments for the rarely granted remedy of stay for an abuse of process have failed. Serious concerns about the widespread uncontrolled use of the Mr. Big strategy were expressed by Timothy Moore, Peter Copeland and Regina Schuller, "Deceit, Betrayal and the search for the Truth: Legal and Psychological perspectives on the 'Mr. Big' Strategy" (2009), 55 Crim. L.Q. 348.

In *R. v. Earhart* (2011), 90 C.R. (6th) 238 (B.C. C.A.) Bennett J.A., relying on *obiter dicta* by the Ontario and British Columbia Courts of Appeal in *R. v. Osmar* (2007), 44 C.R. (6th) 276, 217 C.C.C. (3d) 174 (Ont. C.A.), leave to appeal refused [2007] 2 S.C.R. vii (note), 85 (S.C.C.) and *R. v. Bonisteel* (2008), 61 C.R. (6th) 64, 236 C.C.C. (3d) 170 (B.C. C.A.), suggests that some more extreme versions of the Mr. Big technique might shock the conscience of the community so as to render any resulting statement inadmissible: *Earhart* at para. 84.

In her C.R. annotation Lisa Dufraimont writes:

The community shock test presents a promising avenue for developing possible limitations on the Mr. Big technique for two reasons. First, the courts' power to exclude evidence obtained by shocking tactics has been recognized by the Supreme Court of Canada: *R. v. Oickle*, [2000] 2 S.C.R. 3. Second, the power seems primarily directed at restraining just the kinds of dirty tricks (beatings staged to intimidate suspects, for example) that are sometimes used in Mr. Big operations.

One potential objection to the application of the community shock test to the Mr. Big scenario centres on the person in authority requirement. The community shock test was first articulated by Lamer J. in his concurring judgment in *R. v. Rothman*, [1981] 1 S.C.R. 640, a pre-Charter case concerning a cell plant undercover operation. The test was only adopted by a majority of the Supreme Court in *Oickle*, when it was articulated as one of four factors to be considered in assessing the voluntariness of a confession. Some might argue that if the community shock test is now a part of the confessions rule, then it should not be applicable to the Mr. Big scenario because the confessions rule only applies when the accused knows she is speaking to a person in authority. However, a strong counter argument can be raised that the Supreme Court never intended to subsume the community shock test entirely into the confessions rule. Even in *Oickle*, the Court described the community shock test as a "distinct inquiry. . .related to voluntariness" (at para. 65). Moreover, the Court cited with approval the examples of shocking tactics offered by Lamer J. in *Rothman*, which included undercover operations with police posing as chaplains and legal aid lawyers: *Rothman* at p. 697 cited in *Oickle* at para. 66. Clearly, in these circumstances the confession would not be offered to a known person in authority, but the Supreme Court has affirmed that statements obtained by such unsavoury means should be excluded from evidence under the community shock test.

The community shock test remains under-developed analytically and has rarely been applied in practice. However, the potential exists for the doctrine to be developed as a means of placing some restraint on Mr. Big operations.

In its 2:1 majority judgment in *R. v. Hart* (2012), 97 C.R. (6th) 16 (N.L. C.A.), affirmed [2014] 2 S.C.R. 544, 312 C.C.C. (3d) 250, 12 C.R. (7th) 221 (S.C.C.), the Supreme Court of Newfoundland and Labrador (Court of Appeal) recently became the first Canadian appellate court to seriously criticize the Mr. Big strategy and to exclude self-incriminating statements obtained in a Mr. Big sting. The majority in *Hart* did not rely on the community shock test but instead identified two alternative bases for holding that the Mr. Big statements were obtained in violation of s. 7 of the Charter. First, the majority widened the application of the pre-trial right to silence to cover cases where the accused is not physically in detention but is equivalently in the control of the state. Second, the Court held that the overarching principle against self-incrimination was violated because police abused their power over Mr. Hart in the context of the Mr. Big operations to obtain a confession that was coerced and unreliable. See article by Lisa Dufraimont, "*R. v. Hart*: Building a Screen for Mr. Big Confessions" (2013), 97 C.R. (6th) 104.

The Mr. Big strategy reached the Supreme Court in *Henry* and the Supreme Court decided to address the issue by a new two-pronged approach.

R. v. HART
[2014] 2 S.C.R. 544, 312 C.C.C. (3d) 250, 12 C.R. (7th) 221 (S.C.C.)

The accused was charged with the first-degree murder of his twin three-year-old daughters, who drowned in a lake while under his care. The accused had taken the girls to a lakeside park by car. When questioned by police on the day of the drownings, he claimed that one of his daughters fell into the water and he panicked and drove home to get his wife, leaving his other daughter on the dock. First responders found both girls floating in the lake but it was too late to save their lives. The accused told the same story when interrogated by police about a month later.

Two weeks later, the accused contacted police and volunteered that his previous account of events was untruthful. He explained that he had a seizure at the park after removing his daughters from the car. When he came to and saw one of his daughters in the water, his only thought was to drive home to his wife. The accused explained that he lied in his earlier statements to police because he did not want to lose his driver's licence. The accused suffers from epilepsy and his licence has been suspended in the past because of that condition.

Police were convinced that the accused had murdered his daughters but they did not have sufficient evidence to charge him. More than two years after the girls' deaths, police decided to mount a Mr. Big operation by luring the accused into a fictitious criminal organization and trying to get him to confess to the boss. The operation began with several weeks of lifestyle surveillance, which revealed that the accused rarely left home and did so only when accompanied by his wife. The accused was then befriended by two undercover officers, who hired the accused as a driver. Several weeks into the accused's employment, the officers told the accused that they were part of a criminal organization headed by a boss. From that point, the accused participated in simulated criminal activity, including delivering smuggled alcohol and stolen credit cards.

The accused was paid $4,470 for his work in the first two months of the operation, and the officers also paid for his travel, hotel rooms and frequent dinners. After two months, the accused was fully immersed in his new fictitious life and would tell the undercover officers that he loved them and that they were brothers. At this point, according to one of the officers, the accused spontaneously offered what can be described as his first confession, stating that he had planned to murder his daughters and had carried it out. This admission came in response to the officer claiming to have assaulted a prostitute and explaining that sometimes bad things had to be done for the organization. The admission was not recorded and the accused denied that it occurred.

The operation continued for two more months, during which time the officers constantly emphasized the importance within the organization of trust, honesty and loyalty, indicating that the untrustworthy were met with violence. The accused was told that there was a big deal coming in the future and that if he participated the accused could be paid up to $25,000. The accused was told that he would only be allowed to participate in the deal if Mr. Big approved, and that Mr. Big had checked into him and found a problem that would have to be resolved before he could continue to work for the organization.

The accused met with the undercover officer posing as Mr. Big. The accused expressed his gratitude to Mr. Big, telling him that his life had turned around since he started working for the organization. Mr. Big raised the topic of the accused's daughters and asked why the accused had killed them. The accused stated that he had a seizure, implying that their deaths were accidental. Mr. Big rejected this explanation and told the accused not to lie. After further probing by Mr. Big, the accused gave his second confession, saying that he had killed his daughters because he feared child welfare authorities would remove them from his home. On being pressed for details of their deaths, the accused said he struck his daughters with his shoulder, which caused them to fall in the water.

Two days later, the accused returned with an undercover officer to the scene of the drownings to re-enact the event. In this context the accused gave a third confession. The officer knelt down to play the role of one of the girls and the accused demonstrated how he pushed his daughters into the water by nudging the officer with his knee. Shortly thereafter, the accused was arrested and charged with two counts of first-degree murder.

By the time of his arrest, the accused had participated in 63 "scenarios" with the undercover officers, had been paid $15,720 for his work, travelled to Halifax, Montreal, Ottawa, Toronto and Vancouver, stayed in hotels, and dined in fine restaurants. The total cost of the operation was $413,268.

Evidence of the accused's self-incriminating statements during the Mr. Big operation was admitted at trial. The jury found the accused guilty on both counts of first-degree murder. The accused appealed. The Newfoundland and Labrador Court of Appeal, by a majority, allowed the appeal, quashed the convictions and ordered a new trial. The Crown appealed to the Supreme Court of Canada.

MOLDAVER J (McLachlin C.J. and LeBel, Abella, and Wagner JJ. Concurring): . . .

How Should the Law Respond to the Problems Posed by Mr. Big Confessions? . . .

83 In searching for a response to the concerns these operations raise, we must proceed cautiously. To be sure, Mr. Big operations can become abusive, and they can produce confessions that are unreliable and prejudicial. We must seek a legal framework that protects accused persons, and the justice system as a whole, against these dangers. On the other hand, Mr. Big operations are not necessarily abusive, and are capable of producing valuable evidence, the admission of which furthers the interests of justice. We ought not forget that the Mr. Big technique is almost always used in cold cases involving the most serious crimes. Put simply, in responding to the dangers posed by Mr. Big

confessions, we should be wary about allowing serious crimes to go unpunished.

Summary of a Proposed Solution

84 In this section, I propose a solution that, in my view, strikes the best balance between guarding against the dangers posed by Mr. Big operations, while ensuring the police have the tools they need to investigate serious crime. This solution involves a two-pronged approach that (1) recognizes a new common law rule of evidence, and (2) relies on a more robust conception of the doctrine of abuse of process to deal with the problem of police misconduct.

85 The first prong recognizes a new common law rule of evidence for assessing the admissibility of these confessions. The rule operates as follows. Where the state recruits an accused into a fictitious criminal organization of its own making and seeks to elicit a confession from him, any confession made by the accused to the state during the operation should be treated as presumptively inadmissible. This presumption of inadmissibility is overcome where the Crown can establish, on a balance of probabilities, that the probative value of the confession outweighs its prejudicial effect. In this context, the confession's probative value turns on an assessment of its reliability. Its prejudicial effect flows from the bad character evidence that must be admitted in order to put the operation and the confession in context. If the Crown is unable to demonstrate that the accused's confession is admissible, the rest of the evidence surrounding the Mr. Big operation becomes irrelevant and thus inadmissible. This rule, like the confessions rule in the case of conventional police interrogations, operates as a specific qualification to the party admissions exception to the hearsay rule.

86 Second, I would rely on the doctrine of abuse of process to deal with the problem of police misconduct. I recognize that the doctrine has thus far proved less than effective in this context. While the problem is not an easy one, I propose to provide some guidance on how to determine if a Mr. Big operation crosses the line from skillful police work to an abuse of process.

87 The purposes of this two-pronged approach are to protect an accused's right to a fair trial under the Charter, and to preserve the integrity of the justice system. Those are the ends that must ultimately be achieved. This approach strives to reach them by ensuring that only those confessions that are more probative than prejudicial, and which do not result from abuse, are admitted into evidence.

88 However, it must be remembered that trial judges always retain a discretion to exclude evidence where its admission would compromise trial fairness (see R. v. Harrer, [1995] 3 S.C.R. 562). This is because "the general principle that an accused is entitled to a fair trial cannot be entirely reduced to specific rules" (ibid., at para. 23). It is impossible to predict every factual scenario that could present itself. As such, I do not foreclose the possibility that, in an exceptional case, trial fairness may require that a Mr. Big confession be excluded even where the specific rules I have proposed would see the confession admitted.

89 In practice, this two-pronged approach will necessitate that a voir dire be held to determine the admissibility of Mr. Big confessions. The Crown will bear the burden of establishing that, on balance, the probative value of the confession outweighs its prejudicial effect, and it will be for the defence to establish an abuse of process. Trial judges may prefer to begin their analysis by assessing whether there has been an abuse of process. A finding of abuse makes weighing the probative value and prejudicial effect of the evidence unnecessary.

90 Against this backdrop, I will now elaborate on the main features of this two-pronged solution.

Why Does the Crown Bear the Onus of Establishing that the Probative Value of a Mr. Big Confession Outweighs its Prejudicial Effect?

91 The common law rule of evidence I have proposed creates a presumption that Mr. Big confessions are inadmissible, and places the onus of demonstrating that they ought to be received on the Crown. The onus is justified because of the central role played by the state in creating these confessions. It is the state that designs and implements these operations, expending significant resources and acting as puppeteer in the production of the accused's ultimate confession. The state creates the potent mix of a potentially unreliable confession accompanied by prejudicial character evidence. Given its pivotal role, the state should bear the responsibility of showing that the confession it has orchestrated and produced warrants admission into evidence.

92 Placing the onus on the Crown also works to address concerns with abusive state conduct. Confronted by the reality that the Crown will ultimately bear the burden of justifying reception of a Mr. Big confession, the state will be strongly encouraged to tread carefully in how it conducts these operations. As I will explain, the conduct of the police is a factor to be taken into account in assessing the reliability of a Mr. Big confession. This creates a strong incentive for the state to conduct these operations with restraint.

93 The onus has the added benefit of encouraging the creation of a more thorough record of the operation. At present, many of the key interactions between undercover officers and the accused are unrecorded. This is problematic. Where it is logistically feasible and would not jeopardize the operation itself or the safety of the undercover officers, the police would do well to record their conversations with the accused. With the onus of demonstrating reliability placed on the Crown, gaps in the record may undermine the case for admissibility, which will encourage better record keeping.

How is Probative Value Assessed?

. . .

99 Returning to Mr. Big confessions, their probative value derives from their reliability. A confession provides powerful evidence of guilt, but only if it is true. A confession of questionable reliability carries less probative force, and in deciding whether the probative value of a Mr. Big confession outweighs the

prejudicial effect of the character evidence that accompanies it, trial judges must examine its reliability.

100 What factors are relevant in assessing the reliability of a Mr. Big confession? A parallel can perhaps be drawn between the assessment of "threshold reliability" that occurs under the principled approach to hearsay. Under the principled approach, hearsay becomes admissible where it is both necessary and reliable. Reliability can generally be established in one of two ways: by showing that the statement is trustworthy, or by establishing that its reliability can be sufficiently tested at trial (R. v. Khelawon, 2006 SCC 57, [2006] 2 S.C.R. 787, at paras. 61-63). The latter route to reliability is often met through an opportunity to cross-examine the hearsay declarant, but this has no application in the present context because the accused is not a compellable witness.

101 However, the factors used to demonstrate the trustworthiness of a hearsay statement are apposite. In assessing the trustworthiness of a hearsay statement, courts look to the circumstances in which the statement was made, and whether there is any confirmatory evidence (Khelawon, at paras. 62 and 100).

102 Confessions derive their persuasive force from the fact that they are against the accused's self-interest. People do not normally confess to crimes they have not committed (Hodgson, at para. 60). But the circumstances in which Mr. Big confessions are elicited can undermine that supposition. Thus, the first step in assessing the reliability of a Mr. Big confession is to examine those circumstances and assess the extent to which they call into question the reliability of the confession. These circumstances include – but are not strictly limited to – the length of the operation, the number of interactions between the police and the accused, the nature of the relationship between the undercover officers and the accused, the nature and extent of the inducements offered, the presence of any threats, the conduct of the interrogation itself, and the personality of the accused, including his or her age, sophistication, and mental health.

103 Special note should be taken of the mental health and age of the accused. In the United States, where empirical data on false confessions is more plentiful, researchers have found that those with mental illnesses or disabilities, and youth, present a much greater risk of falsely confessing (Garrett, at p. 1064). A confession arising from a Mr. Big operation that comes from a young person or someone suffering from a mental illness or disability will raise greater reliability concerns.

104 In listing these factors, I do not mean to suggest that trial judges are to consider them mechanically and check a box when they apply. That is not the purpose of the exercise. Instead, trial judges must examine all the circumstances leading to and surrounding the making of the confession – with these factors in mind – and assess whether and to what extent the reliability of the confession is called into doubt.

105 After considering the circumstances in which the confession was made, the court should look to the confession itself for markers of reliability.

Trial judges should consider the level of detail contained in the confession, whether it leads to the discovery of additional evidence, whether it identifies any elements of the crime that had not been made public (e.g., the murder weapon), or whether it accurately describes mundane details of the crime the accused would not likely have known had he not committed it (e.g., the presence or absence of particular objects at the crime scene). Confirmatory evidence is not a hard and fast requirement, but where it exists, it can provide a powerful guarantee of reliability. The greater the concerns raised by the circumstances in which the confession was made, the more important it will be to find markers of reliability in the confession itself or the surrounding evidence.

How is Prejudicial Effect Measured?

106 Weighing the prejudicial effect of a Mr. Big confession is a more straightforward and familiar exercise. Trial judges must be aware of the dangers presented by these confessions. Admitting these confessions raises the spectre of moral and reasoning prejudice. Commencing with moral prejudice, the jury learns that the accused wanted to join a criminal organization and committed a host of "simulated crimes" that he believed were real. In the end, the accused is forced to argue to the jury that he lied to Mr. Big when he boasted about committing a very serious crime because his desire to join the gang was so strong. Moral prejudice may increase with operations that involve the accused in simulated crimes of violence, or that demonstrate the accused has a past history of violence. As for reasoning prejudice – defined as the risk that the jury's focus will be distracted away from the charges before the court – it too can pose a problem depending on the length of the operation, the amount of time that must be spent detailing it, and any controversy as to whether a particular event or conversation occurred.

107 On the other hand, the risk of prejudice can be mitigated by excluding certain pieces of particularly prejudicial evidence that are unessential to the narrative. Moreover, trial judges must bear in mind that limiting instructions to the jury may be capable of attenuating the prejudicial effect of this evidence.

How are Probative Value and Prejudicial Effect Compared?

108 In the end, trial judges must weigh the probative value and the prejudicial effect of the confession at issue and decide whether the Crown has met its burden. In practice, the potential for prejudice is a fairly constant variable in this context. Mr. Big operations are cut from the same cloth, and the concerns about prejudice are likely to be similar from case to case. As a result, trial judges will expend much of their analytical energy assessing the reliability of the confessions these operations generate.

109 Determining when the probative value of a Mr. Big confession surpasses its potential for prejudice will never be an exact science. As Justice Binnie observed in Handy, probative value and prejudicial effect are two variables which "do not operate on the same plane" (para. 148). Probative value is concerned with "proof of an issue", while prejudicial effect is concerned with "the fairness of the trial" (ibid.). To be sure, there will be easy

cases at the margins. But more common will be the difficult cases that fall in between. In such cases, trial judges will have to lean on their judicial experience to decide whether the value of a confession exceeds its cost.

110 Despite the inexactness of the exercise, it is one for which our trial judges are well prepared. Trial judges routinely weigh the probative value and prejudicial effect of evidence. And as mentioned, they are already asked to examine the reliability of evidence in a number of different contexts, as well as the prejudicial effect of bad character evidence. They are well positioned to do the same here. Because trial judges, after assessing the evidence before them, are in the best position to weigh the probative value and prejudicial effect of the evidence, their decision to admit or exclude a Mr. Big confession will be afforded deference on appeal.

What is the Role of the Doctrine of Abuse of Process?

111 The rule of evidence I have proposed goes a long way toward addressing all three of the concerns raised by Mr. Big operations. It squarely tackles the problems they raise with reliability and prejudice. And it takes significant account of the concern regarding police misconduct both by placing the admissibility onus on the Crown, and by factoring the conduct of the police into the assessment of a Mr. Big confession's probative value.

112 I should not, however, be taken as suggesting that police misconduct will be forgiven so long as a demonstrably reliable confession is ultimately secured. That state of affairs would be unacceptable, as this Court has long recognized that there are "inherent limits" on the power of the state to "manipulate people and events for the purpose of ... obtaining convictions" (R. v. Mack, [1988] 2 S.C.R. 903, at p. 941).

113 In my view, this is where the doctrine of abuse of process must serve its purpose. After all, the doctrine is intended to guard against state conduct that society finds unacceptable, and which threatens the integrity of the justice system (R. v. Babos, 2014 SCC 16, at para. 35). Moreover, the doctrine provides trial judges with a wide discretion to issue a remedy – including the exclusion of evidence or a stay of proceedings – where doing so is necessary to preserve the integrity of the justice system or the fairness of the trial (ibid., at para. 32). The onus lies on the accused to establish that an abuse of process has occurred.

114 I acknowledge that, thus far, the doctrine has provided little protection in the context of Mr. Big operations. This may be due in part to this Court's decision in R. v. Fliss, 2002 SCC 16, [2002] 1 S.C.R. 535, where Binnie J., writing for the majority, described the Mr. Big technique as "skillful police work" (para. 21). But the solution, in my view, is to reinvigorate the doctrine in this context, not to search for an alternative framework to guard against the very same problem. The first step toward restoring the doctrine as an effective guard against police misconduct in this context is to remind trial judges that these operations can become abusive, and that they must carefully scrutinize how the police conduct them.

115 It is of course impossible to set out a precise formula for determining when a Mr. Big operation will become abusive. These operations are too varied

for a bright-line rule to apply. But there is one guideline that can be suggested. Mr. Big operations are designed to induce confessions. The mere presence of inducements is not problematic (Oickle, para. 57). But police conduct, including inducements and threats, becomes problematic in this context when it approximates coercion. In conducting these operations, the police cannot be permitted to overcome the will of the accused and coerce a confession. This would almost certainly amount to an abuse of process.

116 Physical violence or threats of violence provide examples of coercive police tactics. A confession derived from physical violence or threats of violence against an accused will not be admissible – no matter how reliable – because this, quite simply, is something the community will not tolerate (see, e.g., R. v. Singh, 2013 ONCA 750, 118 O.R. (3d) 253).

117 Violence and threats of violence are two forms of unacceptable coercion. But Mr. Big operations can become coercive in other ways as well. Operations that prey on an accused's vulnerabilities – like mental health problems, substance addictions, or youthfulness – are also highly problematic (see Mack, at p. 963). Taking advantage of these vulnerabilities threatens trial fairness and the integrity of the justice system. As this Court has said on many occasions, misconduct that offends the community's sense of fair play and decency will amount to an abuse of process and warrant the exclusion of the statement.

118 While coercion is an important factor to consider, I do not foreclose the possibility that Mr. Big operations can become abusive in other ways. The factors that I have outlined, while not identical, are similar to those outlined in Mack, with which trial judges are well-familiar (p. 966). At the end of the day, there is only so much guidance that can be provided. Our trial judges have long been entrusted with the task of identifying abuses of process and I have no reason to doubt their ability to do the same in this context.

Why Use This Two-Pronged Approach?

119 As we have seen, Mr. Big operations raise three interrelated concerns – reliability, prejudice, and police misconduct. I have proposed two separate tests that, taken together, address all three.

120 The reason for this lies in the analytically distinct problems that the three concerns raise. Reliability and prejudice are fundamentally evidentiary issues. They are concerned with the quality of the evidence these operations produce. Indeed, they do not emerge as problems at all until a Mr. Big confession is admitted at trial. The concern that the police may engage in misconduct, by contrast, is focused on the behaviour of the state in eliciting the evidence. To be sure, there is significant overlap between the concerns. Police misconduct is more likely to produce an unreliable confession. But the overlap is not perfect. For example, a confession elicited during a Mr. Big operation where there has been no misconduct may still turn out to be unreliable and prejudicial. Similarly, a confession that is the product of misconduct may turn out to be reliable. Thus, in order to take complete account of both issues, two legal tools are required – one that looks directly at the evidence, and one that serves as a check on the conduct of the police.

121 I have turned to a common law rule of evidence to address the concerns these confessions raise with reliability and prejudice. Without question, unreliable and prejudicial evidence implicate rights under the Charter, including the right to a fair trial and the presumption of innocence. But our common law rules of evidence are, and must be, capable of protecting the constitutional rights of the accused. It is axiomatic that the common law must be developed in a manner consistent with the fundamental values enshrined in the Charter (see RWDSU v. Dolphin Delivery Ltd., [1986] 2 S.C.R. 573, at p. 603). Our rules of evidence have embraced this constitutional imperative and have evolved into principled, flexible tools that are "highly sensitive to the due process interests of the accused" (D. Paciocco, "Charter Tracks: Twenty-Five Years of Constitutional Influence on the Criminal Trial Process and Rules of Evidence" (2008), S.C.L.R. (2d) 309, at p. 311). The common law rule of evidence I have proposed fits comfortably with this Court's approach in the post-Charter era.

122 To deal with the concern regarding police misconduct, I have turned to the doctrine of abuse of process. Doing so makes good sense because, as mentioned, the doctrine is intended to guard against state misconduct that threatens the integrity of the justice system and the fairness of trials. Moreover, a form of abuse of process has long provided a residual protection against unfair police tactics in the context of conventional police interrogations (see Oickle, at paras. 65-67; Rothman v. The Queen, [1981] 1 S.C.R. 640, at p. 697). The doctrine is therefore well suited to providing a check against police misconduct in this context.

123 The two-pronged approach I have articulated is also consistent with the demands of the principle against self-incrimination. The principle against self-incrimination has two purposes: protecting against abusive state conduct, and guarding against unreliable confessions (Hebert, at p. 175; R. v. Jones, [1994] 2 S.C.R. 229, at p. 250). These protections flow from "the value placed by Canadian society upon individual privacy, personal autonomy and dignity" (White, at para. 43). However, the principle does not act as a free-standing legal protection. Rather, the principle is a "general organizing principle of criminal law from which particular rules can be derived" (Jones, at p. 249). Where its underlying rationale suggests that legal protection is needed in a specific context, but the law provides for none, the principle can be used to fashion a "contextually-sensitive" new rule to address the gap in the law (White, at para. 45).9 In my view, the common law rule of evidence I have proposed acts, along with the abuse doctrine, as yet another specific legal protection that derives from the general principle and its underlying rationale...

Justice Moldaver excluded the evidence on the first holding that the limited value of the confession was outweighed by the prejudicial effect. It was held to be not necessary to decide whether there had been an abuse of process. Justices Cromwell and Karakatsanis delivered separate concurring judgments. Whether there was a new trial was left to the Crown Attorney, who later decided not to proceed.

R. v. MACK
[2014] 3 S.C.R. 3, 315 C.C.C. (3d) 315, 13 C.R. (7th) 225 (S.C.C.)

The accused was charged with the first-degree murder of his roommate. The victim disappeared and, about a month later, a friend of the accused reported to police that the accused had confessed to killing the victim and burning his body. Police mounted a Mr. Big operation targeting the accused. The operation began when the accused was introduced to an undercover officer, B., at a nightclub where the accused was working. The accused soon learned that B. was involved in criminal activity and worked for an organization headed by a man named L. The accused did several jobs for the organization over the next few months.

Early on, in a conversation with B., the accused described the victim as a crack head and a drug addict who had stolen from his son's piggy bank. Two months into the operation, the accused met with L., who attempted to question the accused about his missing roommate. The accused asked if he could decline to speak about the victim. L. indicated that it was his choice, but that refusing to speak would mean the accused would remain on the organization's third line. L. told the accused that talking about his roommate was the only way to advance to the organization's first line. During that meeting, the accused continued to refuse to discuss the victim.

Three weeks later, the accused met with B. and said he was willing to do what it took to work for the organization. When B. asked why the accused had killed his roommate, the accused responded that the victim was a liar, a thief and a drug dealer. The accused told B. that he shot the victim five times before burning his body. The accused offered to show B. where he had burned the victim's body and took B. to the fire pit on his father's property. The accused claimed that he had taken the ashes out of the fire pit and that there was nothing left of the victim.

A few days later, the accused again met with L. He described the victim as a crack head who had stolen from his son's piggy bank, and claimed to have shot the victim five times before burning his body on the accused's father's property. Shortly after this second meeting with L., the accused was arrested and charged with first-degree murder. Police searched the father's property and found the victim's remains and shell casings in the fire pit. The Mr. Big operation lasted four months and the accused participated in 30 scenarios with undercover officers. He was paid approximately $5,000 plus expenses for his work with the organization.

The accused's statements in the Mr. Big operation were admitted in evidence against him. The jury found the accused guilty and his appeal to the Alberta Court of Appeal was dismissed. The accused appealed to the Supreme Court of Canada.

Moldaver delivered a unanimous judgment for the Court. The tactics the police had used were distinguishable from those in *Hart* and the confession met the requirements for admission. However, the Court also decided that when Mr. Big confessions are admitted there should be a warning given to juries:

MOLDAVER J.:

43 In *Hart*, this Court identified two evidentiary concerns with confessions that are the product of a Mr. Big operation. The first is that the confessions may be unreliable. Mr. Big operations are intended to induce confessions, and the inducements offered to a suspect may incentivize the suspect to falsely confess. Second, Mr. Big confessions are invariably accompanied by bad character evidence in which the accused has shown a willingness to commit crimes to gain entry into a criminal organization (see *Hart*, at paras. 68-77).

44 The common law rule of evidence that was set out in *Hart* was intended to respond to the evidentiary concerns raised by Mr. Big operations. However, while this rule responds to these two evidentiary concerns, it does not erase them. The focus of the rule is to determine whether a Mr. Big confession should be admitted into evidence. It does not decide the ultimate question of whether the confession is reliable, nor does it eliminate the prejudicial character evidence that accompanies its admission. Thus, even in cases where Mr. Big confessions are admitted into evidence, concerns with their reliability and prejudice will persist. It then falls to the trial judge to adequately instruct the jury on how to approach these confessions in light of these concerns.

50 ...[T]here is no magical incantation that must be read to juries by trial judges in all Mr. Big cases. Instead, trial judges are required to provide juries with the tools they need to address the concerns about reliability and prejudice that arise from these confessions. The nature and extent of the instructions required will vary from case to case.

51 However, there is some guidance – short of a prescriptive formula – that can be provided to trial judges who must instruct juries in cases where a Mr. Big confession has been admitted into evidence.

52 With respect to the reliability concerns raised by a Mr. Big confession, the trial judge should tell the jury that the reliability of the accused's confession is a question for them. The trial judge should then review with the jury the factors relevant to the confessions and the evidence surrounding it. As explained in *Hart*, the reliability of a Mr. Big confession is affected by the circumstances in which the confession was made and by the details contained in the confession itself. Thus, the trial judge should alert the jury to "the length of the operation, the number of interactions between the police and the accused, the nature of the relationship between the undercover officers and the accused, the nature and extent of the inducements offered, the presence of any threats, the conduct of the interrogation itself, and the personality of the accused" – all of which play a role in assessing the confession's reliability (see *Hart*, at para. 102).

53 Moreover, the trial judge should discuss the fact that the confession itself may contain markers of reliability (or unreliability). Jurors should be told to consider the level of detail in the confession, whether it led to the discovery of additional evidence, whether it identified any elements of the crime that had not been made public, or whether it accurately described mundane details of the crime the accused would not likely have known had he not committed it (see *Hart*, at para. 105).

54 This is not to suggest that trial judges are required to provide a detailed catalogue of every piece of evidence that might bear on the reliability of the confession. The task is simply to alert the jury to the concern about the reliability of the confession, and to highlight the factors relevant to assessing it.

55 With respect to the bad character evidence that accompanies a Mr. Big confession, the challenge is a more familiar one. The trial judge must instruct the jury that this sort of evidence has been admitted for the limited purpose of providing context for the confession. The jury should be instructed that it cannot rely on that evidence in determining whether the accused is guilty. Moreover, the trial judge should remind the jury that the simulated criminal activity – even that which the accused may have eagerly participated in – was fabricated and encouraged by agents of the state.

61 In my view, the trial judge's charge left the jury equipped to deal with the concerns of reliability and prejudice that emerged from the Mr. Big confessions. No error has been shown. Accordingly, I would reject this ground of appeal.

Appeal dismissed.

There has been an unmistakeable general trend since *Hart* and *Mack* to admit Mr. Big evidence subject to a cautionary jury instruction in most cases: see *R. v. Balbar*, 2014 BCSC 2285 (B.C. S.C.); *R. v. Keene*, 2014 ONSC 7190 (Ont. S.C.J.); *R. v. Hales*, 2015 SKCA 124 (Sask. C.A.); *R. v. Ledesma*, 2014 ABQB 788 (Alta. Q.B.); and *R. v. Magoon*, 2015 ABQB 351 (Alta. Q.B.). Consider whether the confession should be admitted under the *Hart/Mack* approach in the following three cases:

PROBLEM 13

The accused was charged with first-degree murder and attempted murder after the mother of the accused's child and the mother's boyfriend were shot in their bed. The female victim died but the male victim survived. The Crown's evidence at trial included a confession given by the accused to an undercover police officer posing as a crime boss in a Mr. Big undercover operation.

The operation lasted four months, involved 43 scenarios, and introduced the accused, who was unemployed, to a lifestyle of expensive restaurants and hotels. The accused was paid $8,500 including expenses. He developed deep friendships with two of the undercover officers. It was made clear that the members of the fictitious criminal organization considered each other as family, and were expected to be honest and loyal to each other. The accused never witnessed the organization directing any violence toward its own members. However, he was exposed to violence in two scenarios, including one in which he was told the organization planned to murder a man who owed them money. The accused offered to kill the man the man before the undercover officers simulated the murder within earshot of the accused.

The accused was told there was a big job coming up and that he would be paid $25,000 if he participated, but that his participation depended on the approval of Mr. Big. Mr. Big told the accused that if the accused was completely truthful with him, he could help the accused's past go away so the accused could continue working for the organization. The punishment for lying was never to work for the organization again. The accused confessed to shooting the two victims. There was also evidence that the accused acquired a shotgun and shells prior to the murder and that, after the murder, he told the individuals who gave him these items to tell no one about it.

R. v. *Allgood*, 2015 SKCA 88, 327 C.C.C. (3d) 196, 23 C.R. (7th) 86 (Sask. C.A.); August 7. See CR annotation by Lisa Dufraimont.

PROBLEM 14

The accused was charged with the first-degree murder of a 14-year-old girl. The victim's decomposed and naked body was found in a shallow grave with four large rocks on top of it. The police kept a number of crime scene details from the public, including that the victim's body was naked and that there was a large rock over the head.

The principal evidence against the accused comprised his admissions during a Mr. Big operation. Police determined that the victim knew both the accused and his teenage son, and the two men became targets of separate Mr. Big operations. The operation targeting the accused involved 39 scenarios, many of which included simulated criminal activity. Two of the scenarios included simulated violence against undercover operatives and some of the scenarios included undercover operatives pretending to be involved in producing pornographic movies with teenage girls. The accused was paid in cash for his work for the fictitious criminal organization and reimbursed for his expenses. Over the course of the operation he received $9,000, and shortly before he confessed to Mr. Big he was promised that he would receive $32,000 for "the next big score".

When Mr. Big confronted the accused about the murder of the victim, the accused admitted he had killed her because his son had sexually assaulted her and the accused was concerned that his son could go to jail. The accused said he strangled her to death, removed all her clothing and, with the help of his son, buried her in a shallow grave with large rocks on top of her.

See *R. v. West*, 2015 BCCA 379, 23 C.R. (7th) 107 (B.C. C.A.); Sept. 14.

PROBLEM 15

In December 1976 the victim was found lifeless in her car in the parking lot of a local shopping mall. She was 23 years old at the time, mother to an infant daughter and eight months pregnant. It was the accused, her husband of three years, who alerted passersby to the discovery. That evening, detectives examined the family home but found nothing abnormal. The autopsy revealed that the cause of death was asphyxiation by ligature strangulation but was unable to identify the type of ligature used. Detectives met with the accused five times in the days following the incident. He was suspected but never charged. A subsequent coroner's inquest failed to identify the murderer.

Thirty-two years later, the accused was charged with first-degree murder after he confessed to killing his wife to the boss of a fictitious criminal organization, at the conclusion of a Mr. Big sting operation. The accused confessed that he strangled his wife inside their home, placed her body in the car and drove to the shopping mall with their infant daughter. He then went into Canadian Tire with his daughter only to return to the car and fake the discovery of his wife's lifeless body.

Here the Mr. Big operation lasted four months. During this time, the accused participated in 40 scenarios before ultimately meeting the big boss of the apparent criminal organization. By the time he met Mr. Big for the interview, the accused had been instilled with the image of the gang projected to him over the course of the past months: the gang's members did not hesitate to use violence and threats of violence against their own members or third-party debtors; they are so powerful that they can find anyone easily; they have various contacts, even in the police; and they can even create an alibi to protect a member who committed a murder.

The organization did more than simply encourage a confession from the accused. Deliberately submitting the accused to scenes of violence with the stated purpose of making him understand the gang's power and resolve, combined with threats, hardly veiled, of what would happen to his friend Vince — the primary undercover operative — if the accused were not admitted in the gang and the idea that the big boss would "lose" two guys if the accused did not tell him what he wanted to hear, amount to unacceptable coercive tactics. The pressure placed the accused in a situation where he believed his own safety and that of Vince would be potentially compromised if he were not accepted in the organisation.

At trial, the accused testified to explain that his confession was not truthful and that he lied to Mr. Big under duress. The jury convicted him of first-degree murder.

See *R. v. Laflamme*, 2015 QCCA 1517, 23 C.R. (7th) 137 (C.A. Que.); Sept. 21.

While the new regime laid out in *Hart* and *Mack* is clearly more protective of the accused than the former law, some commentators have taken the view that the Supreme Court still has not gone far enough to protect suspects targeted in Mr. Big operations: see Adriana Poloz, "Motive to Lie? A Critical Look at the 'Mr. Big' Investigative Technique" (2015) 19 *Can Crim. L.R.* 231, and Adelina Iftene, "The Hart of the (Mr.) Big Problem", forthcoming in Crim.

L.Q. See too Jason MacLean and Frances Chapman, "Au Revoir, Monsieur Big? Confessions, Coercion and the Courts" (2015), 23 C.R. (7th) 184.

Although a wide path to admission of Mr. Big-induced confessions now seems the reality in Canada, this is not yet so in the United Kingdom or the United States, where principles against the admission of coerced statements apply equally to confessions to known persons in authority OR to undercover agents. See Chris Hunt and Micah Rankin, "*R. v. Hart*: A New Common Law Confession Rule for Undercover Operations" (2015), 14 Oxford University Commonwealth Law Journal. The authors urge that the new Canadian Mr. Big model not be followed in other jurisdictions. Our own voluntary confession rule does not overlook police threats to persons other than the accused nor does it have a corroboration route to admission. Furthermore, our test for exclusion of evidence obtained in violation of a Charter right under s. 24(2) in *R. v. Grant*, [2009] 2 S.C.R. 353 (see below, chapter 5) does not pivot on reliability. The *Hart/Mack* Mr. Big regime certainly appears to be a pro-State anomaly.

PROBLEM 16

The accused was charged with sexual touching of a person under the age of 14 contrary to s. 151 of the Criminal Code. The complainant was his daughter aged approximately seven or eight at the time. She was 18 at the time of the trial. At the time of the alleged offence the accused had been estranged from his wife for two years and only had weekend access to his two children. The allegation was that, while his daughter was lying on him and he was affectionately rubbing her bottom, his hand moved to touch her vagina.

At trial a *voir dire* was held to determine the admissibility of a letter the accused wrote to his daughter from the police station following the administration of a polygraph test and interrogation. The letter included the following statement:

> Please understand in those times you . . . were my babies and I couldn't be with you. I loved you each so much. On the weekends that I saw you all I wanted to do was hold you close. If I made the mistake of moving my hand inappropriately then I'm very sorry.

The accused consulted his lawyer before consenting to a polygraph test. The lawyer advised him not to participate as he could be manipulated. The test and subsequent interrogation by the same officer lasted five hours from 9:00 a.m. to just before 2:00 p.m. The event was recorded on audiovisual tape. The accused was allowed one 15 to 20 minute break at about 11:00 a.m. and was not offered anything to eat. The officer testified that she merely followed the usual protocol or practice for use of the polygraph. The officer advised him at the outset that she was there to get the truth and would not play games or throw curve balls. The accused was advised that he had failed the test which included three questions as to whether he had touched his daughter's vagina. He continued to protest his innocence. During the five hours the officer tricked him into believing:

(i)   in the infallibility or near infallibility, of the polygraph test by the use of protestations to that effect and a card trick;

(ii)   that his daughter had been hypnotized and that she had given a version of events under hypnosis similar to what she had reported to the police, and that because she was hypnotized, she was unable to lie;

(iii) that the officer would protect his best interests and was an uninvolved party;

(iv)   that no games would be played on him and that the police officer was not there to determine guilt;

(v)   that he was a person who was callous to the safety of others and who was disrespectful of the law;

(vi)   that whether he went to gaol depended on him choosing between whether he had made a mistake, or that he was a monster like Clifford Olsen;

(vii) that his own sexual morality included allegedly perverse sexual practices; and

(viii) that it would be in his best interests to write to his daughter admitting his mistake.

Is the letter admissible? Compare *R. v. N.* (2005), 28 C.R. (6th) 140 (Ont. S.C.).

PROBLEM 17

The accused is charged with murder. The body of the victim was discovered by the victim's ex-boyfriend, Jeff, in her apartment at 1:30 p.m., May 2, 1992. On the mirror in the deceased's living room a three word message was printed in lipstick: "JEFF YOU'RE NEXT." During the course of the investigation the accused became a possible suspect. The police phoned him at his home and asked to speak with him. The police said they could come to his home or he could come downtown. The accused opted for the latter. When he arrived at the police station the police advised him of his right to remain silent but did not advise him of his right to counsel. The accused said: "I've got nothing to hide. I was with her that morning but I left about noon. She was very much alive when I left."

By May 27 the police investigation had reached the stage where they had reasonable and probable grounds to arrest the accused but they elected not to do so. On May 27 the accused advised the police that he had retained counsel and did not wish to speak to the police except with or through his lawyer. The police said they understood but asked him if he would please advise them where he went after leaving the victim's apartment on May 2. The accused said he went straight to his mother's apartment, arriving there about 12:30. The mother is prepared to testify that her son did not arrive at her home that day until 2:00 p.m. She remembers because it was her birthday and her only son was late for the party which began at 1:00 p.m.

On May 28 the police asked the accused's employer to provide samples of the accused's handwriting. The handwriting needed to be printed. The employer, through a pretext caused the accused to do some printing and this was given over to forensic for analysis. Once advised of the positive comparison with the message left on the mirror the accused was arrested.

Was any of the evidence obtained in violation of the accused's Charter rights?

Compare *R. v. Miller* (1991), 9 C.R. (4th) 347, 5 O.R. (3d) 678, 68 C.C.C. (3d) 517 (Ont. C.A.), *R. v. Corak* (1994), 29 C.R. (4th) 388 (B.C. C.A.) and *R. v. Paternack* (1994), 42 C.R. (4th) 292 (Alta. C.A.), reversed on another ground in [1996] 3 S.C.R. 607, 2 C.R. (5th) 119, 110 C.C.C. (3d) 382 (S.C.C.).

PROBLEM 18

Significant circumstantial evidence linked the accused to the murder of his aunt. To obtain additional evidence against him, the police began an undercover operation. Several officers, posing as members of a criminal organization, worked at winning the accused's confidence. The accused thought the criminal enterprise he was dealing with was a large international organization involved in drug trafficking and money laundering. He was led to believe that this organization was moving to Calgary, that he had been chosen as its Calgary contact, and that he could potentially make hundreds of thousands of dollars by participating in the organization's criminal activities. The undercover police engaged the accused in criminal activities, including money laundering, theft, receiving illegal firearms and selling drugs. From the beginning, the undercover officers encouraged their suspect to talk about his aunt's murder, but he consistently refused to do so. By late October, the undercover officers decided a new tactic was necessary. They began trying to convince the accused that they had contacts in the police department who were prepared to act unlawfully, and that they had been able to use those contacts in the past to influence an investigation. The undercover officers suggested to him that they could use their corrupt police contacts to steer the murder investigation away from him. When he continued to balk at talking about the murder, they told him that he might be a liability to their organization because of the ongoing murder investigation. They forcefully suggested he "come clean" with them to protect the organization from possible police interference. This led him to confess. At no time was he aware of the true identities of the undercover officers. Is this confession admissible?

Compare *R. v. Grandinetti*, [2005] 1 S.C.R. 27, 25 C.R. (6th) 1, 191 C.C.C. (3d) 449 (S.C.C.) and Stuart, Annotation, C.R., *ibid.*, at p. 3. For a careful assessments of the use of such sting tactics in four recent murder cases see Christopher Nowlin, "Excluding the Post-offence Undercover Operation from Evidence — Warts and All", (2004) 8 Can. Crim. L. Rev. 382. The author and several trial judges expressed significant concerns as to the reliability of such evidence.

PROBLEM 19

The accused, Pinnock and Robinson were charged with first degree murder. During the investigation the police employed an undercover officer to pretend to be an Obeahman, a spiritual advisor in some Caribbean cultures. The officer befriended the mother of one of the accused and thereby arranged to meet with the two accused numerous times and persuade them that, in accordance with the religious practices of Obeah, they needed to confide to him what they knew about the death of the victim. In this manner he elicited inculpatory statements from the accused as well as investigatively helpful information. All of the meetings were audio and videotaped, and the Crown sought to admit the tapes into evidence. The accused sought the exclusion of the evidence on the basis that there was a violation of their freedom of religious rights, that the police tactic was a dirty trick, that there was a violation of their equality rights, and that the communications were privileged. Rule.

Compare *R. v. Welsh* (2007), 51 C.R. (6th) 33 (Ont. S.C.J.) and see annotation by Stephen Coughlan C.R. *ibid.* 35.

PROBLEM 20

The accused was charged with several offences in connection with a home invasion. He was interrogated by an RCMP officer after his arrest. The interrogation was video-recorded and resulted in a confession. The interrogation was a well planned, well orchestrated exercise. Prior to the interview, police prepared extensive briefing notes on, among other things, the props to be used and the moral themes to be developed during the interrogation. The interviewing officer went into the interrogation familiar with the alleged offences and believing the accused guilty. The interrogation lasted 2 hours 51 minutes, and the accused was allowed two bathroom breaks. The interviewing officer maintained a conversational tone and conducted the interrogation in a skilful and professional manner.

The accused was alert and willing to participate in the interrogation to some extent. However, in the course of the interview, he expressed a wish to remain silent more than 40 times. On 19 such occasions, the interviewing officer responded that he was happy to hear the accused's comment because it indicated that the accused was aware of his right to silence, whereupon the officer immediately continued the interrogation.

The accused's express exercise of his right to silence became increasingly persistent throughout the interrogation but was always ignored. For a substantial period near the end of the interview, the accused said nothing other than repeatedly expressing his refusal to talk.

The Crown applies to have the record of the interrogation admitted into evidence. Admissible?

Compare *R. v. Reader* (2007), 49 C.R. (6th) 301 (Man. Q.B.).

PROBLEM 21

The accused, aged 26, was a daycare worker at a child care centre that the three-year-old complainant attended. The complainant told her mother that the accused put his finger in her "peepee" and in her mouth. After police interviewed the complainant and her mother, they asked the accused to come to the police station. When he arrived he was arrested for sexual assault and sexual interference, read his rights and cautioned. The accused spoke with duty counsel for nine minutes and was then interrogated. The accused was informed that he was alleged to have assaulted a child at the daycare, but he was not at first advised of the details of the alleged offence and indicated on several occasions that he had no idea of the allegations or of what was going on. During the interview, the accused asserted his right to remain silent 28 times on the advice of the lawyer, but the officer continued his questioning. The officer finally stopped the interview on the basis that his aggressive tactics were not being successful. The accused applied to exclude his three-and-a-half hour videotaped statement to police on the basis that the evidence was obtained contrary to ss. 7, 10(a) and 10(b) of the Charter and was also involuntary. Rule.

Compare *R. v. Koivisto* (2011), 87 C.R. (6th) 285 (Ont. C.J.) and see CR annotation by Don Stuart.

Chapter 5

CHARTER REMEDIES

This chapter considers the general remedy provisions available to accused persons in the criminal process. The focus is on remedies under s. 24 of the Charter, particularly s. 24(2), which provides for the power to exclude evidence at trial. We also consider remedies under s. 52 of the Constitution Act, 1982, as well as various other remedies available at common law.

1. Remedies under s. 24

In *R. v. Big M Drug Mart Ltd.,* [1985] 1 S.C.R. 295 (S.C.C.), Dickson C.J.C. for the majority of the Supreme Court held that any provincial court has the power to declare laws to be of no force or effect under s. 52(1) of the Constitution Act, 1982. Apart from this very powerful remedy available for all courts there is, in addition, a wide remedy s. 24 in the Charter for every court of "competent jurisdiction". The "enforcement" provision in s. 24 is as follows:

> **24.**(1) Anyone whose rights of freedoms, as guaranteed by this Charter, have been infringed or denied may apply to a court of competent jurisdiction to obtain such remedy as the court considers appropriate and just in the circumstances.
>
> (2) Where, in proceedings under subsection (1), a court concludes that evidence was obtained in a manner that infringed or denied any rights or freedoms guaranteed by this Charter, the evidence shall be excluded if it is established that, having regard to all the circumstances, the admission of it in the proceedings would bring the administration of justice into disrepute.

For a review of the chequered history of s. 24 as various drafts passed through Parliament, see Stuart, *Charter Justice in Canadian Criminal Law* (6th ed., 2014) chapter 11.

The Supreme Court has yet to pronounce on the range of "appropriate and just" remedies under s. 24(1). Criminal courts have at one time or another resorted to dismissals, stays, costs or, in some cases, reduction of sentence. Recently in *R. v. Nasogaluak,* 2010 SCC 6, [2010] 1 S.C.R. 206, 251 C.C.C. (3d) 293, 72 C.R. (6th) 1 (S.C.C.), the Supreme Court declared a strong preference for any sentence reduction for police abuse to occur under the usual sentencing process of balancing, aggravating, or mitigating factors rather than as a specific Charter remedy. Nevertheless, in his penultimate paragraph, Justice LeBel left a tantalizing hint that there may yet be rare occasions when a sentence may be below the statutory limits:

> I do not foreclose, but do not need to address in this case, the possibility that, in some exceptional cases, sentence reduction outside statutory limits, under s. 24(1) of the Charter, may be the sole effective remedy for some particularly egregious form of misconduct by state agents in relation to the offence and to the offender. In

that case, the validity of the law would not be at stake, the sole concern being the specific conduct of those state agents.

For a criticism of *Nasogaluak* on the basis that the police conduct in arresting an aboriginal suspect was not sufficiently decried, see: H. Archibald Kaiser, "*Nasogaluak*: Foregone Opportunities in an Unduly Restricted Sentencing Decision" (2010), 72 C.R. (6th) 29. There was no mention of force in the arrest report and no medical help was offered. In *R. v. Bellusci* (2012), 94 C.R. (6th) 221 (S.C.C.), the Supreme Court unanimously confirmed the trial judge's stay of criminal charges against a prison inmate because of excessive force used by the prison guard. This may have reduced the impact of the *Nasogaluak* ruling.

In the Saskatchewan Court of Appeal in *Therens* (1983), 33 C.R. (3d) 204 (Sask. C.A.), four of the five judges held that one of the remedies available under s. 24(1) was the exclusion of evidence. In approving that approach taken by the trial judge, Tallis J.A. reasoned:

> The above approach taken by the learned trial judge leans in favour of emphasizing the fundamental rights guaranteed by the Charter. I endorse such an approach because, in my opinion, this court should not balance away the respondent's constitutional guarantee under s. 10(b) to be informed of the right to counsel. If the trial judge in this case cannot exclude the evidence under s. 24(1), then perhaps no other remedy or sanction is available unless the court entertains an application for the far more drastic remedy of a stay of proceedings. The framers of the Charter have clearly specified certain constitutional safeguards for an accused person which courts should strive to uphold rather than balance away on the footing that only minimal risks are involved. I think that it is far safer for the courts to emphasize the constitutional guarantees instead of substituting words not mentioned in ss. 10(b) and 24 so that the constitutional guarantee reads, in effect, that:
>
> Everyone has the right on arrest or detention . . .
>
> (b) to retain and instruct counsel without delay and to be informed of that right, provided however, that evidence obtained in violation of his rights shall be admissible unless he establishes to the satisfaction of the trial court that, having regard to all the circumstances, the admission of such evidence in the proceedings would bring the administration of justice into disrepute.

In the Supreme Court in *Therens*, [1985] 1 S.C.R. 613 (S.C.C.), Le Dain J., with five judges concurring, squarely holds that s. 24(2) is the sole basis for the exclusion of evidence because of an infringement or denial of a right or freedom guaranteed by the Charter. He reasoned as follows:

> It is clear, in my opinion, that in making explicit provision for the remedy of exclusion of evidence in s. 24(2), following the general terms of s. 24(1), the framers of the *Charter* intended that this particular remedy should be governed entirely by the terms of s. 24(2). It is not reasonable to ascribe to the framers of the *Charter* an intention that the courts should address two tests or standards on an application for the exclusion of evidence—first, whether the admission of the evidence would bring the administration of justice into disrepute, and if not, secondly, whether its exclusion would nevertheless be appropriate and just in the circumstances. The inevitable result of this alternative test or remedy would be that s. 24(2) would become a dead letter. The framers of the *Charter* could not have

intended that the explicit and deliberately adopted limitation in s. 24(2) on the power to exclude evidence because of an infringement or a denial of a guaranteed right or freedom should be undermined or circumvented in such a manner. The opening words of s. 24(2) "Where, in proceedings under subsection (1)" simply refer, in my view, to an application for relief under s. 24(1). They reinforce the conclusion that the test set out in s. 24(2) is to be the exhaustive one for the remedy of exclusion of evidence. I conclude, therefore, that the Saskatchewan Court of Appeal erred in law in affirming the exclusion of the evidence provided by the breathalyzer test on the ground that it was appropriate and just in the circumstances, within the meaning of s. 24(1) of the *Charter*.

Dickson C.J.C. and Lamer J. were the only judges who preferred to leave this issue open.

Despite *Therens*, the Supreme Court has since recognised an uncertain discretion to exclude evidence to ensure a fair trial under s. 7, 11(*d*) and, surprisingly, s. 24(1): see *R. v. Harrer*, [1995] 3 S.C.R. 562, 42 C.R. (4th) 269, 101 C.C.C. (3d) 193 (S.C.C.) and *R. v. White*, [1999] 2 S.C.R. 417, 24 C.R. (5th) 201, 135 C.C.C. (3d) 257 (S.C.C.); see too discussion by Michael Davies, "Using s. 24(1) of the Charter to Exclude Evidence: It's Just Not Fair" (2000), 29 C.R. (5th) 225. This discretion usually arises where the Charter is held not to apply. However, this is not always the case. In *R. v. Bjelland*, 67 C.R. (6th) 201, 246 C.C.C. (3d) 129, [2009] 2 S.C.R. 651 (S.C.C.), the Supreme Court held that exclusion of evidence may be granted as a remedy under section 24(1) where, for example, there has been late disclosure of evidence by the Crown. Nevertheless, the Court greatly restricted the remedy by holding that it should be awarded only in the following exceptional circumstances: (a) where the late disclosure renders the trial process unfair and this unfairness cannot be remedied through an adjournment and disclosure order, or (b) where exclusion is necessary to maintain the integrity of the justice system.

In *R. v. Buhay*, [2003] 1 S.C.R. 631, 174 C.C.C. (3d) 97, 10 C.R. (6th) 205 (S.C.C.), there is an *obiter* recognition by Arbour J. of a common law discretion to exclude evidence obtained in circumstances such that it would result in unfairness if the evidence was admitted at trial, or if the prejudicial effect of admitting the evidence outweighs its probative value. For a comment on this aspect of *Buhay*, see Michael Plaxton, "Who Needs Section 24(2)? Or Common Law Sleight of Hand" (2003) 10 C.R. (6th) 236. We will focus in this course on the normal remedy in criminal trials for excluding evidence obtained in violation of the Charter: that under s. 24(2).

2. Exclusion of Evidence

Prior to the Charter, Canadian courts followed English common law in holding that the illegality of the means used to obtain evidence generally has no bearing upon its admissibility. The leading decision is *A.G. Que. v. Begin*, [1955] S.C.R. 593, 21 C.R. 217 (S.C.C.), in which the Supreme Court unanimously held, without any explanation of the policy considerations, that the results of a blood test were admissible in evidence as they were relevant to prove intoxication, even if they had been obtained illegally. The accused's consent to the test had been obtained but he had not been warned that the results might be used in evidence against him. On behalf of the Court, Fautaux J. held:

> Without doubt, the method used in obtaining certain of this evidence can, in certain cases, be illegal and even give rise to appeals of civil or even criminal order against those who have used it, but the proposition will not be discussed further, since in this case, illegality tainting the method of obtaining the evidence does not affect *per se* the admissibility of this evidence in the trial (at 602).

In *R. v. Sang,* [1979] 2 All E.R. 1222, 1225 (H.L.) the English Court of Appeal certified for the House of Lords, as a point of law of general importance, the question:

> Does a trial judge have a discretion to refuse to allow evidence, being evidence other than evidence of admission, to be given in any circumstances in which such evidence is relevant and of more than minimal probative value?

In an apparent unanimous conclusion, the Lords agreed:

> (1) A trial judge in a criminal trial has always a discretion to refuse to admit evidence if in his opinion its prejudicial effect outweighs its probative value.
>
> (2) Save with regard to admissions and confessions and generally with regard to evidence obtained from the accused after commission of the offence, he has no discretion to refuse to admit relevant admissible evidence on the ground that it was obtained by improper or unfair means. The court is not concerned with how it was obtained.

In Scotland a broader discretion to exclude exists. In *Lawrie v. Muir* [(1950), S.C.(J) 19 at pp. 26-27, quoted in *King v. R.,* [1968] 2 All E.R. 610, 615 (P.C.)] Lord Cooper wrote:

> From the standpoint of principle it seems to me that the law must strive to reconcile two highly important interests which are liable to come in conflict—(a) the interest of the citizen to be protected from illegal or irregular invasions of his liberties by the authorities, and (b) the interest of the State to secure that evidence bearing upon the commission of crime and necessary to enable justice to be done shall not be withheld from courts of law on any merely formal or technical ground. Neither of these objects can be insisted upon to the uttermost. The protection of the citizen is primarily protection for the innocent citizen against unwarranted, wrongful and perhaps high handed interference, and the common sanction is an action of damages. The protection is not intended as a protection for the guilty citizen against the efforts of the public prosecutor to vindicate the law. On the other hand, the interest of the State cannot be magnified to the point of causing all the safeguards for the protection of the citizen to vanish, and of offering a positive inducement to the authorities to proceed by irregular methods.
>
> . . .
>
> Irregularities require to be excused, and infringements of the formalities of the law in relation of these matters are not lightly to be condoned. Whether any given irregularity ought to be excused depends upon the nature of the irregularity and the circumstances under which it was committed. In particular the case may bring into place the discretionary principle of fairness to the accused which has been so fully developed in our law in relation to the admission in evidence of confessions or admissions by a person suspected or charged with a crime. That principle would

obviously require consideration in any case in which the departure from the strict procedure had been adopted deliberately with a view to securing the admission of evidence obtained by an unfair trick . . . On the other hand, to take an extreme instance figured in argument, it would usually be wrong to exclude some highly incriminating production in a murder trial merely because it was found by a police officer in the course of a search authorised for a different purpose or before a proper warrant had been obtained.

In 1984 the U.K. Parliament passed the Police and Criminal Evidence Act which reconstructed the voluntary confession rule to read that a confession would be inadmissible where it had been obtained by "oppression" or

in consequence of anything said or done which was likely, in the circumstances existing at the time, to render unreliable any confession which might be made by him in consequence thereof.

As a last minute compromise, Parliament also declared in s. 78(1) a discretion to exclude

if it appears to the court that, having regard to all the circumstances, including the circumstances in which the evidence was obtained, the admission of the evidence would have such an adverse effect on the fairness of the proceedings that the court ought not to admit it.

It is still broadly true to state that in the United States there is an automatic exclusionary rule (the fruit of the poisonous tree doctrine) in terms of which any illegally obtained evidence is forever inadmissible.

In *Weeks v. United States,* 232 U.S. 383 (1914), the United States Supreme Court held that in a federal prosecution the Fourth Amendment to the Constitution barred the use of evidence secured through an illegal search and seizure. In *Wolf v. Colorado,* 338 U.S. 25 (1949), the Court was asked whether the exclusionary rule fashioned in *Weeks* should be made applicable to state prosecutions through the due process clause of the Fourteenth Amendment. At that time thirty states rejected the *Weeks* doctrine, while seventeen states accepted it. The Court declared that the "security of one's privacy against arbitrary intrusion by the police" is "implicit in the concept of ordered liberty and as such enforceable against the States through the Due Process Clause". The Court, however, declined to apply the exclusionary rule saying that the minimum standards of due process could be otherwise satisfied; injured parties could be left to their remedies of private action and internal discipline of the police. In *Mapp v. Ohio,* 367 U.S. 643 (1961), the Court decided the time had come to make the exclusionary rule applicable to the States. Justice Clark, delivering the opinion of the Court wrote:

To hold otherwise is to grant the right but in reality to withhold its privilege and enjoyment.

The Court felt compelled to reach its conclusion because they concluded that other remedies had completely failed to secure compliance with the constitution. Evidence seized improperly would therefore be excluded but also the Court fashioned a doctrine which would exclude not only the evidence seized but also evidence subsequently discovered through information obtained as a result of the search. This became known as the "fruit of the poisonous tree" doctrine. That doctrine, developed in search cases, was later applied to evidence derived from other constitutional infringements.

In recent years various members of the United States Supreme Court have expressed reservations about the automatic operation of the exclusionary rule. While they have restricted the types of proceedings and searches it can apply to (see Bass "The Erosion of the Exclusionary Rule Under the Burger Court", (1981), 33 Baylor L.R. 363), the general rule is still intact. The majority of the United States Supreme Court in *U.S. v. Leon* 104 S. Crt. 3405 (1984) and *Massachusetts v. Sheppard* 104 S. Crt. 3424 (1984), did create a good faith exception but it is narrowly confined to situations where police officers have used a technically defective warrant believing it to be valid. Since *Leon* and *Massachusetts*, however, the good faith exception has been expanded in at least three ways: to admit evidence uncovered by objectively reasonable reliance on a statute later declared unconstitutional (*Illinois v. Krull*, 107 S.Ct. 1160 (1987)), of seizures pursuant to clerical errors by court employees (*Arizona v. Evans*, 115 S.Ct. 1185 (1995)), and where officials conduct a search in objectively reasonable reliance on binding appellate precedent (*Davis v. U.S.*, 131 S.Ct. 2419 (2011)). Clearly the exclusionary rule is far less automatic than it used to be.

In January 2009 in *Herring v. United States*, 555 U.S. 1 (2009) Chief Justice Roberts writing for a 5-4 majority, confirmed that exclusion is not a necessary consequence of a Fourth Amendment violation and that the benefits of deterrence must outweigh the costs of letting guilty and possibly dangerous defendants go free. He held that:

> To trigger the exclusionary rule, police conduct must be sufficiently deliberate that exclusion can meaningfully deter it, and sufficiently culpable that such deterrence is worth the price paid by the justice system. . . . [The] exclusionary rule serves to deter deliberate , reckless , or grossly negligent conduct, or in some circumstances recurring or systemic negligence.

The standard for exclusion had not been reached, the majority ruled in this case of State carelessness. The accused had been arrested on a warrant because county officials had negligently not updated computer records to show that the warrant had actually been rescinded.

The academic debate in the United States rages on unabated. 62 Judicature contains a dialogue between the two leading protagonists, Kamisar and Wilkey, at pp. 70, 215, 337 and 351. See also Wilkey, "Enforcing the Fourth Amendment by Alternatives to the Exclusionary Rule", (1982) 95 F.R.D. 211, and Kamisar, "Search and Seizure of America", (1982) 10 Human Rights 14. There is also an empirical debate as to whether the rule is successful in deterring police violations of the Constitution. The central work is a study by Oakes, "Studying the Exclusionary Rule in Search and Seizure", (1969) 37 U. of Chi. L.R. 665, which found no significant deterrence. It has been severely attacked in some quarters on the grounds of methodology (see, for example, "On the Limitations of Empirical Evaluations of the Exclusionary Rule: A Critique of the Spiotto Research and *U.S. v. Calandra*", (1975) 69 N.W.U. L. Rev. 740) and rebutted by other empirical studies (see Canon, "The Exclusionary Rule: Have Critiques Proven That It Doesn't Deter Police?", (1979) 62 Judicature 398, and Loewenthal, "Evaluating The Exclusionary Rule in Search and Seizure", (1980) 9 Anglo-Amer. L. Rev. 238). The empirical debate in the United States is at a stalemate. It is now focussed on the question of who bears the onus of justifying that the exclusionary rule does or does not deter police misconduct. Others have given up the idea of attempting to justify the exclusionary rule on simple utilitarian grounds. For them, a principled approach is necessary. Instead of arguing deterrence, they would justify exclusion as advancing:

> the twin goals of enabling the judiciary to avoid the taint of partnership in official lawlessness and of assuring the people that the government would not profit from its lawlessness behaviour, thus minimizing the risk of seriously undermining popular trust in government.

> *U.S. v. Calandria,* 414 U.S. 338, 357 (1974), per Brennan J.

Richard M Re, "The Due Process Exclusionary Rule" (2014) 127 *Harv. L.Rev.* 1885, concludes that the exclusionary rule is weak because the Fourth Amendment does not effectively deter police, restore rights to accused, maintain the integrity of the court, or repudiate unconstitutional conduct. He suggests that these functions would be better served under the due process clause.

BLACK, Hugo L., in Green v. United States, 365 U.S. 301
(1961), 309-310

Bad men, like good men, are entitled to be tried and sentenced in accordance with law.

R. v. DUGUAY
(1985), 50 O.R. (2d) 375, 45 C.R. (3d) 140 (Ont. C.A.)

Occupants of a house were asked by youth over the fence whether they kept their dog tied up. When their house was burglarised they told the police of this strange conversation and gave police a description of the three youth. The police identified where they lived and got them to come to the crime scene. They were immediately arrested, placed in a police cruiser and questioned in the vehicle.

MACKINNON A.C.J.O. (Martin J.A. concurring):—

Section 24(2) of the Canadian Charter of Rights and Freedoms
> Section 24(2) reads:
> 24(2) Where, in proceedings under subsection (1), a court concludes that evidence was obtained in a manner that infringed or denied any rights or freedoms guaranteed by this Charter, the evidence shall be excluded if it is established that, having regard to all the circumstances, the admission of it in the proceedings would bring the administration of justice into disrepute.

This is a more difficult issue to determine. It is agreed that the onus was on the respondents to establish that the admission of their statements and their fingerprints, and the fact that the stereo was recovered as a direct result of Murphy's statement, would, under the circumstances, bring the administration of justice into disrepute.

After quoting from Mr. Justice Lamer's statement in *Rothman v. The Queen*, [1981] 1 S.C.R. 640 at p. 696, 59 C.C.C. (2d) 30 at p. 74, 121 D.L.R. (3d) 578 at p. 621, the trial judge went on to say on the point:

> Other than some actual form of torture, I cannot think of anything more shocking to the right-thinking member of the community that the courts would allow police officers to introduce evidence which they have obtained through the nefarious means of an unlawful arrest. To admit such evidence would, in effect mean, that the court sanctions unlawful arrests by the police. Far be it from this court to give that blessing. I therefore rule as inadmissible any utterances or statements made by the accused in this case. I further rule inadmissible, any evidence which the police might have obtained as a result of such utterances or statements. Fingerprint evidence which arises out of the fact that these accused were fingerprinted following their arrest is also ruled inadmissible.

Although the trial judge's language is somewhat excessive in condemning the action of the two detectives, and his statement is too general, in my view, without becoming too overblown in my own language, the manner in which the police proceeded suggested a somewhat incipient Star Chamber attitude.

There are cases where the circumstances satisfy that even if the evidence is "tainted" by some breach of Charter rights the refusal to admit that evidence may cause greater injury to the State and society and to the administration of justice than its admission. In other words, in such cases the refusal to admit the evidence may be more likely to bring the administration of justice into disrepute. But that is not this case. As already indicated, there will also be cases where the breach is a "slight" one and the admission of the evidence would have no effect on the reputation of the administration of justice.

It is repugnant to our concept of the administration of criminal justice and to the rights of citizens in a free and democratic society, to make them subject to arbitrary arrest for investigative purposes. The arbitrary quality of the act with the resultant breach of a Charter right has already been determined in the instant case. The question to be determined is: whether, "having regard to the circumstances", the admission of the inculpatory statements, the evidence of the fingerprints and their relevance and their evidence relative to the recovery of the stereo set would bring the administration of justice into disrepute?

Counsel for the Crown argued that there had to be a "causal connection" established between the breach of the Charter right and the securing of the evidence before one could enter upon a consideration of s. 24(2). He submitted that there was no such causal connection here. The language of s. 24(2) has been described as broad enough to encompass circumstances in which the violation is not a necessary condition to the obtaining of the evidence. Be that as it may, in my view there is in this case a simple, understandable causal connection between the breach of the Charter right and the obtaining of the evidence. The inculpatory statements were a direct result of the illegal arrest—indeed the hoped-for result and purpose of the arrest. The location of the stereo set flowed directly from the respondent Murphy's statement. The securing of the respondent's fingerprints (which were not otherwise available) was under the compulsion of the *Identification of Criminals Act,* R.S.C. 1970, c. I-1, s. 2, which only came into play on the arrest (presumed legal at the time) of the respondents: *Davis v. State of Mississippi* (1969), 89 S. Ct. 1394, 394 U.S. 721.

As there is no suggestion that the police had or would necessarily have discovered the evidence without the breach of the Charter the significance of the breach is great, the evidence being necessary for a successful prosecution.

Counsel for the Crown argues that the trial judge erred in that he considered only the controlling of police conduct and failed to assess other criteria in determining whether the admission of the evidence would bring the administration of justice into disrepute. On a careful reading of the trial judge's analysis of the evidence, however, in my opinion he did balance various factors in considering this issue, and earlier made his findings of fact for that purpose.

What are the factors in this case that need to be considered? First, the finding of fact that, in effect, the arrest was not made in good faith. The trial judge held that these experienced officers could not have believed that they had reasonable and probable grounds for the arrest. There was found to be a deliberate breach of the Charter right for an illegal purpose. Secondly, the offence was not a serious one. As MacDonald J.A. put it in *R. v. Stevens* (1983), 7 C.C.C. (3d) 260 at p. 264, 1 D.L.R. (4th) 465 at p. 469, 35 C.R. (3d) 1:

> In a relatively minor case like the present the violation of the individual's right to privacy might, to some jurists, be considered shocking. In a far more serious case the interests of society might well dictate that similar conduct was not so shocking as to bring the administration of justice into disrepute.

Thirdly, there was no question of urgency which might not excuse but could explain the conduct of the police. Fourthly, the respondents were three 17-year-olds, whose names and addresses were known. They had no criminal record. Indeed, one of them (Duguay) was not even identified as being in the neighbour's backyard on the night of the break-in. Finally, there was clearly no fear of the respondents fleeing the jurisdiction or going into hiding. When these facts are added to the arbitrary actions of the police—which facts I suppose, in part, underline the arbitrary conduct—I conclude that the trial judge was entitled to hold that the admission of the evidence would bring the administration of justice into disrepute and that he made no error in law in so finding.

It has been suggested that the victim of such a crime may wonder why the admitted perpetrator is allowed to go free and that this reaction may very well bring the administration of justice into disrepute. But that is not the test. One could as well ask what the victim's attitude would be if it were his child's Charter rights that were infringed. Long before the Charter there existed the possibility that a guilty person might go free if an inculpatory statement, truthful or not, were held not to be a voluntary one; or if some procedural

defect existed in a wiretap resulting in the exclusion of evidence obtained
thereby. The integrity of the criminal justice system demands these results.
Under the Charter, if to the average citizen interested in the administration of
justice and the protection of the Charter rights, the admission of the objected-
to evidence, *under all the circumstances,* would bring the administration of
justice into disrepute then it must be excluded: *Davis v. State of Mississippi,*
supra.

If the court should turn a blind eye to this kind of conduct, then the police
may assume that they have the court's tacit approval of it. I do not view the
exclusion of the evidence as a punishment of the police for their conduct,
although it is to be hoped that it will act as a future deterrent. It is rather an
affirmation of fundamental values of our society, and the only means in this
case of ensuring that the individual's Charter rights are not illusory. I agree
with the conclusion of the trial judge and would have reached the same
conclusion that, on the facts as found by him, the respondents have satisfied
the burden of establishing that the admission of the evidence would bring the
administration of justice into disrepute.

ZUBER J.A. (dissenting):—

Excluding the evidence

Assuming that there was a violation of the Charter in this case, the
problem remains whether or not the evidence obtained as a result should be
excluded. Section 24(2) of the Charter provides as follows:

> 24(2) Where, in proceedings under subsection (1), a court concludes that evidence
> was obtained in a manner that infringed or denied any rights or freedoms
> guaranteed by this Charter, the evidence shall be excluded if it is established that,
> having regard to all the circumstances, the admission of it in the proceedings would
> bring the administration of justice into disrepute.

It is apparent from the wording of the section itself that the critical
question is whether or not the admission of the evidence in question would
bring the administration of justice into disrepute. It is further apparent from
the words of the section that all of the circumstances must be considered.

In a pre-Charter case, *Rothman v. The Queen,* [1981] 1 S.C.R. 640, 59
C.C.C. (2d) 30, 121 D.L.R. (3d) 578, dealing with the admissibility of a
statement, Lamer J. dealt with the concept of "bringing the administration of
justice into disrepute" and provided some helpful comments and also identified
some of the circumstances which should be considered. He said at p. 697
S.C.R., pp. 74-5 C.C.C., pp. 621-2 D.L.R.:

> The judge, in determining whether under the circumstances the use of the
> statement in the proceedings would bring the administration of justice into
> disrepute, should consider all of the circumstances of the proceedings, the manner
> in which the statement was obtained, the degree to which there was a breach of
> social values, the seriousness of the charge, the effect the exclusion would have on
> the result of the proceedings. It must also be borne in mind that the investigation
> of crime and the detection of criminals is not a game to be governed by the
> Marquis of Queensberry rules. The authorities, in dealing with shrewd and often
> sophisticated criminals, must sometimes of necessity resort to tricks or other forms

of deceit and should not through the rule be hampered in their work. What should be repressed vigorously is conduct on their part that shocks the community. That a police officer pretend to be a lock-up chaplain and hear a suspect's confession is conduct that shocks the community; so is pretending to be the duty legal-aid lawyer eliciting in that way incriminating statements from suspects or the accused; injecting Pentothal into a diabetic suspect pretending it is his daily shot of insulin and using his statement in evidence would also shock the community; but generally speaking, pretending to be a hard drug addict to break a drug ring would not shock the community; nor would, as in this case, pretending to be a truck driver to secure the conviction of a trafficker; in fact, what would shock the community would be preventing the police from resorting to such a trick.

This statement is the origin of what is referred to in later cases dealing with s. 24(2) as the "community shock test".

In *R. v. Simmons* (1984), 45 O.R. (2d) 609, 11 C.C.C. (3d) 193, 7 D.L.R. (4th) 719, 39 C.R. (3d) 223, Howland C.J.O. dealt with the question of what would bring the administration of justice into disrepute and also addressed the community shock test. At p. 634 O.R., p. 218 C.C.C., p. 744 D.L.R., p. 252 C.R., he said:

In my opinion, in determining whether the administration of justice has been brought into disrepute within s. 24(2), the following matters are of importance: the nature and extent of the illegality, the manner in which the evidence was obtained, the good faith or the lack of good faith of the persons who obtained the evidence, whether the accused's rights under the Charter were knowingly infringed, and the seriousness of the charge. This list is not intended to be all-inclusive. There may be other matters of importance which should be considered.

If the evidence is obtained in such a manner as to shock the Canadian community as a whole, it would no doubt be inadmissible as bringing the administration of justice into disrepute. There may, however, be instances where the administration of justice is brought into disrepute within s. 24(2) without necessarily shocking the Canadian community as a whole. In my opinion, it is preferable to consider every case on its merits as to whether it satisfies the requirements of s. 24(2) of the Charter and not to substitute a "community shock" or any other test for the plain words of the statute.

I agree with the Chief Justice of Ontario that courts should not, by a process of redefinition and by the formulation of tests, make the Charter into something that it is not. However, in my respectful opinion, the formulation of a judgment premised on s. 24(2) of the Charter requires more than a recitation of all of the circumstances followed by a selection of the result—admission or exclusion. If this is done by a trial court, it is difficult for an appellate court to know the real reason for the decision. On the other hand, if this process is followed by an appellate court, it is of very little guidance to trial courts.

Bound up in the evaluation of all of the circumstances and the determination of whether the administration of justice will be brought into disrepute are the principles that one brings to the evaluation process. Without a clear appreciation of what these principles are, the evaluation process will become far too subjective and, as a result, the treatment of evidentiary matters pursuant to s. 24(2) will become unacceptably inconsistent. In my view, the Chief Justice of Ontario in *Simmons,* in telling us that we should not substitute tests for the clear words of the Charter, did not exclude the identification of the principles that we bring to the process of evaluation.

I wish, then, to turn to the principles that underlie this process of evaluation and, of course, I cannot pretend that the following is an exhaustive list of such principles.

First, s. 24(2) represents a compromise between the American exclusionary rule and our own pre-Charter law that, generally speaking, evidence illegally obtained was nevertheless admissible. In my view, however, the position arrived at is not a middle position equidistant between the two competing positions. Evidence obtained as a result of a Charter violation is, as a general rule, admissible. The exception to this general rule arises only when the admission of such evidence will bring the administratin of justice into disrepute. I agree with the comment of Ewaschuk J., who said in *R. v. Gibson* (1984), 37 C.R. (3d) 175 at p. 185:

> As a result of that compromise, s. 24(2) of the Charter tilts the balance in favour of truth, so that evidence, even though obtained as a result of constitutional violation, is prima facie admissible. However, the evidence may nonetheless be excluded where an applicant for its exclusion establishes on a balance of probabilities that, having regard to all the circumstances of the individual case, the admission of the evidence would bring the administration of justice into disrepute: see *R. v. Collins* [(1983), 5 C.C.C. (3d) 141, 148 D.L.R. (3d) 40, 33 C.R. (3d) 130, [1983] 5 W.W.R. 43], and *R. v. Chapin* (1983), 43 O.R. (2d) 458 (C.A.).

Section 24(2) is premised on a Charter violation. It is therefore inappropriate to say that courts cannot turn a blind eye to Charter violations or cannot sanction violations by admitting the evidence. The Charter itself contemplates the admission of evidence obtained as a result of a Charter violation. Further, it is not necessary that courts sanction or turn a blind eye to Charter violations. Section 24(1) permits courts to use a wide range of remedies other than the exclusion of evidence to uphold the value of Charter rights.

The logical extension of the blind-eye argument leads to the exclusion of evidence almost automatically and will inevitably lead us to a position very close to the exclusionary rule as it exists in the United States. This would be a result which is clearly inconsistent with the compromise position taken by s. 24(2) itself. On wider grounds, and as a matter of principle, we should be very wary of moving in the direction of an exclusionary rule. The American experience with the exclusionary rule should dampen the ardour of anyone ready to follow that course.

Second, it is important that we understand clearly what is being done when evidence is sought to be excluded pursuant to s. 24(2). Courts are being asked to suppress the truth. Most evidentiary rules of exclusion are based upon the lack of relevance, unreliability or the confusion that could be caused by admission. In the case of exclusion pursuant to s. 24(2), none of these frailties exist. The case at hand is a good example. Evidence in this case is clear, cogent and reliable and is sought to be excluded.

Obviously, the reliability of the evidence is not a reason which, by itself, can defeat the effect of s. 24(2) but it is an important consideration when we come to consider the issue of "bringing the administration of justice into disrepute". The question becomes whether the admission of the truth (albeit discovered as a result of a Charter violation) will bring the administration of justice into disrepute. The converse question is, what will the suppression of the truth do to the repute of the administration of justice?

Section 24(2) of the Charter entitles courts to say that at a certain point the price of truth is too high. When the Charter violation by which the evidence is obtained does more damage to the fabric of society than the crime which is being investigated, then reasonable men will say that the admission of such evidence will bring the administration of justice into disrepute.

Third, in approaching the issue of the repute of the administration of justice, it is of some significance to keep in mind that our criminal justice system from its beginnings until 1982 regularly admitted evidence despite the fact that it was illegally obtained. Had this case taken place prior to 1982, all of the evidence excluded by the trial judge would have been admitted without exciting any notice whatever.

Granted that the Charter has changed the law but it has not, overnight, transformed the healthy repute of the administration of justice into a fragile flower ready to wilt because of the admission of evidence obtained as a result of a violation of the Charter rights of an accused. The regard of the Canadian public for the administration of justice prior to the Charter, despite the fact that evidence illegally obtained was admitted as a matter of course, was, in my view, very high. The repute of the administration of justice has not now suddenly become highly vulnerable.

Fourth, control of the police has no place in the application of s. 24(2). Prior to the enactment of the Charter and when evidence illegally obtained was freely admitted, misconduct of the police could be dealt with either by prosecution or by civil action. Section 24(1) expands this notion and provides courts with a large armoury of remedies whereby Charter violations can be dealt with apart from the exclusion of evidence. Even in the United States, control of the police is not regarded as a strong argument for upholding the exclusionary rule. On a more mundane level, there is no satisfactory evidence that the exclusion of evidence is effective as a mechanism for control of police methods. Whatever penalty there may be in excluding the evidence in a given case does not fall on the police. It falls on the public.

Fifth, it is, I think, obvious that disrepute must rest on the view of the whole community and not just the view of the few no matter how knowledgeable or expert the few may be.

I conclude from all of the foregoing that evidence will be excluded pursuant to s. 24(2) on the grounds that the administration of justice will be brought into disrepute only in highly exceptional cases. As mentioned above, Howland C.J.O. in *Simmons*, has told us that the community shock test should not displace the plain words of the statute. In my view, Lamer J. in *Rothman*, in enunciating the community shock test, did not mean it to be definitive. However, the community shock test retains value as a convenient way of expressing the exceptional quality of the circumstances that will lead to the conclusion that the administration of justice will be brought into disrepute.

Frequent resort to the exclusion of evidence will create a perception by the public that the criminal justice system is a sort of legalistic game in which a misstep by the police confers immunity upon the accused. This perception will most certainly bring the administration of justice into disrepute.

In all of the foregoing, to a large extent I have repeated concepts earlier expressed by Seaton J.A. in *R. v. Collins* (1983), 5 C.C.C. (3d) 141, 148 D.L.R. (3d) 40, 33 C.R. (3d) 130, and Esson J.A. in *R. v. Hamill* (1984), 14 C.C.C. (3d) 338, 13 D.L.R. (4th) 275, 41 C.R. (3d) 123. By repetition I express my agreement.

The facts of this case

I turn now to the circumstances to be considered pursuant to s. 24(2).

Accepting the trial judge's findings that the two detectives did not believe on reasonable and probable grounds that the three accused were the authors of the break-in, there was nevertheless a basis in fact for their arrest. As mentioned earlier, the arrest was neither random nor capricious. Their following detention was neither oppressive nor inhumane. Nothing in the trial record suggests that the detectives were acting in bad faith. The principle criticism of the procedure followed by the two detectives is that they arrested first and took the statements thereafter. Had it been the other way around, there seems to be little doubt that the statements would have been the same and, rather obviously, the rest of the evidence would have been the same.

The crime with which these three accused are charged is a serious one. The break and entry of a dwelling carries a maximum penalty of life imprisonment. In *Colet v. The Queen*, [1981] 1 S.C.R. 2, 57 C.C.C. (2d) 105, 119 D.L.R. (3d) 521, the Supreme Court of Canada was concerned with police powers of search of a dwelling. Ritchie J. said at p. 8 S.C.R., p. 110 C.C.C., p. 526 D.L.R.:

> . . . what is involved here is the longstanding right of a citizen of this country to the control and enjoyment of his own property, including the right to determine who shall and who shall not be permitted to invade it. The common law principle has been firmly engrafted in our law since *Semayne's Case*, 77 E.R. 194, 5 Co. Rep. 91a, in 1604 where it was said "That the house of every one is to him as his castle and fortress, as well for his defence against injury and violence, as for his repose . . .". This famous dictum was cited by my brother Dickson in the case of *Eccles v. Bourque*, [1975] 2 S.C.R. 739, in which he made an extensive review of many of the relevant authorities.

It seems to me that the law of this country which protects a citizen's dwelling against unauthorized police entry should be equally solicitous with respect to a break-in of a dwelling by thieves.

In excluding the evidence, the learned trial judge treated all of the evidence as having been obtained in a manner that infringed or denied Charter rights. In a mechanical way there is a causal link between the arrest and the three accused and all of the evidence that followed. However, in my view, the causal link becomes much weaker with respect to the finding of the stolen goods and very much weaker with respect to the fingerprint evidence. It is argued that without the arrest the sample prints would not have been taken from the three accused. However, this was only the mechanism of identification. The Laframboise premises and the stolen goods bore the fingerprints. Two of the accused had hands and fingers with prints that matched. The procedural act of causing the accused to place their prints on a card to provide the connective link was obtained through a Charter violation only in the most technical sense.

In my view, the plight of the victim is also a relevant circumstance within s. 24(2). His dwelling was broken into and his possessions were stolen. He expended his time and energy by reporting the matter to the police, testifying at the preliminary hearing and apparently by attending at the trial ready to testify again. However, his recourse to the law has yielded him nothing. He, no doubt, has some interesting impressions as to the course of these proceedings.

The last circumstance to be considered is the effect of the exclusion of the evidence and, in this case, it is obvious that the exclusion of the evidence in question led to the collapse of the Crown's case.

The foregoing circumstances evaluated against a background of the principles earlier set out lead me to the conclusion that the respondents fall far short of establishing that the admission of the evidence in this case would bring the administration of justice into disrepute. It is likely not accurate to speak of the burden resting on those who seek to exclude evidence as an onus of proof. In most cases, no evidence will be called respecting the issue of disrepute. This burden may be more aptly referred to as a burden of persuasion and, in my view, this burden was not discharged. On the contrary, I think it more likely that the exclusion of the evidence in this case will bring the administration of justice into disrepute.

Which position do you prefer? Which position do you think found favour in the Supreme Court of Canada? See R. v. Duguay, [1989] 1 S.C.R. 93, 67 C.R. (3d) 252, 46 C.C.C. (3d) 1 (S.C.C.).

Collins remains a foundation case for the consideration of s. 24(2).

R. v. COLLINS
[1987] 1 S.C.R. 265, 56 C.R. (3d) 193, 33 C.C.C. (3d) 1 (S.C.C.)

See earlier, under Warrantless Searches (on p. 120), for a review of the facts and the ruling that s. 8 had been violated.

LAMER J. (Dickson C.J.C., Wilson and La Forest JJ. concurring):—On the record as it now stands, the appellant has established that the search was unreasonable and violated her rights under s. 8 of the Charter. As Seaton J.A. pointed out in the Court of Appeal, s. 24(2) has adopted an intermediate position with respect to the exclusion of evidence obtained in violation of the Charter. It rejected the American rule excluding all evidence obtained in violation of the Bill of Rights and the common law rule that all relevant evidence was admissible regardless of the means by which it was obtained. Section 24(2) requires the exclusion of the evidence "if it is established that, having regard to all the circumstances, the admission of it in the proceedings would bring the administration of justice into disrepute."

At the outset, it should be noted that the use of the phrase "if it is established that" places the burden of persuasion on the applicant, for it is the position which he maintains which must be established. Again, the standard of persuasions required can only be civil standard of the balance of probabilities. Thus, the applicant must make it more probable than not that the admission of the evidence would bring the administration of justice into disrepute.

It is whether *the admission of the evidence* would bring the administration of justice into disrepute that is the applicable test. Misconduct by the police in the investigatory process often has some effect on the repute of the administration of justice, but s. 24(2) is not a remedy for police misconduct, requiring the exclusion of the evidence if, because of his misconduct, the administration of justice was brought into disrepute. Section 24(2) could well have been drafted in that way, but it was not. Rather, the drafters of the Charter decided to focus on the admission of the evidence in the proceedings, and the purpose of s. 24(2) is to prevent having the administration of justice brought into *further disrepute* by the admission of the evidence in the proceedings. This further disrepute will result from the admission of evidence that would deprive the accused of a fair hearing, or from judicial condonation of unacceptable conduct by the investigatory and prosecutorial agencies. It will also be necessary to consider any disrepute that may result from the exclusion of the evidence. It would be inconsistent with the purpose of s. 24(2) to exclude evidence if its exclusion would bring the administration of justice into greater disrepute than would its admission. Finally, it must be emphasized that even though the inquiry under s. 24(2) will necessarily focus on the specific prosecution, it is the long-term consequences of regular admission or exclusion of this type of evidence on the repute of the administration of justice which must be considered: see on this point Gibson, above, p. 245.

The concept of disrepute necessarily involves some element of community views, and the determination of disrepute thus requires the judge to refer to what he conceives to be the views of the community at large. This does not mean that evidence of the public's perception of the repute of the administration of justice, which Professor Gibson suggested could be presented in the form of public opinion polls (above, pp. 236-47), will be determinative of the issue (see *Therens*, supra, pp. 653-54). The position is different with respect to obscenity, for example, where the court must assess the level of tolerance of the community, whether or not it is reasonable, and may consider public opinion polls: *R. v. Prairie Schooner News Ltd.* (1970), 1 C.C.C. (2d) 251 at 266 (Man. C.A.), cited in *Towne Cinema Theatres Ltd. v. R.*, [1985] 1 S.C.R. 494 at 513. It would be unwise, in my respectful view, to adopt a similar attitude with respect to the Charter. Members of the public generally become conscious of the importance of protecting the rights and freedoms of accused only when they are in some way brought closer to the system either personally or through the experience of friends or family. Professor Gibson recognized the danger of leaving the exclusion of evidence to uninformed members of the public when he stated at p. 246:

> The ultimate determination must be with the courts, because they provide what is often the only effective shelter for individuals and unpopular minorities from the shifting winds of public passion.

The Charter is designed to protect the accused from the majority, so the enforcement of the Charter must not be left to that majority.

The approach I adopt may be put figuratively in terms of the reasonable person test proposed by Professor Yves-Marie Morissette in his article "The Exclusion of Evidence under the *Canadian Charter of Rights and Freedoms*: What to Do and What Not to Do" (1984), 29 McGill L.J. 521, at p. 538. In applying s. 24(2), he suggested that the relevant question is: "Would the admission of the evidence bring the administration of justice into disrepute in the eyes of a reasonable man, dispassionate and fully apprised of the circumstances of the case?" The reasonable person is usually the average person in the community, but only when that community's current mood is reasonable.

The decision is thus not left to the untrammelled discretion of the judge. In practice, as Professor Morissette wrote [at p. 538], the reasonable person test is there to require of judges that they "concentrate on what they do best: finding within themselves, with cautiousness and impartiality, a basis for their own decisions, articulating their reasons carefully and accepting review by a higher court where it occurs." It serves as a reminder to each individual judge that his discretion is grounded in community values and, in particular, long-term community values. He should not render a decision that would be unacceptable to the community when that community is not being wrought with passion or otherwise under passing stress due to current events. In effect, the judge will have met this test if the judges of the Court of Appeal will decline to interfere with his decision, even though they might have decided the matter differently, using the well-known statement that they are of the view that the decision was not unreasonable.

In determining whether the admission of evidence would bring the administration of justice into disrepute, the judge is directed by s. 24(2) to consider "all the circumstances". The factors which are to be considered and balanced have been listed by many courts in the country (see in particular Anderson J.A. in *R. v. Cohen* (1983), 33 C.R. (3d) 151 (B.C. C.A.); Howland C.J.O. in *R. v. Simmons* (1984), 45 O.R. (2d) 609 (C.A.); Philp J.A. in *R. v. Pohoretsky; R. v. Ramage; R. v. L.A.R.*, [1985] 3 W.W.R. 289 (C.A.); MacDonald J. in *R. v. Dyment* (1986), 49 C.R. (3d) 338 (P.E.I. C.A.), and Lambert J.A. in *R. v. Gladstone*, [1985] 6 W.W.R. 504 (B.C. C.A.)), and by Seaton J.A. in this case. The factors that the courts have most frequently considered include:

— What kind of evidence was obtained?

— What Charter right was infringed?

— Was the Charter violation serious or was it of a merely technical nature?

— Was it deliberate, wilful or flagrant, or was it inadvertent or committed in good faith?

— Did it occur in circumstances of urgency or necessity?

— Were there other investigatory techniques available?

— Would the evidence have been obtained in any event?

— Is the offence serious?

— Is the evidence essential to substantiate the charge?

— Are other remedies available?

I do not wish to be seen as approving this as an exhaustive list of the relevant factors, and I would like to make some general comments as regard these factors. As a matter of personal preference, I find it useful to group the factors according to the way in which they affect the repute of the administration of justice. Certain of the factors listed are relevant in determining the effect of the admission of the evidence on the fairness of the trial. The trial is a key part of the administration of justice, and the fairness of Canadian trials is a major source of the repute of the system and is now a right guaranteed by s. 11(d) of the Charter. If the admission of the evidence in some way affects the fairness of the trial, then the admission of the evidence would *tend* to bring the administration of justice into disrepute and, subject to a consideration of the other factors, the evidence generally should be excluded.

It is clear to me that the factors relevant to this determination will include the nature of the evidence obtained as a result of the violation and the nature of the right violated and not so much the manner in which the right was violated. Real evidence that was obtained in a manner that violated the Charter will rarely operate unfairly for that reason alone. The real evidence existed irrespective of the violation of the Charter and its use does not render the trial unfair. However, the situation is very different with respect to cases where, after a violation of the Charter, the accused is conscripted against himself through a confession or other evidence emanating from him. The use of such evidence would render the trial unfair, for it did not exist prior to the violation and it strikes at one of the fundamental tenets of a fair trial, the right against self-incrimination. Such evidence will generally arise in the context of an infringement of the right to counsel. Our decisions in *Therens*, supra, and *Clarkson v. R.*, [1986] 1 S.C.R. 383, are illustrative of this. The use of self-incriminating evidence obtained following a denial of the right to counsel will generally go to the very fairness of the trial and should generally be excluded. Several Courts of Appeal have also emphasized this distinction between pre-existing real evidence and self-incriminatory evidence created following a breach of the Charter: see *Dumas v. R.* (1985), 41 Alta. L.R. (2d) 348 (C.A.); *R. v. Strachan* (1986), 49 C.R. (3d) 289 (B.C. C.A.), and *R. v. Dairy Supplies Ltd.*, Man. C.A., 13th January 1987 [now reported [1987] 2 W.W.R. 661]. It may also be relevant, in certain circumstances, that the evidence would have been obtained in any event without the violation of the Charter.

There are other factors which are relevant to the seriousness of the Charter violation and thus to the disrepute that will result from judicial acceptance of evidence obtained through that violation. As Le Dain J. wrote in *Therens* at p. 652:

The relative seriousness of the constitutional violation has been assessed in the light of whether it was committed in good faith, or was inadvertent or of a merely technical nature, or whether it was deliberate, wilful or flagrant. Another relevant consideration is whether the action which constituted the constitutional violation was motivated by urgency or necessity to prevent the loss or destruction of the evidence.

I should add that the availability of other investigatory techniques and the fact that the evidence could have been obtained without the violation of the Charter tend to render the Charter violation more serious. We are considering the actual conduct of the authorities and the evidence must not be admitted on the basis that they could have proceeded otherwise and obtained the evidence properly. In fact, their failure to proceed properly when that option was open to them tends to indicate a blatant disregard for the Charter which is a factor supporting the exclusion of the evidence.

The final relevant group of factors consists of those that relate to the effect of excluding the evidence. The question under s. 24(2) is whether the system's repute will be better served by the admission or the exclusion of the evidence, and it is thus necessary to consider any disrepute that may result from the exclusion of the evidence. In my view, the administration of justice would be brought into disrepute by the exclusion of evidence essential to substantiate the charge, and thus the acquittal of the accused, because of a trivial breach of the Charter. Such disrepute would be greater if the offence was more serious. I would thus agree with Professor Morissette that evidence is more likely to be excluded if the offence is less serious (above, pp. 529-31). I hasten to add, however, that if the admission of the evidence would result in an unfair trial, the seriousness of the offence could not render that evidence admissible. If any relevance is to be given to the seriousness of the offence in the context of the fairness of the trial, it operates in the opposite sense: the more serious the offence, the more damaging to the system's repute would be an unfair trial.

Finally, a factor which, in my view, is irrelevant is the availability of other remedies. Once it has been decided that the administration of justice would be brought into disrepute by the admission of the evidence, the disrepute will not be lessened by the existence of some ancillary remedy: see Gibson, above, at p. 261.

I would agree with Howland C.J.O. in *Simmons*, supra, that we should not gloss over the words of s. 24(2) or attempt to substitute any other test for s. 24(2). At least at this early stage of the Charter's development, the guidelines set out are sufficient and the actual decision to admit or exclude is as important as the statement of any test. Indeed, the test will only take on concrete meaning through our disposition of cases. However, I should at this point add some comparative comment as regards the test I enunciated in *Rothman*, supra, a pre-Charter confession case dealing with the resort to "tricks", which was coined in the profession as the "community shock test". That test has been applied to s. 24(2) by many courts, including the lower courts in this case. I still am of the view that the resort to tricks that are not in the least unlawful, let alone in violation of the Charter, to obtain a statement should not result in the exclusion of a free and voluntary statement unless the trick resorted to is a dirty trick, one that shocks the community. That is a very high threshold, higher, in my view, than that to be attained to bring the administration of justice into disrepute in the context of a violation of the Charter.

There are two reasons why the threshold for exclusion under s. 24(2) is lower. The first, an obvious one, is that, under s. 24(2), there will have been a violation of the most important law in the land, as opposed to the absence of any unlawful behaviour as a result of the resort to tricks in *Rothman*.

The second reason is based on the language of s. 24(2). Indeed, while both the English text of s. 24(2) and *Rothman* use the words "*would* bring the administration of justice into disrepute", the French versions are very different. The French text of s. 24(2) provides "*est susceptible de* déconsidérer l'administration de la justice", which I would translate as "*could* bring the administration of justice into disrepute". This is supportive of a somewhat lower threshold than the English text. As Dickson J. (as he then was) wrote in *Hunter v. Southam Inc.*, supra, at p. 157:

> Since the proper approach to the interpretation of the *Charter of Rights and Freedoms* is a purposive one, before it is possible to assess the reasonableness or unreasonableness of the impact of a search or of a statute authorizing a search, it is first necessary to specify the purpose underlying s. 8: in other words, to delineate the nature of the interests it is meant to protect.

As one of the purposes of s. 24(2) is to protect the right to a fair trial, I would favour the interpretation of s. 24(2) which better protects that right, the less onerous French text. Most courts which have considered the issue have also come to this conclusion: see Gibson at pp. 63 and 234-35. Section 24(2) should thus be read as "the evidence shall be excluded if it is established that, having regard to all the circumstances, the admission of it in the proceedings *could* bring the administration of justice into disrepute". This is a less onerous test than *Rothman*, where the French translation of the test in our reports, "ternirait l'image de la justice", clearly indicates that the resort to the word "would" in the test "would bring the administration of justice into disrepute" means just that.

CONCLUSION

As discussed above, we must determine in this case whether the evidence should be excluded on the record as it stands at present.

The evidence obtained as a result of the search was real evidence and, while prejudicial to the accused as evidence tendered by the Crown usually is, there is nothing to suggest that its use at the trial would render the trial unfair. In addition, it is true that the cost of excluding the evidence would be high: someone who was found guilty at trial of a relatively serious offence will evade conviction. Such a result could bring the administration of justice into disrepute. However, the administration of justice would be brought into greater disrepute, at least in my respectful view, if this court did not exclude the evidence and dissociate itself from the conduct of the police in this case which, always on the assumption that the officer merely had suspicions, was a flagrant and serious violation of the rights of an individual. Indeed, we cannot accept that police officers take flying tackles at people and seize them by the throat when they do not have reasonable and probable grounds to believe that those people are either dangerous or handlers of drugs. Of course, matters might well be clarified in this case if and when the police officer is offered at a new trial an opportunity to explain the grounds, if any, that he had for doing what he did. But if the police officer does not then disclose additional grounds for his behaviour, the evidence must be excluded.

I would allow the appeal and order a new trial.

[McIntyre J. dissented.]

How practical and valid is the distinction of Lamer J. between evidence which affects the fairness of the trial and evidence that does not, such as real evidence? See R.J. Delisle, "*Collins*: An Unjustified Distinction" (1987), 56 C.R. (3d) 216.

For a highly critical analysis of the Supreme Court's record, see David M. Paciocco, "The Judicial Repeal of s. 24(2) and the Development of the Canadian Exclusionary Rule", (1990) 32 Crim. L.Q. 326. For results of an empirical survey of public attitudes to exclusion when presented with various scenarios, see A.W. Bryant, "Public Attitudes to the Exclusion of Evidence", (1990) 69 Can. Bar Rev. 1.

In *Hebert*, considered above under Right to Silence, Justice Sopinka, writing on the exclusionary rule, offered a thought:

> As Lamer J. pointed out in *Collins*, any impingement on trial fairness strikes at the heart of the reputation of the administration of justice. But the Crown has submitted in the present case that the good faith of the police officers who arranged for the deception of the appellant, relying on the authority of *Rothman*, supra, is a significant factor in favour of receiving the evidence. For myself, I fail to see how the good faith or otherwise of the investigating officers can cure, so to speak, an unfair trial. This court's cases on s. 24(2) point clearly, in my opinion, to the conclusion that, where impugned evidence falls afoul of the first set of factors set out by Lamer J. in *Collins* (trial fairness), the admissibility of such evidence cannot be saved by resort to the second set of factors (the seriousness of the violation). These two sets of factors are alternative grounds for the *exclusion* of evidence, and not alternative grounds for the *admission* of evidence. It seems odd indeed to assert that evidence the admission of which would render a trial unfair ought to be admitted because the police officer thought he was doing his job. From the accused's perspective (whose trial is ex hypothesi proceeding unfairly), it makes little difference the the police officer has a clean conscience in the execution of his duty. This no doubt accounts for the language of exclusion in this court's cases on the issue, which seems to contemplate a direct progression from (a) the admission of such evidence, to (b) an adverse effect on the fairness of the trial, to (c) the disrepute of the administration of justice.

This *obiter dictum* was quoted with approval by Justice Iacobucci, speaking for six judges in *R. v. Elshaw*, [1991] 3 S.C.R. 24, 7 C.R. (4th) 333, 67 C.C.C. (3d) 97 (S.C.C.), who, in excluding incriminating statements of the accused taken in violation of his right to counsel, wrote:

A violation of rights which jeopardizes the fairness of the trial cannot be 'saved' by mitigating factors (such as the good faith of the police).

Later, in *R. v. Broyles*, [1991] 3 S.C.R. 595, 9 C.R. (4th) 1, 68 C.C.C. (3d) 308 (S.C.C.), Justice Iacobucci, writing for a unanimous seven person court, excluding statements taken in violation of the accused's right to silence, similarly wrote:

> As I indicated in *Elshaw*, supra, I agree with the reasons of Sopinka J. in *Hebert*, supra, that, at least where the fairness of the trial has been affected by the admission of tainted evidence, good faith on the part of the police cannot reduce the seriousness of the violation.

A leading decision on the meaning of "obtained by" in section 24(2) is *Burlingham:*

R. v. BURLINGHAM
[1995] 2 S.C.R. 206, 38 C.R. (4th) 265, 97 C.C.C. (3d) 385 (S.C.C.)

For the facts and ruling that there had been a s. 10(*b*) violation, see earlier under Right to Counsel. The 6-1 majority, over the sole dissent of L'Heureux-Dubé J., further held that the evidence as to the finding of the gun, including the voluntary statement made by the accused to his girlfriend, should be excluded under s. 24(2):

IACOBUCCI J. (La Forest, Sopinka, Cory, and Major JJ. concurring):—

. . .

It appears that, when the s. 24(2) analysis was first developed by this Court in R. v. Collins, the impact of the evidence on the fairness of the trial was determined to be the most important consideration under s. 24(2) in terms of triggering the exclusionary effect of the Charter remedy.

In *R. v. Collins*, Lamer J. also noted that self-incriminatory evidence obtained as a result of a Charter breach (i.e., evidence where the accused is conscripted against him- or herself through a confession or other evidence emanating from him or her) will generally go to the fairness of the trial and should generally be excluded. It was expressly held that such evidence will generally arise in the context of an infringement of the right to counsel. Trial unfairness strikes at the heart of the reputation of the administration of justice: *R. v. Hebert, supra*, at pp. 207-8; see also J. Sopinka, S.N. Lederman and A.W. Bryant, *The Law of Evidence in Canada* (1992), at p. 407, "[o]nce impugned evidence has been found to come within the trial fairness rationale, exclusion is virtually certain to follow".

On the other hand, Lamer J. noted that the admission of real evidence obtained in a manner that violates the Charter will rarely operate unfairly for that reason alone. This conclusion militates against the exclusion of the gun in the case at bar. However, I find that, in jurisprudence subsequent to *R. v. Collins*, this Court has consistently shied away from the differential treatment of real evidence. For example, in *R. v. Ross*, [1989] 1 S.C.R. 3, at p. 16, Lamer C.J. emphasized that the admissibility of evidence under s. 24(2) depended ultimately not on its nature as real or testimonial, but on whether or not it would only have been found with the compelled assistance of the accused:

> the use of any evidence that could not have been obtained but for the participation of the accused in the construction of the evidence for the purposes of the trial would tend to render the trial process unfair.

These comments are apposite to the case at bar. Further, I draw attention to the conclusions of La Forest J. in *R. v. Colarusso*, [1994] 1 S.C.R. 20, at p. 74, where it was noted that the mere fact that impugned evidence is classified as either real or conscriptive should not in and of itself be determinative.

The exclusion of real evidence was specifically dealt with in the decision of this Court in *R. v. Mellenthin*, [1992] 3 S.C.R. 615. In *R. v. Mellenthin*, the admission into evidence of the drugs—despite their status as real evidence—would have certainly affected the trial's fairness because they would not have been found without the improper conduct. The drugs were consequently deemed inadmissible.

· · ·

I suggest that it is appropriate to commence the consideration of what evidence should or should not be excluded from the trial process with the evidence obtained most proximate to the Charter breach and then work towards evidence arising more remotely therefrom. Since the trial judge deemed Burlingham's confession to be inadmissible, the contested evidence most proximate to the breach is the finding of the gun. As shall become evident, this gun would never have been found were it not for the unconstitutional conduct by the police officers. In any event, in terms of formulating this analysis, it must be kept in mind that there may be times (as in this case) where more remote evidence might not be admitted if its admission would have the same effect as admitting the most proximate evidence.

As mentioned earlier, I find that the derivative real evidence, the gun, would not have been found but for the information improperly obtained through the s. 10(*b*) breach. The question is not even whether such evidence would, on a balance of probabilities, have otherwise been located. The gun was at the bottom of the frozen Kootenay River and the only person who knew of its location was the appellant.

· · ·

I also share McEachern C.J.'s view that the appellant's statement to Ms. Hall that he had directed the police to the location of the gun can be classified as derivative evidence. It is true, as Cumming J.A. points out in his concurring majority opinion below, that the appellant made this statement voluntarily and that Hall was not a person in authority. However, even though the statement may have not have been "caused" directly by the breach, it was certainly made as a result of that breach. The statements to Hall flowed from the appellant's understandably confused state of mind stemming from the 10(*b*) violations and the critical decisions he had made in the absence of counsel. The appellant was still under the erroneous impression that the "deal" was on. The statement was made the morning after the appellant had been unconstitutionally conscripted to provide evidence against himself. He had never been properly informed of his right to counsel and it cannot be said with any degree of conviction that he would have made the same statement to Hall had he been duly advised of his constitutional rights. In fact, he would have had nothing to say to Hall had he not been improperly conscripted to provide evidence against himself by the police in the first place. For this reason, the rights violation had much more than, as characterized by L'Heureux-Dubé, J., simply an incidental effect on the making of the impugned statement.

. . .

It is now necessary to focus more directly on the issues of proximity and remoteness. In this regard, the decision of this Court in *R. v. Strachan*, [1988] 2 S.C.R. 980, at pp. 1005-6, is helpful to this analysis.

R. v. Strachan concerned the admissibility of evidence (marijuana) obtained as a result of a valid search during which the accused's right to counsel was violated. Dickson C.J.C. made it clear that a strict causal analysis is not necessary in a s. 24(2) analysis and that the presence of a temporal connection is not determinative. He stated at pp. 1005-6:

> In my view, all of the pitfalls of causation may be avoided by adopting an approach that focuses on the entire chain of events during which the *Charter* violation occurred and the evidence was obtained... A temporal link between the infringement of the *Charter* and the discovery of the evidence figures prominently in this assessment, particularly where the *Charter* violation and the discovery of the evidence occur in the course of a single transaction . . . [However] [t]here can be no hard and fast rule for determining when evidence obtained following the infringement of a *Charter* right becomes too remote.

Seen in light of Dickson C.J.'s comments in *R. v. Strachan*, it appears that the problem with Cumming J.A.'s reasoning with respect to the statement to Hall is that he fails to recognize the important connection between the content of the statement and the s. 10(*b*) violation. The fact is that the Crown sought to introduce the statement at trial precisely because it allowed it to do indirectly what the trial judge had ruled the Crown could not do directly: introduce evidence that the appellant knew where the gun was hidden. In this regard, the inclusion of the statement to Hall would directly affect the fairness of the trial, which is a key consideration in affecting the repute of the justice system, despite the fact that the statement was but remotely connected to the unconstitutional conduct. In effect, excluding the gun while including the statements effectively eviscerates the Charter of most of its protective value to the accused in this case; including both would totally eliminate any such value.... Furthermore, I note that in two recent decisions this Court has concluded that, in cases of including evidence flowing from a s. 10(*b*) violation, the onus lies upon the Crown to demonstrate on a balance of probabilities that, regarding the unfairness of the trial component of the test under s. 24(2), the accused would not have consulted counsel even if properly advised: *R. v. Bartle, supra*; *R. v. Pozniak*, [1994] 3 S.C.R. 310. The Crown has clearly not met this burden, nor even the less onerous requirements stipulated in earlier jurisprudence.

Moreover, the serious nature of the Charter breach in this case also supports the conclusion that the administration of justice would be brought into disrepute by the admission of the evidence.... In this case, it is clear that the violation was wilful and flagrant. It is also clear, as discussed earlier, that there was no element of urgency. Indeed, as McEachern C.J. notes, the police actually created an artificial situation of urgency in order to trick the accused into accepting the deal without first consulting a lawyer.

As to the third branch of the *Collins* test, I am satisfied that the effect of excluding the evidence on the reputation of the administration of justice will be incidental and far outweighed by the negative consequences that would follow were this unconstitutional evidence to be included. I realize that the appellant stands accused of a serious offence. However, as shall become evident in my disposition of this matter, the end result of allowing this appeal is not the issuance of a stay, but the ordering of a new trial in which the accused will have to meet the lawful evidence adduced against him. All that is required is the holding of the constitutionally mandated fair trial that should have occurred in the first place, and would have occurred were it not for the misconduct of the law enforcement agents.

Consequently, a new trial should be ordered in which the impugned evidence will not be admitted, namely: (1) the Hall testimony regarding the appellant's recounting of the events of the night of January 4, 1985; (2) evidence that police divers had found the gun in the river; (3) the Biddlecome and Lewis testimony identifying the murder weapon at trial; and (4) the gun itself. I add that, as was found at trial, the appellant's confession as well as his gestures and directions to the police with regard to the location of the gun are equally inadmissible. The Crown, if it chooses, can properly introduce the rest of the evidence it has adduced against the accused, including, as noted by McEachern C.J., the evidence of Biddlecome and Lewis that the accused had possession of a sawed off .410 shotgun shortly before the disappearance of Ms. Worms as well as Hall's testimony that the accused had told her he was actually present when Biddlecome had beaten and killed Ms. Worms.

. . .

Given the seriousness of the *Charter* violations, I agree with McEachern C.J. that this is not a case where the curative effect of s. 686(1)(b)(iii) is appropriate since the admission of the unconstitutionally obtained evidence at trial amounted, in my mind, to a "substantial wrong" toward both the accused as well as the administration of justice: *R. v. Elshaw*, supra. After all, the improperly obtained evidence formed a critical component of the Crown's case and it cannot be said that there is no reasonable possibility that the verdict would have been different were this evidence to have been properly excluded at trial: *R. v. Bevan*, [1993] 2 S.C.R. 599. This is not a case that fits into the small exception mentioned in *R. v. Elshaw*, *supra*, at p. 46, where the curative provision could apply notwithstanding that evidence should have been excluded under s. 24(2). Unlike in *R. v. Hodge* (1993), 133 N.B.R. (2d) 240 [C.A.], where the curative provision was applied because the evidence excluded under s. 24(2) could not have factored very significantly in the conviction of the accused, I find that there was a reasonable possibility that the impugned evidence in this case (a murder weapon and evidence that the accused took the police to find that weapon) could have weighed significantly in his conviction.

The trial judge's instruction to the jury reproduced by L'Heureux-Dubé, J. does not alter my view in this regard.

On a broader note, I am reluctant to open the door to the possibility that it shall become commonplace for an accused to prove a *Charter* breach sufficient to impugn the repute of the administration of justice and then have s. 686(1)(b)(iii) deny that person the opportunity to have a fair trial in which he or she shall face evidence obtained in a constitutional manner. Consideration should be given to limiting the *Elshaw* exception only to cases in which it can be shown beyond a reasonable doubt that the impugned evidence excluded under s. 24(2) in light of a *Charter* violation did not contribute at all to the original verdict. Focus is thus made on whether the unconstitutionally conscripted evidence in any way influenced the verdict. See David M. Tanovich, "Can the Improper Admission of Evidence Under the Charter Ever be Cured?" (1994), 32 C.R. (4th) 82.

Since preparing the above, I have had the benefit of reading the reasons of Sopinka J. regarding the manner in which the Court has been applying s. 24(2) of the *Charter* since the *Collins* decision. I concur with his reasons.

L'Heureux-Dubé J. agreed that the police conduct constituted a serious violation of the s. 10(*b*) Charter right to counsel. But she was of the opinion that the voluntary statement of the accused to his girlfriend and the finding of the murder weapon should not be excluded under s. 24(2). According to L'Heureux-Dubé J., a material gap had developed between the views of the community and those of the Court with respect to the exclusion of unconstitutionally obtained evidence. She felt this was attributable to the broad interpretation that the Court had given to the term "trial fairness" in the first branch of the *Collins* test, and the virtually absolute exclusionary consequences that follow from a finding of "trial unfairness". The court was digging itself into a hole. For her, this approach to "trial fairness" was inconsistent with the first principles laid down by the Court in *Collins* and with the courts' obligation under s. 24(2) to adjudicate upon the exclusion of the impugned evidence "having regard to all the circumstances". The Court should adopt an approach to s. 24(2) which looks both to reliability and the integrity of the judicial justice system which found its genesis in Lamer J.'s influential remarks in *Rothman*, its inspiration in the wording and historical context of s. 24(2), and its application in *Collins*. Under the Reliability Principle anything done by the authorities to cast doubt on the reliability of the evidence should almost inevitably be excluded, although consideration should still be had of the other two branches of the *Collins* test. Such evidence would render the trial unfair. Where the evidence is reliable, evidence could still be excluded under the Fairness Principle which relates to the impact of the seriousness of the rights violation on the reputation of the justice system. Contrary to the view of Sopinka J., this distinguished the approach from that in *Wray*. If the judge has concluded that the evidence should be excluded under one of the first two principles, the third branch of the *Collins* test involved an inquiry into whether the value to society of admitting the evidence outweighs the prejudice to societal and individual interests that can flow from admission. Would the long-term values of the community, assuming it to be reasonable, dispassionate and fully informed, be shocked by exclusion? Justice Sopinka responded.

SOPINKA J. (Cory, Iacobucci and Major JJ. concurring):—

. . .

The jurisprudence of this Court with respect to s. 24(2), subsequent to *Collins*, has generally evolved with due respect for stare decisis but also with due regard for the fact that as an early comprehensive statement of principles, it did not purport to be exhaustive or immutable. . . . It is apparent that the words "conscripted against himself through a confession or other evidence emanating from him" [in *Collins*] necessitated further definition in subsequent cases. Whether it was ever so intended, it soon became apparent that real evidence and evidence emanating from the accused were not mutually exclusive categories of evidence. . . . The rationale for this view is that it is unfair for the Crown to make out its case in whole or in part by the use of evidence that it obtained in breach of the rights of the accused and involving his or her participation. The participation of the accused in providing incriminating evidence involving a breach of *Charter* rights is the ingredient that tends to render the trial unfair as he or she is not under any obligation to assist the Crown to secure a conviction. Serious breaches of the *Charter* which do not involve the participation of the accused may result in the exclusion of the evidence under the second branch of the *Collins* test.

. . .

My colleague's criticism is with respect to the kind of evidence that can result in an unfair trial. In her view, only the admission of evidence that is not reliable by reason of some connection with state action amounting to a *Charter* breach can render the trial unfair (the "reliability principle"). . . . I have great difficulty in appreciating how the application of these two principles as suggested by my colleague constitutes a return to *Collins*. Nowhere in *Collins* is the fairness of the trial equated with the reliability of the evidence. The description used in *Collins* as to the kind of evidence that could render a trial unfair was "a confession or other evidence emanating from him". Leaving aside the words "or other evidence emanating from him", even the admissibility of a "confession" is not determined solely on the basis of reliability. Prior to the *Charter* and at common law, reliability ceased to be the exclusive basis for excluding confessions. See *R. v. Rothman*, [1981] S.C.R. 640, *R. v. Hebert*, [1990] 2 S.C.R. 151, especially at p. 207, *R. v. Whittle*, [1994] 2 S.C.R. 914, at p. 932, and *R. v. Sang*, [1980] A.C. 402. It could hardly be suggested that exclusion of involuntary confessions did not relate to the fairness of the trial. The reliability principle would, therefore, impose a more restrictive exclusionary rule than that which existed at common law. Its preoccupation with the probative value of the evidence would also appear to be a close relative of the rule in *R. v. Wray*, [1971] S.C.R. 272 . . . *Wray* was widely criticized, has not been followed by this Court and was not the basis for the exclusionary power adopted by the *Charter* in s. 24(2).

It is not accurate to characterize the first branch of the *Collins* test as an automatic rule of exclusion with respect to all self-incriminating evidence. While a finding that admission of illegally obtained evidence would render the trial unfair will result in exclusion, the Court must first conclude that "in all the circumstances" the admission of the evidence would render the trial unfair.

. . .

The distinction that was made in *Collins* between real evidence and evidence emanating from the accused was based, at least in part, on the rationale that real evidence (or things) can be discovered without the participation of the accused. They pre-existed the state action which is called into question, and were there to be discovered by investigative means not involving the accused. If the evidence was discoverable without the participation of the accused, then it has the attributes of real evidence. Conversely, evidence that clearly emanates from the accused such as statements has not been subjected to the discoverability analysis. While it can be argued that when an accused has been denied the right to counsel under s. 10(*b*), an inquiry could be made as to whether the accused would have acted differently had his *Charter* rights been observed, the Court has generally refused to enter into such an inquiry. Unless the right to counsel is waived by the accused, such a breach generally results in the exclusion of the evidence.

Gonthier J. decided that the reasons of L'Heureux-Dubé J., read together with the comments of Sopinka J., contributed to a proper understanding of the principles governing the exclusion of evidence under s. 24(2). He was not prepared to apply the curative provision of s. 686(1)(B)(iii). For him, the extreme egregious conduct of the police cast a pall on the perception of fairness of the whole trial process and constituted a substantial wrong for which the proper remedy was a new trial.

The L'Heureux-Dubé J. position is not as radical a departure as it first seems as she supports the *Collins* approach. Her major complaint is that all three factors should always be considered. There is indeed much to be said for this point of view. However it seems clear that L'Heureux-Dubé J. *would* ensure that the exclusion of evidence is very rare in her focus on reliability and her view that under the third group of factors the test should be whether exclusion would shock the community. Iacobucci J. and Sopinka J. reply that if there is no real possibility of exclusion of evidence obtained in violation of a Charter right, Charter rights would have little meaning. **With whom do you agree?**

. . .

The issue of the connection between the violation and the obtaining of the evidence has received subsequent attention from the Supreme Court. In particular, the Court has ruled on the issue of whether previous violations may taint the subsequent obtaining of evidence that was on its own obtained in a constitutional fashion. In *R. v. Wittwer*, [2008] 2 S.C.R. 235, 57 C.R. (6th) 205, 231 C.C.C. (3d) 97, there had been two prior interrogations that violated section 10(b) of the Charter. In a third interrogation that was otherwise constitutionally proper, the officer found it necessary to refer to the previous interviews. This was sufficient to taint the third statement and result in its exclusion. The leading passage is now that of Justice Fish speaking for a unanimous Court in *R. v. Wittwer*, as follows:

> In considering whether a statement is tainted by an earlier Charter breach, the courts have adopted a purposive and generous approach. It is unnecessary to establish a strict causal relationship between the breach and the subsequent statement. The statement will be tainted if the breach and the impugned statement can be said to be part of the same transaction or course of conduct: *Strachan*, at p. 1005. The required connection between the breach and the subsequent statement may be "temporal, contextual, causal or a combination of the three": *R. v. Plaha* (2004), 189 O.A.C. 376, at para. 45. A connection that is merely "remote" or "tenuous" will not suffice: *R. v. Goldhart*, [1996] 2 S.C.R. 463, at para. 40; *Plaha*, at para. 45. (para. 21)

As an example of remoteness, see: *R. v. Archambault* (2012), 91 C.R. (6th) 381 (Que. C.A.), application/notice of appeal (2012), 2012 CarswellQue 10764 (S.C.C.) in which the Court found that there was not the requisite link between obtaining the evidence and a denial of the right to counsel. The accused had been detained without counsel for 5 1/2 hours while a search warrant was executed. The trial judge was held to have wrongly excluded the evidence even though the Charter breaches were rightly held to have been serious.

. . .

We have seen that in *Collins*, Chief Justice Lamer identified as a "matter of personal taste" three groups of factors to be considered. Under the first grouping where an accused had been conscripted against himself the trial would be rendered unfair and the evidence should generally be excluded. The second factor was the seriousness of the breach and the third the effect of admission or exclusion on the administration of justice.

Ten years later, Justice Cory, speaking for a 5-4 majority in *R. v. Stillman*, [1997] 1 S.C.R. 607, 5 C.R. (5th) 1, 113 C.C.C. (3d) 321 at para. 80, refused to change course and held that conscriptive evidence is generally inadmissible — because of its presumed impact on trial fairness — unless it would have been independently discovered. For several years, the effect of *Stillman* was the drawing of a bright line: conscripted evidence was almost always excluded and non-conscripted evidence almost always included. A satisfactory definition of conscription also proved elusive. In *Stillman*, Justice Cory described conscription broadly as a process in which the accused is "compelled to participate in the creation or discovery of the evidence," and also as a narrow category approach of compelled incrimination "by means of a statement, the use of the body or the production of bodily samples".

Courts tended to rely on the category test when defining conscription. Especially in the case of statements, this leads to strange results. Where a statement by accused to the police was obtained in violation of the right to counsel guarantee in section 10(b) but there was no issue of voluntariness, in what sense could the accused be said to have been compelled? Similarly, it was difficult to say that an accused was compelled in the case of minor breaches of the right to counsel or where the police had no opportunity to provide the right because the accused made a spontaneous outburst.

The ruling of the Canadian Supreme Court in *R. v. Grant*, 66 C.R. (6th) 1, 245 C.C.C. (3d) 1, [2009] 2 S.C.R. 353 (S.C.C.), handed down on July 17, 2009 after having been on reserve for 15 months, and the companion ruling in *R. v. Harrison*, 66 C.R. (6th) 105, 245 C.C.C. (3d) 86, [2009] 2 S.C.R. 494 (S.C.C.) are bellwether rulings on the approach to deciding whether evidence obtained in violation of the Charter should be excluded under section 24(2). In *Grant* a 6-1 majority abandoned the *Collins/Stillman* approach and asserted a discretionary approach with revised criteria and emphasis. Much of the voluminous prior Supreme Court and lower court jurisprudence on section 24(2) over the past 27 years bacame of little moment. The Court has arrived at a discretionary approach to s. 24(2) free of rigid categories but placing special emphasis on the factor of seriousness of the breach rather than the seriousness of the offence or the reliability of the evidence. The same criteria are to be applied to all cases of Charter breach.

R. v. GRANT
66 C.R. (6th) 1, 245 C.C.C. (3d) 1, [2009] 2 S.C.R. 353 (S.C.C.)

Three officers were on patrol at mid-day in an area in Toronto where four schools had a history of student assaults, robberies and drug offences occurring over the lunch hour. Two plainclothes officers driving an unmarked car noticed the accused, an 18 year-old black man, walk by them in a manner they considered suspicious. He stared at them and fidgeted with his coat and pants. They asked a uniformed officer to have a chat with him. That officer was on directed patrol to maintain high visibility presence to provide student reassurance and to deter crime. The uniformed officer stood in his path, told him to keep his hands in front, and began to question him. He was first asked "what was going on" and for his name and address. The plainclothes officers arrived and stood behind the uniformed officer. The questioning turned to whether or not he had ever been arrested and whether "he had anything on him he that he shouldn't". He responded that he had a small amount of marijuana. When the officer asked if there was anything else, he admitted he had a firearm. The officer arrested him and searched him, finding marihuana and a loaded revolver. Grant was charged with five firearms offences.

We earlier saw that the majority of the Supreme Court held that the accused was detained without reasonable suspicion and that his Charter rights under ss. 9 and 10(b) had been violated.

The Court then turned to a re-consideration of section 24(2) principles.

Per McLACHLIN C.J. and CHARRON J. (LeBel, Binnie, Fish and Abella JJ. concurring):—

B. Exclusion of the Evidence

1. Background

[59] When must evidence obtained in violation of a person's Charter rights be excluded? Section 24(2) of the Charter provides the following answer:

> Where, in proceedings under subsection (1), a court concludes that evidence was obtained in a manner that infringed or denied any rights or freedoms guaranteed by this Charter, the evidence shall be excluded if it is established that, having regard to all the circumstances, the admission of it in the proceedings would bring the administration of justice into disrepute.

[60] The test set out in s. 24(2) — what would bring the administration of justice into disrepute having regard to all the circumstances — is broad and imprecise. The question is what considerations enter into making this determination. In *Collins* and in *R. v. Stillman*, [1997] 1 S.C.R. 607, this Court endeavoured to answer this question. The *Collins / Stillman* framework, as interpreted and applied in subsequent decisions, has brought a measure of certainty to the s. 24(2) inquiry. Yet the analytical method it imposes and the results it sometimes produces have been criticized as inconsistent with the language and objectives of s. 24(2). In order to understand these criticisms, it is necessary to briefly review the holdings in *Collins* and *Stillman*.

[61] In Collins, the Court (per Lamer J., as he then was) proceeded by grouping the factors to be considered under s. 24(2) into three categories: (1) whether the evidence will undermine the fairness of the trial by effectively conscripting the accused against himself or herself; (2) the seriousness of the Charter breach; and (3) the effect of excluding the evidence on the long-term repute of the administration of justice. While Lamer J. acknowledged that these categories were merely a "matter of personal preference" (p. 284), they quickly became formalized as the governing test for s. 24(2).

[62] *Collins* shed important light on the factors relevant to determining admissibility of Charter-violative evidence under s. 24(2). However, the concepts of trial fairness and conscription under the first branch of *Collins* introduced new problems of their own. Moreover, questions arose about what work (if any) remained to be done under the second and third categories, once conscription leading to trial unfairness had been found. Finally, issues arose as to how to measure the seriousness of the breach under the second branch and what weight, if any, should be put on the seriousness of the offence charged in deciding whether to admit evidence.

[63] The admission of physical or "real" evidence obtained from the body of the accused in breach of his or her Charter rights proved particularly problematic. Ten years after *Collins*, the Court revisited this question in *Stillman*. The majority held that evidence obtained in breach of the Charter should, at the outset of the s. 24(2) inquiry, be classified as either "conscriptive" or "non-conscriptive". Evidence would be classified as conscriptive where "an accused, in violation of his Charter rights, is

compelled to incriminate himself at the behest of the state by means of a statement, the use of the body or the production of bodily samples": Stillman, at para. 80, per Cory J. The category of conscriptive evidence was also held to include real evidence discovered as a result of an unlawfully conscripted statement. This is known as derivative evidence.

[64] *Stillman* held that conscriptive evidence is generally inadmissible — because of its presumed impact on trial fairness — unless if it would have been independently discovered. Despite reminders that "all the circumstances" must always be considered under s. 24(2) (see *R. v. Burlingham*, [1995] 2 S.C.R. 206, per Sopinka J., *R. v. Orbanski*, 2005 SCC 37, [2005] 2 S.C.R. 3, per LeBel J.), *Stillman* has generally been read as creating an all-but-automatic exclusionary rule for non-discoverable conscriptive evidence, broadening the category of conscriptive evidence and increasing its importance to the ultimate decision on admissibility.

[65] This general rule of inadmissibility of all non-discoverable conscriptive evidence, whether intended by *Stillman* or not, seems to go against the requirement of s. 24(2) that the court determining admissibility must consider "all the circumstances". The underlying assumption that the use of conscriptive evidence always, or almost always, renders the trial unfair is also open to challenge. In other contexts, this Court has recognized that a fair trial "is one which satisfies the public interest in getting at the truth, while preserving basic procedural fairness to the accused": *R. v. Harrer*, [1995] 3 S.C.R. 562, at para. 45. It is difficult to reconcile trial fairness as a multifaceted and contextual concept with a near-automatic presumption that admission of a broad class of evidence will render a trial unfair, regardless of the circumstances in which it was obtained. In our view, trial fairness is better conceived as an overarching systemic goal than as a distinct stage of the s. 24(2) analysis.

[66] This brief review of the impact of *Collins* and *Stillman* brings us to the heart of our inquiry on this appeal: clarification of the criteria relevant to determining when, in "all the circumstances", admission of evidence obtained by a Charter breach "would bring the administration of justice into disrepute".

2. Overview of a Revised Approach to Section 24(2)

[67] The words of s. 24(2) capture its purpose: to maintain the good repute of the administration of justice. The term "administration of justice" is often used to indicate the processes by which those who break the law are investigated, charged and tried. More broadly, however, the term embraces maintaining the rule of law and upholding Charter rights in the justice system as a whole.

[68] The phrase "bring the administration of justice into disrepute" must be understood in the long-term sense of maintaining the integrity of, and public confidence in, the justice system. Exclusion of evidence resulting in an acquittal may provoke immediate criticism. But s. 24(2) does not focus on immediate reaction to the individual case. Rather, it looks to whether the overall repute of the justice system, viewed in the long term, will be adversely affected by admission of the evidence. The inquiry is objective. It asks whether a reasonable person, informed of all relevant circumstances and the values

underlying the Charter, would conclude that the admission of the evidence would bring the administration of justice into disrepute.

[69] Section 24(2)'s focus is not only long-term, but prospective. The fact of the Charter breach means damage has already been done to the administration of justice. Section 24(2) starts from that proposition and seeks to ensure that evidence obtained through that breach does not do further damage to the repute of the justice system.

[70] Finally, s. 24(2)'s focus is societal. Section 24(2) is not aimed at punishing the police or providing compensation to the accused, but rather at systemic concerns. The s. 24(2) focus is on the broad impact of admission of the evidence on the long-term repute of the justice system.

[71] A review of the authorities suggests that whether the admission of evidence obtained in breach of the Charter would bring the administration of justice into disrepute engages three avenues of inquiry, each rooted in the public interests engaged by s. 24(2), viewed in a long-term, forward-looking and societal perspective. When faced with an application for exclusion under s. 24(2), a court must assess and balance the effect of admitting the evidence on society's confidence in the justice system having regard to: (1) the seriousness of the Charter-infringing state conduct (admission may send the message the justice system condones serious state misconduct), (2) the impact of the breach on the Charter-protected interests of the accused (admission may send the message that individual rights count for little), and (3) society's interest in the adjudication of the case on its merits. The court's role on a s. 24(2) application is to balance the assessments under each of these lines of inquiry to determine whether, considering all the circumstances, admission of the evidence would bring the administration of justice into disrepute. These concerns, while not precisely tracking the categories of considerations set out in *Collins*, capture the factors relevant to the s. 24(2) determination as enunciated in *Collins* and subsequent jurisprudence.

(a) Seriousness of the Charter-Infringing State Conduct

[72] The first line of inquiry relevant to the s. 24(2) analysis requires a court to assess whether the admission of the evidence would bring the administration of justice into disrepute by sending a message to the public that the courts, as institutions responsible for the administration of justice, effectively condone state deviation from the rule of law by failing to dissociate themselves from the fruits of that unlawful conduct. The more severe or deliberate the state conduct that led to the Charter violation, the greater the need for the courts to dissociate themselves from that conduct, by excluding evidence linked to that conduct, in order to preserve public confidence in and ensure state adherence to the rule of law.

[73] This inquiry therefore necessitates an evaluation of the seriousness of the state conduct that led to the breach. The concern of this inquiry is not to punish the police or to deter Charter breaches, although deterrence of Charter breaches may be a happy consequence. The main concern is to preserve public confidence in the rule of law and its processes. In order to determine the effect of admission of the evidence on public confidence in the justice system, the

court on a s. 24(2) application must consider the seriousness of the violation, viewed in terms of the gravity of the offending conduct by state authorities whom the rule of law requires to uphold the rights guaranteed by the Charter.

[74] State conduct resulting in Charter violations varies in seriousness. At one end of the spectrum, admission of evidence obtained through inadvertent or minor violations of the Charter may minimally undermine public confidence in the rule of law. At the other end of the spectrum, admitting evidence obtained through a wilful or reckless disregard of Charter rights will inevitably have a negative effect on the public confidence in the rule of law, and risk bringing the administration of justice into disrepute.

[75] Extenuating circumstances, such as the need to prevent the disappearance of evidence, may attenuate the seriousness of police conduct that results in a Charter breach: *R. v. Silveira*, [1995] 2 S.C.R. 297, per Cory J. "Good faith" on the part of the police will also reduce the need for the court to disassociate itself from the police conduct. However, ignorance of Charter standards must not be rewarded or encouraged and negligence or wilful blindness cannot be equated with good faith: *R. v. Genest*, [1989] 1 S.C.R. 59, at p. 87, per Dickson C.J.; *R. v. Kokesch*, [1990] 3 S.C.R. 3, at pp. 32-33, per Sopinka J.; *R. v. Buhay*, 2003 SCC 30, [2003] 1 S.C.R. 631, at para. 59. Wilful or flagrant disregard of the Charter by those very persons who are charged with upholding the right in question may require that the court dissociate itself from such conduct. It follows that deliberate police conduct in violation of established Charter standards tends to support exclusion of the evidence. It should also be kept in mind that for every Charter breach that comes before the courts, many others may go unidentified and unredressed because they did not turn up relevant evidence leading to a criminal charge. In recognition of the need for courts to distance themselves from this behaviour, therefore, evidence that the Charter-infringing conduct was part of a pattern of abuse tends to support exclusion.

(b) Impact on the Charter-Protected Interests of the Accused

[76] This inquiry focuses on the seriousness of the impact of the Charter breach on the Charter-protected interests of the accused. It calls for an evaluation of the extent to which the breach actually undermined the interests protected by the right infringed. The impact of a Charter breach may range from fleeting and technical to profoundly intrusive. The more serious the impact on the accused's protected interests, the greater the risk that admission of the evidence may signal to the public that Charter rights, however high-sounding, are of little actual avail to the citizen, breeding public cynicism and bringing the administration of justice into disrepute.

[77] To determine the seriousness of the infringement from this perspective, we look to the interests engaged by the infringed right and examine the degree to which the violation impacted on those interests. For example, the interests engaged in the case of a statement to the authorities obtained in breach of the Charter include the s. 7 right to silence, or to choose whether or not to speak to authorities (Hebert) — all stemming from the principle against self-incrimination: *R. v. White*, [1999] 2 S.C.R. 417, at para. 44. The more

serious the incursion on these interests, the greater the risk that admission of the evidence would bring the administration of justice into disrepute.

[78] Similarly, an unreasonable search contrary to s. 8 of the Charter may impact on the protected interests of privacy, and more broadly, human dignity. An unreasonable search that intrudes on an area in which the individual reasonably enjoys a high expectation of privacy, or that demeans his or her dignity, is more serious than one that does not.

(c) Society's Interest in an Adjudication on the Merits

[79] Society generally expects that a criminal allegation will be adjudicated on its merits. Accordingly, the third line of inquiry relevant to the s. 24(2) analysis asks whether the truth-seeking function of the criminal trial process would be better served by admission of the evidence, or by its exclusion. This inquiry reflects society's "collective interest in ensuring that those who transgress the law are brought to trial and dealt with according to the law": *R. v. Askov*, [1990] 2 S.C.R. 1199, at pp. 1219-20. Thus the Court suggested in *Collins* that a judge on a s. 24(2) application should consider not only the negative impact of admission of the evidence on the repute of the administration of justice, but the impact of failing to admit the evidence.

[80] The concern for truth-seeking is only one of the considerations under a s. 24(2) application. The view that reliable evidence is admissible regardless of how it was obtained (see *R. v. Wray*, [1971] S.C.R. 272) is inconsistent with the Charter's affirmation of rights. More specifically, it is inconsistent with the wording of s. 24(2), which mandates a broad inquiry into all the circumstances, not just the reliability of the evidence.

[81] This said, public interest in truth-finding remains a relevant consideration under the s. 24(2) analysis. The reliability of the evidence is an important factor in this line of inquiry. If a breach (such as one that effectively compels the suspect to talk) undermines the reliability of the evidence, this points in the direction of exclusion of the evidence. The admission of unreliable evidence serves neither the accused's interest in a fair trial nor the public interest in uncovering the truth. Conversely, exclusion of relevant and reliable evidence may undermine the truth-seeking function of the justice system and render the trial unfair from the public perspective, thus bringing the administration of justice into disrepute.

[82] The fact that the evidence obtained in breach of the Charter may facilitate the discovery of the truth and the adjudication of a case on its merits must therefore be weighed against factors pointing to exclusion, in order to "balance the interests of truth with the integrity of the justice system": *Mann*, at para. 57, per Iacobucci J. The court must ask "whether the vindication of the specific Charter violation through the exclusion of evidence extracts too great a toll on the truth-seeking goal of the criminal trial": *R. v. Kitaitchik* (2002), 166 C.C.C. (3d) 14 (Ont. C.A.), at para. 47, per Doherty J.A.

[83] The importance of the evidence to the prosecution's case is another factor that may be considered in this line of inquiry. Like Deschamps J., we view this factor as corollary to the inquiry into reliability, in the following limited sense. The admission of evidence of questionable reliability is more likely to bring the

administration of justice into disrepute where it forms the entirety of the case against the accused. Conversely, the exclusion of highly reliable evidence may impact more negatively on the repute of the administration of justice where the remedy effectively guts the prosecution.

[84] It has been suggested that the judge should also, under this line of inquiry, consider the seriousness of the offence at issue. Indeed, Deschamps J. views this factor as very important, arguing that the more serious the offence, the greater society's interest in its prosecution (para. 226). In our view, while the seriousness of the alleged offence may be a valid consideration, it has the potential to cut both ways. Failure to effectively prosecute a serious charge due to excluded evidence may have an immediate impact on how people view the justice system. Yet, as discussed, it is the long-term repute of the justice system that is s. 24(2)'s focus. As pointed out in Burlingham, the goals furthered by s. 24(2) "operate independently of the type of crime for which the individual stands accused" (para. 51). And as Lamer J. observed in *Collins*, "[t] he Charter is designed to protect the accused from the majority, so the enforcement of the Charter must not be left to that majority" (p. 282). The short-term public clamour for a conviction in a particular case must not deafen the s. 24(2) judge to the longer-term repute of the administration of justice. Moreover, while the public has a heightened interest in seeing a determination on the merits where the offence charged is serious, it also has a vital interest in having a justice system that is above reproach, particularly where the penal stakes for the accused are high.

[85] To review, the three lines of inquiry identified above — the seriousness of the Charter-infringing state conduct, the impact of the breach on the Charter-protected interests of the accused, and the societal interest in an adjudication on the merits — reflect what the s. 24(2) judge must consider in assessing the effect of admission of the evidence on the repute of the administration of justice. Having made these inquiries, which encapsulate consideration of "all the circumstances" of the case, the judge must then determine whether, on balance, the admission of the evidence obtained by Charter breach would bring the administration of justice into disrepute.

[86] In all cases, it is the task of the trial judge to weigh the various indications. No overarching rule governs how the balance is to be struck. Mathematical precision is obviously not possible. However, the preceding analysis creates a decision tree, albeit more flexible than the *Stillman* self-incrimination test. We believe this to be required by the words of s. 24(2). We also take comfort in the fact that patterns emerge with respect to particular types of evidence. These patterns serve as guides to judges faced with s. 24(2) applications in future cases. In this way, a measure of certainty is achieved. Where the trial judge has considered the proper factors, appellate courts should accord considerable deference to his or her ultimate determination.

3. Application to Different Kinds of Evidence

[87] We have seen that a trial judge on a s. 24(2) application for exclusion of evidence obtained in breach of the Charter must consider whether admission

would bring the administration of justice into disrepute, having regard to the results of the three lines of inquiry identified above.

[88] We now turn to some of the types of evidence the cases have considered.

(a) Statements by the Accused

[89] Statements by the accused engage the principle against self-incrimination, "one of the cornerstones of our criminal law": *R. v. Henry*, 2005 SCC 76, [2005] 3 S.C.R. 609, at para. 2. This Court in *White*, at para. 44, per Iacobucci J., described the principle against self-incrimination as "an overarching principle within our criminal justice system, from which a number of specific common law and Charter rules emanate, such as the confessions rule, and the right to silence". The principle also informs "more specific procedural protections such as, for example, the right to counsel in s. 10(b), the right to non-compellability in s. 11(c), and the right to use immunity set out in s. 13". Residual protection for the principle against self-incrimination is derived from s. 7.

[90] This case concerns s. 24(2). However, it is important to note at the outset that the common law confessions rule, quite apart from s. 24(2), provides a significant safeguard against the improper use of a statement against its maker. Where a statement is made to a recognized person in authority, regardless of whether its maker is detained at the time, it is inadmissible unless the Crown can establish beyond a reasonable doubt that it was made voluntarily. Only if such a statement survives scrutiny under the confessions rule and is found to be voluntary, does the s. 24(2) remedy of exclusion arise. Most commonly, this will occur because of added protections under s. 10(b) of the Charter.

[91] There is no absolute rule of exclusion of Charter-infringing statements under s. 24(2), as there is for involuntary confessions at common law. However, as a matter of practice, courts have tended to exclude statements obtained in breach of the Charter, on the ground that admission on balance would bring the administration of justice into disrepute.

[92] The three lines of inquiry described above support the presumptive general, although not automatic, exclusion of statements obtained in breach of the Charter.

[93] The first inquiry focusses on whether admission of the evidence would harm the repute of justice by associating the courts with illegal police conduct. Police conduct in obtaining statements has long been strongly constrained. The preservation of public confidence in the justice system requires that the police adhere to the Charter in obtaining statements from a detained accused.

[94] The negative impact on the justice system of admitting evidence obtained through police misconduct varies with the seriousness of the violation. The impression that courts condone serious police misconduct is more harmful to the repute of the justice system than the acceptance of minor or inadvertent slips.

[95] The second inquiry considers the extent to which the breach actually undermined the interests protected by the right infringed. Again, the potential to harm the repute of the justice system varies with the seriousness of the

impingement on the individual's protected interests. As noted, the right violated by unlawfully obtained statements is often the right to counsel under s. 10(b). The failure to advise of the right to counsel undermines the detainee's right to make a meaningful and informed choice whether to speak, the related right to silence, and, most fundamentally, the protection against testimonial self-incrimination. These rights protect the individual's interest in liberty and autonomy. Violation of these fundamental rights tends to militate in favour of excluding the statement.

[96] This said, particular circumstances may attenuate the impact of a Charter breach on the protected interests of the accused from whom a statement is obtained in breach of the Charter. For instance, if an individual is clearly informed of his or her choice to speak to the police, but compliance with s. 10(b) was technically defective at either the informational or implementational stage, the impact on the liberty and autonomy interests of the accused in making an informed choice may be reduced. Likewise, when a statement is made spontaneously following a Charter breach, or in the exceptional circumstances where it can confidently be said that the statement in question would have been made notwithstanding the Charter breach (see *R. v. Harper*, [1994] 3 S.C.R. 343), the impact of the breach on the accused's protected interest in informed choice may be less. Absent such circumstances, the analysis under this line of inquiry supports the general exclusion of statements taken in breach of the Charter.

[97] The third inquiry focusses on the public interest in having the case tried fairly on its merits. This may lead to consideration of the reliability of the evidence. Just as involuntary confessions are suspect on grounds of reliability, so may, on occasion, be statements taken in contravention of the Charter. Detained by the police and without a lawyer, a suspect may make statements that are based more on a misconceived idea of how to get out of his or her predicament than on the truth. This danger, where present, undercuts the argument that the illegally obtained statement is necessary for a trial of the merits.

[98] In summary, the heightened concern with proper police conduct in obtaining statements from suspects and the centrality of the protected interests affected will in most cases favour exclusion of statements taken in breach of the Charter, while the third factor, obtaining a decision on the merits, may be attenuated by lack of reliability. This, together with the common law's historic tendency to treat statements of the accused differently from other evidence, explains why such statements tend to be excluded under s. 24(2).

(b) Bodily Evidence

[99] Bodily evidence is evidence taken from the body of the accused, such as DNA evidence and breath samples. Section 8 of the Charter protects against unreasonable search and seizure, and hence precludes the state from obtaining such evidence in a manner that is unreasonable.

[100] The majority in *Stillman*, applying a capacious definition of conscription, held that bodily evidence is "conscriptive" and that its admission would affect

trial fairness. This resulted in a near-automatic exclusionary rule for bodily evidence obtained contrary to the Charter.

[101] *Stillman* has been criticized for casting the flexible "in all the circumstances" test prescribed by s. 24(2) into a straight-jacket that determines admissibility solely on the basis of the evidence's conscriptive character rather than all the circumstances; for inappropriately erasing distinctions between testimonial and real evidence; and for producing anomalous results in some situations: see, e.g., *Burlingham*, per L'Heureux-Dubé J.; *R. v. Schedel* (2003), 175 C.C.C. (3d) 193 (B.C.C.A.), at paras. 67-72, per Esson J.A.; D. M. Paciocco, "Stillman, Disproportion and the Fair Trial Dichotomy under Section 24(2)" (1997), 2 Can. Crim. L.R. 163; R. Mahoney, "Problems with the Current Approach to s. 24(2) of the Charter: An Inevitable Discovery" (1999), 42 Crim. L.Q. 443; S. Penney, "Taking Deterrence Seriously: Excluding Unconstitutionally Obtained Evidence Under Section 24(2) of the Charter" (2004), 49 McGill L.J. 105; D. Stuart, Charter Justice in Canadian Criminal Law (4th ed. 2005), at p. 581. We will briefly review each of these criticisms.

[102] The first criticism is that the *Stillman* approach transforms the flexible "all the circumstances" test mandated by s. 24(2) into a categorical conscriptive evidence test. Section 24(2) mandates a broad contextual approach rather than an automatic exclusionary rule: D. M. Paciocco, "The Judicial Repeal of s. 24(2) and the Development of the Canadian Exclusionary Rule" (1989-90), 32 Crim. L.Q. 326; A. McLellan and B. P. Elman, "The Enforcement of the Canadian Charter of Rights and Freedoms: An Analysis of Section 24" (1983), 21 Alta. L. Rev. 205, at pp. 205-8; *Orbanski*, at para. 93. As stated in *Orbanski*, per LeBel J., the inquiry under s. 24(2) "amounts to finding a proper balance between competing interests and values at stake in the criminal trial, between the search for truth and the integrity of the trial . . . All the *Collins* factors remain relevant throughout this delicate and nuanced inquiry" (para. 94).

[103] A flexible, multi-factored approach to the admissibility of the evidence is required, not only by the wording of s. 24(2) but by the wide variation between different kinds of bodily evidence. The seriousness of the police conduct and the impact on the accused's rights of taking the bodily evidence, may vary greatly. Plucking a hair from the suspect's head may not be intrusive, and the accused's privacy interest in the evidence may be relatively slight. On the other hand, a body cavity or strip search may be intrusive, demeaning and objectionable. A one-size-fits-all conscription test is incapable of dealing with such differences in a way that addresses the point of the s. 24(2) inquiry — to determine if the admission of the evidence will bring the administration of justice into disrepute.

[104] Recent decisions suggest a growing consensus that the admissibility of bodily samples should not depend solely on whether the evidence is conscriptive: *R. v. Richfield* (2003), 178 C.C.C. (3d) 23 (Ont. C.A.), per Weiler J.A.; *R. v. Dolynchuk* (2004), 184 C.C.C. (3d) 214 (Man. C.A.), per Steel J.A.; *R. v. Banman*, 2008 MBCA 103, 236 C.C.C. (3d) 547, per MacInnes J.A. This Court in *R. v. S.A.B.*, 2003 SCC 60, [2003] 2 S.C.R. 678, dealing with the constitutionality of DNA warrant provisions in the Criminal Code,

acknowledged that the Charter concerns raised by the gathering of non-testimonial evidence are better addressed by reference to the interests of privacy, bodily integrity and human dignity, than by a blanket rule that by analogy to compelled statements, such evidence is always inadmissible. See also: L. Stuesser, "R. v. S.A.B.: Putting 'Self-Incrimination' in Context" (2004), 42 Alta. L. Rev. 543.

[105] The second and related objection to a simple conscription test for the admissibility of bodily evidence under s. 24(2) is that it wrongly equates bodily evidence with statements taken from the accused. In most situations, statements and bodily samples raise very different considerations from the point of view of the administration of justice. Equating them under the umbrella of conscription risks erasing relevant distinctions and compromising the ultimate analysis of systemic disrepute. As Professor Paciocco has observed, "in equating intimate bodily substances with testimony we are not so much reacting to the compelled participation of the accused as we are to the violation of the privacy and dignity of the person that obtaining such evidence involves" ("Stillman, Disproportion and the Fair Trial Dichotomy under Section 24(2)", at p. 170). Nor does the taking of a bodily sample trench on the accused's autonomy in the same way as may the unlawful taking of a statement. The pre-trial right to silence under s. 7, the right against testimonial self-incrimination in s. 11(c), and the right against subsequent use of self-incriminating evidence in s. 13 have informed the treatment of statements under s. 24(2). These concepts do not apply coherently to bodily samples, which are not communicative in nature, weakening self-incrimination as the sole criterion for determining their admissibility.

[106] A third criticism of the conscription test for admissibility of bodily evidence under s. 24(2) is that from a practical perspective, the conscriptive test has sometimes produced anomalous results, leading to exclusion of evidence that should, in principle and policy, be admitted: see Dolynchuk; *R. v. Shepherd*, 2007 SKCA 29, 218 C.C.C. (3d) 113, per Smith J.A. dissenting, aff'd 2009 SCC 35 (released concurrently); and *R. v. Padavattan* (2007), 223 C.C.C. (3d) 221 (Ont. S.C.J.), per Ducharme J. Notably, breath sample evidence tendered on impaired driving charges has often suffered the fate of automatic exclusion even where the breach in question was minor and would not realistically bring the administration of justice into disrepute. More serious breaches in other kinds of cases — for instance, those involving seizures of illegal drugs in breach of s. 8 — have resulted in admission on the grounds that the evidence in question was non-conscriptive. This apparent incongruity has justifiably raised concern.

[107] We conclude that the approach to admissibility of bodily evidence under s. 24(2) that asks simply whether the evidence was conscripted should be replaced by a flexible test based on all the circumstances, as the wording of s. 24(2) requires. As for other types of evidence, admissibility should be determined by inquiring into the effect admission may have on the repute of the justice system, having regard to the seriousness of the police conduct, the impact of the Charter breach on the protected interests of the accused, and the value of a trial on the merits.

[108] The first inquiry informing the s. 24(2) analysis — the seriousness of the Charter-infringing conduct — is fact-specific. Admission of evidence obtained by deliberate and egregious police conduct that disregards the rights of the accused may lead the public to conclude that the court implicitly condones such conduct, undermining respect for the administration of justice. On the other hand, where the breach was committed in good faith, admission of the evidence may have little adverse effect on the repute of the court process.

[109] The second inquiry assesses the danger that admitting the evidence may suggest that Charter rights do not count, thereby negatively impacting on the repute of the system of justice. This requires the judge to look at the seriousness of the breach on the accused's protected interests. In the context of bodily evidence obtained in violation of s. 8, this inquiry requires the court to examine the degree to which the search and seizure intruded upon the privacy, bodily integrity and human dignity of the accused. The seriousness of the intrusion on the accused may vary greatly. At one end of the spectrum, one finds the forcible taking of blood samples or dental impressions (as in *Stillman*). At the other end of the spectrum lie relatively innocuous procedures such as fingerprinting or iris-recognition technology. The greater the intrusion on these interests, the more important it is that a court exclude the evidence in order to substantiate the Charter rights of the accused.

[110] The third line of inquiry — the effect of admitting the evidence on the public interest in having a case adjudicated on its merits — will usually favour admission in cases involving bodily samples. Unlike compelled statements, evidence obtained from the accused's body is generally reliable, and the risk of error inherent in depriving the trier of fact of the evidence may well tip the balance in favour of admission.

[111] While each case must be considered on its own facts, it may be ventured in general that where an intrusion on bodily integrity is deliberately inflicted and the impact on the accused's privacy, bodily integrity and dignity is high, bodily evidence will be excluded, notwithstanding its relevance and reliability. On the other hand, where the violation is less egregious and the intrusion is less severe in terms of privacy, bodily integrity and dignity, reliable evidence obtained from the accused's body may be admitted. For example, this will often be the case with breath sample evidence, whose method of collection is relatively non-intrusive.

(c) Non-bodily Physical Evidence

[112] The three inquiries under s. 24(2) will proceed largely as explained above. Again, under the first inquiry, the seriousness of the Charter-infringing conduct will be a fact-specific determination. The degree to which this inquiry militates in favour of excluding the bodily evidence will depend on the extent to which the conduct can be characterized as deliberate or egregious.

[113] With respect to the second inquiry, the Charter breach most often associated with non-bodily physical evidence is the s. 8 protection against unreasonable search and seizure: see, e.g., *Buhay*. Privacy is the principal interest involved in such cases. The jurisprudence offers guidance in evaluating the extent to which the accused's reasonable expectation of privacy was

infringed. For example, a dwelling house attracts a higher expectation of privacy than a place of business or an automobile. An illegal search of a house will therefore be seen as more serious at this stage of the analysis.

[114] Other interests, such as human dignity, may also be affected by search and seizure of such evidence. The question is how seriously the Charter breach impacted on these interests. For instance, an unjustified strip search or body cavity search is demeaning to the suspect's human dignity and will be viewed as extremely serious on that account: *R. v. Simmons*, [1988] 2 S.C.R. 495, at pp. 516-17, per Dickson C.J.; *R. v. Golden*, 2001 SCC 83, [2001] 3 S.C.R. 679. The fact that the evidence thereby obtained is not itself a bodily sample cannot be seen to diminish the seriousness of the intrusion.

[115] The third inquiry, whether the admission of the evidence would serve society's interest in having a case adjudicated on its merits, like the others, engages the facts of the particular case. Reliability issues with physical evidence will not generally be related to the Charter breach. Therefore, this consideration tends to weigh in favour of admission.

(d) Derivative Evidence

[116] The class of evidence that presents the greatest difficulty is evidence that combines aspects of both statements and physical evidence — physical evidence discovered as a result of an unlawfully obtained statement. The cases refer to this evidence as derivative evidence. This is the type of evidence at issue in this case.

[117] We earlier saw that at common law, involuntary confessions are inadmissible. The common law's automatic exclusion of involuntary statements is based on a sense that it is unfair to conscript a person against himself or herself and, most importantly, on a concern about the unreliability of compelled statements. However, the common law drew the line of automatic inadmissibility at the statements themselves and not the physical or "real" evidence found as a result of information garnered from such statements. Because reliability was traditionally the dominant focus of the confessions rule, the public interest in getting at the truth through reliable evidence was seen to outweigh concerns related to self-incrimination: *Wray* and *R. v. St. Lawrence*, [1949] O.R. 215 (H.C.J.).

[118] Section 24(2) of the Charter implicitly overruled the common law practice of always admitting reliable derivative evidence. Instead, the judge is required to consider whether admission of derivative evidence obtained through a Charter breach would bring the administration of justice into disrepute.

[119] The s. 24(2) jurisprudence on derivative physical evidence has thus far been dominated by two related concepts — conscription and discoverability. Physical evidence that would not have been discovered but for an inadmissible statement has been considered conscriptive and hence is inadmissible: *R. v. Feeney*, [1997] 2 S.C.R. 13, and *Burlingham*. The doctrine of "discoverability" has been developed in order to distinguish those cases in which the accused's conscription was necessary to the collection of the evidence, from those cases where the evidence would have been obtained in any event. In the former cases, exclusion was the rule, while in the latter, admission was more likely.

[120] The conscription-discoverability doctrine has been justifiably criticized as overly speculative and capable of producing anomalous results: D. Stuart, "Questioning the Discoverability Doctrine in Section 24(2) Rulings" (1996), 48 C.R. (4th) 351; *Hogg*, at section 41.8(d). In practice, it has proved difficult to apply because of its hypothetical nature and because of the fine-grained distinctions between the tests for determining whether evidence is "derivative" and whether it is "discoverable": see *Feeney*, at paras. 69-71.

[121] The existing rules on derivative evidence and discoverability were developed under the *Collins* trial fairness rationale. They gave effect to the insight that if evidence would have been discovered in any event, the accused's conscription did not truly cause the evidence to become available. The discoverability doctrine acquired even greater importance under *Stillman* where the category of conscriptive evidence was considerably enlarged. Since we have concluded that this underlying rationale should no longer hold and that "trial fairness" in the *Collins/Stillman* sense is no longer a determinative criterion for the s. 24(2) inquiry, discoverability should likewise not be determinative of admissibility.

[122] Discoverability retains a useful role, however, in assessing the actual impact of the breach on the protected interests of the accused. It allows the court to assess the strength of the causal connection between the Charter-infringing self-incrimination and the resultant evidence. The more likely it is that the evidence would have been obtained even without the statement, the lesser the impact of the breach on the accused's underlying interest against self-incrimination. The converse, of course, is also true. On the other hand, in cases where it cannot be determined with any confidence whether evidence would have been discovered in absence of the statement, discoverability will have no impact on the s. 24(2) inquiry.

[123] To determine whether the admission of derivative evidence would bring the administration of justice into disrepute under s. 24(2), courts must pursue the usual three lines of inquiry outlined in these reasons, taking into account the self-incriminatory origin of the evidence in an improperly obtained statement as well as its status as real evidence.

[124] The first inquiry concerns the police conduct in obtaining the statement that led to the real evidence. Once again, the extent to which this inquiry favours exclusion will depend on the factual circumstances of the breach: the more serious the state conduct, the more the admission of the evidence derived from it tends to undermine public confidence in the rule of law. Were the police deliberately and systematically flouting the accused's Charter rights? Or were the officers acting in good faith, pursuant to what they thought were legitimate policing policies?

[125] The second inquiry focuses on the impact of the breach on the Charter-protected interests of the accused. Where a statement is unconstitutionally obtained, in many cases the Charter right breached is the s. 10(b) right to counsel, which protects the accused's interest in making an informed choice whether or not to speak to authorities. The relevant consideration at this stage will be the extent to which the Charter breach impinged upon that interest in a free and informed choice. Where that interest was significantly compromised

by the breach, this factor will strongly favour exclusion. In determining the impact of the breach, the discoverability of the derivative evidence may also be important as a factor strengthening or attenuating the self-incriminatory character of the evidence. If the derivative evidence was independently discoverable, the impact of the breach on the accused is lessened and admission is more likely.

[126] The third inquiry in determining whether admission of the derivative evidence would bring the administration into disrepute relates to society's interest in having the case adjudicated on its merits. Since evidence in this category is real or physical, there is usually less concern as to the reliability of the evidence. Thus, the public interest in having a trial adjudicated on its merits will usually favour admission of the derivative evidence.

[127] The weighing process and balancing of these concerns is one for the trial judge in each case. Provided the judge has considered the correct factors, considerable deference should be accorded to his or her decision. As a general rule, however, it can be ventured that where reliable evidence is discovered as a result of a good faith infringement that did not greatly undermine the accused's protected interests, the trial judge may conclude that it should be admitted under s. 24(2). On the other hand, deliberate and egregious police conduct that severely impacted the accused's protected interests may result in exclusion, notwithstanding that the evidence may be reliable.

[128] The s. 24(2) judge must remain sensitive to the concern that a more flexible rule may encourage police to improperly obtain statements that they know will be inadmissible, in order to find derivative evidence which they believe may be admissible. The judge should refuse to admit evidence where there is reason to believe the police deliberately abused their power to obtain a statement which might lead them to such evidence. Where derivative evidence is obtained by way of a deliberate or flagrant Charter breach, its admission would bring the administration of justice into further disrepute and the evidence should be excluded.

4. Application to this Case

[129] The issue is whether the gun produced by Mr. Grant after Toronto police stopped and questioned him should be excluded from the evidence at his trial. The trial judge held that had a Charter breach been established, he would not have excluded the evidence. While the trial judge's s. 24(2) conclusion may not command deference where an appellate court reaches a different conclusion on the breach itself (see *R. v. Grant*, [1993] 3 S.C.R. 223, at pp. 256-57, per Sopinka J.; *R. v. Harris*, 2007 ONCA 574, 225 C.C.C. (3d) 193, at p. 212), the trial judge's underlying factual findings must be respected, absent palpable and overriding error.

[130] Here, the admissibility of Mr. Grant's incriminatory statements is not in issue, the statements having no independent evidentiary value. The only issue is the admission or exclusion of the gun. This falls to be determined in accordance with the inquiries described earlier.

[131] At the outset, it is necessary to consider whether the gun was "obtained in a manner" that violated Mr. Grant's Charter rights: see *R. v. Strachan*, [1988] 2

S.C.R. 980, and *R. v. Goldhart*, [1996] 2 S.C.R. 463. As explained above, we have concluded that Mr. Grant's rights under ss. 9 and 10(b) of the Charter were breached. The discovery of the gun was both temporally and causally connected to these infringements. It follows that the gun was obtained as a result of a Charter breach.

[132] Because the gun was discovered as a result of statements taken in breach of the Charter, it is derivative evidence. The question, as always, is whether its admission would bring the administration of justice into disrepute. To answer this question, it is necessary to consider the concerns that underlie the s. 24(2) analysis, as discussed above, in "all the circumstances" of the case, including the arbitrary detention and the breach of the right to counsel.

[133] We consider first the seriousness of the improper police conduct that led to the discovery of the gun. The police conduct here, while not in conformity with the Charter, was not abusive. There was no suggestion that Mr. Grant was the target of racial profiling or other discriminatory police practices. The officers went too far in detaining the accused and asking him questions. However, the point at which an encounter becomes a detention is not always clear, and is something with which courts have struggled. Though we have concluded that the police were in error in detaining the appellant when they did, the mistake is an understandable one. Having been under a mistaken view that they had not detained the appellant, the officers' failure to advise him of his right to counsel was similarly erroneous but understandable. It therefore cannot be characterized as having been in bad faith. Given that the police conduct in committing the Charter breach was neither deliberate nor egregious, we conclude that the effect of admitting the evidence would not greatly undermine public confidence in the rule of law. We add that the Court's decision in this case will be to render similar conduct less justifiable going forward. While police are not expected to engage in judicial reflection on conflicting precedents, they are rightly expected to know what the law is.

[134] The second inquiry under the s. 24(2) analysis focuses on whether the admission of the evidence would bring the administration of justice into disrepute from the perspective of society's interest in respect for Charter rights. This inquiry focuses on the impact of the breach on the accused's protected interests. Because the two infringed Charter rights protect different interests, it is necessary to consider them separately at this stage.

[135] The initial Charter violation was arbitrary detention under s. 9 of the Charter, curtailing Mr. Grant's liberty interest. This interaction, beginning as a casual conversation, quickly developed into a subtly coercive situation that deprived Mr. Grant of his freedom to make an informed choice as to how to respond. This is so, notwithstanding the fact that the detention did not involve any physical coercion and was not carried out in an abusive manner. We therefore conclude that the impact of this breach, while not severe, was more than minimal.

[136] The second Charter violation was breach of Mr. Grant's s. 10(b) right to counsel. Cst. Gomes, by his own admission, was probing for answers that would give him grounds for search or arrest. Far from being spontaneous utterances, the appellant's incriminating statements were prompted directly by

Cst. Gomes' pointed questioning. The appellant, in need of legal advice, was not told he could consult counsel.

[137] As discussed, discoverability remains a factor in assessing the impact of Charter breaches on Charter rights. The investigating officers testified that they would not have searched or arrested Mr. Grant but for his self-incriminatory statements. Nor would they have had any legal grounds to do so. Accordingly, the fact that the evidence was non-discoverable aggravates the impact of the breach on Mr. Grant's interest in being able to make an informed choice to talk to the police. He was in "immediate need of legal advice" (*Brydges*, at p. 206) and had no opportunity to seek it.

[138] Considering all these matters, we conclude that the impact of the infringement of Mr. Grant's rights under ss. 9 and 10(b) of the Charter was significant.

[139] The third and final concern is the effect of admitting the gun on the public interest in having a case adjudicated on its merits. The gun is highly reliable evidence. It is essential to a determination on the merits. The Crown also argues that the seriousness of the offence weighs in favour of admitting the evidence of the gun, so that the matter may be decided on its merits, asserting that gun crime is a societal scourge, that offences of this nature raise major public safety concerns and that the gun is the main evidence in the case. On the other hand, Mr. Grant argues that the seriousness of the offence makes it all the more important that his rights be respected. In the result, we do not find this factor to be of much assistance.

[140] To sum up, the police conduct was not egregious. The impact of the Charter breach on the accused's protected interests was significant, although not at the most serious end of the scale. Finally, the value of the evidence is considerable. These effects must be balanced in determining whether admitting the gun would put the administration of justice into disrepute. We agree with Laskin J.A. that this is a close case. The balancing mandated by s. 24(2) is qualitative in nature and therefore not capable of mathematical precision. However, weighing all these concerns, in our opinion the courts below did not err in concluding that the admission of the gun into evidence would not, on balance, bring the administration of justice into disrepute. The significant impact of the breach on Mr. Grant's Charter-protected rights weighs strongly in favour of excluding the gun, while the public interest in the adjudication of the case on its merits weighs strongly in favour of its admission. Unlike the situation in *R. v. Harrison*, 2009 SCC 34, the police officers here were operating in circumstances of considerable legal uncertainty. In our view, this tips the balance in favour of admission, suggesting that the repute of the justice system would not suffer from allowing the gun to be admitted in evidence against the appellant.

—————————

In lonely dissent Justice Deschamps expresses vigorous opposition to the majority's approach to section 24(2). It was inconsistent with the purpose of s. 24(2) of the Charter: to maintain public confidence in the administration of justice. The proposed test, by focussing the analysis on the conduct of the police in the first branch and on the interest of the accused in the second, and by attaching less importance to the seriousness of the offence in the third, did not give sufficient consideration to the long-term societal interest that must guide the judge in reaching a decision. Whether the evidence is reliable and whether it is essential or peripheral were in her view factors crucial to the maintenance of public confidence, as was the seriousness of the offence (Paras 223-226).

R. v. HARRISON
66 C.R. (6th) 105, 245 C.C.C. (3d) 86, [2009] 2 S.C.R. 494 (S.C.C.)

In *Harrison*, the accused and his friend were driving a rented sports utility vehicle from Vancouver to Toronto. In Ontario, a police officer on highway patrol noticed that the vehicle had no front licence plate. Only after activating his roof lights to pull it over did he realize that, because it was registered in Alberta, the vehicle did not require a front licence plate. The officer was informed by radio dispatch that the vehicle had been rented at the Vancouver airport. Even though he had no grounds to believe that any offence was being committed, the officer testified that abandoning the detention might have affected the integrity of the police in the eyes of observers. Having stopped the vehicle he asked the accused for his driver's license, which the accused was not able to find. The officer performed a CPIC check and found that the accused's license was suspended, and so he arrested him on that basis. He then decided to search the vehicle incident to that arrest, testifying at trial that he thought the license might be in the vehicle. He questioned the accused and the other passenger about the existence of drugs or weapons in the car, and eventually opened two large cardboard boxes in the rear compartment of the vehicle, finding 35 kg (77 pounds) of cocaine.

Per Chief Justice McLachlin (Binnie, LeBel, Fish, Abella and Charron JJ. concurring):—

[20] The Charter breaches in this case are clear. It is common ground that the appellant's rights under ss. 8 and 9 of the Charter were violated by the detention and search, as found by the trial judge. Given that the officer recognized prior to the detention that the appellant's S.U.V. did not require a front licence plate, he should not have made the initial stop. A vague concern for the "integrity" of the police, even if genuine, was clearly an inadequate reason to follow through with the detention. The subsequent search of the S.U.V. was not incidental to the appellant's arrest for driving under a suspension and was likewise in breach of the Charter. While an officer's "hunch" is a valuable investigative tool — indeed, here it proved highly accurate — it is no substitute for proper Charter standards when interfering with a suspect's liberty.

[21] Breaches of the Charter established, the question is whether the evidence thereby obtained should be excluded under s. 24(2) of the Charter. The test set out in s. 24(2) is simply stated: would the admission of the evidence bring the administration of justice into disrepute? *Grant* identifies three lines of inquiry

relevant to this determination. Once again, they are: (1) the seriousness of the Charter infringing state conduct (2) the impact of the breach on the Charter protected interests of the accused, and (3) society's interest in the adjudication of the case on its merits. I will discuss each of these in turn.

(a) Seriousness of the Charter-Infringing State Conduct

[22] At this stage the court considers the nature of the police conduct that infringed the Charter and led to the discovery of the evidence. Did it involve misconduct from which the court should be concerned to dissociate itself? This will be the case where the departure from Charter standards was major in degree, or where the police knew (or should have known) that their conduct was not Charter-compliant. On the other hand, where the breach was of a merely technical nature or the result of an understandable mistake, dissociation is much less of a concern.

[23] The trial judge found that the police officer's conduct in this case was "brazen", "flagrant" and "very serious". The metaphor of a spectrum used in *R. v. Kitaitchik* (2002), 166 C.C.C. (3d) 14 (Ont. C.A.), per Doherty J.A., may assist in characterizing police conduct for purposes of this s. 24(2) factor:

> Police conduct can run the gamut from blameless conduct, through negligent conduct, to conduct demonstrating a blatant disregard for Charter rights... What is important is the proper placement of the police conduct along that fault line, not the legal label attached to the conduct. [Citation omitted; para. 41.]

[24] Here, it is clear that the trial judge considered the Charter breaches to be at the serious end of the spectrum. On the facts found by him, this conclusion was a reasonable one. The officer's determination to turn up incriminating evidence blinded him to constitutional requirements of reasonable grounds. While the violations may not have been "deliberate", in the sense of setting out to breach the Charter, they were reckless and showed an insufficient regard for Charter rights. Exacerbating the situation, the departure from Charter standards was major in degree, since reasonable grounds for the initial stop were entirely non-existent.

[25] As pointed out by the majority of the Court of Appeal, there was no evidence of systemic or institutional abuse. However, while evidence of a systemic problem can properly aggravate the seriousness of the breach and weigh in favour of exclusion, the absence of such a problem is hardly a mitigating factor.

[26] I note that the trial judge found the officer's in-court testimony to be misleading. While not part of the Charter breach itself, this is properly a factor to consider as part of the first inquiry under the s. 24(2) analysis given the need for a court to dissociate itself from such behaviour. As Cronk J.A. observed, "the integrity of the judicial system and the truth seeking function of the courts lie at the heart of the admissibility inquiry envisaged under s. 24(2) of the Charter. Few actions more directly undermine both of these goals than misleading testimony in court from persons in authority" (para. 160).

[27] In sum, the conduct of the police that led to the Charter breaches in this case represented a blatant disregard for Charter rights. This disregard for

Charter rights was aggravated by the officer's misleading testimony at trial. The police conduct was serious, and not lightly to be condoned.

(b) Impact on the Charter Protected Interests of the Accused

[28] This factor looks at the seriousness of the infringement from the perspective of the accused. Did the breach seriously compromise the interests underlying the right(s) infringed? Or was the breach merely transient or trivial in its impact? These are among the questions that fall for consideration in this inquiry.

[29] In this case, the detention and the search had an impact on the appellant's liberty and privacy interests. The question is how that impact should be characterized.

[30] The majority of the Court of Appeal emphasized the relatively brief duration of the detention and the appellant's low expectation of privacy in the S.U.V., and concluded that the effect of the breach on the appellant was relatively minor. It is true that motorists have a lower expectation of privacy in their vehicles than they do in their homes. As participants in a highly regulated activity, they know that they may be stopped for reasons pertaining to highway safety — as in a drinking-and-driving roadblock, for instance. Had it not turned up incriminating evidence, the detention would have been brief. In these respects, the intrusion on liberty and privacy represented by the detention is less severe than it would be in the case of a pedestrian. Further, nothing in the encounter was demeaning to the dignity of the appellant.

[31] This said, being stopped and subjected to a search by the police without justification impacts on the motorist's rightful expectation of liberty and privacy in a way that is much more than trivial. As Iacobucci J. observed in *Mann*, the relatively non-intrusive nature of the detention and search "must be weighed against the absence of any reasonable basis for justification" (para. 56 (emphasis in original)). A person in the appellant's position has every expectation of being left alone — subject, as already noted, to valid highway traffic stops.

[32] I conclude that the deprivation of liberty and privacy represented by the unconstitutional detention and search was therefore a significant, although not egregious, intrusion on the appellant's Charter-protected interests.

(c) Society's Interest in an Adjudication on the Merits

[33] At this stage, the court considers factors such as the reliability of the evidence and its importance to the Crown's case.

[34] The evidence of the drugs obtained as a consequence of the Charter breaches was highly reliable. It was critical evidence, virtually conclusive of guilt on the offence charged. The evidence cannot be said to operate unfairly having regard to the truth-seeking function of the trial. While the charged offence is serious, this factor must not take on disproportionate significance. As noted in *Grant*, while the public has a heightened interest in seeing a determination on the merits where the offence charged is serious, the public also has a vital interest in a justice system that is beyond reproach, particularly where the penal stakes for the accused are high. With that caveat in mind, the

third line of inquiry under the s. 24(2) analysis favours the admission of the evidence as to do so would promote the public's interest in having the case adjudicated on its merits.

(d) Balancing the Factors

[35] I begin by summarizing my findings on the three factors in *Grant*. The police conduct in stopping and searching the appellant's vehicle without any semblance of reasonable grounds was reprehensible, and was aggravated by the officer's misleading testimony in court. The Charter infringements had a significant, although not egregious, impact on the Charter-protected interests of the appellant. These factors favour exclusion, the former more strongly than the latter. On the other hand, the drugs seized constitute highly reliable evidence tendered on a very serious charge, albeit not one of the most serious known to our criminal law. This factor weighs in favour of admission.

[36] The balancing exercise mandated by s. 24(2) is a qualitative one, not capable of mathematical precision. It is not simply a question of whether the majority of the relevant factors favour exclusion in a particular case. The evidence on each line of inquiry must be weighed in the balance, to determine whether, having regard to all the circumstances, admission of the evidence would bring the administration of justice into disrepute. Dissociation of the justice system from police misconduct does not always trump the truth seeking interests of the criminal justice system. Nor is the converse true. In all cases, it is the long-term repute of the administration of justice that must be assessed.

[37] In my view, when examined through the lens of the s. 24(2) analysis set out in *Grant*, the trial judge's reasoning in this case placed undue emphasis on the third line of inquiry while neglecting the importance of the other inquiries, particularly the need to dissociate the justice system from flagrant breaches of Charter rights. Effectively, he transformed the s. 24(2) analysis into a simple contest between the degree of the police misconduct and the seriousness of the offence.

[38] The trial judge placed great reliance on the Ontario Court of Appeal's decision in *Puskas*. However, the impact of the breach on the accused's interests and the seriousness of the police conduct were not at issue in *Puskas*; Moldaver J.A. opined that if there was a breach of s. 8, it was "considerably less serious than the trial judge perceived it to be", the police having fallen "minimally" short of the constitutional mark (para. 16). In those circumstances, the public interest in truth-seeking rightly became determinative.

[39] This case is very different. The police misconduct was serious; indeed, the trial judge found that it represented a "brazen and flagrant" disregard of the Charter. To appear to condone wilful and flagrant Charter breaches that constituted a significant incursion on the appellant's rights does not enhance the long-term repute of the administration of justice; on the contrary, it undermines it. In this case, the seriousness of the offence and the reliability of the evidence, while important, do not outweigh the factors pointing to exclusion.

[40] As Cronk J.A. put it, allowing the seriousness of the offence and the reliability of the evidence to overwhelm the s. 24(2) analysis "would deprive those charged with serious crimes of the protection of the individual freedoms afforded to all Canadians under the Charter and, in effect, declare that in the administration of the criminal law 'the ends justify the means'"(para. 150). Charter protections must be construed so as to apply to everyone, even those alleged to have committed the most serious criminal offences. In relying on *Puskas* in these circumstances, the trial judge seemed to imply that where the evidence is reliable and the charge is serious, admission will always be the result. As *Grant* makes clear, this is not the law.

[41] Additionally, the trial judge's observation that the Charter breaches "pale in comparison to the criminality involved" in drug trafficking risked the appearance of turning the s. 24(2) inquiry into a contest between the misdeeds of the police and those of the accused. The fact that a Charter breach is less heinous than the offence charged does not advance the inquiry mandated by s. 24(2). We expect police to adhere to higher standards than alleged criminals.

[42]   In summary, the price paid by society for an acquittal in these circumstances is outweighed by the importance of maintaining Charter standards. That being the case, the admission of the cocaine into evidence would bring the administration of justice into disrepute. It should have been excluded.

Appeal allowed; acquittal entered.

Deschamps J. delivered a lengthy dissent.

Several of the changes of direction and decisions in these pronouncements on section 24(2) deserve closer examination. Early Canadian commentary has been largely favourable: see especially Professors David Paciocco, Revisions to David Paciocco and Lee Stuesser, *The Law of Evidence* (5th ed., 2008, Irwin Law) (2009), Don Stuart, "Welcome Flexibility and Better Criteria from the Supreme Court of Canada for Exclusion of Evidence Obtained in Violation of the Canadian Charter of Rights and Freedoms" (2009) *Southwestern Journal of International Law* 101 and Tim Quigley, "Was it Worth the Wait? The Supreme Court's Approaches to Detention and Exclusion of Evidence": (2009) 67 C.R. (6th) 88. Professor Hamish Stewart, "The Grant Trilogy and the Right Against Self-incrimination" (2009) 67 C.R. (6th) 97 however expresses concerns that the Court has unduly lessened the right against self-incrimination. See too Penney, Rondinelli and Stribopoulos, *Criminal Procedure in Canada* (LexisNexis, 2011) pp. 557-573. David Paciocco, "Section 24(2): Lottery or Law — The Appreciable Limits of Purposive Reasoning" (2011) 58 Crim. L.Q. 1 is, however, less enthusiastic about the new regime and expresses concerns *inter alia* about too much discretion for trial judges and the discounting of the factor of seriousness of the offence.

Can the decision to exclude in *Harrison* but not in *Grant* be justified?

Abandoning Conscripted/non-conscripted Distinction

The 6-1 majority in *Grant* decided that it was time to abandon the *Collins/Stillman* framework for discretion.

Most Canadian academics and many judges will welcome the abandonment of the distinction between conscripted and non-conscripted evidence. See Paciocco and Quigley above. See also Ron Delisle, "Collins: An Unjustified Distinction" (1987) 56 C.R. (3d) 216, Stephen Coughlan, Criminal Procedure Cases in the Supreme Court of Canada": (1997) 13 *Supr. Court Rev.* (2nd), Michael Davies, "Alternative Approaches to the Exclusion of Evidence under s.24(2) of the Charter" (2002) 46 Crim.L.Q. 21, Steven Penney, "Taking Deterrence Seriously. Excluding Unconstitutionally Obtained Evidence Under Section 24(2) of the Charter", (2004) 49 McGill L.J.6 105. But see Hamish Stewart, above and Kent Roach, "The Evolving Fair Trial Test Under Section 24(2) of the Charter", (1996) 1 *Can.Crim.L.R.* 117. It is overly complex, arbitrary and rigid. Apart from the difficult issue of definition, different approaches had to be followed when considering conscripted and non-conscripted evidence, even in the same trial. Furthermore a breach relating to conscripted evidence is not necessarily more serious than a breach relating to non-conscripted evidence. There was no presumption of exclusion, for example, where a drug squad ransacks a private dwelling without bothering to get a warrant in deliberate violation of s. 8. Exclusion should not be based on artificial categories or inflexible rules. Instead, what should be at stake, as the majority held in *Grant*, is the integrity of the justice system in admitting evidence obtained in breach of the Charter where the breach was serious.

The abandonment of the *Collins/Stillman* trial fairness yardstick has admittedly set up an inconsistency with the separate discretion to exclude under s. 11(d) to ensure a fair trial which the Court recognized in *Harrer*. This rarely exercised discretion is mostly applied in trials in Canada where the Charter breach occurred outside our borders. The *Harrer* jurisprudence needs to be reconsidered and made consistent with *Grant*.

Seriousness of Violation rather than Seriousness of Offence is Key

Whether there will be more or less exclusion in future will likely only become evident after several years of applying *Grant*. The Court has clearly decided that evidence can no longer be excluded simply because it was conscripted — which may well result in less exclusion in breathalyser and bodily sample cases, for example. However favouring exclusion is the Court's important rulings that the seriousness of Charter violation is the first consideration and that the same analysis is to be applied whatever the seriousness of the offence. This is made especially clear by Chief Justice McLachlin speaking for the 6-1 majority in *R. v. Harrison*. **Do you agree with this view?**

Exclusionary Trend since *Grant* and *Harrison*

After some five years there can now be no doubt that the Supreme Court in *Grant* and *Harrison* has put in place a robust discretionary exclusion remedy for s. 24(2). Several surveys have consistently documented that across the country trial judges are likely to exclude for Charter violations in roughly two out of every three cases for all types of Charter breaches and whatever the type of evidence. See Mike Madden "Empirical Data on Section 24(2) under *R. v. Grant*" (2010), 78 C.R. (6th) 278 (see also in (2011), 14 *Can.Crim.L.Rev.* 229) and, for similar findings in Quebec, see Thierry Nadon, "Le paragraphe 24(2) de la Charte au Québec depuis Grant: si la tendance se maintient", (2011), 86 C.R. (6th) 33. The most comprehensive survey is now that of Ariane Asselin, "Trends for Exclusion of Evidence in 2012" (2013), 1 C.R. (7th) 74, which reports the major findings of her LL.M. thesis at Queen's "The Exclusionary Rule in Canada: Trends and Future Directions"; http://hdl.handle.net/1974/8244. Asselin analysed all s. 24(2) rulings in Canada for the year 2012 where Charter violations were found. She found an overall exclusion rate at trials of 73%. Almost half the exclusion occurred in Ontario. There was an 80% exclusion rate in B.C., 90% in Saskatchewan, 91% in Quebec and 100% in Newfoundland and Nova Scotia. There was far less exclusion in Manitoba and Alberta.

Appeal courts are much less likely to exclude although the *Grant* requirement of "considerable deference" to trial judges where there is no error in principle is being largely followed. Justin Milne, "Exclusion of Evidence Trends post *Grant*: Are Appeal Courts Deferring to Trial Judges" (2015) 19 *Can. Crim. L.R.* 373, surveyed appeal decisions between 2011 and 2014. He found that there was deference in only 60% of the cases and a preference to defer where the trial judge had admitted the evidence. The discrepancy between trial and appeal courts may be explained by the reality that courts of appeal are more likely to be confronted by selective Crown appeals against exclusion decisions by trial judges based on unreasonable errors.

The importance of this reality should not be exaggerated. In the vast majority of criminal trials across the country, Charter issues are not even raised and often, where they are, Charter violations are not found. But it is the reality that in hundreds of rulings each year where Charter violations are found, the s. 24(2) remedy of exclusion is now regularly invoked. In s. 24(2) cases it is clear that trial judges are to be concerned not only about truth concerning guilt or innocence, but also about the truth that police officers are often proved to be deliberately flouting, careless or ignorant about Charter standards. If there is a concern about exclusion of highly probative evidence the question should be directed against the apparently lax and ineffective training of police officers respecting Charter standards, even where they are clearly established. If the police learned to apply Charter standards there would be no possibility of exclusion.

There were indeed dangers in softening the exclusion remedy by adopting a test of "proportionality" between the seriousness of the violation and the seriousness of the offence. A criminal trial under a system of entrenched Charter rights for accused has to concern itself with the truth of police abuse and disregard of Charter standards, not just the truth of the accused's guilt. Without the remedy of exclusion in cases where the court considers the crime serious there would be a large number of criminal trials where the Charter will cease to provide protection. This could create public cynicism regarding the integrity of our system of law enforcement. There cannot be a *de facto* two-tier system where one zone is Charter-free and the police ends always justify the means. There must be a real risk of exclusion for serious Charter breaches even in cases of serious crimes, as the Supreme Court has now emphatically determined.

The first *Grant* factor of seriousness of the violation and the second factor of impact on Charter protected interests overlap in that the second factor also addressing the seriousness of the violation. The Court seems to anticipate problems with its new step two and gives extensive advice about how its three-part inquiry might be approached respecting statements by accused, bodily evidence, non-bodily physical evidence, and derivative evidence. However the Court is at pains to emphasise that the three *Grant* factors have to be applied to any type of evidence.

Ariane Asselin finds some surprises in the patterns of exclusion of different types of evidence:

> Particularly noteworthy are the rates of exclusion for specific types of evidence. The survey identifies a high level of exclusion for bodily evidence, including breath samples, and a lower rate of exclusion for testimonial evidence. Moreover, with respect to non-bodily physical evidence, the survey shows that the rate of exclusion for drugs is 20% higher than for guns. These results are surprising given the Supreme Court of Canada's comments in *Grant* about how exclusion could operate in relation to different types of evidence and its anticipation that certain patterns would emerge. The findings of this survey signal that the emerging patterns at the trial court level are perhaps not the ones intended by the SCC.

It seems clear that the Supreme Court did envisage less exclusion where breath evidence is obtained in violation of the Charter. In *Grant*, when dealing with bodily evidence, the Court observed that:

> where the violation is less egregious and the intrusion is less severe in terms of privacy, bodily integrity and dignity, reliable evidence obtained from the accused's body may be admitted. For example, this will often be the case with breath sample evidence, whose method of collection is relatively non-intrusive. [para 111]

A review of a number of 2010 rulings on exclusion of breathalyzer evidence showed some judges relying on para. 111 not to exclude, but that there was a much stronger trend to exclude where the breach was found to be deliberate, negligent or ignorant of Charter rights. In *R. v. Au-Yeung* (2010), 75 C.R. (6th) 78 (Ont. S.C.J.), and cases there referred to, Justice Ducharme of the Ontario Superior Court noted the passing remark in para. 111 but decided that the third *Grant* factor of the public interest in trial on the merits where the evidence is reliable must not trump the key *Grant* factor of seriousness of the breach. The breach in *Au-Yeung* was held to be serious and to result in exclusion as the officers were ignorant of their powers contrary to the rule of law emphasised in *Grant*. Many trial judges across the country have excluded and continue to exclude breath evidence based on serious breaches of ss. 8, 9, 10(a) and 10(b). In *R. v. Taylor*, [2014] 2 S.C.R. 495, 311 C.C.C. (3d) 285, 12 C.R. (7th) 1 (S.C.C.), Justice Abella, speaking for the Supreme Court, excluded blood samples in an impaired driving case because of a violation of s. 10(b). There is no mention of para. 111. But see the judgment of Rosenberg J.A. for the Ontario Court of Appeal in *R. v. MacMillan* (2013), 296 C.C.C. (3d) 277, 1 C.R. (7th) 90 (Ont. C.A.), which relied on para. 111 not to exclude in an impaired driving case and criticism of this trend by Campbell J. in *R. v. Rehill*, 2015 ONSC 6025 (Ont. S.C.J.).

Reliability and Importance of Evidence Not Determinative

Exclusion is also favoured by the Court's determination that although reliability of the evidence and that it is essential to the Crown's case are relevant considerations for admission they are not trumping. This is very evident in the Court's decision in *Harrison* to exclude 35 kilograms of cocaine found in a vehicle search in violation of ss. 8 and 9. **Do you agree?**

Police "Good Faith"

On the important issue of whether police good faith can mitigate the seriousness of the breach the *Grant* majority held that intentional or reckless disregard of Charter rights should normally lead to exclusion and also that ignorance of Charter standards must not be rewarded or encouraged and negligence or wilful blindness cannot be equated with good faith (para75, citing *Buhay* and other authority).

It is unfortunately not clear how demanding our Supreme Court is on this point given the finding in *Grant* that the police's officer's mistake was understandable given "considerable legal uncertainty" as to the meaning of the triggering concept of detention and did not amount to bad faith. Surely Grant was psychologically detained under existing Supreme Court law by the three police officers, who were clearly trying to obtain incriminating evidence. Furthermore there is agreement in *Grant* that there was no reasonable suspicion for investigative detention required in *R. v. Mann*. It is true that there was authority in Ontario (Moldaver J.A. in *R. v. B. (L.)* (2007), 49 C.R. (6th) 245, 227 C.C.C. (3d) 70 (Ont. C.A.)) that the concept of psychological detention did not equally apply to pedestrian stops. That view is now clearly overruled. The Supreme Court in *Grant* also made it clear that aggressive police questioning on the street to gain incriminating evidence in violation of the Charter as in *Grant* should in future result in exclusion:

> We add that the Court's decision in this case will be to render similar conduct less justifiable going forward. While police are not expected to engage in judicial reflection on conflicting precedents, they are rightly expected to know what the law is (para. 133).

As in *Grant*, the Supreme Court has since not excluded for good faith in cases where the Charter standard was uncertain at the time of the police action. *R. v. Cole*, [2012] 3 S.C.R. 34, 290 C.C.C. (3d) 247, 96 C.R. (6th) 88 (S.C.C.) concerned a warrantless search of a school computer and *R. v. Aucoin*, [2012] 3 S.C.R. 408, 290 C.C.C. (3d) 448, 97 C.R. (6th) 294 (S.C.C.)

involved the placing of a person in the police cruiser after a traffic stop while the traffic ticket was being written, which was held to be not reasonably necessary and contrary to s. 9. This is a special meaning of the phrase "good faith". In future cases those standards are now clear and there should be no acceptance of any good faith argument in those contexts.

The B.C. Court of Appeal in *R. v. Dhillon* (2012), 93 C.R. (6th) 260 (B.C. C.A.) reinforces the powerful earlier majority judgment of Frankel J.A. in *R. v. Reddy* (2010), 71 C.R. (6th) 327, 251 C.C.C. (3d) 151 (B.C. C.A.) that police ought to be following the *Mann* regime for investigative detention and furthermore that the s. 8 and 9 violations should result in exclusion under *Grant* and *Harrison*. There is a recent flurry of such exclusions where proactive policing has not shown police compliance with the *Mann* requirements. See *R. v. Chen*, 2012 ONSC 2832 (Ont. S.C.J.), *R. v. Assiu*, 2012 ONCJ 327 (Ont. C.J.), *R. v. Trott*, 2012 BCPC 174 (B.C. Prov. Ct.) and *R. v. Vulic*, 2012 SKQB 221 (Sask. Q.B.). See too *R. v. Brown* (2012), 286 C.C.C. (3d) 481, 92 C.R. (6th) 375 (Ont. C.A.) and Justice Hill in his encyclopedic judgment in *R. v. Thompson* (2013), 1 C.R. (7th) 125 (Ont. S.C.J.). The Courts rarely expressly find racial discrimination as did a judge of the Quebec Municipal Court in *Longueuil (Ville) v. Debellefeuille*, 2012 QCCM 235, 2012 CarswellQue 9363, EYB 2012-211459, [2012] R.J.Q. 1961, [2012] Q.J. No. 9003 (Que. Mun. Ct.), the only such 2012 ruling found by Asselin.

The majority in *Harrison* also suggests courts should exclude to disassociate from police misconduct,

> where the departure from Charter standards was major in degree, or where the police knew (or should have known) that their conduct was not Charter-compliant (para. 22).

It would have been preferable had the Court expressly disavowed the utility of the politically and emotionally charged labels of good or bad faith, which have produced uncertainty and inconsistency. Justice Doherty of the Ontario Court of Appeal has pointed to dangers of such labels in *R. v. Kitaitchik* (2002), 4 C.R. (6th) 38, 166 C.C.C. (3d) 14 (Ont. C.A.) at para. 41. Judges are very familiar with deciding whether conduct was intentional or negligent. A Charter breach should be considered *especially serious* where the police have intentionally breached a Charter standard and *serious* where the breach was negligent. Police misperception or ignorance of Charter standards should only mitigate a Charter breach where the Crown has shown due diligence by the police in their attempt to comply with Charter standards; We should expect police not to be careless about Charter rights (see Stephen Coughlan, "Good Faith and Exclusion of Evidence under the Charter" (1992) 11 C.R. (4th) 304. As in the case of the tort of negligent investigation, the standard should be that "police act professionally and carefully, not just to avoid gross negligence" (*Hill v. Hamilton-Wentworth (Regional Municipality) Police Services Board*, 2007 SCC 41, [2007] 3 S.C.R. 129, 50 C.R. (6th) 279 at para. 70 (per McLachlin C.J. for the majority).

Discoverability

Under *Stillman* only if conscripted evidence would have been discoverable by lawful means would the evidence not make the trial unfair and judges could consider other factors. The *Grant* majority accept that the conscription-discoverability doctrine had been justifiably criticized as overly speculative and capable of producing anomalous results: and that it had proved difficult to apply. The majority declared that discoverability should no longer be determinative of admissibility (para. 122).

This is welcome as the fact that the police could have discovered the evidence without violating the Charter adds an obtuse inquiry. There should be a catch-22 for Crown arguments about discoverability in that the reality police could have found the evidence without violating the Charter surely makes the violation more serious. See Carol Brewer, "Stillman and Section 24(2): Much Ado About Nothing" (1997) 2 Can.Crim.L.R. 240. This was emphasised by Lamer C.J. in *Collins* and re-asserted by Justice Arbour J. for a unanimous Court in *R. v. Buhay*, [2003] 1 S.C.R. 631, 10 C.R. (6th) 205, 174 C.C.C. (3d) 97. Questions of legal remedy should turn on the evidence of what actually happened rather than what might have occurred.

Some academics sought to justify the discoverability doctrine on pragmatic grounds. Professor David Paciocco , "Disproportion and the Fair Trial Dichotomy under Section 24(2)" , (1997) 2 Can. Crim. L.Rev. 163 at 170 wrote that

> Discoverability is a prudent criterion, but it is entirely pragmatic and not the least principled. It is born of the realization that to exclude evidence that the police would have had in any event is to give the accused a windfall, and to require the State to overcompensate.....This has nothing to do with whether the trial is unfair.

Professor Kent Roach "The Evolving Fair Trial Test under Section 24(2) of the Charter", (1996) 1 *Can.Crim.L.R.* 117 at 123. suggests that

> The State, as well as the accused, should not be put in a worse position than if the violation had not occurred.

These views are not persuasive. Surely, as Richard Mahoney,"Problems with the Current Approach to s. 24(2) of the Charter: An Inevitable Discovery" (1999) 42 Crim. L.Q. 240 at 250 puts it

> A proper inquiry under s. 24(2) should never be stultified by any purported rule that the state should never be worse off as a result of having breached one of the accused's Charter rights. There are times when the state should be worse off to the extent of seeing a guilty person acquitted

Most unfortunately the Supreme Court in *Grant* appears to have resuscitated a different form of the discoverability inquiry in the following paragraph:

> Discoverability retains a useful role, however, in assessing the actual impact of the breach on the protected interests of the accused. It allows the court to assess the strength of the causal connection between the Charter-infringing self-incrimination and the resultant evidence. The more likely it is that the evidence would have been obtained even without the statement, the lesser the impact of the breach on the accused's underlying interest against self-incrimination. The converse, of course, is

also true. On the other hand, in cases where it cannot be determined with any confidence whether evidence would have been discovered in absence of the statement, discoverability will have no impact on the s. 24(2) inquiry (para. 123).

The Court here appears to return in part to a doctrine that lacks rationale, especially given the revised focus on the seriousness of the violation. Furthermore it appears to mix up discoverability with the causal inquiry into whether the evidence was obtained by the Charter violation. That issue was not engaged in either *Grant* or *Harrison*. The Supreme Court has previously striven to ensure that the exclusion remedy not be curtailed by an unduly strict causal test (see earlier *Strachan, Burlingham* and *Wittwer*).

In *R. v. Côté* (2011), 87 C.R. (6th) 1, [2011] 3 S.C.R. 215, 276 C.C.C. (3d) 42 (S.C.C.) a 8-1 majority of the Supreme Court strongly re-asserts the approach to s. 24(2) it declared in *Grant* and *Harrison*. Faced with an exclusion decision for multiple Charter violations in an investigation of a domestic murder case, the Quebec Court of Appeal arrived at a compromise along the lines of the now rejected *Collins/Stillman* dichotomy: the conscripted evidence of statements should be excluded but the non-conscripted reliable evidence, here forensic evidence found in a warrantless search contrary to s. 8, was to be admitted as the murder offence was serious. According to Justice Cromwell for the Supreme Court majority, the Quebec Court of Appeal had firstly erred in intervening on the basis that the police had not deliberately acted in an abusive manner. The Court had exceeded its role by its re- characterization of the evidence which departed from express findings by the trial judge of deliberate and systemic police misconduct not tainted by any clear and determinative error. The Court of Appeal had also erred in interfering with the trial judge's s. 24(2) determination by assigning greater importance to the seriousness of the offence. Justice Cromwell powerfully re-asserts that, once there has been a determination on the first and second *Grant* factors that the Charter violation or violations were serious, the factors of the seriousness of the offence, the reliability of the evidence and the importance of the evidence to the Crown's case are not determinative and should not lead to admission.

Justice Cromwell in *Côté* holds that discoverability is a factor relevant to the first two *Grant* factors but not determinative. In this case the fact that the police could have acted in compliance with the Charter made the violation and invasion of privacy more serious. Justice Cromwell repeats a line in *Grant* that trial judges should not speculate about discoverability. Whether the police would have discovered the evidence is necessarily speculative. Surely it would be better for the Court to abandon this unprincipled and confusing inquiry? In practice, trial judges often avoid it. Asselin found that discoverability was only considered in 15 of the 98 trial court rulings on s. 24(2) in 2012.The focus should be on what the police did, not on what they might have done. Discoverability should always, as in *Côté*, amount to a "catch 22" for the Crown: if the police did not have to break the Charter standard this makes their breach more serious.

Canadian and U.S. Supreme Courts: Rowing in Opposite Directions

Another blow against the exclusionary rule in the United States to date came in January 2009 in *Herring v. United States*, 129 S. Ct. 695 (U.S. Sup. Ct., 2009). Chief Justice Roberts writing for a 5-4 majority, confirmed that exclusion is not a necessary consequence of a Fourth Amendment violation and that the benefits of deterrence must outweigh the costs of letting guilty and possibly dangerous defendants go free. He held that,

> To trigger the exclusionary rule, police conduct must be sufficiently deliberate that exclusion can meaningfully deter it, and sufficiently culpable that such deterrence is worth the price paid by the justice system. ...[The] exclusionary rule serves to deter deliberate, reckless , or grossly negligent conduct, or in some circumstances recurring or systemic negligence

The standard for exclusion had not been reached, the majority ruled in this case of State carelessness. The accused had been arrested on a warrant because county officials had negligently not updated computer records to show that the warrant had actually been rescinded.

In marked contrast we have seen that the Supreme Court of Canada in *Grant*, although the majority paid no attention to Unites States jurisprudence, implicitly embraced what Justice Ginsberg dissenting in *Herring* described as the more "majestic" rationale of the remedy of exclusion: to preserve the rule of law and the integrity of the justice system. Our Supreme Court sees deterrence as merely a happy windfall of exclusion. There is some double speak here in that when the Court speaks of not wishing to condone unconstitutional behaviour by the police it seems really to be saying that it wishes to punish police and deter them from continuing to commit such breaches. In any event as a practical matter it will be much easier to argue for exclusion in Canada in that there is no impossible burden of establishing that exclusion will in fact deter police in the future.

There are two other dramatic points of contrast. The Canadian remedy is expressly discretionary. The Supreme Court sees no wisdom in an automatic rule of exclusion however minor the violation. This approach also means that the constitutional standard developed for each Charter right does not have to be watered down by judges for fear of an overreaching exclusionary rule.

Importantly the Supreme Court of Canada sees the need to encourage exclusion where police have deliberately or reckless violated the Charter but also where they have been ignorant or merely careless in disregarding those rights. The Supreme Court of the United States is now clearly far more tolerant of unconstitutionality in putting the good faith bar as low as gross negligence or systemic or recurrent negligence.

Ineffectiveness of Other Remedies

In *Hudson v. Michigan*, 547 U.S. 586 (U.S. S.C., 2006) Justice Scalia, writing for a 5-4 majority, refused to apply the exclusionary rule to a violation of the Fourth Amendment "knock-and-announce" rule. In the course of doing he suggested that exclusion may no longer be necessary because of the increasing professionalism of police forces, with wide-ranging reforms in education, training and supervision, better internal discipline and various forms of citizen review.

Policing and review standards have also improved in Canada as well. However those preferring alternative remedies, such as civil suits and police complaints procedures, now bear a heavy burden of demonstrating their comparative efficacy. In Canada they have thus far generally proved to be a poor and low visibility response to systemic problems of police abuse or ignorance of their powers under an entrenched Charter. Police are rarely, if ever, disciplined for Charter breaches that uncover evidence of criminality. Civil litigation is expensive, uncertain in outcome, and, if successful, likely to be subject to confidentiality agreements. Civil litigation is also highly unlikely where the plaintiff is in prison. In *Ward v. Vancouver (City)*, 76 C.R. (6th) 207, [2010] 2 S.C.R. 28 (S.C.C.) the Supreme Court recently recognized a new right to sue civilly for compensation for a Charter breach but pragmatically restricted the remedy to superior courts.

In Canada, the remedy of exclusion for Charter breaches has proved to be an important vehicle to hold agents of the State indirectly and publicly accountable. On a daily basis defence counsel can challenge the behaviour of police officers. Where there are patterns of inclusion despite police breaches there will be less incentive for police to take the Charter seriously. In considering exclusion remedies Courts must be concerned with the long-term integrity of the justice system if Charter standards for accused are ignored and/or operate unequally against vulnerable groups, such as persons of colour and those who are young.

PROBLEM 1

The accused was charged with possession of a stolen auto. Following his arrest and the usual police cautions he was asked regarding the whereabouts of the keys to the car. He professed ignorance. The police threatened him that he would be kept in custody until the keys were found. The prosecution did not seek to introduce any statements which may have been made following this exchange. The prosecution did, however, lead evidence of the accused taking the police to the place where the keys were hidden. The trial judge excluded the evidence of the accused's involvement in the finding of the keys. The accused was acquitted.

Compare *R. v. Woolley* (1988), 63 C.R. (3d) 333, 40 C.C.C. (3d) 531 (Ont. C.A.) and *R. v. Black*, [1989] 2 S.C.R. 138, 70 C.R. (3d) 97, 50 C.C.C. (3d) 1 (S.C.C.).

PROBLEM 2

The accused was charged with murder. Investigating officers went to his residence and asked him to accompany them to the detachment office at Stellarton for questioning. He was advised that he was not under arrest, but was given the usual police caution and advised of his right to counsel. He went to the detachment office, and the interview lasted one hour. He admitted that he had told people that he intended to rob the victim, but denied saying that he intended to kill him.

The accused agreed to take a polygraph test. He was transported to Halifax for the purpose. He was not advised that he was being taken for questioning, but rather was advised that the only purpose of the trip was to take the polygrah test. The accused was introduced to the polygraph operator, D., who gave him the usual police caution. D. told the accused that the polygraph test was voluntary and he could leave the room at any time. D. testified that the test is divided into three distinct parts: the pre-test interview, the test and the post-test interview. In the case of a truthful subject, the exam is terminated after the test. If the subject proves deceptive and fails the test, the questioning continues. D. advised the accused at 1:00 p.m. that he failed the test, and proceeded to question him until 2:00 p.m., when D. was forced to retire with a headache. W., another polygrapher, immediately took over the qustioning, and it continued until 3:41 p.m., when C. took over the interrogation. During C.'s interrogation the accused confessed to the killing. C. described to the accusd another case where an accused was convicted only of manslaughter because he had admitted to the police his involvement but denied intent. The interrogation by C. continued until 5:22 p.m. All the interrogations were taped. During the interrogations the accused was given the police caution on several occasions. When the accused suggested on a number of occasions that he consult counsel, the requests were ignored by D. and by C.

The accused managed to contact his counsel at 6:00 p.m. Counsel spoke with C., was advised of the statements, and then interviewed the accused. Counsel advised C. that his client would not be giving further statements. C. did not advise counsel that the police planned to take the accused back to the murder scene to do a re-enactment of the crime on video-tape. The accused was taken to the scene and cautioned, but there was no mention of his right to counsel. The accused did a re-enactment of the crime, which was video-taped.

At the trial, following a lengthy voir dire, the trial judge admitted all of the statements and the video-tape into evidence. The accused did not testify on the voir dire or on the trial. No other independent evidence placed the accused at the scene. The remaining evidence tended to confirm the statements. The accused was convicted of second degree murder, and appealed. What result?

Compare *R. v. Nugent* (1988), 63 C.R. (3d) 351, 42 C.C.C. (3d) 431 (N.S. C.A.).

PROBLEM 3

Would *Wray* be decided differently under the Charter?

PROBLEM 4

Late one night police pulled over a van for failure to signal a left turn. The officer approached the vehicle and noticed that the accused, seated in the front passenger seat, was not wearing a seatbelt. He saw the accused lean forward with his left hand down his back. The officer became concerned about safety and ordered everyone in the car to keep their hands where he could see them. They did so. The officer then, as a matter of his routine, asked all of the occupants to identify themselves. They did so. The officer checked the names through the Canadian Police Information Centre ("CPIC") and discovered that the accused was on bail, a term of which required him to abide by a curfew. That curfew had long passed. In fact, the charges giving rise to the bail had been withdrawn six days earlier but the bail information had not been removed from CPIC. The officer returned to the vehicle, arrested Harris for breaching his bail, handcuffed him, took him back to the police cruiser, and searched him. During that search, the officer discovered a quantity of crack cocaine tucked into the waistband of Harris's underwear. He charged the accused with possession of cocaine for the purposes of trafficking and advised him of his right to counsel.

Harris brought a Charter application at the outset of his trial alleging several constitutional violations. The trial judge found that the accused was arbitrarily detained and subjected to an unconstitutional search when he asked him to identify himself while he was detained in the vehicle. She further held that Harris was denied his right to counsel while under arbitrary detention. The trial judge concluded that the cocaine seized from Harris was obtained as the result of these constitutional violations and should be excluded under s. 24(2) of the Charter. The accused was acquitted and the Crown appealed. Give judgment.

Compare *R. v. Harris* (2007), 49 C.R. (6th) 220, 255 C.C.C. (3d) 193 (Ont. C.A.).

PROBLEM 5

At 2:30 p.m. detectives in an unmarked police car noticed two 15-year-old boys, L.B. and F, loitering around the entrance to a high school. They were physically apart but talking to each other, which aroused the officers' suspicions. The officers went up to the youths to question them. Before they reached L.B., he came straight toward them. One of the officers asked L.B. how it was going and L.B. responded "good". He then asked him what they were "doing there" and L.B. replied "just hanging out". They were asked for their names and dates of birth. They complied and the police ran a CPIC check. An officer noticed that L.B. had left behind the black knapsack he had been carrying. The officer went to look for it. At this point L.B. appeared nervous and fidgety. The officer found the knapsack near the stairs where L.B. had been first seen. He opened it and found a gun. The accused was placed under arrest.

At L.B.'s trial on eight firearm related charges, the defence brought a motion to exclude the evidence as having been found in violation of his Charter rights. A *voir dire* was held at which the accused did not testify. The trial judge adopted and applied the legal framework formulated by the trial judge in *R. v. Powell* in determining that L.B. was psychologically detained. L.B. was a pedestrian whom the police questioned in circumstances where they had no right to detain him, even temporarily. Hence, in deciding the issue of psychological detention, L.B. could be presumed to feel compelled to answer the questions put to him by the police, without the need for testimony from him as to his subjective perception of a sense of compulsion. The trial judge held L.B. had been detained from the moment of the CPIC search and that there had been violation of his section 8 and 10(b) Charter rights. The evidence should be excluded under s. 24(2) and the accused acquitted. The Crown appealed. Give judgment.

Compare *R. v. B. (L.)* (2007), 49 C.R. (6th) 245, 227 C.C.C. (3d) 70 (Ont. C.A.).

PROBLEM 6

The accused was charged with possession of marihuana and possession of crack cocaine.

Early one Friday evening, three officers were on foot patrol in a west end part of Toronto in response to resident concerns about drug dealing in alleyways and so on in a general sense, but, as they candidly testified, they were not investigating any particular or specific matters or complaints. At the corner in question they approached the accused, a 21-year-old black man. Officer B recognised him as had arrested him previously on drug charges and had had some other contact. He called out, "Hey Lionel". Williams did not appear to be happy to see the police. He stepped back but stopped when officer B engaged him in conversation. At the same time, the other two officers took positions according to their training, with one behind Williams and the other to his side, so that the officers effectively formed a semi-circle around him. At least one of the officers began filling out a "208" and asking questions relating to date of birth, address etc. Officer B testified that he had not usually seen Williams in this particular part of the Division and asked him what he was doing there and where he was going. He said he was going to a party. Williams seemed "nervous" and "fidgety". He put his hands in his pockets, and was advised to keep his hands out of his pockets. While he complied with the request, his hands returned to his pockets and as a result he was asked a few times in the course of this two-minute brief exchange to take his hands out of his pockets. Williams was wearing dark baggy jeans, a white tee shirt and a hooded sweatshirt referred to as a "hoodie". All three officers testified that the fact that Williams appeared nervous and the fact that he kept putting his hands back in his pockets gave rise to some concern for their safety. For that reason, officer B asked the accused to lift the front of his "hoodie" up so that they could see his waistband. Officer B explained that this was important as weapons are most often concealed around the waist. As Williams complied with this request, a baggie of marihuana fell out of his left pant leg onto the ground. At this point, officer B placed his hand on Williams' arm and advised him he was under arrest for possession of marihuana, to which Williams responded by saying "Man, it's just some weed, you don't have to do this". Before the arrest could be completed and the accused could be read his rights, he "bodychecked" officer B and ran off west along St Clair Ave. As he was running across St Clair, he was seen to throw something away. This turned out to be 4.8 grams of crack cocaine. He was later arrested. The defence counsel brought a motion for exclusion of evidence on the basis that the evidence was found in violation of the accused's ss. 8 and 9 Charter rights. Give judgment.

Compare *R. v. Williams* (2007), 52 C.R. (6th) 98 (Ont. S.C.J.).

PROBLEM 7

A high-school teacher had a work-issued laptop which he was entitled to use for personal purposes. A school technician discovered nude and partly nude photographs of an underage female student on the teacher's laptop while performing maintenance activities. The technician reported this discovery to the principal, who directed the technician to copy the photographs to a CD. The principal seized the laptop from the teacher and school board technicians copied the temporary Internet files onto a second CD. The laptop and both CDs were handed over to the police who, without a warrant, reviewed their contents and then created a mirror image of the hard drive for forensic purposes. The Court has found that s. 8 was violated by the police in not obtaining a warrant before examining the laptop contents. However, the school principal did not violate the accused's s. 8 rights by examining the laptop and copying the CDs. Should the evidence obtained by the police be admitted? Does the fact that the police had the grounds to obtain a warrant but did not make the breach more or less serious?

Compare *R. v. Cole*, 2012 SCC 53, 96 C.R. (6th) 88 (S.C.C.). See CR annotation by Stephen Coughlan.

3. Declarations of Invalidity Under s. 52 of the Charter and Saving Under s. 1

In *R. v. Big M Drug Mart Ltd.*, [1985] 1 S.C.R. 295 (S.C.C.), Chief Justice Dickson for the majority of the Supreme Court held that any court has the power under s. 52(1) of the Constitution Act, 1982, to declare laws contrary to the Charter to be of no force or effect. Such challenge will necessarily raise the possibility of a demonstrably justified reasonable limit under s. 1.

An entrenched Charter would not have been politically attainable without the key compromise in s. 1. This "guarantee" of rights and freedoms reads:

The *Canadian Charter of Rights and Freedoms* guarantees the rights and freedoms set out in it subject only to such reasonable limits prescribed by law as can be demonstrably justified in a free and democratic society.

Deschenes C.J.S.C., in his scholarly judgment in *Quebec Assoc. of Protestant School Bds. v. A.G. Que. (No. 2)*, [1982] C.S. 673, 140 D.L.R. (3d) 33 (Que. S.C.) (an analysis not considered when the matter reached the Supreme Court of Canada), analysed s. 1 to impose four conditions (at 66): (1) prescribed by law; (2) within reasonable limits; (3) demonstrably justified; and (4) in a free and democratic society.

He furthermore drew three basic conclusions as to the meaning of "reasonable limit" (at 77):

1. A limit is reasonable if it is a proportionate means to attain the purpose of the law;

2. Proof of the contrary involves proof not only of a wrong, but of a wrong which runs against common sense; and

3. The courts must not yield to the temptation of too readily substituting their opinion for that of the Legislature.

The blueprint for the interpretation of s. 1 was authoritatively declared by the Supreme Court of Canada in *Oakes*.

(a) *Oakes* **test**

R. v. OAKES
[1986] 1 S.C.R. 103, 50 C.R. (3d) 1, 24 C.C.C. (3d) 321 (S.C.C.)

DICKSON C.J.C. (Chouinard, Lamer, Wilson and Le Dain JJ. concurring):—This appeal concerns the constitutionality of s. 8 of the *Narcotic Control Act*, R.S.C. 1970, c. N-1. The section provides, in brief, that if the Court finds the accused in possession of a narcotic, he is presumed to be in possession for the purpose of trafficking. Unless the accused can establish the contrary, he must be convicted of trafficking. The Ontario Court of Appeal held that his provision constitutes a "reverse onus" clause and is unconstitutional because it violates one of the core values of our criminal justice system, the presumption of innocence, now entrenched in s. 11(*d*) of the *Canadian Charter of Rights and Freedoms*. The Crown has appealed.

. . .

The respondent, David Edwin Oakes, was charged with unlawful possession of a narcotic for the purpose of trafficking, contrary to s. 4(2) of the *Narcotic Control Act*. He elected trial by magistrate without a jury. At trial, the Crown adduced evidence to establish that Mr. Oakes was found in possession of eight one gram vials of *cannabis* resin in the form of hashish oil. Upon a further search conducted at the police station, $619.45 was located. Mr. Oakes told the police that he had bought ten vials of hashish oil for $150 for his own use, and that the $619.45 was from a workers' compensation cheque. He elected not to call evidence as to possession of the narcotic. Pursuant to the procedural provisions of s. 8 of the *Narcotic Control Act*, the trial judge proceeded to make a finding that it was beyond a reasonable doubt that Mr. Oakes was in possession of the narcotic.

Following this finding, Mr. Oakes brought a motion to challenge the constitutional validity of s. 8 of the *Narcotic Control Act*, which he maintained imposes a burden on an accused to prove that he or she was not in possession for the purpose of trafficking. He argued that s. 8 violates the presumption of innocence contained in s. 11(*d*) of the *Charter*.

To interpret the meaning of s. 11(*d*), it is important to adopt a purposive approach. As this Court stated in *R. v. Big M Drug Mart Ltd.*, [1985] 1 S.C.R. 295 at p. 344:

> The meaning of a right or freedom guaranteed by the *Charter* was to be ascertained by analysis of the *purpose* of such a guarantee; it was to be understood, in other words, in the light of the interests it was meant to protect.
>
> In my view this analysis is to be undertaken, and the purpose of the right or freedom in question is to be sought by reference to the character and the larger objects of the *Charter* itself, to the language chosen to articulate the specific right or freedom, to the historical origins of the concepts enshrined, and where applicable to the meaning and purpose of the other specific rights and freedoms.

To identify the underlying purpose of the *Charter* right in question, therefore, it is important to begin by understanding the cardinal values it embodies.

The presumption of innocence is a hallowed principle lying in the very heart of criminal law. Although protected expressly in s. 11(*d*) of the *Charter*, the presumption of innocence is referable and integral to the general protection of life, liberty and security of the person contained in s. 7 of the *Charter* (see *Reference re. s. 94(2) of the Motor Vehicle Act* (1986), 48 C.R. (3d) 289 (S.C.C.). The presumption of innocence protects the fundamental liberty and human dignity of any and every person accused by the State of criminal conduct. An individual charged with a criminal offence faces grave social and personal consequences, including potential loss of physical liberty, subjection to a social stigma and ostracism from the community, as well as other social, psychological and economic harms. In light of the gravity of these consequences, the presumption of innocence is crucial. It ensures that until the State proves an accused's guilt beyond all reasonable doubt, he or she is innocent. This is essential in a society committed to fairness and social justice. The presumption of innocence confirms our faith in humankind; it reflects our belief that individuals are decent and law-abiding members of the community until proven otherwise.

The presumption of innocence has enjoyed longstanding recognition at common law. In the leading case, *Woolmington v. Director of Public Prosecutions*, [1935] A.C. 462 (H.L.), Viscount Sankey wrote at pp. 481-482:

> Throughout the web of the English Criminal Law one golden thread is always to be seen, that it is the duty of the prosecution to prove the prisoner's guilt subject to what I have already said as to the defence of insanity and subject also to any statutory exception. If, at the end of and on the whole of the case, there is a reasonable doubt, created by the evidence given by either the prosecution or the

prisoner, as to whether the prisoner killed the deceased with a malicious intention, the prosecution has not made out the case and the prisoner is entitled to an acquittal. No matter what the charge or where the trial, the principle that the prosecution must prove the guilt of the prisoner is part of the common law of England and no attempt to whittle it down can be entertained.

Subsequent Canadian cases have cited the *Woolmington* principle with approval (see, for example, *Manchuk v. The King*, [1938] S.C.R. 341, at p. 349; *R. v. City of Sault Ste. Marie*, [1978] 2 S.C.R. 1299, at p. 1316).

Further evidence of the widespread acceptance of the principle of the presumption of innocence is its inclusion in the major international human rights documents. Article 11(1) of the *Universal Declaration of Human Rights*, adopted December 10, 1948 by the General Assembly of the United Nations, provides:

Art. 11(1) Everyone charged with a penal offence has the right to be presumed innocent until proved guilty according to law in a public trial at which he has had all the guarantees necessary for his defence.

In the *International Covenant on Civil and Political Rights*, 1966, art. 14(2) states:

Art. 14(2) Everyone charged with a criminal offence shall have the right to be presumed innocent until proved guilty according to law.

Canada acceded to this Covenant, and the Optional Protocol which sets up machinery for implementing the Covenant, on May 19, 1976. Both came into effect on August 19, 1976.

In light of the above, the right to be presumed innocent until proven guilty requires that s. 11(*d*) have, at a minimum, the following content. First, an individual must be proven guilty beyond a reasonable doubt. Second, it is the State which must bear the burden of proof. As Mr. Justice Lamer stated in *Dubois v. The Queen* (November 21, 1985, unreported) at p. 6:

Section 11(*d*) imposes upon the Crown the burden of proving the accused's guilt beyond a reasonable doubt as well as that of making out the case against the accused before he or she need respond, either by testifying or calling other evidence.

Third, criminal prosecutions must be carried out in accordance with lawful procedures and fairness. The latter part of s. 11(*d*), which requires the proof of guilt "according to law in a fair and public hearing by an independent and impartial tribunal", underlines the importance of this procedural requirement.

. . .

The *Woolmington* case was decided in the context of a legal system with no constitutionally entrenched human rights document. In Canada, we have tempered parliamentary supremacy by entrenching important rights and freedoms in the Constitution. Viscount Sankey's statutory exception proviso is clearly not applicable in this context and would subvert the very purpose of the entrenchments of the presumption of innocence in the *Charter*. . . . Section 8 of the *Narcotics Control Act* is not rendered constitutionally valid simply by virtue of the fact that it is a statutory provision.

In general one must, I think, conclude that a provision which requires an accused to disprove on a balance of probabilities the existence of a presumed fact, which is an important element of the offence in question, violates the presumption of innocence in s. 11(*d*). If an accused bears the burden of disproving on a balance of probabilities an essential element of an offence, it would be possible for a conviction to occur despite the existence of a reasonable doubt. This would arise if the accused adduced sufficient evidence to raise a reasonable doubt as to his or her innocence but did not convince the jury on a balance of probabilities that the presumed fact was untrue.

The fact that the standard is only the civil one does not render a reverse onus clause constitutional. As Sir Rupert Cross commented in the *Rede Lectures*, "The Golden Thread of the English Criminal Law: The Burden of Proof", delivered in 1976 at the University of Toronto, at pp. 11-13:

> It is sometimes said that exceptions to the Woolmington rule are acceptable because, whenever the burden of proof on any issue in a criminal case is borne by the accused, he only has to satisfy the jury on the balance of probabilities, whereas on issues on which the Crown bears the burden of proof the jury must be satisfied beyond a reasonable doubt. . . . The fact that the standard is lower when the accused bears the burden of proof than it is when the burden of proof is borne by the prosecution is no answer to my objection to the existence of exceptions to the Woolmington rule as it does not alter the fact that a jury or bench of magistrates may have to convict the accused although they are far from sure of his guilt.

As we have seen, the potential for a rational connection between the basic fact and the presumed fact to justify a reverse onus provision has been elaborated in some of the cases discussed above and is now known as the "rational connection test". In the context of s. 11(*d*), however, the following question arises: if we apply the rational connection test to the consideration of whether s. 11(*d*) has been violated, are we adequately protecting the constitutional principle of the presumption of innocence? As Professors MacKay and Cromwell point out in their article "Oakes: A Bold Initiative" (1983), 32 C.R. (3d) 221, at p. 223:

> The rational connection test approves a provision that *forces* the trier to infer a fact that may be simply rationally connected to the proved fact. Why does it follow that such a provision does not offend the constitutional right to be proved guilty beyond a reasonable doubt?

A basic fact may rationally tend to prove a presumed fact, but not prove its existence beyond a reasonable doubt. An accused person could thereby be convicted despite the presence of a reasonable doubt. This would violate the presumption of innocence.

I should add that this questioning of the constitutionality of the "rational connection text" as a guide to interpreting s. 11(*d*) does not minimize its importance. The appropriate stage for invoking the rational connection test, however, is under s. 1 of the *Charter*. This consideration did not arise under the *Canadian Bill of Rights* because of the absence of an equivalent to s. 1. At the Court of Appeal level in the present case, Martin J.A. sought to combine the analysis of s. 11(*d*) and s. 1 to overcome the limitations of the *Canadian Bill of Rights* jurisprudence. To my mind, it is highly desirable to keep s. 1 and s. 11(*d*) analytically distinct. Separating the analysis into two components is consistent with the approach this Court has taken to the *Charter* to date (see *R. v. Big M Drug Mart Ltd., supra*; *Hunter v. Southam Inc.*, [1984] 2 S.C.R. 145; *Law Society of Upper Canada v. Skapinker*, [1984] 1 S.C.R. 357).

To return to s. 8 of the *Narcotic Control Act*, I am in no doubt whatsoever that it violates s. 11(*d*) of the *Charter* by requiring the accused to prove on a balance of probabilities that he was not in possession of the narcotic for the purpose of trafficking. Mr. Oakes is compelled by s. 8 to prove he is *not* guilty of the offence of trafficking. He is thus denied his right to be presumed innocent and subjected to the potential penalty of life imprisonment unless he can rebut the presumption. This is radically and fundamentally inconsistent with the societal values of human dignity and liberty we espouse, and is directly contrary to the presumption of innocence enshrined in s. 11(*d*). Let us turn now to s. 1 of the *Charter*.

. . .

It is important to observe at the outset that s. 1 has two functions: first, it constitutionally guarantees the rights and freedoms set out in the provisions which follow; and, second, it states explicitly the exclusive justificatory criteria (outside of s. 33 of the *Constitution Act*, 1982) against which limitations on those rights and freedoms must be measured. Accordingly, any s. 1 inquiry must be premised on an understanding that the impugned limit violates constitutional rights and freedoms—Justice Wilson stated in *Singh v. Ministry of Employment and Immigration, supra*, at pp. 218-19: ". . . it is important to remember that the courts are conducting this inquiry in light of a commitment to uphold the rights and freedoms set out in the other sections of the *Charter*."

A second contextual element of interpretation of s. 1 is provided by the words "free and democratic society". Inclusion of these words as the final standard of justification for limits on rights and freedoms refers the Court to the very purpose for which the *Charter* was originally entrenched in the Constitution: Canadian society is to be free and democratic. The Court must be guided by the values and principles essential to a free and democratic society which I believe embody, to name but a few, respect for the inherent dignity of the human person, commitment to social justice and equality, accommodation of a wide variety of beliefs, respect for cultural and group identity, and faith in social and political institutions which enhance the participation of individuals and groups in society. The underlying values and principles of a free and democratic society are the genesis of the rights and freedoms guaranteed by the *Charter* and the ultimate standard against which a limit on a right or freedom must be shown, despite its effect, to be reasonable and demonstrably justified.

The rights and freedoms guaranteed by the *Charter* are not, however, absolute. It may become necessary to limit rights and freedoms in circumstances where their exercise would be inimical to the realization of collective goals of fundamental importance. For this reason, s. 1 provides criteria of justification for limits on the rights and freedoms guaranteed by the *Charter*. These criteria impose a stringent standard of justification, especially when understood in terms of the two contextual considerations discussed above, namely, the violation of a constitutionally guaranteed right or freedom and the fundamental principles of a free and democratic society.

The onus of proving that a limit on a right or freedom guaranteed by the *Charter* is reasonable and demonstrably justified in a free and democratic society rests upon the party seeking to uphold the limitation. It is clear from the text of s. 1 that limits on the rights and freedoms enumerated in the *Charter* are exceptions to their general guarantee. The presumption is that the rights and freedoms are guaranteed unless the party invoking s. 1 can bring itself within the exceptional criteria which justify their being limited. This is further substantiated by the use of the word "demonstrably" which clearly indicates that the onus of justification is on the party seeking to limit: *Hunter v. Southam Inc., supra.*

The standard of proof under s. 1 is the civil standard, namely, proof by a preponderance of probability. The alternative criminal standard, proof beyond a reasonable doubt, would, in my view, be unduly onerous on the party seeking to limit. Concepts such as "reasonableness", "justifiability" and "free and democratic society" are simply not amenable to such a standard. Nevertheless, the preponderous of probability test must be applied rigorously. Indeed, the phrase "demonstrably justified" in s. 1 of the *Charter* supports this conclusion. Within the broad category of the civil standard, there exist different degrees of probability depending on the nature of the case: see Sopinka and Lederman, *The Law of Evidence in Civil Cases* (Toronto: 1974) at p. 385. As Lord Denning explained in *Bater v. Bater*, [1950] 2 All E.R. 458 (C.A.) at p. 459:

> The case may be proved by a preponderance of probability, but there may be degrees of probability within the standard. The degree depends on the subject-matter. A civil court, when considering a charge of fraud, will naturally require a higher degree of probability than that which it would require if considering whether negligence were established. It does not adopt so high a standard as a criminal court, even when considering a charge of a criminal nature, but still it does require a degree of probability which is commensurate with the occasion.

This passage was cited with approval in *Hanes v. Wawanesa Mutual Insurance Co.*, [1963] S.C.R. 154 at 161. A similar approach was put forward by Cartwright J. in *Smith v. Smith & Smedman*, [1952] 2 S.C.R. 312 at pp. 331-32:

> I wish, however, to emphasize that in every civil action before the tribunal can safely find the affirmative of an issue of fact required to be proved it must be satisfied, and that whether or not it will be so satisfied must depend on the totality of the circumstances on which its judgment is formed including the gravity of the consequences.

Having regard to the fact that s. 1 is being invoked for the purpose of justifying a violation of the constitutional rights and freedoms the *Charter* was designed to protect, a very high degree of probability will be, in the words of Lord Denning, "commensurate with the occasion". Where evidence is required in order to prove the constituent elements of a s. 1 inquiry, and this will generally be the case, it should be cogent and persuasive and make clear to the court the consequences of imposing or not imposing the limit. See: *Law Society of Upper Canada v. Skapinker, supra*, at p. 384; *Singh et al v. Ministry of Employment and Immigration, supra*, at p. 217. A court will also need to know what alternative measures for implementing the objective were available to the legislators when they made their decisions. I should add, however, that there may be cases where certain elements of the s. 1 analysis are obvious or self-evident.

To establish that a limit is reasonable and demonstrably justified in a free and democratic society, two central criteria must be satisfied. First, the objective, which the measures responsible for a limit on a *Charter* right or freedom are designed to serve, must be "of sufficient importance to warrant overriding a constitutionally protected right or freedom": *R. v. Big M Drug Mart Ltd., supra* at p. 352. The standard must be high in order to ensure that objectives which are trivial or discordant with the principles integral to a free and democratic society do not gain s. 1 protection. It is necessary, at a minimum, that an objective relate to concerns which are pressing and substantial in a free and democratic society before it can be characterized as sufficiently important.

Second, once a sufficiently significant objective is recognized, then the party invoking s. 1 must show that the means chosen are reasonable and demonstrably justified. This involves "a form of proportionality test": *R. v. Big M Drug Mart Ltd., supra*, at p. 352. Although the nature of the proportionality test will vary depending on the circumstances, in each case courts will be required to balance the interests of society with those of individuals and groups. There are, in my view, three important components of a proportionality test. First, the measures adopted must be carefully designed to achieve the objective in question. They must not be arbitrary, unfair or based on irrational considerations. In short, they must be rationally connected to the objective. Second, the means, even if rationally connected to the objective in the first sense, should impair "as little as possible" the right or freedom in question: *R. v. Big M Drug Mart Ltd., supra*, at p. 352. Third, there must be a proportionality between the *effects* of the measures which are responsible for limiting the *Charter* right or freedom, and the objective which has been identified as of "sufficient importance".

With regard to the third component, it is clear that the general effect of any measure impugned under s. 1 will be the infringement of a right or freedom guaranteed by the *Charter*, and an almost infinite number of factual situations may arise in respect of these. Some limits on rights and freedoms protected by the *Charter* will be more serious than others in terms of the nature of the right or freedom violated, the extent of the violation, and the degree to which the measures which impose the limit trench upon the integral principles of a free and democratic society. Even if an objective is of sufficient importance, and the first two elements of the proportionality test are satisfied, it is still possible that, because of the severity of the deleterious effects of a measure on individuals or groups, the measure will not be justified by the purposes it is intended to serve. The more severe the deleterious effects of a measure, the more important the objective must be if the measure is to be reasonable and demonstrably justified in a free and democratic socity.

Having outlined the general principles of a s. 1 inquiry, we must apply them to s. 8 of the *Narcotic Control Act*. Is the reverse onus provision in s. 8 a reasonable limit on the right to be presumed innocent until proven guilty beyond a reasonable doubt as can be demonstrably justified in a free and democratic society?

The starting point for formulating a response to this question is, as stated above, the nature of Parliament's interest or objective which accounts for the passage of s. 8 of the *Narcotic Control Act*. According to the Crown, s. 8 of the *Narcotic Contral Act* is aimed at curbing drug trafficking by facilitating the conviction of drug traffickers. In my opinion, Parliament's concern with decreasing drug trafficking can be characterized as substantial and pressing. The problem of drug trafficking has been increasing since the 1950's at which time there was already considerable concern. (See *Report of the Special Committee on Traffic in Narcotic Drugs.* Appendix to Debates of the Senate, Canada, Session 1955, pp. 690-700; see also *Final Report, Commission of Inquiry into the Non-Medical Use of Drugs* (Ottawa, 1973). Throughout this period, numerous measures were adopted by free and democratic societies, at both the international and national levels.

At the international level, on June 23, 1953, the *Protocol of Limiting and Regulating the Cultivation of the Poppy Plant, the Production of International and Wholesale Trade in, and Use of Opium*, to which Canada is a signatory, was adopted by the United Nationals Opium Conference held in New York. The *Single Convention on Narcotic Drugs, 1961*, was acceded to in New York on March 30, 1961. This treaty was signed by Canada on March 30, 1961. It entered into force on December 13, 1964. As stated in the Preamble, "addiction to narcotic drugs constitutes a serious evil for the individual and is fraught with social and economic danger to mankind, . . ."

At the national level, statutory provisions have been enacted by numerous countries which, *inter alia*, attempt to deter drug trafficking by imposing criminal sanctions (see, for example, *Misuse of Drugs Act*, 1975, No. 116 (New Zealand; *Misuse of Drugs Act*, 1971, c. 38 (United Kingdom).)

The objective of protecting our society from the grave ills associated with drug trafficking, is, in my view, one of sufficient importance to warrant overriding a constitutionally protected right or freedom in certain cases. Moreover, the degree of seriousness of drug trafficking makes it acknowledgement as a sufficiently important objective for the purposes of s. 1, to a large extent, self-evident. The first criterion of a s. 1 inquiry, therefore, has been satisfied by the Crown.

The next stage of inquiry is a consideration of the means chosen by Parliament to achieve its objective. The means must be reasonable and demonstrably justified in a free and democratic society. As outlined above, this proportionality test should begin with a consideration of the rationality of the provision: is the reverse onus clause in s. 8 rationally related to the objective of curbing drug trafficking? At a minimum, this requires that s. 8 be internally rational; there must be a rational connection between the basic fact of possession and the presumed fact of possession for the purpose of trafficking. Otherwise, the reverse onus clause could give rise to unjustified and erroneous convictions for drug trafficking of persons guilty only of possession of narcotics.

In my view, s. 8 does not survive this rational connection test. As Martin J.A. of the Ontario Court of Appeal concluded, possession of a small or negligible quantity of narcotics does not support the inference of trafficking. In other words, it would be irrational to infer that a person had an intent to traffic on the basis of his or her possession of a very small quantity of narcotics. The presumption required under s. 8 of the *Narcotic Control Act* is overinclusive and could lead to results in certain cases which would defy both rationality and fairness. In light of the seriousness of the offence in question, which carries with it the possibility of imprisonment for life, I am further convinced that the first component of the proportionality test has not been satisfied by the Crown.

Having concluded that s. 8 does not satisfy this first component of proportionality, it is unnecessary to consider the other two components.

. . .

The Ontario Court of Appeal was correct in holding that s. 8 of the *Narcotic Control Act* violates the *Canadian Charter of Rights and Freedoms* and is therefore of no force or effect. Section 8 imposes a limit on the right guaranteed by s. 11(*d*) of the *Charter* which is not reasonable and is not demonstrably justified in a free and democratic society for the purpose of s. 1.

[Estey J. (McIntyre J. concurring) delivered a short concurring judgment.]

Subsequently, in *R. v. Edwards Books & Art Ltd.; R. v. Videoflicks Ltd.*, [1986] 2 S.C.R. 713, 55 C.R. (3d) 193, 30 C.C.C. (3d) 385 (S.C.C.), Chief Justice Dickson restated his *Oakes* test:

Two requirements must be satisfied to establish that a limit is reasonable and demonstrably justified in a free and democratic society. First, the legislative objective which the limitation is designed to promote must be of sufficient importance to warrant overriding a constitutional right. It must bear on a "pressing and substantial concern". Second, the means chosen to attain those objectives must be proportional or appropriate to the ends. The proportionality requirement, in turn, normally has three aspects: the limiting measures must be carefully designed, or rationally connected, to the objective; they must impair the right as little as possible; and their effects must not so severely trench on individual or group rights that the legislative objective, albeit important, is nevertheless outweighed by the abridgement of rights. The Court stated that the nature of the proportionality test would vary depending on the circumstances. Both in articulating the standard of proof and in describing the criteria comprising the proportionality requirement the Court has been careful to avoid the rigid and inflexible standards.

The Supreme Court was deciding whether a provincial Sunday observance law was unconstitutional through a violation of the freedom of religion guaranteed by s. 2(a) of the Charter. The judgment of the Chief Justice is notable for suggesting that the *Oakes* test will vary depending on the context. Furthermore, in applying the test, the Chief Justice saw the question as whether the Act abridged the freedom of religion as "little as is *reasonably* possible". The test was whether there was "some *reasonable* alternative scheme which would allow the province to achieve its objective with fewer detrimental effects on religious freedom".

The need for flexibility is even more evident in the separate judgment of Mr. Justice La Forest:

> . . . in describing the criteria comprising the proportionality requirement, the court has been careful to avoid rigid and inflexible standards. That seems to me to be essential. Given that the objective is of pressing and of substantial concern, the legislature must be allowed adequate scope to achieve that objective. It must be applied on a realistic basis having regard to the nature of the particular area sought to be regulated and not on an abstract theoretical plane. In interpreting the Constitution, Courts must be sensitive to . . . "the practical living facts" to which a legislature must respond. That is especially so in a field of so many competing pressures as the one here in question.

In *R. v. Chaulk*, [1990] 3 S.C.R. 1303, 2 C.R. (4th) 1, 62 C.C.C. (3d) 193 (S.C.C.) it was argued that the presumption of sanity then contained in s. 16(4) of the Criminal Code, placing the onus of proving the defence of insanity on the accused, was a violation of the presumption of innocence in s. 11(*d*). Chief Justice Lamer, writing for himself and four other judges, held that there had been a violation but it could be justified under s. 1. The objective of the presumption was to "avoid placing an impossible burden of proof on the Crown". Citing recent judgments of the Court, indicating that Parliament was not required to adopt the absolutely least intrusive means, Chief Justice Lamer saw the issue as "whether the less intrusive means would achieve the same objective or would achieve the same objective as effectively". The Chief Justice concluded that the alternative of an evidentiary burden requiring that the accused merely raise a reasonable doubt would not be as effective, accepting arguments by Attorneys General that it would be very easy for the accused to "fake" such a defence.

The sole dissent on this point in *Chaulk* was Madam Justice Wilson, who held that this was not the case for relaxing the minimum impairment test. This might be done where a legislature, mediating between competing groups of citizens or allocating scarce resources, had to compromise on the basis of conflicting evidence. But in *Chaulk* the state was acting as "singular Antagonist" of a very basic right of the accused and the strict standard of review in *Oakes* should be applied. The government's objective could be quite readily met by a mere burden on the accused to adduce evidence that made insanity a "live issue fit and proper to be left to the jury".

Do you think that the minimum intrusion test for s. 1 should, in the context of criminal law, be (a) does the limit restrict as little as possible (*Oakes*) or (b) does it restrict as little as reasonably possible (*Edwards Books*) or (c) does it achieve the same objective as effectively (*Chaulk*)?

The Supreme Court has vacillated between these tests and has applied the same test inconsistently: see further Stuart, *Charter Justice in Canadian Criminal Law* (6th ed., 2014) pp. 16-27. In *Ramsden v. Peterborough (City)* (1993), 23 C.R. (4th) 391 (S.C.C.) Iacobucci J., speaking for the full Court, without referring to authority, applied the *Edwards Books* formula in holding that the violation of freedom of expression by a municipal by-law banning posters on utility poles was too wide to be saved under s. 1.

In *R. v. Laba* (1994), 34 C.R. (4th) 360 (S.C.C.) the issue was the constitutionality of a provision under s. 394(1)(b) of the Criminal Code requiring a person charged with possessing or selling minerals to establish the defence of ownership or lawful authority. Sopinka J., for a Court unanimous on this point, held that the Crown could not demonstrably justify this persuasive burden on an accused. In the course of the judgment a reference to *Chaulk* is followed by the remark that

> it is also important to remember that this is not a case in which the legislature has attempted to strike a balance between the interests of competing individuals or groups. Rather it is a case in which the government (as opposed to other individuals or groups) can be characterised as the singular antagonist of an individual attempting to assert a legal right which is fundamental to our system of criminal justice (at 392).

This appears to return to the minority Wilson position in *Chaulk*. **Do you consider that section 1 should always be applied more strictly in the criminal law context?**

In the 30 years of jurisprudence since *Oakes*, section 1 consideration has invariably started with a recitation of the *Oakes* approach, almost as if it were a legislative replacement of the words of section 1. In *R.J.R. MacDonald Inc. v. Canada (Attorney General)*, [1995] 3 S.C.R. 199, a major decision on section 1, McLachlin J. reasserts for the majority that:

> The factors generally relevant to determining whether a violative law is reasonably and demonstrably justified in a free and democratic society remain those set out in *Oakes*. The first requirement is that the objective of the law limiting the Charter right or freedom must be of sufficient importance to warrant overriding it. The second is that the means chosen to achieve the objective must be proportional to the objective and the effect of the law — proportionate, in short, to the good which it may produce. Three matters are considered in determining proportionality: the measures chosen must be rationally connected to the objective; they must impair the guaranteed right or freedom as little as reasonably possible (minimal impairment); and there must be overall proportionality between the deleterious effects of the measures and the salutary effects of the law.

In its very lengthy judgment in *R.J.R. MacDonald*, the Supreme Court held that a federal ban on advertising and promotion of tobacco without health warnings under the Tobacco Products Act violated freedom of expression guaranteed by section 2(*b*) of the Charter. The Court further held, 5:4, that the violation could not be saved under section 1. The judgment turns on section 1 with the degree of deference to be paid to Parliament being the pivotal issue. The majority finds it crucial that the federal government did not tender evidence in support of the need for a total ban. The minority through Mr. Justice La Forest would have allowed Parliament considerable latitude in its decision that a total ban was appropriate. On minimum intrusion the Court again seems agreed that the issue is whether the measure restricted as little as reasonably possible.

One of the majority judgments, by Madam Justice McLachlin, Major J. and Sopinka J. concurring, engages in the most wide-ranging and thoughtful consideration of *Oakes* since that decision. Unfortunately the extent to which she is speaking for the Court is unclear given a much shorter concurring judgement by Justice Iacobucci, Lamer C.J. concurring, which indicates that he differs "somewhat" with McLachlin J.'s section 1 analysis. The extent of the disagreement is left unclear.

Per McLACHLIN J.:—

. . .

First, to be saved under s. 1 the party defending the law (here the Attorney General of Canada) must show that the law which violates the right or freedom guaranteed by the Charter is "reasonable". In other words, the infringing measure must be justifiable by the processes of reason and rationality. The question is not whether the measure is popular or accords with the current public opinion polls. The question is rather whether it can be justified by application of the processes of reason. In the legal context, reason imports the notion of inference from evidence or established truths. This is not to deny intuition its role, or to require proof to the standards required by science in every case, but it is to insist on a rational, reasoned defensibility.

Second, to meet its burden under s. 1 of the Charter, the state must show that the violative law is "demonstrably justified". The choice of the word "demonstrably" is critical. The process is not one of mere intuition, nor is it one of deference to Parliament's choice. It is a process of demonstration. This reinforces the notion inherent in the word "reasonable" of rational inference from evidence or established truths.

The bottom line is this. While remaining sensitive to the social and political context of the impugned law and allowing for difficulties of proof inherent in that context, the courts must nevertheless insist that before the state can override constitutional rights, there be a reasoned demonstration of the good which the law may achieve in relation to the seriousness of the infringement. It is the task of the courts to maintain this bottom line if the rights conferred by our constitution are to have force and meaning. The task is not easily discharged, and may require the courts to confront the tide of popular public opinion. But that has always been the price of maintaining constitutional rights.

. . .

Having set out the criteria determinative of whether a law that infringes a guaranteed right or freedom is justified under s. 1, La Forest J. [in this case] offers observations on the approach the courts should use in applying them. His first point is that the *Oakes* test must be applied flexibly, having regard to the factual and social context of each case. I agree.

. . .

That the s. 1 analysis takes into account the context in which the particular law is situate should hardly surprise us. The s. 1 inquiry is by its very nature a fact-specific inquiry. In determining whether the objective of the law is sufficiently important to be capable of overriding a guaranteed right, the court must examine the actual objective of the law. . . . However, while the impugned law must be considered in its social and economic context, nothing in the jurisprudence suggests that the contextual approach reduces the obligation on the state to meet the burden of demonstrating that the limitation on rights imposed by the law is reasonable and justified. Context is essential in determining legislative objective and proportionality, but it cannot be carried to the extreme of treating the challenged law as a unique socio-economic phenomenon, of which Parliament is deemed the best judge. This would be to undercut the obligation on Parliament to justify limitations which it places on Charter rights and would be to substitute *ad hoc* judicial discretion for the reasoned demonstration contemplated by the Charter.

. . .

Related to context is the degree of deference which the courts should accord to Parliament. It is established that the deference accorded to Parliament or the legislatures may vary with the social context in which the limitation on rights is imposed. For example, it has been suggested that greater deference to Parliament or the Legislature may be appropriate if the law is concerned with the competing rights between different sectors of society than if it is a contest between the individual and the state. However, such distinctions may not always be easy to apply. For example, the criminal law is generally seen as involving a contest between the state and the accused, but it also involves an allocation of priorities between the accused and the victim, actual or potential.

. . .

As with context, however, care must be taken not to extend the notion of deference too far. Deference must not be carried to the point of relieving the government of the burden which the Charter places upon it of demonstrating that the limits it has imposed on guaranteed rights are reasonable and justifiable. Parliament has its role: to choose the appropriate response to social problems within the limiting framework of the Constitution. But the courts also have a role: to determine, objectively and impartially, whether Parliament's choice falls within the limiting framework of the Constitution. The courts are no more permitted to abdicate their responsibility than is Parliament. To carry judicial deference to the point of accepting Parliament's view simply on the basis that the problem is serious and the solution difficult, would be to diminish the role of the courts in the constitutional process and to weaken the structure of rights upon which our constitution and our nation is founded.

. . .

I agree with La Forest J. that proof to the standard required by science is not required. Nor is proof beyond a reasonable doubt on the criminal standard required. As the s. 1 jurisprudence has established, the civil standard of proof on a balance of probabilities at all stages of the proportionality analysis is more appropriate. . . . Care must be taken not to overstate the objective. The objective relevant to the s. 1 analysis is the objective of the infringing measure, since it is the infringing measure and nothing else which is sought to be justified. If the objective is stated too broadly, its importance may be exaggerated and the analysis compromised. As my colleague has noted, the

Tobacco Products Control Act is but one facet of a complex legislative and policy scheme to protect Canadians from the health risks of tobacco use. However, the objective of the impugned measures themselves is somewhat narrower than this. The objective of the advertising ban and trade mark usage restrictions must be to prevent people in Canada from being persuaded by advertising and promotion to use tobacco products. The objective of the mandatory package warning must be to discourage people who see the package from tobacco use.

. . .

I come finally to a fourth general matter discussed by La Forest J. — the degree of deference which appellate courts should accord to the findings of the trial judge under s. 1 of the Charter analysis. The trial judge in these cases concluded that the proportionality test was not met. He based this conclusion on findings that the evidence failed to establish any of the three requirements for proportionality under s. 1. As a general rule, courts of appeal decline to interfere with findings of fact by a trial judge unless they are unsupported by the evidence or based on clear error. This rule is based in large part on the advantage afforded to the trial judge and denied to the appellate court of seeing and hearing the witnesses. La Forest J. concludes that this rule does not apply to the findings of the trial judge in these cases, because those findings were not "adjudicative facts" but rather were "legislative facts".

While this approach sheds some light on the matter, the distinction between legislative and adjudicative facts may be harder to maintain in practice than in theory. Suffice it to say that in the context of the s. 1 analysis, more deference may be required to findings based on evidence of a purely factual nature whereas a lesser degree of deference may be required where the trial judge has considered social science and other policy oriented evidence. As a general matter, appellate courts are not as constrained by the trial judge's findings in the context of the s. 1 analysis as they are in the course of non-constitutional litigation, since the impact of the infringement on constitutional rights must often be assessed by reference to a broad review of social, economic and political factors in addition to scientific facts. At the same time, while appellate courts are not bound by the trial judge's findings in respect of social science evidence, they should remain sensitive to the fact that the trial judge has had the advantage of hearing competing expert testimony firsthand. The trial judge's findings with respect to the credibility of certain witnesses may be useful when the appeal court reviews the record.

LIBMAN v. QUEBEC (ATTORNEY GENERAL)
[1997] 3 S.C.R. 569 (S.C.C.)

The appellant challenged the constitutional validity of certain provisions of the Quebec Referendum Act. The Court found the impugned provisions infringed the freedoms of expression and association guaranteed by ss. 2(b) and (d) of the Charter. In the courts below, the Superior Court and the Court of Appeal held that the impugned provisions infringed freedom of expression but that this infringement was justifiable under s. 1 of the Charter. The

Supreme Court decided the provisions couldn't be saved. In the course of its *per curiam* decision the Court wrote:

. . .

In *R.J.R.-MacDonald*, supra, McLachlin J. explained the application of the minimal impairment test as follows, at p. 342:

> [T]he government must show that the measures at issue impair the right of free expression as little as reasonably possible in order to achieve the legislative objective. The impairment must be "minimal", that is, the law must be carefully tailored so that rights are impaired no more than necessary. The tailoring process seldom admits of perfection and the courts must accord some leeway to thelegislator. If the law falls within a range of reasonable alternatives, the courts will not find it overbroad merely because they can conceive of an alternative which might better tailor objective to infringement.

This Court has already pointed out on a number of occasions that in the social, economic and political spheres, where the legislature must reconcile competing interests in choosing one policy among several that might be acceptable, the courts must accord great deference to the legislature's choice because it is in the best position to make such a choice. On the other hand, the courts will judge the legislature's choices more harshly in areas where the government plays the role of the "singular antagonist of the individual" — primarily in criminal matters — owing to their expertise in these areas (*Irwin Toy*, supra, at pp. 993-94; *McKinney v. University of Guelph*, [1990] 3 S.C.R. 229, at pp. 304-5; *Stoffman v. Vancouver General Hospital*, [1990] 3 S.C.R. 483, at p. 521; *R.J.R.-MacDonald*, supra, at pp. 279 and 331-32). La Forest J.'s comment on the subject in RJR-MacDonald, supra, at p. 277, is perfectly apposite:

> Courts are specialists in the protection of liberty and the interpretation of legislation and are, accordingly, well placed to subject criminal justice legislation to careful scrutiny. However, courts are not specialists in the realm of policy-making, nor should they be. This is a role properly assigned to the elected representatives of the people, who have at their disposal the necessary institutional resources to enable them to compile and assess social science evidence, to mediate between competing social interests and to reach out and protect vulnerable groups.

(b) Prescribed by law

Since s. 1 is expressly designed to consider the possibility of reasonable limits "prescribed by law", it can never be used to justify unconstitutional conduct, for example by police officers. It is now well understood that the prescription by law can be by statute or regulation, express or implied, or by common law. In *R. v. Therens*, [1985] 1 S.C.R. 613 (S.C.C.), the Supreme Court held that the Criminal Code breathalyzer demand power did not involve a limit on the right to counsel. However, in *R. v. Thomsen*, [1988] 1 S.C.R. 640 (S.C.C.), the court held that the power to demand a roadside test *did* involve an implied limit on the right to counsel. In *R. v. Grant*, [1991] 3 S.C.R. 139, 7 C.R. (4th) 388, 67 C.C.C. (3d) 268 (S.C.C.) it was held that there was no significance in the fact that the word "roadside" has now been deleted from the current Criminal Code provision in s. 254(2).

A 7-2 majority of the Supreme Court in *R. v. Orbanski*, [2005] 2 S.C.R. 3 (*sub nom. R. v. Elias*), 196 C.C.C. (3d) 481, 29 C.R. (6th) 205 (S.C.C.) recently extended this implied limit approach to authorise sobriety tests and question as to intoxication following vehicle stops without s. 7 or 10(b) rights.

The Ontario Court of Appeal held in *Ont. Film & Video Appreciation Soc. and Ont. Bd. of Censors* (1984), 38 C.R. (3d) 271 (Ont. C.A.) that a non-binding set of broad guidelines promulgated by pamphlet were not capable of being law and therefore could not be a s. 1 limit on the freedom of expression. Furthermore, it is now clearly established that a Charter right or freedom cannot be subject to a reasonable limit prescribed by law under s. 1 if that law is too vague: see *Ref. re Criminal Code, Ss. 193 & 195.1(1)(c)* (1990), 77 C.R. (3d) 1 (S.C.C.). The Supreme Court expressly adopted the view of the Federal Court of Appeal in *Luscher v. Dep. M.N.R. (Customs & Excise)* (1985), 45 C.R. (3d) 81 (Fed. C.A.) that a customs tariff on an immoral or indecent matter was so vague, ambiguous, uncertain and subject to discretionary determination that it was, for that fact alone, an unreasonable limit.

In early Charter analysis, it was thought that there would be some Charter rights or freedoms that would not be subject to further balancing under s. 1. In *Hunter v. Southam Inc.*, [1984] 2 S.C.R. 145 (S.C.C.), the Supreme Court specifically left open the difficult question of the relationship between the protection in s. 8 against unreasonable search or seizure and s. 1 and, in particular, "what further balancing of interest, *if any,* may be contemplated by s. 1, beyond that envisaged by s. 8." Later, for the Ontario Court of Appeal in *R. v. Noble* (1984), 42 C.R. (3d) 209, 16 C.C.C. (3d) 146 (Ont. C.A.), Mr. Justice Martin indicated that he would have "great difficulty" in concluding that an unreasonable search power was justifiable under s. 1 as a reasonable limit. Likewise, it seems counter-intuitive to justify cruel and unusual punishment contrary to s. 12 or a denial of liberty contrary to principles of fundamental justice in s. 7. However, in the case of s. 7, it is now beyond question that the Supreme Court will consider the possibility of demonstrably justifying violations although it is reluctant to do so.

In *R. v. Heywood* (1994), 34 C.R. (4th) 133 (S.C.C.) the majority of the Court held the loitering offence under what was then s. 179(1)(b) of the Criminal Code was contrary to section 7 of the Charter on the basis of overbreadth and that the violation could not be justified under section 1. Cory J. for the majority noted that in the *Reference re s. 94(2) of the Motor Vehicle Act (B.C.)* case the Court had previously expressed doubt whether any s. 7 violation could ever be justified except perhaps in times of war or national emergencies, and further held that overbroad legislation which infringed section 7 would "appear to be incapable of passing the minimum intrusion branch of the s. 1 analysis" (at 163).

(c) "To the extent of the inconsistency"

Section 52 of the Constitution states that a law which is inconsistent with the Constitution is of no force and effect, "to the extent of the inconsistency". Can the law then be partially saved?

Recall *Hunter v. Southam Inc.*, [1984] 2 S.C.R. 145 (S.C.C.), where the prosecution asked the Court to "read down" the legislation to make it reasonable under s. 8 of the Charter and so compatible with the Charter. The Court declined the invitation and Dickson C.J. wrote:

> While the courts are guardians of the Constitution and of individuals' rights under it, it is the legislature's responsibility to enact legislation that embodies appropriate safeguards to comply with the Constitution's requirements. It should not fall to the courts to fill in the details that will render legislative lacunae constitutional.

In *R. v. Oakes* (1983), 32 C.R. (3d) 193, 2 C.C.C. (3d) 339 (Ont. C.A.), the prosecution asked the court to read the legislation down in such a way that it would be reasonable within s. 11(*d*) of the Charter. The presumptive device, mandating a finding of an intention to traffic on proof of possession, would be reasonable, provided the amount possessed was substantial. The Court declined and Martin J.A. wrote:

> Parliament, if it has wished to do so, might have decided that possession of a specified quantity of a certain drug was more consistent with trafficking than with possession for personal use, and could have made the possession of the specified quantity presumptive evidence that the drug was possessed for the purpose of trafficking. . . . Since, however, Parliament has not addressed that issue, I do not think the courts should undertake to rewrite the statute by applying it on a "case by case" basis even if we were entitled to do so, and I think we are not.

Nevertheless there are indications of a change in attitude. In *R. v. Holmes* (1988), 64 C.R. (3d) 97, 41 C.C.C. (3d) 497 (S.C.C.), the accused was charged with possession "without lawful excuse, the proof of which lies upon him" of housebreaking instruments. Dickson C.J. found the legislative provision to be a violation of s. 11(*d*) and not saved by s. 1 but wrote:

> This does not, however, lead to the conclusion that the whole of s. 309(1) is void. Excising the words "the proof of which lies upon him" from the provision would eliminate the possibility of the conviction of an accused who had a lawful excuse for his or her actions but could not prove that excuse on a balance of probabilties. . . . I would order that the offending words be severed, so that an accused bears only an evidential burden in this regard.

For an excellent discussion of this issue, see A. Manson, "The Charter and Declarations of Invalidity" (1990), 74 C.R. (3d) 95.

R. v. GRANT
[1993] 3 S.C.R. 223, 24 C.R. (4th) 1, 84 C.C.C. (3d) 173 (S.C.C.)

The Supreme Court decided that s. 10 of the Narcotic Control Act (NCA) violated s. 8 because it authorized warrantless searches but there was no requirement in the provision that there had to be exigent circumstances. The

Court then had to decide on the appropriate remedy. Writing for a unanimous court, Justice Sopinka decided to read it down:

> In *Schachter v. Canada*, [1992] 2 S.C.R. 679, Lamer C.J.C. for the court, set out the range of remedies and the basic approach to their selection:
>
>> A court has flexibility in determining what course of action to take following a violation of the *Charter* which does not survive s. 1 scrutiny. Section 52 of the *Constitution Act, 1982* mandates the striking down of any law that is inconsistent with the provisions of the Constitution, but only "to the extent of the inconsistency". Depending upon the circumstances, a court may simply strike down, it may strike down and temporarily suspend the declaration of invalidity, or it may resort to the techniques of reading down or reading in. ... In choosing how to apply s. 52 . . . a court will determine its course of action with reference to the nature of the violation and the context of the specific legislation under consideration. [At pp. 695-96.]
>
> The Crown has admitted that s. 10 of the NCA is unreasonable in so far as it authorizes warrantless searches of places other than a dwelling-house in circumstances in which it would be practicable to obtain a warrant. The Crown further suggested that the appropriate remedy in the circumstances would be to "read down" s. 10 so as not to authorize warrantless searches where it is feasible to obtain a warrant. I am satisfied that this remedy is the appropriate one considering that the concerns generally associated with "reading down" do not arise in the case at bar.

In *Laba*, Sopinka J. for the unanimous Court held that the remedy for the unconstitutional reverse onus in question was to read it as an evidentiary burden. The section was in future to be read as deleting "unless he establishes" and inserting "in the absence of evidence which raises a reasonable doubt". **Is this reading in or reading down? Should the Court be engaged in such legislative redrafting?**

4. Judicial Stay as Abuse of Process

Over a number of years, prior to the Charter, the courts, particularly in Ontario, developed a common law power for judges to stay criminal proceedings as an abuse of process. The power was actually used very sparingly and often to control prosecutorial practices at trial considered by a trial judge to be oppressive. When, however, the matter reached the Supreme Court of Canada in *Rourke v. R.,* the alleged abuse arose from pre-trial delay by the police. The majority of the Supreme Court seemed to reject any notion of the judicial power to stay as an abuse. Identify and evaluate the policy considerations advanced on either side.

ROURKE v. R.

[1978] 1 S.C.R. 1021, 38 C.R.N.S. 268, 35 C.C.C. (2d) 129 (S.C.C.)

PIGEON J. (Martland, Ritchie, Beetz and de Grandpre JJ. concurring):—On 26th February 1973 an information was sworn against the appellant alleging a kidnapping and robbery committed on 5th October 1971. A warrant was issued and the appellant was later arrested on 3rd April 1973. A preliminary inquiry was held in June 1973 and the appellant was committed to trial. When he appeared for trial before a County Court Judge on 21st November 1973 on an indictment preferred by an agent of the Attorney General of British Columbia, he moved for a stay of the proceedings as an abuse of process. His contention was that the delay in bringing him before the court was prejudicial to his defence; a person who would have been a key witness had died in the interval. It was also asserted that the appellant had not been in hiding and could readily have been arrested sooner if the police had acted with reasonable diligence. The County Court Judge accepted those submissions and stayed the proceedings.

An application for mandamus heard by a judge of the Supreme Court of British Columbia [16 C.C.C. (2d) 133] was dismissed on the basis that the County Court Judge had jurisdiction to do what he had done and, having exercised his discretion bona fide and on evidence before him, his decision could not be revised. This judgment was unanimously reversed on appeal, McIntyre J.A. saying for the court [[1975] 6 W.W.R. 591 at 603-604, 25 C.C.C. (2d) 555, 62 D.L.R. (3d) 650]:

> I do not treat lightly the argument that an accused may suffer prejudice by delay even before criminal proceedings commence. It may well be that a case could arise where real prejudice could result from such delay. It is my view, however, that such delay would ordinarily raise a substantive defence. The provisions of the Criminal Code above referred to [ss. 577(3) and 737] would give the trial judge ample power to see the accused received what he is entitled to, that is, a fair trial according to law and in a proper case, where delay has denied the right to make full answer and defence, an acquittal might well result. In my view, however, facts which would give the discretion to the County Court Judge to stay the proceedings had not arisen in the case at bar. Matters should have proceeded and the respondent could have raised had he been so disposed the matters complained of at his trial.

> I now turn to the final question. Is mandamus available to the Crown in this case? With the utmost deference I am unable to share the view of the Judge appealed from that the remedy of mandamus may not be given here. It is well settled in my opinion that where a judge having a jurisdiction to exercise declines to do so because of a decision on a preliminary question, which does not go to the merits as regards either fact or law, mandamus will lie. I refer to such cases as Rex v. Pochrebny, [1930] 1 W.W.R. 139, affirmed [1930] 1 W.W.R. 688, 38 Man. R. 593, 53 C.C.C. 163 (C.A.), where a reference is made to leading authorities on the subject, and to Regina v. Smith (1974), 16 C.C.C. (2d) 11 (N.B. C.A.), and to Regina v. Taylor, 44 C.R. 51, 48 W.W.R. 361, [1964] 3 C.C.C. 363 (Sask.).

> In the case at bar it is clear that the County Court Judge declined to exercise his jurisdiction to hear and to determine the case upon a point clearly preliminary to the proceeding and upon matters which preceded the preferring of the indictment. In my view the preliminary objection was unfounded and mandamus should go.

I cannot find any rule in our criminal law that prosecutions must be instituted promptly and ought not to be permitted to be proceeded with if a delay in instituting them may have caused prejudice to the accused. In fact, no authority was cited to establish the existence of such a principle, which is at variance with the rule that criminal offences generally are not subject to prescription except in the case of specific offences for which a prescription time has been established by statute. I have to disagree with the view expressed by McIntyre J.A. that there could be factual situations giving to a trial judge discretion to stay proceedings for delay. For the reasons I gave in *Regina v. Osborn*, 12 C.R.N.S. 1, [1971] S.C.R. 184, 1 C.C.C. (2d) 482, 15 D.L.R. (3d) 85, I cannot admit of any general discretionary power in courts of criminal jurisdiction to stay proceedings regularly instituted because the prosecution is considered oppressive. In fact, I think the correct view is that which was expressed as follows by Viscount Dilhorne in *D.P.P. v. Humphrys*, [1976] 2 All E.R. 497 at 510-11:

> In *Mills v. Cooper*, [1967] 2 Q.B. 459, [1967] 2 All E.R. 100, where justices had dismissed a summons on the ground that it was oppressive and an abuse of the process of the court, Lord Parker C.J. [at p. 467], while holding that it was not, said:
>
> '. . . every court has undoubtedly a right in its discretion to decline to hear proceedings on the ground that they are oppressive, and an abuse of the process of the court.'
>
> I must confess to some doubt whether this is a correct statement of the law in relation to magistrates' courts. If it is, it appears to me to be fraught with considerable dangers. One bench, thinking a prosecution should not have been brought, will dismiss it as oppressive and vexatious. Other benches on precisely the same facts may take a completely different view, with the result that there is a lack of uniformity in the administration of justice.
>
> Nor is the existence of the power my noble and learned friends, Lord Salmon and Lord Edmund-Davies, think the judge has and its exercise without considerable dangers.
>
> A judge must keep out of the arena. He should not have or appear to have any responsibility for the institution of a prosecution. The functions of prosecutors and of judges must not be blurred. If a judge has power to decline to hear a case because he does not think it should be brought, then it soon may be thought that the cases he allows to proceed are cases brought with his consent or approval.
>
> If there is the power which my noble and learned friends think there is to stop a prosecution on indictment in limine, it is in my view a power that should only be exercised in the most exceptional circumstances.

In considering the situation in the courts of Canada, due weight should be given to the effect of the codification of our criminal law. Here is in what terms s. 7(3) of the Criminal Code, R.S.C. 1970, c. C-34, preserves common law defences:

> (3) Every rule and principle of the common law that renders any circumstance a justification or excuse for an act or a defence to a charge continues in force and applies in respect of proceedings for an offence under this Act or any other Act of the Parliament of Canada, except in so far as they are altered by or are inconsistent with this Act or any other Act of the Parliament of Canada.

This provision refers to a "defence", not to a discretionary stay of proceedings. In this connection, I would point out that in *Kienapple v. The Queen*, 26 C.R.N.S. 1, [1975] 1 S.C.R. 729, 15 C.C.C. (2d) 524, 44 D.L.R. (3d) 351, as in *Doré v. A.G. Can.*, 27 C.R.N.S. 237, [1975] 1 S.C.R. 756, 15 C.C.C. (2d) 542, 1 N.R. 489, 44 D.L.R. (3d) 370, res judicata (rather than issue estoppel) was accepted as a defence on the merits, not as a preliminary plea. This distinction is important. It happens here that the case was not tried before a superior court judge and, therefore, mandamus lay to revise a decision on a preliminary question which did not go to the merits: *Kipp v. A.G. Ont.*, 45 C.R. 1, [1965] S.C.R. 57, [1965] 2 C.C.C. 133. However, if the same decision had been made by a superior court judge, such remedy would clearly not be available and it does not seem that an appeal would lie.

By virtue of ss. 602 and 605(1), there is a right of appeal only if the decision is "a judgment or verdict of acquittal". What is an "acquittal" was considered in *Regina v. Sheets*, 15 C.R.N.S. 232, [1971] 1 W.W.R. 672, [1971] S.C.R. 614, 1 C.C.C. (2d) 508, 16 D.L.R. (3d) 221. It was there held that a judgment quashing an indictment, not on account of "procedural or technical defects", but on the interpretation of the section under which the accused was charged, was in effect an "acquittal". The reasons given for the full court by Fauteux C.J.C. do not seem to contemplate any disposition which would be neither a dismissal of the charge on the merits, nor a quashing on procedural grounds, although it is expressly stated that a quashing on the ground of prescription is an "acquittal". It is obvious that the dismissal of a charge upon one of the special pleas mentioned in s. 535 is a disposition on the merits and, therefore, an "acquittal".

In my view, the absence of any provision in the Criminal Code contemplating the staying of an indictment by a trial judge or an appeal from such decision is a strong indication against the existence of any power to grant such stay. The present legislative policy is clearly in the direction of allowing a right of appeal from final trial court judgments on indictable offences in all cases. Section 9 of the Criminal Code gives a right of appeal against conviction for contempt of court and this was extended in 1972, c. 13, s. 4, to a conviction for contempt in the face of the court. Section 719(5), enacted by 1964-65, c. 53, s. 1, gives a right of appeal in habeas corpus matters. It would hardly be consistent with such policy to have a discretionary jurisdiction that could be exercised by superior court judges in criminal matters where the only possible appeal would be a direct appeal to this court under s. 41(1) of the Supreme Court Act, R.S.C. 1970, c. S-19. Considerations of policy may not be of much importance in the application of explicit statutory provisions because policy decisions are essentially for Parliament. It is quite another matter when we are dealing with unwritten principles.

I would dismiss the appeal.

LASKIN C.J.C. (Spence, Dickson and Judson JJ. concurring):—In a broad sense, pleas of autrefois convict and acquit and of res judicata and issue estoppel may be said to be aspects of abuse of process; they may be regarded as crystallized means of control, having a particular ambit of operation but not exhaustive of the scope of abuse of process. To recognize it as a desirable general notion for judicial control of the criminal process does not mean that its only bounds are the discretion of a trial judge which must inevitably be respected. That discretion must itself be addressed to situations capable of being embraced in the general notion and cannot itself be the touchstone of abuse of process.

One such situation, recognized long ago in case law, arises where use is sought to be made of the criminal courts to collect a debt or to realize on some civil claim: see *Rex v. Leroux*, 62 O.L.R. 336, 50 C.C.C. 52, [1928] 3 D.L.R. 688 (C.A.); *Rex v. Bell*, [1929] 2 W.W.R. 399, 49 B.C.R. 166, 51 C.C.C. 388, [1929] 3 D.L.R. 931 (C.A.); *Regina v. Leclair*, 23 C.R. 216, [1956] O.W.N. 336, 115 C.C.C. 297 (C.A.); *Nebraska v. Morris*, [1971] 1 W.W.R. 53, 2 C.C.C. (2d) 282, 16 D.L.R. (3d) 102 (Man.). Another situation in which there is a spectrum of cases and where their disparate facts do not admit of common treatment, is that which arises when a charge is withdrawn or dismissed for want of prosecution and then re-laid: see *Regina v. Koski*, [1972] 1 W.W.R. 398, 5 C.C.C. (2d) 46 (sub nom. *Regina v. K.*) (B.C.) (where there were numerous delays in proceeding against a juvenile, none of them caused by the accused, and where, after accused appeared for trial with a number of witnesses for the second time, an adjournment was sought by the Crown and was refused by the court which dismissed the charges for want of prosecution and subsequently ordered a stay of proceedings when a new information was sworn containing the same charges); *Regina v. Heric*, [1975] 4 W.W.R. 422, 23 C.C.C. (2d) 410 (B.C.) (where adjournment refused to Crown and charge dismissed when no evidence presented, and where new charge, laid on same facts, held to be abuse of process but res judicata also held to be available to accused); *Regina v. Davis*, [1975] 5 W.W.R. 669, 24 C.C.C. (2d) 218 (B.C.) (stay of proceedings to cure procedural error and relaying of information not an abuse of process); *A.G. Sask. v. McDougall*, [1972] 2 W.W.R. 66 (Sask.) (charge withdrawn after plea of not guilty and several adjournments and then re-laid and after further adjournments accused acquitted after trial; Crown on appeal by way of trial de novo proposing to lead evidence not presented to court of first instance; held to be abuse of process); *Regina v. Kowerchuk*, 15 C.R.N.S. 95, [1971] 4 W.W.R. 564, 3 C.C.C. (2d) 291, reversed 23 C.R.N.S. 55, [1972] 5 W.W.R. 255, which was affirmed 23 C.R.N.S. 55n, [1972] 5 W.W.R. 255n (Alta. C.A.) (proceedings stayed for abuse of process where Crown at time of trial withdrew charge and laid new information for virtually same drug offence because unable to produce analyst as required witness on charge as originally laid); *Regina v. Del Puppo*, [1974] 3 W.W.R. 621, 16 C.C.C. (2d) 462 (B.C.) (abuse of process where, inter alia, after charge dismissed for want of prosecution following delays and adjournment new information sworn on same charge to get around court's refusal to grant another adjournment).

A variation on this situation is the attempt to proceed on a second identical information after the accused has been discharged following a preliminary inquiry: see *Re Sheehan and The Queen* (1973), 14 C.C.C. (2d) 23 (Ont.) (prohibition granted but court recognized indictment could be preferred with consent of judge or Attorney General pursuant to Code s. 505(4)).

Abuse of process has been put forward in a number of Canadian cases as a ground for staying or prohibiting criminal proceedings where there has been excessive and unexplained delay in bringing the accused to trial after the charge or after committal for trial: see *Regina v. Falls and Nobes* (1976), 26 C.C.C. (2d) 541 (Ont.) (frequent delays because of non-appearance of complainant and accused appearing 16 and 17 times respectively over a period of about two years, during which time charge withdrawn and re-laid; delay oppressive and prejudicial to accused and proceedings stayed); *Regina v. Burns, Fairchild and Donnelly,* 30 C.R.N.S. 387, [1975] 4 W.W.R. 305, 25 C.C.C. (2d) 391 (B.C.) (no abuse of process where delay between preliminary hearing and trial not occasioned by Crown); *Regina v. Thorpe* (1973), 11 C.C.C. (2d) 502 (Ont.) (two-year unexplained delay of Crown after committal for trial before trial date fixed held to be prejudicial to fair trial and abuse of process); *Re Vroom and Lacey* (1973), 14 C.C.C. (2d) 10 (Ont.) (no abuse of process by mere fact of repeated delays, although none attributable to the accused, or by reason of the swearing of three successive informations where they all concerned the same charge).

Abuse of process as a ground for quashing charges or staying proceedings was invoked in cases where an accused was removed for trial to a place remote from that where the offences were allegedly committed and was prejudiced in his ability, by reason, for example, of prohibitive cost, to bring witnesses, and thus denied his right to make full answer and defence: see *Regina v. Ittoshat,* 10 C.R.N.S. 385, [1970] 5 C.C.C. 159, 12 D.L.R. (3d) 266 (Que.); *Regina v. Atwood,* [1972] 4 W.W.R. 399, 7 C.C.C. (2d) 116, reversed [1972] 5 W.W.R. 600, 8 C.C.C. (2d) 147 (N.W.T.). Again, abuse of process was made the ground of a stay of proceedings in a case where the accused committed the alleged offence at the instigation of a police officer who instilled the idea and actively persuaded and encouraged the accused to carry it out: see *Regina v. Shipley,* [1970] 2 O.R. 411, [1970] 3 C.C.C. 398. This court dealt with a similar situation, one going beyond the involvement of an agent provocateur, in *Lemieux v. The Queen,* 2 C.R.N.S. 1, [1967] S.C.R. 492, [1968] 1 C.C.C. 187, 63 D.L.R. (2d) 75, where Judson J. for the court held that an accused could not be found guilty of breaking and entering a dwelling house where the scheme to entrap the accused had been set up by the police with an informer and the owner of the dwelling house had co-operated, giving possession of the house to the police who had urged the informer to break in with the assistance of others including the accused.

I have paraded this long list of cases to show how varied are the fact situations in which judges of different levels and different provinces have used abuse of process as a way of controlling prosecution behaviour which operates prejudicially to accused persons. I pass no judgment on the correctness of any of the decisions, but they do indicate, by their very diversity, the utility of a general principle of abuse of process which judges should be able to invoke in appropriate circumstances to mark their control of the process of their courts and to require fair behaviour of the Crown towards accused persons. . . . .

The facts and, indeed, the situation now before us do not, in my view, provide any basis for considering the invocation of the court's power to stay the proceedings against the accused. The appellant is in effect asking the courts to undertake the supervision, through their power to control prosecutions before them, of the operation and efficiency of police departments, departments which vary in organization and in size and in the demands that are made upon them. Absent any contention that the delay in apprehending the accused had some ulterior purpose, courts are in no position to tell the police that they did not proceed expeditiously enough with their investigation, and then impose a sanction of a stay when prosecution is initiated. The time lapse between the commission of an offence and the laying of a charge following apprehension of an accused cannot be monitored by courts by fitting investigations into a standard mould or moulds. Witnesses and evidence may disappear in the short run as well as in the long, and the accused too may have to be sought for a long or short period of time. Subject to such controls as are prescribed by the Criminal Code, prosecutions initiated a lengthy period after the alleged commission of an offence must be left to take their course and to be dealt with by the court on the evidence, which judges are entitled to weigh for cogency as well as credibility. The court can call for an explanation of any untoward delay in prosecution and may be in a position, accordingly, to assess the weight of some of the evidence.

In the result, I see no basis, despite allegations of prejudice, upon which abuse of process could be invoked in this case and hence it did not provide an occasion for the exercise of discretion. *Regina v. Koski*, supra, if it be correctly decided (and, as I said, I pass no judgment on it), is a far different case from the present one. Its invocation by Rae J. shows the danger of generalizing the application of the doctrine of abuse of process.

For the reasons aforesaid, differing in part from those of the British Columbia Court of Appeal with whose conclusion, however, I agree, I would dismiss the appeal.

R. v. JEWITT
[1985] 2 S.C.R. 185, 47 C.R. (3d) 193, 21 C.C.C. (3d) 7 (S.C.C.)

DICKSON C.J.C.:—The principal issue in this appeal is whether a judicially entered stay of proceedings is "a judgment or verdict of acquittal of a trial court" from which the Crown may appeal to the Court of Appeal under s. 605(1)(a) of the Criminal Code. The point, though narrow, is important and contentious. It has given rise to conflicting opinions in Courts of Appeal of this country.

The respondent, Damon Fidel Garfield Jewitt, was charged with unlawfully trafficking in a narcotic, cannabis (marijuana), contrary to the provisions of the Narcotic Control Act. He pleaded not guilty to the charge. He was tried at Vancouver before Wong Co. Ct. J. sitting with a jury. He admitted selling one pound of marijuana but said he was persuaded to sell to the undercover police officer by a fellow employee who was a police informer. The jury found there had been unlawful entrapment and the court thereupon directed the clerk of the court to make an entry on the record staying the proceedings on the indictment.

. . .

Abuse of Process

Before considering whether a stay of proceedings is a judgment or verdict of acquittal or tantamount thereto, it is necessary to determine whether, at common law, a discretionary power to stay proceedings in a criminal case for abuse of process exists, in the words of Laskin C.J.C. in *Rourke v. R.*, [1978] 1 S.C.R. 1021 at 1034, as a means of "controlling prosecution behaviour which operates prejudicially to accused persons".

The inherent jurisdiction of a superior court to stay proceedings which are an abuse of its process was recognized in Canada as early as 1886, in the case of *Re Sproule* (1886), 12 S.C.R. 140. In recent years, however, uncertainty has clouded the question whether Canadian courts, apart from powers given to the Attorney General under s. 508 of the Criminal Code, have a discretion to stay proceedings for abuse of process. This may, in some measure, stem from several decisions of this court, in particular, *R. v. Osborn*, [1971] S.C.R. 184; *Rourke v. R.*, supra; and *Amato v. R.*, [1982] 2 S.C.R. 418.

This court's decision in *Rourke*, supra, was seen by some as a death blow to the doctrine of abuse of process. As Stanley Cohen stated in "Observations on the Re-Emergence of the Doctrine of Abuse of Process" (1981), 19 C.R. (3d) 310: "The strong statements of Pigeon J. in disposing of that appeal led many to believe that any future use of the doctrine had been foreclosed."

In *Rourke*, the abuse alleged stemmed from lengthy delay on the part of the police in arresting the accused. Pigeon J., speaking for the majority of the court, concluded at p. 1043:

> For the reasons I gave in *The Queen v. Osborn*, [1971] S.C.R. 184, I cannot admit of any general discretionary power in courts of criminal jurisdiction to stay proceedings regularly instituted because the prosecution is considered oppressive.

And on the same page:

> I cannot find any rule in our criminal law that prosecutions must be instituted promptly and ought not to be permitted to be proceeded with if a delay in instituting them may have caused prejudice to the accused.

The apparent finality with which Pigeon J. appeared to deny any discretionary power to stay proceedings was tempered by his adoption, as the "correct view", of what was said by Viscount Dilhorne in *D.P.P. v. Humphrys*, [1976] 2 All E.R. 497 at 510-11 (H.L.). The passage quoted by Pigeon J. at pp. 1043-44 concluded with these words:

> If there is the power which my noble and learned friends think there is to stop a prosecution on indictment in limine, it is in my view a power that should only be exercised in the most exceptional circumstances.

The breadth of the decision in *Rourke*, supra, has been the subject of differing views in various provincial appellate courts.

The British Columbia Court of Appeal in *R. v. Lebrun* (1978), 7 C.R. (3d) 93, interpreted *Rourke* widely and declared simpliciter that the doctrine of abuse of process was not available in criminal proceedings. A similar result was reached by the Manitoba Court of Appeal in *R. v. Catagas* (1977), 2 C.R. (3d) 328.

On the other hand, the Ontario and Alberta Courts of Appeal began almost immediately to construe the decision in *Rourke* restrictively and assert the potential for application of the doctrine in exceptional circumstances: see, for example, *Re Ball and R.* (1978), 44 C.C.C. (2d) 532 (Ont. C.A.); *Re Abarca and R.* (1980), 57 C.C.C. (2d) 410 (Ont. C.A.); *Re Abitibi Paper Co. and R.* (1979), 47 C.C.C. (2d) 487 (Ont. C.A.); *R. v. Crneck* (1980), 30 O.R. (2d) 1 (Ont. H.C.); *Orysiuk v. R.* (1977), 37 C.C.C. (2d) 445 (Alta. C.A.).

Several decisions of this court also contained obiter dicta suggesting the doctrine was not entirely moribund.

Pratte J., in *Erven v. R.,* [1979] 1 S.C.R. 926, referred obliquely to the doctrine of abuse of process, remarking on p. 957:

> The normal procedure for determining the voluntariness of a statement of the accused is through a *voir dire* and, the onus being on the Crown to prove voluntariness, a request for a *voir dire* should not be denied save in rare circumstances, where, for instance, the request would be clearly frivolous or *would constitute a demonstrable abuse of process.* [The italics are mine.]

The matter was raised again in *R. v. Krannenburg,* [1980] 1 S.C.R. 1053, where, in reasons in which Pigeon J. concurred, I commented on p. 1061:

> Indeed the laying of another information may amount to nothing less than an abuse of process.

Abuse of process was most recently reviewed by this court in the case of *Amato,* supra. The pivotal issue in *Amato* was the defence of entrapment. Estey J., with Laskin C.J.C. and McIntyre and Lamer JJ. concurring, reviewed the power of the court to stay a prosecution where an abuse of process was found to have occurred. On this matter, Estey J. concluded, on pp. 453-54:

> I come therefore to the conclusion that the decisions of *Osborn* and *Rourke* must be taken as standing on their own facts and limited precisely to the ratio of the judgments disposing of the issues arising on those facts. It follows therefore that the observations of Jessup J.A. in *Osborn* with reference to the origins and breadth of the trial court discretion to protect the processes of the courts from abuse remain substantially unimpaired by succeeding decisions in this Court. Viewed from another perspective the majority in *Rourke* affirms an exceptional jurisdiction to stay proceedings whereas Laskin C.J.C. for the minority takes the view of Lord Devlin in *Connelly* and finds the doctrine of abuse of process a wide-ranging technique for the control by the criminal court of criminal procedure in the protection of the processes of that court; a technique illustrated but not limited by the special pleas of *autrefois acquit* and *convict, res judicata* and issue estoppel (p. 287). In my respectful view, much of what was said by both divisions of this Court in *Rourke* is *obiter dicta,* bearing in mind the precise issue of abuse of process in the form of delay by the prosecution which was then the only issue before the Court. There is a distinction to be drawn where the initiating process is valid and the only issue is delay prejudicial to the accused, as in *Rourke;* and the case where the executive action leading to the charge and its prosecution is offensive to the principles on which the administration of justice is conducted by the courts. It is for this further reason that the judgment in *Rourke* in my view is not here applicable.

Four members of the court, of whom I was one, held that the defence of entrapment, assuming it to be available under Canadian law, did not arise on the facts of the case. Ritchie J. was of the view that, if Amato had been subjected to a threat of violence against himself if he failed to co-operate with the police plan for procuring the drug, this might well have supported a defence of entrapment. Ritchie J. concluded, however, that the evidence did not disclose any such threat.

Although the existence of the power to stay proceedings for abuse of process remained an open question following this court's decision in *Amato,* a number of courts assumed authority to enter a stay in exceptional circumstances: see, for example, *R. v. Miller* (1984), 12 C.C.C. (3d) 54 (B.C. C.A.); *R. v. Boross* (1984), 12 C.C.C. (3d) 480 (Alta. C.A.); and *R. v. Hamm* (1984), 34 Sask. R. 241 (C.A.), leave to appeal to S.C.C. refused [1984] 2 S.C.R. vii.

The Ontario Court of Appeal recently reviewed the authorities in *R. v. Young* (1984), 40 C.R. (3d) 289, per Dubin J.A. (Howland C.J.O. and Martin J.A. concurring), and concluded on p. 329:

> I am satisfied on the basis of the authorities that I have set forth above that there is a residual discretion in a trial court judge to stay proceedings where compelling an accused to stand trial would violate those fundamental principles of justice which underlie the community's sense of fair play and decency and to prevent the abuse of a court's process through oppressive or vexatious proceedings. It is a power, however, of special application which can be exercised only in the clearest of cases.

That the controversy continues, however, can be seen from *R. v. Belton* (1982), 31 C.R. (3d) 223, leave to appeal to S.C.C. refused [1983] 1 S.C.R. v. Monnin J.A., speaking for the court, held that the Manitoba Court of Appeal was bound by the majority decision in *Rourke* to hold that there was no power to stay for an abuse of process. He also stated that the Supreme Court of Canada would have "to give clear indication whether a judicial stay is available or not in the matter of abuse of process". In a subsequent decision, *Balderstone v. R.* (1983), 8 C.C.C. (3d) 532, leave to appeal to S.C.C. refused [1983] 2 S.C.R. v. Monnin C.J.M., again speaking for the court, acknowledged that the abuse of process question was "not free from doubt" and sought further direction from this court.

The New Brunswick Court of Appeal in *R. v. Perry* (1984), 14 C.C.C. (3d) 5, also concluded that a trial court judge is without jurisdiction to stay proceedings for an abuse of process.

It seems to me desirable and timely to end the uncertainty which surrounds the availability of a stay of proceedings to remedy abuse of process. Clearly, there is a need for this court to clarify its position on such a fundamental and wide-reaching doctrine.

Lord Devlin has expressed the rationale supporting the existence of a judicial discretion to enter a stay of proceedings to control prosecutorial behaviour prejudicial to accused persons in *Connelly v. D.P.P.,* [1964] A.C. 1254 at 1354 (H.L.):

Are the courts to rely on the Executive to protect their process from abuse? Have they not themselves an inescapable duty to secure fair treatment for those who come or who are brought before them? To questions of this sort there is only one possible answer. The courts cannot contemplate for a moment the transference to the Executive of the responsibility for seeing that the process of law is not abused.

I would adopt the conclusion of the Ontario Court of Appeal in *R. v. Young*, supra, and affirm that

.... there is a residual discretion in a trial court judge to stay proceedings where compelling an accused to stand trial would violate those fundamental principles of justice which underlie the community's sense of fair play and decency and to prevent the abuse of a court's process through oppressive or vexatious proceedings.

I would also adopt the caveat added by the court in *Young* that this is a power which can be exercised only in the "clearest of cases".

Judgment or Verdict of Acquittal

. . .

I see no logical reason why a decision to quash an indictment on a question of law should be considered a judgment or verdict of acquittal whereas a decision to enter a stay on a question of law should not. Anderson J.A. pointed out it would be an anomolous and absurd result if dismissal of the charges on the basis that the proceedings constituted an abuse of process would permit an appeal but a stay of the proceedings on the basis that they constituted an abuse of process would not. Hence, I would conclude that the administration of criminal justice would be better served by a determination that a stay of proceedings is tantamount to a judgment or verdict of acquittal and subject to appeal by the Crown pursuant to s. 605(1)(*a*).

. . .

The appeal should be allowed, the judgment below set aside and an order go directing the Court of Appeal of British Columbia to hear and determine the Crown's appeal on the merits.

R. v. KEYOWSKI
[1988] 1 S.C.R. 657, 62 C.R. (3d) 349, 40 C.C.C. (3d) 481 (S.C.C.)

The accused's first two trials on charges of criminal negligence causing death ended with the juries failing to agree on a verdict. At the third trial, the trial judge ordered a stay on the grounds that it would constitute both an abuse of process and violation of s. 7 of the Canadian Charter of Rights and Freedoms. The Crown's appeal was allowed and a new trial ordered. The majority held that it was necessary for the accused to show prosecutorial misconduct. The accused appealed further.

WILSON J. (Dickson C.J., Estey, McIntyre, Lamer, La Forest, and L'Heureux-Dubé, concurring):—The legal issue on the appeal is a very narrow one, namely, whether a series of trials could per se constitute an abuse of process or whether it is necessary for the accused to show prosecutorial misconduct. The majority of the Court of Appeal expressed the view that the

accused had to establish prosecutorial misconduct. Vancise J.A., writing for
the majority, stated at p. 68:

> In the absence of evidence that the legal officers of the Crown were guilty of
> prosecutorial misconduct or proceeded for [sic] some ulterior motive, in short that
> the proceedings were oppressive, the continuation of the trial on the indictment is
> not an abuse of process.

To define "oppressive" as requiring misconduct or an improper motive would,
in my view, unduly restrict the operation of the doctrine. In this case, for
example, where there is no suggestion of misconduct, such a definition would
prevent any limit being placed on the number of trials that could take place.
Prosecutorial conduct and improper motivation are but two of many factors to
be taken into account when a court is called upon to consider whether or not in
a particular case the Crown's exercise of its discretion to relay the indictment
amounts to an abuse of process.

While I disagree with the majority of the Court of Appeal that
prosecutorial misconduct must be demonstrated in order to give rise to an
abuse of process, I nevertheless agree with their conclusion that a new trial was
properly ordered in this case. The appellant has, in my view, failed to
demonstrate that this is one of those "clearest of cases" which would justify a
stay. The charge is a serious one. The proceedings have not occupied an undue
amount of time. The accused has not been held in custody, and, while he has
undoubtedly suffered substantial trauma and stigma from the proceedings and
the attendant publicity, he is probably not distinguishable in this respect from
the vast majority of accused. A third trial may indeed stretch the limits of the
community's sense of fair play, but does not of itself exceed them. In these
circumstances, and having regard to the seriousness of the charge, I think that
the administration of justice is best served by allowing the Crown to proceed
with the new trial.

A brief comment on s. 7 of the Charter. The parties to his appeal were
agreed that the common law doctrine of abuse of process was now subsumed in
s. 7. The trial judge accepted this proposition, as did all the members of the
Court of Appeal, although in neither of the courts below was there much
analysis of the relationship between the two. Bayda C.J.S., however, noted, at
pp. 74-75, what he saw as a potential difference in onus:

> Counsel for the Attorney General conceded—and rightly so—that if the
> circumstances of the present case justly give rise to a finding of an abuse of process,
> they would automatically give rise to a finding of violation of s. 7. The converse
> should also be true but for the matter of onus. Had this case been decided on the
> basis of s. 7, it would have been sufficient for the accused to prove *on the balance of
> probabilities* a violation of "the principles of fundamental justice" as that phrase is
> used in s. 7... By deciding the case on the basis of "abuse of process", it would appear
> necessary to apply the "clearest of cases" onus (the *Young-Jewitt* test) in determining
> whether that same violation of "the principles of fundamental justice" occurred. I am
> unable to give a valid explanation for the distinction in onus.

Despite the references to s. 7 in the judgments below, counsel before this
court did not address the s. 7 issue in either written or oral argument. For that

reason I would prefer to leave the issue of the relationship between s. 7 and the common law doctrine of abuse of process to another day.

I would dismiss the appeal.

Appeal dismissed.

R. v. O'CONNOR
[1995] 4 S.C.R. 411, 44 C.R. (4th) 1, 103 C.C.C. (3d) 1 (S.C.C.)

A Bishop was charged with four counts of sexual offences, two involving rape, alleged to have occurred over a three year period some 25 years before. Defence counsel obtained a pre-trial order requiring that the Crown disclose the complainants' entire medical, counselling and school records and that the complainants authorize production of such records. The accused later applied for a judicial stay of proceedings based on non-disclosure of several items. Crown counsel asserted that the non-disclosure of some of the medical records was due to inadvertence on her part, and that she had "dreamt" the transcripts of certain interviews had been disclosed. She submitted that uninhibited disclosure of medical and therapeutic records would revictimize the victims, and suggested that the disclosure order exhibited gender bias. The trial judge dismissed the application for a stay, finding that the failure to disclose certain medical records had been an oversight. He concluded that while the conduct of the Crown was "disturbing", he did not believe that there was a "grand design" to conceal evidence, nor any "deliberate plan to subvert justice". On the second day of the trial, counsel for the accused made another application for a judicial stay of proceedings based largely on the fact that the Crown was still unable to guarantee to the accused that full disclosure had been made. The trial judge stayed proceedings. The Court of Appeal allowed the Crown's appeal and directed a new trial. The accused appealed to the Supreme Court.

We shall return to this decision later when we deal with the topic of disclosure in criminal cases. At this point we consider only the concept of abuse of process. On that point the Court appeared to be unanimous and Justice L'Heureux-Dubé articulated the applicable principles:

L'HEUREUX-DUBÉ J.:—

. . .

The modern resurgence of the common law doctrine of abuse of process began with the judgment of this Court in *R. v. Jewitt*. . . . The general test for abuse of process adopted in that case has been repeatedly affirmed. After considering much of this case law, the Court of Appeal concluded that the preponderance of cases favoured maintaining a distinction between the *Charter* and the common law doctrine of abuse of process. The Court of Appeal may, in my view, have underestimated the extent to which both individual rights to trial fairness and the general reputation of the criminal justice system are fundamental concerns underlying both the common law doctrine of abuse of process and the *Charter*. This, for the following reasons.

First, while the *Charter* is certainly concerned with the rights of the individual, it is also concerned with preserving the integrity of the judicial system. Subsection 24(2) of the *Charter* gives express recognition to this dual role. More significantly, however, this Court has, on many occasions, noted that the principles of fundamental justice in s. 7 are, in large part, inspired by, and premised upon, values that are fundamental to our common law. . . . The common law doctrine of abuse of process is part and parcel of those fundamental values. It is, therefore, not surprising that in *R. v. Potvin*, [1993] 2 S.C.R. 880 at p. 915 (per Sopinka J.), the majority of this Court recognized that the court's power to remedy abuses of its process now has constitutional status.

Conversely, it is equally clear that abuse of process also contemplates important individual interests. . . . What is significant for our purposes, however, is the fact that one often cannot separate the public interests in the integrity of the system from the private interests of the individual accused. In fact, it may be wholly unrealistic to treat the latter as wholly distinct from the former. This Court has repeatedly recognized that human dignity is at the heart of the *Charter*. While respect for human dignity and autonomy may not necessarily, itself, be a principle of fundamental justice (*Rodriguez v. British Columbia (Attorney General)*), [1993] 3 S.C.R. 519 at p. 592, per Sopinka J. for the majority), it seems to me that conducting a prosecution in a manner that contravenes the community's basic sense of decency and fair play and thereby calls into question the integrity of the system is also an affront of constitutional magnitude to the rights of the individual accused. It would violate the principles of fundamental justice to be deprived of one's liberty under circumstances which amount to an abuse of process and, in my view, the individual who is the subject of such treatment is entitled to present arguments under the *Charter* and to request a just and appropriate remedy from a court of competent jurisdiction.

. . .

Second, I would note the beginnings of a strong trend toward convergence between the *Charter* and traditional abuse of process doctrine. In *R. v. Xenos* (1991), 70 C.C.C. (3d) 362 (Que. C.A.), for instance, the accused had been charged with arson and attempting to defraud an insurance company. It emerged in cross-examination that the Crown's key witness had arranged with the insurers to be paid $50,000 by the insurers if the accused was convicted. The trial judge found an abuse of process, but declined to order a stay. Rather, in convicting the accused, he said that he had ignored this evidence. The Court of Appeal agreed in principle with the trial judge that a stay was not the only remedy for an abuse of process and went on to rule that the appropriate remedy was in fact to exclude the witness's testimony in a new trial before a different judge. This case is an excellent example, in my mind, of how courts are becoming increasingly bold and innovative in finding appropriate remedies in lieu of stays for abuses of process. Professor Stuesser points out in "Abuse of Process: The Need to Reconsider" (1994), 29 C.R. (4th) 92 at p. 99, moreover, that the common law in the United Kingdom and Australia urges judges to look at lesser remedies before entering stays of proceedings. He argues that these authorities support the view that even under the common law, the remedy for abuse of process is no longer only a stay of proceedings.

. . .

Remedies less drastic than a stay of proceedings are of course available under s. 24(1) in situations where the "clearest of cases" threshold is not met but where it is proved, on a balance of probabilities, that s. 7 has been violated. In this respect the *Charter* regime is more flexible than the common law doctrine of abuse of process. However, this is not a reason to retain a separate common law regime. It is important to recognize that the *Charter* has now put into judges' hands a scalpel instead of an axe—a tool that may fashion, more carefully than ever, solutions taking into account the sometimes complementary and sometimes opposing concerns of fairness to the individual, societal interests, and the integrity of the judicial system. . . . I see no reason why such balancing cannot be performed equally, if not more, effectively under the *Charter*, both in terms of defining violations and in terms of selecting the appropriate remedy to perceived violations.

For these reasons, I conclude that the only distinction between the two regimes will be those instances in which the Charter, for some reason, does not apply yet where the circumstances nevertheless point to an abuse of the court's process. Because the question is not before us, however, I leave for another day any discussion of when such situations, if they indeed exist, may arise. As a general rule, however, there is no utility in maintaining two distinct approaches to abusive conduct. The distinction is one that only lawyers could possibly find significant. More importantly, maintaining this somewhat artificial dichotomy may, over time, create considerably more confusion than it resolves.

. . .

[The] common law doctrine of abuse of process has found application in a variety of different circumstances involving state conduct touching upon the integrity of the judicial system and the fairness of the individual accused's trial. For this reason, I do not think that it is helpful to speak of there being any one particular "right against abuse of process" within the Charter. Depending on the circumstances, different Charter guarantees may be engaged. For instance, where the accused claims that the Crown's conduct has prejudiced his ability to have a trial within a reasonable time, abuses may be best addressed by reference to s. 11(*b*) of the Charter, to which the jurisprudence of this Court has now established fairly clear guidelines. . . . Alternatively, the circumstances may indicate an infringement of the accused's right to a fair trial, embodied in ss. 7 and 11(*d*) of the Charter. In both of these situations, concern for the individual rights of the accused may be accompanied by concerns about the integrity of the judicial system. In addition, there is a residual category of conduct caught by s. 7 of the Charter. This residual category does not relate to conduct affecting the fairness of the trial or impairing other procedural rights enumerated in the Charter, but instead addresses the panoply of diverse and sometimes unforeseeable circumstances in which a prosecution is conducted in such a manner as to connote unfairness or vexatiousness of such degree that it contravenes fundamental notions of justice and thus undermines the integrity of the judicial process.

It must always be remembered that a stay of proceedings is only appropriate "in the clearest of cases", where the prejudice to the accused's right to make full answer and defence cannot be remedied or where irreparable prejudice would be caused to the integrity of the judicial system if the prosecution were continued. Where life, liberty or security of the person is engaged in a judicial proceeding, and it is proved on a balance of probabilities that the Crown's failure to make proper disclosure to the defence has impaired the accused's ability to make full answer and defence, a violation of s. 7 will have been made out. In such circumstances, the court must fashion a just and appropriate remedy, pursuant to s. 24(1). Although the remedy for such a violation will typically be a disclosure order and adjournment, there may be some extreme cases where the prejudice to the accused's ability to make full answer and defence or to the integrity of the justice system is irremediable. In those "clearest of cases", a stay of proceedings will be appropriate.

On the issue of whether a stay should have been granted on the facts in the *O'Connor* case, a 6-3 majority decided the appeal should be dismissed. L'Heureux-Dubé J., La Forest, Gonthier and McLachlin JJ. concurring, decided that while the Crown's conduct in the case was shoddy and inappropriate, the non-disclosure could not be said to have violated the accused's right to full answer and defence. The order had been issued without any form of inquiry into the relevance of the documents, let alone a balancing of the privacy rights of the complainants and the accused's right to a fair trial, and was thus wrong. Cory J., with Iacobucci J. concurring, decided that although the actions of Crown counsel were extremely high-handed and thoroughly reprehensible, the Crown's misdeeds were not such that, upon a consideration of all the circumstances, the drastic remedy of a stay was merited. Major J., Lamer C.J. and Sopinka J. concurring, dissented on the basis that in their view the Crown's conduct impaired the accused's ability to make full answer and defence and violated fundamental principles of justice underlying the community's sense of fair play and decency. In their view the impropriety of the disclosure order did not excuse the Crown's failure to comply. **Was the majority correct in not confirming the trial judge's stay?**

R. v. L. (W.K.)
[1991] 1 S.C.R. 1091, 6 C.R. (4th) 1, 64 C.C.C. (3d) 321 (S.C.C.)

The accused was charged in 1987 with 17 counts of sexual assault, gross indecency and assault relating to his stepdaughter and two daughters. The first incident was alleged to have occurred in 1957 and the last one in 1985. The victims first complained to the police in 1986. The trial judge stayed the proceedings on the basis a trial now would be contrary to principles of fundamental justice and that the explanation for the 30 year delay in reporting was "ludicrous" and "specious". The British Columbia Court of Appeal held the trial should not have been stayed. On further appeal by the accused, the Supreme Court agreed that this was not a case for a stay.

STEVENSON J. (for the full Court):—

. . .

Does the *Charter* now insulate accused persons from prosecution solely on the basis of the time that has passed between the commission of the offence and the laying of the charge? In my view, it does not.

Staying proceedings based on the mere passage of time would be the equivalent of imposing a judicially created limitation period for a criminal offence. In Canada, except in rare circumstances, there are no limitation periods in criminal law. The comments of Laskin C.J.C. in *Rourke* are equally applicable under the *Charter*.

Sections 7 and 11(*d*) of the *Charter* protect, among other things, an individual's right to a fair trial. The fairness of a trial is not, however, automatically undermined by even a lengthy pre-charge delay. Indeed, a delay may operate to the advantage of the accused, since Crown witnesses may forget or disappear. The comments of Lamer J. (as he then was) in *R. v. Mills*, supra, at p. 945 [[1986] 1 S.C.R.], are apposite:

> Pre-charge delay is relevant under ss. 7 and 11(*d*) because it is not the *length* of the delay which matters but rather the *effect* of that delay upon the fairness of the trial. [Emphasis added.]

Courts cannot, therefore, assess the fairness of a particular trial without considering the particular circumstances of the case. An accused's rights are not infringed solely because a lengthy delay is apparent on the face of the indictment.

I note, additionally, and in response to the trial Judge's specific comments regarding society's attitudes relating to sexual crimes, that the nature of this kind of offence provides additional support for my conclusion. The appellant was charged with several offences which amounted to sexual abuse. It is well documented that non-reporting, incomplete reporting, and delay in reporting are common in cases of sexual abuse. The 1984 *Report of the Committee on Sexual Offences Against Children and Youths* (the "Badgley Report"), vol. 1 (Ottawa: Supply and Services, 1984) (Chair: Robin F. Badgley), explained at p. 187 that:

> Most of these incidents were not reported by victims because they felt that these matters were too personal or sensitive to divulge to others, and because many of them were too ashamed of what had happened.

After reviewing the evidence, the Report concluded that:

> Female victims were more than twice as likely (23.8 per cent) as male victims (11.1 per cent) to have sought assistance. However, a majority of victims of both sexes had not done so. For three in four female victims and about nine in ten male victims, these incidents had been kept as closely guarded personal secrets.

For victims of sexual abuse to complain would take courage and emotional strength in revealing those personal secrets, in opening old wounds. If proceedings were to be stayed based solely on the passage of time between the abuse and the charge, victims would be required to report incidents before they were psychologically prepared for the consequences of that reporting.

That delay in reporting sexual abuse is a common and expected consequence of that abuse has been recognized in other contexts. In the United States, many states have enacted legislation modifying or extending the limitation period for the prosecution of sexual abuse cases, in recognition of the fact that sexual abuse often goes unreported, and even undiscovered by the complainant, for years. This legislation has, to date, withstood constitutional challenges: see, for example, Durga M. Bharam, "Statute of Limitations for Child Sexual Abuse Offenses: A Time for Reform Utilizing the Discovery Rule" (1989), 80 J. Crim. L. & Criminology 842. Establishing a judicial statute of limitations would mean that sexual abusers would be able to take advantage of the failure to report which they themselves, in many cases, caused. This is not a result which we should encourage. There is no place for an arbitrary rule.

Since *O'Connor*, the Supreme Court has continued to vacillate on its approach to abuse of process. In its latest pronouncement in *R. v. Neil* (2002), 6 C.R. (6th) 1, 168 C.C.C. (3d) 321 (S.C.C.), in dismissing the argument for a stay, Binnie J. refers to *Canada (Minister of Citizenship & Immigration) v. Tobiass*, [1997] 3 S.C.R. 391, 10 C.R. (5th) 163, 118 C.C.C. (3d) 443 (S.C.C.), for the propositions that the residual category is a small one and that, in the vast majority of cases, the concern will be about the fairness of the trial.

This contrasts with Binnie J.'s dissenting opinion in *R. v. Regan*, 2002 SCC 12, 49 C.R. (5th) 1, 161 C.C.C. (3d) 97 (S.C.C.) where he states that the observation in *Tobiass* should not be treated as deprecating the importance of the residual category (para. 213). See further comments by H. Archibald Kaiser, "*Regan*: Nearly a Tsunami Out of a Few Ripples", (2002) 49 C.R. (5th) 74 and Nathan Gorham, "*Regan*: The Residual Category of Abuse of Process Continues to Shrink", (2002) 49 C.R. (5th) 87. See earlier David MacAlister, "Does the Residual Category for Abuse of Process Really Exist?" (1999) 28 C.R. (5th) 72.

In *O'Connor*, L'Heureux-Dubé J. for the full Court appeared to determine that the common law doctrine of stay as an abuse of process had now been subsumed under the Charter, except perhaps in cases where the Charter did not apply. In *Neil*, Binnie J. expressly leaves open the question of whether the doctrine of abuse of process can be invoked where there is no state action. According to Binnie J. (para. 43):

At common law, the doctrine of abuse of process was rooted in objectionable conduct by private litigants, for example using the courts for an improper purpose. Although s. 7 of the Charter incorporates the abuse of process doctrine, it does not extinguish the common law doctrine under which the courts have an inherent and residual discretion to control their own processes and prevent their abuse: *Cobb*, *supra*, at para. 37.

In *United States v. Cobb*, [2001] 1 S.C.R. 587, 41 C.R. (5th) 81, Arbour J. stayed an extradition proceedings on the basis that U.S. authorities had been abusive without any mention of the more restrictive approach to the doctrine of stay as an abuse of process set out in *O'Connor*.

The Supreme Court has recently become even more resistant to authorising stays as an abuse of process because of misconduct by the Crown. The Supreme Court has made it clear that the abuse of process doctrine should be only exceptionally applied. In *R. v. Piccirilli* (*sub nom. R. v. Babos*), [2014] 1 S.C.R. 309, 308 C.C.C. (3d) 445, 8 C.R. (7th) 1 (S.C.C.), Moldaver J. decided for the Court over the sole dissent of Abella J. that the stay as an abuse of process under the residual category is to be used in "extremely rare" cases. Justice Moldaver decided that although the abuse doctrine could be invoked against systemic issues, there was a need to balance the interests of society in adjudication on the merits. In *Babos*, a prosecutorial threat to lay more charges if the accused proceeded to trial went without a remedy. See critical comments by Tim Quigley, "*Babos*: Balancing Test Unnecessarily Restricts Residual Category for Stay as Abuse of Process" (2014), 8 C.R. (7th) 55 and Archibald Kaiser "Further Narrowing Access to a Stay of Proceedings Where the Integrity of the Judicial Process Is Implicated" (2014), 8 C.R. (7th) 59. In *R. v. Emms*, [2012] 3 S.C.R. 810, 292 C.C.C. (3d) 533, 98 C.R. (6th) 95 (S.C.C.), non-disclosure to the defence of police jury vetting contrary to a direction from the Crown Attorney's office also went without remedy as there was held to be no evidence of intentional wrongdoing.

In *R. v. Anderson*, [2014] 2 S.C.R. 167, 311 C.C.C. (3d) 1, 11 C.R. (7th) 1 (S.C.C.), the Court made it clear that Crown discretion can only be reviewed under the doctrine of stay as abuse of process. Instead, the Court distinguishes between exercises of prosecutorial discretion in a broad sense and matters of court tactics and conduct. Prosecutorial discretion is held to be only reviewable under the abuse of process doctrine but court tactics and conduct more broadly through the inherent or implied jurisdiction of courts to control their own process. We will consider the judgement in *Anderson* in the next chapter on the role and powers of Crown attorneys.

The Supreme Court has made it even more difficult to review Crown discretion. The need for considerable deference to prosecutorial discretion is said to be justified by the separation of powers doctrine and because courts are not well suited to review such decisions. This restraint is in marked contrast to *PHS Community Services Society v. Canada (Attorney General)* (*sub nom. Canada (Attorney General) v. PHS Community Services Society*), [2011] 3 S.C.R. 134, 272 C.C.C. (3d) 428, 86 C.R. (6th) 223 (S.C.C.), where the Court unanimously decided that the refusal of a federal Minister to grant an exemption for the Insite safe injection site had been arbitrary contrary to s. 7 of the Charter. There was no talk of separation of powers in *PHS*, or long ago in *Operation Dismantle Inc. v. R.*, [1985] 1 S.C.R. 441 (S.C.C.), where the Court held that decisions of the executive branch of government, including Cabinet decisions, are subject to Charter review by the courts. In *R.*

v. Gill, 2012 ONCA 607, 96 C.R. (6th) 172 (Ont. C.A.), Doherty J.A. for the Ontario Court of Appeal sought to apply that wider power to review recognized in *PHS* to review of non-core exercise of prosecutorial discretion on the basis of the Charter principles of arbitrariness and gross disproportionality. But the Court in *Anderson* declared without real explanation that *Gill* should not be followed.

A new restriction was announced in *Anderson*. Apart from the long-established onus on the accused to prove an abuse on a balance of probabilities, the defence now also has an evidentiary burden to meet before the Crown has to give reasons for the exercise of its discretion. In contrast, Justice Rosenberg had suggested that prosecutors should be required to put their reasons for discretion on the record: "The Attorney General in the 21st Century: A Tribute to Ian Scott: The Attorney General and the Administration of Criminal Justice" (2009), 34 Queen's L.J. 813 at para. 78.

None of these limitations apply when courts are reviewing police discretion. Here there is no talk of courts being ill-suited to review, procedural hurdles, presumptions of good faith or suggestion that the remedy under s. 24(2) can only being exercised in the clearest of cases.

The Court in *Anderson* does indicate that prosecutors have no such shield against their exercise of Charter duties such as that of disclosure. The irony is that the abuse of process doctrine has itself long been recognized as a Charter doctrine under s. 7.

The jurisprudence of the Supreme Court on the doctrine of stays for abuse of process has long been resistant, complex and inconsistent. The survival of this power over some 34 years since the majority of the Supreme Court tried to get rid of the doctrine in *R. v. Rourke* is in large measure due because in the trenches trial judges have sometimes found it essential to the integrity of the justice system to be able to sanction various forms of abuse by police and/or Crown. Despite *Babos* and *Anderson* this independent pattern seems unlikely to change.

See also criticism of Micah Rankin, "*R. v. Anderson*: Prosecutorial Discretion and the Expanding Immunity of Crown counsel" (2014), 11 C.R. (7th) 30.

Consider whether a trial judge should exercise his power to stay as an abuse of process in the following cases.

PROBLEM 8

The accused pointed a sawed-off shotgun at another and cocked it. It discharged and the victim died as a result. The accused claimed that he had merely intended to show the victim that he meant business in respect of an attempt to recover a debt. The accused was charged with murder but the information did not specify the charge as being first degree murder. Nevertheless, following a preliminary inquiry, he was committed for trial on a first degree murder charge. A motion to quash the committal for first degree murder failed but a further appeal to the Ontario Court of Appeal was successful. This decision was confirmed

by the Supreme Court of Canada, who ordered that the matter be remitted to the Provincial Judge to commit for trial on the charge of second degree murder. Shortly thereafter the Attorney General preferred an indictment against the accused on a charge of first degree murder invoking its power under s. 507 of the Criminal Code. The accused was later found guilty of first degree murder, the Crown having refused to accept a plea of guilty to a charge of second degree murder.

Compare *R. v. Chabot* (1985), 44 C.R. (3d) 70 (Ont. C.A.).

PROBLEM 9

The accused was charged with various counts relating to trafficking in cocaine. The evidence had been obtained through months of investigation by an undercover police officer and the execution of a search warrant at the accused's premises. Both in initiating the undercover work and executing the warrant, the police relied on the information of an informant. At trial the defence counsel in cross-examination of the investigating officer asked why one "R" had been arrested on the same day. The Crown counsel strongly objected on the basis that the question was irrelevant and would lead to the identification of the police informer. The trial judge ruled against the Crown. Crown counsel responded by entering a stay of proceedings and, shortly thereafter, reinstituting the proceedings before another judge. This judge refused to stay the proceedings as an abuse of process. He later refused to allow the line of questioning in issue. It was unnecessary because there had been no evidence of entrapment.

Should the second proceedings have been stayed as an abuse of process?

Compare *Scott v. R.*, [1990] 3 S.C.R. 979, 2 C.R. (4th) 153, 61 C.C.C. (3d) 300 (S.C.C.).

PROBLEM 10

The accused was found in the possession of a small bag and admitted that it contained cocaine. He was not arrested. More than 14 months later he was summoned to appear on a charge of possession of a narcotic. The information charged him with an indictable offence. The time limit for charging him with a summary conviction offence elapsed before the Crown Office had received the analysis certificate. The first Crown Attorney refused to initiate the prosecution by way of indictment because of the small quantity of narcotics involved. Many months later another Crown Attorney indicted.

Compare *R. v. Quinn* (1989), 73 C.R. (3d) 77, 54 C.C.C. (3d) 157 (Qué. C.A.).

PROBLEM 11

Police officers with the Toronto Police Sevices Emergency Task Force and the Guns and Gangs Task Force executed a drug search warrant at a boarding house in Toronto. When they entered the room, they found the accused naked with a female companion. In arresting him, two officers used tasers on him. With the first taser he fell to the ground and was handcuffed. Another officer then deployed a second taser, cycling it several times. Cocaine was found near the accused and in a nearby shirt. He is charged with possession of cocaine for trafficking.

Compare *R. v. Walcott* (2008), 57 C.R. (6th) 223 (Ont. S.C.J.). See generally David MacAlister, "Reviewing Police Use of Tasers: Recent Developments Include Application of the Abuse of Process Doctrine" (2007) 57 C.R. (6th) 263.

PROBLEM 12

A number of violent robberies of private residences had occurred in the Mississauga area. The three accused, Tran, Dang and Johnson, were charged along with other persons that included Rhodes, Dam and Rodney. The indictment alleged certain substantive offences and two conspiracies alleging that the accused and the others had the common unlawful purpose of targeting homes at night for robberies. Two different houses had been robbed on two occasions, each with considerable violence towards the occupants and the theft of valuables. Rhodes, Dam and Rodney pleaded guilty and testified at the trial of Tran, Dang and Johnson. All testified in a largely exculpatory manner, although their pre-trial statements had implicated the accused.

All three accused were convicted of conspiracy by the jury but acquitted of the substantive charges. At the trial Tran had argued for a stay of proceedings before the trial judge. After a *voir dire*, the trial judge essentially accepted Tran's evidence of what had transpired. Tran had turned himself into police on the advice of counsel. He did so in a different territorial division from where the offences were alleged to have been committed. Two police officers, V and C, transported him and attempted to gain admissions. Tran, however, asserted his right to remain silent. The two officers exerted some force on him and V punched him in the jaw causing a fracture and permanent damage. The officers attempted to cover up the assault by placing him in front of a video camera and unsuccessfully trying to have him state that he had hit his chin on a table. The police testified on the *voir dire* to a different version that was not accepted since it was contrary to independent evidence and especially to expert medical evidence.

During the trial and after the *voir dire*, the Crown sought to have V sit at the prosecution table to assist. When the defence objected, the trial judge removed V and, later, C from assisting. However, V continued to work with witnesses outside the courtroom in preparing them for testimony.

Compare *R. v. Tran* (2010), 76 C.R. (6th) 307 (Ont. C.A.) and see CR annotation by Tim Quigley.

PROBLEM 13

The accused was a prisoner being transported along with other prisoners. He was verbally abusive to a guard, A, who then disclosed to the other prisoners that the accused was a rapist. The accused threatened to rape A's wife and children. A later alleged that he was injured when the accused forced the door open upon him. A assaulted the accused while the latter was handcuffed and shackled, causing injuries, including a head injury for which the accused was kept in observation in hospital.

The accused was charged with assault causing bodily harm, assault of a peace officer and intimidation of a justice system participant. At trial, the trial judge had a reasonable doubt about whether bodily harm had been caused to A and acquitted him of both assaults. He found that the intimidation charge had been proved but held that there had been an abuse of process under s. 7 of the Charter and ordered a stay of proceedings on that charge.

On a Crown appeal of the stay, the Quebec Court of Appeal overturned the stay and ordered the continuation of the trial before the trial judge. The accused appealed that decision to the Supreme Court of Canada.

Compare *R. v. Bellusci* (2012), 94 C.R. (6th) 221 (S.C.C.) and see CR annotation by Tim Quigley.

5. Civil Action

With conspicuous reliance on the highest courts of other jurisdictions such as New Zealand and South Africa, Chief Justice McLachlin, in *Ward v. Vancouver (City)*, 76 C.R. (6th) 207, [2010] 2 S.C.R. 28 (S.C.C.), sets out to establish a principled approach to a Charter remedy distinct from tort law to award damages against the state for Charter breaches. Both in terms of establishing the remedy and quantifying the damages the Court stresses the rationales of compensation, vindication and deterrence. The focus on deterrence contrasts with the Court's resistance to deterring police from Charter breaches as a rationale for excluding evidence under s. 24(2) (see *R. v. Collins*, [1987] 1 S.C.R. 265, 33 C.C.C. (3d) 1, 56 C.R. (3d) 193 (S.C.C.) and now *R. v. Grant*, [2009] 2 S.C.R. 353, 245 C.C.C. (3d) 1, 66 C.R. (6th) 1 (S.C.C.), where the focus is rather on the integrity of the justice system and preserving the rule of law).

Ward certainly supplies new ammunition for civil suits, for example those seeking compensation for allegedly illegal police actions in the G-20 protests in Toronto. Given the flexibility the Supreme Court allows, actions are likely to be framed in tort law with this revamped Charter remedy in the alternative.

The Court, however, makes it clear that a provincial criminal court is not a court of competent jurisdiction for these purposes. The vast majority of those charged with criminal offences face trials in provincial courts and where Charter breaches are established they will still largely have to rely on the remedies of exclusion of evidence under s. 24(2), stays and declarations of invalidity.

Civil suits of any type are notoriously expensive and inaccessible to the poor, as Chief Justice McLachlin has herself emphasised in various speeches. They will likely remain a somewhat remote option for those who have to go through a criminal trial. This is especially so if there is a sentence of imprisonment. The *Ward* remedy will, however, presumably and anomalously be a new option in superior criminal courts given their long-established inherent jurisdiction.

In the literature on the American exclusionary rule, opponents often invoked in aid the fact that Canada has preferred an effective tort remedy. Reliance was often placed on a short commentary written by G. Arthur Martin (now Martin J.A.), "The Exclusionary Rule Under Foreign Law" (1961), 52 J. Crim. L., C. and P.S. 271, in which he stated:

> The problem of deliberate violation of the rights of the citizen by the police in their efforts to obtain evidence has not been as pressing in Canada as in some other countries . . . In addition the remedy in tort has proved reasonably effective; Canadian juries are quick to resent illegal activity on the part of the police and to express that resentment by a proportionate judgment for damages.

Much later, original research in Canada by defenders of the American exclusionary rule cast a different light. Katz, "Reflections on Search and Seizure and Illegally Obtained Evidence in Canada and the United States" (1980), 3 Can.-U.S. L.J. 103 at 128-129, comments wryly as follows:

> An American commentator, James E. Spiotto, has written "Canada's experience with the tort remedy suggests that viable alternatives to the exclusionary rule do exist". Mr. Spiotto offered that conclusion despite his survey of Canadian law which turned up no appellate case involving a tort action against police officers for illegal searches and seizures in the Province of Ontario, only two appellate cases in other Canadian provinces, and a statement from a police commissioner that he could not remember any illegal search and seizure tort suits since the 1950's. In fact, the only suit which the commissioner could remember from the 1950's resulted in a finding against the police officers but the award of damages was only one dollar. Perhaps that damage award is the best explanation for the paucity of tort suits.

The effectiveness of the tort action against police misconduct in Canada was seriously questioned long before the advent of the Charter.

In *Nelles v. Ont.*, [1989] 2 S.C.R. 170, 71 C.R. (3d) 358 (S.C.C.), the court held that while the Crown has absolute immunity against a suit for malicious prosecution in Ontario, the Attorney General and the Crown Attorneys in question did *not* have such immunity. The plaintiff would have to prove absence of reasonable and probable cause for commencing proceedings and an improper purpose or motive.

See also now *Proulx v. Québec (Procureur général)*, [2001] 3 S.C.R. 9, 46 C.R. (5th) 1, 159 C.C.C. (3d) 225 (S.C.C.). The plaintiff had been found guilty of first degree murder. The Quebec Court of Appeal overturned the conviction on the ground that the verdict was unreasonable, and entered an acquittal. The plaintiff then brought an action for malicious prosecution against the Attorney General of Quebec. The trial judge found that there were no reasonable and probable grounds for laying the charge against the plaintiff, that the prosecutor had acted on an improper motive, and therefore, held that the Attorney General was liable. Another judge assessed damages at around $1.18 million. The Attorney General's appeal to the Quebec Court of Appeal was allowed, and the plaintiff appealed to the Supreme Court of Canada. A 4-3 majority held that the appeal should be allowed and the judgment at trial restored.

In *Canada (Attorney General) v. McArthur*, [2010] 3 S.C.R. 626, 81 C.R. (6th) 1 (S.C.C.) the Supreme Court held a provincial court had jurisdiction to hear a s. 24(1) action for damages for Charter violations while in solitary confinement in penitentiary. The Federal Court did not have exclusive jurisdiction.

In *Henry v. British Columbia (Attorney General)* (2014), 8 C.R. (7th) 108 (B.C. C.A.), reversed [2015] 2 S.C.R. 214, 18 C.R. (7th) 338 (S.C.C.), the Supreme Court was unanimous in holding that the civil remedy for breach of a Charter standard recognised in *Ward* does not require proof of "malice" required for the tort of malicious prosecution. The B.C. Court of Appeal in *Henry* in the Court below had seen the tort of malicious prosecution as an "efficacious remedy" against Crown misconduct. Although a one million dollar award for malicious prosecution was confirmed by the Supreme Court in *Proulx* it is clear that this result is the anomaly and that the civil remedy for malicious prosecution in reality rarely succeeds: see David Debenham, "Who is Investigating Your Investigator?" 2012 *Annual Review of Civil Litigation* 351 (Justice Archibald ed, Toronto: Carswell, 2012).

Justice Moldaver for the majority persuasively explains why a civil action against the Crown for non-disclosure in breach of its Charter obligations should not be limited to proof of the restrictive element of "malice" long established for the tort of malicious prosecution. A 4-2 majority decided that there has to be proof of intent to violate the Charter standard as contrasted to malice. It is, however, not clear what the majority have in mind. Justice Moldaver makes it express that negligence or even gross negligence is not enough, lest the Crown become too fearful and restrained in exercising their powers. But he also recognised that knowledge can be imputed to the Crown based on the reasonable standard that they ought to have known that the information was material to a defence. That is not a standard of subjective intent. This uncertainty may well lead to further civil litigation in the future. In partial dissent, the Chief Justice McLachlin, the author of the unanimous judgment in *Ward*, sees no need to impose a requirement of proof on intent on a civil action for breach of non-disclosure.

Hopefully Crown attorneys should take from *Henry* that they would be well advised to be generous in interpreting their Charter obligation to disclose. The Charter right to full Crown disclosure was not established when Ward chose to defend himself against serial sexual assault charges in 1983.

However, in hindsight the egregious non-disclosures by the Crown appear to have resulted in wrongful convictions and 27 years of incarceration.

6. General Review Questions

QUESTION ONE

The accused, Bob, is charged with impaired driving and possession of housebreaking instruments. He has retained you to act for him on his upcoming trial. From your interview with him and the disclosure from the Crown's office you have determined that the evidence at the trial will describe the following scenario:

Bob, a black man, was driving his vehicle late at night in the affluent west end of the City of Kingston. He will testify that he was driving slowly as he was searching for the address of a friend's house. Constable Jones was patrolling the area in an unmarked police vehicle, having been assigned the task by his sergeant because there had been a number of burglaries in that neighbourhood.

The constable drove alongside the accused's vehicle and motioned Bob to pull over. When Bob had done so, the officer asked him to get out of the car. Bob asked the constable why he had been pulled over and Constable Jones said, "Never mind that; put your hands on the roof of the car and spread your legs". The accused acceded to the constable's request and the constable patted him down. In doing so the constable found a screwdriver which he confiscated. The officer then requested Bob to remove his boots and drop his trousers. Bob did so. The constable found nothing more but he glanced through the window into the interior of the vehicle and saw a pair of pliers. He reached in and took them. The constable then asked Bob to walk a few paces along the white line in the middle of the road and to pick up some coins which he dropped on the road in front of him. The constable then told Bob that he was under arrest for impaired driving and that he would be taking him downtown for a breath test. The constable advised Bob of his right to retain and instruct counsel. He then arranged for the vehicle to be towed to the police pound and escorted the accused to the station.

When the accused arrived at the station he was booked in and advised to wait in a room while the breathalyzer officer was sent for. The booking officer then remembered Bob's name as that of a person who had previously been convicted of break and enter. The booking officer advised Constable Jones to check out the vehicle. Constable Jones went to the pound and, using Bob's keys, opened the trunk. He found a flashlight, a jimmy bar, gloves and two VCR's. When he returned to the station he was advised by the breath man that the accused blew a high reading and that, in the opinion of the breath man, Bob was quite drunk.

With reference to appropriate authority, write a legal memorandum on possible Charter violations.

QUESTION TWO

A restaurant was burned to the ground. At the scene of the raging fire, Sergeant Chris asked bystanders whether they knew the owner.

Finally, a man, Bob, is identified to him. The Sergeant asked Bob in the street whether he knew how the fire started. Bob indicates that he has no idea and that he was playing poker with a friend in a nearby bar when somebody told him that his restaurant was on fire. (*Statement 1*)

Three months later, the Fire Marshall reports to Sergeant Chris that the fire was indeed caused by arson—probably a can of gas. Sergeant Chris finds arson a very difficult crime to solve but his experience tells him that insurance fraud is often the motive and that he should start with the owner. He manages to contact Bob over the telephone at about 7:00 p.m. He informs him that arson was involved in the fire and that, since he was in the vicinity when the fire occurred, he is on the suspect list. He asked Bob to come down for an interview at the police station. Bob arrives at the station within 15 minutes and is taken to a small interview room. There Sergeant Chris advises him that it is routine practice in arson cases these days to eliminate suspects through polygraph examinations. He advises Bob that the examination is totally painless and that it is up to him as to whether or not he wishes to undergo the test. Bob indicates that he has nothing to hide and submits to the test. The test takes about an hour and involves the polygraphist asking a series of questions, with Bob's sensory responses measured on a graph. After an hour, the polygraphist informs Bob that he has failed the test. Bob then asks what will happen to him. The officer answers that he did not know, since he still does not know the truth. At this point, the accused breaks down and indicates verbally "I was desperate, I set the fire". (*Statement 2*)

At this point, Sergeant Chris places Bob under arrest, advising him that he will be charged with arson, that he has the right to remain silent and the right to retain and instruct counsel without delay. He asks Bob whether he understands. Bob replies, "I'm finished—I've got no money left". Sergeant Chris shows Bob a list of criminal lawyers in the yellow pages of the telephone directory. He is provided with a telephone and phones the first lawyer listed in the book. It is now about 8:30 in the evening and all Bob gets is an answering machine. He asks Sergeant Chris what he should do now. The Sergeant indicates that he should leave a message that the lawyer should come to the police station. Bob does so. At this point, Bob is lodged in the police cells.

Sergeant Chris reports the results of his investigations to his inspector. The inspector tells him in no uncertain terms that he had just blown an arson investigation. The inspector informs him that the courts have clearly ruled that polygraph tests are inadmissible for any purpose. He tells Sergeant Chris to try to get another statement.

Sergeant Chris arranges to have another officer pose as a janitor sweeping the floor in the cell block. The "janitor" asks Bob, "What are you in for?" "Arson", says Bob. "Good God", exclaims the "janitor". Bob says, "I was desperate and needed the money". (*Statement 3*) There is no further conversation.

The "janitor" reports this conversation to Sergeant Chris. Two hours later, Sergeant Chris gets a break. He is called to the cell block by another accused, Fink, in custody on an unrelated charge. Fink tells him proudly that the booking officer did not detect that he had a small parabolic microphone in his pocket which he has used to record a conversation with Bob, in which Bob has openly admitted that he torched his restaurant. (*Statement 4*)

At about midnight, Sergeant Chris receives a telephone call from the lawyer indicating that he will not come to the police station as he has given up criminal law practice. The officer gives Bob the telephone book again and says that he should call another lawyer. Bob however indicates that he wants to go to sleep and he'll wait until the morning. At this point, the officer indicates that in his view criminal lawyers don't really care and rarely come to the police station anyhow. He asks Bob if he wants a cup of coffee. Bob says yes. Over coffee, the officer strikes up a conversation. He asks Bob how he got himself into such a financial mess. Bob indicates that he gambled away the profits from the restaurant. The officer then asks him how it is possible to set a whole restaurant on fire. Bob replies that it was really quite simple. He just got a can of gas, sprinkled it around the main dining room and lit it. The officer asks what he did with the can. Bob indicates that he hid it in his attic. (*Statement 5*) At this point, Sergeant Chris says, "Are you sure you don't want a lawyer?" Bob says, "Maybe I should have one." Sergeant Chris facilitates a phone call to another lawyer.

Within 15 minutes, this lawyer arrives at the station and strongly advises the accused that he is not to talk at all to any police officer about anything. He advises Sergeant Chris that it should be clearly understood that the police are not to try to get any statements from his client.

As soon as the lawyer has gone, Sergeant Chris returns to the cell and has little difficulty in persuading Bob to record his previous statements in writing. In his signed statement, Bob admits that he set the fire and how he did it. (*Statement 6*) Later that morning, pursuant to a search warrant, Sergeant Chris recovers the gas can from Bob's attic. It is later established that the can has Bob's fingerprints on it. (*Evidence of the can itself*)

Write a legal memorandum for the Crown assessing, with reference to appropriate authorities, whether each of the above six statements and the can will be admitted into evidence at trial.

QUESTION THREE

During a bitter labour dispute at a nickel mine, the mining company hired scabs in an effort to break the union. In addition, some union members crossed the picket lines and continued working. Naturally, the striking miners were upset. After several weeks of the strike, there was a sudden explosion at the mine that killed nine miners. The RCMP began an immediate investigation that lasted several months. Eventually, they began to suspect one Warren Rogers, one of the striking miners and an expert in explosives.

Sergeant Renfrew phoned Rogers and indicated that she would like to speak to him. She stated that he could come to the detachment or she would come to his home. Rogers preferred coming to the detachment and therefore attended there and provided exculpatory answers to the questions. In the succeeding weeks, he came to the detachment office on five more occasions, each time at the request of Sergeant Renfrew. She did not indicate on those occasions that she was willing to come to Rogers' home. On all but the last occasion, Rogers again provided only exculpatory answers to her questions.

On the last visit to the detachment office, Sergeant Renfrew enlisted the aid of a police informant, Mole. While Rogers was waiting to speak to Renfrew, Mole engaged him in conversation. He asked Rogers many questions about the strike, the mine, and the explosion. He showed a great deal of interest in Rogers' knowledge of explosives. During the course of the conversation, Rogers stated that he was having trouble sleeping because of the explosion and the resulting deaths. [Statement A] The Crown would later argue that this statement was post-offence conduct in the sense that it showed consciousness of guilt.

Rogers then went into an interview room to speak with Renfrew. At first, the conversation was of much the same tenor as previous conversations. However, after awhile, Sergeant Renfrew said, "I think everything you have said is a lie. I believe you planted the bomb that killed those men." Rogers appeared very shaken and said in a quiet voice, "You're right. I'm sorry". [Statement B]

Sergeant Renfrew then stated to Rogers, "You're under arrest for the murder of the nine miners. You need not say anything but anything you do say will be taken down and may be used in evidence. You also have the right to retain and instruct counsel without delay. You can phone the legal aid office if you like. Do you want a lawyer?"

Rogers replied that he would like to speak to a lawyer. He was given a phone book and phone. He tried calling the office of a local private lawyer but received no answer, likely because it was 10:00 p.m. Renfrew suggested he call another lawyer but Rogers refused. They continued talking for some time and finally Rogers said, "I want to tell you everything that happened. I don't need a lawyer for that."

Sergeant Renfrew then obtained a lengthy and detailed incriminating statement from Rogers. [Statement C]

Write a legal memorandum in which you discuss whether each of the three statements will be admitted into evidence at trial.

QUESTION FOUR

You are an articled clerk to a justice of the Ontario Superior Court. She is no expert on criminal law. At Don's trial on charges of possessing drugs and a firearm, a *voir dire* has been held into the admissibility of evidence of drugs found following a vehicle stop and search. She is worried because she knows that the defence counsel, Alan Gold, is a leading lawyer who really knows his Charter law and will try anything to get his client off. She asks you for a legal brief discussing in detail whether there have been breach or breaches of sections 8 and 9 of the Charter.

The following picture of the evidence has emerged:

Officer Cronk has been an officer patrolling the Jane-Finch area in Toronto, a notoriously high crime area, for some five years. His experience has taught him that black youth are increasingly responsible for drug crimes in this neighbourhood and that it is increasingly common to find such youth with guns. His sergeant tells him, just before he goes out on patrol one night, "If you really want your promotion to sergeant you should mix it up more and be proactive".

At about 2 a.m. the streets are becoming deserted. Cronk decides to go after every traffic infraction committed by youthful drivers in the hopes that this can lead to crime detection. He stops a car driven by a black youth, which slid through a stop sign without properly stopping. He follows the car with his lights flashing. The vehicle stops and the youth, Don, jumps out of his vehicle. According to Cronk the young man seemed nervous and fidgety and would not look the officer in the eye. Cronk has been trained that such behavioural cues are suspicious. Shining his flashlight into the vehicle the officer sees signs of food cartons, a few small clear plastic bags and a cell phone. Cronk's training and experience suggests to him that he might well be dealing with a drug trafficker. He immediate shouts out "You are being detained for investigation of drugs. Give me your I.D". Don hands over a driver's license, not telling the officer that the licence is actually that of his brother, Ron. Cronk never specifically asked Don for his name. Cronk runs a CPIC check which shows that the license holder, Ron, has a prior criminal record for possessing and trafficking marihuana. Cronk uses his radio to summon a nearby canine officer, who has an experienced and reliable dog, Ian, trained to sniff out drugs and bombs. It takes 15 minutes for the dog handler to arrive. When he does Ian immediately goes to the trunk of the vehicle and sits down - a signal that he has detected drugs. Cronk immediately informs Don, whom he calls Ron, that he is under arrest for drug possession. He resists, so Cronk tasers him. While Don is rolling about on the ground Cronk handcuffs him. He is still shouting so Cronk tasers him again. This subdues Don. Within minutes he fully recovers from the effects of the taser and struggles to his feet. Cronk feels inside Don's pants and finds and seizes a small handgun strapped to the inside of his thigh. Cronk then opens the vehicle's trunk and finds a large quantity of marihuana and other drugs.

Part III

PRE-TRIAL PROCEDURE

This part follows the criminal prosecution into court and focuses on a number of important issues that arise prior to trial, including bail hearings, disclosure and preliminary inquiries. We begin with a consideration of the adversarial system and the ethical limits placed on defence counsel and the Crown.

Chapter 6

ADVERSARIAL SYSTEM AND ROLE OF COUNSEL

1. Adversary System

The method of inquiry in our courts is quite distinct from the scientific method; the method of ascertaining the facts at common law is known as adversarial while the scientific might be labelled inquisitorial. The principal distinguishing characteristic between the two methods resides in the relative passivity of the judge in the adversarial method. Her function is to make the ultimate finding of fact but she does not herself investigate; rather, she judges the merits of two positions that are put before her. The tradition in the English-speaking world is to regard the "over-speaking 'judge as no well-tuned cymbal'" (Bacon L.C. as quoted by Lord Denning in *Jones v. National Coal Board*, [1957] 2 Q.B. 55, [1957] 2 All E.R. 155 (C.A.) at 64 (Q.B.)) and should a trial judge intervene too frequently during the trial she runs the risk of being reversed on appeal and a new trial ordered. A frank description of our method of inquiry by the Ontario Court of Appeal appears in *Phillips v. Ford Motor Company*, [1971] 2 O.R. 637, 18 D.L.R. (3d) 641 at 657 (O.R.) where Evans J.A. wrote:

> Our mode of trial procedure is based upon the adversarial system in which the contestants seek to establish through relevant supporting evidence, before an impartial trier of facts, those events or happenings which form the bases of their allegations. This procedure assumes that the litigants, assisted by their counsel, will fully and diligently present all the material facts which have evidentiary value in support of their respective positions and that these disputed facts will receive from a trial Judge a dispassionate and impartial consideration in order to arrive at the truth of the matters in controversy. A trial is not intended to be a scientific exploration with the presiding Judge assuming the role of a research director; it is a forum established for the purpose of providing justice for the litigants. Undoubtedly a Court must be concerned with truth, in the sense that it accepts as true certain sworn evidence and rejects other testimony as unworthy of belief, but it cannot embark upon a quest for the "scientific" or "technological" truth when such an adventure does violence to the primary function of the Court, which has always been to do justice, according to law.

The adversary method has been justified over the years by many lawyers as capable of promoting the finest approximation to the truth. The diligence of the parties in ferreting out evidence favourable to their side and the vigour with which they attack their opponent's case are seen as finer guarantees of approximating the historical truth than giving the problem for resolution to some government official whose motivation can rarely be of the magnitude of the parties. Also, it is believed that the bias of the decision-maker can be minimized if he plays a much less active role than is demanded in the inquisitorial method. The judge who himself conducts the examination of witnesses is seen as "descend[ing] into the arena and is liable to have his vision clouded by the dust of the conflict. Unconsciously he deprives himself of the advantage of calm and dispassionate observation" (Lord Green M.R. in *Yuill v. Yuill*, [1945] 1 All E.R. 183 (C.A.) at 189).

Whether the adversary method will more closely approximate truth is certainly open to question. The lawyer is trained to seek success for his client, to win the game. The goal is to present the best picture of the client's position and not the most complete picture. Also, the adversary system presupposes for success some equality between the parties and when this is lacking the "truth" becomes too often simply the view of the more powerful. Most judges will confess to the frequent temptation to reach out and "even the match" but the system cautions against such practice. Perhaps most importantly, while it may be true that in deciding between the validity of two competing theories the decision-maker may be considerably aided by advocates on each side presenting their respective position in the strongest arguments possible, it is certainly questionable whether such a technique is valuable in ensuring that all of the available evidence has been presented by the parties for examination. As Professor Peter Brett has noted:

> observe the practice of scientists and historians in carrying out their investigations. . . . [A] lengthy search will fail to reveal one competent practitioner in either discipline who will willingly and in advance confine himself, in deciding any question involving factual data, to a choice between two sets of existing data proferred to him by rival claimants. In short, the inquisitorial method is the one used by every genuine seeker of the truth in every walk of life (not merely scientific and historical investigations) with only one exception . . . the trial system in the common-law world. (Brett, "Legal Decision-Making Bias: A Critique" (1973), 45 U. Col. L. Rev. 1.)

One large impediment to our search for truth is that the facts to be discovered by our courts are almost always past facts. Our method of discovering them is normally through the oral testimony of witnesses who have personal knowledge about what happened. This personal "knowledge" might perhaps better be described as personal beliefs about what they now remember of facts which they believe they observed. The trier of fact then has regard to what the witness says and, based on her observations of what the witness said and of his manner of saying it, she comes to her own opinion as to whether that is an honest belief. She can do no more. She cannot, as the scientist might, duplicate in his laboratory the actual facts and test the hypothesis proposed. Facts as found by the court are really then only guesses about the actual facts. "Subjectivity piled on subjectivity . . . a trial court's finding of fact is, then, at best, its belief or opinion about someone else's belief or opinion" (Frank, *Courts on Trial*, p. 22). Mr. Justice Haines of the Ontario Supreme Court described it this way:

> A trial is not a faithful reconstruction of the events as if recorded on some giant television screen. It is an historical recall of that part of the events to which witnesses may be found and presented in an intensely adversary system *where the object is quantum of proof.* Truth may be only incidental (*R. v. Lalonde*, [1972] 1 O.R. 376, 15 C.R.N.S. 1, 5 C.C.C. (2d) 168 (H.C.), at 4 (C.R.N.S.) emphasis added.)

Besides searching for a different truth than the scientist, our methods are circumscribed by other considerations which require our fact-finding to be done in a way which is acceptable to the parties and to society. Our courts provide a forum for the purpose of resolving disputes between parties which they themselves have been unable to resolve in any other way. Our modern form of trial began simply as a substitute for private duels and feuds which had later been dignified by the process of trial by battle. The resolution of the conflict must be done in a way which ensures social tranquility generally and is also acceptable to the individual parties. The parties should be able to leave the court feeling that they have had their say, that their case has been presented in the best possible light and that they have been judged by an impartial trier. In judging the efficacy of the legal system's method of fact-finding we must remember that:

> A contested law suit is society's last line of defense in the indispensable effort to secure the peaceful settlement of social conflicts—it is a last-ditch process in which something more is at stake than the truth only of the specific matter in contest. There is at stake also that confidence of the public generally in the impartiality and fairness of public settlement and disputes which is essential if the ditch is to be held and the settlements accepted peaceably. . . . While it is important that the court be right . . . a decision must be made now, one way or the other: . . . to require certainty . . . would be impracticable and undesirable. The law thus compromises. (Hart and McNaughton, *Evidence and Inference in the Law*, D. Lerner, ed., (1958), p. 57.)

With these thoughts in mind we *might* better understand, and even accept, some of the rules and procedures at work in a criminal trial. For additional thoughts along this line see Brooks, "The Judge and the Adversary System," *The Canadian Judiciary*, A. Linden, ed. (1976).

Consider the following criticisms of the adversary system by Geoffrey Hazard.

HAZARD, ETHICS IN THE PRACTICE OF LAW
(1978), 127-34

No question of legal ethics is more difficult than the question whether an advocate can help suppress the truth in order to protect his client. In so far as litigation is concerned, the effect is to immobilize the law's enforcement. A lawyer can, within the limits of the law, obstruct its enforcement by advising his client to refuse to testify. At the borderland of the law, and without much risk to himself, he can go a considerable way in helping his client build a coverup. For example, he can advise the client about the consequences of preserving records or indicate to him the legal consequences of a certain line of testimony that the client might give. To the extent that such advice is given and acted upon, the effect is much the same as putting a client on the stand when it is known that his testimony will be false. The truth of the matter, which might have been discovered if the lawyer had not been involved, will less likely be discovered because he is involved. The problem is whether the benefits are worth that cost.

Paradoxically, the primary benefit of the system is often said to be the promotion of truth. For every instance in which truth is suppressed or distorted by the adversary system, it is thought there are more instances in which the system uncovers truth that otherwise would not have been uncovered. There is no practicable way to test this claim. It is worth considering, however, whether the situation would really be much better if we gave up the adversary system in favor of the interrogative system. But even if the claim were false we might want to keep the rule as it is. Under the present system, using ostensibly open competition for discovery of the truth, the law has troubles with suppression and distortion; what sort of troubles would it have if we depended on *ex officio* procedures for getting the evidence? If the truth suffers from our use of the adversary system, we ought to consider how it might suffer if we used some other system. In our political culture, the interrogative system of trial could well turn out to resemble Congressional hearings.

The real value of the adversary system thus may not be its contribution to truth but its contribution to the ideal of individual autonomy. This is the rationale underlying many rules that obscure the truth, such as the privilege against self-incrimination and the rule that private premises may not be searched without a warrant. The proposition, as applied to the adversary system, is that there is good in being able to say what one wants to say, even if it involves the commission of perjury. Stated baldly, the proposition is shocking. The norms of our society condemn lying, although it is perhaps worth noting that the biblical rule is the much narrower proposition that one should not bear false witness against a neighbor. At any rate, conventional morality does not openly recognize the value of being able to lie. Still, our commitment to truthfulness may actually go no further than homily; when it comes to serious business such as negotiation and diplomacy, most people accept the utility, the inevitability, and perhaps even the desirability of dissimulation in various forms.

Why should dissimulation not be acceptable in court? There are many cultures in which it is assumed that parties to legal conflict lie on their own behalf; no pretense is made that they should be expected to do otherwise. The common law formerly exhibited the same attitude, for it did not allow testimony from a criminal defendant or any "party in interest" in civil litigation. The present ethical dilemma in the adversary system may therefore be ultimately traceable to the abolition of the common law rules of witness disqualification.

The reform of the common law rules occurred in the nineteenth century. It was based on the proposition that few injustices would result if interested persons were allowed to testify. It was believed that with cross-examination and the good sense of the jury, the truth will out most of the time. Perhaps it is time that this premise was re-examined, for it seems evident that if the stakes involved in a lawsuit are substantial, if the outcome depends on the truth, and if the parties are authorized to give evidence as to what the truth is, the parties will distort their submissions to the maximum extent possible. The artistry and self-consciousness of the distortion will of course vary. In many cases it may be supposed that at least one party will tell the unvarnished truth, hoping if not trusting that it will be seen as such. But to require a party to choose between imprisonment or financial self-destruction on the one hand, and complete truthfulness on the other, is to impose a moral burden that may simply be too heavy. And, directly to the point of the present discussion, it imposes nearly as difficult a burden on the advocate who must advise the party in making the choice.

There is much ambivalence concerning the advocate's responsibility in this respect. The rules clearly say that, even in the defense of criminal cases, the advocate may not assist his client in committing perjury or in otherwise fabricating or suppressing evidence. In practice, lawyers often wind up violating these rules, some of them quite frequently. But they seek escapes from moral responsibility for having done so.

There are several escapes. It is said that no client is guilty until found so by a court; therefore, one cannot know what the truth is until then; therefore, one cannot conclude that a client's testimony will constitute perjury. This is pure casuistry. Of course there are doubtful situations, but there are also ones that are not doubtful. A thing is not made true or not by a court's pronouncing on it, and a lawyer can reach conclusions about an issue without having a judge tell him what to think.

Another escape is for the advocate to indicate to the client how inconvenient it would be if the evidence were such and so, and leave it to the client to do the dirty work—well illustrated in "the lecture" in *Anatomy of a Murder*. Another is for the advocate to pretend that the rules governing his responsibility are different from what they are—to pretend that duty to client requires aiding him in whatever the client feels he must do to vindicate himself in court. The advocate is then absolved because he is merely an instrument.

As the situation stands, the advocate is supposed to be both the champion of his client and a gatekeeper having a duty to prevent his client from contaminating the courtroom. In principle, these responsibilities are compatible. The duty to the court simply limits the ways in which a lawyer can champion his client's cause. In practice, however, the duties have come to be in perhaps uncontrollable conflict.

The sources of this conflict are located in the depths of our system of advocacy. An important factor in the advocate's ability to control the conflict is the set of rules that describe his relationship to the client and the cause. In other legal systems, these relationships are quite different from what they are in this country. In the English system, for example, the barrister is insulated from the case in several important ways. An English barrister has no continuing relation with any client; his fee is fixed before trial in negotiations to which he is not a party and on a basis unrelated to eventual victory or defeat; the case is placed with a barrister through a solicitor as intermediary; and barristers as a group are small in number, aristocratic, clannish, and closely tied to the judiciary. The barrister thus is strongly identified as an officer of the court and as a gatekeeper concerning what kind of evidence will be offered. In the continental system, the advocate is insulated from the client by somewhat similar conventions; equally important, he has a much more limited responsibility in the trial because the judge and not the advocate is primarily responsible for eliciting the facts.

In the American system, however, the advocate's relationship to his client's cause is much more dependent and intimate. In litigation involving "repeat business" clients, the advocate or his firm usually is also counsel under retainer to the client. In litigation involving "one shot" clients, such as plaintiff's injury claims, the lawyer's fee is usually contingent on the outcome. In any event, the advocate is expected and permitted to investigate the facts and interrogate witnesses before trial, thus becoming a party to the evidence before its presentation in court. A much wider range of harassing tactics is indulged in American litigation. Hence, the advocate's situation in our version of the adversary system is fairly defined by Shaw's description of marriage: it "combines the maximum of temptation with the maximum of opportunity." It is not difficult to see why the lawyer may be relatively ineffective as a source of restraint on his client.

. . .

This brings in view another serious problem of the adversary system. The trial lawyer can become completely immersed in his lawsuits, to the point where they become his identity and their outcome the sole criterion of his professional stature. Indeed, it is often only with difficulty that a modern trial specialist can maintain distance between himself and his craft. The whole tendency of his work leads him to hold, with Vince Lombardi, that winning is not the most important thing but the only thing. And the result can be that he becomes incapacitated to give his client detached advice about the prospects of ultimate victory and the advisability of settling through compromise. The problem can be especially severe in "big" cases for and against big corporations, because one such case can for several years be the vocation of a good part of a firm or agency's litigation staff. But it is inherent in the system. An English barrister is reported to have remonstrated, upon the prospect of compromising a bitter suit between heirs to a large fortune, "What? And allow that magnificent estate to be frittered away among the beneficiaries?"

If it is possible that the adversary system can work satisfactorily, and necessary that it must do so because no other system of adjudication is likely to be any better, it remains true that the system in its present form is pretty sick. The problem can be posed in terms of the attitude with which the advocate should approach a case. One approach, whether in reality or in idealized form we cannot be entirely sure, is that of the English barrister. In this approach, the advocate undertakes a dispassionate analysis of the facts and a magisterial consideration of the law with the aim of establishing common ground with his opposite number and thereupon settling the case on the basis of truth and legal justice, or at worst, isolating for trial the issues of fact or law that prove intractable. A lot of litigation in this country is actually determined this way, when the advocates trust each other's competence, integrity, and judgment. But a lot of litigation is conducted otherwise. In the other approach the advocate is a streetfighter—aggressive, guileful, exploitive. Some clients seem to want it that way, at least until they find out that two can play the game. At any rate many clients suppose that is the way litigation inevitably must be conducted and approach their counsel with a corresponding set of expectations. The advocate in turn can confirm and exploit these expectations, providing fulfillment of the prophecy if he wishes. As the institution of adversary adjudication now stands, the advocate has very strong inducements to oblige.

R. v. FELDERHOF
(2003), 180 C.C.C. (3d) 498, 17 C.R. (6th) 20 (Ont. C.A.)

ROSENBERG, J.A.:—The respondent to this appeal is facing eight counts of violating the Securities Act, R.S.O. 1990, c. S. 5 arising out of the affairs of Bre-X Minerals Ltd. The Ontario Securities Commission charged the respondent, a senior officer in Bre-X, with insider trading and authorizing or acquiescing in misleading press statements. After 70 days of trial, counsel for the prosecution took the unusual step of applying for prohibition and *certiorari* to halt the prosecution. Counsel for the Ontario Securities Commission, who are conducting the prosecution, seek to prohibit the continuation of the proceedings before Hryn J., to quash rulings he made and ask for an order that the trial begin anew before another judge of the Ontario Court of Justice. The prosecution alleges that the trial judge made a number of serious errors that have deprived him of jurisdiction to proceed and undermined the appellant's right to a fair trial. Fundamental to its position is the allegation that the trial judge has failed in his duty to curb the uncivil conduct of the respondent's counsel. The prosecution also alleges that the trial judge has not made evidentiary rulings when he should have and which were necessary to the presentation of the prosecution case and has improperly interfered in the conduct of the prosecution case.

Campbell J. heard the application and in extensive and careful reasons he dismissed the application. He found no jurisdictional error. I agree with that conclusion. The respondent sought costs of the motion. Campbell J. dismissed that application and the respondent appeals from that order. I would dismiss that appeal.

. . .

It is important that everyone, including the courts, encourage civility both inside and outside the courtroom. Professionalism is not inconsistent with vigorous and forceful advocacy on behalf of a client and is as important in the criminal and quasi-criminal context as in the civil context. Morden J.A. of this court expressed the matter this way in a 2001 address to the Call to the Bar: "Civility is not just a nice, desirable adornment to accompany the way lawyers conduct themselves, but, is a duty which is integral to the way lawyers do their work." Counsel are required to conduct themselves professionally as part of their duty to the court, to the administration of justice generally and to their clients. As Kara Anne Nagorney said in her article, "A Noble Profession? A Discussion of Civility Among Lawyers" (1999), 12 Georgetown Journal of Legal Ethics 815, at 816-17, "Civility within the legal system not only holds the profession together, but also contributes to the continuation of a just society. . . Conduct that may be characterized as uncivil, abrasive, hostile, or obstructive necessarily impedes the goal of resolving conflicts rationally, peacefully, and efficiently, in turn delaying or even denying justice." Unfair and demeaning comments by counsel in the course of submissions to a court do not simply impact on the other counsel. Such conduct diminishes the public's respect for the court and for the administration of criminal justice and thereby undermines the legitimacy of the results of the adjudication.

Nothing said here is inconsistent with or would in any way impede counsel from the fierce and fearless pursuit of a client's interests in a criminal or quasi-criminal case. Zealous advocacy on behalf of a client, to advance the client's case and protect that client's rights, is a cornerstone of our adversary system. It is "a mark of professionalism for a lawyer to firmly protect and pursue the legitimate interests of his or her client". As G. Arthur Martin said, "The existence of a strong, vigorous and responsible Defence Bar is essential in a free Society". Counsel have a responsibility to the administration of justice, and as officers of the court, they have a duty to act with integrity, a duty that requires civil conduct. This was a complex case involving experienced counsel who took very different views about the role of the prosecutor and the rules of evidence. There is nothing in this record that shows that the trial judge was biased against the prosecution. The application judge has catalogued the attempts that the trial judge did make to keep the trial and defence counsel on track. The prosecution says he did not do enough but I think it difficult at this stage to second-guess a trial judge who was faced with what would be a very long and difficult case.

. . .

In *Marchand*, this court has commented upon the problems caused by incivility in the courtroom. In that case, the court noted that civility in the courtroom is not only the responsibility of counsel but also "very much the responsibility of the trial judge." The failure of counsel and the trial judge in that case to discharge their responsibilities "tarnished the reputation of the administration of justice". Crown counsel have special responsibilities as "ministers of justice". But, as officers of the court and as barristers and solicitors, defence counsel also have responsibilities to the court and to other counsel and they have a duty to uphold the standards of the profession. As I have said, defence counsel's obligation to his or her client to fearlessly raise every legitimate issue is not incompatible with these duties to the court, to fellow counsel and to the profession. See Arthur Maloney, Q.C., "The Role of the Independent Bar", 1979 Law Society of Upper Canada Special Lectures 49 at 63, and G. Arthur Martin, Q.C., "The Role and Responsibility of the Defence Advocate" (1970), 12 C.L.Q. 376 at 385.

Mr. Maloney and Mr. Martin both referred to the well-known passage from *Rondel v. Worsley*, [1969] 1 A.C. 191 at 227-8 where Lord Reid said, in part that, "[c]ounsel must not mislead the court, [and] he must not lend himself to casting aspersions on the other party or witnesses for which there is no sufficient basis in the information in his possession". As the application judge noted, in this case the core problem was that Mr. Groia did not seem to understand the role of the prosecutor. This led him to make his improper allegations against the prosecutor when the prosecutor simply objected to a question or an attempt to introduce a document. I assume Mr. Groia believed in the merit of these submissions and was not deliberately misleading the court and casting aspersions on counsel and the "government" for which there was no foundation; nevertheless, he was bound by the standards of the profession to keep his rhetoric within reasonable bounds. If he was unable to do so, the trial judge had the responsibility referred to in *Marchand*.

This has nothing to do with trials not being "tea parties". Every counsel and litigant has the right to expect that counsel will conduct themselves in accordance with The Law Society of Upper Canada, Rules of Professional Conduct. Those rules are crystal clear. Counsel are to treat witnesses, counsel and the court with fairness, courtesy and respect. See Rules 4 and 6 and Commentaries. I have set out what seems to have been the genesis for the acrimony between counsel in this case. Even if Mr. Groia honestly believed that the prosecution tactics were excessive and could amount to an abuse of process, this did not give him licence for the kind of submissions he made in this case. As the application judge said, "[a]buse of process and prosecutorial misconduct . . . form part of the arsenal of defence tactics". But, motions based on abuse of process and prosecutorial misconduct can and should be conducted without the kind of rhetoric engaged in by defence counsel in this case.

Joe Groia, the defence lawyer in *Felderhof*, was found guilty of professional misconduct by the Law Society of Upper Canada and suspended for one month. On his appeal to the Divisional Court (*Groia v. Law Society of Upper Canada*, 2015 ONSC 686 (Ont. Div. Ct.), Justice Nordheimer, for the Court, addressed the concerns raised by many advocacy groups about the chilling effect that the civility movement can have on resolute advocacy:

62 I pause at this juncture to address a point made by the intervener, The Criminal Lawyers' Association. The CLA provided us with an article that Don Bayne, a respected criminal defence lawyer, had prepared for a CLA conference in 2013 on the subject of the tension between zealous advocacy

and incivility. [Bayne, "Problems with the Prevailing Approach to the Tension Between Zealous Advocacy and Incivility" (2013) 4 C.R. (7th) 301.] Within that article, the author refers to some data that he had obtained from the respondent, regarding the nature of civility complaints that the respondent receives. According to the author, the data suggested that a disproportionate number of complaints are filed for alleged civility infractions regarding criminal defence lawyers. The CLA relied on this article to support its submission that the Appeal Panel's decision in this case, if sustained, could cast a "chill" on the passion and dedication with which criminal defence lawyers approach their task in the future.

63 I would make two comments in response to that submission. First, as the author himself recognized, the data he received is not statistically reliable. Second, and more importantly, if there is an unjustified and disproportionate pursuit of criminal defence lawyers on the issue of incivility, in the context of allegations of professional misconduct, then that is an issue to be addressed with the profession and not with this court. Those lawyers who believe that they are being unfairly singled out should be raising the issue with the governors of the profession and, through them, with the staff who are responsible for the investigation of such complaints.

68 The reality is that incivility amounting to professional conduct does not allow for a fixed definition. Uncivil words spoken by one lawyer in one case may not cross the line into professional misconduct whereas similar words spoken by another lawyer in a different case may. While the uncertainty that results from the inability to arrive at a comprehensive definition may be unfortunate, this is not the only area of law where uncertainty exists. Indeed, the uncertainty of law is, in one sense, the bread and butter of lawyers who are constantly called upon to advise clients just because there is such uncertainty. If what is right and what is wrong, what is lawful and what is unlawful, was always clear and certain, it is likely that the population of needed lawyers would be considerably decreased.

73 I start with the principle that a lawyer's conduct must first be uncivil to invoke the disciplinary process. Zealous advocacy, including the use of language that may be very tough in its expression, is not, by itself, sufficient to open the door to professional misconduct proceedings. Words that are passionate, or the effect of which may sting, may often be necessary to make the required point, or to persuade the adjudicator towards a certain view. It would be contrary to the recognized role of an advocate to formulate a rule that does not recognize that central reality.

74 Rather, the conduct that engages the incivility concern begins with conduct that it is rude, unnecessarily abrasive, sarcastic, demeaning, abusive or of any like quality. It is conduct that attacks the personal integrity of opponents, parties, witnesses or of the court, where there is an absence of a good faith basis for the attack, or the individual counsel has a good faith basis for the belief but that belief is not an objectively reasonable one. In addition, single instances of such conduct will be less likely to engage the misconduct concern as will repeated instances of the same conduct. In other words, a solitary instance of uncivil conduct will not, generally speaking, be sufficient to ground

a complaint of professional misconduct, unless it is of a particularly egregious form.

75 In my view, however, there must be an additional element attached to the uncivil conduct, in order for it to rise to the level of professional misconduct. For uncivil conduct to rise to the level that would properly engage the disciplinary process, it must be conduct that, in addition to being uncivil, will also bring the administration of justice into dispute, or would have the tendency to do so. It is conduct that calls into question the integrity of the court process and of the players involved in it. It is conduct that risks bringing the administration of justice into disrepute because it is conduct that strikes at the very qualities of what the justice system represents. It is conduct that would make an impartial outside observer question the central tenets upon which the justice system is based. It is the difference between impassioned, but reasoned, disagreements and the uninformed, nasty, personal tirades that too often mark the exchanges we see in political and media exchanges on matters of public importance. It is the hallmark of professionalism that both sides recognize that reasonable people can have strong, but legitimate, disagreements without the need for either side to call into question the honour or integrity of their opponent.

Joe Groia was elected as a Bencher of the LSUC in 2015.

The Supreme Court of Canada has also recognized civility as a professional norm in *Doré c. Québec (Tribunal des professions)*, 2012 SCC 12, [2012] 1 S.C.R. 395 (S.C.C.). In *Doré*, a criminal defence lawyer left an intemperate letter to the judge who presided over his client's bail hearing and who was himself intemperate with Doré in court. For example, on one occasion he noted that "an insolent lawyer is rarely of use to his client". Doré received a 21-day suspension for the letter. Justice Abella, for the Court, observed that:

61 No party in this dispute challenges the importance of professional discipline to prevent incivility in the legal profession, namely "potent displays of disrespect for the participants in the justice system, beyond mere rudeness or discourtesy" (Michael Code, "Counsel's Duty of Civility: An Essential Component of Fair Trials and an Effective Justice System" (2007), 11 Can. Crim. L.R. 97, at p. 101; see also Gavin MacKenzie, *Lawyers and Ethics: Professional Responsibility and Discipline* (5th ed. 2009), at p. 8-1). The duty to encourage civility, "both inside and outside the courtroom", rests with the courts and with lawyers (*R. v. Felderhof* (2003), 68 O.R. (3d) 481 (C.A.), at para. 83).

. . .

68 Lawyers potentially face criticisms and pressures on a daily basis. They are expected by the public, on whose behalf they serve, to endure them with civility and dignity. This is not always easy where the lawyer feels he or she has been unfairly provoked, as in this case. But it is precisely when a lawyer's equilibrium is unduly tested that he or she is particularly called upon to behave with transcendent civility. On the other hand, lawyers should not be expected

to behave like verbal eunuchs. They not only have a right to speak their minds freely, they arguably have a duty to do so. But they are constrained by their profession to do so with dignified restraint.

The target of the letter, Justice Boilard, was reprimanded by the Canadian Judicial Council for his conduct at the bail hearing.

LUBAN, THE ADVERSARY SYSTEM EXCUSE
The Good Lawyer: Lawyers' Rules and Lawyers' Ethics
(Rowman & Allenheld, 1984), 85-87

On February 7, 1973, Richard Helms, the former director of the Central Intelligence Agency, lied to a Senate committee about American involvement in the overthrow of the Allende government in Chile. Santiago proved to be Helms's Waterloo; he was caught out in his perjury and prosecuted. Helms claimed that requirements of national security led him to lie to Congress. We can only speculate, however, on how the court would have viewed this excuse, for in fact the case never came to trial; Helms's lawyer, the redoubtable Edward Bennett Williams, found an ingenious way to back the government down. He argued that national security information was relevant to Helms's defense and must be turned over to Helms, thereby confronting the government with the unpleasant choice of dropping the action or making public classified and presumably vital information. The government chose the first option and allowed Helms to plead guilty to a misdemeanor charge.

I don't know if anyone ever asked Williams to justify his actions; had anyone attempted to do so, they would presumably have been told that Williams was simply doing his job as a criminal defense attorney. The parallel with Helms's own excuse is clear—he was doing his job, Williams was doing his—but it is hard to miss the irony. Helms tried to conceal national security information; therefore he lied. Williams, acting on Helms's behalf, threatened to reveal national security information as part of a tactic that has come to be called "graymailing." One man's ends are another man's means. Neither lying nor graymailing (to say nothing of destabilizing elected regimes) are morally pretty, but a job is a job and that was the job that was. So, at any rate, runs the excuse.

We may want to reject these "good soldier" excuses or we may find them valid and persuasive. That is the issue I shall address here. A second graymailing example will warm us to our topic:

> In instances [of merger cases involving firms in competition with each other] in which the [Federal Trade] commission's legal case looked particularly good and none of the usual defenses appeared likely to work, the staff was confronted several times with the argument that if they did not refrain from prosecution and allow the merger, one of the proposed merger partners would close down its operations and dismiss its employees. . . . Of course, the mere announcement of the threat to close the plant generates enormous political pressure on the prosecutor not to go forward. Ought lawyers to be engaged in such strategies for the purpose of consummating an otherwise anticompetitive and illegal transaction involving the joinder of two substantial competitors?

On the lawyers' advice, the firms played a nice game of chicken: closing down by stages, they laid off a few workers each day until the FTC cried uncle.

What could justify the conduct of these lawyers? A famous answer is the following statement of Lord Henry Brougham:

> An advocate, in the discharge of his duty, knows but one person in all the world, and that person is his client. To save that client by all means and expedients, and at all hazards and costs to other persons, and, amongst them, to himself, is his first and only duty; and in performing this duty he must not regard the alarm, the torments, the destruction which he may bring upon others. Separating the duty of a patriot from that of an advocate, he must go on reckless of consequences, though it should be his unhappy fate to involve his country in confusion.

This speech, made in his 1820 defense of Queen Caroline against King George IV's charge of adultery, was itself an act of graymail. Reminiscing years later, Brougham said that the King would recognize in it a tacit threat to reveal his secret marriage to a Catholic, a marriage that, were it to become public knowledge, would cost him his crown. Knowing this background of Brougham's oft-quoted statement might make us take a dim view of it; it has, nevertheless, frequently been admired as the most eloquent encapsulation of the advocate's job.

Brougham's statement invites philosophical reflection for at first blush it is equally baffling to utilitarianism, and moral rights theory, and Kantianism. The client's utility matters more than that of the rest of the world put together. No one else's moral rights matter. Other people are merely means to the client's ends. Moral theory seems simply to reject Brougham's imperatives.

They are, however, universalizable over lawyers, or so it is claimed. The idea seems to be that the role of lawyer, hence the social institutions that set up this role, reparse the Moral Law, relaxing some moral obligations and imposing new ones. In the words of an Australian appellate court, "Our system of administering justice necessarily imposes upon those who practice advocacy duties which have no analogies, and the system cannot dispense with their strict observance."

The system of which the court speaks is the so-called "adversary system of justice." My main question is this: does the adversary system really justify Brougham's position? I hope that the example of Helms and his lawyers has convinced you that a more general issue is lurking here, the issue of what I shall call institutional excuses. We can state the main question in full generality in this way: can a person appeal to a social institution in which he or she occupies a role in order to excuse conduct that would be morally culpable were anyone else to do it? Plausibly, examples exist in which the answer is yes: we do not call it murder when a soldier kills a sleeping enemy, although it is surely immoral for you or me to do it. There are also cases where the answer is no, as in the job "concentration camp commandant" or "professional strikebreaker." Here, we feel, the immorality of the job is so great that it accuses, not excuses, the person who holds it.

This suggests that an important feature of a successful institutional excuse is that the institution is itself justified. I think that is partly right, but I do not think it is the whole story. I shall argue that the *kind* of justification that can be offered of the institution is germane to the success of the excuses it provides.

In the following extracts it is suggested that the adversary system employed by the criminal justice system is not compatible with female and aboriginal values. Do you agree?

CARRIE MENKEL-MEADOW, PORTIA IN A DIFFERENT VOICE: SPECULATION ON A WOMEN'S LAWYERING PROCESS
(1985), 1 *Berkeley Women's L.J.* 39, at pp. 44-55

In her book, *In a Different Voice: Psychological Theory and Women's Development*, Gilligan observes that much of what has been written about human psychological development has been based on studies of male subjects exclusively. As a consequence, girls and women have either not been described, or they are said to have "failed" to develop on measurement scales based on male norms. Just as Gilligan has observed that studies of human psychological development have been centred on males, feminists have observed the law to be based on male values and behaviours. As Frances Olsen notes:

> Law is supposed to be rational, objective, abstract and principled, like men; it is not supposed to be irrational, subjective, contextualized or personalized like women. The social, political and intellectual practices that constitute "law" were for many years carried out almost exclusively by men. Given that women were long excluded from the practice of law, it should not be surprising that the traits associated with women are not greatly valued by law. Moreover, in a kind of vicious cycle, the "maleness" of law was used as a justification for excluding women from practicing law. While the number of women in law has been rapidly increasing, the field continues to be heavily male dominated.

The male-derived model of moral reasoning and psychological development described by Gilligan values hierarchical thinking based on the logic of reasoning from abstract, universal principles. Gilligan measures her findings against the work of her colleague, Lawrence Kohlberg. His theory of moral development comprised of six "universal" stages is based on a study of eighty-four *boys* from childhood through adulthood. Gilligan explains that when Kohlberg's model is applied to women, they tend to score at a stage three, a stage characterized by seeing morality as a question of interpersonal relations and caring for and pleasing others. In looking at moral judgments and hearing the "women's voice," Gilligan discovered that:

> When one begins with the study of women and derives developmental constructs from their lives, the outline of a moral conception different from that described by Freud, Piaget, or Kohlberg begins to emerge and informs a different description of development. In this conception, the moral problem arises from conflicting responsibilities rather than from competing rights and requires for its resolution a mode of thinking that is contextual and narrative rather than formal and abstract.

An example drawn from Gilligan's work best illustrates the duality of girls' and boys' moral development. In one of the three studies on which her book is based, a group of children are asked to solve Heinz's dilemma, a hypothetical moral reasoning problem used by Kohlberg to rate moral development on his six-stage scale. The dilemma is that Heinz's wife is dying of cancer and requires a drug which the local pharmacist has priced beyond Heinz's means. The question is posed: should Heinz steal the drug?

To illustrate and explain the differences between the ways boys and girls approached this problem, Gilligan quotes from two members of her sample, Jake and Amy. Jake, an eleven-year-old boy, sees the problem as one of "balancing rights," like a judge who must make a decision or a mathematician who must solve an algebraic equation. Life is worth more than property, therefore Heinz should steal the drug. For Amy, an eleven-year-old girl, the problem is different. Like a "bad" law student she "fights the hypo"; she wants to know more facts: Have Heinz and the druggist explored other possibilities, like a loan or credit transaction? Why couldn't Heinz and the druggist simply sit down and talk it out so that the druggist would come to see the importance of Heinz's wife's life? In Gilligan's terms, Jake explores the Heinz dilemma with "the logic of justice" while Amy uses the "ethic of care." Amy scores lower on the Kohlberg scale because she sees the problem rooted in the persons involved rather than in the larger universal issues posed by the dilemma.

In conventional terms Jake would make a good lawyer because he spots the legal issues of excuse and justification, balances the rights, and reaches a decision, while considering implicitly, if not explicitly, the precedential effect of his decision. But as Gilligan argues, and as I develop more fully below, Amy's approach is also plausible and legitimate, both as a style of moral reasoning and as a style of lawyering. Amy seeks to keep the people engaged; she holds the needs of the parties and their relationships constant and hopes to satisfy them all (as in a negotiation), rather than selecting a winner (as in a lawsuit). If one must be hurt, she attempts to find a resolution that will hurt least the one who can least bear the hurt. (Is she engaged in a "deep pocket" policy analysis?) She looks beyond the "immediate lawsuit" to see how the "judgment" will affect the parties. If Heinz steals the drug and goes to jail, who will take care of his wife? Furthermore, Amy is concerned with *how* the dilemma is resolved: the process by which the parties communicate may be crucial to the outcome. (Amy cares as much about procedure as about substance.) And she is being a good lawyer when she inquires whether all the facts have been discovered and considered.

The point here is not that Amy's method or moral reasoning is better than Jake's, nor that she is a better lawyer than Jake. (Some have read Gilligan to argue that the women's voice is better. I don't read her that way.) The point is that Amy does some things different from Jake when she resolves this dilemma, and these things have useful analogies to lawyering and may not have sufficiently credited as useful lawyering skills. Jake and Amy have something to learn from one another.

Thus, although a "choice of rights" conception (life v. property) of solving human problems may be important, it is not the only or the best way. Responsibilities to self and to others may be equally important in measuring moral, as well as legal decision making, but have thus far been largely ignored.

For example, a lawyer who feels responsible for the decisions she makes with her client may be more inclined to think about how those decisions will hurt other people and how the lawyer and client feel about making such decisions. (Amy thinks about Heinz, the druggist, and Heinz's wife at all times in reaching her decision; Jake makes a choice in abstract terms without worrying as much about the people it affects.)

. . .

III. THE ADVOCACY-ADVERSARIAL MODEL

The basic structure of our legal system is premised on the adversarial model, which involves two advocates who present their cases to a disinterested third party who listens to evidence and argument and declares one party a winner. In this simplified description of the Anglo-American model of litigation, we can identify some of the basic concepts and values which underlie this choice of arrangements: advocacy, persuasion. hierarchy, competition, and binary results (win/lose). The conduct of litigation is relatively similar (not coincidentally, I suspect) to a sporting event—there are rules, a referee, an object to the game, and a winner is declared after the play is over. As I have argued elsewhere, this conception of the dispute resolution process is applied more broadly than just in the conventional courtroom. The adversarial model affects the way in which lawyers advise their clients ("get as much as you can"), negotiate disputes ("we can really get them on that") and plan transactions ("let's be sure to draft this to your advantage"). All of these activities in lawyering assume competition over the same limited and equally valued items (usually money) and assume that success is measured by maximizing individual gain. Would Gilligan's Amy create a different model?

By returning to Heinz's dilemma we see some hints about what Amy might do. Instead of concluding that a choice must be made between life and property, in resolving the conflict between parties as Jake does, Amy sees no need to hierarchically order claims. Instead, she tries to account for all the parties' needs, and searches for a way to find a solution that satisfies the needs of both. In her view, Heinz should be able to obtain the drug for his wife and the pharmacist should still receive payment. So Amy suggests a loan, a credit arrangement, or a discussion of other ways to structure the transaction. In short, she won't play by the adversarial rules. She searches outside the system for a way to solve the problem, trying to keep both parties in mind. Her methods substantiate Gilligan's observations that women will try to change the rules to preserve the relationships.

Furthermore, in addition to looking for more substantive solutions to the problem (i.e., not accepting the binary win/lose conception of the problem), Amy also wants to change the process. Amy sees no reason why she must act as a neutral arbiter of a dispute and make a decision based only on the information she has. She "belie[ves] in communication as the mode of conflict resolution and [is convinced] that the solution to the dilemma will follow from its compelling representation. . . ." If the parties talk directly to each other, they will be more likely to appreciate the importance of each other's needs.

Thus, she believes direct communication, rather than third party mediated debate, might solve the problem, recognizing that two apparently conflicting positions can both be simultaneously legitimate, and there need not be a single victor.

The notion that women might have more difficulty with full-commitment-to-one-side model of the adversary system is graphically illustrated by Hilary, one of the women lawyers in Gilligan's study. This lawyer finds herself in one of the classic moral dilemmas of the adversary system: she sees that her opponent has failed to make use of a document that is helpful to his case and harmful to hers. In deciding not to tell him about the document because of what she sees as her "professional vulnerability" in the male adversary system, she concludes that "the adversary system of justice impedes not only the supposed search for truth (the conventional criticism), but also *the expression of concern for the person on the other side*." Gilligan describes Hilary's tension between her concept of rights (learned through legal training) and her female ethic of care as a sign of her socialization in the male world of lawyering. Thus, the advocacy model, with its commitment to one-sided advocacy, seems somehow contrary to "apprehending the reality of the other" which lawyers like Hilary experience. Even the continental inquisitorial model, frequently offered as an alternative to the adversarial model, includes most of these elements of the male system—hierarchy, advocacy, competition and binary results.

So what kind of legal system would Amy and Hilary create if left to their own devices? They might look for ways to alter the harshness of win/lose results; they might alter the rules of the game (or make it less like a game); and they might alter the very structures and forms themselves. Thus, in a sense Amy and Hilary's approach can already be found in some of the current alternatives to the adversary model such as mediation. Much of the current interest in alternative dispute resolution is an attempt to modify the harshness of the adversarial process and expand the kinds of solutions available, in order to respond better to the varied needs of the parties. Amy's desire to engage the parties in direct communication with each other is reflected in mediation models where the parties talk directly to each other and forge their own solutions. The work of Gilligan and Noddings, demonstrating an ethic of care and a heightened sense of empathy in women, suggests that women lawyers may be particularly interested in mediation as an alternative to litigation as a method of resolving disputes.

Even within the present adversarial model, Amy and Hilary might, in their concern for others, want to provide for a broader conception of interested parties, permitting participation by those who might be affected by the dispute (an ethic of inclusion). In addition, like judges who increasingly are managing more of the details of their cases, Amy and Hilary might seek a more active role in settlement processes and rely less on court-ordered relief. Amy and Hilary might look for other ways to construct their lawsuits and remedies in much the same way as court of equity mitigated the harshness of the law court's very limited array of remedies by expanding the conception of what was possible.

The process and rules of the adversary system itself might look different if there were more female voices in the legal profession. If Amy is less likely than Jake to make assertive, rights-based statements, is she less likely to adapt to the male-created advocacy mode? In my experience as a trial lawyer, I observed that some women had difficulty with the "macho" ethic of the courtroom battle. Even those who did successfully adapt to the male model often confronted a dilemma because women were less likely to be perceived as behaving properly when engaged in strong adversarial conduct. It is important to be "strong" in the courtroom, according to the stereotypic conception of appropriate trial behavior. The woman who conforms to the female stereotype by being "soft" or "weak" is a bad trial lawyer; but if a woman is "tough" or "strong" in the courtroom, she is seen as acting inappropriately for a woman. Note, however, that this stereotyping is contextual: the same woman acting as a "strong" or "tough" mother with difficult children would be praised for that conduct. Women's strength is approved of with the proviso that it be exerted in appropriately female spheres.

Amy and Hilary might create a different form of advocacy, one resembling a "conversation" with the fact finder, relying on the creation of a relationship with the jury for its effectiveness, rather than on persuasive intimidation. There is some anecdotal evidence that this is happening already. Recently, several women prosecutors described their styles of trial advocacy as the creation of a personal relationship with the jury in which they urge jurors to examine their own perceptions and values and encourage them to think for themselves, rather than "buying" the arguments of one of the advocates. This is a conception of the relationship between the lawyer and the fact-finder which is based on trust and mutual respect rather than on dramatics, intimidation and power, the male mode in which these women had been trained and which they found unsatisfactory.

In sum, the growing strength of women's voice in the legal profession may change the adversarial system into a more cooperative, less war-like system of communication between disputants in which solutions are mutually agreed upon rather than dictated by an outsider, won by the victor, and imposed upon the loser. Some seeds of change may already be found in existing alternatives to the litigation model, such as mediation. It remains to be seen what further changes Portia's voice may make.

FINAL REPORT OF THE ABORIGINAL HEALING JOINT COMMITTEE, FOR GENERATIONS TO COME; THE TIME IS NOW. A STRATEGY FOR ABORIGINAL FAMILY HEALING
(1993), 10-12

To ensure a common understanding of major terms used in this report, the Aboriginal Family Healing Joint Steering Committee has agreed to the following definitions. These definitions will also apply to any implementation of the Aboriginal Family Healing Strategy.

Aboriginal Community:

The Aboriginal community has been defined as a group of Aboriginal people who share similar beliefs, traditions and cultural identity. These groups exist through shared political, cultural, spiritual and/or other affiliations. Aboriginal communities include but are not limited to, First Nations, people who share a Metis identity, Friendship Centres, community based organizations (locals), political/non-political organizations, or any other collection of Aboriginal individuals who share identity, regardless of geography.

Family Violence:

The Aboriginal People in Ontario define family violence as consequent to colonization, forced assimilation, and cultural genocide, the learned negative, cumulative, multi-generational actions, values, beliefs, attitudes and behavioral patterns practised by one or more people that weaken or destroy the harmony and well-being of an Aboriginal individual, family, extended family, community, or nationhood.

In order to address the issue, government must be clear on the understanding, experience and definition of family violence by Aboriginal People.

This would include understanding the wholistic implication of the issue that Aboriginal family violence refers not to isolated, specific incidents of abuse, but rather to the physical, mental, emotional, and spiritual welfare of Aboriginal individuals, families, extended families, communities, and nations.

The Healing Continuum:

It has been agreed that the Aboriginal Healing Strategy will focus on healing and wellness.

The Healing Continuum is based on wholistic and comprehensive concepts including promotion, prevention, crisis intervention, promotion of stability, curative, rehabilitative, training and supportive services for the individual, family, extended family and community all at once.

The concept of healing, rather than merely responding to incidents of violence, and the focus on wellness demands a strategy that is different from the current response to family violence. There is an inherent conflict between a solution which seeks harmony and balance within the individual, family and community, and one which is crisis oriented, punishes the abuser, and separates the family and community. Aboriginal family violence must be addressed with a strategy that makes sense to Aboriginal communities.

It is understood that the wellness focus includes the physical, mental, emotional and spiritual well-being of Aboriginal People. In this way, it will be possible to address the issue of family healing, rather than the issue of family violence.

The strategy must be ongoing and flexible enough to meet the changing needs and experiences of the Aboriginal community on its path to wellness.

It is understood that the strategy must address the needs of Aboriginal people who reside on and off reserve. It has been stated by the government representatives on the Joint Steering Committee that not all program and service delivery will be able to be provided on a First Nation or community by community basis.

The Life Cycle:

The Healing Continuum is embodied within the Aboriginal paradigm of the Wheel of Life or Life Cycle. The Life Cycle explains that the concept of life means conquering the four main journeys in life: Infancy, Youth, Maturity, and Old Age. These four stages of life are celebrated as the four prime moments in life which correspond to the four directions, the four seasons, the four colours, and the four gifts: physical, mental, emotional and spiritual, including the four elements that make up the world: water, air, mineral and fire. The "Healing Continuum" recognizes the ages and stages of development from birth to death, meaning that the cycle of life never ends.

The Life Cycle incorporates all members of the community, each of whom are at different stages in their journey: infants, toddlers, children, youth, young adults, parents, grandparents, and Elders. Each person has a gift to bring and a role to play in the community as explained in the teachings below. The purpose of healing is to restore life to all members such that they will be able to share their gift and assume their responsibility in the community.

When the Healing Continuum is integrated into the Life Cycle, it ensures that the needs of each person, from infant to Elder, are considered in the continuum of care that constitutes the healing process. Because the Life Cycle itself is a wholistic paradigm, its use here ensures a comprehensive approach to Aboriginal family healing program planning, development, and implementation.

First they arrested the Communists—but I was not a Communist, so I did nothing. Then they came for the Social Democrats—but I was not a Social Democrat, so I did nothing. Then they arrested the trade unionists—and I did nothing because I was not one. And then they came for the Jews and then the Catholics, but I was neither a Jew nor a Catholic and I did nothing. At last they came and arrested me—and there was no one left to do anything about it.

Rev. Martin Niemoller
Nazi Prison Survivor

GREENSPAN AND JONAS, GREENSPAN: THE CASE FOR THE DEFENCE
(1987), 260-265

Whenever a crime is committed (or whenever some people in the community suspect that an act may amount to a crime), a large, impersonal machinery goes into motion. Its initial purpose is to determine if some act or event was, in fact, a crime—and if it concludes that it was, to find the individual (or group of individuals) responsible for it.

Once this appears to be accomplished, the machinery shifts into second gear. It tries to establish the accused individual's *degree* of responsibility. Then, in third gear, his or her appropriate punishment. Sometimes there is a fourth gear: the machinery may turn its attention to some social or legal condition in the hope of making it easier to define, prevent, or detect such crimes in the future.

This process can involve dozens and dozens of people in its various stages. Ideally—and often in actual fact—they are highly trained, intelligent, dedicated, and hard-working human beings: people of great personal integrity. They are police officers, forensic experts, medical doctors, prosecuting attorneys, court officials, judges, jurors, parole officials, prison administrators, and lawmakers. Except for the jurors, they are all professionals. Many of them have the authority to knock on anybody's door and ask for information and assistance. Even when they cannot compel people's co-operation by law, they can expect people to co-operate with them as a civic or moral duty. They also have at their disposal support personnel and sophisticated, expensive equipment, the best society can provide, to help them in their work.

There is nothing wrong with any of this, of course. Crime cannot go undetected, undefined, or unpunished. No community could function without protecting itself from crime.

However, this great, impersonal, awesome machinery has one built-in bias. It is an unconscious, functional bias, somewhat like an aircraft's bias for leaving the ground as soon as it has attained a certain speed. The bias of the justice system is to find guilt. That is, first, to define any human act that comes to its attention as a crime; then, to define any suspect as a person who has probably committed such an act; and finally, to define any human being who has committed such an act as a criminal. That's the way the justice system flies.

Everyone knows that in a given individual case none of this may be true—yet the great machine of the criminal justice system may thunder down the runway and take off regardless.

. . .

Our justice system has tried to counteract this potential by two remedies.

First, on an abstract level, the remedy is the law's presumption that every person is innocent until proven guilty on relevant evidence beyond a reasonable doubt.

By saying "on an abstract level" I don't mean to imply that this presumption is unimportant. On the contrary, it is vital and fundamental. Everything else flows from the presumption of innocence. However, without a second remedy on a concrete level, it could remain as ineffectual as a sheathed sword. Or, to use a more up-to-date methaphor, as an engine without a driver.

This second, concrete remedy is the lawyer for the defence. He drives the abstract engine of the presumption of innocence. He is the one person in the entire world, apart from the accused person's mother, who *starts* with the assumption that the authorities must be mistaken.

To balance the awe-inspiring machinery of the criminal-justice system, the law permits one individual to be the accused person's friend. He is, as the legal expression goes, to be "of counsel" to him. Simply put, his job is to "believe" the accused—or at least not to disbelieve him. His job is to look at every circumstance surrounding the allegations against a defendant with the assumption that they prove, or are consistent with, his innocence.

The defence lawyer is to balance the dozens of powerful professionals whose task is to investigate and prosecute an accused person. We give the defence lawyer this task in the knowledge that a defendant may *be* innocent. Innocent, not just as an abstract legal idea (because in that sense he is innocent anyway until found guilty), but as a matter of plain, actual fact. What he is accused of may not amount to a crime, or he may not have committed it. If it is a crime and he did commit it, it may not be as serious a crime as his adversary, the prosecutor, suggests. And even if it is as serious, there may be something about the circumstances, or about the defendant as a human being, that makes him something else than a criminal deserving the worst punishment.

Since this may be so, our system has decided that there must be one person in the defendant's community who acts as if it were so. One man or woman who is not the defendant's inquisitor, accuser, or judge. One who doesn't merely keep an open mind about him. One person who is the defendant's advocate.

Society assigns this role to the defence lawyer. He is the one person whose duty is to assume the best about a defendant at every step of the way. The defence lawyer alone, among all the defendant's fellow citizens and neighbours, must act on the assumption that whatever the defendant says is true. He must act on the assumption that the defendant's accusers are mistaken. Mistaken—or possibly malicious. They may have their own axe to grind. The defence lawyer must put everything they say about the defendant to the strictest test of proof. In so far as the law permits, he must put the accusers on trial.

This is the defence lawyer's duty. It's a duty not just to his client, but to his society. It is not something the defence lawyer decides in his own mind: it is an obligation the community places on him. The defence lawyer chooses his occupation voluntarily, but he does not choose his role: his society defines his role for him. The moral essence of this role has been distilled by the common experience of our legal tradition over the centuries. It is that a community can retain justice and freedom only as long as it gives standing to one person to take, within the limits of the law, the defendant's side in court.

. . .

The defence lawyer, as many people have pointed out, only defends a client (or a client's act) and not a crime. Central to any defence, other than a submission in mitigation of sentence, is the position that the client *didn't* do something. Or that whatever he did was not wrong in law, or at least not as wrong as the prosecution contends. If a lawyer suggested that yes, my client did shoot this man deliberately and in cold blood, but the victim was a nasty fellow who deserved to be shot, *then* he would be defending a crime—but no lawyer does that. (The only exceptions in our times have been some "activist" lawyers who attempted to gain the acquittal of murderers on the basis of some "higher" political or social motive.)

But these are only aberrations—albeit dangerous ones—and we need not concern ourselves with them here. Like most criminal lawyers, I defend clients, not crimes. Which is why I find questions like: "How can you defend those people?" or "Is there any kind of crime at which you'd draw a line?" meaningless.

I haven't the slightest moral conflict defending people accused of homicide, sexual assault, business fraud, environmental offences, or even crimes against humanity. I don't "draw the line" at anything. If I defended *crimes*, maybe I would—but I don't defend crimes. I only defend innocent people. Until they are found guilty there are no other kinds of people for me to defend, and what difference does it make what an innocent person is accused of?

_____

Would you represent any and all accused?

See Michel Proulx, "The Defence of the Unpopular or Repugnant Client: Some of the Hardest Questions", (2005) 5 Can. Crim. L. Rev. 221.

Helen Conway, a sole practitioner and defence counsel in Windsor writing in the *Law Times* of September 10, 2001 under the title "The Spirit of the Law" points to statistics of disproportionate rates of depression, addiction and suicide for lawyers, financial strain from low legal aid rates, high overheads and collection difficulties, and a bureaucratic and inefficient criminal justice system. She concludes that the practice of criminal law

> is not for the faint of heart. Lawyers take the heat from all directions and most have even grown accustomed to the overall disrespect and disapproval towards them which exists in the community. Ultimately, however, moral affirmation and professional certainty have to come not from society but from within the knowledge and belief that perhaps lawyers have in some small measure protected the rights of an individual or defended a client who has been wronged or treated unfairly.

> The practice of [criminal] law is, first and finally, a vocation, a call to represent and to advance the ideal of justice. While public in practice, it is also and always personal in spirit. (p. 8)

2. Role of Defence Counsel

DENNING, THE TRADITIONS OF THE BAR
(1955), 72 So. Afr. L.J. 43 at 48

The duty of counsel to defend his client ranks so high that laymen are often prone to pose the moral question: How can a barrister consistently urge a jury to find a man not guilty when the barrister himself must know that the man is guilty? The answer to that question is that the barrister is not to set himself up as a judge of his client's case. He is only the mouthpiece of the client to put the case before the jury. No matter how improbable or incredible—or even possible—it may seem for his client's case to succeed, he must put it before the jury for them to judge. The limit is only reached when he actually knows, by the man's own admission to him, that he is guilty. If the barrister gets to know this before the trial starts—and nevertheless the man is determined to plead not guilty—then the barrister must withdraw from the case; because there then comes into play another tradition of the English Bar, which is of equal importance with those I have already mentioned; and that is the tradition of honesty. A barrister must not put forward a case which he knows to be false or assert as a fact that which he knows to be untrue. Dr. Samuel Johnson put it succinctly when he said: 'A lawyer is not to tell what he knows to be a lie; he is not to produce what he knows to be a false deed; but he is not to usurp the province of the jury and of the judge and determine what shall be the effect of evidence—what shall be the result of legal argument'.

G.A. MARTIN, THE ROLE AND RESPONSIBILITY OF THE DEFENCE ADVOCATE
(1970), 12 Crim. L.Q. 376

The defence counsel is not the *alter ego* of the client. The function of defence counsel is to provide professional assistance and advice. He must, accordingly, exercise his professional skill and judgment in the conduct of the case and not allow himself to be a mere mouthpiece for the client.

The Tentative Draft Standards Of The American Bar Association Project On Standards For Criminal Justice with respect to the prosecution and defence function state:

> The "alter ego" concept of a defence lawyer, which sees him as a mouthpiece for his client, is fundamentally wrong, unethical and destructive of the lawyer's image; more important to the accused, perhaps, this pernicious idea is destructive of the lawyer's usefulness. The lawyer's value to each client stems in large part from the independence of his stance, as a professional representative rather than as an ordinary agent.

Even Erskine, that immortal advocate, was reminded of his proper function when he said in the trial of Tom Paine:

> I will now lay aside the role of the advocate and address you as a man.

which evoked the following response from the court:

> You will do nothing of the sort. The only right and licence you have to appear in this Court is as an advocate.

The literature with respect to the duty of the advocate properly and frequently reminds him of his duty to resist any attempt on the part of the court, or anyone else, to override the rights of his client.

It is, of course, fundamental to his role that an advocate should, while acting with proper courtesy to the court, fearlessly uphold the interest of his client without regard to any unpleasant consequence to himself or any other person.

The literature on advocacy, however, is strangely silent with respect to the duty of the advocate, on occasion, to resist the wishes of the client; and yet in order to effectively discharge his duties as an advocate he may be required to conduct the trial in a manner which is contrary to his client's wishes. Nevertheless, this view comes as a surprise to some lawyers. Why should this be so?

The Tentative Draft Standards suggests that the right of the client to plead guilty or not guilty and the right of counsel thereafter to make the decisions (with two exceptions) with respect to the conduct of the trial is analogous to the right of the patient to decide whether to submit to surgery but not to tell the surgeon how to perform the operation.

I think the analogy might be carried still farther. I cannot conceive of a medical practitioner who had killed a patient by grossly improper treatment defending himself before his professional colleagues on a charge of professional misconduct or before a court on a trial for manslaughter by urging that while he was perfectly aware that the treatment was wrong and contrary to accepted medical practice he treated the patient in the way the patient insisted he treat him.

Mr. Justice Blackburn, over a hundred years ago, indicated that it would be unprofessional for a lawyer to undertake the conduct of a case giving up all discretion as to how he should conduct it. He said:

> Few counsel, I hope, would accept a brief on the unworthy terms that he is simply to be the mouthpiece of his client.
>
> If the counsel cannot induce his client to act on his advice in such a case, the proper course is to return his brief.

The later statement of Mr. Justice Blackburn may require qualification to the extent that counsel should only refuse to continue to act where the disagreement between counsel and his client is so fundamental that compliance with the client's wishes would prevent counsel from fulfilling his proper function. Sometimes the proper course to be followed is reasonably open to two different views. Counsel should not refuse to continue to act without good reason.

. . .

It is clear, therefore, that it is defence counsel, not the client, who decides what witnesses to call, whether he should cross-examine a witness, and if so how the cross-examination should be conducted.

It is equally clear that there is at least one decision that only the client can make and that is the decision as to whether to plead guilty or not guilty. The High Court of Australia in *Tuckiar v. The King* said:

> Whether he be in fact guilty or not, a prisoner is, in point of law, entitled to acquittal from any charge which the evidence fails to establish he committed and it is not incumbent on his counsel by abandoning his defence to deprive him of the benefit of such rational arguments that fairly arise on the proofs submitted.

An admission of facts which constitutes guilt to counsel does not preclude counsel from testing the evidence submitted by the prosecution and from submitting that such evidence does not establish the guilt of the defendant beyond a reasonable doubt. Such an admission by the client, however, imposes ethical restrictions on defence counsel with respect to the manner in which he is entitled to conduct the defence of his client. Notwithstanding the right of the accused to require the prosecution to prove his guilt, counsel is under a duty after making a thorough investigation to advise the client as to what, in his considered opinion, the probable outcome of the case is likely to be. He is entitled to present his advice in strong terms. If he thinks that it is to the defendant's advantage to plead guilty he should so advise him. Defence counsel throughout carries a very heavy responsibility. He should never urge a defendant to plead guilty until he has made a thorough investigation of the facts and the relevant law. Indeed, in my view, before urging a defendant to plead guilty he should have conducted the same type of intensive investigation which a lawyer preparing for trial should undertake.

I have heard many unlikely stories in my time from defendants; some surprisingly, turned out to be true. Some cases look impossible; intensive preparation indicates that they are not really so. Others, regrettably, from the defence counsel's point of view, not only look impossible but actually are.

Although counsel is free to advise an accused in strong terms as to the plea that he should enter, the ultimate choice is that of the accused and it must be a free choice. Counsel, however, is not bound to follow instructions which are *unreasonable* and in proper cases is entitled to refuse to act for a client who rejects his advice.

On the other hand, counsel must not allow an accused to plead guilty unless he admits he committed the act and had the mental state necessary to constitute the offence charged. He must not permit an accused, who denies committing the act or possessing the mental state necessary to constitute the offence, to plead guilty because of some hoped for advantage such as a lighter sentence.

Are there other decisions which only the client can make? *The Tentative Draft Standards* reserve two other decisions for the client, namely:

(i) Whether to waive a trial by jury where that is permissible, and

(ii) Whether to testify on his own behalf.

Obviously, neither counsel nor anyone else can deprive an accused of his fundamental rights. If the accused insists on giving evidence or insists on a jury trial, contrary to counsel's advice, counsel cannot, as a matter of law, prevent him from exercising those rights. This is not to say that defence counsel should not endeavour to control the client's decision on these questions where, in the considered opinion of counsel, the course which the client insists be followed would seriously prejudice his interests. These conflicts, however, will rarely arise if a proper lawyer-client relationship is established. Counsel should explain to the client why it is necessary for him to be in control. He should endeavour to obtain the client's confidence, and his concurrence to counsel's exercise of necessary control.

Counsel should also consult with the client and keep him informed with respect to his reasons for following a particular course of action. If, however, there is a conflict between counsel and client on a *fundamental* matter which cannot be resolved, counsel is entitled to withdraw if he does so at a sufficiently early date in accordance with the Law Society's ruling in this respect.

GREENSPAN AND JONAS, GREENSPAN: THE CASE FOR THE DEFENCE
(1987), 59-60

Many people believe . . . that your lawyer is there "to get you off". That's what you hire him for, they think; that's his function. But that's not quite so. Your lawyer's function is to *defend* you.

. . . [Most] professional criminals are likely to appreciate the difference more than ordinary citizens who happen to be charged with some offence once in their lives. Full-time crooks are likely to know better than to say to their lawyers: "Sure, I made this illegal U-turn, but who is to know? I'll deny it, so you can get me off."

Ordinary citizens are sometimes surprised to hear that their lawyer can't put them on the witness stand to say in court that they didn't make an illegal U-turn when, in fact, they made one. Why can't he let them say it? Because it's not true.

A lawyer can't assist his client or anyone else in misleading a court—on the witness stand or in an affidavit. All a lawyer can do is to advise his client of his right to say nothing in answer to a charge. He can advise him to stand mute, then make sure that the prosecution discharges the burden of proof placed on it by law. Sometimes the prosecution can't . . . and if the Crown can't prove its charges beyond a reasonable doubt, then of course the accused must go free.

It is a lawyer's duty to put the Crown to the most rigorous test, but no lawyer can assist a client in the commission of perjury. Accused persons are always presumed innocent, but, even beyond this general presumption, if a lawyer leads an accused's denial of guilt in the witness-box as part of the defence's evidence, then the lawyer himself, in his own mind, must be in a state of doubt about the defendant's guilt. He can't say this to a jury, of course, because a lawyer's state of mind is irrelevant. But though he can't say it, it has to be so, for the simple reason that no lawyer can knowingly allow a client to state falsehoods or deny true facts under oath.

CANADIAN BAR ASSOCIATION'S CODE OF PROFESSIONAL CONDUCT (1987, as amended in 2004)
CONFIDENTIAL INFORMATION

RULE

Maintaining Information in Confidence

1. The lawyer has a duty to hold in strict confidence all information concerning the business and affairs of the client acquired in the course of the professional relationship, and shall not divulge any such information except as expressly or impliedly authorized by the client, required by law or otherwise required by this Code.

Public Safety Exception

2. Where a lawyer believes upon reasonable grounds that there is an imminent risk to an identifiable person or group of death or serious bodily harm, including serious psychological harm that would substantially interfere with health or well-being, the lawyer shall disclose confidential information where it is necessary to do so in order to prevent the death or harm, but shall not disclose more information than is required.

. . .

Commentary

Guiding Principles

1. The lawyer cannot render effective professional service to the client unless there is full and unreserved communication between them. At the same time the client must feel completely secure and entitled to proceed on the basis that, without an express request or stipulation on the client's part, matters disclosed to or discussed with the lawyer will be held secret and confidential.

2. This ethical rule must be distinguished from the evidentiary rule of lawyer and client privilege with respect to oral or written communications passing between the client and the lawyer. The ethical rule is wider and applies without regard to the nature or source of the information or to the fact that others may share the knowledge.

3. The importance of the even broader ethical rule regarding confidential information is illustrated by the Supreme Court of Canada's approach to solicitor-client privilege. The Court has held that solicitor-client privilege must remain as close to absolute as possible if it is to retain its relevance. Solicitor-client privilege is a rule of evidence, an important civil and legal right and a principle of fundamental justice in Canadian law. The public has a compelling interest in maintaining the integrity of the solicitor-client relationship. Confidential communications to a lawyer represent an important exercise of the right to privacy, and they are central to the administration of justice in an adversarial system.

. . .

Disclosure Required by Law

11. When disclosure is required by law or by order of a court of competent jurisdiction, the lawyer should be careful not to divulge more than is required. Legislation in certain jurisdictions imposes a duty on persons to report sexual or physical abuse in specified circumstances. Careful consideration of the wording of such legislation is necessary to determine whether, in such circumstances, communications that are subject to solicitor-client privilege must be disclosed.

THE LAWYER AS ADVOCATE

RULE

When acting as an advocate, the lawyer must treat the tribunal with courtesy and respect and must represent the client resolutely, honourably and within the limits of the law.

Commentary

Guiding Principles

1. The advocate's duty to the client "fearlessly to raise every issue, advance every argument, and ask every question, however distasteful, which he thinks will help his client's case" and to endeavour "to obtain for his client the benefit of any and every remedy and defence which is authorized by law" must always be discharged by fair and honourable means, without illegality and in a manner consistent with the lawyer's duty to treat the court with candour, fairness, courtesy and respect.

Prohibited Conduct

2. The lawyer must not, for example:

    . . .

    (b) knowingly assist or permit the client to do anything that the lawyer considers to be dishonest or dishonourable;

    . . .

    (e) knowingly attempt to deceive or participate in the deception of a tribunal or influence the course of justice by offering false evidence, misstating facts or law, presenting or relying upon a false or deceptive affidavit, suppressing what ought to be disclosed or otherwise assisting in any fraud, crime or illegal conduct.

    . . .

Duties of Defence Counsel

10. When defending an accused person, the lawyer's duty is to protect the client as far as possible from being convicted except by a court of competent jurisdiction and upon legal evidence sufficient to support a conviction for the offence charged. Accordingly, and notwithstanding the lawyer's private opinion as to credibility or merits, the lawyer may properly rely upon all available evidence or defences including so-called technicalities not known to be false or fraudulent.

11. Admissions made by the accused to the lawyer may impose strict limitations on the conduct of the defence and the accused should be made aware of this. For example, if the accused clearly admits to the lawyer the factual and mental elements necessary to constitute the offence, the lawyer, if convinced that the admissions are true and voluntary, may properly take objection to the jurisdiction of the court, or to the form of the indictment, or to the admissibility or sufficiency of the evidence, but must not suggest that some other person committed the offence, or call

any evidence that, by reason of the admissions, the lawyer believes to be false. Nor may the lawyer set up an affirmative case inconsistent with such admissions, for example, by calling evidence in support of an alibi intended to show that the accused could not have done, or in fact had not done, the act. Such admissions will also impose a limit upon the extent to which the lawyer may attack the evidence for the prosecution. The lawyer is entitled to test the evidence given by each individual witness for the prosecution and argue that the evidence taken as a whole is insufficient to amount to proof that the accused is guilty of the offence charged, but the lawyer should go no further than that.

The problem with such rules of professional responsibility is that they clearly often conflict and are less than clear in specific cases. It may be helpful to distinguish between rules of professional responsibility which must be followed to avoid discipline by professional bodies and considerations of personal ethics.

For a most detailed consideration of ethical obligations facing counsel in criminal cases see Michel Proulx and David Layton, *Ethics and Canadian Criminal Law* (Toronto: Irwin Law, 2001).

American legal scholar Professor Monroe Freedman, "Professional Responsibility of the Criminal Defense Lawyer: The Three Hardest Questions", (1966) 64 Mich. L. Rev. 1469, writes that "professional responsibility requires that an advocate have full knowledge of every pertinent fact". **Would you ask your client for full details as to his involvement in the matter that gave rise to the charge?**

On another model, sometimes called "blind person's bluff", the lawyer remains purposively ignorant about potentially embarrassing facts and discourages the client from telling anything. **Which model would you follow and why?**

PROBLEM 1

You have agreed to act on behalf of a client charged with murder. He is wearing a jacket that appears to be bloodstained. He admits to you that it is the jacket that he was wearing on the evening of the incident. He didn't realize the stain was noticeable. He asks your advice as to what he should do with the jacket. You're unsure what to tell him so he removes the jacket and gives it to you. What do you do? Would it make a difference if this initial interview occurred in the interview room at the local police station where your client is being detained?

PROBLEM 2

Do you consider that Bernardo's counsel in a highly publicized sexual assault and double murder case acted unethically in following his client's instructions to

1. **remove videotapes of the events in question from a ceiling in the house where the murders were alleged to have taken place;**

2. not to look at them; and

3. to look at them and use them for his defence after his wife, Karla Homolka, entered into a plea bargain under which she was to plead guilty to manslaughter, to receive a sentence of 12 years concurrent on each count and to testify against him.

Was it unethical for the defence counsel, Mr. Murray, to then keep the tapes which he now knew depicted murders and sexual assault for a further 17 months before being advised by the Law Society to turn them over to the trial judge and withdraw from the case? His explanation was that he wanted to use them to cross-examine Homolka and put the responsibility on her, not Bernardo.

See generally Macdonald and Pink, "Murder, Silence and Physical Evidence: The Dilemma of Client Confidentiality", (1997) 2 Can. Crim. L.R. 111; Kent Roach, "Smoking Guns: Beyond the Murray Case", (2000) 43 Crim. L.Q. 409; and Wayne Renke, "Real Evidence, Disclosure and the Plight of Counsel", (2003) 47 Crim. L.Q. 175.

Murray was later charged with obstruction of justice but was acquitted on the basis of a lack of proof of intent to mislead and because the rules of professional responsibility in such a situation were quite unclear.

PROBLEM 3

John Smith has been charged with assault. He asks you to represent him and you agree. He tells you that he beat on the victim during a drunken rage. He imagines that it was because he has never cared for his manner. He knows that he started this particular fracas but also advises you that the victim himself has two previous convictions of assault, which, he suggests, could be fertile ground for cross-examination. The victim describes the beating in some detail. At the end of the examination-in-chief you turn to your client who advises, "That's exactly what happened. Now go get him. Destroy his credibility." What do you do?

Your client is convicted. Would you inform the Crown about two other assault convictions registered against your client under another name?

PROBLEM 4

Your client is prosecuted for robbery. He committed the crime at 10:45 and has admitted the same to you. The sole prosecution witness indentified your client as the robber but mistakenly placed the time at 10:15. Your client has an airtight alibi for 10:00 to 10:30. Will you present the alibi?

PROBLEM 5

Your client says that he is innocent, but that he wants to plead guilty "to get it over with". He is tired of the court delay and does not want to lose any more time off work. The offence is a minor one. Would you assist him in entering his guilty plea? Would you advise him to indicate remorse to secure a minimal penalty?

PROBLEM 6

John Smith has been charged with the murder of a fourteen-year-old girl and asks you to defend him. You accept his retainer and during the first interview he admits the killing and discloses the whereabouts of the body. The police have been unable to discover the location of the body; the charge against your client rests largely on the fact that the deceased was last seen arguing with your client. Should you advise the police of the body's location? Should you go to the location described by your client and see whether the body is still hidden there? You read in the newspaper of the mental anguish of the deceased's parents who cannot cope with the problem of not knowing whether their child is dead or alive. Should you advise the parents that the child is dead? See Chamberlain, "Confidentiality and the Case of Robert Garrow's Lawyers," (1976), 25 Buffalo L. Rev. 212.

PROBLEM 7

You have just been successful in obtaining the release of your client on the condition that he enter into a recognizance promising to appear on the day set for his trial. The terms of the recognizance required a deposit of $10,000 which deposit was made by your client's invalid mother. Your client thanks you for your services, for which you have not yet been paid, and advises that he is leaving the jurisdiction. He has not yet signed the recognizance. Do you advise anyone?

PROBLEM 8

As the result of questions by the trial judge you believe that her view of the facts is mistaken. The mistake benefits your client. Should you correct the judge? Does it matter whether the mistake is because the judge misinterpreted the evidence led or because certain facts, within your knowledge, were not led in evidence? As the result of her questions you believe the judge is mistaken as to the law, and again the mistake enures to the benefit of your client. Would you correct her?

PROBLEM 9

After about eight weeks of a first degree murder trial, an application was made on behalf of the defence counsel for permission to withdraw from the case. By estimate of counsel, the trial would last another one or two weeks. After an adjournment, the court was advised that following the cross-examination of the accused, information had been provided by the accused to the defence counsel, the nature and particulars of which could not be disclosed without breaching solicitor-client confidentiality. As a result of that information, it was argued that any continued participation by the defence counsel while maintaining the confidentiality of the information would result in a deception of the court. The information was fundamentally inconsistent with the very essence of the case which had been advanced to the jury on behalf of the accused. Should counsel be required to continue his representation of the accused, any active participation whatsoever would raise the potential of counsel misleading the court. Crown counsel, while acknowledging the obligation of solicitor-client confidentiality attaching to the communication, took the position that defence counsel ought not to be permitted to withdraw. Rule and give reasons.

Compare *R. v. Jenkins* (2001), 44 C.R. (5th) 248, 152 C.C.C. (3d) 426 (Ont. S.C.J.). See David Layton, "R. v. Jenkins: Client Perjury and Disclosure by Defence Counsel", (2001) 44 C.R. (5th) 259.

Is it different if the reason for withdrawal is that the client won't or can't pay his lawyer? Should a lawyer require the approval of the judge to withdraw?

Should a different standard apply to withdrawal on ethical grounds as opposed to non-payment of fees? What standard should apply when a legal aid lawyer wishes to withdraw when the client has not complied with the eligibility criteria or requirements of the legal aid administration? See: *Cunningham v. Lilles*, 73 C.R. (6th) 1, [2010] 1 S.C.R. 331, 254 C.C.C. (3d) 1 (S.C.C.).

3. Role of the Prosecutor

GROSMAN, THE PROSECUTOR: AN INQUIRY INTO THE EXERCISE OF DISCRETION
(1969), 10-14, 16-19

AN HISTORICAL PERSPECTIVE

ENGLAND

By the common law of England crimes were committed not against the state but against a particular person or his family and the injured party; hence, the victim or some interested relative stepped forward in person to initiate and conduct the prosecution of the alleged offender. Since it was not the state, but private, aggrieved parties, who prosecuted, the act was carried out with a zeal that turned the law into a tool for private vengeance.

The abuses of private prosecution were acknowledged by Henry VIII who in 1534 suggested that "Those laws have been printed 'in our maternal English tongue' and are so available to all; yet they are not put into force unless it be by malice, rancour and evil will. 'Better it were that they had never been made, unless they should be put in due and perfect execution . . .'" To remedy the imperfect execution of the laws of the realm Henry VIII proposed that the sergeants of the common weal act as police prosecutors to enforce penal statutes throughout the country.

As early as 1243 the sovereign was represented by a professional attorney who prosecuted pleas of particular interest to the king. These interests included, among others, proceedings against churchmen brash enough to pronounce a sentence of excommunication against a royal retainer and the investigation of certain homicides pertaining to the Crown. It later developed that the king's sergeants pleaded the royal cause before the courts and the attorney general gradually took over the general supervision of the king's legal affairs. In the country at large, the public interest and crimes of no particular concern to the sovereign remained to be determined by private litigation in which the Crown generally took no interest.

From the time of Henry VIII's original proposal that prosecutors be appointed throughout the country, a variety of proposals were advanced for the public prosecution of crimes by the Crown and appointed Crown officers. Some supported the public prosecution of penal infractions; others dismissed the idea in favour of a continuation of the English tradition of private prosecution. Although the king's attorneys and the king's sergeants had from the earliest times received payment from the Crown for their services, the fees gained in the private practice of law were substantially greater than those forthcoming from the Crown. It was natural, then, that the suggestion that these eminent lawyers devote themselves solely to Crown interests and forego private practice should meet some strong resistance from the incumbent Crown officers. The debate surrounding the abuses of private prosecution and the desirability of the superintendence and the conduct of criminal prosecutions by the state and state officers continued unabated throughout the nineteenth century.

In 1879, the office of the Director of Public Prosecutions was established and the director charged with devoting his time solely to the public service, acting primarily as senior adviser to police and other prosecuting authorities. At the same time it was made clear that this new and permanent prosecutorial office would not interfere with the right of any private person to institute or carry on any criminal proceeding. Today, the office of the Director of Public Prosecutions advises government departments and the police, but intervenes to conduct only those prosecutions of particular importance or difficulty including cases referred to it by government agencies and all offences formerly punishable by death. In relation to the total number of prosecutions in England only a small proportion are taken by the director.

The English system has remained, in principle, one of private prosecution. When the Director of Public Prosecutions or the police institute or conduct a prosecution, their status and power in law remain those of a private prosecutor. Although in theory each prosecution is private, in practice, as it has developed, individual initiative is removed from the institution and conduct of prosecutions. It is the police who most often initiate the prosecution by the laying of an information and it is they who most often prosecute cases heard in the lower courts. At the higher court levels the "county" or "police" solicitor usually retains a barrister to prosecute the case on behalf of the Crown. The barrister retained is not employed by the police or by any public office, but remains aloof and independent from the investigatory procedures. He is briefed by the police solicitor as he would be by any other solicitor who might retain his services, and he therefore holds no general briefs for the Crown.

UNITED STATES

Unlike the development of the public prosecution in England in the first years of the eighteenth century, most of the American colonies were doing away with private prosecutions, and as early as 1704 the first public prosecution statute was enacted: "Henceforth there shall be in every countie a sober, discreet and religious person appointed by countie courts, to be atturney for the Queen to prosecute and implead in the lawe all criminals and to doe all other things necessary or convenient as an atturney to suppresse vice and immoralitie . . ."

By the end of the nineteenth century official prosecutions in the majority of the newly independent United States were conducted by public prosecutors. This development, so unlike the English common law tradition of private prosecutions, was partly a product of a prevalent hostility towards all things English and a certain enthusiastic interest in French institutions. The American prosecutor, both federal and state, was patterned after both the English Attorney General and the French *avocat général* and *procureur du Roi*.

By statute, in 1789, the office of the United States district attorney was created in order to "prosecute in each district all delinquents for crimes and offences cognizable under the authority of the United States." At the end of the Civil War, the Attorney-General of the United States was given supervisory power over all the United States federal prosecutors, and his office became the law office of government known today as the Department of Justice, responsible for all federal prosecutions.

At the state level, local prosecutors called district attorneys act in their own counties much like local attorneys general with a sense of independence from state control. This may result from the elective nature of the office and the aggressive attitude to crime and criminals displayed in public by the incumbent in order to justify his re-election. In addition to their functions as counsel in the conduct of a trial, but unlike their English counterparts, the district attorneys perform important investigatory functions concurrently with police agencies and exercise a wide discretion over the initiation of investigations, prosecutions, and the arrest of suspects. Once the information has been laid the district attorney takes over the management of the prosecution. Unlike the English system of private prosecutions and the remoteness of counsel retained for the prosecution from the investigatory and initiatory charging processes of the police, the American prosecutor combines the functions of police adviser with those of prosecutor at the trial. The federal prosecuting system in the United States very much resembles the French structure, and yet at the local level in each state the independence of the prosecutor and his freedom from supervisory control is a unique development born of the hardy independence of a young country disenchanted with past attempts at forced centralization.

CANADA

In Canada, the Crown officers were originally located at the seat of government and prosecutions were conducted at this central locale. As the population expanded into areas more remote from the central authority, the Attorney-General and his agents, the law officers of the Crown, could not effectively attend to their duties. By 1857 a county attorney was appointed by the Governor-in-Council for every county in Upper Canada. These were local lawyers who acted as part-time prosecutors appointed and generally supervised by the Attorney-General. Local county attorneys became responsible not only for the prosecution of crimes in their respective counties, but often acted to supervise the administration of criminal justice in their locality.

With Confederation in 1867, criminal law and procedure was designated by the British North America Act as being within federal competence. The Attorney-General of Canada was to regulate, conduct, and defend all criminal proceedings for the Crown or any federal department with respect to any subject matter, apart from the Criminal Code, and within the legislative jurisdiction of the federal government. The provinces through their own Attorneys-General assumed responsibility for the constitution of the criminal courts and the administration of criminal justice. Their jurisdiction included the regulation of provincial courts and law enforcement within the province as well as the prosecution of provincial and criminal code offences and the appointment of local Crown prosecutors and magistrates.

Private prosecutions and those brought by municipal and federal government departments are conducted by specially retained lawyers. The prosecutor specially retained by a federal government department to prosecute locally generally remains remote from the investigatory and charging procedures and prosecution, based as it is on individual case retainers, resembles English practice. Federal prosecutions represent only a small portion of the criminal prosecutions in Canada. But even in these the provincial Attorney-General, through his provincially appointed Crown prosecutor, may intervene where in the interests of justice he deems it appropriate to do so.

In Canada there has been a tradition of part-time Crown prosecutors, often lawyers appointed as a result of political patronage who, in additon to their private practice of law, assume prosecuting duties. The employment of part-time prosecutors has become untenable in the face of growing urban crime and the resulting administrative demands. Familiarity with the system and a certain expertise is coming to be expected from the Crown prosecutor. It is now generally accepted that only with a permanent Crown prosecutor and a permanent Crown prosecuting structure can these new demands be adequately answered in urban areas.

It was the local Crown Attorney or prosecutor appointed by the provincial Attorney-General who conducted and continues to conduct the great bulk of the prosecutions throughout the counties. Every local Crown prosecutor is an agent of the provincial Attorney-General for the purpose of prosecutions under the provisions of the Criminal Code and provincial statutes. Today, in the larger metropolitan areas, the permanent Crown prosecutor is usually a full-time salaried Crown officer. He is prohibited from engaging in private practice and must devote his time to the duties of his office. He takes no part in civil litigation on behalf of the province or municipality. In rural areas he is often a local lawyer carrying on a private practice, appointed as Crown agent for prosecutions in his county and paid by the province on a fee basis. In summary conviction and other minor criminal prosecutions a police officer may appear as agent of the provincial Attorney General to conduct the proceedings, although this practice is generally frowned upon.

The permanent Crown prosecutor is a public officer and a provincial civil servant responsible to the Attorney-General of the province. Although the latter may prefer to appoint members from the ranks of his own political party the full-time Crown prosecutor, once appointed, does not engage in overt political activity. Changes in the government of the day do not affect his tenure as he has become, in the larger urban centres, more a civil servant than a political appointee.

The prosecutor in Canada has come to resemble more his French, Scottish, or American counterpart than his English confederate. But, unlike the American district attorney, once appointed he is non-political and plays little part in initiating criminal prosecutions or in supervising and directing police investigation. Unlike the French *procureur de la République*, the Canadian Crown prosecutor has not been specifically groomed for his duties, but is a lawyer educated as other lawyers. It is expected that he will develop the necessary expertise once he begins prosecuting.

In urban areas today the large bulk of prosecutions is conducted by a permanent professional prosecutor who represents the Crown with a considerable freedom of action. The independence of the prosecutor from the police, and the initiating and investigatory procedures in accord with the traditional concept associated with the English barrister, have been modified by Canadian practice. The Canadian prosecutor often acts not only as an advocate for the Crown at the trial; in addition, his contacts with the police are more substantial than those of his counterpart in England, but are far from reaching the state of interdependence of police and prosecution that prevails in the U.S.

Section 2 of the Criminal Code defines "prosecutor":

"prosecutor" means the Attorney General or, where the Attorney General does not intervene, means the person who institutes proceedings to which this Act applies, and includes counsel acting on behalf of either of them;

"Attorney General"

(a) subject to paragraphs (b.1) to (g), with respect to proceedings to which this Act applies, means the Attorney General or Solicitor General of the province in which those proceedings are taken and includes his or her lawful deputy,

(b) with respect to the Yukon Territory, the Northwest Territories and Nunavut, or with respect to proceedings commenced at the instance of the Government of Canada and conducted by or on behalf of that Government in respect of a contravention of, a conspiracy or attempt to contravene, or counselling the contravention of, any Act of Parliament other than this Act or any regulation made under such an Act, means the Attorney General of Canada and includes his or her lawful deputy,

(b.1) with respect to proceedings in relation to an offence under subsection 7(2.01), means either the Attorney General of Canada or the Attorney General or Solicitor General of the province in which those proceedings are taken and includes the lawful deputy of any of them,

(c) with respect to proceedings in relation to a terrorism offence or to an offence under section 57, 58, 83.12, 424.1 or 431.1 or in relation to an offence against a member of United Nations personnel or associated personnel under section 235, 236, 266, 267, 268, 269, 269.1, 271, 272, 273, 279 or 279.1, means either the Attorney General of Canada or the Attorney General or Solicitor General of the province in which those proceedings are taken and includes the lawful deputy of any of them,

(d) with respect to proceedings in relation to
    (i) an offence referred to in subsection 7(3.71), or
    (ii) an offence referred to in paragraph (a) of the definition "terrorist activity" in subsection 83.01(1), where the act or omission was committed outside Canada but is deemed by virtue of subsection 7(2), (2.1), (2.2), (3), (3.1), (3.4), (3.6), (3.72) or (3.73) to have been committed in Canada,

means either the Attorney General of Canada or the Attorney General or Solicitor General of the province in which those proceedings are taken and includes the lawful deputy of any of them,

(e) with respect to proceedings in relation to an offence where the act or omission constituting the offence
    (i) constitutes a terrorist activity referred to in paragraph (b) of the definition "terrorist activity" in subsection 83.01(1), and
    (ii) was committed outside Canada but is deemed by virtue of subsection 7(3.74) or (3.75) to have been committed in Canada,

means either the Attorney General of Canada or the Attorney General or Solicitor General of the province in which those proceedings are taken and includes the lawful deputy of any of them,

(f) with respect to proceedings under section 83.13, 83.14, 83.28, 83.29 or 83.3, means either the Attorney General of Canada or the Attorney General or Solicitor General of the province in which those proceedings are taken and includes the lawful deputy of any of them; and

(g) with respect to proceedings in relation to an offence referred to in sections 380, 382, 382.1 and 400, means either the Attorney General of Canada or the Attorney General or Solicitor General of the province in which those proceedings are taken and includes the lawful deputy of any of them;

Crown Attorneys have a great deal of discretion in the daily decisions that they make. In Quebec and British Columbia, Crown Attorneys approve charges before they are laid. In other provinces, like Ontario, the police lay charges and seek legal advice from Crown Attorneys when they see fit. Once a charge is laid, Crown Attorneys enjoy a very wide discretion on the issues of when to withdraw charges or when to agree to a plea on less serious offences. To some extent, the discretion of a Crown Attorney is fettered by internally generated policies. In Ontario, the Crown Policy Manual (2005) attempts to control the decision-making powers of Crown Attorneys in certain situations.

By s. 579 in the case of indictable offences, and applicable under s. 795 to summary conviction proceedings, the Attorney-General or his agent may stay any proceedings which have been instituted. Within a year the proceedings may be recommenced without laying a new charge but if no such notice is given the proceedings shall be deemed never to have commenced. Although not provided for in the Code the Crown also has the power to withdraw charges. In *R. v. Osborne* (1975), 33 C.R.N.S. 211, 25 C.C.C. (2d) 405 (N.B. C.A.), the trial judge had purported to refuse the Crown's request to withdraw charges before the Court. The request had been made prior to plea and the appellate Court corrected the trial judge:

> I would point out the refusal of the trial Judge to permit a withdrawal of the original information for assault before any evidence is adduced is an usurpation by the Court of the administrative function of the Crown prosecutor and the Attorney-General to determine who and for what offence any person should be prosecuted. Case law clearly indicates the Courts should distinguish between private prosecutions and those carried on by the Crown. They show the Courts should not interfere with the administration of justice by making the matter of withdrawal a means of controlling the Crown's discretion to prosecute and thereby bring the executive and judicial branches of government into conflict. They point out and emphasize that the business of withdrawals is strictly that of the Attorney-General or his agents before the Court. They equate the right of withdrawal to the right to grant a stay of proceedings. The Crown prosecutor is in a better position than the Judge to know how serious any particular case is. Further the prosecutor is the representative of The Queen and it is inconceivable the Court should refuse the right of Her Majesty to withdraw an information or stay a prosecution.

The dominant view presently is that the situation is different if the prosecutor has led evidence on the charge and the withdrawal must then be with the consent of the trial judge: see *Blasko v. R.* (1975), 33 C.R.N.S. 227 (Ont. H.C.).

The prosecutor also has a supervisory role over private prosecutions: In *R. v. Bradley* (1975), 24 C.C.C. (2d) 482 (Ont. C.A.), the Court held that the role of a private prosecutor, permitted by statute in Canada, is parallel to, but not in substitution for, the role of the Attorney General and that when the two come into conflict, the role of the Crown is paramount, "where in his opinion the interests of justice require that he intervene and take over the private prosecution" In the case of proceedings, the power is expressly given in the Criminal Code definition of "prosecutor" in s. 2. As a result of ss. 579, 579.01, and 579.1 either the provincial or federal prosecutor may intervene and take over a private prosecution or enter a stay to halt such proceedings.

We have noted that Parliament has often attempted to indicate criteria upon which police discretion is to be exercised in a wide variety of contexts. **Do you think the same should be true of prosecutors?**

In *R. v. Smythe*, the open discretion of a Crown to choose proceedings by way of indictment or by way of summary conviction in hybrid offences was challenged under the equality provisions of the Canadian Bill of Rights.

R. v. SMYTHE

[1971] S.C.R. 680, 16 C.R.N.S. 147, 3 C.C.C. (2d) 366 (S.C.C.)

The accused was charged under s. 132 of the Income Tax Act. Pursuant to s. 132(2) of the Act, the Attorney-General of Canada elected that the charges be prosecuted upon indictment. That section provided that when proceeded with by way of summary conviction the accused was liable to a fine and or imprisonment of up to two years. If proceeded with on indictment the maximum term was set at five years but there was also a minimum term of two months. The accused successfully moved before the trial judge to quash the indictment on the ground that s. 132 was inoperative pursuant to the Canadian Bill of Rights as it denied the accused the right to equality before the law.

FAUTEUX C.J.C. [For the Court rejecting this argument]:—In my opinion, appellant's views fail to recognize that the provisions of s. 132(2) do not, by themselves, place any particular person or class of persons in a condition of being distinguished from any other member of the community and that, applicable without distinction to everyone, as indeed they are, these provisions simply confer upon the Attorney-General of Canada the power of deciding, according to his own judgment and in all cases, the mode of prosecution for offences described in s. 132(1). Appellant's arguments also fail to recognize that the manner in which a Minister of the Crown exercises a statutory discretionary power conferred upon him for the proper administration of a statute is irrelevant in the consideration of the question whether the statute, in itself, offends the principle of equality before the law. Obviously, the manner in which the Attorney-General of the day exercises his statutory discretion may be questioned or censured by the legislative body to which he is answerable, but that again is foreign to the determination of the question now under consideration. Enforcement of the law and especially of the criminal law would be impossible unless someone in authority be vested with some measure of discretionary power. The following statements made in the *Lafleur* case at p. 248 [C.C.C.] by Montgomery, J.A., with the concurrence of Tremblay, C.J.Q., and Pratte, J.A., are to the point and I adopt them.

> I cannot conceive of a system of enforcing the law where someone in authority is not called upon to decide whether or not a person should be prosecuted for an alleged offence. Inevitably there will be cases where one man is prosecuted while another man, perhaps equally guilty, goes free. A single act, or series of acts, may render a person liable to prosecution in more than one charge, and someone must decide what charges are to be laid. If an authority such as the Attorney-General can have the right to decide whether or not a person shall be prosecuted, surely he may, if authorized by statute, have the right to decide what form the prosecution shall take. I cannot see that the situation is altered because s. 132(2) provides for a minimum term of imprisonment.

I am also in complete agreement with the view expressed in the present case by Wells, C.J.H.C., who concluded that before the enactment of the *Canadian Bill of Rights,* the discretion of the Attorney-General to elect the mode of prosecution as he saw fit was part of the British and Canadian conception of equality before the law. And I am unable to infer from the provisions of the *Canadian Bill of Rights* any suggestion that Parliament differed from that view or had any intention to depart so radically from that state of the law. Indeed, if appellant's fundamental submission was acceded to, some thirty sections of the *Criminal Code* and others in some forty Canadian statutes where, as in s. 132(2), the power to elect to proceed by way of summary conviction or by way of indictment is conferred, would be rendered inoperative. In brief, appellant's submission is potentially destructive of statutory ministerial discretion conferred upon a Minister of the Crown for the administration of the law in Canada and tantamount to a recognition that Parliament has used an oblique method to paralyse the administration of the law.

With respect to the decision of the Supreme Court of Oregon in the *Pirkey* case, *supra,* as well as that of the Supreme Court of the State of Washington in *Olsen v. Delmore, supra,* I agree that these decisions are of no assistance in view of the differences existing between the systems of Government obtaining in Canada and in the United States of America. And I may, incidentally, point out that, as appears by the following extract of the reasons for judgment delivered by Brand, J., in the *Pirkey* case, this decision rests mainly on the fact that, contrary to what is the case in Canada, the distinction between a felony and a misdemeanour still obtains in the United States of America. The extract can be found at p. 702 of the report:

> Since the provision for punishment constitutes one element in the definition of a crime, it would appear that this statute, in effect, defines two crimes as a matter of substantive law; one a felony, and the other a misdemeanor. And since the statute itself furnishes no criterion by which to determine when an accused is to be charged with felony, and when with a misdemeanor, the statute, at least insofar as it provides for alternative charges, must be void by reason of constitutional mandate, unless a criterion not set forth in the statute can be implied therefrom, and unless the power to apply it can be delegated to the grand jury or magistrate.

In my opinion, the provisions of s. 132(2) of the *Income Tax Act* are not discriminatory and do not offend the principle of equality before the law. It follows that appellant's basic submission must be rejected as ill founded.

We earlier considered the now-leading decision in *Anderson* that Crown discretion may only be considered under a very narrow stay as an abuse of process power. The Court abandoned an emerging distinction between core and non-core decisions as difficult to apply and having led to inconsistency. This was also the suggestion of Ben Snow, "Reviewing Crown Discretion: The Need for a Unified, Principled Approach that Mandates Transparency: (2013), 98 C.R. (6th) 143, who was cited in the arguments in *Anderson* but not referred to by the Court.

Here we consider the Court's judgment and its new distinction between reviewing Crown discretion and reviewing tactical decisions.

R. v. ANDERSON
[2014] 2 S.C.R. 167, 311 C.C.C. (3d) 1, 11 C.R. (7th) 1 (S.C.C.)

The accused was convicted of driving with excessive alcohol in his blood. That offense carries a mandatory minimum sentence of 30 days' imprisonment for a second offence and 120 days' imprisonment for a subsequent offence. These mandatory minimum sentences apply only if the Crown notifies the accused of its intention to seek a greater punishment prior to any plea. Crown counsel served a notice of intent to seek greater punishment as the accused had four previous impaired driving related convictions. The trial judge held that Crown counsel breached ss. 7 and 15(1) of the Charter by serving the Notice without considering the accused's Aboriginal status. The accused was sentenced to a 90-day intermittent sentence followed by two years probation. The Newfoundland and Labrador Court of Appeal dismissed the appeal sentence on the basis of a s. 7 violation. The Court divided as to whether the Crown decision to serve the Notice concerned a core or non-core prosecutorial discretion. The Crown appealed.

The Supreme Court was unanimous. The appeal should be allowed and a term of imprisonment of 120 days should be substituted, with service of the remainder of the sentence stayed in accordance with the concession of the Crown. The Court first ruled that the Crown was not required to consider an accused's Aboriginal status when making decisions that limit the sentencing options available to a judge as that was a matter for the judge. The Court then turned to the matter of review of the Crown's decision.

MOLDAVER J. (for a unanimous Court)

[34] Having concluded that the Crown is not under a constitutional obligation to consider the accused's Aboriginal status when making a decision that limits the sentencing options available to a judge, the next question is whether the Crown's decision to tender the Notice is reviewable in some other way, and if so, under what standard.

(1) Review of Crown Decision Making

[35] There are two distinct avenues for judicial review of Crown decision making. The analysis will differ depending on which of the following is at issue: (1) exercises of prosecutorial discretion; or (2) tactics and conduct before the court.

[36] All Crown decision making is reviewable for abuse of process. However, as I will explain, exercises of prosecutorial discretion are only reviewable for abuse of process. In contrast, tactics and conduct before the court are subject to a wider range of review. The court may exercise its inherent jurisdiction to control its own processes even in the absence of abuse of process.

(a) *Prosecutorial Discretion*

[37] This Court has repeatedly affirmed that prosecutorial discretion is a necessary part of a properly functioning criminal justice system: *Beare*, at p. 410; *R. v. T. (V.)*, [1992] 1 S.C.R. 749, at pp. 758-62; *R. v. Cook*, [1997] 1 S.C.R. 1113, at para. 19. In *Miazga v. Kvello Estate*, 2009 SCC 51, [2009] 3 S.C.R. 339, at para. 47, the fundamental importance of prosecutorial discretion was said to lie, "not in protecting the interests of individual Crown attorneys, but in advancing the public interest by enabling prosecutors to make discretionary decisions in fulfilment of their professional obligations without fear of judicial or political interference, thus fulfilling their quasi-judicial role as 'ministers of justice'". More recently, in *Sriskandarajah v. United States of America*, 2012 SCC 70, [2012] 3 S.C.R. 609, at para. 27, this Court observed that "[n]ot only does prosecutorial discretion accord with the principles of fundamental justice — it constitutes an indispensable device for the effective enforcement of the criminal law".

[38] Unfortunately, subsequent to this Court's decision in *Krieger v. Law Society of Alberta*, 2002 SCC 65, [2002] 3 S.C.R. 372, confusion has arisen as to what is meant by "prosecutorial discretion" and the law has become cloudy. The present appeal provides an opportunity for clarification.

[39] In *Krieger*, this Court provided the following description of prosecutorial discretion:

> "Prosecutorial discretion" is a term of art. It does not simply refer to any discretionary decision made by a Crown prosecutor. Prosecutorial discretion refers to the use of those powers that constitute the core of the Attorney General's office and which are protected from the influence of improper political and other vitiating factors by the principle of independence. [para. 43]

[40] The Court went on to provide the following examples of prosecutorial discretion: whether to bring the prosecution of a charge laid by police; whether to enter a stay of proceedings in either a private or public prosecution; whether to accept a guilty plea to a lesser charge; whether to withdraw from criminal proceedings altogether; and whether to take control of a private prosecution (para. 46). The Court continued:

> Significantly, what is common to the various elements of prosecutorial discretion is that they involve the ultimate decisions as to whether a prosecution should be brought, continued or ceased, and what the prosecution ought to be for. <u>Put differently, prosecutorial discretion refers to decisions regarding the nature and extent of the prosecution and the Attorney General's participation in it.</u> Decisions that do not go to the nature and extent of the prosecution, i.e., the decisions that govern a Crown prosecutor's tactics or conduct before the court, do not fall within the scope of prosecutorial discretion. Rather, such decisions are governed by the inherent jurisdiction of the court to control its own processes once the Attorney General has elected to enter into that forum. [Emphasis added; emphasis in original deleted; para. 47.]

[41] Since *Krieger*, courts have struggled with the distinction between prosecutorial discretion, and tactics and conduct. The use of the word "core" in *Krieger* has led to a narrow definition of prosecutorial discretion,

notwithstanding the expansive language used in Krieger to define the term, namely: ". . . decisions regarding the nature and extent of the prosecution and the Attorney General's participation in it" (para. 47). Difficulty in defining the term has also led to confusion regarding the standard of review by which particular Crown decisions are to be assessed.

[42] The current appeal presents a good illustration of both problems. As noted earlier, the Newfoundland and Labrador Court of Appeal split on the issue of how to characterize the Crown's decision to tender the Notice. Welsh J.A. held that it was a matter of "core" prosecutorial discretion, whereas Green C.J.N.L. and Rowe J.A. (following *R. v. Gill*, 2012 ONCA 607, 112 O.R. (3d) 423, at paras. 54-56), considered it to be a tactical decision and thus "outside [the] core" (para. 49).

[43] The court also diverged on the applicable standard of review. Welsh J.A. held that the distinction between core decisions and decisions falling outside the core was of no consequence as both types of decisions were reviewable on the same standard — the standard articulated in *Gill*, in which the Ontario Court of Appeal held that the decision to tender the Notice was reviewable if it (1) undermined the integrity of the administration of justice; (2) operated in a manner that rendered the sentencing proceedings fundamentally unfair; (3) was arbitrary; or (4) resulted in a limit on the accused's liberty that was grossly disproportionate to the state interest in pursuing a particular course of action (*Gill*, at para. 59). Green C.J.N.L. and Rowe J.A. disagreed. In their view, tactical decisions (decisions "outside the core") were reviewable according to the *Gill* standard, whereas "core" prosecutorial discretion was reviewable solely for abuse of process. The diverging views present in this case, and in many others, demonstrate the unsatisfactory state of the law.

[44] In an effort to clarify, I think we should start by recognizing that the term "prosecutorial discretion" is an expansive term that covers all "decisions regarding the nature and extent of the prosecution and the Attorney General's participation in it" (*Krieger*, at para. 47). As this Court has repeatedly noted, "[p]rosecutorial discretion refers to the discretion exercised by the Attorney-General <u>in matters within his authority</u> in relation to the prosecution of criminal offences" (*Krieger*, at para. 44, citing *Power*, at p. 622, quoting D. Vanek, "Prosecutorial Discretion" (1988), 30 *Crim. L.Q.* 219, at p. 219 (emphasis added)). While it is likely impossible to create an exhaustive list of the decisions that fall within the nature and extent of a prosecution, further examples to those in *Krieger* include: the decision to repudiate a plea agreement (as in *R. v. Nixon*, 2011 SCC 34, [2011] 2 S.C.R. 566); the decision to pursue a dangerous offender application; the decision to prefer a direct indictment; the decision to charge multiple offences; the decision to negotiate a plea; the decision to proceed summarily or by indictment; and the decision to initiate an appeal. All pertain to the nature and extent of the prosecution. As can be seen, many stem from the provisions of the *Code* itself, including the decision in this case to tender the Notice.

[45] In sum, prosecutorial discretion applies to a wide range of prosecutorial decision making. That said, care must be taken to distinguish matters of prosecutorial discretion from constitutional obligations. The

distinction between prosecutorial discretion and the constitutional obligations of the Crown was made in *Krieger*, where the prosecutor's duty to disclose relevant evidence to the accused was at issue:

> In *Stinchcombe, supra*, the Court held that the Crown has an obligation to disclose all relevant information to the defence. While the Crown Attorney retains the discretion not to disclose irrelevant information, disclosure of relevant evidence is not, therefore, a matter of prosecutorial discretion but, rather, is a prosecutorial duty. [Emphasis added; para. 54.]

Manifestly, the Crown possesses no discretion to breach the *Charter* rights of an accused. In other words, prosecutorial discretion provides no shield to a Crown prosecutor who has failed to fulfill his or her constitutional obligations such as the duty to provide proper disclosure to the defence.

(i) The Standard of Review for Prosecutorial Discretion

[46] The many decisions that Crown prosecutors are called upon to make in the exercise of their prosecutorial discretion must not be subjected to routine second-guessing by the courts. The courts have long recognized that decisions involving prosecutorial discretion are unlike other decisions made by the executive: see M. Code, "Judicial Review of Prosecutorial Decisions: A Short History of Costs and Benefits, in Response to Justice Rosenberg" (2009), 34 *Queen's L.J.* 863, at p. 867. Judicial non-interference with prosecutorial discretion has been referred to as a "matter of principle based on the doctrine of separation of powers as well as a matter of policy founded on the efficiency of the system of criminal justice" which also recognizes that prosecutorial discretion is "especially ill-suited to judicial review": *Power*, at p. 623. In *Krieger*, the Court discussed the separation of powers doctrine as a basis for judicial deference to prosecutorial discretion:

> In our theory of government, it is the sovereign who holds the power to prosecute his or her subjects. A decision of the Attorney General, or of his or her agents, within the authority delegated to him or her by the sovereign is not subject to interference by other arms of government. An exercise of prosecutorial discretion will, therefore, be treated with deference by the courts and by other members of the executive . . . . [para. 45]

[47] The Court also noted the more practical problems associated with regular review of prosecutorial discretion:

> The quasi-judicial function of the Attorney General cannot be subjected to interference from parties who are not as competent to consider the various factors involved in making a decision to prosecute. To subject such decisions to political interference, or to judicial supervision, could erode the integrity of our system of prosecution. [para. 32]

[48] Manifestly, prosecutorial discretion is entitled to considerable deference. It is not, however, immune from all judicial oversight. This Court has repeatedly affirmed that prosecutorial discretion is reviewable for abuse of process: *Krieger*, at para. 32; *Nixon*, at para. 31; *Miazga*, at para. 46.

[49] The jurisprudence pertaining to the review of prosecutorial discretion has employed a range of terminology to describe the type of prosecutorial conduct that constitutes abuse of process. In *Krieger*, this Court used the term

"flagrant impropriety" (para. 49). In *Nixon*, the Court held that the abuse of process doctrine is available where there is evidence that the Crown's decision "undermines the integrity of the judicial process" or "results in trial unfairness" (para. 64). The Court also referred to "improper motive[s]" and "bad faith" in its discussion (para. 68).

[50] Regardless of the precise language used, the key point is this: abuse of process refers to Crown conduct that is egregious and seriously compromises trial fairness and/or the integrity of the justice system. Crown decisions motivated by prejudice against Aboriginal persons would certainly meet this standard.

[51] In sum, prosecutorial discretion is reviewable solely for abuse of process. The *Gill* test applied by the Newfoundland and Labrador Court of Appeal was developed at a time when courts were struggling with the post-*Krieger* "core" versus "outside the core" dichotomy. To the extent the *Gill* test suggests that conduct falling short of abuse of process may form a basis for reviewing prosecutorial discretion, respectfully, it should not be followed.

(ii) The Threshold Evidentiary Burden

[52] The burden of proof for establishing abuse of process lies on the claimant, who must prove it on a balance of probabilities: *Cook*, at para. 62; *R. v. O'Connor*, [1995] 4 S.C.R. 411, at para. 69, *per* L'Heureux-Dubé J.; *R. v. Jolivet*, 2000 SCC 29, [2000] 1 S.C.R. 751, at para. 19. However, given the unique nature of prosecutorial discretion — specifically, the fact that the Crown will typically (if not always) be the only party who will know *why* a particular decision was made, this Court in *Nixon* recognized that where prosecutorial discretion is challenged, the Crown may be required to provide reasons justifying its decision where the claimant establishes a proper evidentiary foundation: para. 60.

[53] In *Nixon*, this Court noted the following reasons as to why there must be a "proper evidentiary foundation" before the abuse of process claim should proceed:

> . . . mandating a preliminary determination on the utility of a *Charter*-based inquiry is not new: *R. v. Pires*, 2005 SCC 66, [2005] 3 S.C.R. 343. Similar thresholds are also imposed in other areas of the criminal law, they are not an anomaly. Threshold requirements may be imposed for pragmatic reasons alone. As this Court observed in *Pires* (at para. 35):
>
>> For our justice system to operate, trial judges must have some ability to control the course of proceedings before them. One such mechanism is the power to decline to embark upon an evidentiary hearing at the request of one of the parties when that party is unable to show a reasonable likelihood that the hearing can assist in determining the issues before the court.
>
> Quite apart from any such pragmatic considerations, there is good reason to impose a threshold burden on the applicant who alleges that an act of prosecutorial discretion constitutes an abuse of process. Given that such decisions are generally beyond the reach of the court, it is not sufficient to launch an inquiry for an applicant to make a bare allegation of abuse of process. [Emphasis added; paras. 61-62.]

[54] *Nixon* involved the Crown's repudiation of a plea agreement. The Court held that the repudiation of a plea agreement was "a rare and exceptional event" that met the evidentiary threshold and justified an inquiry into the propriety of the Crown's decision: *Nixon*, at para. 63. Indeed, the evidence in *Nixon* was that only two other plea agreements had been repudiated in Alberta's history. As a result, the Court held that

> to the extent that the Crown is the only party who is privy to the information, the evidentiary burden shifts to the Crown to enlighten the court on the circumstances and reasons behind its decision to resile from the agreement. That is, the Crown must explain why and how it made the decision not to honour the plea agreement. The ultimate burden of proving abuse of process remains on the applicant and, as discussed earlier, the test is a stringent one. However, if the Crown provides little or no explanation to the court, this factor should weigh heavily in favour of the applicant in successfully making out an abuse of process claim. [para. 63]

[55] Requiring the claimant to establish a proper evidentiary foundation before embarking on an inquiry into the reasons behind the exercise of prosecutorial discretion respects the presumption that prosecutorial discretion is exercised in good faith: *Application under s. 83.28 of the Criminal Code (Re)*, 2004 SCC 42, [2004] 2 S.C.R. 248, at para. 95. It also accords with this Court's statement in *Sriskandarajah*, at para. 27, that "prosecutorial authorities are not bound to provide reasons for their decisions, <u>absent evidence</u> of bad faith or improper motives" (emphasis added).

[56] Finally, I note that the content of a Crown policy or guideline may be relevant when a court is considering a challenge to the exercise of prosecutorial discretion. Policy statements or guidelines are capable of informing the debate as to whether a Crown prosecutor's conduct was appropriate in the particular circumstances. See R. J. Frater, *Prosecutorial Misconduct* (2009), at p. 259. For example, a decision by a Crown prosecutor that appears to contravene a Crown policy or guideline may provide some evidence that assists the claimant in establishing the threshold evidentiary foundation. However, as the intervener the Director of Public Prosecutions of Canada submits, Crown policies and guidelines do not have the force of law, and cannot themselves be subjected to *Charter* scrutiny in the abstract: see *R. v. Beaudry*, 2007 SCC 5, [2007] 1 S.C.R. 190, at para. 45 (discussing police practices manuals).

(b) *Tactics and Conduct Before the Court*

[57] The second category in the framework for review of Crown activity was referred to in *Krieger* as "tactics or conduct before the court": para. 47. As stated in *Krieger*, "such decisions are governed by the inherent jurisdiction of the court to control its own processes once the Attorney General has elected to enter into that forum" (para. 47).

[58] Superior courts possess inherent jurisdiction to ensure that the machinery of the court functions in an orderly and effective manner: *R. v. Cunningham*, 2010 SCC 10, [2010] 1 S.C.R. 331, at para. 18; *Ontario v. Criminal Lawyers' Association of Ontario*, 2013 SCC 43, [2013] 3 S.C.R. 3, at para. 26. Similarly, in order to function as courts of law, statutory courts have implicit powers that derive from the court's authority to control its own process:

Cunningham, at para. 18. This jurisdiction includes the power to penalize counsel for ignoring rulings or orders, or for inappropriate behaviour such as tardiness, incivility, abusive cross-examination, improper opening or closing addresses or inappropriate attire. Sanctions may include orders to comply, adjournments, extensions of time, warnings, cost awards, dismissals, and contempt proceedings.

[59] While deference is not owed to counsel who are behaving inappropriately in the courtroom, our adversarial system *does* accord a high degree of deference to the tactical decisions of counsel. In other words, while courts may sanction the conduct of the *litigants*, they should generally refrain from interfering with the conduct of the *litigation* itself. In *R. v. S.G.T.*, 2010 SCC 20, [2010] 1 S.C.R. 688, at paras. 36-37, this Court explained why judges should be very cautious before interfering with tactical decisions:

> In an adversarial system of criminal trials, trial judges must, barring exceptional circumstances, defer to the tactical decisions of counsel . . . . [C]ounsel will generally be in a better position to assess the wisdom, in light of their overall trial strategy, of a particular tactical decision than is the trial judge. By contrast, trial judges are expected to be impartial arbiters of the dispute before them; the more a trial judge second-guesses or overrides the decisions of counsel, the greater is the risk that the trial judge will, in either appearance or reality, cease being a neutral arbiter and instead become an advocate for one party. . . .
>
> The corollary of the preceding is that trial judges should seldom take it upon themselves, let alone be required, to second-guess the tactical decisions of counsel. Of course, trial judges are still required to "make sure that [the trial] remains fair and is conducted in accordance with the relevant laws and the principles of fundamental justice": *Lavallee, Rackel & Heintz v. Canada (Attorney General)*, 2002 SCC 61, [2002] 3 S.C.R. 209, at para. 68.

[60] Crown counsel is entitled to have a trial strategy and to modify it as the trial unfolds, provided that the modification does not result in unfairness to the accused: *Jolivet*, at para. 21. Likewise, as this Court recently held in *R. v. Auclair*, 2014 SCC 6, [2014] 1 S.C.R. 83, a judge may exceptionally override a Crown tactical decision in order to prevent a *Charter* violation.

[61] Finally, as with all Crown decision making, courtroom tactics or conduct may amount to abuse of process, but abuse of process is not a precondition for judicial intervention as it is for matters of prosecutorial discretion.

[The Court held that the Crown's power to serve notice to seek a higher mandatory penalty on an aboriginal offender for impaired driving could only be reviewed under the abuse doctrine and for that there was no evidence in support.]

CANADIAN BAR ASSOCIATION'S CODE OF PROFESSIONAL CONDUCT (1987)

The Lawyer As Advocate

Duties of Prosecutor

9. When engaged as a prosecutor, the lawyer's prime duty is not to seek a conviction, but to present before the trial court all available credible evidence relevant to the alleged crime in order that justice may be done through a fair trial upon the merits. The prosecutor exercises a public function involving much discretion and power and must act fairly and dispassionately. The prosecutor should not do anything that might prevent the accused from being represented by counsel or communicating with counsel and, to the extent required by law and accepted practice, should make timely disclosure to the accused or defence counsel (or to the court if the accused is not represented) of all relevant facts and known witnesses, whether tending to show guilt or innocence, or that would affect the punishment of the accused.

R. v. S. (F.)
(2000), 31 C.R. (5th) 159, 144 C.C.C. (3d) 466 (Ont. C.A.)

The accused was charged with numerous sexual offences against his stepdaughter. He was tried by a court composed of a judge and jury. The accused's position was that the complainant's testimony was all an act. It was part of his defence that because of his work he was rarely at home and had little, if any, opportunity to commit the offences. The accused's wife and his stepson were called as witnesses by the defence and testified that they had never witnessed any sexual improprieties or unusual behaviour.

Crown counsel, in his opening address to the jury, personalized his role in the case. He said his role was to obtain a conviction. Counsel saw it as his duty to inform the jury of what he knew so that the jury could join him in his conclusion that the accused was guilty. In addressing the jury, he twice referred to the complainant as "notre victime", as if she were his client and inferred there was some bond between the jury and himself against the accused. In his closing address to the jury, he stated that his mission was to obtain a conviction and ensure that justice was done for the complainant. He told the jury he was an honest and just person and expressed the view that if the jury was not convinced of the accused's guilt it was because he had failed to successfully do his job. He then added the comment that we ("nous"), he and the jury, would have to live with this sad result. He seemed to have felt the need to ask the jury to excuse his conduct toward the accused.

In his cross-examination of the accused, Crown counsel was sarcastic, flippant and disrespectful towards the accused. The accused's defence was, in part, that for various reasons he did not have the opportunity to commit the alleged offence. At issue was whether he had the opportunity to be alone with the complainant. In cross-examination, in this regard, he allowed that he was, like every father, sometimes alone with the complainant. At times he resisted Crown counsel's suggestions that being alone with her gave him the opportunity to sexually assault the complainant. On the issue of whether the accused was alone with the complainant in the house the transcript showed that he answered in the affirmative or acknowledged that he was alone with her ten times and answered in the negative nine times. In his closing address, Crown counsel incorrectly summarized the cross-examination and on five occasions said that the accused said that he was never alone with the complainant.

Despite telling the accused that he did not have to provide an explanation as to why the complainant made up the allegation of sexual abuse, Crown counsel invited the accused to provide one and then ridiculed the explanation. Also, Crown counsel inquired of the accused whether the complainant was a known liar.

During his closing address to the jury, Crown counsel proceeded to read an excerpt of a Supreme Court of Canada decision dealing with the non-reporting, incomplete reporting and delayed reporting of cases of sexual abuse. Not only did counsel read from the decision, he in fact misrepresented the passage he was purporting to quote by omitting the references made therein by the court that the relevant opinion was attributed to a report and not to the court directly as the Crown represented.

LABROSSE J.A. (Weiler and Charron J.A. concurring): — [In] . . . my view, counsel's conduct seriously prejudiced the appellant.

In *R. v. Henderson* (1999), 44 O.R. (3d) 628, this court recently reviewed the role of Crown counsel during a trial. It is appropriate to quote again what I said at pp. 638-9, speaking for a five-member panel:

> The classic articulation of Crown counsel's role was set out in *R. v. Boucher*, [1955] S.C.R. 16 at pp. 23-24, 110 C.C.C. 263 at p. 270, where Rand J. stated:
>
> It cannot be over-emphasised that the purpose of a criminal prosecution is not to obtain a conviction; it is to lay before a jury what the Crown considered to be creditable evidence relevant to what is alleged to be a crime. Counsel have a duty to see that all available legal proof of the facts is presented: it should be done firmly and pressed to its legitimate strength, but it must also be done fairly. The role of prosecutor excludes any notion of winning or losing; his function is a matter of public duty than which in civil life there can be none charged with greater personal responsibility. It is to be efficiently performed with an ingrained sense of the dignity, the seriousness and the justness of judicial proceedings.
>
> In *Boucher*, Taschereau J. added the following comments which were cited with approval by Lamer C.J.C. in *R. v. Swietlinski*, [1994] 3 S.C.R. 481 at pp. 494-95, 92 C.C.C. (3d) 449:
>
> [Translation] The position held by counsel for the Crown is not that of a lawyer in civil litigation. His functions are quasi-judicial. His duty is not so much to obtain a conviction as to assist the judge and jury in ensuring that the fullest possible justice is done. His conduct before the Court must always be characterised by moderation and impartiality. He will have properly performed his duty and will be beyond all reproach if, eschewing any appeal to passion, and employing a dignified manner suited to his function, he presents the evidence to the jury without going beyond what it discloses.

. . .

Generally, Crown counsel perform all aspects of their functions honourably and fairly, and in most cases the respectable conduct of Crown counsel undoubtedly enhances public confidence in the criminal justice system. To this extent, I note the comments made by Cory J in *R. v. Bain*, [1992] 1 S.C.R. 91, 69 C.C.C. (3d) 481, where he states [at pp. 101-02]: "As a rule the conduct and competence of Crown Attorneys is exemplary. They are models for the Bar and the community." The efforts of Crown counsel are particularly admirable given their significant case loads and considerable resource restrictions.

. . . In the present case, these defining guidelines have all been breached by Crown counsel.

First, he personalized his role in the case. . .

Second, the involvement of his person became even more obvious in his closing address to the jury. . .

Third, Crown counsel was inappropriately sarcastic, flippant and disrespectful towards the appellant. . .

As stated earlier, Crown counsel breached every aspect of the classic articulation of the role of Crown counsel referred to in *R. v. Boucher*. He took this case very personally. He injected his own credibility and belief into the case. His stated goal was to obtain a conviction and justice for the complainant. If the appellant were acquitted by the jury, he would have failed. His conduct was anything but moderate and impartial.

In the present case, as I said in *Henderson*, Crown counsel's conduct, viewed in its totality and with regard to the obligation on Crown counsel to act in a scrupulously fair manner, crossed over the line and must be characterized as improper and unfair. The cumulative effect of the improprieties resulted in serious prejudice.

. . .

Unfortunately the improperties were never diffused or corrected by the trial judge.

The disposition of the issues dealt with in this appeal lead me to conclude that the appellant did not receive a fair trial. As was so succinctly stated in *R. v. F. (A.)*, (supra at 472), "unless and until Crown counsel stop this kind of improper and prejudicial conduct, this court will regrettably have to remit difficult and sensitive cases of this nature back for a new trial at great expense to the emotional well-being of the parties, not to mention the added burden to the administration of justice."

I would allow the appeal, set aside the conviction, and order a new trial.

See generally Paul Taylor and Stephen Byrne, "Reflections on Crown Attorneys and Cross-Examination", (2001) 45 Crim. L.Q. 303.

Nadjari, lecturing fellow prosecutors, as quoted in
LUBAN, LAWYERS AND JUSTICE
Princeton, 1988

Your true purpose is to convict the guilty man who sits at the defense table, and to go for the jugular as viciously and as rapidly as possible. . . . You must never forget that your goal is total annihilation.

GROSMAN, THE PROSECUTOR: AN INQUIRY INTO THE EXERCISE OF DISCRETION
(1969), 63

In the courtroom there is the acknowledged pressure that, once adversarial positions have been taken and a trial takes place, "You can't afford to have too many people found not guilty. Better not to prosecute them in the first place." The pressure to succeed at trial is twofold. To maintain his administrative credibility and to encourage guilty pleas the prosecutor must demonstrate that he is able if forced to take the final adversarial remedy, to succeed consistently at trial. If he were continually defeated the compromises offered in pre-trial negotiations would quickly lose their value. The defence would be risking little by advising the entry of a not guilty plea if a complete acquittal at trial seemed probable. Too many prosecutions lost at trial seriously undermine faith in the competency and decision-making of the initiators. Successes, as well as confirming administrative regularity, are needed to justify the confidence placed by most prosecutors in the professional soundness of the original initiating decision by the police, and to corroborate their conviction that most persons accused of crime are guilty. One prosecutor, when asked whether there was any pressure to produce, replied:

> You mean successes? Yes, I think there is. It stems from the realization of those in office for some time that people before the courts are justly accused of their wrongdoing. By coincidence, once in a while you get a string of not guilty cases but if it persists for too long maybe you are not prosecuting with vigour. The reason for it is a general feeling that before someone is charged there is evidence indicative that they committed the offence with which they are charged. There is a feeling that if you have been going for quite a while with few convictions there is something wrong.

The viability of the administrative perspective that "we don't arrest innocent people" can only be sustained if the vast majority of cases are either disposed of by guilty pleas or convictions at trial. As another prosecutor said: "Ninety-five per cent of the people are guilty as charged. Those cases that are thrown out are thrown out mostly on evidentiary gaps in the Crown's case." In sum, confidence in present administrative practices is maintained only if the acquittal rate is not substantial. In that sense prosecutors see themselves as engaged competing not directly with defence lawyers but to sustain their own record and credibility.

MINISTRY OF ATTORNEY GENERAL FOR ONTARIO, CROWN POLICY MANUAL (2005)

Role of the Crown

Preamble to the Crown Policy Manual

Crown counsel play a pivotal role in the administration of criminal justice. In many respects, the role of the Crown is a cornerstone of the criminal justice system. The Crown Policy Manual facilitates and enhances the performance of that role by communicating the Attorney General's guidance, in important areas of Crown practice and discretion, to Crown counsel. These policies are accessible to the public on the Attorney General's website, thus enhancing public confidence in the operation of the criminal justice system.

Public confidence in the administration of criminal justice is bolstered by a system where Crown counsel are not only strong and effective advocates for the prosecution, but also Ministers of Justice with a duty to ensure that the criminal justice system operates fairly to all: the accused, victims of crime, and the public. The role of Crown counsel has been described on many occasions. The following observations from the Supreme Court of Canada provide a summary of our complex function within the criminal justice system:

> It cannot be overemphasized that the purpose of a criminal prosecution is not to obtain a conviction; it is to lay before a jury what the Crown considers to be credible evidence relevant to what is alleged to be a crime. Counsel have a duty to see that all available legal proof of the facts is presented; it should be done firmly and pressed to its legitimate strength, but it must also be done fairly. The role of prosecutor excludes any notion of winning or losing; his function is a matter of public duty than which in civil life there can be none charged with greater responsibility. It is to be efficiently performed with an ingrained sense of the dignity, the seriousness, and the justness of judicial proceedings. (*R. v. Boucher*)
>
> . . .
>
> While it is without question that the Crown performs a special function in ensuring that justice is served and cannot adopt a purely adversarial role towards the defence, (cites omitted) it is well recognized that the adversarial process is an important part of our judicial system and an accepted tool in our search for truth: See for example, *R. v. Gruenke*, [1991] 3 S.C.R. 263 at 295, 67 C.C.C., (3d) 289; per L'Heureux-Dubé, J. Nor should it be assumed that the Crown cannot act as a strong advocate within this adversarial process. In that regard, it is both permissible and desirable that it vigorously pursue a legitimate result to the best of its ability. Indeed, this is a critical element of this country's criminal law mechanism: (cites omitted). In this sense, within the boundaries outlined above, the Crown must be allowed to perform the function with which it has been entrusted; discretion in pursuing justice remains an important part of that function. (*R. v. Cook*)

Constitutional Foundation for the Role of the Crown

It is a fundamental principle that the Attorney General must carry out prosecution responsibilities independent of any partisan political influences. Crown counsel, as agents of the Attorney General, share the Attorney General's independence from partisan political influence but are not independent themselves of the direction of the Attorney General. Because of the potential for suggestions of political influence and, given that there are hundreds of thousands of criminal cases which flow through the courts every year in Ontario, it would be imprudent and impractical for the Attorney General to become involved in individual cases on a routine basis. The common practice is for the Attorney General to grant broad areas of discretion in criminal prosecutions to Crown counsel (except in those few circumstances where the Criminal Code requires the Attorney's personal involvement or consent). This granting of decision-making latitude reflects respect for the professional judgment of Crown counsel and is consistent with Crown counsel's Minister of Justice role.

The Attorney General is accountable to the Legislature for the entire process through which justice is administered in the province. Because of this accountability, which includes specific cases, a continuum of responsibility within the Ministry has been established. This continuum extends from Crown counsel at the operational level upward to the Deputy Attorney General and the Attorney General. Each Crown counsel or Assistant Crown Attorney reports to a Crown Attorney or Director. Crown Attorneys in turn report to Directors, while Directors report to the Assistant Deputy Attorney General, who reports to the Deputy Attorney General. The Ministry also employs per diem counsel to act as Crown counsel and provincial prosecutors. They are subject to this internal reporting structure.

Crown Counsel as an Advocate

The role of Crown counsel as an advocate has historically been characterized as more a "part of the court" than an ordinary advocate.

A prosecutor's responsibilities are public in nature. As a prosecutor and public representative, Crown counsel's demeanor and actions should be fair, dispassionate and moderate; show no signs of partisanship; open to the possibility of the innocence of the accused person and avoid "tunnel vision." It is especially important that Crown counsel avoid personalizing their role in court. Objectionable cross-examination or immoderate jury addresses are the antithesis of the proper role of the Crown.

The adversarial system in which we operate requires our participation as strong advocates, but it also is seriously flawed if the "adversaries" are not evenly matched. We have, therefore, a special duty to the accused and his counsel so that they may fully and fairly place their evidence and arguments before the courts.

The Role of Crown Counsel in Relation to Victims and Witnesses

Crown counsel owe special duties of candour and respect to all victims. Crown counsel is not and can never function as the victim's lawyer. In circumstances where the fair and impartial exercise of prosecutorial discretion is at odds with the victim's desires, Crown counsel should be sensitive but realistic and candid with victims.

The Role of Crown Counsel in Relation to the Police

Although Crown counsel work closely with the police, the separation between police and Crown roles is of fundamental importance to the proper administration of justice. The police investigate and lay charges where they believe on reasonable grounds that an offence has been committed. Crown counsel will carefully review all charges to ensure they meet the Ministry's screening standard. Crown counsel proceed only with prosecutions which present a reasonable prospect of conviction and where the prosecution is in the public interest. A distinct line between these two functions, which allows both the police and Crown counsel to exercise discretion independently and objectively, forms part of a system of checks and balances. Given the current reality of large and complex police investigations, access to timely advice from Crown counsel in these cases may be crucially important. Special task forces often include and benefit from both Crown and Police participation, necessitating a close working relationship. The independence of roles and responsibilities, upon which the justice system depends, must be respected in any of these special working relationships.

Crown Counsel's Duty of Fairness to the Public

Crown counsel have a responsibility to ensure that every prosecution is carried out in a manner consistent with the public interest. One aspect of the public interest which bears special mention is the challenge facing government and private sector organizations concerning institutional discrimination. Crown counsel, as key participants in the criminal justice system, play an important role in assisting to overcome any forms of discrimination that deny equal access to the criminal justice system. Crown counsel take a leadership role in ensuring that various forms of discrimination, including homophobia, racism and racial profiling, are not reflected in the criminal justice system. Discrimination against child witnesses and women in the criminal justice system existed until changes in the Criminal Code and case law recognized and changed it.

An important aspect of the Crown role relates to community involvement. Crown counsel play an important role in the community as ambassadors for the criminal justice system. Crowns donate generously of their own time and energy to education about the justice system by speaking at schools, to police, at judicial information sessions and to public groups. Crowns participate in mentoring law students and junior Crowns. In performing these activities, Crowns embody the sense of fair play and justice for which they are known in their professional lives.

Crown Policy Manual

One of the chief mechanisms by which the Attorney General for the Province of Ontario provides advice and guidance to Crowns on the exercise of prosecutorial discretion is the Crown Policy Manual which sets out the overall philosophy, direction, and priorities of the Ministry. In carrying out the duties of the Crown Attorney, a natural tension exists between prosecutorial discretion exercised in individual cases and general prosecution policy formulated by the Attorney General.

Crown counsel have a broad discretion to conduct cases to ensure that justice is done in individual circumstances. This prosecutorial discretion is necessary to allow Crown counsel to respond to unique circumstances in cases including victims, offenders, and local conditions. Prosecutorial discretion, when exercised fairly and impartially, is an essential component of the criminal justice system.

Notwithstanding the importance of discretion, it is also necessary in the public interest to have uniform prosecution policies applicable across the province. Policies assist and guide individual prosecutors in exercising their prosecutorial discretion. The policies in this Manual are not intended to replace the sound judgment that Crown counsel exercise. They set out appropriate considerations for prosecutorial decision-making, while supporting flexibility. Crowns are expected to exercise their discretion in accordance with overall priorities in the Manual, keeping in mind the need to see justice done in individual cases. Directives which bind the discretion of Crown counsel in the conduct of individual cases are few and far between.

There are many discretionary decisions made daily by Crown counsel that are not specifically described in these policies. In general, Crown counsel should exercise their discretion in keeping with the spirit of the policies in this Manual.

Purposes of the Crown Policy Manual

The Crown Policy Manual provides consistency of approaches to prosecutions across the province, for example, in such areas as child abuse, sexual assault, and spouse/partner abuse. The Manual conveys the Attorney General's instructions and priorities as well as the rationale for them to Crowns. It provides the public with an indication of the guiding principles for Crowns, thus enhancing public accountability.

Application of the Crown Policy Manual

The Attorney General, Deputy Attorney General, Assistant Deputy Attorney General, Directors, Crown Attorneys, Assistant Crown Attorneys, Crown counsel, per diem crowns, provincial prosecutors (governed by the Criminal Law Division) are all subject to the policies and advice provided in the Crown Policy Manual.

. . .

POLICE: RELATIONSHIP WITH CROWN COUNSEL

Crown counsel and police agencies have separate responsibilities in the criminal justice system. They are required to work in partnership to enforce criminal laws effectively. The working relationship between police and crown counsel should reflect mutual respect and professionalism. These are fostered by appropriate recognition of the boundaries between the investigative and prosecutorial functions.

Police have the sole responsibility for charging decisions except where the consent of the Attorney General is required by statute. Crown counsel are solely responsible for determining whether a charge is to proceed once it has been laid.

Police may seek advice from Crown counsel concerning legal issues arising in the investigation of offences. Crown counsel may ask the assistance of police in conducting further investigations and providing further information. Each agency has a role to play, independent of the other, and neither agency is subordinate. This independence is fundamental to the maintenance of their role as "Ministers of Justice", and is essential to the proper administration of justice.

. . .

Charge Screening

PRINCIPLES

The decision to continue or terminate a prosecution can be one of the most difficult for Crown counsel to make. The community relies upon Crown counsel to vigorously pursue provable charges while protecting individuals from the serious repercussions of a criminal charge where there is no reasonable prospect of conviction. Every charge must be screened in accordance with the charge screening standards of "reasonable prospect of conviction" and "public interest" as outlined in this policy and in Memoranda issued by the Assistant Deputy Attorney General (Criminal Law Division). Further background information about charge screening may be obtained from "Report of the Attorney General's Advisory Committee on Charge Screening Disclosure and Resolution Discussions (the Martin Committee Report)".

Crown counsel are to screen every charge as soon as practicable after the charge arrives at the Crown's office and prior to setting a date for preliminary hearing or trial. The Crown Attorney in each jurisdiction is to set up a protocol for all charges to be screened.

The obligation to screen a charge is ongoing as new information is received by Crown counsel in preparation for and during the conduct of bail hearings, pretrials, preliminary hearings, trials and appeals.

Reasonable Prospect of Conviction: When considering whether or not to continue the prosecution of a charge the first step is to determine if there is a reasonable prospect of conviction. This test must be applied to all cases. If the Crown determines there is no reasonable prospect of conviction, at any stage of the proceeding, then the prosecution of that charge must be discontinued.

The threshold test of "reasonable prospect of conviction" is objective. This standard is higher than a "*prima facie*" case that merely requires that there is evidence whereby a reasonable jury, properly instructed, could convict. On the other hand, the standard does not require "a probability of conviction," that is, a conclusion that a conviction is more likely than not.

Public Interest: If there is a reasonable prospect of conviction, then Crown counsel must consider whether it is in the public interest to discontinue the prosecution, notwithstanding the existence of a reasonable prospect of conviction. The public interest factors must only be considered after the threshold test, a reasonable prospect of conviction has been met. No public interest, however compelling, can warrant the prosecution of an individual if there is no reasonable prospect of conviction.

Scope of Policy: All cases, including child abuse, sexual assaults and spouse/partner offences, must be screened in accordance with the "reasonable prospect of conviction" and "public interest" standards. The personal, professional or "political" consequences of a screening decision should never affect Crown counsel's judgment. Nor should stereotypes about certain categories of witnesses such as child witnesses, witnesses with mental disabilities and complainants of spouse/partner abuse or sexual offences, affect Crown counsel's judgment. Since this is an area of discretion where reasonable people will differ, it is always advisable to consult with experienced colleagues when faced with a difficult charge screening decision. Crown counsel will be supported by the Ministry when they make difficult judgment calls in the proper exercise of their discretion.

Domestic Violence

PRINCIPLES

Domestic Violence is not a private family matter — Domestic Violence offences are criminal acts and should be prosecuted as vigorously as other serious criminal matters. Spousal abuse is a prevalent social problem which affects all of us, including children who have witnessed or been exposed to domestic violence. Spouse/partner offences are often committed in a context where there is a pattern of assaultive and controlling behaviour. This violence goes beyond physical assault and often includes emotional, psychological and sexual abuse that is intended to induce fear, humiliation and powerlessness.

In prosecuting cases of spousal abuse, Crown counsel should be sensitive to the dynamics that exist in families where a spouse is abused. In addition to fear for their personal safety and that of their children, victims of these offences may be under intolerable pressure on account of financial considerations, the need for childcare, disapproval of family members, or fear of being ostracized by the community.

Victims of these offences and their children should be able to live as safely as other members of society. At all stages of the prosecution, including bail hearings, the safety of victims and their families is a paramount factor for Crown counsel to consider in the exercise of discretion.

SCOPE OF POLICY

This policy addresses the prosecution of crimes involving the use of physical or sexual force, actual or threatened, in an intimate relationship! Intimate relationships include those between opposite sex and same sex partners. They vary in duration and legal formality, and include current and former dating, common law and married couples.

Scheduling and Assignment of Cases: The Crown Attorney for each jurisdiction is to ensure that a system is in place to identify these cases. In those jurisdictions where domestic violence courts exist, a small team of Crown counsel will have carriage of all spouse/partner prosecutions and continuity of counsel should be maintained until the conclusion of the case. Although not all cases of spousal abuse can be assigned in all jurisdictions, it is important that all of these cases be given priority in scheduling.

Charge Screening and Resolution Discussions: The policies and practice memoranda on charge screening and resolution discussions apply to cases of spousal abuse just as they do to all other types of charges. The public interest factors in these cases, however, should be weighed in light of the predominant need to protect the victim. Given the prevalence and danger of spouse/partner abuse and the dangers inherent in it, it will usually, although not always, be in the public interest to proceed with these prosecutions in cases where there is a reasonable prospect of conviction.

Counsel should exercise caution in evaluating requests from the victim for withdrawal of charges. Given the dynamics that exist in families where a spouse is abused, victims may be reluctant to continue a prosecution and be under intolerable pressure to withdraw

Sentencing: In cases of spousal abuse, Crown counsel should ensure that full submissions are made at sentencing hearings, including victim impact, and that the court is made aware of all factors relevant to the protection and safety of the victim, the victim's family, and the public.

Do you agree with this screening process?

PROBLEM 10

You have been assigned to prosecute a case of domestic assault. The police laid the charge after they had been called to investigate a disturbance. The wife told the police that her husband had beaten her and that this was not the first time. The trial is to take place tomorrow, three months after the alleged incident. The victim approaches you and wants to withdraw the charge. She tells you that her husband has returned to Alcoholics Anonymous and is participating with her in a marriage-counselling program. The incidence of domestic violence in your community is very high. Will you withdraw?

Compare *R. v. K. (M.)* (1992), 16 C.R. (4th) 121, 74 C.C.C. (3d) 108 (Man. C.A.), leave to appeal to S.C.C. granted (1992), [1993] 1 W.W.R. lix (note), critically reviewed by Anne McGillivray, "K. (M.): Legitimating Brutality", C.R. *ibid.* 125-132.

PROBLEM 11

John is observed slipping a box of mints, value $1.75, into his jacket. He is arrested by store security and, following store policy, a charge is laid. John is in his second year of university and hopes to go to law school. He has no prior record. Your brief indicates that he was co-operative during the investigation. He had told the security officer, "I'm dumbfounded. I don't know why I took them". You are approached by a senior defence counsel, acting for John. He's also a friend of John's family. He tells you that John has been going through some rough times of late. John's older brother was recently killed in a car accident and John has just broken up with his girlfriend. He tells you that John is basically a "good kid" but he's under a lot of pressure because exams are just around the corner. Counsel asks if you'll withdraw the charges. Will you?

Suppose that you decide not to withdraw the charge but just as the case is being called by the court clerk you are advised that the store security officer is not present. You can't prove the charge and the trial judge is known not to grant adjournments in such cases. You know that John is about to plead guilty. What do you do?

Chapter 7

BAIL HEARINGS

This chapter addresses the important question of what happens to an accused after he or she has been arrested, taken into custody and charged with an offence. How does the state ensure that the accused will appear in court and stand trial? Is the public in need of protection from the accused during this period of time? Should the accused person be subject to some form of restraint during the interval of arrest to trial? Will this restraint take the form of detention? If so, how is this squared with the presumption of innocence enshrined in s. 11(d) of the Charter? These are the questions confronted by the law of bail.

The notion of bail pending trial antedates recorded English law and its original purpose is therefore not altogether certain. It may have stemmed from the medieval sheriff's desire to avoid the costly and troublesome burden of personal responsibility for those in his charge. Whether motivated by a concern for their prisoner's well-being or as an economy measure, sheriffs commonly released prisoners either on their own recognizances, with or without requiring the posting of some sort of bond, or on the promise of a third party to assume personal responsibility for the accused's appearance at trial. From ad hoc arrangements by the sheriff we move by the Statute of Westminster of 1275 to a system wherein conditions for pre-trial release are specified and the power of release transferred from sheriff to justice of the peace. To ensure that the accused would reappear on the date set for trial, a third party, or surety, had to assume a personal responsibility for the accused, on penalty of forfeiture of his own property. These sureties, usually local landowners, were given the powers of a jailer to prevent the accused's flight and this system was eminently reasonable in an immobile land-oriented society. See Note, "Bail: An Ancient Practice Re-examined" (1961), 70 Yale L.J. 966.

In England, still, these sureties are called 'bail'; i.e., the bail *is the third party* who is responsible on his recognizance for the due appearance of the person charged. Any contract by which an accused person agrees to indemnify the bail or surety for loss suffered by the accused failing to appear is unenforceable since it is an illegal contract. It is illegal since it is calculated to interfere with the proper administration of justice, i.e., if the *bail*, or surety, has a contract of indemnity to protect him from loss, then he would have no interest whatever in seeing that the accused person was forthcoming to take his trial and criminals, particularly if possessed of means, would very frequently abscond from justice. See *R. v. Porter*, [1910] 1 K.B. 369 (C.A.). This English attitude is reflected in theory in Canadian legislation by s. 139(1)(*b*) of the Criminal Code which makes it an indictable offence for anyone to attempt to obstruct or defeat the course of justice by indemnifying or agreeing to indemnify a surety or, being a surety, agreeing to accept a fee or any form of indemnity in respect of a person being released from custody. So strict, *in theory,* is this attitude that the Law Society of Upper Canada has advised its members that they may be considered to be committing a criminal offence if they post bond for their clients since their legal fee might be interpreted as covering the cost of putting up of bail. Though professional bondsmen are obviously then illegal, the fact of their existence is undeniable; in a study of bail records by Professor Friedland, *Detention Before Trial* (1965), it was found that in a period of five months, more than one-eighth of all the cash put up in Toronto magistrate courts was put up by a single person.

The British attitude towards release pending trial, that money was not to be the guarantee for a person's appearing at his trial, was also incorporated into the legislation in the Canadian Criminal Code governing release by justices of the peace, *prior* to the Bail Reform Act provisions which came into effect in 1971. These now-repealed legislative provisions *did not* require security in advance anymore than the English law of bail required it. In fact, the legislation obviously contemplated payment of money *only,* if and when, the accused failed to appear. Prior to 1971, s. 451 of the Criminal Code provided three alternate modes of release pending trial open to the justice. The justice could order the man admitted to bail by:

1.   release on recognizance in Form 28 with sufficient sureties;

2.   release on recognizance in Form 28 without sureties but with a deposit;

3.   release on accused's own recognizance in Form 28 without any deposit.

Form 28 clearly showed that moneys mentioned in the bond to secure the accused's attendance were to be paid if, and only if, the accused failed to appear: the Form began "[B]e it remembered that on this day the persons named . . . acknowledged themselves to owe to Her Majesty the several amounts set out... to be made . . . of their goods and lands *if* (the accused) fails in the condition hereunder written." Clearly, what was envisaged was the creation of a debt defeasible on the accused's appearance. The second mode of release open to the justice, by requiring security in advance, was enacted as an alternative to the normal method of producing sureties, to protect the liberty of the individual far from home.

> A stranger in the community might not be able to provide sureties and thus might be forced to remain in custody in cases where release on his own recognizance without deposit might be considered inappropriate.

> (Ouimet Committee Report, Ch. 7, "Bail—The Practice of Requiring Security in Advance.")

While the law seems clear, the practice that developed under these provisions was to the exact opposite effect. Perhaps to avoid the task of determining the sufficiency of the surety by inquiry, the justices demanded cash in advance or evidence of property holdings. The evidence of property holdings sometimes required the production of title deeds, solicitor's certificates, real estate valuer's report, tax certificates, and so forth, all of which was time-consuming and not authorized by law. Professor Friedland's study also indicated that the amount of cash required by the justice of the peace to "satisfy the justice respecting the sufficiency of the surety" became standardized according to the crime charged without any real consideration of the status of the surety at all. This inflexible procedure of cash in advance corresponded to the general practice in the United States but was even more productive of detention in Canada when it is remembered that, unlike the American position, professional bail bondsmen are illegal in Canada.

The Ouimet Committee, largely responsible for the Bail Reform Act of 1971, recognized the practice that had grown up and recommended changes in the legislation to ensure a return to the original philosophy of bail. It is important to recognize this: the *new* legislation, though more detailed than the former Code provisions, is *not* new in the sense that it changed the pre-existing *law,* but only new in the sense that it sought to change the *practice.* The new provisions were an attempt to ensure greater compliance with the always announced policy of bail but whether the attempt is regarded as successful is not dependent so much on the statutory language used but rather on the personnel involved in the day-to-day administration.

The Ouimet Committee was persuaded that too many accused persons were being arrested rather than being summoned to a court appearance and, once arrested, the accused were too often detained in custody pending their trial. Professor Friedland's study noted that "the overwhelming majority of accused persons in Toronto charged with offences against the Criminal Code were arrested rather than summoned". In his quite large sample (6,000 cases) the accused was arrested in over ninety-two per cent of the cases. Of those arrested, eighty-four per cent remained in custody until their first court appearance. These figures reflected the practice, despite consistent statements by appellate courts, that a summons should normally be issued with arrest only to take place if absolutely necessary.

We saw earlier under Appearances Notices that the 1971 Bail Reform Act changes to the Criminal Code were aimed at reducing pre-trial custody which Professor Friedland's study had shown to be excessive. The new legislation therefore stressed release pending trial. For certain offences the police officer was commanded to issue an appearance notice rather than arrest unless the public interest dictated otherwise; s. 495(2). The officer who decided that an arrest was necessary was commanded to release such a person as soon as practicable and compel his appearance by way of summons or appearance notice; s. 497. The officer in charge of the lock-up was commanded to release as soon as practicable a person charged with these offences and compel his later attendance by summons, promise to appear or recognizance; ss. 498(1), 499. A person who failed to appear when required by an appearance notice, promise to appear, recognizance, or summons, may be arrested by a warrant; ss. 502, 512. Failing to appear also constituted an offence in its own right, s. 145; previously, failing to respond to a summons was not an offence.

The remainder of this chapter is focused on bail decisions that are made in court, by judges.

Jurisdiction over bail observes some of the distinctions identified in the materials on classification of offences in Chapter 1 of this book. One important distinction is the difference between s. 469 offences and non-section 469 offences. With respect to the former category, in which murder is the most frequently charged offence, s. 522 of the Criminal Code requires that bail hearings are heard by superior court judges. This jurisdiction is historical and is likely meant to reflect the attitude that the release status of someone charged with this type of offence ought to be made by the most senior trial court in the province. Reviews from bail decisions under s. 522 must go to the court of appeal of the province in a cumbersome two-step procedure under s. 680.

The overwhelming majority of offences in the Criminal Code are non-section 469 offences. Bail decisions for these offences are decided in accordance with s. 515, by a "justice." Section 2 of the Code defines as a "justice" as "justice of the peace" or a "provincial court judge." In Ontario, bail hearings for non-section 469 offences are often presided over by justices of the peace. In the rest of the country, provincial court judges hear bail hearings under s. 515. **Do you think it is desirable for bail decisions, sometimes on very serious offences, to be heard by judicial officers who are not necessarily legally trained?** Reviews of the decisions of justices of the peace under s. 515 are heard by judges of the superior court of criminal jurisdiction, pursuant to ss. 520 (review by accused) and 521 (review by Crown) of the Code.

1. Show Cause Hearings

The legislation passed in 1971 emphasized the release of accused persons, and this was made clear by s. 515. Prior to the Act, an accused was required to petition for bail. The legislation originally required that the justice order the release of an accused unless the prosecutor shows cause why release should not be ordered. Under that early version, if conditions were necessary, it was for the prosecution to show why that was so. Recognizances, sureties and cash bail were only to be ordered if the prosecutor persuaded the justice that something less was not sufficient. This was the ladder effect. However, amendments were soon added to the original legislation to reverse the burden of proof in some circumstances. Over time, more and more offences have become the subject of reverse onuses. These are set out in s. 515(6). Where a reverse onus is applicable, it is for the accused to show cause why release should be ordered. The ladder effect still applies but in reverse order. That is, it is now the accused in a reverse onus situation who must satisfy the justice that less restrictive measures should be ordered.

2. Grounds for Detention

Until a 1997 amendment, as to which see below, section 515(10) provided that detention of an accused in custody is justified only on either the primary ground that his detention is necessary to ensure his attendance in court or the secondary ground that his detention is necessary in the public interest or for the protection or safety of the public. The secondary grounds contain the possibilities of abuse that could seriously impair the spirit of reform. The Canadian case law prior to this enactment was divided from province to province as to whether likelihood of the accused committing a crime is a fit criterion for refusing bail. If you confine someone in custody because you feel he may commit other crimes while awaiting his trial, what does this do to the presumption of innocence? We need to bear in mind that the person so confined has not even been *tried,* much less convicted, for the offence with respect to which bail is being considered. If the reasoning in s. 515(10) is sound then perhaps we ought to confine all those convicted of crime for an indefinite period since they may later commit other crimes if set free! The Ouimet Committee concluded that refusing bail for the protection of the public did not violate the Canadian Bill of Rights provision respecting the presumption of innocence.

The Ouimet Committee, in deciding in favour of adding protection of the public as a justification for detention considered the following hypothetical:

> Suppose the case of a man charged with attempting to murder his wife against whom there was overwhelming evidence, and suppose there was the clearest evidence that he would immediately upon his release renew the endeavour; could it be reasonably argued that he had an absolute right to be released as long as the Court was satisfied that he would appear for trial?

Some have strenuously argued that, indeed, even such a man as this must be released as the sole function of bail is to ensure attendance at trial. Do you agree? Should orders of detention for the protection of the public only be given in situations that approximate very closely the hypothetical used in justification by the Ouimet Committee? If the practice develops of making such orders simply on the basis that the accused has a criminal record and might possibly commit other crimes while awaiting trial could there be a successful challenge under s. 11(*e*) of the Charter of Rights? That section provides:

> Any person charged with an offence has the right not to be denied reasonable bail without just cause.

The secondary grounds for detention were "the public interest *or* for the protection or safety of the public". What was meant by "public interest"?

Re POWERS and R.

(1973), 20 C.R.N.S. 23, 9 C.C.C. (2d) 533 (Ont. H.C.)

LERNER J.:—This application is by way of notice of motion to set aside,

> . . . the Detention Order issued on the 15th day of August (sic) 1972 by Provincial Judge Camblin on a charge that the accused did on or about the 15th day of August, 1972 have in her possession a restricted drug (metamphetamine) for the purpose of trafficking . . .

. . .

It is not uncommon for persons charged and released on bail to be subsequently arrested on similar or charges of which the instant case is typical.

An affidavit filed on behalf of the Attorney-General of Canada by one of his counsel, indicated that the applicant was charged on August 15, 1972, with possession of a controlled drug (methamphetamine) for the purpose of trafficking and a detention order was made in connection with that charge. To put it another way, the applicant was refused bail on that charge.

The allegations set out in his affidavit were not disputed by the applicant. It would appear then that when she was before the Provincial Judge on August 15th, the applicant was awaiting trial on five similar offences, each committed on different dates, and that she had been released pending her trials *on each*, even though she had failed to appear on two occasions in violation of her promises to appear, thus necessitating the issue and execution of two Bench warrants. It would also appear that the applicant was awaiting trial on three additional charges which were unrelated in nature to those already mentioned and that she had been released pending her trial on each of them. The first charge was laid on April 22, 1972, and the others in May, June, July and August.

. . .

It was not seriously argued upon this application before me that the applicant, if released, would not appear at trial, even though the affidavit filed on behalf of the Attorney-General indicated that the applicant had failed to appear on two previous occasions. I conclude, on the material before me, that the applicant, if released, would probably appear for her trial.

In cases where ensuring appearance at trial is not the real issue, the most difficult problems are the cases of persons with a history of previous convictions or who are before the Court accused of an offence or offences while upon interim release awaiting trial on an earlier charge or charges. That was the situation on this application. If all of the considerations are met as to appearance at trial, according to s. 457(7)(*a*), [now 515(10)(*a*)] the basis for justification of detention is found in paragraph (*b*) thereof:

> (*b*)   on the secondary ground (the applicability of which shall be determined only in the event that and after it is determined that his detention is not justified on the primary ground referred to in paragraph (*a*)) that his detention is necessary in the public interest or for the protection or safety of the public, having regard to all the circumstances including any substantial likelihood that the accused will, if he is released from custody, commit a criminal offence involving serious harm or an interference with the administration of justice.

It is not too difficult to envisage cases which might fall into the description ". . . any substantial likelihood that the accused will, if he is released from custody, commit a criminal offence involving serious harm or an interference with the administration of justice", *e.g.*, an accused awaiting trial for break, enter and theft, accused of similar offences since release; or bank robbers accused of similar or related offences since release. Evidence of such matters is obviously not too difficult to assess and resolve.

The real problem, as stated earlier, which is the main theme of the instant application stems from situations of which the facts of this case are an example. Where a person is alleged to have committed, as here, a series of similar or related offences (*e.g.* —drugs, etc.) while on interim release, it cannot be said that she will likely commit a criminal offence involving serious harm (*except to herself*) or interference with the administration of justice. A perusal of the history of the outstanding charges herein makes this apparent.

Do the circumstances then fit into the larger area "that this detention is necessary in the public interest"? What is the public interest? Relating to the facts of this application, the only person or persons that may be *directly* affected as stated above if she were released, would be the accused.

"Public interest" involves many considerations, not the least of which is the "public image" of the *Criminal Code, the Bail Reform Act* amendments, the apprehension and conviction of criminals, the attempts at deterrence of crime, and ultimately the protection of that overwhelming percentage of citizens of Canada who are not only socially conscious but law-abiding. This cannot be emphasized too strongly. Much has been written in the public press about the attitude of citizens, juries, law enforcement officers (who some seem to forget are also citizens in our society) concerning accused persons being released and subsequently arrested on allegations of commission of further offences. When weighing the *rights* of the accused in the context that he should not be improperly detained or discriminated against, one is also mindful of the *rights* of the community and remember that in the "public interest" the scales not be tipped in the other direction to the extent that the citizen may, in wonderment and bewilderment, feel that the application of our criminal laws (bail provisions) is a mockery or at least not being administered realistically or in the public interest. When equalizing the treatment before the law of rich and poor, the sophisticated and the artless or the simple, care must be taken that the public interest as I have indicated, not be sacrificed or shrugged off.

The effect on the public interest was considered by Zuber, J., formerly of the County Court of Essex, now a Justice of the High Court, on a bail review in January, 1972 (unreported). The accused had a record from 1956 to 1969 (over a period of 14 years) at which time he was sentenced to four years for break, enter and unlawful possession of stolen property. He was paroled July 15, 1970, the parole to expire in June, 1973. On the bail review application he stood accused of three charges of robbery. The learned Judge refused bail on the premise that there was substantial likelihood that the accused would commit another crime involving serious harm, for example, theft, or break-in or robbery, while awaiting trial and he observed:

> In the past, the accused has proceeded with depressing regularity from one conviction to the next. Even while on parole there is a probable case that he has committed three offences. I think that it would be ignoring the plain lessons of human experience to say that there is not substantial likelihood that this accused will commit another crime involving serious harm, for example theft, break-in or robbery while awaiting trial.

The disposition of that application was the subject of critical comment in Can. Bar. J., vol. 3, No. 2 (N.S.) (1972), to the effect that this was not in keeping with the spirit of the reforms of the *Bail Reform Act*; that it was in fact detaining him because of his previous convictions and assuming that he was guilty now, as charged, before his trial. This, in my view is unrealistic and "ignoring the plain lessons of human experience". Relating this case to the "public interest" as I have expressed it above, the public which has this "public interest" must be allowed to feel safety and security as well as tolerant and enlightened administration of justice. That can only be achieved by recognizing the plain lessons of the citizens' ordinary experiences in life and translating them into realistic as well as humane and enlightened application of these procedures.

In summary, because "the public interest" is, in my view, directly concerned for the reasons expressed above, detention herein is necessary. The application is therefore refused.

Application dismissed.

R. v. GRAHAM
Ont. Dist. Ct., August 2, 1990

FLEURY D.C.J.:—The section contemplates the detention of an accused where it is necessary in the public interest. This somewhat fluid concept was analyzed by Mr. Justice Lerner in *Re Powers and R.* ... In *R. v. Brown*, an unreported decision of my brother Judge Shapiro, released on October 19, 1983, this very experienced judge held that persons who use a handgun are not to be released from custody pending trial. He concluded that this was in the interest of the public. Similarly, Mr. Justice Boilard, one of the most prominent criminal jurists on the Quebec Superior Court, in *R. v. Zelman*, unreported on June 19, 1987, concluded that it was in the interest of the public to detain heroin traffickers without bail. In our modern society, where all sectors have become much more aware of the prevalence of sexual abuse of all kinds, it is clearly in the public interest to discourage any type of sexual abuse. The assault described by the victim in this case probably embodies the worst nightmares of many women. The horrendous circumstances of the assault perpetrated are enough to frighten the most courageous women and to cause panic in the streets. I am well aware that the accused is presumed innocent until proven guilty and that he is entitled to the benefit of proof beyond a reasonable doubt. I am also aware that the Charter of Rights gives him the right "not to be denied reasonable bail without just cause". . . . The concept of reasonable bail as outlined in the Charter must be understood in the context of the present provisions of the Criminal Code of Canada. It is clear that there are circumstances where there is no substantial likelihood of the commission of a criminal offence which might still justify a detention order in the public interest. The case at bar, in my opinion, is one such case. There was so much violence, the assault was so serious and the circumstances so demeaning to the victim, that there is a need to protect the public at large from being exposed to an individual who, on the facts outlined to me, appears to have been the perpetrator. . . . The principles outlined in *Powers*, supra, have not changed despite the advent of the Charter.

R. v. LAMOTHE
(1990), 77 C.R. (3d) 236, 58 C.C.C. (3d) 530 (Qué. C.A.)

According to the Crown, D, M and Lamothe and two others went to a bar where they met the victim, G. They later went to D's house where they consumed alcohol and drugs. The group then got into Lamothe's father's car. D and M stabbed G more than 21 times. Lamothe stayed at the wheel throughout. Later, he wiped the blood off the inside and outside of the car doors and off the seats. D and M were charged with first degree murder and Lamothe with being an accessory after the fact to murder under s. 240. Lamothe's application to be released on bail was rejected. He appealed.

Baudoin J. spoke concerning the judge's power to grant bail.

BAUDOIN J.:—His discretion must be exercised judicially and in conformity with the general principles and general rules of our criminal law, in particular the presumption of innocence and the other fundamental guarantees set out by the Charter.

That this discretion is exercised pursuant to ss. 520, 521, or 522 of the *Criminal Code* does not, and especially must not, make a difference from the point of view of the application of the requisite criteria. In other words, one must not give a different meaning to the presumption of innocence, nor a different application to the legal protections granted to the fundamental human rights, on the basis of the type of offence involved. The type of offence committed may however, given their circumstances, have an influence on the exercise of this discretion. It then becomes one among all the other factors which the judge must, or can, take into consideration. Accordingly, a judge, faced with an individual charged with an offence which puts the safety of the public into jeopardy, and if he considers that there is a probability that the accused may recidivate, may refuse interim release.

. . .

The presumption of innocence, especially since fundamental rights have been entrenched in the Constitution, must not be relegated uniquely to the sole role of determining the guilt of the accused. *It must exist at all stages of the criminal process*. It must also benefit the present accused who is here seeking interim release, having regard however to the fact that, as mentioned above, the burden of proof is reversed in the case of an application under s. 522. However, it is a reversal of a *burden of proof* in a very limited situation and not a *reversal of the presumption of innocence*. This goes to the sufficiency of the evidence offered in order to convince and not to the exercise of a fundamental right.

It would therefore probably not be unhelpful to repeat certain of the principles set out in the *Perron* case.

The first is that even overwhelming evidence of the commission of an offence, or even being caught in flagrant delict, is only one element among others which the judge must consider.

The second is that the probability of a conviction and the seriousness of the crime are also not the only criteria to be taken into consideration.

The third is that a judge hearing the application need not decide at this stage the results of the trial into the guilt or innocence of the accused. He must in every case, and at all stages of the case, first consider the presumption of innocence and take it into consideration, and, not get ahead of the trial on the merits.

What about the protection of the public interest mentioned in s. 515(10)(*b*)?

. . .

The notion of public interest is made up of two aspects. The judge must determine, on the one hand, what the perception of the public will be should the accused be released and, on the other hand, what the reaction of the accused will be. In my view, these two criteria do not have to mean one and the same thing.

With respect to the perception of the public, as we know, a large part of the Canadian public often adopts a negative and even emotional attitude towards criminals or powerful criminals. The public wants to see itself protected, see criminals in prison and see them punished severely. To get rid of a criminal is to get rid of crime. It perceives the judicial system harshly and the administration of justice in general as too indulgent, too soft, too good to the criminal. This perception, almost visceral in respect of crime, is surely not the perception which a judge must have in deciding the issue of interim release. If this were the case, persons charged with certain types of offences would never be released because the perception of the public is negative with respect to the type of crime committed, while others, on the contrary, would almost automatically be released where the public's perception is neutral or more indulgent. The criminal law and its application also has, and must have, an educational value for the public. An *informed* public must understand that the existence of the presumption of innocence at all stages of the criminal process is not a *purely theoretical notion*, but a concrete reality and that, despite what may happen, in its perception, for certain inconveniences with respect to effectiveness in the repression of crime, it is the *price that must be paid for life in a free and democratic society*. Therefore, the perception of the public must be situated at another level, that of a public reasonably informed about our system of criminal law and capable of judging and perceiving without emotion that the application of the presumption of innocence, even with respect to interim release, has the effect that people, who may later be found guilty of even serious crimes, will be released for the period between the time of their arrest and the time of their trial. In other words, the criterion of the public perception must not be that of the lowest common denominator. An informed public understands that there exists in Canada a constitutionally guaranteed presumption of innocence (*s. 11(d) of the Charter*) and the right not to be denied reasonable bail without just cause (*s. 11(e) of the Charter*).

Weighing the public reaction, the judge must then ask whether the release of the accused pending his trial would provoke among a reasonbly informed public a reaction which would discredit the administration of criminal justice.

. . .

[Baudoin J. then quotes Lamer J. in *R. v. Collins*, [1987] 1 S.C.R. 265 (S.C.C.) on disrepute before continuing.]

The dangerousness of the individual, the circumstances of the crime charged, the type of offence, the existence and contents of a criminal record, the probability of recidivism, the situation of the victim are factors which may assist the judge in forming an idea with respect to this reaction. The criminal justice system must not give rise to scandal. It must cultivate an image of serene, impartial and exemplarly justice.

The bail judge conceded that there is no reason to suspect that the accused would not appear at trial, that he is dangerous or that he would intimidate a witness or impede the administration of justice. In refusing bail on the only ground left, the public interest, he based himself too heavily on the seriousness of the offence and the likelihood of a conviction. The accused has properly discharged the burden placed on him by s. 522 and should be released.

R. v. MORALES
[1992] 3 S.C.R. 711, 17 C.R. (4th) 74, 77 C.C.C. (3d) 91 (S.C.C.)

A majority of the Supreme Court held that the criterion of "public interest" as a basis for pre-trial detention violated s. 11(e) of the Charter and should be severed from the section. The Court was unanimous that the "public safety" component was constitutional.

LAMER C.J.C. (La Forest, Sopinka, McLachlin and Iacobucci JJ. concurring):—

. . .

In my view, the criterion of "public interest" as a basis for pre-trial detention under s. 515(10)(*b*) violates s. 11(*e*) of the *Charter* because it authorizes detention in terms which are vague and imprecise. D. Kiselbach, "Pre-trial Criminal Procedure: Preventive Detention and the Presumption of Innocence" (1988-89) 31 Crim. L.Q. 168, at p. 186, describes "public interest" as "the most nebulous basis for detention". I agree with this characterization of the public interest component of s. 515(10)(*b*) and view it as a fatal flaw in the provision.

A very thorough review of the constitutional "doctrine of vagueness" was recently undertaken by Gonthier J. in *Canada v. Pharmaceutical Society (Nova Scotia)*, [1992] 2 S.C.R. 606.... After noting at p. 632 that "the threshold for finding a law vague is relatively high", Gonthier J. held at p. 643 that "a law will be found unconstitutionally vague if it so lacks in precision as not to give sufficient guidance for legal debate."

. . .

In my view, the doctrine of vagueness is applicable to s. 515(10)(*b*) because there cannot be just cause for denial of bail within the meaning of s. 11(*e*) if the statutory criteria for denying bail are vague and imprecise. *Nova Scotia Pharmaceutical Society*, at p. 632 [S.C.R.], identified two rationales for the doctrine of vagueness, namely fair notice to the citizen and limitation of law enforcement discretion. Fair notice is "an understanding that certain conduct is the subject of legal restrictions" (p. 635), a factor which is not relevant to a provision like s. 515(10)(*b*) which does not prohibit conduct. However, limitation of law enforcement discretion is still a relevant factor. In the *Prostitution Reference*, at p. 1157 [S.C.R.], I explained this rationale in terms of a "standardless sweep": "is the statute so pervasively vague that it permits a 'standardless sweep' allowing law enforcement officials to pursue their personal predilections?". In my view the principles of fundamental justice preclude a standardless sweep in any provision which authorizes imprisonment. This is all the more so under a constitutional guarantee not to be denied bail without just cause as set out in s. 11(*e*). Since pre-trial detention is extraordinary in our system of criminal justice, vagueness in defining the terms of pre-trial detention may be even more invidious than is vagueness in defining an offence.

. . .

A provision does not violate the doctrine of vagueness simply because it is subject to interpretation. To require absolute precision would be to create an impossible constitutional standard. As I stated in the *Prostitution Reference* at p. 1157 [S.C.R.]:

> The fact that a particular legislative term is open to varying interpretations by the courts is not fatal. As Beetz J. observed in *R. v. Morgentaler*, [1988] 1 S.C.R. 30, at p. 107, "(f)lexibility and vagueness are not synonymous". Therefore the question at hand is whether the impugned sections of the *Criminal Code* can be or have been given sensible meanings by the courts.

It seems apparent that, at the very least, the term "public interest" is subject to interpretation. It accordingly becomes necessary to determine whether it iscapable of being given a constant and settled meaning by the courts.

. . .

As currently defined by the courts, the term "public interest" is incapable of framing the legal debate in any meaningful manner or structuring discretion in any way.

Nor would it be possible in my view to give the term "public interest" a constant or settled meaning. The term gives the courts unrestricted latitute to define any circumstances as sufficient to justify pre-trial detention. The term creates no criteria to define these circumstances. No amount of judicial interpretation of the term "public interest" would be capable of rendering it a provision which gives any guidance for legal debate.

As a result, the public interest component of s. 515(10)(*b*) violates the s. 11(*e*) of the *Charter* because it authorizes a denial of bail without just cause.

(ii) Section 1

In my view, this violation is not justified under s. 1. The limit cannot be justified under the test in *R. v. Oakes*, [1986] 1 S.C.R. 103, 50 C.R. (3d) 1, 65 N.R. 87, 53 O.R. (2d) 719 (headnote only), 24 C.C.C. (3d) 321, 14 O.A.C. 335, 26 D.L.R. (4th) 200, 19 C.R.R. 308, and may be too vague even to constitute a limit which is "prescribed by law" under s. 1.

Although the term "public interest" may well be so vague that it does not constitute a limit which is "prescribed by law" under s. 1, as Gonthier J. noted in *Nova Scotia Pharmaceutical Society* at p. 627 [S.C.R.], "[t]he Court will be reluctant to find a disposition so vague as not to qualify as 'law' under s. 1 *in limine*, and will rather consider the scope of the disposition under the 'minimal impairment' test". Accordingly, I prefer to proceed immediately to the *Oakes* test.

Even if the term "public interest" is capable of passing the threshold test under s. 1 of being a limit which is "prescribed by law", I am of the opinion that it cannot be justified under the *Oakes* test. I am prepared to accept that the term "public interest" could be justified under the first branch of the *Oakes* test. In my view, s. 515(10)(*b*) has two objectives, both of which are apparent from the wording of the provision. The first objective is to prevent those who have been arrested from committing criminal offences. The second objective is to prevent those who have been arrested from interfering with the administration of justice. This second objective is extremely important. The criminal justice system cannot function properly if it is subverted by the accused's interference with the administration of justice. In my opinion, the objective of preventing such interference is sufficiently important to warrant overriding a constitutionally protected right. The first objective of s. 515(10)(*b*) is also important. The prevention of crime is one objective of all criminal law. I am prepared to accept that the objective of preventing crime by those who have already been accused of criminal conduct is sufficiently important to warrant overriding a constitutionally protected right.

However, in my view the public interest component of s. 515(10)(*b*) does not meet the second branch of the *Oakes* test, the proportionality test. None of the three components of the proportionality test is met. First, there is no rational connection between the measure and the objectives of preventing crime and preventing interference with the administration of justice. As the respondent submits, the provision is so vague that it does not provide any means to determine which accused are most likely to commit offences or interfere with the administration of justice while on bail. It accordingly authorizes pre-trial detention in many cases which are not related to the objectives of the measure. Second, the measure does not impair rights as little as possible. In both *R. v. Keegstra*, supra, at pp. 785-786 [S.C.R.], and *R. v. Seaboyer (sub nom. R. v. S.(S))* [1991] 2 S.C.R. 577, 7 C.R. (4th) 117, 128 N.R. 81, 6 C.R.R. (2d) 35, (sub nom. R. v. S.) 66 C.C.C. (3d) 321, 83 D.L.R. (4th) 193, 48 O.A.C. 81, at p. 626 [S.C.R.], vagueness was a factor relevant to determining whether there had been a minimal impairment of rights. *Nova Scotia Pharmaceutical Society* noted at p. 627 [S.C.R.] that "vagueness as it relates to the 'minimal impairment' branch of s. 1 merges with the related concept of overbreadth". The vague and overbroad concept of public interest permits far more pre-trial detention than is required to meet the limited objectives of preventing crime and preventing interference with the administration of justice by those who are on bail. Accordingly, it does not constitute a minimal impairment of rights. Third, there is no proportionality between the effects of the measure and its objectives. By authorizing excessive pre-trial detention, the effects of the limit far exceed the objectives of the measure.

As a result, the violation of s. 11(*e*) is not justified under s. 1 of the *Charter*.

GONTHIER J. (dissenting in part) (L'Heureux-Dubé J. concurring):—

. . .

In this regard, it is, first, significant to recognize the general sense of the phrase, which is a reference to the special set of values which are best understood from the point of view of the aggregate good and are of relevance to matters relating to the well-being of society. Indeed, in this sense it is at the heart of our legal system and inspires all legislation as well as the administration of justice. Its content is in turn expressed by laws, be they the Constitution, the common law or legislation. The *Charter* is an expression of the fundamental values which direct the public interest. The concept of public interest is indeed broad but it is not meaningless, nor is it vague.

. . .

As the Chief Justice appropriately points out, a bail application differs from other legal determinations in that is does not involve a finding of guilt as to past conduct. Consequently, the general interest of the accused in being able to be informed of which conduct is prohibited by the law does not bear on this type of proceeding. A bail application is rather concerned with governing future conduct during the interim period awaiting trial. What is at issue are the reasons for detention. The criterion set by the *Charter* is that of just cause. This implies two elements: (1) a cause or reason and (2) a proportionality between the reason and the deprivation of liberty that makes the cause "just". Public interest, as used in s. 515(10), must be understood in this context. Under s. 515(10), two main elements exist in relation to the operation of the public interest criterion. One of them is a constraint upon the type of relationship which must exist between the reasons for a refusal to grant bail and the relevant public interest: it must be one of necessity. This is reflected in s. 515(10) by the requirement not only of a public interest but also of necessity for the detention. This element of necessity involves a causal link between the public interest and the detention such as to make the detention necessary and not merely convenient or desirable but also an element of importance, weight or seriousness of the public interest such as to outweigh the accused's right to personal liberty. This necessity of course can only be and indeed must be, by the terms of s. 515(10)(*b*) itself, determined having regard to all the circumstances, that is to the full context both of the accused and the community. The element of seriousness of the public interest to be considered serves to qualify the other element, namely the content of the considerations which may be included within the public interest criterion. Some of these considerations may be covered by the words, in s. 515(10)(*b*), "for the protection or safety of the public". The section expressly includes certain examples of relevant matters. It means that they should relate to the safeguarding of the fundamental values of the rule of law and the *Charter* which include the maintaining of order and security and respect for the fundamental individual and collective rights of others. However, the concept of public interest is broader than that of protection or safety of the public, and includes interests which may not be properly included within the categories of public health or safety. The aim of avoiding interference with the administration of justice is one such example. Other examples of a public interest which have been mentioned as having been actually experienced are the protection of the accused himself from suicide or from the actions of others, the prevention of activities which involve the possession of or dealing in small quantities of illegal narcotics, or the preparation of reports for the court which require the presence of the accused. Also important is the consideration that the criterion of necessity in the public interest is capable of encompassing circumstances which have not been foreseen or, indeed, which may be unforeseeable, yet when they occur, albeit rarely, they obviously make the detention necessary and undoubtedly provide just cause for denying bail within the meaning of s. 11(*e*) of the *Charter*. The courts must be able to deal with such circumstances. The good governance of society and the rule of law itself require that Parliament be allowed to provide for social peace and order even in unforeseen circumstances. The appropriate instrument for doing this is through the administration of justice by the courts and allowing them a measure of discretion which they are bound to exercise judicially, that is, for reasons that are relevant, within the limits provided by law and in accordance with the *Charter*. The importance and the nature of this function of legislative provisions have been recognized by this court in *Nova Scotia Pharmaceutical Society*, supra, at p. 642 [S.C.R.]. It was there stated that:

> One must be wary of using the doctrine of vagueness to prevent or impede State action in furtherance of valid social objectives, by requiring the law to achieve a degree of precision to which the subject-matter does not lend itself. A delicate balance must be maintained between societal interests and individual rights. A measure of generality also sometimes allows for greater respect for fundamental rights, since circumstances that would not justify the invalidation of a more precise enactment may be accommodated through the application of a more general one.

I am in full agreement with the Chief Justice that flexibility and vagueness are not synonymous. The former is a quality necessary to the administration of justice. Section 515(10)(*b*) provides for this. Its dual requirements of public interest and necessity which itself predicates a public interest of a serious nature have meaning, give rise to legal debate and, though broad, are not vague but provide an adequate framework and limit for the exercise of judicial discretion and a means for controlling such exercise while at the same time allowing for the flexibility required for an effective administration of justice and implementation of the rule of law. I underline, as does the Chief Justice in his reasons both in this case and in the case of *R. c. Pearson* (November 19,

1992), Doc. 22173 (C.S.C.) [now reported at (1992), 17 C.R. (4th) 1], that the bail process is subject to very exacting procedural guarantees which both structure and guide the exercise of judicial discretion.

In 1997, five years after the *Morales* decision, Parliament passed a large omnibus bill to amend various aspects of the Criminal Code. This included an amendment to s. 515.

515 (10) For the purposes of this section, the detention of an accused in custody is justified only on one or more of the following grounds:

(a) where the detention is necessary to ensure his or her attendance in court in order to be dealt with according to law;

(b) where the detention is necessary for the protection or safety of the public, having regard to all the circumstances including any substantial likelihood that the accused will, if released from custody, commit a criminal offence or interfere with the administration of justice; and

(c) on any other just cause being shown and, without limiting the generality of the foregoing, where the detention is necessary in order to maintain confidence in the administration of justice, having regard to all the circumstances, including the apparent strength of the prosecution's case, the gravity of the nature of the offence, the circumstances surrounding its commission and the potential for a lengthy term of imprisonment.

The constitutionality of paragraph (c) was challenged in *R. v. Hall*:

R. v. HALL
(2002), 4 C.R. (6th) 197, 167 C.C.C. (3d) 449 (S.C.C.)

In 1999, a woman's body was found with 37 slash wounds to her hands, forearms, shoulder, neck and face. It appeared her assailant had attempted to decapitate her. The murder received much media attention and caused significant public concern and a general fear that a killer was at large. Based on compelling physical and other evidence linking the accused to the crime, he was charged with first degree murder. He applied for bail.

The bail judge held that pre-trial detention was not necessary "to ensure attendance in court" under s. 515(10)(a) of the Criminal Code nor for the "safety of the public" under s. 515(10)(b). He held, however, that detention was necessary to "maintain confidence in the administration of justice" under s. 515(10)(c) in view of the highly charged aftermath of the murder, the strong evidence implicating the accused, and the other factors referred to in subsection (c). A superior court judge dismissed the accused's habeas corpus application challenging the constitutionality of s. 515(10)(c). The Court of Appeal affirmed that decision. The accused appealed.

A 5-4 majority of the Supreme Court upheld the constitutionality of part of s. 515(10)(c).

McLACHLIN C.J.C. (L'Heureux-Dubé, Gonthier, Bastarache and Binnie JJ. concurring):—

. . .

3. Constitutionality of Bail Denial for "Any Other Just Cause"

The first phrase of s. 515(10)(c) which permits denial of bail "on any other just cause being shown" is unconstitutional. Parliament cannot confer a broad discretion on judges to deny bail, but must lay out narrow and precise circumstances in which bail can be denied: *Pearson* and *Morales, supra*. This phrase does not specify any particular basis upon which bail could be denied. The denial of bail "on any other just cause" violates the requirements enunciated in *Morales, supra*, and therefore is inconsistent with the presumption of innocence and s. 11(e) of the Charter. Even assuming a pressing and substantial legislative objective for the phrase "on any other just cause being shown", the generality of the phrase impels its failure on the proportionality branch of the *Oakes* test (*R. v. Oakes*, [1986] 1 S.C.R. 103). Section 52 of the Constitution Act,1982, provides that a law is void to the extent it is inconsistent with the Charter. It follows that this phrase fails. The next phrase in the provision, "without limiting the generality of the foregoing", is also void, since it serves only to confirm the generality of the phrase permitting a judge to deny bail "on any other just cause".

However, this does not mean that all of s. 515(10)(c) is unconstitutional. The loss of the above phrases leaves intact the balance of s. 515(10)(c), which is capable of standing alone grammatically and in terms of Parliament's intention. Whatever the fate of the broad initial discretion para. (c) seems to convey, Parliament clearly intended to permit bail to be denied where necessary to maintain confidence in the administration of justice, having regard to the four specified factors. This leaves the question of whether this latter part of s. 515(10)(c), considered on its own, is unconstitutional.

4. Constitutionality of the Provision for Denying Bail Where Necessary to Maintain Confidence in the Administration of Justice

(a) The Function of this Provision

Underlying much of the accused's argument is the suggestion that the first two grounds for denying bail suffice and that a third ground serves only to permit the denial of bail for vague and unspecified reasons. Accepting this argument, Iacobucci J. concludes, at para. 86, that "the fear that a situation may arise where the bail judge is unable to provide for the protection of the public without relying on the residual ground is without reasonable foundation".

Yet it seems to me that the facts of this case, as well as the facts in such cases as *R. v. MacDougal* (1999), 138 C.C.C. (3d) 38 (B.C.C.A.), and the pre-*Morales* case of *R. v. Dakin*, [1989] O.J. No. 1348 (QL) (C.A.), offer convincing proof that in some circumstances it may be necessary to the proper functioning of the bail system and, more broadly of the justice system, to deny bail even where there is no risk the accused will not attend trial or may re-offend or interfere with the administration of justice. Bolan J., on strong and cogent evidence, concluded that bail could not be denied on either of these grounds. But he also found that detention was necessary to maintain confidence in the administration of justice. The crime was heinous and unexplained. The evidence tying the accused to the crime was very strong. People in the community were afraid. As Proulx J.A., speaking of a similarly inexplicable and brutal murder stated in *R. v. Rondeau* (1996), 108 C.C.C. (3d) 474 (Que. C.A.), at p. 480 [translation] "[t]he more a crime like the present one is unexplained and unexplainable, the more worrisome bail becomes for society". The provision at issue serves an important purpose—to maintain confidence in the administration of justice in circumstances such as these.

Therefore, Parliament provided for denial of bail where paras. (a) and (b) of s. 515(10) are not met but the judge, viewing the situation objectively through the lens of the four factors stipulated by Parliament, has decided that there is "just cause" for refusing bail. To allow an accused to be released into the community on bail in the face of a heinous crime and overwhelming evidence may erode the public's confidence in the administration of justice. Where justice is not seen to be done by the public, confidence in the bail system and, more generally, the entire justice system may falter. When the public's confidence has reasonably been called into question, dangers such as public unrest and vigilantism may emerge.

Public confidence is essential to the proper functioning of the bail system as a whole: see *R. v. Valente (No. 2)*, [1985] 2 S.C.R. 673 (S.C.C.) at p. 689. Indeed, public confidence and the integrity of the rule of law are inextricably linked. As Hall J.A. stated in *MacDougall*, supra, at p. 48:

> To sustain the rule of law, a core value of our society, it is necessary to maintain public respect for the law and the courts. A law that is not broadly acceptable to most members of society will usually fall into desuetude: witness the unhappy prohibition experiment in the United States. *Courts must be careful not to pander to public opinion or to take account of only the overly excitable, but I believe that to fail to have regard to the provisions of s. 515(5)(c) in the relatively rare cases where it can properly be invoked would tend to work against maintaining broad public confidence in the way justice is administered in this country* [emphasis added by the Supreme Court] .....

Bail denial to maintain confidence in the administration of justice is not a mere "catch-all" for cases where the first two grounds have failed. It represents a separate and distinct basis for bail denial not covered by the other two categories. The same facts may be relevant to all three heads. For example, an accused's implication in a terrorist ring or organized drug trafficking might be relevant to whether he is likely to appear at trial, whether he is likely to commit further offences or interfere with the administration of justice, and whether his detention is necessary to maintain confidence in the justice system. But that does not negate the distinctiveness of the three grounds.

I conclude that a provision that allows bail to be denied on the basis that the accused's detention is required to maintain confidence in the administration of justice is neither superfluous nor unjustified. It serves a very real need to permit a bail judge to detain an accused pending trial for the purpose of maintaining the public's confidence if the circumstances of the case so warrant. Without public confidence, the bail system and the justice system generally stand compromised. While the circumstances in which recourse to this ground for bail denial may not arise frequently, when they do it is essential that a means of denying bail be available.

(b) Is the Ground for Denying Bail Unconstitutionally Vague or Overbroad?

The appellant says that maintaining confidence in the administration of justice is vague and overbroad, and amounts to substituting a new phrase for the ground of "public interest" which the Court held unconstitutional in *Morales, supra*. However, the ground of maintaining confidence in the administration of justice as articulated in para. (c) is much narrower and more precise than the old public interest ground. The term "public interest" is imprecise and "has not been given a constant or settled meaning by the courts": *Morales, supra*, at p. 732. The articulated ground of maintaining confidence in the administration of justice, by contrast, relies on concepts held to be justiciable and offers considerable precision.

The test for impermissible vagueness is whether the law so lacks precision that it fails to give sufficient guidance for legal debate: *R. v. Nova Scotia Pharmaceutical Society*, [1992] 2 S.C.R. 606, at pp. 638-40. The test sets a high threshold: *Winko v. British Columbia (Forensic Psychiatric Institute)*, [1999] 2 S.C.R. 625, at para. 68. Laws are of necessity general statements that must cover a variety of situations. A degree of generality is therefore essential, and is not to be confused with vagueness, which occurs when the law is so imprecise that it does not permit legal debate about its meaning and application. As noted in *Morales, supra*, at p. 729: "To require absolute precision would be to create an impossible constitutional standard".

The phrase "proper administration of justice" was held to provide an intelligible standard and hence not overbroad in *Canadian Broadcasting Corp. v. New Brunswick (Attorney General)*, [1996] 3 S.C.R. 480, in the context of preserving openness in the administration of justice. In that case, La Forest J. defined the phrase as including a discretionary power of the courts to control their own process. At para. 59, he states:

> The phrase "administration of justice" appears throughout legislation in Canada, including the Charter. Thus, "proper administration of justice", which of necessity has been the subject of judicial interpretation, provides the judiciary with a workable standard.

If the phrase "administration of justice" is sufficiently precise, it must follow that the phrase "necessary to maintain confidence in the administration of justice", amplified by a direction to consider four specified factors, is not unconstitutionally vague. The inquiry is narrowed to the reasonable community perception of the necessity of denying bail to maintain confidence in the administration of justice, judicially determined through the objective lens of "all the circumstances, including the apparent strength of the prosecution's case, the gravity of the nature of the offence, the circumstances surrounding its commission and the potential for a lengthy term of imprisonment". Even where a standard viewed alone is impermissibly vague, such factors may save it: *Nova Scotia Pharmaceutical Society, supra....*

This leaves the argument that the ground for denial of bail is overbroad, or of whether the means chosen by the state go further than necessary to accomplish its objective: see *R. v. Heywood*, [1994] 3 S.C.R. 761, at pp. 792-93. The meaning of a law may be plain, yet the law may be overbroad: *Heywood, supra*, at pp. 792-93. It is important that a bail provision not trench more than required on the accused's liberty and the presumption of innocence. Denial of bail must be confined to a "narrow set of circumstances" related to the proper functioning of the bail system: *Pearson* and *Morales, supra*.

Section 515(10)(c) sets out specific factors which delineate a narrow set of circumstances under which bail can be denied on the basis of maintaining confidence in the administration of justice. As discussed earlier, situations may arise where, despite the fact the accused is not likely to abscond or commit further crimes while awaiting trial, his presence in the community will call into question the public's confidence in the administration of justice. Whether such a situation has arisen is judged by all the circumstances, but in particular the four factors that Parliament has set out in s. 515(10)(c) — the apparent strength of the prosecution's case, the gravity of the nature of the offence, the circumstances surrounding its commission and the potential for lengthy imprisonment. Where, as here, the crime is horrific, inexplicable, and strongly linked to the accused, a justice system that cannot detain the accused risks losing the public confidence upon which the bail system and the justice system as a whole repose.

This, then, is Parliament's purpose: to maintain public confidence in the bail system and the justice system as whole. The question is whether the means it has chosen go further than necessary to achieve that purpose. In my view, they do not. Parliament has hedged this provision for bail with important safeguards. The judge must be satisfied that detention is not only advisable but *necessary*. The judge must, moreover, be satisfied that detention is necessary not just to any goal, but *to maintain confidence in the administration of justice*. Most importantly, the judge makes this appraisal objectively through the lens of the four factors Parliament has specified. The judge cannot conjure up his own reasons for denying bail; while the judge must look at all the circumstances, he must focus particularly on the factors Parliament has specified. At the end of the day, the judge can only deny bail if satisfied that in view of these factors and related circumstances, a reasonable member of the community would be satisfied that denial is necessary to maintain confidence in the administration of justice. In addition, as McEachern C.J.B.C. (in Chambers) noted in *R. v. Nguyen* (1997), 119 C.C.C. (3d) 269, the reasonable person making this assessment must be one properly informed about "the philosophy of the legislative provisions, Charter values and the actual circumstances of the case" (p. 274). For these reasons, the provision does not authorize a "standardless sweep" nor confer open-ended judicial discretion. Rather, it strikes an appropriate balance between the rights of the accused and the need to maintain justice in the community. In sum, it is not overbroad. . . .

6. *Remedy*

Since the introduction of the Charter, courts have engaged in a constitutional dialogue with Parliament. This case is an excellent example of such dialogue. Parliament enacted legislation that permitted a judge to detain an accused person where detention was "necessary in the public interest" . This Court considered this language and determined that the portion of s. 515(10)(b) that authorized pre-trial detention for reasons of public interest was unconstitutional. At p. 742 of *Morales, supra,* Lamer C.J. severed the "public interest" ground from the rest of s. 515(10)(b) because the provision could still function as a whole. After considering this Court's reasons in *Pearson* and *Morales, supra,* Parliament replaced the "public interest" ground with new language. . . .

I would dismiss the appeal. The phrase in s. 515(10)(c) that permits the denial of bail "on any other just cause being shown and, without limiting the generality of the foregoing," is unconstitutional and should be severed from the paragraph. The portion of the paragraph that permits a judge to deny bail "where the detention is necessary in order to maintain confidence in the administration of justice..." is constitutionally valid.

IACOBUCCI J. (dissenting) (Major, Arbour and LeBel JJ. concurring):—At the heart of a free and democratic society is the liberty of its subjects. Liberty lost is never regained and can never be fully compensated for; therefore, where the potential exists for the loss of freedom for even a day, we, as a free and democratic society, must place the highest emphasis on ensuring that our system of justice minimizes the chances of an unwarranted denial of liberty.

In the context of the criminal law, this fundamental freedom is embodied generally in the right to be presumed innocent until proven guilty, and further in the specific right to bail. When bail is denied to an individual who is merely accused of a criminal offence, the presumption of innocence is necessarily infringed. This is the context of this appeal, one in which the "golden thread" that runs through our system of criminal law is placed in jeopardy. And this is the context in which laws authorizing pre-trial detention must be scrutinized.

Section 11(e) of the Canadian Charter of Rights and Freedoms calls particularly on courts, as guardians of liberty, to ensure that pre-trial release remains the norm rather than the exception to the norm, and to restrict pre-trial detention to only those circumstances where the fundamental rights and freedoms of the accused must be overridden in order to preserve some demonstrably pressing societal interest.

The duty to protect individual rights lies at the core of the judiciary's role, a role which takes on increased significance in the criminal law where the vast resources of the state and very often the weight of public opinion are stacked against the individual accused. Courts must not, therefore, take lightly their constitutional responsibility to scrutinize the manner by which the legislature has authorized the detention of the accused in the absence of a conviction.

In my view, when the impugned s. 515(10)(c) of the Criminal Code, R.S.C. 1985, c. C-46, is held up to the appropriate constitutional standard, a standard which takes into account the fundamental importance of the presumption of innocence, it is impossible to justify the sweeping discretion to abrogate the liberty of the accused that this section affords. Unlike the Chief Justice, whose reasons I have had the benefit of reading, I conclude that s. 515(10)(c) cannot withstand Charter scrutiny and must be struck down in its entirety. As I discuss in these reasons, this conclusion is dictated by principle, precedent, and policy.

After the "public interest" component of s. 515(10)(b) was struck down by this Court in *Morales*, pre-trial detention could be justified only under one of the two traditional grounds, namely, ensuring the accused's attendance in court or protecting the safety of the public. As already mentioned, s. 515(10) was eventually amended to add the tertiary ground in dispute here. The other major change was the removal of the primary/secondary structure of the provision. As a result, bail can now be denied under any one of paras. (a), (b), or (c) of s. 515(10) without consideration of the other paragraphs.

As noted above, Parliament waited five years before reacting to *Morales* by amending s. 515(10), and it is significant that the respondent was unable to point to any evidence that during these five years the pre-trial detention scheme was lacking in any way. Indeed, the only justification for the creation of the tertiary ground that the respondent was able to suggest was that "courts should have the exceptional power to deny bail in limited circumstances not covered by the existing legislation" (respondent's factum, at para. 21). However, in the absence of evidence of any deficiencies in the bail system during the five years after the *Morales* decision, the argument that bail judges require this residual category loses much of its force. Although the lack of an empirical foundation for the provision says nothing, in and of itself, as to its validity under s. 11(e) of the Charter (but it does arise in the s. 1 analysis), it is important to bear in mind the context underlying this appeal, namely, that for five years there was no indication that the bail system was in need of a tertiary ground in addition to the two traditional grounds for denying bail.

On a more theoretical level, in oral argument, counsel were hard pressed to raise even a convincing *hypothetical* scenario which called for pre-trial detention for reasons other than those listed in paras. (a) and (b). On the facts of this case, given that the accused was charged with a seemingly inexplicable and brutal murder, the bail judge might have been justified in denying bail under the second ground on the basis that, without any apparent motive for the crime, there was a substantial risk of re-offence. As pointed out by Proulx J.A. in *R. v. Rondeau* (1996), 108 C.C.C. (3d) 474 (Que. C.A.), at p. 480, in the context of a similarly inexplicable and brutal murder, [translation] "[t]he more a crime like the present one is unexplained and unexplainable, the more worrisome bail becomes for society". Counsel also referred to a hypothetical scenario where granting bail in respect of a highly publicized crime could cause public unrest or rioting. Again, however, in my view, the wording of s. 515(10)(b) is broad enough to encompass any type of threat to "the protection or safety of the public", not just a threat from the accused. The provision states that detention is justified where it is necessary for the protection or safety of the public, having regard to all the circumstances. This includes, but is clearly not limited to, a consideration of the substantial likelihood that the accused will re-offend or interfere with the administration of justice . . .

Even if it were possible to imagine rare and isolated situations where it would be justifiable to deny bail for reasons other than those set out in paras. (a) and (b), we are not here dealing with such narrow specific grounds, but instead with a broad, open-ended provision. It should also be remembered that bail is not an all-or-nothing proposition. The bail judge has the discretion to grant bail under particular terms and conditions which are tailored to meet the facts of an individual case. This flexibility goes a long way to narrow the situations where detention is required. Finally, as pointed out in *Rondeau*, where an accused is charged with murder, s. 515(10) is read in light of s. 522 such that the burden of proof is shifted onto the accused to show cause why pre-trial detention is not necessary with respect to the grounds listed under s. 515(10).

As a result of the above factors, in my view, the fear that a situation may arise where the bail judge is unable to provide for the protection of the public without relying on the residual ground is without reasonable foundation.

. . . It should be remembered that while it may not be appropriate for the Court to address a constitutional question neither squarely raised nor fully argued by the parties to a case, generally the Court ought not to avoid such questions when they are clearly put before the Court with adequate argument on the issues involved by the parties, as is the case here.

In this regard, I agree with the following comments of Professor Don Stuart which, although in reference to the Ontario Court of Appeal decision in this case, apply equally well here:

> Surely if the issue is vagueness or overbreadth, then the whole section is to be considered, otherwise the consideration would be blinkered and distorted? On the narrow approach of the Ontario Court, the umbrella clause will only be reviewable where a bail judge expressly rests on it. Reasons given at show cause hearings are often enigmatic and the approach in *Hall* may well insulate the section from proper review. Courts are the guardians of the constitution and should not be bending over backwards to sidestep fully developed and presented Charter challenges. (D. Stuart, "Hall: The Ontario Court of Appeal Ducks Broader Issues in Upholding the New Public Interest Bail Provision", (2000) 35 C.R. (5th) 219, at p. 220).

(1) "Any Other Just Cause"

As discussed, in *Morales*, this Court held that a restriction on the s. 11(e) right to bail will be valid if it meets the following two conditions:

(1) bail is denied only in a narrow set of circumstances; and,

(2) the denial of bail is necessary to promote the proper functioning of the bail system, and is not undertaken for any purpose extraneous to the bail system.

. . .

(a) Narrow Set of Circumstances

In my view, it is impossible to hold that the words "any other just cause" provide for the denial of bail under a narrow set of circumstances as required by *Morales*. The phrase falls considerably more afoul of the vagueness doctrine than the old "public interest" ground because it fails even to specify a particular basis upon which bail may be denied.

When one looks at the plain language of the provision, it is self-evident that the deliberate open-endedness of the phrase "on any other just cause being shown and, without limiting the generality of the foregoing" must preclude a finding that the phrase only applies in a narrow set of circumstances. How can a set be considered narrow when it is explicitly left open with no criteria to govern or limit its exercise? I agree with the Chief Justice that the phrase "any other just cause" is not sufficiently narrow to meet constitutional standards imposed by *Pearson* and *Morales.*

. . .

(2) "Necessary to Maintain Confidence in the Administration of Justice"

(a) Narrow Set of Circumstances

. . .

At first blush, the fact that the provision includes a list of factors to be considered suggests that the confidence in the administration of justice ground is sufficiently precise; however, upon examination, it is difficult to see how the listed factors contribute to a determination of whether confidence in the administration of justice would be promoted by denying bail. As such, in my opinion, these factors serve as little more than a facade of precision.

The factors listed under s. 515(10)(c) are: "the apparent strength of the prosecution's case, the gravity of the nature of the offence, the circumstances surrounding its commission and the potential for a lengthy term of imprisonment". On their face, these factors seem relevant to a determination of whether bail should be granted or denied; however, one must assume here that the bail decision is not being made in order to ensure the accused attends court or to protect the public, otherwise the decision would be made under either s. 515(10)(a) or (b) which deal specifically with those grounds. . . .

I fail to see how confidence in the administration of justice is promoted by detaining an accused who is not at risk of absconding nor a threat to public safety. On the contrary, to detain an accused in such circumstances solely on the basis that the crime is a serious one and the Crown's case is strong would serve to undermine confidence in the administration of justice when one bears in mind the importance of the presumption of innocence to the proper administration of justice . . .

By enacting s. 515(10)(c), Parliament has essentially revived, albeit with more elaborate wording, the old "public interest" ground that this Court struck down in *Morales.* . . . In my view, s. 515(10)(c) invokes similarly vague notion of the public image of the criminal justice system, the only difference being that in s. 515(10)(c) the public image standard is expressed by the phrase "maintain confidence in the administration of justice" as opposed to the term "public interest".

Professor Trotter, one of the leading experts in this area, comes to a similar conclusion, *supra,* at pp. 145-46:

Section 515(10)(c) is more detailed and refined than its predecessor [the "public interest" ground]. However, it achieves the same objective—it permits the detention of an accused person based upon the anticipated reaction of the public to the decision, free of any concern about the accused person absconding or re-offending.

Given this underpinning in public perceptions, s. 515(10)(c) is ripe for misuse, allowing for irrational public fears to be elevated above the Charter rights of the accused. In the face of a highly publicized serious crime and a strong prima facie case, the importance of the presumption of innocence or the right to bail will not be at the forefront of the minds of most members of the public. Many individuals will instead accept the factors listed in the provision to be a proxy for the accused's guilt, and the release of the accused may very well provoke outrage among certain members of the community. However, this outrage cannot be used by the bail judge as a justification for denying bail, whether or not it is dressed up in administration of justice language. Indeed, the case at bar aptly illustrates this very pitfall.

Bolan J. said:

> This City, like any other small city, looks to its courts for protection. The feelings of the community have been expressed by certain witnesses. Some people are afraid, and some people have voiced their concerns. This is a factor which I will accordingly take into consideration when I assess the third ground.

With respect, the bail judge erred in considering the subjective fears of members of the public when he had already determined that the accused should not be denied bail for fear of flight or threat to the public. Although it may well be that the reaction of the public can play a role in determining the threat posed by the accused's release under the public safety ground, that is not what the bail judge decided in this case. It is the role of courts to guard the Charter rights of the accused when they conflict with irrational and subjective public views, even when sincerely held. The problem with s. 515(10)(c) is that, stripped to its essence, its very purpose is to allow these subjective fears to form the sole basis by which bail is denied. . . .

It does not further our pre-trial release scheme to allow irrational fears and inclinations to distort the proper application of bail requirements. No authority is needed for the proposition that ill-informed emotional impulses are extraneous to our system of bail.

. . .

[Iacobucci J. further held that the provision could not be saved under s. 1. It did not address a pressing and substantial concern and failed the proportionality tests. He then turned to the issue of remedy. He continued:]

. . .

VII. The Relationship Between the Courts and Legislatures

In *Vriend v. Alberta*, [1998] 1 S.C.R. 493, the interaction between the various branches of government was described as a dialogue, with the result, at para. 139, that

... each of the branches is made somewhat accountable to the other. The work of the legislature is reviewed by the courts and the work of the court in its decisions can be reacted to by the legislature in the passing of new legislation (or even overarching laws under s. 33 of the Charter). This dialogue between and accountability of each of the branches have the effect of enhancing the democratic process, not denying it.

A good example of how this process plays out is found in the cases of *R. v. O'Connor*, [1995] 4 S.C.R. 411, and *R. v. Mills*, [1999] 3 S.C.R. 668.... In my view, s. 515(10)(c) demonstrates how this constitutional dialogue can break down. Although Parliament has responded to this Court's decision in *Morales*, it has not done so with due regard for the constitutional standards set out in that case. On the contrary, Parliament has essentially revitalized the "public interest" ground struck down in that case. In my respectful view, by upholding the impugned provision, at least in part, my colleague has transformed dialogue into abdication. The mere fact that Parliament has responded to a constitutional decision of this Court is no reason to defer to that response where it does not demonstrate a proper recognition of the constitutional requirements imposed by that decision.

Finally, I emphasize that the role of this Court, and indeed of every court in our country, to staunchly uphold constitutional standards is of particular importance when the public mood is one which encourages increased punishment of those accused of criminal acts and where mounting pressure is placed on the liberty interest of these individuals. Courts must be bulwarks against the tides of public opinion that threaten to invade these cherished values. Although this may well cost courts popularity in some quarters, that can hardly justify a failure to uphold fundamental freedoms and liberty.

For arguments that s. 515(1)(c) was unconstitutional for reasons including but not limited to vagueness and overbreadth, see Louis Strezos, "Section 515(10)(c) of the Criminal Code: Resurrecting the Unconstitutional Denial of Bail", (1998) 11 C.R. (5th) 43. For critical comments on *Hall*, see annotations by Stuart and Quigley in (2002) 4 C.R. (6th) 1, 81 and H. Archibald Kaiser, "Hall: Erosion of Basic Principles in Bail and Beyond", (2002) 4 C.R. (6th) 241.

The grounds for detention have frequently been amended and now read as follows:

515(10) For the purposes of this section, the detention of an accused in custody is justified only on one or more of the following grounds:

(a) where the detention is necessary to ensure his or her attendance in court in order to be dealt with according to law;

(b) where the detention is necessary for the protection or safety of the public, including any victim of or witness to the offence, or any person under the age of 18 years, having regard to all the circumstances including any substantial likelihood that the accused will, if released from custody, commit a criminal offence or interfere with the administration of justice; and

(c) if the detention is necessary to maintain confidence in the administration of justice, having regard to all the circumstances, including

(i) the apparent strength of the prosecution's case,

(ii) the gravity of the offence,

(iii) the circumstances surrounding the commission of the offence, including whether a firearm was used, and

(iv) the fact that the accused is liable, on conviction, for a potentially lengthy term of imprisonment or, in the case of an offence that involves, or whose subject-matter is, a firearm, a minimum punishment of imprisonment for a term of three years or more.

A close consideration of the majority judgment in *Hall* suggested that the tertiary ground should be used sparingly given that

1.   McLachlin C.J. remarks that that there are "relatively rare cases where it can be properly invoked" (citing Hall J.A. of the B.C.C.A.) (para, 27) and that "the circumstances in which recourse to this ground for bail denial may not arise frequently"(para. 31);

2.   McLachlin C.J. accepts that the reasonable person making the assessment of the need to maintain public confidence must be properly informed about the philosophy of the legislative provisions, Charter values and the actual circumstances of the case (para. 41); and

3.   *Hall* was an especially brutal offence with evidence that the community were fearful about this particular case.

This view that the public confidence ground is to be used sparingly was over the next 13 years widely accepted by Courts of Appeal and many trial judges. However, it was rejected by the Supreme Court in *R. v. St-Cloud.*

R. v. ST-CLOUD
2015 SCC 27, [2015] 2 S.C.R. 328, 321 C.C.C. (3d) 307, 19 C.R. (7th) 223 (S.C.C.)

S was charged, along with two others, with aggravated assault of a bus driver. The attack was extremely violent, leaving the driver with serious long-term injuries. The Crown opposed interim release. A judge of the Court of Quebec found detention was justified for the protection or safety of the public under s. 515(10)(b) and to maintain public confidence in the administration of justice under s. 515(10)(c). Following the preliminary inquiry the accused applied for bail. A judge of the Court of Quebec found that the risk of re-offending had been reduced but that detention of S was still justified under s. 515(10)(c). S then applied under s. 520 of the Criminal Code for a review by a Superior Court judge. He determined that the detention was not necessary under s. 515(10)(c), which had to be used sparingly. The incident was repugnant, heinous and unjustifiable but not unexplainable. He ordered S's release. The Crown appealed.

The Supreme Court allowed the appeal and restored the detention order.

WAGNER J. (McLachlin C.J. and Abella, Rothstein, Moldaver, Karakatsanis, Wagner and Gascon JJ. Concurring):

(3) Principles That Must Guide the Analysis

(a) *Rejecting a Narrow Application of Section 515(10)(c) Cr.C.*

[39] It is true that some decisions reflect a strict application of s. 515(10)(c): see, e.g., *R. v. Thomson* (2004), 21 C.R. (6th) 209 (Ont. S.C.J.); *R. v. B. (A)* (2006), 204 C.C.C. (3d) 490 (Ont. S.C.J.); *R. v. Pichler*, 2009 ABPC 24; *R. v. Teemotee*, 2011 NUCJ 17. This approach has also been adopted by some appellate courts. For example, the British Columbia Court of Appeal and the Ontario Court of Appeal have stated that the use of s. 515(10)(c) is justified only in rare or exceptional circumstances: *R. v. Bhullar*, 2005 BCCA 409, at paras. 62 and 65; *R. v. Brotherston*, 2009 BCCA 431, 71 C.R. (6th) 81, at paras. 30 and 35; *R. v. LaFramboise* (2005), 203 C.C.C. (3d) 492 (Ont. C.A.), at para. 30. A variant of this prerequisite is that s. 515(10)(c) must be used "sparingly": *LaFramboise*, at para. 30; *R. v. D. (R.)*, 2010 ONCA 899, 273 C.C.C. (3d) 7, at paras. 51 53. The Saskatchewan Court of Appeal has also held that s. 515(10)(c) requires that there be "something more", something in addition to the four factors set out in it: *R. v. Blind* (1999), 139 C.C.C. (3d) 87 (Sask. C.A.), at para. 16. Although the latter case predated this Court's decision in *Hall*, this statement has been reiterated since *Hall*, including by the Ontario Court of Appeal: *LaFramboise*, at para. 38. In a judgment subsequent to *LaFramboise*, the Ontario Court of Appeal found instead that the words "something more" were simply a way to convey the need to use s. 515(10)(c) sparingly: *D. (R.)*, at para. 53. However, it expressed the view that the third ground for detention is not limited to the most heinous of offences and can be invoked even if the community has not experienced the same horror and fear as was the case in *Hall*.

[46] I am of the opinion that some courts have misinterpreted this Court's decision in *Hall*. First of all, the Court's comments must be viewed in the context of that case and analyzed in light of the case's very specific circumstances: the crime was an extremely horrific one. It was therefore natural for the Court to take this into account when applying s. 515(10) (c) *Cr.C.* The Court's description of the crime as horrific, heinous and unexplained was simply an observation, a description of the facts considered by the Court in its analysis of s. 515(10) (c) *Cr.C.* It cannot be read as imposing conditions or prerequisites.

[47] In my view, the question whether a crime is "unexplainable" or "unexplained" is not a criterion that should guide justices in their analysis under s. 515(10) (c). Apart from the fact that the provision itself does not even refer to such a criterion, I consider the concept ambiguous and confusing. What is meant by an "unexplainable" crime? Is it a crime against a random victim? A crime that could be committed only by a person who is not rational? An especially horrific crime?

[48] Moreover, many crimes may be "explainable" in one way or another; for example, it may be that the assailant was provoked by the victim or that he or she had a mental illness or was intoxicated. From this perspective, the "unexplainable" crime criterion is of little assistance.

[49] The application of a criterion based on the notion of an "unexplainable" crime could also lead to undesirable conclusions. Crimes that are truly heinous and horrific might not satisfy it. Such a criterion could therefore give the public the impression that justices are "justifying" certain crimes, that is, crimes that are "explainable".... As much as possible, it would also be wise for justices hearing applications for release to avoid attaching such a label to the circumstances of the alleged crimes that come before them so as not to give the public the impression that they are "justifying" them.

[50] Furthermore, I agree with the appellant that detention may be justified only in rare cases, but that this is simply a consequence of the application of s. 515(10) (c) and not a precondition to its application, a criterion a court must consider in its analysis or the purpose of the provision.

[51] This interpretation is consistent with the following comment made by this Court in *Hall*:

> While the circumstances in which recourse to this ground for bail denial may not arise frequently, when they do it is essential that a means of denying bail be available. [Emphasis added; para. 31.]

[52] I am of the view that a "rareness" of circumstances criterion would be vague and unmanageable in practice. How would such a criterion be assessed? Should justices consider how many cases have been heard (in their jurisdictions, in Canada, in the last year, etc.) and, at the same time, ensure that cases of detention based on s. 515(10) (c) will remain "rare" if they order detention in the cases before them? Should a justice review the cases in which detention has been ordered and determine whether the facts of the case before him or her are the same (or nearly the same) as the facts of those cases? In any event, it seems to me that a "rareness" of circumstances criterion would prompt justices to engage in a comparative exercise and thus to move away from the careful examination of the circumstances of individual cases that the situation requires. In my opinion, a comparative approach such as this could potentially undermine the public's confidence in the administration of justice.

[53] Moreover, the appellant correctly points out that s. 515(10) (c) *Cr.C.* is worded clearly and that it does not require exceptional or rare circumstances.

[54] In conclusion, the application of s. 515(10) (c) is not limited to exceptional circumstances, to "unexplainable" crimes or to certain types of crimes such as murder. The Crown can rely on s. 515(10) (c) for any type of crime, but it must prove — except in the cases provided for in s. 515(6) — that the detention of the accused is justified to maintain confidence in the administration of justice.

(b) *Circumstances Set Out in Section 515(10) (c) Cr.C.*

[55] Section 515(10) (c) expressly refers to four circumstances that must be considered by a justice in determining whether the detention of an accused is

necessary to maintain confidence in the administration of justice. The justice must assess each of these circumstances — or factors — and consider their combined effect. This is a balancing exercise that will enable the justice to decide whether detention is justified.

[56] It must be kept in mind that, at this stage of criminal proceedings, the accused is still presumed innocent regardless of the gravity of the offence, the strength of the prosecution's case or the possibility of a lengthy term of imprisonment.

(i) Apparent Strength of the Prosecution's Case

[57] An interim release hearing is a summary proceeding in which more flexible rules of evidence apply. As a result, some of the evidence admitted at this hearing may later be excluded at trial. As Justice Trotter notes, it may be difficult to assess the strength of the prosecution's case at such a hearing: "The expeditious and sometimes informal nature of a bail hearing may reflect an unrealistically strong case for the Crown" (p. 3 7).

[58] Despite these difficulties inherent in the release process, the justice must determine the apparent strength of the prosecution's case. On the one hand, the prosecutor is not required to prove beyond a reasonable doubt that the accused committed the offence, and the justice must be careful not to play the role of trial judge or jury: matters such as the credibility of witnesses and the reliability of scientific evidence must be analyzed at trial, not at the release hearing. However, the justice who presides at that hearing must consider the quality of the evidence tendered by the prosecutor in order to determine the weight to be given to this factor in his or her balancing exercise. For example, physical evidence may be more reliable than a mere statement made by a witness, and circumstantial evidence may be less reliable than direct evidence. The existence of ample evidence may also reinforce the apparent strength of the case.

[59] On the other hand, the justice must also consider any defence raised by the accused. Rather than raising a defence at the initial hearing, the latter will most likely not do so before the release hearing held upon completion of the preliminary inquiry, and may not even raise one before trial. If the accused does raise a defence, however, this becomes one of the factors the justice must assess, and if there appears to be some basis for the defence, the justice must take this into account in analyzing the apparent strength of the prosecution's case. ...

(ii) Gravity of the Offence

[60] For the purposes of s. 515(10) (c), what the justice must determine is the "objective" gravity of the offence in comparison with the other offences in the *Criminal Code*. This is assessed on the basis of the maximum sentence — and the minimum sentence, if any — provided for in the *Criminal Code* for the offence.

(iii) Circumstances Surrounding the Commission of the Offence, Including Whether a Firearm Was Used

[61] Without drawing up an exhaustive list of possible circumstances surrounding the commission of the offence that might be relevant under s. 515(10) (c), I will mention the following: the fact that the offence is a violent, heinous or hateful one, that it was committed in a context involving domestic violence, a criminal gang or a terrorist organization, or that the victim was a vulnerable person (for example, a child, an elderly person or a person with a disability). If the offence was committed by several people, the extent to which the accused participated in it may be relevant. The aggravating or mitigating factors that are considered by courts for sentencing purposes can also be taken into account.

(iv) Fact That the Accused Is Liable for a Potentially Lengthy Term of Imprisonment

[62] The fourth circumstance set out in s. 515(10) (c) is "the fact that the accused is liable, on conviction, for a potentially lengthy term of imprisonment or, in the case of an offence that involves, or whose subject matter is, a firearm, a minimum punishment of imprisonment for a term of three years or more".

[63] Although it is not desirable, for the purposes of s. 515(10) (c) *Cr.C.*, to establish a strict rule regarding the number of years that constitutes a "lengthy term of imprisonment", some guidance is nonetheless required for the exercise to be undertaken by justices in this regard.

[64] First of all, since I have found that no crime is exempt from the possible application of s. 515(10) (c) *Cr.C.*, it is self evident that the words "lengthy term of imprisonment" do not refer only to a life sentence.

[65] Moreover, to determine, on a case by case basis, whether the accused is actually liable for a potentially "lengthy term of imprisonment", the justice must consider all the circumstances of the case known at the time of the hearing, as well as the principles for tailoring the applicable sentence. But this does not mean that the justice would be justified in embarking on a complex exercise to calculate the sentence the accused might receive: it must be borne in mind that interim release occurs at the beginning of the criminal process and that the justice must avoid acting as a substitute for the trial judge. That being said, there will be cases in which a claim of mitigating or aggravating circumstances appears to have sufficient merit for it to be open to the justice to consider it in determining whether the accused is liable for a potentially "lengthy term of imprisonment". As far as possible, therefore, this fourth circumstance is assessed *subjectively*, unlike the second circumstance — the gravity of the offence — which is assessed *objectively*.

(c) *The Listed Circumstances Are Not Exhaustive*

[68] Section 515(10) (c) could not be worded more clearly: it refers to "all the circumstances, including . . . ." In my opinion, Parliament would have worded this provision differently (although I will not comment on the validity of such a wording) if it had intended a detention order to be automatic where

the four listed circumstances weigh in favour of such an order. In fact, Parliament intended the opposite. As the Chief Justice stated in Hall, a justice dealing with an application for detention based on s. 515(10) (c) must consider all the relevant circumstances, but must *focus particularly on the factors Parliament has specified*: para. 41. The automatic detention argument also seems to be inconsistent with the following statement by the Chief Justice, at para. 41:

> At the end of the day, the judge can <u>only</u> deny bail <u>if satisfied that in view of these factors and related circumstances</u>, a reasonable member of the community would be satisfied that denial is necessary to maintain confidence in the administration of justice. [Emphasis added.]

[69] Moreover, the automatic detention argument disregards the fact that the test to be met under s. 515(10) (c) is whether the detention of the accused is necessary to maintain confidence in the administration of justice. The four listed circumstances are simply the main factors to be balanced by the justice, together with any other relevant factors, in determining whether, in the case before him or her, detention is necessary in order to achieve the purpose of maintaining confidence in the administration of justice in the country. This is the provision's purpose. Although the justice must consider all the circumstances of the case and engage in a balancing exercise, this is the ultimate question the justice must answer, and it must therefore guide him or her in making a determination. The argument that detention must automatically be ordered if the review of the four circumstances favours that result is incompatible with the balancing exercise required by s. 515(10) (c) and with the purpose of that exercise.

[70] Finally, it is important not to overlook the fact that, in Canadian law, the release of accused persons is the cardinal rule and detention, the exception: *Morales*, at p. 728. To automatically order detention would be contrary to the "basic entitlement to be granted reasonable bail unless there is just cause to do otherwise" that is guaranteed in s. 11 (e) of the *Charter: Pearson*, at p. 691. This entitlement rests in turn on the cornerstone of Canadian criminal law, namely the presumption of innocence that is guaranteed by s. 11 (d) of the *Charter* (*Hall*, at para. 13). These fundamental rights require the justice to ensure that interim detention is truly justified having regard to all the relevant circumstances of the case.

[71] Although I will not set out an exhaustive list of the circumstances relevant to the analysis required by s. 515(10) (c) *Cr.C.*, I think it will be helpful to give a few examples. Section 515(10) (c)(iii) refers to the "circumstances surrounding the commission of the offence". I would add that the personal circumstances of the accused (age, criminal record, physical or mental condition, membership in a criminal organization, etc.) may also be relevant. The justice might also consider the status of the victim and the impact on society of a crime committed against that person. In some cases, he or she might also take account of the fact that the trial of the accused will be held at a much later date.

(d) *Meaning of "Public"*

[72] I should point out that although the French version of s. 515(10) (c) refers to "*la confiance du public*" (public confidence) — "*sa détention est nécessaire pour ne pas miner la confiance du public envers l'administration de la justice, compte tenu de toutes les circonstances, notamment les suivantes . . .*" — the word "public" does not actually appear in the provision's English version. However, this Court has confirmed that detention under this provision is based on the need to maintain *public* confidence in the administration of justice: *Hall*, at para. 41. This means that the justice's balancing of all the circumstances under s. 515(10) (c) must always be guided by the perspective of the "public".

. . .

[74] In *Hall*, this Court explained that the "public" in question consists of reasonable members of the community who are properly informed about "the philosophy of the legislative provisions, *Charter* values and the actual circumstances of the case": para. 41, quoting *R. v. Nguyen* (1997), 119 C.C.C. (3d) 269 (B.C.C.A.), at para. 18.

. . .

[77] .[.[The] ...word "public" used in the context of the new s. 515(10) (c) does not mean Canadians who tend to react impulsively. This being said, although it is true that the public in question consists of reasonable, well informed persons, and not overly emotional members of the community, it seems to me that some of the decisions have rendered the word "public" meaningless in this context. Parliament made an express choice by using the word "*public*" in the French version of s. 515(10) (c) in requiring that the courts take confidence in the administration of justice into account in deciding whether an accused should be detained pending trial. It referred not to legal experts or judges, but to the "public". Meaning must therefore be given to this legislative choice. Public confidence cannot be equated with the confidence of legal experts in the administration of justice. The Canadian public — even its most knowledgeable members — cannot be expected to have the same level of legal knowledge as judges or lawyers. That would distort the meaning of the word "public". It would also disregard the purpose of this provision, which is to maintain public confidence in the administration of justice.

[78] I note that this position is similar to the one taken by this Court concerning s. 24(2) of the *Charter*, which provides for the exclusion of evidence obtained in violation of the *Charter* if "the admission of it in the proceedings would bring the administration of justice into disrepute". In *R. v. Collins*, [1987] 1 S.C.R. 265, Lamer J., writing for the majority, put the relevant question in figurative terms: "Would the admission of the evidence bring the administration of justice into disrepute in the eyes of the reasonable man, dispassionate and fully apprised of the circumstances of the case?" (p. 282, quoting Y. M. Morissette, "The Exclusion of Evidence under the *Canadian Charter of Rights and Freedoms*: What To Do and What Not To Do" (1984), 29 *McGill L.J.* 521, at p. 538). Lamer J. stated that "[t]he reasonable person is usually the average person in the community, but only when that community's

current mood is reasonable": *Collins*, at p. 282. He explained that the reasonable person test "serves as a reminder to each individual judge that his discretion is grounded in community values, and, in particular, long term community values. He should not render a decision that would be unacceptable to the community when that community is not being wrought with passion or otherwise under passing stress due to current events": *ibid.*, at pp. 282 83; see also *R. v. Burlingham*, [1995] 2 S.C.R. 206, at para. 142.

[79] Thus, a reasonable member of the public is familiar with the basics of the rule of law in our country and with the fundamental values of our criminal law, including those that are protected by the *Charter*. Such a person is undoubtedly aware of the importance of the presumption of innocence and the right to liberty in our society and knows that these are fundamental rights guaranteed by our Constitution. He or she also expects that someone charged with a crime will be tried within a reasonable period of time, and is aware of the adage that "justice delayed is justice denied": *R. v. Trout*, 2006 MBCA 96, 205 Man. R. (2d) 277, at para. 15. Finally, a reasonable member of the public knows that a criminal offence requires proof of culpable intent (*mens rea*) and that the purpose of certain defences is to show the absence of such intent. A well known example of this type of defence is the mental disorder defence. The person contemplated by s. 515(10) (c) *Cr.C.* therefore understands that such a defence, once established, will enable an accused to avoid criminal responsibility. However, it would be going too far to expect the person in question to master all the subtleties of complex defences, especially where there is overwhelming evidence of the crime, the circumstances of the crime are heinous and the accused admits committing it.

[80] In short, the person in question in s. 515(10) (c) *Cr.C.* is a thoughtful person, not one who is prone to emotional reactions, whose knowledge of the circumstances of a case is inaccurate or who disagrees with our society's fundamental values. But he or she is not a legal expert familiar with all the basic principles of the criminal justice system, the elements of criminal offences or the subtleties of criminal intent and of the defences that are available to accused persons.

[81] It is of course not easy for judges to strike an appropriate balance between the unrealistic expectations they might have for the public on the one hand, and the need to refuse to yield to public reactions driven solely by emotion on the other. This exercise may be particularly difficult in this era characterized by the multiplication and diversification of information sources, access to 24 hour news reports and the advent of social media.

[82] Canadians may in fact think they are very well informed, but that is unfortunately not always the case. Moreover, people can also make their reactions known much more quickly, more effectively and on a wider scale than in the past, in particular through the social media mentioned above, which are conducive to chain reactions. The courts must therefore be careful not to yield to purely emotional public reactions or reactions that may be based on inadequate knowledge of the real circumstances of a case.

[83] However, the courts must also be sensitive to the perceptions of people who are reasonable and well informed. This enables the courts to act

both as watchdogs against mob justice and as guardians of public confidence in our justice system. It would therefore be dangerous, inappropriate and wrong for judges to base their decisions on media reports that are in no way representative of a well informed public. Indeed, the Quebec Court of Appeal recognized this risk in its recent decision in *R. v. Turcotte*, 2014 QCCA 2190:

> [TRANSLATION] The press clippings show how risky it is to rely on this mode of proof. They contain several different opinions that vary in the degree to which they are balanced, objective, moderate or superficial. Many of them contain inaccurate facts or do not mention the essential facts. Most of them say nothing about the legal principles that must be applied in making release decisions. Certain opinions stir up anger and distort the debate. Few accurately report the facts and correctly state the applicable principles. On the whole, it must be acknowledged that they do not satisfy the reasonable person test defined in the case law. [para. 68 (CanLII)]

[84] Having said this, I wish to point out that this does not mean the courts must automatically disregard evidence that comes from the news media. It must be recognized that the media are part of life in society and that they reflect the opinions of certain segments of the Canadian public. In *Canadian Broadcasting Corporation v. New Brunswick (Attorney General)*, [1991] 3 S.C.R. 459, at p. 475, this Court noted: "The media have a vitally important role to play in a democratic society. It is the media that, by gathering and disseminating news, enable members of our society to make an informed assessment of the issues which may significantly affect their lives and well being." Such opinion evidence can therefore be considered by the courts when it is admissible and relevant. This will be the case where it corresponds to the opinion of the reasonable person I described above.

. . .

[86] In short, there is not just one way to undermine public confidence in the administration of justice. It may be undermined not only if a justice declines to order the interim detention of an accused in circumstances that justify detention, but also if a justice orders detention where such a result is not justified.

(4) Conclusion on the Application of Section 515(10) (c) Cr.C.

[87] I would summarize the essential principles that must guide justices in applying s. 515(10) (c) *Cr.C.* as follows:

- Section 515(10) (c) *Cr.C.* does not create a residual ground for detention that applies only where the first two grounds for detention ((a) and (b)) are not satisfied. It is a distinct ground that itself provides a basis for ordering the pre trial detention of an accused.
- Section 515(10) (c) *Cr.C.* must not be interpreted narrowly (or applied sparingly) and should not be applied only in rare cases or exceptional circumstances or only to certain types of crimes.
- The four circumstances listed in s. 515(10) (c) *Cr.C.* are not exhaustive.
- A court must not order detention automatically even where the four listed circumstances support such a result.

- The court must instead consider all the circumstances of each case, paying particular attention to the four listed circumstances.
- The question whether a crime is "unexplainable" or "unexplained" is not a criterion that should guide the analysis.
- No single circumstance is determinative. The justice must consider the combined effect of all the circumstances of each case to determine whether detention is justified.
- This involves balancing all the relevant circumstances. At the end of this balancing exercise, the ultimate question to be asked by the court is whether detention is necessary to maintain confidence in the administration of justice. This is the test to be met under s. 515(10) (c).
- To answer this question, the court must adopt the perspective of the "public", that is, the perspective of a reasonable person who is properly informed about the philosophy of the legislative provisions, *Charter* values and the actual circumstances of the case. However, this person is not a legal expert and is not able to appreciate the subtleties of the various defences that are available to the accused.
- This reasonable person's confidence in the administration of justice may be undermined not only if a court declines to order detention where detention is justified having regard to the circumstances of the case, but also if it orders detention where detention is not justified.

[88] In conclusion, if the crime is serious or very violent, if there is overwhelming evidence against the accused and if the victim or victims were vulnerable, pre trial detention will usually be ordered.

Justice Wagner then considered the power of review of detention orders. The Court held that on the basis of the wording of ss. 520 and 521 of the Criminal Code, and comparison with other review proceedings and with sentence appeals, these sections do not confer an open ended discretion on the reviewing judge to vary the initial decision concerning detention or release. They do not establish a *de novo* proceeding but a hybrid remedy. Exercising the power of review will be appropriate in only three situations: (1) where there is admissible new evidence if that evidence shows a material and relevant change in the circumstances of the case; (2) where the impugned decision contains an error of law; or (3) where the decision is clearly inappropriate. The reviewing judge, therefore, does not have the power to interfere with the initial decision simply because he or she would have weighed the relevant factors differently.

In this case, the Supreme Court held that the Superior Court judge erred in stating that the public confidence ground must be interpreted narrowly and applied only in rare cases, and in placing weight on the factor that the offence was explainable. He intervened even though there was no basis for a review, given that there was no change in circumstances and no error of law, and that the initial decision was not clearly inappropriate. When all the relevant circumstances are weighed as required by s. 515(10)(c), the detention of S was necessary to maintain confidence in the administration of justice.

Do you agree with the following criticism of the ruling in *St-Cloud*?

Don Stuart, "*St-Cloud*: Widening the Public Confidence Ground to Deny Bail Will Worsen Deplorable Detention Realities"
(2015) 19 C.R. (7th) 337

The Supreme Court is unanimous in deciding that the public confidence ground to refuse bail should not be used rarely or sparingly, as so many Courts of Appeal and bail judges have determined over the past 10 years since *Hall*. The Court furthermore crafts a more complex and narrower approach to bail review.

In my view this Supreme Court ruling is uncharacteristically law and order in its orientation to one of the most serious issues facing the criminal justice system — that of burgeoning pre-trial detention in poor conditions at a time when crime rates are falling. There seems little point in advancing serious criticism of a unanimous Supreme Court decision but this decision poses challenges for the future that can only be understood and faced by first considering what is wrong with the ruling. In my view there are at least four serious flaws.

1. The Court completely ignored disturbing data about the current realities of pre-trial detention presented by intervenors.

An intervenor, The Canadian Civil Liberties Association, drew the Court's attention to its findings in its report "Set up to Fail": Bail and the Revolving Door of Pre-trial Detention" (July, 2014):

Canada's Jails: The Rising pre-trial detention population

Provincial and territorial jails hold individuals detained before their trial and anyone sentenced to a custodial sentence under two years; federal prisons incarcerate those who are convicted and sentenced to two or more years in custody.

On an average day in 2012/2013, there were 25,208 people behind bars of provincial and territorial jails; 54.5% of these people were in a pre-trial custody, legally innocent, awaiting trial or determination of bail.

Over the past 30 years, the pre-trial detention rate has tripled; 2005 was the first time Canada's provincial and territorial jails held more people who were legally innocent than they did sentenced offenders.

There are significant differences between different provinces and territories. Manitoba has the highest proportion of pre-trial incarceration: 66% of people incarcerated in that province are in pre-trial detention. Other provinces with high percentages of pre-trial detention include Alberta (61%), Yukon (60%) and Ontario (60%). Prince Edward Island has the lowest ratio of pre-trial to sentenced population; 18% of its jailed population is in pre-trial custody.

Two-thirds of those in pre-trial detention are charged with non-violent offences. Violation of a previous bail condition is the most common reason for people to be held for a bail appearance, accounting for just over 1 in 10 cases.

In *St-Cloud* the Supreme Court did not even mention this Report or the argument that deciding that the public confidence ground should not be used sparingly would make these realities worse. Compare the response of Justice O'Neill of the Ontario Superior Court in *R. v. McCormack*, December 17, 2014, in the course of a bail review in Parry Sound:

> In my view, those statistics are shocking, and contrary to the values underlying this country's Constitution. Countless appellate court authorities, the *Morales* decision included, speak to the spirit and intent of Canada's bail laws and the underlying rationale behind s. 515(10) of the *Criminal Code*. [para. 22]

The CCLA Report also documented that in 2011/2012 Aboriginal Canadians made up 25% of admissions to remand, with the figure rising to 37% for Aboriginal women. There are other sources the Supreme Court ought to have considered. The John Howard Society of Canada Reasonable Bail (2013) documented that a disproportionate number of individuals in pre-trial detention in Ontario have substance abuse and/or mental health issues. The Report of the Commission on Systemic Racism in the Ontario Criminal Justice System (1995) found that the bail denial rate for drug trafficking charges was 27 times higher for black accused. In *R. v. Prince* (2006), 41 C.R. (6th) 389 (Ont. C.J.) Justice Reinhardt found conditions in the Don Jail in Toronto did not meet UN Standard Minimum Rules for the Treatment of Prisoners. In a speech Justice Rosenberg "The Attorney General and the Administration of Justice" (2009), 39 Queen's L.J. 813 at 856-859 asserted that such conditions are inconsistent with Charter Rights and Canada's obligations under the International Covenant on Civil and Political Rights.

The troubling context revealed in these and other sources was ignored by the Supreme Court in its pre-occupation with statutory interpretation of our complex Criminal Code provisions and in asserting and re-interpreting the 5-4 majority precedent of *Hall*. Justice Wagner sees his view that the public confidence ground should not be used sparingly as consistent with the remark of McLachlin C.J in *Hall* that "the circumstances in which recourse to this ground may not arise frequently" (quoted at para 51) but he avoids referring to her earlier remark in Hall (para. 27) that there are "relatively rare cases where it can be properly invoked" — citing Hall J.A. of the B.C.C.A.

2. The Court plays only lip service to the presumption of innocence under s.11(d) and the Charter right not to be deprived of bail without just cause under s.11(e).

> Justice Wagner refers to these important Charter standards and notes
> the fact that in Canadian law, the release of accused persons is the cardinal rule and detention, the exception [par. 70]

Yet at the end of his above-quoted summary of a balancing approach to decide on the public confidence ground, which is likely to be widely relied on, Justice Wagner boils the approach down to

> In conclusion, if the crime is serious or very violent, if there is overwhelming evidence against the accused and if the victim or victims were vulnerable, pre trial detention will usually be ordered. [para 88]

He also offers a list of circumstances surrounding the commission of the offence where the public confidence ground may be relied on:

> Those that might be relevant under s. 515(10) (c) include the following: the fact that the offence is a violent, heinous or hateful one, that it was committed in a context involving domestic violence, a criminal gang or a terrorist organization, or that the victim was a vulnerable person. If the offence was committed by several people, the extent to which the accused participated in it may be relevant. The aggravating or mitigating factors that are considered by courts for sentencing purposes can also be taken into account.[para 61]

The danger here is that other judges may well rely on their own perception of what crimes are serious such as break and enter of a dwelling house, hard drugs or any drugs or any form of sexual assault or even theft from an employer. The Supreme Court has substantially expanded the potential for detention where there is no flight risk or present danger to the public.

Although the expanding thrust of *St Cloud* is clear there is an inconsistent point in the judgment where Justice Wagner indicates that even if the four statutory factors support detention the court must not order detention automatically [para. 69]. Does that signify at least some restraint?

As for the meaning of "public" confidence Justice Wagner agrees with earlier pronouncements of Chief Justice Lamer in *R. v. Collins*, [1987] 1 S.C.R. 265, 33 C.C.C. (3d) 1, 56 C.R. (3d) 193 (S.C.C.) and Justice Baudoin in *R. c. Lamothe* (1990), 58 C.C.C. (3d) 530, 77 C.R. (3d) 236 (C.A. Que.) that the public must be informed about Charter rights and the criminal justice system and courts must consider their perspectives when their mood is reasonable and not overly emotional. But then he is quick to say that public opinion is not that of legal experts. Neither of those two earlier jurists made that qualification. Chief Justice Lamer also spoke in *Collins* of the Charter being used to protect the minority against the tyranny of the majority.

3. The Court ignores the reality of most first instance bail hearings

In bail courts, particularly in large cities, many arrestees are unrepresented. It is often left to overworked duty counsel, Crown Attorneys and justices of the peace to scramble to get through the docket and reduce overcrowding in grim holding cells to a more manageably dimension. There is little evidence presented other than Crowns reading out hastily prepared police notes The arresting officer is seldom there for cross-examination.   Such hearings are necessarily short.

The Supreme Court sets up a detailed consideration of the four criteria and furthermore emphasises they are not exclusive. Even if there is a full hearing with evidence led, which is much more likely in bail hearings before a Superior Court judge (who have exclusive jurisdiction in murder cases), the confidence ground will now be much more difficult to apply. In contrast the flight risk and public safety ground are more linear and more amenable to quick adjudication. For at least the past decade at the front line the public confidence ground has usually been reserved for rare cases. It is not "some" cases that interpreted *Hall* in this way but the vast majority of Courts of

Appeal justices and many trial judges. It is hard to find a recent interpretation that even hints at the views expressed on the public confidence ground by the Supreme Court. If *St-Cloud* is followed to the letter, bail hearings will necessarily take longer, delaying other bail hearings and in the end result many more accused will be detained.

4. The review process the Supreme Court puts in place is curiously complex and narrower.

In the case of bail reviews before judges mechanically apply the Supreme Court's more restrictive approach to receiving new evidence for a review they need to take into account the realities of a first bail denial when evidence is often not led. The Supreme Court does recognise the need for flexibility in applying the *Palmer* criteria. The other grounds of errors of law and "clearly inappropriate" also allow more scope for review.

In *McCormack* Justice O'Neill decided that he should undertake a review not limited, as others judges had ruled, to where the trial had been delayed. A drug addict charged with a number of very serious charges was released to live with her parents as sureties. Hopefully such a review will not now be pre-empted.

What of the future?

Hopefully restraint will still be exercised by front line Crown Attorneys, justices of the peace and judges at the first level or on a review. If not the detention rate will grow and an already appalling situation will get worse. One of the major changes of the Bail Reform Act in 1972 which aimed to reduce documented high pre-trial detention rates in Toronto was to place the onus of justification on the Crown Attorney. Although statutory reversals of that onus have been a growth industry in the past years in most cases that onus is still on the Crown. Hopefully Crown Attorneys and bail judges will take their roles seriously and not advance or give in to glib and expedient public confidence arguments that could be spawned by *St-Cloud*.

Justices of the peace and judges who have expressed unease about the public confidence ground will likely still resist such arguments for detention. Others will, however, undoubtedly be more receptive. The reality is that lawyers and judges in the front lines typically care a lot about criminal justice and attitudes and beliefs will differ. Opening up the public confidence ground will undoubtedly lead to further disparities in how bail actually operates and likely make troubling realities worse.

See too criminologist David MacAlister, "*St-Cloud*: Expanding Tertiary Grounds for Denying Judicial Interim release' (2015), 19 C.R. (7th) 344, who documents ever-expanding remand rates across the country and also that a ground to deny bail similar to our public confidence ground is not found in the bail laws of the United Kingdom, Australia, New Zealand or the United States. See too Micah Rankin, "*R. v. St-Cloud*: Searching for a Silver Lining" (2015), 19 C.R. (7th) 359.

3. Onus

While *Morales* and *Hall, supra*, were constitutional cases, the framework for the constitutional analysis was established in *Pearson. Pearson* involved a consideration of so-called "reverse-onus" provisions. Recall that placing the onus on the Crown to justify the detention of the accused person was one of the cornerstones of the Bail Reform Act. In 1976, after only four years with the new provisions, Parliament amended the legislation by creating a number of situations where the onus would be placed on the accused person to justify release. The reverse-onus provisions are now found in s. 515(6) and s. 522 of the Criminal Code. Originally they were restricted to accused charged with murder (s. 522), accused charged with an indictable offence while already on release on an indictable offence (s. 515(6)(a)), an accused not ordinarily resident in Canada (s. 515(6)(b)), an accused charged with an offence under ss. 145(2) to (5) (s. 515(6)(c)), and an accused charged with trafficking drugs under the Narcotic Control Act.

In *Pearson*, the Court confronted the constitutionality of s. 515(6)(d) as it then read. In *Morales*, the Court simultaneously considered the reverse-onus provision in s. 515(6)(a). The Court upheld both provisions as constitutional.

R. v. PEARSON
[1992] 3 S.C.R. 665, 17 C.R. (4th) 1, 77 C.C.C. (3d) 124 (S.C.C.)

A 5-2 majority held that s. 515(6)(*d*) did not violate ss. 7, 9, 11(*d*) or 11(*e*) of the Charter.

LAMER C.J.C. (Sopinka and Iacobucci JJ. concurring):—

. . .

Although s. 515(6)(d) constitutes a denial of bail in certain circumstances, in my opinion there is just cause for this denial of bail. There are two reasons for my conclusion. First, bail is denied only in a narrow set of circumstances. Second, the denial of bail is necessary to promote the proper functioning of the bail system and is not undertaken for any purpose extraneous to the bail system. The effect of s. 515(6)(d) is to establish a set of special bail rules in circumstances where the normal bail process is incapable of functioning properly. In my view, there is just cause for these special rules.

The circumstances in which bail is denied under s. 515(6)(d) are very narrow. Section 515(6)(d) applies only to a very small number of offences, all of which involve the distribution of narcotics. Furthermore, s. 515(6)(d) does not deny bail for all persons who are charged with these offences, but rather denies bail only when these persons are unable to demonstrate that detention is not justified having regard to the specified primary or secondary grounds. The narrow scope of the denial of bail under s. 515(6)(d) is essential to its validity under s. 11(e). The basic entitlement of s. 11(e) cannot be denied in a broad or sweeping exception.

The offences which are included under s. 515(6)(d) have specific characteristics which justify differential treatment in the bail process.

. . .

The unique characteristics of the offences subject to s. 515(6)(d) suggest that those offences are committed in a very different context than most other crimes. Most offences are not committed systematically. By contrast, trafficking in narcotics occurs systematically, usually within a highly sophisticated commercial setting. It is often a business and a way of life. It is highly lucrative, creating huge incentives for an offender to continue criminal behaviour even after arrest and release on bail. In these circumstances, the normal process of arrest and bail will normally not be effective in bringing an end to criminal behaviour. Special bail rules are required in order to establish a bail system which maintains the accused's right to pre-trial release while discouraging continuing criminal activity.

Another specific feature of the offences subject to s. 515(6)(d) is that there is a marked danger that an accused charged with these offences will abscond rather than appear for trial.

. . .

In the Court of Appeal, Proulx J.A. expressed concern about the scope of s. 515(6)(d). He felt that it is inequitable to treat a person who distributes a few joints of marijuana in the same manner as a person running a sophisticated network to traffic cocaine. Proulx J.A.'s concerns are legitimate. The scope of the *Narcotic Control Act* is very broad.

. . .

Although I believe that Proulx J.A.'s concerns about the scope of s. 515(6)(d) are legitimate, in my view they do not lead to a conclusion that s. 515(6)(d) violates s. 11(e). The "small fry" and "generous smoker" will normally have no difficulty justifying their release and obtaining bail.

. . .

The special bail rules in s. 515(6)(d) do not have any purpose extraneous to the bail system, but rather merely establish an effective bail system for specific offences for which the normal bail system would allow continuing criminal behaviour and an intolerable risk of absconding. The scope of these special rules is narrow and carefully tailored to achieve a properly functioning bail system. I therefore conclude that there is just cause for s. 515(6)(d) to depart from the basic entitlement of s. 11(e) and to deny bail in certain circumstances. Accordingly, I conclude that s. 515(6)(d) does not violate s. 11(e).

GONTHIER J. (concurring) (L'Heureux-Dubé J. concurring):—I am in agreement with the reasons of the Chief Justice, subject however to my reasons in the case of *R. v. Morales* (November 19, 1992), Doc. 22404 (S.C.C.) [now reported at (1992), 17 C.R. (4th) 74], in which I conclude that the criterion of public interest in s. 515(10)(b) of the *Criminal Code*, R.S.C. 1985, c. C-46, is not unconstitutional.

. . .

McLACHLIN J. (dissenting in part):—

. . .

As the Chief Justice acknowledges, the section is very broad. First, it applies to everyone who commits the specified offences. Second, the offences are very broad. They catch anyone who "traffics" in a drug, however small the quantity or whatever the circumstances. And "trafficking" itself is a very broad concept. As a result, s. 515(6)(d) catches not only large-scale drug dealers, but the friend who shares a joint of marijuana at a party or gives it to a friend for safekeeping. All trafficking is repugnant and hence criminally punishable. But when the issue is denial of bail, the different dangers associated with the different types of trafficking, may require different treatment.

I agree with my colleague that there may be "just cause" for denying bail to persons charged with serious, large-scale or commercial trafficking. With the greatest respect, however, it seems to me that the reasons he gives for this conclusion do not apply to other traffickers. The reasons he gives are two. First, the trafficker is said to be more likely than persons charged with other offences to continue his or her criminal behaviour in the interval before trial if he or she is released. Second, the trafficker is said to be more likely than persons charged with other offences to abscond and fail to appear at trial.

These distinctions apply only to one category of persons caught by s. 515(6)(d) — the organized commercial trafficker. Let us look first at the argument that the trafficker is more likely than those charged with other offences to continue criminal activity while awaiting trial. My colleague supports this conclusion with the following observations (at p. 30 [p. 62, ante]):

> Most offences are not committed systematically. By contrast, trafficking innarcotics occurs systematically, usually within a highly sophisticated commercial setting. . . . It is highly lucrative, creating huge incentives for an offender to continue criminal behaviour even after arrest and release on bail.

These comments are applicable to a person involved in organized commercial drug trafficking. They do not apply to others. Much trafficking has nothing to do with profit or making money. Profit is not a required element of the offence: see *R. v. Drysdelle* (1978), 22 N.B.R. (2d) 86, 39 A.P.R. 86, 41 C.C.C. (2d) 238 (C.A.). Nor is promotion of future distribution required: see *R. v. Larson*, 18 C.R.N.S. 149, [1972] 2 W.W.R. 705, 6 C.C.C. (2d) 145 (B.C. C.A.). The amounts involved may be minuscule; no money need change hands. In short, the "small- time" trafficker may not be motivated by money or profit, nor be a participant in a "highly sophisticated commercial setting". The argument advanced by my colleague does not apply to him or her.

The second argument is that there is a "marked danger" that an accused charged with the offence of trafficking will abscond and not appear for trial. My colleague supports this conclusion as follows (at p. 31 [p. 62, ante]):

> Drug importers and traffickers . . . have access both to a large amount of funds and to sophisticated organizations which can assist in a flight from justice. These offenders accordingly pose a significant risk that they will abscond rather than face trial.

Again, the same problem arises. Not all accused denied bail under s. 515(6)(d) fall into the category of prosperous drug lords; not all have international organizations willing to help them escape the country. The casual user who gives a joint to a friend provides an obvious example. But even in the commercial drug world, it is far from clear that those charged with trafficking are more able to abscond than people charged with other offences. Those charged with trafficking are often at the bottom of the chain and rarely provide a link to the top.

. . .

If s. 515(6)(e) violates s. 11(e) of the *Charter*, it must be struck down under s. 1 and s. 52 of the *Constitution Act, 1982* unless the Crown establishes that it is "demonstrably justified" in a free and democratic society. To meet this test a law must be directed to an objective of compelling importance and must not exceed what is necessary to achieve that objective. I take as given that s. 515(6)(d) is directed to avoiding repeat offences and absconding. These are important objectives. The problem is that s. 515(6)(d) goes further than is necessary to achieve those objectives. As discussed, there is no reason to conclude that small and casual traffickers pose any particular threat of repeating the offence or fleeing from their trial. Thus violating their constitutional right to bail in the absence of "just cause" does nothing to promote the objectives of the section. Other jurisdictions, like the United States and Australia, distinguish between major and minor trafficking. Canada, for no apparent reason, does not. One may hope that Parliament will revisit the question and consider confining denial of bail to cases where it can be justified. For the present, however, I agree with the Court of Appeal that s. 515(6)(d) cannot be justified and accordingly is of no force and effect under s. 52 of the *Constitution Act, 1982*. Consequently, I would dismiss the appeal.

. . .

LA FOREST J. (dissenting):—I agree with Justice McLachlin, for the reasons she gives, that s. 515(6)(d) of the *Criminal Code*, R.S.C. 1985, c. C-46, violates s. 11(e) of the *Canadian Charter of Rights and Freedoms* and is not saved by s. 1.

Relying on its own empirical research, the *Report of the Commission on Systemic Racism in the Ontario Criminal Justice System* (1995) suggests (p.158) that the practical effect of presuming detention for persons charged with trafficking or importing narcotics is to imprison small-scale offenders and also to result in racism. The black pre-trial admission rate for drug trafficking/importing charges was 27 times higher than the white rate (p. iii). **Should this result in Parliament's repeal of the drugs reverse onus and/or reconsideration by the Supreme Court?**

However, in 1997 Parliament adopted a reverse onus for drugs offences for the new Controlled Drugs and Substances Act (s. 515(6)(d)). Further, under the anti-gang legislation s. 515(6)(a) adds to the list of reverse onus exceptions those charged with the new s. 467.1 offence or an indictable federal offence with at least a five-year maximum sentence of imprisonment committed for the benefit of, at the direction of, or in association with a criminal organization. Parliament has added offences involving firearms to the growing list of bail reverse onus by adding new ss. 515(6) (a)(vi), (vii) and (viii). That certainly means that in borderline cases an accused charged with a firearms offence should be denied bail This assumes that the new reverse onus provisions survive Charter review. This seems likely given the majority ruling in *R. v. Pearson*. But if the Bail Reform Act has any remaining vitality these amendments should not result in automatic detention in firearms cases. The new amendments have reversed the bail onus for firearms offences and will likely result in more detention in such cases.

What, for example, of a case where a young woman tried to wrestle a firearm away from her boyfriend in her apartment because she did not want him to have a gun, it went off and wounded him, and she is now charged with assault causing bodily harm with a firearm? Should she be denied bail?

Should the reverse onus for bail on murder charges also survive Charter challenge? What about a reverse onus for charges of domestic assault? What of reversing the onus for all violent offences? Would such reverse onuses be constitutional?

PROBLEM 1

In a ten-minute interview this morning you have learned that your client, Bob Richardson, is a 19-year-old resident of a nearby town. He has been a labourer on a local construction site for the past two months. He was arrested last night in the city and charged with possession of two capsules of M.D.A. He was previously found guilty of possession of M.D.A. a year ago, for which he received a conditional discharge.

In docket court, on your advice, he has elected trial before a provincial court judge and pleaded not guilty. A date seven days hence has been set for trial. The prosecutor at this point rises to say simply: "The Crown opposes bail on the ground of the protection of society." The provincial judge is nodding.

Argue the case for judicial interim release, starting, "Your Honour, on behalf of my client, I submit . . .".

Suppose the justice is leaning toward release on recognizance with a surety. The accused's mother is prepared to be the surety. What questions would you, as defence counsel, ask? As Crown?

PROBLEM 2

The accused was arrested on a number of offences alleging violence against his girlfriend. The accused carried the burden of proof for release on bail. For a variety of reasons, the matter was adjourned six times before a bail hearing was finally conducted. The accused was denied bail at the bail hearing. Several of the adjournments were due to not reaching the case in the bail docket. The accused had potential sureties available on all but one of the appearances but they were not available on one occasion thus necessitating an adjournment.

Subsequent to the bail hearing, the accused pleaded guilty to some unrelated offences and was sentenced to prison. At the trial for the offences involving his girlfriend, he sought a stay of proceedings due to violations of his rights under sections 7, 9, and 11(e) and for an assessment of costs against the Crown. In addition to evidence related to the delays in this case, the defence provided evidence of the establishment of a committee to deal with delay issues in that York region of Ontario and that the jurisdiction had substantially fewer bail courts than neighbouring jurisdictions.

The trial judge held that the delay was due to insufficient institutional resources and the breach was serious and flagrant and stayed the proceedings. He also ordered costs against the Crown. The Crown appealed to the Ontario Court of Appeal.

Compare *R. v. Zarinchang* (2010), 73 C.R. (6th) 199, 254 C.C.C. (3d) 133 (Ont. C.A.) and R. v. Simpson, [1995] 1 S.C.R. 449, 95 C.C.C. (3d) 96 (S.C.C.). See CR annotation to *Zarinchang* by Tim Quigley.

Chapter 8

DISCLOSURE AND DISCOVERY

This chapter deals with the question of discovery in the criminal process. To what extent are the Crown and the accused required to share information or evidence with each other? Except for a few very narrow and specific rules, an accused person is generally not required to disclose his or her case to the Crown. The main focus is on the obligations of the Crown. This is justified as a matter of basic fairness in the criminal process. Also, recent history in Canada and England has further demonstrated that the lack of, or inadequate disclosure, has contributed to miscarriages of justice.

There is an important distinction, now recognized in the cases, between "disclosure" and "production". The disclosure cases typically involve questions of whether the Crown properly shared with the accused evidence in its possession or control. The production cases involve potentially relevant materials not in the possession or control of the Crown or the police, but in the hands of so-called third parties (such as complainants, doctors, psychiatrists, hospitals, social agencies, etc.). A typical example of a third-party record case is a request for disclosure of the complainant's diary or a request to produce notes and clinical records kept by the complainant's psychotherapist. Different issues arise, and tailored procedures are created, to deal with these records and the claims of privacy that are often made over these records.

We will learn in this chapter that, in relation to the production of third-party records, there is both a statutory regime in the Criminal Code that applies to sexual offences and a common law regime that applies in other contexts.

The charging instrument, together with any particulars that have been ordered, gives the accused an outline of the case that he will have to meet at trial. In civil matters the opposing parties can be orally examined so that each side can *discover* exactly what the facts are that each side intends to establish and rely on. Each party is required to testify on oath and so define his position with some particularity. The party is thus tied down to a statement of facts and the opposing party can prepare to meet that case. In addition to oral discovery the rules of civil procedure provide for the discovery of documents to determine whether the adversary has any documents which might be used against him. Also the parties may call for the production and inspection of tangible items involved in the matter, including the physical examination of the party himself.

In 1985, in partial response to recommendations of the Law Reform Commission of Canada, Parliament amended the Criminal Code to provide for pre-hearing conferences.

625.1 (1) Subject to subsection (2), on application by the prosecutor or the accused or on its own motion, the court before which, or the judge, provincial court judge or justice before whom, any proceedings are to be held may, with the consent of the prosecutor and the accused, order that a conference between the prosecutor and the accused or counsel for the accused, to be presided over by the court, judge, provincial court judge or justice, be held prior to the proceedings to consider such matters as will promote a fair and expeditious hearing.

(2) In any case to be tried with a jury, a judge of the court before which the accused is to be tried shall, prior to the trial, order that a conference between the prosecutor and the accused or counsel for the accused, to be presided over by a judge of that court, be held in accordance with the rules of court made under section 482 to consider such matters as will promote a fair and expeditious trial.

1. Disclosure

ROYAL COMMISSION ON THE DONALD MARSHALL JR. PROSECUTION
(1989), vol. 1, 238-242

2.5.12 Prosecutorial discretion in the conduct of trials

Once the Crown has determined that a prosecution will proceed, the adversarial aspects of the criminal justice system are evident. The accused is normally represented by defence counsel, the Crown's case is presented by the prosecutor and the trial is conducted before an independent justice with or without a jury.

While the courtroom setting is adversarial, the Crown prosecutor must make sure the criminal justice system itself functions in a manner that is scrupulously fair. The phrase "criminal justice system" is not a mistake of history—we do not have a "criminal convictions systems". Justice is an ideal that requires strict adherence to the principles of fairness and impartiality. The Crown prosecutor as the representative of the State is responsible for seeing that the State's system of law enforcement works fairly. This is nowhere more apparent that in the Crown's obligation to disclose its case to the accused.

2.5.13 Disclosure

We discussed earlier the critical failure of the Crown to disclose its case against Marshall. Both before and after trial, the Crown's failure to disclose information to Marshall's counsel contributed to his conviction and continued imprisonment.

In discussing disclosure, it is opportune to remind ourselves of the comments of U.S. Supreme Court Justice Brandeis in *Burdeau v. McDowell*, 256 U.S. 465 (1921) at 476:

> And in the development of our liberty insistence upon procedural regularity has been a large factor. Respect for law will not be advanced by resort, in its enforcement, to means which shock the common man's sense of decency and fair play.

As will become apparent in this section, our view is that anything less than complete disclosure by the Crown falls short of decency and fair play.

What is the Crown's obligation to disclose its case against the accused? In its written submission to the Royal Commission, the Nova Scotia Branch of the Canadian Bar Association stated the problem as follows:

What information to disclose to an accused in a criminal matter is a question that has long vexed the legal profession. The answer to this question requires a balancing between the interests of the State in the administration of criminal justice and the right of the accused to a fair trial. On one hand, Crown prosecutors are understandably reticent to release information that, if misused, could result in justice not being done. Witness tampering, fabrication of evidence and alibis to meet the Crown's stated case and the elimination of surprise are just three of the concerns Crown prosecutors raise when asked to broaden the scope of information to be disclosed to lawyers for an accused. On the other hand, lawyers for the defence need sufficient information for the preparation of their case and it is the State that generally controls access to that information. Defence counsel need to know not just the evidence against the accused, but the evidence in his or her favour along with evidence that is apparently neutral, suggesting neither guilt nor innocence. Only with full and timely access to the information gathered by agents of the State can defence lawyers properly discharge their burden of holding the State to the criminal burden of proof.

It has long been accepted as indispensable for the fair administration of justice in our society that some access by the accused to the State's case against him or her is required. But what type of access? To statements? To witnesses? To an accused's entire file? And when should access take place? Before the trial? During the trial? Or after the trial if relevant evidence subsequently comes to the attention of the Crown?

It continued at page 69 of its submission:

Were the Crown disclosure problems in the Marshall case a rarity or were they symptomatic of a general reluctance of the State to provide more information to the accused? Clearly the latter is the case. The issue of State disclosure to the accused, balanced against the accused's right to make full answer and defence, goes beyond Canadian borders.

The Canadian Bar Association brief contains an excellent summary of disclosure practices in Canada, the United States, Europe, Australia and New Zealand. Some of the material that follows is extracted from this brief. (We commend to the reader Volume 1 of the brief which has been appended to this Report as Appendix 15).

The current debate about disclosure has concerned itself with the extent of disclosure and its timing. Mr. Justice David Watt reviewed extensively the case law on this subject in the recent decision of *R. v. Belanger*, a decision which was upheld upon appeal to the Ontario Court of Appeal. ([1987] O.J. No. 850, Action No. 471/87) Mr. Justice Watt held that:

. . . There is neither common law principle nor statutory enactment which imposes upon Crown Counsel in charge of a prosecution a general obligation or duty to make full pre-trial disclosure to the accused or his Counsel of the entirety of the Prosecution's case....

Crown Counsel making pre-trial disclosure of the Prosecution's case to defending Counsel ought to do so in a way that is consonant with rather than inimical to his or her role as a representative of the Minister of Justice. Such disclosure as is given must, in a timely and fair manner, apprise the accused of the case to be met and be sufficiently substantial so as not to in any way impair the right of the accused to make full answer and defence at his or her trial. Section 7, as well perhaps as the fair hearing component of paragraph 11(d) of the Charter, provides the constitutional standard against which the prosecutorial conduct in the present case falls to be adjudged.

There is a clear recognition in this case, and in many others, that the accused's right to make full answer and defence, a right provided for in the *Criminal Code*, is one of the principles of fundamental justice referred to in Section 7 of the Charter. There is also a recognition in Canadian case law that the Crown's failure to provide adequate disclosure may impair or even prevent the accused from making a full answer and defence. If this happens, the courts recognize there has been an infringement of Sections 7 and 11(*d*) Charter rights to fundamental justice and a fair hearing. Similarly, in the United States, the common law of disclosure was developed on the basis of constitutional principles. The failure to disclose exculpatory evidence was held to be a violation of the defendant's right to due process and a fair trial. In *United States v. Bagley*, 473 U.S. 667 (1985), the United States Supreme Court concluded that due process was violated only if there was "a reasonable probability that, had the evidence been disclosed to the defence, the result of the proceeding would have been different". The majority of American States have enacted their own rules regarding criminal disclosure. While there is a wide variety of specific enactments, more require a request by defence counsel, and generally the specific material to be disclosed is delineated.

This decision of most American States to codify disclosure requirements is a good one. The approach reflected in current case law involves assessing each individual case of real or alleged non-disclosure to determine if it actually impairs the accused's constitutional right to make full answer and defence. We believe that such an *ad hoc* approach to disclosure means uncertainty and possible unfairness. The inability of an accused to adequately prepare a defence threatens the fairness of the criminal justice system, and it is desirable that as much discretion and subjectivity as possible be removed from decisions concerning disclosure.

The fundamental interest in a fair trial of the accused requires that the accused receive from the Crown all information known to the Crown that might reasonably be considered useful to the accused. The Crown should have a positive and continuing duty to provide this information to the defence. It is immaterial whether or not defence counsel fails to request disclosure of the information in possession of the Crown, or indeed whether defence counsel is negligent in failing to do so. The circumstances of non-disclosure should not be permitted to affect adversely the fairness of the trial received by the accused. The focal point of the issue of fairness is the fact of disclosure of material evidence.

The role of the prosecutor and the obligation of the Crown to disclose its case against the accused has been the subject of considerable comment. Mr. Justice Thomas Zuber, for example, made the point on behalf of the Ontario Court of Appeal in *R. v. Savion and Mizrahi* (1980), 52 C.C.C. (2d) 276 that "... a Crown prosecutor is more than an advocate, he is a police officer engaged in the administration of justice . . .". Mr. Justice Patrick Kerwin of the Supreme Court of Canada in *Lemay v. The King*, [1952] 1 S.C.R. 232 at 241 added that the Crown prosecutor's responsibility for the proper administration of justice means, in part at least, that "the Crown must not hold back evidence because it would assist an accused." In the same case, Mr. Justice John Cartwright put the obligation more positively: "I wish to make it perfectly clear that I do not intend to say anything which might be regarded as lessening the duty which rests upon counsel for the Crown to bring forward evidence of every material fact known to the prosecution whether favorable to the accused or otherwse . . ." (*ibid.* at 257)

The *Canadian Bar Association Code of Professional Conduct* (1987) provides that the prosecutor's prime duty is:

> . . . to see that justice is done through a fair trial upon the merits. The prosecutor exercises a public function involving much discretion and power, and must act fairly and dispassionately. He should not do anything which might prevent the accused from being represented by counsel or communicating with counsel and to the extent required by law and accepted practice, he should make timely disclosure to the accused or his counsel (or the Court if the accused is not represented) of all relevant facts and witnesses known to him, whether tending towards guilt or innocence.

When the Law Reform Commission of Canada considered this question in "Disclosure By The Prosecution" (Report 22, 1984), it stated that:

> It cannot be said that Canadian criminal law enforces a policy of pre-trial disclosure by the prosecution. Apart from specific and limited requirements currently prescribed by law, pre-trial disclosure in Canada is characteristically an informal process, predicated upon the Crown's discretion in the management of its case. To the extent that it exists, pre-trial disclosure is subject to the vagaries of regional practice, plea bargaining and personal relations among members of the Criminal Bar; for these reasons alone it defies systematic analysis as an integral feature of Canadian criminal procedure.

The Crown prosecutor occupies a dual role, being obligated on the one hand to prosecute vigorously those accused of crime, and on the other hand to ensure that the power of the State is used only in the pursuit of impartial justice. But it is not realistic to believe that the prosecutor does not have an interest in the outcome of a criminal trial. To expect any prosecutor to evaluate with any degree of objectivity whether certain evidence in his or her possession will be of use to the accused may be too much to expect in everyday practice.

An obligation to disclose all relevant information is not inconsistent with the proper working of the adversary system. For this system to work, and for justice to be attained, equal parties must participate on an equal basis. This means that the accused must have access to the information in possession of the Crown in order to properly prepare his or her case. Whether or not to disclose information is not a decision that should be left to the discretion of the prosecutor. A statutory obligation to disclose is necessary, and we believe that sufficient protections can be built in to such a statutory obligation to minimize most of the concerns that Crown prosecutors generally raise when considering the issue of full disclosure. For example, the existence of possible witness intimidation can be considered and ruled upon by a justice on an application by the Crown. The policy must be in favour of disclosure, unless the Crown is able to satisfy a justice that there are good reasons for not disclosing in any particular case.

There are two steps in the disclosure process. Initially, the police must be required to place all evidence collected before the prosecutor, so that he or she may evaluate it in order to determine whether the prosecution should be continued; secondly, the Crown must make full disclosure to the accused or his or her counsel.

We have discussed elsewhere in our Report the issue of the police making disclosure to the Crown. The wilful failure of the police to make full disclosure to the Crown must be made the subject of sanctions sufficiently severe to guarantee compliance.

If disclosure is effected on the basis of the statutory obligation which we recommend, there should be noticeable improvements in the pre-trial process generally. A full, timely and continuing disclosure procedure on behalf of the Crown should lead to a shorter and limited form of preliminary inquiry, a productive pre-trial conferrence to resolve evidentiary and legal issues which are anticipated to arise in the course of a trial, and a meaningful forum for a structured plea discussion. It is accepted that the onus is on the Crown to prove its case beyond a reasonable doubt and that the accused is not required to aid in his or her conviction. However, some experienced defence counsel, in advance of the trial, consistently advise Crown counsel as to the general nature of the defences upon which they propose to rely. This practice is commendable. It narrows the issues in dispute and provides a more orderly trial.

An analysis of our criminal law jurisprudence reveals two opposing, although not irreconcilable positions. The law exists to protect society against lawbreakers, and at the same time, to safeguard the liberty and freedom of the individual against the power of the State. Our system of justice must strive simultaneously to guarantee that the rights of the accused will be respected without sacrificing the interests of society. Improving the efficiency of procedures will not impair the balance between those rights and interests. If the integrity of the judicial system in criminal law is to be maintained, we must eliminate those anachronistic and outmoded procedures which breed contempt for the law and which, if left unchecked, will continue to impede the administration of justice. An obligation on the Crown to make full disclosure to the defence is the foundation upon which a fair and efficient system of administration of criminal justice can be built and maintained.

Comprehensive federal legislation is needed to provide an accused with legally enforceable rights.

The Marshall inquiry analysis was a principal source relied on by the Supreme Court in its recognition of the accused's constitutional right to disclosure of the Crown case under s. 7 of the Charter.

R. v. STINCHCOMBE
[1991] 3 S.C.R. 326, 8 C.R. (4th) 277, 68 C.C.C. (3d) 1 (S.C.C.)

SOPINKA J. (La Forest, L'Heureux-Dubé, Gonthier, Cory, McLachlin and Iacobucci JJ. concurring):—This appeal raises the issue of the Crown's obligation to make disclosure to the defence. A witness who gave evidence at the preliminary inquiry favourable to the accused was subsequently interviewed by agents for the Crown. Crown counsel decided not to call the witness and would not produce the statements obtained at the interview. The trial judge refused an application by the defence for disclosure on the ground that there was no obligation on the Crown to disclose the statements. The Court of Appeal affirmed the judgment at trial and the case is here with leave of this court.

. . .

Production and discovery were foreign to the adversary process of adjudication in its earlier history when the element of surprise was one of the accepted weapons in the arsenal of the adversaries. This applied to both criminal and civil proceedings. Significantly, in civil proceedings this aspect of the adversary process has long since disappeared, and full discovery of documents and oral examination of parties and even witnesses are familiar features of the practice. This change resulted from acceptance of the principle that justice was better served when the element of surprise was eliminated from the trial and the parties were prepared to address issues on the basis of complete information of the case to be met. Surprisingly, in criminal cases in which the liberty of the subject is usually at stake, this aspect of the adversary system has lingered on. While the prosecution bar has generally co-operated in making disclosure on a voluntary basis, there has been considerable resistance to the enactment of comprehensive rules which would make the practice mandatory. This may be attributed to the fact that proposals for reform in this regard do not provide for reciprocal disclosure by the defence (see 1974 working paper at pp. 29-31; 1984 report at pp. 13-15; Marshall Commission Report, infra, vol. 2, at pp. 242-44).

It is difficult to justify the position which clings to the notion that the Crown has no legal duty to disclose all relevant information. The arguments against the existence of such a duty are groundless while those in favour are, in my view, overwhelming. The suggestion that the duty should be reciprocal may deserve consideration by this court in the future but is not a valid reason for absolving the Crown of its duty. The contrary contention fails to take account of the fundamental difference in the respective roles of the prosecution and the defence.

. . .

I would add that the fruits of the investigation which are in the possession of counsel for the Crown are not the property of the Crown for use in securing a conviction but the property of the public to be used to ensure that justice is done. In contrast, the defence has no obligation to assist the prosecution and is entitled to assume a purely adversarial role toward the prosecution. The absence of a duty to disclose can, therefore, be justified as being consistent with this role.

. . .

The prosecutor must retain a degree of discretion in respect of these matters. The discretion, which will be subject to review, should extend to such matters as excluding what is clearly irrelevant, withholding the identity of persons to protect them from harassment or injury, or to enforce the privilege relating to informers. The discretion would also extend to the timing of disclosure in order to complete an investigation.

. . .

The right to make full answer and defence is one of the pillars of criminal justice on which we heavily depend to ensure that the innocent are not convicted. Recent events have demonstrated that the erosion of this right due to non-disclosure was an important factor in the conviction and incarceration of an innocent person. In the *Royal Commission on the Donald Marshall, Jr., Prosecution*, vol. 1: Findings and Recommendations (1989) (the "Marshall Commission Report"), the commissioners found that prior inconsistent statements were not disclosed to the defence. This was an important contributing factor in the miscarriage of justice which occurred and led the commission to state that "anything less than complete disclosure by the Crown falls short of decency and fair play" (vol. 1 at p. 238).

. . .

As indicated earlier, however, this obligation to disclose is not absolute. It is subject to the discretion of counsel for the Crown. This discretion extends both to the withholding of information and to the timing of disclosure. For example, counsel for the Crown has a duty to respect the rules of privilege. In the case of informers the Crown has a duty to protect their identity. In some cases serious prejudice or even harm may result to a person who has supplied evidence or information to the investigation. While it is a harsh reality of justice that ultimately any person with relevant evidence must appear to testify, the discretion extends to the timing and manner of disclosure in such circumstances. A discretion must also be exercised with respect to the relevance of information. While the Crown must err on the side of inclusion, it need not produce what is clearly irrelevant. The experience to be gained from the civil side of the practice is that counsel, as officers of the court and acting responsibly, can be relied upon not to withhold pertinent information. Transgressions with respect to this duty constitute a very serious breach of legal ethics. The initial obligation to separate "the wheat from the chaff" must therefore rest with Crown counsel. There may also be situations in which early disclosure may impede completion of an investigation. Delayed disclosure on this account is not to be encouraged and should be rare. Completion of the investigation before proceeding with the prosecution of a charge or charges is very much within the control of the Crown. Nevertheless, it is not always possible to predict events which may require an investigation to be reopened and the Crown must have some discretion to delay disclosure in these circumstances.

The discretion of Crown counsel is, however, reviewable by the trial judge. Counsel for the defence can initiate a review when an issue arises with respect to the exercise of the Crown's discretion. On a review the Crown must justify its refusal to disclose. Inasmuch as disclosure of all relevant information is the general rule, the Crown must bring itself within an exception to that rule.

The trial judge on a review should be guided by the general principle that information ought not to be withheld if there is a reasonable possibility that the withholding of information will impair the right of the accused to make full answer and defence, unless the non-disclosure is justified by the law of privilege. The trial judge might also, in certain circumstances, conclude that the recognition of an existing privilege does not constitute a reasonable limit on the constitutional right to make full answer and defence and thus require disclosure in spite of the law of privilege. The trial judge may also review the decision of the Crown to withhold or delay production of information by reason of concern for the security or safety of witnesses or persons who have supplied information to the investigation. In such circumstances, while much leeway must be accorded to the exercise of the discretion of the counsel for the Crown with respect to the manner and timing of the disclosure, the absolute withholding of information which is relevant to the defence can only be justified on the basis of the existence of a legal privilege which excludes the information from disclosure.

The trial judge may also review the Crown's exercise of discretion as to relevance and interference with the investigation to ensure that the right to make full answer and defence is not violated. I am confident that disputes over disclosure will arise infrequently when it is made clear that counsel for the Crown is under a general duty to disclose *all* relevant information. The tradition of Crown counsel in this country in carrying out their role as "ministers of justice" and not as adversaries has generally been very high. Given this fact, and the obligation on defence counsel as officers of the court to act responsibly, these matters will usually be resolved without the intervention of the trial judge. When they do arise, the trial judge must resolve them. This may require not only submissions but the inspection of statements and other documents and indeed, in some cases, viva voce evidence. A voir dire will frequently be the appropriate procedure in which to deal with these matters.

Counsel for the accused must bring to the attention of the trial judge at the earliest opportunity any failure of the Crown to comply with its duty to disclose of which counsel becomes aware. Observance of this rule will enable the trial judge to remedy any prejudice to the accused if possible and thus avoid a new trial: see *R. v. Caccamo*, [1976] 1 S.C.R. 786, 29 C.R.N.S. 78, 4 N.R. 133, 21 C.C.C. (2d) 257, 54 D.L.R. (3d) 685. Failure to do so by counsel for the defence will be an important factor in determining on appeal whether a new trial should be ordered.

These are the general principles that govern the duty of the Crown to make disclosure to the defence. There are many details with respect to their application that remain to be worked out in the context of concrete situations. It would be neither possible nor appropriate to attempt to lay down precise rules here. Although the basic principles of disclosure will apply across the country, the details may vary from province to province and even within a province by reason of special local conditions and practices. It would, therefore, be useful if the under-utilized power conferred by s. 482 of the *Criminal Code*, R.S.C. 1985, c. C-46, which empowers superior courts and courts of criminal jurisdiction to enact rules, were employed to provide further details with respect to the procedural aspects of disclosure.

The general principles referred to herein arise in the context of indictable offences. While it may be argued that the duty of disclosure extends to all offences, many of the factors which I have canvassed may not apply at all or may apply with less impact in summary conviction offences. Moreover, the content of the right to make full answer and defence entrenched in s. 7 of the *Charter* may be of a more limited nature. A decision as to the extent to which the general principles of disclosure extend to summary conviction offences should be left to a case in which the issue arises in such proceedings. In view of the number and variety of statutes which create such offences, consideration would have to be given as to where to draw the line. Pending a decision on that issue, the voluntary disclosure which has been taking place through the co-operation of Crown counsel will no doubt continue. Continuation and extension of this practice may eliminate the necessity for a decision on the issue by this Court.

There are, however, two additional matters which require further elaboration of the general principles of disclosure outlined above. They are: (1) the timing of disclosure, and (2) what should be disclosed. Some detail with respect to these issues is essential if the duty to disclose is to be meaningful. Moreover, with respect to the second matter, resolution of the dispute over disclosure in this case requires a closer examination of the issue.

With respect to timing, I agree with the recommendation of the Law Reform Commission of Canada in both of its reports that initial disclosure should occur before the accused is called upon to elect the mode of trial or to plead. These are crucial steps which the accused must take which affect his or her rights in a fundamental way. It will be of great assistance to the accused to know what are the strengths and weaknesses of the Crown's case before committing on these issues. As I have pointed out above, the system will also profit from early disclosure as it will foster the resolution of many charges without trial, through increased numbers of withdrawals and pleas of guilty. The obligation to disclose will be triggered by a request by or on behalf of the accused. Such a request may be made at any time after the charge. Provided the request for disclosure has been timely, it should be complied with so as to enable the accused sufficient time before election or plea to consider the information. In the rare cases in which the accused is unrepresented, Crown counsel should advise the accused of the right to disclosure and a plea should not be taken unless the trial judge is satisfied that this has been done. At this stage, the Crown's brief will often not be complete and disclosure will be limited by this fact. Nevertheless, the obligation to disclose is a continuing one and disclosure must be completed when additional information is received.

With respect to what should be disclosed, the general principle to which I have referred is that all relevant information must be disclosed subject to the reviewable discretion of the Crown. The material must include not only that which the Crown intends to introduce into evidence but also that which it does not. No distinction should be made between inculpatory and exculpatory evidence.

. . .

A special problem arises in respect to witness statements and is specifically raised in this case. There is virtually no disagreement that statements in the possession of the Crown obtained from witnesses it proposes to call should be produced. In some cases the statement will simply be recorded in notes taken by an investigator, usually a police officer. The notes or copies should be produced. If notes do not exist then a "will say" statement, summarizing the anticipated evidence of the witness, should be produced based on the information in the Crown's possession. A more difficult issue is posed with respect to witnesses and other persons whom the Crown does not propose to call. In its 1974 working paper, the Law Reform Commission of Canada recommended disclosure of not only the names, addresses and occupations of all "persons who have provided information to investigation or prosecution authorities" (p. 41), but the statements obtained or, if these did not exist, "a summary of the information provided by those persons not intended to be called at trial, along with a statement of the manner in which the information in each summary has been obtained. . ." (p. 41). In its 1984 report, the commission seemed to have changed its mind. It stated (at pp. 27-28):

> With respect to potential witnesses we do not recommend, on a mandatory basis, the type of thorough disclosure that we recommend with respect to proposed witnesses. Complete disclosure would entail not only the identification of such persons, but the disclosure of any statement they made and in some cases their criminal records. In our view a recommendation to this effect would be excessive and disproportionate to the needs of the defence. In many instances these people are of no use, or of marginal use, to the case for either side. Their statements are not evidence, although they may be effectively used by the prosecution for purposes of impeachment in cross-examination in the event the witness is called by the accused. Prosecutors are understandably reluctant to disclose these statements because to do so would imperil their principal utility. It is our view that the interests of the defence are adequately served by the mandatory disclosure of the identity of such persons, although we would not wish our comments to discourage prosecutors from disclosing statements and other relevant information on a voluntary basis.

The Marshall Commission Report recommended disclosure of "any statement made by a person whom the prosecutor proposes to call as a witness or anyone who may be called as a witness". Although not entirely clear, this recommendation appears to extend to anyone who has relevant information and who is either compellable or prepared to testify whether proposed to be called by the Crown or not.

This court, in *R. v. C. (M.H.)*, supra, dealt with the failure to disclose either the identity or statement of a person who provided relevant information to the police but who was not called as a witness. McLachlin J., speaking for the court, indicated that failure to disclose in such cases could impair the fairness of the trial.

I am of the opinion that, subject to the discretion to which I have referred above, all statements obtained from persons who have provided relevant information to the authorities should be produced notwithstanding that they are not proposed as Crown witnesses. Where statements are not in existence, other information such as notes should be produced, and, if there are no notes, then in addition to the name, address and occupation of the witness, all information in the possession of the prosecution relating to any relevant evidence that the person could give should be supplied. I do not find the comments of the commission in its 1984 Report persuasive. If the information is of no use then presumably it is irrelevant and will be excluded in the exercise of the discretion of the Crown. If the information is of some use then it is relevant and the determination as to whether it is sufficiently useful to put into evidence should be made by the defence and not the prosecutor. Moreover, I do not understand the commission's statement that "their statements are not evidence". That is true of all witness statements. They themselves are not evidence but are produced not because they will be put in evidence in that form but will enable the evidence to be called viva voce. That prosecutors are reluctant to disclose statements because use of them in cross-examination is thereby rendered less effective is understandable. That is an objection to all forms of discovery and disclosure. Tactical advantage must be sacrificed in the interests of fairness and the ascertainment of the true facts of the case.

For contrasting views on *Stinchcombe*, see Gerry Ferguson, "Judicial Reform of Crown Disclosure" (1991), 8 C.R. (4th) 295 and Brian Gover, "Stinchcombe: Bad Case, Good Law?" (1991), 8 C.R. (4th) 307.

Stinchcombe discusses but does not decide the question of whether discovery should be a two-way street with a reciprocal obligation of disclosure on the defence. **Do you believe that the Court should declare such a duty?** In *R. v. Brouillette* (*sub nom. R. v. Peruta*) (1992), 78 C.C.C. (3d) 350 (Que. C.A.), leave to appeal to S.C.C. refused (1993), 81 C.C.C. (3d) vi (note) (S.C.C.), the Quebec Court of Appeal read *Stinchcombe* as having impliedly decided, at least in *obiter*, that the defence should not have a duty to disclose. Defence counsel in a murder trial had been under no obligation to disclose written statements obtained from the defence witnesses by a private investigator. Tyndale J.A. added two reasons to those considered by the Supreme Court:

> First, the fact that the power and resources for investigation and litigation available to the prosecution are out of all proportion to those normally available to the defence. Secondly, the long and flourishing tradition in the British system of justice, if not of making things difficult for the prosecution, at least of making things less difficult for the defence, on the excellent ground that it is better that a guilty man go unpunished than that an innocent man be convicted".

For a scheme for a limited defence duty to disclose, see David Tanovich and Lawrence Crocker, "A Modest Proposal for Reciprocal Defence Disclosure"

(1994), 26 C.R. (4th) 333 but compare the rebuttal by Charles B. Davison, "Putting Ghosts to Rest" (1996), 43 C.R. (4th) 105. See too Gil D. McKinnon, "Accelerating Defence Disclosure: A Time for Change" (1996), 1 Can. Crim. L.R. 59 and Suzanne Costom, "Disclosure By The Defence: Why Should I Tell You?" (1996), 1 Can. Crim. L.R. 73.

A 2002 amendment to the Criminal Code (s. 657.3(3)) requires defence counsel to give notice of an expert it intends to call plus, once the Crown has closed its case, a report or summary of the report on which the opinion is to be based. There are growing notice requirements where defence counsel wishes to bring a Charter application to exclude evidence. The extent of the notice and the procedure to be followed is often a matter left to judicial discretion: see the review of jurisprudence by Fradsham J. in *R. v. Coles* (2005), 28 C.R. (6th) 167 (Alta. Prov. Ct.).

The *Stinchcombe* duty on the Crown to disclose is not absolute. The duty is only triggered on request and is subject to Crown discretion not to disclose material that is not clearly irrelevant or is subject to privilege. In *R. v. Morris*, [1983] 2 S.C.R. 190, 36 C.R. (3d) 1, 7 C.C.C. (3d) 97 (S.C.C.) the Supreme Court held that the test of relevance was that provided by Professor Thayer requiring only that the evidence be logically probative of some matter required to be proved; relevance was not dictated by the law but by logic and general experience. The Court expressly rejected the Wigmorean view of legal relevance that something more than a minimum of probative value was required before the jury could hear the evidence. The only class privilege recognized at common law is that for solicitor-client communications, with the privilege being that of the client. There is also an uncertain "case by case" privilege discussed by Wigmore and applied by the courts for certain confidential communications. This privilege may be found if (1) the communication originated in confidence, (2) confidence is essential to the relationship, (3) the relationship is one we ought to foster and, most importantly, (4) the injury to the relationship through disclosure must be greater than the benefit gained for the correct disposal of the litigation. There has recently emerged a new class privilege for police informers: *R. v. Leipert*, [1997] 1 S.C.R. 281, 4 C.R. (5th) 259, 112 C.C.C. (3d) 385 (S.C.C.). See also Ian Carter, "Chipping Away at Stinchcombe: the Expanding Privilege Exception to Disclosure", (2002) 50 C.R. (5th) 332. It has been held that the *Stinchcombe* obligation on the Crown to disclose extends to material in the hands of the police, whether or not the Crown knows of such information (see, for example, *R. v. Vokey* (1992), 14 C.R. (4th) 311 (Nfld. C.A.) and *R. v. T. (L.A.)* (1993), 14 O.R. (3d) 378, 84 C.C.C. (3d) 90 (Ont. C.A.)), but that the Crown is not a research aid to the defence, obliged to inquire as to the possibility of evidence favourable to the defence (see, for example, *R. v. Gingras* (1992), 11 C.R. (4th) 294, 71 C.C.C. (3d) 53 (Alta. C.A.)). In *R. v. Chaplin* (1994), [1995] 1 S.C.R. 727, 36 C.R. (4th) 201, 96 C.C.C. (3d) 225 (S.C.C.), the Supreme Court made it clear that the right to disclosure is confined to material in the possession or control of the Crown.

From the defence point of view, the *Stinchcombe* disclosure obligation was substantially weakened in *R. v. Dixon*, [1998] 1 S.C.R. 244, 122 C.C.C.

(3d) 1, (*sub nom. R. v. McQuaid*) 13 C.R. (5th) 217, where the Supreme Court emphasized that defence counsel must not remain passive and must diligently pursue disclosure. Negligence or a tactical decision not to pursue full disclosure might well jeopardize the success of an appeal based on non-disclosure. According to Cory J., speaking for the five justice Court:

> If defence counsel knew or ought to have known on the basis of other disclosures that the Crown, through inadvertence, had failed to disclose information yet remained passive as a result of a tactical decision or lack of due diligence, it would be difficult to accept a submission that the failure to disclose affected the fairness of the trial (para. 38).

This *Dixon* obligation on defence counsel clearly seeks to prevent defence ambush and other tactics resulting in new trials. However, the defence obligation seems onerous and to saddle accused with the sins of their lawyers. It certainly carries the message that defence counsel are well advised to pursue disclosure with rigour at every point.

In *R. v. Trotta* (2004), 23 C.R. (6th) 261 (Ont. C.A.) it was confirmed that the Crown's duty to disclose continues throughout the appeal process. However, Doherty J.A. stiffened the test to require the defence to demonstrate the reasonable possibility that the evidence would be linked to a fresh evidence application on appeal and that the evidence would be admitted. In *Dixon*, the Court formulated the test as whether the accused was deprived of a reasonably possible avenue of investigation. It may be that this is no different from the formulation in *Trotta* but it is a different formulation. Indeed, the test in *Trotta* might be more stringent since it encompasses the requirements for the admission of fresh evidence, rather than merely whether the defence was deprived of an opportunity to investigate. The *Dixon* test seems to be more consistent with the disclosure threshold at the trial stage: whether there was a reasonable possibility that the material not disclosed could have assisted the defence.

Sometimes it is necessary to reconcile competing claims of an accused whose fair trials are implicated with the interests of the state in international relations, national defence, or national security. Under s. 38 and succeeding sections of the Canada Evidence Act, there is an elaborate process by which the Federal Court is assigned the jurisdiction and authority to determine whether it would be injurious to these state interests to disclose information. This process is not always invoked in a criminal prosecution but, where it is, the Supreme Court of Canada has provided some guidance for reconciling the competing claims. In *R. v. Ahmad*, [2011] 1 S.C.R. 110, 264 C.C.C. (3d) 345, 81 C.R. (6th) 201 (S.C.C.), the Court upheld the constitutionality of the provisions but nevertheless placed the responsibility of the trial judge in criminal proceedings to consider the effect on trial fairness of any non-disclosure ordered by the Federal Court. In order to meet this responsibility, the trial judge will require some information about the non-disclosed material in the form of a summary available only to her or him. Any doubt about trial fairness is to be resolved in the accused's favour with remedies ranging from dismissal of some counts on the indictment, a finding against the Crown on any issue involving the undisclosed information, or, in extreme cases, a stay of proceedings. As well, a special advocate with security clearance is to be appointed to represent the accused's interests in the Federal Court proceedings. It is clear that the Supreme Court expects a great deal of co-operation and negotiation between the Crown and the defence to attempt to avoid the collapse of prosecutions.

LOST EVIDENCE CASES: FROM *CAROSELLA* TO *LA, VU,* AND *McNEIL*

In *R. v. Carosella*, [1997] 1 S.C.R. 80, 4 C.R. (5th) 139, 112 C.C.C. (3d) 289 (S.C.C.), the accused, a teacher, was charged with gross indecency against a former student in 1964. The complainant went to the Windsor Sexual Assault Centre in 1992 for advice as to how to lay charges. She was interviewed by a social worker for about one to two hours. The social worker took notes and advised the complainant that whatever she said could be subpoenaed to court. The complainant said that was all right. Shortly afterwards, the complainant went to the police and the charge was laid. Following a preliminary inquiry the accused was committed to trial. At the trial the accused brought an application for production of the Sexual Assault Centre file. The Crown, complainant and Centre consented to the order. However the produced material did not contain the notes or anything of substance. Before the production order was received, the Centre had destroyed the documents. It had been unsuccessful in opposing applications for production of records in the past and, to protect the privacy interests of its clients, had instituted a policy of taking misleading notes or shredding files with police involvement.

The trial judge stayed the charges. The judge decided the notes were likely relevant and the accused's Charter right to full answer and defence had been breached. The Ontario Court of Appeal set aside the stay on the basis that there had to be evidence that disclosed something more than a mere risk to a Charter right.

The Supreme Court of Canada restored the stay in a very lengthy decision. For the 5-4 majority Sopinka J. held (Lamer C.J., Cory, Iacobucci and Major JJ. concurring) that there had been a breach of the accused's section 7 right to production from the Crown or third parties. Prejudice was relevant at the stage of remedy rather than when considering whether there had been a breach. Here the relevance standard of *Stinchcombe* had been met and also the higher likely relevant test of *O'Connor* for production of third party records. Balancing of interests before production was not in issue as the complainant had consented to the disclosure of the notes. The stay was warranted as the prejudice to the accused's right to make full answer and defence could not be remedied or, alternatively, irreparable prejudice would be caused to the integrity of the judicial system if the prosecution were continued. The majority did not address abuse of process.

L'Heureux-Dubé J. for the minority (La Forest, Gonthier and McLachlin JJ. concurring) held that, where evidence is unavailable, the accused must demonstrate that a fair trial, not a perfect one, cannot be held as a result of the loss. The accused has to demonstrate a real likelihood of prejudice. It is not enough to speculate that there was a potential for harm. Materials can be easily lost and setting too low a standard for dismissal would bring the justice system to a halt. In any event the notes would not meet the likely relevant test of *O'Connor* as there had merely been an assertion that the material would be useful in cross-examination. Also there was no abuse of process.

Following *Carosella*, the Supreme Court considered a series of lost evidence cases culminating in *R. v. La*; *R. v. Vu*, [1997] 2 S.C.R. 680, 8 C.R. (5th) 155, 116 C.C.C. (3d) 97 (S.C.C.). It appears that the Court has adopted a different course where evidence has been lost rather than deliberately destroyed. At around midnight police found a 13-year-old runaway girl they were looking for in a vehicle driven by the accused, known to be a pimp. The girl later became the complainant in a charge of sexual assault against the accused. At the police station an officer made a 45-minute tape recording of one of his conversations with her relating to her life on the run and her being forced into prostitution. The tape was referred to by the officer at Family Court in an application for a secure treatment order. When the matter was handed over to the vice unit to investigate various complaints of prostitution and sexual assault the tape was not turned over. By the time of the accused's preliminary inquiry the officer testified that he had searched for but lost the tape.

When the matter reached the Supreme Court the Court was unanimous that the trial judge had wrongly stayed the charges. The 5:4 split was only as to the reasons.

Sopinka J. (Lamer C.J., Cory, Iacobucci and Major JJ. concurring) gave separate consideration to the section 7 issues of disclosure, abuse of process and full answer and defence. Here none of these rights had been breached.

As for disclosure, according to the majority, the Crown's duty to disclose all relevant evidence in its possession gives rise to a duty on the Crown and the police to preserve evidence known to be relevant. Where evidence is lost, the Crown has a duty to explain the loss. Where the Crown's explanation satisfies the trial judge that the evidence has not been destroyed or lost owing to unacceptable negligence, the duty to disclose has not been breached. Where the Crown is unable to satisfy the judge in this regard, it has failed to meet its disclosure obligations, and there has accordingly been a breach of s. 7 of the Charter. One circumstance that must be considered is the relevance that the evidence was perceived to have at the time. The police cannot be expected to preserve everything that comes into their hands on the off-chance that it will be relevant in the future. Even the loss of relevant evidence will not result in a breach of the duty to disclose if the conduct of the police is reasonable. As the relevance of the evidence increases, so does the degree of care for its preservation that is expected of the police. Here the Crown explanation was satisfactory. There was no evidence of negligence. The conversation had not been taped for the purposes of a criminal investigation. The officer had not failed to take reasonable steps to preserve the tape.

Conduct that will amount to an abuse of process, held Sopinka J., includes conduct on the part of governmental authorities that violates those fundamental principles that underlie the community's sense of decency and fair play. The deliberate destruction of material by the police or other officers of the Crown for the purpose of defeating the Crown's obligation to disclose the material would, typically, fall into this category. An abuse of process was not limited to conduct of officers of the Crown which proceeds from an improper motive. Accordingly, other serious departures from the Crown's duty to preserve material subject to production might also amount to an abuse of process, notwithstanding that a deliberate destruction for the purpose of evading disclosure was not established. In some cases, an unacceptable degree of negligent conduct might suffice. Here the loss did not amount to an abuse of process.

According to the majority, in extraordinary circumstances, the loss of a document may be so prejudicial to the right to make full answer and defence that it impairs the right of an accused to receive a fair trial. In such circumstances, a stay may be the appropriate remedy. This was not so here. The interview recorded was not regarded by the officer as a detailed conversation and alternative information was available to attack the witness's credibility.

L'Heureux-Dubé J. (La Forest, Gonthier and McLachlin JJ. concurring) dissented, mainly on the basis that the duty to disclose resting upon the Crown does not constitute a separate and distinct right operating on its own as a principle of fundamental justice. To establish the very process of disclosure as a distinct constitutional right would be a substantial departure from the jurisprudence in this area and would needlessly complicate this area of law. Disclosure, as a process, engaged different aspects of fundamental justice under s. 7. Not every error or omission by the Crown in making disclosure should automatically lead to a violation of the Charter. The majority's lower threshold for establishing a violation of the "right to disclosure" than for demonstrating an abuse of process was an unacceptable development in the law.

The Supreme Court has subsequently unanimously confirmed that, contrary to the views of L'Heureux-Dubé J., the right to disclosure of the Crown case is indeed a free-standing s. 7 right: see *Dixon* above and *R. v. Taillefer*, [2003] 3 S.C.R. 307, 17 C.R. (6th) 57, 179 C.C.C. (3d) 353 (S.C.C.).

THE ONTARIO ATTORNEY-GENERAL'S ADVISORY COMMITTEE, CHARGE SCREENING, DISCLOSURE, AND RESOLUTION DISCUSSIONS
(1993), 4-6

This Committee, chaired by the former Mr. Justice G. Arthur Martin, has made a number of sweeping recommendations for better administration of criminal justice in Ontario. The Committee proposes that the Attorney-General issue a comprehensive directive on disclosure. In the light of

Stinchcombe the Committee makes the following general recommendations on disclosure:

Disclosure

General Recommendations With Respect to Disclosure Disclosure

Recommendations Pertaining to Investigations

26. The Committee recommends that the Attorney General request that the Solicitor General issue a statement to all police officers emphasizing the importance of taking careful, accurate, and contemporaneous notes during their investigations. (The statement should emphasize that disclosure requirements after Stinchcombe cannot be thwarted by making less accurate or less comprehensive notes.)

27. The Committee recommends that, upon request, copies of relevant original notes should be disclosed, subject to editing or non-disclosure where the public interest requires it, including editing or non-disclosure, where necessary, to protect confidential informants, the existence of on-going investigations, and the integrity of police investigative techniques.

28. The Committee recommends that statements of suspects or accused persons taken at the police station or wherever such persons are detained, be video taped or audio taped, preferably video taped. It is recognized that this may not always be practical or technically feasible.

Ethical and Legal Obligations Relating to Disclosure

The Police

29. The Committee recommends that s. 1(c)(viii) of the Code of Offences, a Schedule to Regulation 791 under the Police Services Act, R.S.O. 1990, c. P-15, be amended to read as follows:

> *Any chief of police, other police officer or constable commits an offence against discipline if he is guilty of*
>
> *(c) NEGLECT OF DUTY, that is to say, if he,*
>
> *where a charge is laid fails to disclose to the officer in charge of the prosecution or the prosecutor any information that he or any person within his knowledge can give for or against any prisoner or defendant.*

Crown Counsel

30. The Committee recognizes that it is a serious disciplinary offence for the Crown not to disclose to the defence as required.

31. The Committee recommends that it is inappropriate for Crown counsel to limit or refuse disclosure in a case, unless defence counsel agrees to limit a preliminary inquiry so as to ensure efficient use of court time. This does not preclude counsel from agreeing to shorten or waive a preliminary inquiry.

32. The Committee recommends that it is inappropriate for the Attorney General to withhold disclosure, unless defence counsel gives an undertaking not to share the information with his or her client.

Defence Counsel

33. The Committee acknowledges that, at present, there is no obligation upon the defence to disclose any part of its case before trial. The Committee makes no further recommendation in this respect.

34. The Committee is of the opinion that it is inappropriate for any counsel to give disclosure materials to the public. Counsel would not be acting responsibly as an officer of the Court if he or she did so.

35. The Committee is of the opinion that defence counsel should maintain custody or control over disclosure materials, so that copies of such materials are not improperly disseminated. Special arrangements may be made between defence and Crown counsel, with respect to maintaining control over disclosure materials where an accused is in custody, and where the volume of material disclosed makes it impractical for defence counsel to be present while the material is reviewed.

Disclosure and Summary Conviction Offences

36. The Committee recommends that the nature and extent of disclosure should not vary based on whether the charge was prosecuted by way of indictment, summary conviction procedure, or prosected under the *Provincial Offences Act.*

37. The Committee recommends that in all summary conviction matters under the Criminal Code which are commenced by a private complainant, the Crown should intervene to either withdraw the charge or to conduct the prosecution. If the Attorney General intervenes and conducts the prosecution, disclosure should be made in the same way as any other prosecution. Nothing herein is to be construed as precluding the Attorney General from assuming carriage of prosecutions under the *Provincial Offences Act* in appropriate cases, for example, under the *Environmental Protection Act.*

Other Recommendations

38. The Committee recommends that the Attorney General should require reasonable efforts from his or her agents to determine the sufficiency of disclosure. It is recognized that the obligation to provide disclosure is on-going.

39. The Committee recommends that all accused persons be advised of their right to disclosure, and where disclosure may be obtained, by written notice on all release forms or summonses.

40. As a general rule, the Committee is in favour of disclosure in writing.

In *Charkaoui, Re*, [2008] 2 S.C.R. 326, 58 C.R. (6th) 45 (S.C.C.) the Supreme Court held routine destruction by CSIS of notes respecting the obtaining of security certificates violated the right to disclosure under section 7 given the serious consequences of the procedure on rights and liberties. The application for a stay was held to be premature on an interlocutory motion.

Sometimes, more than one Crown agency or department may have information that is potentially relevant in a criminal case. This then raises the issue of the role of the prosecution and police in providing Crown disclosure to the defence. In other words, does Crown disclosure apply to Crown entities other than the prosecution? This was clarified by the Court of Canada in *R. v. McNeil*, [2009] 1 S.C.R. 66, 62 C.R. (6th) 1, 238 C.C.C. (3d) 353 (S.C.C.), in which the Court rejected the proposition that all state authorities constitute a single indivisible Crown entity for disclosure purposes, largely because of the impracticality that such a position would entail. Therefore, the police investigating an offence and the Crown prosecuting that offence are separate components of the Crown.

Nevertheless, Charron J. for the Court in *McNeil* confirmed that the police have a corollary duty to the Crown's duty to disclose its case. The duty on the police is to disclose to the Crown any information relating to the investigation of that offence. Moreover, the Court decided for the first time that the corollary duty obliges the police to provide to the Crown any information relating to findings of serious misconduct by police offences if "related to the investigation or if they could reasonably impact on the case against the accused" (para. 15). Any other information in the hands of the police that falls outside these parameters would be governed by the rules respecting production of records held by third parties as discussed in section 2 of this Chapter. Thus, information of police misconduct that is peripheral to the investigation in question or that does not have any realistic effect on an officer's testimony need not be disclosed as a part of Crown disclosure but may be the subject of an application for production under the third party regime.

The Court in *McNeil* made an attempt to bridge the gap between Crown disclosure of the fruits of an investigation and production of third party records. Accordingly, building on *R. v. Arsenault* (1994), 93 C.C.C. (3d) 111 (N.B. C.A.) and *R. v. L. (R.D.)* (1994), 155 A.R. 225 (C.A.), the Court confirmed that the Crown is under a duty to make reasonable inquiries and to obtain such information from other state authorities whenever put on notice of its existence. This represents an extension of the disclosure obligation established in *Stinchcombe*. David Paciocco, "*Stinchcombe* on Steroids: The Surprising Legacy of *McNeil*" (2009), 62 C.R. (6th) 26 has suggested that this aspect of the decision might operate as a surrogate for seeking production of third party records. See also: Don Stuart, "Annotation" (2009), 62 C.R. (6th) 1 and H. Archibald Kaiser, "*McNeil*: A Welcome Clarification and Extension of Disclosure Principles: "the adversary system has lingered on" (2009), 62 C.R. (6th) 36. If the other state authority refuses or fails to provide the information, the Crown must provide this information to the defence, who then may make an application for the production of these third party records.

The remedies for a breach of disclosure can vary according to both the severity and the time of the discovery of the breach. If the breach is found earlier enough, the remedy will often simply be an adjournment of the proceedings to permit the defence to obtain the disclosure, although additional remedies, such as costs, might be ordered. If the breach is not discovered until later in the trial, a mistrial or, perhaps, a stay of proceedings may be ordered, although a stay is reserved for the most extreme situations where the fairness of the trial has been affected or there has been an abuse of process, probably where the evidence has been lost due to unacceptable negligence (*La; Vu*) or deliberately destroyed (*Carosella*). Occasionally, exclusion of evidence is considered as a remedy under section 24(1). However, in *R. v. Bjelland* (2009), 67 C.R. (6th) 201, 246 C.C.C. (3d) 129, [2009] 2 S.C.R. 651 (S.C.C.), the Supreme Court greatly restricted this remedy. In a case involving late disclosure by the Crown, the Court held that this remedy should be awarded only in the following exceptional circumstances: (a) where the late disclosure renders the trial process unfair and this unfairness cannot be remedied through an adjournment and disclosure order, or (b) where exclusion is necessary to maintain the integrity of the justice system. At the appeal stage, and provided that the defence has been duly diligent, a new trial will be ordered if disclosure is still viable. Where it is not, again likely where the evidence has been lost or destroyed, there will be a strong argument for a stay.

2. Production of Third Party Records

These new principles of disclosure have been highly controversial when a defence counsel in a sexual assault case seeks discovery of medical and counselling records of the complainant. It has been suggested that such demands further erode the privacy of victims and make it even less likely that they will come forward. In *R. v. O'Connor* (1992), 18 C.R. (4th) 98 (B.C. S.C.), a Bishop was charged with four counts of a sexual nature, two involving rape, alleged to have occurred over a three-year period some 25 years ago. The charges were stayed when during the trial it became clear that the Crown had not fully complied with a sweeping pre-trial trial order to disclose which included the following:

> THE COURT ORDERS that Crown counsel produce names, addresses, and telephone numbers of therapists, counsellors, psychologists or psychiatrists whom have treated any of the complainants with respect to allegations of sexual assault or sexual abuse.

> THIS COURT FURTHER ORDERS that the complainants authorize all therapists, counsellors, psychologists and psychiatrists whom have treated any of them with respect to allegations of sexual assault or sexual abuse to produce to the Crown copies of their complete file contents and any other related material including all documents, notes, records, reports, tape recordings and video tapes, and the Crown to provide copies of all of this material to counsel for the accused forthwith.

R. v. O'CONNOR
[1995] 4 S.C.R. 411, 44 C.R. (4th) 1, 103 C.C.C. (3d) 1 (S.C.C.)

We have already examined the Supreme Court ruling respecting the reversal of the stay. The Supreme Court also made an important pronouncement on the issue of discovery of medical records in the possession of third parties. Through the judgment of L'Heureux-Dubé J. in *L.L.A. v. A.B.*, handed down with *O'Connor*, the Court unanimously decided that production should not be determined by class or case-by-case privilege.

According to L'Heureux-Dubé J., the creation of a class privilege in favour of private records in criminal law raised concerns relating to

(1) the truth-finding process of our adversarial trial procedure; (2) the possible relevance of some private records; (3) the accused's right to make full answer and defence; (4) the categories of actors included in a class privilege; and (5) the experience of other countries.

L'Heureux-Dubé J. carefully examines case law dealing with privilege and confidential information, including that relating to police informants, solicitor-client privilege and public interest immunity, and points out that the courts have consistently ordered production where necessary to establish innocence. While there was ground to recognize a case-by-case privilege along *Wigmore* lines for private records in some instances, such exceptions to the general evidentiary rule of admissibility and disclosure "should not be encouraged". The better approach was one of balancing competing Charter rights.

L'Heureux-Dubé J., La Forest, Gonthier and McLachlin JJ. concurring, saw the need to balance the accused's right to a fair trial and full answer and defence with the complainant's rights to privacy and to equality without discrimination. The majority through a joint judgment by Lamer C.J. and Sopinka J., with Cory, Iacobucci and Major JJ. concurring, determined that the accused's right to full answer and defence should be balanced against the complainant's rights to privacy under ss. 7 and 8. However, the majority, in not referring to a section 15 equality right for complainants, although it was fully argued, implicitly reject it.

The Court agreed that there should be a two-stage procedure but divided 5-4 as to the precise tests. Lamer C.J., Sopinka, Cory, Iacobucci and Major, JJ. decided that when the defence seeks information in the hands of a third party the onus should be on the accused to satisfy a judge that the information is likely to be relevant. The application for disclosure should be made to the judge seized of the trial, but might be brought before the trial judge prior to the empanelling of the jury. In the context of disclosure, the meaning of relevance was whether the information might be useful to the defence. In the context of production, the test of relevance should be higher: the presiding judge must be satisfied that there is a reasonable possibility that the information is logically probative to an issue at trial or the competence of a witness to testify. While likely relevance was the appropriate threshold for the first stage of the two-step procedure, the judges said it should not be interpreted as an onerous burden upon the accused. The crux of the majority *O'Connor* regime was that the first stage of establishing likely relevance had to be a low threshold as the accused might often be in a Catch-22 situation where he was disadvantaged by arguing relevance of a document he had not seen. The majority disagreed with L'Heureux-Dubé J.'s position that such records would only be relevant in rare cases. The majority gave as examples of possible relevance records which may contain information about the unfolding of the complaint, the use of therapy to influence memory and information bearing on credibility. A relevance threshold, at this stage, was simply a requirement to prevent the defence from engaging in speculative, fanciful, disruptive, unmeritorious, obstructive and time-consuming requests for production. Upon their production to the court, the judge should examine the records to determine whether, and to what extent, they should be produced to the accused. In making that determination, the judge must examine and weigh the salutary and deleterious effects of a production order and determine whether a non-production order would constitute a reasonable limit on the ability of the accused to make full answer and defence.

For L'Heureux-Dubé J., with La Forest, Gonthier and McLachlin JJ. agreeing, the burden on an accused to demonstrate likely relevance should be a significant one and if it could not be met the application for production should be dismissed as amounting to no more than a fishing expedition. The mere fact that the complainant had received treatment or counselling could not be presumed to be relevant to the trial as therapy generally focuses on emotional and psychological responses rather than being oriented to ascertaining historical truth. For the minority at the second stage of deciding whether to order production of private records, the court needed to exercise its discretion in a manner that was respectful of the Charter values of the right to privacy and the right to equality without discrimination. The difference of opinion at the production stage is highlighted by the following passage:

LAMER C.J. and SOPINKA J. (Cory, Iacobucci and Major JJ. concurring):—

. . .

We agree with L'Heureux-Dubé J. that, in balancing the competing rights in question, the following factors should be considered: (1) the extent to which the record is necessary for the accused to make full answer and defence; (2) the probative value of the record in question; (3) the nature and extent of the reasonable expectation of privacy vested in that record; (4) whether production of the record would be premised upon any discriminatory belief or bias" and (5) "the potential prejudice to the complainant's dignity, privacy or security of the person that would be occasioned by production of the record in question. However, L'Heureux-Dubé J. also refers to two other factors that she believes must be considered. She suggests that the judge should take account of "the extent to which production of records of this nature would frustrate society's interest in encouraging the reporting of sexual offences and the acquisition of treatment by victims" as well as "the effect on the integrity of the trial process of producing, or failing to produce, the record, having in mind the need to maintain consideration in the outcome". This last factor is more appropriately dealt with at the admissibility stage and not in deciding whether the information should be produced. As for society's interest in the reporting of sexual crimes, we are of the opinion that there are other avenues available to the judge to ensure that production does not frustrate the societal interests that may be implicated by the production of the records to the defence. A number of these avenues are discussed by the Nova Scotia Court of Appeal in *R. v. Ryan* (1991), 69 C.C.C. (3d) 226 at p. 230:

As the trials of these two charges proceed, there are a number of protective devices to allay the concerns of the caseworkers over the contents of their files. The trial judge has considerable discretion in these matters. It is for the trial judge to determine whether a ban shall be placed on publication. It is for the trial judge to decide whether spectators shall be barred when evidence is given on matters that the trial judge deems to be extremely sensitive and worth excluding from the information available to the public. High on the list is, of course, the matter of relevance. Unless the evidence sought from the witness meets the test of relevancy, it will be excluded. The trial judge is able to apply the well-established rules and tests to determine whether any given piece of evidence is relevant.

We are also of the view that these options are available to the judge to further protect the privacy interests of witnesses if the production of private records is ordered. Consequently, the societal interest is not a paramount consideration in deciding whether the information should be provided. It is, however, a relevant factor which should be taken into account in weighing the competing interests.

In applying these factors, it is also appropriate to bear in mind that production of third party records is always available to the Crown provided it can obtain a search warrant. It can do so if it satisfies a Justice that there is in a place, which includes a private dwelling, anything that there are reasonable grounds to believe will afford evidence of the commission of an offence. Fairness requires that the accused be treated on an equal footing.

Lamer C.J., Sopinka, Cory, Iacobucci and Major JJ. were of the view that the Crown's disclosure obligations established in *Stinchcombe* were unaffected by the confidential nature of therapeutic records when the records were in the possession of the Crown. When that was the case the complainant's privacy interests in the records need not be balanced against the right of the accused to make full answer and defence; concerns relating to privacy or privilege disappeared when the documents were in the Crown's possession. If the records were in the possession of the Crown their relevance was to be presumed. It was seen as unfair in the adversarial process for the Crown to have knowledge that was not shared with the accused; when the records have been shared with the Crown, an agent of the state, the records had become the property of the public to be used to ensure that justice was done. Also where the records were in the possession of the Crown the complainant may be taken to have waived any privilege claim. L'Heureux-Dubé, La Forest, Gonthier and McLachlin JJ. decided that the appeal did not concern the extent of the Crown's obligation to disclose private records in its possession and that any comment on such a question would be strictly obiter. **Do you agree with the majority?**

Bill C-46 (1997)

Following *O'Connor*, the Parliament of Canada passed the comprehensive Bill C-46 to restrict the production of records in sexual offence proceedings. In essence, the legislation now contained in ss. 278.1 to 278.9 of the Criminal Code in large measure reflects the minority position of L'Heureux-Dubé J. in *O'Connor*. In particular:

1. The preamble asserts a section 15 equality right for women and children who are complainants in sexual cases.

2. Although the *O'Connor* likely relevance test is maintained, section 278.3(4) specifies ten assertions which are declared not sufficient on their own to establish that a record is likely relevant to an issue at trial or to the competence of a witness to testify.

3. Under s. 278.5 a trial judge has to balance privacy and other issues before deciding whether to order the production of a record for review by the Court.

4. Under s. 278.7, the trial judge may only order production to the accused on consideration of all seven factors listed by L'Heureux-Dubé J. rather than the five adopted by the *O'Connor* majority.

5. Under s. 278.2, the two-stage balancing process must be applied to records in the possession of the Crown.

In *Mills* a joint judgment by Justices McLachlin and Iacobucci holds constitutional the more comprehensive Parliamentary scheme for access to complainants' records in sexual assault cases, which had enacted word for word the minority approach in *O'Connor*. Of the *O'Connor* majority only Lamer C.J. dissented in *Mills* and only on the issue of applying the balancing of complainants' rights approach to records in the possession of the Crown. Justice Cory chose not to participate before his retirement and Justices Iacobucci and Major no longer supported their earlier positions. One suspects that Justice Sopinka, had he still been alive, may well not have capitulated so easily.

The *Mills* decision also makes broader pronouncements on the need for dialogue with Parliament and on its assertion of equality rights for complainants without reference to current section 15 tests or the implications of its ruling.

R. v. MILLS

[1999] 3 S.C.R. 668, 28 C.R. (5th) 207, 139 C.C.C. (3d) 321 (S.C.C.)

Per McLACHLIN and IACOBUCCI JJ. (L'Heureux-Dubé, Gonthier, Major, Bastarache and Binnie JJ. concurring):—

. . .

The law develops through dialogue between courts and legislatures: see *Vriend v. Alberta*, [1998] 1 S.C.R. 493. Against the backdrop of *O'Connor*, Parliament was free to craft its own solution to the problem consistent with the Charter. Turning to the legislation at issue in this appeal, we find it constitutional. It is undisputed that there are several important respects in which Bill C-46 differs from the regime set out in *O'Connor*. However, these differences are not fatal because Bill C-46 provides sufficient protection for all relevant Charter rights. There are, admittedly, several provisions in the Bill that are subject to differing interpretations. However, in such situations we will interpret the legislation in a constitutional manner where possible: see *Slaight Communications Inc. v. Davidson*, [1989] 1 S.C.R. 1038, at p. 1078. By so doing, we conclude that Bill C-46 is a constitutional response to the problem of production of records of complainants or witnesses in sexual assault proceedings.

. . .

Like *O'Connor*, Parliament has set up a two-stage process: (1) disclosure to the judge; and (2) production to the accused. At the first stage, the accused must establish that the record sought is "likely relevant to an issue at trial or to the competence of a witness to testify" and that "the production of the record is necessary in the interests of justice" (s. 278.5(1)). Bill C-46 diverges from *O'Connor* by directing the trial judge to consider the salutary and deleterious effects of production to the court on the accused's right to full answer and defence and the complainant or witness's right to privacy and equality. A series of factors is listed that the trial judge is directed to take into account in deciding whether the document should be produced to the court (s. 278.5(2)). If the requirements of this first stage are met, the record will be ordered produced to the trial judge. At the second stage, the judge looks at the record in the absence of the parties (s. 278.6(1)), holds a hearing if necessary (s. 278.6(2)), and determines whether the record should be produced on the basis that it is "likely relevant to an issue at trial or to the competence of a witness to testify" and that its production is "necessary in the interests of justice" (s. 278.7). Again at this stage, the judge must consider the salutary and deleterious effects on the accused's right to make full answer and defence and on the right to privacy and equality of the complainant or witness, and is directed to "take into account" the factors set out at s. 278.5(2): s. 278.7(2). When ordering production, the judge may impose conditions on production: s. 278.7(3).

The respondent and several supporting interveners argue that Bill C-46 is unconstitutional to the extent that it establishes a regime for production that differs from or is inconsistent with that established by the majority in *O'Connor*. However, it does not follow from the fact that a law passed by Parliament differs from a regime envisaged by the Court in the absence of a statutory scheme, that Parliament's law is unconstitutional. Parliament may build on the Court's decision, and develop a different scheme as long as it remains constitutional. Just as Parliament must respect the Court's rulings, so the Court must respect Parliament's determination that the judicial scheme can be improved. To insist on slavish conformity would belie the mutual respect that underpins the relationship between the courts and legislature that is so essential to our constitutional democracy: *Vriend*, supra....

RELATIONSHIP BETWEEN THE COURTS AND THE LEGISLATURE GENERALLY

A posture of respect towards Parliament was endorsed by this Court in *Slaight Communications*, supra, at p. 1078, where we held that if legislation is amenable to two interpretations, a court should choose that interpretation that upholds the legislation as constitutional. Thus courts must presume that Parliament intended to enact constitutional legislation and strive, where possible, to give effect to this intention. This Court has also discussed the relationship between the courts and the legislature in terms of a dialogue, and emphasized its importance to the democratic process. In Vriend, supra, at para. 139, Iacobucci J. stated:

> To my mind, a great value of judicial review and this dialogue among the branches is that each of the branches is made somewhat accountable to the other. The work of the legislature is reviewed by the courts and the work of the court in its decisions can be reacted to by the legislature in the passing of new legislation (or even overarching laws under s. 33 of the Charter). This dialogue between and accountability of each of the branches have the effect of enhancing the democratic process, not denying it.

See also Peter W. Hogg and Allison A. Bushell, "The Charter Dialogue Between Courts and Legislatures" (1997), 35 Osgoode Hall L.J. 75. If the common law were to be taken as establishing the only possible constitutional regime, then we could not speak of a dialogue with the legislature. Such a situation could only undermine rather than enhance democracy. Legislative change and the development of the common law are different....

Courts do not hold a monopoly on the protection and promotion of rights and freedoms; Parliament also plays a role in this regard and is often able to act as a significant ally for vulnerable groups. This is especially important to recognize in the context of sexual violence. The history of the treatment of sexual assault complainants by our society and our legal system is an unfortunate one. Important change has occurred through legislation aimed at both recognizing the rights and interests of complainants in criminal proceedings, and debunking the stereotypes that have been so damaging to women and children, but the treatment of sexual assault complainants remains an ongoing problem. If constitutional democracy is meant to ensure that due regard is given to the voices of those vulnerable to being overlooked by the majority, then this court has an obligation to consider respectfully Parliament's attempt to respond to such voices.

Parliament has enacted this legislation after a long consultation process that included a consideration of the constitutional standards outlined by this Court in O'Connor. While it is the role of the courts to specify such standards, there may be a range of permissible regimes that can meet these standards. It goes without saying that this range is not confined to the specific rule adopted by the Court pursuant to its competence in the common law. In the present case, Parliament decided that legislation was necessary in order to address the issue of third-party records more comprehensively. As is evident from the language of the preamble to Bill C-46, Parliament also sought to recognize the prevalence of sexual violence against women and children and its disadvantageous impact on their rights, to encourage the reporting of incidents of sexual violence, to recognize the impact of the production of personal information on the efficacy of treatment, and to reconcile fairness to complainants with the rights of the accused. Many of these concerns involve policy decisions regarding criminal procedure and its relationship to the community at large. Parliament may also be understood to be recognizing "horizontal" equality concerns, where women's inequality results from the acts of other individuals and groups rather than the state, but which nonetheless may have many consequences for the criminal justice system. It is perfectly reasonable that these many concerns may lead to a procedure that is different from the common law position but that nonetheless meets the required constitutional standards.

We cannot presume that the legislation is unconstitutional simply because it is different from the common law position. The question before us is not whether Parliament can amend the common law; it clearly can. The question before us is whether in doing so Parliament has nonetheless outlined a constitutionally acceptable procedure for the production of private records of complainants in sexual assault trials....

TENSIONS AMONG FULL ANSWER AND DEFENCE, PRIVACY, AND EQUALITY

(a) Balancing Interests and Defining Rights

At play in this appeal are three principles, which find their support in specific provisions of the Charter. These are full answer and defence, privacy, and equality. No single principle is absolute and capable of trumping the others; all must be defined in light of competing claims. As Lamer C.J. stated in *Dagenais*, [1984] 3 S.C.R. 835 at p. 877:

> When the protected rights of two individuals come into conflict . . . Charter principles require a balance to be achieved that fully respects the importance of both sets of rights.

. . . Whether or not all the rights involved are "principles of fundamental justice", Charter rights must always be defined contextually

(b) Nature of the Charter Principles

(i) Full Answer and Defence

It is well established that the ability of the accused to make full answer and defence is a principle of fundamental justice protected by s. 7.... Many of these principles of fundamental justice are informed by the legal rights outlined in ss. 8 to 14 of the Charter .... Our jurisprudence has recognized on several occasions "the danger of placing the accused in a "Catch-22" situation as a condition of making full answer and defence". This is an important consideration in the context of records production as often the accused may be in the difficult position of making submissions regarding the importance to full answer and defence of records that he or she has not seen. Where the records are part of the case to meet, this concern is particularly acute as such a situation very directly implicates the accused's ability to raise a doubt concerning his or her innocence. As the Court stated in *R. v. Leipert*, [1997] 1 S.C.R. 281, at para. 24, "[t]his Court has consistently affirmed that it is a fundamental principle of justice, protected by the Charter, that the innocent must not be convicted". Where the records to which the accused seeks access are not part of the case to meet, however, privacy and equality considerations may require that it be more difficult for accused persons to gain access to therapeutic or other records.

That said, the principles of fundamental justice do not entitle the accused to "the most favourable procedures that could possibly be imagined": *R. v. Lyons*, [1987] 2 S.C.R. 309, per La Forest J., at p. 362. This is because fundamental justice embraces more than the rights of the accused. For example, this Court has held that an assessment of the fairness of the trial process must be made "from the point of view of fairness in the eyes of the community and the complainant" and not just the accused: *R. v. E. (A.W.)*, [1993] 3 S.C.R. 155, per Cory J., at p. 198.... This spectrum of interests reflected in the principles of fundamental justice highlights the need to avoid viewing any particular principle in isolation from the others....

Several principles regarding the right to make full answer and defence emerge from the preceding discussion. First, the right to make full answer and defence is crucial to ensuring that the innocent are not convicted. To that end, courts must consider the danger of placing the accused in a Catch-22 situation as a condition of making full answer and defence, and will even override competing considerations in order to protect the right to make full answer and defence in certain circumstances, such as the "innocence at stake" exception to informer privilege. Second, the accused's right must be defined in a context that includes other principles of fundamental justice and Charter provisions. Third, full answer and defence does not include the right to evidence that would distort the search for truth inherent in the trial process.

(ii) Privacy

Since *Hunter v. Southam Inc.*, [1984] 2 S.C.R. 145, this Court has recognized that s. 8 of the Charter protects a person's reasonable expectation of privacy. This right is relevant to the present appeal, as an order for the production of documents is a seizure within the meaning of s. 8 of the Charter [citations omitted]. Therefore an order for the production of records made pursuant to ss. 278.1 to 278.91 of the Criminal Code, falls within the ambit of s. 8. . . .

This Court has most often characterized the values engaged by privacy in terms of liberty, or the right to be left alone by the state.... This interest in being left alone by the state includes the ability to control the dissemination of confidential information. These privacy concerns are at their strongest where aspects of one's individual identity are at stake, such as in the context of information "about one's lifestyle, intimate relations or political or religious opinions"....

In fostering the underlying values of dignity, integrity and autonomy, it is fitting that s. 8 of the Charter should seek to protect a biographical core of personal information which individuals in a free and democratic society would wish to maintain and control from dissemination to the state. This would include information which tends to reveal intimate details of the lifestyle and personal choices of the individual. That privacy is essential to maintaining relationships of trust was stressed to this Court by the eloquent submissions of many interveners in this case regarding counselling records. The therapeutic relationship is one that is characterized by trust, an element of which is confidentiality. Therefore the protection of the complainant's reasonable expectation of privacy in her therapeutic records protects the therapeutic relationship. . . .

Given that s. 8 protects a person's privacy by prohibiting unreasonable searches or seizures, and given that s. 8 addresses a particular application of the principles of fundamental justice, we can infer that a reasonable search or seizure is consistent with the principles of fundamental justice. Moreover, as we have already discussed, the principles of fundamental justice include the right to make full answer and defence. Therefore a reasonable search and seizure will be one that accommodates both the accused's ability to make full answer and defence and the complainant's privacy right.

From our preceding discussion of the right to make full answer and defence, it is clear that the accused will have no right to the records in question insofar as they contain information that is either irrelevant or would serve to distort the search for truth, as access to such information is not included within the ambit of the accused's right.... The values protected by privacy rights will be most directly at stake where the confidential information contained in a record concerns aspects of one's individual identity or where the maintenance of confidentiality is crucial to a therapeutic, or other trust-like, relationship.

(iii) Equality

Equality concerns must also inform the contextual circumstances in which the rights of full answer and defence and privacy will come into play. In this respect, an appreciation of myths and stereotypes in the context of sexual violence is essential to delineate properly the boundaries of full answer and defence. As we have already discussed, the right to make full answer and defence does not include the right to information that would only distort the truth-seeking goal of the trial process. In *R. v. Osolin*, [1993] 4 S.C.R. 595, Cory J., for the majority on this issue, stated, at pp. 669 and 670:

> The provisions of ss. 15 and 28 of the Charter guaranteeing equality to men and women, although not determinative should be taken into account in determining the reasonable limitations that should be placed upon the cross-examination of a complainant.... A complainant should not be unduly harassed and pilloried to the extent of becoming a victim of an insensitive judicial system.

The reasons in *Seaboyer* make it clear that eliciting evidence from a complainant for the purpose of encouraging inferences pertaining to consent or the credibility of rape victims which are based on groundless myths and fantasized stereotypes is improper. The accused is not permitted to "whack the complainant" through the use of stereotypes regarding victims of sexual assault.....

When the boundary between privacy and full answer and defence is not properly delineated, the equality of individuals whose lives are heavily documented is also affected, as these individuals have more records that will be subject to wrongful scrutiny. Karen Busby cautions that the use of records to challenge credibility at large will subject those whose lives already have been subject to extensive documentation to extraordinarily invasive review. This would include women whose lives have been documented under conditions of multiple inequalities and institutionalization such as Aboriginal women, women with disabilities, or women who have been imprisoned or involved with child welfare agencies.

("Discriminatory Uses of Personal Records in Sexual Violence Cases" (1997), 9 C.J.W.L.148, at pp. 161-62.)

These concerns highlight the need for an acute sensitivity to context when determining the content of the accused's right to make full answer and defence, and its relationship to the complainant's privacy right.

SUMMARY

In summary, the following broad considerations apply to the definition of the rights at stake in this appeal. The right of the accused to make full answer and defence is a core principle of fundamental justice, but it does not automatically entitle the accused to gain access to information contained in the private records of complainants and witnesses. Rather, the scope of the right to make full answer and defence must be determined in light of privacy and equality rights of complainants and witnesses. It is clear that the right to full answer and defence is not engaged where the accused seeks information that will only serve to distort the truth-seeking purpose of a trial, and in such a situation, privacy and equality rights are paramount. On the other hand, where the information contained in a record directly bears on the right to make full answer and defence, privacy rights must yield to the need to avoid convicting the innocent. Most cases, however, will not be so clear, and in assessing applications for production courts must determine the weight to be granted to the interests protected by privacy and full answer and defence in the particular circumstances of each case. Full answer and defence will be more centrally implicated where the information contained in a record is part of the case to meet or where its potential probative value is high. A complainant's privacy interest is very high where the confidential information contained in a record concerns the complainant's personal identity or where the confidentiality of the record is vital to protect a therapeutic relationship.

With this background in mind, we now proceed to discuss the statutory provisions under attack.

. . .

THE STATUTORY PROVISIONS

Section 278.3(4) lists a series of "assertions" that cannot "on their own" establish that a record is likely relevant. The respondent submits that on a plain reading, this provision prevents the accused from relying on the listed factors when attempting to establish the likely relevance of the records. This, he argues, interferes with the right to make full answer and defence by restricting what the judge can consider in determining whether the records must be produced to the defence. The legislation raises the bar for production, he asserts, making it difficult if not impossible for the accused to meet the likely relevance test of ss. 278.5 and 278.7. The Respondent contends that it is unconstitutional to exclude the assertions listed in s. 278.3(4) as irrelevant.

This submission forgets that when legislation is susceptible to more than one interpretation, we must always choose the constitutional reading. See *Slaight*, supra, at p. 1078. This mistake leads the respondent to overstate the purpose and effect of s. 278.3(4). As has frequently been held, its purpose is to prevent speculative and unmeritorious requests for production [citations omitted].It does not entirely prevent an accused from relying on the factors listed, but simply prevents reliance on bare "assertions" of the listed matters, where there is no other evidence and they stand "on their own".

The purpose and wording of s. 278.3 does not prevent an accused from relying on the assertions set out in subsection 278.3(4) where there is an evidentiary or informational foundation to suggest that they may be related to likely relevance. . . . The section requires only that the accused be able to point to case specific evidence or information to show that the record in issue is likely relevant to an issue at trial or the competence of a witness to testify, see *Leipert*, supra, at para. 21. Conversely, where an accused does provide evidence or information to support an assertion listed in s. 278.3(4), this does not mean that likely relevance is made out. Section 278.3(4) does not supplant the ultimate discretion of the trial judge. Where any one of the listed assertions is made and supported by the required evidentiary and informational foundation, the trial judge is the ultimate arbiter in deciding whether the likely relevance threshold set out in s. 278.5 and 278.7 is met. We conclude that s. 278.3(4) does not violate ss. 7 or 11(d) of the Charter.

. . .

Both the majority and minority of this Court in *O'Connor*, supra, held that records must be produced to the judge for inspection if the accused can demonstrate that the information is "likely to be relevant": *O'Connor*, supra, at para. 19, per Lamer C.J. and Sopinka J., and at para 138, per L'Heureux-Dubé J. The Court defined the standard of likely relevance as "a reasonable possibility that the information is logically probative to an issue at trial or the competence of a witness to testify". Although the majority recognized that complainants have a constitutional right to privacy it held that no balancing of rights should be undertaken at the first stage. This conclusion was premised on the finding that: (1) to require the accused to meet more than the likely relevance stage would be to "put the accused in the difficult situation of having to make submissions to the judge without precisely knowing what is contained in the records"; and (2) there is not enough information before a trial judge at this initial stage of production for an informed balancing procedure to take place. To this end, the majority held that the analysis should be confined to determining "likely relevance"and "whether the right to make full answer and defence is implicated by information contained in the records". In contrast, the minority held that once the accused meets the "likely relevance" threshold, he must then satisfy the judge that the salutary effects of ordering the documents produced to the court for inspection outweigh the deleterious effects of such production, having regard to the accused's right to make full answer and defence, and the effect of such production on the privacy and equality rights of the subject of the records. L'Heureux-Dubé J. found that a sufficient evidentiary basis could be established at this stage through Crown disclosure, defence witnesses, the cross-examination of Crown witnesses at both the preliminary inquiry and the trial and, on some occasions, expert evidence. Parliament, after studying the issue, concluded that the rights of both the complainant and the accused should be considered when deciding whether to order production to the judge. In coming to this conclusion, Parliament must be taken to have determined, as a result of lengthy consultations, and years of Parliamentary study and debate, that trial judges have sufficient evidence to engage in an informed balancing process at this stage. . . . As a result of the consultation process, Parliament decided to supplement the "likely relevant" standard for production to the judge proposed in *O'Connor* with the further requirement that production be "necessary in the interests of justice". The result was s. 278.5. This process is a notable example of the dialogue between the judicial and legislative branches discussed above. This Court acted in *O'Connor*, and the legislature responded with Bill C-46. As already mentioned, the mere fact that Bill C-46 does not mirror *O'Connor* does not render it unconstitutional.

The question comes down to this: once likely relevance is established, is it necessarily unconstitutional that a consideration of the rights and interests of those affected by production to the court might result in production not being ordered? The answer to this question depends on whether a consideration of the range of rights and interests affected, in addition to a finding of likely relevance, will ultimately prevent the accused from seeing documents that are necessary to enable him to defend himself — to raise all the defences that might be open to him at trial. The non-disclosure of third party records with a high privacy interest that may contain relevant evidence will not compromise trial fairness where such non-disclosure would not prejudice the accused's right to full answer and defence.

Section 278.5(1) is a very wide and flexible section. It accords the trial judge great latitude. Parliament must be taken to have intended that judges, within the broad scope of the powers conferred, would apply it in a constitutional manner — a way that would ultimately permit the accused access to all documents that may be constitutionally required. Indeed, a production regime that denied this would not be production "necessary in the interests of justice".

. . .

While this Court may have considered it preferable not to consider privacy rights at the production stage, that does not preclude Parliament from coming to a different conclusion, so long as its conclusion is consistent with the Charter in its own right. As we have explained, the Bill's directive to consider what is "necessary in the interests of justice", read correctly, does include appropriate respect for the right to full answer and defence.

This leaves the argument that the judge cannot consider the factors listed in s. 278.5(2) without looking at the documents. However, s. 278.5(2) does not require that the judge engage in a conclusive and in-depth evaluation of each of the factors. It rather requires the judge to "take them into account"— to the extent possible at this early stage of proceedings — in deciding whether to order a particular record produced to himself or herself for inspection. Section 278.5(2) serves as a checklist of the various factors that may come into play in making the decision regarding production to the judge. Therefore, while the s. 278.5(2) factors are relevant, in the final analysis the judge is free to make whatever order is "necessary in the interests of justice" — a mandate that includes all of the applicable "principles of fundamental justice" at stake.

Furthermore, contrary to the respondent's submissions, there is a sufficient evidentiary basis to support such an analysis at this early stage. This basis can be established through Crown disclosure, defence witnesses, the cross-examination of Crown witnesses at both the preliminary inquiry and the trial, and expert evidence, see: *O'Connor*, supra, at para. 146, per L'Heureux-Dubé J. As noted by Taylor J. for the British Columbia Supreme Court, "the criminal process provides a reasonable process for the acquisition of the evidentiary basis", *Hurrie*, supra, at para. 39. To this end, as the Attorney of British Columbia submitted: "Laying the groundwork prior to trial, or comprehensive examination of witnesses at trial, will go a long way to establishing a meritorious application under this legislation".

The nature of the records in question will also often provide the trial judge with an important informational foundation. For example, with respect to the privacy interest in records, the expectation of privacy in adoption or counselling records may be very different from that in school attendance records, see for example, *R. v. J.S.P.*, B.C.S.C., Vancouver Registry Nos. CC970130 & CC960237, May 15, 1997. Similarly, a consideration of the probative value of records can often be informed by the nature and purposes of a record, as well as the record taking practices used to create it. As noted above, many submissions were made regarding the different levels of reliability of certain records. Counselling or therapeutic records, for example, can be highly subjective documents which attempt merely to record an individual's emotions and psychological state. Often such records have not been checked for accuracy by the subject of the records, nor have they been recorded verbatim. All of these factors may help a trial judge when considering the probative value of a record being sought by an accused.

As discussed above in the context of defining the right to full answer and defence, courts must as a general matter ensure that the accused can obtain all pertinent evidence required to make full answer and defence, and must be wary of the danger of putting the accused in a Catch-22 situation in seeking to obtain such evidence. Where there is a danger that the accused's right to make full answer and defence will be violated, the trial judge should err on the side of production to the court. We conclude that s. 278.5 is constitutional.

Once the first hurdle is passed and the records are produced to the judge, the judge must determine whether it is in the interests of justice that they be produced to the defence. Again the judge must be satisfied that the records are "likely relevant" and that production, this time to the accused, is necessary in the interests of justice. In making this decision, the judge must once again consider the factors set out in s. 278.5(2).

The respondent accepts that weighing competing interests is appropriate at this second stage of the analysis. However, the respondent contends that the requirement under s. 278.7(2), that the trial judge take the factors specified in paragraphs s. 278.5(2)(a) to (h) into account, inappropriately alters the constitutional balance established in *O'Connor*. Specifically, the respondent contends that ss. 278.5(2)(f) and (g) elevate the societal interest in encouraging the reporting of sexual offences and encouraging of treatment of complainants of sexual offences, to a status equal to the accused's right to make full answer and defence. This, he suggests, alters the constitutional balance established in *O'Connor*, where the majority specifically determined these factors to be of secondary importance to defence interests in any balancing of competing interests and better taken into account through other avenues. The respondent also contends that s. 278.5(2)(h) unfairly requires trial judges to consider the effect of disclosure on the integrity of the trial process. The respondent submits that this is a question going to admissibility.

These concerns are largely answered by the analysis advanced under s. 278.5(2), discussed at greater length above. Trial judges are not required to rule conclusively on each of the factors nor are they required to determine whether factors relating to the privacy and equality of the complainant or witness "outweigh" factors relating to the accused's right to full answer and defence. To repeat, trial judges are only asked to "take into account" the factors listed in s. 278.5(2) when determining whether production of part or all of the impugned record to the accused is necessary in the interest of justice, s. 278.7(1).

The respondent argues that the inclusion of the societal interest factors in ss. 278.5(2)(f) and (g) alters the constitutional balance established by the *O'Connor* majority. With respect, this argument is unsound. . . . As noted above, when preparing Bill C-46 Parliament had the advantage of being able to assess how the *O'Connor* regime was operating. From the information available to Parliament and the submissions it received during the consultation process, Parliament concluded that the effect of production on the integrity of the trial was a factor that should be included in the list of factors for trial judges to "take into account" at both stages of an application for production. Several interveners have interpreted this factor as requiring courts to consider, along with the other enumerated factors, whether the search for truth would be advanced by the production of the records in question; that is, the question is whether the material in question would introduce discriminatory biases and beliefs into the fact-finding process. We agree with this interpretation of the inquiry required by s. 278.5(2)(h) and believe it to be in keeping with the purposes set out in the preamble of the legislation.

By giving judges wide discretion to consider a variety of factors and requiring them to make whatever order is necessary in the interest of justice at both stages of an application for production, Parliament has created a scheme that permits judges not only to preserve the complainant's privacy and equality rights to the maximum extent possible, but also to ensure that the accused has access to the documents required to make full answer and defence.

LAMER C.J. (dissenting in part):—

. . .

While I agree with McLachlin and Iacobucci JJ.'s finding that Bill C-46 complies with ss. 7 and 11(d) of the Canadian Charter of Rights and Freedoms as it applies to the production of records in the possession of third parties, I take a different view of the legislative regime's approach to records in the hands of the Crown. In my opinion, Bill C-46's treatment of records that form part of the case to meet tips the balance too heavily in favour of privacy to the detriment of the accused's right to make full answer and defence.

Do you think there should be a presumption of constitutionality in Charter cases?

What are the advantages and disadvantages of the new approach of dialogue and deference? What of Chief Justice Dickson's view in *Hunter v. Southam* that the courts should be the guardians of the Constitution?

On the issue of equality, why was there no reference to the ten-part test for judging section 15 claims established in *Law v. Minister of Human Resources Development*, [1999] 1 S.C.R. 497 by Justice Iacobucci J. for a unanimous Court, as recently as March, 1999 (later to be drastically modified in *R. v. Kapp*, [2008] 2 S.C.R. 483, 58 C.R. (6th) 1, 232 C.C.C. (3d) 349 (S.C.C.))?

For an analysis that *O'Connor* applications were used almost always against female complainants, see Karen Busby, "Third Party Records Cases Since R. v. O'Connor", (2000) 27 Man. L.J. 355.

The implications of an enforceable section 15 claim for complainants in sexual assault cases is left unexplored. The policy issues are far wider than establishing privacy rights for therapeutic and other records of complainants. Can complainants now seek status to be represented throughout a sexual assault trial? How about rights to cross-examine the accused, to challenge the similar fact evidence rule or to reverse the presumption of innocence?

For critical comments on *Mills*, see Stuart, "*Mills*: Dialogue with Parliament and Equality by Assertion at What Cost?", (2000) 28 C.R. (5th) 275 and Peter Sankoff, "Crown Disclosure After *Mills*: Have the Ground Rules Suddenly Changed?", (2000) 28 C.R. (5th) 285.

For a view that *Mills* allows for discretion such that little has changed, see Steve Coughlan, "Complainants' Records After *Mills*: Same As It Ever Was", (2000) 33 C.R. (5th) 300.

The Code provisions for production of third party records as interpreted in *Mills* apply only to sexual offences.

In *R. v. McNeil*, [2009] 1 S.C.R. 66, 62 C.R. (6th) 1, 238 C.C.C. (3d) 353 (S.C.C.) Charron J. speaking for a unanimous Court made it clear that the common law regime set out in *O'Connor* is applicable to applications for the production of third party records for offences other than sexual offences whether or not there is a privacy interest in the record. The Court also provided welcome clarification of the distinction between an *O'Connor* application and an application under the statutory regime for sexual offences. The Court made clear that *O'Connor* applications are different from those under the statutory regime. First, the likely relevance standard serves a different purpose. Where a sexual offence is involved, the standard is intended to counter myths and stereotypes regarding sexual assault victims; in the case of *O'Connor* applications, it is intended only to screen out unmeritorious applications so as to avoid wasting valuable court time and resources. It reaffirmed that the likely relevance burden to be met to get courts to inspect third party records had to be realistic. The accused could not be expected to identify the precise use to which the record would be put if counsel hadn't seen the record. Second, under the *O'Connor* regime, much more balancing of the interests of the accused and that of the third party occurs at the second stage of determining whether production to the defence should occur, rather than at the likely relevance stage under the statutory regime. The Court finally streamlined the two part inquiry for *O'Connor* applications with the remarks that the relevancy assessment will usually be largely determinative of the production issue (para. 30) and,

> If the claim of likely relevance is borne out on inspection, the accused's right to full answer and defence will, with few exceptions, tip the balance in favour of allowing the application for production (para. 41).

Indeed, the Court further offered a simple test at the second stage: If the third party record happened to be in the Crown's file, would there be any basis for refusing to disclose it under *Stinchcombe* disclosure obligations? If not, the record should be produced to the defence.

Recently the majority of the Supreme Court may have changed the balance again in favour of rights of accused. The context was a cross-examination regarding a diary in the possession of the accused as to why the complainant had not mentioned abuse by the accused.

R. v. SHEARING

(2002), 2 C.R. (6th) 213, 165 C.C.C. (3d) 225 (S.C.C.)

The accused was charged with 20 counts of sexual offences alleged to have occurred between 1965 and 1989. As a cult leader he had preached that sexual experience with him was the way to a higher level of conscience. One of the complainants kept a daily diary for eight months in 1970. When the complainant left the group home her mother put some of her belongings in a cardboard box in a storage area shared with other residents. About 18 months later, after the accused had been indicted, another resident of the house opened the cardboard box, found the complainant's diary and gave it to the defence. At trial, the defence sought to use the diary to contradict the complainant on the basis of entries arguably inconsistent with her evidence-in-chief, and by showing the absence of any entry chronicling physical or sexual abuse. The complainant objected and, at the voir dire into the admissibility of the diary, asserted a privacy interest. The trial judge permitted the accused to use the diary to cross-examine the complainant on entries the defence considered probative but did not permit cross-examination on the absence of any entries recording physical abuse by the complainant's mother or sexual abuse by the accused. The jury convicted the accused of sexually assaulting his housekeeper's two teenage daughters, one of whom was the diarist, KWG. The accused was acquitted of all charges in respect of the other complainants. The Court of Appeal allowed the accused's appeal with respect to two counts, but otherwise dismissed the appeal.

Per BINNIE J. (McLachlin C.J. and Iacobucci, Major, Bastarache, Arbour and LeBel JJ. concurring):

. . .

B. Limiting the Scope of Cross-examination

The critical importance of cross-examination is not doubted. The appellant stood before the court accused of crimes by numerous complainants but he was presumed to be innocent of each and every count. All of the alleged sexual misconduct, by its very nature, was in private. At trial, it was his word against the credibility of his accusers, individually and (by virtue of the similar fact evidence) collectively. If the complainants were untruthful about what happened in the privacy of their encounters, the most effective tool he possessed to get at the truth was a full and pointed cross-examination. The general principle was stated in *Seaboyer*, per McLachlin J. at p. 611:

> Canadian courts, like courts in most common law jurisdictions, have been extremely cautious in restricting the power of the accused to call evidence in his or her defence, a reluctance founded in the fundamental tenet of our judicial system that an innocent person must not be convicted. It follows from this that the prejudice must substantially outweigh the value of the evidence before a judge can exclude evidence relevant to a defence allowed by law.

It has been increasingly recognized in recent years, however, that cross-examination techniques in sexual assault cases that seek to put the complainant on trial rather than the accused are abusive and distort rather than enhance the search for truth. Various limitations have been imposed. One of these limits is the privacy interest of the complainant, which is not to be needlessly sacrificed. This was explored by Cory J. writing for the majority in *Osolin*, at pp. 669 and 671, as follows:

> A complainant should not be unduly harassed and pilloried to the extent of becoming a victim of an insensitive judicial system. Yet a fair balance must be achieved so that the limitations on the cross-examination of complainants in sexual assault cases do not interfere with the right of the accused to a fair trial.

> . . .

> In each case the trial judge must carefully balance the fundamentally important right of the accused to a fair trial against the need for reasonable protection of a complainant, *particularly where the purpose of the cross-examination may be directed to the "rape myths"* [Emphasis added].

I underline the reference to "rape myths" because in my view it is a concern about a potential revival of the shibboleth of "recent complaint" in sexual assault cases rather than a privacy concern as such, that lies at the heart of the trial judge's ruling.

In *Seaboyer*, the accused sought to cross-examine the complainant on her sexual conduct on other occasions to explain the "bruises and other aspects of the complainant's condition which the Crown had put in evidence". In *Osolin*, the accused sought to cross-examine a notation in the complainant's medical record of a concern she had expressed to her therapist that her attitude and behaviour may have influenced the accused to some extent. This case is different. The focus is not private information as such because, as stated, the trial judge allowed cross-examination by the defence on each of the specific diary entries the defence sought to utilize. The defence objection is to the restriction on its ability to cross-examine on the significance (if any) of what was not recorded. It is common ground that KWG's diary contains no references to beatings by the mother or to sexual abuse by the appellant.

The cogency of this line of questioning rested on the premise that if these assaults had happened, they would have been recorded, and because the events were not recorded, they did not happen. That, in the Crown's view, is where one of the "rape myths" surfaces. The trial judge agreed:

> In essence, [the appellant] wants to go to the jury and argue that the witness has made no "complaint", if I may use that word, to her private, confidential diary about the sexual assaults that she now testifies to.
>
> . . .
>
> [Counsel for KWG] argues strongly that there is no probative value in a lack of complaint in these circumstances, and that to allow cross-examination and argument on the issue is premised upon a discriminatory belief or bias.

The trial judge's trade-off of permitting questions on actual entries but disallowing questions on the absence of entries was criticized in about equal measure by the appellant and the Criminal Lawyers' Association on the one hand, who thought it too restrictive on the defence, and on the other hand by the Crown and Women's Legal Education and Action Fund ("LEAF"), who thought it went too far against the complainant.

The Crown and LEAF took the position that KWG's diary was and remained her property, and that the appellant came into possession of it without colour of right. That being the case, the trial judge ought to have ignored the reality of the appellant's possession (a sort of constructive dispossession) and required the appellant to make an application for compelled production of documents under ss. 278.1 to 278.9, just as if KWG rather than the appellant had possession of it.

I will deal with these points in turn.

(1) Surprise Disclosure of the Diary

In her evidence-in-chief and in the initial cross-examination KWG committed herself to having experienced a profoundly unhappy childhood (a "chamber of horrors" is how the defence put it, somewhat sarcastically), lack of friends at school, prohibition on participation in extracurricular school activities, and not being allowed to wear ordinary teenager clothing. All of this was the background to alleged constant physical abuse by the mother and alleged sexual abuse by the appellant, the latter occurring mainly in the appellant's den at the Centre.

She was asked by the defence about the possible existence of a diary and she said she thought she had received one as a present at Christmas in her early teens, but had only made entries for two weeks or so.

At this point in the trial, counsel for the defence flourished KWG's original diary which she had not seen for 22 years, and announced that it contained day-by-day entries for a period of eight months (not the two weeks she had recalled) commencing January 1970, in the midst of the period of alleged abuse. It recorded what KWG herself described as "mundane" entries about schoolmates, participation in school functions, family outings to see films, Easter presents and some positive references to the appellant (e.g., "Stayed home from school today and had a nice talk with Ivon. He makes you want to work harder"). The defence wished to raise a doubt about the reliability and completeness of KWG's memory by contradicting her testimony with what the defence viewed as inconsistent entries written under her own hand in the diary, and the omission of any entry chronicling physical or sexual abuse.

KWG's response to the surprise disclosure of her 1970 diary was to obtain a short adjournment, and to retain her own Counsel who argued that (1) the diary was the property of KWG and should be returned forthwith and (2) thereafter dealt with under the documentary production provisions of ss. 278.1 to 278.9 of the Criminal Code.

(2) Wrongful Possession of the Diary

KWG testified on the voir dire that she did "not at all" intend to give up her privacy rights. She was "appalled" and wanted the diary and all the copies returned to her as the defence had no right to "the little bit of privacy that [she] had". On cross-examination, KWG described the diary entries as "very mundane", "[b]ut it's still mine. . . . I don't understand what that has to do with anything. This is still mine. Whether it's mundane or exciting or boring, it's still mine". The trial judge found that KWG had never waived or abandoned her privacy interest in the diary and I agree with him.

The voir dire included a lengthy legal debate about whether KWG had or had not abandoned her property interest in her diary, and whether the appellant's possession of it amounted to conversion. I do not think KWG was illegally deprived of possession of the diary (unlike the Chinese restaurateurs whose safe containing private documents was stolen by thieves in *R. v. Law*, 2002 SCC 10). She simply left it behind in a common storage room with other possessions no longer required for day-to-day living. When her mother forwarded her possessions to her in 1995, the diary was not among them. When the diary fell into the appellant's possession 22 years after KWG left home, it was not a "wrongful" taking in any legal sense, although I agree with KWG that it underlined the extent of his unwelcome access to KWG's private life as a by-product of her mother's adherence to the cult.

I do not propose to pursue the property ownership debate. The issue for present purposes is not the "ownership of the diary" (which could be the subject of a civil cause of action) but the status of information contained within the diary. Return of the diary, as proposed by my colleague L'Heureux-Dubé J. at para. 161, would seem to me to shut the barn door after the horse had escaped.

(3) Applicability of Sections 278.1 to 278.9 of the Criminal Code

Sections 278.1 to 278.9 on their face address the *production* not the *use* or *admissibility* of personal information, as stated by Parliament itself in the Preamble (S.C. 1997, c. 30):

> WHEREAS the Parliament of Canada recognizes that the *compelled production* of personal information may deter complainants of sexual offences from reporting the offence to the police and may deter complainants from seeking necessary treatment, counselling or advice;
>
> WHEREAS the Parliament of Canada recognizes that the work of those who provide services and assistance to complainants of sexual offences is detrimentally affected by the *compelled production* of records and by the process to compel that production;
>
> AND WHEREAS the Parliament of Canada recognizes that, while *production* to the court and to the accused of personal information regarding any person may be necessary in order for an accused to make a full answer and defence, *that production* may breach the person's right to privacy and equality and *therefore the determination as to whether to order production should be subject to careful scrutiny....* [Emphasis added.]

The text of ss. 278.1 to 278.9 that follows is consistent with such a purpose. Counsel for KWG at trial and LEAF before this Court, argued that the machinery of ss. 278.1 to 278.9 can be put into reverse, i.e., it contemplates taking documents already in the hands of the defence and restoring these to the complainant, thus requiring the defence to make a fresh application for the document just removed from its possession. In my view, this interpretation is unduly contrived and does violence to the statutory language.

(4) The Issue Here is Admissibility of Evidence, Not Production and Disclosure

The confusion between production (*O'Connor*) and admissibility (*Osolin*) took hold at an early stage of the voir dire in this case.

Having rightly rejected the applicability of ss. 278.1 to 278.9 on the ground that there was no issue here of production or disclosure, the trial judge prefaced the opening of submissions on admissibility as "what I'll call an *O'Connor* application at this stage".

Although well aware of *Seaboyer* (1991) and *Osolin* (1993), the trial judge (and eventually the Court of Appeal) seems to have concluded that these earlier authorities had been overtaken by this Court's subsequent pronouncements in *O'Connor* (1995). I do not agree that *O'Connor* can substitute for *Osolin* or indeed that the two tests are equivalent or interchangeable.

The trial judge heard several days of argument from counsel for KWG as well as counsel for the prosecution and the defence on the use that would be made of KWG's diary in cross-examination before the jury. Much of this argument was directed explicitly to various dicta in *O'Connor, supra*. In his ruling on the permissible scope of the cross-examination, the trial judge "applied" the *O'Connor* principles. . . .

In my view, the trial judge erred in extrapolating the *O'Connor* test from the issue of production of information not previously disclosed to the defence and applying it to the admissibility (or use in cross-examination) before the jury of evidence already in the possession of the defence.

A simple "balancing of interests" test (*O'Connor, supra*, at paras. 129 and 150) cannot be equated to "substantially outweighs" (*Seaboyer, Osolin*). Under *O'Connor*, the default position is that the third party information is not produced to the defence. Under *Seaboyer* and *Osolin*, the default position is that the defence is allowed to proceed with its cross-examination.

(5) *The Proper Limits of Cross-examination*

In *Seaboyer*, McLachlin J. noted that "our courts have traditionally been reluctant to exclude even tenuous defence evidence" (p. 607) and affirmed that the defence has a right to use evidence in its possession unless its prejudicial effect "substantially outweighs" (p. 611) its probative value. The reason for the different orientation is apparent. In the *O'Connor* situation, the accused is not entitled to disclosure, and seeks the intervention of the state to put aside the privacy of a third party complainant. In the *Seaboyer* situation, the state is asked by the complainant to intervene against the accused to deny him the use of information already in his possession. It is true that some of the same values must be weighed (e.g., full answer and defence, privacy, equality rights, etc.) but both the purpose and the context are quite different.

The issue for the trial judge here, therefore, was whether cross-examination on the diary would create prejudice to the complainant that "substantially outweighed" its potential probative value to the appellant, and in that regard whether cross-examination on the absence of entries recording abuse relied upon "rape myths" or the equivalent.

(6) *KWG's Privacy Concerns*

The fact KWG conceded that the diary contained "mundane" sorts of information is not, in my view, fatal to her wish to keep private the entries she did choose to record in her private diary, but the fact KWG freely acknowledged that her teenage diary was not written in any kind of confessional spirit does go to the weight of the privacy interest.

On this point, however, it is KWG not the appellant who might be expected to complain of the trial judge's ruling. He allowed the defence to put to KWG whatever entries it wished where specific entries arguably contradicted KWG on some of the statements she had made in her evidence-in-chief.

All that was left to explore was what she did not write down. Cross-examination on that point would be a high-risk tactic for the defence capable of generating some devastating answers, to put it mildly. However, the appellant considered pursuit of that point to be crucial to his defence.

(7) Omission of Entries Recording Abuse

We arrive then at the appellant's real grievance. He was not allowed to challenge the credibility of KWG based on the absence of any entries dealing with physical or sexual abuse in an important and relevant 8-month period in 1970.

In fact, the jury was never told the omissions existed.

The Crown contends that the effect of this restriction was marginal at best:

> The Respondent submits that the non-recording of an event is generally of much lower probative value than the recording of an event. If an event is recorded which a witness denies, that contradiction cries out for an explanation. Where an event is not recorded, however, that fact is not in itself logically inconsistent with the event having occurred.

The Crown's argument assumes the point in issue, of course. If we assume KWG intended a type of diary that would not be expected to contain entries recording abuse, the omissions would be irrelevant. It is that assumption, however, which the defence sought to explore in cross-examination.

The courts have recognized, no doubt belatedly, that certain techniques of cross-examination traditionally employed in sexual assault cases have distorted rather than advanced the search for truth. This case illustrates one of the problem areas. The omission to record some piece of information is only probative if there is a reasonable expectation that such a record would be made (*R. v. R.M.* (1997), 93 B.C.A.C. 81, at paras. 45-49; *Wigmore on Evidence*, Vol. IIIA (Chadbourn rev. 1970), at para. 1042). A pilot's log will record relevant flight information, because that is its purpose, but not what he or she had to eat for breakfast over the Atlantic Ocean. Hospital records will include medical observations but not what television station the patient happened to be watching that evening. What was objectionable about the defence approach here was that it overlooked (or perhaps resolutely resisted) the need to lay before the jury a rational basis for the inference it ultimately wished to draw, namely that the non-recording of a certain type of information was circumstantial evidence that the alleged abuse never happened.

The problem lies in the unspoken and unproven premise. KWG was obviously under no legal or other duty to record such observations. She clearly did not follow a regular practice of making such entries because no entries of any kind of abuse were made. All sides agree that the diary entries were "mundane". Why assume that a diary devoted to "mundane" entries would necessarily report on episodes of physical and sexual abuse? On what logical basis would such a non-record give rise to an inference of testimonial deficiency or fabrication? In the absence of some evidentiary basis for the premise that abuse ought to have been recorded, the result of allowing the cross-examination to proceed as proposed by the defence ("the entire contents are fair game") would be to allow the defence to go to the jury at the end of the trial and to point to the absence of entries in an effort to suggest—nod nod wink wink—that women and children who are sexually and physically abused do not suffer in silence, but must and do confide their inner hurt even if only to their private diaries.

(8) Legitimate Scope for Cross-examination

This does not turn persons accused of sexual abuse into second class litigants. It simply means that the defence has to work with facts rather than rely on innuendoes and wishful assumptions. This means, in turn, that the defence should not be prevented from getting at the facts. As L'Heureux-Dubé J. wrote in *O'Connor, supra*, at para. 124:

> Although the defence must be free to *demonstrate*, without resort to stereotypical lines of reasoning, that such information is actually relevant to a live issue at trial, it would mark the triumph of stereotype over logic if courts and lawyers were simply to *assume* such relevance to exist, without requiring any evidence to this effect whatsoever. [Emphasis in original]

At the time of the trial, KWG was a mature and well-spoken 42-year-old adult. She was (or had been) an airline stewardess. She was not a child in need of any special protection from the court. There were arguably some contradictions between her testimony as an adult and what she had written as a teenager 27 years before, as the trial judge recognized. These arguable contradictions nourished the defence argument that the diary (including omissions) provided a more accurate picture of events in 1970 than KWG's unaided recollection. I therefore do not, with respect, agree with my colleague L'Heureux-Dubé J. at para. 176 that cross-examination on such issues would serve "no legitimate purpose".

A witness's powers of recall and the reliability of his or her memory are important issues in a trial of events that took place 27 years previously.

(9) The Trial Judge's Ruling with Respect to the Absence of Entries

The trial judge's ruling was certainly understood by Donald J.A. in the British Columbia Court of Appeal, as based on *O'Connor*. He concluded that *Mills, supra*, following on *O'Connor, supra*, "casts a new light on the question of the complainant's privacy and supports the impugned ruling" (para. 83). Further, "*Mills* ... shifted the balance away from the primary emphasis on the rights of the accused" (para. 93), and again, "[t]he majority in *Mills* emphasized the need to concentrate on the context in which the competing rights arise in order to strike the right balance in each case" (para. 94).

Mills, of course, dealt with the constitutional validity of the procedure set out in ss. 278.1 to 278.9 of the Criminal Code for the production of third party records. It did not purport to deal with the proper limits of cross-examination using evidence already in the possession of the defence.

Moreover, even in terms of *production* of third party documents, I do not, with respect, agree that "*Mills* has shifted the balance away from the *primary* emphasis on the rights of the accused" (para. 93 (emphasis added)) because *Mills* itself affirms the primacy—in the last resort — of the requirement of a fair trial to avoid the wrongful conviction of the innocent. *Mills* states in para. 94 that where the information contained in a record directly bears on the right to make full answer and defence, privacy rights must yield to the need to avoid convicting the innocent.

I agree with Donald J.A. that the trial judge applied *O'Connor* to limit the defence cross-examination of the complainant but I do not agree, with respect, that this Court in *O'Connor* or *Mills* either intended to or did substitute a test intended for the production of third party documents to the quite different problem of imposing limits on cross-examination as laid down in *Seaboyer* and *Osolin*.

. . .

The appeal is therefore allowed with respect to the counts pertaining to KWG but is dismissed with respect to the other convictions of the appellant, the validity of which is affirmed.

L'HEUREUX-DUBÉ J. (Gonthier J. concurring, dissenting):—I respectfully disagree that the defence should have been permitted to question KWG on the absence of reference to abuse in her diary. The reasons for my disagreement are twofold. First, the trial judge should have ordered the diary returned to KWG, its rightful owner, and required the appellant to seek production of it through the appropriate statutory channels. Second, even if the appellant had acquired the diary through the proper channels in the first place, the prejudicial effect of the proposed line of questions on the absence of entries substantially outweighs its probative value.

Like my colleague, however, I do not think it is necessary to dwell on the property ownership debate. Even if we assume, in the appellant's favour, that the diary came into his hands in a manner consistent with the statutory scheme, I believe both the trial judge and the Court of Appeal were nonetheless correct to prohibit the proposed line of cross-examination on the diary.

. . .

The test for admissibility of defence evidence is whether the prejudicial effect of that evidence substantially outweighs its probative value: *R. v. Seaboyer*, [1991] 2 S.C.R. 577, 66 C.C.C. (3d) 321, 83 D.L.R. (4th) 193; *R. v. Osolin*, [1993] 4 S.C.R. 595, 86 C.C.C. (3d) 481, 109 D.L.R. (4th) 478. In weighing prejudicial and probative value, the trial judge must consider not only the accused's right to full answer and defence, but also the importance of the complainant's and other witnesses' privacy and equality rights, as outlined in *R. v. O'Connor*, [1995] 4 S.C.R. 411, 103 C.C.C. (3d) 1, 130 D.L.R. (4th) 235, and *R. v. Mills*, [1999] 3 S.C.R. 668, 139 C.C.C. (3d) 321, 180 D.L.R. (4th) 1. The majority decision in *Osolin*, *supra*, clearly held that, similar to *O'Connor*, *supra*, and *Mills*, *supra*, the privacy and equality rights of the complainant as protected by the Charter should inform the trial judge's decision on whether to restrict the defence's cross-examination.

On this point, I disagree with my colleague that "the nature and scope of KWG's diary did not raise privacy or other concerns of such importance as to 'substantially outweigh' the appellant's fair trial right to cross-examine on the [absence of entries in the diary] . . . to test the accuracy and completeness of KWG's recollection of events 27 years previously" (para. 150). Instead, I believe that such cross-examination would introduce a high potential of prejudice. That possibility substantially outweighs the minimal probative value of questions concerning the absence of entries in the complainant's diary.

Proper consideration of the complainant's equality rights also requires an appreciation of myths and stereotypes in the context of sexual violence: see *Mills, supra*; *O'Connor, supra*; *Osolin, supra*; *Seaboyer, supra*. Allowing questioning on the absence of the mention of sexual assault in the diary would be to endorse the same discriminatory beliefs that underlie the "recent complaint" myth. As I explained in *Osolin, supra*, at p. 625, the recent complaint myth "suggest[s] that the presence of certain emotional reactions and immediate reporting of the assault, despite all of the barriers that might discourage such reports, lend credibility to the assault report, whereas the opposite reactions lead to the conclusion that the complainant must be fabricating the event". Similarly, questioning the complainant as to why certain reactions are not present in her diary or why she did not "report" the incident by recording it in her diary, implies that the absence of such writings is support for the conclusion that she fabricated the events.

The rape myth of "recent complaint" has long been dismissed by this Court and, if used to draw a negative inference about the complainant's credibility, constitutes a reversible error: see *R. v. D.D.*, [2000] 2 S.C.R. 275, 2000 SCC 43, 148 C.C.C. (3d) 41, 191 D.L.R. (4th) 60, at para. 63. As this Court firmly explained in *Mills, supra*, at para. 90: "The accused is not permitted to 'whack the complainant' through the use of [such] stereotypes regarding victims of sexual assault." Oftentimes, merely posing a question that may be directed to myths and stereotypes in the sexual assault context is enough to distort the truth-seeking goal of the trial process because the prejudice derives from the innuendo imbedded in the question.

In summary, an application of the *Seaboyer/Osolin, supra*, test that cross-examination should be restricted if the prejudicial impact substantially outweighs the probative value, reveals that the trial judge and Court of Appeal in this case were correct to prohibit the particular line of questioning proposed by the defence. In applying this test, we must consider the accused's right to full answer and defence and the complainant's privacy and equality rights. In the case at bar, the prejudicial effect is very high, while the probative value is, at best, minimal. The diary is an intimate record of the complainant's life during that period of time and the proposed line of cross-examination would necessarily open up much of the diary's contents to scrutiny.

Besides constituting a wide-ranging violation of the complainant's privacy rights, the proposed cross-examination also has potential equality implications, as victims would naturally be loath to report sexual assaults if they feared that their entire private lives would be intensely scrutinized at trial. Given that a diary is an individualistic exercise, questioning a complainant on the failure to record a sexual assault is akin to questioning a complainant as to why she failed to raise a "hue and cry" immediately after the assault. As the proposed line of questioning is animated by a discriminatory belief, the prejudice is high and the potential probative value is very low, if anything. In addition, the defence has the benefit of getting evidence by directly cross-examining the complainant on her version of events, and thus does not require the additional evidence that would result from questioning the complainant on why she did not write about the assaults. Therefore, the evidence is neither relevant nor necessary for the accused to exercise his right to full answer and defence. A review of all of these factors strongly indicates that the trial judge and Court of Appeal were correct to prohibit the proposed line of cross-examination on the diary, as the potential prejudice substantially outweighs the probative value of such an exercise.

See Stuart, "Shearing: Admitting Similar Fact Evidence and Re-asserting the Priority of Rights of Accused in Sexual Assault Trials", (2002) 2 C.R. (6th) 268 and "Zigzags on Rights of Accused: Brittle Majorities Manipulate Weasel Words of Dialogue, Deference and Charter Values", (2003) 20 Sup. Ct. L. Rev. 267.

For strong arguments opposing and supporting Charter rights for victims, see respectively David Paciocco, "Why the Constitutionalisation of Victims Rights Should Not Occur", (2005) 49 Crim. L.Q. 393 and Alan Young, "Crime Victims and Constitutional Rights", (2005) 49 Crim. L.Q. 432. See also Kent Roach, "Victims' Rights and the Charter", (2005) 49 Crim. L.Q. 474, who concludes that "a workable victims' rights amendment to the Charter would not benefit crime victims to a significant extent" (at p. 514).

The retention of the O'Connor common law regime alongside the statutory regime has largely occurred in the context of seeking information about misconduct by police officers involved with the investigation of an accused. In R. v. Quesnelle, [2014] 2 S.C.R. 390, 312 C.C.C. (3d) 187, 11 C.R. (7th) 221 (S.C.C.), the Supreme Court clarified by holding that police occurrence reports unrelated to the charges against the accused are subject to the third-party production regime, either Mills or O'Connor, depending on the offence involved. The Supreme Court recognized that police occurrence reports unrelated to the accused's charges were subject to the privacy interests of those making a complaint to the police. Nevertheless, the Court reiterated what it said in McNeil, namely that the Crown is under a duty to make reasonable inquiries about such reports and to obtain them if they are potentially relevant.

Chapter 9

PRELIMINARY INQUIRY

1. Generally

Prior to the trial of certain indictable offences, a justice of the peace, usually a Provincial Court Judge, will inquire into the charge and determine whether there is sufficient evidence to warrant placing the accused on his trial. The procedure for these preliminary inquiries is set out in Part XVIII of the Criminal Code.

If the indictable offence is listed in s. 553 of the Code, e.g., theft under five thousand dollars, the jurisdiction of the Provincial Court Judge to try the accused is absolute and does not depend on the consent of the accused. In that case, the accused will not have a preliminary hearing prior to his trial. If the indictable offence is listed in s. 469, e.g., murder, under s. 536(2), the offence cannot be tried except by a superior court of criminal jurisdiction and, if either party requests, a preliminary inquiry will be held. With respect to all other indictable offences the accused has the option as to how he will be tried. If he elects to be tried by a Provincial Court Judge, there will be no preliminary hearing but if he elects to be tried by a judge of another court, he will be entitled to a preliminary inquiry.

In 1980, it was estimated by the Department of Justice that there were preliminary inquiries in 5% of trials involving Criminal Code offences. There are even fewer preliminary inquiries given the strong recent trend to create hybrid offences where a Crown may elect to proceed by way of summary conviction and thereby deny the accused a preliminary inquiry. Recall, too, that in 1995 Parliament increased the maximum penalty for several hybrid offences when proceeded against by way of summary conviction, to 18 months, for example, assault causing bodily harm and sexual assault.

Empirical data clearly shows that the number of trials occurring in superior courts across Canada is quickly declining: Webster and Doob, "The Superior/Provincial Criminal Court Distinction: Historical Anachronism or Empirical Reality" (2003) 48 Crim. L.Q. 77. Less than two percent of criminal trials now occur in superior courts. Clearly there are fewer jury trials and less preliminary inquiries. The authors suggest that, with the exception of murder trials which occur in superior courts, provincial judges also now deal with equally serious offences.

For some 10 years, the Department of Justice issued a series of proposals to abolish preliminary inquiries largely based on considerations of cost and efficiency and also on concerns that a principal witness should not have to testify and be cross-examined twice — at the preliminary inquiry and then again at trial. The defence bar has stoutly resisted abolition firmly of the view that cross-examination of the Crown witness on oath at the preliminary inquiry is the best way to ensure a fair trial in serious cases.

The Criminal Code was amended in 1985 and the first section of Part XVIII now provides:

> **535.** If an accused who is charged with an indictable offence is before a justice, and a request has been made for a preliminary inquiry under subsection 536(4) or 536.1(3), the justice shall, in accordance with this Part, inquire into the charge and any other indictable offence, in respect of the same transaction, founded on the facts that are disclosed by the evidence taken in accordance with this Part.

2. Preferring the Indictment

The Criminal Code provides that, following the preliminary, the Crown may prefer an indictment against the person ordered to stand trial, in respect of any charge on which that person was ordered to stand trial or any charge founded on the facts disclosed by the evidence taken on the preliminary; see ss. 566 and 574.

The power of the Crown to prefer an indictment under s. 574 ("founded on the facts disclosed by the evidence taken at the preliminary inquiry") is markedly broader than the power of the Justice presiding at a preliminary inquiry ("in respect of the same transaction"). **Is there any justification for this distinction? Is it fair to provide the Crown with this power?**

In addition, the Crown may prefer an indictment where a preliminary has not been held or where a preliminary has been held and the accused discharged. This is sometimes referred to as "direct" indictment.

> **577.** Despite section 574, an indictment may be preferred even if the accused has not been given the opportunity to request a preliminary inquiry, a preliminary inquiry has been commenced but not concluded or a preliminary inquiry has been held and the accused has been discharged, if
>
> (a) in the case of a prosecution conducted by the Attorney General or one in which the Attorney General intervenes, the personal consent in writing of the Attorney General or Deputy Attorney General is filed in court; or
>
> (b) in any other case, a judge of the court so orders.

It has been held that there is no absolute right for an accused to be given a hearing or to submit representations before the preferment of a direct indictment and that the power does not infringe s. 7 of the Charter: see, for example, *R. v. Stolar* (1983), 32 C.R. (3d) 342 (Man. C.A.) and *R. v. Arviv* (1985), 51 O.R. (2d) 551, 45 C.R. (3d) 354 (Ont. C.A.). However, the finding of constitutionality hinged on the requirement that the accused be provided with adequate disclosure prior to trial. Note that the Ministry of the Attorney General, Crown Policy Manual (2005), says the following about direct indictments:

> This power is one that is used infrequently in Ontario.
>
> Generally, counsel may make a request for the Attorney General's consent to a direct indictment where there exist compelling circumstances which require, in the

interest of justice, that the matter be brought to trial forthwith, bearing in mind the strength of the Crown's case and the seriousness of the charge.

Before requesting the Attorney General or Deputy Attorney General's consent, Crown counsel must have concluded that there is a reasonable prospect of conviction and that the continuation of the prosecution is not contrary to the public interest.

3. Preliminary Inquiry as a Discovery Vehicle

SKOGMAN v. R.
[1984] 2 S.C.R. 93, 41 C.R. (3d) 1, 13 C.C.C. (3d) 161 (S.C.C.)

A majority judgment rested on the question of the reviewability of a committal.

ESTEY J.:—The purpose of a preliminary hearing is to protect the accused from a needless, and indeed, improper, exposure to public trial where the enforcement agency is not in possession of evidence to warrant the continuation of the process. In addition, in the course of its development in this country, the preliminary hearing has become a forum where the accused is afforded an opportunity to discover and to appreciate the case to be made against him at trial where the requisite evidence is found to be present. The status of the preliminary inquiry in the United Kingdom is discussed by Patrick Devlin in *The Criminal Prosecution in England* (1960), at p. 10:

> The preliminary inquiry before the magistrates is now a purely legal proceeding; it was designed as an instrument of the prosecution for finding the culpritandpreparing the evidence against him; it has become a shield for the defence, allowing the defendant to ascertain precisely what the material is that is to be used against him and relieving him from the expense and odium of a trial if in the judgment of impartial persons there is not enough evidence to justify it.

The development of the institution of the preliminary hearing has taken a slightly different course in our country:

> The Canadian preliminary inquiry stems from an inquisitorial system of criminal investigation and prosecution in England, in which justices of the peace originally performed all of the investigative functions now performed by the police. The role of the justice of the peace gradually changed and eventually began to take on judicial characteristics. At the same time the inquiry over which the justice of the peace presided also changed, becoming mainly a judicial examination of the justification and need for pre-trial detention of the accused as well as an examination of the need for a trial itself. In this proceeding the prosecution was required to present its case, or at least to present sufficient evidence to establish a *prima facie* case.

(Canada, Law Reform Commission Study Report: "Discovery in Criminal Cases" (1974), pp. 8-9 (footnotes omitted)). It is interesting to go back to a description applied by G. Arthur Martin, Q.C., as he then was, to the preliminary hearing in Canada:

> The preliminary hearing has two aspects. Its primary purpose, of course is to ascertain whether or not there is sufficient evidence to warrant the accused being

placed upon his trial. In determining this, a magistrate, who is conducting a preliminary hearing is not determining whether or not the accused is guilty or not guilty. His function is to ascertain whether or not there is sufficient evidence to induce the belief in the mind of a cautious man that the accused is probably guilty. Therefore, considerations of reasonable doubt have no application at this stage of the proceedings.

. . .

From the point of view of defence counsel the preliminary hearing has another aspect. It affords counsel an opportunity of ascertaining the nature and the strength of the case against his client and it may be likened in that respect to an Examination for Discovery. (G. Arthur Martin, Q.C.: 1955 Special Lectures of the Law Society of Upper Canada, p. 1).

4. Test for Committal: Sufficiency of Evidence

Section 548 provides that the justice shall order the accused to stand trial "if in his opinion there is sufficient evidence to put the accused on trial". In assessing sufficiency should the justice be allowed to assess the credibility of the witnesses? Is sufficiency assessed against some standard?

For many years, the test for committal at a preliminary inquiry was held to be the same as that declared by the Supreme Court in *United States v. Shephard* (1976), [1977] 2 S.C.R. 1067, 30 C.C.C. (2d) 424 (S.C.C.) for extradition (applying also for a motion for a directed verdict). The judge was not to weigh the evidence by assessing credibility and was to decide whether a properly instructed jury could convict if it believed the evidence. In *Shephard* it was held that the judge had wrongly refused to extradite because the principal witness was a paid informant who was manifestly unreliable.

Do you think that Vanek J. improperly weighed the evidence in discharging Susan Nelles, a nurse charged with multiple murders of newborn infants by digoxin poison at the Hospital for Sick Kids in Toronto?

R. v. NELLES
(1982), 16 C.C.C. (3d) 97 (Ont. Prov. Ct.)

VANEK PROV. CT. J.:—In accordance with the foregoing principles of law, I have directed myself that in arriving at a decision whether or not to commit the accused for trial, it is not my function as a "justice" at a preliminary inquiry to weigh the evidence for the purpose of determining whether it is credible or trustworthy; that these matters fall within the sphere of the jury; and that I must consider, apart from credibility and accepting the evidence on the basis that it is true, whether it is "sufficient", under s. 475 of the *Criminal Code* and in accordance with the test of sufficiency laid down by Ritchie J. in *Sheppard*, to warrant committing the accused for trial.

In a judgment of my brother, Belobradic Prov. Ct. J., in *R. v. Genereux* (dated June 2, 1981), unreported) a distinction is made between two senses in which the concept of "weighing" is used in relation to evidence which I find helpful. It is his opinion that a justice at a preliminary inquiry is bound to weigh the evidence in the sense of analyzing the same and considering the inferences that may reasonably be drawn therefrom for the purpose of judging the sufficiency of the evidence for committal. It this sense, pehaps one might substitute for "weighing" the word "assessing". The process, however, is the same.

From my assessment of the evidence before me in this case I come to the following conclusions:

1. The evidence is entirely circumstantial.

2. There is no evidence of any motive.

3. In the case of Janice Estrella, there is no evidence to go before a jury that the accused was the person who murdered this child.

4. While the accused had access to each of Pacsai, Miller and Cook and therefore an opportunity to administer the dosage of digoxin that caused death, in none of these cases did she have exclusive access and opportunity; in each case other persons also had access to each of these infants at relevant times and the opportunity to administer the digoxin to them that caused death.

5. There is no evidence of any acts or conduct on the part of the accused in relation to any of the four babies that is out of the usual course of her duties as a registered nurse at the hospital, or which isolates and identifies her as the person who caused death by the administration of overdoses of digoxin to any of them.

6. The accused is an excellent nurse and enjoys an excellent reputation among her peers.

7. Each item or piece of evidence in support of the Crown's case, if consistent with guilt, is equally consistent with a rational conclusion, grounded in the evidence, that the accused is not the guilty person.

8. In addition, there is powerful evidence in disproof of the allegation that the accused is the person who caused the death of the four babies. This evidence is composed of proof that the accused could not be the person who caused the death of Janice Estrella or who administered an overdose of digoxin to baby Lombardo that likely caused his death, together with the strong likelihood that one person caused the death of all five children: Lombardo, Estrella, Pacsai, Miller and Cook.

9. There is evidence that points in a different direction.

Upon the whole of the evidence, it is my conclusion that there is no evidence to go before a jury on the count of murder in connection with Janice Estrella; that on each of the remaining counts, the evidence against the accused is at least equally consistent with the rational conclusion, grounded in the evidence, that the accused is innocent of the offence charged as it is that the accused is the guilty person. The evidence viewed in its entirety is either of too dubious a nature or amounts to no evidence at all to go before a jury; in either case, a reasonable jury, properly instructed, could not find beyond a reasonable doubt that the guilt of the accused is the only reasonable inference to be drawn from the proven facts.

In my opinion, therefore, upon the whole of the evidence, no sufficient case is made out to put the accused on trial on any of the four charges included in the three informations before me.

Accordingly, with respect to each count, the accused must be discharged.

Accused discharged.

In *Arcuri*, the Supreme Court introduced a concept of "limited weighing" of circumstantial evidence.

R. v. ARCURI

[2001] 2 S.C.R. 828, 44 C.R. (5th) 213, 157 C.C.C. (3d) 21 (S.C.C.)

The accused was charged with first degree murder. At the preliminary inquiry, the Crown's case was entirely circumstantial. The preliminary inquiry judge rejected the accused's contention that he must weigh the evidence and, after viewing the evidence as a whole, determined that the accused should be committed to trial for second degree murder. The accused's certiorari application was dismissed and that decision was affirmed by the Court of Appeal. The issue before the Supreme Court was whether the preliminary inquiry judge, in determining whether the evidence was sufficient to commit the accused to trial, erred in refusing to weigh the Crown's evidence.

McLACHLIN C.J. (L'Heureux-Dubé, Gonthier, Iacobucci, Major, Bastarache, Binnie, Arbour and LeBel JJ. concurring):—

. . .

The question to be asked by a preliminary inquiry judge under s. 548(1) of the Criminal Code is the same as that asked by a trial judge considering a defence motion for a directed verdict, namely, "whether or not there is any evidence upon which a reasonable jury properly instructed could return a verdict of guilty": *Shephard*. Under this test, a preliminary inquiry judge must commit the accused to trial "in any case in which there is admissible evidence which could, if it were believed, result in a conviction": *Shephard*.

The test is the same whether the evidence is direct or circumstantial: see *Mezzo* and *Monteleone*. The nature of the judge's task, however, varies according to the type of evidence that the Crown has advanced. Where the Crown's case is based entirely on direct evidence, the judge's task is straightforward. By definition, the only conclusion that needs to be reached in such a case is whether the evidence is true. . . . It is for the jury to say whether and how far the evidence is to be believed: *Shephard*. Thus if the judge determines that the Crown has presented direct evidence as to every element of the offence charged, the judge's task is complete. If there is direct evidence as to every element of the offence, the accused must be committed to trial.

The judge's task is somewhat more complicated where the Crown has not presented direct evidence as to every element of the offence. The question then becomes whether the remaining elements of the offence—that is, those elements as to which the Crown has not advanced direct evidence — may reasonably be inferred from the circumstantial evidence. Answering this question inevitably requires the judge to engage in a limited weighing of the evidence because, with circumstantial evidence, there is, by definition, an inferential gap between the evidence and the matter to be established—that is, an inferential gap beyond the question of whether the evidence should be believed. It is any fact from the existence of which the trier of fact may infer the existence of a fact in issue"); *McCormick on Evidence, supra*, at pp. 641-42 ("[c]ircumstantial evidence ... may be testimonial, but even if the circumstances depicted are accepted as true, additional reasoning is required to reach the desired conclusion"). The judge must therefore weigh the evidence, in the sense of assessing whether it is reasonably capable of supporting the inferences that the Crown asks the jury to draw. This weighing, however, is limited. The judge does not ask whether she herself would conclude that the accused is guilty. Nor does the judge draw factual inferences or assess credibility. The judge asks only whether the evidence, if believed, could reasonably support an inference of guilt.

. . .

Notwithstanding certain confusing language in *Mezzo* and *Monteleone* nothing in this Court's jurisprudence calls into question the continuing validity of the common law rule: see M. Bloos and M. Plaxton, "An Almost-Eulogy for the Preliminary Inquiry: 'We Hardly Knew Ye'" (2000), 43 Crim. L.Q. 516, at p. 526. In *Mezzo*, the issue was whether the Crown had proffered sufficient evidence as to identity. McIntyre J., writing for the majority, stated that a trial judge can direct an acquittal only if there is "no evidence" as to an essential element of the offence. He also stated that the judge has no authority to "weigh and consider the quality of the evidence and to remove it from the jury's consideration". Those statements, taken alone, might be understood to suggest that a preliminary inquiry judge must commit the accused to trial even if the Crown's evidence would not reasonably support an inference of guilt. However, as the dissent in *Charemski* discusses, the remainder of McIntyre J.'s reasons make clear that by "no evidence" McIntyre J. meant "no evidence capable of supporting a conviction", and by "weighing" McIntyre J. was referring to the ultimate determination of guilt (a matter for the jury), as distinguished from the determination of whether the evidence can reasonably support an inference of guilt (a matter for the preliminary inquiry judge). His concern was to reject the argument that the judge must determine whether guilt is the only reasonable inference. His reasons cannot be read to call into question the traditional rule, namely, that the judge must determine whether the evidence can reasonably support an inference of guilt.

In *Monteleone*, the accused was charged with setting fire to his own clothing store. The evidence was entirely circumstantial. The question was whether the trial judge had erred in directing an acquittal on the grounds that the "cumulative effect [of the evidence] gives rise to suspicion only, and cannot justify the drawing of an inference of guilt": *Monteleone*. In ordering a new trial, McIntyre J. wrote that "[i]t is not the function of the trial judge to weigh the evidence, [or] ... to draw inferences of fact from the evidence before him":

Monteleone. Again, however, the remainder of the reasons make clear that by "weighing" McIntyre J. was referring to the final drawing of inferences from the facts (which task, again, is within the exclusive province of the jury), not to the task of assessing whether guilt could reasonably be inferred. Indeed, the reasons explicitly reaffirm the common law rule that the judge must determine whether "there is before the court any admissible evidence, whether direct or circumstantial, which, if believed by a properly charged jury acting reasonably, would justify a conviction".

Contrary to the appellant's contention, *Charemski* did not evidence disagreement in this Court as to the proper approach. The appellant in *Charemski* had been charged with the murder of his wife. The trial judge directed a verdict of acquittal, principally because the forensic evidence did not affirmatively suggest that the deceased had been murdered. The question in this Court was whether the Court of Appeal erred in setting aside the trial judge's directed verdict of acquittal. There was no disagreement between the majority and the dissent as to the test that the preliminary inquiry justice must apply. On the contrary, both the majority and the dissent clearly reaffirmed *Shephard* and its progeny. Any disagreement concerned not the test for sufficiency but the question of whether sufficient evidence was led in that case. The majority conceded that forensic evidence had not affirmatively indicated that the deceased had been murdered, but reasoned that a properly instructed jury could reasonably infer guilt from the other evidence that the Crown had led. The dissent argued that, as it had not been established that the deceased had been murdered, it was meaningless to discuss identity and causation, two of the other essential elements of the offence. The dissent also argued that the accused's presence in the deceased's apartment could not reasonably be inferred from the accused's conceded presence in the lobby. The dissenting justices concluded that the circumstantial evidence could not reasonably support an inference of guilt.

. . .

In performing the task of limited weighing, the preliminary inquiry judge does not draw inferences from facts. Nor does she assess credibility. Rather, the judge's task is to determine whether, if the Crown's evidence is believed, it would be reasonable for a properly instructed jury to infer guilt. Thus, this task of "limited weighing" never requires consideration of the inherent reliability of the evidence itself. It should be regarded, instead, as an assessment of the reasonableness of the inferences to be drawn from the circumstantial evidence.

. . .

With those principles in mind, I turn, then, to the question of whether Lampkin Prov. J. properly interpreted and applied the law in this case. . . I am not persuaded that Lampkin Prov. J. reached the wrong result. Before committing the appellant to trial, the preliminary inquiry justice thoroughly surveyed the circumstantial evidence that had been presented by the Crown. . . Only after considering "the evidence as a whole" did Lampkin Prov. J. commit the appellant to trial. . . For the foregoing reasons, I conclude that the appeal should be dismissed.

UNITED STATES v. FERRAS

[2006] 2 S.C.R. 77, 39 C.R. (6th) 207, 209 C.C.C. (3d) 353 (S.C.C.)

The accused was charged in the United States with fraud. The extradition proceedings against him was brought by the "record of the case" method under sections 32(1)(a) and 33 of the Extradition Act, S.C. 1999, c. 18. In a companion case, *United Mexican States v. Ortega*, [2006] 2 S.C.R. 120, 39 C.R. (6th) 237, 209 C.C.C. (3d) 387, the extradition proceedings were brought by the "treaty" method provided in section 32(b) of the Act. The issue was whether these methods violated section 7 of the Charter because of the possibility that a person might be extradited on inherently unreliable evidence. In deciding this issue, the Supreme Court had to confront whether its earlier ruling in *United States v. Shephard* (1976), [1977] 2 S.C.R. 1067, 30 C.C.C. (2d) 424, which had stood the test of time until the modification made in *Arcuri*, was still good law in extradition cases.

McLachlin C.J. (for the Court)—

. . .

On [the *Shephard*] view of the law, the combined effect of the relevant provisions (ss. 29, 32 and 33 of the Act) may be to deprive the person sought of the independent hearing and evaluation required by the principles of fundamental justice applicable to extradition. If the extradition judge possesses neither the ability to declare unreliable evidence inadmissible nor to weigh and consider the sufficiency of the evidence, committal for extradition could occur in circumstances where committal for trial in Canada would not be justified. I take as axiomatic that a person could not be committed for trial for an offence in Canada if the evidence is so manifestly unreliable that it would be unsafe to rest a verdict upon it. It follows that if a judge on an extradition hearing concludes that the evidence is manifestly unreliable, the judge should not order extradition under s. 29(1). Yet, under the current state of the law in *Shephard*, it appears that the judge is denied this possibility. Similarly, I take it as axiomatic that a person could not be committed to trial for an offence in Canada if the evidence put against the person is not available for trial. As Donald J.A., dissenting in *Ortega* stated, at para. 51:

> If evidence is not available for trial it should not be used as a basis for committal. The concern goes well beyond modalities and rules of evidence, it goes to the heart of the question for the judge: whether there is enough evidence to put the requested person on trial.

Yet on the majority view in *Shephard*, committal may be ordered in the absence of certification that the evidence is available for trial. This raises particular concerns in an extradition context because the committal becomes the final judicial determination that sends the subject out of the country.

. . .

Section 29(1) of the *Extradition Act*, as discussed, requires the extradition judge to be satisfied that the evidence would justify committal for trial in Canada, had the offence occurred here. Canadian courts in recent decades have adopted the practice of leaving a case or defence to the jury where there is any evidence to support it, and have discouraged trial judges from weighing the evidence and refusing to put a matter to the jury on the basis that the evidence is not sufficiently reliable or persuasive: see *Arcuri*, at para. 30; and *R. v. L. (D.O.)*, [1993] 4 S.C.R. 419, at pp. 454-55. This may explain the conclusion in *Shephard* that the extradition judge has no discretion to refuse to extradite if there is any evidence, however scant or suspect, supporting each of the elements of the offence alleged. This narrow approach to judicial discretion should not be applied in extradition matters, in my opinion. The decision to remove a trial judge's discretion reflects confidence that, given the strict rules of admissibility of evidence on criminal trials, a properly instructed jury is capable of performing the task of assessing the reliability of the evidence and weighing its sufficiency without the assistance of the judge. The accused is not denied the protection of the trier of fact reviewing and weighing the evidence. The effect of applying this test in extradition proceedings, by contrast, is to deprive the subject of any review of the reliability or sufficiency of the evidence. Put another way, the limited judicial discretion to keep evidence from a Canadian jury does not have the same negative constitutional implications as the removal of an extradition judge's discretion to decline to commit for extradition. In the latter case, removal of the discretion may deprive the subject of his or her constitutional right to a meaningful judicial determination *before* the subject is sent out of the country and loses his or her liberty.

It is important as well to note the differences between extradition hearings and domestic preliminary inquiries. Both are pre-trial screening devices and both use the same test of sufficiency of evidence for committal: whether evidence exists upon which a reasonable jury, properly instructed, could return a verdict of guilty: *Shephard*. Previously, the *Extradition Act* cemented the analogy between the two proceedings by directing that an extradition judge "hear the case, in the same manner, as nearly as may be, as if the fugitive was brought before a justice of the peace, charged with an indictable offence committed in Canada": *Extradition Act*, R.S.C. 1985, c. E-23, s. 13. The new Act, however, does not maintain this close parallel in proceedings. Section 24(2) of the Act states: "For the purposes of the hearing, the judge has, subject to this Act, the powers of a justice under Part XVIII of the *Criminal Code*, with any modifications that the circumstances require." This grants the extradition judge the same powers as a preliminary inquiry judge, but requires the judge to exercise those powers in a manner appropriate to the extradition context. The judge no longer follows "as nearly as may be" the procedure of a preliminary inquiry. A second difference comes from the different rules for admitting evidence. Evidence is admitted on a preliminary inquiry according to domestic rules of evidence, with all the inherent guarantees of threshold reliability that those rules entail. In contrast, evidence adduced on extradition may lack the threshold guarantees of reliability afforded by Canadian rules of evidence. A third difference comes from the ability of extradition judges to grant *Charter* remedies. These differences make it inappropriate to equate the task of the extradition judge with the task of a judge on a preliminary inquiry.

I conclude that to deny an extradition judge's discretion to refuse committal for reasons of insufficient evidence would violate a person's right to a judicial hearing by an independent and impartial magistrate — a right implicit in s. 7 of the *Charter* where liberty is at stake. It would deprive the judge of the power to conduct an independent and impartial judicial review of the facts in relation to the law, destroy the judicial nature of the hearing, and turn the extradition judge into an administrative arm of the executive. The process of assessing whether all the boxes are ticked and then ordering committal is not an adjudication, but merely a formal validation. In so far as the majority view in the pre-*Charter* case of *Shephard* suggests a contrary view, it should be modified to conform to the requirements of the *Charter*.

I conclude that s. 32(1)(*a*) and (*b*) and s. 33 of the 1999 Act do not violate the right of a person sought under s. 7 of the *Charter*, because the requirements for committal of s. 29(1), properly construed, grant the extradition judge discretion to refuse to extradite on insufficient evidence such as where the reliability of the evidence certified is successfully impeached or where there is no evidence, by certification or otherwise, that the evidence is available for trial.

In *M. (M.) v. United States of America*, 2015 SCC 62 (S.C.C.), a 6-3 majority decided that in both extradition and preliminary inquiries defences where an accused has the evidentiary burden in contrast to essential elements of the offence are not to be considered. In this extradition hearing the judge discharged MM on the basis of exculpatory evidence indicating that she had harboured her children for their own protection from their father who was abusive but had legal custody. The majority held that a committal to the United States should have been ordered.

PROBLEM 1

The accused is charged with second degree murder in the death of his estranged wife. The deceased was found in her bathtub in the early hours of Christmas Day. Her lungs were heavy, which was consistent with drowning. There were no signs of strangulation. There was no evidence of foul play in her apartment. Everything was neat and in order. No fingerprints of the accused were found in the apartment. The forensic evidence failed to establish definitively that the deceased had died from natural causes, or as a result of accident, suicide or homicide. In support of its theory of homicide, the Crown relied on a number of pieces of circumstantial evidence, including animus and motive. The accused and the deceased had a difficult marriage marked by periods of separation. During one such period, the deceased began a relationship with another man, which the accused found "shameful" and which had made him feel like an "idiot". On one occasion, the deceased told her doctor that she was afraid of staying with her husband and wanted to move away from him. The deceased also once told a friend that the accused was verbally abusive and that she was afraid of him. There was also evidence of a $50,000 life insurance policy on the deceased. The accused admitted to the police that he was present at the deceased's apartment building on the night she died. He had travelled from Vancouver to London, Ontario. The accused also telephoned her. He asked her whether she was alone. Finally, three days after her death, the accused told the police that the deceased had complained about being short of money, being sick and forgetting things. He also volunteered that the deceased had complained to him about falling asleep in the bathtub sometimes for an hour or two and that she had almost drowned on a couple of occasions.

If you are the preliminary inquiry judge would you commit the accused to stand trial on this evidence? If there was no further evidence lead at trial, would you convict? See *R. v. Charemski*, [1998] 1 S.C.R. 679, 15 C.R. (5th) 1, 123 C.C.C. (3d) 225 (S.C.C.).

In *R. v. Hynes*, [2001] 3 S.C.R. 623, 47 C.R. (5th) 278, 159 C.C.C. (3d) 359 (S.C.C.) a narrow 5-4 majority confirmed an earlier position that a justice presiding at a preliminary inquiry is not a court of competent jurisdiction to consider whether evidence obtained in violation of the Charter should be excluded. McLachlin C.J.C., for the majority, held that this would change the screening function to one of a forum for determining Charter breaches, undermine the expeditious nature of the preliminary inquiry and expand costs and delays. Major J. for the dissent suggested that Charter breaches should be considered at the earliest opportunity and that not being able to do so at the preliminary inquiry was inconsistent with the recognized jurisdiction to apply the voluntary confession rule.

Given that the accused now has a constitutional right to disclosure of the Crown's case shouldn't preliminary inquiries be abolished? For strong arguments to the contrary, see Alan Gold and Jill Presser, "Let's Not Do Away with the Preliminaries: A Case in Favour of Retaining the Preliminary Inquiry", (1996) 1 Can. Crim. L.R. 145.

In *The Lawyers Weekly*, May 27, 1988, p. 22, Mr. Edelson, an Ottawa defence counsel, is quoted by the reporter, Cristin Schmitz, as having advised other defence counsel on how to "slice and dice" complainants:

> You have to go in there as defence counsel and whack the complainant hard at the preliminary.... and you've got to attack the complainant with all you've got so that he or she will say I'm not coming back in front of 12 good citizens to repeat this bullshit story that I have just told that judge.

This denigrating remark was referred to by Professor Elizabeth Sheehy, of the Faculty of Law at Ottawa University in *Preliminary Inquiries: Gender Analysis* (1994), a report prepared for Status of Women Canada. She recommends, in the best interests of women, the abolition of preliminary inquiries for sexual and wife assault cases. The same author, however, seeks the retention of preliminaries for women accused of serious crimes in the interests of justice. **Do you agree with these views?**

Many sexual assault trials across Canada are now proceeded with, through Crown election, by way of summary proceedings where there is no preliminary (and no jury trial).

In 2002 a complex series of Criminal Code amendments were enacted which came into force in 2004. See the comprehensive discussion by David Paciocco, "A Voyage of Discovery: Examining the Precarious Condition of the Preliminary Inquiry", (2003) 48 Crim. L.Q. 151. There are three major changes, all intended to restrict preliminaries:

1. Apart from murder cases, where preliminaries are still automatic, defence counsel or the Crown must now request a preliminary to get one: s. 536(4). Paciocco points out that this right will now depend on the competence of defence counsel to assert it. He also raises issues about the situation of an unrepresented accused.

2. If the defence has requested a preliminary inquiry, defence counsel must now indicate which issues they want addressed and provide a list of witness to be called. This may involve pre-hearings: see s. 536.3. Paciocco suggests that these proposals may backfire with further delays resulting from complexity and the new steps to be followed.

3. Crown counsel may conduct preliminaries on the basis of hearsay and other inadmissible evidence subject to a discretion in the justice to order the attendance of the witness for cross-examination: ss. 540(7)-(9) This may well produce inconsistencies in interpretation. In one of the first rulings on these sections, Johnson J. in *R. v. I. (S.P.)* (2005), 193 C.C.C. (3d) 240, 27 C.R. (6th) 112 (Nun. C.J.), announced that preliminaries for sexual assault in that jurisdiction would normally proceed on filing of taped interviews with complainants but that a transcript would have to be provided to the defence and cross-examination allowed.

In some cases, the entire case for the prosecution may be presented at the preliminary inquiry by means of documentation and affidavits. For example, in *R. v. Rao*, 2012 BCCA 275, 288 C.C.C. (3d) 507, 94 C.R. (6th) 109 (B.C. C.A.), the majority and dissenting justices disagreed on whether jurisdictional error was committed by the preliminary inquiry judge in permitting the entire Crown case to be adduced in this fashion and in refusing the defence the right to either call or cross-examine the Crown witnesses who supplied the information that was admitted.

5. Reviewing Decision at Preliminary Inquiry

Following a preliminary inquiry, both the accused and Crown may seek to review the decision of the preliminary inquiry judge. Both may bring an application for *certiorari* to quash the decision of the preliminary inquiry judge. In either case, the only ground for action by the reviewing court is lack of jurisdiction. Thus, neither the accused nor the Crown can complain of errors of law (such as evidentiary rulings) that were made while the preliminary inquiry judge was properly exercising his or her jurisdiction. The typical ground of review for an accused person is that the judge committed him or her for trial in the absence of evidence on one or more charges. See for example, *R. v. Dubois*, [1986] 1 S.C.R. 366, 51 C.R. (3d) 193, 25 C.C.C. (3d) 221 (S.C.C.), reconsideration refused (1986), 22 Admin. L.R. xxviii (S.C.C.). The Supreme Court of Canada has held that the superior court may quash a discharge when it is demonstrated that the preliminary inquiry judge failed to commit an accused to stand trial when there was some evidence on each element of an offence: see *R. v. Sazant*, [2004] 3 S.C.R. 635, 193 C.C.C. (3d) 446 (S.C.C.) and *R. v. DesChamplain*, [2004] 3 S.C.R. 601, 196 C.C.C. (3d) 1 (S.C.C.). However, in this latter situation, instead of making the order for committal that ought to have been made by the preliminary inquiry judge, the reviewing judge can only quash the discharge and remit the matter back to the preliminary inquiry judge: see *R. v. Thomson* (2005), 196 O.A.C. 39 (Ont. C.A.). **Does this make sense, especially in light of the fact that in the converse situation (where the accused challenges a committal), the reviewing judge may quash the committal as ordered (*i.e.*, on a charge of murder) but substitute a committal for trial on a lesser and included offence (*i.e.*, manslaughter)?**

Chapter 10

PLEAS AND PLEA BARGAINING

"You mean," he said, this look of absolute unbelief working across his face, "you mean, if I'm guilty I get out today?"

"Right."

"And if I'm innocent I stay locked up?"

"You got it, man. So what are you gonna be, guilty or innocent?"

Mills, *One Just Man,* Simon and Schuster, New York

A definition that I like and that I think might be useful would be as follows. Plea negotiations are:

A proceeding whereby competent and informed counsel openly discuss the evidence in a criminal prosecution with a view to achieving a disposition which will result in the reasonable advancement of the administration of justice.

Perras, "Plea Negotiations", (1979-80), 22 Crim. L.Q. 58

This chapter addresses the legal aspects of pleas and plea-bargaining. While the practice was at one time controversial, it is now a widely-accepted part of the criminal process. Still, individual cases of plea-bargaining attract public criticism, especially where it is perceived that the accused person was the beneficiary of undeserved leniency. The notorious case of Karla Homolka is the best modern-day example of this phenomenon.

While we have placed this chapter in Part III — Pre-Trial Procedure, guilty pleas and plea-bargaining can and does occur at virtually any juncture of the criminal trial process. Plea negotiations can occur very soon after a charge is laid and they can commence or linger well into the trial.

1. Pleas

In respect of offences tried on indictment, the general statutory provisions are as follows:

606. (1) An accused who is called on to plead may plead guilty or not guilty, or the special pleas authorized by this Part and no others.

(1.1) A court may accept a plea of guilty only if it is satisfied that the accused

(a) is making the plea voluntarily; and

(b) understands

(i) that the plea is an admission of the essential elements of the offence,

(ii) the nature and consequences of the plea, and

(iii) that the court is not bound by any agreement made between the accused and the prosecutor.

(1.2) The failure of the court to fully inquire whether the conditions set out in subsection (1.1) are met does not affect the validity of the plea.

(2) Where an accused refuses to plead or does not answer directly, the court shall order the clerk of the court to enter a plea of not guilty.

(3) An accused is not entitled as of right to have his trial postponed but the court may, if it considers that the accused should be allowed further time to plead, move to quash, or prepare for his defence or for any other reason, adjourn the trial to a later time in the session or sittings of the court, or to the next of any subsequent session or sittings of the court, upon such terms as the court considers proper.

(4) Notwithstanding any other provision of this Act, where an accused or defendant pleads not guilty of the offence charged but guilty of any other offence arising out of the same transaction, whether or not it is an included offence, the court may, with the consent of the prosecutor, accept that plea of guilty and, if the plea is accepted, the court shall find the accused or defendant not guilty of the offence charged and find him guilty of the offence in respect of which the plea of guilty was accepted and enter those findings in the record of the court.

(4.1) If the accused is charged with a serious personal injury offence, as that expression is defined in section 752, or with the offence of murder, and the accused and the prosecutor have entered into an agreement under which the accused will enter a plea of guilty of the offence charged—or a plea of not guilty of the offence charged but guilty of any other offence arising out of the same transaction, whether or not it is an included offence—the court shall, after accepting the plea of guilty, inquire of the prosecutor if reasonable steps were taken to inform the victims of the agreement.

(4.2) If the accused is charged with an offence, as defined in section 2 of the *Canadian Victims Bill of Rights*, that is an indictable offence for which the maximum punishment is imprisonment for five years or more, and that is not an offence referred to in subsection (4.1), and the accused and the prosecutor have entered into an agreement referred to in subsection (4.1), the court shall, after accepting the plea of guilty, inquire of the prosecutor whether any of the victims had advised the prosecutor of their desire to be informed if such an agreement were entered into, and, if so, whether reasonable steps were taken to inform that victim of the agreement.

(4.3) If subsection (4.1) or (4.2) applies, and any victim was not informed of the agreement before the plea of guilty was accepted, the prosecutor shall, as soon as feasible, take reasonable steps to inform the victim of the agreement and the acceptance of the plea.

(4.4) Neither the failure of the court to inquire of the prosecutor, nor the failure of the prosecutor to take reasonable steps to inform the victims of the agreement, affects the validity of the plea.

(5) For greater certainty, subsections 650(1.1) and (1.2) apply, with any modifications that the circumstances require, to pleas under this section if the accused has agreed to use a means referred to in those subsections.

In the case of summary convictions proceedings, the general section is:

801. (1) Where the defendant appears for the trial, the substance of the information laid against him shall be stated to him, and he shall be asked,

(a) whether he pleads guilty or not guilty to the information, where the proceedings are in respect of an offence that is punishable on summary conviction; or

(b) whether he has cause to show why an order should not be made against him, in proceedings where a justice is authorized by law to make an order.

The special pleas of autrefois acquit and autrefois convict, expressed only in the case of proceedings on indictment will be considered in the chapter on Res Judicata.

Can a trial judge vacate an adjudication of guilt?

R. v. MOSER
(2002), 163 C.C.C. (3d) 286 (Ont. S.C.J.)

HILL J.:—

General Principles

An accused's plea of guilt is a fundamentally significant step in the criminal trial process. The plea relieves the Crown of the burden to prove guilt beyond a reasonable doubt — the presumption of innocence, the right to silence, and the right to make full answer and defence to the charge are at an end: *Adgey v. The Queen* (1973), 13 C.C.C. (2d) 177 at 183 per Laskin J. (as he then was) (in dissent in the result); *Regina v. T. (R.)* (1992), 17 C.R. (4th) 247 (Ont. C.A.) at 252 per Doherty J.A.; *Regina v. Ross*, [1997] O.J. No. 1034 (C.A.) at para. 6 *per curiam*.

Where the offender is represented by counsel in a guilty plea proceeding, the trial court has a discretion, as a matter of law, to hold no further inquiry into the factual circumstances alleged in support of the offences charged: *Adgey v. The Queen, supra* at 188-9 per Dickson J. (as he then was); *Brosseau v. The Queen*, [1969] 3 C.C.C. 129 (S.C.C.) at 137-9 per Cartwright C.J.C.; *Regina v. T. (R.), supra* at 258. If the circumstances raise doubt as to the validity of the plea, the trial judge has a discretion to undertake an inquiry, the extent of which will vary according to the particular facts of each case: *Regina v. Meers* (1991), 64 C.C.C. (3d) 221 (B.C. C.A.) at 224-6 per Hinds J.A. Where the accused is self-represented, common law notions of fairness, if not constitutional concerns, mandate more extensive judicial involvement in the plea process.

A guilty plea, to be considered valid, must have minimally sufficient characteristics in order to provide an assurance that the forfeiture of a trial is fair.

To be valid, the plea must be unequivocal — the circumstances should not be such that the plea was unintended or confusing, qualified, modified, or uncertain in terms of the accused's acknowledgement of the essential legal elements of the crime charged: *Regina v. T. (R.), supra* at 252-4; *Regina v. C. (N.)*, [2001] O.J. No. 4484 (C.A.) at para. 6 *per curiam*. The accused's personal entry of the plea is a factor tending to demonstrate the unequivocal character of the plea: *Regina v. Eastmond*, [2001] O.J. No. 4353 (C.A.) at para. 6 *per curiam*.

A plea of guilty must be voluntary in the sense that the plea is a conscious volitional decision of the accused to plead guilty for those reasons which he or she regards as appropriate: *Regina v. T. (R.)*, *supra* at 253; *Regina v. Acorn*, [1996] O.J. No. 3423 (C.A.) at para. 3 *per curiam*. Ordinarily a plea of guilty involves certain inherent and external pressures: *Regina v. Tryon*, [1994] O.J. No. 332 (C.A.) at para. 1 *per curiam*. Plea negotiations in which the prosecution pursues a plea of guilt in exchange for forgoing legal avenues open to it, or agrees not to pursue certain charges, do not render the subsequent plea involuntary: *Regina v. Hector* (2000), 146 C.C.C. (3d) 81 (Ont. C.A.) at 84, 88-9; *Regina v. Lewis*, [1997] O.J. No. 2656 (C.A.) at para. 1-2 *per curiam*. What is unacceptable is coercive or oppressive conduct of others or any circumstance personal to the individual which unfairly deprives the accused of free choice in the decision not to go to trial: *Regina v. T. (R.)*, *supra* at 253; *Laperrière v. The Queen* (1996), 109 C.C.C. (3d) 347 (S.C.C.) at 347-8 per La Forest J. (adopting the dissent of Bisson J.A. at (1995), 101 C.C.C. (3d) 462 (Que. C.A.) at 470-1); *Regina v. Rajaeefard* (1996), 27 O.R. (3d) 323 (C.A.) at 331-4 per Morden A.C.J.O. (as he then was). There is, of course, no closed list of circumstances calling into question the voluntariness of a guilty plea: pressure from the court (*Regina v. Djekic* (2000), 147 C.C.C. (3d) 572 (Ont. C.A.) at 575-6 per curiam; *Regina v. Rajaeefard*, *supra* at 131-4); pressure from defence counsel (*Laperrière v. The Queen, supra*; *Regina v. Tiido*, [1996] O.J. No. 3798 (C.A.) at para. 1 *per curiam*); incompetence of defence counsel (*Regina v. Armstrong*, [1997] O.J. No. 45 (C.A.) at para 2-4 *per curiam*); cognitive impairment or emotional disintegration of the accused (*Regina v. Djekic, supra*; *Regina v. Thissen*, [1998] O.J. No. 1982 (C.A.) at para. 5, 7 *per curiam*); effect of illicit drugs or prescribed medications (*Regina v. Ross, supra*; *Regina v. Hann*, [1997] O.J. No. 5157 (C.A.) at para. 2-3 *per curiam*).

Finally, a guilty plea's validity depends on the plea being informed: *Regina v. T. (R.)*, *supra* at 254-7. It is essential that the accused understand the nature of the charges faced, the legal effect of a guilty plea, and the consequences of such a plea. Where an accused understands the factual basis for the allegations, counsel is able to give advice and take instructions respecting existence of the essential ingredients of the crimes charged. As stated, the legal effect of a guilty plea is to surrender the presumption of innocence and alleviate the prosecution's burden of establishing guilt beyond a reasonable doubt. The accused must generally know the jeopardy faced by way of possible punishment. Often the seriousness of the offences is self-evident and therefore so too is the exposure to a stiff custodial disposition. However, incorrect legal advice as to sentencing options may call into question whether the plea was truly informed: *Regina v. Armstrong, supra* at para. 2-4.

The prior experience of the accused in the criminal justice system is one factor weighing toward the validity of the accused's plea as he or she has had the opportunity to participate in the process: *Regina v. T. (R.)*, *supra* at 256, 260; *Regina v. Eastmond, supra* at para. 4 *per curiam*; *Regina v. Hector, supra* at 85; *Regina v. Sode* (1974), 22 C.C.C. (2d) 329 (N.S.S.C. — A.D.) at 334 per Coffin J.A.

· · ·

In the absence of any circumstances in the record, or a challenge to the competence and professionalism of trial counsel, a trial judge is justified in drawing the inference that counsel took the necessary steps to ensure the client understood the nature and consequences of a guilty plea: *Regina v. Eastmond, supra* at para. 7. Where counsel is experienced in defending criminal cases, it can be safely assumed there exists a professional discharge of counsel responsibilities: *Regina v. Dallaire*, [2001] O.J. No. 1722 (C.A.) at para. 2 *per curiam*; *Regina v. Hector, supra* at 85; *Regina v. Eastmond, supra* at para. 6. This is particularly so where the accused seeks out counsel who has previously acted on his or her behalf: *Regina v. Hector, supra* at 85.

. . .

It may be that following a plea of guilt, otherwise appearing valid when entered, circumstances arise which call into question the actual validity of the plea. Where the circumstances are made known to the trial court, the presiding justice is empowered with a discretion to conduct an inquiry into whether the plea should be rejected or struck and the case proceed to trial: *Adgey v. The Queen, supra* at 189-191 per Dickson J.; *Regina v. C. (N.), supra* at para. 10. Frequently referred to as an *Adgey* hearing, the inquiry focuses on that feature of the existing record, or as amplified, which may reasonably hold real potential to conflict with an unequivocal, voluntary, and informed plea. There is no absolute or unrestricted right to have a guilty plea withdrawn. The onus, in the sense of the burden of persuasion, is upon the accused: *Regina v. Eastmond, supra* at para. 6, 7; *Regina v. Djekic, supra* at 575; *Regina v. C. (N.), supra* at para. 6, 9.

Statements made in the course of the court's inquiry into the facts supporting the allegations immediately following a plea of guilt, although not admitted by the Crown, may justify the court in rejecting the guilty plea: *Adgey v. The Queen, supra* at 189; *Regina v. C. (N.), supra* at para. 10. At times, subsequent statements by the accused to others my raise the spectre of conflict with the guilty plea: *Regina v. Eastmond, supra* (statement to pre-sentence report author); *Regina v. T. (R.), supra* (statement to newspaper reporter).

We must have finality to proceedings unless the demands of justice dictate otherwise: *Regina v. Closs* (1998),105 O.A.C. 392 (C.A.) at para. 394 per Carthy J.A. Exceptional circumstances calling into question the validity of a guilty plea warrant a judicious exercise of discretion to inquire into the legitimacy of the plea. At the same time, the court must be vigilant that an experienced criminal not be allowed to abandon a position when matters "did not play out as expected": *Regina v. Dallaire, supra* at para. 5-6. In other words, a valid guilty plea must not be disturbed by a calculated scheme designed to manipulate the system: *Regina v. Gurney*, [2001] O.J. No. 2227 (C.A.) at para. 1 *per curiam*.

While the accused carries the burden of persuading the court the plea is invalid and ought to be withdrawn, the jurisprudence is not clear as to the standard of persuasion. Some authorities advocate a balance of probabilities standard (*Regina v. C. (S.), supra* at para. 13; *Regina v. Thawer*, [1996] O.J. No. 989 (Prov. Div.) at para. 36 per Omatsu, J.; *Regina v. Mikalishen*, [1996] B.C.J. No. 2541 (Prov. Ct.) at para. 51 per Stansfield J.) while other cases apply a "heavy onus" or "heavy burden" hurdle for the accused (*Regina v. Dallaire, supra* at para. 7; *Regina v. Lamoureux* (1984), 13 C.C.C. (3d) 101

(Que. C.A.) at 106 per Rothman J.A.; *Regina v. Samms*, [1992] N.J. No. 344 (S.C.) at para. 8 per Gushue J.A. (as he then was)). While the quality of the evidence prompting the striking or withdrawal of a guilty plea cannot be speculative, suspect, or lacking in credibility and reliability, I would hesitate to place the burden of persuasion at a point threatening adjudicative fairness. Whatever the standard for appellate intervention, I am content that where a trial judge has a real doubt as to the plea's validity, the court should strike the plea and send the case to trial.

Application to this Case

The totality of the evidence warrants the following findings of fact.

Gregory Moser was charged with serious criminal offences committed August 4th, 2000. He was stoned on crack cocaine when he attacked the young complainant.

The applicant retained a senior barrister experienced in the defence of criminal cases. There was a continued relationship of trust with Mr. Sintzel who had represented Mr. Moser when he faced serious charges in 1998.

The Crown provided disclosure. The complainant's videotaped statement clearly described the applicant ambushing her in the apartment hallway armed with a knife.

By the occasion of the last judicial pre-trial, the applicant was aware the prosecution intended to seek a s. 752.1 Criminal Code assessment as a step toward a dangerous offender application.

Mr. Moser decided to plead guilty. He was experienced in the criminal justice system including participation in prior guilty plea proceedings. There is no evidence that, on the date of pleading guilty, the applicant was cognitively impaired, ill, confused, under pressure, on drugs or medication, or without time to formulate decisions and instructions. On arraignment, Mr. Moser unambiguously entered his own pleas of guilt.

The applicant paid attention as Crown counsel narrated the factual allegations said to support the offences charged. He heard the prosecutor state that he was armed with a knife when he accosted the complainant in the apartment hallway. Cocaine consumption affected the applicant's memory of events.

After consulting with counsel, and aware that he could dispute the facts read out, Mr. Moser requested Mr. Sintzel object to the factual assertion that he had deliberately removed some of the complainant's clothing. The objection was made and submissions heard. The applicant elected not to challenge the allegation that he had a knife when in the hallway. The factual circumstances relating to count #2 as described by the prosecutor fully supported existence of the legal elements of the crime of assault with a weapon.

Defence counsel agreed that the narrated facts were otherwise accurate. This amounted to a statement by Mr. Moser himself. Mr. Sintzel was, of course, unable to report this agreement with the alleged facts, or indeed participate in the guilty plea proceeding at all, unless his client had admitted to him guilt on the assault with a weapon charge. The sole prosecution theory, on its evidence, was that the assault with a weapon involved the use of the knife in the hallway as an instrument designed to terrorize compliance with Mr. Moser's objectives.

The applicant's submission for dislodging his guilty plea on count #2, a plea otherwise appearing on the record to be valid, relies on the dubious assertion that the plea was not truthful. In other words, because the applicant did not want to put the complainant "through the ordeal of giving evidence", he chose to conceal his innocence from the court. I am unable to accept the applicant's evidence or argument as raising a real doubt as to the validity of the plea of guilt to the s. 267(a) Criminal Code offence.

To follow Mr. Moser's approach, one would need to accept that he chose as well to withhold from his own counsel the true facts relating to count #2. To this end, he acknowledged to Mr. Sintzel having a knife in the apartment hallway as part of his plan to ensure D.P. would not be called to testify. It strains belief that the applicant would deceive counsel whom he trusted and who previously represented him in guilty plea proceedings. If Mr. Moser had the secret agenda he maintains, why would he jeopardize keeping the complainant out of the courtroom by disputing the facts relating to the removal of her clothes thereby risking the prosecution responding with her testimony? It cannot seriously be suggested the applicant's plan was so finely calibrated that while unprepared to risk an *Adgey* hearing, he assumed the risk the Crown would not pursue a Gardiner hearing relating to proof of the circumstances in which D.P.'s clothing was removed.

At the time of the arraignment, Mr. Moser either recalled he had a knife in the confrontation at the elevator or, because of the heavy consumption of crack cocaine, did not have sufficient memory to dispute the disclosure material relating to the complainant's account of events and accordingly chose not to deny the alleged facts. Once in custody at the correctional facility, the applicant became increasingly concerned about the potential for a dangerous offender finding. In an effort at self-help to avoid this result, the applicant minimized the extent of his unlawful conduct in the psychiatric interviews. Faced with a court-initiated inquiry as to the validity of the guilty plea to count #2, and psychiatric testimony now in the record predicting future re-offence, the applicant seized the convenient opportunity to lay out a transparently revisionist view of history as part of his effort to avoid the potential for a dangerous offender consequence in his sentencing hearing.

Gregory Moser's pleas of guilt were unequivocal, voluntary, and informed. There is no cause to doubt the validity of the guilty pleas.

Should the Court of Appeal vacate the guilty plea and order a new trial in the following cases?

PROBLEM 1

The accused pleaded guilty to a charge of theft. At the sentence hearing defence counsel stated that he had pressured the accused to plead guilty and moved to withdraw the plea. The trial judge felt that the accused had not been taken by surprise, that he knew what was happening and that his plea of guilty was free and voluntary. Represented by different counsel the accused appealed. Compare *Lamoureux v. R.* (1984), 40 C.R. (3d) 369 (Que. C.A.).

PROBLEM 2

The accused, represented by counsel, pleaded guilty to charges of extortion and conspiracy to commit extortion. He was sentenced to twelve months' imprisonment. He appealed his conviction and asked to be permitted to withdraw his plea of guilty, contending that he did not really understand the nature and consequences of his plea, that he did not really intend to admit guilt and that he was convinced by his counsel to do so on the promise that he would receive a lenient sentence and would be immediately released from prison. Compare *Antoine v. R.* (1984), 40 C.R. (3d) 375 (Que. C.A.); *R. v. Saddlemire* (2007), 46 C.R. (6th) 61, 216 C.C.C. (3d) 119 (Ont. C.A.) and *R. v. Tyler* (2007), 218 C.C.C. (3d) 400 (B.C. C.A.).

PROBLEM 3

The accused was charged with assaulting his wife. The accused went to student legal aid. The student assigned to the case agreed to represent the accused for the purposes only of granting an adjournment as he had not yet received disclosure and was not prepared to proceed as the accused's agent for the purposes of a trial. When the case was called and the student requested an adjournment, the judge directed Crown counsel and the student into the hallway outside the courtroom and began to discuss the case. The judge told the student that the accused could expect a suspended sentence and probation with counselling if he pleaded guilty but that if he were convicted following trial the judge would impose a 10 to 15 day jail term. He also said that he would not grant an adjournment. The student relayed the judge's statements to his client. When the court resumed, the student told the court that he had advised his client in accordance with the judge's advice and that, as a result, the client was prepared to plead guilty. In response the judge remarked, "That's good counselling".

Compare *R. v. Rajaeefard* (1996), 46 C.R. (4th) 111, 104 C.C.C. (3d) 225 (Ont. C.A.).

PROBLEM 4

The accused was charged with break and enter, and assault. Initially, he pleaded not guilty but, despite maintaining his innocence to his lawyer, changed his plea because he feared a more severe sentence. Some years later, the notorious Paul Bernardo was found to have committed the offence. The accused, with the consent of the Crown, was granted an extension of time to appeal the conviction.

Should the Court of Appeal grant his application to expunge the guilty pleas? Compare *R. v. Hanemaayer* (2008), 234 C.C.C. (3d) 3 (Ont. C.A.).

2. Plea Bargaining

A large percentage of accused plead guilty. The subject of plea bargaining concerns those pleas where there is an agreement by the accused to plead guilty with a view to some consideration usually related to charge or sentence. The agreement may be reached quite formally after protracted discussion or may involve a hurried hallway discussion. Usually the plea bargain is entered into following a discussion between the Crown and the defence counsel but sometimes, although less frequently in Canada, the judge is involved. Perhaps the least talked about variety of plea bargain occurs following discussions between the accused and the police. We have earlier seen, however, that the Supreme Court in *Burlingham* interpreted s. 10(*b*) to require consultation with counsel in such cases. Klein obtained a unique perspective on this problem when he interviewed 115 inmates at Prince Albert Maximum-Security Penitentiary.

KLEIN, LET'S MAKE A DEAL
(1976) (unpublished Ph.D. thesis)

In looking at the system of negotiated justice from the offender's perspective, the reader who is familiar with the related literature may judge the extent to which there is a correspondence between the views of offenders and officials. At the very least, we suggest that the offender's view is logically consistent with the more "respectable" portrayals of the working of the criminal justice system in general and the negotiation process in particular.

While the benefits obtained by offenders and officials were sometimes more apparent than real, the deals themselves were none the less consistent with descriptions of the criminal justice system that emphasize the goals of crime control and bureaucratic efficiency.

We have discovered, from another perspective, a view of a complex process. In the course of considering the offender's view, the reader has had the opportunity to have a glimpse of offenders as human beings with needs and desires that are not unlike those of persons with noncriminal identities. In most of the preceding accounts of negotiations there has been an implicit awareness of process, structure, and norms vis-à-vis the criminal justice system. It is out of this awareness that basic patterns of negotiations emerged.

From the standpoint of the offender, the kickback is generally the most beneficial type of deal. Deals involving the kickback of stolen property or material used in the commission of criminal acts may result in significant concessions to offenders while furthering the achievement of the legitimate goals of crime prevention and control. However, it was suggested that the benefits obtained by officials are sometimes more apparent than real. Taken to its logical conclusion, the possibility of making such a deal may actually encourage crime as offenders commit criminal acts to acquire the material needed to bolster their bargaining positions.

Information is the lifeblood of any police department. Offenders who can supply the police with information may be able to obtain worthwhile concessions from the authorities. However, most offenders perceive the costs—both mental and physical—of acting as an informer as outweighing whatever benefits they might accrue.

A deal in which the focus is a plea of guilty in exchange for concessions is the focus of most literature on negotiated justice. Such deals are designed to increase bureaucratic efficiency in appearance or in actuality. While common, they are of questionable benefit to most offenders.

Deals for bail generally involve a kickback. The benefits to offenders making such deals are twofold: They are out of jail while awaiting trial, and they may return to crime to raise money for their defence. When the latter is an offender's motivation for making a deal for bail, it is obvious that the official goal of crime prevention is not furthered.

The offender's perspective has drawn attention to some aspects of the negotiation process that hitherto have been generally ignored. One such aspect is that of justice by negotiation as an ongoing process. For the offender who is aware of the possibilities for manipulation present in the system, the negotiation process may extend from the initial encounter with the police through the time of sentencing. This view of the negotiation process suggests that descriptions of this process that have been confined to the interactional boundaries of the role of the prosecutor may be analogous to the presentation of only the second act of a three act play.

Unlike previous descriptions of the negotiation process, the police emerged as frequent, and often significant, actors. The police are the gatekeepers to the criminal justice system. In large measure, their actions have a direct influence upon the stance taken by the prosecutor in dealing with a defendant and help to define the boundaries of the disposition of a case. The police were involved in 79 percent of the 202 cases of bargaining described by our informants. In fact, they were the *only* officials directly involved in conducting the negotiation with the offender in 52 percent of these cases.

Some would maintain that it is in no way proper for the police to engage in any type of bargaining with an accused. Given the role of the prosecutor in the criminal justice system, prosecutorial bargaining may be more easily justified. However, it has been suggested in our analysis that if there is justification for bargaining by the police, such justification may reside in the need for crime prevention, law enforcement, and the conservation of limited resources.

ERICSON, MAKING CRIME: A STUDY OF DETECTIVE WORK
(1981), 90

The organization of the courts also facilitates plea transactions, and the primacy of police involvement in these transactions. As we have already mentioned, a guilty plea typically ensures that the judge will make no inquiry into how it was produced, thus leaving detectives to construct a case with a concern only for how it can be "sold" in plea transactions with the defence and Crown attorneys. More fundamentally, the Bench in Canada has done little more than assert their disapproval of "plea bargaining" in individual cases (Cousineau and Verdun-Jones, 1979: 294). This has probably contributed to a belief that the practice is sporadic rather than established and widespread. This belief may in turn be one reason why, in contrast to the United States, there has been no systematic inquiry into the phenomenon which might lead to a developed policy.

Among the detective cases followed through to the point of disposition in court, none were known to have involved judges in plea transactions. However, judges making statements in court indicated that they gave tacit approval to plea transactions worked out among detectives, defence attorneys and Crown attorneys. For example, during a court hearing of DC 228 the judge called an early recess for lunch, stating to the Crown attorney, the lawyer for one accused, and the lawyer for the other two accused: "You're all buddies now—we'll take an early lunch and you can discuss this matter over lunch to expedite this matter." The Crown attorney and two lawyers went out to lunch, and were later joined for a brief period by the investigating detective. They negotiated a plea settlement, which included a reduction to attempted theft from attempted robbery for one accused. After lunch they returned to court, where the pleas were duly registered in accordance with this settlement.

In making their case to the Crown attorney, detectives could rely upon several organizational elements which allow them to effect considerable control. One element was that the Crown attorney was dependent upon detectives for the production and construction of evidence. The detectives were obviously more knowledgeable about the details of a case because they had made it, literally. This made Crown attorneys dependent upon detectives, having to trust the detectives' work in order to get on with their own work (cf. Skolnick, 1966: 179).

At the Provincial Court level, Crown attorneys involved in the cases we studied were generally assigned to a courtroom rather than to a case. In consequence, one case could be worked on by a different Crown attorney at each hearing date. This resulted in a Crown attorney being less informed than he would have been if he was assigned a case at the beginning and followed it through to its conclusion. Typically, a Crown attorney would have 20-25 case files on the morning of the court appearance for those cases without having much detailed knowledge of them. Indeed, in many cases the Crown attorney had not even read the case file by the time he was approached by a defence attorney and/or detective about a possible plea transaction (cf. Montagnes, 1978; Ericson, 1980: Ch. 6). In these circumstances, Crown attorneys were very likely to defer to the judgments of detectives in making a deal for guilty pleas.

In *Santobello v. New York,* 404 U.S. 264, Douglas J. noted:

These "plea bargains" are important in the administration of justice both at the state and at the federal levels and, as the Chief Justice says, they serve an important role in the disposition of today's heavy calendars.

However important plea bargaining may be in the administration of criminal justice, our opinions have established that a guilty plea is a serious and sobering occasion inasmuch as it constitutes a waiver of the fundamental rights to a jury trial, to confront one's accusers, to present witnesses in one's defense, to remain silent, and to be convicted by proof beyond all reasonable doubt.

The accused in pleading guilty waives many rights and accommodates the State. **What benefits is he or she entitled to?**

FERGUSON and ROBERTS, PLEA BARGAINING: DIRECTIONS FOR CANADIAN REFORM
(1974), 52 Can. Bar Rev. 497, 513

. . . The range of benefits discussed in the legal literature are: (1) a reduction in the charge to a lesser or included offence; (2) a withdrawal of other charges or a promise not to proceed on other possible charges; (3) a recommendation or a promise as to the type of sentence that can be expected (fine, probation, imprisonment, and so on); and (4) a recommendation or a promise as to the severity of the sentence (amount of fine or length of imprisonment). Other possible benefits mentioned less often are: (5) the use of summary conviction procedure rather than indictable procedure in offences where the Crown has a choice; (6) a promise not to apply for a sentence of preventive detention; (7) a promise not to apply for a harsher penalty in accordance with sections 592 and 740 of the Criminal Code where the accused has a previous conviction for the same offence; (8) a promise not to force trial by jury under section 498 of the Criminal Code where the accused wishes to avoid that mode of trial; (9) a promise not to charge friends or family of the accused; (10) a promise not to mention at the time of sentencing any aggravating circumstances of the offence, or not to mention a previous criminal record, or not to make public any embarrassing circumstances of the offence; (11) a promise or a recommendation as to the place of imprisonment, the type of treatment, or the time of parole; (12) a promise to arrange for sentencing before a particular judge, who is generally lenient, or a threat to have the accused sentenced by a certain judge who is considered very harsh; (13) a promise not to oppose release on bail or release after conviction but before sentence.

See also *R. v. Johnston,* [1970] 2 O.R. 780 (Ont. C.A.)

In the circumstances we believe that there was an error in principle on the part of the learned Judge in settling upon those two terms. Believing as we do that 14 years might very well be regarded as a maximum sentence for the offences involved, it is obvious that little, if any, consideration was given by the trial Judge to the fact that these two men pleaded guilty and thus saved the community a great deal of expense. In this respect reference to the case of *R. v. de Haan*, [1967] 3 All E.R. 618, might be made.

MINISTRY OF ATTORNEY GENERAL FOR ONTARIO, CROWN POLICY MANUAL (2005)

Resolution discussions are an essential part of the criminal justice system in Ontario. When properly conducted, the provide a form of dispute resolution that can benefit all of the participants in that system, including victims, witnesses, the accused, counsel, police, and the people of Ontario. The proper administration of justice, including consideration of the public interest, is the primary concern of any resolution discussion.

. . .

In conducting resolution discussions, Crown counsel should attempt to balance the interests of the victim, the protection of the public, and the rights of the accused in the framework of the optimal use of limited resources. Reference may be made to the preamble of the Crown Policy Manual for a more detailed discussion of the role of Crown counsel.

A resolution agreement with respect to charge and/or sentence should adequately reflect the public interest and the gravity of the provable offence or offences. Crown counsel should ensure that the interests of the victim are considered in reaching a resolution.

There are some fundamental principles of resolution discussions that are binding directives:

- Crown counsel must not accept a guilty plea to a charge knowing that the accused is innocent
- Crown counsel must not knowingly accept a guilty plea to a charge when a material element of that charge can never be proven unless that fact is fully disclosed to the defence
- Crown counsel must not purport to bind the Attorney General's right to appeal any sentence
- Unless there are exceptional circumstances, Crown counsel must honour agreements reached during resolution discussions.

When a plea has been bargained for, is it voluntary? In what sense? Is an accused entitled to know, with some certainty, the sentence? Should the judge be involved? Should the victim?

KIPNIS, CRIMINAL JUSTICE AND THE NEGOTIATED PLEA
(1975/76), 86 Ethics 93, 104

I think that the appeal that plea bargaining has is rooted in our attitude toward bargains in general. Where both parties are satisfied with the terms of an agreement, it is improper to interfere. Generally speaking, prosecutors and defendants are pleased with the advantages they gain by negotiating a plea. And courts, which gain as well, are reluctant to vacate negotiated pleas where only "proper" inducements have been applied and where promises have been understood and kept. Such judicial neutrality may be commendable where entitlements are being exchanged. But the criminal justice system is not such a context. Rather it is one in which persons are justly given, not what they have bargained for, but what they deserve, irrespective of their bargaining position.

To appreciate this, let us consider another context in which desert plays a familiar role; the assignment of grades in an academic setting. Imagine a "grade bargain" negotiated between a grade conscious student and a harried instructor. A term paper has been submitted and, after glancing at the first page, the instructor says that if he were to read the paper carefully, applying his usually rigid standards, he would probably decide to give the paper a grade of D. But if the student were to waive his right to a careful reading and conscientious critique, the instructor would agree to a grade of B. The grade-point average being more important to him than either education or justice in grading, the student happily accepts the B, and the instructor enjoys a reduced workload.

One strains to imagine legislators and administrators commending the practice of grade bargaining because it permits more students to be processed by fewer instructors. Teachers can be freed from the burden of having to read and to criticize every paper. One struggles to envision academicians arguing for grade bargaining in the way that jurists have defended plea bargaining, suggesting that a quick assignment of a grade is a more effective influence on the behavior of students, urging that grade bargaining is necessary to the efficient functioning of the schools. There can be no doubt that students who have negotiated a grade are more likely to accept and to understand the verdict of the instructor. Moreover, in recognition of a student's help to the school (by waiving both the reading and the critique), it is proper for the instructor to be lenient. Finally, a quickly assigned grade enables the guidance personnel and the registrar to respond rapidly and appropriately to the student's situation.

What makes all of this laughable is what makes plea bargaining outrageous. For grades, like punishments, should be deserved. Justice in retribution, like justice in grading, does not require that the end result be acceptable to the parties. To reason that because the parties are satisfied the bargain should stand is to be seriously confused. For bargains are out of place in contexts where persons are to receive what they deserve. And the American courtroom, like the American classroom, should be such a context.

. . .

In its coercion of criminal defendants, in its abandonment of desert as the measure of punishment, and in its relaxation of the standards for conviction, plea bargaining falls short of the justice we expect of our legal system. I have no doubt that substantial changes will have to be made if the institution of plea bargaining is to be obliterated or even removed from its central position in the criminal justice system. No doubt we need more courts and more prosecutors. Perhaps ways can be found to streamline the jury trial procedure without sacrificing its virtues. Certainly it would help to decriminalize the host of victimless crimes—drunkenness and other drug offenses, illicit sex, gambling, and so on—in order to free resources for dealing with more serious wrongdoings. And perhaps crime itself can be reduced if we begin to attack seriously those social and economic injustices that have for too long sent their victims to our prisons in disproportionate numbers. In any case, if we are to expect our citizenry to respect the law, we must take care to insure that our legal institutions are worthy of that respect. I have tried to show that plea bargaining is not worthy, that we must seek a better way. Bargain justice does not become us.

In general, our Courts have been reluctant to give any legal effect to a plea bargain.

R. v. NIXON
2011 SCC 34, 271 C.C.C. (3d) 36, 85 C.R. (6th) 1 (S.C.C.)

The accused drove her vehicle through a stop sign and collided with another vehicle, killing two people and seriously injuring their young child. She was charged with seven offences, including impaired driving causing death, impaired driving causing bodily harm, dangerous driving causing death, and dangerous driving causing bodily harm. However, a plea resolution agreement was reached, under which she would plead guilty to the provincial offence of careless driving and the criminal charges would be dropped. Before the guilty plea was entered, the Assistant Deputy Minister (ADM) determined that the plea resolution agreement was not in the best interests of administration of justice. The Crown therefore withdrew the agreement. At trial, after the trial judge ruled that the revocation of the plea agreement was not reasonable, the accused pleaded guilty to careless driving and was acquitted on the remaining counts. The Crown's appeal to the Alberta Court of Appeal was allowed and the accused then appealed to the Supreme Court of Canada, which dismissed her appeal.

CHARRON J. (for the Court):—

[44] As stated earlier, it is argued that a plea agreement should be regarded as a contractual undertaking and enforced just as any other lawyers' undertaking. This argument cannot be sustained. It completely ignores the public dimension of a plea agreement. Indeed, contrary to Ms. Nixon's contention, the Law Society of Alberta specifically recognizes in the comment to Rule 27 of its *Code of Professional Conduct* that "[a]n agreement between the prosecution and defence regarding the plea to be entered is not considered a usual lawyers' undertaking due to the policy considerations involved" (updated 2009 (online)). Vitiating factors, such as mistake, misrepresentation or fraud, which usually inform a private party's right to resile from a bargain, do not fully capture the public interest considerations which are at play in any decision to repudiate a plea agreement.

[45] A plea agreement cannot be summarily enforced by the court as any other lawyers' undertaking, as Ms. Nixon contends. It is also wrong to suggest that repudiation, in and of itself, warrants a judicial remedy even in the absence of prejudice (as the application judge concluded, at para. 55), or in the absence of

conduct amounting to an abuse of process. This argument is founded on the erroneous premise that the decision to repudiate a plea agreement falls outside the scope of prosecutorial discretion and, as such, is not subject to the constitutional principles set out in *Krieger*.

[46] However, to the extent that the lawyers' undertaking analogy underscores the importance of honouring plea agreements, it can usefully contribute to the analysis. Indeed, in the oft-quoted Ontario *Report of the Attorney General's Advisory Committee on Charge Screening, Disclosure, and Resolution Discussions* (1993) (the "*Martin Committee Report*"), the Committee found resolution agreements in criminal proceedings to be "in the nature of undertakings". The duty of counsel to honour resolution agreements was regarded as "a particular example of the duties of integrity and responsibility" that lie "at the heart of counsel's professional obligations". Honouring resolution agreements was not only "ethically imperative", but also a "practical necessity", as these agreements "dispose of the great bulk of the contentious issues that come before the criminal courts in Ontario" (commentary to Recommendation 53, at pp. 312-13 of the *Martin Committee Report*).

[47] In light of this practical necessity, the *binding effect* of plea agreements is a matter of utmost importance to the administration of justice. It goes without saying that plea resolutions help to resolve the vast majority of criminal cases in Canada and, in doing so, contribute to a fair and efficient criminal justice system.

[48] Of course, there may be instances where different Crown counsel will invariably disagree about the appropriate plea agreement in a particular case. Given the number of complex factors that must be weighed over the course of plea resolution discussions, this reality is unsurprising. However, the vital importance of upholding such agreements means that, in those instances where there is disagreement, the Crown may simply have to live with the initial decision that has been made. To hold otherwise would mean that defence lawyers would no longer have confidence in the finality of negotiated agreements reached with front-line Crown counsel, with whom they work on a daily basis. Further, if agreements arrived at over the course of resolution discussions cannot be relied upon by the accused, the benefits that resolutions produce for *both* the accused and the administration of justice cannot be achieved. As a result, I reiterate that the situations in which the Crown can properly repudiate a resolution agreement are, and must remain, very rare.

[49] All Attorneys General who have participated in this appeal agree that a plea agreement should only be repudiated in exceptional and rare circumstances. However, the lawyers' undertaking analogy can only go so far on the question that occupies us. The analogy can usefully underscore the importance of honouring plea agreements, but it cannot inform the standard against which any repudiation conduct is to be measured. The *Martin Committee Report* made this clear in the same commentary quoted above, stating the following:

> Thus, it is plain that resolution agreements must not undermine the integrity of the court, or otherwise bring the administration of justice into disrepute. While the

> sanctity of agreements entered into is an important principle of the administration of justice, Crown counsel's primary duty is to the integrity of the system. Accordingly, in the rare cases where these two values clash, the latter must prevail. [p. 314]

As a result, the argument that a plea agreement can simply be characterized as a contractual undertaking must fail.

. . .

[68] As discussed earlier, the ADM's decision to resile from the plea agreement falls within the scope of prosecutorial discretion. In the absence of any prosecutorial misconduct, improper motive or bad faith in the approach, circumstances, or ultimate decision to repudiate, the decision to proceed with the prosecution is the Crown's alone to make. Reasonable counsel may indeed, and often do, differ on whether a particular disposition is in the public interest in the circumstances of the case. The ADM, in good faith, determined that Crown counsel's assessment of the strength of the evidence was erroneous and, on that basis, having regard to the seriousness of the offences, concluded that it would not be in the public interest to terminate the prosecution on the criminal charges. This can hardly be regarded as evidence of misconduct.

[69] This does not mean that plea agreements can be overturned on a whim. The method by which the decision was reached can itself reveal misconduct of a sufficient degree to amount to abuse of process. But that is not what occurred here. The act of repudiation was indeed a rare and exceptional occurrence. The evidence revealed that there have been only two prior occurrences in Alberta, "one in the 1980s and one within the year prior to the trial in this matter" (Court of Appeal decision, at para. 48). There was also no evidence of abusive conduct in the process leading to the decision to repudiate. I agree with the analysis of Paperny J.A. in this regard (at para. 50):

> Further, this is not a case where the repudiation was done "unfairly" or when the discretion of the Attorney General was exercised "irrationally, unreasonably or oppressively". The ADM carefully reviewed the evidence that was the subject of concern and relied on legal opinions and took guidance from the Ontario Attorney General's policy to instruct himself on the relevant considerations. Having satisfied himself that the original view of the trial prosecutor was incorrect and that the resulting plea resolution agreement would bring the administration of justice into disrepute, he acted expeditiously in communicating the decision to withdraw the plea resolution agreement to the respondent. He also considered possible prejudice to the respondent and concluded that there would be no such prejudice. The ADM's conduct, viewed in its totality, cannot be characterized as unfair, unreasonable, oppressive or irrational. The high threshold to find abuse of process has not been met here.

[70] Finally, Ms. Nixon was returned to the position she was in at the conclusion of the preliminary hearing before the plea agreement was entered into. There is no merit to the contention that she suffered prejudice as a result of the repudiation.

Appeal dismissed.

See CR Annotation by Tim Quigley.

PROBLEM 5

You as assistant Crown Attorney are about to begin a trial of sexual assault. The complainant advises that the experience of cross-examination at the preliminary inquiry was so horrific that she cannot proceed to trial. She advises that if called as a witness she will refuse to testify even though threatened with contempt proceedings. You are convinced of the accused's guilt. May you suggest to defence counsel that though you regard your case as solid you will recommend a reformatory term if his client pleads guilty? See Hooper, "Discovery in Criminal Cases" (1972), 50 Can. Bar Rev. 445, 469 and Alschuler, "The Prosecutor's Role in Plea Bargaining" (1968-69), 36 Univ. of Chi. L.R. 49, 62.

PROBLEM 6

You are acting for an accused charged with sexual assault. The accused entered a corner store and at knife point ordered the young female clerk to disrobe. He touched her breast, panicked and fled. Nothing was taken from the store. He asks you to negotiate a plea to armed robbery. He realizes the penalty may be greater but he fears his own treatment if incarcerated as a sex offender. Would you seek the arrangement?

A Committee of the Law Reform Commission of Canada proposed the abolition of plea bargaining.

LAW REFORM COMMISSION OF CANADA; WORKING PAPER NO. 15: CRIMINAL PROCEDURE—CONTROL OF THE PROCESS
(1975), 39-60

Plea bargaining is now an established practice in many parts of the country. Some regard it as a perversion of justice. Others welcome it as an alternative to the adversary system. Still others claim that, whatever its merits or defects, it is essential to the efficient administration of the criminal law. Detailed information on the prevalence of plea bargaining and on the manner in which it operates does not exist. Enough is known of the practice, however, to enable us to conclude that it has become a significant factor in the administration of justice. What we know also compels us to condemn plea bargaining.

Much of the controversy surrounding plea bargaining results from disagreement as to what the practice is. We define a plea bargain as any agreement by the accused to plead guilty in return for the promise of some benefit. The parties to the agreement will usually be the accused and Crown counsel, but it is also possible for the police or the court to be party to the bargain. We shall concentrate our discussion on the form of plea bargaining that appears to be most common, namely, a bargain made with Crown counsel, and then briefly state our position on police and judicial bargaining.

A plea bargain between the Crown and the accused is made possible by the accused's right to plead guilty, and by the Crown's discretionary powers, particularly in charging. The accused relinquishes his right to trial by pleading guilty in return for some concession by the Crown. The Crown has a variety of inducements to offer; these include: reducing the number or seriousness of the charges, proceeding by summary conviction rather than by indictment on mixed offences, and making recommendations as to sentence favourable to the accused. The accused's motive in striking a bargain will usually be to obtain a lighter sentence; the Crown's motive will usually be its desire to dispose of the case with a minimum of delay, cost and effort.

We believe that the objections to plea bargaining are overwhelming. It detracts from the pursuit of the legitimate goals of the criminal justice system. It destroys the appearance and the reality of justice.

So long as the practice exists, parties will adopt tactics to maximize their bargaining strength. The Crown will be tempted to overcharge, or to exaggerate the strength of its case. The defence may use delaying tactics, elect a jury trial to obtain a bargaining advantage, exaggerate the strength of the defence, or refuse to plead guilty even where there is no hope of an acquittal. The entire pre-plea process thus becomes a ritual bearing no relationship to the realities of the case. The sentencing process is also distorted. In so far as the Crown has adopted tactics that guarantee a lenient sentence to the accused, the court has been deprived of its power to impose a sentence appropriate to the offence and the offender. If the Crown has made promises as to sentence that depend on the discretion of the judge, the accused may be deprived of the benefit he hoped to purchase by his guilty plea.

Neither the public interest, nor the interests of the parties can be properly served by a system in which the merits of the case take second place to the bargaining strength and skills of the parties. The accused's interest will not be served if he is pressured to plead guilty by his lawyer's failures in negotiation. In extreme cases he may even be persuaded to plead guilty to an offence he did not commit. The public's interests will not be protected if administrative expediency is the principal factor governing the exercise of Crown counsel's discretion. A dangerous criminal should not be let-off with a minor conviction and penalty just because he is willing to plead guilty, and thus save the state the time and expense of a trial. Nor does society benefit from a negotiated plea of guilty by a petty offender who should not have been prosecuted.

The evils of plea bargaining are magnified by the fact that it is generally conducted in secret. Involuntary pleas by accused persons, or unethical conduct by counsel can occur in the bargaining process. These will not be brought to light in court. What is disclosed in court will, at best, be an incomplete story; at worst, it will be an inaccurate story. Nor can the interests of the public or of the victim be protected if all major decisions in a case are made in secret negotiations.

Above all, we object to plea bargaining because it is contrary to the entire notion of justice. Justice should not be, and should not be seen to be, something that can be purchased at the bargaining table. Neither the public nor the offender can respect such a system. Once the Crown has decided in the public interest to prosecute a charge, bargaining for a plea should not be used as a substitute for judicial adjudication on guilt or sentence.

Plea bargaining is supported by some as a desirable method of achieving compassion and flexibility in the administration of the law by providing an alternative to the "all or nothing" adversary contest. We do not agree. Flexibility, compassion, and non-adversarial methods of disposition are essential. They may be achieved, without resorting to plea bargaining, by the rational use of Crown discretionary powers. If, for example, it is in the interests of the accused and of society to charge a minor offence, carrying a light penalty, then the Crown should so charge; it has the power to do so without exacting the price of a guilty plea by threatening the accused with a more serious, less appropriate charge. We are not condemning the exercise of prosecutorial discretion. We are condemning, as unnecessary and as wrong in principle, the practice of making the exercise of the discretion dependent on the accused's plea of guilty, and on administrative expediency.

It is urged by many that plea bargaining is necessary in order to maintain a high proportion of guilty pleas, without which the administration of justice would grind to a halt.

A significant decrease in the number of guilty pleas would place strains on the resources of the criminal justice system. Long delays and "assembly line" justice are evils that must be avoided. Plea bargaining may give us a quick and cheap method of avoiding these problems, but it also impairs the quality of the system. If society places a value on justice, it should be prepared to pay the price by allocating sufficient resources to the criminal justice system. Also, within the limits of available resources, there are many procedures not involving plea bargaining, such as diversion, that may be employed to reduce the work of the courts.

Furthermore, we suspect that the casual connection between plea bargaining and a high percentage of guilty pleas has been exaggerated. Persons plead guilty for a variety of reasons. There are many ways in which guilty pleas can be encouraged without resorting to plea bargaining. As indicated above, some of the pressures encouraging plea bargaining are generated by the expectation of bargaining. Both sides adopt extreme positions to increase their bargaining strength. The attitude of the parties would be more realistic if they did not have to prepare for negotiations. If the Crown refrains from overcharging and adopts a positive, non-punitive approach to sentencing, guilty pleas will be more readily entered. Full discovery of the Crown's case before trial may also induce more guilty pleas by persuading the accused of the futility of going to trial.

We are not convinced, therefore, that plea bargaining is an administrative necessity. The evidence is scarce and inconclusive. Even if the necessity of the practice were conclusively demonstrated, we would legitimize it as part of the procedural law only with that reluctance that inevitably accompanies any sacrifice of principle to expediency. Plea bargaining may save time and money. We doubt that the saving is worth the cost.

The objections to plea bargaining by the Crown apply also to bargaining by the police. In addition, bargaining by the police has the added disadvantage of involving the police in charging and other prosecutorial decisions that should be the responsibility of the Crown.

Judicial participation in plea bargaining is rare. Some critics of Crown bargaining have proposed, however, that judicial supervision of the practice might eliminate its undesirable features. Many forms of judicial involvement have been suggested. None in our view is satisfactory. Some of the proposals would imperil judicial impartiality, and require the judiciary to decide matters that are properly the political responsibility of the Crown. Certain forms of judicial review might have the merit of eliminating the secrecy surrounding plea bargains, and of protecting the rights of the accused. But these and other possible advantages are minor improvements that would not compensate for the basic evils of the practice. In a sense, judicial involvement in plea bargaining is the worst possible approach to the problem. It is an approach that would legitimize as a legal institution a practice which degrades the administration of justice.

We recommend, therefore, that plea bargaining be eliminated. This can be accomplished without legislation, if the Attorneys General issue directives to this effect to their agents, and if judges use their influence to discourage the practice.

The legal profession widely rejected these recommendations. The former Attorney-General of Ontario, Roy McMurtry, for example, suggested that the authors of the Working Paper were looking at the subject "in a rarefied atmosphere which I think is somewhat detached from the real world" and said that there was nothing wrong with the practice of plea bargaining if it was controlled by responsible people (*The Globe and Mail*, February 26, 1976).

Part IV

THE TRIAL PROCESS

Chapter 11

PRELIMINARY CONSIDERATIONS AND PRE-TRIAL MOTIONS

This chapter deals with a number of issues that must be dealt with prior to the commencement of the trial. While this chapter might well have been placed in the previous Part (Pre-Trial Procedure), in most jurisdictions, it is preferable (if not required) that these types of motions be dealt with by the actual trial judge. This is done for reasons of efficiency by avoiding the fragmentation of the trial process that would be caused by interlocutory appeals. When the types of decisions that are addressed in the following pages are decided by the trial judge, appeals from these decisions are absorbed in the ultimate verdict and can be adjudicated through the general appeal process (addressed later in this book, in Chapter 14).

In the chapters in Part II — Investigation, the elements of rights under numerous sections of the Charter (ss. 7, 8, 9, 10 and 11) were addressed. The determination of whether there any of those rights were violated in any given case, and the related question of whether there should any remedy under s. 24 of the Charter or s. 52 of the Constitution Act, 1982 will be determined at trial, usually after a pre-trial motion. These motions are brought before the trial judge. Sometimes they can be dealt with at the beginning of trial, prior to any evidence on the merits of the charges being adduced. This is the case with claims that s. 11(b) (trial within a reasonable time) has been infringed and a number of other rights. Other claims need, such as the impact of lost evidence and s. 7 of the Charter, sometimes need to be evaluated in the light of all evidence adduced at trial. Provincial Rules of Court must be consulted in order to determine the proper procedure to be followed before an application for a Charter remedy can be brought: see *R. v. Blom* (2002), 167 C.C.C. (3d) 332, 6 C.R. (6th) 181 (Ont. C.A.).

There are some pre-trial motions that should be made well before trial and, consequently, cannot wait until there is a specific trial judge. A good example of this is an application for a change of venue.

In efforts to streamline the trial process and to avoid lengthy evidentiary and procedural hearings at trial, Parliament has made several amendments to the Criminal Code. Section 625.1 allows for pre-hearing conferences for all trials and requires them for jury trials. The language of the provision is fairly general but permits the parties, with the assistance of the pre-hearing judge (who may not be the trial judge), to consider any matters that might contribute to a fair and expeditious trial. Then, the *Fair and Efficient Criminal Trials Act*, S.C. 2011, c. 16 was enacted to permit the appointment of a case management judge at any time before jury selection in a jury trial or before the hearing of evidence in a non-jury trial. The case management judge may not necessarily become the trial judge. The role of a case management judge is to assist the parties in resolving various issues, including identifying which witnesses might be necessary, encouraging admissions of fact in order to dispense with proof thereof, and sometimes taking guilty pleas and imposing sentences. In some cases, the case management judge may also adjudicate such issues as disclosure, admissibility of evidence, Charter issues, expert evidence matters, and severance of counts or accuseds. (For the latter, see s. 5 of this chapter.) Rulings made at this stage may apply at trial unless the trial judge is satisfied that it would not be in the interests of justice to do so. Where there are separate but related trials to be held in the same jurisdiction, it is possible for a single case management judge to conduct a joint hearing that is applicable to some or all of those trials: s. 551.7.

1. Right to Counsel at Trial (Charter, s. 7)

There is a traditional common law right to make full answer and defence. This is the usual vehicle, largely in the control of the trial judge, to guarantee the right to counsel at trial. Express provisions have long been in the Criminal Code (see ss. 650(3), 684 and 802).

The right to make full answer and defence is now constitutionally enshrined by the right in s. 7 of the Charter not to be deprived of life, liberty and security except in accordance with the principles of fundamental justice and in s. 11(*d*) which guarantees a fair and public hearing. **Can you have a fair hearing if you do not have counsel at your trial?**

DEUTSCH v. LAW SOCIETY OF UPPER CANADA
(1986), 47 C.R. (3d) 166 (Ont. Div. Ct.)

CRAIG J.:—Upon the submissions and arguments before me in the instant case it is my opinion that (except in a limited and indirect way, to be mentioned later), the right to a funded counsel has not been entrenched by s. 7 and/or s. 11(*d*) of the *Charter*. With the exception of the language provisions, most of the rights guaranteed by the *Charter* are expressed in negative terms in the sense that they require that the state refrain from certain activities. To impose a constitutionally entrenched positive duty on the government to expend public funds on the defence of persons accused of crimes would require a specific guarantee in express language.

Counsel for the respondent has referred me to the Minutes of the proceedings of the *Special Joint Committee of the Senate and House of Commons on the Constitution of Canada* (the Minutes) as an aid to interpretation of the *Charter* on this issue. The minutes of January 27th, 1981, reveal that an amendment to s. 10 of the *Charter* was proposed which would have added the following clause:

> (d)   if without sufficient means to pay for counsel and if the interests of justice so require, to be provided with counsel.

The members of the Committee considered Article 14(3) of the *International Covenant on Civil and Political Rights*, Article 6 of the *European Convention on Human Rights* and the *Sixth Amendment to the American Constitution*. Mr. Chretien, the then Minister of Justice submitted to the Committee that the provincial legal aid programmes were adequate to deal with the problem. The proposed amendment was defeated.

To date, there appear to be at least four reported decisions where the Minutes have been admitted and considered. For example, in *Re Federal Republic of Germany and Rauca* (1983), 41 O.R. (2d) 225, the Ontario Court of Appeal referred to the Minutes while interpreting s. 6 of the *Charter* without particularly addressing the issue of its admissibility. (See also *R. v. Konechny*, [1984] 2 W.W.R. 481, 25 M.V.R. 132, 38 C.R. (3d) 69, 10 C.C.C. (3d) 233, 6 D.L.R. (4th) 350 (B.C. C.A.)). The Minutes were admitted with some reservation as an aid to interpretation of the *Charter* in *Public Service Alliance of Can. v. R.*, [1984] 2 F.C. 562, 9 C.R.R. 248 (F.C. T.D.); affirmed (1984), 84 C.L.L.C. 14,054 (*sub nom. P.S.A.C. v. Can.*), 11 C.R.R. 97, 55 N.R. 285, 11 D.L.R. (4th) 387 (Fed. C.A.) and in *R. v. R. (T.)* (1983), 28 Alta. L.R. (2d) 383 at p. 393, 50 A.R. 56 at p. 63 (Alta. Q.B.). In both cases counsel had sought to rely on comments of Liberal cabinet ministers regarding the meaning of certain sections of the *Charter*. While the minutes were admitted in both cases, little weight was accorded them. Reed J. in the Federal Court in the *Public Service Alliance* cases summarized her position on this issue succinctly [at p. 263]:

> At one time records of such debates were not even admissible as relevant to the interpretation of legislation. Now that the rule has become more liberalized, we must not go too far the other way in terms of assuming that such comments should always be given significant weight. It should not be forgotten that statements made in such circumstances have an advocacy character. An attempt is made to convince the members of the Committee of the soundness of the Minister's proposal.
>
> Accordingly, I am not willing, in this case, to give much weight to the Minister's interpretation of the section unless there are other indicia leading to the same conclusion.

In the case at bar the respondent seeks to rely principally upon a vote defeating a proposed amendment before the Joint Committee. The weight of authority suggests that the Minutes should be admitted into evidence. Although the cautionary words of Reed J. above regarding the reliability of comments mde by cabinet ministers make good sense, it is reasonable to hold that the result of a vote on an amendment to the *Charter* should be given greater weight. It cannot be discarded on the basis that it is adversarial in nature. When viewed in this way the Minutes become persuasive authority for the proposition that the *Charter* was not intended to entrench a right to funded counsel.

In conclusion as to this issue, under the common law the accused has a right to a fair trial and the trial judge is bound to ensure that an accused person receives a fair trial. Here the accused faces possible imprisonment. Pursuant to s. 7 of the *Charter* the accused has an entrenched right not to be deprived of his liberty except in accordance with the principles of fundamental justice. Also pursuant to s. 11(*d*) he has an entrenched right to a "fair and public hearing . . .". The right to fundamental justice and a fair and public hearing includes the right to a fair trial There may be rare cases where legal aid is denied to an accused person facing trial, but where the trial judge is satisfied that, because of the seriousness and complexity of the case, the accused cannot receive a fair trial without counsel. In such a case it seems to follow that there is an entrenched right to a funded counsel under the *Charter*. As indicated earlier that is not new; it is the same right enjoyed by an accused at common law. It may still be a difficult question for a judge (or judge in Weekly Court) to decide whether a funded counsel shall be appointed. First, because an accused has an absolute right to proceed without counsel regardless of the complexity of the case; second, where an accused has been denied legal aid without error in law or jurisdiction on the part of the Legal Aid authorities, and/or where the accused refuses to comply with reasonable requirements of those authorities, his appearance in court without counsel *may* be construed as an exercise by him of his right to proceed without counsel: *R. v. Ciglen*, (1979), 10 C.R. (3d) 226 (Ont. H.C.). It is unnecessary for me to deal with the administrative details. I assume they would be dealt with on a case by case basis through the Department of the Attorney General of Ontario; and thus might require the adjournment of a trial to make the necessary arrangements.

The Alberta Court of Appeal in *R. v. Robinson* (1989), 73 C.R. (3d) 81, 51 C.C.C. (3d) 452 (Alta. C.A.) ruled that as there was no general right to the provision of funded counsel at trial, there would be no unqualified constitutional right to counsel for an appeal.

In *New Brunswick (Minister of Health & Community Services) v. G. (J.),* [1999] 3 S.C.R. 46, 26 C.R. (5th) 203 (S.C.C.) the Supreme Court determined that a government application for custody of children implicates the right to security of the person and the right to a fair hearing such that an indigent parent may have a s. 7 right to a state-funded counsel. The judge would have to consider the seriousness of the issue, the complexity of the proceeding and the capacity of the parent. Speaking for the majority, Lamer C.J. expressly distinguished his judgment for the Court in *Prosper* where he had held there was no positive right to state-funding under s. 10. This did not preclude a limited right to state-funded counsel under s. 7. In 2002, courts in Alberta and Quebec relied on this precedent to substantially raise the legal aid tariff in complex and lengthy gangsterism trials. However, on further appeal the Courts of Appeal denied such a jurisdiction to raise legal aid tariffs:

R. v. PETERMAN
(2004), 19 C.R. (6th) 258, 185 C.C.C. (3d) 352 (Ont. C.A.)

The accused was charged with two counts of arson in Perth. Legal Aid Ontario issued him a legal aid certificate. A lawyer in Newmarket, some four hours drive distant who had acted for the accused before, agreed to act for the accused on the certificate. The lawyer's application for travel funds was declined given the availability of local counsel. The lawyer brought an application against Legal Aid Ontario *inter alia* seeking payment for travel time and preparation time and junior counsel. The application judge granted this part of the request as reasonable and required for fair representation.

She ordered costs of $500 against the Crown. Legal Aid and the Crown appealed.

The Ontario Court of Appeal allowed appeals by the Crown and Legal Aid Ontario quashed the order of the application judge, including the costs order.

ROSENBERG J.A. (Borins and Feldman JJ.A. concurring):—

. . .

Defence counsel who undertake to defend indigent accused through the legal aid system perform an invaluable service to the community and to the administration of justice in this province. The state has a constitutional obligation to ensure that indigent accused receive a fair trial, and in many cases that means ensuring that the accused is represented by counsel. Under the Ontario legal aid certificate system, it is because defence lawyers are willing to accept legal aid certificates and provide competent and effective counsel to accused facing criminal charges that the state is able to fulfil its constitutional obligation. The importance of the work that defence counsel perform for legal aid clients cannot be underestimated. Moreover, defence counsel agree to perform these services at rates, and in accordance with conditions, that mean they will not always be fully reimbursed for all the work they do to ensure that clients caught up in the criminal justice system receive fair treatment and an effective defence. See the comments of Nicholas J. in *R. v. G.L.*, [2002] O.J. No. 3898 (C.J.).

However, under our system the obligation for setting legal aid rates and policies relating to retention of out-of-town counsel and of junior or co-counsel lies with Legal Aid Ontario, not the court. See *New Brunswick (Minister of Health and Community Services v. G.(J.))*, [1999] 3 S.C.R. 46 at paras. 102-8 and *R. v. Cai* (2002), 170 C.C.C. (3d) 1 (Alta. C.A.), application for leave to appeal to the Supreme Court of Canada dismissed [2003] S.C.C.A. No. 253, at paras. 8-18. A criminal trial court has no jurisdiction to review those policies and, having determined that they are unreasonable, impose other arrangements on Legal Aid Ontario. A criminal trial court's jurisdiction rests solely on the obligation to ensure that an accused person receives a fair trial. In some cases, the court will be satisfied that if an accused is not represented by counsel, his or her right to a fair trial as guaranteed by ss. 7 and 11(d) of the Canadian Charter of Rights and Freedoms will be infringed. If such an accused lacks the means to employ counsel privately, but has nevertheless been refused legal aid, the court can make an order staying the proceedings until the necessary funding for counsel is provided by the state. The trial will then not proceed until either the government or Legal Aid Ontario provides funding for counsel. This is a so-called *Rowbotham* order based on this court's decision in *R. v. Rowbotham* (1988), 41 C.C.C. (3d) 1. The court explained the legal basis for this order at p. 66:

> In our opinion, those who framed the Charter did not expressly constitutionalize the right of an indigent accused to be provided with counsel, because they considered that, generally speaking, the provincial legal aid systems were adequate to provide counsel for persons charged with serious crimes who lacked the means to employ counsel. However, in cases not falling within provincial legal aid plans,

ss. 7 and 11(d) of the Charter, which guarantee an accused a fair trial in accordance with the principles of fundamental justice, require funded counsel to be provided if the accused wishes counsel, but cannot pay a lawyer, and representation of the accused by counsel is essential to a fair trial.

In some cases, legal aid has been refused because in accordance with legal aid guidelines, the person does not qualify financially for legal aid. Where the accused seeks a *Rowbotham* order, the court, while giving appropriate deference to the decision of Legal Aid, must reach its own decision about whether the accused can afford counsel. As was said in *Rowbotham* at p. 69, "there may be rare circumstances in which legal aid is denied but the trial judge, after an examination of the means of the accused, is satisfied that the accused, because of the length and complexity of the proceedings or for other reasons, cannot afford to retain counsel to the extent necessary to ensure a fair trial". However, when a court makes a *Rowbotham* order, it is not conducting some kind of judicial review of decisions made by legal aid authorities. Rather, it is fulfilling its independent obligation to ensure that the accused receives a fair trial. . . .

The Charter guarantees to a fair trial and fundamental justice mean that the state must provide funds so that an indigent accused can be represented by counsel where counsel is required to ensure that the accused person has a fair trial. Further, within reason, the court will protect an accused's right to choose his or her counsel. As this court said in *R. v. Speid* (1984), 43 O.R. (2d) 596 at 598:

> The right of an accused to retain counsel of his choice has long been recognized at common law as a fundamental right. It has been carried forth as a singular feature of the Legal Aid Plan in this province and has been inferentially entrenched in the Charter of Rights which guarantees everyone upon arrest or detention the right to retain and instruct counsel without delay. However, although it is a fundamental right and one to be zealously protected by the Court, it is not an absolute right and is subject to reasonable limitations.

Absent compelling reasons, such as a disqualifying conflict of interest or incompetence, the courts will not interfere with an accused's choice of counsel. Further, the courts will avoid actions that result in accused persons being improperly or unfairly denied the opportunity to be represented by their counsel of choice. See *R. v. McCallen* (1999), 131 C.C.C. (3d) 518 (Ont. C.A.) at 531-32.

However, the right of an accused person to be free of unreasonable state or judicial interference in his or her choice of counsel does not impose a positive obligation on the state to provide funds for counsel of choice. See *R. v. Prosper* (1994), 92 C.C.C. (3d) 353 (S.C.C.) at p. 374, *R. v. Rockwood* (1989), 49 C.C.C. (3d) 129 (N.S.C.A.), *R. v. Ho*, [2004] 2 W.W.R. 590 (B.C.C.A.), and *Attorney General of Quebec v. R.C.* (2003), 13 C.R. (6th) 1 (Que. C.A.).

There would appear to be two exceptions to this general proposition. First, in some unique situations it may be that an accused can establish that he or she can only obtain a fair trial if represented by a particular counsel. In those unusual circumstances, the court may be entitled to make an order to ensure that the accused is represented by that counsel. This was the case in *R. v.*

Fisher and the genesis of the so-called *Fisher* order. But in making the order, Milliken J. recognized that he was faced with a unique case, and he suggested at para. 20 that the circumstances that led him to make the order might not occur in Saskatchewan "in another thirty years".

Second, in unusual circumstances, the court may find that the accused simply cannot find competent counsel to represent him or her on conditions imposed by Legal Aid. One would expect those cases to be exceedingly rare. For example, if the accused was unable to retain local counsel, Legal Aid would inevitably grant authorization to retain out-of-town counsel. See *R. v. Swearengen* (December 5, 2002, unreported Ont. S.C.J.). Courts in Ontario have, with few exceptions, rejected the proposition that enhanced rates above those authorized by Legal Aid are necessary to ensure that accused receive competent counsel. See *R. v. Abu-Taha*, [2001] O.J. No. 4278 (S.C.J.), *R. v. Montpellier*, [2002] O.J. No. 4279 (S.C.J.), *R. v. Swearengen*, and *R. v. Magda*, [2001] O.J. No. 1861 (S.C.J.).

The respondent's case is not unique and it is not of the same order of complexity as the *Fisher* case. It is an arson case expected to last seven days in which there may be up to thirty Crown witnesses, one of whom was a former accomplice. If this is the level of complexity that would justify a *Fisher* order, virtually every accused facing a jury trial could claim an entitlement to state-funded counsel of choice. That is simply not the law. As to the respondent's relationship with his counsel, it is not unusual for accused to have prior professional relationships with a lawyer. The fact that counsel had a prior relationship with the respondent and that the respondent had confidence in him similarly did not demonstrate an entitlement to state-funded counsel of choice. See *R. v. Bruha*, [2003] 1 W.W.R. 339 (N.W.T.S.C.). I have set out earlier a paragraph from the affidavit of junior counsel where he attempts to explain the basis for the application. There is nothing in that paragraph that could justify a conclusion that this case was so difficult, and that counsel's relationship with the respondent was so special, that only Mr. Wrock could handle it.

This was also not a case where a *Fisher*-type order was required because the respondent could not otherwise obtain competent counsel. There was no evidence before the application judge that other competent counsel were not available to take the case and to do so on the conditions imposed by Legal Aid. Oral submissions from counsel at the hearing about the number of lawyers in the county was no basis for finding that there were no other competent lawyers available to take the case.

. . .

There was . . . no evidence that no other lawyer was available to proceed with the trial on the scheduled trial date. Even if there had been such evidence, it would not follow that the respondent was entitled to the order made by the application judge. The application judge could have adjourned the case to permit the respondent time to retain local counsel. Subsequent events have demonstrated that the respondent is not concerned with or prejudiced by delay of his trial. At his request the trial has in fact now been adjourned for over a year pending the outcome of this appeal.

Alternatively, having regard to the circumstances, the application judge could have required Mr. Wrock to proceed with the case since he was on the record and had undertaken to defend the respondent. Rule 2.09(5) of the Rules of Professional Conduct of the Law Society of Upper Canada is clear on this issue:

> Where a lawyer has agreed to act in a criminal case and where the date set for trial is not far enough removed to enable the client to obtain another lawyer or to enable another lawyer to prepare adequately for trial and an adjournment of the trial date cannot be obtained without adversely affecting the client's interests, *the lawyer who agreed to act may not withdraw because of non-payment of fees.* [Emphasis added.]

The order made by the application judge was not necessary to ensure that the respondent was properly represented and received a fair trial. There was therefore no basis for making that order and it must be set aside.

———————

For a review of the differing approaches by Courts of Appeal, see Guy Cournoyer, "Canada's Gideon's Trumpets and the Limits of Financial Remedies: Courts as Funambulists", (2004) 19 C.R. (6th) 273.

It is now well established that a court may appoint counsel where it is necessary to protect the right to make full answer and defence under s. 7. Courts do not set the fees, however, but will often resort to a temporary stay of the proceedings. The Supreme Court of Canada, in the context of the appointment of an *amicus curiae*, has held that a court may appoint the *amicus* but may not set the rate of the fees because of the longstanding principle that it is unconstitutional to permit judges to allocate public funds: *R. v. Imona-Russell* (*sub nom. Ontario v. Criminal Lawyers' Association of Ontario*), [2013] 3 S.C.R. 3, 300 C.C.C. (3d) 137, 4 C.R. (7th) 1 (S.C.C.). The Court left room for a judge to set the rate of pay as a Charter remedy. The Court also recognized the possibility of a stay of proceedings until the Attorney General and *amicus* can agree on the fees. Presumably, these rulings are also applicable to the appointment of counsel.

Courts now frequently acknowledge that the right to make full answer and defence protected under ss. 7 and 11(*d*) of the Charter includes a right to effective assistance of counsel: see, for example, *R. v. Silvini*, later under "Joint Trials" and *R. v. Joanisse* (1995), 44 C.R. (4th) 364 (Ont. C.A.). However, courts of appeal have been most reluctant to order new trials on the basis of incompetence of counsel and often rely on the necessity to not second-guess tactical decisions made at trial (see, however, an order of a new trial in a sexual assault case on the basis that incompetent cross-examination may have affected the outcome: *R. v. P. (T.)* (2002), 4 C.R. (6th) 369, 165 C.C.C. (3d) 281 (Ont. C.A.)).

When the issue of the right to competent counsel reached the Supreme Court in *R. v. B. (G.D.)*, [2000] 1 S.C.R. 520, 32 C.R. (5th) 207, 143 C.C.C. (3d) 289 (S.C.C.), the Court was uncharacteristically terse. For the Court, Major J. adopted the *Strickland* approach as justified by Doherty J.A. in *Joanisse.* The right to effective assistance of counsel extended to all accused as a principle of fundamental justice. It is derived from the evolution of the common law, s. 650(3) of the Criminal Code of Canada and ss. 7 and 11(d) of the Charter. An appellant had to establish incompetence and that a miscarriage of justice resulted.

> Incompetence is determined by a reasonableness standard. The analysis proceeds upon a strong presumption that counsel's conduct fell within the wide range of reasonable professional assistance. The onus is on the appellant to establish the acts or omissions of counsel that are alleged not to have been the result of reasonable professional judgment. The wisdom of hindsight has no place in this assessment (para. 27).

Major J. added that miscarriages of justice could take many forms but could include procedural unfairness or compromise the trial's result. Where no prejudice had occurred, appellate courts should refrain from grading counsel's performance or professionalism which was a matter best left to the profession's self-governing body. In *B. (G.D.)*, the defence counsel's failure to introduce an audio-taped conversation between the complainant and her mother had been tactical and had not resulted in a miscarriage of justice.

It is unfortunate that the Court did not justify its resort to the low level *Strickland* test or its focus on prejudice. See further criticism by Charles Davison, "Importing Strickland: Some Concerns in Light of the Supreme Court's Adoption of the American Test for Ineffective Counsel", (2000) 32 C.R. (5th) 220. In *Strickland* there is a strong dissent by Justice Marshall who points to disparities in representation and asks whether the test is a reasonably competent adequately paid retained lawyer or a reasonably competent appointed attorney.

With legal aid budgets slashed across the country, this was a matter the Court ought to have addressed. For rulings on the right to effective assistance of counsel, see Dale Ives, "The Role of Counsel and the Courts in Safeguarding the Accused's Opportunity to Decide whether to Testify", (2006) 51 Crim. L.Q. 508, Hill J. in *R. v. Furtado* (2006), 43 C.R. (6th) 305 (Ont. S.C.J.), *R. v. G. (D.M.)* (2011), 84 C.R. (6th) 420, 275 C.C.C. (3d) 295 (Ont. C.A.) (new trial ordered in sexual assault case due to inadequate preparation by defence counsel respecting entry of guilty plea), *R. v. Carr* (2010), 266 C.C.C. (3d) 235 (Alta. C.A.) (not calling physician who had evidence of concussion in impaired driving case) and *R. v. Ross* (2012), 290 C.C.C. (3d) 555 (N.S. C.A.) (not giving advice as to risk of not testifying where defence based on mistake as to age of complainant). Where an accused is unrepresented there are important but uncertain obligations imposed on trial judges: see, for example, *R. v. Tran* (2001), 44 C.R. (5th) 12, 156 C.C.C. (3d) 1 (Ont. C.A.), *R. v. Moghaddam* (2006), 37 C.R. (6th) 110, 206 C.C.C. (3d) 497 (B.C. C.A.), annotation, *ibid.*, by Tim Quigley and *R. v. Imona-Russell* (2011), 86 C.R. (6th) 407, 270 C.C.C. (3d) 256 (Ont. C.A.), reversed (*sub nom. Ontario v. Criminal Lawyers' Association of Ontario*), [2013] 3 S.C.R. 3, 300 C.C.C. (3d) 137, 4 C.R. (7th) 1 (S.C.C.).

2. Adjournments

There are numerous provisions scattered across the Criminal Code dealing with adjournment powers of presiding judicial officers. For instance, s. 516 permits a justice to adjourn a bail hearing and s. 537 permits a justice to adjourn a preliminary inquiry from time to time. With respect to charges tried on indictment, s. 571 (relating to non-jury trials) and s. 645 (jury trials) confers power on a trial judge to adjourn the trial from time to time. Section 803 of the Criminal Code permits the trial judge of a summary conviction matter to adjourn the proceedings.

R. v. G. (J.C.)

(2004), 189 C.C.C. (3d) 1 (Que. C.A.), leave to appeal refused (2005), 2005 CarswellQue 841 (S.C.C.)

The accused was charged with robbery offences and aggravated assault. On the date set for trial, the Crown sought an adjournment because the complainant was not present in court. The complainant had been subpoenaed (by ordinary mail), as permitted by s. 20.1 of the Code of Penal Procedure, R.S.Q. c. C-25.1. Crown counsel advised the trial judge that the complainant lived with her parents, but that her parents had not heard from her for four days. The trial judge refused to grant the adjournment. The accused was acquitted. The Crown's first appeal to the summary conviction appeal court was dismissed. A majority of the Court allowed the Crown's further appeal.

DALPHOND J.A. (Morin J.A. concurring):—

. . .

I

It is undisputed that whether an adjournment or a postponement should be granted or not is a discretionary matter for the trial judge (*Manhas v. The Queen*, [1980] 1 S.C.R. 591; *R. v. Barrette*, [1977] 2 S.C.R. 121; *R. v. Darville* (1956), 116 C.C.C. 113 (S.C.C.); *R. v. MacDonald*, [1998] N.J. No. 340 (QL) (C.A.)).

Such judicial discretion can however be reviewed on appeal if it has not been exercised judicially (*R. v. Darville, supra; R. v. Ash*, [1993] N.S.J. No. 395 (QL) (C.A.) [reported 125 N.S.R. (2d) 235]). The test for appellate review is whether the trial judge has given sufficient weight to all relevant considerations (*Reza v. Canada*, [1994] 2 S.C.R. 394). Of course, if the judgment is based on reasons that are not well founded in law, a court of appeal may intervene.

On the elements to be considered by a judge when asked to grant an adjournment of a criminal trial due to the absence of a witness, the Supreme Court of Canada provided some guidelines in 1956 in *R. v. Darville, supra*. They can be summarized as follows:

(a)   that the absent witness is a material witness in the case;

(b)   that the party applying for an adjournment has been guilty of no laches or neglect in omitting to endeavour to procure the attendance of this witness; and

(c)   that there is a reasonable expectation that the witness can be procured at the future time to which it is sought to put off the trial.

Moreover, as pointed out by Cartwright J. in his concurring opinion in *Darville*, a trial judge errs in law by refusing a request for an adjournment without having given the party seeking it an opportunity to demonstrate that the conditions described above are met. I agree with this principle of law, which has been applied by numerous courts of appeal (see for examples: *R. v. T. (A.)* (1991), 69 C.C.C. (3d) 107 (Alta. Q.B.); *R. v. Ash*, [1993] N.S.J. No. 395 (QL) (C.A.) [reported 125 N.S.R. (2d) 235]; *R. v. Casey*, [1987] N.S.J. No. 340 (QL) (C.A.) [reported 80 N.S.R. (2d) 247]; *R. v. Fahey*, [2003] B.C.J. No. 2331 (QL) (C.A.) [reported 308 W.A.C. 36]; *R. v. MacDonald*, [1998] N.J. No. 340 (QL) (C.A.) [reported 132 C.C.C. (3d) 205]). In other words, before concluding that a party has been negligent, the trial judge must give that party an opportunity to establish all the relevant facts.

Finally, I believe that it is proper for a trial judge when asked for a postponement to consider other relevant circumstances such as the gravity of the charges, the number of previous postponements and the consequences of a postponement for the accused.

Briefly stated, the decision whether or not to grant the adjournment must be made in light of the realities of each case and shall be consistent with the interests of justice.

II

There is no doubt that the first criterion mentioned in *Darville* was met. The witness who did not appear was the complainant in the case, a minor girl. Her presence was critical to establish the case against the respondent.

I deal now with the second criterion: was the Crown negligent? This has to be decided according to the evidence made before the trial judge, which in this file, consists of the Crown counsel's short oral representations. Only two facts were represented then to the judge:

1)   A subpoena was served to the complainant by ordinary mail:

The Court:

We'll see . . . did you prepare a subpoena? Did you serve her with a subpoena?

Me Maria-Giustina Corsi (for the Crown):

The subpoena was sent. Your Honour . . .

Me Emile Benamor (for the accused):

There's a subpoena (inaudible) you have to have it, c'est dans votre dossier.

Me Maria-Giustina Corsi:

The subpoena, I believe, was sent by mail if you verify in your file, your Honour; the subpoena for this date was sent, however I don't have any return, so I assume that it was sent by mail. Your Honour. It was (inaudible).

2) A few days before the trial, the complainant ran away from her parents'
    home, a fact discovered by the Crown further to police calls to the parents
    the day of the hearing and a few days before:

    Me Maria-Giustina Corsi (for the Crown):

    So, Your Honour, in this file concerning Mr. C, Your Honour, as the Crown was
    telling you in French earlier on, is that the victim by the name of A. B. is a person
    that has a particular train of life, Your Honour, the parents . . . she still lives with
    the parents, however following the verification by the sergeant detective
    McKay(ph) this morning and over the week, it's been four days since the parents
    have seen Mrs.B. Your Honour, for these reasons — it's the first time that it comes
    to trial today — I would ask you a postponement in this file and I would ask you
    to postpone it to the 13th of June of this year . . . [Emphasis added.]

If the trial judge was unsatisfied with this recital of the facts, he should
have said so and then ordered an adjournment to provide the Crown the
opportunity to bring before him proper evidence of what really happened, such
as an affidavit from the parents attesting that their daughter received the
subpoena and ran away a few days before the scheduled date of the trial, the
testimony of the police officer on the various steps undertaken before the trial,
etc. He did not; so these facts stand.

As pointed out by my colleague Hilton, no one can seriously challenge
that the Crown acts in accordance with the law when it sends a subpoena by
ordinary mail in accordance with s. 20.1 of the Code of Penal Procedure,
R.S.Q. c. C-25.1. In other words, service of a subpoena by ordinary mail is a
valid procedure to summon a witness in criminal proceedings. Thus, there
ought to be no presumption either that such a method of service constituted
neglect or that it did not.

In this case, the judge seems to think that using this method for the victim
constituted neglect by the Crown:

    The Court:

    I deny the postponement; I think that knowing the person, the kind of person, a
    special effort should be made supporting the . . . everybody . . . the cases have to
    proceed, it was fixed for half a day, it's a serious matter. [Emphasis added.]

With respect, this is a clearly unreasonable ratio since there was no
evidence whatsoever made before the trial judge that if the complainant had
been personally served with a subpoena, she would not have run away. Thus,
the Crown could not be found negligent for having sent the subpoena by
ordinary mail instead of by bailiff or by another mode of personal service.

In fact, nobody knew why the complainant took off: Was she afraid of
testifying? Did she simply forget about the subpoena? Or was it for some other
reason?

To be sure, the Crown which had just found out about the disappearance
of the complainant, could not then be blamed by the trial judge for not
knowing the answer; only an adjournment could have provided an opportunity
to find out.

In brief, based on the sole evidence before him, the trial judge could not reasonably conclude that the Crown had been guilty of neglect in omitting to endeavour to procure the attendance of the complainant.

As for the submission of counsel for the respondent made before us that, somehow, prior to the trial, the Crown should have been aware of the fact that the complainant was not going to appear and should have done something about it, is not sustainable, since she was not required to be present before the time set for the trial (*R. v. MacDonald, supra*).

The third criterion is the most difficult, particularly where, as here, it is not known before the time set for trial that the witness will not be appearing. . .

Again, I think, with respect, that the trial judge erred in law by refusing the Crown's request for an adjournment without having given it an opportunity to demonstrate that this condition was met.

All that being said, was it nevertheless in the interests of justice to order an acquittal in this case? I think definitely not. The charges were serious (aggravated assault, robbery and conspiracy to commit a robbery), there was no prior postponement and the defence attorney did not mention any specific adverse consequence for the accused (he was not detained at the time).

In these circumstances, the trial judge should not have refused the Crown's request for a postponement of the trial and should not have subsequently acquitted the respondent. Instead, he should have considered issuing a warrant, or if unsatisfied with the facts alleged by the Crown, he should have adjourned to give the Crown an opportunity to adduce proper evidence.

. . .

HILTON J.A. (dissenting):— The sole issue in this appeal is whether a judge sitting in the Youth Division of the Court of Quebec properly exercised his discretion when he denied a request for the postponement of a trial and acquitted the respondent when the victim, who Crown counsel affirmed had been sent a subpoena by ordinary mail, did not appear to testify. This Court is thus called upon to consider the application of the principles that have governed this issue since the judgment of the Supreme Court of Canada in 1956 in *R. v. Darville*, as those principles have been applied in Quebec and elsewhere by appellate courts.

. . .

In its factum, the Crown contends that the trial judge abused his discretion by denying it a postponement since it acted in accordance with the law by sending a subpoena to the victim by ordinary mail. This is all the more so the case, the Crown says, because this was the first request for a postponement, and no prejudice was shown to or claimed by the respondent. In short, the Crown argues in its factum that its conduct of the case was beyond reproach, and that the gravity of the offences with which the respondent was charged weighed against denying a postponement and against entering a verdict of acquittal.

. . .

In this case, the trial judge focused in the main on what he perceived to be the Crown's negligence in not having taken adequate steps to ensure the presence of the victim, who he knew was a material witness, especially in light of what Crown counsel described as the young witness' "particular train of life". He also listened to the request of Crown counsel to adjourn the matter to a specified date approximately three weeks later, at which time she expected the witness to be back in court for another case.

In support of its position that the trial judge did not properly exercise his discretion by refusing the adjournment and acquitting the respondent, the Crown has cited a number of cases from courts across Canada, including Quebec, where courts exercising appellate jurisdiction under the Criminal Code have intervened to quash verdicts of acquittal entered by trial judges when material witnesses, usually the victim, did not appear at trial. Most of these cases cited by the Crown, however, are ones where the witnesses in question actually did receive a subpoena. The others are distinguishable on the facts.

. . .

No one can seriously challenge that the Crown acts in accordance with the law when it sends a subpoena by ordinary mail in accordance with s. 20.1 of the Code of Penal Procedure. It runs a consequential risk, however, such as the circumstances of this case and that of *Bissonnette* show, when it cannot adequately demonstrate if the subpoena was sent and if so when, or if it was in fact received when the intended recipient does not appear in response to the summons. To compound the problem, the Crown makes no effort on a timely basis to verify whether the subpoena was sent or whether or not it was received.

From what the Court was told at the hearing, the sending of subpoenas by ordinary mail is the rule rather than the exception. There does not appear to be any independent judgment exercised as to whether a subpoena should be sent in a more effective manner if the circumstances warrant. Undoubtedly, that practice may work in many instances, but it can hardly be doubted that using the ordinary mail to reach a 16-year old girl with a "particular" lifestyle and then not following up to insure the subpoena was received was conduct replete with risk.

. . .

The Crown also contends that the Court should forgive its acknowledged negligence because of the gravity of the charges: conspiracy to commit robbery, robbery and aggravated assault.

Gravity, however, is a two-way street.

The Crown did not consider that the gravity of the charges against the accused warranted any particular consideration when it came time to compel the attendance of its only witness to the trial. On the contrary, by its conduct, it took a casual approach and treated the case as if it was a simple run-of-the-mill affair.

The gravity of the charges also weighs on the accused, who had pleaded not guilty to them, and whose liberty was at risk once he had entered a plea of not guilty. It is precisely because of the gravity of the charges that the accused is entitled to expect that absent special circumstances which are not present here, the Crown will be ready to proceed on the date fixed for the trial. This it could not do, and I see no compelling reason why the accused should be faced anew with the prospect of a new trial.

Finally, the Crown makes much of the fact that its request for a postponement was the first one of the case, and that for that reason as well, the trial judge should have acceded to its request for an adjournment to another date. No party, be it the Crown or the accused, is entitled to a postponement simply because one has not been previously requested, as if somehow such a request was analogous to the peremptory challenge of a juror which must be granted as a matter of course. Any application for a postponement must stand or fall on its merits, and for no other reason.

In conclusion, I cannot say that the trial judge abused his discretion in disposing of the case in the manner he did. He took account of the submissions made to him, and having determined that the Crown had not prosecuted the case with sufficient diligence by failing to take more appropriate steps to ensure the presence at trial of its only witness, he refused to grant a postponement. Such a decision can hardly be criticized when the Crown did not even have an attestation that a subpoena had been sent by ordinary mail, and its counsel merely affirmed, without any supporting evidence, that one had been sent. When the Crown offered no evidence, the trial judge acquitted the accused. . . .

I would dismiss the appeal.

---

3. Trial Within a Reasonable Time (Charter, s. 11(b))

Motions to stay proceedings for unreasonable delay contrary to s. 11(b) of the Charter are generally made to the trial judge, at the outset of trial. As demonstrated in the following cases, the trial judge must decide the complicated question of unreasonable delay in light of the way the case has proceeded from the time of charge, through a preliminary inquiry (if applicable) to the opening of trial.

The Charter of Rights provides:

11. Any person charged with an offence has the right . . .

(b) to be tried within a reasonable time.

The s. 11(b) right is triggered by a charge of an offence, which has been held to include a provincial offence: *R. v. Wigglesworth*, [1987] 2 S.C.R. 541, 60 C.R. (3d) 193, 37 C.C.C. (3d) 385 (S.C.C.). This does not include professional disciplinary proceedings nor assigned forfeiture under the Customs Act: *Martineau v. Ministre du Revenu national*, [2004] 3 S.C.R. 737, 24 C.R. (6th) 207, 192 C.C.C. (3d) 129 (S.C.C.), based on allegations of false statements in exporting goods.

R. v. ASKOV

[1990] 2 S.C.R. 1199, 79 C.R. (3d) 273, 59 C.C.C. (3d) 449 (S.C.C.)

After a number of very split rulings on the proper test for s. 11(*b*) the Supreme Court arrived at a majority opinion in *Askov*. For the first time the Court also spoke on the issue of institutional delay: delay caused by lack of resources such as courtrooms, judges and Crown counsel. Extortion and weapons charges against four accused had taken almost three years to come to trial. The Court held that, even if a delay of one year prior to the preliminary could be discounted as being in large part attributable to defence adjournments, the delay of almost two years between the preliminary and trial had been caused by a lack of facilities in Brampton, in the Ontario Judicial District of Peel. There had been a breach of s. 11(*b*) and the charges had to be stayed.

CORY J. (Dickson C.J.C. and La Forest, L'Heureux-Dubé and Gonthier JJ. concurring):—

. . .

JUDICIAL CONSIDERATION OF THE PRINCIPLE OF PROVIDING A TRIAL WITHIN A REASONABLE TIME

The United States

In the United States the Sixth Amendment ensures that "In all criminal prosecutions, the accused shall enjoy the right to a speedy and public trial". The United States Supreme Court considered the issue in *Barker v. Wingo*, 407 U.S. 514, 33 L. Ed. 2d 101, 92 S. Ct. 2182 (1972). In that case Barker, who was charged with murder, was brought to trial five years after the murder was committed. The delay was caused by the necessity of trying an accomplice beforehand. This prerequisite trial was extremely complicated; the accomplice was tried no less than six times. During this ongoing process, Barker initially had agreed to continuances or adjournments. He began to assert his right to a speedy trial only 31/2 years after the charges were laid.

The court held that a flexible approach should be taken to cases involving delay and that the multiple purposes or aims of the Sixth Amendment must be appreciated. Powell J., giving the reasons for the court, recognized the general concern that all persons accused with crimes should be treated according to fair and decent procedures. He particularly noted that there were three individual interests which the right was designed to protect. They were:

(i) to prevent oppressive pre-trial incarceration;

(ii) to minimize the anxiety and concern of the accused; and

(iii) to limit the possibility that the defence will be impaired or prejudiced.

However, Powell J. went on to observe that, unlike other constitutional rights which only have an individual interest, the right to a speedy trial involved the added dimension of a societal interest. He found that a delay could result in increased financial cost to society and, as well, could have a negative effect upon the credibility of the justice system. Further, it was noted that a delay could work to the advantage of the accused. For example, the fostering of a delay could become a defence tactic designed to take advantage of failing memories or missing witnesses or could permit the accused to manipulate the system in order to bargain for a lesser sentence. Specifically, he stated at p. 521 that the right to a speedy trial was:

> . . . a more vague concept than other procedural rights. It is, for example, impossible to determine with precision when the right has been denied. We cannot definitely say how long is too long in a system where justice is supposed to be swift but deliberate. As a consequence, there is no fixed point in the criminal process when the State can put the defendant to the choice of either exercising or waiving the right to a speedy trial.

In order to balance the individual right and the communal aspect of the Sixth Amendment, the United States Supreme Court adopted an approach of ad hoc balancing "in which the conduct of both the prosecution and the defendant are weighed" (p. 530). The balancing is undertaken by reference to four factors identified by Powell J. as the test for infringement of the right to a "speedy trial". They are as follows:

(i)   the length of the delay;

(ii) the reason for the delay;

(iii) the accused's assertion of the right; and

(iv) prejudice to the accused

The first factor is the triggering mechanism or threshold determination of the excessiveness of the delay. If that delay appears prima facie excessive, the court must then consider the three remaining factors to determine whether the accused has been deprived of the Sixth Amendment right.

Position in Canada subsequent to the passing of the Charter

. . .

[Justice Cory reviewed the Court's earlier decisions on s. 11(b).]

Purpose of s. 11(b)

I agree with the position taken by Lamer J. that s. 11(b) explicitly focusses upon the individual interest of liberty and security of the person. Like other specific guarantees provided by s. 11, this paragraph is primarily concerned with an aspect of fundamental justice guaranteed by s. 7 of the Charter. There could be no greater frustration imaginable for innocent persons charged with an offence than to be denied the opportunity of demonstrating their innocence for an unconscionable time as a result of unreasonable delays in their trial. The time awaiting trial must be exquisite agony for accused persons and their immediate family. It is a fundamental precept of our criminal law that every individual is presumed to be innocent until proven guilty. It follows that, on the same fundamental level of importance, all accused persons, each one of whom is presumed to be innocent, should be given the opportunity to defend themselves against the charges they face and to have their name cleared and reputation re-established at the earliest possible time.

Although the primary aim of s. 11(*b*) is the protection of the individual's rights and the provision of fundamental justice for the accused, nonetheless there is, in my view, at least by inference, a community or societal interest implicit in s. 11(*b*). That community interest has a dual dimension. First, there is a collective interest in ensuring that those who transgress the law are brought to trial and dealt with according to the law. Second, those individuals on trial must be treated fairly and justly. Speedy trials strengthen both those aspects of the community interest. A trial held within a reasonable time must benefit the individual accused, as the prejudice which results from criminal proceedings is bound to be minimized. If the accused is in custody, the custodial time awaiting trial will be kept to a minimum. If the accused is at liberty on bail and subject to conditions, then the curtailments on the liberty of the accused will be kept to a minimum. From the point of view of the community interest, in those cases where the accused is detained in custody awaiting trial, society will benefit by the quick resolution of the case either by reintegrating into society the accused found to be innocent or, if found guilty, by dealing with the accused according to the law. If the accused is released on bail and subsequently found guilty, the frustration felt by the community on seeing an unpunished wrongdoer in their midst for an extended period of time will be relieved.

There are as well important practical benefits which flow from a quick resolution of the charges. There can be no doubt that memories fade with time. Witnesses are likely to be more reliable testifying to events in the immediate past, as opposed to events that transpired many months or even years before the trial. Not only is there an erosion of the witnesses' memory with the passage of time, but there is bound to be an erosion of the witnesses themselves. Witnesses are people; they are moved out of the country by their employer; or for reasons related to family or work they move from the east coast to the west coast; they become sick and unable to testify in court; they are involved in debilitating accidents; they die, and their testimony is forever lost. Witnesses too are concerned that their evidence be taken as quickly as possible. Testifying is often thought to be an ordeal. It is something that weighs on the minds of witnesses and is a source of worry and frustration for them until they have given their testimony.

It can never be forgotten that the victims may be devastated by criminal acts. They have a special interest and good reason to expect that criminal trials take place within a reasonable time. From a wider point of view, it is fair to say that all crime disturbs the community and that serious crime alarms the community. All members of the community are thus entitled to see that the justice system works fairly, efficiently and with reasonable dispatch. The very reasonable concern and alarm of the community which naturally arises from acts of crime cannot be assuaged until the trial has taken place. The trial not only resolves the guilt or innocence of the individual but acts as a reassurance to the community that serious crimes are investigated and that those implicated are brought to trial and dealt with according to the law.

The failure of the justice system to deal fairly, quickly and efficiently with criminal trials inevitably leads to the community's frustration with the judicial system and eventually to a feeling of contempt for court procedures. When a trial takes place without unreasonable delay, with all witnesses available and memories fresh, it is far more certain that the guilty parties who committed the crimes will be convicted and punished and those that did not will be acquitted and vindicated. It is no exaggeration to say that a fair and balanced criminal justice system simply cannot exist without the support of the community. Continued community support for our system will not endure in the face of lengthy and unreasonable delays.

Further, implicit support for the concept that there is a societal aspect to s. 11(*b*) can be derived from the observation that the last thing that some wish for is a speedy trial. There is no doubt that many accused earnestly hope that the memory of a witness will fail and that other witnesses will become unavailable.

. . .

Factors to be taken into account in determining whether or not there has been an infringement of s. 11(b)

(i)   The Length of the Delay

It is clear that the longer the delay, the more difficult it should be for a court to excuse it. This is not a threshold requirement as in the United States, but rather is a factor to be balanced along with the others. However, very lengthy delays may be such that they cannot be justified for any reason.

(ii)   Explanation for the Delay

This category, referred to by Sopinka J. in *Smith*, supra, may be usefully subdivided with the aspects of systemic delay and conduct of the accused amplified.

(a)   The Conduct of the Crown (or Delay Attributable to the Crown):

Generally speaking, this category will comprise all of the potential factors causing delay which flow from the nature of the case, the conduct of the Crown, including officers of the state, and the inherent time requirements of the case. Delays attributable to the actions of the Crown or its officers will weigh in favour of the accused. For example, the 19 adjournments initiated by the trial judge in *Rahey*, supra, or the unavailability of judges because of holidays in *Smith*, supra, are examples where the actions or the lack of actions of Crown officers weighed against the state in the assessment of the reasonableness of the delay.

It is under this heading that the complexity of the case should be taken into account. Complex cases which require longer time for preparation, a greater expenditure of resources by Crown officers and the longer use of institutional facilities will justify delays longer than those that would be acceptable in simple cases.

(b)   Systemic or Institutional Delays:

On a more specific level, the question of delays caused by systemic or institutional limitations should also be discussed under the heading of delays attributable to the Crown. This factor will often be the most difficult to assess. A careful and sensitive balancing will be required in order to properly assess the significance of this aspect of delay. First, let us consider the problem from the point of view of society. Section 11(*b*) applies to all Canadians in every part of our land. In a country as vast and diverse as ours, the institutional problems are bound to differ greatly from province to province and from district to district within each province. Differences of climate, terrain, population and financial resources will require different solutions for the problem of providing adequate facilities and personnel. Lack of financial resources may require imaginative answers to difficult problems, including the provision of temporary facilities. The problems presented and the solutions required will vary between heavily-populated centres such as Toronto and Montreal and the sparsely-populated districts bordering on Hudson Bay.

Wise political decisions will be required with regard to the allocation of scarce funds. Due deference will have to be given to those political decisions, as the provisions of courtroom facilities and Crown attorneys must, for example, be balanced against the provision of health care and highways. Yet solutions must be found, as indeed they have been in many jurisdictions outside Ontario. Similarly-situated communities can provide a rough comparison and some guidance as to what time period constitutes an unreasonable delay of the trial of an accused person. That comparison should always be made with the more efficient of the comparable jurisdictions.

The right guaranteed by s. 11(*b*) is of such fundamental importance to the individual and of such significance to the community as a whole that the lack of institutional resources cannot be employed to justify a continuing unreasonable postponement of trials. In *Mills*, supra, Lamer J. noted at p. 935:

> In an ideal world there would be no delays in bringing an accused to trial and there would be no difficulties in securing fully adequate funding, personnel and facilities for the administration of criminal justice. As we do not live in such a world, some allowance must be made for limited institutional resources.

However, the lack of institutional facilities can never be used as a basis for rendering the s. 11(*b*) guarantee meaningless.

. . .

Where inordinate delays do occur, it is those who are responsible for the lack of facilities who should bear the public criticism that is bound to arise as a result of the staying of proceedings which must be the inevitable consequence of unreasonable delays. Members of the community will not and should not condone or accept a situation where those alleged to have committed serious crimes are never brought to trial solely as a result of unduly long delays. It is a serious consequence with potentially dangerous overtones for the community. It is right and proper that there be criticism of the situation when it occurs.

The response to the question of "How long is too long?" as it applies to institutional delay will always be difficult to fashion in our country. The question must be answered in light of the particular facts of each case. There can be no certain standard of a fixed time which will be applicable in every region of the country. Nonetheless, an inquiry into what is reasonable in any region should not be taken in isolation and must, of necessity, involve a comparison with other jurisdictions. Consideration must be given to the geography, the population and the material resources of the province and district. The comparison of similar and thus comparable districts must always be made with the better districts and not with the worst.

. . .

To summarize, when considering delays occasioned by inadequate institutional resources, the question of how long a delay is too long may be resolved by comparing the questioned jurisdiction to the standard maintained by the best comparable jurisdiction in the country. The comparison need not be too precise or exact. Rather, it should look to the appropriate ranges of delay to determine what is a reasonable limit. In all cases it will be incumbent upon the Crown to show that the institutional delay in question is justifiable.

(c)   The Conduct of the Accused (or Delay Attributable to the Accused):

As Lamer J. so cogently observed in *Mills*, it is a fundamental precept of our criminal justice system that it is the responsibility of the Crown to bring the accused to trial. Further, the right to be tried within a reasonable time is an aspect of fundamental justice protected by s. 7 of the Charter. It follows that any inquiry into the conduct of the accused should in no way absolve the Crown from its responsibility to bring the accused to trial. Nonetheless, there is a societal interest in preventing an accused from using the guarantee as a means of escaping trial. It should be emphasized that an inquiry into the actions of the accused should be restricted to discovering those situations where either the accused's acts directly caused the delay (as in *Conway*, supra) or the acts of the accused are shown to be a deliberate and calculated tactic employed to delay the trial. These direct acts on the part of the accused, such as seeking an adjournment to retain new counsel, must of course be distinguished from those situations where the delay was caused by factors beyond the control of the accused, or a situation where the accused did nothing to prevent a delay caused by the Crown.

In addition, since the protection of the right of the individual is the primary aim of s. 11(*b*), the burden of proving that the direct acts of the accused caused the delay must fall upon the Crown. This would be true except in those cases where the effects of the accused's action are so clear and readily apparent that the intent of the accused to cause a delay is the inference that must be drawn from the record of his or her actions.

(iii)   Waiver

While the question of waiver could be discussed under factor (ii)(c) above (delay attributable to the accused), for reasons of clarity I prefer to examine the issue separately.

The accused should not be required to assert the explicitly-protected individual right to trial within a reasonable time. It is now well established that any waiver of a Charter right must be "clear and unequivocal . . . with full knowledge of the rights the procedure was enacted to protect and of the effect the waiver will have on those rights in the process": see *Korponay v. Can. (A.G.)*, [1982] 1 S.C.R. 41 at 49, 26 C.R. (3d) 343, 65 C.C.C. (2d) 65, 134 D.L.R. (3d) 354, 44 N.R. 103 (sub nom. *R. v. Korponey*) [Que.]. The failure of an accused to assert the right does not give the Crown licence to proceed with an unfair trial. Failure to assert the right would be insufficient in itself to impugn the motives of the accused, as might be the case with regard to other s. 11 rights. Rather there must be something in the conduct of the accused that is sufficient to give rise to an inference that the accused has understood that he or she had a s. 11(b) guarantee, understood its nature and has waived the right provided by that guarantee. Although no particular magical incantation of words is required to waive a right, nevertheless the waiver must be expressed in some manner. Silence or lack of objection cannot constitute a lawful waiver.

. . .

If the Crown is relying upon actions of the accused to demonstrate waiver, then the onus will lie upon the Crown to prove that a specific waiver can be inferred. It may well be that the setting of trial dates and the agreement to those dates by counsel for the accused may be sufficient to constitute waiver.

. . .

In sum, the burden always rests with the Crown to bring the case to trial. Further, the mere silence of the accused is not sufficient to indicate a waiver of a Charter right; rather, the accused must undertake some direct action from which a consent to delay can be properly inferred. The onus rests upon the Crown to establish on a balance of probabilities that the actions of the accused constitute a waiver of his or her rights.

(iv)   Prejudice to the Accused

The different positions taken by members of the court with regard to the prejudice suffered by an accused as a result of a delayed trial are set forth in *Mills* and *Rahey*, both supra. Perhaps the differences can be resolved in this manner. It should be inferred that a very long and unreasonable delay has prejudiced the accused. As Sopinka J. put it in *Smith*, at p. 1138:

> Having found that the delay is substantially longer than can be justified on any acceptable basis, it would be difficult indeed to conclude that the appellant's s. 11(b) rights have not been violated because the appellant has suffered no prejudice. In this particular context, the inference of prejudice is so strong that it would be difficult to disagree with the view of Lamer J. in *Mills* and *Rahey* that it is virtually irrebuttable.

Nevertheless, it will be open to the Crown to attempt to demonstrate that the accused has not been prejudiced. This would preserve the societal interest by providing that a trial would proceed in those cases where, despite a long delay, no resulting damage had been suffered by the accused. Yet the existence of the inference of prejudice drawn from a very long delay will safely preserve the pre-eminent right of the individual. Obviously, the difficulty of overcoming the inference will of necessity become more difficult with the passage of time, and at some point will become irrebuttable. Nonetheless, the factual situation presented in *Conway*, supra, serves as an example of an extremely lengthy delay which did not prejudice the accused. However, in most situations, as Sopinka J. pointed out in *Smith*, the presumption will be "virtually irrebuttable".

Furthermore, the option left open by Sopinka J. in the *Smith* case whereby accused persons who have suffered some additional form of prejudice are permitted to adduce evidence of prejudice on their own initiative in order to strengthen their position in seeking a remedy under s. 24(1) of the Charter is consistent with the primary concern of protecting the individual's right under s. 11(b).

. . .

[In applying these principles Justice Cory noted the following.]

It is apparent that the situation in Peel district has been in a deplorable state for many years. Something is terribly wrong. As Zuber J.A. noted, the situation is "enormously complex" and there is no "magic solution" or "quick fix". Nonetheless, something must be done. Urgent attention to the situation is required. The response of the government of Ontario has been neither overwhelming nor particularly successful.

. . .

The only conclusion which can be drawn from an analysis of the material filed is that the problem of systemic delay in Peel has not and cannot be resolved simply by introducing a more efficient caseflow management system. More resources must be supplied to this district, perhaps by way of additional Crown attorneys and courtrooms. This conclusion cannot come as a surprise. The problem has existed for many years, back at least as far as 1981.

. . .

The extent and gravity of the problem in Peel is brought home by reference to the comparative study done in 1987 by Professor Baar. The study illustrated that, in Canada, New Brunswick and Quebec were best able to bring their cases to trial within the 30- to 90-day range. In terms of the time taken to completely dispose of a case from committal to disposition, the median total time in New Brunswick's lower courts (Provincial Courts) was 152 days. The median total time in upper courts (s. 96 courts) was 72 days. By comparison, in Ontario the best district was London, with a median total time of 239 days, and the median upper court time of 105 days. Toronto, Ottawa and St. Catharines were all close together, with median total times of between 315 and 349 days and upper court times between 133 and 144 days.

Professor Baar wrote that: "[b]y all measures used in the study, Brampton District Court was significantly slower than any other location studied: median total time was 607 days and median upper court time was 423 days." Nor can any comfort be drawn by comparison to the United States. Professor Baar concluded that the Peel district is generally substantially slower than the slowest United States jurisdictions. Further, he noted that the delay in the present case was longer than 90 per cent of all cases in terms of median total time among those heard, even in Peel district. This case therefore represents one of the worst from the point of view of delay in the worst district not only in Canada but, so far as the studies indicate, anywhere north of the Rio Grande.

. . .

Making a very rough comparison and more than doubling the longest waiting period to make every allowance for the special circumstances in Peel would indicate that a period of delay in a range of some six to eight months between committal and trial might be deemed to be the outside limit of what is reasonable. The usual delays in Peel are more than four times as long as those of busy metropolitan districts in the province of Quebec, and the delay in this case is more than eight times as long. The figures from the comparable districts demonstrate that the Peel district situation is unreasonable and intolerable.

The delay in this case is such that it [is] impossible to come to any other conclusion than that the s. 11(b) Charter rights guaranteed to the individual accused have been infringed. As well, the societal interest in ensuring that these accused be brought to trial within a reasonable time has been grossly offended and denigrated. Indeed, the delay is of such an inordinate length that public confidence in the administration of justice must be shaken. Justice so delayed is an affront to the individual, to the community and to the very administration of justice. The lack of institutional facilities cannot in this case be accepted as a basis for justifying the delay.

I am well aware that, as a consequence of this decision, a stay of proceedings must be directed. This is, to say the least, most unfortunate and regrettable. It is obvious that the charges against the appellants are serious. Extortion and threatened armed violence tear at the basic fabric of society. To accede to such conduct would constitute a denial of the rule of law and an acceptance of a rule that unlawful might makes right. The community has good reason to be alarmed by the commission of serious crimes. There can be no doubt that it would be in the best interest of society to proceed with the trial of those who are charged with posing such a serious threat to the community. Yet that trial can be undertaken only if the Charter right to trial within a reasonable time has not been infringed. In this case that right has been grievously infringed and the sad result is that a stay of proceedings must be entered. To conclude otherwise would render meaningless a right enshrined in the Charter as the supreme law of the land.

In brief concurring opinions Lamer C.J., Wilson and Sopinka JJ. each rejected the majority position that s. 11(b) protected a societal as well as an individual interest. Lamer J. continued to insist that prejudice, in the sense of the fairness of the trial being affected, was irrelevant to s. 11(b). Wilson J. expressed the opinion that there should be no finding of prejudice without evidence being led.

In R. v. Bennett (1991), 3 O.R. (3d) 193, 6 C.R. (4th) 22, 64 C.C.C. (3d) 449 (Ont. C.A.) Madam Justice Arbour for the Ontario Court of Appeal described the impact of Askov in Ontario as "staggering". In one six-month period over 34000 charges had been stayed, dismissed or withdrawn. This included 8600 impaired driving charges, 6000 theft under $1000, a substantial number of assaults and frauds, 500 sexual assaults, more than 1000 drug offences and thousands of parking and other provincial offences. The Court held that the 6-8 month period mentioned in Askov had been wrongly interpreted as a mechanical limitation period and that in future judges should exercise judgment and properly balance the factors mentioned in Askov.

In July 1991, Mr. Justice Cory told a legal conference in Cambridge, England, that although the Court knew that *Askov* would have an impact "quite frankly we were not aware of the extent of that impact" (*Lawyer's Weekly*, July 26, 1991). The justice's further remark that the Court had not been made aware of the number of cases which could potentially be affected was later challenged by the defence counsel in *Askov*, who pointed to extensive statistical data filed by the Ontario Attorney-General (*Lawyer's Weekly*, August 2, 1991).

It was not long before the Supreme Court changed direction.

R. v. MORIN

[1992] 1 S.C.R. 771, 12 C.R. (4th) 1, 71 C.C.C. (3d) 1 (S.C.C.)

On January 9, 1988, the accused was charged with driving with an excess amount of alcohol. When she appeared in Provincial Court on February 23, her counsel explicitly requested "the earliest possible trial date". The trial was set for March 28, 1989. On her scheduled trial date, the accused brought a motion to stay the proceedings arguing that the 141/2-month delay infringed her right to be tried within a reasonable time. The motion was dismissed and the accused was convicted on the "over 80" charge. On appeal, the summary conviction appeal court stayed the charge. The Ontario Court of Appeal allowed the Crown's appeal and restored the conviction. The accused appealed.

SOPINKA J. (La Forest, Stevenson, Iacobucci JJ. concurring):—The issue in this appeal concerns the right of an accused to be tried within a reasonable time. This right is enshrined in s. 11(*b*) of the *Canadian Charter of Rights and Freedoms* which states:

> 11. Any person charged with an offence has the right...
>
> (b) to be tried within a reasonable time; . . .

Though beguiling in its simplicity, this language has presented the court with one of its most difficult challenges in search of an interpretation that respects the right of the individual in an era in which the administration of justice is faced both with dwindling resources and a burgeoning case load. We are asked in this appeal to re-examine the problem in light of the effect on the administration of justice of our decision in *R. v. Askov*, [1990] 2 S.C.R. 1199, 79 C.R. (3d) 273, 113 N.R. 241, 49 C.R.R. 1, 59 C.C.C. (3d) 449, 74 D.L.R. (4th) 355, 75 O.R. (2d) 673, 42 O.A.C. 81. Evidence presented to us indicates that between October 22, 1990 and September 6, 1991, over 47,000 charges have been stayed or withdrawn in Ontario alone. The reaction to this has been mixed. On the one hand, many applaud the result which has in their view unclogged the system of much dead wood in the form of charges that should not have been laid or having been laid ought to have been dropped. This, they say, will enable the system to more quickly accommodate cases that are more pressing and lessen the period during which alleged criminals are free to roam the streets while awaiting trial. On the other hand, many others deprecate what in their opinion amounts to an amnesty for criminals, some of whom were charged with very serious crimes. They assert that accused persons are discharged when they have suffered no prejudice to the complete dismay of victims who have suffered, in some cases, tragic losses.

. . .

The development of the jurisprudence relating to s. 11(b) is instructive in that it underscores the importance of avoiding rigidity in the interpretation of new constitutional rights early in the life of a constitutional document. The court could have simply adopted the American approach articulated in *Barker v. Wingo*, 407 U.S. 514 (1972), which has resulted in only the most egregious delays being proscribed. Instead, in accordance with the intent of the *Charter*, this court has attempted to develop a Canadian approach with due regard for the American experience. Embarking as we did on uncharted waters it is not surprising that the course we steered has required, and may require in the future, some alteration in its direction to accord with experience.

. . .

Finally, in *Askov*, we dealt with a case which came to us from the Court of Appeal for Ontario and originated in Brampton, Ontario, a notorious sore spot in relation to unreasonable delay. Applying the basic criteria in *Smith*, the court was unanimous that the delay was unreasonable. The court went on to suggest that "a period of delay in a range of some six to eight months between committal and trial might be deemed to be the outside limit of what is reasonable" (p. 1240 [S.C.R.]). It is the interpretation and application of this statement that resulted in the large number of stays and withdrawals to which I have referred.

. . .

The primary purpose of s. 11(b) is the protection of the individual rights of accused. A secondary interest of society as a whole has, however, been recognized by this court. I will address each of these interests and their interaction.

The individual rights which the section seeks to protect are: (1) the right to security of the person, (2) the right to liberty, and (3) the right to a fair trial.

The right to security of the person is protected in s. 11(b) by seeking to minimize the anxiety, concern and stigma of exposure to criminal proceedings. The right to liberty is protected by seeking to minimize exposure to the restrictions on liberty which result from pre-trial incarceration and restrictive bail conditions. The right to a fair trial is protected by attempting to ensure that proceedings take place while evidence is available and fresh.

The secondary societal interest is most obvious when it parallels that of the accused. Society as a whole has an interest in seeing that the least fortunate of its citizens who are accused of crimes are treated humanely and fairly. In this respect trials held promptly enjoy the confidence of the public. . . . In some cases, however, the accused has no interest in an early trial and society's interest will not parallel that of the accused.

There is, as well, a societal interest that is by its very nature adverse to the interests of the accused. In *Conway*, a majority of this court recognized that the interests of the accused must be balanced by the interests of society in law enforcement. This theme was picked up in *Askov* in the reasons of Cory J. who referred to "a collective interest in ensuring that those who transgress the law are brought to trial and dealt with according to the law" (pp. 1219-1220 [S.C.R.]). As the seriousness of the offence increases so does the societal demand that the accused be brought to trial. The role of this interest is most evident and its influence most apparent when it is sought to absolve persons accused of serious crimes simply to clean up the docket.

The Approach To Unreasonable Delay — The Factors

The general approach to a determination as to whether the right has been denied is not by the application of a mathematical or administrative formula, but rather by a judicial determination balancing the interests which the section is designed to protect against factors which either inevitably lead to delay or are otherwise the cause of delay. . . . While the court has at times indicated otherwise, it is now accepted that the factors to be considered in analyzing how long is too long may be listed as follows:

1.   the length of the delay;

2.   waiver of time periods;

3.   the reasons for the delay, including

    (a)   inherent time requirements of the case,

    (b)   actions of the accused,

    (c)   actions of the Crown,

    (d)   limits on institutional resources, and

    (e)   other reasons for delay; and

4.   prejudice to the accused.

. . .

The role of the burden of proof in this balancing process was set out in the unanimous judgment of this court in *Smith*, supra [at pp. 1132-1133 S.C.R.], as follows:

> I accept that the accused has the ultimate or legal burden of proof throughout. A case will only be decided by reference to the burden of proof if the court cannot come to a determinate conclusion on the facts presented to it. Although the accused may have the ultimate or legal burden, a secondary or evidentiary burden of putting forth evidence or argument may shift depending on the circumstances of each case. For example, a long period of delay occasioned by a request of the Crown for an adjournment would ordinarily call for an explanation from the Crown as to the necessity for the adjournment. In the absence of such an explanation, the court would be entitled to infer that the delay is unjustified. It would be appropriate to speak of the Crown having a secondary or evidentiary burden under these circumstances. In all cases, the court should be mindful that it is seldom necessary or desirable to decide this question on the basis of burden of proof and that it is preferable to evaluate the reasonableness of the overall lapse of time having regard to the factors referred to above.

I do not read the *Askov* decision as having departed from this statement although portions of the reasons of Cory J. emphasized certain aspects of the evidentiary burden on the Crown.

A definition of each of these factors and their interaction follows. I will deal with them in the order that they should be considered by a trial court.

1.   *The Length of the Delay*

As I have indicated, this factor requires the court to examine the period from the charge to the end of the trial. Charge means the date on which an information is sworn or an indictment is preferred (see *Kalanj*, supra, at p. 1607 [S.C.R.]). Pre-charge delay may in certain circumstances have an influence on the overall determination as to whether post-charge delay is unreasonable but of itself it is not counted in determining the length of the delay.

An inquiry into unreasonable delay is triggered by an application under s. 24(1) of the *Charter*. The applicant has the legal burden of establishing a *Charter* violation. The inquiry, which can be complex (as may be illustrated by the proceedings in the Court of Appeal in this case), should only be undertaken if the period is of sufficient length to raise an issue as to its reasonableness. If the length of the delay is unexceptional, no inquiry is warranted and no explanation for the delay is called for unless the applicant is able to raise the issue of reasonableness of the period by reference to other factors such as prejudice. If, for example, the applicant is in custody, a shorter period of delay will raise the issue.

2.   *Waiver of Time Periods*

If the length of the delay warrants an inquiry into the reasons for delay, it appears logical to deal with any allegation of waiver before embarking on the more detailed examination of the reasons for delay. If by agreement or other conduct the accused has waived in whole or in part his or her rights to complain of delay then this will either dispose of the matter or allow the period waived to be deducted.

This court has clearly stated that in order for an accused to waive his or her rights under s. 11(*b*), such waiver must be clear and unequivocal, with full knowledge of the rights the procedure was enacted to protect and of the effect that waiver will have on those rights (*Korponay v. Canada (Attorney General)*, [1982] 1 S.C.R. 41, 26 C.R. (3d) 343, 65 C.C.C. (2d) 65, 132 D.L.R. (3d) 354, (sub nom. *R. v. Korponey*) 44 N.R. 103, at p. 49 [S.C.R.]; see also *R. v. Clarkson*, [1986] 1 S.C.R. 383, 50 C.R. (3d) 289, 66 N.R. 114, 69 N.B.R. (2d) 40, 177 A.P.R. 40, 25 C.C.C. (3d) 207, 26 D.L.R. (4th) 493, 19 C.R.R. 209, at pp. 394-396 [S.C.R.]; *Askov*, supra, at pp. 1228-1229 [S.C.R.]). Waiver can be explicit or implicit. If the waiver is said to be implicit, the conduct of the accused must comply with the stringent test for waiver set out above. As Cory J. described it in *Askov*, supra, [at p. 1228 S.C.R.]:

> . . . there must be something in the conduct of the accused that is sufficient to give rise to an inference that the accused has understood that he or she had a s. 11(*b*) guarantee, understood its nature and has waived the right provided by that guarantee.

Waiver requires advertence to the act of release rather than mere inadvertence. If the mind of the accused or his or her counsel is not turned to the issue of waiver and is not aware of what his or her conduct signifies, then this conduct does not constitute waiver. Such conduct may be taken into account under the factor "actions of the accused" but it is not waiver. As I stated in *Smith*, supra, which was adopted in *Askov*, supra, consent to a trial date can give rise to an inference of waiver. This will not be so if consent to a date amounts to mere acquiescence in the inevitable.

. . .

3.   *The Reasons for the Delay*

If the application by an accused is not resolved by reason of the principles of waiver, the court will have to consider the other explanations for delay. Some delay is inevitable. Courts are not in session day and night. Time will be taken up in processing the charge, retention of counsel, applications for bail and other pre-trial procedures. Time is required for counsel to prepare. Over and above these inherent time requirements of a case, time may be consumed to accommodate the prosecution or defence. Neither side, however, can rely on their own delay to support their respective positions. When a case is ready for trial a judge, courtroom or essential court staff may not be available and so the case cannot go on. This latter type of delay is referred to as institutional or systemic delay. I now turn to a closer examination of each of these reasons and the role each plays in determining what delay is unreasonable.

(a)   *Inherent time requirements*

All offences have certain inherent time requirements which inevitably lead to delay. Just as the fire truck must get to the fire, so must a case be prepared. The complexity of the trial is one requirement which has often been mentioned.

. . .

As well as the complexity of a case, there are inherent requirements which are common to almost all cases. The respondent has described such activities as "intake requirements". Whatever one wishes to call these requirements, they consist of activities such as retention of counsel, bail hearings, police and administration paperwork, disclosure, etc. All of these activities may or may not be necessary in a particular case but each takes some amount of time. As the number and complexity of these activities increase, so does the amount of delay that is reasonable.

. . .

Another inherent delay that must be taken into account is whether a case must proceed through a preliminary inquiry. Clearly a longer time must be allowed for cases that must proceed through a "two-stage" trial process than for cases which do not require a preliminary hearing.

. . .

(b)   *Actions of the accused*

This aspect of the reasons for the delay should not be read as putting the "blame" on the accused for certain portions of delay. There is no necessity to impute improper motives to the accused in considering this factor. Included under this heading are all actions taken by the accused which may have caused delay. In this section I am concerned with actions of the accused which are voluntarily undertaken. Actions which could be included in this category include change of venue motions, attacks on wiretap packets, adjournments which do not amount to waiver, attacks on search warrants, etc. I do not wish to be interpreted as advocating that the accused sacrifice all preliminary procedures and strategy, but simply point out that if the accused chooses to take such action, this will be taken into account in determining what length of delay is reasonable.

. . .

(c)   *Actions of the Crown*

As with the conduct of the accused, this factor does not serve to assign blame. This factor simply serves as a means whereby actions of the Crown which delay the trial may be investigated. Such actions include adjournments requested by the Crown, failure or delay in disclosure, change of venue motions, etc. . . . [T]here is nothing wrong with the Crown seeking such adjournments but such delays cannot be relied upon by the Crown to explain away delay that is otherwise unreasonable.

(d)   *Limits on institutional resources*

Institutional delay is the most common source of delay and the most difficult to reconcile with the dictates of s. 11(*b*) of the *Charter*. It was the major source of the delay in *Askov*. As I have stated, this is the period that starts to run when the parties are ready for trial but the system cannot accommodate them. In utopia, this form of delay would be given zero tolerance. There, resources would be unlimited and their application would be administratively perfect so that there would be no shortage of judges or courtrooms and essential court staff would always be available. Unfortunately, this is not the world in which s. 11(*b*) was either conceived or in which it operates. We live in a country with a rapidly growing population in many regions and in which resources are limited. In applying s. 11(*b*), account must be taken of this fact of life.

. . .

How are we to reconcile the demand that trials are to be held within a reasonable time in the imperfect world of scarce resources? While account must be taken of the fact that the state does not have unlimited funds and other government programs compete for the available resources, this consideration cannot be used to render s. 11(*b*) meaningless. The court cannot simply accede to the government's allocation of resources and tailor the period of permissible delay accordingly. The weight to be given to resource limitations must be assessed in light of the fact that the government has a constitutional obligation to commit sufficient resources to prevent unreasonable delay which distinguishes this obligation from many others that compete for funds with the administration of justice. There is a point in time at which the court will no longer tolerate delay based on the plea of inadequate resources. This period of time may be referred to as an administrative guideline. I hasten to add that this guideline is neither a limitation period nor a fixed ceiling on delay. Such a guideline was suggested in *Askov* and was treated by some courts as a limitation period. I propose therefore to examine in some detail the purpose of a guideline commencing with an examination of its role in *Askov*.

In *Askov* we were dealing with a period of delay of approximately 2 years subsequent to committal for trial. All of this delay was institutional o[r] systemic delay. Applying the factors that had crystallized in *Smith*, supra, we concluded that the delay was clearly unreasonable. In his reasons, which in this respect were unanimous, Cory J. did go on to state (at p. 1240 [S.C.R.]):

> ... a period of delay in a range of some six to eight months between committal and trial might be deemed to be the outside limit of what is reasonable.

With respect to institutional factors, he stated (at p. 1226 [S.C.R.]):

> The question must be answered in light of the particular facts of each case. There can be no certain standard of a fixed time which will be applicable in every region of the country.

The purpose of the suggested period was not therefore that it was to be treated as a limitation period and inflexible. The purpose in expressing a guideline is two-fold. First, as I have already indicated, it is to recognize that there is a limit to the delay that can be tolerated on account of resource limitations. Second, it is to avoid each application pursuant to s. 11(*b*) being turned into a trial of the budgetary policy of the government as it relates to the administration of justice. The flavour of such a proceeding can be appreciated by a perusal of the voluminous record before the court in this case.

A number of considerations enter into the adoption of a guideline and its application by trial courts. A guideline is not intended to be applied in a purely mechanical fashion. It must lend itself and yield to other factors. This premise enters into its formulation. The court must acknowledge that a guideline is not the result of any precise legal or scientific formula. It is the result of the exercise of a judicial discretion based on experience and taking into account the evidence of the limitations on resources, the strain imposed on them, statistics from other comparable jurisdictions and the opinions of other courts and judges, as well as any expert opinion. With respect to the use of statistics, care must be taken that a comparison of jurisdictions is indeed a comparative analysis. For example, in *Askov* we were given statistics with respect to Montreal in an affidavit by Professor Baar. Subsequently, it was brought to our attention that this was a misleading comparison. Evidence was led in this appeal showing that the manner in which criminal charges are dealt with in Montreal and Brampton is sufficiently dissimilar so as to make statistics drawn from the two jurisdictions of limited comparative value. Comparison with other jurisdictions is therefore to be applied with caution and only as a rough guide. These then are the factors which enter into the formulation by an appellate court of a guideline with respect to administrative delay. I now turn to its application in the trial courts.

. . .

The application of a guideline will also be influenced by the presence or absence of prejudice. If an accused is in custody or, while not in custody, subject to restrictive bail terms or conditions or otherwise experiences substantial prejudice, the period of acceptable institutional delay may be shortened to reflect the court's concern. On the other hand, in a case in which there is no prejudice or prejudice is slight, the guideline may be applied to reflect this fact.

In this case we are dealing with the Provincial Court. The suggested period of institutional delay ranges from 6 to 10 months. The respondent suggests that 8 to 10 months of purely systemic delay would not be unreasonable in the Provincial Court. It admits, however, that it is aiming at institutional delay of no more than 6 to 8 months in Provincial Court.

. . .

In *Askov*, Cory J., after reviewing comparative statistics suggested that a period in the range of 6 to 8 months between committal and trial would not be unreasonable. Based on the foregoing, it is appropriate for this court to suggest a period of institutional delay of between 8 to 10 months as a guide to provincial courts. With respect to institutional delay after committal for trial, I would not depart from the range of 6 to 8 months that was suggested in *Askov*. In such a case, this institutional delay would be in addition to the delay prior to committal.

. . .

The application of these guidelines under the supervision of the court of appeal is subject to the review of this court to ensure that the right to trial within a reasonable time is being respected.

. . .

4.   *Prejudice to the Accused*

Section 11(*b*) protects the individual from impairment of the right to liberty, security of the person, and the ability to make full answer and defence resulting from unreasonable delay in bringing criminal trials to a conclusion. . . . While the observation of Dubin C.J.O. in *Bennett* that many, perhaps most, accused are not anxious to have an early trial may no doubt be accurate, s. 11(*b*) was designed to protect the individual, whose rights are not to be determined on the basis of the desires or practices of the majority. Accordingly, in an individual case, prejudice may be inferred from the length of the delay. The longer the delay the more likely that such an inference will be drawn. In circumstances in which prejudice is not inferred and is not otherwise proved, the basis for the enforcement of the individual right is seriously undermined.

This court has made clear in previous decisions that it is the duty of the Crown to bring the accused to trial (see *Askov*, supra, at pp. 1225, 1227, 1229 [S.C.R.]). While it was not necessary for the accused to assert her right to be tried within a reasonable time, strong views have been expressed that in many cases an accused person is not interested in a speedy trial and that delay works to the advantage of the accused. This view is summed up by Doherty J. (as he then was) in a paper given to the National Criminal Law Program in July 1989 which was referred to with approval by Dubin C.J.O. in *Bennett* (at p. 52 [C.R.]) and echoes what has been noted by numerous commentators:

> An accused is often not interested in exercising the right bestowed on him by s. 11(*b*). His interest lies in having the right infringed by the prosecution so that he can escape a trial on the merits. This view may seem harsh but experience supports its validity.

As also noted by Cory J. in *Askov*, supra, "the s. 11(*b*) right is one which can often be transformed from a protective shield to an offensive weapon in the hands of the accused" (p. 1222 [S.C.R.]). This right must be interpreted in a manner which recognizes the abuse which may be invoked by some accused. The purpose of s. 11(*b*) is to expedite trials and minimize prejudice and not to avoid trials on the merits. Action or non-action by the accused which is inconsistent with a desire for a timely trial is something that the court must consider. . . . Inaction may, however, be relevant in assessing the degree of prejudice, if any, that an accused has suffered as a result of delay.

Apart, however, from inferred prejudice, either party may rely on evidence to either show prejudice or dispel such a finding. For example, the accused may rely on evidence tending to show prejudice to his or her liberty interest as a result of pre-trial incarceration or restrictive bail conditions. Prejudice to the accused's security interest can be shown by evidence of the ongoing stress or damage to reputation as a result of overlong exposure to "the vexations and vicissitudes of a pending criminal accusation", to use the words adopted by Lamer J. in *Mills*, supra, at p. 919 [S.C.R.]. The fact that the accused sought an early trial date will also be relevant. Evidence may also be adduced to show that delay has prejudiced the accused's ability to make full answer and defence.

Conversely, the prosecution may establish by evidence that the accused is in the majority group who do not want an early trial and that the delay benefited rather than prejudiced the accused. Conduct of the accused falling short of waiver may be relied upon to negative prejudice. As discussed previously, the degree of prejudice or absence thereof is also an important factor in determining the length of institutional delay that will be tolerated. The application of any guideline will be influenced by this factor.

[The Court then dealt with the application of the above principles to its particular case. After dealing with the length of the delay, waiver, inherent time requirements and the actions of the accused and the Crown, it dealt with the issue of institutional resources.]

Perhaps the single most important factor in this case is the limit on institutional resources. It appears that from some time in March 1988 until March 1989, the parties were prepared for trial but the judicial system could not accommodate them. It is somewhat unclear whether a date in early 1989 could have been made available as a result of the letter from the Crown's office but I am prepared to infer from the totality of the facts that an institutional delay of about 12 months was involved. This time period is the time from which the parties were ready for trial until the point at which the courts were able to accommodate this case.

In considering the reasonableness of this delay, the court must consider the facts surrounding this institutional delay. It must be remembered that this appeal arises from Ontario Provincial Court and arises from a region which has experienced significant growth in recent years.

I will deal first with the consideration which must be given to the fact that we are dealing with a Provincial Court. The Ontario Provincial Court disposes of approximately 95 per cent of criminal cases in Ontario. Evidence led by the Crown in this appeal shows that the caseload of this Provincial Court increased more than 125 per cent from 1985/86 to 1989/90. After several years in which the caseload was stable at 80,000 cases, the caseload of the Provincial Court in Ontario increased from 80,000 to 180,000 from 1985/86 to 1989/90. This rapid increase in caseload cannot, of course, always be predicted, nor can the government respond immediately to the inevitable strain on resources. While this court has made it clear that there is no longer any general transitional period in which to allow the government to comply with its constitutional obligations to provide sufficient facilities, this does not remove the issue of changing local circumstances from consideration.

In the jurisdiction in which this case arose, the District of Durham, the increase in caseload from 1985/86 to 1990/91 was approximately 70 per cent in adult court and an astounding 143 per cent in youth court. This was only partially caused by a population increase of 40 per cent during the previous decade. Thus, it is not surprising that the provision of institutional resources may have lagged somewhat behind the demand. Since some time in July 1990, however, it appears that the Durham Provincial Court has been able to dispose of cases at a more rapid rate than it has received new cases. While one cannot use institutional resources to nullify the right to be tried within a reasonable time, one also cannot use rapidly changing local conditions to compel a general amnesty. Based on the above factors, I would allow a period for systemic delay which is in the upper range of the guideline. In my view, a period in the order of 10 months would not be unreasonable. While I have suggested that a guideline of 8 to 10 months be used by courts to assess institutional delay in Provincial Courts, deviations of several months in either direction can be justified by the presence or absence of prejudice.

. . .

4. *Prejudice to the Accused*

The accused led no evidence of prejudice. The court must still consider what, if any, prejudice is to be inferred from the delay. In this regard the Crown relies on the fact that several months prior to trial, counsel in the Durham region received a letter dated January 16, 1989 from the Crown Attorney's office which stated in part:

> [i]f you wish to move any of your cases up or *feel that any clients are suffering prejudice as a result of delay please give Audrey or I a shout and we'll try to locate an earlier date.* Thank you for your co-operation. [Emphasis added.]

It may be unrealistic to suggest that a trial set for approximately two months from the date of this letter could have been significantly moved up but we will never know what would have happened as the accused did not request any action. While the accused was not *required* to do anything to expedite her trial, her inaction can be taken into account in assessing prejudice. I conclude for this reason that the accused was content with the pace with which things were proceeding and that therefore there was little or no prejudice occasioned by the delay.

Disposition

Applying the guideline to which I have referred and taking into account the strain on institutional resources, the reasons of the Court of Appeal in regard thereto and the absence of any significant prejudice, I am of the opinion that the delay in this case was not unreasonable. I have come to this conclusion without the necessity of resorting to the burden of proof.

In view of the result at which I have arrived, it is unnecessary to consider the argument of the Attorney General of Canada that a stay is not the only remedy available for an infringement of the right protected by s. 11(*b*). The appellant's rights under s. 11(*b*) have not been violated and the appeal is dismissed.

[Gonthier J. and McLachlin J. delivered concurring opinions.]

. . .

LAMER C.J.C. (dissenting):—...I would allow the appeal and restore the stay entered by Murphy D.C.J. of the summary conviction appeal court.

I agree with the principles and guidelines set out by my brother Sopinka J., except as regards proof of prejudice.

. . .

My understanding of Cory J.'s reasons (in *Askov*) is that the onus is on the applicant as regards prejudice only when the applicant is seeking a remedy additional to a stay.

. . .

While I dissented as regards the approach of Cory J. on prejudice, that approach was concurred in by six other judges. My views on the issue which I have held since *R. v. Mills*, [1986] 1 S.C.R. 863, 52 C.R. (3d) 1, 26 C.C.C. (3d) 481, 29 D.L.R. (4th) 161, 21 C.R.R. 76, 67 N.R. 241, 16 O.A.C. 81, and throughout s. 11(*b*) judgments in this court, have conclusively been put to rest by *Askov* and I here on in feel bound by it. Furthermore, as *Askov* is a very recent decision of this court, I do not think it desirable that it be revisited in this case.

Both of my colleagues in their reasons, McLachlin J. somewhat more so than Sopinka J., place the onus on the accused to prove prejudice. This is a fundamental change to the position that this court has taken. While I have never changed my mind as regards my dissenting position, I will, as I should, apply *Askov* to the facts of this case. Leaving the onus on the Crown, it has shown that Ms. Morin's liberty and fair trial interests have not been affected.

But it has not even attempted to show that her security interests have not been affected; by that I mean the kind of prejudice I described in *Mills*, supra, at p. 920 [S.C.R.], "stigmatization of the accused, loss of privacy, stress and anxiety resulting from a multitude of factors, including possible disruption of family, social life and work, legal costs, uncertainty as to the outcome and sanction". I conclude that this kind of prejudice has been suffered beyond the length of time that can be legitimately supported on the basis of limited institutional resources.

The immediate effect of *Morin* was to drastically reduce the number of s. 11(b) stays. Although at first glance the *Morin* ruling seems to re-state *Askov*, adding a new 8 to 10 month guideline for trials in provincial courts, there are at least four important differences.

1.   The more serious the charge the less likely it is to be stayed.

2.   The Crown no longer has the burden of proving that delay was caused by the accused, that institutional delay was justified, that there was no prejudice, or that the accused has waived his s. 11(b) right.

3.   The comparative jurisdiction test is much less important.

4.   Whether the accused has been prejudiced is crucial.

Do you agree with these changes?

See Stuart, *Charter Justice in Canadian Criminal Law* (6th ed., 2014) chapter 6. The Court's analysis of prejudice is carefully assessed by Stephen Coughlan, "Trial Within a Reasonable Time: Does the Right Still Exist?" (1992), 12 C.R. (4th) 34. He raises troubling issues about the stress on prejudice to security interests:

> It is difficult to believe the court really intends that an accused should lead evidence of prejudice to a security interest. It is easy to see how an accused would show prejudice to liberty or fair trial interests — by showing that bail conditions were onerous, or that evidence was lost due to delay. But is an accused also required to call neighbours who became stand-offish to testify about their lower opinion of the accused? Should an accused call medical evidence to show that he or she found the waiting period especially stressful? Inviting evidence on these points imports the "thin skull" doctrine into Canadian litigation: a particularly nervous and sensitive accused will have greater rights. Such an approach is possible but does not immediately seem desirable (at 40).

Section 11(b) stays tend to increase where judges become concerned by excessive delays resulting from lack of resources. It is used as a political tool to get more resources.

R. v. PUSIC
(1996), 30 O.R. (3d) 692 (Gen. Div.)

The accused were charged with a number of theft offences. It was agreed that it was not an unduly complex case. It was also agreed that there had been no waiver. The application for a stay was granted.

HILL J.: —

. . .

In the instant case, by agreement of counsel, the relevant time period may be described as July 27, 1993, date of charge, to September 9, 1996, scheduled trial date. This is a period of approximately 37 months. All counsel agree that this is an exceptional delay clearly raising the issue of reasonableness.

. . .

We do not have the luxury of a system which can provide instant access to litigants, in terms of courtrooms, judges and jury panels. Some institutional or systemic delay must be tolerated in recognition of the limited resources available. This situation of tolerance itself has limits or the s. 11(*b*) protection would be entirely eviscerated. Whatever the competition for fiscal resources, the government has a constitutional obligation to try an accused within a reasonable time.

. . .

The scheduling of criminal cases is of course governed to a significant degree by the courtroom space and judicial officers available. Since 1978, the population of Peel has increased dramatically from about 421,618 to a projected 1996 population base of 903,400 or an increase of nearly 115 per cent. It is important, in understanding the feeder group for the criminal courts in Peel, that Canada's busiest airport, the Toronto or Pearson International Airport, is within this jurisdiction. Therefore, above the current 903,400 population base there exists a transient population within Peel, on a daily basis, at this airport facility. In 1990, 22 million passengers used the facility, an increase of 38 per cent since 1986. Since 1990, a third terminal has been constructed and the consumer use of the airport has continued to increase. In *R. v. Askov*, Cory J. noted the evidence in that case that the airport "generates a great many drug-related offences".

. . .

There is startling evidence before me that, as of May 31, 1996, in the General Division for Peel, nearly one-third of the outstanding criminal indictments exceeded eight months in age at this court level. Of the total number of pending indictments, over 14 per cent exceeded one year in the General Division. Adduced in this court was further evidence that, in the General Division in Peel, in the 1995-1996 time period, there was a markedly higher indictment to judge ratio of newly added indictments than in several other large urban centres in Ontario. Such material and information as the court has before it, raises a real question of the level of courtroom and judicial resources committed to Peel. The judicial rebuke of the dilemma in Peel was unequivocal in the *Askov* decision. Alarming signals of institutional endangerment of constitutional rights have emerged in this case. To the extent that there exists institutional, governmental recklessness with respect to the s. 11(*b*) rights of accused persons in Peel, arising from insufficient resources, this cannot be condoned by the courts.

On December 2, 2003 the Auditor General of Ontario reported that criminal charges pending for more than eight months had increased from 60,000 to almost 100,000 in the past five years. According to recent Canadian Centre for Justice Statistics, well over half of those in gaol in Ontario are awaiting trial.

In *R. v. M. (R.)* (2003), 19 C.R. (6th) 325, 180 C.C.C. (3d) 49 (Ont. C.A.) the Ontario Court of appeal upheld a s. 11(b) stay of sexual assault charges given a delay of 61 months between arrest and trial.

MacPherson J.A., Doherty and Feldman JJ.A. concurring, held that as the pages of the calendar turn from months to years there was a duty on all participants in the case — Crown, defence counsel and the trial judge — to formally recognise that the case was in jeopardy of being stayed and to discuss fully on the record how to deal with it. Stephen Coughlan, Annotation to M.R., *ibid.*, sees this ruling as having the potential to breathe new life into institutional delay claims. He points to disturbing data since *Morin:*

> Statistics Canada reports that the average time for a case with a single charge has increased from 121 days in 1994/95 to 185 days in 2002/2003. In cases where multiple charges are concerned, the average over that same nine year period has gone from 157 to 209 days (relying on Statistics Canada, The Daily, November 28, 2003: //www.statcan.ca:80/Daily/English/031127/d031127e.htm)

In the period from 2004-2007 the trickle of successful section 11(b) claims became a steady drip, especially in Ontario, Saskatchewan and British Columbia, where institutional shortfalls are again becoming evident. In the last four years the rate of successful 11(b) applications markedly increased especially in Ontario but also in other provinces; see Don Stuart, "Annotation" (2009), 67 C.R. (6th) 95. A February 13, 2012, CBC report by Kathy Tomlinson, "Disgusting court backlog may free hit and run accused" found that in 2011, 109 cases were stayed in B.C. courts, many involving impaired driving, and there were 2,500 pending cases that had passed the 18-month mark into the danger zone of being tossed. The causes of delay were said to be too few judges and Crown, and too many unrepresented accused.

The decision of the Supreme Court in *R. v. Godin* has the potential to further revitalise the s. 11(b) right in several respects. The Court is far more accepting of the realities facing defence counsel seeking an early trial where court and Crown resources are lacking, places a strong burden of justification of delay back on the Crown (in marked contrast to the approach in *Morin*) and does not require evidence of actual prejudice (again in contrast to the ruling in *Morin* on the facts).

R. v. GODIN

(2009), 67 C.R. (6th) 95, 245 C.C.C. (3d) 271, [2009] 2 S.C.R. 3 (S.C.C.)

In May 2005, the accused was charged with sexual assault, unlawful confinement, and threatening to kill his ex-girlfriend. The Crown elected to proceed summarily. In mid September, the trial date was fixed for three days in mid February 2006, some nine months after the charges were laid. Four days before the trial, the Crown received the forensic report indicating that the DNA of the sperm sample obtained from the complainant the day after the alleged offences did not match the accused. As a result, the Crown and defence agreed that the Crown would re-elect to proceed by indictment in order to give the defence the opportunity to explore the complainant's evidence and the forensic report at a preliminary inquiry. The earliest court day available was September 2006. In late February defence counsel wrote to the court and the Crown proposing 31 earlier alternative dates on which he would be available. The Crown did not respond. The one-day preliminary inquiry was adjourned at the September date for want of sufficient court time. It was re-scheduled to February 5, 2007 because defence counsel was unavailable at a December date proposed by the Crown. The one day preliminary inquiry was completed 21 months after the charges were laid. The trial was set for November 2007, 30 months after the charges were laid. In June 2007, the accused successfully brought an application for a stay of proceedings on the ground that his right to be tried within a reasonable time guaranteed by s. 11(b) of the Canadian Charter of Rights and Freedoms was violated.

On the Crown appeal, a majority of the Court of Appeal (per MacPherson J., Cronk J.A. concurring and Glithero J. (ad hoc) dissenting) set aside the stay and remitted the matter to trial. The trial judge had erred in his analysis of the conduct of the defence and the issue of prejudice to the accused. On the further appeal the Supreme Court restored the stay.

Justice Cromwell noted that the delays substantially exceeded the guidelines set out by the Court in *R. v. Morin* of 8 to 10 months for institutional delay in the provincial courts and of 6 to 8 months from committal to trial, for a total guideline period of between 14 and 18 months. That, on its own, did not make the delay unreasonable. According the Cromwell J. the difficulty in this case, arose from the considerable delay coupled with three additional facts: (1) the case was a straightforward one with few complexities and requiring very modest amounts of court time; (2) virtually all of the delay was attributable to the Crown and unexplained, let alone justified; and (3) defence counsel attempted, unsuccessfully, to move the case ahead faster. There was some evidence of prejudice to the accused and, when defence counsel tried to get earlier dates, his correspondence was ignored. In the result, what had started out as a summary conviction prosecution had not yet gone to trial more than two years later. In all of the circumstances, the trial judge was correct to conclude that this delay was unreasonable.

In contrast to the judgment of the Court in *Morin* where little of the burden is placed on the Crown in *Godin* the Court is more demanding. Cromwell J. finds that virtually all of the delay, in particular the 9 month delay in obtaining and disclosing the forensic analysis and the delay resulting from the adjournment of the preliminary inquiry, was attributable to the Crown. The Crown is seen to have the burden of explaining unusual delays caused by the forensic investigators. It had offered no explanation in this case. The Crown had also failed to explain why the defence counsel's request for an earlier date for the preliminary inquiry was ignored and why more priority was not given to this case which, by then, was in obvious s. 11(b) difficulty. Contrary to the view of the majority of the Ontario Court of Appeal the Supreme Court is far more accepting of the conduct of the defence counsel. The defence counsel did not significantly contribute to the delays. Although the defence agreed to the Crown re-election, had the Crown obtained the forensic evidence within a reasonable amount of time, the re-election to proceed by indictment and the subsequent preliminary inquiry could have happened much sooner. The accused was entitled to timely disclosure, and he did not receive it. There was also no suggestion that defence counsel was unreasonable in rejecting the earliest date offered to re-schedule the preliminary inquiry. In the words of Justice Cromwell,

> While scheduling requires reasonable availability and reasonable cooperation, it does not for s. 11(b) purposes require defence counsel to hold themselves in a state of perpetual availability [para. 23]

The Supreme Court of Canada also rebuked the majority of the Ontario Court of Appeal for finding that the trial judge had erred in his assessment of prejudice. The Court importantly clarified how the assessment of prejudice should occur.

CROMWELL J.: —

. . .

(ii) Prejudice

[29] The Court of Appeal disagreed with the trial judge's analysis of prejudice and found that any prejudice to the accused's interest in a fair trial was too speculative to be considered. Partly on this basis, the Court of Appeal found that the delay was not unreasonable. I respectfully disagree. In light of the length of the delay, of the Crown's failure to explain the multiple delays adequately, and of the prejudice to the accused's liberty and security interests — if not also to his interest in a fair trial — the delay in this case was unreasonable.

[30] Prejudice in this context is concerned with the three interests of the accused that s. 11(*b*) protects: liberty, as regards to pre-trial custody or bail conditions; security of the person, in the sense of being free from the stress and cloud of suspicion that accompanies a criminal charge; and the right to make full answer and defence, insofar as delay can prejudice the ability of the defendant to lead evidence, cross-examine witnesses, or otherwise to raise a defence. See *Morin*, at pp. 801-3.

[31] The question of prejudice cannot be considered separately from the length of the delay. As Sopinka J. wrote in *Morin*, at p. 801, even in the absence of specific evidence of prejudice, "prejudice may be inferred from the length of the delay. The longer the delay the more likely that such an inference will be drawn". Here, the delay exceeded the ordinary guidelines by a year or more, even though the case was straightforward. Furthermore, there was some evidence of actual prejudice and a reasonable inference of a risk of prejudice.

[32] This approach was reflected in the trial judge's reasons, where he wrote that the delay in this case was "well beyond any reasonable

interpretation of the [*Morin*] guidelines" (2007 CarswellOnt 5364, at para. 20) and that the appellant had suffered prejudice as a result. The judge referred specifically to the fact that the charges had been hanging over the appellant's head for a long time and that he was subject to "fairly strict" bail conditions (para. 22).

[33] The Court of Appeal disagreed with the sequence in which the trial judge addressed the issue of prejudice, noting that the trial judge only turned to his consideration of prejudice after he had already concluded that s. 11(*b*) had been infringed. Respectfully, I cannot accept that the trial judge erred in this regard. It is in my respectful view clear from reading the judge's reasons as a whole that he considered the relevant factors.

[34] The majority of the Court Appeal acknowledged that these charges had been hanging over the appellant's head for a long time. It was reasonable, in my view, to infer as the trial judge did that the prolonged exposure to criminal proceedings resulting from the delay gave rise to some prejudice. The majority of the Court of Appeal appears to have given no weight to this consideration. The majority of the Court of Appeal also disagreed with the trial judge's findings relating to prejudice flowing from restrictive bail conditions. The appellant had been on judicial interim release for more than two years. It is true that his bail conditions were relaxed as the delay lengthened, but the trial judge did not err in the circumstances of this case by taking this consideration into account as one aspect relevant to his overall assessment of whether the long delay was unreasonable.

[35] The majority of the Court of Appeal rejected as speculative the appellant's contention that his ability to make full answer and defence had been prejudiced. There was evidence, however, that there was a risk of prejudice to his defence because of the delay. In my respectful view, the majority of the Court of Appeal erred by failing to accord any weight to this risk of prejudice.

[36] The nature of the risk to the appellant's ability to make full answer and defence was well set out by Glithero R.S.J., dissenting in the Court of Appeal, at paras. 69-74. He noted that the case was likely to turn on credibility and, in particular, on cross-examination of the complainant and her boyfriend in light of the DNA test results and prior statements. The dissenting judge concluded that the extra passage of time made it more likely that the ability of the appellant to cross-examine effectively had been diminished.

[37] It is difficult to assess the risk of prejudice to the appellant's ability to make full answer and defence, but it is also important to bear in mind that the risk arises from delay to which the appellant made virtually no contribution. Missing from the analysis of the majority of the Court of Appeal, in my respectful view, is an adequate appreciation of the length of the delay in getting this relatively straightforward case to trial. As noted already, prejudice may be inferred from the length of the delay.

[38] Moreover, it does not follow from a conclusion that there is an unquantifiable risk of prejudice to the appellant's ability to make full answer and defence that the overall delay in this case was constitutionally reasonable.

Proof of actual prejudice to the right to make full answer and defence is not invariably required to establish a s. 11(*b*) violation. This is only one of three varieties of prejudice, all of which must be considered together with the length of the delay and the explanations for why it occurred.

IV. Conclusion

[39] This was not a complex case. A delay of 30 months in bringing it to trial is striking, given that the delay was virtually entirely attributable to the Crown or institutional delay and was largely unexplained. Critical evidence was disclosed some nine months after the tests which produced it, the appellant's request for earlier dates was ignored, and when the case was clearly in s. 11(*b*) trouble, the matter was not proceeded with on the date set for the long-awaited preliminary hearing. The length of the delay and the evidence supported the trial judge's inference that some prejudice to the appellant resulted from the delay.

[40] As McLachlin J. (as she then was) put it in her concurring reasons in *Morin*, at p. 810, "[w]hen trials are delayed, justice may be denied. Witnesses forget, witnesses disappear. The quality of evidence may deteriorate. Accused persons may find their liberty and security limited much longer than necessary or justifiable. Such delays are of consequence not only to the accused, but may affect the public interest in the prompt and fair administration of justice."

[41] Of course, there is a strong societal interest in having serious charges tried on their merits. However, the progress of this case was delayed to such a degree that the appellant's constitutional right to be tried within a reasonable time was violated. In my respectful opinion, the Court of Appeal erred in reversing the trial judge's conclusion to that effect.

[42] I would allow the appeal and restore the order of the trial judge.

Stephen Coughlan, in the CR's review "30th Anniversary of the Canadian Charter of Rights and Freedoms: The Impact on Criminal Justice" (2012) 91 C.R. (6th) 71, writes as follows:

Godin is aimed at remedying that watering down of the right, by discouraging reliance on a minute breakdown of time periods and by not insisting on prejudice to fair trial or liberty interests in addition to an impact on security interests. It is disheartening, therefore, to see how frequently courts conducting an 11(b) analysis still refer back twenty years to *Morin* rather than taking *Godin* as the source of fresh guidance it was meant to be. *Godin* did not change the relevant factors, but it did pull out for special emphasis the admonition in *Morin* that section 11(b) claims are not to be determined "by the application of a mathematical or administrative formula". Nonetheless it remains common to see delay analyses breaking the total time into periods of two months and twenty-nine days, one month and five days, and so on. See for example *R. v. Lahiry*, 2011 ONSC 6780 (cited with approval in *R. v. Tran*, 2012 ONCA 18) or *R. v. Khan*, 2011 ONCA 173.

A specific issue awaiting resolution by the Supreme Court is the difference in approach to section 11(b) taken by courts in Ontario, which hinges on the meaning of the word "delay". In *Askov*, for example, the accused were committed for trial on September 21 1984 and made his section 11(b) application on September 2 1986. The Supreme Court described this in *Morin* as "a period of delay of approximately two years subsequent to committal for trial" and noted that "a period of delay in a range of some six to eight months between committal and trial might be deemed to be the outside limit of what is reasonable." In other words, for the Supreme Court "delay" was the total time taken. In Ontario, however, courts consider "delay" to be the time taken <u>beyond</u> that which is justified. For example in *R. v. Khan*, a case which took twenty months to reach the preliminary inquiry, was found to have involved only three-and-a-half months of "delay" and therefore to be within the *Morin* eight-to-ten month guideline. There is a clear difference between "taking ten months is reasonable" and "taking ten months more than needed is reasonable", and so this is a matter which ought to be clarified by the Court.

Some Ontario courts are, however, paying heed to *Godin*. See, e.g.: *R. v. Niro* (2015), 21 C.R. (7th) 352 (Ont. C.J.), C.R. comment by Steve Coughlan and *R. v. Swaminathan* (2015), 21 C.R. (7th) 372 (Ont. C.J.).

For purposes of section 11(*b*) when does time begin to run?

R. v. KALANJ
[1989] 1 S.C.R. 1594, 70 C.R. (3d) 260, 48 C.C.C. (3d) 459 (S.C.C.)

Following a police investigation respecting an allegation of theft, the accused were arrested without warrant. They were released the same day, having been told that charges would be laid. Informations alleging the offences of theft and conspiracy to commit theft, respectively, were sworn only some eight months later. The Crown explained the delay by the time necessary to prepare its case, including reviewing a large number of electronically-intercepted communications. The trial was set to commence only some two years after the information had been sworn. The trial judge quashed the indictment on the basis that the delay had violated the accused's right to be tried within a reasonable time under s. 11(*b*) of the Canadian Charter of Rights and Freedoms. The trial judge found that both accused and their families had suffered serious trauma and public embarrassment because of the arrests. While the time from the swearing of the information to the date of trial did not amount to an unreasonable delay, the delay of some eight months between arrest and release and the swearing of the information had been unreasonable. The British Columbia Court of Appeal allowed the appeal by the Crown, holding that the trial judge had erred in considering the pre-information delay in the s. 11(*b*) decision. The order quashing the indictment was vacated and a trial on the merits directed. The accused appealed.

MCINTYRE J. (L'Heureux-Dubé, and LaForest JJ. concurring):—The general issue on these appeals is whether the rights of the appellants under s. 11(*b*) of the Canadian Charter of Rights and Freedoms "to be tried within a reasonable time" have been infringed. More specifically, the question is whether pre-charge delays should be included in the calculation of whether there was an unreasonable delay in bringing the appellants to trial.

. . .

In dealing with s. 11, it must first be recognized that it is limited in its terms to a special group of persons, those "charged with an offence". It deals primarily with matters relating to the trial. It is to be noted that s. 11 is distinct from s. 10 and serves a different purpose: the two sections must not be equated. The framers of the Charter made a clear distinction between the rights guaranteed to a person arrested and those of a person upon charge. Sections 8 and 9, as well, guarantee essential rights ordinarily of significance in the investigatory period, separate and distinct from those covered in s. 11. It has been said that the purpose of s. 11 should be considered in deciding upon the extent of its application. This purpose, it has been said, is to afford protection for the liberty and security interests of persons accused of crime. While it is true that s. 11 operates for this purpose, I emphasize that it does so within its own sphere. It is not, nor was it intended to be, the sole guarantor and protector of such rights. As stated above, s. 7 affords broad protection for liberty and security, while the other sections, particularly those dealing with legal rights, apply to protect those rights in certain stated circumstances. Section 11 affords its protection after an accused is charged with an offence. The specific language of s. 11 should not be ignored, and the meaning of the word "charged" should not be twisted in an attempt to extend the operation of the section into the pre-charge period. The purpose of s. 11(*b*) is clear. It is concerned with the period between the laying of the charge and the conclusion of the trial and it provides that a person charged with an offence will be promptly dealt with.

The length of the pre-information or investigatory period is wholly unpredictable. No reasonable assessment of what is, or is not, a reasonable time can be readily made. Circumstances will differ from case to case and much information gathered in an investigation must, by its very nature, be confidential. A court will rarely, if ever, be able to fix in any realistic manner a time limit for the investigation of a given offence. It is notable that the law — save for some limited statutory exceptions — has never recognized a time limitation for the institution of criminal proceedings. Where, however, the investigation reveals evidence which would justify the swearing of an information, then for the first time the assessment of a reasonable period for the conclusion of the matter by trial becomes possible. It is for that reason that s. 11 limits its operation to the post-information period. Prior to the charge, the rights of the accused are protected by general law and guaranteed by ss. 7, 8, 9 and 10 of the Charter.

I acknowledge that in taking this position it may be said that I am departing from the earlier judgments of this Court which have said that there will be exceptional cases where pre-charge delays will be relevant under s. 11(b). In my view, however, the departure is more apparent than real. The exception referred to by Lamer J. in *Carter* — where two indictments are preferred because of successful appeals after a first trial — has been dealt with in *R. v. Antoine* (1983), 5 C.C.C. (3d) 97 (Ont. C.A.), and *Re Garton and Whelan* (1984), 14 C.C.C. (3d) 449 (Ont. H.C.). These cases support the proposition that pre-charge delay is not relevant under s. 11(b), by holding that the time commences to run from the date the original information was sworn.

It has been considered that special circumstances could arise which, in the interests of justice, would require some consideration of pre-charge delay because of prejudice which could result from its occurrence. In my view, however, the exceptional cases should be dealt with by reliance on the general rules of law and, where necessary, the other sections of the Charter. This approach would take account of and meet the concerns caused by the possibility of pre-charge delays. Delays which occur at the pre-charge stage are not immune from the law outside the scope of s. 11(b). The Criminal Code itself in ss. 577(3) [now s. 650(3)] and 737(1) [now s. 802(1)] protects the right to make full answer and defence should it be prejudiced by pre-charge delay. Section 455.1 [now s. 505] provides for a prompt swearing of an information where an appearance notice has been issued or an accused has been released from custody under ss. 452 [now s. 497] or 453 [now s. 498]. As well, the doctrine of abuse of process may be called in aid, and as early as 1844 the common law demonstrated that it was capable of dealing with pre-information delays. Baron Alderson B. in *R. v. Robins* (1844), 1 Cox C.C. 114, in a case where nearly two years had elapsed from the alleged commission of an offence before the complaint was made to the justices, said [p. 114]:

> I ought not to allow this case to go further. It is monstrous to put a man on his trial after such a lapse of time. How can he account for his conduct so far back? If you accuse a man of a crime the next day, he may be enabled to bring forward his servants and family to say where he was and what he was about at the time; but if the charge be not preferred for a year or more, how can he clear himself? No man's life would be safe if such a prosecution were permitted. It would be very unjust to put him on his trial.

> His Lordship then directed the jury to acquit the prisoner.

In additon, given the broad wording of s. 7 and the other Charter provisions referred to above, it is not, in my view, necessary to distort the words of s. 11(b) in order to guard against a pre-charge delay. In my view, the concerns which have moved the court to recognize the possibility of special circumstances which would justify a consideration of pre-charge delay under s. 11(b) will thus be met.

In the case at bar, both the courts below considered that the post-charge delays were not such that they could be said to deprive the appellants of trial within a reasonable time. I am in agreement with this finding. The trial judge, however, considered the pre-charge delay of some eight months and concluded that it was unreasonable and upon that conclusion found that s. 11(b) had been infringed. In this, I, in agreement with the Court of Appeal, considered that he was in error. I would accordingly dismiss the appeals.

LAMER J. (dissenting):—[I]t seems that both appellants were released under the condition that they would not leave the area. However, neither of them was formally charged until 14th January 1983, although on the day of the arrest, Kalanj was told that he was being arrested for theft and Pion was told that he was being arrested for conspiracy to commit theft. In the months following the arrest, both accused suffered financial, familial, social and health problems. It is obvious that in such a small community, they were "the talk of the town", and that their conduct was, as of the moment they were arrested, of common knowledge to the people of the area. I note that they tried to expedite the laying of charges but could not persuade the prosecution to do so. They suffered without a doubt a breach of their liberty as well as a restraint of their security. Concerning the concept of security of the person, I stated in *Mills*, supra, at pp. 919-20:

> Additionally, under s. 11(b), the security of the person is to be safeguarded as jealously as the liberty of the individual. In this context, the concept of security of the person is not restricted to physical integrity; rather, it encompasses protection against "overlong subjection to the vexations and vicissitudes of a pending criminal accusation" . . . These include stigmatization of the accused, loss of privacy, stress and anxiety resulting from a multitude of factors, including possible disruption of family, social life and work, legal costs, uncertainty as to the outcome and sanction. These forms of prejudice cannot be disregarded nor minimized when assessing the reasonableness of delay.

Applying the above definitions and comments to these instant cases, I am of the view that the delay started when the appellants were first arrested and released under the condition they would not leave the area. This period is in fact the only period on which the lower courts diverged as they both stated that all the other delays were reasonable. This is also the only time-span that my brother McIntyre considered which may have violated the s. 11(b) right. With my discussion in *Mills* in mind, it is obvious that the eight months elapsed between the arrest and the "formal charge" were in violation of s. 11(b). Not only can it not be said that the appellants consented to the delay occurring between the arrest and the moment they were taken to court, as both accused tried to expedite the laying of charges, although they could not persuade the prosecution to do so, but the Crown has not given any reasonable explanation to justify the said delay before taking the appellants to court. In fact, the Crown tells us that the investigation was not over, which, far from being a justification of what they did, is, in my respectful view, an admission to the fact that they were not ready to charge and therefore should not have arrested. But, as I said, in different terms, the Charter is there precisely to protect the citizen from this kind of situation and we would be remiss if, by a definition, we were to put the victim of such conduct beyond the shield of the Charter while protecting those who are in no need of its protection because the police proceeded lawfully.

As this disposes of these cases, I do not need to analyze whether the subsequent period has been satisfactorily explained or not.

With the greatest of respect, I am of the view that the Court of Appeal for British Columbia erred in law by considering the eight-month period elapsed between the arrest and the laying of the charges as pre-charge delay. The said period should have been computed in determining whether or not the accused have been tried within reasonable time. I would consequently allow both appeals and order a stay of proceedings against Pion and Kalanj.

WILSON J. (dissenting):—I have had the benefit of the reasons of my colleagues, Justices McIntyre and Lamer, in these appeals and find myself in agreement with the position of Lamer J. on the main issue as to the time from which the appellants' right to a trial within a reasonable time starts to run under s. 11(b) of the Canadian Charter of Rights and Freedoms. I believe that if s. 11(b) is designed to protect the liberty and security interests of the accused, and I think it is, then the relevant starting point for the running of time under the section should not be upon the ex parte laying of the information before the justice of the peace, but rather when the impact of the criminal process is felt by the accused through the service of process upon him in the form of a summons or notice of appearance or an arrest with or without warrant. This flexible approach to s. 11(b) seems to me most adequately to give effect to the obvious purpose of the provision.

I do, however, have a significant point of disagreement with Lamer J. which I feel obliged to address very briefly. I do not agree with my colleague that prejudice to the security interests of the appellants arising purely from the fact of the imposition of the process upon them, i.e., that they became, in Lamer J.'s colourful phrase, "the talk of the town", should be considered in assessing the reasonableness of the delay. As I indicated in *Mills v. R.*, [1986] 1 S.C.R. 863, and again in *R. v. Rahey*, [1987] 1 S.C.R. 588, it is my view that the prejudice we are concerned with is that arising from the delay and not from the imposition of the process. The latter prejudice arises whether there is delay or not. I do, however, think that the appellants were prejudiced by the delay between the arrest and the laying of the information and that this prejudice can be attributed to the delay and not simply to the imposition of the process. After their highly publicized arrests the appellants were forced to live under a generalized cloud of suspicion and stigma for over eight months. Although an arrest and the subsequent laying of charges would have affected their broad security interests at any time, the unjustified delay in the bringing of specific charges, in my view, substantially aggravated that prejudice beyond what is acceptable or inherent in the criminal process itself.

I accordingly concur with Lamer J. in his proposed disposition of the appeals.

The 3-2 decision in *Kalanj* was accepted as settled law in *Morin*, above. Nevertheless, some nuances remain. For example, in *R. v. Lanteigne* (2010), 81 C.R. (6th) 240, 265 C.C.C. (3d) 123 (N.B. C.A.), it was held that an accused continues to be charged with an offence during the time between the entry of a stay by the Crown and recommencement of the proceedings. This decision may, however, be in doubt due to the Ontario Court of Appeal decision in *R. v. Milani* (2014), 314 C.C.C. (3d) 101, 12 C.R. (7th) 429 (Ont. C.A.), leave to appeal refused 2015 CarswellOnt 262, 2015 CarswellOnt 263 (S.C.C.). The Court held that, during the time of the entering of the stay and the resurrection of the charges, the accused was not charged with an offence.

R. v. POTVIN
[1993] 2 S.C.R. 880, 23 C.R. (4th) 10, 83 C.C.C. (3d) 97 (S.C.C.)

The accused was charged with criminal negligence causing death. The information was sworn on September 15, 1988. He was released from custody on an undertaking. A series of lengthy delays occurred, to accommodate both the Crown and the defence, and a trial date was finally set on December 3, 1990. Accused applied on that date for and was granted a stay of proceedings under s. 24(1) of the Charter on the ground that his right to trial within a reasonable time in s. 11(*b*) of the Charter had been infringed.

On December 24, 1990, the Attorney General appealed against the stay. The appeal was heard in the Court of Appeal for Ontario on April 24, 1992 during which the issue of appellate delay was raised. On June 22, 1992, the Court of Appeal allowed the appeal, set aside the stay and remitted the matter for trial on an expedited basis. The accused appealed. The authority of *Morin* was accepted by all the justices in the Supreme Court. A majority of the Court further held that appellate delay could not be considered under s. 11(*b*).

Per SOPINKA J. (L'Heureux-Dubé, Gonthier, Cory and Iacobucci JJ. concurring):— To determine whether the delay was unreasonable, the Court of Appeal weighed the explanation for the delay and prejudice to the accused to determine whether the appellant's constitutional right to be tried within a reasonable time had been breached. Osborne J.A. noted that this court had held in *R. v. Morin*, [1992] 1 S.C.R. 771, that, although prejudice is only one factor to be taken into account in the balancing process, a conclusion that prejudice was absent or that it was minimal is significant. The rationale for the pre-eminent position given to prejudice was held to be consistent for the purposes of s. 11(*b*) — to protect the rights of the accused and the dual societal interest in seeing an accused treated humanely and fairly and in seeing those accused of crimes be brought to trial.

Weighing all the factors, Osborne J.A. found that the delay was not unreasonable. He concluded that the prejudice that may be inferred was minimal, and that there was nothing on the record to suggest that the respondent ever sought an earlier date for the pre-trials, the preliminary hearing or the trial. While noting that "there may be a fine line between acceptance of the inevitability of the pace of proceedings and contentment with the speed of the process," Osborne J.A. held that the guidelines set out in *Morin* do not establish a limitation period and that a balancing of all aspects of the delay in this case led to the conclusion that the delay was not unreasonable.

. . .

I would adopt the conclusions and reasons of Osborne J.A. and dismiss this ground of appeal.

Appellate Delay

This issue was raised in the Court of Appeal but was not dealt with. I have concluded that s. 11(*b*) does not apply to delay in respect of an appeal from conviction by the accused nor an appeal from an acquittal by the Crown. Moreover, in my opinion, there is no distinction in this regard between an acquittal after trial and a judicial stay.

. . .

The general objects and purposes of s. 11(*b*) were recently restated in *R. v. Morin*.

. . .

If these purposes and objects were embodied in s. 11(*b*) without restriction, it would be difficult to argue that the section had no application to appeals. The section has, however, been interpreted in a manner that does not extend its protection of these interests against the consequences of delay at large, but only from the consequences of delay flowing from a formal charge. Short of a formal charge, similar consequences proceeding from other aspects of governmental activity in the criminal process do not trigger the protection of the provision. Accordingly, in *Kalanj*, supra, this court dealt with a situation in which the accused were arrested after a lengthy investigation. On the day of the arrest the accused were fingerprinted and released but were advised not to leave town, that they would be charged and that a summons would issue. More than eight months later charges were laid. This court was invited to hold that, because of the involvement of the interests that underlie s. 11(*b*), it should extend to the pre-charge delay. The invasion of the interests protected by s. 11 in the broad sense could certainly be equated to the consequences of a charge. The stigma and anxiety resulting from arrest and fingerprinting would exceed the consequences flowing from laying of a charge followed by a summons. The restraint on liberty was the equivalent to that which occurs when a charge is laid and the accused is released on bail. The delay pre-trial has the same effect on the freshness of the evidence as post-charge delay. Nonetheless, this court held that the accused were not persons charged until a formal charge was laid and that s. 11(*b*) did not apply. This judgment has been applied to rule out review of pre-charge delay unless the accused can establish a breach under s. 7. See *R. v. L. (W.K.)*, [1991] 1 S.C.R. 1091.

. . .

Clearly, during the period after an acquittal and the service of a notice of appeal, the person acquitted is not a person charged. No proceeding is on foot which seeks to charge the person acquitted. Upon the appeal's being filed there is a possibility, the strength of which will vary with each case, that the acquittal will be set aside and the charge will be revived. The plight of the acquitted person is that of one against whom governmental action is directed which may result in a charge. In this respect the former accused is like the suspect against whom an investigation has been completed and charges are contemplated awaiting a decision by the prosecutor.

. . .

There is even less reason to extend the protection of s. 11(*b*) to a convicted person who appeals. The appeal itself is not governmental action.

. . .

The conclusion I have reached applies to appeals from acquittals and convictions. Furthermore, I see no valid reason to distinguish between an acquittal on the merits and a judicial stay. In light of the interest protected under s. 11(*b*), the differences between an acquittal and a judicial stay are purely technical. In both cases the accused can plead autrefois acquit and no proceedings may be brought in respect of the same charge unless the acquittal or stay is set aside on appeal. No restraints can be placed on the liberty of the former accused pending appeal. There is no basis on which to assume that the theoretical existence of a charge that has been stayed carries any greater stigma or causes greater anxiety to the respondent in an appeal from a judicial stay than an appeal from acquittal. Certainly there is no evidence on this point. I doubt that the public understands the difference. An unpopular acquittal generates as much public indignation as a stay. The degree of anxiety is dictated more by the strength of the grounds of appeal than by the form of the verdict.

. . .

This conclusion does not leave the criminal appellant or respondent without a remedy when delay of appeal proceedings affect the fairness of the trial. While s. 11(*b*) does not apply, s. 7 may in appropriate circumstances afford a remedy. In *R. v. L. (W.K.)*, supra, this court held that, in respect of pre-charge delay, if the particular circumstances of the case indicated that the fairness of the trial had been affected by the delay, s. 7 can be resorted to. This is simply the application to delay of the court's power to remedy an abuse of process which is enshrined in s. 7 as a principle of fundamental justice.

[The majority did, however, make it clear that the s. 11(b) clock would start to run again were a Court of Appeal to order a new trial.]

. . .

McLACHLIN J. (Lamer C.J.C. and Major J. concurring):— . . . The rights protected by s. 11(*b*), as noted earlier are the right to security of the person, the right to liberty, and the right to a fair trial: *R. v. Morin*, [1992] 1 S.C.R. 771.

. . .

The rights which s. 11(*b*) seeks to protect are all engaged in the period between a verdict or a stay and the final disposition of the criminal charges. Security of the person and the right to liberty are engaged. The acquitted person, having been found not guilty, faces the prospect of conviction and incarceration. The person against whom a stay has been entered faces the same possibility. The convicted person, if the appeal succeeds and the conviction is found to be invalid, can equally argue that the law's delay in arriving at that conclusion has deprived him or her of his or her liberty and security of the person during the appellate interval. The right to a fair trial is engaged as well. In all three situations, the acquittal, conviction and stay, the subject of the criminal proceedings faces the prospect of a new trial, whose fairness may be jeopardized by excessive delay.

The narrow remedy proposed by my colleague for post-stay, post-verdict delay would not, with respect, provide a remedy capable of meeting these concerns. He concludes that s. 7 applies where the delay is so long that it constitutes abuse of process. The accused would be entitled to a remedy only where he or she could show that a new trial would be so unfair as to amount to an abuse of the court's process. I have several problems with this conclusion.

. . .

The abuse of process doctrine is a narrow doctrine which has only on rare occasions provided a remedy to accused persons caught overlong in the meshes of the criminal process. Its primary aim is not the rights of the accused person, but the repute of the system of justice. . . . Moreover, it has repeatedly been held that the doctrine of abuse of process should be applied only in the clearest of cases. . . . This has been taken to impose a higher standard of proof than would face an accused relying on a breach of rights under the *Charter*. . . . Without definitively ruling on that question, the fact remains that abuse of process has seldom, in its long history, served as a remedy for delay in the criminal process. It has been stringently and sparingly applied.

. . .

This brings me to the matter of remedy. This court has held in cases of pre-verdict, non-appellate delay, that a stay of proceedings is the minimum and generally appropriate remedy: *R. v. Rahey*, supra, at p. 614. However, where a verdict has been entered, a stay may not be appropriate. For example, a stay of proceedings would be useless to a convicted person complaining of appellate delay; indeed, it would deny him or her a just remedy by preventing him or her from proceeding with his or her appeal. The nearest alternative to a stay of proceedings, quashing the conviction, might seem inappropriate given that one would be releasing, not a person presumed to be innocent as at the pre-trial stage, but a convicted felon who has not served his or her sentence. To release a convicted killer into society, for example, without having served his or her sentence, solely because the appeal he or she chose to bring took more time than reasonable, would be to grant a remedy which far outstrips the wrong and which overlooks the important societal interest in the safety and security of members of the public. Confronted with these alternatives, a judge finding unreasonable delay in such a case might wish instead to make a different order. He or she might order that the appeal be expedited, for example. Nor would I rule out other remedies such as damages to compensate for loss of liberty or mental suffering, although I would leave the question of what remedies may be appropriate for resolution on a case-by-case basis.

The many different circumstances which may prevail at the post-verdict, post-stay stage require a flexible approach to remedies. In some cases stays of proceedings may be appropriate. In other cases, other remedies will necessarily arise for consideration.

. . .

LA FOREST J. (concurring in the result):— I agree with Justice Sopinka that s. 11(*b*) of the *Canadian Charter of Rights and Freedoms* does not apply to appellate delay. . . . (However) a stay should not as often be used as the appropriate remedy for appellate delay as for trial delay. On these matters, it will be obvious that I generally share the views of Justice McLachlin.

For a critical review of *Potvin*, see Graeme Mitchell, "Potvin: Charter-proofing Criminal Appeals" (1993), 23 C.R. (4th) 37.

In *MacDougall*, [1998] 3 S.C.R. 45, 19 C.R. (5th) 275, 128 C.C.C. (3d) 483, the Supreme Court held that delay in sentencing at trial is encompassed within the s. 11(*b*) protection.

PROBLEM 1

In the mid-1950s the accused was a member of an R.C.M.P. surveillance unit whose task was to detect Russian espionage operating from the Soviet Embassy. He was dismissed from the R.C.M.P. in 1958 after pleading guilty to Criminal Code offences relating to fraudulent cheques. In 1982 he gave interviews to television and news media respecting his R.C.M.P. intelligence work.

In 1983 he was charged with offences under the Official Secrets Act relating to incidents which occurred in the 1950s. You believe these incidents were known to the R.C.M.P. long before the telecast. Can you complain about the delay?

Compare *R. v. Morrison* (1984), 38 C.R. (3d) 351 (Ont. Prov. Ct.), later overruled on jurisdictional grounds: see (1984), 47 O.R. (2d) 700, 44 C.R. (3d) 85 (Ont. C.A.) and see *R. v. L. (W.K.)* (1991), 6 C.R. (4th) 1 (S.C.C.) (discussed later under "Abuse of Process").

PROBLEM 2

Accused was charged in September 1981 with six counts of making false returns under the Income Tax Act. His trial before a provincial court judge began six months later. The Crown closed its case in November 1982 and, after an adjournment, the defence made a motion for a directed verdict on December 13, 1982. Over the next eleven months, there were nineteen adjournments each initiated by the trial judge. For nine of those months, appellant raised no objection to the delay. On September 13, 1983, he wrote to the Crown requesting that it seek a decision from the judge. The judge ordered further adjournments. The accused wrote again to the Crown on several occasions alleging a violation of his constitutional rights and demanding the withdrawal of the charges. The requests were refused. Instead, the Crown filed a motion for mandamus. On November 14, 1983, one day prior to the trial judge's decision dismissing the motion for a directed verdict, accused made an application pursuant to s. 24(1) of the Charter to the Supreme Court of Nova Scotia for an order dismissing the charges. The application was based on an alleged violation of s. 11(b) of the Charter. Rule on the application. Compare *Rahey v. R.*, [1987] 1 S.C.R. 588, 57 C.R. (3d) 289, 33 C.C.C. (3d) 289 (S.C.C.).

PROBLEM 3

In 1989 accusations of misconduct by a school teacher against his female students were made public. He was suspended and later dismissed by the school board. Three former students testified at a subsequent arbitration hearing, which ended in October, 1990. In December, 1990, an information was sworn containing five counts alleging sexual offences against these three between September, 1979, and June, 1984. A series of procedural delays occurred totaling over 23 months from the information date to the scheduled trial date. The delay from committal to the trial date was over 15 months. The Crown's case evolved from one to be disposed of within five days to one where expert evidence and similar fact evidence would be significant. Three weeks was seen to be necessary. The first available trial date for a three week trial was April, 1993. An application to stay the proceedings on the basis that they violated the accused's right to be tried within a reasonable time under s. 11(b) of the Canadian Charter of Rights and Freedoms has been made. Rule.

Compare *R. v. Armstrong* (1993), 22 C.R. (4th) 286 (B.C. C.A.).

PROBLEM 4

On June 23, 1996, the accused was driving his vehicle southbound when a northbound vehicle being driven by B made a U-turn in front of the accused and a violent collision occurred. A passenger in the B vehicle was thrown to the road and died of her injuries. It was alleged that both drivers were impaired and that the accused was driving without his headlights on. On September 9, 1998—26 months later—a motion was brought to stay based on a violation of s.11(b). The motions judge finds two periods assignable to the accused—a four-month intake period to obtain counsel and two months to hear the s. 11(b) motion. This left 21 months attributable to the Crown, about half of which was institutional delay through lack of resources. In the meantime, restrictive bail conditions had been imposed, including weekly reporting to police, a curfew, no drinking and no driving. Considering the *Morin* tests, should there be a stay entered?

Compare *R. v. Williamson* (2000), 34 C.R. (5th) 152, 144 C.C.C. (3d) 540 (Ont. C.A.), leave to appeal refused (2000), 262 N.R. 398 (note) (S.C.C.).

PROBLEM 5

The accused physician was charged with two counts of sexual assault against two former male patients. He was charged in November, 1998. His preliminary inquiry started in November, 1999. It was adjourned to February, 2000, at which time he was discharged. The Crown proceeded by direct indictment. The trial was scheduled for November 2000 but was adjourned to February 2001 as a result of late disclosure by the Crown. Assuming a period of delay in apparent breach of s. 11(b), do you think that the proceedings should be stayed because of prejudice in the form of evidence by defence lawyers, the accused's psychiatrist, and his family as to stress that the delay had caused the accused?

Compare *R. v. Christie* (2001), 160 C.C.C. (3d) 192 (N.S. C.A.).

PROBLEM 6

The accused were charged on September 24, 1999 in an information charging 36 persons with 21 offences including gangsterism and conspiracy. The charges resulted from an investigation that had involved 400 police officers, 20 to 30 of them having substantial involvement. All of the accused were initially remanded into custody pending trial. The Crown chose to make disclosure by electronic means and a police officer was assigned to act as disclosure coordinator. The amount of evidence involved in the case, involving hundreds of thousands of pages, made the magnitude and complexity of the prosecution unprecedented within the province. Over the subsequent 40 months there were difficulties with disclosure, as orders were made for disclosure to be made by hard copy, court rulings in other cases affected what evidence was seen as relevant, additional issues were seen as being relevant, further boxes of evidence were found after disclosure was said to be nearly complete, and information relating to additional individuals was seen as being relevant to the prosecution. Several orders were made for the completion of disclosure but in each case more material was found after the set date had passed. Over 70,000 pages of material were disclosed to the defence after the trial had commenced. Eventually the original 36 accused were severed into two separate groups for trial, and all charges except a count of conspiracy were dropped against the accused in this case. A number of motions had yet to be considered which would potentially require a further 14 to 21 months before a jury would be empanelled. On January 13, 2003, the accused applied for a stay of proceedings based on a denial of their right to a trial within a reasonable time. Rule?

Compare *R. v. Chan* (2003), 15 C.R. (6th) 53 (Alta. Q.B.). Similar delay problems arose in trials of biker gang members in Quebec see *R. v. Callocchia* (2000), 39 C.R. (5th) 374, 149 C.C.C. (3d) 215 (Que. C.A.) and see Anne-Marie Boisvert, "Mega-trials: The Disturbing Situation in Quebec", (2003) 15 C.R. (6th) 178.

PROBLEM 7

Suppose that the date of alleged offences that include serious drug trafficking charges was October 1, 2002 but that the accused was neither arrested nor charged on that date. Suppose also that the informations were not sworn until May 18, 2003. On June 1, 2003, the accused was arrested and first appeared in court on these matters. On that date, the charges were read but no other action taken because the accused requested an opportunity to hire counsel.

The matters were adjourned at his request to June 4, 2003, at which time he was granted bail. One of the bail conditions required him to turn in his passport. The matter was then adjourned to June 14, 2003. On the next appearance on June 14, 2003, the prosecutor was sick, with the result that the matter was once again adjourned to July 11, 2003. On that date, the only things that occurred were the election of the accused of trial by jury and the setting of a preliminary inquiry date. Defence counsel requested the earliest possible date which, she was informed, was November 18, 2003. That date, unfortunately, was the only date in the succeeding months on which Crown counsel was unavailable. As a consequence, the preliminary inquiry was set for January 4, 2004. On January 4, the arresting officer was unexpectedly out of town at an anti-gun control rally. The preliminary inquiry was therefore adjourned to February 7, 2004. Defence counsel reluctantly agreed to the adjournment, saying, "I suppose that's okay, although my client doesn't like this hanging over his head."

On February 7, 2004, the preliminary inquiry was held and the accused was committed for trial in the superior court. Because of shortages of staff, the transcript of the proceedings was not prepared until July, 2004. The accused was then arraigned in the superior court and a trial date arranged. Defence counsel requested the earliest possible date, which turned out to be October 21, 2004. However, due to a shortage of judges and courtrooms, the case was not reached on that date and was further adjourned until March 29, 2005.

Prior to that date, the accused launched a pre-trial motion in which he argued that there had been unreasonable trial delay and, further, that the Court lacked the jurisdiction to try these offences.

Indicate all bases for the arguments and assess the likelihood of their succeeding. If the arguments succeed, what remedies are available?

4. Formal Attacks on the Information or Indictment

It will be recalled that there are only two types of proceeding: those on indictment and those by way of summary conviction proceeding. In the case of either type of trial before a provincial court judge the charge is contained in the information. If the trial is on indictment the information is treated for all purposes as an indictment (ss. 2 and 554). In the case of proceedings on indictment before a superior court the information which commenced the process is replaced by another document called the indictment which becomes the charging instrument in the trial (s. 566) (see Form 4).

In any trial there is only one indictment or information for each accused but the document may contain more than one accused or more than one count (i.e., charge). A formal attack may be against one or all of the counts.

A formal objection is sometimes introduced by general language such as a motion to quash for a formal defect, that the charge is void for uncertainty or that the charge does not name an offence known to law. However it is preferable to be more precise and to distinguish between three distinct types of objections: insufficiency, duplicity and improper joinder. Here we will consider each defect in turn and then consider savings devices that may be used to rectify the defect without the necessity of starting the process again. In the case of summary conviction proceedings a successful formal objection may act as a full defence since new proceedings may be barred by the six-month time limitation.

Two points should be made clear. First, overwhelmingly, the tendency is to deal with sufficiency and duplicity issues through amendment if possible. Second, if a charge contains defects that cannot be remedied through amendment and the challenge is made, as it should be, before plea, the Crown is not prevented from re-laying the charge in proper form because the accused was never in jeopardy of conviction on the defective charge. For a discussion of the concept of "jeopardy," see *R. v. Moore* below.

(a) Grounds

(i) Insufficiency

A charge in an indictment will be insufficient if it does not comply with the general Criminal Code requirements as set out in ss. 581 and 583:

581. (1) Each count in an indictment shall in general apply to a single transaction and shall contain in substance a statement that the accused or defendant committed an indictable offence therein specified.

(2) The statement referred to in subsection (1) may be

(a) in popular language without technical averments or allegations of matters that are not essential to be proved,

(b) in the words of the enactment that describes the offence or declares the matters charged to be an indictable offence, or

(c) in words that are sufficient to give to the accused notice of the offence with which he is charged.

(3) A count shall contain sufficient detail of the circumstances of the alleged offence to give to the accused reasonable information with respect to the act or omission to be proved against him and to identify the transaction referred to, but otherwise the absence or insufficiency of details does not vitiate the count.

(4) Where an accused is charged with an offence under section 47 or sections 49 to 53, every overt act that is to be relied upon shall be stated in the indictment.

(5) A count may refer to any section, subsection, paragraph or subparagraph of the enactment that creates the offence charged, and for the purpose of determining whether a count is sufficient, consideration shall be given to any such reference.

(6) Nothing in this Part relating to matters that do not render a count insufficient shall be deemed to restrict or limit the application of this section.

. . .

583. No count in an indictment is insufficient by reason of the absence of details where, in the opinion of the court, the count otherwise fulfils the requirements of section 581 and, without restricting the generality of the foregoing, no count in an indictment is insufficient by reason only that

(a) it does not name the person injured or intended or attempted to be injured;

(b) it does not name the person who owns or has a special property or interest in property mentioned in the count;

(c) it charges an intent to defraud without naming or describing the person whom it was intended to defraud;

(d) it does not set out any writing that is the subject of the charge;

(e) it does not set out the words used where words that are alleged to have been used are the subject of the charge;

(f) it does not specify the means by which the alleged offence was committed;

(g) it does not name or describe with precision any person, place or thing; or

(h) it does not, where the consent of a person, official or authority is required before proceedings may be instituted for an offence, state that the consent has been obtained.

The same provisions apply to summary conviction proceedings (s. 795). A motion to quash based on a "defect apparent on the face" of an indictment or information must be brought before the plea or thereafter only by leave of the court (s. 601(1)). There is no indication given as to the basis upon which leave may be given. **Can you imagine situations when such leave would be granted?**

These provisions obviously strive to compromise between ensuring that the accused gets adequate notice of the charge so that he can prepare his defence and avoiding undue technicalities. In the early common law, technical attacks were a necessity to give the courts a device to avoid an excessive penalty such as the death penalty for a relatively minor offence.

For many years, counsel have turned to the unanimous decision of the Supreme Court of Canada in *Brodie v. R.*, [1936] S.C.R. 188 (S.C.C.) to support an argument that a particular charge does not give the accused adequate notice. In *Brodie* the charge read as follows:

> The Attorney-General of the Province of Quebec charges that: during the months of September and October in the year of Our Lord one thousand nine hundred and thirty-three, at the city of Quebec, in the District of Quebec, and elsewhere in the province of Quebec, George H. Brodie, of Toronto, and G.C. Barrett, of Belleville, Ontario were party to a seditious conspiracy, in conspiring together with the W.F. Greenwood, W.G. Brown, Mrs. Charles Alton and Mrs. A.M. Rose and also with other persons unknown, thereby committing the crime of seditious conspiracy.

It was held that a charge must identify the act "by specifying the time, the place and the matter" (at 193) and that this particular indictment should be quashed as it did not describe the offence "in such a way as to lift it from the general to the particular" (at 198). Rinfret J. held on behalf of the Court (at 194-5):

It is not sufficient in a count to charge an indictable offence in the abstract. Concrete facts of a nature to identify the particular act which is charged and to give the accused notice of it are necessary ingredients of the indictment. An accused person may not be charged merely of having committed murder; the statement must specify the manner. In the same way, in the present case, the appellants could not be charged merely with having been "parties to a seditious conspiracy", or having "committed the crime of seditious conspiracy". The particular agreement . . . ought to have been specified in the charge preferred.

What is sometimes called the paramountcy s. 581(6) can be invoked in aid of the *Brodie* interpretation. There is, however, a marked recent tendency for our courts to avoid the rigour of *Brodie* and to reject insufficiency arguments on the basis that they are unduly technical and an unnecessary holdover of earlier times.

R. v. McKENZIE
[1972] S.C.R. 409, 16 C.R.N.S. 374 (S.C.C.)

RITCHIE J.:—This is an appeal brought by the Attorney General of British Columbia pursuant to the provisions of the Criminal Code, 1953-54 (Can.), c. 51, s. 598(1)(*a*) [re-en. 1960-61, c. 44, s. 12; 1968-69, c. 38, s. 65] from a judgment of the Court of Appeal of that province, [1971] 2 W.W.R. 716, 14 C.R.N.S. 104, 2 C.C.C. (2d) 28 (Davey C.J.B.C. dissenting), which set aside the conviction of the respondent for theft and directed his acquittal.

On the night of 30th-31st March 1970 the respondent, who is a taxi-driver, was employed by Dominic Louis Christian to drive one of his taxis upon terms which entitled the respondent to retain 45 per cent of the daily receipts and required him to account for the balance and to pay 55 per cent of the total receipts, less the cost of gasoline, to his employer. The accounting was carried out by means of what has been referred to as a "trip sheet" on which is recorded the starting point, destination and fare charged for each trip, and a record is also made of the amount retained by the driver, which is referred to as "wages", the amount paid for gas and oil and the "net cash" due to the owner.

At about 3:30 a.m. on 31st March the respondent had driven Christian's car to the airport where he picked up five passengers, two of whom were destined for addresses in the City of Vancouver, two for West Vancouver and one for North Vancouver. The two Vancouver passengers were charged $4.50 and $4.75 respectively, and the West Vancouver passengers were charged $8.55 and $9.50. The North Vancouver passenger, who was dropped last, did not give evidence, but I think the learned trial Judge was justified in expressing the hope "that she had a good purse full of money with her".

In accounting for the 3:30 a.m. trip from the airport, the respondent only recorded one trip for one passenger with a total cash fare of $6.35. It is quite apparent that, without giving any consideration to the North Vancouver passenger, the respondent received cash charges of at least $26.95 for the use of Christian's car in making this trip and I agree with the learned Provincial Judge that the evidence supports the conclusion that the respondent failed to account for or pay approximately $16.50 to his employer for which he was required to account under the terms of his employment.

The respondent was charged that he:

> At the City of Vancouver, on the 31st day of March, A.D. 1970, unlawfully did commit theft of the approximate sum of $16.50 the property of Dominic Louis Christian contrary to the form of the statute in such case made and provided.

Tysoe J.A. in the course of the reasons for judgment, which he delivered on behalf of the majority of the Court of Appeal, expressed the view that this form of charge lacks any averment of the essential ingredients of an offence under s. 276(1) [s. 330] of the Code and he concluded by saying [p. 728]:

> My opinion is that it does not charge an offence under s. 276 and a conviction for such an offence cannot rest upon it. The fact is the appellant was not charged with the offence of which the evidence shows that he might perhaps have been found guilty.

In so holding, the majority of the Court of Appeal gave effect to the contention, made on behalf of the respondent, that in the case of "theft", which is described in one way in s. 269 [s. 322] and in another in s. 276 [s. 330], an indictment or information is invalid as failing to comply with s. 492(3) unless it contains an averment of all the essential ingredients contained in this section of the Code describing the offence disclosed by the evidence.

. . .

In the course of his dissenting reasons for judgment, Davey C.J.B.C. pointed out that theft is not the only offence which is capable of being committed in more ways than one under the provisions of the Code, and he referred to s. 135 describing four different kinds of behaviour which may constitute the crime of "rape". In this latter regard he cited the case of *Regina v. LeBlanc*, B.C. C.A., 15th November 1966 (not yet reported), where the indictment charged that at a certain time and place he, LeBlanc "did rape (a named woman) contrary to the form of statute in such cases made and provided" and Lord J.A., speaking on behalf of the Court of Appeal of British Columbia, said:

> Counsel has referred to s. 135 of the Code, which is the section dealing with rape, and submits that inasmuch as the section describes more than one aspect of sexual intercourse with a female person which would constitute rape, that there should have been an averment in the charge as to the manner in which the accused is alleged to have committed the offence. Was it by impersonating her husband or by fear of bodily harm or in any of the other ways in which rape can be an offence. As my brother Branca pointed out during the course of argument, surely this is a matter for particulars.

. . .

I am of the opinion that the charge in the present case complies with the Code in that it is in the words of s. 280 [s. 334] which declares "theft" to be an indictable offence and the respondent's failure to account to his employer was, in my opinion, "theft" within the meaning of s. 276(1). It follows that I agree with the dissenting view expressed by Davey C.J.B.C. that this "was a good charge of theft" under that section.

If there had been any genuine doubt as to the conduct to which the charge related, further particulars describing the means by which the offence was alleged to have been committed could have been sought under s. 497(1)(*f*) of the Code, but this was not the course which was followed.

. . .

In allowing this appeal in the Court of Appeal, Tysoe J.A. relied on a line of cases such as *Regina v. Leclair,* [1956] O.W.N. 336, 23 C.R. 216, 115 C.C.C. 297 (C.A.); *Rex v. Connors* (1923), 51 N.B.R. 247 (C.A.); *Rex v. Fraser,* 11 Sask. L.R. 209, [1918] 2 W.W.R. 324, 30 C.C.C. 70, 40 D.L.R. 691 (C.A.); and *Regina v. Tepoorten* (1961), 37 C.R. 299, 131 C.C.C. 356 (B.C. C.A.). In each of these cases the charge was framed "in the words of the enactment that describes the offence" and failure to allege some essential ingredient of the offence so charged was found to be fatal. As I have indicated, different considerations apply to a case such as the present one where the charge is framed in the words declaring the matter charged to be an indictable offence. I accordingly share the opinion of Davey C.J.B.C. that the cases last referred to are clearly distinguishable and have no application to the question here raised.

I should observe also that there is a fundamental difference between the present case and that of *Brodie and Barrett v. The King,* [1936] S.C.R. 188, 65 C.C.C. 289, [1936] 3 D.L.R. 81, upon which much reliance was placed by the respondent's counsel. That was a case in which the charge alleged that the two accused "were party to a seditious conspiracy *in conspiring*" with certain named persons and with persons unknown, but there was no allegation of what the conspirators had conspired to do. At p. 199 Rinfret J. (as he then was), speaking on behalf of the Court said:

> . . . although conspiracy to commit a crime, being in itself an indictable offence, may be charged alone in an indictment and independently of the crime conspired to be committed, it does not follow that the count charging conspiracy alone, without the setting out of any overt act, must not describe it in such a way as to contain in substance the fundamental ingredients of the particular agreement which is charged, or, in other words, in such a way as to specify, in substance, the specific transaction intended to be brought against the accused.

This was the ground on which the charge was found to be insufficient and it cannot, in my view, be seriously contended in the present case that the charge did not specify the specific transaction intended to be brought against McKenzie or that he could have been in any doubt as to what the complaint was.

. . .

For all these reasons I would allow this appeal and restore the conviction entered by the learned Provincial Judge.

R. v. CÔTÉ
[1978] 1 S.C.R. 8, 40 C.R.N.S. 308, 33 C.C.C. (2d) 353 (S.C.C.)

The accused was charged in an information that on a specified day at a specified place he "did refuse to comply with a demand by a peace officer to provide a sample of breath suitable for analysis to determine if any, the proportion of alcohol in his blood, contrary to section 235(2) of the Criminal Code". The Saskatchewan Court of Appeal quashed the conviction on the basis that the information did not allege the essential element that the refusal was "without reasonable excuse". However the Supreme Court of Canada was unanimous in holding that there was no defect in the information.

DE GRANDPRE J.:—Appellant submits that [no defect] exists, the words "without reasonable excuse" being brought to the attention of the accused by the specific reference to the section of the Criminal Code creating the offence. Appellant invokes [subsection] (4) of s. 510, which also applies to informations:

> 510.(5) A count may refer to any section, subsection, paragraph or subparagraph of the enactment that creates the offence charged, and for the purpose of determining whether a count is sufficient, consideration shall be given to any such reference.

I agree with that submission; the golden rule is for the accused to be reasonably informed of the transaction alleged against him, thus giving him the possibility of a full defence and a fair trial. When, as in the present case, the information recites all the facts and relates them to a definite offence identified by the relevant section of the Code, it is impossible for the accused to be misled. To hold otherwise would be to revert to the extreme technicality of the old procedure.

In contrast, in *R. v. WIS Dev. Corp.* the Supreme Court held that an information containing thirty-two counts alleging breaches of the Aeronautics Act and its regulations were void *ab initio* for want of sufficient details required by s. 581(3).

R. v. WIS DEV. CORP.
[1984] 1 S.C.R. 485, 40 C.R. (3d) 97 (S.C.C.)

The form of the sixteen counts alleging breaches of the Aeronautics Act was as follows:

> AND FURTHER THAT on or between the 27th day of March, A.D. 1980 and the 29th day of March, A.D. 1980, at or near the City of Calgary, in the Province of Alberta, did unlawfully operate a commercial air service without holding a valid and subsisting licence issued under Section 16 of the *Aeronautics Act,* Revised Statutes of Canada 1970, c. A-3, contrary to section 17(1) of the said Act, and did thereby commit an offence under the said section 17.

and the form of the sixteen counts alleging breaches of the regulations was as follows:

> AND FURTHER THAT on or between the 27th day of March, A.D. 1980 and the 29th day of March, A.D. 1980, at or near the City of Calgary, in the Province of Alberta, did unlawfully operate a commercial air service in Canada, while not holding a valid and subsisting certificate issued by the Minister certifying that the holder thereof is adequately equipped and able to conduct a safe operation as an air carrier, contrary to section 700 of the Consolidated Regulations of Canada 1978, c. 2 (formerly the Air Regulations) as amended.

In concluding that the charges were void, Lamer J. for the Court, was content to adopt the accused's arguments, expressed in their factum.

LAMER J.:—The information at bar is in the express words of the language contained in s. 17 of the *Aeronautics Act,* R.S.C. 1970, c. A-3 and s. 700 of the Regulations thereunder. In each instance, the gravamen of the offence is the operation of a 'commercial air service' without the requisite licence or certificate. Regard must be had to s. 9(1) of the *Aeronautics Act,* which defines 'commercial air service' as 'any use of aircraft in or over Canada for hire or reward'. 'Hire or reward' is defined as 'any payment, consideration, gratuity or benefit directly or indirectly charged, demanded, received or collected by any person for the use of an aircraft'.

The operation of a 'commercial air service' within the meaning of s. 9(1) of the *Aeronautics Act* could therefore relate to a multitude of activities or usages of aircraft in Canada, for example the use of an aircraft to haul passengers or freight, the use of an aircraft as a demonstrator by a dealer or manufacturer, or indeed even the use of the aircraft in a photo session for the purposes of advertisement of another product such as liquor or cigarettes. The statute under which the information at bar has been laid casts a broad net and the prohibition is directed at many diverse and unrelated uses of aircraft in Canada which by the language of s. 9(1) are deemed to be the operation of a 'commercial air service'.

R. v. B. (G.)

[1990] 2 S.C.R. 30, 56 C.C.C. (3d) 200, 77 C.R. (3d) 347 (S.C.C.)

Each accused youth was charged with committing a sexual assault on a child between December 2 and December 20, 1985. The child was 7 years old at that time and 8 when testifying at the trial. The child's testimony appeared to put the date of the assault in late 1984. The trial judge decided that the testimony of the child's mother and that of an expert on child abuse could not accurately establish the date of the offence. He acquitted on the basis that the date of the offence, an essential element of the offence, had not been established beyond a reasonable doubt. He refused to amend the information. When the matter reached the Supreme Court, the highest Court decided that the charge was adequate and should have been amended to accord with the evidence.

WILSON J. (L'Heureux-Dubé, Gonthier, Cory and McLachlin JJ. concurring):—

. . .

(a) *Time of the offence*

The appellants take issue with the Court of Appeal's conclusion that the trial judge erred in finding that the time of the offence was an essential element of the offence and in refusing to amend the information in light of the evidence presented at trial. In support of this ground the appellants advance three main propositions:

1. An information must specify the time, place and matter of an offence in order to afford an accused a full defence and fair trial.

2. If the time specified on the information conflicts with that of the evidence, the information must be quashed.

3. Time is an essential element of any offence, but particularly so when the accused leads alibi evidence. Therefore the time of the offence must be proven beyond a reasonable doubt in order for a conviction to result, and if the evidence is conflicting with respect to time, and the date of the offence cannot be determined, the information must be quashed.

While these three propositions are not entirely separable, and each bears on the balance that must be maintained between eschewing unnecessary technicalities and the right of an accused to make full answer and defence, it is, in my view, most convenient to deal with each proposition individually.

. . .

The appellants rely on the statement in *Brodie* that the time, place and matter of the offence must be specified in support of their argument that the time of the offence is an essential ingredient and must be clearly identified and proven. However, since *Brodie* there has been an increased tendency for the courts, including this court, to reject insufficiency arguments on the basis that they are overly technical and an unnecessary holdover from earlier times. Thus the earlier authorities called for a greater degree of specifity than seems to be required today, but there are also more extensive corrective measures available to the Crown in the present Criminal Code.

. . .

[The Court then reviewed *Côté and WIS Dev. Corp.*]

What the above cases do not address, however, is with what degree of particularity the time of the offence must be spelled out in order to constitute adequate information. The usual practice in alleging the time of the offence is to state the day on which, or a particular time period during which, the offence was committed. The Crown contends, however, that, while time must be specified, the *exact* time need not be identified or proved. The precedential authority from various provincial appellate courts supports the Crown's position.

In *R. v. Colgan* (1986), 54 C.R. (3d) 167, 30 C.C.C. (3d) 183, 43 Man. R. (2d) 101, affirmed [1987] 2 S.C.R. 686, 61 C.R. (3d) 290, 38 C.C.C. (3d) 576, 50 Man. R. (2d) 128, 79 N.R. 350, the accused was charged with unlawfully stealing money "[b]etween the first day of JANUARY, A.D., 1979 and the 31st day of MARCH, A.D., 1985". Prior to plea, counsel for the accused objected to the insufficiency of the information and the trial judge quashed the information on the basis that it did not give the accused enough detail to enable her to identify the transactions alleged to have occurred between the dates specified. Monnin C.J.M., for the majority of the Manitoba Court of Appeal, noted that the main difficulty confronting the trial judge was that the time period was more than six years. He reviewed this court's decisions in *Brodie, Côté,* and *WIS Dev.,* all supra, and concluded that the wording of the count did lift the offence from the general to the particular and that no essential element of the offence was missing. In doing so he noted that the accused had been told the time period, the place, the victim and the offence in terms that were sufficient to describe the nature of the offence although not the specific details of it. In addressing the lengthy time period Monnin C.J.M. said at p. 189:

> There are and have been many similar charges in this jurisdiction. The only difference in this one is that the period of the alleged theft extends over 63 months and as a result it may be difficult for the defence to prepare its case. That is not sufficient ground to invalidate an otherwise proper and complete count. Fairness or difficulty to prepare a defence are matters to be presented to the trier of fact when the evidence is tendered.

Chief Justice Monnin's decision was upheld in this court.

In *Re R. and C. (R.I.)* (1986), 32 C.C.C. (3d) 399, 17 O.A.C. 354, the majority of the Ontario Court of Appeal upheld the validity of an information charging the accused with sexually assaulting a 9-year-old child over a period of six months. The trial judge of his own motion had quashed the information on the ground that it failed to specify the acts constituting the alleged offence of sexual assault and also because of the period of time over which the offence was alleged to have been committed. Krever J.A., with Brooke J.A. concurring, pointed out that, due to the nature of the charge and the age of the victim, complete particularity with respect to time would likely be impossible. Krever J.A. stated at p. 403 that "to require it would make prevention of a serious social problem exceedingly difficult". He concluded that the sufficiency requirements in the Criminal Code were met. See also *R. v. Ryan; R. v. Charbonneau* (1985), 37 M.V.R. 296, 23 C.C.C. (3d) 1, 120 O.A.C. 172, leave to appeal to S.C.C. refused [1986] 1 S.C.R. xiii, 15 O.A.C. 237, 65 N.R. 244, and *R. v. Fox* (1986), 50 C.R. (3d) 370, 24 C.C.C. (3d) 366, leave to appeal to S.C.C. refused [1986] 1 S.C.R. ix, 50 C.R. (3d) xxv [B.C.], which both dealt with offences of impaired driving and held that the exact time need not be specified in the information.

It is apparent from these cases that what constitutes reasonable or adequate information with respect to the act or omission to be proven against the accused will of necessity vary from case to case. The factual matters which underlie some offences permit greater descriptive precision than in the case of other offences. Accordingly, a significant factor in any assessment of the reasonableness of the information furnished is the nature and legal character of the offence charged. It is also apparent, however, that in general an information or indictment will not be quashed just because the exact time of the offence is not specified. Rather, the matter will continue on to trial on the merits. While it is obviously important to provide an accused with sufficient information to enable him or her to identify the transaction and prepare a defence, particularity as to the exact time of the alleged offence is not in the usual course necessary for this purpose. It goes without saying, of course, that there may be cases where it is.

In this case the only particular at issue is the time, place, victim and offence alleged to have been committed all being clearly identified in the information. The appellants submit, however, that time is an essential element of any offence and must be specified and proven. Given the tenor of the decisions referred to, the appellants cannot succeed on this ground. Having regard to the nature of the offence charged and the age of the victim, the information provided was, in my view, adequate.

. . .

In my view, the following conclusions can be drawn from the authorities:
1. While time must be specified in an information in order to provide an accused with reasonable information about the charges brought against him and ensure the possibility of a full defence and a fair trial, exact time need not be specified. The individual circumstances of the particular case may, however, be such that greater precision as to time is required, for instance if there is a paucity of other factual information available with which to identify the transaction.
2. If the time specified in the information is inconsistent with the evidence and time is not an essential element of the offence or crucial to the defence, the variance is not material and the information need not be quashed.
3. If there is conflicting evidence regarding the time of the offence, or the date of the offence cannot be established with precision, the information need not be quashed and a conviction may result, provided that time is not an essential element of the offence or crucial to the defence.
4. If the time of the offence cannot be determined and time is an essential element of the offence or crucial to the defence, a conviction cannot be sustained.

Accordingly, when a court is faced with circumstances in which the time of the offence cannot be determined with precision or the information conflicts with the evidence, the first question that must be asked is whether time is either an essential element of the offence or crucial to the defence. It will be only in cases where this first question is answered affirmatively that the trier of fact must then determine whether the time of the offence has been proven beyond a reasonable doubt. If the answer to the first question is in the negative, a conviction may result even though the time of the offence is not proven, provided that the rest of the Crown's case is proven beyond a reasonable doubt.

In the present case, however, the trial judge failed to address the first question. He found on the evidence before him that the date of the offence had not been established beyond a reasonable doubt, and acquitted the accused. In doing so he erred. . . . Had the trial judge directed himself to the first question, he would have been forced to conclude that time was not an essential element of the offence or crucial to the defence. Indeed, the date of the offence is not generally an essential element of the offence of sexual assault. It is a crime no matter when it is committed. From the record in this case it is also clear that the date of the offence was not crucial to the defence. The appellants' claim on appeal that the date was crucial because alibi evidence was led cannot, in my view, be seriously maintained. At trial each appellant testified and put forward only general denials. They did not lead alibi evidence at that time. Moreover, since the alleged assault took place in the school washroom during recess, the only possible alibi would seem to be that one or more of the appellants was not in attendance at school during the relevant period specified in the information or suggested by the evidence. There is nothing in the record to support this.

I conclude, therefore, that the Court of Appeal was correct in holding that the time of the offence was not an essential element in the circumstances of this case and need not be proven beyond a reasonable doubt. I also agree with the Court of Appeal that, if the assault took place as alleged, the evidence supports the conclusion that it occurred some time between November 1, 1985 and 20th December, 1985 and that amending the information to this effect would not cause irreparable harm to the appellants. Since the trial judge made no findings of fact apart from the time element, the Court of Appeal was correct in concluding that a new trial was necessary.

[The Court later addressed the issue of the credibility of the child witnesses.]

While children may not be able to recount precise details and communicate the when and where of an event with exactitude, this does not mean that they have misconceived what happened to them and who did it. In recent years we have adopted a much more benign attitude to children's evidence, lessening the strict standards of oath-taking and corroboration, and I believe that this is a desirable development. The credibility of every witness who testifies before the courts must, of course, be carefully assessed, but the standard of the "reasonable adult" is not necessarily appropriate in assessing the credibility of young children.

After *B.(G.)*, the Code was amended to insert s. 601(4.1), which makes it clear that a variance between the time or place of an offence is not material.

Under s. 11(*a*) of the Charter "[A]ny person charged with an offence has the right to be informed without unreasonable delay of the specific offence". Decisions so far have been cautious.

Re WARREN
(1983), 35 C.R. (3d) 173 (Ont. H.C.)

LINDEN J.:—

I. THE APPLICATION

This is an application by four accused charged with offences under s. 163 of the Criminal Code, R.S.C. 1970, c. C-34, for an order in lieu of certiorari quashing the informations laid against them and for an order in lieu of prohibition prohibiting any judge of the Provincial Court (Criminal Division) from taking any further proceedings in this matter.

. . .

II. THE FACTS

On 23rd November 1982 the applicants were charged with offences under s. 163 of the Code. Such offences are "hybrid" by virtue of s. 165, which sets out two alternative modes of prosecution:

165. Every one who commits an offence under section 159, 161, 162, 163 or 164 is guilty of

(a) an indictable offence and is liable to imprisonment for two years, or

(b) an offence punishable on summary conviction.

The informations charging the accused make no reference to s. 165(*a*) or (*b*). The Crown did not indicate whether it would be proceeding summarily or by indictment until 5th April 1983, when the applicants appeared for preliminary inquiry. On that date, an assistant Crown attorney informed the applicants that he intended to proceed summarily, with the result that a trial rather than a preliminary inquiry would be held.

At the outset of the proceedings, the applicants applied to DiCecco Prov. J. for an order quashing the informations and preventing the Crown from electing to proceed summarily. His Honour dismissed the application and permitted the Crown to make its election. DiCecco Prov. J. found that s. 165 is merely a procedural provision, that s. 11(*a*) of the Canadian Charter of Rights and Freedoms, Constitution Act, 1982, Pt. I, which provides that an accused has the right "to be informed without unreasonable delay of the specific offence", does not apply, and that s. 11(*a*) guarantees the accused's right to be informed of the acts constituting the offence with which he is charged, but does not grant any rights with respect to how a charge is to be proceeded with. His Honour noted, however, that preparation for a preliminary inquiry differs from preparation for trial. There could be unfairness to the accused as a result of the Crown waiting until the date set for the preliminary inquiry to make an election. As a result, His Honour permitted the calling of the defence to be adjourned, although he required the Crown to present its case that day.

III. THE LAW

One of the grounds for this application is that the informations charging the applicants fail to disclose specific offences, and thus contravene s. 11(*a*) of the Charter of Rights. The applicants submit that the words "specific offence" encompass the substantive elements of an offence, the procedure to be followed in prosecuting the offence, and penal consequences following conviction. In other words, an accused "must be informed without unreasonable delay" of, among other things, whether the Crown is proceeding by way of summary conviction or by indictment. Since s. 165 sets out two possible modes of procedure, two separate offences are created, even though the substantive elements of both offences are the same. The Crown right of election thus is part of the "specific offence".

The meaning of the phrase "specific offence" has been considered in only one reported decision. In *R. v. Nijhar* (1982), 70 C.C.C. (2d) 318, 2 C.R.R. 43 (B.C. Co. Ct.), Perry Co. Ct. J. dismissed an application by an accused to quash an indictment charging him with alternative offences. His Honour concluded that the words "specific offence" in s. 11(*a*) cannot be extended to take away the Crown's right to lay several alternative charges (p. 319). In obiter, Perry Co. Ct. J. noted that, even if an accused is not informed of the specific offence with which he is charged within a reasonable time, any prejudice "can be dealt with by an application to adjourn in order to allow time to rectify any alleged unreasonable delay" (p. 319).

Nijhar is of some assistance on this application because it indicates that the words "specific offence" in s. 11(*a*) are not intended to fetter the Crown's discretionary powers with respect to the procedure to be followed in the prosecution of criminal charges. In his article "The Role of the Accused in the Criminal Process" in The Canadian Charter of Rights and Freedoms: Commentary (1982), edited by W.S. Tarnopolsky and G.-A. Beaudoin, at p. 335, E. Ratushny appears to confirm that those words should be construed to mean only the substantive elements of an offence. His commentary upon the importance of the guarantee in s. 11(*a*) makes no reference to an accused's "right" to be told of how the Crown intends to proceed. At p. 352:

> It is easy to see why the requirement of a proper accusation is an important protection to an accused. A specific accusation presupposes a specific offence in law. It, therefore, provides an opportunity at the outset for the accused to challenge the authority of the officials of the state to subject him to the criminal process. If no offence exists in law, the accusation can be attacked and quashed, thereby terminating the proceeding.
>
> It is also important in specifying the exact conduct which is said to constitute the offence. The accused must be aware of such details as the specific time and place, when and where the offence occurred, the manner in which it is alleged to have been committed and the identity of the victim, if any, so that he may prepare his defence. It could be argued that s. 11(*a*) requires only that the 'offence' be specified (for example, rape, robbery, etc.) since it makes no reference to identifying the details of the act or transaction. However, once again, to take such a narrow interpretation would render the protection a sham.
>
> The accused should also know his accuser so that he might be aware of any improper motives and bring legal action against that accuser if the prosecution is malicious.
>
> The accusation provides another important protection to the accused. It defines the scope of the proceedings against him. The evidence and argument must relate to the specific charge. It is generally not permissible, for example, to bring in evidence of other unlawful or immoral conduct on the part of the accused which does not relate to the accusation which he is facing. The accused is to be tried with respect to specific alleged misconduct and not for the kind of person he is.

Canada's international obligations also are of assistance in determining the meaning of s. 11(*a*) of the Charter. Although legislation has not been enacted to incorporate the United Nations International Covenant on Civil and Political Rights into the domestic law of Canada, the Covenant can be used to help construe ambiguous provisions of a domestic statute, if there are no provisions of the domestic statute contrary to the portions of the Covenant being relied upon: M. Cohen and A. Bayefsky, "The Canadian Charter of Rights and Freedoms in Public International Law" (1983), 61 Can. Bar Rev.

265, at pp. 295-96. Since the meaning of s. 11(*a*) is not completely clear on its face, resort should be had to the Covenant as a tool of statutory interpretation.

Article 14, para. 3(*a*) of the Covenant grants a right very similar to that guaranteed by s. 11(*a*):

> Art. 14-3. In the determination of any criminal charge against him, everyone shall be entitled to the following minimum guarantees, in full equality:
>
> (a) To be informed promptly and in detail in a language which he understands of the *nature and cause of the charge* against him. (The italics are mine.)

Surely the words "nature and cause of the charge" do not include the mode of procedure to be employed in prosecuting the offence. Since the Parliament of Canada is presumed not to act in violation of its international obligations, s. 11(*a*) of the Charter should be construed in a manner consistent with art. 14 of the Covenant. As a result, I must conclude that the right to be informed of the "specific offence" means the right to be informed of the substantive offence and the acts or conduct which allegedly form the basis of that charge. It does not give an accused the right to be informed of how the Crown will exercise its discretion with respect to the manner of prosecution. There are not two offences set out here, but only one. DiCecco Prov. J. thus was correct in dismissing the application to quash the informations laid against the applicants. Consider whether the following charges are sufficient.

Application dismissed.

In *R. v. S. (A.)* (1998), 19 C.R. (5th) 393, 130 C.C.C. (3d) 320 (Ont. C.A.), leave to appeal refused (1999), 137 C.C.C. (3d) 393 (S.C.C.), the court relied on s. 11(a) for the proposition that a trial requires a specified charge. Here, the offence charged of anal intercourse had been declared unconstitutional so the accused was entitled to an acquittal.

Are the following charges sufficient?

PROBLEM 8

The accused is charged that he "did on the twelfth day of February, 1984, in the City of Trail, County of Kootenay, Province of British Columbia, while his ability to drive a motor vehicle was impaired by alcohol or a drug did drive a motor vehicle, contrary to the form of Statutes in such case made or provided". Compare *R. v. Nadin* (1971), 14 C.R.N.S. 201 (B.C. C.A.). See too *R. v. Fox* (1986), 50 C.R. (3d) 370, 24 C.C.C. (3d) 366, leave to appeal refused (1987), 50 C.R. (3d) xxv (note) (S.C.C.), *R. v. Colgan* (1986), 54 C.R. (3d) 167, 30 C.C.C. (3d) 183, affirmed [1987] 2 S.C.R. 686, 61 C.R. (3d) 290, 38 C.C.C. (3d) 576 (S.C.C.) and *G.B.*, above.

PROBLEM 9

The accused is charged with trafficking a drug contrary to s. 5(1) of the Controlled Drugs and Substances Act, S.C. 1996, c. 19 as amended. The definition section in the Act defines "traffic" *inter alia* as "to sell, administer, give, transfer, transport, send or deliver the substance".

Can the accused successfully argue that not specifying which of these acts is charged is void for insufficiency? Compare *Mills v. R.* (1972), 16 C.R.N.S. 382 (Sask. Q.B.); reversed without reasons in (1972), 18 C.R.N.S. 400 (Sask. C.A.), *R. v. Peebles* (1975), 24 C.C.C. (2d) 144 (B.C. C.A.), and *R. v. Labine* (1975), 23 C.C.C. (2d) 567 (Ont. C.A.). Must the Crown particularize the specific drug? See *R. v. Saunders*, [1990] 1 S.C.R. 1020, 77 C.R. (3d) 397, 56 C.C.C. (3d) 220 (S.C.C.).

PROBLEM 10

The information reads that the accused "on or about the ninth day of September, 1984, at the City of Brantford in the said County, did wrongfully and without lawful authority for the purpose of compelling another person to abstain from doing anything that he has a lawful right to do, unlawfully obstruct a highway, contrary to s. 423(1)(g) of the Criminal Code of Canada". Compare *R. v. Rowley* (1972), 7 C.C.C. (2d) 230 (Ont. C.A.).

PROBLEM 11

The accused is charged that he "on or about the eleventh day of April, A.D. 1984 at or near the City of Penticton, County of Yale, Province of British Columbia, did unlawfully steal a pizza from William Eggli and at the time thereof did use threats of violence to William Eggli, contrary to the form of statute in such case made and provided". Section 343 of the Criminal Code specifies four types of robbery including under subsection (a) one who "steals, and for the purpose of extorting whatever is stolen or to prevent or overcome resistance to the stealing, uses violence or threats of violence to a person or property".

This charge follows the form of a charge of robbery under s. 343(a) suggested in Martin's Annual Criminal Code as follows:

A.B. on .... at .... did steal [*specify property stolen, e.g., the sum of fifty dollars*] from C.D. and at the time thereof did use violence [*or threats of violence*] to C.D. contrary *etc.*

However the form suggested in Snow's Annotated Criminal Code is more specific:

A.B., at ...., on ...., did steal [*specify what*], and for the purpose of extorting what was stolen [*or* to prevent (*or* overcome) resistance to the stealing], did use violence [*or* threats of violence], to wit [*specify*], against C.D. [*or* the property of C.D.], contrary to section 303 of the Criminal Code.

Martin's Criminal Code, but not Snow's, contains a suggested general charge of robbery as follows:

A.B. on .... at .... did rob C.D. of [*specify property taken, e.g., a wallet containing personal papers and the sum of fifty dollars*] contrary *etc.*

Would your answer be any different had the Crown chosen to use this alternative form instead? What if the Crown had chosen to use the more specific version in Snow's but had got the section number wrong, specifying section 343(*b*)?

Compare *Re Livingstone and R.* (1975), 29 C.C.C. (2d) 557 (B.C. S.C.).

PROBLEM 12

The accused is charged that "on or about the 7th day of August, 1983, at or near Parksville, in the Province of British Columbia, he did commit a sexual assault on M.M. contrary to the Criminal Code". Compare *R. v. Cook* (1985), 46 C.R. (3d) 129 (B.C. C.A.) and see *R. v. B. (G.)* above and *R. v. W. (A.G.)*, [1993] 1 S.C.R. 3, 78 C.C.C. (3d) 302, 17 C.R. (4th) 393 (S.C.C.).

Compare *Myhren v. R.* (1985), 48 C.R. (3d) 270 (N.W.T. S.C.) and *R. v. Atatahak* (1986), 51 C.R. (3d) 286 (N.W.T. S.C.). See too *R. v. C. (R.I.)* (1986), 32 C.C.C. (3d) 399 (Ont. C.A.).

PROBLEM 13

By information sworn April 20, 1993, the accused are charged that between the 10th day of September, 1991 and the 10th day of May, 1992, at or near Plymouth, in the County of Pictou, Province of Nova Scotia, they did:

(1) By means of unlawful acts or omissions cause the deaths of Larry Arthur Bell, Robert Steven Doyle, Earle Eric McIsaac, Harry Alliston McCallum, Romeo Andrew Short, Ferris Todd Dewan, Adonis Joseph Dollimont, Charles Robert Fraser, Trevor Martin Jahn, Eugene William Johnson, Myles Daniel Gillis, Remi Joseph Drolet, Lawrence Elwyn James, Peter Francis Vickers, George James Monroe, John Thomas Bates, Bennie Joseph Benoit, Wayne Michael Conway, Roy Edward Feltmate, John Phillip Halloran, Randolph Brian House, Stephen Paul Lilley, Michael Frederick MacKay, Angus Joseph MacNeil, Glenn David Martin and Danny James Poplar, and did therefore commit the offence of manslaughter, contrary to Section 236 of the Criminal Code; and

(2) By the manner in which they operated a coal mine under the company name of Westray Coal, also known as Westray Coal Mine, or in omitting to do anything that it was their duty to do, show wanton or reckless disregard for the lives or safety of other persons and did thereby cause the deaths of Larry Arthur Bell, Robert Steven Doyle, Earle Eric McIsaac, Harry Alliston McCallum, Romeo Andrew Short, Ferris Todd Dewan, Adonis Joseph Dollimont, Charles Robert Fraser, Trevor Martin Jahn, Eugene William Johnson, Myles Daniel Gillis, Remi Joseph Drolet, Lawrence Elwyn James, Peter Francis Vickers, George James Monroe, John Thomas Bates, Bennie Joseph Benoit, Wayne Michael Conway, Roy Edward Feltmate, John Phillip Halloran, Randolph

Brian House, Stephen Paul Lilley, Michael Frederick MacKay, Angus Joseph MacNeil, Glenn David Martin and Danny James Poplar, and did thereby commit the offence of criminal negligence causing death, contrary to Section 220 of the Criminal Code.

See *R. v. Curragh Inc.* (1993), 124 N.S.R. (2d) 59, 345 A.P.R. 59 (N.S. Prov. Ct.). Compare *R. v. Curragh Inc.* (1993), 125 N.S.R. (2d) 185 (*sub nom. R. v. Curragh Inc. (No. 2)*), 349 A.P.R. 185 (N.S. Prov. Ct.).

(ii) Duplicity

Duplicity is really another aspect of sufficiency.

The common law against duplicity prohibits alternative charges in a single count. There is nothing duplicitous about alternative counts. A duplicitous charge is confusing to the accused and prejudices a fair defence. In the case of proceedings on indictment the relevant Code provisions are s. 581(1) and the apparently contradictory s. 590(1) (compare, however, Teplitsky, "Duplicity and the Single Transaction: A Reconciliation" (1977), 37 C.R.N.S. 265). In the case of summary conviction proceedings there is a distinct s. 789(1)(*b*) (although s. 581(1) and (6) still apply). Again it is important to remember that a motion to quash in respect of a defect apparent on the face of the charge must be brought before the plea and thereafter only by leave of the Court (s. 601(1)).

R. v. SAULT STE. MARIE
[1978] 2 S.C.R. 1299, 3 C.R. (3d) 30 (S.C.C.)

DICKSON J.:—The appeal raises a preliminary issue as to whether the charge, as laid, is duplicitous and, if so, whether ss. 732(1) and 755(4) [re-en. 1974-75-76, c. 93, s. 94] of the Criminal Code, R.S.C. 1970, c. C-34, preclude the accused city of Sault Ste. Marie from raising the duplicity claim for the first time on appeal. It will be convenient to deal first with the preliminary point and then consider the concept of liability in relation to public welfare offences.

The city of Sault Ste. Marie was charged that it did discharge or cause to be discharged or permitted to be discharged or deposited, materials into Cannon Creek and Root River, or on the shore or bank thereof, or in such place along the side that might impair the quality of the water in Cannon Creek and Root River, between 13th March and 11th September 1972. The charge was laid under s. 32(1) of the Ontario Water Resources Act, R.S.O. 1970, c. 332 [title am. 1972, c. 1, s. 70(1)], which provides, so far as relevant, that every municipality or person that discharges or deposits or causes or permits the discharge or deposit of any material of any kind into any water course or on any shore or bank thereof or in any place that may impair the quality of water, is guilty of an offence and, on summary conviction, is liable on first conviction to a fine of not more than $5,000 and on each subsequent conviction to a fine of not more than $10,000 or to imprisonment for a term of not more than one year or to both fine and imprisonment.

Although the facts do not rise above the routine, the proceedings have to date had the anxious consideration of five courts. The city was acquitted in Provincial Court (Criminal Division) but was convicted following a trial de novo on a Crown appeal. A further appeal by the city to the Divisional Court was allowed and the conviction was quashed [30 C.C.C. (2d) at 260]. The Court of Appeal for Ontario on yet another appeal directed a new trial [30 C.C.C. (2d) 257 at 283]. Because of the importance of the legal issues, this court granted leave to the Crown to appeal and leave to the city to cross-appeal.

To relate briefly the facts, the city on 18th November 1970 entered into an agreement with Cherokee Disposal and Construction Co. Ltd. for the disposal of all refuse originating in the city. Under the terms of the agreement, Cherokee became obligated to furnish a site and adequate labour, material and equipment. The site selected bordered Cannon Creek which, it would appear, runs into the Root River. The method of disposal adopted is known as the "area" or "continuous slope" method of sanitary land fill, whereby garbage is compacted in layers which are covered each day by natural sand or gravel.

Prior to 1970, the site had been covered with a number of fresh-water springs that flowed into Cannon Creek. Cherokee dumped material to cover and submerge these springs and then placed garbage and wastes over such material. The garbage and wastes in due course formed a high mound sloping steeply toward, and within 20 feet of, the creek. Pollution resulted. Cherokee was convicted of a breach of s. 32(1) of the Ontario Water Resources Act, the section under which the city has been charged. The question now before the court is whether the city is also guilty of an offence under that section.

In dismissing the charge at first instance, the judge found that the city had had nothing to do with the actual disposal operations, that Cherokee was an independent contractor and that its employees were not employees of the city. On the appeal de novo Judge Vannini found the offence to be one of strict liability and he convicted. The Divisional Court in setting aside the judgment found that the charge was duplicitous. As a secondary point, the Divisional Court also held that the charge required mens rea with respect to causing or permitting a discharge. When the case reached the Court of Appeal that court held that the conviction could not be quashed on the ground of duplicity because there had been no challenge to the information at trial. The Court of Appeal agreed, however, that the charge was one requiring proof of mens rea. A majority of the court (Brooke and Howland JJ.A.) held there was not sufficient evidence to establish mens rea and ordered a new trial. In the view of Lacourciere J.A., dissenting, the inescapable inference to be drawn from the findings of fact of Judge Vannini was that the city had known of the potential impairment of waters of Cannon Creek and Root River and had failed to exercise its clear powers of control.

The divers, and diverse, judicial opinions to date on the points under consideration reflect the dubiety in these branches of the law.

The duplicity point

Turning then to the question of duplicity, and whether the information charged the city with several offences or merely one offence which might be committed in different modes. The argument is that s. 32(1) of the Ontario Water Resources Act charges three offences: (i) discharging; (ii) causing to be discharged; (iii) permitting to be discharged, deleterious materials. The applicable principle is well established: if the information in one count charges more than one offence, it is bad for duplicity: *Kipp v. A.G. Ont.,* [1965] S.C.R. 57, 45 C.R. 1, [1965] 2 C.C.C. 133.

The rule against multiplicity of charges in an information is contained in s. 724(1) of the Code, which reads as follows:

> 724. (1) In proceedings to which this Part applies, the information . . .
>
> (b) may charge more than one offence or relate to more than one matter of complaint, but where more than one offence is charged or the information relates to more than one matter of complaint, each offence or matter of complaint, as the case may be, shall be set out in a separate count.

Section 731(a) provides, however, that no information shall be deemed to charge two offences by reason only that it states that the alleged offence was committed in different modes.

Several tests have been suggested for determining whether an indictment or information is multiplicitous. Probably the best known test is that enunciated by Avory J. in *R. v. Surrey Justices; Ex parte Witherick,* [1932] 1 K.B. 450 at 452 (D.C.). The charge was that of driving without due care and attention and without reasonable consideration for other persons. Avory J. said that if a person may do one without the other, it followed as a matter of law that an information which charged him in the alternative would be bad. In *R. v. Madill,* [1943] 1 W.W.R. 365, 79 C.C.C. 206 at 210, [1943] 2 D.L.R. 570 (Alta. C.A.), Ford J.A. applied the test of "whether evidence can be given of distinct acts, committed by the person charged, constituting two or more offences", and in *R. v. Internat. Nickel Co.* (1972), 10 C.C.C. (2d) 44 at 48 (Ont. C.A.), Arnup J.A. expressed the view that if a section containing two or more elements is to be construed as containing only one offence, one must be able to state with precision the essence of the single offence.

Each of these tests is helpful as far as it goes, but each is too general to provide a clear demarcation in concrete instances. This is shown by the variety of cases and the diversity of opinion in this case itself. To resolve the matter one must recall, I think, the policy basis of the rule against multiplicity and duplicity. The rule developed during a period of extreme formality and technicality in the preferring of indictments and laying of informations. It grew from the humane desire of judges to alleviate the severity of the law in an age when many crimes were still classified as felonies, for which the punishment was death by the gallows. The slightest defect made an indictment a nullity. That age has passed. Parliament has made it abundantly clear in those sections of the Criminal Code having to do with the form of indictments and informations that the punctilio of an earlier age is no longer to bind us. We must look for substance and not petty formalities.

The duplicity rule has been justified on two grounds: to be fair to the accused in the preparation of his defence and to enable him to plead autrefois convict in the future. As Avory J. said in *R. v. Surrey Justices; Ex parte Witherick,* supra, at p. 452:

> It is an elementary principle that an information must not charge offences in the alternative, since the defendant cannot then know with precision with what he is charged and of what he is convicted and may be prevented on a future occasion from pleading autrefois convict.

The problem of raising a defence of autrefois convict is illusory even when there is duplicity. It is difficult to see as a practical matter why the Crown would begin new proceedings after having just concluded a successful prosecution. Even if there were a prosecution, it could not succeed. Assume conviction of the city on a charge of (i) discharging, (ii) causing discharge of or (iii) permitting discharge of a pollutant at a stated time and place. If another charge were laid at a later date in respect of (i) or (ii) or (iii), as related to the same pollutant and the same time and place, the new charge would be based on the same cause or matter which had already formed the basis of a conviction, and a further conviction would be barred: *Kienapple v. R.,* [1975] 1 S.C.R. 729, 26 C.R.N.S. 1, 15 C.C.C. (2d) 524, 1 N.R. 322, 44 D.L.R. (3d) 351. It is equally clear that no problem of autrefois acquit arises, even where there is duplicity, because an acquittal means acquittal on all the offences charged, and thus there is no difficulty in raising the defence of autrefois acquit to a later charge of one of the same offences alone.

In my opinion, the primary test should be a practical one, based on the only valid justification for the rule against duplicity: does the accused know the case he has to meet, or is he prejudiced in the preparation of his defence by ambiguity in the charge? Viewed in that light, as well as by the other tests mentioned above, I think we must conclude that the charge in the present case was not duplicitous. There was nothing ambiguous or uncertain in the charge. The city knew the case it had to meet. Section 32(1) of the Ontario Water Resources Act is concerned with only one matter, pollution. That is the gist of the charge and the evil against which the offence is aimed. One cognate act is the subject of the prohibition. Only one generic offence was charged, the essence of which was "polluting", and that offence could be committed in one or more of several modes. There is nothing wrong in specifying alternative methods of committing an offence, or in embellishing the periphery, provided only one offence is to be found at the focal point of the charge. Furthermore, although not determinative, it is not irrelevant that the information has been laid in the precise words of the section.

I am satisfied that the legislature did not intend to create different offences for polluting, dependent upon whether one deposited or caused to be deposited or permitted to be deposited. The legislation is aimed at one class of offender only, those who pollute.

In *R. v. Matspeck Const. Co.,* [1965] 2 O.R. 730, [1965] 4 C.C.C. 78, Hughes J. considered the very section now under study and, adopting the approach I favour, concluded that the charge was not duplicitous. The judge said, p. 732:

There can be no doubt in the mind of accused that he is charged with having in one mode or another, discharged or deposited material into water and that this material may have impaired its quality.

On the other hand, in the English case of *Ross Hillman Ltd. v. Bond*, [1974] Q.B. 435, 59 Cr. App. R. 42, [1974] 2 All E.R. 287 (D.C.), where very similar language was used, May J. said, p. 291, that the Act (in that case s. 40(5)(*b*) of the Road Traffic Act, 1972) created three distinct types of offence. I think that the authority of the English cases in this area of the law must be carefully considered and their aid discounted to the extent that the statutory provisions applicable differ from those contained in our Code.

I conclude that the charge in this case is not duplicitous. It is unnecessary, therefore, to consider whether a defendant can raise a duplicity objection for the first time on appeal.

Consider whether the following charges are duplicitous.

PROBLEM 14

The accused is charged with driving a motor vehicle or having care or control of that motor vehicle while impaired. Compare *R. v. Phillips* (1958), 29 C.R. 127 (Sask. Q.B.).

PROBLEM 15

The Crown has laid a single count of possession of child pornography alleging conduct over a period of time. During that period of time, there have been statutory amendments that changed the possible defences during the continuous transaction. Compare *R. v. Katigbak*, 2011 SCC 48, [2011] 3 S.C.R. 326, 276 C.C.C. (3d) 1, 88 C.R. (6th) 1 (S.C.C.).

In *R. v. Greenfield*, [1973] 1 W.L.R. 1151, [1973] 3 All E.R. 1050 (C.A.) it was held that duplicity in a count is a matter of form and cannot relate to the evidence called in support of the count. This is not true in Canada as there is authority holding a count duplicitous not because it is objectionable on its face but because the evidence adduced at trial relates to the commission of more than one offence: see *R. v. Hulan* (1969), 6 C.R.N.S. 296, [1970] 1 C.C.C. 36 (Ont. C.A.); *R. v. Rafael* (1972), 7 C.C.C. (2d) 325 (Ont. C.A.), and *R. v. Barnes* (1975), 2 C.R. (3d) 310, 26 C.C.C. (2d) 112 (N.S. C.A.).

(iii) Improper Joinder of Counts

An indictment or information can contain any number of counts (ss. 591(1) and 789(1)(*b*)). The only exception used to be a provision in s. 589 that, where there is a count of murder, the only additional count that could be joined was a further count of murder. However, in 1991, s. 589 was amended to allow other counts arising from the same transaction as the murder or on consent of the accused.

In *R. v. Phillips*, [1983] 2 S.C.R. 161, 35 C.R. (3d) 193, 8 C.C.C. (3d) 118 (S.C.C.) it was held that a trial judge is without jurisdiction to try together separate informations or indictments, even if the parties consent. *Phillips* was strongly criticized as excessively technical: see David Doherty, "Phillips: An Unwarranted Return to the Punctilio of an Earlier Age" (1983), 35 C.R. (3d) 203. In *R. v. Clunas*, [1992] 1 S.C.R. 595, 11 C.R. (4th) 238, 6 O.R. (3d) 672 (note), 70 C.C.C. (3d) 115 (S.C.C.) the Supreme Court reversed *Phillips* and held that there can be joinder of offences or of accused charged in separate informations on consent or where the offences or accused could initially have been jointly charged. The Court also held that summary conviction offences can be joined with indictable offences where the trial is in a provincial court without preliminary inquiry. Now, thankfully, where there are separate informations the trials may proceed jointly on consent of the parties and even sometimes without their consent. It will no longer be necessary for the Crown to lay new information to put separate charges on one piece of paper or for trial judges to resort to the device of deeming evidence taken during one trial to have been tendered at the second.

(b) Saving Devices

(i) Particulars

In response to an attack for insufficiency or to a demand by a defence counsel the court may order that the Crown furnish particulars under s. 587. Alternatively, particulars may be forthcoming from the Crown as a result of an informal dialogue or exchange of correspondence. If this informal process is considered satisfactory by the defence it is imperative for the protection of the accused that these particulars be placed on the court record by order of the court. This is because the Crown is bound by particulars ordered and must prove the particularized charge. This was always clear at common law and s. 587(3)(*c*) now provides that the "trial shall proceed in all respects as if the indictment has been amended to conform with the particular".

Whether particulars are ordered is in the discretion of the trial judge. The only limiting phrase, and not much of a limitation at that, appears in s. 587(1), which refers to the trial judge being "satisfied that it is necessary for a fair trial".

The function of particulars in a conspiracy trial was held by Pennell J. in *R. v. C.G.E. Co.* (1974), 17 C.C.C. (2d) 433 at 443 (Ont. H.C.) to be twofold:

> Primarily their function is to give such exact and reasonable information to the accused respecting the charge against him as will enable him to establish fully his defence. The second purpose is to facilitate the administration of justice .... The secondary purpose can be illustrated quite simply. When a conspiracy count involves an alleged widespread complicated conspiracy for the accomplishment of a purpose going beyond the performance of individual acts, the particulars furnished will assist the Judge in ruling on the relevancy of the evidence. To adopt a homely form of words, a trial circumscribed by particulars will not wander all over the shop and will foreclose an unreal controversy.

The same court, however, held that the Crown should not be encumbered with an order to particularize the precise date and, "to a lesser degree", the precise time. It subsequently held that 38 pages of fairly general particulars sufficed, approval being given to the opinion of Boyd McBride J. in *R. v. McGavin Bakeries* (1950), 99 C.C.C. 330 at 339 (Alta. S.C.) that:

> the intention of [s. 516] is not, in my opinion, that a fair trial requires the Crown to give as particulars, details of all the minutiae of acts or omissions over nearly 17 years likely to be adduced in evidence in support of the charge. (at pp. 448-9)

In *R. v. WIS Dev. Corp.,* [1984] 1 S.C.R. 485, 40 C.R. (3d) 97 (S.C.C.) the Supreme Court held that the insufficiency in respect of factual details vitiated the charge brought by way of summary conviction and furthermore, reluctantly, that this was a defect of substance which could not be remedied by particulars or amendment in view of the particular statutory provisions applying to summary conviction proceedings. These provisions were repealed in 1985 so, presumably, such a deficient charge could now be saved.

THATCHER v. R.
(1984), 42 C.R. (3d) 259 (Sask. Q.B.)

MAHER J.:—Following a preliminary inquiry held at Regina, Saskatchewan, the accused, W. Colin Thatcher, was on 28th June 1984 committed for trial on a charge that he did unlawfully cause the death of JoAnn Kay Wilson, and did thereby commit first degree murder contrary to s. 218 [re-en. 1974-75-76, s. 105, s. 5] of the Criminal Code, R.S.C. 1970, c. C-34. Counsel on behalf of Mr. Thatcher has launched the present motion seeking the following relief:

> (1) an order directing the prosecutor to furnish particulars to the accused, such particulars to further describe the means by which the accused is alleged to have caused the death of JoAnn Kay Wilson, the order being sought pursuant to s. 516(1)(*f*) of the Criminal Code.

. . .

No indictment has as yet been filed but the application proceeded on the understanding, accepted by counsel on behalf of the Crown, that the indictment intended to be preferred against the accused would be in substantially the same terms as the information upon which he was committed for trial.

It is the contention of Mr. Allbright that from a perusal of the preliminary inquiry it appears to be the theory of the Crown that the accused, Thatcher, did the act that caused the death of JoAnn Kay Wilson. There was, however, further evidence adduced on behalf of the Crown from which a jury could possibly conclude that the killing was done by a person or persons unknown. If such is the evidence at the trial Thatcher would have to face the possibility of a jury finding him to be a party to and therefore guilty of the offence of murder as an aider or abetter pursuant to the provisions of s. 21 of the Criminal Code.

Mr. Allbright takes the position that he has the right to know the case he has to meet and that his approach and manner of defence could vary and would depend upon whether the position of the Crown is that Thatcher committed the act himself or that it was done by a person or persons unknown. Accordingly, he asks the court to order the Crown to decide whether the accused is alleged to have committed the offence or is a party to an offence that was committed by others, and to so state in the form of particulars that will be binding upon the Crown.

Mr. Kujawa admits that the position of the Crown is that the majority of the evidence points to the accused having done the act, but that an intervening person is not excluded. He contends that the indictment as proposed is good in law and questions the right of the court to make the order requested by counsel for the defence.

Section 516 of the Code empowers the court to order the prosecution to furnish particulars when it is satisfied that it is necessary for a fair trial, and the application is sought in this case under subs. (1)(f), which empowers the court to make an order for particulars "further describing the means by which an offence is alleged to have been committed".

There are a number of authorities that deal with applications for particulars in circumstances similar to the facts in the present case. In *R. v. Lukich*, 2 C.R. 73, [1946] 2 W.W.R. 508, 87 C.C.C. 83, the Appellate Division of the Alberta Supreme Court directed a new trial on a charge against an accused of keeping a common gaming house when the justices who tried the matter ordered the Crown to specify which of the different kinds of gaming houses specified in the Code was the one to which the charge related. Speaking on behalf of the court, Harvey C.J.A. said at p. 85:

> It seems clear that the Justices were in error in compelling the prosecutor to charge the offence, by particulars or otherwise, under some one of the different definitions of s. 226 [of the Criminal Code, R.S.C. 1927, c. 36].

> Particulars are only for the purpose of seeing that justice is done and to give an opportunity to the accused to make a proper defence, but they should not be required when the result would be an injustice in preventing the prosecution from establishing proof of an offence.

A case almost directly on point is *R. v. Govedarov* (1975), 3 O.R. (2d) 23, 25 C.R.N.S. 1, 16 C.C.C. (2d) 238, affirmed (sub nom. *R. v. Popovic*) [1976] 2 S.C.R. 308, 32 C.R.N.S. 54, 25 C.C.C. (2d) 161, 62 D.L.R. (3d) 56, 7 N.R. 231, a decision of the Ontario Court of Appeal. The accused were convicted of non-capital murder arising out of the death of a restaurant dishwasher during a breaking and entering. The jury were instructed on s. 213 of the Criminal Code, providing for constructive murder in the course of, inter alia, burglary and robbery. One of the grounds of appeal was the failure of the trial judge to order particulars as to which of the offences enumerated in s. 213 [am. 1974-75-76, c. 93, s. 13; c. 105, s. 29; 1980-81-82-83, c. 125, s. 15] the Crown relied on. In rejecting this ground of appeal, Martin J.A. said at pp. 269-70:

> The indictment had been preceded by a preliminary hearing lasting several days. Clearly, the purpose of the application for particulars was not to require the prosecution to provide the accused with additional details with respect to matters referred to in the indictment in order that the accused might be more fully informed of the act or omission charged against them *but was to restrict the*

> *prosecution to reliance on a part only of the definition of murder contained in the Criminal Code.*

(The italics are mine.)

Martin J.A. went on to review the authorities relating to the providing of particulars, which hold that the true function of particulars is to give such information as is sufficient to enable a defendant fairly to defend himself when in court, but on the other hand are not to fetter the prosecutor in the conduct of his case. He concluded at p. 271:

> The accused in the instant case were charged with murder. The Crown was entitled to rely upon any part or parts of the definition of murder which were applicable to the facts which it was open to the jury to find were proved.

This decision was referred to and applied later by Martin J.A. in delivering the unanimous decision of the Ontario Court of Appeal in *R. v. Khan* (1982), 36 O.R. (2d) 399, 66 C.C.C. (2d) 32. Therein it was held that particulars of the offence alleged to have been committed should not be ordered on a charge of breaking and entering with intent to commit an indictable offence under s. 306(1)(*a*) of the Criminal Code. It was open to the Crown to lead evidence as to the indictable offence or offences that may have been committed by the accused, and it would be inappropriate

> to require particulars to be furnished particularizing the particular indictable offence alleged to be intended to be committed in an indictment under s. 306(1)(*a*) [p. 37].

And finally there is to be found in the recently published text Criminal Pleadings and Practice in Canada (1983), by Eugene G. Ewaschuk (now Ewaschuk J. of the Ontario High Court), two statements by the learned author on this particular point. He says at para. 9.135 [p. 219]:

> A court will not order the Crown to particularize which underlying or predicate offence it relies on to establish liability for the offence charged . . .

And, after quoting the authorities to which I have referred, concludes [at p. 219]:

> It would be inappropriate in such cases to order particulars as to the Crown's theory of the accused's liability since to do so would nullify the scope of the accused's liability as provided by statute.

From the foregoing authorities I am satisfied that the accused is not entitled to an order for the particulars he seeks. If there is evidence upon which a properly instructed jury could find that the accused committed the offence or that he was a party to the commission of an offence by a person or persons unknown, it must be left to the jury to make either of such findings and their right to do so may not be restricted by an order for particulars. The application for particulars is accordingly dismissed.

(ii) Amendment

Since amendments to the Criminal Code in 1955, a trial judge has had a very wide discretion to amend an indictment or an information (ss. 601, 795). See too ss. 590(2) and (3).

601. (1) An objection to an indictment preferred under this Part or to a count in an indictment, for a defect apparent on its face, shall be taken by motion to quash the indictment or count before the accused enters a plea, and, after the accused has entered a plea, only by leave of the court before which the proceedings take place. The court before which an objection is taken under this section may, if it considers it necessary, order the indictment or count to be amended to cure the defect.

(2) Subject to this section, a court may, on the trial of an indictment, amend the indictment or a count therein or a particular that is furnished under section 587, to make the indictment, count or particular conform to the evidence, where there is a variance between the evidence and

(a) a count in the indictment as preferred; or

(b) a count in the indictment

    (i) as amended, or

    (ii) as it would have been if it had been amended in conformity with any particular that has been furnished pursuant to section 587.

(3) Subject to this section, a court shall, at any stage of the proceedings, amend the indictment or a count therein as may be necessary where it appears

(a) that the indictment has been preferred under a particular Act of Parliament instead of another Act of Parliament;

(b) that the indictment or a count thereof

    (i) fails to state or states defectively anything that is requisite to constitute the offence,

    (ii) does not negative an exception that should be negatived,

    (iii) is in any way defective in substance,

and the matters to be alleged in the proposed amendment are disclosed by the evidence taken on the preliminary inquiry or on the trial; or

(c) that the indictment or a count thereof is in any way defective in form.

(4) The court shall, in considering whether or not an amendment should be made to the indictment or a count in it, consider

(a) the matters disclosed by the evidence taken on the preliminary inquiry,

(b) the evidence taken on the trial, if any;

(c) the circumstances of the case;

(d) whether the accused has been misled or prejudiced in his defence by any variance, error or omission mentioned in subsection (2) or (3), and

(e) whether, having regard to the merits of the case, the proposed amendment can be made without injustice being done.

(4.1) A variance between the indictment or a count therein and the evidence taken is not material with respect to

(a) the time when the offence is alleged to have been committed, if it is proved that the indictment was preferred within the prescribed period of limitation, if any; or

(b) the place where the subject-matter of the proceedings is alleged to have arisen, if it is proved that it arose within the territorial jurisdiction of the court.

(5) Where, in the opinion of the court, the accused has been misled or prejudiced in his defence by a variance, error or omission in an indictment or a count therein, the court may, if it is of the opinion that the misleading or prejudice may be removed by an adjournment, adjourn the proceedings to a specified day or

sittings of the court and may make such an order with respect to the payment of costs resulting from the necessity for amendment as it considers desirable.

(6) The question whether an order to amend an indictment or a count thereof should be granted or refused is a question of law.

(7) An order to amend an indictment or a count therein shall be endorsed on the indictment as part of the record and the proceedings shall continue as if the indictment or count had been originally preferred as amended.

(8) A mistake in the heading of an indictment shall be corrected as soon as it is discovered but, whether corrected or not, is not material.

(9) The authority of a court to amend indictments does not authorize the court to add to the overt acts stated in an indictment for high treason or treason or for an offence against any provision in sections 49, 50, 51 and 53.

(10) In this section, "court" means a court, judge, justice or provincial court judge acting in summary conviction proceedings or in proceedings on indictment.

(11) This section applies to all proceedings, including preliminary inquiries, with such modifications as the circumstances require.

There can be no question that these provisions are far too complicated. Note differences between various subsections, for example, as to what stage an amendment can be made, whether evidence must have been adduced and whether the amendment power applies to a defect of substance or form (a difficult distinction which is not defined).

In practice it would appear that there is a power of amendment in most cases but that trial courts are sometimes reluctant to exercise them. However, courts now commonly remedy duplicity by resort to an amendment: the Crown is asked to choose one offence on which to proceed and any other is deleted.

You may wish to consider whether there should have been an amendment in the case of the problems noted under insufficiency above.

R. v. MOORE
[1988] 1 S.C.R. 1097, 65 C.R. (3d) 1, 41 C.C.C. (3d) 289 (S.C.C.)

The accused was charged with a count of possession of stolen property which did not allege that he knew the property was obtained by the commission of an offence punishable by indictment. After the accused entered a not guilty plea, the court, before taking any evidence, quashed the information as failing to disclose an offence in law. A new information containing the previously omitted averment was sworn against the accused to which he pleaded autrefois acquit. This plea was rejected and he was convicted at trial. He appealed and the appeal was allowed. The Crown appealed.

LAMER J. (McIntyre, Le Dain and La Forest JJ. concurring): —

The Chief Justice has set out the facts, analyzed the judgments below [[1984] 2 W.W.R. 362, 9 C.C.C. (3d) 1], and identified the issue to be decided in this case, namely [p. 4] "whether quashing an information, after plea, for failure to allege a material averment constitutes a verdict of acquittal for the purpose of pleading autrefois acquit to a new information."

There appears to be no disagreement, either between ourselves or with the judges below, as regards the fact that, acting under s. 529 of the Code, the judge erred in quashing the information. Indeed, the information was not a nullity but only voidable and the accused was clearly in jeopardy of being convicted when the judge quashed the information. On this it is without any reservation that I agree with the reasons of the Chief Justice. I also agree with his analysis of s. 537 and that, added to the requirement that the accused must have been put in jeopardy, there must also have been a final determination equivalent to an acquittal.

My respectful disagreement with the Chief Justice is in the qualification to be given to a quashing by a judge when he does so acting, at trial, under the authority of s. 529 [now s. 601]....

Since the enactment of our Code in 1892 there has been, through case law and punctual amendments to s. 529 and its predecessor sections, a gradual shift from requiring judges to quash to requiring them to amend in the stead; in fact, there remains little discretion to quash. Of course, if the charge is an absolute nullity, an occurrence the conditions of which the Chief Justice has set out clearly in his reasons, no cure is available as the matter goes to the very jurisdiction of the judge. In such a case, the doctrine of autrefois acquit is never a bar to the re-laying of the charge because the accused was never in jeopardy and the disposition of the charge through quashing was for lack of jurisdiction. Also, if and when a charge is laid before that or another judge, it will be the first time the accused is in jeopardy before a judge having jurisdiction on the accused and the subject matter. There was nothing to be acquitted of, and for this reason, there is no "autrefois", as there was no offence, and no "acquit" as there was no jurisdiction to acquit or convict. But, if the charge is only voidable, the judge has jurisdiction to amend. Even failure to state something that is an essential ingredient of the offence (and I am referring to s. 529(3)(b)(i)) is not fatal; in fact, it is far from being fatal, as the section commands that the judge "shall" amend.

My understanding of s. 529, when read in its entirety, is that it commands the following to the trial judge: absent absolute nullity and subject to certain limits set out in subs. (9), the judge has very wide powers to cure any defect in a charge by amending it; if the mischief to be cured by amendment has misled or prejudiced the accused in his defence, the judge must then determine whether the misleading or prejudice may be removed by an adjournment. If so, he must amend, adjourn and thereafter proceed. But, if the required amendment cannot be made without injustice being done, then and only then the judge is to quash. Therefore, a judge must not quash a charge, and it is reversible error of law if he does, unless he has come to that conclusion, namely, that "the proposed amendment" cannot "be made without injustice being done". However, if having determined, as a matter of law (see subs. (6)), that an amendment cannot be made without causing irreparable prejudice, his quashing of the charge at the trial is then, in my view, tantamount to an acquittal. This is equally true whether, to terminate the proceedings under s. 529, the judge uses the word "quash", "dismiss", "discharge" or "acquit". With respect, this to me is obvious, because re-laying before another judge an amended charge would be no less prejudicial to the accused than the amendment of the first one by the previous judge. Section 529(4) and (5) would then be a useless exercise of judgment.

It has been suggested that the factors, other than those related to prejudice, to be considered by the trial judge under s. 529(4) are indicative of the fact that irreparable prejudice is not necessarily the ultimate factor to determine whether to amend or quash. This with respect is to read s. 529 with an "all-or-nothing" approach, that is, that the judge must either amend or quash. The factors listed under s. 529(4) are, as the opening words of the subsection indicate, relevant to determine whether there should be an amendment, and not whether the judge should amend or quash. Quashing will occur only if there is irreparable prejudice. A judge may well come to the conclusion that there is no need to quash because there is no prejudice to the accused, without necessarily concluding that there need be an amendment. Such could be the case where the defect is one of pure form as contemplated by s. 529(3)(c). If there is irreparable prejudice, there is no amendment available. A contrario, however, there need not always be an amendment. In other words, the question whether one quashes or not is not on all fours with whether one, absent irreparable prejudice, amends or not.

What is misleading here is that it is clear to us, as it was to the Court of Appeal, that the judge quashed when he clearly should not have, as an amendment would not have caused any prejudice to the accused. However, this is no reason to allow the Crown to lay an amended charge once the accused has been acquitted, albeit by error. The trial judge's decision is open to appeal. Assuming error is found, the Court of Appeal will direct him to amend and hear the case, or will amend the charge itself and then return the file to the judge for trial on the amended charge. The fact that this will result in the accused being tried on the amended charge in any event is no reason for downgrading the "quashing" so as to permit the Crown to re-lay an amended charge without facing a special plea. When a judge quashes under s. 529, that decision is deemed without error until reversed by a court of appeal. Otherwise the second judge, ordinarily of the same jurisdiction, when assessing whether the "quashing" is or is not tantamount to an acquittal for the purpose of determining whether there is autrefois acquit, would have to determine whether his colleague was or was not in error in deciding to quash.

Finally, I have not changed my mind as regards the concurrence I gave to my brother McIntyre in *Petersen v. R.*, [1982] 2 S.C.R. 493, [1982] 6 W.W.R. 498, 30 C.R. (3d) 165, 69 C.C.C. (2d) 385, 140 D.L.R. (3d) 480, 18 Sask. R. 162, 44 N.R. 92. I have, with respect, no difficulty whatsoever reconciling our court's decision in *Petersen* with our previous decision in *Doyle v. R.*, [1977] 1 S.C.R. 597, 35 C.R.N.S. 1, 29 C.C.C. (2d) 177, 68 D.L.R. (3d) 270, 10 Nfld. & P.E.I.R. 45, 9 N.R. 285 [Nfld.]. *Petersen* was dealing with the termination of proceedings at a trial, albeit a summary conviction, while in *Doyle* the proceedings were terminated at a preliminary inquiry. The latter lacks the required "jeopardy", amongst other differences in nature between the two types of proceedings. Furthermore, in *Petersen*, as in the case at bar, the Crown simply ignored the disposition of a case in a court of record and commenced new proceedings on the same information, alleging the same cause, while leaving the record in the court below unchallenged. I would therefore dismiss this appeal.

R. v. TREMBLAY
[1993] 2 S.C.R. 932, 23 C.R. (4th) 98, 84 C.C.C. (3d) 97 (S.C.C.)

The accused was charged with keeping a common bawdy-house for the purpose of the practice of acts of indecency contrary to what is now s. 210(1) of the Criminal Code. At the premises nude dancers would perform for their clients in private rooms with a mattress and a chair. The majority of clients masturbated. Very late in the trial, after all the defence evidence had been called, the Crown sought to amend the charge by deleting the words "the practice of indecency" to include the words "practice of prostitution". The trial judge rejected both motions on the basis the amendments would cause serious prejudice to the accused.

On the final appeal the Supreme Court agreed with the trial judge.

CORY J. (La Forest, L'Heureux-Dubé, Gonthier, and McLachlin JJ. concurring):— By virtue of this section, [s. 601], the courts now possess reasonably wide powers of amendment. Yet, it remains an important principle of criminal law that persons accused of a crime must know the charge brought against them in order to present a full answer and defence (*R. v. Côté* (sub nom. *Vézina v. R.; Côté v. R.; R. v. Côté*) [1986] 1 S.C.R. 2). A court cannot amend an information or indictment where to do so would cause irreparable prejudice (*R. v. Moore*, [1988] 1 S.C.R. 1097). Moreover, a court cannot amend an information unless the evidence tendered is capable of supporting such a charge.

In the present case it is not necessary to consider whether evidence of prostitution was disclosed during the trial. The prejudice that granting the amendment would cause the appellants is determinative of the issue.

When the motion for the amendment was brought it was obvious that the appellants had prepared their defence on the basis that the acts performed were not indecent. In light of the wording of the original charge the appellants quite properly prepared their entire defence on this issue. This can be seen from the careful and lengthy testimony provided by the expert witness on this very question. To have permitted the amendment at this stage would have caused irreparable prejudice to the appellants. Perhaps much earlier in the trial proceedings it might have been appropriate to allow the proposed amendment provided an adequate adjournment was granted to the appellants to prepare their defence to meet the amended charges. Undoubtedly, the appellants would have needed time to consider their position and to consult and retain experts with regard to the issue as to whether the acts constituted prostitution. That, of course, is speculation. It is sufficient to say that, in the circumstances of this case, the trial judge was correct in his conclusion that to grant the amendment at this late stage would have caused irreparable prejudice to the appellants.

. . .

In *R. v. P. (M.B.)*, [1994] 1 S.C.R. 555, 29 C.R. (4th) 209, 89 C.C.C. (3d) 289 (S.C.C.), a case alleging sexual assault against the accused's niece, the trial judge allowed the Crown to reopen its case to counter a defence of alibi based on the 1982 date specified in the indictment and confirmed by the complainant's mother. The mother now testified that the date was in fact 1983 and the trial judge allowed an amendment of the indictment to conform to the evidence. A 5:4 majority of the Supreme Court confirmed that the conviction should be quashed. According to Chief Justice Lamer, for the majority, where the Crown has closed its case and the defence has started to answer the case, the trial judge's discretion is very restricted and it will only be in the narrowest of cases that the Crown should be permitted to reopen. According to the dissenting justices, neither the reopening nor the amendment had prejudiced the accused by altering the case to meet.

In *R. v. D. (S.)* (2011), 270 C.C.C. (3d) 287, [2011] 1 S.C.R. 527 (S.C.C.) the trial judge convicted an accused of sexual interference with his daughter four months after the date alleged by the complainant. The indictment was never amended. The majority of the Quebec Court of Appeal ordered a new trial but the Supreme Court, over the sole dissent of Fish J., reversed and restored the conviction. In a brief judgment the Court held that the defence turned on credibility and the defence had not been prejudiced.

In *R. v. McCune* (1998), 131 C.C.C. (3d) 152, 21 C.R. (5th) 247 (B.C. C.A.), the Court quashed a conviction for manslaughter. The Crown had been permitted to change its theory in its closing address to the jury from manslaughter by unlawful act in the form of assault of the accused's elderly mother to that of manslaughter by criminal negligence through poor maintenance of the house. The accused was held to have been denied the right to make full answer and defence.

(iii)   On Appeal

Motions to quash indictments or informations for defects apparent on their face must be brought before an accused has pleaded and thereafter only by leave of the court. Appeal courts are most reluctant to consider such formal objections raised for the first time on appeal. This is generally felt to be a matter for the trial judge and also there is a fear that technical objections might otherwise be deliberately left for appeal. The attitude has hardened. For example de Grandpré J. in *R. v. Côté,* [1978] 1 S.C.R. 8, 40 C.R.N.S. 308, 33 C.C.C. (2d) 353 (S.C.C.) held that, even if there had been a defect apparent on the face, there would have been no necessity to amend the information since no objection was made at trial and "the matter ends there".

5. Application for Severance

As amended in 1985, s. 591(3) of the Criminal Code provides:

(3) The court may, where it is satisfied that the interests of justice so require, order

(a) that the accused or defendant be tried separately on one or more of the counts; and

(b) where there is more than one accused or defendant, that one or more of them be tried separately on one or more of the counts.

Thus, it can be seen that the subsection refers to both severing counts and severing accused persons. Such applications must be made to the trial court and are usually done by means of a pre-trial motion prior to trial or at the beginning of the trial. In both cases, if severance is granted, separate trials must be held for the severed counts or defendants. However, the same rather vague criterion "the interests of justice" applies to both types of severance application. First, let us consider severance of counts:

Section 590(3) gives the court a wide jurisdiction "where it is satisfied that the ends of justice require it" to order that the count in an indictment be divided into two or more counts. The same wide discretion is given to the trial judge to grant a motion made before or during a trial to separate the trial of an accused upon one or more counts (s. 591(3)). Section 591(4) permits an order for severance either before or during the trial. The former is preferred, either through a pre-trial motion to the trial judge or through the use of a case management judge under s. 551.3 of the Code. If the order is made during the trial, the trial judge or jury, as the case may be, does not render a verdict on charges or accused persons that have been severed from that trial. Consider whether the court was correct in refusing to exercise such a discretion in *R. v. Racco (No. 1)*.

R. v. RACCO (NO. 1)
(1975), 29 C.R.N.S. 303 (Ont. Co. Ct.)

GRABURN CO. CT. J.:—This is an application by Giuseppe Racco to sever the counts in an indictment preferred against him and for a separate trial of those counts.

Mr. Racco is charged in Count 1 of the indictment that on 1st August 1971, at Toronto, without lawful justification or excuse, he had in his possession counterfeit money, to wit, seven counterfeit United States $20 federal reserve notes, and in Count 2 he is charged that at the same time and the same place, without lawful excuse, he had in his possession an explosive substance, one ground burst projectile simulator, for other than a lawful purpose, both counts being laid pursuant to the Criminal Code, R.S.C. 1970, c. C-34.

The application is made under s. 520 [now s. 591] of the Criminal Code, the relevant subsections of which provide in subs. (1):

520. (1) Subject to section 518

which is not relevant here

. . . any number of counts for any number of indictable offences may be joined in the same indictment, but the counts shall be distinguished in the manner shown in Forms 3 and 4.

Subsection (3) provides:

(3) The court may, where it is satisfied that the ends of justice require it, direct that the accused be tried separately upon one or more of the counts.

And subs. (4) provides that:

(4) An order for the separate trial of one or more counts in an indictment may be made before or during the trial, but if the order is made during the trial the jury shall be discharged from giving a verdict on the counts on which the trial does not proceed.

It is common ground that whether an order will be made severing the counts in the indictment on an application under s. 520 is a discretionary matter so far as the trial court is concerned.

Mr. Greenspan submits, and I agree with this submission, that in order to determine whether a severance ought to be granted, the facts, as expected to be disclosed in the evidence, are relevant.

I am told that the circumstances are that in August 1971 police officers went to the residence or the premises of Mr. Racco and observations were made on his home. A vehicle drove into the accused's driveway. The occupants of this vehicle entered the home of the accused. The accused was seen to come out of his home with an object, which apparently was described or will be described by the witnesses as a white object, and disappeared, returning in a few moments with what I am told the witnesses will describe as a green object and this green object was placed in a position underneath certain steps, I believe, at the front of the premises. This object subsequently turned out to be the ground burst projectile simulator which is the subject of Count 2.

Shortly after this, officers entered the premises and in the course of searching them a brown envelope was found in a bedroom dresser drawer and in the brown envelope were a number of United States $20 federal reserve notes which are apparently counterfeit.

The first obvious point which arises from the short recital of the facts I have just given is that there is certainly, in terms of time and in terms of place, a nexus between the finding of the simulator and the finding of the counterfeit United States federal reserve notes. The nexus as to time and place is, as far as time is concerned, within minutes and, of course, the place involves a section of the interior and the exterior of the same premises.

It is clear so far as the authorities are concerned that even though s. 520(1) permits any number of counts for any number of indictable offences to be joined in the same indictment, the courts are loath, for example, to permit the joinder of a count of bigamy with a count of break and enter, for reasons which I think are so obvious that they do not require elaboration. Different considerations apply, however, where there is a nexus between the offences alleged and it is in those circumstances that s. 520(3) becomes significant.

The position taken by Mr. Greenspan on this application is this: First, he submits that notwithstanding any direction that this Court would give in relation to considering the evidence pertinent to each count separately, a jury would be unconsciously influenced, for example, on Count 1 by the finding of the projectile on Count 2, and on Count 2 by the finding of the counterfeit money on Count 1. Mr. Greenspan's position is, as the jury would be unconsciously influenced accordingly, that the accused would be embarrassed in his defence in relation to a trial of Counts 1 and 2 together.

Mr. Greenspan further submits that the issue in relation to both counts is going to be one of credibility because the position of the defence is, in relation to the counterfeit money, substantially that the money was planted by the police, and in relation to Count 2, the simulator, the defence is explicitly that the simulator was planted by the police. Mr. Greenspan's position therefore is that if the accused is obliged to defend both counts contemporaneously on the issue of credibility, the accused would also be embarrassed.

Mr. Greenspan takes a further position that if the evidence on one count were relevant to the other he would not have made this application, but he contends that the evidence in relation to the projectile simulator is not relevant to the count of possession of counterfeit money and vice versa.

I think at this juncture that I should deal with Mr. Chasse's contention that the evidence of the finding of the projectile simulator is relevant to the issue of the counterfeit money. I am not satisfied that it is necessary for me to decide this issue at this stage of the trial. It may be necessary, perhaps, for me to decide it at some other stage but at this point I do not believe I am called upon to decide that issue and I think that I will say no more about that at the present time.

It seems to me that the issue here resolves itself into a question of what is the meaning of the words "the ends of justice" in s. 520(3). Certainly, where an accused is facing more than one count and evidence on one may not be prima facie relevant on another count, it would appear that an accused may well be prejudiced or embarrassed in his defence, but I query whether the words "ends of justice" mean only the interests of the accused and, in my judgment, they embrace both the interests of the accused and the interests of the administration of justice generally.

It seems to me that where the issue is substantially credibility and where there is a close nexus in time and place in relation to the counts as exists in this case, it is in the interests of justice that both of these counts be tried together and I say this particularly for this reason: Mr. Greenspan has indicated that the defence in both instances is that of a plant on the part of the police. In my view, the interests of justice require that this issue of a plant by the police be resolved by one tribunal and not by two tribunals.

It is realistic in the circumstances of this case that either the accused will be acquitted or he will be convicted of both counts because, again, in view of the nexus in time and in place, common sense dictates to me that if the jury has a reasonable doubt as to a plant of one item they will have a reasonable doubt as to the plant of the other, and if they do not have a reasonable doubt as to the plant of one item it is reasonable to suppose, in view of the circumstances outlined to me, they would not have a reasonable doubt about the other.

In my judgment, to permit a severance here could lead to the following undesirable result. A jury on a trial of Count 1 could have a reasonable doubt whether the counterfeit money has been planted and acquit the accused. A different jury might come to a different conclusion in relation to the simulator and convict the accused. In the light of the identical nature of the defence to both offences, it seems to me that such a result is not in the interests of the administration of justice and is not a criterion on which a court should act under subs. (3).

I have considered Mr. Greenspan's point as to the difficulty of the jury being influenced on one count by the evidence relating to the other but I am satisfied that I can adequately instruct the jury so as to negate this danger. Therefore, for the reasons I have given, at this stage of the trial, I am of the view that the ends of justice require the counts to be tried together and I so order and I dismiss the application.

Severance of counts has historically been relatively rare. However, the recent decision of the Supreme Court of Canada in *R. v. Last* may indicate a change in this position:

R. v. LAST
(2009), 69 C.R. (6th) 1, 247 C.C.C. (3d) 449 (S.C.C.)

Last was charged with the sexual assault of two women in unrelated incidents occurring one month apart. In both cases he met the women in the company of a mutual acquaintance and then insisted on being alone with them. Both women claimed that they were repeatedly sexually assaulted and terrorized over a number of hours by Last. The second complainant alleged the assaults took place after she had been choked into unconsciousness. Last took the position that the sexual activity with the first complainant was consensual and that he was not the person who had assaulted the second woman. The Crown proceeded to try both counts on a single indictment. Last applied to sever the counts but Justice Killeen rejected this application. The jury convicted Last on both counts. An appeal to the Ontario Court of Appeal was dismissed, Justice Juriansz dissenting. Last appealed as of right to the Supreme Court of Canada.

DESCHAMPS J.: —

1. Introduction

1 The Crown enjoys a large discretion in deciding to include more than one count in an indictment (s. 591(1) of the *Criminal Code*, R.S.C. 1985, c. C-46). On an application to sever a multi-count indictment, the overarching criteria are the interests of justice. This appeal raises the issue of whether a trial judge erred in dismissing an application to sever. In my view, he did.

. . .

3.1 *The Severance Application*

. . .

As noted by this Court in *R. v. Litchfield*, [1993] 4 S.C.R. 333 (S.C.C.), the absence of specific guidelines for granting severance requires that deference be afforded to a trial judge's ruling to the extent that he or she acts judicially and the ruling does not result in an injustice (at pp. 353-54):

> The criteria for when a count should be divided or a severance granted are contained in ss. 590(3) and 591(3) of the *Code*. These criteria are very broad: the court must be satisfied that the ends or interests of justice require the order in question. Therefore, in the absence of stricter guidelines, making an order for the division or severance of counts requires the exercise of a great deal of discretion on the part of the issuing judge. The decisions of provincial appellate courts have held, and I agree, that *an appellate court should not interfere with the issuing judge's exercise of discretion unless it is shown that the issuing judge acted unjudicially or that the ruling resulted in an injustice.*
>
> [Emphasis added.]

15 The Court in Litchfield integrated the long accepted two separate grounds for intervention: an unjudicial severance ruling or a ruling that resulted in an injustice (see, for example, *R. v. Kestenberg* (1959), 126 C.C.C. 387 (Ont. C.A.), leave to appeal refused, [1960] S.C.R. x (S.C.C.); and *R. v. Grandkowski* (1946), 31 Cr. App. R. 116 (Eng. C.A.), at pp. 119-20). These two grounds involve different inquiries. While the determination of whether the judge acted unjudicially calls for an inquiry into the circumstances prevailing at the time it was made, the review of whether the ruling resulted in an injustice will usually entail scrutiny that includes the unfolding of the trial and of the verdicts (*R. v. Rose* (1997), 100 O.A.C. 67 (Ont. C.A.), at para. 17).

16 The ultimate question faced by a trial judge in deciding whether to grant a severance application is whether severance is required in the interests of justice, as per s. 591(3) of the *Code*. The interests of justice encompass the accused's right to be tried on the evidence admissible against him, as well as society's interest in seeing that justice is done in a reasonably efficient and cost-effective manner. The obvious risk when counts are tried together is that the evidence admissible on one count will influence the verdict on an unrelated count.

17 Courts have given shape to the broad criteria established in s. 591(3) and have identified factors that can be weighed when deciding whether to sever or not. The weighing exercise ensures that a reasonable balance is struck between the risk of prejudice to the accused and the public interest in a single trial. It is important to recall that the interests of justice often call for a joint trial. Litchfield, where the Crown was prevented from arguing the case properly because of an unjudicial severance order, is but one such example. Severance can impair not only efficiency but the truth-seeking function of the trial.

18 The factors identified by the courts are not exhaustive. They simply help capture how the interests of justice may be served in a particular case, avoiding an injustice. Factors courts rightly use include: the general prejudice to the accused; the legal and factual nexus between the counts; the complexity of the evidence; whether the accused intends to testify on one count but not another;

the possibility of inconsistent verdicts; the desire to avoid a multiplicity of proceedings; the use of similar fact evidence at trial; the length of the trial having regard to the evidence to be called; the potential prejudice to the accused with respect to the right to be tried within a reasonable time; and the existence of antagonistic defences as between co-accused persons: *R. v. E. (L.)* (1994), 94 C.C.C. (3d) 228 (Ont. C.A.), at p. 238; *R. c. Cross* (1996), 112 C.C.C. (3d) 410 (Que. C.A.), at p. 419; *R. v. C. (D.A.)* (1996), 106 C.C.C. (3d) 28 (B.C. C.A.), at para. 9, aff'd [1997] 1 S.C.R. 8 (S.C.C.)).

. . .

21 Since the trial judge enjoys a broad discretion in deciding whether to sever or not, a reviewing court should only intervene on the ground of unjudicial ruling if the judge erred on a question of law or made an unreasonable decision. I will review first the accused's submission that the dismissal of his intention to testify resulted in an unjudicial ruling and then turn to the prejudicial effect of trying all counts together, and the minimal benefits of a joint trial to the administration of justice. I will end the analysis by reviewing the weighing exercise conducted by the trial judge.

3.2 The Accused's Intention to Testify

. . .

25 In assessing the accused's testimonial intention on a severance application the underlying concern is for the accused's ability to control his defence, and, more specifically, his right to decide whether or not to testify with respect to each of the counts unimpaired by inappropriate constraints.

26 Both the Crown and the defence submit that the accused's intention should be objectively justifiable. This requirement is, indeed, a threshold. The accused's expression should have both a subjective and an objective component. However, while a formulaic expression of a subjective intention is not sufficient in and of itself to discharge the accused's burden to have the counts severed, the trial judge should not substitute his or her own view for that of the accused and determine that the accused should testify or not. Rather, the trial judge must simply satisfy him- or herself that the circumstances objectively establish a rationale for testifying on some counts but not others. The burden on the accused is to provide the trial judge with sufficient information to convey that, objectively, there is substance to his testimonial intention. The information could consist of the type of potential defences open to the accused or the nature of his testimony: *Cross*, at p. 421. However, the accused is not bound by his stated intention; he remains free to control his defence, as the case unfolds, in a manner he deems appropriate.

27 While an accused's provisional intention with respect to testifying is certainly a consideration which should be given significant weight, it is but one factor to be balanced with all the others. An accused's stated and objectively justifiable intention to testify on some but not all counts is not necessarily determinative of a severance application. It can be counterbalanced by other circumstances that the judge finds may prevent the accused from testifying, or

be outweighed by factors that demonstrate that the interests of justice require a joint trial.

28 During the severance hearing counsel for the defence explained to the trial judge, albeit briefly, that Mr. Last was more likely to testify in respect of the S.M. counts since the issue was whether the sexual intercourse was consensual or not, and was therefore highly dependent on S.M.'s word against Mr. Last's. Defence counsel at trial did not further elaborate on Mr. Last's position, other than to say that the M.A. counts were "dependent more heavily on other evidence". However, the suggestion before the Court of Appeal and this Court was that Mr. Last was less likely to testify with respect to the M.A. counts since they involved an issue of identification.

29 While defence counsel could reasonably argue that the M.A. counts called for a distinct theory of the case from the S.M. counts, it is to be noted that the likelihood Mr. Last may feel strategically compelled to testify with respect to the M.A. counts as well as the S.M. counts could not be discounted. The Crown's evidence implicating Mr. Last on the M.A. counts was not insignificant given Mr. Last's admission that he was in her apartment just prior to the assault and M.A.'s identification of Mr. Last as her assailant. It was thus fairly probable he would have to testify in order to put forward his theory of the case — that it was someone else who entered M.A.'s apartment and committed the assault. Such a testimonial outcome was discernable at the time of the severance application.

30 I conclude that although Mr. Last's intention to testify on one set of counts and not the other was objectively justifiable, it did not constitute, in this case, a significant factor in view of the likelihood that his decision whether or not to testify would be the same in relation to both sets of counts.

3.3 Nexus Between the Two Incidents

31 Another factor to be considered on a severance application is whether there is any legal or factual nexus between the counts. The trial judge found there was a nexus in time and place between the two sets of charges because the two assaults giving rise to the charges occurred in the city of London, approximately one month apart. The dissent in the Court of Appeal, however, found the nexus between the two counts to be "exceedingly weak":

> Factually, the two cases involve different complainants. They occurred in different locations. They occurred approximately one month apart.
>
> Legally, both sets of counts relate to sexual assault, but they raise different legal issues. In the S.M. case, the legal issue was consent, and in the M.A. case the issue was identification.
>
> None of the evidence on one set of cases was relevant or admissible on the other. At trial, the Crown agreed that none of the evidence qualified as similar fact evidence. [paras. 127-29]

32 I agree with the dissenting judge that the factual and legal nexus between the two sets of counts is extremely thin. The fact that the two incidents occurred in London approximately one month apart is of very limited significance in this case. This was the city where Mr. Last resided and worked. The attacks on the women were not closely connected in any meaningful way. While the charges

were similar, the theory of the defence was completely different: consent was at issue in one and identification in the other. The theory of the Crown that the two incidents were part of the same transaction was not supported by the facts. Rather, the attacks were separate incidents. The trier of fact would not need to know about one in order to understand the other. The circumstances surrounding the charges were not sufficiently similar in character to have supported a similar fact evidence application. Accordingly, there was no truth-seeking interest in trying the counts together.

33 In many cases a ruling allowing similar fact evidence will favour a joint trial since the evidence on all incidents would have to be introduced in any event. However, in view of the different burden in a similar fact evidence application, the issue has to be considered carefully in the context of a severance motion.

34 In the case at bar, an issue facing the trial judge at the time of the severance hearing was the fact that the Crown indicated that it wanted to wait until the conclusion of its evidence before making a similar fact evidence application. There is no procedural rule requiring the Crown to bring the similar fact evidence application at the time of the severance application: see D. Watt, *Watt's Manual of Criminal Evidence* (2009), at § 34.02. Given that the assessment of the similar fact evidence application can be a difficult task, in many cases such an assessment may be best done once all of the Crown's evidence has been tendered. However, in this case, the acts complained of did not come close to having the requisite "high degree of similarity" that would have rendered "the likelihood of coincidence objectively improbable": Arp, at para. 43; see also *R. v. Handy*, 2002 SCC 56, [2002] 2 S.C.R. 908 (S.C.C.). Therefore it was clear at the severance motion that a similar fact application was not likely to succeed. Indeed, in his reasons, the trial judge did not rely on the possibility of a similar fact evidence application for denying severance.

35 In summary, the nexus in this case was so tenuous as to hardly bear any weight in favour of a joint trial.

3.4 Risk of Prejudice to the Accused

36 Mr. Last identifies two sources of prejudice in trying the counts together, and submits that the trial judge's failure to accord significant weight to this factor constituted an error in principle. First, joinder created the potential for cross-pollination on credibility assessments. The existence of two complainants who had no relation to each other alleging two separate incidents of sexual assault created a risk that the credibility of each complainant would be bolstered. Similarly, if the jury found Mr. Last not credible while testifying with respect to one set of counts, the jury might presume that he was also not credible with respect to the other. Second, the joinder created a risk that the jury would engage in prohibited propensity reasoning. If the jury were to find that the Crown had satisfied the burden of proof for one set of offences, the jury might infer that Mr. Last was the kind of person who would commit these types of crimes and thereby convict him of the second set of offences.

. . .

40 The significant risk of propensity reasoning to the accused cannot be understated. The severity of the injuries in M.A.'s case and the telling pictural representation of those injuries, together with the testimonies of the experts, made the evidence in this case much more visual than in S.M.'s case. On the other hand, the alleged threat with a gun and repeated sexual assault on the night of S.M.'s 19th birthday with the ensuing inherent psychological and emotional distress, if joined with the counts in M.A.'s case, seriously invited the possibility that the jury would engage in impermissible credibility bolstering and prohibited propensity reasoning. As pointed out by defence counsel, the jury would inevitably wonder why two complainants who did not know each other would independently accuse Mr. Last of sexual assault. Furthermore, if the jury was convinced beyond a reasonable doubt that Mr. Last had committed sexual assault on one victim, the jury would be inclined to reason that Mr. Last had the propensity for committing this type of offence and convict on the other. Indeed, the trial judge implicitly recognized the potential prejudice to the accused, but felt that he could cure any resulting prejudice with a limiting instruction (A.R., at p. 79). I will later comment further on the limiting instruction.

3.5 Minimal Benefit to the Administration of Justice

41 Another factor to consider is the benefit enuring to the administration of justice from holding a joint trial. As mentioned earlier, this is not a case where the evidence of one assault would have to be introduced at the trial of the other. The assaults did not bear the markers of similar fact evidence. Consequently, considering the unlikelihood of a successful similar fact application, the gains in judicial economy usually achieved from avoiding multiple proceedings were absent in this case.

42 Moreover, there was no overlap in evidence or key witnesses, such as complainants or expert witnesses. Indeed, only some of the investigating officers would likely have testified on both sets of counts and even then their evidence would not have overlapped. The benefits to the administration of justice in trying the counts together were thus minimal.

3.6 Balancing the Factors and Assessing the Interests of Justice

44 It was incumbent upon the trial judge to consider and weigh cumulatively all the relevant factors to determine whether the interests of justice require severance. In this case, although Mr. Last was likely to testify on both incidents, the risk of prejudice to Mr. Last in having a joint trial was nevertheless significant because of the dangers of credibility cross-pollination and prohibited propensity reasoning. In other circumstances, after balancing all relevant factors, the interests of justice may have nevertheless required a joint trial. However, in this case, there was an absence of compelling countervailing reasons for having a joint trial. This case did not pose a risk of inconsistent verdicts, nor did it involve substantial overlap in witness testimony or other evidence. As stated by the dissenting judge, "the nature of the nexus between the counts in this case did not provide a reason why it was necessary, desirable or convenient to try the cases together" (para. 130).

Indeed, a joint trial in the circumstances of this case did not serve any truth-seeking interest, and brought few if any benefits to the administration of justice.

45 While the Crown argued that it was open to the trial judge to decide that a proper jury instruction can overcome any potential prejudice to Mr. Last, I agree with the dissenting judge below that this should be done only where there are sufficient countervailing factors providing a rationale for a joint trial (at para. 155):

> Here, the countervailing factors in favour of trying these two sets of charges together were negligible and the reasons to sever were compelling. As a result, this was not a case to attempt to address the risk of prejudice by a jury instruction.

46 Indeed, if a proper jury instruction were all that was needed to deal with potential prejudice to the accused, then prejudice would in a sense cease to be a relevant factor in the analysis. While a limiting instruction can limit the risk of inappropriate cross-pollination or propensity reasoning, courts should not resort to a limiting instruction unless there is a valid reason to do so. As with the accused's intention to testify, the limiting instruction is but one factor in the balancing exercise.

47 As previously stated, all the factors must be considered and weighed cumulatively. Here, most of the factors militated in favour of separate trials. Consequently, the significant risk of prejudice to the accused clearly outweighed any benefits to the administration of justice in trying the counts together. Failing to conduct a proper balancing of the relevant factors, the trial judge made an unreasonable decision. I therefore conclude that the trial judge acted unjudicially and that intervention is warranted.

4. Conclusion

49 Since I have found that the trial judge acted unjudicially in denying severance, I would allow the appeal, set aside the convictions, and remit the matter to the Superior Court for the S.M. and the M.A. counts to be retried separately.

Appeal allowed.

Is this judgment troubling? Consider the views of Professor Janine Benedet of the Faculty of Law. U.B.C. in the following C.R. annotation:

> These sexual assaults were unrelated events in the sense that there was little common evidence between them. Certainly the trial judge treated them as separate incidents, sentencing the accused to two consecutive sentences of imprisonment. There is also little doubt that these were extremely serious charges; the accused in this case had no prior sexual assault convictions and was only 19 years of age when the offences occurred, yet the trial judge sentenced him to over 22 years of imprisonment.

> Yet the cases had more factual similarities than the courts may have recognized. Both women testified that Last was a bare acquaintance. In both cases the women agreed to be in Last's company in the presence of a third person, and Last refused to leave with that mutual friend, insisting on being alone with the complainant. In both cases the women were choked before they were assaulted vaginally and anally. While there were also distinctive factual features of each assault, the

Supreme Court's reliance on the accused's differing defences as a point of dissimilarity is puzzling. A more realistic appraisal of the accused's claims is that he chose to put the Crown to the proof of its case on the issue of non-consent in the first count because it was possible to do so in light of the relative scarcity of corroborating evidence. On the second count, there was little point in insisting that the Crown prove non-consent because the complainant's physical injuries were so profound. The accused's tactical decision to contest certain elements and not others does not enhance the dissimilarity of the counts.

It is worth considering why the Crown wanted these cases tried together. There is no doubt that the credibility of a sexual assault complainant is enhanced every time another victim comes forward to accuse the same perpetrator. A so-called "he said — she said" case is always less attractive for the Crown than a "he said — they said" case. This is why similar fact evidence is so powerful. The problem, of course, is that society continues to be more sceptical of women who report sexual assault than of other victims who report victimization through other criminal acts. One might argue that this historic bias actually supports a generous approach to joint trials in sexual assault cases. Alternatively, it points to a need to reexamine the rules on similar fact evidence with more attention to the context in which such applications are made.

Canadian criminal law has always contemplated the possibility of separate counts tried jointly on the same indictment even where a similar fact evidence application would not be successful. It has been assumed that a proper caution to the jury is sufficient to diminish the risk of prejudice. That category of cases seems to have been narrowed considerably by this decision. We can expect to see an increasing number of successful severance applications in sexual assault prosecutions involving multiple victims.

Whether the charges are admissible as similar fact evidence often determines whether a motion of improper joinder will be granted. It has been held that two counts of first-degree murder 17 years apart and strikingly dissimilar should have resulted in severance (*R. v. Jeanvenne* (2010), 261 C.C.C. (3d) 462, 80 C.R. (6th) 182 (Ont. C.A.)) but not where the alleged first-degree murder counts were based on evidence showing a consistent pattern of luring, restraint with handcuffs and disposal of the bodies (*R. v. Pickton* (2009), 260 C.C.C. (3d) 132 (B.C. C.A.)).

An application to sever the trial of an accused person from that of a co-accused is governed by the same criterion in s. 591(3). However, in evaluating whether that criterion has been met, there are somewhat different considerations. There is a classic pronouncement by Wurtele J. in *R. v. Weir* (1899), 3 C.C.C. 351 (Qué . Q.B.):

The discretion of the presiding judge must not be exercised in a desultory or immethodical manner, but it must be guided and regulated by judicial principles and fixed rules.

The usual grounds for a severance are:—

(1.)—That the defendants have antagonistic defences;

(2.)—That important evidence in favor of one of the defendants which would be admissable on a separate trial would not be allowed on a joint trial;

(3.)—That evidence which is incompetent against one defendant, is to be introduced against another, and that it would work prejudicially to the former with the jury;

(4.)—That a confession made by one of the defendants, if introduced and proved, would be calculated to prejudice the jury against the other defendants; and

(5.)—That one of the defendants could give evidence for the whole or some of the other defendants and would become a competent and compellable witness on the separate trials of such other defendants.

However, motions to sever are rarely successful. The attitude is best expressed in the leading decision in the English case of *R. v. Grondkowski* (1946), 31 Crim. App. Rep. 116 (C.C.A.), often applied in Canada. Lord Goddard C.J. held that there will usually be a joint trial where the prisoners were engaged in a common enterprise and went on to hold (at 120) that:

> the discretion [to sever] no doubt, must be exercised judicially, that is, not capriciously. The Judge must consider the interests of the justice as well as the interests of the prisoners. It is too often now-a-days thought, or seems to be thought, that "the interests of justice" means only "the interests of the prisoners". If once it were taken as settled that every time it appeared that one prisoner, as part of his defence, means to attack another, a separate trial must be ordered, it is obvious there is no room for discretion and a rule of law substituted for it. There is no case in which this has ever been laid down, and in the opinion of the Court it would be most unfortunate and contrary to the true interests of justice if it were.

Applying this reasoning in a conspiracy trial in *R. v. Miller* (1952), 36 Crim. App. R. 169, [1952] 2 All E.R. 667 (C.C.A.), Devlin J. concluded [36 Crim. App. R. 169 at 174] that it must follow that "cases must be rare in which further conspirators can properly in the interests of justice be granted a separate trial". Clearly the issue of severance raises difficult policy issues.

One contentious situation in which severance becomes important is where the Crown is contemplating introducing similar fact evidence against the accused. In *R. v. Blacklaws* (2012), 93 C.R. (6th) 83, 285 C.C.C. (3d) 132 (B.C. C.A.), reversed [2013] 1 S.C.R. 403, 297 C.C.C. (3d) 305 (S.C.C.), the trial judge refused an application by the accused severance of counts and then later denied a Crown application to introduce similar fact evidence. The Court of Appeal allowed the subsequent appeal from conviction, holding that the approach taken by the trial judge ran the risk of impermissible propensity reasoning by the jury. In *R. v. Dorsey* (2012), 93 C.R. (6th) 65, 288 C.C.C. (3d) 62 (Ont. C.A.), the trial judge granted the defence severance motion but later permitted the evidence of the complainant relating to the severed charge to be admitted as similar fact evidence. The Court of Appeal allowed this appeal as well. In an annotation (2012), 93 C.R. (6th) 83, Quigley suggests that the solution would be to call upon the Crown to advance its application to admit similar fact evidence at the same time as the defence application for severance of counts is heard. That approach would avoid speculation about whether a subsequent similar fact evidence application would possibly succeed or not.

VAMPLEW, JOINT TRIALS?
(1969-1970), 12 Crim. L.Q. 30 at 42-4

Now, what is the public interest factor that has been previously referred to? I believe it is a number of things which I shall enumerate as follows:

1. In case of a joint venture, a number of common issues such as identity, intent, *actus reus,* etc., would have to be decided by the triers of fact. If separate trials were granted, two different triers of fact would have to decide in the main the same basic issues with the decided risk of inconsistent verdicts. All one has to do is read the law reports to find that this is not uncommon.

2. Compounding the aforementioned problem is the additional feature of two different charges to two different triers of fact. The effect of this would have immeasurable consequence giving rise to a further inconsistency.

3. One accused would not have to face up to his co-accused and stand the test of cross-examination by his counsel. One must bear in mind also that counsel for the accused are in a much better position to cross-examine and bring out the whole truth than counsel for the Crown because they receive instructions through their respective clients. Accordingly, they are both in the same position and there is no imbalance.

4. The risk of convicting an innocent man is always more probable than in a joint trial. For example, if one accused is acquitted, the triers of fact, notwithstanding firm directions on this, may take this into account. Without comparing the two stories, they cannot reach a fair and just conclusion. The issue of a red herring is always there. Joseph Sedgwick, Q.C., in a lecture made such a personal observation:

    As to severance of accused, it must be borne in mind that there are dangers as well as advantages. Separately tried, one accused can be called against the other, and I well remember a murder case of some 37 years ago where the two accused moved for a severance, which was granted and they were tried separately with each blaming the other. Both were convicted and hanged. Tried together I think one of them, somewhat less implicated, would have had a fair chance of acquittal.

5. As outlined earlier in the *Miller* case, each accused can blame the other and thereby raise a reasonable doubt in absence of the other. Someone must be committing perjury yet they cannot be tried jointly on a perjury charge. The rule in *R. v. Philips et al.,* that two cannot be jointly indicted for perjury applies only where both are indicted as principals in the first degree: there is no reason why the suborner should not be tried with his principal. I can conceivably see two persons being charged separately with homicide with reference to the same offence, each blaming the other and thereby winning an acquittal. Then, when tried for perjury, they reverse their positions and thereby compound the original issue, giving some substance to the doctrine "the law is an ass" and not a very innocent one either.

In addition to this, one accused calls the other, who can testify with impunity under the Evidence Act taking the whole blame. In a homicide case, where the issue of separate trials is usually raised, this may automatically make him liable to perjury later on, which is a less serious offence.

6. The triers of fact would be determining only half of the main issue, which is highly undesirable.

7. The hallmark of a guilty person involved in a joint enterprise is to blame the other party to the offence. By separation of trials, this vital issue is not before the triers of fact.

8. In a small community, if a separate trial is granted and the attendant publicity is forthcoming, a built-in argument for a change of venue application is made out. Accordingly, the local members of the community who are the ones most concerned are no longer seized of the matter as triers of the fact. Reports of the first trial in the press cannot be curtailed but with it, the evil of prejudice coming in, affecting the second triers of fact, cannot be discounted.

9. While not a paramount factor, the added expense, inconvenience of witnesses, jurors, etc., is not entirely to be discounted.

10. Last but not least, on a show cause application for separate trials, the necessary presumption must arise that one accused is innocent as charged or else the application is not being made *bona fide* and only for the ulterior motive that it would be easier to defend the accused. Presuming the application is made in good faith. Therefore, would it not be better for the innocent party, as well as the general administration of justice, that the same jury hear "all the evidence" and be in a position to fix guilt where it belongs?

In conclusion, therefore, it must be rare indeed where a factual situation demands that two accused be tried separately, and when that does occur, it is so obvious that the question does not beg debate.

Another view is that it is by no means certain that a joint trial can adequately protect the co-accused from being wrongfully implicated by evidence which is in fact admissible only against another accused, particularly if one retains a healthy skepticism about the ability of a trier of facts, judge or jury, to eradicate from consideration inadmissible evidence.

Glanville Williams, *Criminal Law: The General Part* (2nd ed., 1961), p. 683 makes the following interesting suggestions:

> Something can be done to alleviate the position if the judge sums up and takes the verdict of each defendant separately, as he has cause to do: unfortunately, the practice is not obligatory. Wherever possible, each defendant should be separately represented, for juries tend to convict in a bunch those who engage the same counsel. It is also desirable that too many defendants should not be tried together.

From the point of view of an accused, can you identify situations in which a joint trial would, however, be beneficial to the accused?

R. v. SAVOURY
(2005), 31 C.R. (6th) 1, 200 C.C.C. (3d) 94 (Ont. C.A.)

The accused were jointly tried on a three count indictment. Savoury was charged with attempted murder and Savoury and Shaw with robbery with a firearm and aggravated assault. Shaw offered to sell a gold chain to N, whom he knew from junior high. They got into a car driven by N. At Shaw's direction they picked up a man from among a group of men. He sat in the back seat. Shaw directed N to drive off and then to park on an adjoining street. There the man in the back seat pulled a gun, pointed it at N and demanded his jewellery. He instructed Shaw to search the glove compartment. He then instructed N to get into the back seat, removed his jewellery and placed a bag over his head. N thought he was about to be shot and grabbed for the gun. In the ensuing struggle the gun discharged. N was shot in the stomach. N saw the man in the back seat and Shaw exchange congratulatory hand gestures when they left the car. N later identified Savoury from a photo line-up as the man in the back seat. Savoury's left palm print was also found on the outside of the right rear door of the vehicle. The accused were convicted on all counts and appealed. Savoury appealed against the trial judge's decision not to allow his trial to be severed.

DOHERTY J.A. (Feldman and LaForme JJ.A. concurring):—

. . .

(iv) The severance argument

At the conclusion of the Crown's case, counsel for Shaw elected to call no evidence. Counsel for Savoury indicated that he intended to call a defence and moved for an order severing his trial from Shaw's. Counsel indicated that he wanted to call Shaw as a witness. Shaw was, of course, not a compellable witness as long as he was a co-accused. There is no indication that Savoury knew before Shaw elected to call no evidence that Shaw would not testify. Shaw had testified at the first trial on the same charges.

Savoury's counsel advised the trial judge that he anticipated that if Shaw were compelled to testify, he would state that Savoury was not the person in the back seat who had robbed and shot N. To support this submission, counsel for Savoury relied on Shaw's videotaped statement made under oath to the police at the time of his arrest and Shaw's testimony in his own defence at the first trial on these charges. That trial had resulted in a mistrial when the members of the jury were unable to agree on their verdicts. In the videotaped statement, Shaw identified the person in the back seat as a man known to him as "Buju". Shaw described "Buju" and that description was not consistent with Savoury's appearance. In the statement, Shaw said he had no knowledge that "Buju" planned to rob N. Shaw insisted he had nothing to do with the robbery. In his evidence at the first trial, Shaw testified that the person in the back seat was a man known to him as "Buju". He further testified that he was also a victim of the robbery and had been threatened by "Buju" during the robbery. Shaw testified that he knew Savoury and that while Savoury was present outside of the house when he and N drove up in his girlfriend's car, Savoury did not get into the vehicle and had nothing to do with the robbery.

The trial judge refused to order severance. In detailed reasons, the trial judge acknowledged that one accused's desire to call a co-accused to give evidence that could assist the accused in his or her defence could justify a severance order. She went on to consider the substance of Shaw's videotaped statement to the police and his testimony at the prior trial. After noting many inconsistencies in Shaw's account of the relevant events, she said:

> As for evidence not available in joint trials, courts have attempted to gauge the actual prejudice to the accused as opposed to hypothetical possibilities. The practical result of Seymour Shaw testifying in a trial in favour of Travis Savoury is that he has given so many prior inconsistent statements under oath that he would very likely be found not to be a reliable witness

A trial judge may order severance of the trial of a co-accused only if satisfied that "the interests of justice so require": Criminal Code, s. 591(3). The interests of justice encompass those of the accused, the co-accused, and the community as represented by the prosecution. The trial judge must weigh these sometimes competing interests and will direct severance only if the accused seeking severance satisfies the trial judge that severance is required. To satisfy that burden, the accused must overcome the presumption that co-accused who are jointly charged and are said to have acted in concert, should be tried together. The policy behind this presumption was described by D.W. Elliot in his article "Cut Throat Tactics: The Freedom of an Accused to Prejudice a Co-Accused", [1991] Crim. L. Rev. 5 at 17, and cited with approval by Sopinka J. in *R. v. Crawford*, [1995] 1 S.C.R. 858, 96 C.C.C. (3d) 481 at 397:

> [I]t is undeniable that the full truth about an incident is much more likely to emerge if every alleged participant gives his account on one occasion. ....

In the present case, the co-accused Shaw did not allege that he would be prejudiced by a severance order, or by a joint trial. The competing interests are, therefore, those of Savoury and the Crown. Savoury did not argue that his fair trial right would be prejudiced in the sense that at a joint trial the jury would hear evidence that was inadmissible against Savoury and that could prejudice his case. Savoury did argue, however, that his right to make full answer and defence was prejudiced by a joint trial in that it rendered his co-accused Shaw a non-compellable witness. Savoury contended that Shaw had direct exculpatory evidence to give and that Savoury could make full answer and defence only if he could compel Shaw to give that evidence.

The Crown opposed severance relying on factors such as the extra costs and delay associated with separate trials, as well as the added imposition on N, the victim who had already been required to testify three times.

The Crown did not, and could not, rely on the danger of inconsistent verdicts described in cases like *R. v. Suzack* (2000), 141 C.C.C. (3d) 449 (Ont. C.A.). In *Suzack*, the two co-accused blamed each other for the murder. Where "cut throat" defences are advanced, there is a real danger that if severance is granted, each accused may successfully point the finger at the other accused in their separate trials. Two acquittals based on directly contradictory versions of the relevant events hardly encourage respect for the criminal justice process. The defences advanced by Shaw and Savoury were not antagonistic and there was no suggestion that if severance were ordered, two juries would hear two very different versions of the relevant events.

The trial judge's decision to refuse severance was an exercise of her discretion. Like any other discretionary decision, the trial judge's refusal to grant severance is entitled to deference: *R. v. Litchfield*, [1993] 4 S.C.R. 333, 86 C.C.C. (3d) 97 at 113-114 (S.C.C.). This court will interfere with the exercise of that discretion where the trial judge had failed to consider the relevant principles, or has considered an irrelevant principle. If the trial judge has erred in principle, it falls to this court to decide, according to the proper principles, whether severance should have been granted. Even if a trial judge has considered the relevant principles, this court will review the trial judge's exercise of her discretion against a reasonableness standard. . . .

The trial judge correctly recognized that an accused's desire to call his co-accused as a witness for his defence could provide the basis for a successful severance application, but that the mere assertion of a desire to call the co-accused did not make severance automatic: *R. v. Chow* (2005), 195 C.C.C. (3d) 246 at 255-56 (S.C.C.); *R. v. Boulet* (1987), 40 C.C.C. (3d) 38 at 42 (Que. C.A.); *R. v. Torbiak and Gillis* (1978), 40 C.C.C. (2d) 193 at 199 (Ont. C.A.); *R. v. Agawa and Mallet* (1975), 28 C.C.C. (2d) 379 at 387 (Ont. C.A.).

Where an accused seeking severance contends that this right to make full answer and defence will be prejudiced unless the co-accused can be compelled to testify, two factors must be addressed by the trial judge:

- Is there a reasonable possibility that the co-accused, if made compellable by severance, would testify?
- If the co-accused would testify, is there a reasonable possibility that the co-accused's evidence could affect the verdict in a manner favourable to the accused seeking severance?

If the accused seeking severance can convince the trial judge that there is a reasonable possibility that the co-accused will testify and that his testimony could affect the verdict by creating a reasonable doubt as to the accused's guilt, the trial judge may properly grant severance. It is nonetheless open to the trial judge to exercise her discretion against severance if there are other factors of significant cogency that outweigh the potential impairment of the accused's right to make full answer and defence occasioned by a joint trial. An accused is entitled to a fair trial, but not necessarily the ideal trial from the defence perspective: *R. v. Cross* (1996), 112 C.C.C. (3d) 410 at 419 (Que. C.A.), leave to appeal to S.C.C. refused [1997] C.S.C.R. No. 15, 114 C.C.C. (3d) vi.

The trial judge's reasons refusing severance focused on the two criteria identified above. Although the Crown argued, based on Shaw's refusal to testify in an unrelated proceeding, that there was reason to doubt Shaw's willingness to testify if severance was granted, I read the trial judge's reasons as assuming that he would testify if rendered compellable. Shaw had testified at the first trial and had given a sworn videotaped statement to the police. In addition, counsel, who had presumably spoken with Shaw, had indicated that

Shaw was prepared to testify. Counsel's representations are entitled to some weight: *R. v. Boulet, supra*, at p. 42.

There was good reason to believe that Shaw would testify if compelled to do so. In reaching that conclusion, I place no weight on Shaw's decision not to testify in the joint trial. His decision not to testify in his own trial casts little, if any, light on whether he would testify if compelled to do so at a trial in which he was not an accused. This is particularly true in a case like this where the evidence that Savoury wanted to elicit from Shaw had little or no relevance to the defence advanced by Shaw. Shaw did not hurt his cause by testifying in a separate trial that Savoury was not the person in the back seat.

I am, however, satisfied that the trial judge erred in principle when considering the possible effect of the evidence that Shaw could give if compelled to testify. The trial judge went beyond the limited inquiry into Shaw's reliability and credibility that is contemplated on a severance application. Martin J.A. described that inquiry in these terms in *R. v. Torbiak, supra*, at p. 199:

> If the evidence of a co-accused sought to be elicited on behalf of another co-accused is such that, when considered in the light of the other evidence, it might reasonably affect the verdict of the jury by creating a reasonable doubt as to the guilt of the latter, then precluding him from having the benefit of that evidence may require a separate trial, [emphasis added] . . .
>
> . . .

The trial judge failed to consider what the jury might reasonably take from Shaw's evidence considered in the context of the rest of the evidence. Instead, the trial judge asked herself: "How reliable is Mr. Shaw going to be as a witness?" She then undertook a detailed examination of Shaw's videotaped statement and his prior testimony, highlighting several inconsistencies between the videotaped statement and his testimony, and between different parts of his testimony.

The trial judge's reasons refusing severance reveal potential difficulties with Shaw's credibility and reliability. He had, however, from the moment of his arrest consistently asserted that Savoury was not the person in the back seat who committed the robbery. While some of the inconsistencies alluded to by the trial judge are potentially significant, they are the standard fare that juries regularly grapple with when assessing the reliability and credibility of both Crown and defence witnesses.

The trial judge made her own assessment of Shaw's reliability and credibility, having never seen him testify, and she found both wanting. On that basis, she refused severance. In doing so, she went beyond her limited responsibilities on the severance application and intruded on the domain of the jury. Provided that Shaw's evidence, considered in the context of the rest of the evidence, could reasonably have left the jury with a reasonable doubt as to Savoury's involvement in the robbery, the trial judge was required to leave the ultimate assessment of Shaw's credibility and reliability with the jury: see *R. v. Buric* (1996), 106 C.C.C. (3d) 97 (Ont. C.A.), aff'd [1997] 1 S.C.R. 535, 114 C.C.C. (3d) 95 (S.C.C.).

The circumstances of this case can be usefully compared to those found in *R. v. Agawa and Mallet, supra.* In that case, the co-accused sought severance so that he could compel Mallet, his co-accused, to testify. In affirming the trial judge's refusal to grant severance, Martin J.A. noted at pp. 387-88 that the proposed evidence of Mallet was "simply not believable" and was "patently unbelievable" when placed alongside the incontrovertible physical and forensic evidence.

I find nothing "patently unbelievable" in Shaw's assertion that Savoury was not the person in the back seat. The fingerprint evidence, although a significant arrow in the Crown's quiver, does not render Shaw's evidence sufficiently incredible to allow the conclusion that it could not possibly affect the deliberations of a reasonable jury. In fact, Shaw's testimony provides some modest support for the contention that Savoury may have touched the car when it was parked in front of the house. It is also noteworthy that at the first trial, at which Shaw testified, the jury was unable to reach a verdict on any count.

Having concluded that the trial judge erred in principle in weighing the credibility and reliability of Shaw, I turn next to the question of whether severance was warranted on a proper application of the relevant principles. Not without some hesitation, I have concluded that severance should have been granted. For the reasons set out above, Savoury's inability to call Shaw as a witness prejudiced his right to make full answer and defence. While there were some considerations weighing against severance, such as the requirement that Mr. Noel would have to testify for a fourth time, those considerations were not sufficiently cogent to trump Savoury's interest in having potentially exculpatory evidence presented to the jury. The interests of justice required severance.

Crown counsel referred to Savoury's failure to testify in his own defence to support Crown counsel's submission that the failure to order severance did not occasion a miscarriage of justice. Savoury's failure to testify is irrelevant to the determination of whether on an application of the proper principles, the interests of justice required severance. His failure to testify could be relied on by the Crown to support a contention that the Crown's case was so strong that the failure to order severance could not have affected the verdict and, therefore, did not occasion a miscarriage of justice. The case presented by the Crown here does not carry the kind of weight required to support this argument. Savoury may have secured an acquittal or at least, as occurred at the first trial a hung jury, if he could have compelled Shaw to testify.

The convictions entered against Savoury must be quashed and a new trial ordered on all counts.

. . .

[Shaw's appeal was dismissed.]

It has also been held that it is reversible error for a trial judge not to sever an accused's trial when his counsel was required to withdraw during the trial for ethical reasons: *R. v. Al-Enzi* (2014), 313 C.C.C. (3d) 417, 14 C.R. (7th) 161 (Ont. C.A.), leave to appeal refused 2014 CarswellOnt 17353, 2014 CarswellOnt 17354 (S.C.C.).

PROBLEM 16

A drug conspiracy trial involving five accused has lasted eight weeks. At the conclusion of the Crown's case the accused B calls two witnesses but does not himself take the stand. Counsel for the next accused M calls B as a witness but he refuses to testify. Counsel for M then applies for a separate trial at which he can call B. He tenders an affidavit that B will corroborate the testimony which M will give as to his own acts and intentions and that B will also give independent evidence which M himself could not give in view of B's knowledge of chemistry. There is also an affidavit from B that he will testify at a separate trial. At this point, counsel for the other three accused indicate that they are in the same position and also make motions for severance. Compare *R. v. Bradley* (1980), 57 C.C.C. (2d) 542 (Que. S.C.).

R. v. SILVINI
(1991), 9 C.R. (4th) 233, 5 O.R. (3d) 545, 68 C.C.C. (3d) 251 (Ont. C.A.)

The accused S and M were jointly charged with conspiracy to traffic in heroin. They were represented by the same counsel. M did not testify at trial. Until the opening of trial, he had planned to plead guilty and to testify in S's defence. S expected M to testify and claimed that he did not learn until after he himself had testified that he could not call M as a witness. The accused and M were convicted. The accused appealed.

LACOURCIÈRE J. (McKinlay and Osborne JJ.A., concurring):—

. . .

The appellant's first ground of appeal is that he was deprived of his right to make full answer and defence to the charge, because his counsel was in a position of conflict as between him and his co-accused Mangiapane. He contends that this resulted in a miscarriage of justice and in a breach of his rights under ss. 7, 10(b) and 11(*d*) of the *Canadian Charter of Rights and Freedoms*. In addition, he claims that trial counsel failed to provide effective assistance at the trial and that this ineffectiveness, in all reasonable probability, affected the verdict of the jury.

. . .

In the present case, trial counsel should have recognized immediately that, as a result of Mangiapane's change of plea, a position of conflict had arisen which could undermine the appellant's right to a fair trial. I accept the appellant's submission that trial counsel's effectiveness was seriously impaired in the following way. The appellant was prevented from compelling Mangiapane to testify, and trial counsel was unable to advise Mangiapane whether or not to testify without potentially harming the interests of one of his two clients. In addition, trial counsel could not cross-examine Crown witnesses so as to show that the case against Mangiapane was much stronger than was that against the appellant, since to do so would compromise Mangiapane's position. Trial counsel was also precluded from arguing during his address to the jury that, whereas Mangiapane—in whose apartment the concealed heroin had been found—was clearly guilty, the appellant was merely a visitor who had arrived in order to go with Mangiapane to pick up food for the restaurant where the appellant worked as a bookkeeper and singer.

By reason of the conflict of interest, it is further submitted that trial counsel was precluded from arguing before the jury that, unlike the appellant who had testified and denied his guilt, the co-accused Mangiapane had not testified. Counsel submits that, accordingly, the jury could have drawn an adverse inference against Mangiapane and a positive inference regarding the appellant.

The law permits counsel for a co-accused to comment on the failure of the other accused to testify. Section 4(6) of the *Canada Evidence Act*, R.S.C. 1985, c. C-5, only prohibits a judge or counsel for the prosecution from making such a comment. Moreover, this type of comment by counsel does not violate the accused's constitutional right, under s. 11(c) of the Charter, not to be compelled to be a witness in proceedings against himself: see *R. v. Naglik* (1991), 3 O.R. (3d) 385, 46 O.A.C. 81, 65 C.C.C. (3d) 272 (C.A.), at pp. 393-397 [O.R.]. However, trial counsel, by reason of his conflict of interest, was precluded from asking the jury to draw an adverse inference against one of the accused. The legitimate and often effective strategy of shifting the blame to one's co-defendant was not available to counsel in this common defence. While it is doubtful that the jury would have translated Mangiapane's guilt as tending to cast doubt on the appellant's guilt, it certainly was not open to counsel for the appellant, even if the appellant had been separately represented, to invite the jury to draw a positive inference by reason only of the appellant's decision to testify. In any event, the appellant's right to effective assistance of counsel entitled him to the competent advice of counsel unburdened by a conflict of interest.

. . .

Because of the difficulty of assessing the effect of the conflict of interest on the defence of the appellant, I am not prepared to apply the curative proviso of s. 686(1)(*b*)(iii) [am. R.S.C. 1985, c. 27 (1st Supp.), ss. 145, 203] of the *Criminal Code*. The appellant has satisfied the burden of showing that the conflict of interest had an adverse effect on the performance of defence counsel at trial.

. . .

B. *Actual Ineffectiveness of Counsel*

The appellant contends that, apart from the conflict of interest issue, his trial counsel failed to provide him with reasonably effective legal assistance, and that there is a reasonable probability that the result of the trial would have been different, but for that lapse.

In *R. v. Garofoli*, supra, at pp. 150-152 [C.C.C., pp. 242-245 C.R.], this court considered the argument that the performance of counsel for an accused was so inadequate as to deprive the accused of the effective assistance of counsel. Martin J.A., referring to counsel's submission that the accused's right to the effective assistance of counsel was protected by ss. 7, 10(*b*) and 11(*d*) of the *Charter*, was prepared to assume for the purpose of that appeal that an accused has a constitutional right to such assistance. The court applied the principles enunciated in *Strickland*, supra. In that case, the court held that the proper standard for counsel's performance is that of reasonably effective assistance to protect the accused's fundamental right to a fair trial guaranteed through the due process clauses and largely defined through the Sixth Amendment. Counsel's role at trial is "to ensure that the adversarial testing process works to produce a just result under the standards governing decision": *Strickland*, supra, at p. 2064. The two components required to show counsel's deficient performance are stated in *Strickland*, supra, on the same page, and were quoted by Martin J.A. in *Garofoli*, supra, at p. 152 [C.C.C., p. 245 C.R.], as principles which "can usefully be applied in this jurisdiction".

> First, the defendant must show that counsel's performance was deficient. This requires showing that counsel made errors so serious that counsel was not functioning as the "counsel" guaranteed the defendant by the Sixth Amendment. Second, the defendant must show that the deficient performance prejudiced the defense. This requires showing that counsel's errors were so serious as to deprive the defendant of a fair trial, a trial whose result is reliable. Unless a defendant makes both showings, it cannot be said that the conviction or death sentence resulted from a breakdown in the adversary process that renders the result unreliable.

Thus, in order to show that the defence was prejudiced by the deficient performance, it must be shown "that there is a reasonable probability that, but for counsel's unprofessional errors, the result of the proceeding would have been different": *Strickland*, supra, at p. 2068.

. . .

[The Court then considered the accused's argument that the counsel was ineffective in failing to apply for a severance, in failing to secure the attendance of a witness, one Principato, and in making an extremely brief address to the jury.]

. . .

When evaluating counsel's performance, the court must always keep in mind that an accused bears the burden of overcoming a strong presumption that counsel's conduct falls within the wide range of reasonable professional assistance: see *Strickland*, supra, at p. 2065. In that case, O'Connor J., delivering the opinion of the court, said at p. 2066:

> Thus, a court deciding an actual ineffectiveness claim must judge the reasonableness of counsel's challenged conduct on the facts of the particular case, viewed as of the time of counsel's conduct. A convicted defendant making a claim of ineffective assistance must identify the acts or omissions of counsel that are alleged not to have been the result of reasonable professional judgment. The court must then determine whether, in light of all the circumstances, the identified acts or omissions were outside the wide range of professionally competent assistance. In making that determination, the court should keep in mind that counsel's function,

as elaborated in prevailing professional norms, is to make the adversarial testing process work in the particular case. At the same time, the court should recognize that counsel is strongly presumed to have rendered adequate assistance and made all significant decisions in the exercise of reasonable professional judgment.

In my respectful view, adhering to the caution expressed in *Strickland*, supra, and adopted in *Garofoli*, supra, at p. 151 [C.C.C., p. 244 C.R.], and accordingly applying a highly deferential scrutiny of counsel's performance, I am unable to say that counsel's conduct in respect of these two latter complaints was ineffective or unprofessional. Further, I am not satisfied that a different course of conduct with respect to securing the attendance of Principato would reasonably have affected the verdict.

In summary, on this ground of appeal, I am satisfied that trial counsel failed to provide reasonably effective legal assistance to the appellant, by reason only of the failure to apply for a severance. The performance of trial counsel was adversely affected, impairing the appellant's right to present full answer and defence. Thus, the proper functioning of the adversarial process was undermined and the verdict resulting from a trial lacking in fairness cannot be relied upon.

6. Application for Change of Venue

As discussed in Chapter 1, there is a strong presumption that the trial will occur in the place where the offence was alleged to have been committed. However, s. 599 of the Criminal Code permits a judge to order that the venue of the trial be changed "if it appears expedient to the ends of justice." The typical reason for this type of order is that prejudicial pre-trial publicity makes it impossible to select an impartial jury necessary to ensure a fair trial. These types of orders are rarely made, reliance being placed on the protections afforded to the parties at trial, including recently expanded jury selection procedures. When a change of venue order is made, there is an important limit on this power — the venue of the trial can only be changed to another territorial division in the *same province* in which the offence is alleged to have been committed. Therefore, a judge cannot decide that the venue of the trial should be changed and then order that it take place in an adjoining province.

Although applications for change of venue are most often made by the accused, it is open to the prosecution as well. The prosecution was successful in its second application following a hung jury in the following case.

R. v. PONTON
(1899), 2 C.C.C. 417 (Ont. H.C.)

ROBERTSON, J.:—This is a second application to change the place of trial, and is made, as the former was, on behalf of the Crown. The accused, William H. Ponton and one Robert Mackie, were charged at the last Napanee Assizes with having robbed the Dominion Bank at its branch office in Napanee.

Before the Assizes commenced, an application was made before me to change the place of trial, under sec. 651 of the Criminal Code, upon the ground that the sympathy felt for the accused Ponton and Mackie in the town of Napanee and in the county of Lennox and Addington, of which it was the county town, was such that a fair trial could not be had. There were a great number of affidavits filed pro and con, but the result was that I was obliged to refuse the motion, the grounds of which refusal are fully set forth in my former judgment. Since then, at the Assizes holden at Napanee in November last, the trial took place and resulted in the conviction of Mackie, but the jury could not agree as to Ponton, and they were discharged. Ponton's trial was then traversed to the then next Assizes at Napanee, which are fixed for the 24th April instant.

This motion is now made on the same material as was used on the former application, supplemented by the affidavits of Mr. Sheriff Hawley; William Greer, inspector of the criminal investigation department of Ontario; Samuel C. McElwain, of Toronto, provincial constable, who was in charge of the jury at and during the time they were sent to their room to consider their verdict; Samuel Adams, chief of police of Napanee; and Mr. Hector Charlesworth, of Toronto, news reporter for "The Mail and Empire," reporting the proceedings for that paper at the trial. And from these affidavits it appears that the jury retired to consider their verdict at 4.40 o'clock p.m., and the Court adjourned about 6 o'clock p.m., to reassemble at 8 o'clock the same evening. During the interval a very large crowd congregated in and about the court house, a portion of which numbering 200 to 300 persons, could be seen from a window at the end of the corridor on which the jury room was situated, and could plainly be heard at the door of the jury room. They were swearing, hooting, shouting, and behaving in a most disorderly manner, and some of them shouted out: "Don't you fellows bring Billy Ponton in guilty! He is not guilty. What's the matter with Billy Ponton? He's all right." This was shouted by a large number of voices, and could be distinctly heard in the jury room by the jurors. This hooting, yelling, and shouting continued for at least one and one-half hours, and, in the opinion of these deponents, "such disorderly conduct, shouting, hooting, and yelling must have had an intimidating effect upon the said jury, and that the deponents are of opinion that had the said jury that evening returned a verdict of guilty against the prisoner Ponton, they could not have safely passed through the said crowd assembled in and about the said court house." On the morning of the 3rd of December, after the jury had been discharged, the constable McElwain says he was appealed to, in his capacity as a constable, by one of the jurors who was supposed to have been one of those who had stood out for conviction, as he (the juror) feared that the crowd, who had again gathered round the streets, and who were making threatening remarks as he passed them, would do him bodily harm. The crowd so assembled were in a very excited condition, and from the remarks made, and their general behaviour, it was perfectly evident that their sympathies were strongly with the prisoner Ponton. That the inspector (Greer) mingled with and in the said crowd, so far as it was possible to do, but, owing to its being so dense, it was only with great difficulty that he succeeded in doing so. The remarks which he heard were of the most grossly insulting character in regard to the learned Judge, and many of such remarks were threatening to the person of the Judge, but, owing to the darkness of the corridors and the density of the crowd, it was impossible to "locate the parties" making them.

Order changing venue.

In *R. v. Fatt* (1986), 54 C.R. (3d) 281, 30 C.C.C. (3d) 69 (N.W.T. S.C.), the venue of a second degree murder charge was changed because of bias in a small native community against the victim and in favour of the accused.

R. v. SUZACK

(2000), 30 C.R. (5th) 346, 141 C.C.C. (3d) 449 (Ont. C.A.), leave to appeal refused (2001), 270 N.R. 193 (note) (S.C.C.)

The accused were charged with the first degree murder of a police constable. The constable was murdered in the course of the execution of his duties. The accused advanced cutthroat defences, each saying the other had done the actual shooting. Each accused was convicted and on their appeals separate grounds were argued. Both argued that the trial judge had erred in refusing to grant a change of venue.

DOHERTY J.A.:—The appellants unsuccessfully sought a change of venue. They relied on pre-trial publicity beginning with the shooting in October 1993 and extending through to September 1994 when the change of venue application was made.

The media coverage was extensive and, in parts, highly emotional. It evinced the community's understandable outrage at the murder of a police officer and its deep sympathy for his family. Some of the coverage suggested that the criminal justice system had failed Constable MacDonald and the community. These references were primarily a reaction to Suzack's release on parole, despite strong opposition, shortly before the murder.

The media reports made many references to the heinous nature of the murder, the criminal antecedents of both appellants, particularly Suzack, and the fact that Suzack was a parole violator when he participated in the killing of Constable MacDonald.

The media coverage linked Constable MacDonald's death to broader issues such as:

- the circulation of a petition referred to as the "MacDonald petition" calling for the return of the death penalty. Some 12,000 people signed the petition; and
- calls for tougher criminal laws and better armed police. These calls were supported by a lobby group which organized a "black ribbon campaign" in memory of Constable MacDonald. Some 40,000 black ribbons were distributed in the Sudbury area.

The media coverage also reflected the community's strong sympathy for Constable MacDonald's family. Constable MacDonald was a well-liked and respected young officer. A trust fund for his children and a scholarship for disadvantaged children were established in his memory. A youth football league was also named in his honour.

The appellants advanced two arguments in support of their contention that the trial judge should have ordered a change of venue. The first submission accepts the law as it presently exists and argues that the trial judge failed to exercise his discretion in a judicial manner. The second, and more ambitious, submission contends that the principles under which change of venue applications have been determined must be recalibrated in the light of the Charter guarantee of the right to a fair trial. The appellants submit that the Charter right to a fair trial requires that the Crown demonstrate that an accused's right to a fair trial can be preserved without a change of venue....

It is a well-established principle that criminal trials should be held in the venue in which the alleged crime took place. This principle serves both the interests of the community and those of the accused. There will, however, be cases where either or both the community's interests and the accused's interests in a fair trial are best served by a trial in some other venue. Section 599(1)(*a*) of the Criminal Code provides in part:

> A court . . . upon the application of the prosecutor or the accused [may] order the trial to be held in a territorial division in the same province other than that in which the offence would otherwise be tried if
>
> (a)   it appears expedient to the ends of justice,...

As the section indicates, a change of venue should be ordered where the judge is satisfied that it "appears expedient to the ends of justice". This determination will depend on the judge's assessment of the evidence led on the application and the weighing of the various factors which favour or tell against a change of venue. In short, the trial judge's decision requires an exercise of discretion. . . .

A review of the case law in which change of venue applications have been made in cases involving the murder of a police officer demonstrates that in similar cases the discretion created by s. 599(1)(*a*) may properly be exercised in different ways. . . .

The appellants accept, for the purposes of their first submission on this ground of appeal, that this court can interfere with the trial judge's exercise of his discretion only if the trial judge erred in principle or if it can be said that the exercise of his discretion was unreasonable in all of the circumstances. An error in principle encompasses a failure to consider relevant factors, the taking into account of irrelevant factors, and a failure to properly weigh the various applicable factors: *R. v. Rezaie* (1996), 112 C.C.C. (3d) 97 at 103 (Ont. C.A.).

Trainor J., the trial judge, described his approach to the discretion vested in him by s. 599(1) in terms that are consistent with the case law:

> .... The obligation or onus is on the defence to show, on a balance of probabilities, that there is a fair and reasonable likelihood of partiality or prejudice in the Sudbury area, that cannot be overcome by the safeguards in jury selection,

including the oath, instructions from the trial judge to the jury panel including jury screening, peremptory challenges, challenges for cause and the rules of evidence.

In deciding against ordering a change in venue, Trainor J. gave considerable weight to the three factors. He stressed the numerous safeguards available to protect the appellants' rights to a fair trial within the trial process, including their right to an extensive challenge for cause process. He also observed that most of the potentially prejudicial media coverage concerning the criminal activities of the appellants had appeared in the media over a year before the scheduled trial date. Finally, Trainor J. identified the real source of potential prejudice to the appellants as the evidence to be adduced in the trial rather than the pre-trial publicity. Trainor J. observed that by the end of the Crown's opening address, the jury selected to try the case, wherever the venue, would be apprised of facts that could prejudice them against the appellants. Counsel for the appellants submit that this factor supported their claim for a change of venue and Trainor J. erred in principle in relying on that factor in refusing the change of venue.

Trainor J. was correct in identifying exposure to the facts of this case as the strongest source of potential prejudice. On any version of events, this was a cold-blooded murder of a helpless police officer acting in the execution of his duties. Further, on any version of events, both appellants were implicated in the attack and one or both had committed murder. Any jury, no matter where the venue, would hear that Suzack was a parole violator and that both appellants were involved in criminal activity. Wherever the trial was to take place, the jury selected would have their ability to act impartially and dispassionately severely tested by the evidence they would hear.

Where the real potential for prejudice lies in the evidence which the jury eventually selected to try the case will hear, a change of venue does not assist in protecting an accused's right to a fair trial. The many safeguards built into the trial process itself must provide that protection. Trainor J. properly considered the real source of the potential prejudice to the appellants' fair trial interests in considering whether a change of venue would serve the ends of justice.

The appellants also submit that Trainor J. failed to give sufficient weight or gave too much weight to other relevant factors in deciding that a change of venue should not be granted. It is difficult to marry the concept of an error in principle based on a failure to give appropriate weight to relevant factors with the concept of deference to the decision of the trial judge. It seems to me that the weight to be assigned to particular factors is the essence of the exercise of the discretion vested in the trial judge. In any event, the argument as framed in this case amounts to an attempt to re-argue the change of venue application in the hope that this court would exercise its discretion differently than did Trainor J. I see no error in principle in the weight assigned by Trainor J. to the various relevant factors and I would not take up the appellants' invitation to engage in a de novo assessment of the evidence led on the application. . . .

There can be no doubt that s. 599(1) must operate in a manner that is consistent with Charter rights and in particular, the right to a fair trial. I regard s. 599(1) as one of many mechanisms designed to protect an accused's right to a fair trial. If a judge is satisfied, having regard to the various mechanisms available to protect an accused's right to a fair trial, that an accused cannot receive a fair trial in the assigned venue, then the interests of justice would clearly require a change of venue under s. 599(1)(*a*).

There is nothing inconsistent with an accused's right to a fair trial and the placing of the onus on an accused to demonstrate that a change of venue is "expedient to the ends of justice." Placing the onus on the accused, if he is the applicant on the change of venue motion, is nothing more than an application of the traditional and well-established rules of the adversarial process. A party who seeks a remedy bears the onus of showing the need for that remedy....

Nor in my view does the right to a fair trial require a change of venue wherever pre-trial publicity poses a risk to that right. The risk will exist to some extent in virtually every case where there has been pre-trial publicity. The right to a fair trial is compromised where despite the available safeguards there is a reasonable likelihood that an accused cannot receive a fair trial in the local venue.

. . .

The application for a change of venue raised difficult problems. Trainor J. gave them careful consideration. I think he was in a much better position to make the subtle assessment required by the change of venue motion than is this court. I would not give effect to this ground of appeal.

PROBLEM 17

The accused is charged with three counts of date rape (sexual assault) against three different women in university residences. The trial before judge alone is highly publicized with detailed daily reports in the local newspapers and television newscasts. While the trial is in progress there are demonstrations outside the court by groups of university students and others demanding that justice be served by a conviction. The accused's family residence is vandalised by slogans indicating that the accused is a rapist. The trial judge acquits on all three counts. As the accused is driven from the court some of the crowd lunge at him and pound the car. The Crown appeals to the Court of Appeal. Assuming that a new trial was ordered, now some 2 years after the first trial, would you as a judge grant a defence motion for a change of venue?

PROBLEM 18

The accused is a lawyer of Aboriginal descent. He has many Aboriginal clients in the venue where he is to be tried. He seeks a change of venue. The trial judge orders a change of venue to a different location within the same judicial district. The reasoning was that to change the venue to a completely different judicial district could have the effect of excluding virtually all Aboriginal people from being potential jurors because of the accused's personal and professional relationships. Was the ruling correct?

Compare *R. v. Robinson* (2009), 261 C.C.C. (3d) 184 (Ont. S.C.J.).

Chapter 12

JURY TRIALS

This chapter addresses the specialized procedures that apply to trials by judge and jury. Specific emphasis is given to the method by which juries are selected.

1. General

R. v. BRYANT
(1984), 48 O.R. (2d) 732, 42 C.R. (3d) 312 (Ont. C.A.)

BLAIR J.A.:—

HISTORY AND SIGNIFICANCE OF TRIAL BY JURY

Trial by jury is an institution unique to common law countries. It is more than a mere incident of criminal procedure. It has been described as a pillar of the Constitution and praised as a palladium of liberty. This is because the rights and freedoms of individuals in our society have been protected from the power of the state to launch prosecutions and control the appointment of judges by the requirement that guilt on any charge must be proved to the satisfaction of 12 ordinary citizens. The true significance of the right of trial by jury can only be understood by reference to its history because, as Lord Devlin has written in "Trial by Jury", Hamlyn lecture (1966), at p. 4:

> The English jury is not what it is because some lawgiver so decreed but because that is the way it has grown up.

I propose, therefore, to review the history of the right of trial by jury in the criminal law in England, the United States of America and Canada.

ENGLAND

In England, the history of trial by jury can be traced more than 900 years to the time of William the Conqueror: see Holdsworth, A History of English Law, 5th ed. (1931), vol. 1, pp. 312-50. Juries were first used by the Norman Kings as inquisitorial bodies to obtain information from the community important to the administration of the Kingdom. Holdsworth states at p. 313 that:

> Domesday Book, which was . . . an enquiry into the extent, value, and tenure of the greater part of the land of England, was compiled from the verdicts of jurors.

The jurors thus chosen from the community were themselves the source of the information required by the Sovereign and were sworn upon oath to disclose what they knew of the facts. Juries became a powerful instrument in extending the influence of the Royal courts of justice. Under the direction of the Royal judges on circuit, juries were used from early times to determine facts and their use for this purpose was systematized in criminal proceedings in the reign of

Henry II. The Assize of Clarendon of 1166 provided for the summoning of juries of presentment or accusation to discover and report on persons in their neighbourhood suspected of serious crimes.

The modern jury system evolved over the next five centuries. The judicial role of the petit jury was separated from the accusatory role of the grand jury. Jurors ceased to be witnesses and by 1650 it was established that they could not act on any evidence which was not given under oath in court: see *Bennet v. Hartford Hundred* (1650), Sty. 233, 82 E.R. 671; Holdsworth, p. 336.

The independence of the jury from control by the judiciary and the Crown was secured later in the same century. *Bushell's Case* (1670), 1 Freem. 2, Vaug. 135, 89 E.R. 2, 124 E.R. 1006, held that jurors could not be fined or imprisoned for bringing in a verdict contrary to the direction of a judge. Once the immunity of juries for judicial acts was established, the only way in which the Crown could exert pressure for favourable verdicts was by controlling the selection of jurors. This was one of the grievances which led to the Revolution of 1688. The Bill of Rights, 1688 (1 Will. & Mar. Sess. 2), c. 2, forbade the practice of the selection of "partial, corrupt and unqualified persons" as jurors. Historians are agreed that a major objective of the revolutionary settlement expressed in the Bill of Rights was the preservation of the jury as a protection against arbitrary rule.

The evolution of trial by jury in criminal cases in England proceeded concurrently with the development of democratic parliamentary institutions and came to be regarded as a basic right essential to the operation of a free political system. The constitutional importance of the jury was described by Blackstone in Commentaries on the Laws of England, Lewis ed. (1902), vol. 4, pp. 349-50, as follows:

> Our law has therefore wisely placed this strong and twofold barrier, of a presentment and a trial by jury, between the liberties of the people and the prerogative of the crown. It was necessary, for preserving the admirable balance of our constitution, to vest the executive power of the laws in the prince; and yet this power might be dangerous and destructive to that very constitution, if exerted without check or control by justices of *oyer* and *terminer* occasionally named by the crown; who might then, as in France or Turkey, imprison, despatch, or exile any man that was obnoxious to the government, by an instant declaration that such is their will and pleasure. But the founders of the English law have with excellent forecast contrived that . . . the truth of every accusation, whether preferred in the shape of indictment, information, or appeal, should afterwards be confirmed by the unanimous suffrage of twelve of his equals and neighbours, indifferently chosen and superior to all suspicion.

In modern times, the constitutional significance of the jury continues to be recognized, as illustrated by Lord Devlin's description of it as the "lamp of freedom" in "Trial by Jury" at p. 164:

> Each jury is a little parliament. The jury sense is the parliamentary sense. I cannot see the one dying and the other surviving. The first object of any tyrant in Whitehall would be to make Parliament utterly subservient to his will; and the next to overthrow or diminish trial by jury, for no tyrant could afford to leave a subject's freedom in the hands of twelve of his countrymen. So that trial by jury is

more than an instrument of justice and more than one wheel of the constitution: it is the lamp that shows that freedom lives.

Trial by jury remains a basic feature of the criminal law of England and has been little altered by statute. The Criminal Justice Act, 1967 (Eng.), c. 80, s. 13, relaxed the unanimity rule by permitting majority verdicts of eleven to one or ten to two, subject to the proviso that the jury must attempt to reach a unanimous verdict for at least two hours or such longer period as the court considers reasonable. As in Canada, the right to jury trial varies with the type of offence. The most serious offences must be tried on indictment before a jury. For the majority of other offences, the accused may be tried by jury or, at his election, by some other mode of trial. Only for minor offences is provision made for summary trial without a jury: see Archbold, Pleading, Evidence and Practice in Criminal Cases, 40th ed. (1979), pp. 5-23.

UNITED STATES OF AMERICA

The English colonists brought trial by jury with them to America and they were quick to establish that right in their colonial courts and legislatures: see Moore, The Jury: Tool of Kings, Palladium of Liberty (1974). One of the grievances against England listed in the Declaration of Independence of 1776 was that the people had been deprived "in many cases, of the benefits of Trial by Jury".

The United States Constitution reflected the high value attached to trial by jury by providing in art. 3 that "The Trial of all Crimes, except in Cases of Impeachment, shall be by Jury". This was reinforced by the Sixth Amendment, which formed part of the Bill of Rights. It provided that: "In all criminal prosecutions, the accused shall enjoy the right to a speedy and public trial, by an impartial jury of the State and District wherein the crime shall have been committed . . ."

In *Duncan v. Louisiana,* 391 U.S. 145, 20 L. Ed. 2d 491, 88 S. Ct. 1444, rehearing denied 392 U.S. 947, 20 L. Ed. 2d 1412, 88 S. Ct. 2270 (1968), White J. stated at pp. 153-54 that the "skeletal history" to which I have referred "is impressive support for considering the right to jury trial in criminal cases to be fundamental to our system of justice". Later, he emphasized the constitutional importance of jury trial as a guarantee of the people's liberties in the following passage at pp. 155-56:

> The guarantees of jury trial in the Federal and State Constitutions reflect a profound judgment about the way in which law should be enforced and justice administered. A right to jury trial is granted to criminal defendants in order to prevent oppression by the Government. Those who wrote our constitutions knew from history and experience that it was necessary to protect against unfounded criminal charges brought to eliminate enemies and against judges too responsive to the voice of higher authority. The framers of the constitutions strove to create an independent judiciary but insisted upon further protection against arbitrary action. Providing an accused with the right to be tried by a jury of his peers gave him an inestimable safeguard against the corrupt or overzealous prosecutor and against the compliant, biased, or eccentric judge. If the defendant preferred the commonsense judgment of a jury to the more tutored but perhaps less sympathetic reaction of the single judge, he was to have it. Beyond this, the jury trial provisions

in the Federal and State Constitutions reflect a fundamental decision about the exercise of official power—a reluctance to entrust plenary powers over the life and liberty of the citizen to one judge or to a group of judges. Fear of unchecked power, so typical of our State and Federal Governments in other respects, found expression in the criminal law in this insistence upon community participation in the determination of guilt or innocence. The deep commitment of the Nation to the right of jury trial in serious criminal cases as a defense against arbitrary law enforcement qualifies for protection under the Due Process Clause of the Fourteenth Amendment, and must therefore be respected by the States.

In the *Duncan* case, the Supreme Court declared unconstitutional a Louisiana law which denied the right of trial by jury for simple battery, a misdemeanor punishable by a maximum of three years' imprisonment. In doing so, it confirmed that the Fourteenth Amendment, which provides that states cannot "deprive any person of life, liberty, or property, without due process of law", incorporated the Sixth Amendment right to trial by jury. White J. categorically rejected earlier Supreme Court decisions that had countenanced limitations of the traditional right of trial by jury, holding that only petty crimes, which in general appear to call for a maximum sentence not exceeding six months, do not require jury trial if they otherwise qualify as petty offences. Subsequent to *Duncan,* incursions upon the right of trial by jury have been few in number and limited to the "mechanics", as opposed to the substance, of the system. For example, state laws providing for juries of less than 12 and dispensing with the requirement of unanimity have been upheld: *v. Florida,* 399 U.S. 78, 26 L. Ed. 2d 446, 90 S. Ct. 1893 (1970), and *Apodaca v. Oregon,* 406 U.S. 404, 32 L. Ed. 2d 184, 92 S. Ct. 1628 (1972). Moreover, the right to jury trial does not extend to military tribunals, as is the case in Canada under s. 11(*f*) of the Charter: *Ex Parte Quirin; Ex parte Haupt; Ex parte Kirling,* 317 U.S. 1, 87 L. Ed. 3, 63 S. Ct. 1, 2 (1942).

CANADA

The right of trial by jury existed in the four original provinces of Canada before Confederation: see Whyte and Lederman, Canadian Constitutional Law, 2nd ed. (1977), pp. 2-7 to 2-9. It was received as part of the common law of England by the colonies of Nova Scotia in 1758 and New Brunswick in 1784.

Its history in Quebec and Ontario is more complicated and demonstrates the importance attached to the jury from the earliest times in this province. After the British conquest, the Royal Proclamation of 1763, R.S.C. 1970, App. II, no. 1, established the law of England as the law of the colony of Quebec, with the result that the right of trial by jury existed in both criminal and civil proceedings. The British Parliament by the Quebec Act, 1774 (14 Geo. 3), c. 38 (also R.S.C. 1970, App. II, no. 2) restored the pre-conquest French law in civil matters, which made no provision for juries, but continued the application of English criminal law :see Edwards, "The Advent of English (Not French) Criminal Law and Procedure into Canada—A Close Call in 1774" (1984), 26 Cr. L.Q. 464. The Quebec Act applied to the enlarged colony of Quebec, which then included most of what is now southern Ontario. The Act was passed over the strong opposition of Edmund Burke and other members of the British

House of Commons, who protested against the withdrawal of the right of civil jury trials: "Debates in the British Parliament on the Quebec Act", in W.P.M. Kennedy, Statutes, Treaties and Documents of the Canadian Constitution, 2nd ed. (1930), pp. 94-135. After the American Revolution, the loyalists who came to Canada objected to the provisions of the Quebec Act, including its denial of the right of trial by jury: "Petition for House of Assembly November 24, 1784" in Kennedy, pp. 172-74. This was one of the grievances of the loyalist settlers which led to the separation of the provinces of Upper and Lower Canada by the Constitutional Act, 1791 (31 Geo. 3), c. 31 (also R.S.C. 1970, App. II, no. 3). Significantly, the first Acts passed by the new legislature of Upper Canada replaced the French civil law by the civil law of England and provided for jury trials in civil cases: An Act respecting Property and Civil Rights, 1792 (U.C.), c. 1, and 1792 (U.C.), c. 2.

At Confederation, jurisdiction over criminal law passed to the federal Parliament, which continued the entrenched right to jury trial of the four original provinces: see Taschereau, The Criminal Statute Law of the Dominion of Canada (1888), pp. 805-806. When the Criminal Code, 1892 (Can.), c. 29, was enacted in 1893, it preserved the existing right to trial by jury and provided basically the same classification of criminal offences with respect to jury trials as is to be found in today's Code: Taschereau, at pp. 756, 844 and 877.

The Criminal Code now provides that an accused has the right to jury trial except for minor offences, as is the case in England and the United States. Section 427 makes trial by jury mandatory for a limited number of serious offences, including treason, murder, sedition and piracy, except in Alberta, where s. 430 permits an accused charged with any offence to be tried with his consent by a judge without a jury. An accused charged with any other serious indictable offence has the right to be tried by jury unless he consents by his election to be tried by a magistrate or judge without a jury: ss. 429 and 484. There are a limited number of indictable offences where a magistrate has absolute jurisdiction and the accused is not entitled to trial by jury. These include minor thefts and fraud where the value of the property involved does not exceed $200, as well as some gaming offences: s. 483 [am. 1972, c. 13, s. 40; 1974-75-76, c. 93, s. 62]. In addition, an accused charged with an offence punishable upon summary conviction is not entitled to trial by jury. Section 722(1) provides that the maximum penalty for summary conviction offences is a fine of not more than $500 or imprisonment for six months or both. Canada has made fewer modifications of the jury than either England or the United States. No provision is made in the Criminal Code for exceptions to the unanimity rule and, except for the Yukon and Northwest Territories, where six jurors suffice, 12 persons are required to constitute a jury: ss. 560 and 561. Section 429 of the Code is in fact broader than the Charter by providing for jury trial for all indictable offences, in contrast to s. 11(f) of the Charter, which only guarantees trial by jury for indictable offences carrying a maximum punishment of five years' imprisonment or more.

CONCLUSION

This history demonstrates that the right of trial by jury not only is an essential part of our criminal justice system but also is an important constitutional guarantee of the rights of the individual in our democratic society. In all common law countries it has, for this reason, been treated as almost sacrosanct and has been interfered with only to a minimal extent....

Largely because of the growth of Crown election offences and elections by Crown counsel to deny the accused the choice of preliminary inquiries and trial by jury, there are now far fewer jury trials. As a result many serious offences, such as many sexual assault trials, now take place without juries. **Is this cause for concern?**

Van Dyke, *Jury Selection Procedures* (1977), suggests that trial by jury is "the fairest instrument of justice because of a belief that the danger of bias is even greater when 'experts' are used" (at p. xii) and that it is only "when the decision-makers come from the population at large, and return to it, will their decisions reflect the collective conscience of the community and be accepted by the community" (at p. xiii). The author invokes in aid G.K. Chesterton, "Twelve Wise Men" in *Tremendous Trifles* (12th ed., 1930), p. 50, penned after Chesterton had served on a jury:

> Now, it is a terrible business to mark a man out for the vengeance of men. But it is a thing to which a man can grow accustomed, as he can to other terrible things; he can even grow accustomed to the sun. And the horrible thing about all legal officials, even the best, about all judges, magistrates, barristers, detectives and policemen, is not that they are wicked (some of them are good), not that they are stupid, several of them are quite intelligent, it is simply that they have got used to it. Strictly they do not see the prisoner in the dock; all they see is the usual man in the usual place.
>
> They don't see the awful Court of judgment; they only see their own workshop. Therefore, the instinct of Christian civilization has most wisely declared that into their judgments there shall upon every occasion be infused fresh blood and fresh thoughts from the streets. Men shall come in who can see the Court, and see it all as one sees a new picture or a play hitherto unvisited. Our civilization has decided, and very justly decided, that determining the guilt or innocence of men is a thing too important to be trusted to trained men. It wishes for light upon that awful matter, it asks men who know no more law than I know, but who can feel the things that I felt in the jury box. When it wants a library catalogued or the solar system discovered, or any trifle of that kind, it uses up its specialists. But when it wishes anything done which is really serious, it collects twelve of the ordinary men standing around. The same thing was done, if I remember right, by the Founder of Christianity.

What do you think is the rationale of trial by jury today?

R. v. SHERRATT

[1991] 1 S.C.R. 509, 3 C.R. (4th) 129, 63 C.C.C. (3d) 193 (S.C.C.)

L'HEUREUX-DUBÉ J. (Sopinka, Gonthier and Cory JJ. concurring):—

The Evolution of the Modern Jury

A brief overview of the evolution of the jury serves to bring into sharp relief the important functions that juries serve. These functions and the principles that inform them, play a crucial role in the consideration of the issue presently before this Court.

While the exact origin of the jury as we now know it is difficult to trace, it is commonly believed that most early societies possessed some sort of adjudicative structure similar in form and purpose to that which serves our system today. Lloyd E. Moore, in a comprehensive examination of the history of the jury, *The Jury, Tool of Kings, Palladium of Liberty* (Cincinnati: W.H. Anderson Co., 1973), records the use of jury-like bodies as early as the time of Solon in the 7th and 6th centuries B.C. The most democratic of these early institutions were the Athenian general assemblies. The forebearer of our modern jury, however, is widely thought to be the Frankish inquisitio whereby local men, with knowledge of the matter in dispute, swore to tell the truth upon a question put to them by the Judge. Only matters in which the Crown had an interest were resolved in this fashion.

. . .

However, as the function of the jury evolved and its domain narrowed, principles not unlike those underlying our challenge procedure evolved. (See Moore at p. 56; J.H. Baker, *An Introduction to English Legal History*, 2nd ed. (London: Butterworths, 1979) at pp. 64-66; Schulman and Meyers, supra, at p. 423, and Sir Patrick Devlin, *Trial by Jury*, (London: Stevens, 1965) at p. 67).

Moore informs us that much of what constitutes our present procedure in challenging prospective jurors, and the grounds upon which such challenges could take place, developed in the 16th and 17th centuries in England. Thus, the number of challenges, the types of challenge allocated to each party, and the grounds upon which such challenges could be based, were formalized early in the modern development of the jury. (See also Schulman and Meyers at pp. 425-428.)

Importantly, the development of the institution known as the jury, and the process through which it came to be selected, was neither fortuitous nor arbitrary, but proceeded upon the strength of a certain vision of the role that that body should play. Most of the early rationales for the use of the jury are as compelling today as they were centuries ago while other, more modern, rationales have developed. The Law Reform Commission of Canada in its 1980 Working Paper, *The Jury in Criminal Trials*, sets out numerous rationales for the past and continued existence of the jury. The jury, through its collective decision making, is an excellent fact finder; due to its representative character, it acts as the conscience of the community; the jury can act as the final bulwark against oppressive laws or their enforcement; it provides a means whereby the public increases its knowledge of the criminal justice system and it increases, through the involvement of the public, societal trust in the system as a whole.

These rationales or functions of the jury continue to inform the development of the jury and our interpretation of legislation governing the selection of individual jurors. The modern jury was not meant to be a tool in the hands of either the Crown or the accused and indoctrinated as such through the challenge procedure, but rather was envisioned as a representative cross-section of society, honestly and fairly chosen. Any other vision may run counter to the very rationales underlying the existence of such a body. As Moore comments, it is only recently that any real representation of society by juries has been achieved in most Western nations. He describes the American experience in these words at p. 231:

> In 1791, a party to a civil or a criminal case was entitled to a 12 member, male, white, unanimous jury.

Increasingly, however, many countries have since repealed property, sex, and race qualifications for jurors, and have legislated other expansions in the number of citizens eligible for jury duty. (For the English legislative experience see the Morris Committee, Report of the Departmental Committee on Jury Service, Command Paper No. 2627; see also N. Blake, "The Case for the Jury", in M. Findlay and P. Duff, eds., *The Jury Under Attack* (London: Butterworths, 1980), at p. 142.) These later developments only serve to underscore the previously articulated rationales for the existence of the jury.

The importance of the jury in our system of criminal justice past and present is eloquently described by Sir William Blackstone in his *Commentaries on the Law of England*, Book 4 (Chicago: University of Chicago Press, 1979), at pp. 349-359:

> So that the liberties of England cannot but subsist so long as this palladium remains sacred and inviolate; not only from all open attacks, (which none will be so hardy as to make,) but also from all secret machinations which may sap and undermine it; by introducing new and arbitrary methods of trial; . . . And, however convenient these may appear at first, (as doubtless all arbitrary powers, well executed, are the most convenient) yet let it be again remembered that delays and little inconveniences in the forms of justice are the price that all free nations must pay for their liberty in more substantial matters; that these inroads upon this sacred bulwark of the nation are fundamentally opposite to the spirit of our constitution.

Section 11(*f*) of the *Canadian Charter of Rights and Freedoms* enshrines the right to trial by jury with these words:

> 11. Any person charged with an offence has the right
>
> . . .
>
> (f) except in the case of an offence under military law tried before a military tribunal, to the benefit of trial by jury where the maximum punishment for the offence is imprisonment for five years or a more severe punishment.

The perceived importance of the jury and the Charter right to jury trial is meaningless without some guarantee that it will perform its duties impartially and represent, as far as is possible and appropriate in the circumstances, the larger community. Indeed, without the two characteristics of impartiality and representativeness, a jury would be unable to perform properly many of the functions that make its existence desirable in the first place. Provincial legislation guarantees representativeness, at least in the initial array. The random selection process, coupled with the sources from which this selection is made, ensures the representativeness of Canadian criminal juries. (See the provincial *Jury Acts*.) Thus, little if any objection can be made regarding this crucial characteristic of juries. Schulman and Myers make this clear at p. 408 of their discussion:

> Jury qualification requirements in Canadian provinces are considerably different than those in the United States or England. The American Bar Association standards for trial by jury, as recommended by the Advisory Committee on the Criminal Trial, say that — 'The names of those persons who may be called for jury service should be selected at random from sources which will furnish a representative cross-section of the community.' *Canadian laws by and large have long met the standard.* [Citations omitted, emphasis added.]

However, the "in-court" selection procedure, set out in the *Criminal Code*, can impact on the representativeness of the jury in some situations. The impartiality of the jury is controlled in the main through the *Criminal Code* procedure. Section 11(*d*) of the *Charter* further buttresses the requirement of impartiality:

11. Any person charged with an offence has the right

. . .

(d) to be presumed innocent until proven guilty according to law in a fair and public hearing by an independent and impartial tribunal.

In order, then, to be meaningful, the application of the *Criminal Code* provisions must be informed by these larger expressions of principle.

Under s. 11(*f*) of the Canadian Charter of Rights and Freedoms "[A]ny person charged with an offence has the right, except in the case of an offence under military law tried before a military tribunal, to the benefit of trial by jury where the maximum punishment for the offence is imprisonment for five years or more severe punishment".

2. Number and Qualifications of Jurors

The number is set at twelve (s. 631(5)) for all provinces and territories.

The Criminal Code (s. 626) delegates to the provinces the power to determine the appropriate qualifications for somebody to serve on a jury in a criminal matter, except that since 1972, s. 626(2) expressly precludes sex discrimination. No woman could serve on a jury in Ontario until 1951, Manitoba until 1952, and Quebec until 1971. The jury qualifications thus differ from province to province. In Ontario, for example, the Juries Act, R.S.O. 1990, c. J.3 sets the following qualifications:

2. Subject to sections 3 and 4, every person who,

(a) resides in Ontario;

    (b) is a Canadian citizen; and

    (c) in the year preceding the year for which the jury is selected had attained the age of eighteen years or more,

is eligible and liable to serve as a juror on juries in the Superior Court of Justice in the county in which he or she resides.

3.(1) The following persons are ineligible to serve as jurors:

1. Every member of the Privy Council of Canada or the Executive Council of Ontario.

2. Every member of the Senate, the House of Commons of Canada or the Assembly.

3. Every judge, and every justice of the peace.

4. Every barrister and solicitor and every student-at-law.

5. Every legally qualified medical practitioner and veterinary surgeon who is actively engaged in practice and every coroner.

6. Every person engaged in the enforcement of law including, without restricting the generality of the foregoing, sheriffs, wardens of any penitentiary, superintendents, jailers or keepers of prisons, correctional institutions or lockups, sheriff's officers, police officers, firefighters who are regularly employed by a fire department for the purposes of subsection 41(1) of the *Fire Protection and Prevention Act, 1997* and officers of a court of justice..

. . .

(3) Every person who has been summoned as a witness or is likely to be called as a witness in a civil or criminal proceeding or has an interest in an action is ineligible to serve as a juror at any sittings at which the proceeding or action might be tried.

(4) Every person who, at any time within three years preceding the year for which the jury roll is prepared, has attended court for jury service in response to a summons after selection from the roll prepared under this Act or any predecessor thereof is ineligible to serve as a juror in that year.

4. A person is ineligible to serve as a juror who,

    (a) has a physical or mental disability that would seriously impair his or her ability to discharge the duties of a juror; or

    (b) has been convicted of an indictable offence, unless the person has subsequently been granted a pardon.

    In *R. v. Church of Scientology* (1997), 33 O.R. (3d) 65, 7 C.R. (5th) 267, 116 C.C.C. (3d) 1 (Ont. C.A.) it was held that the exclusion of non-citizens from jury trials did not violate ss. 7, 11(*d*), 11(*f*) or 15 of the Charter. **Do you think there should be a uniform set of qualifications applying across Canada and inserted in the Criminal Code?** This was tentatively recommended by the Law Reform Commission of Canada, *Working Paper 27: The Jury in Criminal Trials* (1980), but not pursued in their final report to Parliament, *Report 16: The Jury,* (1982).

    It is clear that the Canadian practice is to provide lawyers with limited information as to personal details of prospective jurors. In *R. v. Caldough* (1961), 36 C.R. 248, 131 C.C.C. 336 (B.C. S.C.) the defence counsel arranged to have prospective members of the jury panel telephoned and asked whether they invested in the stock market, what their religion was and finally whether they had any objections to social drinking. When the trial judge discovered this he dismissed the panel, holding that there had been improper conduct. Any communication, it was held, would interfere with the course of justice. **Do you agree? Should counsel receive more information about prospective jurors?**

In *R. v. Latimer*, [1997] 1 S.C.R. 217, 4 C.R. (5th) 1, 112 C.C.C. (3d) 193 (S.C.C.), the accused had been convicted of second degree murder of his severely disabled daughter. By the time the matter reached the Supreme Court it had been established that before the trial the Crown counsel and a police officer had prepared a questionnaire asking prospective jurors for their views on a number of issues, including religion, abortion and mercy killing. The questionnaire was administered to some 30 prospective jurors either on the telephone or at various police stations. Of these persons, five served on the jury which convicted the accused. The Attorney General of Saskatchewan acknowledged that the accused was entitled to a new trial. The Supreme Court of Canada, in dismissing the appeal concerning an alleged breach of the accused's s. 10(*b*) rights, noted that the conduct of the Crown respecting the prospective jurors had been a flagrant abuse of process and interference with the administration of justice.

TIM QUIGLEY, HAVE WE SEEN THE END OF IMPROPER JURY VETTING?

In *R. v. Yumnu*, *R. v. Davey*, and *R. v. Emms*, handed down on December 20, 2012, the Supreme Court of Canada has seemingly settled the issue of the extent to which jury panel vetting may take place and the approach to be taken by the courts in analyzing such conduct. The salient points of the judgments might be summarized as follows:

- Because the Criminal Code and provincial jury eligibility statutes exclude persons with certain types of criminal convictions from serving on juries and some provinces also exclude those charged with criminal offences, and because self-reporting by prospective jurors has proven to be unreliable, it is permissible for the Crown to request the police to conduct criminal record checks and, where relevant, criminal charges (*Yumnu*; *Emms*);

- This vetting must be disclosed to the defence (*Yumnu*; *Emms*);

- This limited form of vetting does not extend to determining whether prospective jurors are disreputable (or, presumably, other features about them that infringe their privacy but might be useful in jury selection) (*Yumnu*; *Emms*);

- Nevertheless, the Crown is permitted to seek the opinions of police officers who are part of the prosecution team about such matters as the partiality, eligibility or suitability of prospective jurors. Relevant information must be disclosed to the defence (*Davey*);

- Where the Crown seeks the opinion of police officers, general impressions, personal or public knowledge in the community, rumours or hunches need not be disclosed (*Davey*);

- In advancing an argument that the trial was unfair because of the jury vetting process, the defence must show (1) that the Crown failed to disclose relevant information that it was obliged to disclose and (2) that had disclosure been made, there was a reasonable possibility that the jury would have been differently constituted. If the defence succeeds, the Crown may rebut the argument by showing that the jury was nonetheless impartial (all three cases);

- If the defence cannot show that the trial was rendered unfair, it may succeed by showing that there was the appearance of injustice in the sense that there was a serious interference with the administration of justice or that the conduct was so offensive to the community's sense of fair play and decency that the proceedings led to a miscarriage of justice (all three cases).

Several aspects of the approach taken by the Court are worthy of comment.

First, the manner in which appellate review of cases takes place had an effect in this case. The analysis by the Court is focused on the non-disclosure by the Crown of its vetting practices, rather than more squarely on the question of whether jury vetting should be permitted at all. Therefore, although the Court in all three cases (*Yumnu*, at paragraph 15; *Emms*, at paragraph 50; *Davey*, at paragraphs 8, 25, and 34) made strong statements about the impropriety of any vetting beyond determining criminal records, this message is diluted by the greater focus on non-disclosure and the approach to be taken in assessing whether the non-disclosure should result in the overturning of a verdict. As well, the deferential standard of review accorded the Court of Appeal decisions contributes to a more weakened statement of the impropriety of jury vetting apart from determining the criminal record of prospective jurors. A requirement of disclosure of jury vetting practices is quite different from a clear statement that jury vetting is impermissible: it is the difference between a confession of wrongdoing and the wrongdoing itself.

That some provinces exclude those facing criminal charges from jury service is also a complication in that it requires more extended database searches that may well uncover other impermissible information about potential jurors. The practical reality that self-reporting by jurors is problematic and that database searches are therefore necessary may be something that we must tolerate but it leaves open the possibility of abuses. Some thought might go into developing better practices. For instance, would it be feasible for court officials to have access to police databases for the limited purposes of checking criminal records so as to avoid even the appearance of the police acting at the behest of the Crown? It is also questionable why some provinces exclude those charged with offences from jury service. Because such persons are presumed innocent, why should they be ineligible to serve as jurors?

Because of the focus on non-disclosure and the jurisprudence that has arisen on that topic, the Court has attempted to align the issue in that broader context. A breach of disclosure that is discovered after the trial has been governed by the approach taken in *R. v. Dixon* (1998) 13 C.R. (5th) 217 (S.C.C.). Consequently, consistent with that approach, the Court in these cases has established the test of whether there is a reasonable possibility that the jury would have been differently constituted. However, this gives rise to further problems. In *Emms*, at para. 23, Justice Moldaver acknowledged that speculation is involved in assessing whether this test can be met. Yet, he went on to find that the test had not been met in that case—surely, on a speculative basis. The exercise of peremptory challenges is frequently an intuitive, almost entirely subjective, and spontaneous process. Speculative post-trial scrutiny is a rather unruly criterion by which to assess the effects of a failure to disclose jury vetting. This will be especially more difficult where there have been both peremptory challenges and challenges for cause because a peremptory challenge may be exercised when the challenge for cause has failed.

Similarly, the distinction drawn in *Davey* by Justice Karakatsanis between seeking opinions from police officers associated with the prosecution for concrete information relating to juror partiality, eligibility or suitability as opposed to general impressions, rumours or hunches is far from a bright line. In the first place, it is not obvious why police should be asked to express opinions at all. Even though the police provide necessary assistance to prosecutions, the Court made it clear in *R. v. McNeil* (2009), 62 C.R. (6th) 1 (S.C.C.) that the Crown and police are separate entities. Connecting them for the purpose of fulfilling a disclosure obligation as was done in *McNeil* is quite different from establishing the police as a resource in jury selection. Second, opinions as to partiality or suitability run the risk of straying into the forbidden categories. Finally, excluding general impressions, etc., from the disclosure obligation invites placing information in that category so as to avoid disclosure. Opinion input from the police might have been prohibited altogether instead of running these risks.

The major weakness of the decisions, however, is the failure to place enough stress on the appearance of justice. Even if there may be confidence that the fairness of each trial was not actually jeopardized, to many people there will be a lingering appearance of unfairness. The appearance of justice has even more importance in the context of jury trials because juries provide the only official input from citizens in our criminal justice system. Thus, scrupulous adherence to fair, impartial and transparent procedures for selecting jurors is required. It is therefore disappointing that none of the nine justices saw fit to elevate this concern to the level of finding a miscarriage of justice, at least in *Emms*.

It might have been thought after *R. v. Latimer* that prosecutors throughout the land would be wary of improper solicitation of information about potential jurors. Sadly, this has proven to be wrong. These three decisions have missed an opportunity to send a very strong message that such conduct is not tolerable. Of the three decisions, *Emms* must be the most egregious because the memorandum from the Crown Attorney's office was ignored by the local Crown office. Perhaps more disturbing than the conduct itself, however, is the Court's failure to find that at least this case resulted in the appearance of injustice. Instead, there is this extraordinary statement:

> The record is silent as to why that memorandum was not complied with. Whatever the reason, it is apparent that the Barrie Crown Attorney's Office simply continued to carry on the practice it had been following for some years. That is unacceptable — but I do not put it down to malevolence or intentional wrongdoing. While disconcerting, the evidence falls well short of establishing that the police and the Crown conspired to obtain a jury favourable to their cause *(Emms,* at para. 44).

Requiring that a conspiracy be established sets the bar far too high. Blatant disregard for a direction from a superior justice official surely merits judicial condemnation.

These decisions leave the law in an unsatisfactory state. Verdicts were overturned in *Latimer, R. v. Hobb,* 2010 NSCA 62, leave to appeal refused [2010] 3 S.C.R. vi, and *R. v. Spiers* 2012 ONCA 798, 293 C.C.C. (3d) 17, 98 C.R. (6th) 114 (Ont. C.A.). A distinguishing point in all of them is that the police provided more information than was requested by the Crown (and, in *Latimer,* directly contacted potential jurors without having been requested to do so). *Spiers* was decided while the Supreme Court trilogy was pending. Thus far, it has not been appealed.

Although the provinces and territories are delegated the authority to determine jury qualifications, ss. 11(d) and (f) of the Charter have been interpreted to require at least a degree of representativeness of the characteristics of the community from which the jury poll is to be drawn. The interpretation and content given these rights by the majority in *Kokopenace* below provide very little scope for successful challenges against an unrepresentative jury roll.

R. v. KOKOPENACE

2015 SCC 28, [2015] 2 S.C.R. 398, 321 C.C.C. (3d) 153, 20 C.R. (7th) 1 (S.C.C.)

The accused was charged with second-degree murder in the District of Kenora, Ontario. He was an Aboriginal man from a First Nations reserve in the jurisdiction. After trial by jury, he was convicted of manslaughter. The accused appealed his conviction to the Ontario Court of Appeal and raised the issue on appeal. Fresh evidence was admitted about the efforts made by the province in preparing the jury rolls. This included a report prepared by former Supreme Court of Canada Justice Frank Iacobucci on the same issue: *First Nations Representation on Ontario Juries: Report of the Independent Review Conducted by The Honourable Frank Iacobucci* (Toronto: Ontario Ministry of the Attorney General, 2013). The Iacobucci report indicated that another major factor was the alienation from the justice system felt by Aboriginal peoples.

In Ontario, jury rolls are compiled through municipal assessment rolls except in the case of First Nations, where the sheriff may obtain the names of residents from any source. In the Kenora District, provincial staff had used band lists provided by the federal government but these had become outdated after the federal government quit providing them due to privacy concerns. The province attempted to obtain lists directly from First Nations. By the time of the accused's trial, membership lists from 42 reserves in the District had been obtained but many were several years old. Notices were sent to residents on reserves via General Delivery but the rate of response was very low amounting to less than one-fifth of the non-reserve population. Although the Aboriginal on-reserve proportion of the population was between 21% and 31% of the District's population, only 4.1% of the jury roll consisted of such residents. In attempting to deal with the problem, the province had focused on the lists and the delivery and response rates.

The Ontario Court of Appeal held that in this case the jury roll was not representative because of a substantial departure from what random selection of all potentially eligible jurors in the district would have produced. Of the four factors contributing to the under-representation of Aboriginal on-reserve residents, two—the lists and the delivery of jury notices—were the state's responsibility and within its power to comply. The other two—the low return rate of notices and Aboriginal disengagement from the criminal justice system—were matters within some capacity of the state to address but it failed to make reasonable efforts to do so. There was therefore a sufficient connection between state action and inaction and the lack of a representative jury roll to find a breach of ss. 11(d) and (f).

The Court also held that the honour of the Crown and *Gladue* principles were applicable and found that ss. 11(d) and 11(f) of the Charter had been violated. That Court ordered a new trial. The Court declined to determine whether s. 15 of the Charter had been violated. The Crown appealed to the Supreme Court of Canada.

The Court delivered a very lengthy divided judgment. A 5-2 majority of the Supreme Court allowed the appeal and reinstated the conviction.

MOLDAVER J. (Rothstein, Wagner, and Gascon JJ., concurring):

A. *How Is Representativeness Defined and How Does It Factor Into Sections 11(d) and 11(f) of the Charter?*

(1) Defining Representativeness

[39] Representativeness is an important feature of the jury; however, its meaning is circumscribed. What is required is a "representative cross-section of society, honestly and fairly chosen": *R. v. Sherratt*, [1991] 1 S.C.R. 509, at p. 524. There is no right to a jury roll of a particular composition, nor to one that proportionately represents all the diverse groups in Canadian society. Courts have consistently rejected the idea that an accused is entitled to a particular number of individuals of his or her race on either the jury roll or petit jury...

[40] As this statement indicates, representativeness is about the process used to compile the jury roll, not its ultimate composition. To date, the jurisprudence has discussed two key features of the jury roll process that ensure representativeness: the use of source lists that draw from a broad cross-section of society, and random selection from those sources: *R. v. Find*, 2001 SCC 32, [2001] 1 S.C.R. 863, at para. 20; *Sherratt*, at p. 525; *Church of Scientology*, at p.

121. I would add a third feature to this list, namely, the delivery of notices to those who have been randomly selected. A jury roll is representative when these three features are present, provided that the state has not deliberately excluded members of a particular group. This process aims to ensure that there is an opportunity for individuals with varied perspectives to be included on the jury: *Church of Scientology*, at p. 122. It also seeks to preclude systemic exclusion of segments of the population: *ibid.*, at pp. 122-24.

[41] The first feature — the use of source lists that draw from a broad cross-section of society — aims to capture as many eligible jurors in each district as possible. A perfect source list would capture all eligible jurors and would therefore proportionately represent all eligible groups in the district. However, the *Charter* does not mandate a proportionately representative list, nor would such a requirement be feasible. Indeed, it would be virtually impossible to find a source list that meets this requirement.

[42] The second feature — random selection — focuses on the manner in which individuals are selected from the source lists for inclusion on the jury roll. It ensures that everyone captured on the source lists has an equal chance of being selected for the jury roll. Consequently, representativeness cannot require a jury roll of a particular composition. This would necessitate a selection process that inquired into prospective jurors' backgrounds — a concept that is incompatible with random selection. Indeed, no province requires that its jury rolls proportionately represent the cultures, races, religions, or other individual characteristics of its inhabitants. Requiring that a jury roll proportionately represent the different religions, races, cultures, or individual characteristics of eligible jurors would create a number of insurmountable problems....

[43] ...Even if a perfect source list were used, it would be impossible to create a jury roll that fully represents the innumerable characteristics existing within our diverse and multicultural society.

(2) The Role of Representativeness Within Sections 11(d) and 11(f) of the *Charter*

[47...]

(a) *Section 11(d)*

[48] Since s. 11(d) focuses on the independence and impartiality of the tribunal, the role of representativeness under this guarantee is necessarily limited to its effect on these concepts. A problem with representativeness that does not undermine independence or impartiality will not violate s. 11(d). The parties in this case focused on the impartiality aspect of s. 11(d). Accordingly, I will limit my comments to this concept.

[49] To determine whether a tribunal is impartial, the question is whether a reasonable person, fully informed of the circumstances, would have a reasonable apprehension of bias: *Valente v. The Queen*, [1985] 2 S.C.R. 673, at pp. 684-91; *R. v. Bain*, [1992] 1 S.C.R. 91, at pp. 101, 111-12 and 147-48. A tribunal must be impartial at both the institutional and individual levels. Even if the petit jury does not appear to be biased, s. 11(d) will be violated if the

process used to compile the jury roll raises an appearance of bias at the systemic level: *R. v. Lippé*, [1991] 2 S.C.R. 114, at p. 140.

(b) *Section 11(f)*

[55] In contrast to its limited role in s. 11(d), the role of representativeness in s. 11(f) is broader. Representativeness not only promotes impartiality, it also legitimizes the jury's role as the "conscience of the community" and promotes public trust in the criminal justice system: *Sherratt*, at pp. 523-25; *Church of Scientology*, at pp. 118-20. Representativeness is thus a necessary component of an accused's s. 11(f) right to a jury trial.

[56] To be able to act as the "conscience of the community" as required by s. 11(f), the jury must be representative. For the purposes of s. 11(f), the meaning of representativeness is the same as it is under s. 11(d): it protects the accused's right to an adequate jury selection process.

[57] Although both provisions incorporate the same definition of representativeness, the broader role it plays in s. 11(f) creates an important point of distinction: while a problem with representativeness will not necessarily violate s. 11(d), the same cannot be said about s. 11(f). Because representativeness is a key characteristic of the jury, its absence will automatically undermine the s. 11(f) right to a trial by jury. ...

[58] For these reasons, a problem with representativeness will violate s. 11(f) even if it is not so serious as to undermine impartiality. That said, if a problem with representativeness does undermine impartiality, it will violate both ss. 11(d) and 11(f).

(3) The Legal Test for Representativeness

(a) *The Appropriate Test Focuses on the Process Used to Compile the Jury Roll*

[61] As a result, I would reframe the test as follows. To determine if the state has met its representativeness obligation, the question is whether the state provided a fair opportunity for a broad cross-section of society to participate in the jury process. A fair opportunity will have been provided when the state makes reasonable efforts to: (1) compile the jury roll using random selection from lists that draw from a broad cross-section of society, and (2) deliver jury notices to those who have been randomly selected. In other words, it is the act of casting a wide net that ensures representativeness. Representativeness is not about targeting particular groups for inclusion on the jury roll.

(3) Conclusion on the Sufficiency of Ontario's Efforts

[125] Ontario made reasonable efforts to include Aboriginal on-reserve residents in the jury process. I therefore conclude that there was no violation of ss. 11 (d) or 11 (f) of the *Charter*.

[126] As we now know, the problem runs much deeper than flawed lists. The Iacobucci Report concludes, at para. 209, that "the most significant systemic barrier to the participation of First Nations peoples in the jury system in Ontario is the negative role the criminal justice system has played in their

lives, culture, values, and laws throughout history". This is a serious policy concern that merits attention. But the accused's ss. 11 (d) and 11 (f) *Charter* rights are not the appropriate vehicle to redress this concern. The accused's right to be tried by a jury of his peers is a right aimed at securing a fair adjudicative process. It cannot be used to dictate to the government how it should — let alone *must* — resolve important policy questions of this nature. For the purposes of ss. 11 (d) and 11 (f), the state's constitutional obligation stops when it has provided a fair opportunity for a broad cross-section of society to participate in the jury process. It has done so.

[127] In coming to this conclusion, I wish to emphasize that nothing in these reasons should be taken as suggesting that it would be appropriate for Ontario to stall its efforts to address the problem of the underrepresentation of Aboriginal on-reserve residents in the jury system. As this Court has noted on many occasions, the estrangement of Aboriginal peoples from the justice system is a pressing matter. If reconciliation is ever to be achieved, the state's efforts must not only continue; they must increase. But this Court is not a commission of inquiry, and its role is not to dictate to the government how to resolve this issue. The question facing us is whether the accused's ss. 11 (d) and 11 (f) *Charter* rights were violated. Viewed through that narrow lens, the state's efforts were sufficient.

C. *Did Ontario Violate the Section 15 Rights of Mr. Kokopenace or of Aboriginal On-Reserve Residents Who Were Potential Jurors?*

[128] For the reasons given by the Court of Appeal, I would dismiss Mr. Kokopenace's s. 15 claims. With respect to his personal s. 15 claim, he has not clearly articulated a disadvantage. This is fatal to his claim. With respect to his request for public interest standing to advance a s. 15 claim on behalf of Aboriginal on-reserve residents who were potential jurors, I would not accede to this request. As an accused person, Mr. Kokopenace may have different, potentially conflicting interests from those of potential jurors. If a challenge is to be raised on their behalf, there must be an opportunity for their views to be represented. Like the Court of Appeal, I would therefore decline to grant public interest standing and dismiss his claim on behalf of potential jurors.

Although differing on the basis for doing so, Justice Karakatsanis concurred in the result.

Cromwell J. (dissenting) (McLachlin C.J. concurring) dissented in a strongly worded opinion. In the view of the dissenters, the selection of a properly constituted jury is the foundation for a fair trial and public confidence in the administration of justice. The fundamental conception of a properly selected jury is that it be drawn randomly from a sample of eligible people in the district and who, because of that random selection, are representative of the population of the district. There is no stand-alone right to a representative jury but representativeness is a component of the rights under ss. 11(d) and (f). Along with impartiality, it is one of the fundamental characteristics of a properly constituted jury and essential for the jury to perform its function as a conscience of the community as a part of s. 11(f) and of an independent and impartial tribunal under s. 11(d). Defects in the formation of a jury therefore affect its representative character and must be considered in determining whether either Charter right has been infringed. The rights belong to persons charged with an offence and there is no corresponding right under them for the community at large or any particular group to be included on a jury roll, jury array or petit jury.

The dissent and Justice Iacobucci in his Report were surely on good ground to say that the state bears a significant responsibility to deal with the systemic issues, including reluctance to serve on juries, that have occurred as a consequence of Canada's historical and contemporary treatment of Aboriginal peoples. There is, of course, no Charter right to have a jury that bears the same characteristics as the actual accused.

Tim Quigley, "*Kokopenace*: Charter Rights to Jury Representation for Aboriginal Accused are Obliterated for Expediency" (2015), 20 C.R. (7th) 99 at 105, proposes an approach different from those taken by the Court:

It seems to me that one way of working through the difficulties outlined by the majority, yet giving meaningful content to both the nature of the section 11 rights in question and Aboriginal estrangement is to frame the issue differently and more narrowly. Rather than focus on representativeness in the sense of mirroring the community, I suggest turning the question around to ask whether a consistent deficiency in the representativeness of a particular group rises to the level of a Charter violation. Thus, rather than wrestling with the admittedly difficult issues of what groups and in what proportion they should be represented, the question becomes whether there is a deficiency in the representativeness of a definable group. This question can only be answered if there are sufficient data to both demonstrate the discrete nature of the group in issue and its proportion in the district that is being assessed. It might also be necessary to consider whether it is a systemic issue in that jurisdiction or simply a one-time blip in the compilation of the jury roll. For the moment, it is likely that the only group for whom there is the necessary definability and the data consists of Aboriginal people who live on reserves. For example, I doubt that the data even exist to show whether or not Aboriginal people living off-reserve are underrepresented. The question of other definable groups being underrepresented also would require sufficient empirical evidence to require constitutional scrutiny.

This case provided a factual basis for determining that on a chronic basis Aboriginal reserve residents are systemically excluded from being on the jury roll in this particular judicial district. Apart from a viable remedy, nothing more needed to be decided in this case. Indeed, that is the thrust of the common law—to make incremental changes in the law as required by the exigencies of the particular case. This would have left for another day in a different set of factual circumstances whether other violations of representativeness under sections 11(d) and (f) were made out.

3. Empanelling the Jury

See generally Tanovich, Paciocco and Skurka, *Jury Selection in Criminal Trials* (Toronto: Irwin Law, 1997).

(a) Challenge to Array

A court official, usually described as the sheriff, must assemble for each court sitting approximately 100 people from whom twelve must be chosen for a particular trial. The process of gathering these 100 people is called the array. The exact process differs from province to province but is usually done from a centralized data list such as the census or assessment rolls.

Once the 100 people have been assembled in the courtroom, it is open for counsel for the accused or the Crown to challenge the array. The procedure is set out in the Criminal Code:

> **629.**(1) The accused or the prosecutor may challenge the jury panel only on the ground of partiality, fraud or wilful misconduct on the part of the sheriff or other officer by whom the panel was returned.
>
> (2) A challenge under subsection (1) shall be in writing and shall state that the person who returned the panel was partial or fraudulent or that he wilfully misconducted himself, as the case may be.
>
> (3) A challenge under this section may in in Form 40.
>
> **630.** Where a challenge is made under section 629, the judge shall determine whether the alleged ground of challenge is true or not, and where he is satisfied that the alleged ground of challenge is true, he shall direct a new panel to be returned.

Successful challenges to the array are rare.

R. v. BORN WITH A TOOTH
(1993), 22 C.R. (4th) 232, 81 C.C.C. (3d) 393 (Alta. Q.B.)

O'LEARY J.:—Prior to the commencement of jury selection the Crown filed a written challenge to the array summoned by the Sheriff. The grounds alleged are partiality and wilful misconduct. I have considered the evidence and the submissions of Counsel and my ruling on the validity of the challenge follows.

The accused is an aboriginal person and is charged with several *Criminal Code* offences alleged to have been committed September 7, 1990 on the Peigan Indian Reservation near Brocket, Alberta. He has elected trial by judge and jury. The Sheriff of the Judicial District of Calgary has returned a jury panel in accordance with his duty under s. 7 of the *Jury Act*, S.A. 1982, ch. J-2.1, the relevant part of which states:

> 7(1) When a jury is required, the clerk shall immediately direct the sheriff to summon a sufficient number of persons from which the jury is to be selected.
>
> (2) The persons to be summoned shall be selected at random in accordance with the regulations.

The regulations concerning the sources of names for the list of eligible residents from which panels are selected are not involved in this inquiry. The regulations say nothing about the mechanics of the random selection procedure prescribed by s. 7(2).

The substance of the challenge is that the array was not selected at random as required by s. 7(2) of the *Jury Act*.

The Sheriff issued jury summonses to 252 individuals residing in the Judicial District of Calgary. Two hundred were selected "at random" from the list of voters for the City of Calgary. The remaining members of the panel are aboriginal persons residing on the three reservations located within the judicial district. The Manager of the Sheriff's office in Calgary, the individual responsible for assembling the panel, said in an Affidavit and confirmed in oral testimony that he had been directed to have a number of individuals of native origin on the jury panel. He made efforts to comply by contacting responsible individuals and organizations and by referring to customer lists of TransAlta Utilities. He was able to secure the names of 52 people. All of them were included in the jury panel.

The selection procedure used by the Sheriff to choose the 200 prospective jurors was not truly random as he followed a recently-adopted practice of selecting males and females alternately so as to ensure that every panel returned is composed equally of men and women. The lack of randomness inherent in this practice has not as yet, to my knowledge, been advanced as a ground for challenging an array and is not the basis of the present challenge.

The prosecutor says that the Sheriff was wrong in selecting and including the 52 individuals of native origin on the panel. He maintains that the panel must be randomly selected from the community at large and no portion of it can legally be chosen or appointed from a particular segment of society.

Counsel for the accused supports the propriety of the panel as summoned. She concedes that the panel was not selected at random, but submits that the procedure used is a form of affirmative action which is justified in light of the conclusion reached in a number of recent studies that native Canadians have been and continue to be discriminated against by the justice system.

. . .

In *R. v. Sherratt* (1991), 3 C.R. (4th) 129, L'Heureux-Dubé J., writing for the majority of the Supreme Court of Canada, identified the two fundamental elements of the criminal jury system - impartiality and representativeness. At p. 141 she said:

> The perceived importance of the jury and the *Charter* right to jury trial is meaningless without some guarantee that it will perform its duties impartially and represent, as far as is possible and appropriate in the circumstances, the larger community. Indeed, without the two characteristics of impartiality and representativeness, a jury would be unable to perform properly many of the functions which make its existence desirable in the first place.

. . .

Representativeness is guaranteed, firstly, by ensuring that as far as possible and practicable the pool or population from which jury panels are selected is representative of the whole community, and, secondly, by selecting jury panels from that pool on a random basis. In her article, "Charter Equality

Rights: Some General Issues and Specific Applications In British Columbia To Elections, Juries and Illegitimacy" (1984), 18.2 U.B.C. Law Rev. 351, Dean Lynn Smith examined efforts in England and the United States to ensure that juries contained more members of minority groups. After concluding that it is impractical to expect individual juries to reflect the demographic composition of the community, she makes a comment with which I agree. She says at p. 495:

> If our continued use of juries reflects a belief that representatives of the community can and should decide certain matters, then it must be the case that arrays are drawn from the community as a whole at random, promiscuously and indiscriminately, otherwise juries in individual cases are not truly representative of the community.

Artificially skewing the composition of jury panels to accommodate the demands of any of the numerous distinct segments of Canadian society would compromise the integrity of the jury system. The effectiveness of the criminal jury system is based on its widespread acceptance by the community as a fair and just method of deciding issues of criminal responsibility. That confidence, and thus the value of the system, would be seriously eroded if manipulation of the composition of juries were permitted, regardless of how well-intentioned the practice might be.

An unarticulated premise of the argument supporting affirmative action in the jury selection process is that some otherwise qualified members of Canadian society are incapable of judging the conduct of other members of the same community in a fair and impartial manner in accordance with the solemn oath taken by jurors. There is no justification for such an assumption.

In my view, the condonation of a process other than random selection from a representative population will lead inevitably to the demise of the jury system. The selective inclusion of members of one group of citizens in a jury panel necessarily discriminates against others. It is a small step from the calculated inclusion of members of one distinct group to the express exclusion of those of other such groups.

There is no provision in the present law for jury panels which are "tailor-made" to suit the race, national or ethnic origin, colour, religion, sex, age, mental or physical disability or other discrete characteristics of accused persons. The ruling sought by the accused could not be made without rejecting a cardinal principle of the criminal jury system. Such a fundamental change should be made only by legislation.

I am satisfied that the challenge is true. As required by s. 630 of the Code, I direct the Sheriff to return a new panel of prospective jurors. I intend to discharge the panel which has been challenged.

Before concluding I wish to make it clear that my finding of "partiality" does not imply any morally blameworthy conduct by the Sheriff or any member of his staff. The expression is not used in the Code in a pejorative sense. Everyone involved in the selection of the array acted in good faith and with the best of intentions.

Three black men were charged with first degree murder following a 1994 shooting in the course of a botched robbery in a Toronto restaurant called "Just Deserts". By the time of the trial, the killing had become a subject of notoriety and significant racially charged media coverage. The victim was a young white woman. The trial judge, Justice Trafford, ordered that the massive 1000-person jury pool be divided randomly into groups of 25 individuals and that the groups be called in an order giving preference to those lots containing black persons. Two of the jurors ultimately selected were black. Following his conviction, one of the accused appealed on the basis that the trial had been unfair due to the judge's procedure in jury selection, which had been laden with stereotypes. Justice Rosenberg, speaking for the Ontario Court of Appeal, dismissed the appeal: *R. v. Brown* (2006), 45 C.R. (6th) 22, 215 C.C.C. (3d) 330 (Ont. C.A.). The trial judge had not erred in exercising his inherent jurisdiction to adopt a process in accordance with the spirit of the Code provisions. Having the jurors return in groups of 25 was a reasonable decision — one which did not require the consent of the parties. However, it was held to have been ill-advised to have the groups containing people of colour return to court first. There are, reasoned the Court, an almost infinite number of characteristics one might consider should be represented and it would not be possible to ensure representation in every jury. However, the error was not a reversible one. The approach taken was meant to foster representativeness and had not resulted in prejudice as it had virtually no real impact on the make-up of the group called forward when compared to census data as to the racial make-up of Toronto.

(b) Challenge to Poll

At this stage the weeding-out process begins to arrive at the actual jury of twelve which will try the accused. There is a very detailed procedure set out in ss. 631-644. **Although twelve jurors ultimately render a verdict, s. 631 permits the trial judge to order that thirteen or fourteen jurors may be selected and sworn. This is designed to ensure that in case any jurors must later be excused for any reason, there will remain sufficient jurors to decide the case. The minimum number of jurors required to render a legal verdict is ten: s. 644(2). In the event that more than twelve jurors remain at the point of being instructed to begin their deliberations, the trial judge must determine which twelve persons are to render the verdict. This is done by drawing cards: s. 652.1(2).** The most usual type of challenge in a jury trial in Canada is the peremptory challenge for which a reason does not have to be given.

632. The judge may, at any time before the commencement of a trial, order that any juror be excused from jury service, whether or not the juror has been called pursuant to subsection 631(3) or (3.1) or any challenge has been made in relation to the juror, for reasons of

(a) personal interest in the matter to be tried;

   (b) relationship with the judge presiding over the jury selection process, the judge before whom the accused is to be tried, the prosecutor, the accused, the counsel for the accused or a prospective witness; or

   (c) personal hardship or any other reasonable cause that, in the opinion of the judge, warrants that the juror be excused.

633. The judge may direct a juror whose name has been called pursuant to subsection 631(3) or (3.1) to stand by for reasons of personal hardship or any other reasonable cause.

634. (1) A juror may be challenged peremptorily whether or not the juror has been challenged for cause pursuant to section 638.

(2) Subject to subsections (2.1) to (4), the prosecutor and the accused are each entitled to

   (a) twenty peremptory challenges, where the accused is charged with high treason or first degree murder;

   (b) twelve peremptory challenges, where the accused is charged with an offence, other than an offence mentioned in paragraph (a), for which the accused may be sentenced to imprisonment for a term exceeding five years; or

   (c) four peremptory challenges, where the accused is charged with an offence that is not referred to in paragraph (a) or (b).

(2.01) If the judge orders under subsection 631(2.2) that 13 or 14 jurors be sworn in accordance with this Part, the total number of peremptory challenges that the prosecutor and the accused are each entitled to is increased by one in the case of 13 jurors or two in the case of 14 jurors.

(2.1) If the judge makes an order for alternate jurors, the total number of peremptory challenges that the prosecutor and the accused are each entitled to is increased by one for each alternate juror.

(2.2) For the purposes of replacing jurors under subsection 644(1.1), the prosecutor and the accused are each entitled to one peremptory challenge for each juror to be replaced.

(3) Where two or more counts in an indictment are to be tried together, the prosecutor and the accused are each entitled only to the number of peremptory challenges provided in respect of the count for which the greatest number of peremptory challenges is available.

(4) Where two or more accused are to be tried together,

   (a) each accused is entitled to the number of peremptory challenges to which the accused would be entitled if tried alone; and

   (b) the prosecutor is entitled to the total number of peremptory challenges available to all the accused.

An amendment to the Code in 2008 has modified the procedure for challenges for cause. The amendment inserted ss. 640(2.1) and 2(2) which permit an accused to apply to have the two triers of the issue make the determination for all prospective jurors and that those two triers then may never become jury members in that trial. It has been held that, since the provisions expressly require the application to be made by the defence, the trial judge has no inherent authority to resort to such "static" triers if the defence has made no application: *R. v. Noureddine*, 2015 ONCA 770 (Ont. C.A.). A new trial was ordered in this murder case.

> **635.**(1) The accused shall be called on before the prosecutor is called on to declare whether the accused challenges the first juror, for cause or peremptorily, and thereafter the prosecutor and the accused shall be called on alternately, in respect of each of the remaining jurors, to first make such a declaration.
>
> (2) Subsection (1) applies where two or more accused are to be tried together, but all of the accused shall exercise the challenges of the defence in turn, in the order in which their names appear in the indictment or in any other order agreed on by them,
>
> (a) in respect of the first juror, before the prosecutor; and
>
> (b) in respect of each of the remaining jurors, either before or after the prosecutor, in accordance with subsection (1).

Note that the defence counsel and Crown have an equal number of peremptory challenges, the number depending on the type of offence. The equality of peremptory challenges was only established by Criminal Code amendment in 1992. Prior to that date the Crown had only four peremptory challenges for any type of offence but also a power to stand by up to 48 prospective jurors. In *R. v. Bain*, [1992] 1 S.C.R. 91, 10 C.R. (4th) 257, 69 C.C.C. (3d) 481 (S.C.C.), the majority of the Supreme Court held that this gave an unfair advantage to the Crown which violated s. 11(*d*). The Crown's stand aside provision was declared invalid but the declaration was suspended for 6 months to avoid a hiatus. Parliament later responded with the Criminal Code amendments equalizing peremptory challenges.

The Crown and defence counsel may also make any number of challenges for cause:

> **638.**(1) A prosecutor or an accused is entitled to any number of challenges on the ground that
>
> (a) the name of a juror does not appear on the panel, but no misnomer or misdescription is a ground of challenge where it appears to the court that the description given on the panel sufficiently designates the person referred to;
>
> (b) a juror is not indifferent between the Queen and the accused;
>
> (c) a juror has been convicted of an offence for which he was sentenced to death or to a term of imprisonment exceeding twelve months;
>
> (d) a juror is an alien;
>
> (e) a juror even with the aid of technical, personal, interpretative or other support services provided to the juror under section 627, is physically unable to perform properly the duties of a juror; or
>
> (f) a juror does not speak the official language of Canada that is the language of the accused or the official language of Canada in which the accused can best give testimony or both official languages of Canada, where the accused is required by reason of an order under section 530 to be tried before a judge and jury who speak the official language of Canada that is the language of the accused or the official language of Canada in which the accused can best give testimony or who speak both official languages of Canada, as the case may be.

Recently a psychologist, an expert on jury selection in the United States, appeared on a CBC program and advised that it is impossible to have an impartial jury in a criminal trial since everyone is biased to some degree against an accused. **Should Canadian courts sanction jury selection experts to aid lawyers in challenging on the basis of demographic surveys, jury simulations and/or general attitudinal research?**

PROBLEM 1

The accused was charged with conspiracy to procure an illegal abortion. The defence counsel mounted a general challenge for cause of every member of the jury panel. Following lengthy submissions between the judge, defence counsel and the Crown, the trial judge determined that prospective jurors would be asked the following questions in determining whether they were impartial between the Crown and the accused:

(a)   "Do you have any religious, moral or other beliefs relating to abortion such that you would convict or acquit regardless of the law or the evidence? Answer yes or no.

(b)   Have you, because of religious or moral beliefs or because of what you have read or seen in the media, formed any opinion as to the guilt or innocence of the accused? Answer yes or no.

(c)   Despite any beliefs or opinions would you be able to set aside those beliefs or opinions and reach a verdict of guilty or not guilty solely on the evidence and the law you receive in this courtroom? Yes or no."

As counsel on behalf of the Catholic Women's League of Canada objecting to this method of selection what argument would you make? Is it material that the permitted questions were suggested by Crown counsel? In *R. v. Morgentaler* (1985), 44 C.R. (3d) 189 (Ont. C.A.), the league was denied leave to intervene on the appeal. The manner of selection was not considered on the appeal.

The selection of jurors in *Morgentaler* has been criticized by I.A. Hunter in (1986-87), 29 Crim. L.Q. 176.

Both *Morgentaler* (1985), 44 C.R. (3d) 189 (Ont. C.A.) and *Crosby* (1979), 49 C.C.C. (2d) 555 (Ont. H.C.) were addressed by the Ontario Court of Appeal in *R. v. Zundel*. It was held that the trial judge had erred in refusing the defence application to challenge potential jurors for cause in view of prejudicial pre-trial publicity generated by the prosecution.

R. v. ZUNDEL

(1987), 58 O.R. (2d) 129, 56 C.R. (3d) 1, 31 C.C.C. (3d) 97 (Ont. C.A.)

Per Curiam

The appellant, Ernst Zundel, was charged with the commission of two offences contrary to s. 177 of the Criminal Code, R.S.C. 1970, c. C-34. The indictment read as follows:

1. ERNST ZUNDEL stands charged that he, during the year 1981, at the Municipality of Metropolitan Toronto in the Judicial District of York, did publish a statement or tale that he knows is false, namely the article "The West, War, and Islam", and the said article is likely to cause mischief to the public interest in social and racial tolerance, contrary to the Criminal Code.

2. ERNST ZUNDEL stands further charged that he, in or about the year 1981, at the Municipality of Metropolitan Toronto in the Judicial District of York, did publish a statement or tale, namely "Did Six Million Really Die?" that he knows is false and that is likely to cause mischief to the public interest in social and racial tolerance, contrary to the Criminal Code.

. . .

On a motion made by defence counsel following the appellant's arraignment but before any plea was taken, the presiding judge conducted a pre-trial voir dire. In the course of the voir dire the appellant was sworn and testified, as the sole witness, regarding the pretrial publicity concerning him. Section 567(1)(*b*) of the Criminal Code was invoked. It reads as follows:

567.(1) A prosecutor or an accused is entitled to any number of challenges on the ground that . . .

(*b*) a juror is not indifferent between the Queen and the accused . . .

On the voir dire the appellant filed many articles published before the trial in the Globe and Mail which identified the appellant as a distributor of neo-Nazi, anti-Semitic hate literature. One such article quoted political personalities describing the appellant as "one of the world's big purveyors of Nazi propaganda" (Globe and Mail, 15th June 1983).

Other articles, taken from the Toronto Sun and the Ottawa Citizen, were filed. They described action by the Postmaster General to suspend the appellant's mail privileges (later reinstated) and included comments by the federal Minister of Justice on proposed legislation to curb hate literature, with particular reference to the appellant.

Other materials filed included two articles reporting picketing by the appellant and his group of the film "The Boys from Brazil", which is said to describe the cloning of Hitler, and a number of articles in different publications referring to large demonstrations by Jewish groups at the appellant's home in Toronto and referring to the views of a group known as the "Canadian Holocaust Rememberance Association" which focussed on the appellant. The appellant described these materials "as standard Zionist rhetoric".

In addition, the appellant produced media reports of confrontations between the appellant's group and hostile demonstrators at the earlier court proceedings, and the explosion of a pipe bomb, causing considerable property damage, near the appellant's garage in September 1984. The appellant also produced on the voir dire a tape-recording of a C.B.C. broadcast on the television program "The National", which he claims was a distortion of a press conference that he had given. There was also evidence of a large demonstration of up to 2,000 people outside of the appellant's home, and of demonstrations at the courthouse on the occasion of earlier appearances, which culminated in a violent confrontation outside the Metropolitan Courthouse on the first morning of the trial.

The evidence presented on the voir dire was meant to support the appellant's endeavour to establish his right to question the prospective jurors on their potential prejudice. The appellant's purpose was to demonstrate that members of identifiable groups entertained ill will towards him and therefore could not be dispassionate and impartial jurors.

A.   *The Question*

In his reasons for ruling, given orally after the first ruling on the Charter, the learned trial judge summarized the evidence given by the appellant on the voir dire and referred to the scenes of physical violence between the appellant and his followers and members of the Jewish Defence League. He quoted the questions which counsel for the appellant proposed to ask of each juror.

1. Can you consider and will your mind allow considerations of the question of whether there were gas chambers in Germany for the extermination of Jews? Yes or no.

2. Can you impartially consider the question of gas chambers and the Holocaust and remove from your mind the massive publicity of it to decide the case on the evidence put before you in this court, and only on such evidence? Yes or no.

3. Do you believe that the Jews of today are God's chosen people or especially favoured by God? Yes or no.

4. Do you believe the Holocaust happened as depicted by the media, and would you be able to remove that idea from your mind and consider the question solely on the evidence presented in court? Yes or no.

5. Do you have any moral, religious or other beliefs relating to Jews or the Holocaust such that you would convict or acquit regardless of the law or evidence? Yes or no.

6. Do you have any moral, religious, or other beliefs relating to Freemasons such that you would convict or acquit regardless of the law or evidence? Yes or no.

7. Have you, because of religious or moral beliefs, or because of what you have heard, read or seen in the media, formed any opinion as to the guilt or innocence of the accused? Yes or no.

8. Despite any beliefs or opinions, would you be able to set aside those beliefs or opinions and reach a verdict of guilty or not guilty solely on the evidence and the law you receive in this courtroom? Yes or no.

9. Do you have any abiding prejudices against German people?

In addition, counsel for the accused had asked the trial judge, in his opening remarks to the jury panel, to excuse anyone from the jury panel who:

(1)   is a Jewish person or is employed by Jewish persons or is a close relative of a Jewish person;

(2)   is a Freemason or is employed by a Freemason or is a close friend or relative of a Freemason;

(3)   is personally acquainted with the accused in such a way that he favours or dislikes the accused so much that he would be unable, through prejudice to look impartially upon the accused or judge his guilt or innocence solely on the evidence in court;

(4)   speaks or understands some English, but has difficulty understanding it fully.

After making reference to the decision of Osler J. in *R. v. Crosby* (1979), 49 C.C.C. (2d) 255 (Ont. H.C.), the learned trial judge noted that there had not been any " 'notorious episode' in the community". In that case, Osler J., in refusing to permit counsel to challenge for cause on the grounds of racial prejudice, said at p. 256:

> It seems to me that, in the absence of any notorious episode in a community of the type I have mentioned, to permit challenges of this kind to go forward simply on the ground that man is prejudiced and that black and white may frequently be prejudiced against each other is to admit to a weakness in our nation and in our community which I do not propose to acknowledge.

> Should the fact that an accused belongs to a particular, even a highly visible minority group lead automatically to a searching examination of prospective jurors on their views there would be few criminal cases today in which such challenges would not be justified.

The learned trial judge concluded that allowing the proposed questions would prevent a substantial segment of the community from sitting as jurors. After quoting excerpts from the leading case in this province on the subject of challenge for cause, *R. v. Hubbert* (1975), 11 O.R. (2d) 464, 31 C.R.N.S. 27, 29 C.C.C. (2d) 279, affirmed [1977] 2 S.C.R. 267, 15 O.R. (2d) 324, 38 C.R.N.S. 381, 33 C.C.C. (2d) 207, 15 N.R. 139, the learned trial judge concluded as follows:

> I conclude with the observation that the evidence I have heard and read shows that the accused, perhaps through his own deliberate acts, has attracted much publicity and notoriety upon himself. His position on sensitive, emotion-provoking subjects certainly achieved that result, in my view. That alone, however, should not compel the exercise of my judicial discretion to permit any of these questions to be put. Each and every proposed question, I find, offends the principles set out in *R. v. Hubbert*. There is no evidentiary connection between the attracted notoriety and the reasonable prospect that any prospective juror, regardless of his or her racial origin, or religious belief, or for any other reason, would be unable to impartially return a verdict in this trial based solely and only upon the evidence led thereat . . .

> Mr. Zundel elected trial by jury. No one forced him to elect that mode of trial. He has an absolute right to be tried by a jury of his peers. Having so elected, the public notoriety he has attracted to himself does not of itself, in the absence of anything further, entitle him to use any of these questions to challenge his prospective jurors for cause in order to tailor his own jury to suit him.

Following the dismissal of his application, the appellant was arraigned and pleaded not guilty to the charges. In his opening remarks to the panel the learned trial judge then gave the following caution:

> If there is any prospective juror here who is a member of, or who is related by blood or marriage to anyone else who is a member of, any group or organization

which uses violent confrontation in public places in support of or in opposition to the ideas of other groups, and if by the reason of that membership or your relationship you feel that you would be unable to judge and act as a judge or as a juror who, as a judge, impartially, and solely and only upon the evidence that you have heard, then you will please so indicate in the same manner as I have already indicated.

If there is anything that you have heard, seen or read about this case that would prevent you from impartially deciding a verdict solely and only upon the evidence led in this courtroom, then of course you don't come to the case free of preconceived notions or prejudice, and you will please so indicate.

Notwithstanding anything I have said, if there is any member of your number who is a prospective juror whose present views concerning the guilt or innocence of this accused are so strongly fixed that an impartial assessment of the evidence heard only in this trial would be impossible or difficult, if the answer to this question or to any of the other questions I have posed is "Yes", if your name is called please indicate that when you come to the book to be sworn.

It is clear from the analysis made by this court in *R. v. Hubbert*, supra, at pp. 291-92, that, where the suggestion is made that publicity concerning the alleged offence has been widespread, there may be a danger that the mind of a prospective juror may be influenced and biased in such a way that he would be unable to give an impartial verdict.

There is no doubt, and the learned trial judge found as a fact in the instant case, that there had been considerable pre-trial publicity in the media, generally adverse to the appellant. In our respectful view, the learned trial judge erred in stressing the absence of a notorious episode and elevating it as a sine qua non requirement to a successful application to allow the proposed question in the challenge for cause. While a notorious episode would be a factor to be considered in an application of this kind, we do not think that Osler J. ever intended it to be an absolute requirement. In the present case, in any event, the series of well-publicized confrontations continuing up to the time of trial would, in our view, qualify as notorious episodes.

Similarly, the fact that the appellant's conduct attracted publicity and notoriety upon himself is not sufficient to automatically disallow certain questions to be put to the jury. The judge's discretion must be exercised judicially. The real question is whether the particular publicity and notoriety of the accused could potentially have the effect of destroying the prospective juror's indifference between the Crown and the accused. In this context "indifference" means "Absence of feeling for or against": the Shorter Oxford English Dictionary, 3rd ed. (1944). The equivalent is a now rare expression, "indifferency", meaning "Absence of bias, prejudice, or favour".

The reference in the judge's ruling to the absence of an evidentiary connection between the publicity and notoriety and the challenge to the prospective juror's lack of indifference is, with respect, based on a misconception. It is not for the presiding judge to rule on the "evidentiary connection", but for the trier selected for that purpose. In addition, the trial judge's statement that the accused "would not be allowed to tailor-make his own jury" was incorrect, inasmuch as any challenge for cause by the defence would have been tried by the triers selected from the jury panel pursuant to the provisions of s. 569(2) of the Criminal Code.

Having recognized these errors, it is only fair to point out that counsel for the appellant, in his recorded submissions and in framing the questions, was in large part responsible for the adverse ruling. It is apparent on the record that Crown counsel at trial was prepared to concede that certain questions could properly be asked of each prospective juror. In particular, QQ.7 and 8, if the reference to "religous or moral belief" or "opinions" had been deleted, would have been appropriate questions in seeking to determine whether the pre-trial publicity and the accused's notoriety had made it impossible for the prospective juror to render an impartial verdict. This near-agreement was referred to by the trial judge in his ruling in the following passage:

> As I understand it, Crown counsel and defence counsel may well have come close to agreement that, subject to my order, QQ.7 and 8 might be permitted, but they have been totally unable to agree with respect to the balance of the questions that I have just read.

It appears from his submissions and proposed questions that defence counsel at trial was attempting to disqualify all Freemasons and Jewish members of the panel as jurors in the case. The assumption that Jewish people or Freemasons form part of a homogenous group with an identity of interest capable of subverting their impartiality in a criminal case is unwarranted, and formed the basis of proposed QQ. 3, 5 and 6 in the first group of questions and grounds 1 and 2 in the proposed remarks to the jury panel. It is contrary to established practice in this province to attempt to challenge jurors for cause on general grounds such as race, religion, political belief, or opinions: see *R. v. Hubbert*, supra, at p. 290. Similarly, a challenge on the basis of membership in a minority group is not permissible in Canada.

Mr. Christie, counsel for the appellant, defended the propriety of these questions by referrring to questions which were approved by the then Associate Chief Justice of the High Court in the 1984 prosecution against Dr. Henry Morgentaler and others: *R. v. Morgentaler*, 15th October 1984 (not yet reported). We were provided with a certified transcript of the three main questions, which were framed following a long discussion in chambers and which were asked of each prospective juror in the case. All three questions inquired of the prospective juror whether he or she had any religious, moral or other beliefs or opinions relating to abortion that would interfere with the juror's ability to render a true verdict. Mr. Christie also relied on the ruling made by Ewaschuk J. in *R. v. Rowbotham* (1984), 12 C.C.C. (3d) 189 (Ont. H.C.), where prospective jurors were asked first, by defence counsel, whether they had a strong dislike for the narcotic marijuana or hashish. As a corollary to this question the Crown then asked whether they had a strong view in favour of the legalization or use of marijuana or hashish. In either case, the jurors were asked whether their views would prevent them from rendering a true verdict based on the evidence given at trial. The rationale for the ruling was given at p. 192:

> A general as opposed to a particular challenge may arise because of extensive pretrial publicity or, as here, because of strong personal views held by various

members of the public on such controversial matters as drugs, obscenity or abortion. The goal is to obtain a fair trial for both sides based only on the evidence at trial and not on juror's personal prejudices.

Counsel for the appellant relied on the rulings in *Morgentaler* and *Rowbotham*, made since the *Hubbert* decision, supra, as supporting his proposed set of questions on the challenge for cause. In particular, he claims to have framed his questions by reference to the questions allowed by Parker A.C.J.H.C. in *Morgentaler*. There is some similarity in the questions' reference to religious, moral or other beliefs. We must point out, however, that the propriety of the questions used in the challenge for cause in the *Morgentaler* case was never made an issue and thus was not reviewed in the Crown appeal to this court.

In the present case, the defence motion was directed in part towards the exclusion of Jewish people on the grounds that they would not render a true verdict as to the occurrence of the Holocaust. The majority of the proposed questions were improperly worded, and therefore properly rejected by the learned trial judge. This rejection should not have been the end of the matter, so as to foreclose any challenge for cause.

In our view, although the presiding judge correctly refused the questions as framed, he ought, in the circumstances, to have advised counsel that he was not precluded from rephrasing certain of the proposed questions in a manner which would have been in accordance with the guidelines laid down in *R. v. Hubbert*, supra.

There is a denial of a fundamental right to a fair and proper trial where the accused is not allowed to challenge any number of jurors for cause, when the grounds of challenge are properly specified in accordance with s. 567(1)(*b*) of the Criminal Code and made before the juror is sworn. We are concerned that the failure of the presiding judge to advise counsel that he was at liberty to amend some of the questions may have resulted in the denial of a fundamental right; counsel was entitled to determine whether any potential juror was, by reason of the pre-trial publicity and the notoriety of the appellant, sufficiently impartial. In our opinion the appellant was effectively denied that fundamental right.

It was conceded by counsel, in the course of the argument that the challenge for cause was not repeated when each juror came forward to be sworn, according to the correct practice. We agree, however, that, once the trial judge had refused the defence permission to ask any of the proposed questions and failed to give an opportunity to amend, the defence was, in effect, prevented from exercising its right to challenge for cause. A trial judge cannot, in the exercise of a discretion which he undoubtedly possesses in the area of admitting grounds of challenge for cause and settling the questions, effectively curtail the statutory right to challenge for cause.

The warning later given by the trial judge, requesting that individual members of the panel disqualify themselves under certain circumstances, was insufficient to correct the erroneous denial of the statutory right of challenge for cause. The issue of impartiality or indifference is one that Parliament has entrusted to the two tiers, not to the conscience of the individual prospective juror.

We are all of the view that the appellant was deprived of his right to have a jury selected according to law, whose impartiality or appearance of impartiality could not be impugned. This error was compounded by the judge's refusal to order a ban on the publication both of the submissions made and of the ruling on the motion, as was done in *R. v. Keegstra*, 9th April 1985 (not yet reported), which may have also prejudiced the appellant's right to an impartial jury.

In a Criminal Reports annotation to the *Zundel* decision, John Rosen commented:

Judicial prejudice against challenge for cause remains intact. Both judgments (*Zundel* and *Hubbert*) commence with the presumption that a juror will abide by his oath regardless of any preconceived ideas or personal prejudices, and that it is somehow unfair to the juror and costly to the system to ask whether the presumption is true. Accepting the proposition that the average juror will honestly attempt to fulfull his sworn duty, what harm is there in asking prospective jurors about their prior knowledge of the case and their possible lack of partiality, particularly when the object of the exercise is to ensure that a constitutionally-entrenched right is not violated by strangers to the judicial system? . . . The court (in *Zundel*) reiterated its opinion in *Hubbert* that an attempt to challenge jurors for cause on general grounds such as race, religion, political belief or opinions, and particularly membership in a minority group, is not permissible in Canada. Clearly, it would be offensive to suggest that anyone, simply because of a non-majoritarian belief or background, should be disqualified from participating in the judicial process. However, the evidence relating to such factors may in some circum-stances be relevant evidence for the triers of fact to consider, in light of the whole of the evidence before them, in determining the impartiality of any prospective juror. In *Zundel*, for example, it would have been acceptable to ask a potential juror whether he or she was Jewish and to inquire into whether this factor would inhibit an impartial verdict on the evidence. At issue was a pamphlet denouncing the Holocaust. For many Jews, the Holocaust has become more than an historical account of persecution and death. It has become a symbolic focus for religious, ethic and cultural survival which lies at the heart of a community's self-identity and aspirations. Regardless of the repugnance of Zundel's conduct, like all accused persons in Canada he was entitled to be tried by an impartial jury.

SHERRATT v. R.

[1991] 1 S.C.R. 509, 3 C.R. (4th) 129, 63 C.C.C. (3d) 193 (S.C.C.)

The accused was charged and convicted of the murder of a pimp. After his arrest, he told the police about the killing and where in Winnipeg he had disposed of the body. The commercial garbage bin had been emptied and the search for the body received media publicity including questions about the victim, his background and involvement in killings in the United States. The accused's background was also the subject of media speculation. These reports appeared about 9 to 10 months before the trial. The accused sought to challenge for cause each potential juror because of the potential for partiality as a result of the pre-trial publicity. The trial judge rejected the challenge.

The Supreme Court held that the trial judge had not erred and took the opportunity to re-examine the principles of challenging prospective jurors.

L'HEUREUX-DUBÉ J. (Sopinka, Gonthier and Cory JJ. concurring):—

In rationalizing these various judicial expressions, it is necessary to reflect on what was in fact said by the Ontario Court of Appeal in *Hubbert*. While certain broad statements in that case may warrant comment, the Court's discussion of the pre-screening procedure and the proper course for a trial judge to follow in an application for a challenge for cause due to alleged partiality, in the main, cannot be challenged. Generally, the Court correctly states the law as it is understood in this country when dealing with an application for a challenge for cause based upon partiality. Certain comments may, however, be appropriate in light of the coming into force of the *Charter*. While it is no doubt true that trial judges have a wide discretion in these matters, and that jurors will usually behave in accordance with their oaths, these two principles cannot supercede the right of every accused person to a fair trial, which necessarily includes the empanelling of an impartial jury. (See The Law Reform Commission of Canada, *The Jury in Criminal Trials*, Working Paper 27, 1980.)

This, however, does not mean that an accused has the right to a favourable jury, or that the selection procedure can be used to thwart the representativeness that is essential to the proper functioning of a jury. While it may be, in some instances, that the peremptory challenges allocated to the accused and the Crown, and the Crown's additional right to stand aside, will be used by the parties to alter somewhat the degree to which the jury represents the community, peremptory challenges are justified on a number of grounds. The accused may, for example, not have sufficient information to challenge for cause a member of the panel he/ she feels should be excluded. Peremptory challenges can also, in certain circumstances, produce a more representative jury depending upon both the nature of the community and the accused. Challenges of this nature also serve to heighten an accused's perception that he/she has had the benefit of a fairly selected tribunal.

As to challenges for cause, they are properly used to rid the jury of prospective members who are not indifferent or who otherwise fall within s. 567 (now s. 638), of the Code, but they stray into illegitimacy if used merely, without more, to over- or under-represent a certain class in society, or as a "fishing expedition" in order to obtain personal information about the juror. As previously mentioned, information obtained on an ultimately unsuccessful challenge for cause may, however, lead the challenger to exercise the right to challenge peremptorily or to stand aside the particular juror. If the challenge process is used in a principled fashion, according to its underlying rationales, possible inconvenience to potential jurors or the possibility of slightly lengthening trials is not too great a price for society to pay in ensuring that accused persons in this country have, and appear to have, a fair trial before an impartial tribunal — in this case the jury.

This being said, some words of caution are in order as to the nature of the pre-screening that can be legitimately engaged in by trial judges. If one harkens back to the actual words used by the Court of Appeal in *Hubbert*, it becomes clear, in my opinion, that the procedure envisioned is inoffensive and falls outside of the warnings delivered in *Barrow*, and *Guérin c. R.; Pimparé c. R.*, as evidenced by the following, at pp. 292-293 [C.C.C., pp. 40-44 C.R.N.S.]:

> Turning to the practical consideration of the methods by which the process should be carried out, we deal first with the kind of *obvious partiality* dealt with in the English practice direction. Some trial Judges make a practice of saying to the jury panel, before the selection process begins, something of this nature:
>
> If there is anyone on this panel who is closely connected with a party to this case or with a witness who is to testify, will you please stand?
>
> . . .
>
> *To take obvious examples, if the juror is the uncle of the accused, or the wife of a witness, or the brother of the investigating police officer, he ought not to serve.*
>
> In our view, the trial Judge on his own should excuse that prospective juror from the case, without more ado. . . . *We think the practice of excusing jurors of obvious partiality is a desirable one in all cases.* [Emphasis added.]

I agree. And, as pointed out by the Ontario Court of Appeal, if the trial Judge does not excuse a juror at this stage, that juror is still subject to challenge or to a direction to stand aside. Nothing said by the Court of Appeal relates to cases of disputed partiality. The initial procedure outlined by the Court of Appeal goes only to such clear-cut cases of partiality that, as said in *Guérin c. R.; Pimparé c. R.*, and *Barrow*, the consent of counsel is and can be presumed. Once out of obvious situations of non-indifference, as in *Guérin c. R.; Pimparé c. R.*, and *Barrow*, the procedure takes on a different colour: consent can no longer be presumed and the procedure must conform to that which is set out in the *Criminal Code*. There is absolutely no room for a trial Judge to increase further his/her powers and take over the challenge process by deciding controversial questions of partiality. If there exist legitimate grounds for a challenge for cause, outside of the obvious cases addressed by the *Hubbert* procedure, it must proceed in accordance with the Code provisions — the threshold pre-screening mechanism is a poor, and more importantly, an illegal substitute in disputed areas of partiality. (See Vidmar and Melnitzer, "Juror Prejudice: An Empirical Study of a Challenge for Cause" (1984) 22 Osgoode Hall L.J. 487.) After this initial, narrowly drawn procedure is complete, the process as set out in the *Criminal Code* must be adhered to. I will refer again to the clear words of Dickson C.J.C. in *Barrow* at p. 714 [S.C.R., p. 319 C.R.], which, though addressing a somewhat different question, are apposite here:

> The *Code* sets out a detailed process for the selection of an impartial jury. It gives both parties substantial powers in the process and sets up a mechanism to try the partiality of a potential juror when challenged for cause. The trier of partiality is not the judge but a mini-jury of two potential or previously selected jurors. . . . Parliament has decided that the issue of partiality is a question of fact that must be decided by two of the jurors themselves, not by the judge. . . . Any judge who attempts to participate in such decisions usurps the function of the jurors.

Perhaps more pertinent to the issue here is the question of what degree of pre-trial publicity or, more generally, non-indifference, is necessary to lead to the right to challenge for cause and thus have the trial of the issue proceed before the "mini-jury". The example of pre-trial publicity arises on the facts of this case, and the existence of publicity prior to trial would appear to be the most frequent cause for a challenge based upon non-indifference.

A number of factors need to be addressed in answering this question. To begin with, s. 567 (now s. 638) of the *Criminal Code* places little, if any, burden on the challenger. On the other hand, a reasonable degree of control must be retained by the trial judge and, thus, some burden placed upon the challenger to ensure that the selection of the jury occurs in a manner that is in accordance with the principles I have previously articulated, and also to ensure that sufficient information is imparted to the trial judge such that the trial of the truth of the challenge is contained within permissible bounds. Thus, while there must be an "air of reality" to the application, it need not be an "extreme" case, as were, for example, the cases of *Zundel*, supra, and *Guérin c. R.*; *Pimparé c. R.* The Ontario Court of Appeal in *Zundel* provided a useful guide in this regard, at p. 132 [C.C.C., p. 37 C.R.]:

> The real question is whether the particular publicity and notoriety of the accused could potentially have the effect of destroying the prospective juror's indifference between the Crown and the accused.

Postulating rigid guidelines is obviously an impossible task. Lawton J. in *R. v. Kray* (1969), 53 Cr. App. R. 412 (C.A.), draws a valuable distinction in pre-trial publicity cases between mere publication of the facts of a case, and situations where the media misrepresents the evidence, dredges up and widely publicizes discreditable incidents from an accused's past, or engages in speculation as to the accused's guilt or innocence. It may well be that the pre-trial publicity or other ground of alleged partiality will, in itself, provide sufficient reasons for a challenge for cause. The threshold question is not whether the ground of alleged partiality will create such partiality in a juror, but rather whether it could create that partiality which would prevent a juror from being indifferent as to the result. In the end, there must exist a realistic *potential* for the existence of partiality, on a ground sufficiently articulated in the application, before the challenger should be allowed to proceed.

Application to the Facts of the Case

Applying these principles to the facts of this case, given the whole of the circumstances, the procedure followed by the trial Judge was correct. It is unfortunate, however, in my view, that the trial Judge used the word "extraordinary" to describe the challenge for cause procedure. As I have hopefully made clear throughout these reasons, the right to challenge for cause is an important one designed to ensure a fair trial. It is of great assistance in the selection of a jury that can properly fulfill those duties accorded it. Further, the ability to challenge for cause rests upon a showing by the challenger of a realistic potential for partiality. The process is neither "extraordinary" nor "exceptional".

Notwithstanding his seeming misapprehension of the nature of the process, the trial Judge was correct, in my view, in deciding that there was nothing before him in the present instance that satisfied the requirement set out above. The pre-trial publicity did not satisfy the query, "whether the particular publicity and notoriety of the accused could potentially have the effect of destroying the prospective juror's indifference." Based on the information given to the Judge, there was no realistic potential for the existence of partiality on the basis of pre-trial publicity. The trial occurred a substantial period of time after the publicity in question and, more importantly, it appears that the media reports were concerned more with the search and subsequent discovery of the remains of the victim and the victim's reputation, than with the accused or subsequent proceedings against him. As Huband J.A. said at p. 149 [C.C.C.], the pre-trial publicity here "was not of the type to occasion partiality towards an accused". In addition, Jewers J. did not close off the challenge procedure at this point, but rather invited continued challenges based on more appropriate information. Such information was not forthcoming despite the representation by accused's counsel that he had material to substantiate his allegations.

Having so concluded, I am nonetheless of the view that the majority of the Court of Appeal interpreted *Hubbert* too broadly. I refer particularly to the comments of Huband J.A. at p. 150, regarding the pre-screening of prospective jurors for partiality undertaken by the trial Judge. This initial process in my view only applies, as is evidenced by the words used in *Hubbert*, to consensual, uncontested matters of partiality, and not where the challenge for cause is grounded on some pertinent allegation as in *Barrow*, and *Guérin c. R.*; *Pimparé c. R.*

In 1993 Mr. Justice Doherty for the Ontario Court of Appeal delivered two controversial judgments on jury selection. **Are his positions consistent and what are the further implications flowing from the change of direction in *Parks*?**

R. v. BIDDLE
(1993), 24 C.R. (4th) 65, 14 O.R. (3d) 756 (Ont. C.A.)

Per DOHERTY J.A. (Osborne and Austin JJ.A. concurring):—The appellant was convicted, after a trial before a court composed of a judge and jury of two counts of assault causing bodily harm (counts 2 and 5) and two counts of choking with intent to commit an indictable offence (counts 3 and 6). He was acquitted on two other charges.

. . .

The appellant received sentences totalling 12 years. He appeals only his convictions.

Identity was the only issue at trial. Both victims were attacked immediately after leaving the underground parking area of their respective apartment buildings. Both victims were choked and suffered bodily harm. The victims' descriptions of the attacks were not disputed. Their identification of the appellant as their attacker was, however, strenuously challenged. Neither victim knew the appellant.

. . .

II. *Did the Jury Selection Process Create a Reasonable Apprehension of Bias?*

The appellant was tried by an all female jury. A review of the trial record makes it clear that Crown counsel at trial set out to empanel an all female jury. I do not understand Crown counsel in this court to have suggested otherwise.

The jury selection process proceeded under the then operative provisions of the *Criminal Code*, R.S.C. 1970, c. C-34. Those sections gave the Crown four peremptory challenges and 48 stand asides. The accused had twelve peremptory challenges and no stand asides. Assuming a jury could be chosen without exhausting the entire jury panel, the Crown could unilaterally eliminate 52 prospective jurors as opposed to the twelve which the defence could unilaterally reject.

Defence counsel peremptorily challenged eleven jurors, ten women and one man. In total, 42 prospective jurors (28 men and 14 women) were suitable to the defence. No prospective male juror was suitable to the Crown. Of the 30 persons stood aside by the Crown, 28 were male. One of the two women was stood aside at her request.

The Crown was able to achieve its goal of an all female jury in part because of the numerical advantage bestowed on it by the then operative provisions of the *Criminal Code*. That advantage allowed the Crown to unilaterally reject almost three times as many potential jurors as the defence. It also put the Crown in the position, when the last juror was being selected, of having the right to unilaterally reject another 22 jurors as opposed to the one peremptory challenge remaining to the defence. The numerical superiority both in relation to the jurors actually rejected and the potential to reject further jurors allowed the Crown the predominant role in shaping the gender constitution of the jury.

In *R. v. Bain*, [1992] 1 S.C.R. 91, 69 C.C.C. (3d) 481 [10 C.R. (4th) 257] the sections of the *Criminal Code* giving the Crown the advantage it used in this case were held to violate s. 11(*d*) of the *Charter*. The court, however, suspended the declaration of invalidity for a period of six months from the date of the judgment in *Bain*. This trial took place well before Bain was released. Consequently, according to the order made in *Bain*, the jury selection provisions were operative when this jury was selected.

The two judgments constituting the majority in *Bain* took different approaches to its application to cases tried before *Bain* was released. At p. 109 S.C.R., p. 513 C.C.C. [p. 266 C.R.], Cory J., for three members of the four person majority held that a verdict returned by a jury empanelled under the former provisions of the Code could only be set aside if the appellant could demonstrate an "abuse" of the stand aside provisions by the Crown. This court has adopted the position advanced by Cory J.: *R. v. Sedore*, released June 30, 1993 at 6-11.

Cory J. referred to *R. v. Pizzacalla* (1991), 69 C.C.C. (3d) 115, 7 C.R. (4th) 294 (Ont. C.A.), as an example of a case where the stand aside provisions had been "abused" by the Crown. In *Pizzacalla* this court looked to the effect of the prosecution's use of its stand asides on the perceived impartiality of the jury ultimately selected. I understand *Pizzacalla* to have applied the well-known reasonable apprehension of bias test in assessing whether the end product of the Crown's use of its stand aside powers was an impartial or partial jury.

In my view, the "abuse" described by Cory J. in *Bain* refers to both the misuse of the stand aside power and the resultant negative consequences on the impartiality of the jury selected as a result of that misuse. Consequently in pre-*Bain* cases the court must address the Crown's use of its numerical advantage to shape the composition of the jury, and must also decide whether the jury selected by that process is one which would create a reasonable apprehension of bias in the mind of a reasonable observer.

The question of bias must be addressed from the vantage point of the reasonable, well-informed observer. The apprehension of bias must be objectively based. Obviously, some jurors are stood aside because Crown counsel sees some tactical advantage in standing them aside. In this case it could be concluded that Crown counsel believed that an all female jury would work to his advantage, although counsel might well argue that he believed that the advantage rested not in their partiality, but in their ability to impartially try the case. Crown counsel's intention in exercising stand asides and his or her belief with respect to the disposition of the jury ultimately selected are not determinative of the bias issue. The composition of the jury must be such as to leave the well-informed observer with a reasonable apprehension of bias in favour of the Crown. That reasonable apprehension is not established by showing that Crown counsel, through the use of stand asides, was able to get the kind of jury he or she believed would work to the Crown's advantage.

In holding that the prosecutor's motives for exercising his or her stand asides are not conclusive with respect to the jury's perceived impartiality, I do not intend to countenance the use of stand asides to gain some perceived tactical advantage. Clearly, the prosecutor should not so employ that power: *R. v. Bain*, supra, per Gonthier J. in dissent at 119 S.C.R., at 497 C.C.C. [p. 301 C.R.]. The danger of just such misuse figured prominently in the court's declaration of unconstitutionality in *Bain*. The Crown's abuse of its stand aside power (or its peremptory challenge power), may give rise to remedies at trial, if unlike here, the alleged abuse is raised at trial. Exclusion of potential jurors based on their sex may also implicate an accused's rights under s. 15 of the *Charter*: *Batson v. Kentucky*, 476 U.S. 79 (1985). That issue is not before this court. This appeal was argued solely on the basis that the conclusion reached in *Pizzacalla* applied with equal force to this case and necessitated the quashing of the convictions.

The fact that a jury is unisexual does not establish a reasonable apprehension of bias: *R. v. Pizzacalla*, supra, at 116 C.C.C., 296 C.R.; *R. v. B. (F.F.)* (1991), 69 C.C.C. (3d) 193 at 222, 11 C.R. (4th) 56 at 89 (N.S.C.A.), appeal allowed on other grounds, [1993] 1 S.C.R. 697. The impugned aspect of the jury's make up must be assessed in the context of the particular case.

In *Pizzacalla*, counsel for the accused at trial objected to the manner in which Crown counsel used his stand asides. In this court the Crown conceded the appeal, acknowledging that in light of the nature of the allegations, an all female jury gave "the appearance that the prosecutor secured a favourable jury" (at 116 C.C.C., 296 C.R.). This court agreed with that concession. No such concession is made here.

In this case both victims were women. More importantly, they were victims of the kind of random violence to which women are all too frequently exposed to in our society. It is regrettable, but true, that women know all too well, and much better than men, the terror that can be associated with that nightly walk through a lonely parking area to one's apartment or home. Since women are more likely than men to be victims of the type of assault involved in this case, it is understandable that they may be more inclined to see themselves as victims of this kind of assault.

This potential identification by female jurors with the victims should not, however, be overstated. A strong association with the plight of the victim does not equate with bias in favour of the prosecution. Any reasonable person would sympathize with these women. They were the entirely innocent victims of vicious unprovoked assaults. Any juror would have to be careful not to let sympathy interfere with their objective assessment of the evidence.

This case turned entirely on the question of identification. The victims' honesty was not in issue. The reliability of their identification evidence was very much in issue. I am not prepared to hold, because women may be particularly sensitive to the plight of the victims, that an all female jury would be unable to objectively assess the reliability of the identification evidence provided by the victims. More to the point, I am not prepared to find that the reasonable, well-informed observer would reasonably apprehend that an all female jury would be favourably disposed to find for the Crown on the issue of identification.

It is dangerous and contrary to our concepts of equality and individuality to make findings of partiality on the basis of assumed stereotypical reactions based on gender. At heart, the appellant's submission rests on just such assumptions. There is nothing in the circumstances of this case which lifts it above the level of unwarranted stereotyping. In this regard, it is instructive that trial counsel apparently perceived no bias as he did not object during the jury selection process.

This ground of appeal fails.

R. v. PARKS
(1993), 24 C.R. (4th) 81, 15 O.R. (3d) 324 (Ont. C.A.)

Per DOHERTY J.A. (Krever and Abella JJ.A. concurring):—

The appellant was tried on a charge of second degree murder and convicted of manslaughter by the jury. The trial judge imposed a sentence of seven years. The appellant appeals his conviction and sentence.

The grounds of appeal do not require a detailed recitation of the evidence. The appellant was a drug dealer and the deceased was a cocaine user. The deceased approached the appellant and discussed the purchase of cocaine. The deceased gave the appellant some money but the appellant did not produce any cocaine. The deceased then grabbed the appellant and demanded his money back. This confrontation occurred in an elevator. Several other persons, including friends of the appellant, were in the elevator. The deceased produced a knife. The appellant had that knife (or some other knife) at some point during the struggle. The two men wrestled and eventually a group of people, including the appellant and the deceased, moved from the elevator to a hallway. Moments later the deceased was lying in the stairwell bleeding to death from a stab wound in the heart. The appellant fled the scene. He was arrested later the same day. He had been stabbed in the left hand during the altercation with the deceased.

. . .

C. *The Challenge for Cause*

At the outset of the jury selection, defence counsel indicated that he intended to challenge prospective jurors for cause. He had reduced to writing the two questions which he wished to put to each potential juror. They were:

As the judge will tell you, in deciding whether or not the prosecution has proven the charge against an accused a juror must judge the evidence of the witnesses without bias, prejudice or partiality:

(1) In spite of the judge's direction would your ability to judge witnesses without bias, prejudice or partiality be affected by the fact that there are people involved in cocaine and other drugs?

(2) Would your ability to judge the evidence in the case without bias, prejudice or partiality be affected by the fact that the person charged is a black Jamaican immigrant and the deceased is a white man?

The trial judge refused to permit either question. On appeal, counsel for the appellant argued that both questions should have been allowed. I see no merit in the argument as it relates to the first question. The question implies that a witness's involvement in the drug trade and his or her personal use of illicit drugs should have no relevance in "judging witnesses". To the contrary, those factors could properly be considered by the jury in its assessment of the credibility and reliability of witnesses. I need say no more than to indicate my agreement with the trial judge's ruling on the first question posed by defence counsel.

The propriety of the second question does require detailed consideration.

The appellant is black and the deceased was white. There was, however, no suggestion that the homicide was racially motivated or that race-related matters had anything to do with the events to be placed before the jury. Further, while the question referred to the accused as "a black Jamaican immigrant", it does not appear that his nationality or immigration status were relevant, or would be made known to the jury. In this Court (and in the trial judge's reasons) the question was approached on the basis that it referred to a black accused without regard to his country of origin or his status in Canada.

Counsel for the accused did not call any evidence in support of the proposed challenge. He argued that anti-black racism in Toronto was a "notorious fact" which could assert itself through one or more members of the jury drawn from that community who were charged with the responsibility of determining the fate of a black man charged with murdering a white man. Counsel contended that the extent of race-based prejudice in Metropolitan Toronto and the interracial nature of the homicide provided a sufficient foundation for the limited inquiry he proposed.

The trial judge disagreed. He relied on the "presumption" that duly chosen and sworn jurors can be relied on to do their duty and decide the case on the evidence without regard to personal biases and prejudices. The trial judge held there was nothing particular in this case which negated that "presumption".

The "presumption" relied on by the trial judge is well established, both as a fundamental premise of our system of trial by jury, and as an operative principle during the jury selection process. The trial judge's conclusion that the "presumption" could be relied on to overcome potential racial prejudice against a minority accused is consistent with rulings made by other trial judges in this province. [*R. v. Racco (No. 2)* (1975), 23 C.C.C. (2d) 205 at 208 [29 C.R.N.S. 307 at p. 310] (Ont. G.S.P.); *R. v. Crosby* (1979), 49 C.C.C. (2d) 255 (Ont. H.C.); *R. v. McCollin* (7 December 1992), Toronto, (Ont. Gen. Div.), Dunnet J. [unreported].]

. . .

Before turning to the principles controlling the challenge for cause process, the nature and ambit of the proposed question must be clearly understood. Counsel did not seek to challenge for cause based on race. He did not suggest that a person could be successfully challenged on the basis of his or her colour, or that only persons of a particular race would be challenged for cause. The question as posed was race neutral and did not assume that only non-blacks would be subject to the challenge. The question also did not seek to challenge prospective jurors based only on their opinions, beliefs or prejudices. The question went beyond that and was directed to the jurors' ability to set aside certain beliefs, opinions or prejudices when performing their duty as a juror. The appellant does not challenge the proscription against challenges based on race or the beliefs, opinions or prejudices of potential jurors set down in *Hubbert*, [Supra, note 2 at 475-76 O.R., 289-290 C.C.C. [p. 37 C.R.N.S.].] and reiterated in *R. v. Zundel*. [(1987), 58 O.R. 129 at 165, 31 C.C.C. (3d) 97 at 133 [56 C.R. (3d) 1 at p. 38] (C.A.), leave to appeal to S.C.C. refused (1987), 61 O.R. (2d) 588 (note).]

The question which counsel wanted to put to potential jurors cannot be criticized as either an effort to obtain a favourable jury or an attempt to indoctrinate prospective jurors with the position to be advanced by the defence at trial. A "no" answer to the question would hardly suggest that the potential juror would be more likely to side with the defence than the Crown. A "yes" answer to the question could be based on a racial bias in favour of the accused in which case, a defence initiated challenge would result in the loss of a juror who was potentially favourable to the defence. Similarly, as race played no part in the defence to be advanced, it could not be said that counsel sought to use the challenge for cause process to fire the first volley in a race-based defence.

I would not characterize the question as a device designed by counsel to gain some insight into the personality of potential jurors so as to enable counsel to more effectively use his peremptory challenges. The proposed inquiry involved a single question focused on a specific issue. It asked only the potential juror's own evaluation of his or her ability to abide by the juror's oath despite the colour of the accused and the interracial nature of the homicide. Counsel did not seek to inquire into individual jurors' lifestyles, antecedents, or personal experiences with a view to exposing underlying racial prejudices. He did not propose the kind of wide-ranging personalized disclosure involved in voir dire inquiries into potential racial prejudice permitted in some American jurisdictions. [E.g. see E. Krauss & B. Bonora, eds., *Jurywork: Systematic Techniques*, 2d ed. (New York: Clark Boardman, 1983) at 10-53 - 10-56.] Canadian courts have resisted that approach to jury selection. [*R. v. Hubbert*, supra, note 2 at 474-76 O.R., 289-90 C.C.C. [p. 37 C.R.N.S.].] Attempts to introduce that methodology in the context of challenges for cause based on racial prejudice raise very difficult problems, which need not be addressed here, given the single and very specific question counsel wished to ask potential jurors.

Nor do I agree with Crown counsel's submission that the question proposed could be counterproductive in that it would "inject racial . . . overtones into a case where none existed previously". This submission is borrowed from the concurring opinion of Powell J. in *Turner v. Murray* [476 U.S. 28 at 49 (1986); see also *People v. Mack*, 473 N.E. 2d 880 at 892-93 (Ill. S. Ct. 1985).] The argument, however, only has validity if one assumes that none of the prospective jurors is racially biased. If one or more are biased, their presence in the array, and their potential role as jurors "injects" racial overtones into the proceeding. A question directed at revealing those whose bias renders them partial does not "inject" racism into the trial, but seeks to prevent that bias from destroying the impartiality of the jury's deliberations.

I also cannot agree with the Crown's submission that in a case like the present it is somehow fairer to a black accused to prohibit a challenge premised on race based partiality. Where that accused wishes to make that inquiry, presumably because of a perceived danger of partiality based on race, I do not think it lies with the Crown to argue that the accused should be protected from himself or herself by denying the request in the interest of fairness to the accused.

. . .

I turn now to the relevance of the question posed by counsel for the accused. To determine relevancy, one must define partiality in the context of the challenge for cause process. Partiality has both an attitudinal and behavioural component. It refers to one who has certain preconceived biases, and who will allow those biases to affect his or her verdict despite the trial safeguards designed to prevent reliance on those biases. [J.E. Pfeifer, "Reviewing the Empirical Evidence on Jury Racism: Findings of Discrimination or Discriminatory Findings?" (1990) 69 Nebraska L.R. 230.]

A partial juror is one who is biased and who will discriminate against one of the parties to the litigation based on that bias. To be relevant to partiality, a proposed line of questioning must address both attitudes and behaviour flowing from those attitudes.

Partiality cannot be equated with bias. [S.L. Johnson, "Black Innocence and the White Jury" (1985) 83 Michigan L.R. 1611 at 1649-1651; D.L. Suggs & B.D. Sales, "Juror Self-Disclosure in the Voir Dire: A Social Science Analysis" (1981) 56 Indiana L.J. 245 at 248.] Questions which seek to do no more than establish that a potential juror has beliefs, opinions or biases which may operate for or against a particular party cannot establish partiality. A diversity of views and outlooks is part of the genius of the jury system and makes jury verdicts a reflection of the shared values of the community. It is inevitable that with diversity come views which can be described as biases or prejudices for or against a party to the litigation. Those biases will take various forms and be of varying degrees. Some biases, such as the presumption of innocence, are crucial to the rendering of a true verdict. Others, by their very nature, will be irrelevant to the case in point. Those biases which can be set aside when a person assumes his or her role as juror are also irrelevant to the partiality of the juror. A juror's biases will only render him or her partial if they will impact on the decision reached by that juror in a manner which is immiscible with the duty to render a verdict based only the evidence and an application of the law as provided by the trial judge. [*Wainright v. Witt*, 469 U.S. 412 at 423-24 (1985); *Murphy v. Florida*, 421 U.S. 794 at 799-800 (1975); *Irvin v. Dowd*, 366 U.S. 717 at 722-23 (1961); *U.S. v. Burr*, 25 F. Cas. 49 at 50-51 (1807); B.J. Gurney, "The Case for Abolishing Peremptory Challenges in Criminal Trials" (1986) 21 Harvard Civil Rights — Civil Liberties L.R. 227 at 246-48, 257-51; J.J. Gobert, "In Search of the Impartial Jury" (1988) 79 (2) J. Crim. L. & Criminology 269 at 313.]

In this case, the issue to be determined on a challenge for cause was not whether a particular potential juror was biased against blacks, but whether if that prejudice existed, it would cause that juror to discriminate against the black accused in arriving at his or her verdict.

The question framed by counsel for the accused captured both components of the partiality requirement. It asked whether a prospective juror's ability to act in accordance with the trial judge's directions would be affected by the colour of the accused and the interracial nature of the violence alleged. Its relevance to a juror's partiality is obvious if one contemplates the position of a juror who answered "yes" to the question as framed by counsel for the accused. Surely the triers of impartiality would be virtually compelled to reject that juror. [*Aldridge v. U.S.*, 283 U.S. 308 at 312 (1931), quoting with approval, *State v. McAfee*, 64 N.C. 339 (1870)].

Having concluded that the question as put by counsel was relevant to the potential partiality of jurors, I must now determine whether the appellant satisfied the threshold test referred to in *Sherratt*. Was there a realistic possibility that one or more prospective jurors would, because of racial prejudice, not be impartial as between the Crown and the accused?

This question raises two discrete issues:

- Was there a realistic possibility that a potential juror would be biased against a black accused charged with murdering a white person?

AND

- Was there a realistic possibility that a prospective juror would be influenced in the performance of his or her judicial duties by racial bias?

Both questions must be addressed. Just as the mere existence of prejudicial pre-trial publicity does not give an automatic right to challenge for cause, the existence of racial prejudice within the community from which jurors are drawn does not entitle an accused to challenge for cause. Counsel's right to challenge for cause on the basis put forward in this case is not resolved by accepting the self-evidence [sic] proposition that there are people in Metropolitan Toronto who are racially biased. The inquiry must go further. The nature and extent of the bias, the dynamics of jury adjudication, and the effect of directions intended to counter any jury bias must all be considered. In other words, the presumption that jurors will perform their duty according to their oath must be balanced against the threat of a verdict tainted by racial bias.

The existence and the extent of racial bias are not issues which can be established in the manner normally associated with the proof of adjudicative facts. Unlike claims of partiality based on pre-trial publicity, the source of the alleged racial prejudice cannot be identified. There are no specific media reports to examine, and no circulation figures to consider. There is, however, an ever growing body of studies and reports documenting the extent and intensity of racist beliefs in contemporary Canadian society. Many deal with racism in general, others with racism directed at black persons. Those materials lend support to counsel's submission that wide-spread anti-black racism is a grim reality in Canada and in particular in Metropolitan Toronto.

That racism is manifested in three ways. There are those who expressly espouse racist views as part of a personal credo. There are others who subconsciously hold negative attitudes towards black persons based on stereotypical assumptions concerning persons of colour. Finally, and perhaps most pervasively, racism exists within the interstices of our institutions. This systemic racism is a product of individual attitudes and beliefs concerning blacks and it fosters and legitimizes those assumptions and stereotypes.

[The Court then reviewed several studies on racism in Canada.]

. . .

I do not pretend to essay a detailed critical analysis of the studies underlying the various reports to which I have referred. Bearing that limitation in mind, however, I must accept the broad conclusions repeatedly expressed in these materials. Racism, and in particular anti-black racism, is a part of our community's psyche. A significant segment of our community holds overtly racist views. A much larger segment subconsciously operates on the basis of negative racial stereotypes. Furthermore, our institutions, including the criminal justice system, reflect and perpetuate those negative stereotypes.

These elements combine to infect our society as a whole with the evil of racism. Blacks are among the primary victims of that evil.

In my opinion, there can be no doubt that there existed a realistic possibility that one or more potential jurors drawn from the Metropolitan Toronto community would, consciously or subconsciously, come to court possessed of negative stereotypical attitudes toward black persons.

The trial judge did not deal directly with the possibility that one or more potential jurors would harbour anti-black bias. I do not suggest that he was not alive to that possibility, although absent an opportunity to examine the relevant materials, he may not have appreciated the nature and extent of those biases within our community. The trial judge proceeded directly to the second issue raised by the proposed challenge. His reliance on the "presumption" referred to earlier indicates that he was satisfied that any concerns referable to anti-black bias could be effectively dealt with by the safeguards present in the post-jury selection phase of the trial. Many such safeguards exist. The juror's oath or affirmation no doubt binds the conscience of many who might otherwise be disposed to decide matters based on assumptions and preconceptions including racial biases. The seriousness of the jury's task and the solemnity of the occasion may have the same effect. [*Pfeifer*, supra, note 15 at 245.] The "diffused impartiality" produced by the melding of twelve diverse and individual perspectives into a single decision making body may also counter personal prejudices. [*Thiel v. Southern Pacific Co.*, 328 U.S. 217 (1946), per Frankfurter J. (dissenting) at 227; *Commonwealth v. Soares*, 387 N.E. 2d 499 at 515 (Mass. S. Ct. 1979), cert. denied, *Massachusetts v. Soares*, 444 U.S. 881 (1979); see also *R. v. Mackow* (1975), 28 C.R.N.S. 87 at 94 (B.C. C.A.).] Similarly, the dynamics of jury deliberations where minds are focused on the evidence, and individual opinions and conclusions must withstand the scrutiny of fellow jurors, offer protection against discriminatory behaviour. [M.F. Kaplan and C. Schersching, "Reducing Juror Bias: An Experimental Approach" in P.D. Lipsitt & B.D. Sales, eds., *New Directions in Psycholegal Research* (New York: Van Nostrand Reinhold, 1980) 149 at 166; *Guerney*, supra, note 17 at 247-48; see also *Gobert*, supra, note 17 at 279 where the author suggests that the reliance on the cleansing effect of group dynamics is suspect.]

Finally, the trial judge's warnings to the jury that they must not resort to preconceptions or biases, including racial biases, in arriving at their verdict will no doubt have a salutory effect. [Pfeifer, supra, note 15 at 247-48; Gobert, supra, note 17 at 325; Johnson, supra, note 16 at 1678-79 suggests judicial warnings against resort to bias have little positive value.] This safeguard is particularly significant in that it brings to the surface of the proceedings, at a crucial point, the danger of allowing racial biases to influence the verdict. In doing so, it alerts jurors to the need to closely examine their own assessments and conclusions to ensure that such bias has not seeped into their deliberations. This trial judge gave a strong warning against resort to prejudices or biases during the deliberation process.

There is a longstanding debate about the effectiveness of these trial safeguards. That debate is part of the wider dispute concerning the effectiveness of the jury system as an adjudicative process. [See Chapter 1 in H. Kalven Jr. & H. Zeisel, *The American Jury* (Boston: Little, Brown & Co., 1966), where the authors survey the competing contentions; R. Hastie, S.D. Penrod & N. Pennington, *Inside the Jury* (Cambridge, Mass: Harvard University Press, 1984); Law Reform Commission of Canada, *The Jury in Criminal Trials*, Working Paper No. 27 (Ottawa: Supply & Services Canada, 1980) (Chair: F.C. Muldoon) at Chapter II.] Our system requires that I accept that the jury system is effective, and that the safeguards are effective, and generally produce verdicts based only on an application of the law as provided by the trial judge to the evidence adduced at trial. The availability of the right to challenge for cause based on partiality, however, demonstrates that in some situations these safeguards are seen to be insufficient, and must be supplemented by the challenge process.

In deciding whether the post-jury selection safeguards against partiality provides a reliable antidote to racial bias, the nature of that bias must be emphasized. For some people, anti-black biases rest on unstated and unchallenged assumptions learned over a lifetime. Those assumptions shape the daily behaviour of individuals, often without any conscious reference to them. In my opinion, attitudes which are engrained in an individual's subconscious, and reflected in both individual and institutional conduct within the community, will prove more resistant to judicial cleansing than will opinions based on yesterday's news and referable to a specific person or event. [Johnson, supra, note 16 at 1679.]

Justice McLachlin recently described both the danger and potential power of bias in the decision making process:

> Racial stereotypes serve a similar purpose to that served by gender stereotypes. We may decide to reject a person's opinion or refuse their application for employment on the basis of race because it saves us the trouble of really analyzing whether we should be accepting the person's point of view or candidature. I am not suggesting that people consciously decide to apply inappropriate racial stereotypes on the ground that they provide easier solutions than rational decision-making. The matter is more complicated, less express than that. In fact, the racial or sexual stereotypes are there, in our minds, bred by social conditioning and encouraged by popular culture and the media. Sometimes they are embedded in our institutions. We tend to accept them as truths. When faced by a problem, we automatically apply them because it is natural and easy — much easier than really examining the problem and coming to a rational conclusion by the process of thought and listening and evaluation. ["Stereotypes: Their Uses and Misuses" (Address to the McGill University Faculty of Law Human Rights Form, 25 November 1992) at 11.]

Others suggest that perceptions based on racial bias are particularly influential in the decision-making process because they tend to filter or even alter the information provided to the decision maker. Bias shapes the information received to conform with those biases. In doing so, it gives the decision reached, at least in the eyes of the decider, an air of logic and rationality. [American Bar Association Advisory Committee on Fair Trial and Free Press, "Standards Relating to Fair Trial and Free Press" (Chicago, 1968) (Chair: P.C. Reardon) at 62; Gobert, supra, note 17 at 320-21.]

The criminal trial milieu may also accentuate the role of racial bias in the decision making process. Anti-black attitudes may connect blacks with crime and acts of violence. A juror with such attitudes who hears evidence describing a black accused as a drug dealer involved in an act of violence may regard his attitudes as having been validated by the evidence. That juror may then readily give effect to his or her preconceived negative attitudes towards blacks without regard to the evidence and legal principles essential to a determination of the specific accused's liability for the crime charged. [Johnson, supra, note 16 at 1644-47]

Extensive social science research in the United States gives further reason to believe that racially prejudiced attitudes translate into discriminatory verdicts within the jury room....

Subsequent empirical studies in the United States using mock juries suggest that juries are more inclined to convict defendants who are not of the same race as the juror. This is especially so where the evidence against the accused is not strong, or where the victim of the offence is of the same race as the juror. Archival studies based on the results of actual cases are said to support this view. [Many of these studies are referred to and analyzed by Pfeifer, supra, note 15, and Johnson, supra, note 16. Johnson finds them persuasive; Pfeifer does not.]

. . .

Case law from the Supreme Court of the United States is also instructive.

. . .

There are relatively little Canadian data relating to the impact of racial bias on jury verdicts. Section 649 of the *Criminal Code* effectively bars research into the effect of racial bias on actual jury deliberations. [The Law Reform Commission of Canada has recommended that s. 649 be amended to permit exceptions in the case of specific research projects approved by the Chief Justice of the province: Law Reform Commission of Canada, *Report 16: The Jury* (Ottawa: Supply & Services, 1982) at 82. In Working Paper No. 27, supra, note 37 at 143 the Commissioners supported such research as perhaps "the only way" to understand the jury process.] I have located only one Canadian mock jury study. [R.M. Bagby & N.A. Rector, "Prejudicial Attitudes in a Simulated Legal Context" (1991) 11 Health L. Can. 94.] That study attempted to determine whether white jurors discriminated against a West Indian black accused on the basis of colour. The authors reported:

> It was found that (a) prejudicial attitudes were not replicated in this simulated legal setting; (b) there was an absence of prejudicial, subjective perceptions of the victim and the defendant; (c) the perception of the victim was not affecting the subject's perception of the defendant; and (d) guilt ratings and sentencing decisions were not prejudiced by the ethnic background of either the defendant or victim. [Ibid. at 95.]

The authors did, however, refer to a second Canadian study (not available to this writer) which reached a contrary conclusion. [J.E. Pfeifer & R.P. Ogloff, "Prejudicial Sentencing Trends in Simulated Jurors in Canada" (Paper presented at the 49th Annual Meeting of the Canadian Psychological Association, 1988.] The study concluded: [Supra, note 65 at 96.]

We present this interpretation of the results with caution. Further investigation of prejudicial attitudes both within and outside of the legal context in Canada is necessary before any national comparison can be drawn with the United States.

Despite the lack of empirical data, Canadian commentators have no doubt that racist attitudes do impact on jury verdicts where the accused is a member of a racial minority. . . .

. . .

The ever-developing awareness of the nature and extent of racism, and in particular anti-black racism in Metropolitan Toronto, suggests that the insights provided by the American material, and the conclusions of Canadian commentators have at least some application to juries selected from among the residents of Metropolitan Toronto. I am satisfied that in at least some cases involving a black accused there is a realistic possibility that one or more jurors will discriminate against that accused because of his or her colour. In my view, a trial judge, in the proper exercise of his or her discretion, could permit counsel to put the question posed in this case, in any trial held in Metropolitan Toronto involving a black accused. I would go further and hold that it would be the better course to permit that question in all such cases where the accused requests the inquiry.

There will be circumstances in addition to the colour of the accused which will increase the possibility of racially prejudiced verdicts. It is impossible to provide an exhaustive catalogue of those circumstances. Where they exist, the trial judge must allow counsel to put the question suggested in this case.

In my opinion, the interracial nature of the violence involved in this case, and the fact that the alleged crime occurred in the course of the black accused's involvement in a criminal drug transaction, combined to provide circumstances in which it was essential to the conduct of a fair trial that counsel be permitted to put the question. [Even though reference to the factual context of the case must be made to assess the possibility of a racially biased verdict, the inquiry is still aimed at impartiality at the time of the challenge; see *R. v. Hubbert, supra,* note 2 at 481-82 O.R., 295-96 C.C.C. [pp. 43-44 C.R.N.S.].] With respect, I must conclude that the trial judge erred in refusing to allow counsel to ask the question.

In reaching my conclusion I have not relied on a costs/benefits analysis. Fairness cannot ultimately be measured on a balance sheet. That kind of analysis, however, supports my conclusion. [*Ham v. South Carolina, supra,* note 51 at 533-34, per Marshall J. (dissenting).] The only "cost" is a small increase in the length of the trial. There is no "cost" to the prospective juror. He or she should not be embarrassed by the question; nor can the question realistically be seen as an intrusion into a juror's privacy.

There are at least three benefits to allowing the question. Some potential jurors who would discriminate against a black accused are eliminated. [This benefit depends on the truthfulness of the answers given by the prospective jurors. There is considerable debate about the reliability of answers provided by jurors during a challenge for cause inquiry: Videmar & Melnitzer, *supra,* note 69 at 502; Gobert, *supra,* note 17 at 317; Suggs & Sales, *supra,* note 16 at

268-69; Gurney, supra, note 17 at 266-67.] Prospective jurors who can arrive at an impartial verdict are sensitized from the outset of the proceedings to the need to confront potential racial bias and ensure that it does not impact on their verdict. In this regard, the challenge process would serve the same purpose as the trial judge's directions to the jury concerning the basis on which they must approach their task and reach their verdict. Lastly, permitting the question enhances the appearance of fairness in the mind of the accused. As indicated earlier, many blacks perceive the criminal justice system as inherently racist. A refusal to allow a black accused to even raise the possibility of racial discrimination with prospective jurors can only enhance that perception. By allowing the question, the court acknowledges that the accused's perception is worthy of consideration.

III   Conclusion

I have no reason to doubt the fairness of this trial, the impartiality of this jury or the validity of their verdict. However, the appellant was denied his statutory right to challenge for cause. That right is essential to the appearance of fairness and the integrity of the trial. The improper denial of this right necessitates the quashing of the conviction without any demonstration of actual prejudice. [*R. v. Cloutier*, [1979] 2 S.C.R. 709 at 724, 48 C.C.C. (2d) 1 at 23 [12 C.R. (3d) 10 at p. 46], per Pratte J.] I would allow the appeal, quash the conviction, and direct a new trial on the charge of manslaughter.

The Supreme Court denied leave to appeal *Parks*. However it heard an appeal in *Biddle*.

R. v. BIDDLE
[1995] 1 S.C.R. 761, 36 C.R. (4th) 321, 96 C.C.C. (3d) 321 (S.C.C.)

Sopinka J. for the Court, over the sole dissent of L'Heureux-Dubé J., ordered a new trial on the basis that the Crown had improperly split its case. Only three justices dealt with the issue of whether the way the all-women jury was chosen created a reasonable apprehension of bias. The other six justices decided that since the provision which the Crown had used to stand aside prospective jurors had been repealed, the issue of law involving its use could not recur and therefore was of academic interest only.

GONTHIER J.:—

. . . Beyond the more immediate repercussions, the first ground raised by the appellant essentially brings into scrutiny the fundamental element of the conduct of the Crown in the unfolding of the trial . . . As I emphasized in *R. v. Bain*, the Crown is party to the fairness of the trial which it also has an obligation to promote. Even though, practically speaking, the trial judge is the ultimate guardian of the fairness of the trial, this does not authorize the prosecution to neglect this obligation nor to undermine its importance.

In the context of the selection of jurors, this obligation of the Crown is discharged through the wise use which it must make of the means at its disposal in order to select a jury which is impartial, representative and competent. In the same way as this power of selection must not be used for the purpose of obtaining a finding of guilt, the right to stand by must not be used to skew the composition of the jury or to gain a tactical advantage, but rather, only for the purpose of choosing the jury best qualified to judge a case. One must conscientiously strive to ensure that a jury possess the above-mentioned qualities.

Of these three elements, impartiality is without doubt the most important. While plainly the jury's competence is a fundamental requirement, one must acknowledge that it is more difficult to exercise a direct influence on it through a mechanism such as stand-bys. Representativeness, on the other hand, is more susceptible to being affected by the selection process. The present case is an excellent example of this. As I observed in *R. v. Bain*, representativeness is a characteristic which furthers the perception of impartiality even if not fully ensuring it. While representativeness is not an essential quality of a jury, it is one to be sought after. The surest guarantee of jury impartiality consists in the combination of the representativeness with the requirement of a unanimous verdict. Consequently, an apparent attempt by the prosecution to modify the composition of the jury so as to exclude representativeness, as occurred in this case, in itself undermines the impartiality of a jury.

For these reasons, I would allow the appeal and order a new trial.

McLACHLIN J.:—

. . .

Gonthier J. suggests that a jury must be "impartial, representative and competent". I agree that a jury must be impartial and competent. But, with respect, the law has never suggested that a jury must be representative. For hundreds of years, juries in this country were composed entirely of men. Are we to say that all these juries were for that reason partial and incompetent?

To say that a jury must be representative is to confuse the means with the end. I agree that representativeness may provide extra assurance of impartiality and competence. I would even go so far as to say that it is generally a good thing. But I cannot accept that it is essential in every case, nor that its absence automatically entitles an accused person to a new trial.

To say that a jury must be representative is to set a standard impossible of achievement. The community can be divided into a hundred different groups on the basis of variants such as gender, race, class and education. Must every group be represented on every jury? If not, which groups are to be chosen and on what grounds? If so, how much representation is enough? Do we demand parity based on regional population figures? Or will something less suffice? I see no need to start down this problematic path of the representative jury, provided the impartiality and competence of the jury are assured. Representativeness may be a means to achieving this end. But it should not be elevated to the status of an absolute requirement.

In the case at bar there is no evidence that the Crown used its stand-by powers to the end of achieving a jury which would be favourable to the Crown. It is at least equally open to infer, as Doherty J.A. suggests, that its aim was to secure a jury which would be capable of judging the issues in an impartial and unbiased manner. So the suggestion of deliberate Crown abuse of the system is not made out.

Nor is there any evidence that the jury chosen was, or could reasonably be perceived to be, other than impartial and competent. Indeed, one must presume the contrary, given that each party had the right to test each juror and object to any juror who might be partial or incompetent. The defence, in suggesting partiality, asks in essence that we infer from the fact that the jury was composed entirely of women that it would be partial to the Crown, or would be seen by a reasonable person to be partial to the Crown. These are inferences which I cannot draw. I see no reason to suppose that an all-woman jury cannot be as impartial as all-male juries have been presumed to be for centuries. Nor can I see any reason to suppose that an all-woman jury would be seen by a reasonable member of the public as favouring the Crown. The question is not whether people, or even a number of people, might for irrational reasons object to an all-woman jury. The question is rather whether such people could reasonably object to an all-woman jury, each member of which has been judged to be impartial and competent and, apart from gender, fit to judge the issues in the case. That question must, in my view, be answered in the negative. Therefore, I agree with the Court of Appeal below that no error was demonstrated in the selection of the jury.

L'HEUREUX-DUBÉ J. (dissenting):—

. . .

In my view all three grounds of appeal fail and the appeal should be dismissed. In this respect, I adopt the reasons of Doherty J.A. for the unanimous Court of Appeal of Ontario . . . In the result, Doherty J.A. concluded that there was no reasonable apprehension of bias. I agree and therefore reject this first ground of appeal . . . Before concluding, I note that since first writing these reasons I have had the opportunity to read the reasons of my colleagues Justices Gonthier and McLachlin, who both discuss the issue of jury representativeness. On this issue, I agree with the comments of McLachlin J. and respectfully disagree with those of Gonthier J.

Justice Judge Trafford of the Ontario Court of Justice, General Division, in *R. v. Kerr* (1995), 42 C.R. (4th) 118 (Ont. Gen. Div.), allowed a challenge for cause to include the following two questions in addition to that allowed in *Parks*:

Do you have any beliefs or opinions about black men from Jamaica and the commission of crimes, particularly crimes involving drugs, that would prevent you from judging the evidence in this case, without bias, prejudice or partiality?

Do you have any beliefs or opinions about the reliability of police officers, either in support of or in opposition to them, that would prevent you from judging the evidence in this case without bias, prejudice, or partiality?

The accused, young black men from Jamaica, were charged with trafficking in crack cocaine. The defence for both accused would be a denial of the allegation and an assertion that the white police officers were mistaken or deliberately fabricating the evidence. Trafford J. allowed the two additional questions in the challenges for cause given the evidence tendered in support. This included a number of affidavits and newspaper articles, on the consent of the Crown. The articles tended to establish recent and widespread media coverage in Toronto questioning police integrity, including the arrest of four Toronto police officers on a charge of obstructing justice by fabricating evidence in a drugs trial and comments of an American law professor related to the O.J. Simpson trial that police officers are trained to lie. A defence expert, whose expertise was not contested by the Crown, relying in part on an 1995 Angus Reid survey of 400 randomly chosen Toronto residents, testified as to the existence of a stereotypical assumption amongst a significant portion of the Toronto population linking black males from Jamaica to crimes of violence and drugs.

In Ontario there has been a variety of judicial opinion as to whether a *Parks*-type screening process should be available to screen potential jurors for other potential biases such as those based on gender and/or the experience of a victim. See the review by David Tanovich, "Rethinking Jury Selection: Challenge for Cause and Peremptory Challenges" (1994), 30 C.R. (4th) 310. However a pointed *obiter* by Galligan J.A. for the Ontario Court of Appeal in *R. v. Cameron* (1995), 96 C.C.C. (3d) 346 (Ont. C.A.) had the effect of narrowly limiting *Parks* to screening for racial bias in Toronto:

> Before leaving this ground of appeal I should recount the concern expressed by counsel for the Crown that the decision in *Parks* has been followed by a dramatic increase in the number and breadth of questions which trial judges have been allowing counsel to put to jurors upon challenges for cause. *Parks* has been badly misinterpreted if it is being taken as authorization for using the challenge for cause process to ask wide-ranging questions of prospective jurors. Parks reaffirmed the presumption that duly sworn jurors can be relied upon to do their duty and decide cases on the evidence without regard to personal biases or prejudices. In *Parks*, Doherty J.A. said:
>
> > The "presumption" relied on by the trial judge is well established, both as a fundamental premise of our system of trial by jury, and as an operative principle during the jury selection process.
>
> *Parks* is a case which applied long-settled and well-established principles to a particular case. This court was satisfied in that case that the articulated ground for challenge did show the existence of a realistic potential partiality. For that reason, it ruled that a very narrow, precisely restricted question ought to have been permitted to be asked .... Thus, it must be accepted that *Parks* was a particular case decided upon a specific issue. It must not be taken as a point of departure....

In *R. v. Wilson*, reasons released March 19, 1996, the Ontario Court of Appeal changed course on the issue of racial bias and now requires a *Parks* screening process across Ontario whenever an accused is black. According to Chief Justice McMurtry for the Court, any distinction based on a geographic boundary between Metropolitan Toronto and other Ontario communities would be arbitrary and should not form the basis of a judicial exercise of discretion to refuse the challenge. It was, suggested the Chief Justice, unrealistic and illogical to assume that anti-black attitudes stop at the borders of Metropolitan Toronto.

In *R. v. Alli* (1996), 110 C.C.C. (3d) 283 (Ont. C.A.), the accused was convicted of sexual assault. He was found to have sexually assaulted another male prisoner while both were confined in the drunk tank of a local lockup. The accused was Guyanese and the complainant was Vietnamese. The accused complained that the trial judge had improperly denied him his right to challenge prospective jurors for cause. The accused had sought to challenge for cause on two grounds: the potential prejudice against homosexuals and the potential prejudice against the accused because he was a member of a visible minority. The accused had called no evidence in support of either proposed ground. Justice Doherty wrote:

> In *Parks*, this court went outside the trial record and beyond the material submitted by the parties to find sociological and empirical support for its conclusions. That form of appellate activism, while appropriate in some cases, should be used sparingly: *Willick v. Willick*, [1994] 3 S.C.R. 670, per L'Heureux-Dubé J. (concurring) at 699-705. Appellate analysis of untested social science data should not be regarded as the accepted means by which the scope of challenges for cause based on generic prejudice will be settled. This court is now asked to extend the automatic right to challenge for cause recognized in *Parks* to a much broader concept of racial prejudice and to prejudice based on sexual preference. No evidentiary basis for the extension is provided. Any proposed extension of *Parks* should be approached with caution. Where, as in this case, there was no evidence offered at trial to support the proposed extension, the court should decline to interfere with the trial judge's exercise of his or her discretion. Any extension of *Parks* should await a case in which an adequate evidentiary foundation has been laid at trial to permit an informed determination of whether the ratio of *Parks* should be extended to other forms of generic prejudice.

R. v. WILLIAMS
(1994), 30 C.R. (4th) 277, 90 C.C.C. (3d) 194 (B.C. S.C.)

The accused, an Aboriginal person, was charged with robbery of a pizza parlour in Victoria. The accused brought an application to challenge each potential juror for cause. His defence counsel proposed to ask each prospective juror whether the juror's ability to judge the evidence in the case without bias, prejudice or partiality would be affected by the fact that the accused was Aboriginal or by the fact that the accused was Aboriginal and the complainant white. Evidence in the form of commission reports and other writings and the oral evidence of four witnesses was tendered to establish widespread bias and prejudice toward Aboriginal people. Chief Justice Esson denied the application. The existence of widespread bias and prejudice toward Aboriginal people did not in itself establish a realistic potential for the existence of partiality on behalf of prospective jurors such as to displace the presumption that jurors can be relied on to do their duty and decide the case without regard to their personal biases and prejudices. The decision of the

Ontario Court of Appeal in *R. v. Parks* was based on a particular set of conditions existing in Metropolitan Toronto, in particular the attitudes held by many regarding the link between black persons and serious crime. The cost/benefit analysis did not support such challenges. There would be heavy expense in time, money and convenience of jurors. Challenging for cause based on systemic racism was a step toward the wide open examination of jurors in American trials and an illegitimate step in the direction of using the challenge as a fishing expedition. Granting the application would not result in using the challenge process in a principled fashion and would not ensure a fair trial to any greater degree than hitherto. The court was being asked to legislate a new procedure inconsistent with the language and rationale of the legislation. If such additional costs were to be imposed on the system it should be by Parliament not the court. **Do you agree with this approach?**

The *Williams* ruling was accepted on further appeal to the British Columbia Court of Appeal on April 29, 1996. The Court ruled that the Chief Justice had not erred in principle. The Chief Justice properly addressed the two important questions of the realistic possibility of bias and the realistic possibility that a juror by reason of such bias might not be indifferent between the Queen and the accused. He had properly relied on the presumption that jurors will discharge their duty in accordance with their oath. While the evidence tendered at trial and on appeal established a deep-rooted dissatisfaction by Aboriginals with the existing system of the administration of justice it did not support a finding that the nature and extent of racial tensions between Aboriginal and non-Aboriginal persons is such that there is a potential that a prospective juror may not be impartial in trying a charge against an Aboriginal person.

The argument that a challenge for cause should flow automatically from the fact of inter-racial tensions was not a legal principle recognized by the authorities. The argument rests on the premise that it is to be expected that minorities will not be treated fairly by their fellow citizens. It assumes that a fair trial can be assured only if Canada adopts the American system of detailed questioning of prospective jurors. Canadian authorities do not support that proposition.

The stereotype upon which *Parks* was based is that of a Black person, who, in the light of American and Canadian experience, is perceived as being linked with serious urban crime. The stereotype that arose from the evidence in this case was different. It was of a disadvantaged person, often in conflict with the law, but no more inclined to serious criminal activity than any other similarly disadvantaged person.

The cost/benefit analysis of the Chief Justice had been *obiter*.

R. v. WILLIAMS
[1998] 1 S.C.R. 1128, 15 C.R. (5th) 227, 124 C.C.C. (3d) 581 (S.C.C.)

Per McLACHLIN J. (Lamer C.J. and L'Heureux-Dubé, Gonthier, Cory, Iacobucci, Major, Bastarache and Binnie JJ. concurring):—

. . .

WHAT IS THE RULE?

The Prevailing Canadian Approach to Jury Challenges for Lack of Indifference Between the Crown and the Accused

The prosecution and the defence are entitled to challenge potential jurors for cause on the ground that "a juror is not indifferent between the Queen and the accused". Lack of "indifference" may be translated as "partiality", the term used by the Courts below. "Lack of indifference" or "partiality", in turn, refer to the possibility that a juror's knowledge or beliefs may affect the way he or she discharges the jury function in a way that is improper or unfair to the accused. A juror who is partial or "not indifferent" is a juror who is inclined to a certain party or a certain conclusion. The synonyms for "partial" in Burton's *Legal Thesaurus* (2nd ed. 1992), at p. 374, illustrate the attitudes that may serve to disqualify a juror:

> bigoted, discriminatory, favorably disposed, inclined, influenced, interested, jaundiced, narrow-minded, one-sided, partisan, predisposed, prejudiced, prepossessed, prone, restricted, subjective, swayed, unbalanced, unequal, uneven, unfair, unjust, unjustified, unreasonable.

The predisposed state of mind caught by the term "partial" may arise from a variety of sources. Four classes of potential juror prejudice have been identified— interest, specific, generic and conformity: see Neil Vidmar, "Pretrial prejudice in Canada: a comparative perspective on the criminal jury" (1996), 79 Jud. 249, at p. 252. Interest prejudice arises when jurors may have a direct stake in the trial due to their relationship to the defendant, the victim, witnesses or outcome. Specific prejudice involves attitudes and beliefs about the particular case that may render the juror incapable of deciding guilt or innocence with an impartial mind. These attitudes and beliefs may arise from personal knowledge of the case, publicity through mass media, or public discussion and rumour in the community. Generic prejudice, the class of prejudice at issue on this appeal, arises from stereotypical attitudes about the defendant, victims, witnesses or the nature of the crime itself. Bias against a racial or ethnic group or against persons charged with sex abuse are examples of generic prejudice. Finally, conformity prejudice arises when the case is of significant interest to the community causing a juror to perceive that there is strong community feeling about a case coupled with an expectation as to the outcome.

. . .

To guide judges in the exercise of their discretion, this Court formulated a rule in *Sherratt*: the judge should permit challenges for cause where there is a "realistic potential" of the existence of partiality. *Sherratt* was concerned with the possibility of partiality arising from pre-trial publicity. However, as the courts in this case accepted, it applies to all requests for challenges based on bias, regardless of the origin of the apprehension of partiality. Applying *Sherratt* to the case at bar, the enquiry becomes whether in this case, the evidence of widespread bias against aboriginal people in the community raises a realistic potential of partiality.

Identifying the Evidentiary Threshold

Esson C.J. and the Court of Appeal applied the test of "realistic potential" of partiality. However, they took a different view from that of Hutchison J. as to when the evidence establishes a realistic potential of partiality. The debate before us divided on the same lines. The Crown argues that evidence of widespread racial bias against persons of the accused's race does not translate into a "realistic potential" for partiality. There is a presumption that jurors will act impartially, whatever their pre-existing views. Evidence of widespread bias does not rebut that presumption. More is required. The Crown does not detail what evidence might suffice. However, it emphasizes that the evidence must point to not only bias, but also partiality, or bias that may affect the outcome. What is required, in the Crown's submission, is concrete evidence showing prejudice that would not be capable of being set aside at trial. The Crown interprets *Parks*, where challenges for cause for racial bias in the community were permitted, as being an exceptional case where the nature and extent of the racial bias was sufficiently extreme to establish a reasonable possibility of partiality.

The defence takes a different view. First, it argues that *Sherratt* establishes that the right to challenge for cause is not exceptional or extraordinary or extreme. Second, it suggests that evidence of widespread prejudice against aboriginals in the community suffices to raise a "realistic potential" for partiality, entitling the accused to question potential jurors as to their prejudices as to whether they will be able to set them aside in discharging their duty as jurors. In the defence submission, the evidentiary threshold proposed by the Crown, Esson C.J. and the Court of Appeal is too high.

In my respectful view, the positions of the Crown, Esson C.J. and the Court of Appeal reflect a number of errors that lead to the evidentiary threshold for challenges for cause being set too high. I will discuss each of these in turn.

(1) The Assumption that Prejudice Will be Judicially Cleansed

Underlying the Crown's submissions (as well as the judgments of Esson C.J. and the Court of Appeal) is the assumption that generally jurors will be able to identify and set aside racial prejudice. Only in exceptional cases is there a danger that racial prejudice will affect a juror's impartiality. .... To suggest that all persons who possess racial prejudices will erase those prejudices from the mind when serving as jurors is to underestimate the insidious nature of racial prejudice and the stereotyping that underlies it. ..... For this reason, it cannot be assumed that judicial directions to act impartially will always effectively counter racial prejudice. .... Racial prejudice and its effects are as invasive and elusive as they are corrosive. We should not assume that instructions from the judge or other safeguards will eliminate biases that may be deeply ingrained in the subconscious psyches of jurors. Rather, we should acknowledge the destructive potential of subconscious racial prejudice by recognizing that the post-jury selection safeguards may not suffice. Where doubts are raised, the better policy is to err on the side of caution and permit prejudices to be examined. Only then can we know with any certainty whether they exist and whether they can be set aside or not. It is better to risk allowing what are in fact unnecessary challenges, than to risk prohibiting challenges which are necessary.

. . .

(2) Insistence on the Necessity of a Link Between the Racist Attitude and the Potential for Juror Partiality

Racial prejudice against the accused may be detrimental to an accused in a variety of ways. The link between prejudice and verdict is clearest where there is an interracial element to the crime or a perceived link between those of the accused's race and the particular crime. But racial prejudice may play a role in other, less obvious ways. Racist stereotypes may affect how jurors assess the credibility of the accused. Bias can shape the information received during the course of the trial to conform with the bias. Jurors harbouring racial prejudices may consider those of the accused's race less worthy or perceive a link between those of the accused's race and crime in general. In this manner, subconscious racism may make it easier to conclude that a black or aboriginal accused engaged in the crime regardless of the race of the complainant: see Kent Roach, "Challenges for Cause and Racial Discrimination" (1995), 37 Crim. L.Q. 410, at p. 421.

Again, a prejudiced juror might see the Crown as non-aboriginal or non-black and hence to be favoured over an aboriginal or black accused. The contest at the trial is between the accused and the Crown. Only in a subsidiary sense is it between the accused and another aboriginal. A prejudiced juror might be inclined to favour non-aboriginal Crown witnesses against the aboriginal accused. Or a racially prejudiced juror might simply tend to side with the Crown because, consciously or unconsciously, the juror sees the Crown as a defender of majoritarian interests against the minority he or she fears or disfavours. Such feelings might incline the juror to resolve any doubts against the accused. Ultimately, it is within the discretion of the trial judge to determine whether widespread racial prejudice in the community, absent specific "links" to the trial, is sufficient to give an air of reality to the challenge in the particular circumstances of each case.

(3) Confusion Between the Two Phases of the Challenge for Cause Process

Section 638(2) requires two inquiries and entails two different decisions with two different tests. The first stage is the inquiry before the judge to determine whether challenges for cause should be permitted. The test at this stage is whether there is a realistic potential or *possibility* for partiality. The question is whether there is reason to suppose that the jury pool *may* contain people who are prejudiced and whose prejudice *might not* be capable of being set aside on directions from the judge. The operative verbs at the first stage are "may" and "might". Since this is a preliminary inquiry which may affect the accused's *Charter* rights, a reasonably generous approach is appropriate.

If the judge permits challenges for cause, a second inquiry occurs on the challenge itself. The defence may question potential jurors as to whether they harbour prejudices against people of the accused's race, and if so, whether they are able to set those prejudices aside and act as impartial jurors. The question at this stage is whether the candidate in question *will* be able to act impartially. To demand, at the preliminary stage of determining whether a challenge for cause should be permitted, proof that the jurors in the jury pool will not be able to set aside any prejudices they may harbour and act impartially, is to ask the question more appropriate for the second stage. The Crown conflates the two stages of the process.

. . .

(4) Impossibility of Proving That Racism in Society Will Lead to Juror Partiality

To require the accused to present evidence that jurors will in fact be unable to set aside their prejudices as a condition of challenge for cause is to set the accused an impossible task. It is extremely difficult to isolate the jury decision and attribute a particular portion of it to a given racial prejudice observed at the community level. Jury research based on the study of actual trials cannot control all the variables correlated to race. Studies of mock juries run into external validity problems because they cannot recreate an authentic trial experience: see Jeffrey E. Pfeiffer, "Reviewing the Empirical Evidence on Jury Racism: Findings of Discrimination or Discriminatory Findings?" (1990), 69 Neb. L. Rev. 230. As recognized by Doherty J.A. in *Parks*, [(1993), 84 C.C.C. (3d) 353 (Ont. C.A.)] at p. 366, "[t]he existence and extent of [matters such as] racial bias are not issues which can be established in the manner normally associated with the proof of adjudicative facts". "Concrete" evidence as to whether potential jurors can or cannot set aside their racial prejudices can be obtained only by questioning a juror.

. . .

(5) Failure to Read s. 638(1)(b) Purposively

The object of s. 638(1)(b) must be to prevent persons who may not be able to act impartially from sitting as jurors. This object cannot be achieved if the evidentiary threshold for challenges for cause is set too high. As discussed above, to ask an accused person to present evidence that some jurors will be unable to set their prejudices aside is to ask the impossible. We may infer in many cases, however, from the nature of racial prejudice, that some prospective jurors, in a community where prejudice against people of the accused's race is widespread, may be both prejudiced and unable to identify completely or free themselves from the effects of those prejudices. It follows that the requirement of concrete evidence that widespread racism will cause partiality would not fulfil the purpose of s. 638(1)(b).

. . .

A rule that accords an automatic right to challenge for cause on the basis that the accused is an aboriginal or member of a group that encounters discrimination conflicts from a methodological point of view with the approach in *Sherratt*, that an accused may challenge for cause only upon establishing that there is a realistic potential for juror partiality. For example, it is difficult to see why women should have an automatic right to challenge for cause merely because they have been held to constitute a disadvantaged group under s. 15 of the *Charter*. Moreover, it is not correct to assume that membership in an aboriginal or minority group always implies a realistic potential for partiality. The relevant community for purposes of the rule is the community from which the jury pool is drawn. That community may or may not harbour prejudices against aboriginals. It likely would not, for example, in a community where aboriginals are in a majority position. That said, absent evidence to the contrary, where widespread prejudice against people of the accused's race is demonstrated at a national or provincial level, it will often be reasonable to infer that such prejudice is replicated at the community level. On the understanding that the jury pool is representative, one may safely insist that the accused demonstrate widespread or general prejudice against his or her race in the community as a condition of bringing a challenge for cause. It is at this point that bigoted or prejudiced people have the capacity to affect the impartiality of the jury. To say that widespread racial prejudice in the community can suffice to establish the right to challenge for cause in many cases is not to rule out the possibility that prejudice less than widespread might in some circumstances meet the *Sherratt* test. The ultimate question in each case is whether the *Sherratt* standard of a realistic potential for partiality is established.

(6) Failure to Interpret s. 638(1)(b) in Accordance with the Charter

The challenge for cause is an essential safeguard of the accused's s. 11(d) *Charter* right to a fair trial and an impartial jury. A representative jury pool and instructions from counsel and the trial judge are other safeguards. But the right to challenge for cause, in cases where it is shown that a realistic potential exists for partiality, remains an essential filament in the web of protections the law has woven to protect the constitutional right to have one's guilt or innocence determined by an impartial jury. If the *Charter* right is undercut by an interpretation of s. 638(1)(b) that sets too high a threshold for challenges for cause, it will be jeopardized.

. . .

(7) The Slippery Slope Argument

The Crown concedes that practical concerns cannot negate the right to a fair trial. The Court of Appeal also emphasized this. Yet behind the conservative approach some courts have taken, one detects a fear that to permit challenges for cause on the ground of widespread prejudice in the community would be to render our trial process more complex and more costly, and would represent an invasion of the privacy interests of prospective jurors without a commensurate increase in fairness. Some have openly expressed the fear that if challenges for cause are permitted on grounds of racial prejudice, the Canadian approach will quickly evolve into the approach in the United States of routine and sometimes lengthy challenges for cause of every juror in every case with attendant cost, delay and invasion of juror privacy.

In the case at bar, the accused called witnesses and tendered studies to establish widespread prejudice in the community against aboriginal people. It may not be necessary to duplicate this investment in time and resources at the stage of establishing racial prejudice in the community in all subsequent cases. The law of evidence recognizes two ways in which facts can be established in the trial process. The first is by evidence. The second is by judicial notice. Tanovich, Paciocco and Skurka observe that because of the limitations on the traditional forms of proof in this context, "doctrines of judicial notice [will] play a significant role in determining whether a particular request for challenge for cause satisfies the threshold test": see *Jury Selection in Criminal Trials* (1997), at p. 138. Judicial notice is the acceptance of a fact without proof. It applies to two kinds of facts: (1) facts which are so notorious as not be the subject of dispute among reasonable persons; and (2) facts that are capable of immediate and accurate demonstration by resorting to readily accessible sources of indisputable accuracy: see Sopinka, Lederman and Bryant, *The Law of Evidence in Canada* (1992), at p. 976. The existence of racial prejudice in the community may be a notorious fact within the first branch of the rule. As Sopinka, Lederman and Bryant note, at p. 977, "[t]he character of a certain place or of the community of persons living in a certain locality has been judicially noticed". Widespread racial prejudice, as a characteristic of the community, may therefore sometimes be the subject of judicial notice. Moreover, once a finding of fact of widespread racial prejudice in the community is made on evidence, as here, judges in subsequent cases may be able to take judicial notice of the fact. "The fact that a certain fact or matter has been noted by a judge of the same court in a previous matter has precedential value and it is, therefore, useful for counsel and the court to examine the case law when attempting to determine whether any particular fact can be noted": see Sopinka, Lederman and Bryant, *supra*, at p.977.

SUMMARY

There is a presumption that a jury pool is composed of persons who can serve impartially. However, where the accused establishes that there is a realistic potential for partiality, the accused should be permitted to challenge prospective jurors for cause under s. 638(1)(b) of the *Code*: see *Sherratt*. Applying this rule to applications based on prejudice against persons of the accused's race, the judge should exercise his or her discretion to permit challenges for cause if the accused establishes widespread racial prejudice in the community.

CONCLUSION

Although they acknowledged the existence of widespread bias against aboriginals, both Esson C.J. and the British Columbia Court of Appeal held that the evidence did not demonstrate a reasonable possibility that prospective jurors would be partial. In my view, there was ample evidence that this widespread prejudice included elements that could have affected the impartiality of jurors. Racism against aboriginals includes stereotypes that relate to credibility, worthiness and criminal propensity. .... In these circumstances, the trial judge should have allowed the accused to challenge prospective jurors for cause. Notwithstanding the accused's defence that another aboriginal person committed the robbery, juror prejudice could have affected the trial in many other ways. Consequently, there was a realistic potential that some of the jurors might not have been indifferent between the Crown and the accused. The potential for prejudice was increased by the failure of the trial judge to instruct the jury to set aside any racial prejudices that they might have against aboriginals. It cannot be said that the accused had the fair trial by an impartial jury to which he was entitled. I would allow the appeal and direct a new trial.

Given *Williams*, Rosenberg J.A. decided for the Ontario Court of Appeal in *R. v. Koh* (1998), 21 C.R. (5th) 188, 131 C.C.C. (3d) 257 (Ont. C.A.) that trial judges in Ontario were to allow challenges for cause by members of any visible minority accused without strict compliance with the requirement of an evidentiary foundation.

The Supreme Court did not address the merits or details of the actual *Parks* question for racial screening. Recently, justices of the Ontario Superior Court have felt the need for modification:

In *R. v. Sinclair* (2009), 67 C.R. (6th) 344, 245 C.C.C. (3d) 203 (Ont. S.C.J.) Murray J. wrote:

47 The purpose of the Parks questions is to endeavour to determine whether a person who thinks in terms of Them and Us, Somebodies and Nobodies, would be influenced in the performance of his or her judicial duties by such thinking. Quite apart from the fact that the convenient setting aside of prejudice is unlikely, the *Parks* questions do not sound like questions asked to achieve this purpose. Many people do not hear them this way. Regrettably, given the importance of their purpose, the *Parks* questions sound like questions which unintentionally validate the unwanted distinction between Them and Us. Perhaps somewhat perversely, and to make a point, I have put the questions differently:

1) (In an interracial crime) Is there a realistic possibility that a potential juror (i.e., one of Us) would be biased against a black (one of Them) charged with committing a serious crime against a white (one of Us)?

OR

2) Is there a realistic possibility that a prospective juror (i.e., one of Us) would be influenced in the performance of his or her judicial duties by bias against a black (one of Them)?

48 In 2008, it is no exaggeration to suggest that this is how the Parks questions sounds to many people. This is how "We" hear it. In short, in 2008, the *Parks* questions sounds like an embedded institutional recognition of the distinction between Us and Them, between Somebodies and Nobodies. It sounds like an

acknowledgement that the institution understands the distinction even if it does not condone it. What we hear when the *Parks* questions are asked is different than what we were intended to hear.

49 Notwithstanding that the Court of Appeal in *Parks* acknowledges that the questions are intended to be asked of non-white jurors, they are questions which, for the most part, are designed to be asked of non-black jurors. Asking a black member of the jury panel one of the *Parks* questions is embarrassing and undignified. Asking either of the *Parks* questions causes discomfort to many people involved in the administration of justice and is not restricted to black jurors who are asked a *Parks* question or to black court officers who ask it. It is often embarrassing and undignified for the judge, for the questioner and for the potential juror. In fact, one wonders, if all the assumptions on which the *Parks* questions are based are correct, why not ask potential jurors if they are prepared to accept directions from a black judge?

50 When a *Parks* question is asked, the discomfort felt by many involved in the judicial process is palpable and is not restricted to men and women of a particular race. "We" are discomfited by the form of the question. "We" are discomfited by the sound of the question.

51 Apart from how it sounds, the *Parks* question feels wrong in the pit of one's stomach. *To Kill a Mockingbird*, the famous American novel by Harper Lee, as a consciousness-raiser, is of and for the early 1960's. In 2008, as one critic has stated, its portrayal of blacks seems condescending and off-balance. As one teacher said, for every white student who is inspired by the book, one black student is demoralized. We live in the world of Spike Lee - not that portrayed by Harper Lee. In the world of Spike Lee and Barack Obama, the *Parks* questions too feel condescending and off-balance.

52 In 2009 we live in a different time and in a different place than we did in 1993 when the *Parks* questions were approved by the Court of Appeal. Our communities have changed and continue to change. Our challenge for cause procedures must change too.

The challenge for cause question should be asked in generic form.

. . .

55 Our judicial system should be prepared to do what it reasonably can in any case to eliminate the risk of a juror taking into account a prohibited factor in his/her deliberations. No accused should have to meet a threshold test to enable a challenge for cause procedure based on concerns of potential juror impartiality based on race, national or ethnic origin, color, religion, sex, age, and mental or physical disability.

56 Trial judges should have the ability to approve a question based on the unique characteristics of the accused if requested by counsel to do so. For example, if an accused is concerned that racial bias may have an impact on jury deliberations, one of the following questions might be asked:

Will you judge the evidence and apply the law as you are directed by the judge without regard to the race of the accused as required by our law?

Or

Will you judge the evidence and apply the law as you are directed by the judge without regard to the race of the accused as required by the Canadian Charter of Rights and Freedoms?

57 Of course a generic inquiry could also be made with respect to national or ethnic origin, color, religion, sex, age or mental or physical disability if requested by an accused. Indeed, I see no disadvantage in allowing a question which may combine a number of factors prohibited by the Charter. The question permitted by the trial judge should be informed by the context of a particular case in consultation with counsel. In some circumstances, this may result in self-identification by an individual accused that would not otherwise occur until after the commencement of trial, if at all. For example, counsel for an accused may ask a judge to advise a jury panel that if selected as a juror during the course of the trial they will hear evidence that the accused is from a certain (identified) country and is of a certain (named) faith. Then, in the challenge for cause procedure, a generic question could be put asking whether the juror will apply the law as directed by the judge without regard to the national or ethnic origin or the religion of the accused.

58 Permitting trial judges to fashion a more generic question will not in any way trivialize or diminish the recognition by the judiciary that the implications of prejudice are devastating and profound. Quite the contrary, the benefits of a more generic and more accessible challenge for cause procedure are that it:

[1] Avoids judicial recognition that racially identified categories of people require special procedures and special protection thus reinforcing institutional recognition of the pervasiveness of the particular bias;

[2] Eliminates the Us and Them sound of the current questions;

[3] Extends the protection of challenge for cause procedures to help ensure absence of any prohibited motives in juror deliberations;

[4] Removes the requirement for an accused to meet a threshold before being entitled to seek equality before and under the law;

[5] Treats all accused people as equally entitled to the protections of s. 15 of the Charter in a jury trial; and

[6] Recognizes that any prejudice informed by a factor prohibited by s.15 of the Charter is intolerable in the application of the criminal law — regardless of whether such prejudice is pervasive in the community.

59 Undoubtedly there has been, and will continue to be, vigorous debate about the wisdom of being restricted to one question in a challenge for cause proceeding. It is not my intention in criticizing the *Parks* questions in favour of a more flexible and generic approach to make any comment on the advantages/ disadvantages of being restricted to one question in a challenge for cause proceeding.

In *R. v. Douse* (2009), 246 C.C.C. (3d) 227, 69 C.R. (6th) 289 (Ont. S.C.J.), defence counsel called expert testimony seeking to justify having each potential juror answer a twelve item questionnaire with the results being analyzed by computer and the results used to determine how much more or less prejudiced the potential juror was than the average person. The degree of prejudice of average persons was to be determined through a random telephone survey conducted by a marketing firm. Potential jurors would then be asked questions that were modified from the approved questions.

In a very lengthy judgment Justice Durno refused to allow the survey and questioning. He did modify the *Parks* question. The applicant would be permitted to offer the following preamble and question:

As the judge will tell you, in deciding whether or not the prosecution has proven the charge against an accused a juror must judge the evidence of the witnesses without bias, prejudice or partiality.

Would your ability to judge the evidence in the case without bias, prejudice or partiality be affected by the fact that the person charged is a black and the victim is a white woman? Which answer most accurately reflects your answer to that question?:

> (a) I would not be able to judge the case fairly.
>
> (b) I might be able to judge the case fairly.
>
> (c) I would be able to judge the case fairly.
>
> (d) I do not know if I would be able to judge the case fairly.

Most Ontario judges still prefer a version of the *Parks* question with an answer of "yes" or "no", although some emphasise that another answer is permitted: *R. v. Wright* (2013), 6 C.R. (7th) 108 (Ont. S.C.J.). For a discussion of the jurisprudence since *Parks*, see: R. Ruperlia, "Erring on the Side of Ignorance: Challenges for Cause Twenty Years after *Parks*" (2013), 92 *Can. Bar. Rev.* 267.

Prior to *Williams*, in *R. v. B. (A.)* (1997), 7 C.R. (5th) 238, 115 C.C.C. (3d) 421 (Ont. C.A.), Justice Moldaver for the Court rejected the possibility of challenges for cause based on the nature of the offence or generic prejudice based on gender in sexual assault cases. Apart from policy issues, such as the difficulty of distinguishing types of offences, Moldaver J.A. ruled that an evidentiary foundation for such challenges had not been laid. In *R. v. K. (A.)* (1999), 27 C.R. (5th) 226, 137 C.C.C. (3d) 225 (Ont. C.A.), he revised his position to allow such challenges on the basis that *Williams* had lowered the evidentiary burden. However his two fellow judges did not agree and re-asserted *B. (A.)*. When the matter reached the Supreme Court, the Court flatly rejected such challenges.

R. v. FIND

[2001] 1 S.C.R. 863, 42 C.R. (5th) 1, 154 C.C.C. (3d) 97 (S.C.C.)

The accused was charged with 21 counts of sexual offences against complainants ranging between 6 and 12 years of age at the time of the alleged offences. Prior to jury selection, he applied to challenge potential jurors for cause, arguing that the nature of the charges against him gave rise to a realistic possibility that some jurors might be unable to try the case against him impartially and solely on the evidence before them. The trial judge rejected the application. The accused was tried and convicted on 17 of the 21 counts. The majority of the Ontario Court of Appeal dismissed the accused's appeal, upholding the trial judge's ruling not to permit the accused to challenge prospective jurors for cause. The Supreme Court dismissed the accused's appeal.

McLACHLIN C.J.:—At stake are two important values. The first is the right to a fair trial by an impartial jury under s. 11(d) of the Canadian Charter of Rights and Freedoms. The second is the need to maintain an efficient trial process, unencumbered by needless procedural hurdles. Our task is to set out guidelines that ensure a fundamentally fair trial without unnecessarily complicating and lengthening trials and increasing the already heavy burdens placed on jurors.

Defence counsel proposed that the following questions be put to potential jurors:

> Do you have strong feelings about the issue of rape and violence on young children?
>
> If so, what are those feelings based on?
>
> Would those strong feelings concerning the rape and violence on young children prevent you from giving Mr. Find a fair trial based solely on the evidence given during the trial of this case?

The trial judge, in a brief oral ruling, dismissed the application on the basis that it simply "doesn't fall anywhere near the dicta of the Court of Appeal in *Regina v. Parks*". . . .

Later, during the process of empanelling the jury, a potential juror spontaneously offered that he had two children, stating "I just don't think I could separate myself from my feelings towards them and separate the case". This prospective juror was peremptorily challenged, and defence counsel renewed the request to challenge for cause, to no avail.

. . .

IV Issue

Did the nature of the charges against the accused give rise to the right to challenge jurors for cause on the ground of partiality?

. . .

One ground for challenge for cause is that a prospective juror is "not indifferent between the Queen and the accused": Criminal Code, s. 638(1)(b). If the judge is satisfied that a realistic potential for juror partiality exists, he or she may permit the requested challenges for cause. If challenged for cause, the impartiality of the candidate is tried by two triers of fact, usually two previously sworn jurors: Criminal Code, s. 640(2). Absent elimination, the juror is sworn and takes his or her place in the jury box. After the full complement of 12 jurors is empanelled, the accused is placed in their charge, and the trial commences.

The Canadian system of selecting jurors may be contrasted with procedures prevalent in the United States. In both countries the aim is to select a jury that will decide the case impartially. The Canadian system, however, starts from the presumption that jurors are capable of setting aside their views and prejudices and acting impartially between the prosecution and the accused upon proper instruction by the trial judge on their duties. This presumption is displaced only where potential bias is either clear and obvious (addressed by judicial pre-screening), or where the accused or prosecution shows reason to suspect that members of the jury array may possess biases that cannot be set aside (addressed by the challenge for cause process). The American system, by contrast, treats all members of the jury pool as presumptively suspect, and hence includes a preliminary voir dire process, whereby prospective jurors are frequently subjected to extensive questioning, often of a highly personal nature, to guide the respective parties in exercising their peremptory challenges and challenges for cause.

The respective benefits and costs of the different approaches may be debated. With respect to benefits, it is unclear that the American system produces better juries than the Canadian system. As Cory J. observed in *R. v. G. (R.M.)*, [1996] 3 S.C.R. 362, at para. 13, we possess "a centuries-old tradition of juries reaching fair and courageous verdicts". With respect to costs, jury selection under the American system takes longer and intrudes more markedly into the privacy of prospective jurors. It has also been suggested that the extensive questioning permitted by this process, while aimed at providing an impartial jury, is open to abuse by counsel seeking to secure a favourable jury, or to indoctrinate jurors to their views of the case.

. . .

In order to challenge for cause under s. 638(1)(b), one must show a "realistic potential" that the jury pool may contain people who are not impartial, in the sense that even upon proper instructions by the trial judge they may not be able to set aside their prejudice and decide fairly between the Crown and the accused. As a practical matter, establishing a realistic potential for juror partiality generally requires satisfying the court on two matters: (1) that a widespread bias exists in the community; and (2) that some jurors may be incapable of setting aside this bias, despite trial safeguards, to render an impartial decision. These two components of the challenge for cause test reflect, respectively, the attitudinal and behavioural components of partiality.

. . .

Trial procedure has evolved over the centuries to counter biases. The jurors swear to discharge their functions impartially. The opening addresses of the judge and the lawyers impress upon jurors the gravity of their task, and enjoin them to be objective. The rules of process and evidence underline the fact that the verdict depends not on this or that person's views, but on the evidence and the law. At the end of the day, the jurors are objectively instructed on the facts and the law by the judge, and sent out to deliberate in accordance with those instructions. They are asked not to decide on the basis of their personal, individual views of the evidence and law, but to listen to each other's views and evaluate their own inclinations in light of those views and the trial judge's instructions. Finally, they are told that they must not convict unless they are satisfied of the accused's guilt beyond a reasonable doubt and that they must be unanimous. It is difficult to conceive stronger antidotes than these to emotion, preconception and prejudice. It is against the backdrop of these safeguards that the law presumes that the trial process will cleanse the biases jurors may bring with them, and allows challenges for cause only where a realistic potential exists that some jurors may not be able to function impartially, despite the rigours of the trial process.

. . .

Ultimately, the decision to allow or deny an application to challenge for cause falls to the discretion of the trial judge. However, judicial discretion should not be confused with judicial whim. Where a realistic potential for partiality exists, the right to challenge must flow: *Williams*. If in doubt, the judge should err on the side of permitting challenges. Since the right of the accused to a fair trial is at stake, "[i]t is better to risk allowing what are in fact unnecessary challenges, than to risk prohibiting challenges which are necessary": *Williams*.

2. *Proof: How a Realistic Potential for Partiality May Be Established*

A party may displace the presumption of juror impartiality by calling evidence, by asking the judge to take judicial notice of facts, or both. In addition, the judge may draw inferences from events that occur in the proceedings and may make common sense inferences about how certain biases, if proved, may affect the decision-making process.

The first branch of the inquiry — establishing relevant widespread bias — requires evidence, judicial notice or trial events demonstrating a pervasive bias in the community. The second stage of the inquiry — establishing a behavioural link between widespread attitudes and juror conduct — may be a matter of proof, judicial notice, or simply reasonable inference as to how bias might influence the decision-making process: *Williams*.

In this case, the appellant relies heavily on proof by judicial notice. Judicial notice dispenses with the need for proof of facts that are clearly uncontroversial or beyond reasonable dispute. Facts judicially noticed are not proved by evidence under oath. Nor are they tested by cross-examination. Therefore, the threshold for judicial notice is strict: a court may properly take judicial notice of facts that are either: (1) so notorious or generally accepted as not to be the subject of debate among reasonable persons; or (2) capable of immediate and accurate demonstration by resort to readily accessible sources of indisputable accuracy.

The scientific and statistical nature of much of the information relied upon by the appellant further complicates this case. Expert evidence is by definition neither notorious nor capable of immediate and accurate demonstration. This is why it must be proved through an expert whose qualifications are accepted by the court and who is available for cross-examination. As Doherty J.A. stated in *R. v. Alli* (1996), 110 C.C.C. (3d) 283 (Ont. C.A.), at p. 285: "[a]ppellate analysis of untested social science data should not be regarded as the accepted means by which the scope of challenges for cause based on generic prejudice will be settled".

C. Were the Grounds for Challenge for Cause Present in this Case?

. . .

The appellant called no evidence, expert or otherwise, on the incidence or likely effect of prejudice stemming from the nature of the offences with which he is charged. Instead, he asks the Court to take judicial notice of a widespread bias arising from allegations of the sexual assault of children.

The Crown, by contrast, argues that the facts on which it agrees do not translate into bias, much less widespread bias.

The appellant relies on the following: (a) the incidence of victimization and its effect on members of the jury pool; (b) the strong views held by many about sexual assault and the treatment of this crime by the criminal justice system; (c) myths and stereotypes arising from widespread and deeply entrenched attitudes about sexual assault; (d) the incidence of intense emotional reactions to sexual assault, such as a strong aversion to the crime or undue empathy for its victims; (e) the experience of Ontario trial courts, where hundreds of potential jurors in such cases have been successfully challenged as partial; and (f) social science research indicating a "generic prejudice" against the accused in sexual assault cases. He argues that these factors permit the Court to take judicial notice of widespread bias arising from charges of sexual assault of children.

(a) Incidence of Victimization

The only social science research before us on the issue of victim empathy is a study by R. L. Wiener, A. T. Feldman Wiener and T. Grisso, "Empathy and Biased Assimilation of Testimonies in Cases of Alleged Rape" (1989), 13 Law & Hum. Behav. 343. The appellant cites this study for the proposition that those participants acquainted in some way with a rape victim demonstrated a greater tendency, under the circumstances of the study, to find a defendant guilty. However, as the Crown notes, this study offers no evidence that victim status *in itself* impacts jury verdicts. In fact, the study found no correlation between degree of empathy for rape victims and tendency to convict, nor did it find higher degrees of victim empathy amongst those persons acquainted with rape victims. Further, the study was limited to a small sample of participants. It made no attempt to simulate an actual jury trial, and did not involve a deliberation process or an actual verdict. In the absence of expert testimony, tested under cross-examination, as to the conclusions properly supported by this study, I can only conclude that it provides little assistance in establishing the existence of widespread bias arising from the incidence of sexual assault in Canadian society.

. . .

(b) Strongly Held Views Relating to Sexual Offences

The appellant submits that the politicized and gender-based nature of sexual offences gives rise to firmly held beliefs, opinions and attitudes that establish widespread bias in cases of sexual assault. This argument found favour with Moldaver J.A. in *K. (A.)*. Moldaver J.A. judicially noticed the tendency of sexual assault to be committed along gender lines. He also took judicial notice of the systemic discrimination women and children have faced in the criminal justice system, and the fact that recent reforms have gone too far for some and not far enough for others. From this foundation of facts, he inferred that the gender-based and politicized nature of sexual offences leads to a realistic possibility that some members of the jury pool, as a result of their political beliefs, will harbour deep-seated and virulent biases that might prove resistant to judicial cleansing. Quoting from the work of Professor Paciocco, Moldaver J.A. emphasized that strong political convictions and impartiality are not necessarily incongruous, but that for some "feminists" "commitment gives way to zealotry and dogma". The conviction that the justice system and its rules are incapable of protecting women and children, it is argued, may lead some potential jurors to disregard trial directions and rules safeguarding the presumption of innocence.

The appellant supports this reasoning, adding that the polarized, politically charged nature of sexual offences results in two prevalent social attitudes: first, that the criminal justice system is incapable of dealing with an "epidemic" of abuse because of its male bias or the excessive protections it affords the accused; and second, that conviction rates in sexual offence cases are unacceptably low. These beliefs, he alleges, may jeopardize the accused's right to a fair trial. For example, jurors harbouring excessive political zeal may ignore trial directions and legal rules perceived as obstructing the "truth" of what occurred, or may simply "cast their lot" with the victim. All this, the appellant submits, amounts to widespread bias in the community incompatible with juror impartiality.

The appellant does not deny that jurors trying any serious offence may hold strong views about the relevant law. Nor does he suggest such views raise concerns about bias in the trial of most offences. Few rules of criminal law attract universal support, and many engender heated debate. The treatment of virtually all serious crimes attracts sharply divided opinion, fervent criticism, and advocacy for reform. General disagreement or criticism of the relevant law, however, does not mean a prospective juror is inclined to take the law into his or her own hands at the expense of an individual accused.

The appellant's submission reduces to this: while strong views on the law do not ordinarily indicate bias, an exception arises in the case of sexual assaults on children. The difficulty, however, is that there is nothing in the material that supports this contention, nor is it self-evident. There is no indication that jurors are more willing to cross the line from opinion to prejudice in relation to sexual assault than for any other serious crime. It is therefore far from clear that strongly held views about sexual assault translate into bias, in the required sense of a tendency to act in an unfair and prejudicial manner.

The material before the Court offers no measure of the prevalence in Canadian society of the specific attitudes identified by the appellant as corrosive of juror impartiality. Some people may indeed believe that the justice system is faltering in the face of an epidemic of abuse and that perpetrators of this crime too often escape conviction; yet, it is far from clear that these beliefs are prevalent in our society, let alone that they translate into bias on a widespread scale.

(c) Myths and Stereotypes About Sexual Offences

The appellant suggests that the strong views that surround the crime of sexual assault may contribute to widespread myths and stereotypes that undermine juror impartiality. In any given jury pool, he argues, some people may reason from the prevalence of abuse to the conclusion that the accused is likely guilty; some may assume children never lie about abuse; and some may reason that the accused is more likely to be guilty because he is a man.

Again, however, the proof falls short. Although these stereotypical beliefs clearly amount to bias that might incline some people against the accused or toward conviction, it is neither notorious nor indisputable that they enjoy widespread acceptance in Canadian society. Myths and stereotypes do indeed pervade public perceptions of sexual assault. Some favour the accused, others the Crown. In the absence of evidence, however, it is difficult to conclude that these stereotypes translate into widespread bias.

(d) Emotional Nature of Sexual Assault Trials

The appellant asks the Court to take judicial notice of the emotional nature of sexual assault trials and to conclude that fear, empathy for the victim, and abhorrence of the crime establish widespread bias in the community. His concern is that jurors, faced with allegations of sexual assaults of children, may act on emotion rather than reason. This is particularly the case, he suggests, for past victims of abuse, for whom the moral repugnancy of the crime may be amplified. He emphasizes that the presumption of innocence in criminal trials demands the acquittal of the "probably" guilty. An intense aversion to sexual crimes, he argues, may incline some jurors to err on the side of conviction in such circumstances. Undue empathy for the victim, he adds, may also prompt a juror to "validate" the complaint with a guilty verdict, rather than determine guilt or innocence according to the law.

Crimes commonly arouse deep and strong emotions. They represent a fundamental breach of the perpetrator's compact with society. Crimes make victims, and jurors cannot help but sympathize with them. Yet these indisputable facts do not necessarily establish bias, in the sense of an attitude that could unfairly prejudice jurors against the accused or toward conviction. Many crimes routinely tried by jurors are abhorrent. Brutal murders, ruthless frauds and violent attacks are standard fare for jurors. Abhorred as they are, these crimes seldom provoke suggestions of bias incompatible with a fair verdict.

One cannot automatically equate strong emotions with an unfair and prejudicial bias against the accused. Jurors are not expected to be indifferent toward crimes. Nor are they expected to remain neutral toward those shown to have committed such offences. If this were the case, prospective jurors would be routinely and successfully challenged for cause as a preliminary stage in the trial of all serious criminal offences. Instead, we accept that jurors often abhor the crime alleged to have been committed — indeed there would be cause for alarm if representatives of a community did not deplore heinous criminal acts. It would be equally alarming if jurors did not feel empathy or compassion for persons shown to be victims of such acts. These facts alone do not establish bias. There is simply no indication that these attitudes, commendable in themselves, unfairly prejudice jurors against the accused or toward conviction. They are common to the trial of many serious offences and have never grounded a right to challenge for cause.

. . .

(e) The History of Challenges for Cause in Ontario

The appellant refers this Court to the experience of Ontario trial courts where judges have allowed defence counsel to challenge prospective jurors for cause in cases involving allegations of sexual assault: see Vidmar, *supra*, at p. 5; D. M. Tanovich, D. M. Paciocco, S. Skurka, Jury Selection in Criminal Trials: Skills, Science, and the Law (1997), at pp. 239-42. These sources, cataloguing 34 cases, indicate that hundreds of potential jurors have been successfully challenged for cause as not indifferent between the Crown and the accused. It is estimated that 36 percent of the prospective jurors challenged were disqualified.

The appellant argues that the fact that hundreds of prospective jurors have been found to be partial is in itself sufficient evidence of widespread bias arising from sexual assault trials. This is proof, he asserts, that the social realities surrounding sexual assault trials give rise to prejudicial beliefs, attitudes and emotions on a widespread scale in Canadian communities.

The Crown disagrees. It argues first, that the survey lacks validity because of methodological defects, and second, that even if the results are accepted, the successful challenges do not demonstrate a widespread bias, but instead may be attributed to other causes.

The first argument against the survey is that its methodology is unsound. The Crown raises a number of concerns: the survey is entirely anecdotal, not comprehensive or random; not all of the questions asked of prospective jurors are indicated; there is no way in which to assess the directions, if any, provided by the trial judge, especially in relation to the distinction between strong opinions or emotions and partiality; and no comparative statistics are provided contrasting these results with the experience in other criminal law contexts. The intervener CLA concedes that the survey falls short of scientific validity, but contends that it nevertheless documents a phenomena of considerable significance. Hundreds of prospective jurors disqualified on the grounds of bias by impartial triers of fact must, it is argued, displace the presumption of juror impartiality. Nonetheless, the lack of methodological rigour and the absence of expert evidence undermine the suggestion that the Ontario experience establishes widespread bias.

The second argument against the survey is that the questions asked were so general, and the information elicited so scarce, that no meaningful inference can be drawn from the responses given by challenged jurors or from the number of potential jurors disqualified. Charron J.A., for the majority in *K. (A.)*, observed that prospective jurors in that case received no meaningful instruction on the nature of jury duty or the meaning and importance of impartiality.

Further, they often indicated confusion at the questions posed to them or asked that the questions be repeated. In the end, numerous prospective jurors were disqualified for offering little more than that they would find it difficult to hear a case of this nature, or that they held strong emotions about the sexual abuse of children.

The challenge for cause process rests to a considerable extent on self-assessment of impartiality by the challenged juror, and the response to questions on challenge often will be little more than an affirmation or denial of one's own ability to act impartially in the circumstances of the case. In the absence of guidance, prospective jurors may conflate disqualifying bias with a legitimate apprehension about sitting through a case involving allegations of sexual abuse of children, or the strong views or emotions they may hold on this subject.

Where potential jurors are challenged for racial bias, the risk of social disapprobation and stigma supports the veracity of admissions of potential partiality. No similar indicia of reliability attach to the frank and open admission of concern about one's ability to approach and decide a case of alleged child sexual abuse judiciously. While a prospective juror's admission of racial prejudice may suggest partiality, the same cannot be said of an admission of abhorrence or other emotional attitude toward the sexual abuse of children. We do not know whether the potential jurors who professed concerns about serving on juries for sexual assault charges were doing so because they were biased, or for other reasons. We do not know whether they were told that strong emotions and beliefs would not in themselves impair their duty of impartiality, or whether they were informed of the protections built into the trial process.

It follows that the survey of past challenge for cause cases involving charges of sexual assault does not without more establish widespread bias arising from these charges.

(f) Social Science Evidence of "Generic Prejudice"

The appellant argues that social science research, particularly that of Vidmar, supports the contention that social realities, such as the prevalence of sexual abuse and its politically charged nature, translate into a widespread bias in Canadian society.

In *Williams, supra*, the Court referred to Vidmar's research in concluding that the partiality targeted by s. 638(1)(b) was not limited to biases arising from a direct interest in the proceeding or pre-trial exposure to the case, but could arise from any of a variety of sources, including the "nature of the crime itself". However, recognition that the nature of an offence may give rise to "generic prejudice" does not obviate the need for proof. Labels do not govern the availability of challenges for cause. Regardless of how a case is classified, the ultimate issue is whether a realistic possibility exists that some potential jurors may try the case on the basis of prejudicial attitudes and beliefs, rather than the evidence offered at trial. The appellant relies on the work of Vidmar for the proposition that such a possibility does in fact arise from allegations of sexual assault.

Vidmar is known for the theory of a "generic prejudice" against accused persons in sexual assault trials and for the conclusion that the attitudes and beliefs of jurors are frequently reflected in the verdicts of juries on such trials. However, the conclusions of Vidmar do not assist in finding widespread bias. His theory that a "generic prejudice" exists against those charged with sexual assault, although in the nature of expert evidence, has not been proved. Nor can the Court take judicial notice of this contested proposition. With regard to the behaviour of potential jurors, the Court has no foundation in this case to draw an inference of partial juror conduct, as discussed in more detail below, under the behavioural stage of the partiality test.

Vidmar himself acknowledges the limitations of his research. He concedes that the notion of "generic prejudice" lacks scientific validity, and that none of the studies he relies on actually asked the questions typically asked of Canadian jurors, including whether they can impartially adjudicate guilt or innocence in a sexual assault trial. . . . The attempt of Vidmar and others to conduct scientific research on jury behaviour is commendable. Unfortunately, research into the effect of juror attitudes on deliberations and verdicts is constrained by the almost absolute prohibition in s. 649 of the Criminal Code against the disclosure by jury members of information relating to the jury's proceedings. More comprehensive and scientific assessment of this and other aspects of the criminal law and criminal process would be welcome. Should Parliament reconsider this prohibition, it may be that more helpful research into the Canadian experience would emerge. But for now, social science evidence appears to cast little light on the extent of any "generic prejudice" relating to charges of sexual assault, or its relationship to jury verdicts.

(g) Conclusions on the Existence of a Relevant, Widespread Bias

Do the factors cited by the appellant, taken together, establish widespread bias arising from charges relating to sexual abuse of children? In my view, they do not. The material presented by the appellant, considered in its totality, falls short of grounding judicial notice of widespread bias in Canadian society against the accused in such trials. At best, it establishes that the crime of sexual assault, like many serious crimes, frequently elicits strong attitudes and emotions.

However, the two branches of the test for partiality are not watertight compartments. Given the challenge of proving facts as elusive as the nature and scope of prejudicial attitudes, and the need to err on the side of caution, I prefer not to resolve this case entirely at the first, attitudinal stage. Out of an abundance of caution, I will proceed to consider the potential impact, if any, of the alleged biases on juror behaviour.

2. Is it Reasonable to Infer that Some Jurors May Be Incapable of Setting Aside Their Biases Despite Trial Safeguards?

The applicant need not always adduce direct evidence establishing this link between the bias in issue and detrimental effects on the trial process. Even in the absence of such evidence, a trial judge may reasonably infer that some strains of bias by their very nature may prove difficult for jurors to identify and eliminate from their reasoning.

This inference, however, is not automatic. Its strength varies with the nature of the bias in issue, and its amenability to judicial cleansing. In *Williams*, the Court inferred a behavioural link between the pervasive racial prejudice established on the evidence and the possibility that some jurors, consciously or not, would decide the case based on prejudice and stereotype. Such a result, however, is not inevitable for every form of bias, prejudice or preconception. In some circumstances, the appropriate inference is that the "predispositions can be safely regarded as curable by judicial direction": *Williams*.

Fundamental distinctions exist between the racial prejudice at issue in *Williams* and a more general bias relating to the nature of the offence itself. These differences relate both to the nature of these respective biases, and to their susceptibility (or resistance) to cleansing by the trial process. It may be useful to examine these differences before embarking on a more extensive consideration of the potential effects on the trial process, if any, of the biases alleged in the present case.

The first difference is that race may impact more directly on the jury's decision than bias stemming from the nature of the offence. By contrast, the aversion, fear, abhorrence, and beliefs alleged to surround sexual assault offences may lack this cogent and irresistible connection to the accused. Unlike racial prejudice, they do not point a finger at a particular accused.

Second, trial safeguards may be less successful in cleansing racial prejudice than other types of bias, as recognized in *Williams*. The nature of racial prejudice — in particular its subtle, systemic and often unconscious operation — compelled the inference in *Williams* that some people might be incapable of effacing, or even identifying, its influence on their reasoning. In reaching this conclusion, the Court emphasized the "invasive and elusive" operation of racial prejudice and its foundation "on preconceptions and unchallenged assumptions that unconsciously shape the daily behaviour of individuals".

The biases alleged in this case, by contrast, may be more susceptible to cleansing by the rigours of the trial process. They are more likely to be overt and acknowledged than is racial prejudice, and hence more easily removed. Jurors are more likely to recognize and counteract them. The trial judge is more likely to address these concerns in the course of directions to the jury, as are counsel in their addresses. Offence-based bias has concerned the trial process throughout its long evolution, and many of the safeguards the law has developed may be seen as a response to it.

Against this background, I turn to the question of whether the biases alleged to arise from the nature of sexual assault, if established, might lead jurors to decide the case in an unfair and prejudicial way, despite the cleansing effect of the trial process.

First, the appellant contends that some jurors, whether victims, friends of victims, or simply people holding strong views about sexual assault, may not be able to set aside strong beliefs about this crime — for example, that the justice system is biased against complainants, that there exists an epidemic of abuse that must be halted, or that conviction rates are too low — and decide the case solely on its merits. Some jurors, he says, may disregard rules of law that are perceived as obstructing the "truth" of what occurred. Others may simply "cast their lot" with groups that have been victimized. These possibilities, he contends, support a reasonable inference that strong opinions may translate into a realistic potential for partial juror conduct.

This argument cannot succeed. As discussed, strongly held political views do not necessarily suggest that jurors will act unfairly in an actual trial. Indeed, passionate advocacy for law reform may be an expression of the highest respect for the rule of law, not a sign that one is willing to subvert its operation at the expense of the accused.

In the absence of evidence that such beliefs and attitudes may affect jury behaviour in an unfair manner, it is difficult to conclude that they will not be cleansed by the trial process. Only speculation supports the proposition that jurors will act on general opinions and beliefs to the detriment of an individual accused, in disregard of their oath or affirmation, the presumption of innocence, and the directions of the trial judge.

The appellant also contends that myths and stereotypes attached to the crime of sexual assault may unfairly inform the deliberation of some jurors. However, strong, sometimes biased, assumptions about sexual behaviour are not new to sexual assault trials. Traditional myths and stereotypes have long tainted the assessment of the conduct and veracity of complainants in sexual assault cases — the belief that women of "unchaste" character are more likely to have consented or are less worthy of belief; that passivity or even resistance may in fact constitute consent; and that some women invite sexual assault by reason of their dress or behaviour, to name only a few. Based on overwhelming evidence from relevant social science literature, this Court has been willing to accept the prevailing existence of such myths and stereotypes: see, for example, *Seaboyer, supra; R. v. Osolin,* and *R. v. Ewanchuk.*

Child complainants may similarly be subject to stereotypical assumptions, such as the belief that stories of abuse are probably fabricated if not reported immediately, or that the testimony of children is inherently unreliable: *R. v. W. (R.),* [1992] 2 S.C.R. 122; *R. v. D.D.,* [2000] 2 S.C.R. 275, 2000 SCC 43; N. Bala, "Double Victims: Child Sexual Abuse and the Canadian Criminal Justice System", in W. S. Tarnopolsky, J. Whitman and M. Ouellette, eds., *Discrimination in the Law and the Administration of Justice* (1993), 231.

These myths and stereotypes about child and adult complainants are particularly invidious because they comprise part of the fabric of social "common sense" in which we are daily immersed. Their pervasiveness, and the subtlety of their operation, create the risk that victims of abuse will be blamed or unjustly discredited in the minds of both judges and jurors.

Yet the prevalence of such attitudes has never been held to justify challenges for cause as of right by Crown prosecutors. Instead, we have traditionally trusted the trial process to ensure that such attitudes will not prevent jurors from acting impartially. We have relied on the rules of evidence, statutory protections, and guidance from the judge and counsel to clarify potential misconceptions and promote a reasoned verdict based solely on the merits of the case.

Absent evidence to the contrary, there is no reason to believe that stereotypical attitudes about accused persons are more elusive of these cleansing measures than stereotypical attitudes about complainants. It follows that the myths and stereotypes alleged by the appellant, even if widespread, provide little support for any inference of a behavioural link between these beliefs and the potential for juror partiality.

. . .

It follows that even if widespread bias were established, we cannot safely infer, on the record before the Court, that it would lead to unfair, prejudicial and partial juror behaviour. This is not to suggest that an accused can never be prejudiced by the mere fact of the nature and circumstances of the charges he or she faces; rather, the inference between social attitudes and jury behaviour is simply far less obvious and compelling in this context, and more may be required to satisfy a court that this inference may be reasonably drawn. The nature of offence-based bias, as discussed, suggests that the circumstances in which it is found to be both widespread in the community and resistant to the safeguards of trial may prove exceptional. Nonetheless, I would not foreclose the possibility that such circumstances may arise. If widespread bias arising from sexual assault were established in a future case, it would be for the court in that case to determine whether this bias gives rise to a realistic potential for partial juror conduct in the community from which the jury pool is drawn. I would only caution that in deciding whether to draw an inference of adverse effect on jury behaviour the court should take into account the nature of the bias and its susceptibility to cleansing by the trial process.

VI Conclusion

The case for widespread bias arising from the nature of charges of sexual assault on children is tenuous. Moreover, even if the appellant had demonstrated widespread bias, its link to actual juror behaviour is speculative, leaving the presumption that it would be cleansed by the trial process firmly in place. Many criminal trials engage strongly held views and stir up powerful emotions — indeed, even revulsion and abhorrence. Such is the nature of the trial process. Absent proof, we cannot simply assume that strong beliefs and emotions translate into a realistic potential for partiality, grounding a right to challenge for cause. I agree with the majority of the Court of Appeal that the appellant has not established that the trial judge erred in refusing to permit him to challenge prospective jurors for cause.

For very different views on *Find*, see Stephen Coughlan, "R. v. Find: Preserving the Presumption of Innocence" (2001) 42 C.R. (5th) 31 and Michael Plaxton, "The Biased Juror and Appellate Review: A Reply to Professor Coughlan" (2001) 44 C.R. (5th) 294.

Recently a spate of appeal rulings have ordered new trials on the basis of lack of direction on the nature of challenges for cause. Juries must be told that the triers are to decide the question on a balance of probabilities, the decision must be by both of them, they have the right to disagree they can retire to consider the matter, and they must be given assistance in the understanding of partiality: see, for example, *R. v. Li* (2004), 183 C.C.C. (3d) 48 (Ont. C.A.).

In *R. v. Spence*, [2005] 3 S.C.R. 458, 33 C.R. (6th) 1, 202 C.C.C. (3d) 1 (S.C.C.) a black accused was charged with robbery of an East Indian pizza deliveryman in the hallway of an apartment block. The trial judge permitted the defence to challenge potential jurors for cause on the basis of potential bias against a black accused but refused to allow a question addressing the interracial nature of the crimes. He held that the "interracial" element was irrelevant on the facts of this case. The accused was convicted.

On appeal, the accused argued that he was deprived of his right to an impartial jury and therefore to a fair trial. The majority of the Ontario Court of Appeal set aside the conviction. The majority held that where an accused entitled to challenge the jury for cause on the basis of race wishes to include the interracial nature of the crime in the question for potential jurors, he is entitled to have the question posed in that way.

On further appeal the Supreme Court allowed the appeal and restored the conviction.

Justice Binnie wrote the unanimous judgment of the Court. He held it was up to the defence to show an "air of reality" to the assertion that the complainant's East Indian origin had the realistic potential of aggravating jurors' prejudice against the black accused because of natural sympathy for the victim by jurors who might be East Indian. This burden was not met. While it was open to the trial judge to include the "interracial" aspect of the crime in the challenge for cause, neither the case law, nor the studies on which the case law was based, supported the need for a broad entitlement in every case to challenge for cause based on racial sympathy as distinguished from potential racial hostility. The majority in the court below had pushed judicial notice beyond its proper limits. It was within the trial judge's discretion to allow the interracial question but it was not an error of law for the trial judge to draw the line where he did. This had not resulted in an unfair trial.

4. Opening Address to Jury

A jury trial generally begins by an opening address to the jury by the Crown counsel. The tradition is described in Salhany, *Canadian Criminal Procedure* (5th ed.), at p. 274:

> . . . In his address, the counsel will lay before the jury a brief summary of the facts upon which the Crown is relying to establish its case and of the evidence of each witness to be called. Since the prosecution counsel is the representative of the Crown imbued with the duty of assisting the jury in arriving at the truth, he must be fair in his opening address as well as in his address to the jury. His duty is to be impartial and excludes any notion of winning or losing. He must guard against injecting comments likely to excite and inflame the jury against the accused. Nor may he express a personal opinion that the accused is guilty or state that the Crown investigators and experts are satisfied as to the accused's guilt. This duty was summoned up succinctly in *Sugarman*:
>
> > It cannot be too often made plain that the business of counsel for the Crown is fairly and impartially to exhibit all the facts to the jury. The Crown has no interest

in procuring a conviction. Its only interest is that the right person should be convicted, that the truth should be known, and that justice should be done.

What are the advantages and disadvantages of this traditional beginning?

5. Closing Address to Jury

Section 651 determines whether the prosecutor or the defence counsel sums up first. If the defence or any one of the defendants adduces evidence the defence must address the jury before the Crown. If no defence evidence is called the order is the Crown, then the accused.

Is it tactically advantageous to address the jury first or last? Why?

In *R. v. Rose*, [1998] 3 S.C.R. 262, 20 C.R. (5th) 246, 129 C.C.C. (3d) 449 (S.C.C.) a 5-4 majority of the Supreme Court decided that this rule in s. 651(3) and (4) did not violate sections 7 and 11(d) of the Charter. However the majority through Cory J. held that the accused would in exceptional circumstances have a right of reply. See Allan Manson, "The Claim of the Rose case: Jury Addresses and Humble Echoes of Reply" (1999), 20 C.R. (5th) 300 and Sankoff and Hendel, "Creating a Right of Reply: Rose is Not Without a Few Thorns" (1999), 20 C.R. (5th) 305.

G.A. MARTIN, CLOSING ARGUMENT TO THE JURY FOR THE DEFENCE IN CRIMINAL CASES
(1967-1968), 10 Crim. L.Q. 34

It is a commonly accepted viewpoint that the address to the jury is not as important as cross-examination or as strategy in a criminal trial.

While there may be an element of truth in this assertion, I am convinced, after practising in the field of criminal law for almost thirty years, that the address to the jury often exerts a decisive influence on the outcome of a criminal prosecution. It is very seldom indeed that cross-examination, however skilfully conducted, *obviously* destroys or answers the case for the prosecution.

The Preparation

The preparation of a good jury address begins long before the trial. As the preparation of a case proceeds, beginning with the initial attorney-client interview, and passing on through the stage of the preliminary hearing and the interviewing of witnesses, counsel must inevitably, if he is to conduct a successful defense, form a theory upon which the defense is to be conducted. He should constantly be thinking about the case, formulating in his mind how he will explain this particular piece of apparently adverse evidence or how to place this particular fact before the jury so that they will feel its full impact from the defense point of view. He should, above all, be considering the order in which he will marshal the facts at his disposal for presentation to the jury. This type of thinking should continue up until the moment he commences his address.

. . .

The Form the Jury Address Should Take

Every good jury address from the time of Cicero has had the same construction, namely: (*a*) the introduction; (*b*) the argument; and (*c*) the peroration.

The Introduction

The purpose of the introduction is to awaken the jury to the grave responsibilities they have assumed, to impress upon them the fact that if they erroneously convict the accused it is almost impossible to correct their error. They should be made to feel that the presumption of innocence and the requirement of proof beyond a reasonable doubt are vital living principles which exist for their protection as well as that of the accused. The language used to achieve this purpose must depend upon the style and creativity of the particular counsel.

Assemble your facts in such a way that the defendant is placed in a sympathetic light. Dwell on the terrible provocation your client endured before reacting to it, how hard he worked to support his wife and family. But emphasize those things in the appropriate part of the address, not at the beginning. The appeal to the emotions is much better made not at the beginning but later on in the address as you deal with topics calculated to arouse the feelings of the jury: the accomplice trying to escape the consequences of his crime by shifting the blame to the accused; the father trying to give his children sound moral instruction and schooling while the unfaithful wife that he killed in the heat of sudden provocation was neglecting her sacred obligations.

During your address it is advisable to refer to your client on occasion as "Tom Jones", or "Mr. Jones", rather than continously as the "prisoner", or "the accused". In that way you personalize him; he is then associated with the man who has the nice little wife and of whom the five neighbors spoke so highly. It is harder to hang Tom Jones than to hang "the prisoner". In your peroration, however, it is better to refer to your client as "this man", "this woman", or "the defendant".

. . .

In your opening remarks you should define with great clarity and simplicity the issues before the jury—the elements of the offense with which the defendant is charged, and which the prosecution must prove beyond a reasonable doubt.

. . .

RIGHT TO DEAL WITH THE LAW APPLICABLE

The rule which prevails in most jurisdictions is that although counsel may not quote from decided cases he may state the principle of law which he deems applicable insofar as it is necessary to do so to make clear what the defense is.

. . .

IMPROPRIETY OF EXPRESSING PERSONAL OPINION

It is improper to express a personal opinion as to the innocence of your client or your belief in the truthfulness or otherwise of a witness. The reason for this is obvious. If it were permissible for defense counsel to express his opinion that the defendant was innocent, it would equally be proper for prosecuting counsel to express his opinion that the accused was guilty. The verdict of the jury might thus depend not on the evidence but on the prestige or stature of counsel making the declaration. If it were ever to become accepted practice for defense counsel to express a personal opinion as to the innocence of the defendant, the failure to express such an opinion on any occasion would be construed as an admission on the part of counsel that he believed his client guilty.

The Argument

In my early years at the Bar I would spend about forty minutes of a forty-five minute speech on the introduction and the last five minutes on the facts. I traced the history of the jury system back to a period before the Norman Conquest and I dwelt at length on the sad fate of my client pacing up and down in a prison cell for years if the jury found against him. Experience has taught me that jury verdicts are won by a convincing argument on the facts, the specific facts; they are not, as a general rule, swayed by broad sweeping declamation. I am consequently of the opinion that after dealing briefly with those fundamentals of justice that should be called to the attention of the jury, and after outlining the issues before them, counsel should then commence his argument.

One of the most effective ways of commencing the argument of the case is by stating, or rather re-stating, the case for the prosecution. The statement must be absolutely accurate, but the prosecution's case is stated in such a way as to highlight any improbabilities in the case and to bring within the statement every fact favorable to the defense.

. . .

There are several ways in which argument may be presented:

(a) by stating the facts and submitting that certain conclusions should be drawn from those facts;

(b) by stating the facts and inviting the jury to draw the desired conclusion;

(c) by stating the facts and asking the jury what conclusions they draw from them. (This, however, is a rare art. The facts must be accurately stated but marshalled in such a way that the only conclusion the jury can draw is the desired one.)

All three methods of argument are usually used at different times during the address. You should never attempt to force your conclusions upon the jury, but rather to lead them to come to the desired conclusion by their own effort.

The usual order of argument in defending a criminal case is:

(a) the destruction of the case for the prosecution;

(b) the marshalling of the evidence for the defense.

It is inevitable and sometimes desirable that there should be some intermingling of both parts of the argument. This is done by exposing the inherent improbability of the testimony for the prosecution, attacking the credibility of prosecution witnesses, scrutinizing their motives, pointing out inconsistences in their evidence, and then directing the argument to assembling the facts which support the defense. I have found that sometimes in difficult criminal cases it may be preferable as soon as the opening remarks are concluded to summarize what the defense is and then proceed in the usual manner. Lawyers often talk about the "theory of the defense". You should not do this before a jury. The jury is liable to equate "the theory of the defense", with something the defense lawyer has concocted in his mind.

In your argument to the jury you should endeavour to explain every adverse fact. You should endeavour to answer the arguments that you feel sure will be made by the prosecution. Tell the jury that under the law [if it be so in your jurisdiction] once the accused says one word in his own defense or calls a single witness to testify on his behalf the prosecution has the right to address the jury last and you will have no opportunity to answer him. Therefore you must, as best you can, anticipate the argument he may make having regard to the line of cross-examination he has pursued and the questions he has put to his own witnesses. You see it is well to suggest you are using his conduct of the case as a means of anticipating his probable arguments, otherwise the jury may think you are able to anticipate his arguments because you recognize the weaknesses in your own case.

It is always a good thing to have some one to attack in a criminal case. It takes the spotlight off the accused. It does not usually pay to attack the prosecutor unless he has done something manifestly unfair, which would be rare. Sometimes   the conduct of the police merits an attack, but do not attack them unless it is warranted. The motives of important prosecution witnesses should be scrutinized with care and whenever possible made the subject of attack. This is particularly true of accomplices.

. . .

ARGUMENT FROM PROBABILITIES

In arguing a case to a jury, one of the strongest arguments is that which is based on probability. People will believe that which accords with their own experience and the recorded experience of others. They will be reluctant to believe that which they regard as improbable. If there are any improbabilities in the prosecution's case you should marshal those improbabilities to the fullest extent.

Another persuasive type of argument is based upon what the prosecution has not proved. Sometimes you do not have too much to go on in the way of affirmative argument. In that case you list all the things the prosecution should have been able to prove if your client was in fact guilty. The failure to prove those things is an indication that they could have the wrong man.

. . .

MOTIVE

It is, of course, trite law that if the case against the accused is fully proved the failure to prove a motive is not fatal. There may be a motive which is not known. Nevertheless, where the case depends on circumstantial evidence, proof of a motive strengthens the case for the prosecution and, conversely, the apparent absence of a motive raises doubts as to the guilt of the accused.

It is more probable that men are killed by those who have some motive for killing them than by those who have not.

. . .

GOOD CHARACTER

Evidence of good character is cogent evidence of the improbability of the accused being guilty. You should explain to the jury what character is. You might say something like the following:

What is character? Character is the sum total of a man's habits. Habit is one of the strongest forces in the world. That is why parents are at such pains to teach their children the good habits of honesty, decency and truthfulness. They know that those habits once formed will govern the course of their lives. It takes years to build good habits; they cannot be changed in a day. You have heard from the testimony of his neighbors the kind of character this man has for honesty. Do you think it probable or even possible that he would suddenly depart from that character, from those settled habits of honesty and decency and commit this crime?

FAILURE TO CALL THE ACCUSED

One of the difficult questions upon which counsel has to make up his mind in his address to the jury is whether to endeavour to explain his failure to call the accused when he has not done so, or to make no reference to it. Now, there are different views upon this subject. My own view is that it is better to make no reference to the fact that the accused has not been called, with one possible exception. The exception applies where the prosecution has put in a statement made by the accused which contains his defense. It then might be appropriate to say that since the accused has given his explanation there is nothing more he can say. You can enhance the value of that explanation by pointing out that it was given by your client at the earliest opportunity he had to give it, namely, when the police interviewed him. His explanation is not something he thought up long after.

Under normal circumstances, to mention your client's failure to testify merely magnifies that failure, and if, in addition, the reasons advanced by counsel for that failure are not convincing to the jury, they are apt to assume the worst. My instinct tells me that this is so, although others hold different views and they may be right.

. . .

AN ACCUSED TESTIFYING ON HIS OWN BEHALF

Where the accused has testified on his own behalf, you should make the most of that fact in your argument. You should point out that accused has told the jury in the only way he can that he is innocent, namely, by taking the witness stand, giving his evidence under oath and submitting to cross-examination. Point out that is all that any member of the jury could do to prove his innocence under like circumstances. If he has been a good witness you will, of course, infer that only an innocent man could have withstood the skilful cross-examination to which he was subjected. If there are flaws in his testimony you will point out the strain that even an innocent man charged with a serious crime is under; perhaps the strain is even greater in the case of an innocent man. You will thus explain any shortcomings in his testimony.

The Peroration

The purpose of the peroration is to bring the speech to a climax and to appeal to the emotions of the jury in a way that will strengthen the arguments addressed to their intellects. The peroration or conclusion of a good jury address should not be stereotyped; it should fit in with the nature of the trial, the issues involved, and the mood that you believe has been created in the courtroom. A peroration which might be suitable in one kind of murder case might not be suitable in another. A peroration which might be suitable in a murder case might be quite unsuitable in a case of receiving stolen goods.

. . .

Pre-eminent among modern perorations is that of Sir Norman Birkett in his defense of the accused Mancini,

> Defending counsel have a most solemn task, as my colleagues and myself know only too well. We have endeavoured, doubtless with many imperfections, to perform that task to the best of our ability. The ultimate responsibility—that rests upon you, and never let it be said, never let it be thought, that any word of mine shall seek to deter you from doing that which you feel to be your duty. But now that the whole of the case is laid before you, I think I am entitled to claim for this man a verdict of not guilty. And, members of the Jury, in returning that verdict you will vindicate a principle of law—that people are not tried by newspapers, not tried by rumour, not tried by statements born of a love of notoriety, but tried by British juries, called to do justice and decide upon the evidence. I ask you for, I appeal to you for, and I claim, from you, a verdict of not guilty. *Stand firm.*

MURRAY, PROSECUTION OF A CRIMINAL JURY TRIAL
(1967-1968), Crim. L.Q. 68 at 74-5

The question of the prosecutor's address to the jury is a subject on which much case law exists (see *Boucher v. The Queen,* 110 C.C.C. 263, 20 C.R. 1, [1955] S.C.R. 16). The prosecutor should endeavour to maintain a sense of fairness in his address, but, on the other hand, it is his duty fully, firmly and fairly to put all of the facts before the jury on which the Crown relies in support of its case. If the Crown addresses the jury first, the prosecutor should endeavour to anticipate the arguments to be advanced by the defence and to deal with such anticipated defences. The question of the length of an address to a jury is always important as it is the writer's observation that jurors tend to become bored and distracted by an overly-long address. Repetition is delay. In other extraordinarily long cases the prosecutor, in the writer's opinion, should not take more than an hour to sum up the Crown's case concisely.

It has become the custom in British Columbia, in cases where the accused is not defended by counsel, for Crown counsel to waive his right of addressing the jury. This is not a universal custom and there are cases where such waiver should not be exercised. In the case of very long trials, for example, Crown counsel owes a duty to the court to assist it in reviewing the evidence even though the accused is undefended. Again, in cases where there are difficult points of law involved which require a sorting out of evidence, Crown counsel, in the writer's view, is not justified in waiving his address....

After the close of all the evidence and during the course of the judge's charge to the jury it is advisable for counsel to have a check list. This check list should be made up of various headings such as "reasonable doubt", "the presumption of innocence", "unanimous verdict" and so on. It occasionally happens that a trial judge will, through oversight, omit a portion of his charge on the law and in these circumstances the check list proves invaluable in drawing the matter to the attention of the judge at the close of his charge. One of the most common oversights is for a judge to forget to tell the jury that if they can reach a verdict it must be a unanimous verdict. Such an oversight would automatically constitute a ground for a new trial.

Again, at the conclusion of the judge's charge, the prosecutor is faced with the question of whether or not he should take objection to the charge and ask the judge to direct or re-direct the jury with respect to any matters he does not feel have been properly covered. If the prosecutor considers the judge has erred during the charge it is important that he take his objection at the conclusion of the charge as the law appears to be clear that the Crown cannot succeed on an appeal if it has not raised the matters it complains of at the trial.

BOUCHER v. R.
[1955] S.C.R. 16, 20 C.R. 1, 110 C.C.C. 263 (S.C.C.)

CARTWRIGHT J.:—This is an appeal from a unanimous judgment of the Court of Queen's Bench, Appeal Side, pronounced on June 15, 1954, dismissing the appeal of the appellant from his conviction on a charge of murder at his trial before Sevigny C.J. and a jury on January 15, 1954.

. . .

As to the third question of law on which leave to appeal was granted, it appears that in the course of his address to the jury counsel for the Crown said:

(Translation) The doctor spoke to us about blood,—we were taken to task gentlemen because we had an analysis of the blood made. But the Crown is not here for the pleasure of having innocent people convicted.

It is the duty of the Crown, when an affair like that happens, no matter what affair, and still more in a serious affair, to make every possible investigation, and if in the course of these investigations with our experts, the conclusion is come to that the accused is not guilty or that there is a reasonable doubt, it is the duty of the Crown, gentlemen, to say so or if the conclusion is come to that he is not guilty, not to make an arrest. That is what was done here.

Counsel for the Crown concluded his address to the jury as follows:

(Translation) Every day we see more and more crimes than ever, thefts and many another thing, at least one who commits armed robbery does not make his victim suffer as Boucher made Jabour suffer. It is a revolting crime for a man with all the strength of his age, of an athlete against an old man of 77, who is not capable of defending himself. I have a little respect for those who steal when they at least have given their victim a chance to defend himself, but I have no sympathy, none, and I tell you not to have any sympathy for these dastards who strike men, friends. Jabour was perhaps not a friend, but he was a neighbour, at least they knew each other.

In a cowardly manner, with blows of an axe. . . . And, if you bring in a verdict of guilty, for once it will almost be a pleasure to me to ask the death penalty for him.

There are a number of other passages in the address of this counsel to the jury which I do not find it necessary to quote as I think they can be fairly summarized by saying that counsel made it clear to the jury not only that he was submitting to them that the conclusion which they should reach on the evidence was that the accused was guilty, a submission which it was of course proper for him to make, but also that he personally entertained the opinion that the accused was guilty.

There is no doubt that it is improper for counsel, whether for the Crown or the defence to express his own opinion as to the guilt or innocence of the accused.

The grave objection to what was said by counsel is that the jury would naturally and reasonably understand from his words first quoted above that he, with the assistance of other qualified persons, had made a careful examination into the facts of the case prior to the trial and that if as a result of such investigation he entertained any reasonable doubt as to the accused's guilt a duty rested upon him as Crown counsel to so inform the Court. As, far from expressing or suggesting the existence of any such doubt in his mind, he made it clear to the jury that he personally believed the accused to be guilty, the jury would reasonably take from what he had said that as the result of his investigation outside the courtroom Crown counsel had satisfied himself of the guilt of the accused. The making of such a statement to the jury was clearly unlawful and its damaging effect would, in my view, be even greater than the admission of illegal evidence or a statement by Crown counsel to the jury either in his opening address or in his closing address of facts as to which there was no evidence.

I conclude that in regard to both the second and third questions on which leave to appeal was granted there was error in law at the trial and that accordingly the appeal should be allowed unless this is a case in which the Court should apply the provisions of s. 1014(2) of the *Code*.

New trial ordered.

PISANI v. R.
[1971] S.C.R. 738, 1 C.C.C. (2d) 477 (S.C.C.)

LASKIN, J.:—This appeal, from the affirmation by the Court of Appeal of Ontario of the conviction of the accused on a charge of possession of counterfeit money, is here by leave on two questions of law that were formulated as follows:

1. Did the Court of Appeal err in failing to hold that the learned trial judge should have declared a mistrial on the motion of counsel for the accused by reason of the nature of Crown counsel's address to the jury?

2. Did the Court of Appeal err in not holding that the address to the jury by Crown counsel was of such a nature as to deprive the accused of a fair trial and hence resulted in a miscarriage of justice?

Counsel for the Crown contended that these questions did not disclose any issue of law, and hence that this Court was without jurisdiction to entertain the appeal. It is sufficient to get to the merits to found jurisdiction on Q. 2, and to rely in this respect on the views of this Court on such a question as expressed in *Boucher v. The Queen*, 110 C.C.C. 263, [1955] S.C.R. 16, 20 C.R. 1.

The reasons for judgment given separately in *Boucher* by Kerwin, C.J.C., Rand, Locke and Cartwright, JJ., amply point up the obligation of Crown counsel to be accurate, fair and dispassionate in conducting the prosecution and in addressing the jury. Over-enthusiasm for the strength of the case for the prosecution, manifested in addressing the jury, may be forgivable, especially when tempered by a proper caution by the trial Judge in his charge, where it is in relation to matters properly adduced in evidence. A different situation exists where that enthusiasm is coupled with or consists of putting before the jury, as facts to be considered for conviction, matters of which there is no evidence and which come from Crown counsel's personal experience or observations. That is the present case.

At the conclusion of Crown counsel's address in this case, counsel for the accused moved for a declaration of a mistrial. The trial Judge did not act on the motion but proceeded to charge the jury. There was nothing in his charge that can be regarded as directed to the serious breaches of duty exhibited by Crown counsel. The charge was in the general pattern that is followed when there is no untoward situation that demands particular consideration and instruction to the jury. I do not consider that the familiar observation or reminder to the jury that they alone are judges of the facts and that they may disregard any comments, whether of the trial Judge or of counsel, on the facts in evidence, can meet a situation where Crown counsel, who addresses the jury last, puts extraneous prejudicial matters to the jury as if such matters were part of the record of evidence.

Of course, there can be no unyielding general rule that an inflammatory or other improper address to the jury by Crown counsel is *per se* conclusive of the fact that there has been an unfair trial and that a conviction thereat cannot stand. The issues in a case and the evidence that is presented are highly relevant in this connection, as is the supervision exercised by the trial Judge in relation to the addresses of counsel and in the course of his charge. In the present case, I am satisfied that what Crown counsel at the trial improperly said to the jury bore so directly on the central issue in the case, namely, knowing possession, and was so prejudicial in respect of that issue and of the related question of credibility of the accused, of whose criminal record the jury were aware, as to deprive the accused of his right to a fair trial. I have already observed that the trial Judge did nothing to erase the effect of Crown counsel's remarks, and I should add that nothing said by defence counsel in his preceding address can be regarded as justifying what Crown counsel intruded into the trial.

I wish to refer to some of the facts of the case and to portions of Crown counsel's address as reproduced in the transcript. The accused was a man with a record not related to any offence involving counterfeit money, and he gave evidence in denial of knowledge of the presence in his car of a package consisting of three tightly rolled up counterfeit notes. They were found by the police wedged among the wires under the dashboard next to the steering column. He had $700 in cash on his person in genuine notes. There was evidence that his wife and two relatives had access to his car. He denied police evidence that he said, when the counterfeit notes were found, "I don't know. It looks like funny money", but admitted that he said to the police, "I guess you've got me good. I want to see a lawyer."

The Crown's theory was that the accused was a "distributor" rather than a "pusher" of counterfeit bills; that is, that he was, so to speak, a wholesaler who showed samples to "pushers" who would buy from the samples and then "sell" to the public. In opening to the jury before any evidence was led Crown counsel spoke as follows:

> So the essence of the charge as you heard from the indictment is that he had it in his custody or possession. It was his car. He had the car for some time; apparently nobody had access to it—that he had placed this money in this hiding place, and he had it for some purpose. I will explain the purpose to you when I address you later.

No evidence was adduced as to any purpose, nor was there any evidence as to how counterfeit bills are distributed or marketed. There was no evidence as to any association of the accused with so-called distributors or pushers.

The transcript of Crown counsel's address to the jury includes the following passages:

> All right, so what happens. The officers found it, and he has all his notes. He is going underneath like that. Now, if a person knew, if somebody in fact had put it there—I suggest he did—you would know where it is. You would be able to put your hand underneath, probably while you are still sitting there and pull it out notwithstanding that it was wedged in; you would know where it is, so you would measure it up and if you needed it—and I will explain why he needed it—you are not going to carry three ten dollar counterfeit bills on your person because in fact you may be stopped by the police. They stop people and they interview people and check people, and he is not going to carry the bills on him; that is for sure. He is not going to put it in his car. You heard the evidence about the $700 on his person at that time, and this comes to the reason why I had Corporal Dore explain what type and quality this money was, going from fair to good to fairly deceptive. He said they were at the top range, deceptive, the best at that time.
>
> Now, I suggest to you that what in fact Pisani had these bills for, was for specimens, for samples, and he would go out, and he was a distributor. He would

not carry any of this money on him. It was too dangerous. The police might stop him, so he hides it in this very unusual hiding place in the car; somewhere where he could get it out fast if he wanted to show somebody, but he wouldn't carry it on his person. He would try to find pushers. People with records don't push counterfeit money. They are distributors. They sell it to people without records and they push it. Pisani wouldn't be caught dead pushing ten dollar bills. It is not worth it to him. He has got a record, so he goes, he finds his pusher, he brings it to wherever the pusher is and then calls them as he reaches underneath the dashboard where it is. He tries to persuade the pusher. He says, "Look, it is good quality ten dollar bills." Here is the sales pitch. He takes the three ten dollar bills, he goes in and he says to the man, and he will take one or two perhaps; he will say: all right, take a look at this. The person looks at it, and if he has another ten dollar bill he would look at it, and he would say: It looks pretty good. Then he would say, all right take a look at this, and then lo and behold they have the same serial number; they have got to be counterfeit. He looks at it and says: This is pretty good; these are top-notch counterfeit, I probably could get rid of this. Maybe that person wouldn't do it, he pushes it through his girlfriend or an associate. He says: Take another look at this. This is another sample. This is another of the batch with a different serial number; have a look at it. That is pretty good too. So that is the sales pitch. He has one. He shows them to everyone. It has to be counterfeit, because it has the same serial number. So he has three samples, and they are top-notch quality and people want it. It is good quality. The type of people that would push them say: Yes, I could fool a person with them.

How many of you people know what a counterfeit looks like? My Dad owns a store. He doesn't know. I work in a store. I don't know what counterfeit is unless there is something drastically wrong with the bill. That is when he questions it.

I suggest to you that Pisani had secreted these three counterfeit ten dollar bills, and he wouldn't touch it. He probably figured the police aren't going to find it there. You will recall that it took the officer quite some time. He would put it there knowing that it was dangerous to have it on his person, on his physical person, and only at the last minute when he arrives where the pusher is, whether it be in a store or an apartment, and he would park, look around and make sure there are no police officers, no detectives that he recognizes, he would take it out and would show the samples to the person who is doing the pushing. Then when he comes back he would hide it in the same place.

Later on in the address, Crown counsel, after referring to Pisani's seven previous convictions and to the legal limitation that these convictions could only be used to assess his credibility, said this:

He had $700 in his possession at that time made up of hundreds, fifties, twenties and tens. Is it possible that he got that as down payment from one of his pushers? He wouldn't bring money to the pusher. The pusher would have to go to somebody else, another person or party that has no record to get money. Pisani wouldn't be caught dead with the money. He would arrange for the pusher to get the money. He wouldn't be caught dead with large quantities of counterfeit money.

Again, in a succeeding portion of the address he spoke as follows:

You heard the evidence that if you put the bills through the silver nitrate processing solution you would ruin the paper itself. It would turn to dark brown as we have heard, and they handle this money gingerly in Ottawa. You don't lift prints off counterfeit; that was known to Pisani. Pisani is, as I suggest to you he is not a pusher, but a distributor. He knows these technical things. He knows you can't lift a print, so I suggest to you that there is a matter of credibility. The story at the scene contrast. There is no one that he mentions. No person that he mentioned that would plant this money, and I suggest to you if that was so there would be a good quantity of money put there instead of three ten dollar bills.

There was no evidence that Pisani knew that fingerprints cannot be lifted from counterfeit money, and Crown counsel was also again repeating as facts matters not in evidence.

Two more passages of the address should be quoted:

I would ask you then to disbelieve Pisani entirely when he says he didn't know who put it there. I suggest to you exactly that he put it there. He might have been on a selling jaunt at that time. He might have gotten a deposit to line up the place where the pusher would have got the money from a third party who had no record and he was coming back. He had a large quantity of money and unfortunately he was stopped and his car was searched.

There is no direct evidence in this case that anyone saw Pisani put it there. There is no statement, and you don't expect statement from a person like this, do you really? A person, I suggest to you, that a person without a record may give a statement, not a person like this. There is no statement: Yes, I put it there. There is nothing like that, so I ask you—I am going to have to ask you to draw your conclusion that he put it there on the basis of circumstantial evidence.

The foregoing passages bear out the assessment I made of the effect of the address.

In my view, no case was made out for the application of s. 592(1)(*b*)(iii) of the *Criminal Code*. In the result, I would allow the appeal, set aside the conviction and direct a new trial.

MORGENTALER v. R.
[1988] 1 S.C.R. 30, 62 C.R. (3d) 1, 37 C.C.C. (3d) 449 at 481-483

On appeal, the Supreme Court confirmed the view of the Ontario Court of Appeal that the defence counsel has been wrong in saying to the jury that if they did not like the law, they need not enforce it.

DICKSON C.J.C.:—

Defence counsel's address to the jury

In his concluding remarks to the jury at the trial of the appellants, defence counsel asserted:

The judge will tell you what the law is. He will tell you about the ingredients of the offence, what the Crown has to prove, what the defences may be or may not be, and you must take the law from him. But I submit to you that it is up to you and you alone to apply the law to this evidence and you have a right to say it shouldn't be applied.

The burden of his argument was that the jury should not apply s. 251 if they thought that it was a bad law, and that, in refusing to apply the law, they could send a signal to Parliament that the law should be changed. Although my disposition of the appeal makes it unecessary, strictly speaking, to review Mr.

Manning's argument before the jury, I find the argument so troubling that I feel compelled to comment.

It has long been settled in Anglo-Canadian criminal law that in a trial before judge and jury, the judge's role is to state the law and the jury's role is to apply that law to the facts of the case. In *Joshua v. The Queen*, [1955] A.C. 121 at p. 130 (P.C.), Lord Oaskey enunciated the principle succintly:

> It is a general principle of British law that on a trial by jury it is for the judge to direct the jury on the law and in so far as he thinks necessary on the facts, but the jury, whilst they must take the law from the judge, are the sole judges on the facts.

The jury is one of the great protectors of the citizen because it is composed of 12 persons who collectively express the common sense of the community. But the jury members are not expert in the law, and for that reason they must be guided by the judge on questions of law.

The contrary principle contended for by Mr. Manning, that a jury may be encouraged to ignore a law it does not like, could lead to gross inequities. One accused could be convicted by a jury who supported the existing law, while another person indicted for the same offence could be acquitted by a jury who, with reformist zeal, wished to express disapproval of the same law. Moreover, a jury could decide that although the law pointed to a conviction, the jury could simply refuse to apply the law to an accused for whom it had sympathy. Alternatively, a jury who feels antipathy towards an accused might convict despite a law which points to acquittal. To give a harsh but I think telling example, a jury fueled by the passions of racism could be told that they need not apply the law against murder to a white man who had killed a black man. Such a possibility need only be stated to reveal the potentially frightening implications of Mr. Manning's assertions. The dangerous argument that a jury may be encouraged to disregard the law was castigated as long ago as 1784 by Lord Mansfield in a criminal libel case, *R. v. Shipley* (1784), 4 Dougl. 73 at pp. 170-1, 99 E.R. 774 at p. 824:

> So the jury who usurp the judicature of law, though they happen to be right, are themselves wrong, because they are right by chance only, and have not taken the constitutional way of deciding the questions. It is the duty of the Judge, in all cases of general justice, to tell the jury how to do right, though they have it in their power to do wrong, which is a matter entirely between God and their own consciences.
>
> To be free is to live under a government by law. . . . Miserable is the condition of individuals, dangerous is the condition of the State, if there is no certain law, or, which is the same thing, no certain administration of law, to protect individuals, or to guard the State.
>
> . . .
>
> In opposition to this, what is contended for?—That the law shall be, in every particular cause, what any twelve men, who shall happen to be the jury, shall be inclined to think; liable to no review, and subject to no control, under all the prejudices of the popular cry of the day, and under all the bias of interest in this town, where thousands, more or less, are concerned in the publication of newspapers, paragraphs, and pamphlets. Under such an administration of law, no man could tell, no counsel could advise, whether a paper was or was not punishable.

I can only add my support to that eloquent statement of principle.

It is no doubt true that juries have a *de facto* power to disregard the law as stated to the jury by the judge. We cannot enter the jury room. The jury is never called upon to explain the reasons which lie behind a verdict. It may even be true that in some limited circumstances the private decision of a jury to refuse to apply the law will constitute, in the words of a Law Reform Commission of Canda working paper, "the citizen's ultimate protection against oppressive laws and the oppressive enforcement of the law" (Law Reform Commission of Canada, Working Paper 27, *The Jury in Criminal Trials* (1980)). But recognizing this reality is a far cry from suggesting that counsel may encourage a jury to ignore a law they do not support or to tell a jury that it has a *right* to do so. The difference between accepting the reality of *de facto* discretion in applying the law and elevating such discretion to the level of a right was stated clearly by the United States Court of Appeals, District of Columbia Circuit, in *U.S. v. Dougherty*, 473 F. 2d 1113 (1972), *per* Leventhal J., at p. 1134:

> The jury system has worked out reasonably well overall, providing "play in the joints" that imparts flexibility and avoid[s] undue rigidity. An equilibrium has evolved—an often marvelous balance—with the jury acting as a "safety valve" for exceptional cases, without being a wildcat or runaway institution. There is reason to believe that the simultaneous achievement of modest jury equity and avoidance of intolerable caprice depends on formal instructions that do not expressly delineate a jury charter to carve out its own rules of law.

To accept Mr. Manning's argument that defence counsel should be able to encourage juries to ignore the law would be to disturb the "marvelous balance" of our system of criminal trials before a judge and jury. Such a disturbance would be irresponsible. I agree with the trial judge and with the Court of Appeal that Mr. Manning was quite simply wrong to say to the jury that if they did not like the law they need not enforce it. He should not have done so.

Recall from Chapter 6 — The Adversarial System and the Role of Counsel — the special ethical duties that are placed on Crown counsel in the conduct of trials. In *R. v. S. (F.)* (2000), 31 C.R. (5th) 159, 144 C.C.C. (3d) 466 (Ont. C.A.), a conviction for child sexual assault was quashed because of Crown counsel's improper questioning of the accused and his inflammatory address to the jury.

Compare G. Huscroft, "The Right to Seek and Return Perverse Verdicts" (1988), 62 C.R. (3d) 123.

PROBLEM 2

In his address to the jury in a murder trial the Crown counsel said the following:

> We have a person here who is a jilted lover. There are thousands, countless thousands I would submit, of jilted lovers walking the streets of Toronto

today, ordinary jilted lovers. If all those jilted lovers did what the accused did the streets would be red with blood, would they not?

He later added:

You will have to leave this courtroom, if you find him guilty of manslaughter and not guilty of murder, and say to the community, "In the face of that evidence, members of the community, we find that this man did not mean to do what he did". You tell that to the community. You tell that to the three-year-old son down there in the kitchen that night who saw his father being shot down in front of him. You have a duty to the community and to the accused. In my submission, your duty is clear on these facts.

Do you think there should be a new trial? Compare *R. v. Roberts* (1973), 14 C.C.C. (2d) 368 (Ont. C.A.).

PROBLEM 3

In his final address to the jury in a trial on a charge of assaulting a peace officer, a defence counsel makes extensive reference to decided cases summarizing the law and repeatedly mentions that this is a more serious assault which attracts an actual penalty of five years. The accused is acquitted and the Crown appeals. Are there grounds for a new trial? Compare *R. v. Cashin* (1981), 49 N.S.R. (2d) 653 (N.S. C.A.).

PROBLEM 4

The accused was charged and convicted, following a trial before judge and jury, of the second degree murder of his wife. The trial judge instructed the jury that the accused's belief that the victim was going to telephone the police to report mental and physical abuse and incest by the accused with his daughter could constitute provocation. The sole ground of appeal against the second degree murder conviction was that the inflammatory closing address of the Crown counsel had deprived the accused of a fair trial. On the first day of the trial defence counsel raised a concern about the family of the deceased wearing white ribbons in the courtroom. Such ribbons are worn annually as a reminder of the murder of young women by Marc Lepine at l'ecole Polytechnique in Montreal. The trial judge declined to rule on the point but asked the Crown attorney to let those individuals know that it was the responsibility of the trial judge to ensure a fair trial. Specific objection was taken to the Crown counsel's statements that if the jury accepted the defence of provocation every wife, husband and child who provoked their father better take cover because it would be open season, that the defence of provocation was not available unless the jury would not have cornered their wife and throttled her, that the murder rate in the region would treble if the defence succeeded, that when Marc Lepine killed the 14 women he was filled with the rage and hatred that the accused felt, and that the jury should not be like persons who stand by and allow a rape or murder to occur. Was this address inflammatory? If so, should there be a new trial?

Compare *R. v. Munroe* (1995), 38 C.R. (4th) 68 (Ont. C.A.), appeal to Supreme Court dismissed in brief oral judgment: (1996), 43 C.R. (4th) (S.C.C.).

6. Charging Jury

Following counsel's address to the jury, the trial judge is then obliged to instruct the jury their duties, the applicable law, how to apply the evidence to the law and the respective positions of the Crown and the defence. Failure to properly explain the theory of the defence to the jury is a common ground of appeal from conviction after a jury trial.

The law relating to instructions is an enormous and complex area of the criminal law. Most appeals from a jury verdict involve complaints about the manner in which the jury was instructed. Sometimes, these complaints are very exacting of the way trial judges have approached their task. In *R. v. Jacquard*, [1997] 1 S.C.R. 314, 113 C.C.C. (3d) 1, 4 C.R. (5th) 280 (S.C.C.), Chief Justice Lamer said:

This appeal raises questions about the standard to which this Court should hold trial judges in charging juries. It is undoubtedly important that jurors try the right facts according to the appropriate legal principles in each case. However, we must ensure that the yardstick by which we measure the fitness of a trial judge's directions to the jury does not become overly onerous. We must strive to avoid the proliferation of very lengthy charges in which judges often quote large extracts from appellate decisions simply to safeguard verdicts from appeal. Neither the Crown nor the accused benefits from a confused jury. Indeed justice suffers.

These comments are not meant to suggest that we sanction misdirected verdicts. This Court has stated on repeated occasions that accused individuals are entitled to properly instructed juries. There is, however, no requirement for perfectly instructed juries. As I specifically indicated at the hearing of this case, a standard of perfection would render very few judges in Canada, including myself, capable of charging juries to the satisfaction of such a standard.

The Supreme Court, as well as the provincial appellate courts, have echoed this sentiment on many occasions. However, it has not prevented them from ordering new trials to rectify injustices.

LAW REFORM COMMISSION, WORKING PAPER 27: THE JURY IN CRIMINAL TRIALS
(1980), 76

Introduction

Questions of law are decided by the judge; questions of fact are decided by the jury. This well-known dichotomy of functions raises the problem of who applies the law to the facts. Because the jury in criminal cases returns a general verdict of guilty or not-guilty, it must discharge this responsibility. Thus, to enable the jury to carry out its duties, the judge instructs the jury on the law which governs the case. In reaching a verdict the jury must then apply those instructions to the facts as it finds them.

Jury instructions must therefore, satisfy two conflicting requirements: the need to state accurately the relevant law and the need to state the law so that the jury understands it. The need to state the law accurately is, of course, an obvious requirement. If the case is appealed, counsel will scrutinize the charge for all possible errors in the statement of law. The court of appeal will hold the instructions to be in error unless the judge has correctly stated the law in all respects. (Of course, not every error causes a substantial wrong or miscarriage of justice.) Because strict legal correctness is the primary concern of the appellate courts, it is naturally the concern of trial judges as well. Indeed, to eliminate the possibility of error from their statements of the law, trial judges will sometimes include long quotations from appellate court judgments in their instructions and in other ways generally attempt to "boiler-plate" them. This often results in instructions which are long, repetitious, and disjointed.

The need to state the law correctly may thus often conflict with the other important requirement of jury instructions: that they be understandable to the jury. The allocation of responsibility between the judge and jury is premised on the jury's ability to understand and apply the law. It is often alleged that one of the most serious deficiencies of trial by jury, and indeed an aspect of it which is sometimes said to place the institution of the jury in jeopary, is the jury's inability to follow and comprehend the instructions given by the judge. If jurors are confused about the law they are to apply, they cannot perform their function properly, and a just verdict will be reached only by chance.

Our survey of judges also led us to the conclusion that something to improve the quality of jury instructions ought to be attempted. Only 23 per cent of the judges were quite certain that juries generally understand the judge's instructions. And while most (82 per cent) felt that it was at least probable that juries understood what was being told to them, a significant minority (18 per cent) felt that it was probable that juries did not understand what was being told them. Not surprisingly, judges who felt that juries probably did not understand judge's instructions were more likely to prefer judges over juries on the question of who is more likely to arrive at a just and fair verdict (74 versus 10 per cent of such judges). They were also much less likely to have a very favourable overall attitude toward the jury (28 versus 90 per cent of such judges).

We found further evidence that jurors have difficulties with the present instructions on the law given to them by judges in an experimental study we undertook. That study is more fully described later on in this chapter.

From time to time, proposals have been made in an attempt to reconcile the goal of stating the law accurately with that of making the charge comprehensible to the jury. In this chapter a number of such proposals will be explored: the adoption of jury instruction guidelines; the use of lay persons and communication experts in the preparation of jury instructions; the improvement of the procedure for the preparation and delivery of jury instructions in particular cases; and the use by the jury of written instructions.

The goal is to develop a process of jury instruction which is expeditious, reduces the number of appeals, and results in instructions which are understandable and accurate.

The Adoption of Jury Instruction Guidelines

The recommendation that judges have available to them jury instruction guidelines should have broad support from the Canadian judiciary. In our survey of judges, 78 per cent of the respondents felt that "a collection of standardized instructions drawn up by leading members of the bench and bar would be useful to [them] in explaining the law to the jury". In fact, in all regions of the country except British Columbia, over 80 per cent of the respondents favoured such instructions. In British Columbia only 13 of the 23 judges responding (56 per cent) wanted such instructions.

In a recent book on instructing the jury, pattern jury instructions are described as "the greatest modern improvement in trial by jury." They were first used over thirty years ago in California, and are now used in the majority of United States jurisdictions. Pattern jury instructions were, and continue to be, employed in most American jurisdictions in response to three problems, all of which are present in Canada. First, judges, particularly newly appointed judges, spend an inordinate amount of time preparing jury instructions. Sometimes they borrow a "precedent" from another judge or quote passages out of a form book, but often they have to prepare instructions by researching case law and formulating their own charges. Much of this time and effort is wasted because judges duplicate each other's work. As well, because the wording of individually prepared charges varies, counsel are also forced to spend extra time examining the wording of each charge instead of being able to concentrate on whether the appropriate instructions were given.

Second, when each judge prepares his or her own instructions on the law, a great number of reversals result because of misdirections. The 1976 volumes of Canadian Criminal Cases reveal that in the sixty-two reported appeals from trials by jury, misdirection to the jury was an issue in fifty of them. The misdirection resulted in a new trial in thirty of these cases. Indeed, the rate of reversals would likely be even higher if it were not for a liberal application of the "no substantial wrong or miscarriage of justice" doctrine, and the appellate court practice of overlooking an error by insisting that the instructions must be read as a whole. Of course the sixty-two cases were reported only because they were appeal cases. They do not represent the totality of jury trials in Canada during the pertinent period.

Reversals result in an enormous and often needless waste of time and money. More accurate instructions would result if, instead of having individual judges research the law and prepare instructions, resources were pooled and instructions prepared in a systematic fashion. Although jury instruction guidelines would not eliminate all appeals based on alleged misdirections, because judges could still err in selecting which instructions to use in a particular case or because some guidelines might be incorrect in the court of appeal's view, their use should substantially reduce the number of these appeals.

A third problem which justifies the development of jury instruction guidelines is that even if a judge in preparing his or her own instructions states the law correctly, in some cases he or she will not have the time or the ability to render them understandable to the jury. Clear and simple writing, particularly about legal concepts, is enormously time consuming and extremely difficult. The incomprehensibility of many jury instructions is a matter of grave concern.

. . .

Advantages

There are five major advantages to the use of jury instruction guidelines: time-saving, accuracy, uniform treatment, impartiality, and, intelligibility.

. . .

If jury instruction guidelines are adopted, the following procedure for instructing the jury would speed up and simplify the process and reduce the possibilities of error.

Submissions by Counsel

At some time before the close of the evidence, counsel should be permitted to request that the judge give particular instructions to the jury. The judge will have a series of standard instructions on such subjects as reasonable doubt, the credibility of witnesses, and the difference between direct and circumstantial evidence. Thus, counsel's request for particular instructions will serve, in the main, to point up issues of law peculiar to the case. To preserve a record for appeal, these requests may be submitted to the judge in writing. If so, copies should also be supplied to all other parties so that they have notice of the requested instructions and, if they disagree with them, they could argue that such instructions should not be given.

This rule is simply one of convenience. The practice would inform the judge of the instructions which counsel feel are relevant to the case and thus assist the judge in preparing the instructions that he or she will deliver. The rule would not relieve the judge of his or her responsibility for instructing the jury on all relevant points of law. And, of course, the judge would not be bound to use the exact language which appeared in the written submissions, or indeed be required to give the requested instructions at all.

Many judges at present invite counsel to make submissions on the law prior to the charge, and our survey of judges indicates that most judges (79 per cent) are in favour of such a practice. Typical comments by judges included the following: "It is very useful to have the opinion of counsel on particular points which they wished to have drawn to the attention of the jury. It is much more efficient to have these comments prior to the charge. There will be circumstances where counsel asks for further instruction following the charge so that it is not a foolproof method. But it is of great assistance and helps to clarify the issues for the jury. The judge, of course, must exercise his discretion in deciding whether he will accept the suggestions of the counsel." "I think it is important for counsel to bring any relevant law or cases to the judge's attention so that, if it is appropriate, it can be included in the judge's charge. This is done sometimes now or on *ad hoc* basis."

Pre-address Conference

Some Canadian judges hold a conference with counsel prior to counsel's closing addresses to the jury. At this time, that portion of the charge relating to the law is discussed with counsel. However, this is not common practice. Thus, in the vast majority of cases, counsel do not know what will be contained in the instructions on the law until the judge delivers his charge to the jury at the end of the case. Even under the present practice, but particularly if jury instruction guidelines were adopted, a pre-address conference would have numerous advantages.

· · ·

Timing of Instruction

We gave much consideration to whether having the judge deliver his charge to the jury prior to counsels' argument has any obvious advantages: true, it would permit counsel to refer to the law as stated by the judge in their closing arguments and relate the evidence to it; and it would permit the jury to evaluate the evidence intelligently as summarized by counsel in light of the law that they will have to apply to it.

The suggestion is that the judge instruct the jury only on the law prior to counsels' address. Following the closing arguments, the judge would then re-state the law and summarize and comment on the evidence, as in the present practice. We rejected this consideration, at last, because: it would protract proceedings unnecessarily; it would serve to present a verbose element of confusion to the minds of the jury; and it might impose a psychological detriment upon the arguments of counsel by seeming to have the judge return to rebut counsel. However, we should welcome readers' opinions about this.

Admittedly, it is extremely difficult for counsel to make an effective closing address to the jury if strictly confined to mentioning the evidence only, and forbidden to mention the applicable law. A few judges do so confine and forbid counsel. However, we have already proposed two possible antidotes for this occasional great difficulty. We have proposed a mandatory preliminary instruction to the newly sworn jury, which instruction includes reference to: a verdict based on the evidence only; the presumption of innocence; burden of proof; reasonable doubt; credibility; and the elements of the crime(s) charged. Such an address at the trial's commencement would surely permit counsel to refer in their closing arguments to the law as stated by the judge. We have also proposed an optional pre-argument conference which, if held, would give the judge ample opportunity to define how far counsel might describe the applicable law to the jury, before counsel could get into difficulty.

Of course the judge must remain the authoritative explainer and interpreter of the law insofar as the jury is concerned. Our recommendations do not accord to counsel any scope for unsurping the judge's role in this regard. Our recommendations would effect a salutary reform by requiring the judge to have the trial's first word and the trial's last word to the jury.

Objections to the Judge's Instructions on the Law

Under the present law, counsel's failure to object to the charge at trial does not prevent him or her from appealing on the ground that the charge contained a misdirection. However, the court of appeal may consider that counsel did not make a timely objection at trial in determining whether the misdirection caused a substantial wrong or miscarriage of justice requiring a new trial. Counsel's failure to object during the trial is taken to be some evidence that the misdirection was not serious.

Strong arguments can be put forward for the position that a failure to object to a misdirection should result in a waiver of the error for the purposes of appeal. Such a rule would act as a strong incentive for counsel to scrutinize the charge carefully, thereby saving the time and expense of at least some new trials. It would also inhibit counsel, even though he or she suspects a misdirection, from deliberately failing to object to the charge on a gamble that a more favourable verdict will be obtained but if not, a ground for appeal will be preserved.

Two reasons are commonly put forward as justifications for the rule that a misdirection can be raised on appeal even though no objection to it was raised at trial. One argument states that it is the duty of the judge rather than of counsel properly to direct the jury, and that the judge must discharge the duty irrespective of the actions of counsel. The other reason is more substantial. That is, if a serious error were made in the judge's instructions to the jury, the accused's right to appeal should not be irrevocably prejudiced because of the incompetence of counsel. An accused has a right to trial according to law. These reasons are reflected in the tentative recommendation which actually proposes no change.

While these reasons might justify a rule that the failure of defence counsel to object to the charge at trial ought not to constitute waiver of the accused's right to appeal, different considerations apply with respect to the Crown. If the Crown is successful on appeal in arguing that there has been a misdirection at trial, the accused must undergo a new trial on the same facts. That the accused should not be placed in jeopardy twice for the same matter is, of course, a basic principle of our criminal law. In the words of Rand J. in *Cullen v. The King* :

> It is the supreme invasion of the rights of the individual to subject him by the physical power of the community to a test which may mean the loss of his liberty or his life; and there is a basic repugnance against the repeated exercise of that power on the same facts unless for strong reasons of public policy.

As Justice Rand further pointed out, "The position of the accused is in sharp contrast to that of the prosecution". The Crown has unlimited resources, while the accused must defend himself in many cases at his own expense. More importantly, the possibility of a new trial can cause the accused grave anxiety, further humiliation and the uncertainty of not being able to plan for his future. The Crown does not bear similarly proportionate detriments when a new trial is ordered. Indeed, in most jurisdictions, the principles underlying the concept of double jeopardy are held in such regard that the prosecution is never able to appeal on acquittal, even on questions of law.

Since the time at which Mr. Justice Rand expressed his opinion, the introduction of legal aid has occurred in Canada. Those who would not diminish the Crown's right of appeal point to the reduction, if not elimination, of financial cost to the accused. Those who would indeed reduce the Crown's right to seek new trials point to the financial cost to the public. The same question is viewed through different optics.

In terms of double jeopardy it may not seem unfair to place a higher burden on the Crown to avoid the possibility of new trials. Prohibiting the Crown from appealing from a misdirection to which it did not object at trial, and thus for which it did not provide the judge with an opportunity for correction, should do two things. First, it should provide an incentive for the Crown to review carefully the instructions at trial; second, it should prevent the Crown from ignoring errors at trial and taking a chance on a favourable verdict knowing that if a favourable verdict is not returned, it might be able to obtain a new trial on appeal. Despite the form of our earlier tentative recommendation which would preserve the *status quo,* the Commission is divided on this issue, and earnestly seeks readers' opinions about it. . . .

Summarizing the Evidence

Under the present law, at the end of counsel's address to the jury, the judge in most cases has a duty to summarize fairly the evidence to the jury. The standard that is applied in determining whether the trial judge has fairly summarized the evidence is most frequently derived from a quotation by Taschereau J. in *Azoulay v. The Queen*:

> The rule which has been laid down, and consistently followed is that in a jury trial the presiding judge must, except in rare cases where it would be needless to do so, review the substantial parts of the evidence and give the jury the theory of the defence, so that they may appreciate the value and effect of that evidence, and how the law is to be applied to the facts as they find them.

The standard of fairness is also frequently derived from a quotation by Spence J. in *Colpitts v. The Queen*:

> Recent decisions in this Court and elsewhere have also emphasized the duty of the trial Judge in his charge to go further and to not only outline the theory of the defence but to give to the jury matters of evidence essential in arriving at a just conclusion in reference to that defence.

While the law is not in doubt, the court of appeal cases in which the issue is whether the trial judge has fairly summarized the evidence are legion.

Under the present law, if the issues in a case are clear and the evidence simple, some courts have held that the trial judge does not need to summarize the evidence. However, even in such cases, court of appeal judges have remarked that it would be preferable for the trial judge to summarize the evidence. The recommendation provides that in all cases the trial judge should summarize the evidence.

In most cases the judge will be most effective in assisting the jury by his summary of the evidence if he or she delineates the essential issues and relates the evidence to them. For example, it has been said that, "The function of a trial judge in a charge to the jury is to explain the law relevant to the issues and to relate the evidence thereto in such a manner that the jury is able to appreciate the pivotal issues upon which the case turns." An often repeated statement as to the trial judge's responsibility was made by O'Halloran J.A.:

> The jury has a right to expect from the judge something more than a mere repetition of the evidence. They have a right to expect that his trained legal mind will employ itself in stripping the statement of non-essentials, and in presenting the evidence to them in its proper relation to the matters requiring factual decisions, and directed also to the case put forward by the prosecution and the answer of the defence, or such answer as the evidence permits.

Thus, while the trial judge does not need to repeat to the jury all the evidence and discrepancies in the evidence (indeed, it might be an error if he or she did, since it might only serve to confuse the jury), he or she must remind them of, and explain to them, the contentions of the parties, and summarize the essential evidence for them. Normally, the best method of doing this will be for the judge to relate the essential evidence to the important facts in issue. However, in some cases, if he or she feels it will be more understandable to the jury, the judge might adopt some other manner of describing the evidence.

2. Commenting on the Evidence

. . .

Under the present law it is well established that the trial judge has the right to comment upon the credibility of witnesses and the strength of the evidence. In this way he or she is able to give the jury the benefit of his or her experience and expertise in evaluating evidence. The recommendation thus preserves this right in the trial judge.

The recommendation imposes two limitations upon the judge's right to comment on the evidence, the first of which is supported by present case authority, the second of which is supported at least by dicta in some cases. The first limitation on the judge's right to comment on the evidence is that he or she must make it unequivocally clear to the jury that fact-finding is their function and that they are free to accept or reject his or her opinion on the evaluation of the evidence. This limitation is well recognized in the jurisprudence.

The second limitation imposed by the recommendation is that "the judge may not directly express an opinion on the guilt or innocence of the accused or that certain testimony is worthy or unworthy of belief". A direct expression by the judge that, for example, "I am of the opinion that the accused is guilty" goes beyond the purpose of permitting the judge to comment on the evidence. The purpose of permitting the judge to comment on the weight of the evidence is to provide the jury with the benefit of the judge's insights in evaluating evidence based upon his or her experience. A statement by the judge that in his or her opinion the accused is guilty is of little assistance to the jury in making their own independent assessment of the evidence. In addition it places the judge in the role of an advocate, a role unbecoming to the position. Under the present law an expression of the judge's belief in the accused's guilt would not appear to be absolutely barred; however, some courts of appeal, particularly recently, have spoken disapprovingly of it.

The recommendation would also prohibit the trial judge from making a direct statement that certain testimony is worthy or unworthy of belief. The reasoning described in the above paragraph also applies to this type of comment. The judge can be most helpful to the jury if he or she describes to them the possible factors which might have affected a particular witness' perception, memory, narration or sincerity and which they should consider in determining that witness' credibility. A bald statement that the judge feels a particular witness is or is not worthy of belief is of little assistance to them in making an independent evaluataion of the witness' credibility. While under present law judges are permitted to express a direct opinion on a witness' credibility, it is clear that it might be an error if he or she presses such an opinion too strongly.

R. v. LEVENE

(1983), 36 C.R. (3d) 386 (Ont. C.A.)

BROOKE J.A.:—The appellant was convicted by Cartwright Co. Ct. J. and a jury at Toronto on two counts on an indictment which charged him with robbery and the use of a firearm in the commission of an offence. At the conclusion of the argument the court pronounced its decision that for reasons to follow the appeal was allowed, the convictions set aside and a new trial ordered.

In our view, there were errors made in the conduct of the trial and the charge to the jury that were so fundamental that the convictions could not stand. The Crown quite properly conceded that this was so. Because there is to be a new trial, it is unnecessary to go into the facts led in evidence, save to say that both counts arose out of one transaction, when the appellant, allegedly armed with a firearm, forcibly took the complainant's jewellery from her person.

We agree with the appellant's submission that the trial judge erred in refusing to permit the appellant to cross-examine certain of the Crown witnesses as to criminal charges outstanding and pending against them at the time of the trial. While the trial judge was referred to the judgment of the Supreme Court of Canada in *Titus v. R.* (1983), 33 C.R. (3d) 17, 2 C.C.C. (2d) 321, 144 D.L.R. (3d) 577, 46 N.R. 477, he was wrong in attempting to distinguish it and was bound to follow it and permit the defence to cross-examine. In this court the Crown concedes the error and that it was such that we could not apply the provisions of s. 613(1)(b)(iii) of the Criminal Code, R.S.C. 1970, c. C-34.

It was contended by the appellant, and the Crown concedes, that there was non-direction amounting to misdirection in the charge to the jury in relation to the issue of whether or not the appellant used a "firearm". We agree. The trial judge simply read to the jury the definition of "firearm" from the Criminal Code. He did not instruct the jury as to the elements of the definition, nor did he attempt to relate the evidence to the elements of the definition. In the circumstances of this case it was important that he should do so, and his failure may have been seriously prejudicial to the appellant.

Finally, at the conclusion of the evidence, rather than permitting counsel to address the jury, the trial judge proceeded by splitting his charge, so that one part preceded counsel's address and the balance of the charge was delivered after counsel had finished. Crown counsel drew to the attention of the trial judge the judgment of this court in *R. v. Coughlin* (1982), 3 C.C.C. (3d) 259. That case was an appeal from a conviction by a court with a jury presided over by the same trial judge. Delivering the reasons for this court, our brother Martin said [p. 263]:

> There is one matter upon which we wish to comment. The trial judge, in his charge to the jury, adopted the somewhat unusual course of first instructing the jury as to the general principles of criminal law applicable to all criminal trials and then interrupting his charge while counsel for the defence and counsel for the Crown, respectively, addressed the jury. The judge then resumed his charge and dealt with the evidence and the case for the prosecution and the defence. We do not think that this procedure resulted in a miscarriage of justice or an unfair trial in the present case, but we think that it is a practice which should not be followed in the future.

When the matter was drawn to his attention, the trial judge said:

> You know, I have talked to other counsel about this. I am fully aware of the view of the members of the Court of Appeal in that case about the split charge.
>
> It is very distressing for a judge to apparently not only ignore but—I don't want to use the word 'defy'—but to go contrary to an express view of the Court of Appeal, but with the greatest respect to the Court of Appeal I am going to do it.
>
> No. I am grateful. I hope you don't mind me sort of telling the two of you about it first when I simply announced I was going to proceed in that fashion. But I made up my mind, after really considering the reasons of the Court of Appeal, as to what I would do, and I will face the music later.

Traditionally, when the evidence is concluded counsel address the jury and make their submissions and then the trial judge sums up. Crown counsel in this case was properly concerned about the procedure. Uniform procedure in the trial of criminal cases is important; it is fundamental to a fair and proper trial in our system. The procedure cannot be varied from place to place or county to county or because of the notions of a particular judge. There may be some very special circumstances or special cases where it is necessary for the proper administration of justice that there be some variation in the procedure in the presentation of a case to the jury, but this was clearly not so in this case. Counsel expect, and in our view are entitled, to go to the jury with their submissions when the evidence is completed and fresh in the minds of the jurymen and not to find themselves bracketed, as it were, by a charge from the bench. We think s. 578(1) of the Criminal Code anticipates this and the significance of who goes first or last when all of the evidence is concluded.

We feel it necessary to observe that the failure of the trial judge to follow the direction of this court on an important matter of procedure can only be regarded as a serious departure from a fundamental principle underlying the proper administration of justice. This verdict cannot stand.

The appeal is allowed. The convictions are set aside and a new trial is ordered.

Various Courts of Appeal have debated whether or not a trial judge can give the jury law books to read, for example, relevant definition sections of the Criminal Code.

R. v. VAWRYK
(1979), 46 C.C.C. (2d) 290 (Man. C.A.)

MATAS J.A. (Hall J.A., concurring):—I have read the reasons for judgment prepared for delivery by Monnin and O'Sullivan, JJ.A. There is no need for me to repeat the facts here. I agree, for the reasons given by O'Sullivan, J.A., that the appeal of Vawryk must be dismissed. With respect to Appleyard, it is my view that the appeal must be allowed and a new trial ordered.

Four provincial appellate tribunals have considered the question of a trial Judge giving the jury printed material on the law: *R. v. Schimanowsky* (1973), 15 C.C.C. (2d) 82, 25 C.R.N.S. 332, [1974] 1 W.W.R. 738 (Sask. C.A.); *R. v. Tennant and Naccarato* (1975), 23 C.C.C. (2d) 80, 7 O.R. (2d) 687, 31 C.R.N.S. 1 (Ont. C.A.); *R. v. Stanford* (1975), 27 C.C.C. (2d) 520 (Que. C.A.); *R. v. Wong* (1978), 41 C.C.C. (2d) 196, [1978] 4 W.W.R. 468 *sub nom. R. v. Wong (No. 2)* (B.C. C.A.).

As might be expected, there were significant factual differences in each of the cases.

In *Schimanowsky,* Culliton, C.J.S., for himself, Woods and Hall, JJ.A., dismissed the appeal from conviction on the grounds that [p. 337 C.R.N.S.] "not only was the evidence such that the jury could properly find the appellant guilty of the charge of robbery, but that any other conclusion would not be a rational one". After making that disposition, the learned Chief Justice dealt with the practice of giving typed sections of the *Criminal Code* to the jury. The learned trial Judge, in giving the sections of the *Code* to the jury, had said, at p. 83 C.C.C., p. 338 C.R.N.S.:

> I will have that typed for you on a separate sheet of paper. It's pretty hard to grasp by my simply reading it to you once, twice or three times. I'll have it typed. *You will be able to look at it and study it in the jury room* when you retire to consider your verdict.

Culliton, C.J.S., said at p. 84 C.C.C., p. 339 C.R.N.S.:

> In my respectful view, the practice of giving to the jury, for their study and consideration, sections of the *Criminal Code,* is one which should not be followed. To do so, in my view, is contrary to the basic principles underlying a jury trial. In a jury trial the jury has a distinct responsibility and the Judge has a distinct responsibility. The jury is the sole judge of the facts. *The Judge has the sole responsibility of instructing the jury on all questions of law and his instruction in that respect the jury is bound to accept and follow.* While a member of a jury may call upon his common-sense and experience in the determination of facts, he cannot do so in the determination of the applicable law. In that sphere he must accept the instructions given by the learned trial Judge whether he personally agrees or disagrees. He has no right to question these instructions. If any member of the jury is not clear as to the instructions in law given by the trial Judge, his remedy is to request the Judge to give further instructions; he cannot apply or adopt his own

interpretation of the law. By giving to the jury the sections of the *Criminal Code* for their study and review, the door is open to the possibility of the jury placing thereon its own interpretation rather than that given by the trial Judge. There should not be provided an opportunity for such a possibility.

The Court held that there had not been a substantial wrong or miscarriage of justice and applied s. 613(1)(*b*)(iii) of the *Code*.

In *Tennant*, the Court, in a *per curiam* judgment, ordered a new trial on several grounds, not relevant to the question before us. It was held, *inter alia*, that the error of the learned trial Judge in setting out the ingredients of the definition of "murder" in s. 212(*a*)(ii) could not be safely paraphrased and that the error was not cured by the learned trial Judge acceding to the jury's request in providing it with a typewritten copy of several sections of the *Code*. The Court dealt separately with the question of the propriety of acceding to the jury's request that they be given typed copies of the sections of the *Code*. Despite the submissions of Crown and defence counsel, the learned trial Judge had declined to instruct the jury that the typed sections of the *Code* must be read subject to his charge.

The first distinction between *Schimanowsky* and *Tennant* was said to be that in *Tennant* the jury requested copies of sections of the *Code* while in *Schimanowsky* the trial Judge of his own initiative had copies of several sections prepared and delivered to the jury for their study and consideration.

In *Tennant*, at p. 103 C.C.C., p. 26 C.R.N.S., the Court said that in its view an important feature of the *Schimanowsky* case was the instruction to the jury: " 'You will be able to look at it and study it in the jury room' " and the Court said this:

> The danger in inviting the jury to study the sections and the implication that they should interpret them is an important feature in that case and notwithstanding the distinction in the facts, it is an important feature in the submissions now before us, for it seems to us that it would be inevitable that the jury or at least some of them might fall into the same error unless they were firmly instructed to the contrary. This is the danger which was foreseen by Chief Justice Culliton and caused him to underscore the basic principle:
> "*The Judge has the sole responsibility of instructing the jury on all questions of law and his instruction in that respect the jury is bound to accept and follow.*"

The Court in *Tennant* held that it was not prepared to say in the circumstances of that case that any substantial wrong or miscarriage of justice had occurred and made the following comments at pp. 102-3 C.C.C., p. 26 C.R.N.S.:

> With the greatest deference to the Saskatchewan Court of Appeal, while we do not think that juries should be encouraged to seek copies of sections of the *Criminal Code* or other related statutes, in our opinion it is entirely a matter in the discretion of the trial Judge in each case, which discretion he must exercise with great caution and care and with clear instructions as to the limited use which can be made of such copies.
>
> . . .
>
> In any case in which copies of sections of the *Criminal Code* or related statutes are provided, the jury must be carefully instructed as to the limited use which can be

made of them, and reminded in the clearest terms that they must accept the law as it has been given to them in the charge and are not to engage in their own interpretation of the sections.

In *Stanford,* Bernier, J.A. (Owen, Lajoie and Bélanger, JJ.A., concurring), said that he could not subscribe to the general statement of principle expressed by Culliton, C.J.S., in *Schimanowsky.* At pp. 525-6, Bernier, J.A. said:

> If a Judge takes the trouble to read and reread to the members of the jury the text of sections of the *Criminal Code* pertinent to the trial, it is because he believes that it is important for them to know it; indeed, the text of the sections which he has read is part of the rules of law which the jury must follow. When, because of the length of the text or the numerous details contained in the text, the Judge believes that in order for them to follow his rules and to reach a verdict knowingly, it would be useful for them to consult the text, I am of the opinion that it is not only permissible but even prudent to give them the text rather than let them use their memory, the reliability of which is questionable in such a foreign area.

And at pp. 526-7, Bernier, J.A., made the following comment on the facts of the case before the Court:

> In my opinion, the fact that it was inadvertently an annotated *Code* does not change anything in the rule. Everything took place while the Court was sitting, in the presence of the accused and his attorney who did not oppose it; it is admitted that the annotations conformed to the rule given by the Judge. It is therefore my opinion that in this case, considering the great care taken by the Judge to explain and repeat completely and explicitly the question, and the great impartiality shown, the irregularity was only a minor one which was of no consequence to the accused. Section 613(1)(*b*)(iii) of the *Criminal Code* applies here and this ground is dismissed.

Crete, J.A., in dissent, said that the practice of giving the jury copies of the *Criminal Code* should neither be approved nor followed.

In *Wong,* McFarlane, J.A., delivered the judgment of the Court, consisting of Taggart, J.A., and McIntyre, J.A. (as he then was). In the opinion of the Court, the charge to the jury was not adequate and a new trial was ordered. In dealing with the question of written extracts of the law being given to the jury, McFarlane, J.A., said at p. 204 C.C.C., p. 476 W.W.R.:

> There has been some diversity of opinion among Canadian Court about the propriety of giving juries written extracts from evidence or from a Judge's charge, memoranda of law, or copies of relevant sections of a statute. The predominant view appears to disapprove. I do not think absolute condemnation is justified. On the other hand, it is no doubt a dangerous procedure and should, I think, be adopted only in very special circumstances and with great care.

I would respectfully adopt the principle that under stringent safeguards it would not be improper, within the discretion of a trial Judge, to give a jury typed extracts of specific sections of the *Code.* But, in my respectful opinion, the necessary safeguards were not followed in the case at bar.

It is true that the learned trial Judge opened his remarks by telling the members of the jury that they were to take the instructions on the law from him. But the effect of that preliminary observation was nullified by what happened later in the charge.

Deniset, J., after explaining to the members of the jury that it would be helpful to them if they had typed copies of relevant *Code* sections, reviewed the sections and made comments on them. When he completed his review, he said:

> That is the law as defined in the Criminal Code. I cannot change it and neither can you. Parliament is the only body that can change that. Having resorted to this particular device of supplying you with the text itself, I feel that I do not have to deal with the subject very much because you have it there in plain English. You understand the English language as well as I do. Why should I try and substitute my interpretation of these particular sections to your particular interpretation of these particular sections. I could be wrong. I prefer to let you decide what it means. I think you are just as capable as I am to do that. I have been watching you throughout these proceedings and you appear to me as a general body of persons who are I would say intelligent and who can understand what goes on.

At the conclusion of the charge, Crown counsel and defence counsel expressed their concern about providing the jury with typed portions of the *Code*. The learned trial Judge responded to the objections by explaining to counsel his reasons for having adopted that procedure. The objections were rejected.

It is my view that telling the jury members that they could decide what the sections mean could have been taken by them as an invitation to interpret the law even if their interpretation was different from the Judge's instructions. This goes further than what was done in any of the cases mentioned above and could well have set the jury in a wrong direction.

In the case of Appleyard, I am not able to say that the jury, charged as it should have been, could not as reasonable men have done otherwise than find him guilty of second degree murder: *Ambrose v. The Queen* (1976), 30 C.C.C. (2d) 97, 69 D.L.R. (3d) 673, [1977] 2 S.C.R. 717 (S.C.C.). In my view, the situation here is different from Vawryk where the evidence was so overwhelming that the jury could not have failed to convict, regardless of the error in the charge.

I would, accordingly, allow the appeal of Appleyard, set the conviction aside and order a new trial on a charge of murder in the second degree.

The concurring judgment of O'Sullivan J.A. is omitted.

MONNIN J.A. (dissenting) (Guy J.A. concurring):—Vawryk and Appleyard were charged with murder in the first degree; Vawryk was found guilty of the crime. Appleyard was found guilty of murder in the second degree.

The learned trial Judge was correct in ruling that the statement of Vawryk to the police was admissible. Once that statement went before the jury, the case of Vawryk was over, since in it he admitted "that we had planned killing him before we even went into his suite". The evidence was overwhelming and the jury could reach no other verdict. I would dismiss Vawryk's appeal.

In the matter of Appleyard, Deniset, J., in what he thought was a first in Canada, handed to each member of the jury two sheets of paper, as follows:

Murder is first degree murder when it is planned and deliberate. All murder that is not first degree murder is second degree murder. And if you decide that the culpable homicide was not planned and deliberate, you look at what murder is according to sec. 212(*a*)(i) and (ii).

Sec. 217. "Culpable homicide that is not murder or infanticide is manslaughter."

Sec. 21.(1) "Every one is a party to an offence who "(a) actually commits it,

"(b) does or omits to do anything for the purpose of aiding any person to commit, or

"(c) abets any person in committing it.

"(2) Where two or more persons form an intention in common to carry out an unlawful purpose and to assist each other therein and any one of them, in carrying out an unlawful purpose, commits an offence, each of them who knew or ought to have known that the commission of the offence would be a probable consequence of carrying out the common purpose is a party to that offence."

The Criminal Code when it deals with murder starts off by stating *sec. 205(1)*

"A person commits homicide when, directly or indirectly, by any means, he causes the death of a human being.

"(2) Homicide is culpable or not culpable.

"(3) Homicide that is not culpable is not an offence.

"(4) Culpable homicide is murder or manslaughter or infanticide."

Then it goes on to say (and I am reading only the essential parts dealing with this case):

Sec. 205(5) "A person commits culpable homicide when he causes the death of a human being,

"(a) by means of an unlawful act," (such as assault).

Then *sec. 212* "Culpable homicide is murder

"(a) where the person who causes the death of a human being

"(i) means to cause his death, or

"(ii) means to cause him bodily harm that he knows is likely to cause his death, and is reckless whether death ensues or not;"

Then *sec. 214.(1)* "Murder is first degree murder or second degree murder.

(2) Murder is first degree murder when it is planned and deliberate.

(7) All murder that is not first degree murder is second degree murder."

During his charge to the jury he said:

Now I come back to the charge which is first degree murder. Here I have taken the liberty of typing out portions of the Criminal Code which pertain to this charge of first degree murder and also the charge of murder generally and also the charge of second degree murder. I have had some copies made of it and I will ask the clerk to distribute a copy of that to each member of the jury and a copy to counsel also.

What I have distributed to you has been copied directly from the Criminal Code. The Criminal Code is of course a public document and I see no reason why the public and the members of the jury and anybody should not be permitted access to what is a public document enacted by the Parliament of Canada. What I am doing now is to my knowledge possibly a first in Canada as far as I know. But, I have decided to do that because in my experience I have found that very often the jury ask questions in which they want the text of one particular section that has been cited over to them by the Judge when he makes his address to the jury and I find that a particularly normal request. After all, why should we expect the jury to hear a series of sections from the Criminal Code and then go back in the jury room and remember them all. It is a pretty fair assumption that you would not remember them all, that some of your discussions may be on what the sections were all about and I don't see anything wrong in it at all by giving you a copy of what is actually published in the Criminal Code as enacted by Parliament. That is why I have done it. I will read this with you.

Later on, after having read various provisions of the *Code*, he told the jury:

> That is the law as defined in the Criminal Code. I cannot change it and neither can you. Parliament is the only body that can change that. Having resorted to this particular device of supplying you with the text itself, I feel that I do not have to deal with the subject very much because you have it there in plain English. You understand the English language as well as I do. Why should I try and substitute my interpretation of these particular sections to your particular interpretation of these particular sections. I could be wrong. I prefer to let you decide what it means. I think you are just as capable as I am to do that. I have been watching you throughout these proceedings and you appear to me as a general body of persons who are I would say intelligent and who can understand what goes on.

It is at least the third time in reported decisions that written extracts of the *Criminal Code* have been given to juries in Canada. In *R. v. Schimanowsky* (1973), 15 C.C.C. (2d) 82, 25 C.R.N.S. 332, [1974] 1 W.W.R. 738, the Court of Appeal of Saskatchewan, speaking through the voice of Culliton, C.J.S., condemned the practice.

In *R. v. Tennant and Naccarato* (1975), 23 C.C.C. (2d) 80, 7 O.R. (2d) 687, 31 C.R.N.S. 1, the Ontario Court of Appeal, consisting of Gale, C.J.O., Brooke and Martin, JJ.A., in a *per curiam* judgment, disagreed with Culliton, C.J.S. in *R. v. Schimanowsky, supra,* and though the three Ontario appellate Judges did not think that juries should be encouraged to seek copies of sections of the *Criminal Code,* they thought the matter was entirely one in the discretion of the trial Judge. While in the Ontario case both defence and Crown counsel requested the trial Judge to remind the jury in the clearest terms that they must accept the law as it is given to them in the Judge's charge and that the learned trial Judges failed to abide by this eminently fair request, nevertheless the Ontario appeal tribunal was not prepared to say that in the circumstances of that case any substantial wrong or miscarriage of justice had occurred. More recently the British Columbia Court of Appeal was faced with the same question in *R. v. Wong* (1978), 41 C.C.C. (2d) 196, [1978] 4 W.W.R. 468 *sub nom. R. v. Wong (No. 2).* McFarlane, J.A., speaking for the Court, at p. 204 had this to say:

> There has been some diversity of opinion among Canadian Courts about the propriety of giving juries written extracts from evidence or from a Judge's charge, memoranda of law, or copies of relevant sections of a statute. The predominant view appears to disapprove. I do not think absolute condemnation is justified. On the other hand, it is no doubt a dangerous procedure and should, I think, be adopted only in very special circumstances and with great care. In this case I am convinced that it must have added to the prominence of the common purpose aspect of the trial and to have concentrated the attention of the jury on the memorandum itself, very probably adding to the confusion, if not actually misleading.

There is some divergence of opinion.

In this case the memorandum of law given to the jury was proper and to the point; it could not have confused them or misled them. I personally do not favour the practice as I think it is fraught with danger, but I cannot condemn it outright in the manner that the Saskatchewan Court of Appeal has done. I think it may be used sparingly and with clear explanation that the jury must accept the law from the trial Judge as he gives it to them. In the instant case Deniset, J., properly instructed them to that extent in the very beginning of his remarks in these words:

> Now, my first duty as a Judge in this case, is to tell you what law is; that you have to follow. You are to follow what I say the law is.

However, upon discussing the two pages of law which he was leaving with them, he indicated that they knew English as well as he did and he left it with them to decide what the law means. He was in error but in the context of the case and the charge as a whole, though I certainly would not have followed this practice, I am unable to say that in itself it is defective and constitutes misdirection. I do not approve of the practice but I am unable to condemn it as being totally erroneous. It certainly is not misdirection which warrants a new trial.

. . .

Both accused received a fair trial and the theory of their respective defences was adequately put to the jury. The verdicts should, therefore, be affirmed and the appeals dismissed.

———————

Another matter which has provoked discussion is the extent to which the jury may make notes of what transpires during the trial.

R. v. BENGERT (NO. 3)
(1979), 48 C.C.C. (2d) 413, (*sub nom. R. v. Bengert No. 13*) 15 C.R. (3d) 62
(B.C. S.C.)

BERGER J. (orally):—Crown counsel proposes, during the course of his address to the jury, to hand them a copy of a chronological record of the dates and events which he claims have been established by the evidence. The chronology is lengthy, 31 pages. It encompasses the whole period of the conspiracy alleged in the indictment; that is, January 1, 1976, to April 12, 1978. There is room at the side of each page for the jury to make notes. Crown counsel says that they should take the chronology into the jury room with them when they retire. The chronology consists of references to the evidence upon which Crown counsel will seek to erect his argument.

Defence counsel object. They say that the chronology gives the impression that there was only one conspiracy—the conspiracy alleged in the indictment. They will urge it upon the jury that this is a case of separate conspiracies, and that none of them has been shown to be the conspiracy alleged in the indictment. They say that the chronology is, in certain instances, misleading, because it does not reflect what emerged on cross-examination.

This trial is now in its seventh month. There are 12 accused. At the outset there were 14. The Crown entered a stay against one of them, Oda, and I directed the jury to bring in a verdict of not guilty against another, McClellan. There are 21 unindicted co-conspirators. Thus, the evidence for the Crown attempts to track the movements of 35 or more persons over a period of 27 months.

We have heard from 185 witnesses. There are 316 exhibits. There are tapes of 41 telephone calls, many of them lengthy. There are 13 affidavits admitted pursuant to s. 30 of the *Canada Evidence Act,* R.S.C. 1970, c. E-10. All of this evidence has been adduced by the Crown. The defence has elected to call no evidence.

The issues in this case have been sharply defined, but the evidence bearing on those issues is voluminous. I think it is right to allow Crown counsel to place his chronology in the hands of each juror to allow them to follow his argument. In this Province we allow jurors to take notes in the course of a trial. In long trials we supply them with looseleaf notebooks for the purpose. In this case I have urged the jury to confine their notetaking to matters they feel may turn out to be especially important so that they will be sure to listen to and observe the witnesses, leaving the transcription of the evidence to the official Court reporter. We find that jurors take such notes as each of them, in his own fashion, finds useful. This brings me to the point. The jury would have every right to take notes during Crown counsel's address. He would have the right to urge them to take a note from time to time as he comes to what he will submit are particularly vital dates or events. So why not let the jury have the chronology while Crown counsel is addressing them?

Defence counsel, when they address the jury, may decide to draw the attention of the jury to dates and events referred to in the Crown's chronology in order to urge that these references do not conform to the evidence, or to urge that these references are not to be relied upon in light of other evidence. Defence counsel will have the right, in any event, to place their own chronology before the jury. I have no doubt that it will be laid out in such a way it will give the impression that this is a case of separate conspiracies, but in their addresses they will seek to persuade the jury of that very thing. I cannot see why a chronology handed to the jury is objectionable on the ground that it reflects what counsel intends to say. It must if the jury are to find it useful in following his address.

It is said, well, the jury will attach inordinate weight to the chronologies. I do not think that there is anything in this argument. The jury have sat here for seven months. They understand the role of counsel is to make submissions, not to give evidence. In any event, I will tell them that the chronologies are not evidence and that they must not substitute them in any way for their own recollection of the evidence. They will have an awful lot of paper with them in the jury room. It would, in my view, be absurd to say that they are likely to treat the chronologies as anything more than a handy guide to the dates and events that counsel allege have been established on the evidence and which they particularly wish to bring to their notice.

Would it be preferable merely to have counsel put a chronology up on the wall and refer the jury to it during the course of counsel's address but not to allow them to take it into the jury room? I do not think so. They would be entitled to copy down the chronology in their notebooks. Better to give each of them a true copy of the chronology in the first place, and let them make notes beside dates and events they think may be important as counsel proceed with their addresses.

During the course of the motion for a directed verdict made at the conclusion of the Crown's case, which took many days, defence counsel handed up to me chronologies of dates and events they had prepared. These were of great assistance to me, yet I relied upon my own recollection and my own notes of the evidence. I cannot doubt that the jury will do the same, especially as I shall tell them that they must.

There are 12 accused left, and defence counsel are entitled altogether to make six speeches. The accused, McNaughton, who is representing himself, is also entitled to make a speech. What if, they say, each of them insists on placing his own chronology before the jury? Won't that create confusion? I do not think so. I think it will assist the jury in comprehending the vital points of counsel's submissions in turn. At the end the jury will have a great deal of paper, but so would a Judge sitting by himself in such a case.

It is said there is no authority for this procedure. That may or may not be so, but in these long trials it is essential that we offer juries the means of organizing the mass of evidence they are confronted with. I reject the notion that they should sit for months without taking a note, as they apparently must do in some other jurisdictions; equally, I reject the notion that they should sit throughout many days of addresses by counsel without having before them a chronology which will enable them to follow Crown counsel's address and then another chronology or chronologies to enable them to follow the addresses of defence counsel. To refuse to allow this to be done when the jury are about to hear a series of addresses that will extend over many days would be to consign them to a judicial never-never land.

Ruling accordingly.

See the following case where the trial judge took the unorthodox approach to charging the jury at various stages of the trial and then providing hard copies of his instructions to the jury for their consideration in jury deliberations:

R. v. MÉNARD
[1998] 2 S.C.R. 109, 125 C.C.C. (3d) 416, 16 C.R. (5th) 226 (S.C.C.)

MAJOR J.:—

. . .

The format of the jury charge in this case was unorthodox. In particular, the trial judge departed from common practice by discussing substantive law at the outset of the trial, by distributing transcripts of his instructions to the members of the jury, and by declining at the end of the trial to review his preliminary remarks regarding basic evidentiary principles. The Court of Appeal expressed concern about the format of the trial judge's instructions, but determined that no miscarriage of justice was occasioned in the circumstances of this case.

I agree with that conclusion and would dismiss this ground of appeal. However, a few general comments are appropriate with regard to the structure of the jury charge in this case. The Criminal Code does not dictate the manner in which a trial judge is to instruct a jury. Rather, the organization of the jury charge is a matter of common law and, like any area of common law, it is subject to innovation in the trial courts and may evolve over time. There are, necessarily, certain fundamental issues which every jury charge must address; these have been elaborated in various doctrines of this Court and do not have to be reviewed. As a general proposition the format of the charge is a matter of discretion. Trial judges have great latitude in deciding how to charge juries, and the structure of the charge may vary from one case to another. It is no secret that long and detailed instructions at the end of a trial may be more confusing than helpful. Trial judges should not be discouraged from taking new approaches in an effort to make their instructions more accessible to the jury. What is crucial is that at the conclusion of the charge the members of the jury understand the nature of their task and have the necessary help from the instructions to carry it out.

The innovations undertaken by the trial judge in this case were designed to improve the overall clarity of his instructions. As he told the members of the jury: "I've been sitting as a judge for about 15 years and I've become increasingly aware of the fact that we are making things difficult for our juries in criminal trials, particularly when trials are lengthy as this one is going to be. Accordingly, I've decided — and this is over the past year — to resort to different methods in order to make your task easier. For all I know, I don't know if any other judges doing [sic] this in Canada."

See also Soubliere J. [ed. note: the trial judge in *Ménard*], "Instructing the jury: A plea for better trials", Law Times, vol. 6, No. 36, October 30-November 5, 1995, at p. 6.

Notwithstanding that laudable intention, certain aspects of the jury charge here raise serious concerns that may create as many problems as they solve. As the Court of Appeal noted at p. 432, the distribution of transcripts, though not erroneous in itself, can easily give rise to reversible error in the event the jury receives only part of the trial judge's instructions in written form: *Cathro v. The Queen*, [1956] S.C.R. 101 at pp. 114-15, 113 C.C.C. 225. Any trial judge adopting such an approach must take care to ensure that the entire charge is provided to the jury in a clear and legible form, and that all members of the jury are capable of reading the materials. It may well be that the dangers associated with such an approach outweigh the potential benefits.

Likewise, instructing the jury in segments throughout the trial does not necessarily constitute error, and may in fact be beneficial in certain circumstances. However, it does increase the risk that the jury might be confused by erroneous statements of law at the outset of the trial or by instructions which are not ultimately related to any of the evidence introduced in the case. Of course, an error contained in a jury charge need not be fatal; the propriety of the charge is a question to be decided based on the charge as a whole, and it is open to the trial judge to attempt to correct any errors that he or she may previously have made. Indeed, juries are frequently recharged as a result of counsel's submissions at the conclusion of the judge's instructions, and potentially fatal errors are often avoided in this way. However, when the jury charge is delivered piecemeal over the course of the trial, such corrections become markedly more difficult. In particular, if the trial judge errs on a point of substantive law at the start of the trial, and the jury members subsequently hear the evidence with that error in their minds, the damage to the fairness of the trial might well be irreparable.

In this case, the trial judge did commit an error in his preliminary instructions regarding the substantive law of murder. In addition, the second segment of his charge was overinclusive, since it addressed the use of prior inconsistent statements of an accused, even though it was not yet known whether Ménard would testify, let alone whether he would be confronted with prior statements. The trial judge made efforts to correct those problems in his closing address. With regard to his charge on prior inconsistent statements by an accused, he directed the jury to disregard his earlier comments. With respect to his discussion of murder, he instructed the jury as follows: The law as to this offence: I have already charged you on the elements of this offence. I have nothing to add. The evidence is such that clearly, Velasquez was the victim of a second degree murder. The issue before you is whether Ménard did it.

Ultimately, the Court of Appeal concluded that the trial judge's errors did not merit a reversal of Ménard's conviction, and I agree. It is worth emphasizing, however, that this result was largely fortuitous — had the question of murder been a live issue in the trial, the judge's misdirection regarding that offence at the outset of the proceedings might have vitiated the entire charge. To instruct a jury on substantive law at the outset of a trial is to walk on thin ice, and any trial judge who chooses to do so must exercise caution to ensure that his or her instructions are correct. I endorse the Court of Appeal's comments at p. 433: [T]here may be considerable benefit in instructing the jury, as the trial judge did in this case, about the trial process and some of the fundamental evidentiary principles right at the outset of the trial. However, before embarking on an expose of the substantive law, the trial judge should wait to hear the evidence, unless counsel agree to a proposed set of instructions tailored to the facts of the case. Even there, the dangers always exist that the evidence will not match these early expectations, and that an error may prove impossible to cure.

As a final note, the trial judge's closing address to the jury was troubling in that it did not bring together the earlier portions of his instructions, and in particular it did not re-emphasize the fundamental principles of reasonable doubt, the presumption of innocence and the burden of proof. Those principles are too important to be referred to in passing at the conclusion of the trial. Even if it is assumed that the jury followed the trial judge's instructions and reread their written transcripts concerning those matters, it would have been better, in the unusual circumstances of this case, for the trial judge to repeat that portion of his instructions and thereby ensure that he was sending the jury into deliberations with those principles fresh in their minds. In spite of these criticisms, the charge taken in its entirety in the circumstances of this case did not result in any miscarriage of justice.

When a trial judge is satisfied that there should be a directed verdict of acquittal, does he or she simply instruct the jury to acquit? The common law tradition was that this was a matter to be left to the jury with an instruction to acquit. In *R. v. Rowbotham*, [1994] 2 S.C.R. 463, 30 C.R. (4th) 141, 90 C.C.C. (3d) 449 (S.C.C.) the jury had resisted such an instruction and wished to consider convicting. When the matter reached the Supreme Court, Chief Justice Lamer decided that the procedure should be changed to avoid such conflict with the jury. The trial judge should now say "As a matter of law, I am withdrawing the case from you and I am entering the verdict I would otherwise direct you to give as a matter of law".

Can a trial judge instruct the jury to convict where he or she is satisfied of the accused's guilt beyond a reasonable doubt?

R. v. KRIEGER
[2006] 2 S.C.R. 501, 41 C.R. (6th) 201, 213 C.C.C. (3d) 303 (S.C.C.)

The accused suffered from a debilitating illness and used marijuana for medicinal purposes. He produced his own supply and also supplied it to others for use. The accused admitted all of the elements of the offence and relied on a defence of necessity. The trial judge held that necessity was not a live issue and directed the jury to convict. During deliberations, two jurors asked to be excused, one on religious grounds, the other on grounds of conscience. The trial judge denied the requests. The jury convicted.

FISH J. (for the Court) —

A clear distinction must in any event be drawn between admissions of fact covering all of the prosecution's allegations and the ultimate question of guilt or innocence that is answered by the verdict alone. This was well explained by Sir Patrick (later Lord) Devlin:

> It [referring to the British precedent of *Stonehouse v. D.P.P.*] could not be said that the whole question of innocence or guilt was taken out of the jury's hands. If it had been, would it have made a difference? Logically it should not. If a single issue can be withdrawn from the jury on the ground that the facts relating to it lead in the eyes of the judge to one conclusion only, then, if the same thing can be said of all the other issues, they too should be withdrawn. But suppose that at the end of the evidence in such a case the judge was, without summing up at all, simply to direct the verdict of Guilty in the same way as he directs a verdict of Not Guilty when the prosecution has failed to make out a case. *This would mean that there had not been even the semblance of a trial by jury.* Whatever formula may be devised to facilitate the application of the proviso, the statutory requirement is that there should be no miscarriage of justice. It would be going very far to say that there was no

miscarriage in a process which deprived an accused entirely of his constitutional right to trial by jury. ("The Judge and the Jury", in *The Judge*, 1979, at pp. 142-43)

And later:

In my idea no conviction can stand that is not based on the verdict of a jury given after a full and proper trial. No matter that the guilt of the accused cries out to the heavens through the voices of all the judges of England. This is the first and traditional protection that the law gives to an accused. The second and more recent protection, given in the way I have chronicled, is that even such a verdict will not be enough if on the evidence the appellate judges find the lurking doubt which they consider that the jury has missed. But the second is an addition to the first and not a substitute for it. (p. 157)

I share these views and consider them to be a complete answer to both points raised by the Crown.

The overwhelming nature of the evidence can hardly justify a directed verdict of guilty. When, if not in such cases, would a verdict of guilty be directed? Would it be permitted whenever the evidence is overwhelming *in the eyes of the judges*? Under our Constitution, the plain answer to this last question is "no".

. . .

In another era, the usual enticement to quick agreement consisted of locking the jury up without "meat, drink, fire and tobacco". Jurors who gave verdicts thought unacceptable by the court were punished in Star Chamber or by the trial judge himself: see Devlin, *Trial by Jury*, at pp. 68-69, 76. In *Bushell's Case* (1670), 6 St. Tr. 999, the jurors were fined and imprisoned for their verdict of "not guilty".

It has since then been well-established that under the system of justice we have inherited from England juries are not entitled *as a matter of right* to refuse to apply the law — but they do have the *power* to do so when their consciences permit of no other course.

The matter was put this way long ago by Lord Mansfield in *R. v. Shipley* (1784), 4 Dougl. 73, 99 E.R. 774, at p. 824 (cited by Dickson C.J. in *R. v. Morgentaler*, [1988] 1 S.C.R. 30, at p. 78):

It is the duty of the Judge, in all cases of general justice, to tell the jury how to do right, though they have it in their power to do wrong, which is a matter entirely between God and their own consciences.

In this case, with the sole intention of "showing the jury how to do right", the trial judge unfortunately deprived the jurors of the responsibility that was by law theirs alone. The appellant was thereby deprived of his constitutional right, in virtue of s. 11(*f*) of the *Charter*, "to the benefit of trial by jury".

I would therefore allow the appeal, quash the appellant's conviction and order a trial before judge and jury in accordance with his election on the indictment that concerns us here.

For comment, see Lisa Dufraimont "Krieger: The Supreme Court's Guarded Endorsement of Jury Nullification" (2007) 41 C.R. (6th) 209. See also *R. v. Gunning*, [2005] 1 S.C.R. 627, 29 C.R. (6th) 17, 196 C.C.C. (3d) 123 (S.C.C.) where the Court held that the trial judge had erred in directing the jury that the Crown had proved an essential element of the offence.

7. Jury Deliberations and Unanimity

Sections 647, 648 and 649 of the Code deal with the discretion of a trial judge to keep the jury separate and also with jury secrecy, which is the rule in Canada.

Indeed, violating jury secrecy is a criminal offence except in certain circumstances:

649. Every member of a jury, and every person providing technical, personal, interpretative or other support services to a juror with a physical disability, who, except for the purposes of

(a) an investigation of an alleged offence under subsection 139(2) in relation to a juror, or

(b) giving evidence in criminal proceedings in relation to such an offence,

discloses any information relating to the proceedings of the jury when it was absent from the courtroom that was not subsequently disclosed in open court is guilty of an offence punishable on summary conviction.

In *R. v. Pan*, [2001] 2 S.C.R. 344, 43 C.R. (5th) 203, 155 C.C.C. (3d) 97, s. 649 was held not to violate s. 7 of the Charter. The Court reiterated that the opinions, arguments, and votes during deliberations are inadmissible in any court proceedings. However, extrinsic evidence, whether from a juror or a third party, of facts, statements, or events that might have tainted the verdict are admissible.

See Paul Quinlan, "Secrecy of Jury Deliberations — Is the Cost Too High?" (1993), 22 C.R. (4th) 127.

Do you think there should be a new trial ordered in each of the following circumstances?

PROBLEM 5

The accused is appealing his rape conviction. There is an affidavit of the foreman of the jury that the Crown told the jurors at the end of the trial that he had gone into the jury room and erased from the blackboard the words "assault and battery" in order to put them out of the jurors' minds. The jurors had written a list of offences on the board in the order of rape, conspiracy, assault and battery and aggravated theft. Compare *R. v. Mercier* (1973), 12 C.C.C. (2d) 377 (Que. C.A.).

PROBLEM 6

The accused is appealing his murder conviction. There is an affidavit from the defence counsel that the sheriff outside the jury room overheard a discussion by the jury in the jury room as follows:

— **Let's do it the democratic way.**

— Let's decide by majority vote.

— Is everyone agreed that we do this in the democratic way?

— What if somebody abstains?

Then, a short time later, the words "eight for". The sheriff also said that the jury returned their verdict five minutes later. Compare *R. v. Perras (No. 2)* (1974), 18 C.C.C. (2d) 47 (Sask. C.A.).

PROBLEM 7

The accused is appealing his conviction for possession of stolen property. There is evidence that police officers were discussing the criminal records of the accused on one occasion in the corridor of the courtroom and were quite probably overheard by one or more members of the jury. There is also evidence that on several occasions the foreman of the jury had social discussions with the police officers who were acquaintances of his. Compare *R. v. Mayhew* (1975), 29 C.R.N.S. 242 (Ont. C.A.).

Section 644 of the Criminal Code states:

(1) Where in the course of a trial the judge is satisfied that a juror should not, by reason of illness or other reasonable cause, continue to act, the judge may discharge the juror.

(1.1) A judge may select another juror to take the place of a juror who by reason of illness or other reasonable cause cannot continue to act, if the jury has not yet begun to hear evidence, either by drawing a name from a panel of persons who were summoned to act as jurors and who are available at the court at the time of replacing the juror or by using the procedure referred to in section 642.

(2) — Where in the course of a trial a member of the jury dies or is discharged pursuant to subsection (1), the jury shall, unless the judge otherwise directs and if the number of jurors is not reduced below ten, be deemed to remain properly constituted for all purposes of the trial and the trial shall proceed and a verdict may be given accordingly.

Should there be a new trial in view of the discretion exercised under s. 644 in the following three problems?

PROBLEM 8

The accused pleaded not guilty to a charge of second degree murder. After twelve jurors had been sworn, but before the accused had been given in charge of the jury and before the Crown had been called upon to present its case, the court was informed that one of the jurors was a fellow employee of the brother of the alleged victim. After hearing the argument, the trial judge discharged that one juror. The trial proceeded before the other eleven jurors who eventually returned a verdict of guilty. Compare *Basarabas v. R.*, [1982] 2 S.C.R. 730, 31 C.R. (3d) 193 (S.C.C.).

PROBLEM 9

The accused was charged with conspiracy to import cocaine. Soon after the jury had been empanelled the trial judge was informed that one of the jurors had smiled at one of the accused. The accused addressed that juror in the presence of counsel, with the balance of the jury excluded. The juror agreed that she had smiled and that she could not remain impartial. She was excused. Defence counsel applied for an order that another juror be empanelled or, failing that, for a mistrial. Both applications were refused. The remainder of the jury panel were brought in and the judge told them that a juror had been excused and that they should not draw any inference adverse to the accused. The eleven person jury convicted. Compare *R. v. Andrews* (1984), 41 C.R. (3d) 82 (B.C.C.A.).

PROBLEM 10

The trial judge recorded a verdict of "not guilty" following the accused's trial on a charge of attempted murder, and discharged the jury. The verdict of the jury had in fact been "guilty", but the trial judge had misheard the foreperson. The judge discovered his mistake approximately seven to nine minutes after the jury's exit from the courtroom and reconvened court with both counsel, the foreperson and one other juror, but without the accused. The trial judge ordered a hearing for the next day at which the full jury was present but the accused was absent. The trial judge held that he had jurisdiction to inquire into the actual verdict and whether an error had occurred. Four days later that inquiry was held, and the trial judge heard testimony from the court reporter and each juror as to what had happened in court. The trial judge did not permit cross examination of the jurors on the issue of bias, but he asked each juror whether he or she had been influenced by anything they had heard or read in the intervening period since the trial had ended. He determined that the jury verdict had in fact been "guilty" and that no jurors had been tainted between the time the verdict was announced and the jurors were reconvened. He entered a conviction. The accused appealed to the Court of Appeal, which upheld the trial judge's decision. The accused appealed to the Supreme Court of Canada.

Compare *R. v. Burke*, [2002] 2 S.C.R. 857, 2 C.R. (6th) 1, 164 C.C.C. (3d) 385 (S.C.C.). The Court was divided 5-4. Which way did they decide? See annotation by Stephen Coughlan, C.R. *ibid.*, 3.

A jury must be unanimous in Canada and the judge's direction on this point is frequently the ground of an appeal.

R. v. G. (R.M.)

[1996] 3 S.C.R. 362, 1 C.R. (5th) 199, 110 C.C.C. (3d) 26 (S.C.C.)

The accused was charged with sexual assault. The jury began their deliberations in mid-afternoon. The next day the jury sent the judge a message that they had reached an impasse. The trial judge recalled them and urged them to consider the public expense of a new trial, the inconvenience which a new trial would cause to all participants and the hardship to the accused and the complainant that a new trial would engender and suggested that the minority might want to reconsider what the majority were saying. The jury returned a guilty verdict 15 minutes later. The verdict was upheld on appeal. On further appeal the conviction was overturned. After criticizing the trial judge's exhortation, the Court offered a model.

Per CORY J. (Lamer C.J. and La Forest, Sopinka, McLachlin, Iacobucci and Major JJ. concurring):—I put forward the following example as one way in which an exhortation could be given to a jury. It is not meant to be followed slavishly as a magic incantation, but rather it is simply a suggestion that may be helpful to trial judges confronted with the need to give some direction to a jury which appears to be deadlocked. The direction might be given along these lines:

> Members of the Jury, you are having difficulty reaching a unanimous verdict. While it is not imperative that you do so, it is obviously desirable. You have sworn to give a true verdict based upon the evidence and that you must do your utmost to achieve. I have the discretion to discharge you from giving a verdict where it appears that further deliberation would be futile. However, this power should not be exercised lightly or too quickly. Frequently when juries are given more time to deliberate they are able to reach an agreement.

> My objective is not to convince you to change your minds but rather, to encourage you to present your own view of the evidence to your fellow jurors to ensure that everyone's opinion has been duly considered. While you may have already formed an opinion as to the proper verdict I would ask that you still keep an open mind and carefully consider your colleagues' viewpoints. However, in reconsidering your position I remind you that at the beginning of the trial each of you took an oath to return a true verdict according to the evidence. It is crucial that no one betray that oath. Therefore, your verdict must be based on the evidence alone and you must not allow yourselves to be influenced by any extraneous considerations.

> The essence of the jury system is the process of reasoning together by exchanging views and deliberating together. It is expected that you will pool your views of the evidence and listen carefully to one another. This means that there must be some give and take in the exchange of opinions. I must emphasize that this does not mean you should subordinate your own genuinely held view of the evidence for the sake of reaching a consensus. It is of course desirable that a unanimous verdict be rendered; yet this may be one of those occasions where you are unable to do so. This will not reflect badly upon you provided that you have made an honest effort to try the case to the best of your abilities.

> Therefore, I would ask you to try once again to reach a verdict. This is a time to reflect further on the evidence to see if, by listening to each other, by carefully

considering the various positions, and by reasoning together, you can come to an agreement and render a unanimous verdict.

I would add that although such a direction would be appropriate in this case and others like it, the situation presented in another case may require a different type of direction.

The judge's discretion in the event of a disagreement of the jury is set out in s. 653.

Section 650 of the Code requires that the accused be present during the whole of his trial. In *R. v. Dunbar* (1982), 28 C.R. (3d) 324 (Ont. C.A.), it was held that the absence of the accused during discussions between the trial judge and counsel, which included discussion of a question by the jury, would require a new trial.

LAW REFORM COMMISSION, WORKING PAPER 27: THE JURY IN CRIMINAL TRIALS
(1980), 19-32

A. The Unanimity Requirement

Recommendation 1

The requirement that the jury be unanimous before it renders a verdict should continue to be an essential characteristic of the jury.

COMMENT

One of the most characteristic features of the criminal jury in Canada is the requirement that all jurors must be unanimous before a verdict can be returned. If, after a reasonable period of deliberation, the jurors are unable to agree on a verdict—either of conviction or acquittal—a hung jury results. A mistrial is declared in such a case, and the charges must be dropped or the accused retried.

The requirement of jury unanimity has an ancient history. As early as 1367, a recorded case noted that unanimity was a necessity. The historical reasons for the rule are obscure. Explanations range from the theory that it developed to compensate for the lack of other rules ensuring that a defendant received a fair trial to the theory that it arose out of the medieval concept of consent, which implied unanimity. Given the changed role of the jury, however, the original reasons for the rule are irrelevant in any debate of its merits in a contemporary legal system.

Despite its ancient roots, the unanimity requirement has come under scrutiny, particularly in recent years, and in many jurisdictions has been abandoned. Pressures for change have been generated by concern that one or two obstinate or corrupt jurors may prevent guilty persons from being convicted; that hung juries cause intolerable delays and expense in the administration of criminal justice; that 'unanimous' verdicts are often compromise verdicts; and that the unanimity requirement makes jury decision-making anomalous in a society which generally proceeds by some form of majority vote.

In 1967, England enacted legislation permitting a jury in a criminal proceeding to return a majority verdict of 10:2 or 11:1. The only prerequisite is that the jury must first deliberate and attempt to reach a unanimous verdict for at least two hours or such longer period as the court thinks reasonable having regard to the nature and complexity of the case.

In 1972, the United States Supreme Court in two five-to-four decisions upheld the constitutionality of non-unanimous jury verdicts in state criminal trials (9:3 decisions in Louisiana for certain crimes, and 10:2 decisions in Oregon for crimes other than first degree murder.)

Juries can return non-unanimous verdicts in specified cases in at least six states in the United States, four states in Australia, and in other such Commonwealth countries as England, Scotland, and Trinidad and Tobago. In most of these jurisdictions, the change from unanimity was made apparently with little prior study. In England, for example, the introduction of majority verdicts sparked a heated debate in both Houses of Parliament, the popular press and the legal literature. Those opposing the change argued that there was "no evidence on which to base a change"; that the House would be taking "a leap in the dark"; that there was "no proof that the unanimity rule needed altering"; and that "the Home Secretary has not made out the case". "What is the mischief ?" asked Lord Denning. Several members of the House of Commons quoted with approval the statement of Sir Patrick Devlin that "it is wise not to tamper with it [the unanimity principle] until the need for alteration is shown to be overwhelming".

In the United States, the Supreme Court decisions holding non-unanimous verdicts constitutional in state criminal cases provoked immediate controversy. Social scientists, in particular, joined in the debate. Many took issue with the assumptions upon which the Court had rested its decision.

In the preparation of this working paper we commissioned two empirical studies and undertook a number of surveys relating to the question of whether we should retain the unanimity requirement. These studies have been collected and published in one volume, a Study Paper, "The Jury". Here we shall briefly review the arguments for and against the unanimity requirement, and the reasons upon which we recommend its retention.

Arguments in Favour of Majority Verdicts

1. The Problem of the Hung Jury

Majority verdicts will result in fewer hung juries than unanimous verdicts and will therefore save the time and expense of retrials.

How serious is the hung jury problem in Canada? In our survey of judges, only 8 per cent of the judges felt that hung juries were a serious problem. The statistical evidence would tend to bear out the impressionistic hunch of the great majority of Canadian judges that in terms of numbers, hung juries are not a problem, let alone a serious problem. Hung juries rarely occur in Canada.

Certainly, by no stretch of the imagination do they occur frequently enough to pose a serious economic problem to the system.

In 1970, juries disagreed about the guilt or innocence of only about 1.1 per cent of the persons who were tried by trial by jury (the trials of 14 persons resulted in a hung jury). In 1971, this percentage dropped to .7 (8 persons) and in 1972 to .4 per cent (5 persons). The persons involved represented respectively, .027, .015 and .009 per cent of the persons charged with an indictable offence in those years. Thus, in 1972 only .009 per cent of the persons charged with an indictable offence had to be retried because of a hung jury.

Statistics Canada has not yet published the figures for the disposition of jury cases for more recent years. Therefore, to get more recent statistics on the number of hung juries, this Commission requested the relevant statistics from the Chief Justice of each province for the period September 1976 to September 1977. The responses were as follows:

	Total Jury Trials	Hung Juries
Newfoundland	10	0
Nova Scotia	64	1
New Brunswick	78	2
Quebec	339	2
Ontario	326	4
Manitoba	44	0
Saskatchewan	95	3
Alberta	83	2
British Columbia	331	—
TOTAL	1370	14

Thus, in 1976-77, only 1.02 per cent of the jury cases resulted in a hung jury.

These figures might be compared to the figures from the United States where it appears that about 5 to 5.5 per cent of jury cases result in a hung jury, and in England where, before the recent change to majority verdicts, about 3.5 to 4 per cent of the cases which went to the jury resulted in disagreement.

Not only is the number of cases in Canada in which there is jury disagreement negligible, but relaxing the unanimity requirement would not eliminate hung juries. The University of Chicago Jury Project found that those states that allowed majority verdicts had only about 45 per cent fewer hung juries than those that required unanimity. In states where a unanimous verdict was required, a hung jury occurred in 5.6 per cent of jury cases. Where a majority verdict was permitted a hung jury occurred in 3.1 per cent of the cases. Adopting a rule for less than unanimous verdicts in Canada would mean that there would be a need in 1972, for example, to retry only .1 per cent of all persons who elect trial by jury instead of about .3 per cent. Thus, a saving of only .2 per cent fewer jury trials would result. Even this figure overstates the savings since prosecutors do not retry all cases in which there has been a hung jury.

It seems clear that abolishing the unanimity requirement will do little to relieve the work load of the criminal courts and the cost of maintaining the criminal justice system. Compared to other potential cost-saving changes and considering the benefits of the unanimity requirement, which will be discussed below, this economic argument becomes inconsequential. The *Report of the Morris Committee on Jury Service* considered that jury disagreements were inevitable if jurors were performing their task conscientiously. And the Committee concluded that "this need cause no concern, unless disagreements occur so frequently as to indicate that the orderly administration of justice is being prejudiced". No evidence exists that this point has been reached in Canada.

Also, in deciding whether the present number of hung juries is a problem we should not forget that the right of one or two jurors to hang a jury is an extremely important one because of the protection it affords to minorities and because of its symbolic value with respect to the worth of the individual. As expressed by an American judge:

> . . . as history reminds us, a succession of juries may legitimately fail to agree until, at long last, the prosecution gives up. But such juries, perhaps more courageous than any other, have performed their useful, vital functions in our system. This is the kind of independence which should be encouraged. It is in this independence that liberty is assured.

2. The Problem of the Corrupt Juror

Even if hung juries occur infrequently they are an unnecessary expense and also pose the threat of releasing guilty persons since it is usually one or two unreasonable or corrupt individuals who hold out and hang a jury that would otherwise have reached a verdict.

Both the premise and the soundness of this argument can be questioned. The argument assumes that hung juries are caused by one or two obstinate or corrupt jurors. Overwhelming evidence suggests this is not the case. In England, where the abolition of unanimous verdicts was opposed vigorously, time and time again members of the House of Commons asked for evidence that the problem of the corrupt juror was serious, but none was forthcoming. It appears that the government was responding to one or two highly publicized trials in which attempts to interfere with jurors was alleged. Subsequent research revealed that the evidence of nobbling (intimidating jurors) was "infinitesimal".

There is no compelling evidence in Canada from actual reported cases to support the fear that corrupt or obstinate jurors pose a serious threat to the criminal justice system. Indeed, an analysis of the kinds of cases in which hung juries occur reveals that they involve a wide range of offences. They are in no way concentrated in those cases in which jury intimidation might be a strong likelihood.

Two lines of data collected by the University of Chicago Jury Project also tend to confirm that the corrupt juror is not a problem. First, in over 200 hung jury cases, not once did the trial judge suggest that there was anything suspicious about the jury deadlock. Second, in no case in which only one, two or three jurors voted for not guilty on the first ballot did the jury fail to reach agreement. In almost every case in which the jury was hung there was a minority of four or five at the beginning of the deliberations. The following table shows the first ballot votes and final outcomes of 155 juries for which the researchers were able to obtain this information:

Per Cent of Deadlocked Juries as
Related to their first Ballot

First Ballot		Per Cent of Juries which:	
Guilty	Not Guilty	Reached a Verdict	Disagreed
11	1	100	—
10	2	100	—
9	3	100	—
8	4		
7	5		
7	5		
6	6	85	15
5	7		
4	8		
3	9	93	7
2	10		
1	11	100	—

These statistics show that jury deadlock results only where a substantial minority viewpoint is prevalent in the first polling of the jury. Consequently, the most likely explanation for jury deadlock is not one or two stubborn, unreasonable, prejudiced or corrupt jurors, but rather "if one may take the first ballot vote as a measure of the ambiguity of the case, then it follows that the case itself must be the primary cause of a hung jury". The authors of the University of Chicago Jury Project conclude by saying, "Hence in the absence of direct and specific evidence of scandal, there is nothing in the hung jury phenomenon, even when a small minority finally deadlocks the jury, which compels, or is even compatible with the view that hung juries are caused by a lone corrupt juror holding out against the objective weight of the evidence".

Even if the assumption that hung juries are frequently caused by a corrupt juror were true, the argument that unanimous verdicts should therefore be abandoned is unsound. It is unsound because the more sensible way to deal with such a problem is the careful screening of jurors, and the vigilant pursuit of any allegations of interference with jurors. In our review of the jury selection process, we will make recommendations which should ensure the opportunity of eliminating the eccentric or prejudiced individual from jury service. In another part of the paper, the problem of jury tampering will be discussed. Furthermore, it must be remembered that a corrupt juror who hangs a jury does not secure the acquittal of the accused. The worst he can do is create a disagreement and put the state to the expense of a new trial.

3. Unanimous Verdicts are Anomalous

A third argument often made in support of majority verdicts is that the requirement of unanimity is inconsistent with, or at least anomalous when compared with decision-making rules for other democratic institutions. Legislative bodies, appellate courts, administrative tribunals and practically every other body in which group decisions must be made, decide on the basis of some form of majority vote. Why not jury verdicts?

Generalizing by analogy is always potentially dangerous. The fallacy inherent in such a form of argumentation is that two things will be made to appear more similar than they really are. That fallacy is present in this argument for majority jury verdicts. Except for the fact that they are all illustrations of group decision-making in a democratic society, jury decision-making bears no resemblance to the other group decision-making processes mentioned in the analogy. Certainly, they do not share sufficient similarities to lead us to conclude that they should be modified to conform in all respects. Numerous differences are obvious: (1) An accused is not convicted unless the jury is satisfied of his guilt beyond a reasonable doubt (for an argument as to the relationship between this burden of proof and the unanimity requirement, see below); (2) The jury has very little time within which to reach a decision, and the only information upon which they can rely is that presented to them; (3) Individual jurors are unskilled in evaluating litigious evidence, it is the juror's collective experience and the deliberative process which result in accurate fact-finding; (4) Jurors must determine essentially factual questions, while most other tribunals also deal with questions of law and policy or both.

4. The Unanimity Rule is a Sham

The unanimity rule is a sham. While receiving the apparent concurrence of all jurors, many verdicts in fact represent either a compromise among the jurors, or a verdict in which a minority acquiesced because of coalition or verbal pressure.

The argument that the unanimity rule ought to be abandoned because it is a sham has two aspects. First, it has been argued that some verdicts are compromises in the sense that the jurors agreed to a result after a period of "negotiation" so that the final verdict did not represent the most satisfactory verdict to any, or at most to only a few of them. However, this aspect of the argument does not lead inexorably or even logically to the conclusion that we should have majority verdicts. For one thing, compromise verdicts may not be an undesirable way to resolve cases. At least it is not clear that they are less just than a verdict reached by a majority that did not have to compromise. Indeed, many people argue that the jury's strength is the fact that its verdict is the result of the interaction of twelve individuals. Furthermore, abandoning the requirement for unanimous verdicts would not necessarily eliminate this problem. A compromise verdict might still be returned in slightly fewer cases, but compromise might still be necessary in order to obtain a verdict of ten or whatever number the majority requirement might be.

The second aspect of this argument is that the unanimity rule is a sham because in many cases a minority of jurors consent to the verdict in order simply to end the deliberations or because they have yielded to coalition or verbal pressure. Intuitively, one suspects that his must occur in some cases. Again, however, the inference that the unanimity requirement should be abandoned does not necessarily follow from this argument. All of the arguments given below which support the unanimity requirement retain their validity even though some verdicts may not reflect true unanimity. It is on the basis of a careful weighing of the benefits of unanimity against the costs that a decision for its retention or abandonment must be made. If the unanimity requirement has important benefits, the fact that it sometimes leads individual jurors to acquiesce in a decision which they might not support would not appear to be a serious cost. Indeed, this phenomenon would also be present in majority verdicts.

Arguments in Favour of Unanimity

The most fundamental rule of criminal procedure is that the accused can be found guilty only if a trier of fact is convinced of his guilt beyond a reasonable doubt. Many people argue that the unanimity requirement is necessary to preserve the integrity of this basic concept. Sir James Stephen propounded the argument in the following way:

> . . . [n]o one is to be convicted of a crime, unless his guilt is proved beyond reasonable doubt. How can it be alleged that this condition has been fulfilled, so long as some of the judges, by whom the matter to be determined, do in fact doubt.

The concept of proof beyond a reasonable doubt performs at least two functions in the criminal justice system. First, it eliminates to the greatest possible extent the chance that an innocent person will be convicted because of an error in the evaluation of the evidence. Second, it ensures the moral acceptability of convictions because the public is not left in doubt as to whether innocent persons are being convicted. The unanimity requirement would appear to further both of these goals.

1. Increased Accuracy of Fact-Finding

The unanimity requirement reduces the risk that innocent people will be convicted by increasing the accuracy of jury fact-finding.

The risk that an innocent person might be convicted could of course be reduced by having 100 people on the jury or by eliminating all trials. The unanimity requirement, however, decreases this risk, not by imposing an unreasonable limitation on conviction, but by increasing the accuracy of the jury's fact-finding.

A jury is assumed to be an accurate fact-finder because it brings to bear on the decision-making process the collective experience and recall of twelve persons, and because the deliberative process in which they engage encourages a give-and-take by which ideas and arguments are tested, refined, confirmed or rejected. The unanimity requirement would appear to be necessary to ensure that these attributes of jury decision-making are present. Empirical research relating to the jury's deliberative process suggests: first, that minority views are more likely to be expressed and considered under the unanimity rule; and second, that the quality of discussion is superior. From these findings, the greater likelihood of an accurate decision under the unanimity rule can be inferred.

2. More Acceptable Verdicts

The unanimity rule leads to verdicts which are more acceptable than majority verdicts.

The maxim, "justice must not only be done but must be seen to be done", embodies an ultimate value in the criminal justice system. Indeed, the public acceptance of and confidence in jury verdicts is an important reason for retaining juries. In this context, then, it must be asked: which are likely to be more acceptable, unanimous or majority verdicts? There is no dearth of unsupported speculation on this topic. Sir Patrick Devlin, for example, stated: "The sense of satisfaction, obtainable from complete unanimity, is itself a valuable thing".

The appearance of justice is important from the point of view of the jurors (if jury duty is to have the desired educative effect); the public (if the criminal trial is to continue to be a morally acceptable method of reinforcing value judgments); and the accused (if rehabilitation is to be possible).

The best data available on this general question relate to the perception of jurors about the two kinds of decision-making rules. The two studies which have sought an answer to this question have found that jurors under the unanimity requirement were more satisfied with the way the decision was made, and were more likely to perceive that justice had been administered.

Our survey of Canadian jurors also suggests that jurors, based on their experience, prefer the unanimity requirement. For example, before serving on the jury, the members of the jury panel were fairly evenly split on the question of unanimity. It was felt by 40.5 per cent that "it would be a good idea to allow less than unanimous verdicts", while 38.5 per cent felt it would not. However, after serving there was a shift toward wanting to maintain the unanimity requirement. While 40.4 per cent still felt it would be a good idea to allow less than unanimous verdicts, about 10 per cent of those who were undecided before serving, were convinced after serving that it would not be a good idea to allow less than unanimous verdicts, thus raising the percentage of jurors who held this view to 48.6 per cent.

The issue of whether the unanimity rule is essential in order to maintain public confidence in the jury system is more difficult to resolve. However, one cannot help but feel that the unanimity requirement, like the proof-beyond-a-reasonable-doubt standard, has an important symbolic value in informing people that the State has taken all possible safeguards to ensure that innocent persons are not convicted. In an effort to obtain some empirical data about the public's awareness of and opinion about the unanimity rule, two questions relating to this issue were included in our opinion poll of the Canadian public.

If few people knew about the unanimity rule, then the argument that it is an essential characteristic of the jury and is required to maintain public confidence in the system would be hard to sustain. However, 75 per cent of people across the country answered "yes" to the question. "Before finding an accused person guilty of a criminal offence in Canada, must all 12 people on the jury agree that he is guilty?" Given the general lack of public awareness about the exact workings of the criminal justice system, this is an impressive percentage of respondents.

Another question asked was whether people felt that the jury should be unanimous before convicting the accused. A list of possible answers were given, including "for all criminal offences" and "for no criminal offences". Approximately one-third of the respondents (33.1 per cent) thought that the jury should be unanimous for all criminal offences, while very few people (3.7 per cent) opposed unanimity for all criminal cases. For serious offences (*e.g.*, murder) as many as 90 per cent of the respondents felt the jury should have to be unanimous. This percentage declined with the seriousness of the offence until, for impaired driving, for example, only 40 per cent of the respondents felt that a jury (if the offence were tried by jury) should have to be unanimous. Thus it appears that for offences presently tried by a jury the great majority of Canadians are in favour of unanimous verdicts.

Finally, what would be the effect of the majority rule on accused's perception of the criminal justice system? Again, although there is no data, one cannot help but think that the accused would be more willing to accept the verdict, and less likely to attempt to rationalize his conviction, if he knew that the jurors had to be unanimous in their findings. Indeed, introducing majority verdicts would result in three kinds of verdicts: acquittal, conviction by a majority, and conviction by a unanimous jury. This concern was emphasized by many judges who corresponded with us on this issue. For example, an Ontario judge claims that "Psychologically, it would be disastrous for an accused to know he was found guilty by simple majority vote." Expanding on this, a judge from British Columbia says that, "There would remain in the accused's mind after his trial the thought that the minority believed in his innocence and he would be dissatisfied with the system."

Another important way in which the unanimity requirement would appear to contribute to the moral acceptability of jury verdicts is by ensuring that the jury discharges its function of bringing community standards to bear on the decision-making process. So that the jury performs this function, jury selection procedures are structured to ensure that minority groups are not excluded from jury service. Yet, it is possible that it will be the views held by these minorities that will be ignored if the jury can reach its verdict on the basis of a majority vote. The effect of such a rule would be to make our commitment to the possibility of a representative jury a hollow promise.

THATCHER v. R.

[1987] 1 S.C.R. 652, 57 C.R. (3d) 97, 32 C.C.C. (3d) 481 (S.C.C.)

In the Supreme Court it was determined that the Crown need not specify whether the accused was charged as a party or principal and that jury unanimity was not required as to the particular nature of the participation.

DICKSON C.J.C.:—The appellant, relying on a recent article by Mark A. Gelowitz entitled "The *Thatcher* Appeal: A Question of Unanimity" (1986), 49 C.R. (3d) 129, argues that, just as in *Brown*, where the English court of Appeal held that "Each ingredient of the offence must be proved to the satisfaction of each and every member of the jury", the court ought to hold that the nature of Thatcher's participation must be proved to each and every juror before he can be convicted of "unlawfully causing" JoAnn Wilson's death.

The appellant accepts, as any reasonable person must, that the jurors need not be unanimous with respect to their acceptance or rejection of each individual piece of evidence. In a long, complicated trial it is absurd to suppose that 12 people could form the same opinion of each item of evidence, and it is absurd to suppose that the Crown could ever prove or explain beyond a reasonable doubt every detail of a murder. A defendant at a murder trial should obviously not be acquitted if some jurors think a .38-calibre bullet was used and others think that a .327-calibre bullet was used. The appellant submits, however, that the jurors ought to be unanimous as to the "material facts" making out the offence. He does not provide a definition of "material facts", except to rely on Mr. Gelowitz for the proposition that jurors must be "in substantial agreement as to just what an accused has done" [p. 136]. This argument, however, overlooks the whole point of s. 21, as I have said, which make the distinction between principals and aiders and abetters legally irrelevant.

Moreover, if *Brown* is correct, and this need not be decided in the present appeal, I am far from convinced that it lays down a proposition as sweeping as the appellant suggests. Eveleigh L.J. acknowledged that jurors could arrive at their conclusions by different routes. Jurors "may be able to say that, whichever way one looks at it, the case is proved" [p. 119]. To be sure, Eveleigh L.J. also articulated the propositions referred to previously. But, in my opinion, s. 21 does not create "ingredients" in the offence of murder, in the same way that each particular "misrepresentation" was an ingredient in the offence of *Brown*. As I read Eveleigh L.J.'s remarks, his second proposition is restricted to cases in which "a number of matters are specified in the charge". This would be analogous to the case when there were several counts in an indictment. If Thatcher had been charged on two counts, of course unanimity would be required in respect of any count for which he is convicted. Such a conclusion flows from the proposition that a verdict stands for guilt, beyond a reasonable doubt, of that for which the accused has been charged. In the present case, Thatcher was charged that he did "unlawfully cause the death of JoAnn Kay Wilson and did thereby commit first degree murder". The charge was carefully worded, and there is no injustice in his conviction on the indictment irrespective of whether the jurors shared the same view as to the most likely manner in which Thatcher committed the murder.

When one considers the implications of the appellant's submission, it becomes even clearer that it is without merit. In the present case there were doubtless three alternatives in the minds of each of the jurors:

(a) Thatcher personally killed his ex-wife;

(b) he aided and abetted someone else to do so;

(c) he is innocent of the crime.

The jurors were told that if any of them had a reasonable doubt regarding (c), Thatcher should be acquitted. Every single juror was, evidently, solidly convinced that (c) was simply not what occurred. Each one was certain that the true statement of affairs was (a) or (b). Even if we suppose, as the appellant would have us do, that the juror individually went beyond thinking in terms of (a) or (b) and specifically opted for one theory, and that some jurors thought only (a) could have occurred and other though only (b) could have occurred, I am far from convinced that there would have been any injustice from convicting Thatcher. As stated, there is no legal difference between the two. Much is made of the fact that (a) and (b) are *factually* inconsistent theories, in the sense that evidence proving (a) tends to disprove (b). But this is really only true of one category of evidence, namely, identification and alibi evidence. The overwhelming mass of evidence tracing the murder weapon to Thatcher was highly probative, as were his statements to various witnesses (prior to the murder) of his intention to kill JoAnn Wilson, and his statement to Lynn Mendell (after the murder) that he had "blown away" his wife.

The appellant's suggestion would fail to achieve justice in a significant number of cases. Suppose the evidence in a case is absolutely crystal clear that when X and Y entered 'Zs house, Z was alive, and when X and Y left, Z was dead. Suppose that in their evidence each of X and Y says that the other of them murdered Z but each admits to having aided and abetted. Are X and Y each to be acquitted if some of the jurors differ as to which of X and Y actually committed the offence? I can see absolutely no reason in policy or law to uphold such an egregious conclusion. The appellant's submission ignores the very reason why Parliament abolished the old common law distinctions: namely, they permitted guilty persons to go free. As Professor Peter MacKinnon points out in "Jury Unanimity" A Reply to Gelowitz and Stuart" (1986), 51 C.R. (3d) 134, at p. 135, if an accused is to be acquitted in situations when every juror is convinced that the accused committed a murder in one of two ways, merely because the jury cannot agree on *which* of the two ways, "it is difficult to imagine a situation more likely to bring the administration of justice into disrepute — and deservedly so."

The full Gelowitz article was later published: "Jury Unanimity on Questions of Material Fact: When Six and Six Do Not Equal Twelve" (1987), 12 Q.L.J. 66.

The following case of *Lawrence* places a further gloss on this issue. In *Thatcher*, it was not necessary to determine how each juror arrived at the conclusion of guilt on first degree murder because, however one reached that conclusion, the sentence was mandatory (life imprisonment without eligibility for parole for 25 years). In *Lawrence*, the Court confronted a manslaughter verdict that could have been reached in one of two ways. However, it was the view of the trial judge that the accused's actual role in the killing mattered for the purposes of sentencing. A trial judge is generally considered to be bound by the jury's implied or express findings of fact: see *R. v. Brown*, [1991] 2 S.C.R. 518, 66 C.C.C. (3d) 1, 6 C.R. (4th) 353 (S.C.C.) and *R. v. Ferguson*, [2008] 1 S.C.R. 96, 54 C.R. (6th) 197, 228 C.C.C. (3d) 385 (S.C.C.).

R. v. LAWRENCE

(1987), 58 C.R. (3d) 71 (Ont. H.C.)

CAMPBELL J. (orally):—This is the sentencing for manslaughter of Terrance Woodrow Lawrence in the brutal killing of Jade Wilson, a little girl of about 20 months. Lawrence and his common law wife, Charlene McLeod, the girl's mother, were originally charged with second degree murder in the child's death. McLeod pleaded guilty to the lesser offence of criminal negligence causing death, and was sentenced by Evans J. on 7th April 1987 to imprisonment for two years less a day plus probation for three years and a mandatory firearm prohibition under s. 98 of the Criminal Code. McLeod was a Crown witness against Lawrence at his trial. On 14th May 1987, after a five-week trial, the jury convicted Lawrence of manslaughter.

The jury had a choice of two different bases of manslaughter. The first basis was that the accused shook the child to death. The second basis was that McLeod shook the child to death and he was criminally negligent in failing to prevent her. In *R. v. Speid* (1985), 46 C.R. (3d) 22 (Ont. C.A.), the learned trial judge in a similar case asked the jury to indicate on which basis they found manslaughter. In that case, the evidence of the second kind of manslaughter arose from the testimony of the accused himself, and the jury after deliberating for some time had asked for clarification of the difference between the two kinds of manslaughter. In this case there was no such basis to penetrate the deliberations of the jury by asking how they had reached their conclusion. I did not do so. I must therefore determine the findings of fact upon which the accused must be sentenced.

I am satisfied, beyond a reasonable doubt, that Lawrence shook the little girl to death.

. . .

I conclude, on this evidence, that the shaking administered by Lawrence to the little girl was violent and sustained and pitiless. The extreme violence of the attack on the child is difficult to visualize, let alone to understand. It is only after some reflection on the evidence of Dr. Wilson and Dr. Smith, together with the evidence of McLeod, that one can develop a picture of the prolonged and unremitting savagery of that attack.

. . .

Mr. Lawrence, would you stand up please? Considering the evidence at trial, the evidence and submissions that I have heard today, the unchallenged portions of the pre-sentence report, the particular pattern of your criminal record as it discloses your lack of interest in rehabilitation, the possibility nonetheless that, if you do apply yourself during your imprisonment, considering the supportive nature of your family, who have so admirably stood behind you, you do have a good deal of potential for change, hopefully, although you have demonstrated very little of this so far, considering the evidence of the time spent in custody, for which I credit you two years, considering again the fact that you did try to resuscitate Jade after your attack, considering your previous pattern of assault on her, considering her age of 20 months, considering the savage and cruel and repeated nature of your brutal attack on her, considering the need to deter others, and considering the need to impose a punishment that adequately reflects the community's revulsion for your crime, I sentence you to imprisonment for 14 years. In addition I make the order required by s. 98(1) of the Criminal Code that you be prohibited from having in your possession any ammunition, firearms or explosive from now until the end of five years following your release.

The accused on a charge of manslaughter is given his choice of how he or she wants to be tried, by judge alone or by judge and jury. The accused in *Lawrence* opted to be tried by judge and jury. The accused thus asked for the facts to be assessed by a jury. Section 11(f) of the Canadian Charter of Rights and Freedoms says that he is entitled to a jury assessment, and yet the judge here substitutes his own view of the facts, on a most critical issue, instead of canvassing the jury. In a civil suit for negligence it is common for the judge to ask the jury to decide: first, whether the defendant was negligent; second, in what his negligence consisted; and third, whether the plaintiff was contributorily negligent and, if so, to what extent. The judge is then better able to determine his award. So too in a criminal case, when the evidence discloses alternate theories of guilt, the judge would be better equipped to determine the proper punishment if he asked the jury for a special rather than a general verdict. The accused would then be tried on the facts by the jury and the judge could then determine the best sentence to fit those facts and society's needs.

A special verdict would not be new to the criminal law, of course, although, to be fair, it did fall into dispute in the 19th century. More recently, English and Canadian jurisprudence has condemned special verdicts in criminal cases: see *R. v. Solomon* (1984), 6 Cr. App. R. (S.) 120 at 126, and *R. v. Tuckey; R. v. Baynham; R. v. Walsh* (1985), 46 C.R. (3d) 97 at 110 (Ont. C.A.). In the English case cited, the court allowed, however:

> The only instance we have been able to find in which it might be said to be common practice to go behind the general verdict and to enquire from the jury the basis upon which it was reached is in the case of a verdict of manslaughter, when the jury may have reached their decision on alternative grounds which have been left to them by the judge. . . . [T]his court [has] said that in such circumstances the judge

may, and generally should, seek guidance from the jury concerning the basis of their verdict.

In the Ontario case cited, the court referred to the English exception but said:

> In our view, such an inquiry after the verdict and for the purpose of sentence can raise more difficulties than it solves, in that the jury may not be unanimous on the evidential basis of the verdict. . . . The jury are entitled to arrive at a unanimous verdict for different reasons and on separate evidential bases. They need not be unanimous in anything but the actual verdict. To require them to state particulars of the offence found is a practice fraught with potential danger and contrary to traditional practice.

Is this a satisfactory reason for failing to follow the English practice in manslaughter cases? That the jury need not be unanimous was confirmed by the Supreme Court of Canada in *Thatcher v. R.*, [1987] 1 S.C.R. 652, 57 C.R. (3d) 97 (S.C.C.). Since it's perfectly proper to find guilt along different paths, what's wrong with disclosing that fact? What is the "potential danger"? If six jurors joined in the unanimous verdict of guilt but were persuaded only of the lesser form of guilt, shouldn't that be known and shouldn't the sentence then be limited to the lesser version?

Section 724(2) now states that the trial judge is to draw his/her own conclusions about aggravating/mitigating circumstances so long as the conclusions are consistent with the jury's verdict.

Chapter 13

VERDICTS

In this section, we consider options that are open to the trier of fact in terms of verdicts. These considerations are equally applicable to trial by judge and jury, and trial by judge alone. Triers of fact are not always locked into a binary choice between guilt or innocence.

1. Included Offences

The accused faces the possibility of conviction not only on the offence specifically charged but on any included offences. Indeed, the trial judge has a duty to charge the jury with respect to included offences which can be supported by the evidence: *Smith v. R.,* [1979] 1 S.C.R. 215, 43 C.C.C. (2d) 417 (S.C.C.). This is so even where the defence expressly states that the lesser offence should not be put to the jury: *R. v. MacLeod,* [2014] 3 S.C.R. 619, 320 C.C.C. (3d) 326 (S.C.C.). In the case of proceedings on indictment there is a general section.

662. (1) A count in an indictment is divisible and where the commission of the offence charged, as described in the enactment creating it or as charged in the count, includes the commission of another offence, whether punishable by indictment or on summary conviction, the accused may be convicted

    (a) of an offence so included that is proved, notwithstanding that the whole offence that is charged is not proved; or

    (b) of an attempt to commit an offence so included.

(2) For greater certainty and without limiting the generality of subsection (1), where a count charges first degree murder and the evidence does not prove first degree murder but proves second degree murder or an attempt to commit second degree murder, the jury may find the accused not guilty of first degree murder but guilty of second degree murder or an attempt to commit second degree murder, as the case may be.

(3) Subject to subsection (4), where a count charges murder and the evidence proves manslaughter or infanticide but does not prove murder, the jury may find the accused not guilty of murder but guilty of manslaughter or infanticide, but shall not on that count find the accused guilty of any other offence.

(4) Where a count charges the murder of a child or infanticide and the evidence proves the commission of an offence under section 243 but does not prove murder or infanticide, the jury may find the accused not guilty of murder or infanticide, as the case may be, but guilty of an offence under section 243.

(5) For greater certainty, where a count charges an offence under section 220, 221 or 236 arising out of the operation of a motor vehicle or the navigation or operation of a vessel or aircraft, and the evidence does not prove such offence but does prove an offence under section 249 or subsection 249.1(3), the accused may be convicted of an offence under section 249 or subsection 249.1(3), as the case may be.

(6) Where a count charges an offence under paragraph 98(1)(*b*) or 348(1)(*b*) and the evidence does not prove that offence but does prove an offence under, respectively, paragraph 98(1)(*a*) or 348(1)(*a*), the accused may be convicted of an offence under that latter paragraph.

Section 662 does not provide a general definition of an "included" offence. This is an issue which has been the subject of protracted and somewhat technical case law.

LUCKETT v. R.
[1980] 1 S.C.R. 1140, 20 C.R. (3d) 393, 50 C.C.C. (2d) 489 (S.C.C.)

CHOUINARD J.: —

Charged with robbery, the appellant was found guilty of common assault. His conviction was upheld by a majority judgment of the Court of Appeal for British Columbia.

The question in issue is whether the offence of common assault is included in that of robbery as described in the enactment creating it, in the Criminal Code, R.S.C. 1970, c. C-34. Included offences are governed by s. 589 [now s. 662]....

As it appears, there are two circumstances under which an offence is included in another: it can be included in the offence "as described in the enactment creating it" or "as charged in the count".

We are concerned here only with the first of these circumstances. It is not in dispute that common assault is not included in the offence as charged in the count, which reads:Indictment: William Eric Luckett stands charged:

That, at the City of Vancouver, County of Vancouver, Province of British Columbia, on the 23rd day of July, 1977, he unlawfully did commit robbery of Walter Leibel, of a quantity of cigarettes and approximately $4.00 in cash contrary to the form of the statute in such case made and provided and against the peace of our Lady the Queen her Crown and dignity.

Robbery is defined by s. 302 of the Criminal Code as follows:

302. Every one commits robbery who

(a) steals, and for the purpose of extorting whatever is stolen or to prevent or overcome resistance to the stealing, uses violence or threats of violence to a person or property;

(b) steals from any person and, at the time he steals or immediately before or immediately thereafter, wounds, beats, strikes or uses any personal violence to that person;

(c) assaults any person with intent to steal from him; or

(d) steals from any person while armed with an offensive weapon or imitation thereof.

It is the appellant's submission that to be considered as an included offence under s. 589(1) the offence must be a necessary ingredient in the description of the offence charged. It is not a necessary ingredient in para. (d) of s. 302, nor is it in para. (a), when the violence or threats of violence used are to property as opposed to a person. The appellant therefore concludes that common assault is not included when the charge is one of robbery without any specific reference to one or the other of the subsections of s. 302.This was the view held by the dissenting members of the Court of Appeal, expressed as follows in the formal judgment:

> That, having regard for the form of the indictment, it was not open to the trial judge to convict of common assault and in the circumstances if the Crown wishes the court to be able to convict of an included offence, it must so frame its indictment as to show upon which of the subsections of s. 302 it intends to rely, so as to give notice to the accused not only of the principal offence with which he is charged but as well of the possible included offences of which he may be convicted if proof of the principal offence fails.

In support of his submission the appellant relied on *R. v. Manuel* (1960), 33 W.W.R. 406, 128 C.C.C. 383 (B.C.C.A.); *R. v. Harmer* (1976), 15 O.R. (2d) 84, 33 C.C.C. (2d) 17, 75 D.L.R. (3d) 20 (C.A.); *R. v. Maika* (1974), 27 C.R.N.S. 115, 17 C.C.C. (2d) 110 (Ont. C.A.); and *Fergusson v. R.*, [1962] S.C.R. 229, 36 C.R. 271, 132 C.C.C. 112.

In *R. v. Manuel* the Court of Appeal for British Columbia held that a charge that the accused "did attempt to murder Joe Manuel" [W.W.R. p. 407] did not include the offences of assault causing bodily harm and common assault.

Delivering the judgment of the court, Sheppard J.A. said at p. 407:

> It follows that in order to be an included offence within sec. 569 [now s. 662] the essential constituent of the included offence must necessarily be 'included or involved' in the offence as described in the enactment creating it or as charged in the count.

And at p. 408 he added:

> Further, to be an included offence the inclusion must form such an apparent and essential constituent of the offence charged that the accused in reading the offence charged will be fairly informed in every instance that he will have to meet not only the offence charged but also the specific offences to be included. Such apparent inclusion must appear from 'the enactment creating' the offence or 'from the offence as charged in the count;' either of those two may be considered under sec. 569 but not the opening by counsel or the evidence.
>
> The crown contended that these assaults were included offences under sec. 210 [now s. 239]; 'the enactment creating the offence.' The difficulty arises in the case at bar in that the offence charged, attempt to murder, may be carried out 'by any means' (sec. 210) and therefore may be by assault or by other means. Hence, in a particular case the attempt to murder as opened by crown counsel or as sought to be proven may be an attempt not carried out by assault.
>
> That is the difficulty in the crown's contention here. Under sec. 569, to determine whether assault is an included offence, regard may be had to sec. 210, the enactment creating the offence charged. But sec. 210 does not necessarily include the offence of assault by reason that under that section the attempt assigned in a particular case may be 'by any means,' and hence may be by means which do not come within 'assault' as defined in sec. 230. It follows that sec. 210 does not make assault such apparent and essential constituent of the offence of attempt to murder that the accused in reading the section would be fairly informed in every instance that he would have to meet the offence of assault.

In *R. v. Harmer, supra*, the issue was whether assault causing bodily harm was included in robbery as charged in the count, and it was found to be included in that particular indictment. It nevertheless appears from the judgment delivered by Evans J.A. that the court was of the opinion that it is not an included offence in a charge of robbery. He wrote at p. 86: "If the trial Judge was of the view that assault causing bodily harm was an included offence in a charge of robbery then on the authorities he was in error." From a previous statement on p. 85-86 it follows that [there] would be included in an indictment charging an offence:

> ....all offences which as a matter of law are necessarily committed in the commission of the principal offence as described in the enactment creating it, as well as those offences of which the accused may be convicted by virtue of express s statutory provisions.

In *R. v. Maika*, supra, the Court of Appeal for Ontario held that common assault was not an included offence within the description of robbery in s. 302. This decision was based on the English case of *R. v. Springfield* (1969), 53 Cr. App. R. 608, [1969] Crim. L.R. 557, in which the Court of Appeal interpreted s. 6(3) of the Criminal Law Act, 1967, c. 58 [quoted at Cr. App. R. p. 610]:

> Where, on a person's trial on indictment for any offence except treason or murder, the jury find him not guilty of the offence specifically charged in the indictment, but the allegations in the indictment amount to or include (expressly or by implication) an allegation of another offence falling within the jurisdiction of the court of trial, the jury may find him guilty of that other offence or of an offence of which he could be found guilty on an indictment specifically charging that other offence.

This section is different from s. 589(1) of our Criminal Code and deals only with offences included in the offence "as charged in the count". It does not deal with offences included in the offence "as described in the enactment creating it", which is what we are concerned with here. For this reason, *R. v. Springfield*, supra, is, in my view, of no assistance in this case.

The appellant has quoted the following extract from the judgment of Taschereau J. (as he then was), speaking for the court in *Fergusson v. R.,* supra, at p. 274:

> In the present case, there was only one count in the indictment, and the charge was for robbery in violation of s. 288 (b) [now s. 302(b)] of the Criminal Code [1953- 54 (Can.), c. 51]. A count in an indictment is divisible and where the commission of the offence charged includes the commission of another offence, whether punishable by indictment or on summary conviction, the accused may be convicted of an offence so included that is proved, notwithstanding that the whole offence that is charged is not proved, or of an attempt to commit an offence so included: Criminal Code, s. 569 [now s. 589]. Thus, a man charged with robbery may be found guilty of theft, but a person charged with robbery may not be found guilty of receiving stolen goods, as was held by the Court of Queen's Bench in the present instance. Receiving stolen goods is a less serious offence, but is not included in a charge of robbery.
>
> The count must therefore include but not necessarily mention the commission of another offence, but the latter must be a lesser offence than the offence charged.

The expression 'lesser offence' is a 'part of an offence' which is charged, and it must necessarily include some elements of the 'major offence', but be lacking in some of the essentials, without which the major offence would be incomplete: *R. v. Louie Yee*, [1929] 1 W.W.R. 882, 24 Alta. L.R. 16, 51 C.C.C. 405, [1929] 2 D.L.R. 452 (C.A.).

Relying on the last sentence of the above extract, the appellant concludes that to be an included offence "an offence must necessarily be included in the description of the offence in the Code". And he goes on to say that where no reference is made to one specific subsection, this means it must be included in all four subsections of s. 302.

With respect, I do not think that the latter proposition is supported by *Fergusson v. R.*, supra, which did not consider this question.

On the other hand, *Fergusson v. R.*, supra, does not support the opposite view either because in that case the accused was specifically charged under s. 288 (b), now s. 302 (b).

Nor is *R. v. George*, [1960] S.C.R. 871, 34 C.R. 1, directly in point. There it was held that common assault was included in robbery, but in that case the charge read that the accused did [p. 9] "unlawfully and by violence steal", which made it fall under s. 288 (b).

To hold, however, that the lesser offence must be included in every subsection of the section referred to would seem to me to impose a requirement beyond those of s. 589. Robbery is one offence which can be committed in different ways and a reference to the relevant section is a reference to it in its entirety.

Section 302 [now s. 343] was s. 288 of the Criminal Code, 1953-54 (Can.), c. 51, which, together with s. 289, replaced ss. 445-448 of the Criminal Code, R.S.C. 1927, c. 36. As put in Crankshaw's Criminal Code of Canada, 7th ed. (1959), at p. 431:

> ROBBERY. The law of robbery was revised in the new Criminal Code by combining together ss. 445, 446 and 448 into one comprehensive section 288 (above). It will be noted that s. 288 (above) contains four clauses (a), (b), (c) and (d). The offence of robbery is punishable under s. 289 which provides that 'every one who commits robbery is guilty of an indictable offence and is liable to imprisonment for life and to be whipped.' There is, therefore, one offence only 'robbery' which may be committed in different ways. These ways of committing robbery are set out in s. 288 (above.).

I would therefore conclude that the lesser offence must be included in the offence charged as described in the enactment, albeit not in all the subsections and that "it is sufficient if the other offence is included in the enactment creating it", as was held in this case by the Court of Appeal for British Columbia, following its own decision in *R. v. Brown* (1959), 124 C.C.C. 127.

This is consistent, in my view, with the decision of this court in *R. v. McKenzie*, [1972] S.C.R. 409, [1972] 1 W.W.R. 451, 16 C.R.N.S. 374, 4 C.C.C. (2d) 296, 21 D.L.R. (3d) 215, where it was held that an accused charged with theft without reference to a specific section, in that case s. 276(1), now s. 290(1), could be found guilty of theft committed in the way described in that section.

The appellant further submitted:

...that the effect of the decision of the majority of the Court of Appeal in the present case will be to require an accused charged with robbery simpliciter to seek particulars from the Crown as to the particular method in which the offence is alleged to have been committed. It is submitted that the onus of describing the offence in particulars should rest with the Crown and not the accused.

This seems to me of little relevance if assault is included in a charge of robbery and, as submitted by counsel for the respondent, an accused charged with robbery will at the outset know that he is faced with a charge of robbery and a charge of assault as well as of theft.

To hold otherwise would, in the respondent's submission, cause the inclusion in the indictment of multiple counts of robbery and of the specific actions under one or more of the subsections of s. 302, as the case may be.

Furthermore, it was the respondent's submission that an accused acquitted of robbery would not be able to plead autrefois acquit within the meaning of s. 537 and would be subject to further prosecution on one or more other charges. In this respect however it can be queried whether in the case of an offence punishable on summary conviction all this could be done within the limitation period of six months.

Appeal dismissed.

R. v. R. (G.)
[2005] 2 S.C.R. 371, 198 C.C.C. (3d) 161, 30 C.R. (6th) 201 (S.C.C.)

G.R. was charged with committing the offence of incest against his daughter. His daughter testified to various sexual acts with her father, which started when she was four or five years old, and continued until she was nine. The accused's daughter was uncertain about whether the accused had ever put his penis into her vagina. Expert evidence was also inclusive on this point. A doctor testified that, while there was evidence of penetration, it could not be determined whether the penetration was with a penis, a finger or some other object. G.R. testified and denied the allegations.

The trial judge found that the accused's penis touched the top of his daughter's "vulva." However, the offence of incest requires proof of actual sexual intercourse. Because it could not be proved that actual intercourse occurred, the accused was acquitted of incest, but convicted of attempted incest.

G.R. appealed. In the Quebec Court of Appeal, the Crown conceded that there was insufficient evidence to support a conviction for attempted incest. On this basis, the Court of Appeal allowed the appeal from conviction. The Court refused the Crown's invitation to substitute convictions for the offences of sexual interference and sexual assault, holding that neither were included offences. The appeal was dismissed by a divided Supreme Court.

BINNIE J. (McLachlin C.J. and Major, Fish and Charron JJ., concurring):—

. . .

It is fundamental to a fair trial that an accused knows the charge or charges he or she must meet. The proper focus is on what the Crown alleges, not on what the accused already knows. An accused will often know a good deal more about the circumstances of an offence than the police or Crown will ever know, but it is not enough for the Crown to say to an accused "you know perfectly well what you're guilty of". The basis of our criminal law is that he or she is only called upon to meet the charge put forward by the prosecution. In this case, lack of consent (or the age of the daughter) was not part of the charge put against the respondent.

Defence counsel cannot give informed advice to an accused person about defence preparation, trial strategy or a possible guilty plea unless and until the full range of the client's legal jeopardy can be ascertained. The Crown too must be able to know with clarity after an acquittal what further charges may be laid, if any, without confronting the defence of *autrefois acquit* or *autrefois convict* (ss. 607-610 of the Criminal Code) (see, e.g., *R. v. Plank* (1986), 28 C.C.C. (3d) 386 (Ont. C.A.)). On the view taken by my colleague Abella J., what may be found to be an included offence in this case may not necessarily be so found in different circumstances. "Included offences" on this view will vary with the facts established in the courtroom and the personal knowledge of each accused. In my view, on the contrary, the exigencies of *autrefois acquit* or *autrefois convict* impose a more solid foundation. Legal jeopardy must be readily ascertainable on the face of the formal proceedings. It is not desirable for such purposes to have to ferret around to determine (if it is determinable) the state of personal knowledge of a previously acquitted or convicted accused. Here, for whatever reason, the Crown did not charge the respondent with sexual assault and sexual interference with a person under the age of fourteen years at the same time as it charged him with incest. The Crown now belatedly wishes to avail itself of these alternative and different offences only because of the respondent's acquittal on the incest charge it *did* proceed with.

In my view, the Quebec Court of Appeal was correct to reject the Crown's position. At no time in these proceedings did the Crown allege against the respondent that his daughter did not consent, or was too young to consent, to sexual activity. Such elements are not "included" in the definition of incest in s. 155(1) of the Criminal Code, nor are they described by apt words in the indictment. It is well established that a person can be convicted of incest as a result of a consensual sexual relationship. The Crown thus seeks to have the respondent convicted of charges which require the prosecution to establish elements (non-consent in the case of assault or the age of the victim in the case of sexual interference) which were not part of the allegations against him at trial. The Crown's surmise that it might have obtained a conviction for sexual assault or sexual interference if it had prosecuted those charges in the first place, or if it had framed the incest case differently, cannot now deprive the respondent of his procedural rights.

. . .

II. Analysis

An important function of an indictment is to put the accused on formal notice of his or her potential legal jeopardy. It is equally important, of course, that if the Crown can establish some but not all of the facts described in the indictment or set out in the statutory definition of the offence, and such partial proof satisfies the constituent elements of a lesser and included offence, that the result be not an acquittal but a conviction on the included offence. As Professor Glanville Williams wrote, "an included offence is one that is made out of bits of the offence charged" ("Included Offences" (1991), 55 *J. Crim. L.* 234, at p. 234). Any other outcome would result in a waste of the resources expended on the trial.

The Crown's argument in this appeal triggers the notice issue. An accused is entitled to be *properly apprised* of the charge or charges he or she is required to meet: *R. v. Guérin*, [1996] Q.J. No. 3746 (C.A.), at para. 36. The question is not what the respondent knew or did not know about his daughter's age. It would be remarkable if he *did not* know her age. He may also know of other aspects of the events at issue that could have given rise to additional charges, but the question is what charges did the Crown allege in the indictment. The answer is that the Crown did not allege that the daughter was below the age of consent, and there is nothing in the nature of the offence of incest as described in the Criminal Code or the wording of the indictment to put the respondent on notice that he was in jeopardy of a conviction for sexual assault or sexual interference.

In other words, the same set of facts may give rise to different charges. An accused is entitled to know which amongst those available charges he or she is required to answer. The indictment is a written accusation that fulfills this function. The rules governing which charges are "included" in "the offence charged, as described in the enactment creating it or as charged in the count" are set out in s. 662 of the Criminal Code.

As my colleague notes, the indictment must go further than simply specifying the offence charged. The indictment must "contain sufficient detail of the circumstances of the alleged offence to give to the accused reasonable information with respect to the act or omission to be proved against him and to identify the transaction referred to" (s. 581(3) of the Code). In short, it is not sufficient simply to charge an accused with "incest contrary to s. 155(1) of the Criminal Code". The accused in this case was entitled to know in "sufficient detail" the circumstances or "the transaction" that gave rise to the Crown allegation that he committed incest to enable him to mount a full answer and defence, or to decide to plead guilty. In this case the respondent was fully informed of "the transaction" that gave rise to the charge. That is not, with respect, the problem here.

It is important not to confuse the requirement to specify the charge with the need to provide sufficient supporting detail of the underlying transaction or circumstances. In *Brodie v. The King*, [1936] S.C.R. 188, cited by my colleague, the charge of seditious conspiracy was clearly made in the indictment, but the transaction that gave rise to the charge was not sufficiently identified. The

Court accepted as correct "the apt words of counsel for the appellants: 'it does not describe the offence in such a way as to lift it from the general to the particular'" (p. 198). Since *Brodie*, the courts, encouraged by amendments to the Criminal Code, have taken a broader view of sufficiency and of the exercise of the courts' powers of amendment, but such a relaxation has nothing to do with the fundamental requirement that the accused be able clearly to ascertain from the offence charged (as described in the enactment creating it or as charged in the count or as expressly stated to be an included offence in the Criminal Code itself), the charges for which he or she risks conviction. In the more recent case of *R. v. Douglas*, [1991] 1 S.C.R. 301, for example, there was no question but that the *charge* was specified in the indictment. The question was whether the underlying *transaction* was identified in sufficient detail to permit a full answer and defence. In my view, it is important to keep separate and distinct the different issues of the offence(s) charged and the sufficiency of notice of the underlying circumstances or transaction to which the charge(s) relate. It is on this point, it seems, that my colleague Abella J. and I find ourselves in disagreement.

Turning to the offence charged here, it is well established that an allegation of incest is not directed to assaultive behaviour. Consent is irrelevant to the charge and irrelevant to the defence. On the other hand, the prohibition against sexual assault is very much concerned with consent but not at all concerned with the "forbidden degrees of consanguinity or affinity". Sexual interference is related to the age of the victim; incest is indifferent to the age of the victim (or willing partner). Historically, incest was dealt with by the ecclesiastical courts, sexual assault and sexual interference were prosecuted in the criminal courts (M. Ingram, *Church Courts, Sex and Marriage in England, 1570-1640* (1990), at p. 366). The elements of the offences were and are different.

A. *The Prohibition Against Incest*

Incest may or may not be consensual. Proof of consent makes no difference to the result: *R. v. S. (M.)* (1996), 111 C.C.C. (3d) 467 (B.C. C.A.), leave to appeal refused, [1997] S.C.C.A. No. 26, [1997] 1 S.C.R. ix). In Queens County, Nova Scotia, for example, a mother was charged with incest with her two adult sons, one of whom in turn was charged with sex with his two adult half-sisters, all of it consensual. Nevertheless, convictions were upheld: *R. v. F. (R.P.)* (1996), 105 C.C.C. (3d) 435 (N.S. C.A.). The court rejected the argument that consensual "'recreational' sexual activity with blood relations should be legalized and constitutionally protected" (p. 441) because the prohibition against incest has nothing to do with consent but is directed to preserving the integrity of the family by avoiding the confusion in roles that would result from incestuous sex . . . there is a "heavy physiological penalty imposed by inbreeding", that is, the sharply increased risk of genetic defects in the children born of incestuous relationships. [pp. 443-44]

The prohibition against incest is also associated with "protection of vulnerable family members" (p. 445). Writing for the court, Roscoe J.A. concluded that incest, whether consensual or non-consensual, is unacceptable, incomprehensible and repugnant to the vast majority of people, and has been for centuries in many cultures and countries. [p. 445]

. . .

B. *The Prohibition Against Sexual Assault*

Sexual assault, on the other hand, is very much concerned with consent. Its purpose is to protect the "personal integrity, both physical and psychological, of every individual": *R. v. Ewanchuk*, [1999] 1 S.C.R. 330, at para. 28. "The inclusion of assault and sexual assault in the *Code*", Major J. continued, "expresses society's determination to protect the security of the person from any <u>non-consensual</u> contact or threats of force" (emphasis added). See also *R. v. Bernier* (1997), 119 C.C.C. (3d) 467 (Que. C.A.), *per* Deschamps. J.A., at p. 474:

> [TRANSLATION] In fact, the assault component in a sexual assault comes rather from the lack of consent on the part of the victim in relation to the touching....
> (aff'd [1998] 1 S.C.R. 975)

C. *The Prohibition Against Sexual Interference*

A critical element of this offence is that the victim be under the age of fourteen years. Unless that fact is proven there can be no conviction: *R. v. Hess*, [1990] 2 S.C.R. 906. By contrast, proof of incest does not require an underage victim.

D. *Effect of the Respondent's Acquittal on the Charge of Incest*

Conviction for incest requires proof beyond a reasonable doubt that "sexual intercourse" occurred (s. 155(1) of the Code). The respondent was acquitted of the only charge brought against him. In light of that acquittal, he can only be convicted of sexual assault or sexual interference as "included offences" if the Crown is able to bring the case within the terms of s. 662 of the Criminal Code.

E. *The Law Governing "Included" Offences*

An offence is "included" if its elements are embraced in the offence charged (as described in the enactment creating it or as charged in the count) or if it is expressly stated to be an included offence in the Criminal Code itself. The test is strict. It must "necessarily" be included, *per* Martland J. in *Lafrance v. The Queen*, [1975] 2 S.C.R. 201, at pp. 213-14:

> . . . the offence created by s. 281 [joy-riding] is not *necessarily included* in the charge of theft . . . and it is not included in the count as charged in the present case. [Emphasis added.]

What is not "necessarily included" is excluded. . . .

The strict interpretation of s. 662 is linked to the requirement of fair notice of legal jeopardy, as emphasized by Sheppard J.A. in *R. v. Manuel* (1960), 128 C.C.C. 383 (B.C. C.A.):

> Further, to be an included offence the inclusion must form such an <u>apparent and essential constituent of the offence charged</u> that the accused in reading the offence charged will be <u>fairly informed in every instance that he will have to meet not only</u>

the offence charged but also the specific offences to be included. Such apparent inclusion must appear from "the enactment creating" the offence or "from the offence as charged in the count"; either of those two may be considered under [s. 662(1)] but not the opening by counsel or the evidence. [Emphasis added; p. 385.]

Martin J.A. of the Ontario Court of Appeal also insisted on making clear to an accused the precise extent of his or her legal jeopardy:

The offence charged as described either in the enactment creating the offence, or as charged in the count, must contain the essential elements of the offence said to be included.

. . .

. . . the offence charged, as described either in the enactment creating the offence or as charged in the count, must be sufficient to inform the accused of the included offences which he must meet. [Emphasis added.]

(*R. v. Simpson (No. 2)* (1981), 58 C.C.C. (2d) 122 (Ont. C.A.), at p. 133 (leave to appeal refused, [1981] 1 S.C.R. xiii); see also *R. v. Harmer and Miller* (1976), 33 C.C.C. (2d) 17 (Ont. C.A.), at p. 19). The principles set out in Martin J.A.'s encyclopaedic reasons for judgment in *Simpson* have since been adopted and applied across Canada. . .

At common law, where an offence consisted of several ingredients ("divisible") the jury could convict of any offence "the elements of which were included in the offence charged, subject to the rule that on an indictment for felony the jury could not convict of a misdemeanour" (*Simpson*, at p. 132). The subject is now governed by statute, and s. 662 authorizes convictions for "included" offences in only three categories:

(a) offences included by statute, e.g. those offences specified in s. 662(2) to (6), and attempts provided for in s. 660;

(b) offences included in the enactment creating the offence charged, e.g. common assault in a charge of sexual assault;

(c) offences which become included by the addition of apt words of description to the principal charge.

In none of these categories is there reference to the "sufficiency" of the factual particulars of the transaction underlying the charge. That is a wholly different subject and is dealt with in s. 581 of the Code.

In terms of the need for fair notice, "included" offences in the first category can be ascertained from the Criminal Code itself: see, e.g., *R. v. Wilmot*, [1941] S.C.R. 53. Cases in the second category also meet the test of fair notice because "an indictment charging an offence also charges all offences which as a matter of law are necessarily committed in the commission of the principal offence as described in the enactment creating it" (*Harmer and Miller*, at p. 19; emphasis added)....

With respect to the second category, it may be said that "[i]f the whole offence charged can be committed without committing another offence, that other offence is *not* included" (P. J. Gloin, "Included Offences" (1961-62), 4 *Crim. L.Q.* 160, at p. 160; emphasis added). This proposition was endorsed by the Manitoba Court of Appeal in *R. v. Carey* (1973), 10 C.C.C. (2d) 330, at p.

334, *per* Freedman C.J.M.; by the Ontario Court of Appeal in *Simpson*, at p. 139, *per* Martin J.A., and by the Quebec Court of Appeal in *Colburne*, at p. 243, to which Proulx J.A. added:

> [TRANSLATION] For my part, I would add that an offence would be included where the essential elements of this offence are *part* of the offence charged. [Emphasis in original.]

Clearly the offence of incest can be committed without committing sexual assault or sexual interference.

It is the third category of cases that is more likely to cause difficulty. What is required are words of description in the count itself of facts which put an accused on notice that, if proven, such facts taken together with the elements of the charge, disclose the commission of an "included" offence: *Allard*. For example, in *Tousignant v. The Queen* (1960), 130 C.C.C. 285 (Que. Q.B. (App. Side)), the indictment charged the accused with attempting to murder the victim *"by hitting him on the head with a blunt instrument"* (p. 291; emphasis added). The italicized words were not essential to the charge of an attempt to murder, but their inclusion in any event permitted conviction on the lesser and (thereby) included offence of causing bodily harm with intent to wound, or assault: see *Simpson*, at p. 139. Similarly in *R. v. Kay*, [1958] O.J. No. 467 (C.A.), the indictment charged manslaughter "by a blow or blows". The addition of these words of description to the indictment disclosed the allegation of an assault, and a conviction of the accused of the included offence of assault causing bodily harm was upheld on appellate review.

. . .

The question in this case is whether the Crown can bring sexual assault and/ or sexual interference within any of the three categories of included offences.

F.   *Application of the Law to the Facts*

In my view, it cannot be said that the respondent in this case was fairly notified that in meeting the charge of incest he was also required to defend against sexual assault or sexual interference as "included" offences. I would apply to this case what was said by Phillimore L.J. in *R. v. Woods*, [1969] 1 Q.B. 447 (C.A.), at p. 451:

> It is of the first importance that a man charged with an offence should know with certainty what it is he may be convicted of. No court should be encouraged to cast around to see whether somehow or other the words of the indictment can be found to contain by some arguable implication the seeds of some other offence.

The fact of the matter is that the Crown *could* have charged the respondent with sexual assault and sexual interference but in the exercise of its prosecutorial discretion refrained from doing so. On the facts of this case, the rules governing "included" offences do not provide a remedy for this omission.

As to the first category, there is nothing in the Criminal Code that explicitly makes sexual assault or sexual interference an offence included in incest.

As to the second category, it cannot be said that incest as "described in the enactment creating it" includes sexual assault or sexual interference. As discussed earlier, incest can be committed without any assault whatsoever. Consent is no defence: *S. (M.)*, *F. (R.P.)*. Nor must the victim be under fourteen years of age. The five accused persons in *F. (R.P.)* were all adults. The age of the complainant constitutes merely a factual circumstance which is irrelevant to whether or not the offence of incest is committed.

As to the third category, it cannot be said that the wording of the count charging the respondent with incest described a sexual assault, or indeed gave any information from which an issue of non-consent could fairly be inferred, or suggested that the victim was underage and therefore was incapable of consenting. It is true, of course, that an allegation of incest includes the allegation of a physical act which, if done without consent, would be an assault. However, if the Crown wished to dispense with proof of non-consent by relying on s. 150.1(1), it was incumbent upon it to allege the factual condition precedent to the operation of s. 150.1(1), namely the fact that the victim was under fourteen years old. This was not done. The age of the victim would be for the Crown to prove, not for the defence to disprove. . ..

The Crown says the evidence subsequently led in the case shows that commission of incest in this case would necessarily have involved the commission of sexual interference and a sexual assault due to the age of the daughter, and that the age of the daughter must have been within the knowledge of the respondent, but there is nothing in s. 662 that permits the Crown to supplement the allegations in the charge, or the elements of the enactment creating the offence, by reference to the personal knowledge of an accused.

The corollary, to what I have said above however, is that acquittal on the charge of incest would not provide the respondent in these circumstances with a defence of *autrefois acquit* to a charge of sexual assault or sexual interference. The rule against double jeopardy requires that the accused at the earlier trial have been in jeopardy of conviction of the subsequent charge: *Cullen v. The King*, [1949] S.C.R. 658, at p. 668; *R. v. Rinnie*, [1970] 3 C.C.C. 218 (Alta. C.A.). The respondent here was in no such jeopardy.

Whether or not the Crown chooses to proceed with other charges against the respondent is for the Crown to decide.

III. *Disposition*

I would dismiss the appeal.

ABELLA J. (Bastarache, LeBel and Deschamps JJ., concurring) (dissenting):—I have had the benefit of reading the reasons of Justice Binnie. With respect, I do not agree with his conclusion that sexual assault is not included in the offence of incest as charged in this case.

The charge of incest put the father, G. R., on notice that the Crown would seek to prove that he had committed an act of sexual intercourse with his daughter during a specified period of time. At the relevant times, his daughter was between five and nine years of age. The issue therefore is whether he could have committed incest without committing sexual assault. Demonstrably, he could not.

The father acknowledged, not surprisingly, that he knew that his daughter was under the age of fourteen at the relevant times. It follows that the indictment provided him with sufficient information to enable him to make full answer and defence to offences arising out of, and included in, the alleged acts of sexual intercourse with his daughter during the time frame specified.

. . .

II.   *Analysis*

The issue before this Court is whether the Court of Appeal ought to have rejected the Crown's submission that sexual assault and sexual interference were included offences in the offence of incest in this case.

. . .

The fundamental principle underlying included offences is that an accused is entitled to know from the indictment or information the offence or offences with which he or she is charged so that there will be no prejudice to the defence. For the majority, the principal issue is one of notice. As Binnie J. points out in his reasons, the accused must be given reasonable notice of the offence or the offences alleged to be included in the principal offence charged. Binnie J. concludes that in the present case "the Crown did not allege that the daughter was below the age of consent, and there [was] nothing in the nature of the offence of incest as described in the *Criminal Code* or the wording of the indictment to put the respondent on notice that he was in jeopardy of a conviction for sexual assault or sexual interference" (para. 12).

Unlike my colleague, I am of the view that the father had reasonable notice. This is based on the premise that the requirement of reasonable notice is satisfied if the following can be shown: the accused could not have committed the offence charged without committing the purported included offence, and the accused knows what offences he or she must be prepared to meet. The test is not a hypothetical one. The question is whether this particular accused had a full opportunity to know and meet the case against him.

. . .

Where it is argued that an offence is included in the charge by reason of the words used, the issue becomes one of the sufficiency of information in the indictment. Words in that indictment sufficient to identify a particular criminal transaction may also serve to identify any included offences (see, e.g., *Tousignant v. The Queen* (1960), 130 C.C.C. 285 (Que. Q.B. (App. side)); *R. v. Manuel* (1960), 128 C.C.C. 383 (B.C. C.A.); *Simpson (No. 2)*.

. . .

As with included offences, the fundamental principle which governs the interpretation of the information or indictment is that the accused must be provided with enough information to make full answer and defence. At common law, and particularly by the beginning of the 19th century, the indictment had become a highly technical document. Strictly proper language was required when framing the charges against an accused and all the facts and circumstances of the offence, including the intent, were required to be set out in the indictment in great detail and with meticulous certainty. . .

. . .

The question then is whether the father's ability to make full answer and defence to a charge of sexual assault, based on the information in the indictment and his own knowledge, has been compromised. In *R. v. Ewanchuk*, [1999] 1 S.C.R. 330, this Court considered the elements of sexual assault. Writing for the majority, Major J. held that sexual assault is a crime of general intent. In order to satisfy the basic *mensrea* requirement, the Crown need only prove that the accused intended to touch the complainant in a sexual manner. The *actus reus* of sexual assault is established by proof of three elements: (i) touching, (ii) the sexual nature of the contact, and (iii) the absence of consent. As with incest, however, s. 150.1 of the Code provides that the consent of the complainant is no defence to a charge of sexual assault where the complainant is under fourteen years of age.

The trial judge found that he had evidence of sexual assault by the accused and evidence that the complainant was under the age of fourteen. These findings were not contested. This father could not have committed the crime of incest, namely having sexual intercourse with his young daughter commencing when she was five years old, without also committing the included crime of sexual assault. By specifying the complainant, the time frame, and the act, the father was put on sufficient notice of the age of the child and provided with enough information to make full answer and defence to the included charge of sexual assault.

No one disputes that the victim was under the age of fourteen during the specified time frame, nor do they dispute that the accused knew that his daughter was under the age of fourteen at that time. The acts put in evidence to establish incest and attempted incest on the one hand and sexual assault on the other were the same.

There was, moreover, no impact on the defence in this case. The father did not raise the issue of consent. His defence was to deny any touching of his daughter in a sexual manner. His defence was based not on lack of penetration, but on the absence of sexual touching. He was therefore in no way prejudiced in his defence by the failure of the indictment to refer to his daughter's age, since her age was, aside from being a fact within his knowledge since her birth, and sufficiently particularized by the designation of the time frame in the indictment, entirely irrelevant to his defence.

III. *Conclusion*

Pursuant to s. 686(4)*(b)*(ii) of the Code, I would allow the appeal and enter a verdict of guilty with respect to the included offence of sexual assault. In view of my conclusion that sexual assault is an included offence, I see no practical purpose in examining whether sexual interference is similarly included.

R. v. MORTON
(1975), 37 C.R.N.S. 42, 29 C.C.C. (2d) 518 (N.S. C.A.)

The Court reviewed the conflicting case law as to whether the offence of having care and control of a motor vehicle while impaired is necessarily included in the offence of impaired driving; both offences falling under s. 234. In adopting the view that it was, the Court pointed out that the Code does not specify that an included offence must necessarily be of lesser gravity in terms of penalty.

MACDONALD J.A.:—With deference to those authorities to the contrary and as stated earlier, I am of the opinion that an included offence need not be a lesser one in the sense of gravity although admittedly they practically always are. Nowhere in the *Criminal Code* is it stated that included offences cannot be of equal severity or gravity to the offences within which they are included. Thus in determining whether offence A is included in offence B it matters not, in my opinion, whether offence A is as grave or serious as offence B. All that matters is whether in order to commit offence B is it necessary to commit offence A. If it is then A is included in B, or as said in *Maika* it is a "necessary step" in offence B. Putting it another way, it is the ingredients of an offence not its gravity that determine whether or not it is included in another offence.

[He furthermore upheld the view that, although s. 589 [now s. 662] appears in the part of the Code dealing only with proceedings on indictment, it is declaratory of fundamental law and applies also in the case of summary conviction proceedings.]

. . .

The question whether s. 589 applies to summary conviction offences was considered by Campbell, C.J., of the Supreme Court of Prince Edward Island in *R. v. Connolly*, [1970] 2 C.C.C. 144 at pp. 147-9, 6 C.R.N.S. 239, he said:

> The question which really gives me considerable difficulty is whether the "included offence" rule is a basic doctrine which extends to summary conviction proceedings, or whether it is purely a statutory provision of the *Cr. Code*, Part XVII, s. 569, and is limited in its operation to procedure by indictment.

> In the case of *R. v. Louie Yee*, 51 C.C.C. 405, [1929] 2 D.L.R. 452, 24 Alta. L.R. 16, Harvey C.J.A., speaking for a five-man Appellate Division, said at p. 406:
> ". . . s. 951 is contained in Part XIX which as the caption states relates to 'Procedure by Indictment,' and, therefore, is not applicable to the case of a summary conviction."

> That was a case stated by the Crown, when a Magistrate had convicted Yee of smoking opium on an information charging possession of the drug. The Court of Appeal remitted the case to the Magistrate to convict and sentence the respondent of the offence originally charged, which had been amply proven, and Harvey, C.J.A., remarked that "smoking" is not included in "having in possession" because "certainly one can have in possession without smoking".

> The issue of the availability of the then s. 951 in summary conviction proceedings did not, therefore, directly arise, and the opinion of the appellate Court on that point is in the borderland of *obiter dictum*. I should, however, accord at least very

persuasive authority to that pronouncement if it had been made under the present *Criminal Code.*

The general effect of Part XXIV of the present *Criminal Code,* 1953-54, as compared with that of its counterpart, XV, of the former *Criminal Code,* 1927, seems to be to approximate the law of summary conviction proceedings much more closely to that of procedure by indictment. I may refer particularly to the content of an information, which under the former *Code* was strictly and technically confined to "one offence only, and not for two or more offences", s. 710 [am. 1960-61, c. 43, s. 42]. Under the present *Code,* the information is less technically constituted. By s. 696(1)(*b*) the information

"(*b*) may charge more than one offence or relate to more than one matter of complaint, but where more than one offence is charged or the information relates to more than one matter of complaint, each offence or matter of complaint, as the case may be, shall be set out in a separate count."

This new provision brings the content of an information under Part XXIV substantially in line with that of an indictment under ss. 492 *et seq.* of Part XVII. Consequently, an information for an offence or group of offences punishable alternatively by indictment or on summary conviction may now be laid in the same form, whichever of the two methods of prosecution is intended.

It is true that s. 596 refers specifically to procedure by indictment, and is not explicitly imported in to the structure of Part XXIV; but the same is true of a great many provisions of Part XVII, which is declaratory principles of law equally applicable to summary conviction proceedings. I may instance the provisions of Part XVII respecting contents of counts, to which I have referred; amendment, division, joinder, or severance of counts; amendment in general; the right of an accused to inspect documents and receive copies; pleas of *autrefois acquit, autrefois convict,* or pardon, and the evidence relative to such pleas; the effect of a plea of not guilty; etc.

It seems to me that s. 569 is such a declaratory statement of fundamental law.

In *R. v. Hollingberry et al.* (1825), 4 B. & C. 329, 107 E.R. 1081, the Court of Queen's Bench held (*per* Curiam) [at p. 1082]:

"In criminal cases it is sufficient for the prosecutor to prove so much of the charge as constitutes an offence punishable by law. This was an indictment for conspiring falsely to indict a person for the purpose of extorting money. The jury found the defendants guilty of conspiring to prefer an indictment for the purpose of extorting money, and that is a misdemeanor, whether the charge be or be not false."

That judgment appears to have been based on a recognized principle of criminal law, and not on any statutory enactment.

I therefore find that s. 569 is declaratory of a fundamental doctrine of law and that (as obviously assumed by the Ontario Court of Appeal, and by Hall, C.J.Q.B., in the *Fischer* and *Phillips* cases respectively) its provisions are applicable by analogy to proceedings under Part XXIV of the present *Criminal Code.* The obvious advantage is to relieve the necessity of repeating, in separate counts, matters of complaint or offences which are not substantially separate from, but are completely included in, the allegations of the main charge or charges.

In *Rickard v. The Queen* (1970), 1 C.C.C. (2d) 153, [1970] S.C.R. 1022, 12 C.R.N.S. 172, the Supreme Court of Canada held that s. 569(4) (now s. 589(5)) of the *Criminal Code* although appearing in Part XVII of the *Criminal Code* which is headed "Procedure by Indictment" applied as well to summary conviction offences. Fauteux, J. (Judson, J., concurring), dissented on other grounds but said with respect to the argument that s. 569(4) of the *Criminal Code* was not applicable to summary conviction proceedings (p. 158 C.C.C., p. 183 C.R.N.S.):

> In *R. v. Connolly, supra*, a similar argument was made by the appellant but was rejected by Chief Justice Campbell who concluded that the provisions of s. 569(4) amount to a declaratory statement of fundamental law. With this conclusion, I am in respectful agreement.

The opinion of Campbell, C.J., on this point as set out in *R. v. Connolly, supra*, was expressly adopted by the Appellate Division of the Alberta Supreme Court in *R. v. Handy* (1971), 3 C.C.C. (2d) 298, 15 C.R.N.S. 300, [1971] 4 W.W.R. 289.

Subsequently, the Supreme Court of Canada held in similar fashion that care and control over 80 is a "lesser included offence" to driving while over 80: *R. v. Drolet*, [1990] 2 S.C.R. 1107, 26 M.V.R. (2d) 169 (S.C.C.).

In *R. v. Haughton*, [1994] 3 S.C.R. 516, 34 C.R. (4th) 22, 93 C.C.C. (3d) 99 (S.C.C.) the Supreme Court held that where an included offence is not left with a jury, a conviction by the jury of the more serious offence cannot generally be relied upon as it may be a reaction against a complete acquittal.

PROBLEM 1

Does a charge of attempted murder contrary to s. 239 of the Code, which does not specify the means, include the offences of causing bodily harm with intent to wound, assault causing bodily harm or unlawfully causing bodily harm? Is the offence of unlawfully attempting to cause bodily harm included? Compare *Simpson v. R.* (1981), 20 C.R. (3d) 36 (Ont. C.A.).

PROBLEM 2

Is the offence of using a firearm in a careless manner or without reasonable precautions for the safety of other persons contrary to s. 86(2) of the Code an included offence in a charge of criminal negligence causing death by pointing and discharging a firearm without lawful excuse contrary to s. 220 of the Code? Compare *R. v. Morehouse* (1982), 65 C.C.C. (2d) 231 (N.B. C.A.).

PROBLEM 3

Is the offence of possession of marijuana included in a charge of unlawfully cultivating marijuana? Compare *R. v. Powell* (1983), 36 C.R. (3d) 396 (B.C. C.A.).

PROBLEM 4

Is the offence of assault causing bodily harm included in a charge of "robbery"? Compare *R. v. Horsefall* (1990), 61 C.C.C. (3d) 245 (B.C. C.A.).

2. Res Judicata

(a) General

A res judicata is a final decision pronounced by a judicial tribunal having competent jurisdiction over the matter in dispute and over the parties thereto. It has long been a doctrine of Anglo-Canadian jurisprudence that the same ought not to be impeached. The justifications usually advanced for the doctrine are grounded in principles of public policy and private justice: the societal interest in a speedy and final conclusion of disputes in order to avoid undue expense and to maintain respect for the judicial system, and the right of the individual to be preserved from a vexatious series of prosecutions, instituted by one of greater position and resources, which could eventually wear down the individual's resistance. In the criminal law, the individual actually needs protection from two evils. First, the harassment of multiple trials for a single anti-social course of conduct, and second, the infliction of multiple punishment for the same matter. The first protection is often expressed in the Latin maxim "nemo debet bis vexari pro una et eadem causa" and the latter as "nemo debet bis puniri pro una delicto". The United States Supreme Court expressed themselves:

> The underlying idea, one that is deeply ingrained in at least the Anglo-American system of jurisprudence, is that the State with all its resources and power should not be allowed to make repeated attempts to convict an individual for an alleged offence, thereby subjecting him to embarrassment, expense and ordeal and compelling him to live in a continuing state of anxiety and insecurity, as well as enhancing the possibility that even though innocent he may be found guilty.
>
> *Green v. U.S.* (1957), 355 U.S. 184, 187.

The doctrine of res judicata operates, in both civil and criminal law, in two distinct ways. In the first instance a final judgment is said to subsume and extinguish the cause of action or offence on which it was based, leaving nothing available to a plaintiff or prosecutor for later prosecution; if the party is successful in his suit his cause of action is said to have *merged* in his judgment, and if unsuccessful he is spoken of as being *barred* from later pursuit thereof. This aspect of res judicata then prevents a second trial of the same cause of action or offence. In the criminal context this aspect is commonly referred to as double jeopardy. The second area of operation for the doctrine occurs when the second trial is of a different cause of action or offence than that first tried, and it then acts to estop any party thereto from disputing the correctness of any issue which can be shown to have been previously litigated and determined. This is usually referred to as issue estoppel.

The principle of double jeopardy is embodied in Canada in the special pleas described in the Criminal Code:

607. (1) An accused may plead the special pleas of

  (a) *autrefois acquit*,

  (b) *autrefois convict*, and

  (c) pardon.

(2) An accused who is charged with defamatory libel may plead in accordance with sections 611 and 612.

(3) The pleas of *autrefois acquit*, *autrefois convict* and pardon shall be disposed of by the judge without a jury before the accused is called to plead further.

(4) When the pleas referred to in subsection (3) are disposed of against the accused, he may plead guilty or not guilty.

(5) Where an accused pleads *autrefois acquit* or *autrefois convict*, it is sufficient if he

  (a) states that he has been lawfully acquitted, convicted or discharged under subsection 730(1), as the case may be, of the offence charged in the count to which the plea relates; and

  (b) indicates the time and place of the acquittal, conviction or discharge under subsection 730(1).

(6) A person who is alleged to have committed an act or omission outside Canada that is an offence in Canada by virtue of any of subsections 7(2) to (3.1) or(3.7), or an offence under the *Crimes Against Humanity and War Crimes Act*, and in respect of which the person has been tried and convicted outside Canada, may not plead *autrefois convict* with respect to a count that charges that offence if

  (a) at the trial outside Canada the person was not present and was not represented by counsel acting under the person's instructions, and

  (b) the person was not punished in accordance with the sentence imposed on conviction in respect of the act or omission,

notwithstanding that the person is deemed by virtue of subsection 7(6), or subsection 12(1) of the *Crimes Against Humanity and War Crimes Act*, as the case may be, to have been tried and convicted in Canada in respect of the act or omission.

and in s. 11(*h*) of the Charter of Rights:

Any person charged with an offence has . . . the right, if finally acquitted of the offence, not to be tried for it again and, if finally found guilty and punished for the offence, not to be tried and punished for it again.

The principle of issue estoppel is found in the common law. Affecting this concept is the doctrine of privity and the doctrine of mutuality. As Lord Denning described it [*McIlkenny v. Chief Constable of West Midlands*, [1980] 2 All E.R. 227 at 235]:

The doctrine of *privity* says that the only persons who can take advantage of the estoppel or be bound by it are the two parties to the proceedings themselves or their privies. . . . The doctrine of *mutuality* says that, in order that there should be an estoppel, it must be such that both of the two parties and their privies must be bound by the estoppel, whichever way it goes.

In *McIlKenny*, Lord Denning notes the abundance of criticism directed over the years against the doctrine of mutuality and praises the American rejection of same. He describes the U.S. position [2 All E.R. 227 at 235]:

> They take a distinction between a decision in favour of a man and a decision against him. If a decision has been given against a man on the identical issue arising in previous proceedings and he had a full and fair opportunity of defending himself in it, then he is estopped from contesting it again in the subsequent proceedings. Not only is he estopped but so are those in privity with him. But there is no corresponding estoppel on the person in whose favour it operates.

Lastly affecting the principle is the doctrine of finality. Finality, according to Lord Denning, should be approached in the following way [2 All E.R. 227 at 238]:

> . . . when an issue has been decided by a competent court *against* a party in an earlier proceeding, it should only be regarded as final if he has had a full and fair opportunity of defending himself therein and the circumstances are such that it would not be fair or just to allow him to re-open it in subsequent proceedings.

It may be that the principle of issue estoppel and the rule against multiple punishment are both constitutionally protected as well. In a dissenting opinion in *Travers v. R.* (1984), 64 N.S.R. (2d) 113, 41 C.R. (3d) 339 (N.S. C.A.), Jones J.A. wrote:

> . . . the plea of res judicata is a principle of fundamental justice. I cannot accept that the framers of the Charter intended to include the pleas of autrefois and at the same time exclude the principles of res judicata or issue estoppel. Assuming that the principle is not included in s. 11(*h*), then, in my view, it clearly falls within s. 7 of the Charter. I agree . . . that s. 7 of the Charter is not restricted simply to procedural matters. Parliament can no longer override the principle and provide for multiple convictions for the same delict. [41 C.R. (3d) 339 at 345].

Unfortunately, the Supreme Court of Canada has not provided thorough guidance on whether ss. 7 or 11(h) provide constitutional protection for either *res judicata* or issue estoppel. In *R. v. Wigglesworth*, [1987] 2 S.C.R. 541, 37 C.C.C. (3d) 385, 60 C.R. (3d) 193 (S.C.C.), the Court appeared to suggest that *res judicata* is covered by s. 11(h) although the Court did not accept the defence argument on its applicability in that case. Later, however, in *Corp. professionnelle des médecins (Québec) v. Thibault*, [1988] 1 S.C.R. 1033, 42 C.C.C. (3d) 1 (*sub nom. Thibault v. Corp. professionnelle des médecins (Qué.)*), 63 C.R. (3d) 273 (S.C.C.) at 292, the Court appeared to suggest that only the *autrefois* pleas are covered by s. 11(h). Moreover, the majority of the Court in *R. v. Mahalingan*, [2008] 3 S.C.R. 316, 237 C.C.C. (3d) 417, 61 C.R. (6th) 207 (S.C.C.), in the course of retaining the doctrine of issue estoppel, did not comment on whether these concepts have constitutional protection.

To determine the amount of protection from multiple trials and multiple punishment it is necessary to examine the court's usage of *both* branches of the res judicata doctrine. Our first concern will be double jeopardy and its limitations.

(b) Double Jeopardy

Two preliminary points: Are the special pleas noted above available in summary conviction proceedings? For the accused to have been vexed, must there be a trial on the merits in the first proceeding? Both matters were considered in the following case.

R. v. RIDDLE
[1980] 1 S.C.R. 380, 48 C.C.C. (2d) 365 (S.C.C.)

DICKSON, J.:—Two questions of considerable practical importance emerge in this appeal: Can an accused raise the special plea of *autrefois acquit* in a summary conviction Court? If so, is the plea available when in the earlier proceeding the charge is dismissed following non-appearance of the informant and refusal of an adjournment? Judicial authority and textbook opinion have been divided on both issues. Thus far, the respondent Riddle has succeeded in three Courts in Alberta.

Judicial history

Riddle was charged with common assault. He pleaded not guilty and the matter was adjourned for trial. On the appointed date, a provincial Judge endorsed the information: "Accused here. I prefer not to hear this case. Trial October 22/75 at 10:00 a.m. by consent."

On October 22nd, Riddle appeared with his counsel, and the proceedings were as follows:

MR. DUNCAN; (appearing for the Crown)	Sir, this matter is set for trial this morning. I believe the Crown witness is here on this. Is Mr. DeBruin in the courtroom? Mr. Cairn? Is Mr. DeBruin here today? Sir, it appears that the informant, the complainant in this case is not present. The Crown would make an application for an adjournment at this time.
THE COURT:	What is the position of the Defence?
MR. DAINES: (appearing for the accused)	Your Honour, we are here and prepared to proceed. We were prepared to proceed on the last occasion when this was set down for trial and at that time the case wasn't reached before Judge Harvie. There were too many cases on. I wish to state I think it should be dismissed at this point because we are prepared to proceed.
THE COURT:	Is there any explanation why the witness is not present?
MR. DUNCAN:	No information at all, sir, why he is not here.
THE COURT:	I would not grant an adjournment. I would ask the Crown to call evidence. Is the Crown in a position to do so?
MR. DUNCAN:	No, sir, the Crown is calling no evidence.

THE COURT: I would dismiss the charge and discharge the accused.

MR. DAINES: Thank you, your honour.

A week later, the complainant swore a new information in terms identical to the first information. When the matter came on before another Provincial Court Judge, Riddle entered a plea of *autrefois acquit* and the charge was dismissed. A Crown appeal by stated case was heard by Laycraft, J., who in a carefully considered judgment held that the plea was available in respect of a summary conviction offence and that it was applicable in the present case. The Crown took a further, unsuccessful appeal to the Appellate Division of the Supreme Court of Alberta [36 C.C.C. (2d) 391, [1977] 5 W.W.R. 58] and finally sought leave to appeal to this Court. Leave was granted on the following grounds:

1. That the Appellate Division of the Supreme Court of Alberta erred in law in holding that an order of dismissal issued pursuant to Section 743 of the *Criminal Code* does not supplant the common law right to raise the special plea of *autrefois acquit* in a summary conviction court.

2. That the Appellate Division of the Supreme Court of Alberta erred in law in holding that the Information was dealt with on the merits.

The plea of autrefois acquit at common law

One of the fundamental rules of the criminal law is expressed in the maxim, *nemo debet bis vexari pro una et eadem causa,* no person shall be placed in jeopardy twice for the same matter. By the special plea of *autrefois acquit,* founded upon that maxim, the accused says simply that he has been previously acquitted of the offence with which he is now charged; that offence is *res judicata, i.e.,* it has passed into a matter adjudged. A second prosecution is, therefore, not open. In the case at bar, the respondent says that the assault alleged in the first information has become converted into *res judicata* or judgment.

The classic statement of the principle is found in Hawkins' *Pleas of the Crown* (1726), vol. II, c. 35, p. 368:

That a Man shall not be brought into Danger of his Life for one and the same Offence, more than once. From whence it is generally taken, by all the Books, as an undoubted Consequence, that where a Man is once found *Not guilty* on an Indictment or Appeal free from Error, and well commenced before any Court which hath Jurisdiction of the Cause, he may by the Common Law in all Cases whatsoever plead such Acquittal in Bar of any subsequent Indictment or Appeal for the same Crime.

[Emphasis added.] In short, when a criminal charge has been once adjudicated by a Court having jurisdiction, the adjudication is final and will be an answer to a later information founded on the same ground of complaint.

. . .

With respect, it would seem that those finding *autrefois acquit* not available in summary conviction cases at common law give to that term its narrow and specialized meaning. Professor Friedland in his book, *Double Jeopardy* (1969), describes the special pleas at pp. 113-4, noting the need for a formal record of the former judgment, carefully engrossed on parchment. Supported by the older case of *Wemyss v. Hopkins* (1875), L.R. 10 Q.B. 378, and the more recent case of *Flatman v. Light et al.*, [1946] 1 K.B. 414 (C.C.A.), Friedland continues:

> The special pleas are not strictly appropriate for cases tried by courts of summary jurisdiction, but the same result is reached by giving effect to the maxim *Nemo debet bis vexari pro una et eadem causa.*

A technical approach was rejected by Lord Goddard in *Flatman* and such a narrow approach was dismissed by Blackburn, J., in *Wemyss* in these words (p. 381):

> I think the fact that the jurisdiction of the justices is created by statute makes no difference. Where the conviction is by a Court of competent jurisdiction, it matters not whether the conviction is by a summary proceeding before justices or by trial before a jury.

Further down the same page, Blackburn, J., makes reference to the availability of a certificate "freeing [a person] from further proceedings, civil or criminal, for the same cause", which goes further than the common law, but states explicitly that "in this case we must rely upon the common law" and this is in relation to a summary conviction matter.

In his perceptive article, "Res Judicata in the Criminal Law", 3 Mel. U. L. Rev. 101 (1961), Professor Howard states at p. 112:

> At the present day the distinction between the courts of summary jurisdiction and superior courts occasions no difficulty. Although it is pedantically true that an *autrefois* plea can be made only to an indictment, there never has been any real doubt that an equivalent objection can be set up in summary proceedings.

. . .

The formal status of the plea of *autrefois acquit* and the pleading and procedural technicalities of an earlier day should not stand in the way of an accused raising as a defence the fact that he has been previously acquitted of the offence with which he now stands charged. The proper procedure in summary conviction matters is not to raise the special plea of *autrefois acquit,* but simply to enter a general plea of not guilty embracing the concept of *res judicata.* Technically, such a general plea is not one of *autrefois acquit* but, as Lord Goddard was moved to say in *Flatman v. Light, supra,* at p. 419, ". . . that does not matter". The Court gives effect to the broad maxim, *nemo debet bis vexari pro una et eadem causa.* The charge has been dismissed by a Court of competent jurisdiction and the accused shall not be charged again with the same matter.

Criminal Code provisions

The foregoing discussion has been concerned with the plea of *autrefois acquit* at common law. What concerns the Court in large measure in this appeal, however, are special statutory provisions found in the *Criminal Code* and their effect. I turn then to the *Code.*

The first reference should be to ss. 534 to 537 [now ss. 606 to 605] inclusive, coupled with s. 502 [now s. 572]. Section 535(1) provides specifically that an accused may plead the special plea of (a) *autrefois acquit*, (b) *autrefois convict*, and (c) pardon. The *Code* provides further that the pleas shall be disposed of by the Judge without a jury before the accused is called upon to plead further. Sections 534 to 537 are found in Part XVII of the *Code*, headed "Procedure by Indictment", and this has given rise to the argument that the special pleas are not available in respect of summary conviction offences, provision for which is contained in Part XXIV of the *Code*.

I do not think this submission can prevail. Something akin to the pleas of *autrefois acquit* was available at common law to a defendant accused of an offence punishable by summary conviction. That being so, it would take language other than that found in ss. 534 to 537 to manifest an intent on the part of Parliament to take away such defence. The *Code* does not contain all the criminal law and Part XXIV does not contain all of the law relating to summary convictions. No authority is needed for the proposition that common law rights are not to be held to be taken away or affected by statute unless such an intent is made manifest by clear language or necessary implication. In the absence of irreconcilable conflict, full effect should be given to both common law and statute. Section 7(3) of the *Code* expressly continues in force every rule and principle of the common law that renders any circumstance a defence to a charge, except in so far as altered by, or inconsistent with, the *Code* or any other act of Parliament. Thus, while the special plea of *autrefois acquit* is not mentioned in the summary conviction provisions of the *Code*, one would have to take an unduly technical and narrow interpretation of that objection and ignore the common law of *Flatman* and *Wemyss* in order to accept the position urged by the Crown.

Part XXIV of the *Code* contains two sections, ss. 734 and 743 [now ss. 799 and 808], which, for ease of reference, I will set out below:

> 734. Where, in proceedings to which this Part applies, the defendant appears for the trial and the prosecutor, having had due notice, does not appear, the summary conviction court may dismiss the information or may adjourn the trial to some other time upon such terms as it considers proper.

> . . .

> 743. (1) Where the summary conviction court dismisses an information it may, if requested by the defendant, draw up an order of dismissal, and shall give to the defendant a certified copy of the order of dismissal.
> (2) A copy of an order of dismissal, certified in accordance with subsection (1) is, without further proof, a bar to any subsequent proceedings against the defendant in respect of the same cause.

The *Code* is clear in providing that where, as here, the defendant appears for the trial and the prosecutor does not appear, the summary conviction Court may dismiss the information. It is then open to the defendant to request the Court to draw up an order of dismissal, a certified copy of which, without further proof, is a bar to any subsequent proceedings against him in respect of the same cause. No certificate was requested in the present case. It is the position of the Crown that failure to obtain a certificate is fatal to the position of the defendant. The Crown relies on the argument, reflected in the first question upon which leave to appeal was granted, that s. 743 supplants the common law right to raise the special plea of *autrefois acquit* in a summary conviction Court. The effect of the argument is that a successful defendant must obtain a certificate of dismissal at the time of trial, failing which he has no protection from a second information. Nothing in the language of the *Code* leads to that conclusion. Section 743 is intended in my view to supplement, and not to supplant, common law rights. It is in aid, rather than in derogation, of those rights. The certificate affords a mechanism, borrowed from English statute law of some antiquity, facilitating proof of dismissal of an information.

. . .

On the merits

In some circumstances, it may be difficult to say whether the defendant has, indeed, been "*bis vexatus*"; for example, where an information has been withdrawn or dismissed on technical grounds, or, the Crown contends, as in the case at bar, where there was no disposition "on the merits". It will be recalled that the second question upon which leave to appeal was granted raises the issue of whether the information was dealt with "on the merits".

I am not at all certain of what is meant by the term "on the merits", or indeed whether the terminology of "on the merits" furthers in any way our understanding of the effect of the dismissal of an information. Section 734 specifically empowers the summary conviction Court to dismiss upon non-appearance of the prosecutor...

. . .

In *R. v. Hatherley* (1971), 4 C.C.C. (2d) 242, [1971] 3 O.R. 430 (leave to appeal to the Supreme Court of Canada refused 1971 S.C.R. xi), the Ontario Court of Appeal held (p. 243):

> On a subsequent charge in which the serial number of the saw in question was changed, a plea of *autrefois acquit* was accepted, and it is the acceptance of that plea which forms the subject-matter of this appeal. We think the plea was properly substantiated and that the appeal fails. We think the accused, once a plea had been entered, was in jeopardy and that if the Crown elected not then to call any evidence, the disposition by acquittal was a disposition on the merits of the case.

In the case of *Haynes v. Davis,* [1915] 1 K.B. 332, an information was preferred against the appellant for having sold milk which was deficient in natural fat. When the case came on for hearing the Magistrate was informed that no certificate of analysis had been served with the summons in pursuance of the applicable legislation, whereupon he dismissed the summons. No evidence of the facts was given. A second summons was then taken out in respect of the same alleged offence. The Court held (Lush, J., dissenting) that the appellant had been in peril of being convicted on the first summons and, therefore, entitled to plead *autrefois acquit* to the second summons. Ridley, J., said, p. 335:

> I think he was in peril and therefore that he was entitled to plead autrefois acquit. The magistrate had jurisdiction unless objection was taken at the proper time to the informality, and unless that objection was taken there was a possibility, and indeed a probability, that the magistrate would proceed to a decision and convict the appellant. The appellant was thus in peril. It is not quite correct to say,

although it is rather an attractive phrase, that there must have been an acquittal upon the merits in order that there may be a good plea of autrefois acquit. In whatever way a person obtains an acquittal, whether it be by the verdict of a jury on the merits or by some ruling on a point of law without the case going to the jury, he is entitled to protection from further proceedings. Once there is an acquittal he cannot be tried again for the same offence.

Avory, J., had this to say at p. 337:

I agree, but I prefer to rest my judgment upon the one ground that the plea of res judicata or autrefois acquit depends for its validity upon this one question, whether the accused on the former occasion was in peril of being convicted of the same offence. If he was, the plea of autrefois acquit is good.

and

The question whether the one or the other is in peril is to be ascertained by inquiring whether the magistrate had jurisdiction to deal with the offence.

In my view, a criminal trial commences and an accused is normally in jeopardy from the moment issue is joined before a Judge having jurisdiction and the prosecution is called upon to present its case in Court. The person accused continues in jeopardy until final determination of the matter by rendering of the verdict.

Should the accused avail himself of the certificate provided for in s. 743(1), s-s. (2) bars any subsequent proceedings in respect of the same cause, without reference to the events giving rise to the dismissal. In principle, there is no reason why a different situation ought to prevail where the defendant has not obtained the certified copy. Nor, in principle, is it easy to distinguish between the situation where the Crown leads evidence which fails to make out a case for the defendant to answer and the situation where, as here, no evidence is led. So long as the case has proceeded to a verdict and a dismissal, that should be sufficient. See *Re Rex v. Ecker; Re Rex v. Fry* (1929), 51 C.C.C. 409 at p. 411, [1929] 3 D.L.R. 760 at p. 761, 64 O.L.R. 1 at p. 3, where Chief Justice Latchford said, in a passage adopted by Taschereau, J., in *Welch v. The King* (1950), 97 C.C.C. 177 at p. 181, [1950] 3 D.L.R. 641 at pp. 644-5, [1950] S.C.R. 412 at p. 417:

This Court was of opinion that "in jeopardy twice"—the *bis vexari* of the legal maxim—has not the meaning of subjection twice to a trial for the same offence except in cases where the first trial has been concluded by an adjudication or judgment declaring the accused acquitted or convicted. Not otherwise could the plea of *autrefois acquit* or *autrefois convict* prevail.

The term "on the merits" does nothing to further the test for the application of the *bis vexari* maxim. There is no basis, in the *Code* or in the common law, for any superadded requirement that there must be a trial "on the merits". That phrase merely serves to emphasize the general requirement that the previous dismissal must have been made by a Court of competent jurisdiction, whose proceedings were free from jurisdictional error and which rendered judgment on the charge.

Speaking generally, it is not readily apparent why the Crown should have the right to decline to adduce evidence in support of its charge and then assert the irrelevance of a dismissal consequent thereon, or why the Crown should be enabled to avoid the effect of refusal of an adjournment by declining to lead evidence and laying a fresh information following dismissal of the first charge. It is the intent of the *Code* that summary conviction matters be disposed of with despatch. No good purpose is served by introducing unwarranted complexities into what are, or should be, simple and straightforward and expeditious procedures.

In the result, I would dismiss the appeal.

Appeal dismissed.

PROBLEM 5

Accused is charged with the provincial offence of unlawfully operating an overweight vehicle. The accused pleads not guilty and the Crown withdraws the charge. The Crown subsequently lays another information charging the identical offence. Is the accused entitled to plead *autrefois acquit*? Compare *R. v. Conrad* (1983), 34 C.R. (3d) 320 (N.S. C.A.), leave to appeal to S.C.C. refused (1983), 59 N.S.R. (2d) 180 (S.C.C.), and *R. v. Karpinski*, [1957] S.C.R. 343, 25 C.R. 365 (S.C.C.). See also *Blasko v. R.* (1975), 33 C.R.N.S. 227 (Ont. H.C.).' Suppose the information was quashed as a nullity prior to plea? See *R. v. Pretty* (1989), 47 C.C.C. (3d) 70 (B.C. C.A.).

The cornerstone of the double jeopardy protection, both in the Criminal Code provision and in the Charter, resides in the meaning of the word "offence". Must the offences be identical? If not, how similar must they be? The criminal law of necessity describes offences in the abstract and, with the ever increasing statutory prohibitions, the risk of a single anti-social act or course of conduct violating more than one provision looms large. For which offence and on how many occasions shall the accused be prosecuted?

Should the protection be available only when the offences require the same evidence for conviction or ought it to be sufficient to establish that the offences arose out of the same course of conduct or transaction? Should the state be allowed to prosecute for an offence factually and legally included in an offence previously tried; *e.g.,* allowed to prosecute first for robbery and later for its necessary ingredient assault? Is it permissible if the order of such prosecutions is reversed?

The Criminal Code provides:

608. Where an issue on a plea of *autrefois acquit* or *autrefois convict* is tried, the evidence and adjudication and the notes of the judge and official stenographer on the former trial and the record transmitted to the court pursuant to section 551 on the charge that is pending before that court are admissible in evidence to prove or to disprove the identity of the charges.

609. (1) Where an issue on a plea of *autrefois acquit* or *autrefois convict* to a count is tried and it appears

(a) that the matter on which the accused was given in charge on the former trial is the same in whole or in part as that on which it is proposed to give him in charge, and

(b) that on the former trial, if all proper amendments had been made that might then have been made, he might have been convicted of all the offences of which he may be convicted on the count to which the plea of *autrefois acquit* or *autrefois convict* is pleaded,

the judge shall give judgment discharging the accused in respect of that count.

(2) The following provisions apply where an issue on a plea of *autrefois acquit* or *autrefois convict* is tried:

(a) where it appears that the accused might on the former trial have been convicted of an offence of which he may be convicted on the count in issue, the judge shall direct that the accused shall not be found guilty of any offence of which he might have been convicted on the former trial; and

(b) where it appears that the accused may be convicted on the count in issue of an offence of which he could not have been convicted on the former trial, the accused shall plead guilty or not guilty with respect to that offence.

The language here employed, enunciating a same evidence test for identity as opposed to a same transaction test, was first articulated in *R. v. Vandercomb and Abbott* (1796), 168 E.R. 455, 2 Leach 708 at 720 (Ex. Ct.) where Buller J., in refusing relief to the accused, wrote:

. . . unless the first indictment were such as the prisoner might have been convicted upon by proof of the facts contained in the second indictment, an acquittal in the first indictment can be no bar to the second.

PROBLEM 6

Accused was acquitted on a charge of robbery. A certificate of acquittal recited that he had been found not guilty of the charge that he did on August 24, 1984 unlawfully steal from John Ashford $300.00 and at the time did use violence. Accused was later charged with the offence that he did, on August 24, 1984 unlawfully assault John Ashford causing him bodily harm. Accused pleads autrefois acquit. Rule on the issue. Compare *Basque v. R.* (1975), 34 C.R.N.S. 264 (N.B. C.A.). See also *Van Rassel v. R.*, [1990] 1 S.C.R. 225, 75 C.R. (3d) 150, 53 C.C.C. (3d) 353 (S.C.C.).

PROBLEM 7

The accused was tried on a charge of attempted murder contrary to s. 239 of the Code and was acquitted. He was then charged with causing bodily harm with intent to wound contrary to s. 244 and when the matter came on for trial he entered a plea of autrefois acquit. How would you rule? Compare *R. v. Rinnie*, [1970] 3 C.C.C. 218 (Alta. C.A.).

R. v. WIGGLESWORTH
[1988] 1 S.C.R. 541, 60 C.R. (3d) 193, 11 C.C.C. (3d) 27 (S.C.C.)

The accused, W., an R.C.M.P. constable, while on duty brought in a suspect for a breathalyzer test. The suspect denied that he was the driver of the car, and W. grabbed him, pushed him and slapped him. As a result of this incident, W. was charged with assault under what is now s. 266(1) of the

Criminal Code and an offence under s. 25 of the Royal Canadian Mounted Police Act. This offence was charged as being "unnecessarily violent towards a prisoner" by grabbing and slapping him. This was a "major service offence", and W. was found guilty by an R.C.M.P. service court and fined. Subsequently, W. appeared before a Provincial Judge on the assault charge. His counsel argued that proceeding on the charge, in light of the service offence conviction, would violate s. 11(h) of the Canadian Charter of Rights and Freedoms. The court accepted the argument and quashed the information. On appeal to the Court of Queen's Bench it was held that the two charges constituted different offences and hence the trial judge had erred in applying s. 11(h) of the Charter. W. was found guilty, and his appeal to the Court of Appeal was dismissed. He obtained leave to appeal to the Supreme Court of Canada on the questions: (1) whether s. 11(h) precluded a prosecution for assault after a conviction and fine for the service offence of being unnecessarily violent; and, if so, (2) whether the Criminal Code prosecution was justified under s. 1 of the Charter.

WILSON J. (Dickson C.J.C., Beetz, McIntyre, Lamer and La Forest JJ. concurring):—The rights guaranteed by s. 11 of the Charter are available to persons prosecuted by the state for public offences involving punitive sanction, i.e., criminal, quasi-criminal and regulatory offences, either federally or provincially enacted.

. . .

While it is easy to state that those involved in a criminal or penal matter are to enjoy the rights guaranteed by s. 11, it is difficult to formulate a precise test to be applied in determining whether specific proceedings are proceedings in respect of a criminal or penal matter so as to fall within the ambit of the section. The phrase "criminal and penal matters" which appears in the marginal note would seem to suggest that a matter could fall within s. 11 either because by its very nature it is a criminal proceeding or because a conviction in respect of the offence may lead to a true penal consequence. I believe that a matter could fall within s. 11 under either branch.

There are many examples of offences which are criminal in nature but which carry relatively minor consequences following conviction. Proceedings in respect of these offences would nevertheless be subject to the protections of s. 11 of the Charter. It cannot be seriously contended that just because a minor traffic offence leads to a very slight consequence, perhaps only a small fine, that offence does not fall within s. 11. It is a criminal or quasi-criminal proceeding. It is the sort of offence which by its very nature must fall within s. 11. I would agree, therefore, with the comments made by Linden J. in *McCutcheon v. Toronto (City)* (1983), 41 O.R. (2d) 652, 20 M.V.R. 267, 22 M.P.L.R. 139, 147 D.L.R. (3d) 193 (H.C.). In that case, the accused claimed the benefit of s. 11 following the alleged commission of a parking offence. At p. 205 Linden J. said:

> This provision of the Charter is available only to persons charged with an offence. On my reading of the by-laws and the legislation, the applicant is such a person, having been charged with offences when the summonses were issued against her . . .

There can be no question that parking infractions are "offences" as that word is used in s. 11 of the Charter. The respondents contend that these are not the types of transgressions against society s. 11 of the Charter is directed at, since there is virtually no stigma attached to a parking ticket. In my view, however, the degree of stigma is of no significance.

In my view, if a particular matter is of a public nature, intended to promote public order and welfare within a public sphere of activity, then that matter is the kind of matter which falls within s. 11. It falls within the section because of the kind of matter it is. This is to be distinguished from private, domestic or disciplinary matters which are regulatory, protective or corrective and which are primarily intended to maintain discipline, professional integrity and professional standards or to regulate conduct within a limited private sphere of activity: see, for example, *Law Soc. of Man. v. Savino*, at p. 292; *Malartic Hygrade Gold Mines (Can.) Ltd. v. Ont. Securities Comm.* (1986), 54 O.R. (2d) 544 at 549, 19 Admin. L.R. 21, 9 O.S.C.B. 2286, 27 D.L.R. (4th) 112, 24 C.R.R. 1, 15 O.A.C. 124 (Div. Ct.); and *Re Barry and Alta. Securities Comm.*, supra, at p. 736, per Stevenson J.A. There is also a fundamental distinction between proceedings undertaken to promote public order and welfare within a public sphere of activity and proceedings undertaken to determine fitness to obtain or maintain a licence. Where disqualifications are imposed as part of a scheme for regulating an activity in order to protect the public, disqualification proceedings are not the sort of "offence" proceedings to which s. 11 is applicable. Proceedings of an administrative nature instituted for the protection of the public in accordance with the policy of a statute are also not the sort of "offence" proceedings to which s. 11 is applicable. But all prosecutions for criminal offences under the Criminal Code and for quasi-criminal offences under provincial legislation are automatically subject to s. 11. They are the very kind of offences to which s. 11 was intended to apply.

This is not to say that if a person is charged with a private, domestic or disciplinary matter which is primarily intended to maintain discipline or integrity or to regulate conduct within a limited private sphere of activity, he or she can never possess the rights guaranteed under s. 11. Some of these matters may well fall within s. 11, not because they are the classic kind of matter intended to fall within the section, but because they involve the imposition of true penal consequences. In my opinion, a true penal consequence which would atract the application of s. 11 is imprisonment or a fine which by its magnitude would appear to be imposed for the purpose of redressing the wrong done to society at large rather than to the maintenance of internal discipline within the limited sphere of activity. In "Annotation to *R. v. Wigglesworth*" (1984), 38 C.R. (3d) 388, at p. 389, Professor Stuart states:

> . . . other *punitive* forms of disciplinary measures, such as fines or imprisonment, are indistinguishable from criminal punishment and should surely fall within the protection of s. 11(*h*).

I would agree with this comment but with two caveats. First, the possibility of a fine may be fully consonant with the maintenance of discipline and order within a limited private sphere of activity and thus may not attract the application of s. 11. It is my view that if a body or an official has an unlimited power to fine, and if it does not afford the rights enumerated under s. 11, it cannot impose fines designed to redress the harm done to society at large. Instead, it is restricted to the power to impose fines in order to achieve the particular private purpose. One indicium of the purpose of a particular fine is how the body is to dispose of the fines that it collects. If, as in the case of proceedings under the Royal Canadian Mounted Police Act, the fines are not to form part of the Consolidated Revenue Fund but are to be used for the benefit of the force, it is more likely that the fines are purely an internal or private matter of discipline: Royal Canadian Mounted Police Act, s. 45. The second caveat I would raise is that it is difficult to conceive of the possibility of a particular proceeding failing what I have called the "by nature" test but passing what I have called the "true penal consequence" test. I have grave doubts whether any body or official which exists in order to achieve some administrative or private disciplinary purpose can ever imprison an individual. Such a deprivation of liberty seems justified as being in accordance with fundamental justice under s. 7 of the Charter only when a public wrong or transgression against society, as opposed to an internal wrong, is committed. However, as this was not argued before us in this appeal I shall assume that it is possible that the "by nature" test can be failed but the "true penal consequence" test passed. Assuming such a situation is possible, it seems to me that in cases where the two tests conflict the "by nature" test must give way to the "true penal consequence" test. If an individual is to be subject to penal consequences such as imprisonment—the most severe deprivation of liberty known to our law—then he or she, in my opinion, should be entitled to the highest procedural protection known to our law.

Before turning to the application of the law to the facts of this case, I want to emphasize that nothing in the above discussion takes away from the possibility that constitutionally guaranteed procedural protections may be available in a particular case under s. 7 of the Charter even although s. 11 is not available. The appellant in this case has chosen to base this case solely on s. 11 of the Charter. In view of this I make no comment on the applicability of s. 7.

It is clear that the R.C.M.P. Code of Discipline is concerned with the maintenance of discipline and integrity within the force. It is designed to regulate conduct within a limited private sphere of activity, i.e., conduct relevant to one's position as a member of the R.C.M.P.

. . .

It would therefore seem that the proceedings before the R.C.M.P. service court fail what I have called the "by nature" test. They are neither criminal proceedings nor quasi-criminal proceedings. They do not appear to be the kind of proceedings which fall within the ambit of s. 11. But it is apparent that an officer charged under the Code of Discipline faces a true penal consequence. He or she may be imprisoned for one year pursuant to s. 36(1) of the Royal Canadian Mounted Police Act if he or she is found guilty of a major service offence. As was stated by Joyal J. in *Van Rassel v. Can. (Commr. of R.C.M.P.)*, [1987] 1 F.C. 473 at 484, 31 C.C.C. (3d) 10, 7 F.T.R. 187 (*sub nom. Van. Rassel v. R.C.M.P.*) (T.D.), a case which also dealt with a s. 11(*h*) claim with respect to proceedings for a major service offence under the Royal

Canadian Mounted Police Act, "The statute as a consequence [of the provision for imprisonment] is as much a penal statute as is the *Criminal Code*". This would seem, therefore, to be that unusual case where proceedings have failed the "by nature" test but have passed the "true penal consequence" test. As I have indicated above in a case of conflict the "by nature" test must give way to the "true penal consequence" test. I find, therefore, that s. 11 applies to proceedings in respect of a major service offence before the R.C.M.P. service court. Is the appellant entitled then to have the prosecution for the alleged criminal assault stayed on the ground that punishment for that offence would result in double punishment of the appellant for the same offence contrary to s. 11(*h*) of the Charter?

This court in *R. v. Prince*, [1986] 2 S.C.R. 480, [1987] 1 W.W.R. 1, 54 C.R. (3d) 97, 30 C.C.C. (3d) 35, 33 D.L.R. (4th) 724, 45 Man. R. (2d) 93, 70 N.R. 119, recently examined the scope of the rule against multiple convictions enunciated in *Kienapple*.

. . .

In the context of proceedings before disciplinary tribunals there is ample authority for the view that disciplinary offences are separate and distinct from criminal offences for the purpose of the rule against multiple convictions: see *Re Pelissero and Loree* (1982), 140 D.L.R. (3d) 676 (Ont. Div. Ct.); *MacDonald v. Marriott* (1984), 52 B.C.L.R. 346, 7 D.L.R. (4th) 697 (S.C.); *Van Rassel v. Can.*, supra; *Re Bridges and Bridges*, Ont. Prov. Ct., per Colter Prov. J. (unreported); *R. v. DeBaie* (1983), 60 N.S.R. (2d) 78, 128 A.P.R. 78 (C.A.); and *R. v. Belliveau; Belliveau v. Dorchester Penitentiary (Warden)* (1984), 55 N.B.R. (2d) 82 at 86, 144 A.P.R. 82 (C.A.). In their text on The Doctrine of Res Judicata, 2nd ed. (1969), Spencer Bower and Turner state at pp. 279-80:

> An example is readily found in an inquiry instituted by the disciplinary authority of a professional body, with a view to the expulsion of one against whom conduct infamous in a professional respect is alleged. In such a case it may be that the conduct alleged is no more and no less than conduct in respect of which the accused person has already been acquitted by a criminal court on a criminal charge. Neither a conviction nor an acquittal before a criminal court on a criminal charge will bar the use of the same conduct before such a tribunal on an application to suspend or expel; for the purpose of the proceeding is not to punish the practitioner for the commission of an offence as such, but to exercise disciplinary power over the members of a profession so as to ensure that their conduct conforms to the standards of the profession.

I would hold that the appellant in this case is not being tried and punished for the same offence. The "offences" are quite different. One is an internal disciplinary matter. The accused has been found guilty of a major offence and has, therefore, accounted to his profession. The other offence is the criminal offence of assault. The accused must now account to society at large for his conduct. He cannot complain, as a member of a special group of individuals subject to private internal discipline, that he ought not to account to society for his wrongdoing. His conduct has a double aspect as a member of the R.C.M.P. and as a member of the public at large. To borrow from the words of the Chief Justice [in *Prince*], I am of the view that the two offences were "two different 'matters', totally separate one from the other and not alternative one to the other". While there was only one act of assault there were two distinct delicts, causes or matters which would sustain separate convictions.

ESTEY J. (dissenting in part):—The distinguishing feature of the tribunal sitting under the Royal Canadian Mounted Police Act is that this tribunal was equipped by Parliament to apply, following the registration of a conviction, a scale of punishment ranging from a reprimand through a fine up to $500 to an ultimate penalty of one year's imprisonment. The statute in addition (s. 38) empowers the convicting officer of the accused to recommend his removal from the force upon conviction. It can hardly be said, given the power under the Royal Canadian Mounted Police Act to couple a one-year imprisonment sentence with a virtually inevitable dismissal from the force upon conviction, that Parliament intended that the scale of punishment would reflect only the internal disciplinary interest of the R.C.M.P. and not the larger community interest in the suppression of the crime of assault wherever committed.

. . .

The facts in *Prince* are quite different from the circumstances in this case. Not only were there two victims of the one stabbing action but, also, the two offences under consideration, viz., causing bodily harm and manslaughter, required proof of different elements. The first required proof of bodily harm and the second required proof of the death of the baby. Cleary there was an insufficient legal nexus to apply the rule against multiple convictions in that case.

This case is completely different. Only one factual assault has occurred for which the appellant has been tried and punished. The potential imposition of a one-year imprisonment pursuant to a "trial" by the tribunal clearly points to this procedure as being in the nature of punishment to redress a social wrong and not only in the nature of disciplinary proceedings. The possibility of dismissal from the force pursuant to s. 38 of the statute reinforces this view. With respect, I cannot agree with the view of Wilson J. that the two offences are in any way totally separate from or different from each other.

The test must be the practical one of determining whether the first court upon registering a conviction was performing a task assigned by Parliament which by the scale of punishment available to the tribunal is readily recognizable as a process in which the general public's interest in the administration of criminal law is recognized over and above the limited interest of internal discipline.

For the reasons given above it is my view that this test is met in this case. The subsequent proceeding under s. 245(1) of the Criminal code falls squarely within the prohibition in s. 11(h) of the Charter that any person "finally found guilty and punished for the offence" has the right "not to be tried or punished for it again". Furthermore, a breach of s. 11(h) rights cannot be justified by any conceivable s. 1 reasonable limits analysis. In any case, the Crown here has made no attempt to do so. The right to be tried and punished only once for an offence cannot, in my view, be fettered or circumscribed by Parliament.

PROBLEM 8

On April 1 an inmate of a provincial jail fails to return from a temporary absence leave. He is arrested and charged with being unlawfully at large contrary to the Criminal Code. Following a trial in provincial court he is found guilty and sentenced to thirty days in prison. A month later he is brought before the prison disciplinary panel on a charge of "disobeying prison regulations in that he did not return from day parole on April 1". He is found guilty and sentenced to a loss of thirty days remission.

With reference to authority examine whether the inmate has any remedy at common law or under the Charter.

Compare *Knockaert v. Canada (Commissioner of Corrections)* (1987), 55 C.R. (3d) 171, 32 C.C.C. (3d) 288 (Fed. C.A.) and *R. v. Shubley* (1990), 74 C.R. (3d) 1 (S.C.C.). See Allan Manson, "Solitary Confinement, Remission and Prison Discipline" (1990), 75 C.R. (3d) 356.

PROBLEM 9

A university student is convicted for being drunk in a public place and for causing a disturbance. He is fined $10 for the first offence and placed on six months probation for the second. He has now been served with a notice from the student Alma Mater Society Court calling on him to show cause why he should not be disciplined for that conduct which occurred on university grounds. Discipline available to the court ranges from a small fine to recommendation for expulsion. Advise him.

(c) Multiple Punishment

Should the permissibility of multiple trials be determined by the same yardstick as used when ascertaining multiple punishment? If the evils are distinct should they be guarded against by the same shield? Some of the confusion in the cases stems from a failure to adequately recognize the distinction in objectives to be pursued. The mission of the multiple trial policy, founded on private justice and public policy, is properly a matter for procedural law and the courts should look primarily to the fairness of the second prosecution, bearing in mind the resources of the adversaries and the ability of the state to have had the second question determined on a previous occasion. The policy forbidding multiple punishment has as its aim the assurance that a wrongdoer receives an adequate penalty but no more. This then presents a problem for substantive law; to fit the proper category of offence to the act of the individual. While it may be of some merit to look to the number of substantive offences violated in a given instance, examine their language for differences, and by seeking the intent of the Legislature in creating the same, determine the amount of punishment an individual deserves for his criminal behaviour, it is difficult to understand how these considerations have any bearing on the correctness of subjecting a defendant to repeated criminal prosecutions.

It is often difficult to ascertain when the rule against multiple punishments is applicable. *Prince* had the effect of narrowing the concept but its determination remains elusive. For example, contrast the decisions in *R. v. Rocheleau* (2013), 5 C.R. (7th) 397 (Ont. C.A.) and *R. v. Meszaros* (2013), 309 C.C.C. (3d) 392, 5 C.R. (7th) 415 (Ont. C.A.). Although the decisions are supportable and undoubtedly correct, they are difficult to explain. See: T. Quigley, "Annotation" (2013), 5 C.R. (7th) 397.

R. v. KINNEAR
(2005), 30 C.R. (6th) 1, 198 C.C.C. (3d) 232 (Ont. C.A.)

R.K., an 18-year-old drug dealer with a lengthy youth court record, was caught shoplifting socks in a department store in downtown Toronto. He and an accomplice were arrested by two security officers who took them to a room at the back of the store. When one of the officers began a "pat down" search, R.K. pulled out a sawed-off shotgun he had hidden under his coat, pointed it at the security officers, threatened to shoot them and his accomplice and instructed the officers to let him out of the room. As R.K. ran from the room, he encountered a third security officer and he pointed the sawed-off shotgun at this officer. R.K. fled through the crowded store with the weapon in full view, and exited the store. The trigger mechanism of the sawed-off shotgun was broken and it would not fire. R.K. knew this, but the people he pointed it at did not and were terrified.

R.K. was charged with eight offences:

- theft (count 1);
- two counts of threatening death (counts 2 and 3);
- possession of a weapon, to wit a sawed-off shotgun,
- for a purpose dangerous to the public peace (count 4)
- escape lawful custody (count 5);
- two counts of using an imitation firearm while committing the indictable offence of threatening
- death (counts 6 and 7); and
- using an imitation firearm while committing the indictable offence of escape custody (count 8).

R.K. pleaded guilty to four of the charges (counts 1, 4, 5 and 8). He maintained that he had not threatened to kill either security guard and pleaded not guilty to counts 2, 3, 6 and 7 relating to threatening. After hearing the evidence of the guards and R.K., the trial judge found that R.K. had threatened to kill the guards and convicted on all eight charges. He refused to stay the two charges of using a firearm while committing the offence of threatening (counts 6 and 7) in accordance with the rule against multiple convictions. R.K. appealed from some of the convictions. He argued that the two convictions for threatening, and the two convictions for using a firearm while committing the offence of threatening should be set aside and those charges should be stayed pursuant to the *Kienapple* rule against multiple convictions.

DOHERTY J.A. (Moldaver and Gillese JJ.A. concurring):—

. . .

(b) The *Kienapple* Principle

In *R. v. Kienapple* (1974), 15 C.C.C. (2d) 524,[1975] 1 S.C.R. 729 (S.C.C.), the court recognized and arguably expanded the common law rule prohibiting more than one conviction for the same criminal wrong. Laskin J. explained that the principle foreclosed more than one conviction for offences arising out of the same delict. He said at pp. 538-39:

> The relevant inquiry so far as res judicata is concerned is whether the same cause or matter (rather than the same offence) is comprehended by two or more offences.

The principle that emerged from *Kienapple* provides that where the transaction gives rise to two or more offences with substantially the same elements and an accused is found guilty of more than one of those offences, that accused should be convicted of only the most serious of the offences: *R. v. Kienapple, supra*, at p. 540. The other charges should be stayed: *R. v. P. (D.W.)* (1989), 49 C.C.C. (3d) 417, [1989] 2 S.C.R. 3 (S.C.C.).

Laskin J. at p. 540 linked the "*Kienapple*" rule to the court's power to protect against abuses of its process. He described the rule as designed to "protect an individual from an undue exercise by the Crown of its power to prosecute and punish".

In *R. v. Prince* (1986), 30 C.C.C. (3d) 35 at 42, [1986] 2 S.C.R. 480 (S.C.C.), Dickson C.J.C. identified the same rationale for the rule:

> [T]he Canadian courts have long been concerned to see that multiple convictions are not without good reason heaped on an accused in respect of a single criminal delict.

Kienapple, like most seminal authorities, left uncharted the full scope of the principle it created. It fell to the court in *Prince, supra*, to take up the task of designing an analytical framework to guide the application of the *Kienapple* rule in specific circumstances.

Dickson C.J.C. for a unanimous court in *Prince*, held that the *Kienapple* rule precluded multiple convictions for different offences only where there was both a factual and a legal nexus connecting the offences. The factual nexus is established where the charges arise out of the same transaction. The legal nexus exists if the offences constitute a single wrong or delict.

The factual nexus is most obvious where offences arise out of the same act. *Kienapple* and *Prince* are examples of a single act leading to multiple charges. A transaction can, however, include more than a single isolated act: *Prince* at p. 44. The adequacy of the factual nexus between offences for the purposes of invoking the rule in *Kienapple* cannot be determined in the abstract, but must be resolved on a case-by-case basis. In describing the factual nexus inquiry, Dickson C.J.C. said in *Prince* at p. 44:

Such difficulties will have to be resolved on an individual basis as cases arise, having regard to factors such as the remoteness or proximity of the events in time and place, the presence or absence of relevant intervening events (such as the robbery conviction in Côté), and whether the accused's actions were related to each other by a common objective. In the meantime, it would be a mistake to emphasize the difficulties. In many cases, including the present appeal, it will be clear whether or not the charges are founded upon the same act.

While there will inevitably be close cases, the factual nexus inquiry dictated by the *Kienapple* rule is relatively straightforward. The legal nexus inquiry, however, is more nuanced. A comparison of the constituent elements of the offences in issue is an essential part of the legal nexus inquiry. However, the mere fact that offences share common elements does not establish a sufficient legal nexus between those offences to warrant the application of the *Kienapple* rule. The legal nexus inquiry is directed not at finding common elements between offences, but at determining whether there are different elements in the offences which sufficiently distinguish them so as to foreclose the application of the *Kienapple* rule. As indicated in *Prince* at p. 49:

> [T]he requirement of sufficient proximity between offences will only be satisfied if there is no additional and distinguishing element that goes to guilt contained in the offence for which a conviction is sought to be precluded by the *Kienapple* principle.

I stress that Dickson C.J.C. referred to an "additional and distinguishing element". Not every difference in the elements of the offences will preclude the *Kienapple* rule. Indeed, if the elements of the offences are identical or if the elements of one offence are all included in the other offence, the pleas of *autrefois convict* or *autrefois acquit* will apply and there is no need to resort to the *Kienapple* rule.

When will it be said that there are no "additional and distinguishing elements" between offences? As indicated in *Prince* at pp. 49-50, there can be "no precise answer" to this question. The sufficiency of the legal nexus between offences will depend on an interpretation of the statutory provisions that create the offences and the application of those statutory definitions to the circumstances of the case.

In *Prince* at pp. 49-51, Dickson C.J.C. provided guidance as to the situations in which there will be a sufficient legal nexus to justify the application of the *Kienapple* rule. He described three categories of cases where the legal nexus between offences will be established. I need not repeat those categories here. In essence, each presents a situation in which the offences charged do not describe different criminal wrongs, but instead describe different ways of committing the same criminal wrong.

Dickson C.J.C. in *Prince* at pp. 51-54 further elucidated the legal nexus inquiry by referring to three factors that will defeat any claim that different offences have a sufficient legal nexus to warrant the application of the *Kienapple* rule. These factors do bear repeating in these reasons. First, where the offences are designed to protect different societal interests, convictions for both offences will not offend the *Kienapple* rule. Second, where the offences allege personal violence against different victims, *Kienapple* will not foreclose convictions for offences relating to each victim. Third, where the offences proscribe different consequences, the *Kienapple* rule will not bar multiple convictions.

I think the three factors identified in *Prince* as severing any possible legal nexus between offences provide further support for the view that the crucial distinction for the purposes of the application of *Kienapple* rule is between different wrongs and the same wrong committed in different ways. If the offences target different societal interests, different victims, or prohibit different consequences, it cannot be said that the distinctions between the offences amount to nothing more than a different way of committing the same wrong.

One final and important point must be made in outlining the *Kienapple* rule. It is subject to the dictates of Parliament. If a statutory provision expressly or by clear implication provides for multiple convictions for offences arising out of the same delict, the court must give effect to the legislative intention subject to a successful Charter challenge: *Kienapple* at p. 540; *R. v. McGuigan* (1982), 66 C.C.C. (2d) 97 at 123-24, [1982] 1 S.C.R. 284 (S.C.C.); *Prince* at pp. 48-49. The post-Charter jurisprudence establishes that multiple convictions for offences arising out of the same delict is not a per se violation of the Charter: *R. v. Krug* (1985), 21 C.C.C. (3d) 193 at 202-203, [1985] 2 S.C.R. 255 (S.C.C.); *R. v. Brown* (1994), 93 C.C.C. (3d) 97, [1994] 3 S.C.R. 749 (S.C.C.). The constitutionality of a provision overriding the *Kienapple* rule will depend on the specifics of that provision and its application to a particular fact situation.

(c) The Application of *Kienapple* to this Case

Counsel for R.K.'s submissions require a consideration of the *Kienapple* rule as it applies to:

- the three convictions on the two charges of threatening and the one charge of escape lawful custody; and
- the three convictions on the charges of using an imitation firearm while committing an indictable offence.

Counsel's contention that R.K. should not have been convicted of two counts of threatening and a charge of escape custody cannot be sustained. While there is a clear factual nexus since the threats were part of the means used by R.K. to effect his escape, there is no legal nexus among the offences justifying the application of the *Kienapple* rule. The legal distinction between the threatening charges and the escape custody charge lies in the societal purpose underlying the offences. The prohibition against death threats seeks to protect the security of the individual. The prohibition against escaping lawful custody seeks to protect the due and effective administration of justice. These very distinct purposes render the offence of threatening and the offence of escape separate delicts, even though both were committed in the course of the same transaction.

I would add, and counsel did not suggest otherwise, that the convictions on the two threatening charges were proper since there were two different victims.

I am satisfied, however, there is merit to counsel's contention that the rule in *Kienapple* forecloses convictions on all three of the charges involving the use of an imitation firearm while committing an indictable offence. I think those charges represent a single criminal wrong justifying only one conviction.

The factual nexus connecting the three offences is obvious. The uses of the firearm referred to in the three charges all arose at the same time and place. There were no intervening events capable of severing the factual nexus. All three offences were motivated by a single common objective, R.K.'s desire to escape custody.

. . .

Section 85(2) creates the generic offence of using an imitation firearm while committing an indictable offence. The specific indictable offence alleged to have been committed is but a particular, albeit an essential particular, of the charge. The essence of the offence lies in the use of an imitation firearm while committing another indictable offence.

Based on the language of s. 85(2), there is no legal distinction to be drawn among the three charges in counts 6, 7 and 8. They describe different ways of committing the offence set out in s. 85(2). The three charges do not promote different societal interests, protect different victims, or prohibit different consequences. Looked at realistically, counts 6, 7 and 8 are akin to snapshots of scenes taken from a videotape depicting a single ongoing use of an imitation firearm in the course of committing several indictable offences.

. . .

The rule in *Kienapple* applies unless Parliament has clearly indicated otherwise. In my view, s. 85(4) is intended to impose an additional penalty for the use of an imitation firearm beyond the penalty imposed for the underlying indictable offences that were committed as part of the same transaction. It does not go so far as to preclude the operation of the *Kienapple* rule to multiple charges of using a firearm while committing an indictable offence that arise out of the same transaction.

. . .

[It] cannot be said that the use of the firearm to threaten the two security guards and the use of the firearm to escape the lawful custody of the security guards involved separate transactions. They were all part and parcel of the same transaction.

. . .

The three charges of using the firearm while committing an indictable offence are equally serious. I think the appropriate order would have been to enter a conviction on count 8, the charge of using a firearm to escape custody, and to enter a stay on counts 6 and 7.

PROBLEM 10

Accused is convicted of robbery and sentenced to three years. On his release from prison he was found in possession of bonds and debentures which had been the subject of the robbery. The accused is now charged with possession of stolen goods. Res judicata?

Compare *Côté v. R.* (1974), 26 C.R.N.S. 26 (S.C.C.).

PROBLEM 11

Accused is charged with impaired driving and also with driving with an excess of alcohol in his blood. On a conviction of the first charge must he be acquitted of the second? Compare *R. v. Houchen* (1976), 31 C.C.C. (2d) 274 (B.C. C.A.). Suppose the two charges are impaired driving and driving while suspended? Compare *R. v. Logeman* (1978), 5 C.R. (3d) 219 (B.C. C.A.). Impaired driving and refusing to provide a breath sample? Compare *R. v. Schilbe* (1976), 30 C.C.C. (2d) 113 (Ont. C.A.). Hunting out of season and hunting with a night-light?

Compare *R. v. McKinney* (1979), 46 C.C.C. (2d) 566 (Man. C.A.); affirmed [1980] 1 S.C.R. 401 (S.C.C.).

PROBLEM 12

The accused was convicted of using a firearm while attempting to commit an indictable offence, contrary to s. 85 of the Code. He now stands charged with attempted murder as a result of the same incident. Res judicata?

Compare *McGuigan v. R.* [1982] 1 S.C.R. 284, 66 C.C.C. (2d) 97 (S.C.C.), *Travers v. R.* (1984), 41 C.R. (3d) 339 (N.S. C.A.) and *Krug v. R.* (1985), 48 C.R. (3d) 97 (S.C.C.).

PROBLEM 13

The accused was convicted of manslaughter arising out of the shooting of her husband. The trial judge placed the accused on probation for two years with conditions: abstain from consumption of alcohol, report to probation officer, and keep the peace and be of good behaviour. Fourteen months later she was convicted of assault causing bodily harm and breach of probation. The breach was for being intoxicated. For the assault she was sentenced to fourteen months' imprisonment and for the breach of probation 45 days consecutive. The accused was then taken before the trial judge who had placed her on probation. He believes it would be appropriate to impose a sentence of three years on the manslaughter charge. Can you persuade him otherwise?

Compare *R. v. Linklater* (1983), 9 C.C.C. (3d) 217 (Y.T. C.A.).

PROBLEM 14

The accused was convicted of aggravated assault and of the offence of using a firearm while committing an indictable offence. Both convictions were based on the fact that she had shot and wounded her sister with a rifle. She appealed her firearm conviction on the basis that it infringed the rule against multiple convictions. Make a ruling.

Compare *R. v. Switzer* (1987), 56 C.R. (3d) 107, 32 C.C.C. (3d) 303 (Alta. C.A.).

PROBLEM 15

As a result of an R.C.M.P. undercover operation, the accused were arrested for their involvement in a conspiracy to import cocaine. One accused was a customs officer whose role was to arrange for the cocaine to clear customs. An indictment was preferred against them jointly by the Crown in right of Canada, charging them with conspiracy to import cocaine. The accused were found guilty, the trial judge rejecting their argument that they should be acquitted by virtue of res judicata. A few weeks before their conviction they had pleaded guilty to a charge of corruptly accepting a bribe laid by the Crown in right of Quebec, and had been sentenced to one year's imprisonment. Those charges were based on the exact same facts as those which led to the conspiracy charges. On appeal by the accused, the Quebec Court of Appeal quashed the conviction for importing cocaine. Which court was correct? Why?

Compare *R. v. Borelli; R. v. Iuculano*, [1988] 1 S.C.R. 667, 62 C.R. (3d) 399, 41 C.C.C. (3d) 288 (S.C.C.).

PROBLEM 16

The accused, charged with drug offences, is granted judicial interim release which includes a condition that he undertake to keep the peace and be of good behaviour. He is already subject to a probation order requiring him to keep the peace and be of good behaviour, especially towards his former wife. He drives up and down a road in the vicinity of his former wife and her companion and waves his arms at them from his car in an apparently offensive manner. On the basis of this evidence he is convicted on a charge of breach of probation. The Crown now wants to use the same evidence to convict him on a charge of breach of recognizance. Is this precluded by the rule against multiple convictions?

Compare *R. v. Furlong* (1993), 81 C.C.C. (3d) 449, 22 C.R. (4th) 193 (Nfld. C.A.).

(d) Issue Estoppel

The use of issue estoppel in the criminal law alternately eases and heightens an accused's burden in attempting to escape a second prosecution. While relieving him of the double jeopardy sine qua non of establishing that the second prosecution is indeed for the same offence as that previously tried, it presents him with an equally difficult task: demonstrating that an issue essential to his conviction has been previously determined in his favour. This often insurmountable hurdle of deciphering a general verdict of not guilty severely restricts the doctrine's ability to act as a substantial limitation on repetitive trials. The defence of issue estoppel, ofttimes confusingly called res judicata in the cases, while held to be applicable in the criminal law, will rarely be of any use.

In *Wright, McDermott and Feeley v. R.,* [1963] S.C.R. 539, 40 C.R. 261 (S.C.C.), Judson J. commented on defence's submission on issue estoppel:

> The weakness in this submission is in trying to read too much into the verdict of not guilty on count 1 where the two counts charge conspiracy. At the first trial, the jury found that the proven facts did not amount to the conspiracy charged. At the second trial, the jury found that the same or substantially identical facts did amount to the conspiracy charged in count 2. An acquittal on a charge of conspiracy does not pronounce against every part of it. On what issue is there an estoppel against the Crown? Is it on the agreement or the corruptly giving or the intent in count 1? All that a judge or a jury, if it becomes fit matter for submission to a jury at the second trial, can determine is that the evidence fell short of warranting a conviction on the precise charge. There is no issue on which it can be said that the Crown is estopped in the second trial. This distinguishes the defence of res judicata in this case from the comparatively simple examples of its application in cases where there is an estoppel on issues such as identity of the accused: *Rex v. Quinn* (1905), 11 O.L.R. 242, 10 C.C.C. 412, 13 Can. Abr. 31, 1277; possession: *Sambasivam v. Public Prosecutor of Malaya,* [1950] A.C. 459, 11 C.R. 55, [1950] 2 W.W.R. 817, 3 Abr. Con. (2nd) 10; responsibility for the death of two persons as a result of the same catastrophe, where an acquittal on a charge of manslaughter of A must result in an acquittal on the same charge for the death of B, the whole matter having been litigated adversely to the prosecution in the first trial: *R. v. Sweetman,* [1939] O.R. 131, 71 C.C.C. 171, [1939] 2 D.L.R. 70, 3 Abr. Con. (2nd) 776; *Gill v. The Queen,* 38 C.R. 122, 1962 Can. Abr. 177.

> These simplicities do not arise when the two counts charge two conspiracies with different component elements. It is impossible in the present case to say that the substantial basic facts common to both counts have been determined in favour of the accused in the first trial. The trial judge was right in his ruling that there was nothing to submit to the jury on this defence and I agree with the reasons of the Court of Appeal in affirming his ruling.

GUSHUE v. R.

[1980] 1 S.C.R. 798, 16 C.R. (3d) 39, 50 C.C.C. (2d) 417 (S.C.C.)

LASKIN, C.J.C.:—The main question in this appeal, which is here by leave of this Court, is whether the appellant may invoke issue estoppel in respect of two charges of which he was convicted, namely, giving contradictory evidence in different judicial proceedings, contrary to s. 124 of the *Criminal Code,* and robbery, contrary to s. 302(*c*) of the *Criminal Code.* These charges and the convictions thereon followed his acquittal on a charge of non-capital murder of the victim of the robbery, one Morris Mayzel.

The appellant gave evidence at his trial for murder and being asked directly "Did you shoot Morris Mayzel?", he answered, "No, I did not". The appellant was associated in a robbery scheme with one Edward McDonald who testified for the Crown. Gushue's evidence was that he did not enter the victim's tailor shop but rather that he withdrew from the scheme and that it was McDonald who entered the tailor shop alone. McDonald testified that it was he who withdrew and that Gushue had entered the tailor shop where the proprietor was shot and killed. I am not concerned here to elaborate on the evidence given at the trial for murder. I add merely that there was evidence that after the killing, Gushue sold a revolver which, according to expert evidence, was the murder weapon. Gushue maintained that he got it from McDonald after the killing of Mayzel.

About four years after his acquittal, the appellant accused, while under investigation for other offences, made statements to the police that he had attempted to steal from Mayzel and had shot him when he resisted. A few months later Gushue pleaded guilty to a charge of robbery of Mayzel. At the same time he was charged with perjury in denying under oath at the murder trial that he had shot Mayzel. He pleaded guilty to that charge as well, but the Provincial Judge after hearing the facts, ordered that a plea of not guilty be entered and proceeded to hold a preliminary inquiry at which Gushue testified on a *voir dire* as to the admissibility of his statements to the police. When asked about the statements, he said that the statements that he had shot Mayzel were true. The Provincial Judge none the less discharged Gushue, holding that the Crown could not relitigate the issue of the shooting in view of the acquittal of murder.

Six months later the Crown applied for and obtained the consent of a County Court Judge to prefer an indictment against Gushue for perjury, contrary to s. 121 of the *Criminal Code* and for making contradictory statements in judicial proceedings contrary to s. 124. The perjury charge was based on the accused's evidence at the murder trial that he did not shoot Mayzel. The charge of making contradictory statements in judicial proceedings was based on Gushue's denial at his murder trial that he had shot Mayzel and his assertion on the *voir dire* at the subsequent preliminary inquiry on the charge of perjury that his statements to the police that he shot Mayzel were true.

At his trial on these charges before Graburn, Co. Ct. J., and a jury, the Judge directed the jury to acquit the accused of perjury because, in view of the finding of the jury on the trial for murder, a second jury would have to make a contrary finding and it was precluded from doing so. The accused was, however, found guilty of the charge under s. 124.

Appeals were launched by the Crown against the acquittal of perjury and by the accused against his conviction of robbery on his plea of guilty and against his conviction of the charge under s. 124. Martin, J.A., who spoke for a five-Judge Court of Appeal, affirmed the convictions of the accused [32 C.C.C. (2d) 189, 74 D.L.R. (3d) 473, 14 O.R. (2d) 620]; and, although of the opinion on the Crown's appeal that the prior acquittal of murder did not preclude conviction of perjury at that trial, and that a new trial would therefore be in order, he concluded that in view of the conviction under s. 124, a conviction of perjury would be contrary to the principle laid down by this Court in *Kienapple v. The Queen* (1974), 15 C.C.C. (2d) 524, 44 D.L.R. (3d) 351, [1975] S.C.R. 729. The appeal from the acquittal of perjury was thereupon dismissed and that matter is not before this Court.

As to the two convictions which are here, and the assertion of the accused that they are properly met by issue estoppel, I think it desirable to say at the outset that issue estoppel is part of the criminal law of Canada, and I would affirm the position of this Court in the matter, as expressed in *McDonald v. The Queen* (1959), 126 C.C.C. 1, [1960] S.C.R. 186, 32 C.R. 101, and *Feeley, Wright and McDermott v. The Queen*, [1963] 3 C.C.C. 201, 40 D.L.R. (2d) 563, [1963] S.C.R. 539. The Court accepted the statement of law of the availability of issue estoppel in criminal proceedings made by the Privy Council in *Sambasivam v. Public Prosecutor, Federation of Malaya*, [1950] A.C. 458, 11 C.R. 55.

There are thin but nonetheless discernible lines between issue estoppel and inconsistent verdicts and double jeopardy. I prefer to take *Sealfon v. United States* (1948), 332 U.S. 575, as involving a recognition of issue estoppel in the criminal law by the Supreme Court of the United States, rather than as resting merely on double jeopardy, that is on an attempt by the prosecution to retry an accused of an offence of which he had previously been acquitted. So, too, there is recognition of issue estoppel by the High Court of Australia in *Mraz v. The Queen (No. 2)* (1956), 96 C.L.R. 62, even though it may be urged that it rests on inconsistent verdicts. In so far as the House of Lords in the recent case of *Director of Public Prosecutions v. Humphrys*, [1976] 2 All E.R. 497, denied that issue estoppel could be raised in criminal proceedings, it does not commend itself to me. I prefer, as compatible with the view taken by this Court, the *obiter* acceptance of issue estoppel in the earlier House of Lords' judgment in *Connelly v. Director of Public Prosecutions*, [1964] 2 All E.R. 401. I think it important to note, however, that on the assumed acceptance of issue estoppel in criminal proceedings, the House of Lords in the *Humphrys* case, *supra*, saw a prosecution for perjury as an exception on the policy ground that although an accused cannot be retried for an offence of which he has been acquitted, he is not to be permitted to escape the consequences of having testified falsely at his trial.

The question before this Court is, therefore, not whether issue estoppel is recognized in Canadian criminal law but whether, as in the *McDonald* case, *supra*, and in the *Feeley, Wright and McDermott* case, *supra*, it has any application to the two convictions of the accused in this case on the relevant facts. There is always, of course, an initial difficulty in giving effect to a plea of issue estoppel where it is directed to the verdict of a jury which consists either of a bare finding of guilty or one of not guilty. How can it be ascertained on what issue or issues the finding rested for the purpose of foreclosing a relitigation of that issue or those issues in a subsequent criminal prosecution?

Counsel for the accused conceded that there cannot be any scrutiny of the evidence to determine what issues were before the jury. A surer guide may be found in the charge of the trial Judge. There were, however, several issues left to the jury and not only the issue whether Gushue alone shot Mayzel in the course of a robbery. Martin, J.A., in the Court of Appeal, gave the following summary of the charge [at p. 202 C.C.C., pp. 486-7 D.L.R.]:

> The Judge who presided over the trial of Gushue for the murder of Mayzel instructed the jury that if Gushue fired the shot which killed Mayzel while committing the offence of robbery, he was guilty of murder or, alternatively, he was guilty of murder if he and MacDonald formed a common intention to rob Mayzel and to assist each other in the robbery, and in carrying out the common

intention MacDonald killed Mayzel and Gushue *knew or ought to have known that the killing of Mayzel* would be a probable consequence of the carrying out or attempting to carry out the proposed robbery. I observe that this latter direction was more favourable to Gushue than the direction to which by law he was entitled, as it was not necessary in the circumstances in order to find him guilty of murder that the jury should find that he knew or ought to have known that the killing of Mayzel was a probable consequence of carrying out the common purpose to rob him.

If the jury followed the instruction which they were given by the trial Judge (as I think we must assume they did), they may have acquitted Gushue either because:

(a) they found that he had withdrawn from the plan to rob Mayzel, or entertained a reasonable doubt on this question, or

(b) although they were satisfied that Gushue was a party to the robbery, they entertained a reasonable doubt whether MacDonald, rather than Gushue, killed Mayzel, and whether Gushue knew or ought to have known that the killing of Mayzel by MacDonald was a probable consequence of the common intention to commit robbery.

I draw particular attention to the misdirection in favour of the accused, imposing as it did a larger burden on the Crown than was warranted in law. Counsel for the accused invoked the *Mraz* case, *supra,* and especially the judgment of Chief Justice Dixon, at pp. 68-9, where that learned Judge said the following:

It is nothing to the point that the verdict may have been the result of a misdirection of the judge and that owing to the misdirection the jury may have found the verdict without understanding or intending what as a matter of law is its necessary meaning or its legal consequences. The law which gives effect to issue estoppels is not concerned with the correctness or incorrectness of the finding which amounts to an estoppel, still less with the processes of reasoning by which the finding was reached in fact; it does not matter that the finding may be thought to be due to the jury having been put upon the wrong track by some direction of the presiding judge or to the jury having got on the wrong track unaided. It is enough that an issue or issues have been distinctly raised and found. Once that is done, then, so long as the finding stands, if there be any subsequent litigation between the same parties, no allegations legally inconsistent with the finding may be made by one of them against the other. *Res judicata pro veritate accipitur* . . . And, as has already been said, this applies in pleas of the Crown.

It was the further contention of counsel for the accused that the acquittal of murder was a positive determination that Gushue did not kill Mayzel, that there was no evidence that Gushue was a party to a killing by McDonald and, consequently, it was wrong to leave it to a second jury on the charge under s. 124 to second guess the jury that acquitted him of murder. It was submitted that if this was allowed, it would mean that a collateral attack could be made on jury verdicts, that the policy of finality of jury verdicts which are not appealed would be circumvented and that the accused would lose the benefit of the presumption of innocence.

I do not think that these submissions are telling in favour of the application of issue estoppel in respect of the charge under s. 124. The gist of the charge under that provision is making the contradictory statement with intent to mislead the Court, that is at the murder trial. The accused is not placed in double jeopardy because he cannot be retried for murder; indeed, it is enough for him to rely on *autrefois acquit*. The surfacing of his subsequent admission under oath that he lied at the trial for murder adds a new element and gives rise to a situation outside of the ambit of the trial for murder. It was contended, however, that the logic of the situation is in favour of the accused, that the jury finding that the accused did not kill Mayzel must be regarded as conclusively true, and the fact of the later contrary admission cannot give rise to a contradiction and there could not, therefore, be an intent to mislead the Court.

Logical as this submission may appear to be, what we have to resolve here is a question of policy based on the premise that issue estoppel cannot be founded on false evidence where the falsity is disclosed by subsequent evidence not available at the trial from which issue estoppel is alleged to arise. In my view, unless it can be said that the subsequent prosecution is an attempt by the Crown to retry the accused—and that is not the case here—the preferable policy is to exclude issue estoppel, especially when the contradictory statements on which the charge under s. 124 is founded consist of admissions of the accused himself.

In the result, I agree with Martin, J.A., that the conviction of the accused under s. 124 should be affirmed.

The charge of robbery and the conviction thereon raised related but also different considerations. I would not in this case foreclose reliance on issue estoppel simply because the accused pleaded guilty to a charge of robbery. It must be noted, however, that robbery is not an included offence on a charge of murder (see s. 589(3) of the *Criminal Code*), and hence the accused, as Martin, J.A., pointed out, was not put in jeopardy of a conviction of robbery when he was tried for murder. What was urged by counsel for the accused was that, on any view of the facts, the killer and robber of Mayzel were one and the same person, and since the accused was acquitted of the killing he could not be guilty of robbery. The accused's evidence that he did not enter the tailor shop must have been accepted by the jury, so it was contended, in order to acquit him of the killing and, correlatively, this excluded any possibility of his implication in the robbery.

However, the trial Judge's charge to the jury left to them not only the issue whether the accused himself killed Mayzel while intending to rob him. He also left to them the issue whether he was associated with McDonald in a common intention to rob Mayzel and to assist each other in carrying it out and whether in that connection McDonald killed Mayzel and Gushue knew or ought to have known that the killing would be a probable consequence of carrying out or attempting to carry out the robbery. Accepting for present purposes that the misdirection on this point, to which I referred earlier, is no bar to issue estoppel, it does not follow that the accused's acquittal of murder, which could have been by reason of the misdirection, necessarily meant that he was not a party to the robbery.

I am of opinion that the question of issue estoppel in respect of the robbery conviction is put to rest by the following statement, which I adopt, in Friedland, *Double Jeopardy* (1969), p. 134:

> The possibility or even the probability that the jury found in the accused's favour on a particular issue is not enough. A finding on the relevant issue must be the only rational explanation of the verdict of the jury.

The point has already been made that the accused could not have been convicted of robbery on his trial for murder. Moreover, it is not the same conduct that is involved in the charge of robbery as in the charge of murder under the alternative direction to the jury given by the trial Judge. In the circumstances, I do not think it is correct to say that the accused was being subjected to a second prosecution for a different aspect of the same conduct which was necessarily involved in his trial for murder. I agree, therefore, with Martin, J.A., that the contentions on behalf of the accused in respect of the robbery conviction fail.

In the result, the appeals are dismissed.

Appeals dismissed.

Jury verdicts result in a more difficult assessment of the merits of an issue estoppel argument. For the doctrine to apply, the issue in question must have be the only rational conclusion for the verdict. Moreover, any findings of fact made at the first trial by the trial judge for sentencing purposes are not binding for the purpose of adjudicating the issue estoppel claim:

R. v. PUNKO
2012 SCC 39, 284 C.C.C. (3d) 285, 94 C.R. (6th) 285 (S.C.C.)

Deschamps J. (McLachlin C.J.C. and Rothstein, Cromwell, Moldaver and Karakatsanis JJ. concurring):—

[1] These appeals concern the application of the doctrine of issue estoppel, as clarified by this Court in *R. v. Mahalingan*, 2008 SCC 63, [2008] 3 S.C.R. 316, in the context of a multi-issue jury trial. The specific question may be stated as follows: Is the Crown estopped from seeking to prove that the East End Chapter of the Hells Angels ("Hells Angels") is a criminal organization, on the basis that the issue was decided adversely to the Crown in a prior jury trial? For the reasons that follow, I would answer this question in the negative and dismiss the appeals.

I. Facts and Judicial History

[2] A multi-faceted, multi-year investigation by the Royal Canadian Mounted Police into the activities of the Hells Angels led to the identification of a broad range of acts that could constitute criminal offences. Some of the offences fell within the prosecutorial jurisdiction of the provincial Crown, while others fell within that of the federal Crown.

[3] The provincial prosecutions proceeded to trial in 2008 in the British Columbia Supreme Court before Romilly J. and a jury. The appellants, John Virgil Punko and Randall Richard Potts, and two others, Jean Joseph Violette and Ronaldo Lising, were tried jointly on varying charges of extortion, uttering threats, counselling mischief and unlawful possession of explosive substances and firearms. Some of the offences were allegedly committed for the benefit of, at the direction of, or in association with a criminal organization, namely the Hells Angels. In July 2009, following a ten-month trial, a jury found each of the accused guilty of a number of offences; however, it acquitted all four of them on all the criminal organization counts. Romilly J. delivered two sets of sentencing reasons, the first concerning Messrs. Punko, Potts and Lising (*R. v. Violette*, 2009 BCSC 1025, [2009] B.C.J. No. 1940 (QL)) and the second, Mr. Violette (*R. v. Violette*, 2009 BCSC 1557 (CanLII), [2009] B.C.J. No. 2262 (QL)).

[4] Meanwhile, a federal prosecution had been authorized. The appellants were charged individually with various drug-related offences, and on some of the counts — to the effect that they had produced and trafficked in a controlled substance (methamphetamine) — it was again alleged that they had done so for the benefit of, at the direction of, or in association with a criminal organization (the Hells Angels). A trial for the drug-related offences was scheduled before Leask J. of the British Columbia Supreme Court without a jury. On November 26, 2009, Leask J. heard pre-trial motions made by the appellants, who contended that the Crown should be estopped from leading evidence that the Hells Angels was a criminal organization, because the issue had already been decided by the jury in the provincial prosecution.

[5] Leask J. granted the appellants' motions (2010 BCSC 70, 251 C.C.C. (3d) 232). He held that the standard to be applied in answering the question whether an issue was decided in a prior proceeding for the purposes of issue estoppel is that of "proof on a balance of probabilities" (para. 28). To determine whether issue estoppel applied, Leask J. considered the general circumstances of the case. First, he considered the fact that the jury had resolved its deliberations shortly after asking Romilly J. a question concerning the definition of a criminal organization (para. 43). Second, Leask J. noted that Romilly J. had found in his reasons for sentence that Mr. Potts had been holding weapons for the Hells Angels (at para. 57) and that Mr. Violette had acted on behalf of the Hells Angels (para. 69). On this second point, Leask J. was of the view that Romilly J. had found that the jury had acquitted Mr. Punko and Mr. Potts on the criminal organization counts because it was not satisfied that the Hells Angels was a criminal organization (para. 75). Leask J. held that the Crown should be estopped from seeking to prove that the Hells Angels was a criminal organization in the trial before him. The Crown appealed.

[6] The Court of Appeal allowed the appeals and ordered a new trial (2011 BCCA 55, 299 B.C.A.C. 235). Kirkpatrick J.A., writing for the court, found that Leask J. had erred in casting the question whether an issue was resolved in a prior proceeding in terms of burden of proof, as it is actually "a question of logic and law" (para. 82). According to Kirkpatrick J.A., because individual

jurors may have reached their decisions on the verdict by different routes, it could not be said that the only rational explanation for the verdict of acquittal was that the jury found that the Hells Angels was not a criminal organization (para. 85). Nor did the nature and timing of the jury's question, or the sentencing judge's reasons, support a conclusion by a court in a subsequent proceeding that the issue of whether the Hells Angels was a criminal organization had necessarily been resolved by the jury. In Kirkpatrick J.A.'s opinion, the sentencing reasons did not "unequivocally state the relevant finding on which the issue estoppel is based" (para. 93).

II.   The Scope of the Doctrine of Issue Estoppel in the Criminal Context

[7] In *Mahalingan*, this Court had to decide whether the doctrine of issue estoppel should be retained as part of Canadian criminal law. A majority of the Court favoured retaining it in the criminal law, but in a narrow form. Not all issues raised in a previous trial can be the subject of issue estoppel. Rather, the Crown is precluded from relitigating only those issues that were *decided in favour of the accused* at the earlier trial (paras. 22, 31 and 33). Moreover, the resolution of an issue in favour of the accused must be "a necessary inference from the trial judge's findings or from the fact of the acquittal" (para. 52).

[8] In applying the doctrine of issue estoppel where the prior proceeding was before a jury, "[t]he question is whether a finding in favour of the accused is logically necessary to the verdict of acquittal" (*Mahalingan*, at para. 53 (emphasis added)), not whether the general circumstances of the case tend to indicate that the jury resolved the issue in favour of the accused. Thus, factors such as questions asked by the jury, the timing of the jury's verdict or findings made by the sentencing judge are not directly relevant to whether the jury resolved an issue in favour of the accused. They can be used only to reinforce a conclusion reached through reasoning based on logical necessity. Where, in light of the record and the parties' allegations, there is more than one logical explanation for the jury's verdict, and if one of these explanations does not depend on the jury's resolving the relevant issue in favour of the accused, the verdict cannot successfully be relied on in support of issue estoppel. An approach that encourages judges to inquire into the jurors' mental deliberations and reasoning processes should be rejected.

[9] I therefore agree with the Court of Appeal that Leask J. erred in law in drawing inferences on a balance of probabilities — a question of burden of proof — rather than considering whether a finding regarding the criminal nature of the organization was logically necessary to the acquittal — a question of logic and law.

[10] Mr. Potts submits that the doctrine of issue estoppel can be applied on the basis of findings of fact made by a sentencing judge under s. 724 of the *Criminal Code*, R.S.C. 1985, c. C-46 ("*Cr. C.*"). That section provides as follows:

> **724.** (1) In determining a sentence, a court may accept as proved any information disclosed at the trial or at the sentencing proceedings and any facts agreed on by the prosecutor and the offender.
>
> (2) Where the court is composed of a judge and jury, the court

    (a) shall accept as proven all facts, express or implied, that are essential to the jury's verdict of guilty; and

    (b) may find any other relevant fact that was disclosed by evidence at the trial to be proven, or hear evidence presented by either party with respect to that fact.

. . .

In support of his submission, Mr. Potts refers to a passage from *Mahalingan* in which the Court held that "an accused should not be called upon to answer allegations of law or fact already resolved in his or her favour by a judicial determination on the merits" (para. 39). In the context of a multi-issue jury trial, I cannot accept that the findings of fact made by the sentencing judge are determinative for the purposes of issue estoppel.

[11] Where a fact is necessary for the purpose of determining the appropriate sentence but is not express or implied in the jury's verdict, the sentencing judge must make his or her own finding (s. 724(2)(*b*) *Cr. C.*). However, such a finding does not constitute a judicial determination *on the merits* of the case; rather, it constitutes a judicial determination only for the purpose of sentencing. The merits of the case in a jury trial pertain to the issues the jurors can take into consideration in reaching a verdict. It is the role of the jury, not the sentencing judge, to make judicial determinations on the merits. The jurors must arrive at a unanimous result on the basis of the evidence. In doing so, it is their prerogative to make their own determinations on the merits. Issue estoppel will apply only where unanimity of the jury on an issue can be discerned through reasoning based on logical necessity.

[12] A sentencing judge must also accept as proven facts that are implicit in the jury's verdict of guilty (s. 724(2)(*a*) *Cr. C.*). These are not determinations of the sentencing judge, but simply his elucidation of the facts the jury must have relied on to convict the accused. The sentencing judge has no duty to elucidate or make findings with respect to a jury's verdict of acquittal. Any observation the sentencing judge makes in that regard may indicate his or her own views, but it is not a determination that binds a judge sitting on a subsequent motion based on issue estoppel. In every case, the judge in the subsequent proceeding must determine whether the sentencing judge's elucidation of the jury's verdict meets the standard of logical necessity. Findings made by a sentencing judge regarding a jury's determinations in a multi-issue trial cannot be used to circumvent the standard of logical necessity established in *Mahalingan*, but only to confirm a conclusion reached by applying that standard.

III. Application to the Facts

[13] In the original trial presided by Romilly J., the jury acquitted the four accused on all the criminal organization counts. Leask J. stated that he was satisfied on a balance of probabilities, on the basis of Romilly J.'s sentencing reasons, the jury's question and the timing of the jury's verdict, that the jury must have acquitted the accused on the basis that the Hells Angels was not a criminal organization. In light of *Mahalingan*, however, the question is whether a finding that the Hells Angels is not a criminal organization is the only logical inference a judge can draw from the jury's verdict. A review of the relevant portions of the transcript of the jury trial reveals that it is not.

[14] In their closing arguments on the criminal organization counts, counsel for Mr. Punko, Mr. Potts and Mr. Lising each advanced two distinct defences: first, that the Crown had failed to prove that the Hells Angels was a criminal organization and, second, that none of the substantive offences were committed for the benefit of, at the direction of, or in association with the Hells Angels.

[15] In his charge, Romilly J. informed the jury that, on all the criminal organization counts, the Crown had to prove the following five elements beyond a reasonable doubt:

> (i) that the accused committed the substantive offence;
>
> (ii) that during the period specified in the count, the Hells Angels was a criminal organization;
>
> (iii) that the accused knew that the characteristics of the Hells Angels were those of a criminal organization during the time period specified in the count;
>
> (iv) that the accused committed the offence for the benefit of, at the direction of, or in association with the Hells Angels; and
>
> (v) that the accused committed the offence with the intent to do so for the benefit of, at the direction of, or in association with the Hells Angels.

Romilly J. instructed the jury that, if it was not satisfied of each element beyond a reasonable doubt, it had to deliver a verdict of not guilty. He also told the jurors that, if they acquitted the accused of the underlying substantive offence, they had to find him not guilty on the associated criminal organization count. The fact that there were five elements the Crown had to prove meant that, if the jury convicted the accused of the substantive offence, there were still four possible reasons for delivering a verdict of not guilty on the associated criminal organization count.

[16] According to the arguments advanced by the defence, which Romilly J. summarized for the jury, there were two main issues the jury had to decide in relation to each criminal organization count once it had found the accused guilty of the predicate offence: (1) whether the Hells Angels was a criminal organization, and (2) whether the predicate offence was committed for the benefit of, at the direction of or in association with the Hells Angels.

[17] It was not argued that Romilly J. had submitted defences to the jury that lacked an evidential foundation, or "air of reality" (see *R. v. Cinous*, 2002 SCC 29, [2002] 2 S.C.R. 3). In this Court, Mr. Punko stated that his "primary defence" to the criminal organization charges was that the Crown had failed to prove that the Hells Angels was a criminal organization (A.F., at para. 21), but that

> [a]s an alternate route to acquittal on the criminal organization counts the Appellants and Lising submitted to the jury that if they committed the substantive offences it was not for "the benefit of, at the direction of, or in association with" the [Hells Angels]. [A.F., at para. 23]

[18] In sum, there are at least two logical explanations for the not guilty verdict on each of the criminal organization counts. This means that a judge cannot infer from the jury verdict, as required by *Mahalingan*, that the jurors

necessarily found that the Hells Angels was not a criminal organization. There was, as counsel for Mr. Punko pointed out, an alternate route to the verdict.

[19] Leask J. placed considerable weight on Romilly J.'s finding that Mr. Potts had been holding weapons for the Hells Angels and that Mr. Violette had been acting on behalf of the Hells Angels. However, regardless of whether Romilly J. was making his own finding of fact under s. 724(2)(b) Cr. C. or was interpreting the jury's verdict, this finding does not assist the appellants in their issue estoppel argument. First, as I mentioned above, findings of fact made by the sentencing judge for the purpose of sentencing under s. 724(2)(b) cannot be relied on in support of issue estoppel. Second, no finding of fact that is implicit in a jury's verdict as elucidated by the sentencing judge is a substitute for a conclusion by a judge hearing a motion based on issue estoppel, applying the standard of logical necessity, that the issue was previously decided in favour of the accused. It bears mentioning here that, because Romilly J.'s findings would have flowed from the jury's decision to *acquit* on the criminal organization counts, they could not have been made under s. 724(2)(a). In any event, it cannot be said that Romilly J.'s findings were a necessary inference from the fact of the acquittal, as there were at least two logical explanations for the jury's decisions to acquit on the criminal organization counts. In considering the motions based on issue estoppel, Leask J. could not conclude that a finding that the Hells Angels was not a criminal organization was logically necessary to the jury's verdict of acquittal. Romilly J.'s findings of fact simply shed light on his own reasoning, not on that of the jurors, and do not provide the support Leask J. attributed to them.

[20] Mr. Punko invokes a policy reason to justify applying the doctrine of issue estoppel in this case. He argues that because the provincial Crown successfully argued at the sentencing hearing before Romilly J. that the conduct of the accused was for or on behalf of the Hells Angels, as a matter of policy the federal Crown should be bound to accept that the jury acquitted them because it had a reasonable doubt that the Hells Angels was a criminal organization. In his opinion, the fact that the federal Crown is now arguing that the Hells Angels is a criminal organization is unfair to the accused (A.F., at paras. 122-24).

[21] In my view, if an issue of unfairness does arise from the positions of the federal and provincial Crowns, it cannot be resolved on the basis of the narrow doctrine of issue estoppel. In Canadian criminal law, issue estoppel merely ensures that an accused will not be required to answer questions that *have already been determined* in his or her favour. If the Crown's conduct in this case were found to be sufficiently egregious, the doctrine of abuse of process could provide protection against relitigation. Moreover, if any guilty verdicts are returned in respect of the federal prosecution, the sentencing judge will be in a position to take into consideration all the circumstances of the conviction, including the sentence imposed by Romilly J., if he finds that the charges are interconnected (s. 725(1)(c) Cr. C.).

[22] In conclusion, it is worth recalling the point made in *Mahalinghan* (paras. 24 and 54) that, in a multi-issue jury trial, it will be rare for an acquittal to ground issue estoppel, because such an acquittal will often have more than one

possible basis and different jurors may have reached a unanimous verdict by different routes. These appeals are an illustration of that point.

[23] I would dismiss the appeals.

In a judgment concurring in the result, Justice Fish preferred to leave open the question of whether there might be reliance on facts determined by the trial judge in sentencing.

In England, the House of Lords has said that it would be better to restrict the use of the phrase "issue estoppel" to civil actions. For them, the concept "abuse of process" was a much more meaningful device. See *Hunter v. Chief Constable of West Midlands Police,* [1982] A.C. 529, [1981] 3 All E.R. 727 (H.L.) 540; followed *Demeter v. Br. Pac. Life Ins. Co.* (1983), 43 O.R. (2d) 33 (Ont. H.C.); affirmed (1984), 48 O.R. (2d) 266 (Ont. C.A.). It may be that the broader concept of abuse of process, with argument based on, and in terms of, its underlying philosophy would be a preferable approach to these problems than the apparent complexity and narrowness of issue estoppel.

In *R. v. Mahalingan,* [2008] 3 S.C.R. 316, 61 C.R. (6th) 207, 237 C.C.C. (3d) 417, a majority of the Court held that the doctrine of issue estoppel should remain a part of Canadian criminal law. The accused had appealed a conviction for aggravated assault. At trial, a witness testified that the accused had sought to dissuade him from testifying. After the trial but before the appeal was heard, the accused was acquitted of obstruction of justice in respect of the allegation by the witness. The Court of Appeal admitted fresh evidence of the acquittal on appeal and ordered a new trial, holding that the acquittal operated as an issue estoppel to render the witness's testimony inadmissible. However, the Supreme Court held that retroactive effect could not be given to issue estoppel. The majority thus modified the doctrine slightly so that its application is limited to precluding the Crown from relitigating an issue that was determined in the accused's favour in a *prior* proceeding, whether the issue was determined on the basis of a positive finding or due to a reasonable doubt.

For criticism of the Supreme Court's narrow approach see Anne London-Weinstein, "Déjà Vu All Over Again: Issue of Estoppel Post *Punko*" (2014) 61 Crim. L.Q. 227.

PROBLEM 17

The accused was tried and acquitted of robbery of a convenience store. A principal piece of evidence tendered against him was his alleged confession in which he described his involvement in that offence and also admitted to a robbery of a tavern. Following a *voir dire* the statement was rejected as involuntary. The accused is now charged with the robbery of the tavern. Is the admissibility at the second trial res judicata?

Compare *Duhamel v. R.,* [1984] 2 S.C.R. 555, 43 C.R. (3d) 1 (S.C.C.).

PROBLEM 18

The accused's motor vehicle struck two individuals who were crossing the street. The accused was indicted separately for each of the deaths. In the first trial the accused was acquitted of manslaughter. At the second trial for manslaughter involving the death of the other he pleads autrefois acquit. What result? He pleads res judicata. He pleads not guilty and raises res judicata as a defence. What result?

Compare *R. v. Sweetman*, [1939] O.R. 131 (Ont. C.A.) and *State v. Fredlund*, 273 N.W. 353 (Minn.) (1937). See also the gross example of *Ciucci v. Illionos*, 356 U.S. 571 (1958).

PROBLEM 19

The accused was charged with impaired driving. He testified to an alibi defence and was acquitted. The accused was later charged with perjury arising out of that testimony. Issue estoppel?

Compare *R. v. Grdic* (1982), 29 C.R. (3d) 395 (B.C. C.A.). Suppose the accused testifies at his perjury trial and he is acquitted. May the Crown lay a charge of perjury relating to his testimony at the first perjury trial?

Compare *Com. v. Spivey* (1932), 48 S.W. 2d 1076 (Ky.). Suppose the accused is convicted at his impaired driving trial. Can he later be charged with perjury regarding his alibi defence?

Compare *R. v. Rothenberg* (1984), 46 C.R. (3d) 18 (Ont. H.C.).

PROBLEM 20

The accused was charged with the manslaughter of his son. The deceased, a three-year-old child, died from severe head injuries. The principal prosecution witness, the child's mother, described the accused's actions of repeatedly striking the deceased. The accused's version was that he had witnessed the mother repeatedly striking the deceased. The child's mother had earlier pleaded guilty to manslaughter on the basis that she had failed to discharge her legal duty as a parent to protect the child from mistreatment by the accused. The trial judge has advised that he intends to leave it open to the jury to find manslaughter either on the basis of acts of commission by the accused or by his omission to act. Do you have any objection?

Compare *R. v. Speid* (1985), 46 C.R. (3d) 22 (Ont. C.A.).

PROBLEM 21

On August 18, 1985, the three children in the Smith family died in a fire at their residence. The children's father pleaded guilty on October 18, 1985, to causing the death of Joy Smith by criminal negligence and was sentenced to imprisonment for two years less one day. Further police investigation suggests that the father was not intoxicated on the evening in question as first believed and you, as an assistant Crown

Attorney, have been asked for advice as to whether the police should pursue the investigation any further leading to a possible successful murder prosecution. Advise.

PROBLEM 22

The accused pleads guilty to a charge of breaking, entering and committing robbery. He is subsequently charged with attempted murder arising from injuries inflicted during the same incident. Has he a *Kienapple* defence on the basis of its interpretation in *Prince*?

Compare *R. v. Wigman*, [1987] 1 S.C.R. 246, 56 C.R. (3d) 289, 33 C.C.C. (3d) 97 (S.C.C.).

PROBLEM 23

A recreation instructor employed by the City of Toronto is convicted of sexually assaulting a young boy and sentenced to 15 months' imprisonment. His appeal is dismissed. His employment is then terminated on the basis that the offence was directly linked to his employment. He grieves his dismissal. The arbitrator holds that the conviction was admissible evidence but not conclusive. The instructor, but not the complainant, testifies. The arbitrator decides that the complainant was a liar and orders that the instructor be re-instated. The employer seeks judicial review. Should the arbitrator have been bound by the principle of finality absent exceptional circumstances?

Compare *Toronto (City) v. C.U.P.E., Local 79* (2001), 45 C.R. (5th) 354 (Ont. C.A.), affirmed [2003] 3 S.C.R. 77, 17 C.R. (6th) 276 (S.C.C.).

Part V

POST-TRIAL REVIEW

Chapter 14

APPEALS

This chapter covers what remedies are available to the Crown and the defence once the trial and/or sentencing phase of the proceedings have been completed. It explores what avenues of relief are available to both the Crown and the defence. For the Crown, the options are an appeal from an acquittal or from the sentence imposed. The Crown may appeal an outright acquittal on the offence as charged, or an acquittal on the offence as charged, but not a conviction on an included offence (*i.e.*, where the accused is charged with murder, but convicted of manslaughter). Similarly, the accused person may appeal conviction, as well as the sentence imposed.

There are other junctures in the criminal process where the Crown or the accused may seek relief by applying to a higher court for relief. The common law and the Criminal Code provide a complicated web of procedures known as extraordinary remedies or prerogative remedies. These remedies are *certiorari*, *mandamus*, *prohibition* and *habeas corpus*. These are highly specialized aspects of criminal procedure that extend beyond the scope of this book. Passing reference is made to certain aspects of extraordinary remedies in the previous chapters. For example, in Chapter 9 on Preliminary Inquiries, reference is made to the *certiorari* procedure used to review decisions of preliminary inquiry judges.

1. Appeals Against Conviction and Acquittal

The Criminal Code separates the procedure for appealing cases proceeded by indictment (Part XXI) and by summary conviction (Part XXVII). Summary conviction appeals are heard by an "appeal court", which is defined as a judge of the superior court of the province (s. 812). Both the Crown and the accused have the ability to appeal convictions, acquittals and sentences (s. 813). Appeals from decisions of the summary conviction appeal court may be taken to the Court of Appeal of the province, but only on a question of law alone and with leave of that court or a judge thereof (s. 839): see *R. v. R. (R.)* (2008), 234 C.C.C. (3d) 463, 59 C.R. (6th) 258 (Ont. C.A.).

The major focus of this chapter is appeals from cases proceeded with by way of indictment. The major provisions relating to the right of the accused and the Crown to appeal and the powers of an appeal court to hear and dispose of appeals are set out below.

675. (1) A person who is convicted by a trial court in proceedings by indictment may appeal to the court of appeal

(a) against his conviction

(i) on any ground of appeal that involves a question of law alone,

(ii) on any ground of appeal that involves a question of fact or a question of mixed law and fact, with leave of the court of appeal or a judge thereof or on the certificate of the trial judge that the case is a proper case for appeal, or

(iii) on any ground of appeal not mentioned in subparagraph (i) or (ii) that appears to the court of appeal to be a sufficient ground of appeal, with leave of the court of appeal; or

(b) against the sentence passed by the trial court, with leave of the court of appeal or a judge thereof unless that sentence is one fixed by law.

(2) A person who has been convicted of second degree murder and sentenced to imprisonment for life without eligibility for parole for a specified number of years in excess of ten may appeal to the court of appeal against the number of years in excess of ten of his imprisonment without eligibility for parole.

(2.1) A person against whom an order under section 743.6 has been made may appeal to the court of appeal against the order.

(3) Where a verdict of not criminally responsible on account of mental disorder or unfit to stand trial is rendered in respect of a person, that person may appeal to the court of appeal against that verdict on any ground of appeal mentioned in subparagraph (1)(a)(i), (ii) or (iii) and subject to the conditions described therein.

(4) Where a judge of the court of appeal refuses leave to appeal under this section otherwise than under paragraph (1)(b), the appellant may, by filing notice in writing with the court of appeal within seven days after the refusal, have the application for leave to appeal determined by the court of appeal.

676. (1) The Attorney General or counsel instructed by him for the purpose may appeal to the court of appeal

(a) against a judgment or verdict of acquittal or a verdict of not criminally responsible on account of mental disorder of a trial court in proceedings by indictment on any ground of appeal that involves a question of law alone;

(b) against an order of a superior court of criminal jurisdiction that quashes an indictment or in any manner refuses or fails to exercise jurisdiction on an indictment;

(c) against an order of a trial court that stays proceedings on an indictment or quashes an indictment; or

(d) with leave of the court of appeal or a judge thereof, against the sentence passed by a trial court in proceedings by indictment, unless that sentence is one fixed by law.

(2) For the purposes of this section, a judgment or verdict of acquittal includes an acquittal in respect of an offence specifically charged where the accused has, on the trial thereof, been convicted or discharged under section 730 of any other offence.

(3) The Attorney General or counsel instructed by the Attorney General for the purpose may appeal to the court of appeal against a verdict that an accused is unfit to stand trial, on any ground of appeal that involves a question of law alone.

(4) The Attorney General or counsel instructed by him for the purpose may appeal to the court of appeal in respect of a conviction for second degree murder, against the number of years of imprisonment without eligibility for parole, being less than twenty-five, that has been imposed as a result of that conviction.

(5) The Attorney General or counsel instructed by the Attorney General for the purpose may appeal to the court of appeal against the decision of the court not to make an order under section 743.6.

(6) The Attorney General or counsel instructed by the Attorney General for the purpose may appeal to the court of appeal against the decision of the court not to make an order under subsection 745.51(1).

. . .

There are also important ancillary powers granted to courts of appeal and the Supreme Court of Canada in s. 683. Chief among these is an application to adduce fresh evidence. The leading cases on the criteria and procedure for an application to admit fresh evidence are *R. v. Palmer* (1979), 14 C.R. (3d) 22, [1980] 1 S.C.R. 759, 50 C.C.C. (2d) 193 (S.C.C.) and *R. v. Nielsen*, 62 C.R. (3d) 313, [1988] 1 S.C.R. 480, 40 C.C.C. (3d) 1 (S.C.C.). The provisions reproduced above provide wide powers of the Court to intervene and to make remedial orders. For instance, in *R. v. Bellusci* (2012), 94 C.R. (6th) 221 (S.C.C.), it was held that, rather than ordering a new trial when overturning a verdict, the appellate court may, in some circumstances where there is no prejudice to the parties and it is in the interests of justice, simply order the continuation of the trial. The scope of some of the powers given to appellate courts is explained in the excerpts below.

R. v. BERNARDO
(1997), 121 C.C.C. (3d) 123, 12 C.R. (5th) 310 (Ont. C.A.)

This aspect of the infamous case against Paul Bernardo dealt with an application to the Court of Appeal to appoint counsel to represent Bernardo, even though his application to legal aid had been refused. Section 684 of the Criminal Code provides for this procedure. In the course of dealing with this case, the Court makes some important observations about the appeal process in Canada.

DOHERTY J.A.:—

Section 684(1) appears in Part XXI of the Criminal Code which controls appeals in indictable matters. Section 675(1) affords an accused an opportunity to appeal his or her conviction to the Court of Appeal on virtually any ground. I recognize that the accused only has a right to appeal on questions of law alone (s. 675(1)(a)(i)). The accused must obtain leave to argue other grounds. In practice, however, at least in Ontario, all grounds of appeal raised by an accused are considered on their merits. There is no separate inquiry into whether leave to appeal should be granted. In effect, the appeal, while on the record, is unlimited. The wide ambit of appeals from convictions is matched by the broad remedial powers granted to the Court of Appeal by s. 686(1)(a). The court may quash a conviction where the verdict is unreasonable, there has been an error in law, or there has been a miscarriage of justice.

When ss. 675 and 686 are considered in combination, it is clear that Parliament contemplated that persons convicted of an indictable offence would have unobstructed access to a wide-ranging review of the trial record at a first level of appeal: *R. v. Morrissey* (1995), 97 C.C.C. (3d) 193 (Ont. C.A.). Liberal access to appellate review, coupled with broad remedial appellate powers, not only protects the obvious interests of the accused, but it also enhances the fairness and reliability of the entire criminal process. In doing so, it promotes public confidence in the reliability of the results of that process and public respect for the justness of the means by which those results are achieved.

Appellate review as provided for by Part XXI of the Criminal Code is not an indulgence to be doled out to those who are somehow seen as deserving of the opportunity to challenge their conviction. The salutary purposes underlying broad appellate review on appeals from convictions are engaged and must be served no matter how heinous the crime or despicable the accused. Detached and reflective appellate review of the trial process is perhaps most important in notorious, emotion-charged cases involving the least deserving accused. It is in those cases that the public eye is most closely focused on the process and the mettle of the criminal justice system undergoes its severest test. By giving the most repugnant appellant full recourse to meaningful appellate review, and by subjecting the apparently most deserving convictions to careful appellate scrutiny the integrity of the process is maintained and a commitment to the unbending application of the rule of law is affirmed.

The "interests of justice" referred to in s. 684(1) must take cognizance of the broad access to appellate review contemplated by s. 675 and the wide remedial powers of the court of appeal set out in s. 686. Justice demands that an accused who appeals under s. 675 be afforded a meaningful opportunity to establish the merits of the grounds of appeal advanced by that appellant. That same interest also insists that the court be able to fully and properly exercise its broad jurisdiction at the conclusion of the appeal. Anything less is inconsistent with the statutory scheme created by Part XXI of the Criminal Code.

Most accused who appeal their convictions in indictable proceedings are represented by counsel and most of those counsel are funded by legal aid. Section 684(1), however, recognizes that there will be cases where even though legal aid has been refused, the assistance of counsel is necessary to the exercise of a meaningful right of appeal.

R. v. MORRISSEY
(1995), 38 C.R. (4th) 4, 97 C.C.C. (3d) 193 (Ont. C.A.)

The accused, a former Christian Brother, was convicted of sexual offences and other offences against a number of former training school residents. In allowing the appeal, the Court discusses the nature of the appeal powers pertaining to appeals against conviction by an accused person.

DOHERTY J.A.:—

. . .

Section 675(1)(a) gives this court jurisdiction to consider grounds of appeal which allege any type of error in the trial proceedings. The wide sweep of s. 675(1)(a) manifests Parliament's intention to provide virtually unobstructed access to a first level of appellate review to those convicted of indictable offences.

The scope of this court's power to quash convictions is commensurate with the broad jurisdiction given to it by s. 676(1)(a). Section 686(1)(a) provides that:

686. (1) On the hearing of an appeal against a conviction or against a verdict that the appellant is unfit to stand trial or not criminally responsible on account of mental disorder, the court of appeal

(a) may allow the appeal where it is of the opinion that

(i) the verdict should be set aside on the ground that is unreasonable or cannot be supported by the evidence,

(ii) the judgment of the trial court should be set aside on the ground of a wrong decision on a question of law, or

(iii) on any ground there was a miscarriage of justice;

The powers granted in that section are qualified to some extent by s. 686(1)(b)(iii) and (iv). For present purposes I need reproduce only s. 686(1)(b)(iii):

(b) [the Court of Appeal] may dismiss the appeal where

(iii) notwithstanding that the court is of the opinion that on any ground mentioned in subparagraph (a)(ii) the appeal might be decided in favour of the appellant, it is of the opinion that no substantial wrong or miscarriage of justice has occurred . . .

While s. 686(1)(a) provides three distinct bases upon which this court may quash a conviction, each shares the same underlying rationale. A conviction which is the product of a miscarriage of justice cannot stand. Section 686(1)(a)(i) is concerned with the most obvious example of a miscarriage of justice, a conviction which no reasonable trier of fact properly instructed could have returned on the evidence adduced at trial. Section 686(1)(a)(ii) read along with s. 686(1)(b)(iii) presumes that an error in law produces a miscarriage of justice unless the Crown can demonstrate the contrary with the requisite degree of certainty. Section 686(1)(a)(iii) addresses all other miscarriages of justice not caught by the two preceding subsections. In so far as the operation of s. 686(1)(a) is concerned, the distinction between errors of law and all other types of error has only one significance. Where the error is one of law the Crown bears the burden of demonstrating that the error did not result in a miscarriage of justice. Where the error is not one of law alone the appellant bears that burden.

In my opinion, on appeals from convictions in indictable proceedings where misapprehension of the evidence is alleged, this court should first consider the reasonableness of the verdict (s. 686(1)(a)(i)). If the appellant succeeds on this ground an acquittal will be entered. If the verdict is not unreasonable, then the court should determine whether the misapprehension of evidence occasioned a miscarriage of justice (s. 686(1)(a)(iii)). If the appellant is able to show that the error resulted in a miscarriage of justice, then the conviction must be quashed and, in most cases, a new trial ordered. Finally, if the appellant cannot show that the verdict was unreasonable or that the error produced a miscarriage of justice, the court must consider the vexing question of whether the misapprehension of evidence amounted to an error in law (s. 686(1)(a)(ii)). If the error is one of law, the onus will shift to the Crown to demonstrate that it did not result in a miscarriage of justice (s. 686(1)(b)(iii)).

In considering the reasonableness of the verdict pursuant to s. 686(1)(a)(i), this court must conduct its own, albeit limited, review of the evidence adduced at trial: *R. v. Burns*. This court's authority to declare a conviction unreasonable or unsupported by the evidence does not depend upon the demonstration of any errors in the proceedings below. The verdict is the error where s. 686(1)(a)(i) is properly invoked. A misapprehension of the evidence does not render a verdict unreasonable. Nor is a finding that the judge misapprehended the evidence a condition precedent to a finding that a verdict is unreasonable. In cases tried without juries, a finding that the trial judge did misapprehend the evidence can, however, figure prominently in an argument that the resulting verdict was unreasonable. An appellant will be in a much better position to demonstrate the unreasonableness of a verdict if the appellant can demonstrate that the trial judge misapprehended significant evidence: *R. v. Burns*.

I need not pursue the relationship between a misapprehension of the evidence and an unreasonable verdict any further. On the evidence adduced in this case and bearing in mind the errors made by the trial judge in his appreciation of that evidence, I cannot say that the convictions of counts 1, 2, 3, and 6 were unreasonable.

I turn next to s. 686(1)(a)(iii). This subsection is not concerned with the characterization of an error as one of law, fact, mixed fact and law or something else, but rather with the impact of the error on the trial proceedings. It reaches all errors resulting in a miscarriage of justice and vindicates the wide jurisdiction vested in this court by s. 675(1). The long reach of s. 686(1)(a)(iii) was described by McIntyre J., for a unanimous court, in *Fanjoy v. R.*, [1985] 2 S.C.R. 233:

> A person charged with the commission of a crime is entitled to a fair trial according to law. Any error which occurs at trial that deprives the accused of that entitlement is a miscarriage of justice.

Fanjoy, like most cases where s. 686(1)(a)(iii) has been invoked, involved prosecutorial or judicial misconduct in the course of the trial: e.g., see *R. v. Stewart* (1991), 62 C.C.C. (3d) 289 (Ont. C.A.); *R. v. R. (A.J.)* (1994), 94 C.C.C. (3d) 168 (Ont. C.A.). Such conduct obviously jeopardizes the fairness of a trial and fits comfortably within the concept of a miscarriage of justice. Nothing in the language of the section, however, suggests that it is limited to any particular type of error. In my view, any error, including one involving a misapprehension of the evidence by the trial judge, must be assessed by reference to its impact on the fairness of the trial. If the error renders the trial unfair, then s. 686(1)(a)(iii) requires that the conviction be quashed.

When will a misapprehension of the evidence render a trial unfair and result in a miscarriage of justice? The nature and extent of the misapprehension and its significance to the trial judge's verdict must be considered in light of the fundamental requirement that a verdict must be based exclusively on the evidence adduced at trial. Where a trial judge is mistaken as to the substance of material parts of the evidence and those errors play an essential part in the reasoning process resulting in a conviction then, in my view, the accused's conviction is not based exclusively on the evidence and is not a "true" verdict. Convictions resting on a misapprehension of the substance of the evidence adduced at trial sit on no firmer foundation than those based on information derived from sources extraneous to the trial. If an appellant can demonstrate that the conviction depends on a misapprehension of the evidence then, in my view, it must follow that the appellant has not received a fair trial, and was the victim of a miscarriage of justice. This is so even if the evidence, as actually adduced at trial, was capable of supporting a conviction.

In *R. v. Sarrazin* (2011), 88 C.R. (6th) 88, [2011] 3 S.C.R. 505, 276 C.C.C. (3d) 210 (S.C.C.) Justice Binnie held for a 6-3 majority that the purpose of the curative proviso is to avoid a retrial that would be superfluous and unnecessary but requires a high burden on the Crown of satisfying the standard of an overwhelming case or a harmless error. The burden, held the Court, should not be relaxed as had been suggested by Moldaver J.A. (as he then was) dissenting in the Ontario Court of Appeal. See C.R. annotation by Tim Quigley.

R. v. H. (J.M.)
[2011] 3 S.C.R. 197, 87 C.R. (6th) 213 (S.C.C.)

Cromwell J. (for a unanimous Court):—

B. *Under What Circumstances Do Alleged Shortcomings in a Trial Judge's Assessment of the Evidence Constitute an Error of Law and Thereby Allow Appellate Review of an Acquittal?*

[1] The Crown's right of appeal from an acquittal of an indictable offence is limited to "any ground of appeal that involves a question of law alone": *Criminal Code*, s. 676(1)(*a*). This limited right of appeal engages the vexed question of what constitutes, for jurisdictional purposes, an error of law alone. This appeal raises once again the issue of when the trial judge's alleged shortcomings in assessing the evidence constitute an error of law giving rise to a Crown appeal of an acquittal. The jurisprudence currently recognizes four such situations. While this may not be an exhaustive list, it will be helpful to review these four situations briefly.

(1) It Is an Error of Law to Make a Finding of Fact for Which There Is No Evidence — However, a Conclusion That the Trier of Fact Has a Reasonable Doubt Is Not a Finding of Fact for the Purposes of This Rule

[2] It has long been recognized that it is an error of law to make a finding of fact for which there is no supporting evidence: *Schuldt v. The Queen*, [1985] 2 S.C.R. 592, at p. 604. It does not follow from this principle, however, that an acquittal can be set aside on the basis that it is not supported by the evidence. An acquittal (absent some fact or element on which the accused bears the

burden of proof) is not a finding of fact but instead a conclusion that the standard of persuasion beyond a reasonable doubt has not been met. Moreover, as pointed out in *R. v. Lifchus*, [1997] 3 S.C.R. 320, at para. 39, a reasonable doubt is logically derived from the evidence or absence of evidence. Juries are properly so instructed and told that they may accept some, all or none of a witness's evidence: *Lifchus*, at paras. 30 and 36; Canadian Judicial Council, Model Jury Instructions, Part III, Final Instructions, 9.4 Assessment of Evidence (online).

[3] The principle that it is an error of law to make a finding of fact for which there is no supporting evidence does not, in general, apply to a decision to acquit based on a reasonable doubt. As Binnie J. put it in *R. v. Walker*, 2008 SCC 34, [2008] 2 S.C.R. 245, at para. 22:

> A major difference between the position of the Crown and the accused in a criminal trial, of course, is that the accused benefits from the presumption of innocence. . . . [W]hereas a conviction requires the prosecution to establish each of the factual elements of the offence beyond a reasonable doubt, no such requirement applies to an acquittal which, unlike a conviction, can rest simply on the absence of proof. [Emphasis deleted.]

[4] The point was expressed very clearly in *R. v. Biniaris*, 2000 SCC 15, [2000] 1 S.C.R. 381, at para. 33: ". . . as a matter of law, the concept of 'unreasonable acquittal' is incompatible with the presumption of innocence and the burden which rests on the prosecution to prove its case beyond a reasonable doubt."

(2) The Legal Effect of Findings of Fact or of Undisputed Facts Raises a Question of Law

[5] *R. v. Morin*, [1992] 3 S.C.R. 286, lists this as one category of cases in which the trial judge's assessment of the evidence may give rise to an error of law. As Sopinka J. put it, at p. 294:

> If a trial judge finds all the facts necessary to reach a conclusion in law and in order to reach that conclusion the facts can simply be accepted as found, a Court of Appeal can disagree with the conclusion reached without trespassing on the fact-finding function of the trial judge. The disagreement is with respect to the law and not the facts nor inferences to be drawn from the facts. The same reasoning applies if the facts are accepted or not in dispute.

In short, the appellate court can simply apply the trial judge's findings of fact to the proper legal principles; the trial judge's error, if there is one, may safely be traced to a question of law rather than to any question about how to weigh the evidence.

(3) An Assessment of the Evidence Based on a Wrong Legal Principle Is an Error of Law

[6] This is another category mentioned in *Morin*. In that case, Sopinka J. stated at p. 295, "Failure to appreciate the evidence cannot amount to an error of law unless the failure is based on a misapprehension of some legal principle." In *B. (G.)*, Wilson J. added important cautionary words concerning this basis for appellate intervention:

. . . it will be more difficult in an appeal from an acquittal to establish with certainty that the error committed by the trial judge raised a question of law alone because of the burden of proof on the Crown in all criminal prosecutions and the increased importance of examining critically all evidence that may raise a reasonable doubt. [p. 75]

[7] This proposition was said by Lamer J. (as he then was) in *Schuldt* to constitute the proper basis for the Court's decision in *Wild v. The Queen*, [1971] S.C.R. 101. In *Schuldt*, at p. 610, it was affirmed that except in the rare cases in which a statutory provision places an onus upon the accused, it can sometimes be said as a matter of law that there is no evidence on which the court can convict, but never that there is no evidence on which it can acquit as there is always the rebuttable presumption of innocence. This approach was also adopted in *B. (G.)* by Wilson J., at pp. 69-70, and the point was further underlined in the concurring reasons of McLachlin J. (as she then was), at p. 79, where she wrote: "In the absence of . . . misdirection the law is clear that doubts about the reasonableness of the trial judge's assessment of the evidence [in the context of a Crown appeal of an acquittal] do not constitute questions of law alone . . . ."

(4) The Trial Judge's Failure to Consider All of the Evidence in Relation to the Ultimate Issue of Guilt or Innocence Is an Error of Law

[8] This was Sopinka J.'s last category in *Morin* (pp. 295-96). The underlying legal principle is set out in another decision called *R. v. Morin*, [1988] 2 S.C.R. 345. The principle is that it is an error of law to subject individual pieces of evidence to the standard of proof beyond a reasonable doubt; the evidence must be looked at as a whole: see, e.g., *B. (G.)*, at pp. 75-77 and 79. However, Sopinka J. sounded an important warning about how this error may be identified. It is a misapplication of the *Morin* principle to apply it whenever a trial judge fails to deal with each piece of evidence or record each piece of evidence and his or her assessment of it. As noted in *Morin* (1992), at p. 296, "A trial judge must consider all of the evidence in relation to the ultimate issue but unless the reasons demonstrate that this was not done, the failure to record the fact of it having been done is not a proper basis for concluding that there was an error of law in this respect." This was the basis of intervention relied on by the Court of Appeal, but as noted earlier, a fair reading of the trial judge's reasons does not support this finding of legal error.

[9] A trial judge is not required to refer to every item of evidence considered or to detail the way each item of evidence was assessed. As Binnie J. pointed out in *Walker*, "Reasons are sufficient if they are responsive to the case's live issues and the parties' key arguments. Their sufficiency should be measured not in the abstract, but as they respond to the substance of what was in issue" (para. 20). *Walker* also clearly holds that the adequacy of a trial judge's reasons is informed by the limited grounds for Crown rights of appeal from acquittals (paras. 2 and 22). As Binnie J. succinctly put it, "Caution must be taken to avoid seizing on perceived deficiencies in a trial judge's reasons for acquittal to create a ground of 'unreasonable acquittal' which is not open to the court under the provisions of the *Criminal Code*" (para. 2).

[10] Having reviewed four types of cases in which an alleged mishandling of the evidence may constitute an error of law alone, I return to the appellant's submissions. He argues that on a Crown appeal from an acquittal, where the error of law is alleged to be a defect in the trial judge's assessment of the evidence, a reviewable error arises only where four conditions are met: (a) an error of law has been committed; (b) the misapprehension of the evidence is not properly characterized as either an unreasonable verdict or a miscarriage of justice; (c) the Crown can show with a high degree of certainty that the error affected the verdict; and (d) there has been a shift in a legal burden to the accused. For reasons I will develop, I cannot accept this submission.

[11] The appellant's first condition — that an error of law has been committed— simply restates the question. The question is under what circumstances may an alleged mishandling of the evidence by the trial judge constitute an error of law alone giving the Crown a right of appeal from an acquittal. I have reviewed four types of situations, which may not be an exhaustive list, in which this may be the case.

[12] The appellant's second condition, relating to whether the alleged misapprehension of the evidence is "not properly characterized" as an unreasonable verdict or a miscarriage of justice, is not a helpful way of approaching the issue. Unreasonable verdict and miscarriage of justice are bases for appellate intervention in the case of conviction appeals; reference to them does not help identify errors of law alone for the purposes of Crown appeals from acquittals.

[13] The appellant's third condition, that the Crown can show a high degree of certainty that the error affected the verdict, similarly does not assist in identifying a question of law alone. This condition relates not to whether an error is one of law, but to when, in the presence of an error of law, appellate intervention is justified.

[14] The appellant's fourth point is that a trial judge's treatment of the evidence can never constitute an error of law for the purposes of permitting a Crown appeal unless there has been a shifting of the burden of proof. He bases this position on a statement by Lamer J. in *Schuldt*, at p. 604:

> . . . a finding of fact that is made in the absence of any supportive evidence is an error of law. I must say, however, that that will happen as regards an acquittal only if there has been a transfer to the accused by law of the burden of proof of a given fact.

[15] The appellant contends that the Court's decision in *Wild* should now be considered to have been wrongly decided.

[16] Respectfully, I do not accept either of these submissions. As I explained earlier, the principle set out in *Schuldt* (and many other cases) is that a reasonable doubt does not need to be based on the evidence; it may arise from an absence of evidence or a simple failure of the evidence to persuade the trier of fact to the requisite level of beyond reasonable doubt. The Court has twice, in *Schuldt* and *B. (G.)*, explained the proper basis of the decision in *Wild*. It is only where a reasonable doubt is tainted by a legal error that appellate intervention in an acquittal is permitted.

C. *Application to This Case*

[17] As noted, while it is an error of law for a trial judge to assess the evidence piecemeal, the trial judge's reasons in this case do not, in my view, disclose any such error.

V. Disposition

[18] I would allow the appeal and restore the acquittals entered at trial.

One of the most commonly argued grounds of appeal is that found in s. 686(1)(a)(i) — that the verdict of guilty is unreasonable or not supported by the evidence. The Supreme Court has tried to inject clarity into the definition of this ground of appeal.

R. v. SHEPPARD

[2002] 1 S.C.R. 869, 50 C.R. (5th) 68, 162 C.C.C. (3d) 298 (S.C.C.)

BINNIE J.: —

In this case, the Newfoundland Court of Appeal overturned the conviction of the respondent because the trial judge failed to deliver reasons in circumstances which "cried out for some explanatory analysis". Put another way, the trial judge can be said to have erred in law in failing to provide an explanation of his decision that was sufficiently intelligible to permit appellate review. I agree with this conclusion and would therefore reject the Crown's appeal.

Twenty-four-year-old Colin Sheppard, an unemployed carpenter from Spaniard's Bay, Newfoundland and Labrador, was charged with possession of stolen property, being two casement windows with a value of $429. No stolen windows were ever found in his possession. The case against Mr. Sheppard rested entirely on an accusation by his estranged girlfriend who took her story to the police two days after the termination of their tempestuous relationship saying that "she would get him". He testified in his own defence. He was convicted by a provincial court judge after a summary trial and fined $1,000 and ordered to "repay" the cost of two windows to a local builder's supply yard. He still does not understand the basis of his conviction and neither do we. The sum total of the trial judge's reasons consists of the following statement:

> Having considered all the testimony in this case, and reminding myself of the burden on the Crown and the credibility of witnesses, and how this is to be assessed, I find the defendant guilty as charged.

Defence counsel says that he was able to sum up his argument in two or three minutes (46 lines of transcript) and Crown counsel rather more succinctly (15 lines of transcript) and questions why less should be expected of a trial judge.

The appellant Crown contends that "[i]t has been a settled principle of Canadian law that a trial judge does not have to give reasons" (factum, at para. 13 (emphasis in original)). This proposition is so excessively broad as to be erroneous. It is true that there is no general duty, viewed in the abstract and divorced from the circumstances of the particular case, to provide reasons "when the finding is otherwise supportable on the evidence or where the basis of the finding is apparent from the circumstances" (*R. v. Barrett*, [1995] 1 S.C.R. 752 (S.C.C.), at p. 753). An appeal lies from the judgment, not the reasons for judgment. Nevertheless, reasons fulfill an important function in the trial process and, as will be seen, where that function goes unperformed, the judgment itself may be vulnerable to be reversed on appeal.

At the broadest level of accountability, the giving of reasoned judgments is central to the legitimacy of judicial institutions in the eyes of the public. Decisions on individual cases are neither submitted to nor blessed at the ballot box. The courts attract public support or criticism at least in part by the quality of their reasons. If unexpressed, the judged are prevented from judging the judges. The question before us is how this broad principle of governance translates into specific rules of appellate review.

. . .

Reasons for judgment are the primary mechanism by which judges account to the parties and to the public for the decisions they render. The courts frequently say that justice must not only be done but must be seen to be done, but critics respond that it is difficult to see how justice can be seen to be done if judges fail to articulate the reasons for their actions. Trial courts, where the essential findings of facts and drawing of inferences are done, can only be held properly to account if the reasons for their adjudication are transparent and accessible to the public and to the appellate courts.

. . .

There are, of course, significant differences between the criminal courts and administrative tribunals. Each adjudicative setting drives its own requirements. If the context is different, the rules may not necessarily be the same. These reasons are directed to the criminal justice context.

Even in the criminal law context, Parliament has intervened to require the giving of reasons in specific circumstances. Section 276.2(3) of the Criminal Code requires trial judges to give reasons for their determination of the admissibility of a complainant's prior sexual history. All the factors affecting the decision must be referred to as well as the manner in which the proposed evidence is considered to be relevant. In the same way, s. 278.8(1) states that trial judges shall provide reasons for ordering or refusing to order the production of certain records that contain personal private information. Section 726.2 provides that when imposing a sentence the court shall state the reasons for it. The only discernable purpose for these provisions is to facilitate appellate review of the correctness of the conviction or acquittal or sentence. It would be strange to impose a more rigorous standard of judicial articulation on an evidentiary ruling or sentence than on the conviction whose correctness is equally before the appellate court for review.

The task is not so much to extol the virtues of giving full reasons, which no one doubts, but to isolate those situations where deficiencies in the trial reasons will justify appellate intervention and either an acquittal or a new trial.

There is a general sense in which a duty to give reasons may be said to be owed to the public rather than to the parties to a specific proceeding. Through reasoned decisions, members of the general public become aware of rules of conduct applicable to their future activities. An awareness of the reasons for a rule often helps define its scope for those trying to comply with it. The development of the common law proceeds largely by reasoned analogy from established precedents to new situations. Few would argue, however, that failure to discharge this jurisprudential function necessarily gives rise to appellate intervention. New trials are ordered to address the potential need for correction of the outcome of a particular case. Poor reasons may coincide with a just result. Serious remedies such as a new trial require serious justification.

On a more specific level, within the confines of a particular case, it is widely recognized that having to give reasons itself concentrates the judicial mind on the difficulties that are presented (*R. v. G. (M.)* (1994), 93 C.C.C. (3d) 347 (Ont. C.A.), at p. 356; *R. v. N. (P.L.F.)* (1999), 138 C.C.C. (3d) 49 (Man. C.A.), at pp. 53-56 and 61-63; *R. v. Hache* (1999), 25 C.R. (5th) 127 (N.S. C.A.), at pp. 135-39; *R. v. Graves* (2000), 189 N.S.R. (2d) 281, 2000 NSCA 150 (N.S. C.A.), at paras. 19-23; *R. v. Gostick* (1999), 137 C.C.C. (3d) 53 (Ont. C.A.), at pp. 67-68). The absence of reasons, however, does not necessarily indicate an absence of such concentration. We are speaking here of the articulation of the reasons rather than of the reasoning process itself. The challenge for appellate courts is to ensure that the latter has occurred despite the absence, or inadequacy, of the former.

A) Functional Test

In my opinion, the requirement of reasons is tied to their purpose and the purpose varies with the context. At the trial level, the reasons justify and explain the result. The losing party knows why he or she has lost. Informed consideration can be given to grounds for appeal. Interested members of the public can satisfy themselves that justice has been done, or not, as the case may be.

The issue before us presupposes that the decision has been appealed. In that context the purpose, in my view, is to preserve and enhance meaningful appellate review of the correctness of the decision (which embraces both errors of law and palpable overriding errors of fact). If deficiencies in the reasons do not, in a particular case, foreclose meaningful appellate review, but allow for its full exercise, the deficiency will not justify intervention under s. 686 of the Criminal Code. That provision limits the power of the appellate court to intervene to situations where it is of the opinion that (i) the verdict is unreasonable, (ii) the judgment is vitiated by an error of law and it cannot be said that no substantial wrong or miscarriage of justice has occurred, or (iii) on any ground where there has been a miscarriage of justice.

The appellate court is not given the power to intervene simply because it thinks the trial court did a poor job of expressing itself.

. . .

D) A Proposed Approach

My reading of the cases suggests that the present state of the law on the duty of a trial judge to give reasons, viewed in the context of appellate intervention in a criminal case, can be summarized in the following propositions, which are intended to be helpful rather than exhaustive:

1. The delivery of reasoned decisions is inherent in the judge's role. It is part of his or her accountability for the discharge of the responsibilities of the office. In its most general sense, the obligation to provide reasons for a decision is owed to the public at large.

2. An accused person should not be left in doubt about why a conviction has been entered. Reasons for judgment may be important to clarify the basis for the conviction but, on the other hand, the basis may be clear from the record. The question is whether, in all the circumstances, the functional need to know has been met.

3. The lawyers for the parties may require reasons to assist them in considering and advising with respect to a potential appeal. On the other hand, they may know all that is required to be known for that purpose on the basis of the rest of the record.

4. The statutory right of appeal, being directed to a conviction (or, in the case of the Crown, to a judgment or verdict of acquittal) rather than to the reasons for that result, not every failure or deficiency in the reasons provides a ground of appeal.

5. Reasons perform an important function in the appellate process. Where the functional needs are not satisfied, the appellate court may conclude that it is a case of unreasonable verdict, an error of law, or a miscarriage of justice within the scope of s. 686(1)(a) of the Criminal Code, depending on the circumstances of the case and the nature and importance of the trial decision being rendered.

6. Reasons acquire particular importance when a trial judge is called upon to address troublesome principles of unsettled law, or to resolve confused and contradictory evidence on a key issue, unless the basis of the trial judge's conclusion is apparent from the record, even without being articulated.

7. Regard will be had to the time constraints and general press of business in the criminal courts. The trial judge is not held to some abstract standard of perfection. It is neither expected nor required that the trial judge's reasons provide the equivalent of a jury instruction.

8. The trial judge's duty is satisfied by reasons which are sufficient to serve the purpose for which the duty is imposed, i.e., a decision which, having regard to the particular circumstances of the case, is reasonably intelligible to the parties and provides the basis for meaningful appellate review of the correctness of the trial judge's decision.

9. While it is presumed that judges know the law with which they work day in and day out and deal competently with the issues of fact, the presumption is of limited relevance. Even learned judges can err in particular cases, and it is the correctness of the decision in a particular case that the parties are entitled to have reviewed by the appellate court.

10. Where the trial decision is deficient in explaining the result to the parties, but the appeal court considers itself able to do so, the appeal court's explanation in its own reasons is sufficient. There is no need in such a case for a new trial. The error of law, if it is so found, would be cured under the s. 686(1)(b)(iii) proviso.

E) Application of These Principles to the Facts

The majority judgments of the Newfoundland Court of Appeal found the trial decision unintelligible and therefore incapable of proper judicial scrutiny on appeal. I agree with this conclusion.

(i)   Intelligibility to the Parties and Counsel

A distinction may be drawn for these purposes between a situation of no reasons and an allegation of inadequate reasons.

In the present case the trial judge stated his conclusion (guilt) essentially without reasons. In the companion appeal in *R. v. Braich*, 2002 SCC 27 (S.C.C.) [reported at (2002), 50 C.R. (5th) 92 (S.C.C.)], the trial judge gave 17 pages of oral reasons, but the accused individuals argued that the reasons overlooked important issues and should be considered inadequate. The two types of situation raise somewhat different problems.

In this case, the trial judge says he "reminded himself" of various things including the burden on the Crown and the credibility of witnesses, but we are no wiser as to how his reasoning proceeded from there. The respondent was convicted of possession of stolen goods. It was central to Ms. Noseworthy's evidence that the "stolen" windows were to be incorporated into the respondent's house, but there was no evidence that a search had been made of his premises. The allegedly stolen property was never found in his possession. The respondent flatly asserted his innocence.

The trial judge's reasons were so "generic" as to be no reasons at all. Speaking of the Crown's attempt to excuse the "boilerplate" reasons by the busy nature of Judge Barnable's courtroom, Green J.A. commented:

> Reasons also relate to the fairness of the trial process. Particularly in a difficult case where hard choices have to be made, they may provide a modicum of comfort, especially to the losing party, that the process operated fairly, in the sense that the judge properly considered the relevant issues, applied the appropriate principles and addressed the key points of evidence and argument submitted.
>
> . . .
>
> It is cold comfort, I would suggest, to an accused seeking an explanation for being convicted in a case where there was a realistic chance of success, to be told he is not entitled to an explanation because judges are "too busy".

I agree, provided it is kept in mind that in the vast majority of criminal cases both the issues and the pathway taken by the trial judge to the result will likely be clear to all concerned. Accountability seeks basic fairness, not perfection, and does not justify an undue shift in focus from the correctness of the result to an esoteric dissection of the words used to express the reasoning process behind it.

Given the weaknesses of the Crown's evidence in this case, even the most basic notion of judicial accountability for the imposition of a criminal record would include accountability to the accused (respondent) as well as to an appellate court: *R. v. Ying*, [1930] 3 D.L.R. 925 (Ont. C.A.); *R. v. McCullough*, [1970] 1 C.C.C. 366 (Ont. C.A.).

The respondent's expressed bewilderment about the trial judge's pathway through the evidence to his decision is not contrived. The majority of the Newfoundland Court of Appeal shared the bewilderment, as do I.

The next question is whether this failure of clarity, transparency and accessibility to the legal reasoning prevented appellate review of the correctness of the decision.

(ii)   Meaningful Appellate Review

The majority of the Newfoundland Court of Appeal found the absence of reasons prevented them from properly reviewing the correctness of the unknown pathway taken by the trial judge in reaching his conclusion, but which remained unexpressed.

Their problem, clearly, was their inability to assess whether the principles of *R. v. W. (D.)*, [1991] 1 S.C.R. 742 (S.C.C.), at p. 757, had been applied, namely, whether the trial judge had addressed his mind, as he was required to do, to the possibility that despite having rejected the evidence of the respondent, there might nevertheless, given the peculiar gaps in the Crown's evidence in this case, be a reasonable doubt as to the proof of guilt. The ultimate issue was not whether he believed Ms. Noseworthy or the respondent, or part or all of what they each had to say. The issue at the end of the trial was not credibility but reasonable doubt.

Where a party has a right of appeal, the law presupposes that the exercise of that right is to be meaningful. This obvious proposition is widely supported in the cases. In *R. v. Richardson* (1992), 74 C.C.C. (3d) 15 (Ont. C.A.), for example, the accused was convicted of two counts of sexual assault. On appeal, in an argument that to some extent anticipates the present case, the accused submitted that the trial judge had concentrated solely on the credibility of the complainant and ignored the totality of evidence, particularly the evidence of five other witnesses that corroborated his version of events. In allowing the appeal, Carthy J.A., with whom Finlayson J.A. concurred, stated at p. 23:

> There is no need that the reasons of a trial judge be as meticulous in attention to detail as a charge to a jury. In moving under pressure from case to case it is expected that oral judgments will contain much less than the complete line of reasoning leading to the result. Nevertheless, if an accused is to be afforded a right of appeal it must not be an illusory right. An appellant must be in a position to look to the record and point to what are arguably legal errors or palpable and

overriding errors of fact. If nothing is said on issues that might otherwise have brought about an acquittal, then a reviewing court simply cannot make an assessment, and justice is not afforded to the appellant.

To the same effect, see *R. v. Dankyi* (1993), 86 C.C.C. (3d) 368 (Que. C.A.); *R. v. Anagnostopoulos* (1993), 20 C.R. (4th) 98 (Nfld. C.A.); *R. v. Davis* (1995), 98 C.C.C. (3d) 98 (Alta. C.A.); and *Hache*, supra. In each of these cases, the lack of reasons prevented the reviewing court from effectively addressing important grounds of appeal.

V. CONCLUSION

Cameron J.A., in dissent, protested that "if Ms. Noseworthy's version of events is accepted by the trier of fact, there is evidence upon which a trier of fact could reasonably convict" (para. 85). I agree that this case does not amount to an "unreasonable verdict" within the meaning of s. 686(1)(a)(i) of the Criminal Code. That conclusion, however, did not exhaust the powers of the Court of Appeal. In my opinion, the failure of the trial judge to deliver meaningful reasons for his decision in this case was an error of law within the meaning of s. 686(1)(a)(ii) of the Criminal Code. The Crown has not sought to save the conviction under the proviso in s. 686(1)(b)(iii), and rightly so.

VI. DISPOSITION

The appeal is dismissed. Whether or not to hold a new trial is in the discretion of the Attorney General of Newfoundland and Labrador.

R. v. BINIARIS
[2000] 1 S.C.R. 381, 143 C.C.C. (3d) 1, 32 C.R. (5th) 1 (S.C.C.)

The accused was convicted of murder and appealed his conviction, arguing among other things that the verdict was unreasonable. The British Columbia Court of Appeal dismissed the appeal and the accused appealed to the Supreme Court of Canada. The Court was asked to reconsider its decision in *Yebes*, both in terms of whether a ground of appeal based on s. 686(1)(a)(i) raises a question of law and the appropriate standard of review for an unreasonable verdict. The following excerpt focuses on the second question.

ARBOUR J.:—

. . .

The test for an appellate court determining whether the verdict of a jury or the judgment of a trial judge is unreasonable or cannot be supported by the evidence has been unequivocally expressed in *Yebes* as follows: [C]urial review is invited whenever a jury goes beyond a reasonable standard . . . the test is "whether the verdict is one that a properly instructed jury acting judicially, could reasonably have rendered".

That formulation of the test imports both an objective assessment and, to some extent, a subjective one. It requires the appeal court to determine what verdict a reasonable jury, properly instructed, could judicially have arrived at, and, in doing so, to review, analyze and, within the limits of appellate disadvantage, weigh the evidence. This latter process is usually understood as referring to a subjective exercise, requiring the appeal court to examine the weight of the evidence, rather than its bare sufficiency. The test is therefore mixed, and it is more helpful to articulate what the application of that test entails, than to characterize it as either an objective or a subjective test.

The *Yebes* test is expressed in terms of a verdict reached by a jury. It is, however, equally applicable to the judgment of a judge sitting at trial without a jury. The review for unreasonableness on appeal is different, however, and somewhat easier when the judgment under attack is that of a single judge, at least when reasons for judgment of some substance are provided. In those cases, the reviewing appellate court may be able to identify a flaw in the evaluation of the evidence, or in the analysis, that will serve to explain the unreasonable conclusion reached, and justify the reversal. . . . In trials by judge alone, the court of appeal often can and should identify the defects in the analysis that led the trier of fact to an unreasonable conclusion. The court of appeal will therefore be justified to intervene and set aside a verdict as unreasonable when the reasons of the trial judge reveal that he or she was not alive to an applicable legal principle, or entered a verdict inconsistent with the factual conclusions reached. These discernible defects are themselves sometimes akin to a separate error of law, and therefore easily sustain the conclusion that the unreasonable verdict which rests upon them also raises a question of law.

The exercise of appellate review is considerably more difficult when the court of appeal is required to determine the alleged unreasonableness of a verdict reached by a jury. If there are no errors in the charge, as must be assumed, there is no way of determining the basis upon which the jury reached its conclusion. But this does not dispense the reviewing court from the need to articulate the basis upon which it finds that the conclusion reached by the jury was unreasonable. It is insufficient for the court of appeal to refer to a vague unease, or a lingering or lurking doubt based on its own review of the evidence. This "lurking doubt" may be a powerful trigger for thorough appellate scrutiny of the evidence, but it is not, without further articulation of the basis for such doubt, a proper basis upon which to interfere with the findings of a jury. In other words, if, after reviewing the evidence at the end of an error-free trial which led to a conviction, the appeal court judge is left with a lurking doubt or feeling of unease, that doubt, which is not in itself sufficient to justify interfering with the conviction, may be a useful signal that the verdict was indeed reached in a non-judicial manner. In that case, the court of appeal must proceed further with its analysis.

When a jury which was admittedly properly instructed returns what the appeal court perceives to be an unreasonable conviction, the only rational inference, if the test in *Yebes* is followed, is that the jury, in arriving at that guilty verdict, was not acting judicially. This conclusion does not imply an impeachment of the integrity of the jury. It may be that the jury reached its verdict pursuant to an analytical flaw similar to the errors occasionally incurred in the analysis of trial judges and revealed in their reasons for judgment. Such error would of course not be apparent on the face of the verdict by a jury. But the unreasonableness itself of the verdict would be apparent to the legally trained reviewer when, in all the circumstances of a given case, judicial fact-finding precludes the conclusion reached by the jury. Judicial appreciation of the evidence is governed by rules that dictate the required content of the charge to the jury. These rules are sometimes expressed in terms of warnings, mandatory or discretionary sets of instructions by which a trial judge will convey the product of accumulated judicial experience to the jury, who, by definition, is new to the exercise. For instance, a judge may need to warn the jury about the frailties of eyewitness identification evidence. Similarly, years of judicial experience has revealed the possible need for special caution in evaluating the evidence of certain witnesses, such as accomplices, who may, to the uninitiated, seem particularly knowledgeable and therefore credible. Finally, judicial warnings may be required when the jury has heard about the criminal record of the accused, or about similar fact evidence. But these rules of caution cannot be exhaustive, they cannot capture every situation, and cannot be formulated in every case as a requirement of the charge. Rather, after the jury has been adequately charged as to the applicable law, and warned, if necessary, about drawing possibly unwarranted conclusions, it remains that in some cases, the totality of the evidence and the peculiar factual circumstances of a given case will lead an experienced jurist to conclude that the fact-finding exercise applied at trial was flawed in light of the unreasonable result that it produced.

When an appellate court arrives at that conclusion, it does not act as a "thirteenth juror", nor is it "usurping the function of the jury". In concluding that no properly instructed jury acting judicially could have convicted, the reviewing court inevitably is concluding that these particular jurors who convicted must not have been acting judicially. In that context, acting judicially means not only acting dispassionately, applying the law and adjudicating on the basis of the record and nothing else. It means, in addition, arriving at a conclusion that does not conflict with the bulk of judicial experience. This, in my view, is the assessment that must be made by the reviewing court. It requires not merely asking whether twelve properly instructed jurors, acting judicially, could reasonably have come to the same result, but doing so through the lens of judicial experience which serves as an additional protection against an unwarranted conviction.

It is not particularly significant to describe this judicial oversight as either objective or subjective. It is exercised by an appeal court and therefore it will invariably draw on a collection of judicial experiences. Because of its judicial character, and because it purports to identify features of a case that will give experienced jurists cause for concern, it is imperative that the reviewing court articulate as precisely as possible what features of the case suggest that the verdict reached by the jury was unreasonable, despite the fact that it was not tainted by any erroneous instructions as to the applicable law. In some cases, the articulation of the grounds upon which an appellate court concludes that a conviction was unreasonable may elucidate previously unidentified dangers in evidence and give rise to additional warnings to the jury in subsequent cases. Most of the time, it will simply point to a case that presented itself with several causes for concern, none of which, in isolation, might have required that the jury be warned in any particular way. There are many illustrations from the case law of verdicts having been found unreasonable essentially on the strength of accumulated judicial experience. Concerns about various aspects of the frailty of identification evidence have been a recurrent basis, by itself or together with other considerations, for overturning verdicts as unreasonable Judicial experience has also been relied upon to question the reasonableness of verdicts in cases of sexual misconduct presenting troubling features such as allegations of sexual touching of a bizarre nature or the possibility of collusion between witnesses. Finally, the experience of the courts has occasionally been brought to bear, although not always explicitly, on the assessment of verdicts rejecting a defence with respect to which there may be unjustified skepticism or even prejudice because those relying on such justifications or excuses may be viewed as simply trying to avoid responsibility for their actions

It follows from the above that the test in *Yebes* continues to be the binding test that appellate courts must apply in determining whether the verdict of the jury is unreasonable or cannot be supported by the evidence. To the extent that it has a subjective component, it is the subjective assessment of an assessor with judicial training and experience that must be brought to bear on the exercise of reviewing the evidence upon which an allegedly unreasonable conviction rests. That, in turn, requires the reviewing judge to import his or her knowledge of the law and the expertise of the courts, gained through the judicial process over the years, not simply his or her own personal experience and insight. It also requires that the reviewing court articulate as explicitly and as precisely as possible the grounds for its intervention. I wish to stress the importance of explicitness in the articulation of the reasons that support a finding that a verdict is unreasonable or cannot be supported by the evidence. Particularly since this amounts to a question of law that may give rise to an appeal, either as of right or by leave, the judicial process requires clarity and transparency as well as accessibility to the legal reasoning of the court of appeal. When there is a dissent in the court of appeal on the issue of the reasonableness of the verdict, both the spirit and the letter of s. 677 of the Criminal Code should be complied with. This Court should be supplied with the grounds upon which the verdict was found to be, or not to be, unreasonable.

Do you think that the standard articulated above for "unreasonable verdicts" is sufficient to guard against potential miscarriages of justice? See the discussion and plea for a lower standard of review based upon a "lurking doubt" in Don Stuart, Ronald J. Delisle and Allan Manson, eds, *Towards a Clear and Just Criminal Law* (Scarborough: Carswell, 1999). **Should the Crown be permitted to argue that an *acquittal* is unreasonable and against the weight of the evidence? Is this feasible in a country with a constitutionally-enshrined presumption of innocence?**

2. Appeals Against Sentence

Once the sentencing phase of the proceedings has been completed, if the accused or the Crown is unhappy with the result, an appeal may be taken to the appropriate appeal court. Procedurally, appeals against sentence follow the same structure as appeals against conviction or acquittal — summary conviction appeals are government by Part XXVII of the Criminal Code, whereas appeals against sentences imposed in indictable proceedings are governed by Part XXI.

For appeals in indictable matters, the key provision is s. 687 of the Criminal Code, which provides:

687. (1) Where an appeal is taken against sentence, the court of appeal shall, unless the sentence is one fixed by law, consider the fitness of the sentence appealed against, and may on such evidence, if any, as it thinks fit to require or to receive,

(a) vary the sentence within the limits prescribed by law for the offence of which the accused was convicted; or

(b) dismiss the appeal.

(2) A judgment of a court of appeal that varies the sentence of an accused who was convicted has the same force and effect as if it were a sentence passed by the trial court.

Section 687 says very little about the scope of review. It has been left to the appellate courts to determine when it is appropriate to intervene. For the longest time, the appellate courts were divided on whether they should take a more interventionist approach by substituting its own view and imposing the sentence that it thinks should have been imposed or whether they should be deferential and only intervene in the face of an error in principle or when the sentence was manifestly excessive or clearly inadequate: see G. Trotter, "Appellate Review of Sentencing Decisions", in Julian V. Roberts and David P. Cole, eds, *Making Sense of Sentencing* (Toronto: University of Toronto Press, 1999). The Supreme Court chose the latter of these two options, as evidenced in the excerpts below.

R. v. SHROPSHIRE
[1995] 4 S.C.R. 227, 102 C.C.C. (3d) 193, 43 C.R. (4th) 269 (S.C.C.)

The accused was convicted of second-degree murder and sentenced to the mandatory term of life imprisonment. The trial judge increased the period of parole ineligibility to 12 years. The British Columbia Court of Appeal allowed the accused's appeal and reduced the period of parole ineligibility to the minimum. The Crown successfully appealed. The following passage sets out the Supreme Court's new approach to appellate review of sentencing decisions.

IACOBUCCI J.:—

. . .

In my view, the British Columbia Court of Appeal not only erred in law regarding the factors justifying the issuance of an extended period of parole ineligibility order, but also in the standard of appellate review it espoused.

Lambert J.A. suggested that an appellate court should reduce the period of parole ineligibility imposed by the trial judge unless the trial judge has given specific reasons which, in the opinion of the appeal court, justify the increased period. This is a very broad standard of review, focusing in an exact manner on the appellate court's assessment of the correctness of the sentencing judge's decision. In my opinion, this standard of review is inappropriate.

Orders made under s. 744 are defined by s. 673 of the Criminal Code as forming part of the "sentence". They are thus to be appealed pursuant to the statutory right of appeal provided by s. 687(1) of the Criminal Code. . . .

The question, then, is whether a consideration of the "fitness" of a sentence incorporates the very interventionist appellate review propounded by Lambert J.A. With respect, I find that it does not. An appellate court should not be given free reign to modify a sentencing order simply because it feels that a different order ought to have been made. The formulation of a sentencing order is a profoundly subjective process; the trial judge has the advantage of having seen and heard all of the witnesses whereas the appellate court can only base itself upon a written record. A variation in the sentence should only be made if the Court of Appeal is convinced it is not fit. That is to say, that it has found the sentence to be clearly unreasonable.

I would adopt the approach taken by the Nova Scotia Court of Appeal in the cases of *R. v. Pepin* (1990), 57 C.C.C. (3d) 355 and *R. v. Muise* (1994), 94 C.C.C. (3d) 119. In *Pepin*, it was held that:

> In considering whether a sentence should be altered, the test is not whether we would have imposed a different sentence; we must determine if the sentencing judge applied wrong principles or [if] the sentence is clearly or manifestly excessive...

> In considering the fitness of a sentence imposed by a trial judge, this court has consistently held that it will not interfere unless the sentence imposed is clearly excessive or inadequate. . . .

The law on sentence appeals is not complex. If a sentence imposed is not clearly excessive or inadequate it is a fit sentence assuming the trial judge applied the correct principles and considered all relevant facts. . . . My view is premised on the reality that sentencing is not an exact science; it is anything but. It is the exercise of judgment taking into consideration relevant legal principles, the circumstances of the offence and the offender. The most that can be expected of a sentencing judge is to arrive at a sentence that is within an acceptable range. In my opinion, that is the only basis upon which Courts of Appeal review sentences when the only issue is whether the sentence is inadequate or excessive. . . .

Unreasonableness in the sentencing process involves the sentencing order falling outside the "acceptable range" of orders; this clearly does not arise in the present appeal. An error of law involves a situation such as that found in *R. v. Chaisson* (1995), 99 C.C.C. (3d) 289, in which a sentencing judge, while calculating the total time-period of incarceration for the purposes of a "half-time" parole ineligibility order under s. 741.2 of the Criminal Code, erroneously included two offences in the calculations notwithstanding the fact that these specific offences were not listed in the schedule of offences to which the s. 741.2 orders apply.

Regarding the issuance of reasons for extending the period of parole ineligibility, it is clear that the provision of reasons by the trial judge will help an appellate court assess the reasonableness of the sentencing decision. In a case where no reasons (either oral or written) are issued, the appellate court may be more inclined to find unreasonableness. However, the fact that no reasons are given should not automatically trigger a decision by appeal or appellate courts to reduce (or, for the matter, increase) the period of parole ineligibility imposed by the trial judge. Generally, although it is always preferable, in a matter as important as sentencing, for a trial judge to give reasons, a trial judge does not err merely because no reasons are given for deciding one way or the other: *R. v. Smith*, [1990] 1 S.C.R. 991; *R. v. Burns*, [1994] 1 S.C.R. 656. In any event, this discussion is, to a large extent, unnecessary in so far as the instant appeal is concerned since McKinnon J. clearly indicated why a period of 12 years was appropriate.

. . .

In the following case of *R. v. M. (C.A.)*, the Supreme Court applied the *Shropshire* approach to appellate review of sentences beyond the specialized murder context. It also refined its reasons for preferring a more deferential standard of review.

R. v. M. (C.A.)
[1996] 1 S.C.R. 500, 46 C.R. (4th) 269, 105 C.C.C. (3d) 327 (S.C.C.)

The accused was convicted of a number of violent and sexually violent offences against his children over a number of years. The trial judge imposed a sentence of 24 years imprisonment. The British Columbia Court of Appeal allowed the accused's appeal and reduced the sentence to 18 years and eight months imprisonment. The Crown successfully appealed to the Supreme Court. The Court wrote about many aspects of sentencing, including the role of retribution and fixed-term sentences. The following excerpt is restricted to the proper scope of appellate review.

LAMER C.J.C.:—

. . .

In *Shropshire*, supra, this Court recently articulated the appropriate standard of review that a court of appeal should adopt in reviewing the fitness of sentence under s. 687(1)....

Put simply, absent an error in principle, failure to consider a relevant factor, or an overemphasis of the appropriate factors, a court of appeal should only intervene to vary a sentence imposed at trial if the sentence is demonstrably unfit. Parliament explicitly vested sentencing judges with a discretion to determine the appropriate degree and kind of punishment under the Criminal Code. As s. 717(1) reads:

> 717. (1) Where an enactment prescribes different degrees or kinds of punishment in respect of an offence, the punishment to be imposed is, subject to the limitations prescribed in the enactment, in the discretion of the court that convicts the person who commits the offence.

This deferential standard of review has profound functional justifications. As Iacobucci J. explained in *Shropshire*, where the sentencing judge has had the benefit of presiding over the trial of the offender, he or she will have had the comparative advantage of having seen and heard the witnesses to the crime. But in the absence of a full trial, where the offender has pleaded guilty to an offence and the sentencing judge has only enjoyed the benefit of oral and written sentencing submissions (as was the case in both *Shropshire* and this instance), the argument in favour of deference remains compelling. A sentencing judge still enjoys a position of advantage over an appellate judge in being able to directly assess the sentencing submissions of both the Crown and the offender. A sentencing judge also possesses the unique qualifications of experience and judgment from having served on the front lines of our criminal justice system. Perhaps most importantly, the sentencing judge will normally preside near or within the community which has suffered the consequences of the offender's crime. As such, the sentencing judge will have a strong sense of the particular blend of sentencing goals that will be "just and appropriate" for the protection of that community. The determination of a just and appropriate sentence is a delicate art which attempts to balance carefully the societal goals of sentencing against the moral blameworthiness of the offender and the circumstances of the offence, while at all times taking into account the needs and current conditions of and in the community. The discretion of a sentencing judge should thus not be interfered with lightly.

Appellate courts, of course, serve an important function in reviewing and minimizing the disparity of sentences imposed by sentencing judges for similar offenders and similar offences committed throughout Canada. . . . But in exercising this role, courts of appeal must still exercise a margin of deference before intervening in the specialized discretion that Parliament has explicitly vested in sentencing judges. It has been repeatedly stressed that there is no such thing as a uniform sentence for a particular crime. . . . Sentencing is an inherently individualized process, and the search for a single appropriate sentence for a similar offender and a similar crime will frequently be a fruitless exercise of academic abstraction. As well, sentences for a particular offence should be expected to vary to some degree across various communities and regions in this country, as the "just and appropriate" mix of accepted sentencing goals will depend on the needs and current conditions of and in the particular community where the crime occurred. For these reasons, consistent with the general standard of review we articulated in *Shropshire*, I believe that a court of appeal should only intervene to minimize the disparity of sentences where the sentence imposed by the trial judge is in substantial and marked departure from the sentences customarily imposed for similar offenders committing similar crimes....

With the greatest respect, I believe the Court of Appeal erred in this instance by engaging in an overly interventionist mode of appellate review of the "fitness" of sentence which transcended the standard of deference we articulated in *Shropshire*.

In a third case, *R. v. McDonnell* [1997] 1 S.C.R. 948, 114 C.C.C. (3d) 436, 6 C.R. (5th) 231 (S.C.C.), the Supreme Court again confirmed its approach to appellate review of sentencing decisions.

It is probably fair to say that the *Shropshire* line of cases has had a revolutionary effect on sentence appeals in Canada. With the bar now set so high, appellate courts are far less likely to intervene in sentencing decisions, thereby creating a reduced incentive to appeal these types of decisions. Commentary on this jurisprudential development has been very critical: see John Norris, "Sentencing for Second-Degree Murder: *Regina v. Shropshire*" (1996) 1 Can. Crim. L. Rev. 199; Allan Manson, "The Supreme Court Intervenes in Sentencing" (1996) 43 C.R. (4th) 306; Tim Quigley, "New Horizons in Sentencing?" (1996) 1 Can. Crim. L. Rev. 279; and Gary Trotter, "*Regina v. Shropshire*: Sentencing, Murder and the Supreme Court of Canada" (1996) 43 C.R. (4th) 288. **Do you find the justifications offered by the Court for a deferential standard to be persuasive? Does such a deferential standard unduly risk the perpetuation of injustice at the sentencing phase of the proceedings?**

The Harper Conservative government introduced a number of new mandatory minimum prison sentences for various offences, particularly for firearms and drug offences. Kent Roach "Rates of Imprisonment and Criminal Justice Policy" (2008) 53 Crim. L.Q. 273 raises concerns that this will substantially increase Canada's imprisonment rates. He notes that Canada's current rate of imprisonment is 110 per 100,000 whereas that in the United States is a staggering 738 per 100,000. By 2013/2014, Canada had dropped to 18th place amongst Organisation for Economic Co-operation and Development countries (Correctional Services Program, *Adult correctional statistics in Canada, 2013/2014* (Ottawa: Statistics Canada, 2014) http://www.statcan.gc.ca/pub/85-002-x/2015001/article/14163-eng.htm?fpv=2693), the rate of incarceration had remained nearly the same.

In *R. v. Ferguson*, 54 C.R. (6th) 197, [2008] 1 S.C.R. 96, 228 C.C.C. (3d) 385 (S.C.C.) the Supreme Court added further rigidity in deciding that constitutional exemptions were not available in the case of minimum sentences. See C.R. comments by Steve Coughlan and Paul Calarco. Coughlan sees the decision as consistent with the rule of law. Calarco suggests that the rigidity may make cruel and unusual punishment under s. 12 of the Charter more likely to succeed.

The message of the 3-2 majority Court of Appeal *R. v. Arcand* (2010), 83 C.R. (6th) 199, 264 C.C.C. (3d) 134 (Alta. C.A.) delivered at the start of a lengthy analysis of Canadian sentencing policies and realities, is that courts of appeal need to be far more aggressive in intervening to control rampant sentencing disparity through a scheme of starting point prison sentences for particular crimes:

> We must face up to five sentencing truths. First, it is notorious amongst judges, of whom there are now approximately 2,100 in this country at three court levels, that one of the most controversial subjects, both in theory and practical application, is sentencing. That takes us to the second truth. The proposition that if judges knew the facts of a given case, they would all agree, or substantially agree on the result, is simply not so. The third truth. Judges are not the only ones who know truths one and two, and thus judge shopping is alive and well in Canada - and fighting hard to stay that way. All lead inescapably to the fourth truth. Without reasonable uniformity of approach to sentencing amongst trial and appellate judges in Canada, many of the sentencing objectives and principles prescribed in the Code are not attainable. This makes the search for just sanctions at best a lottery, and at worst a myth. Pretending otherwise obscures the need for Canadian courts to do what Parliament has asked: minimize unjustified disparity in sentencing while maintaining flexibility. The final truth. If the courts do not act to vindicate the promises of the law, and public confidence diminishes, then Parliament will. [para. 8]

This is a concern not evident in sentencing judgments of other courts of appeal. See, for example, *R. v. Tuglavina* (2011), 83 C.R. (6th) 356, 267 C.C.C. (3d) 401 (N.L. C.A.) and *R. v. Kummer* (2011), 83 C.R. (6th) 379, 266 C.C.C. (3d) 32 (Ont. C.A.), which assert an approach of setting flexible guidelines and accept and justify the Supreme Court's approach that appeal courts should show deference to sentencing decisions of trial judges. The message of the majority of the Alberta Court of Appeal can be read as encouraging the current Parliamentary trend to fixed minimum sentences. Although this would make sentencing easier it is likely that many judges at all levels, and including Alberta judges, would not favour such rigidity or lack of trust in the judiciary. Not all crimes are the same and minimum sentences allow for no individual factors to be taken into account. Ironically, the Alberta Court of Appeal revisited *Arcand* in *R. v. Lee*, 2012 ABCA 17, 290 C.C.C. (3d) 506 (Alta. C.A.) and, by a majority, rejected its reasoning. Thus, most of our appellate courts accept that sentencing is an individualized process and that, as a result, some variability in sentences will inevitably occur. Whether the acceptance of sentencing discretion in this context will influence the judicial attitude towards the mandatory minimum sentences remains to be seen.

3. Appeals to the Supreme Court of Canada

The route to the Supreme Court of Canada is not an easy one in criminal cases. It is determined by an examination of the interaction of sections of the Criminal Code and the Supreme Court Act (R.S.C. 1985, c. S-26). The main provisions in the Criminal Code are ss. 691 and 693, which provide:

> **691.** (1) A person who is convicted of an indictable offence and whose conviction is affirmed by the court of appeal may appeal to the Supreme Court of Canada
>
> (a) on any question of law on which a judge of the court of appeal dissents; or

(b) on any question of law, if leave to appeal is granted by the Supreme Court of Canada.

(2) A person who is acquitted of an indictable offence other than by reason of a verdict of not criminally responsible on account of mental disorder and whose acquittal is set aside by the court of appeal may appeal to the Supreme Court of Canada

(a) on any question of law on which a judge of the court of appeal dissents;

(b) on any question of law, if the Court of Appeal enters a verdict of guilty against the person; or

(c) on any question of law, if leave to appeal is granted by the Supreme Court of Canada.

693. (1) Where a judgment of a court of appeal sets aside a conviction pursuant to an appeal taken under section 675 or dismisses an appeal taken pursuant to paragraph 676(1)(a), (b) or (c) or subsection 676(3), the Attorney General may appeal to the Supreme Court of Canada

(a) on any question of law on which a judge of the court of appeal dissents; or

(b) on any question of law, if leave to appeal is granted by the Supreme Court of Canada.

(2) Where leave to appeal is granted under paragraph (1)(b), the Supreme Court of Canada may impose such terms as it sees fit.

The most important provisions of the Supreme Court Act relating to criminal appeals are ss. 35 and 40, which provide:

35. The Court shall have and exercise an appellate, civil and criminal jurisdiction within and throughout Canada.

40. (1) Subject to subsection (3), an appeal lies to the Supreme Court from any final or other judgment of the Federal Court of Appeal or of the highest court of final resort in a province, or a judge thereof, in which judgment can be had in the particular case sought to be appealed to the Supreme Court, whether or not leave to appeal to the Supreme Court has been refused by any other court, where, with respect to the particular case sought to be appealed, the Supreme Court is of the opinion that any question involved therein is, by reason of its public importance or the importance of any issue of law or any issue of mixed law and fact involved in that question, one that ought to be decided by the Supreme Court or is, for any other reason, of such a nature or significance as to warrant decision by it, and leave to appeal from that judgment is accordingly granted by the Supreme Court.

(2) An application for leave to appeal under this section shall be brought in accordance with paragraph 58(1)(a).

(3) No appeal to the Court lies under this section from the judgment of any court acquitting or convicting or setting aside or affirming a conviction or acquittal of an indictable offence or, except in respect of a question of law or jurisdiction, of an offence other than an indictable offence.

. . .

It is clear from the combination of these provisions that the Supreme Court of Canada exercises great control over its own docket. Under ss. 691 and 693 above, a litigant in a criminal case may sometimes appeal directly to the Court as a matter of right. Members of the Court, particularly Chief Justices, have made *ex cathedra* statements that it would prefer appeals as of right to be abolished. In the United States, no case is considered by the Supreme Court unless *certiorari* has been granted (a process similar to leave to appeal): see Edward Lazarus, *Closed Chambers: The Rise, Fall, and Future of the Modern Supreme Court* (New York: Penguin Books, 1999). To date, Parliament has not responded. In appeal as of right cases, the Court often delivers terse one or two line oral judgments, which seemingly generate the appearance of disinterest in this group of cases. See the criticism of Don Stuart, "The Supreme Court's Duty to Give Reasons in Appeals as of Right" (2003) 10 C.R. (6th) 4.

All other cases are determined by the leave to appeal standard. Section 40 of the Supreme Court Act has been interpreted to be restricted to cases raising questions of national importance: see John Sopinka and Mark Gelowitz, *The Conduct of an Appeal* (Toronto: Butterworths, 1993). Generally speaking, the Court is not concerned with error-correction; it is more concerned with legal issues that transcend the circumstances of any particular case. Still, the standard articulated in s. 40 does permit the Court to redress injustices in compelling cases.

There was a time when the Supreme Court was reluctant to hear appeals from sentence. As a matter of self-imposed policy, the Court will not hear appeals that raise only the issue of fitness of sentence. In more recent years, however, and perhaps in response to statutory changes to the sentencing regime in Canada (such as the creation of the conditional sentence of imprisonment), the Court has granted leave on and decided a sentencing appeals. For examples of the Court's interest in hearing sentencing cases that raise important issues, see the cases referred to early in section 2 of this Chapter.

Chapter 15

MINISTERIAL REVIEW AND CLAIMS OF INJUSTICE

1. Generally

Once the criminal appeal process has been exhausted, there are still avenues by which an accused person may seek to redress injustice, whether it be a wrongful conviction or otherwise. Anglo-Canadian law recognizes the concept of the sovereign to grant "mercy" to accused persons in appropriate cases. This power is now exercised by the Federal Cabinet. While the power exists at common law, the power is preserved and recognized through ss. 748 and 749 of the Criminal Code, which provide:

> **748.** (1) Her Majesty may extend the royal mercy to a person who is sentenced to imprisonment under the authority of an Act of Parliament, even if the person is imprisoned for failure to pay money to another person.
>
> (2) The Governor in Council may grant a free pardon or a conditional pardon to any person who has been convicted of an offence.
>
> (3) Where the Governor in Council grants a free pardon to a person, that person shall be deemed thereafter never to have committed the offence in respect of which the pardon is granted.
>
> (4) No free pardon or conditional pardon prevents or mitigates the punishment to which the person might otherwise be lawfully sentenced on a subsequent conviction for an offence other than that for which the pardon was granted.
>
> **749.** Nothing in this Act in any manner limits or affects Her Majesty's royal prerogative of mercy.

The exercise of the Royal Prerogative of Mercy is largely shrouded in secrecy. There is no fixed, formal process by which an accused person may seek this form of relief. Moreover, the concept of "mercy" in this context means different things. Mercy may apply to extend compassion to a person by refusing to exact the full weight of punishment imposed by the courts. Historically, it has also been use as an error-conviction mechanism to redress wrongful convictions. This use of mercy powers has faded with the creation and extension of appellate courts and formal procedures for Ministerial review: see Gary T. Trotter, "Justice, Politics and the Royal Prerogative of Mercy: Examining the Self-Defence Review" (2001) 26 Queen's L.J. 339.

Existing side-by-side with the nebulous Royal Prerogative of Mercy, are Criminal Code provisions focused more squarely on redressing wrongful convictions. These provisions permit applications to the Minister of Justice in cases of alleged wrongful convictions. Under these provisions, if the Minister was satisfied that an injustice had occurred, he or she could direct a new trial or refer a case to a provincial Court of Appeal or the Supreme Court of Canada. Over the last two decades or so, Canada has been confronted with the fact that its justice system is fallible. Cases like Donald Marshall, Guy Paul Morin and David Milgaard have proven that we should be far from complacent with the criminal trial and appellate process. Similar concerns abound in both the United States and in England: see, for example, Kent Roach and Gary Trotter, "Miscarriages of Justice in the War Against Terror" (2005) 109 Penn State Law Review 967.

The recent Canadian experience with miscarriages of justice also shed light on a flawed system of Ministerial review under what was formerly s. 690 of the Criminal Code. Advocates, activists and academics lamented that, among other things, the process suffered from a lack of independence, inadequate transparency and a general inability to effectively confront claims of injustice: see Patricia Braiden and Joan Brockman, "Remedying Wrongful Convictions Through Applications to the Minister of Justice Under Section 690 of the Criminal Code" (1999) 17 Windsor Y.B. Access Just. 3. The Federal government responded by repealing s. 690 and creating the following new Part of the Criminal Code:

PART XXI.1 — APPLICATIONS FOR MINISTERIAL REVIEW — MISCARRIAGES OF JUSTICE

696.1 (1) An application for ministerial review on the grounds of miscarriage of justice may be made to the Minister of Justice by or on behalf of a person who has been convicted of an offence under an Act of Parliament or a regulation made under an Act of Parliament or has been found to be a dangerous offender or a long-term offender under Part XXIV and whose rights of judicial review or appeal with respect to the conviction or finding have been exhausted.

(2) The application must be in the form, contain the information and be accompanied by any documents prescribed by the regulations.

696.2 (1) On receipt of an application under this Part, the Minister of Justice shall review it in accordance with the regulations.

(2) For the purpose of any investigation in relation to an application under this Part, the Minister of Justice has and may exercise the powers of a commissioner under Part I of the Inquiries Act and the powers that may be conferred on a commissioner under section 11 of that Act.

(3) Despite subsection 11(3) of the Inquiries Act, the Minister of Justice may delegate in writing to any member in good standing of the bar of a province, retired judge or any other individual who, in the opinion of the Minister, has similar background or experience the powers of the Minister to take evidence, issue subpoenas, enforce the attendance of witnesses, compel them to give evidence and otherwise conduct an investigation under subsection (2).

696.3 (1) In this section, "the court of appeal" means the court of appeal, as defined by the definition "court of appeal" in section 2, for the province in which the person to whom an application under this Part relates was tried.

(2) The Minister of Justice may, at any time, refer to the court of appeal, for its opinion, any question in relation to an application under this Part on which the Minister desires the assistance of that court, and the court shall furnish its opinion accordingly.

(3) On an application under this Part, the Minister of Justice may

(a) if the Minister is satisfied that there is a reasonable basis to conclude that a miscarriage of justice likely occurred,

    (i) direct, by order in writing, a new trial before any court that the Minister thinks proper or, in the case of a person found to be a dangerous offender or a long-term offender under Part XXIV, a new hearing under that Part, or

    (ii) refer the matter at any time to the court of appeal for hearing and determination by that court as if it were an appeal by the convicted person or the person found to be a dangerous offender or a long-term offender under Part XXIV, as the case may be; or

(b) dismiss the application.

(4) A decision of the Minister of Justice made under subsection (3) is final and is not subject to appeal.

696.4 In making a decision under subsection 696.3(3), the Minister of Justice shall take into account all matters that the Minister considers relevant, including

(a) whether the application is supported by new matters of significance that were not considered by the courts or previously considered by the Minister in an application in relation to the same conviction or finding under Part XXIV;

(b) the relevance and reliability of information that is presented in connection with the application; and

(c) the fact that an application under this Part is not intended to serve as a further appeal and any remedy available on such an application is an extraordinary remedy.

696.5 The Minister of Justice shall within six months after the end of each financial year submit an annual report to Parliament in relation to applications under this Part.

Section 696.4 underscores the intention of Parliament that the procedure under this Part of the Criminal Code is not meant to serve as another level of appellate review. Consistent with the practice that developed under former s. 690, the Minister of Justice is unlikely to act on anything less than new and compelling evidence. Experience under this new provision is too limited to tell whether it is an improvement on the provisions that were repealed. Andrew Guaglio, "Proving Innocence After Appeals – A Call for Uniform Post-Appeal Disclosure Policies" (2015), 62 Crim. L.Q. 88, points to the lack of Crown and police duty to disclose. There have been repeated calls for the establishment of an independent commission in Canada like the Criminal Cases Review Commission, which operates in the United Kingdom: see the special edition on Wrongful Convictions in (2012) 58 Crim. L.Q. 135-302.

2. Wrongful Convictions

In spite of the procedural safeguards that are available in Canada, including extensive appellate review and constitutional protection, mistakes do occur. In several high-profile cases, there have been serious miscarriages of justice that resulted in wrongful convictions. These include the cases of Donald Marshall, Guy Paul Morin, Thomas Sophonow, David Milgaard, Gregory Parsons, Ronald Dalton, Randy Druken, James Driskell, Romeo

Phillion, Robert Baltovich and, although by far the oldest, Steven Truscott. (The relevant reports are: Royal Commission on the Donald Marshall Jr. Prosecution, *Commissioner's Report: Findings and Recommendations* (Halifax: The Commission, 1989); Fred Kaufman (Commissioner), *The Commission on Proceedings Involving Guy Paul Morin: Report* (Toronto: Queen's Printer, 1988); Peter Cory (Commissioner), *The Inquiry Regarding Thomas Sophonow: The Investigation, Prosecution and Consideration of Entitlement to Compensation* (Winnipeg: Manitoba Justice, 2001); Antonio Lamer (Commissioner), *The Lamer Commission of Inquiry Pertaining to the Cases of Ronald Dalton, Gregory Parsons and Randy Druken* (St. John's: Newfoundland, 2006) *http://www.justice.gov.nl.ca/just/lamer/LamerReport .pdf;* Manitoba (Patrick J. Lesage, Q.C., Commissioner), *Report of the Commission of Inquiry into Certain Aspects of the Trial and Conviction of James Driskell* (Winnipeg: Manitoba Justice, 2007), *http://www.driskell inquiry.ca/pdf/final report jan2007.pdf.* An inquiry has been underway for some time in the *Milgaard* case *(http://www.milgaardinquiry.ca/)* but has not yet reported. The five justice panel of the Ontario Court of Appeal in *R. v. Truscott,* 2007 CarswellOnt 5305, 50 C.R. (6th) 1 (*sub nom. Reference re: Truscott*), 225 C.C.C. (3d) 321 (Ont. C.A.) held in a very lengthy ruling that Truscott ought to be acquitted for a 1959 murder but that he had not demonstrated his factual innocence. Thus the Court held there could be no declaration of innocence in that case. It is unknown whether any further inquiry will take place, although the province of Ontario has indicated that compensation will be provided to Mr. Truscott. The Court of Appeal is to be congratulated for bringing some finality to what must have been a grueling experience for Steven Truscott and his family. The approach taken to determining whether an acquittal or a new trial should be ordered is particularly commendable in light of the inability to actually hold a new trial.

At the same time, there must be some disappointment in the Truscott camp that a declaration of innocence was not issued. The Court pointed to the relative lack of interpretation of s. 686(2) of the Criminal Code which establishes the choice of remedies. The Court is probably on solid legal ground to hold that Truscott carried the burden of demonstrating that an acquittal, rather than a new trial, should be ordered. That being so, it is not surprising that the Court went on to conclude that he had not (and could not) affirmatively establish his innocence. Nevertheless, this is a gap that remains in the jurisprudence concerning wrongful conviction cases. At present, there is no legal mechanism whereby a declaration of innocence may be made. Therefore, unless the true perpetrator is caught and convicted or conclusive evidence of innocence through DNA evidence is available, there is the possibility that in some people's minds a wrongfully convicted person remains guilty.

The Driskell Inquiry Report (Manitoba (Patrick J. Lesage, Q.C., Commissioner), *Report of the Commission of Inquiry into Certain Aspects of the Trial and Conviction of James Driskell* (Winnipeg: Manitoba Justice, 2007), at 123-145, especially 138-143 (*http://www.driskellinquiry.ca/pdf/ final report jan2007.pdf)* also dealt with this issue but concluded that, in the absence of careful thought and a legislative framework, a declaration of innocence could not be contemplated. Chris Sherrin, "Declarations of Innocence" (2010), 35 Queen's L.J. 437, however, sets out a strong case for such declarations.

The tainted blood prosecution trial in Toronto in *Armour Pharmaceutical et al.* (2007), 226 C.C.C. (3d) 438, 50 C.R. (6th) 197 (Ont. S.C.J.), lasted some 18 months. The case concerned the supply of HIV infected blood products to haemophilia sufferers. The U.S. supply company and several doctors involved in the blood distribution process in Canada were charged with criminal negligence causing bodily harm. The defence did not call evidence. Benotto J. pronounced that it would be damning with faint praise to acquit those charged in the tainted blood prosecution on the basis of lack of proof beyond a reasonable doubt. She held that the accused had disproved the allegations. This amounted to a declaration of factual innocence although Benotto J. did not use this terminology.

Fourteen days later, the Ontario Court of Appeal in *R. v. Mullins-Johnson* decided that criminal courts have no jurisdiction to enter a verdict of a finding of factual innocence. It also found policy reasons against such a verdict in that it would degrade the meaning of a not guilty verdict.

R. v. MULLINS-JOHNSON
(2007), 50 C.R. (6th) 265, 228 C.C.C. (3d) 505 (Ont. C.A.)

In 1993 parents found their four-year-old daughter lying dead on her bed. Her uncle, the accused, who had babysat her the night before, was arrested and charged with first degree murder. He was convicted. He had protested his innocence from the very outset but his appeals to the Ontario Court of Appeal and Supreme Court were rejected. He spent 12 years in jail from the time of his arrest until he was released in 2005 on bail. The Minister of Justice referred the matter to the Court of Appeal under s. 696.3(3)(a)(ii) of the Criminal Code, R.S.C. 1985, c. C-46, to determine the case as if it were an appeal on the issue of fresh evidence. The Court heard a number of experts who re-examined the earlier evidence that had led to conviction.

The Ontario Court of Appeal allowed the appeal, quashed the murder conviction and acquitted.

Per O'CONNOR A.C.J.O. (Rosenberg and Sharpe JJ.A concurring): —

...There is no doubt that the new expert opinions in this case are credible and highly cogent. They go to the very core of whether there was an offence committed in this case. The opinions have been provided by some of the leading Canadian and international experts in forensic pathology and pathology. The opinions not only have a profound impact on the reliability of the jury verdict reached at trial, it is submitted that they are dispositive of the result. Finally, in their excellent factums the parties have fully reviewed for us the entire body of evidence aside from the expert evidence. In short, without the expert evidence there is no case against the appellant and no evidence of a crime. The non-expert evidence, if anything, is inconsistent with guilt and, again, is not indicative of a crime. Now that the trial expert evidence has been completely discredited, there is no case against the appellant and he is clearly entitled to an acquittal.

THE DECLARATION OF INNOCENCE

The fresh evidence shows that the appellant's conviction was the result of a rush to judgment based on flawed scientific opinion. With the entering of an acquittal, the appellant's legal innocence has been re-established. The fresh evidence is compelling in demonstrating that no crime was committed against Valin Johnson and that the appellant did not commit any crime. For that reason an acquittal is the proper result.

There are not in Canadian law two kinds of acquittals: those based on the Crown having failed to prove its case beyond a reasonable doubt and those where the accused has been shown to be factually innocent. We adopt the comments of the former Chief Justice of Canada in The Lamer Commission of Inquiry Pertaining to the Cases of: Ronald Dalton, Gregory Parsons, Randy Druken, Annex 3, pp. 342:

> [A] criminal trial does not address "factual innocence". The criminal trial is to determine whether the Crown has proven its case beyond a reasonable doubt. If so, the accused is guilty. If not, the accused is found not guilty. There is no finding of factual innocence since it would not fall within the ambit or purpose of criminal law.

Just as the criminal trial is not a vehicle for declarations of factual innocence, so an appeal court, which obtains its jurisdiction from statute, has no jurisdiction to make a formal legal declaration of factual innocence. The fact that we are hearing this case as a Reference under s. 696.3(3)(a)(ii) of the Criminal Code does not expand that jurisdiction. The terms of the Reference to this court are clear: we are hearing this case "as if it were an appeal". While we are entitled to express our reasons for the result in clear and strong terms, as we have done, we cannot make a formal legal declaration of the appellant's factual innocence.

In addition to the jurisdictional issue, there are important policy reasons for not, in effect, recognizing a third verdict, other than "guilty" or "not guilty", of "factually innocent". The most compelling, and, in our view, conclusive reason is the impact it would have on other persons found not guilty by criminal courts. As Professor Kent Roach observed in a report he prepared for the Commission of Inquiry into Certain Aspects of the Trial and Conviction of James Driskell, "there is a genuine concern that determinations and declarations of wrongful convictions could degrade the meaning of the not guilty verdict" (p. 39). To recognize a third verdict in the criminal trial process would, in effect, create two classes of people: those found to be factually innocent and those who benefited from the presumption of innocence and the high standard of proof beyond a reasonable doubt.

Nothing we have said in these reasons should be taken as somehow qualifying the impact of the fresh evidence. That evidence, together with the other evidence, shows beyond question that the appellant's conviction was wrong and that he was the subject of a terrible miscarriage of justice. We conclude these reasons by paraphrasing what the president of the panel said to Mr. Mullins-Johnson at the conclusion of the oral argument after entering the verdict of acquittal: it is profoundly regrettable that as a result of what has been shown to be flawed pathological evidence Mr. Mullins-Johnson was wrongly convicted and has spent such a very long time in jail.

The matter was not addressed by the Supreme Court in *Trotta* (2007), 50 C.R. (6th) 273, 225 C.C.C. (3d) 97, [2007] 3 S.C.R. 453 (S.C.C.), which ordered a new trial of the parents in the death of the child. *Trotta* and *Mullins-Johnson* were cases requiring remedies because the convictions involved reliance on the opinions of the now discredited work of the child pathologist, Dr. Charles Smith, once considered a leading light in that field in Ontario. A formal review of 45 of Smith's autopsies has already found he made questionable conclusions of foul play in 20 of the cases, 12 of which resulted in criminal convictions and one in a finding of not criminally responsible. On November 12, 2007, Justice Goudge of the Ontario Court of Appeal commenced a judicial inquiry.

Most of the Canadian wrongful conviction cases have been murder cases. There have been three wrongful sexual assault convictions in Alberta: *R. v. Kaminskli, R. v. L.G.P.* and *R. v. D.S.*: Criminal Conviction Review Group, Department Of Justice, December 3, 2015. In each case, it has taken years for the wrongfully convicted person to clear his name. When that has finally occurred, commissions of inquiry have been struck to assess where the case went wrong. Compensation has then been awarded to these unfortunate persons although it is obvious that no monetary payment can properly compensate for the stigma of being convicted of murder, imprisonment for long periods of time (23 years in the case of Milgaard), the stress and expense of attempting to establish innocence, and the frustration that the legal system has such difficulty in admitting to errors. Romeo Phillion spent 31 years in prison for murder before being released in 2003 on bail. The murder charge was finally withdrawn in 2010. In February 2015 the Supreme Court declined to hear an appeal attempting to block his outstanding civil suit against the Ottawa police and Crown. He died at the age of 76 in November of that year.

Perhaps more troubling is the likelihood that there are many more cases of wrongful conviction that have not come to light, probably for offences much less serious than murder, yet wrongful all the same. The relatively generous appeal rights and the process set out in Part XXI.1 of the Criminal Code may assist in rectifying errors, but they do not prevent them. There is now a burgeoning literature on the factors that contribute to wrongful convictions of the innocent and recommendations for reducing or eliminating those factors. A report, The Federal, Provincial and Territorial (FPT) Ministers Responsible for Justice, *Report on the Prevention of Miscarriages of Justice* (Ottawa: Justice Canada, 2005) (*http://canada.justice.gc.ca/en/dept/pub/hop/*) and an academic article, Christopher Sherrin, "Comment on the Report on the Prevention of Miscarriages of Justice" (2007), 52 Crim. L.Q. 140 provide very good summaries of these factors and recommendations for improvement. The discussion that follows draws heavily on these sources.

The following factors have been identified as contributing to the convictions of innocent persons:

(a)   Failure of Crown and/or police to disclose;

(b)   Frailties in eyewitness identification evidence;

(c)   False confessions;

(d)   The use of jailhouse informants;

(e)   Tunnel vision by the police and prosecution;

(f)   Scientific and expert opinion evidence.

(a) Failure of Crown and/or police to disclose

From the first established wrongful conviction case of Donald Marshall, the failure to disclose has often turned out to be a key factor. Many of these cases were before the Charter obligation to disclose established in *R. v. Stinchcombe*.

(b) Frailties in eyewitness identification evidence

Eyewitnesses are often honest but mistaken in their identification of an accused person and their errors have been identified as perhaps the leading factor in wrongful convictions. Their errors fall into two categories: estimator variables (quality of eyesight, opportunity to observe, attention to detail) and system variables (the identification process used by police and others, such as identification line-ups, photo spreads, etc.). Recommendations to standardize and improve the system processes would undoubtedly reduce errors or, at least, reliance on those errors that lead to wrongful convictions. In particular, videotaping these processes would greatly assist in determining whether the process was contaminated or improperly conducted. Nevertheless, honest and careful witnesses will still make errors. Therefore, scepticism about resting a conviction on identification evidence should remain.

(c) False confessions

Surprising though it may seem, people do sometimes falsely confess to a crime and thereby become part of the wrongfully convicted. Some false confessions may be due to underlying psychiatric or psychological problems that cause a person to want to gain notoriety or attention. However, the role of interrogation is a strongly contributing factor. Even those without apparent psychiatric or psychological problems may have personalities susceptible to certain interrogation techniques. Videotaping all such interrogations from beginning to end would do much to uncover situations where the suspect was influenced to confess through the interrogation process. Training the police and prosecutors to detect signs of susceptibility would also be helpful.

In the meantime, additional research is required to learn more about how false confessions occur.

(d) Jailhouse informers

Several of the wrongful conviction cases mentioned above resulted in part from evidence provided by informers who were themselves in custody, and almost always looking for some personal advantage. Despite calls for outlawing such evidence, public authorities are reluctant to move that far. Ontario and some other provinces now have committees that screen all such evidence to see that it meets at least minimum standards of reliability. Vigorous prosecution of informers who have lied and regulation of the benefits accorded them have also been recommended.

(e) Tunnel vision

Tunnel vision — the focussing by police and prosecutors on one suspect to the exclusion of other possible suspects and/or lines of inquiry — has been a major cause of wrongful convictions. It was, to a greater or lesser extent, an important factor in each of the cases cited above. Review of the results of police investigations by prosecutors is one mechanism for avoiding tunnel vision. However, this must come at a very early stage in the process, before its effects have caused the accumulation of self-fulfilling evidence against a suspect and before other lines of inquiry have been foreclosed. Care must also be taken to have an objective review by someone who is not possessed of the same mindset or subject to the same workplace culture. Education of all personnel in the legal system about the dangers of tunnel vision and how to avoid it are also necessary measures.

(f) Scientific and expert opinion evidence

This category of factors in wrongful convictions is a mé lange of evidentiary issues. Judges and juries are very prone to rely on scientific and expert opinion evidence, particularly because of the apparent infallibility of such techniques in popular culture, such as television and movies. But errors in fingerprint evidence, hair and other bodily samples, fibre comparisons, and forensic pathology have contributed to convicting the innocent. Establishment and possible expansion of the DNA databank may assist in providing conclusive evidence for or against a suspect, provided, of course, that the DNA analysis itself has been properly done. Retention of samples for a lengthy time is also important (had evidence been retained in Steven Truscott's case, he might have been able to conclusively demonstrate his innocence). Perhaps even more important is the availability of scientists and experts independent from the police and prosecution since, at the moment, it is very difficult to find such personnel to assess the work of those in the employ of the state. Less subservience to scientific opinion on the part of judges and juries, the latter perhaps through better jury instructions, would also be of assistance.

TABLE OF CASES

Names of cases substantially reproduced in the text are set in bold face type.